PSYCHOLOGY

PSYCHOLOGY

A BIOPSYCHOSOCIAL APPROACH

SECOND EDITION

Christopher Peterson

UNIVERSITY OF MICHIGAN

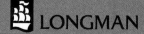

LONGMAN

An imprint of Addison Wesley Longman, Inc.

New York • Reading, Massachusetts • Menlo Park, California • Harlow, England
Don Mills, Ontario • Sydney • Mexico City • Madrid • Amsterdam

Acquisitions Editor: Rebecca Dudley
Developmental Editor: Michael Kimball
Supplements Editor: Donna Campion
Project Coordination, Electronic Page Makeup, and Text Design:
    Thompson Steele Production Services
Cover Designer: Paul Agresti
Cover Illustration: *Female Torso II* by Kasimir Malevich, Russian State Museum,
    St. Petersburg/A. Burkatousky/SuperStock
Artists: Nancy Jean Anderson, Nadine Sokol, Kevin Somerville
Photo Researcher: Julie Tesser
Electronic Production Manager: Eric Jorgensen
Manufacturing Manager: Hilda Koparanian
Printer and Binder: RR Donnelley & Sons Company
Cover Printer: Phoenix Color Corp.

For permission to use copyrighted material, grateful acknowledgment is made to the copyright holders on p. 759, which are hereby made part of this copyright page.

Library of Congress Cataloging-in-Publication Data
Peterson, Christopher, 1950–
        Psychology: A biopsychosocial approach/Christopher Peterson.
                p.   cm.
        ISBN 0-673-52414-0
        1. Psychology.   I. Title.
    BF121.P435   1997
    150—dc20   96-24666
                                                                        CIP

ISBN 0-673-52414-0

12345678910—DOW—99989796

Brief Contents

Detailed Contents

CHAPTER 2   Research in Psychology   30

Evolution and Behavior 60 CHAPTER 3

CHAPTER 4 The Brain and the Nervous System   94

Sensation and Perception   136   CHAPTER 5

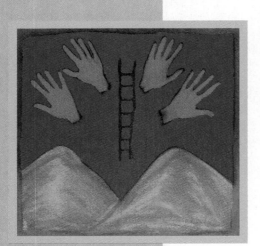

Learning 262   CHAPTER 8

CHAPTER *9*   *Cognition   306*

Development   350

CHAPTER 11 Intelligence 396

Personality   438

C H A P T E R 13 *Psychological Disorders* 480

Therapy 520

Social Cognition and Social Influence 558

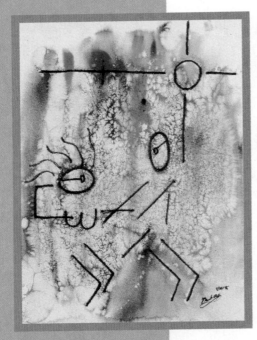

Health Psychology   604

CHAPTER **17** *Industrial-Organizational and Other Applied Psychologies 642*

Preface

TO THE INSTRUCTOR

I had several goals that I wanted to achieve when I wrote this second edition of *Psychology: A Biopsychosocial Approach*. My first goal was to give students a framework with which to think critically about psychology. I believe psychology can best be understood with the **biopsychosocial approach**—in terms of biological mechanisms, psychological processes, and social influences. I am convinced that this approach captures the essence of psychology today, even more so than when I wrote the first edition of this text some years ago.

The biopsychosocial approach helps make sense of theory, research, and application, as well as accommodate the unity and diversity of psychology. From my discussions with colleagues around the country, I know that many instructors are already using a biopsychosocial approach in their introductory classes. Discussion of evolutionary approaches to behavior, for example, is much more common in college classrooms than it was just five years ago. So too is discussion of how behavior differs across social contrasts like gender, ethnicity, and culture. These movements in the field convinced me to revise this text in the way that I have, just as they have already led so many instructors to change their lectures and discussions. My hope is that instructors will find *Psychology: A Biopsychosocial Approach* a novel text that is organized in a way that already fits how they teach.

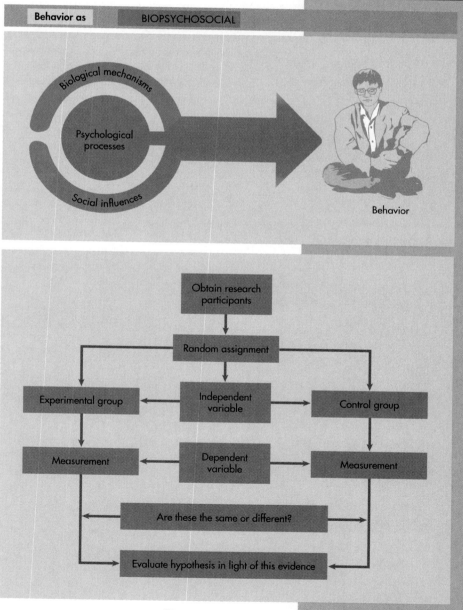

My second goal was to encourage an appreciation and understanding of psychology as a science. Only a small proportion of students in our classes today will themselves become psychologists. However, all of them will encounter ideas from psychology throughout their lives. The newest concepts and findings in psychology are routinely reported in the popular media. Ideas from psychology have spread to literature, to the arts, to other sciences, to health care, and to public policy. If we are to educate today's introductory psychology students properly, then we must give them the tools to evaluate the concepts they will later encounter. I try to emphasize not just the conclusions of research, but also how research is conducted.

My third goal was to cover the applied fields of psychology in a way that does justice to their importance within the discipline. Many texts segregate applications from their discussions of basic psychology by relegating all mention of applications to brief boxes or postscripts. Such a strategy gives a false view of psychology as it really exists, obscuring the reason why psychology is so important in today's world. In *Psychology: A Biopsychosocial Approach,* applications are an integral part of the story I tell.

My fourth and final goal was to update thoroughly the text's coverage of psychology. Of the 2,600 references, more than 1,200 are to articles, chapters, or books written since 1990. My other goals for the text—especially its incorporation of the biopsychosocial approach—dictated when and how updating should occur. Classic references are frequent as well, because it is important for students to understand that psychology has been shaped by its history. Even when contemporary psychologists disagree with their intellectual predecessors, they use the work of previous generations as their point of departure.

The Biopsychosocial Approach

I explain psychological phenomena in terms of relevant biological mechanisms, psychological processes, and social influences. The biopsychosocial approach is a powerful one that can be applied to all topics of concern in psychology. In some cases, we have a good idea what the biopsychosocial details of a given phenomenon might be; in other cases, much more thought and research are required to identify the appropriate biopsychosocial ingredients. Regardless, I have used the biopsychosocial approach to organize the entire text, both what is known and what needs to be known. Psychology is a diverse field, but the biopsychosocial approach provides a unifying framework.

THE BIOPSYCHOSOCIAL APPROACH MANY OF THE EXAMPLES IN THE LIST ON P. XXV AND ELSEWHERE IN THE TEXT ARE ILLUSTRATED WITH SIMILAR BIOPSYCHOSOCIAL FIGURES.

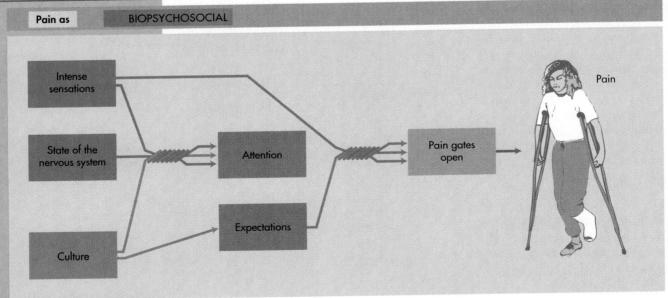

Pain as   BIOPSYCHOSOCIAL

Intense sensations

State of the nervous system

Culture

Attention

Expectations

Pain gates open

Pain

Chapter 1 thoroughly introduces the biopsychosocial approach. Each subsequent chapter begins by presenting an overview of how this approach applies to the subject matter of that chapter and concludes by examining a specific topic in biopsychosocial terms. For example, **Chapter 5, Sensation and Perception,** begins by discussing how perception results from an interplay of the neurological mechanisms responsible for sensation, psychological processes such as attention and adaptation level, and culturally provided labels and expectations. It ends by examining pain and pleasure in these same terms.

Briefly, some of the other discussions of the biopsychosocial approach focus on:

- the contributions to theory and research of individual psychologists (Chapter 2)
- why people age and eventually die (Chapter 3)
- the determinants of sexual orientation (Chapter 4)
- the experience of Haitian zombies (Chapter 6)
- Maslow's hierarchy of motives and Izard's emotion activation systems (Chapter 7)
- Asian versus American elementary education (Chapter 8)
- gender differences in cognition and language (Chapter 9)
- cross-generational effects of the Japanese American internment (Chapter 10)
- Sternberg's triarchic theory of intelligence (Chapter 11)
- gender differences in personality (Chapter 12)
- culture-bound syndromes (Chapter 13)
- cross-cultural and cross-historical approaches to healing (Chapter 14)
- selection and training of professional torturers (Chapter 15)
- shamanism and alternative medicine (Chapter 16)
- psychological mindedness (Chapter 17)

These are some examples of the important and interesting new research that can be more fully explored and explained through the use of the biopsychosocial approach.

Evolution and Human Diversity

The biopsychosocial approach facilitates coverage of two of the most exciting developments in contemporary psychology: the increasing recognition of the role of biological and evolutionary mechanisms in behavior and the increasing appreciation of the role of culture and history in creating human diversity. At first glance, these new developments may seem at odds with one another—another take on the venerable nature-nurture debate—but a biopsychosocial approach allows them to be united. People are products of evolution and culture; the task of psychologists is not to play one viewpoint off against another, but rather to explain when and how both matter.

Chapter 3, Evolution and Behavior, and subsequent chapters discuss how evolved psychological mechanisms are involved in specific behaviors. For example, different species learn in different ways. These differences make sense when we consider them in terms of what was needed for these species to survive in the situations in which they evolved (Chapter 8, Learning). People in different cultures apparently experience and recognize a set of basic emotions, and again, these make sense in terms of the common survival problems our ancestors had to confront and solve (Chapter 7, Motivation and Emotion).

Other discussions of the evolutionary basis of behavior include:

- the evolution of the brain (Chapter 4)
- the fit between sensory systems and the niche of a species (Chapter 5)
- the capacity for consciousness (Chapter 6)
- attachment of infants to their caretakers (Chapter 10)
- multiple intelligences (Chapter 11)
- why personality differences exist (Chapter 12)

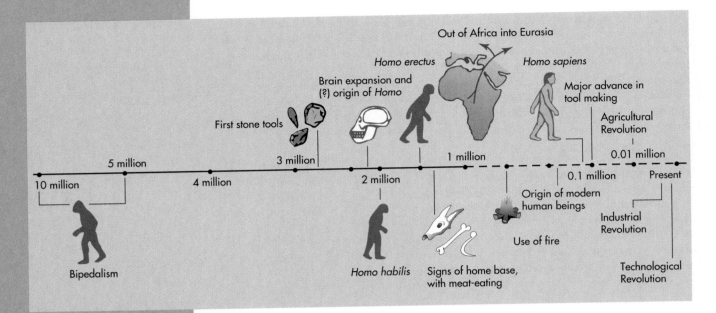

EVOLUTION AND HUMAN BEHAVIOR
BESIDES THE FULL CHAPTER ON
EVOLUTION AND HUMAN
BEHAVIOR, EACH CHAPTER DIS-
CUSSES HOW EVOLVED PSYCHOLOG-
ICAL MECHANISMS ARE INVOLVED
IN SPECIFIC BEHAVIORS.

- why psychopathology exists (Chapter 13)
- biomedical therapies (Chapter 14)
- the pervasiveness of social influence (Chapter 15)
- why and how physical health declines (Chapter 16)
- product design (Chapter 17)

The text also covers examples of what is now known about behavior across lines of gender, culture, and ethnicity. For example, what differences exist between the brains of men and women, and do these differences have any consequences for behavior? See **Chapter 5, Sensation and Perception.** Other discussions of gender differences include:

GENDER, CULTURE, AND ETHNICITY
EVERY CHAPTER HAS INTEGRATED
EXAMPLES AND DISCUSSIONS OF
GENDER, CULTURE, AND ETHNICITY.
ON THE LEFT IS A MALE'S BRAIN,
AND ON THE RIGHT IS A FEMALE'S
BRAIN. BOTH ARE ENGAGED IN THE
SAME TASK. THE FEMALE'S BRAIN
SHOWS ACTIVITY ON BOTH SIDES,
SUGGESTING THAT SKILLS ARE DIS-
TRIBUTED MORE EQUALLY BETWEEN
THE TWO HEMISPHERES FOR
FEMALES THAN FOR MALES.

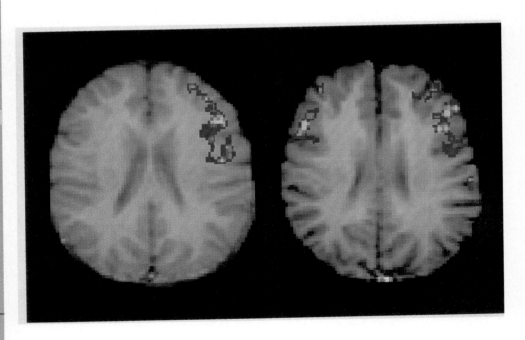

- mate selection (Chapter 3)
- sensory system thresholds (Chapter 5)
- substance abuse (Chapter 6)
- emotional experience and expression (Chapter 7)
- conditioning and modeling (Chapter 8)
- cognition and language (Chapter 9)
- socialization of infants and children (Chapter 10)
- types of intelligence (Chapter 11)
- personality traits (Chapter 12)
- prevalence of different psychopathologies (Chapter 13)
- therapist effectiveness (Chapter 14)
- extent of social influence (Chapter 15)
- mortality and morbidity (Chapter 16)
- meaning of work and reasons for retirement (Chapter 17)

Doing Research

Other texts point out that psychology is a science but then offer conclusions without describing exactly how they were reached. **Chapter 2** focuses on research and every subsequent chapter has *Doing Research*, a specific section that discusses how studies are conducted in a given area. In **Chapter 3,** *Doing Evolution Research* addresses how psychologists use the fossil record to understand human evolution. To encourage critical thinking by students, I also note the limitations of this strategy. Indeed, one of the recurring points I make about research is that all methods have drawbacks. My intent is not to dismiss research but to convey the excitement involved in the ongoing attempts to make conclusions more valid.

Some examples of studies discussed in the *Doing Research* feature include:

- imaging techniques to study the brain (Chapter 4)
- psychophysics techniques to study sensation and perception (Chapter 5)
- introspective reports to study consciousness (Chapter 6)
- projective tests to study motives and emotions (Chapter 7)
- experiments with animals to study learning (Chapter 8)
- artificial intelligence to study cognition (Chapter 9)
- cross-sectional and longitudinal designs to study development (Chapter 10)
- group-administered tests to study intelligence (Chapter 11)
- experience sampling to study personality (Chapter 12)
- research diagnostic criteria to study psychopathology (Chapter 13)
- outcome research to study the effectiveness of psychotherapy (Chapter 14)
- deception experiments to study social influence (Chapter 15)

---

126   CHAPTER 4   *The Brain and the Nervous System*

Table 4.3   Neuropsychological Research Techniques

Technique	Strategy
Lesions and ablations	Damage or destroy parts of the nervous system and determine the consequences
Electrical stimulation	Stimulate the nervous system with electricity and determine the consequences
Chemical stimulation	Stimulate the nervous system with chemicals and determine the consequences
Electrical recording	Record electrical activity in the brain during different activities
Imaging	Take pictures of brain structures and/or functions during different activities
Computer modeling	Simulate functioning of the nervous system with a computer program and compare the consequences with what actually happens

DOING *Neuropsychology* RESEARCH

Neuropsychologists face a daunting task. As you have seen, the nervous system is incredibly complex, and the details of its functioning reside at a microscopic level. Research strategies are indirect, allowing inferences but rarely direct views. Investigators have devised various approaches to aid these inferences (see Table 4.3), and the results described in the previous sections of this chapter reflect their ingenuity.

■ lesion
wound or injury to a particular part of the brain or nervous system

■ ablation
complete destruction or removal of some part of the brain or nervous system

Lesion and Ablation Techniques

Lesion and ablation studies provide an important way to see how damage to the nervous system is linked to subsequent behavior. A **lesion** is a wound or injury to a particular part of the brain or nervous system; an **ablation** is the complete destruction or removal of some structure. Lesions and ablations may be deliberately created by researchers working with animals, or they may be studied as they naturally occur in accidents and illnesses.

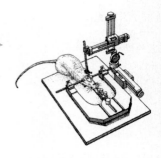

In order to make a lesion in the intended part of the brain, a researcher places an animal in a device like this one that holds the animal's head still and allows a lesion to be made in a specific location.

DOING NEUROPSYCHOLOGICAL RESEARCH DOING RESEARCH IS FOUND IN EVERY CHAPTER, DISCUSSING HOW STUDIES ARE CONDUCTED IN A GIVEN AREA.

■ surveys to study risk factors for illness (Chapter 16)
■ field experiments to study applications of psychology (Chapter 17)

These research discussions are intended to be general, accessible, and critical.

Application

Specific chapters are devoted to applications such as **Chapter 14, Therapy, Chapter 16, Physical Health and Illness,** and **Chapter 17, Industrial-Organizational and Other Applied Psychologies.** Incorporated into virtually all other chapters are discussions of other applications. What do psychologists know about ways of reducing prejudice and discrimination (Chapter 15, Social Cognition and Social Influence)? How can we help people cope with stress (Chapter 16, Physical Health and Illness)?

Here is a sample of the other applications on focus:

■ rehabilitation following brain damage (Chapter 4)
■ method acting (Chapter 7)
■ classroom education (Chapter 8)
■ the improvement of everyday memory (Chapter 9)
■ the creation of "intelligent" machines (Chapter 9)
■ the improvement of everyday problem solving (Chapter 9)
■ the psychological effects of day care (Chapter 10)
■ the psychological effects of divorce (Chapter 10)
■ intelligence testing (Chapter 11)
■ personality assessment (Chapter 12)
■ psychiatric diagnosis (Chapter 13)
■ advertising (Chapter 17)
■ athletic performance (Chapter 17)
■ the insanity plea (Chapter 17)

APPLICATION IN PSYCHOLOGY AN EXAMPLE OF AN INTEGRATED APPLICATION IS THIS SHAMAN. SHAMANS VIEW PHYSICAL PROBLEMS AS STEMMING FROM SPIRITUAL DIFFICULTIES. HERE IS A MEXICAN-AMERICAN CURANDERA.

As I have already mentioned, discussion of these and other applications is integrated with the text, not set aside in boxes or postscripts.

Unique Chapters

Organizational innovations that followed from my goals for the text include: **Chapter 2, Research in Psychology,** which is devoted to research and incorporates both statistics and research ethics into the text. Many other texts relegate statistics to an appendix, and some ignore ethics altogether. Both topics matter and need to be discussed in the context of research.

Chapter 3, Evolution and Behavior, is devoted to evolution and behavior. Other texts cover evolution in a few pages, as an afterthought to consideration of the nervous system, but evolutionary ideas can shed light on the whole of psychology. Given the importance of such fields as sociobiology and evolutionary psychology, students need to be introduced to evolutionary ideas in a thorough way that encourages appropriate appreciation and skepticism.

Psychology: A Biopsychosocial Approach gives expanded coverage of applied psychology and includes two chapters not found in many other texts. **Chapter 16, Physical Health and Illness,** is devoted to health psychology, and **Chapter 17, Industrial-Organizational and Other Applied Psychologies,** focuses on industrial-organizational psychology. Also included in **Chapter 17** are discussions of applied fields such as engineering psychology, consumer psychology, environmental psychology, and sports psychology.

The Pedagogical System

In *Psychology: A Biopsychosocial Approach*, pedagogical techniques were chosen because they reinforced the goals of the text. The most important part of this system is the deliberate presentation of theory, research, and application in a consistent way across chapters, as I have already noted. As students move from one chapter to another, they will find the strategy of coverage increasingly familiar.

Here are some of the specific pedagogical techniques featured in each chapter. Some are standard, and some are unique to this text and follow from its biopsychosocial approach:

■ **Chapter Opening Outlines.** It is helpful to call these outlines to the attention of your students as a way for them to understand the internal structuring of chapters and the relative space devoted to different topics.

■ **Chapter Opening Vignettes.** Each chapter begins with a vignette that highlights the concerns of the chapter. These vignettes are of high interest and should draw students into the chapter. I refer to each vignette throughout the relevant chapters. For example, **Chapter 15, Social Cognition and Social Influence,** begins with the story of Rodney King and the rioting in Los Angeles that followed the acquittal of the police officers who beat him. References to this vignette are then made when the chapter discusses causal attributions, obedience, and conformity.

CHAPTER OPENING PEDAGOGY A CHAPTER OPENING TABLE OF CONTENTS AND VIGNETTE DRAW THE STUDENT INTO THE CHAPTER CONTENT.

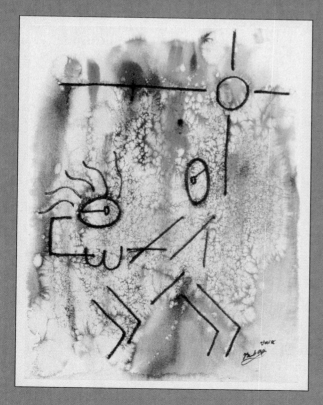

CHAPTER 15

Social Cognition and Social Influence

On March 3, 1991, Rodney King unwillingly participated in one of the most frequently viewed incidents ever captured on film. On that day, King, a black male, was stopped for a traffic violation by Los Angeles police officers. A passerby with a video camera captured the beating to which King was then subjected. Two officers, who were white, repeatedly hit King with their nightsticks for more than two minutes, even after he had fallen to the ground. Another officer, also white, kicked him several times. According to King's testimony later, the officers made racial slurs while beating him. King suffered numerous injuries, among them a broken leg, a shattered cheekbone, and a ruptured eye socket.

The police officers were subsequently charged with using excessive force, and when on April 29, 1992, a jury found them innocent, widescale rioting erupted in Los Angeles, resulting in $1 billion in property damages. Businesses owned by Korean Americans were frequent targets of the mostly black rioters. The riots also produced numerous injuries. For example, Reginald Denny, a white truck driver, was dragged from his vehicle and severely beaten by several black men.

UNDERSTANDING SOCIAL COGNITION AND SOCIAL INFLUENCE: DEFINITION AND EXPLANATION

The field of psychology that is concerned with people as social beings is **social psychology:** "an attempt to understand and explain how the thought, feeling, and behavior of individuals are influenced by the actual,

■ **Overview: A Biopsychosocial Context.** Following the chapter opening vignette, each chapter provides a brief overview of the topics on focus. Typically, important definitions are provided along with a sketch of how the biopsychosocial approach is brought to bear in the chapter. For example, **Chapter 5, Sensation and Perception,** defines some basic terms and concepts and then sketches the philosophical debate between rationalism and empiricism, explaining how the biopsychosocial approach helps resolve the debate.

■ **Stop and Think Questions.** Students should do more than plunge relentlessly through a chapter, a highlighter in hand and an eye on the clock. They should pause and reflect on what they have read. These Stop and Think questions appear after each major section in the text. Some of the questions are straightforward, intended to provide a quick check for the student to assess how well he or she has learned important terms and concepts. Others are more probing and require critical thinking. Answers to the Stop and Think questions are located at the end of the text.

STOP AND THINK QUESTIONS
STOP AND THINK QUESTIONS
APPEAR AFTER EACH MAJOR
SECTION TO PROVIDE STU-
DENTS WITH A CONCEPT
CHECK.

Stop and Think

1 How can a researcher demonstrate an instinct?

2 Are there motives that do not have a corresponding physiological need?

3 Think of an example from your everyday life of a motive that is well explained in cognitive terms.

■ **Summary Tables.** I have created Summary Tables for every chapter. These summary tables help students to synthesize and to assimilate large chunks of information. There are, for example, Summary Tables covering Evolutionary Explanations of Human Behavior in **Chapter 3,** Approaches to Emotion in **Chapter 7,** and Psychodynamic Approaches After Freud in Chapter 12.

SUMMARY TABLE
SUMMARY TABLES APPEAR IN
EVERY CHAPTER TO HELP
STUDENTS SYNTHESIZE AND
ASSIMILATE LARGE CHUNKS
OF INFORMATION.

Table 3.2   Summary: Evolutionary Explanations of Human Behavior

Approach	Key emphasis
Social Darwinism	"Evolution" of societies as a whole
Comparative psychology	Comparisons and contrasts across species
Ethology	Behavior in the natural environments
Behavior genetics	Genetic influences on individual differences
Sociobiology	Complex social behavior
Evolutionary psychology	Evolved psychological mechanisms

■ **Marginal Glossary.** To reinforce the way psychologists use specific words, key terms appear in boldface in the text. These terms, along with their definitions, are repeated in the margins. An overall glossary appears at the end of the book.

■ **Topics in a Biopsychosocial Context.**   Each chapter concludes with a section that examines a specific topic from a biopsychosocial approach. I have tried to choose topics that are provocative. For example, **Chapter 6, Consciousness,** closes with a discussion of Haitian zombies; **Chapter 12, Personality,** discusses gender differences in traits; and **Chapter 16, Health Psychology,** addresses shamanism and alternative medicine. The intent of these and other closing discussions is to reinforce the use of the biopsychosocial approach throughout the chapter.

I have also illustrated the biopsychosocial approach with figures throughout the text. These figures have a recurring color scheme that visually represents the biological mechanisms, psychological processes, and social influences needed to fully explain certain behavior.

■ **Summary.**   The summary is a bulleted list organized under headings that correspond to the major sections of the chapter. This will help students as they preview and review a given chapter.

■ **Key Terms.**   The boldface terms introduced in the chapter are listed at the end of the chapter, along with relevant page numbers. These appear in the order they were introduced in the chapter and provide another summary of the chapter's content, this time in terms of the key concepts. Again, these should be helpful to your students as they try to take away the major message of a chapter or study for an exam.

PERSONALITY IN A BIOPSYCHOSOCIAL CONTEXT

To study people in their entirety, personality psychologists have drawn on broad perspectives—specifically, psychodynamic, trait, phenomenological, and social learning approaches. Each approach emphasizes different components of personality, and all are in principle compatible.

Indeed, recent theoretical extensions of each approach usually acknowledge the importance of other approaches. For example:

■ Biologically minded theorists have attempted to specify the neurological basis for Freudian concepts (Gaillard, 1992; Katz, 1991; Thompson, Baxter, & Schwartz, 1992; Zuelzer & Maas, 1994).
■ Contemporary object relations theorists stress the importance of people's thoughts and beliefs about the social environment (Westen, 1991).
■ Trait theorists are interested in the specific settings where traits are (or are not) displayed (Van heck, Perugini, Caprara, & Froger, 1994).
■ Phenomenological theorists recognize that at least some of the cognitive processes giving rise to personality exist outside conscious awareness (Kihlstrom, 1990).
■ Social learning theorists now attempt to describe the idiosyncratic ways in which a person interprets situations (Shoda, Mischel, & Wright, 1993, 1994).

As these integrative attempts continue, a biopsychosocial perspective on personality will result.

Gender and Personality: Theory and Evidence

Let me conclude by examining a question of scientific and popular interest: Do men and women have different personalities? Psychodynamic theories, particularly Freud's original account, usually posit broad gender differences because men and women take different routes through the stages of psychosexual development. Trait theories expect to find gender differences in characteristics reflecting evolved psychological mechanisms related to reproduction. Phenomenological and social learning theories are neutral with regard to gender differences: Men and women may or may not have different personalities, depending on the circumstances they have encountered that lead to characteristic thoughts and habits (Bussey & Bandura, 1992).

Figure 12.1
Personality as Biopsychosocial. Although most theories of personality acknowledge its biopsychosocial nature, these theories have traditionally emphasized one particular aspect of personality and its determinants. Trait theories focus on biological aspects of personality, psychodynamic theories and phenomenological theories focus on psychological aspects (motivation and emotion in the first case and cognition in the second case), and social learning theories focus on social aspects.

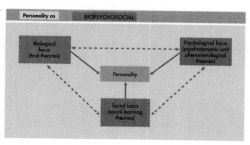

TOPICS IN A BIOPSYCHOSOCIAL CONTEXT EACH CHAPTER CONCLUDES WITH TOPICS IN A BIOPSYCHOSOCIAL CONTEXT TO REINFORCE CHAPTER CONTENT.

Ancillaries For the Instructor

Instructor's Resource Manual. Written by Margaret F. Lynch of San Francisco State University, the Instructor's Resource Manual (IRM) contains a wealth of teaching aids for each chapter: chapter outlines, lecture supplements, classroom demonstrations, critical thinking exercises, mini-experiments, self-test exercises, suggestions for additional readings, and an extensive guide to audiovisual materials. The IRM comes in a three-ring binder for easy reproduction of student handouts; the binder can also serve as a storage unit for collecting favorite lecture supplements and teaching materials.

Test Bank. The Test Bank is particularly appropriate for this second edition because it was written by the author, Christopher Peterson. The Test Bank features an assortment of multiple-choice, short-answer, true/false, and essay items that test applied, factual, and conceptual knowledge. Items are referenced by chapter, topic, skill, and text page.

TestMaster Computerized Testing System. This flexible, easy-to-master computer test bank includes all of the test items in the Test Bank. The Testmaster software allows you to edit existing questions and add your own items. Tests can be printed in several different formats and can include figures, such as graphs and tables. TestMaster is available in Macintosh and IBM-compatible formats.

Lecture Shell. The chapter outlines of the entire text are available on disk for use in creating your own lecture outlines.

Transparencies. A new Introductory Psychology Transparency Package contains 200 full-color acetates designed to accompany the text. The package features many transparencies specifically designed for large lecture halls.

Other Media. Fully updated CD-ROM, laserdiscs, electronic transparencies, presentation software, and videos are also available to qualified adopters of *Psychology: A Biopsychosocial Approach*, Second Edition. Please contact your Longman sales representative for more information.

Ancillaries For the Student

Study Guide. Written by Todd Zakrajsek, Southern Oregon State College, this manual has been extensively updated to reflect the new coverage in the second edition. It includes learning objectives, chapter outlines, critical thinking questions that illustrate concepts in the text, three sets of practice tests with suggested answers, key-term reviews, and a How to Study section.

Biopsychosocial Workbook and Practice Tests. Written by the author of the text and the Test Bank, this ancillary is designed to help students to think critically about the biopsychosocial approach and to prepare for exams. The workbook consists of a series of behavioral phenomena that involve biological mechanisms, psychological processes, and social influences; students are helped to see how these are involved in each example. The practice tests consist of 20 or more multiple-choice questions per chapter, with annotated answers.

Interactive Media for the Student

SuperShell Computerized Tutorial.   Created by Carolyn Meyer, Lake Sumter Community College, this interactive program helps students learn important psychological facts and concepts through drill and practice exercises and diagnostic feedback. SuperShell provides immediate correct answers and the text page numbers on which the material is discussed. A running score of the student's performance is maintained on the screen throughout the session. SuperShell is available for both Macintosh and IBM-compatible computers.

Journey II.   Students are guided through a concept-building tour of the experimental method, the nervous system, learning, development, and psychological assessment with this program, developed by Intentional Educations. Each module is self-contained and comes complete with step-by-step pedagogy. This program is available in Macintosh and IBM-compatible formats.

Acknowledgments

Texts have histories in which particular people figure prominently, and *Psychology: A Biopsychosocial Approach* is no exception. My efforts would have amounted to little without the assistance of many other people. The editors at Longman who worked with me throughout this revision helped me articulate my goals and then achieve them. Special thanks need to be conveyed to editorial assistants Jennifer Wingertzahn and Karen Helfrich; to designer Sally Steele, for creating a look that fits the text's message; to photo researcher Julie Tesser, for her help in choosing apt illustrations; to production editor Elinor Stapleton, for her attention to detail; to copyeditor Roberta A. Winston, for maintaining yet improving my style of writing; and to marketing manager Mark Paluch, for seeing to it that instructors noticed the products of my labor.

Leslie Carr helped immensely in her role as an adjunct editor. Rebecca Dudley, my current acquisitions editor, was able to bring to this text a tender heart and a tough mind, which I appreciated in equal measure. Editor-in-chief Marcus Boggs has been my publishing godfather for longer than either one of us would like to admit, and the very existence of this text is the result of his role in my professional life.

I express special gratitude to Michael Kimball, my developmental editor throughout the entire process of revising the book. Once upon a time, I expressed a wish for an editor who indeed would edit, using a heavy pencil as needed. In Michael, I encountered not just an appropriately heavy pencil but also a keen ear for language, as well as unflagging support for my work on the book and for me. Texts and people can have crises, and these are best navigated with a little help from one's friends, among whom I am privileged to include Michael.

Reviewers galore were consulted while this text was being revised. Particularly helpful, and not just because she was enthusiastic, was Dr. Margaret F. Lynch of San Francisco State University. Dr. Lynch read my drafted chapters with exceeding care and provided countless tips for improvement. The comments of all the reviewers, individually and collectively, did much to correct the substance and improve the style of *Psychology: A Biopsychosocial Approach*. Much thanks to:

Ira B. Albert, Dundalk Community College
Don Allen, Langara College
Betty Andrews, Jefferson Community College
Carol M. Baldwin, University of Arizona
Terence W. Barrett, North Dakota State University
John J. Boswell, University of Missouri-St. Louis
Saundra Y. Boyd, Houston Community College System
David Buss, University of Michigan

Christian J. Buys, Mesa State College

Jim Calhoun, University of Georgia

Sally S. Carr, Lakeland Community College

George A. Cicala, University of Delaware

June Madsen Clausen, University of San Francisco

Richard F. Dean, Anne Arundel Community College

Mary K. Devitt, Oklahoma State University

Ismael Dovalina, Palo Alto College

William O. Dwyer, Memphis State University

Val Farmer-Dougan, Illinois State University

Deborah Frisch, University of Oregon

William Rick Fry, Youngstown State University

Solomon M. Fulero, Sinclair College

Dashiel J. Geyen, University of Houston -Downtown

Harvey J. Ginsburg, Southwest Texas State University

Myra Heinrich, Mesa State College

Tracy B. Henley, Mississippi State University

Jennifer Higa, Duke University

David K. Hogberg, Albion College

Don Jacob, Odessa College

Mary Janssen, Indiana University

Gary G. Johnson, Normandale Community College

James Johnson, University of North Carolina-Wilmington

Edward Kardas, Southern Arkansas University

Stanley K. Kary, St. Louis Community College

Jane Kestner, Youngstown State University

Debra King-Johnson, Clemson University

Gerald Koff, Walsh College

Michael J. Lambert, Brigham Young University

Gary Levy, University of Wyoming

Paul E. Levy, University of Akron

Sanford Lopater, Christopher Newport University

Steven Maier, University of Colorado-Boulder

David G. McDonald, University of Missouri

Linda Mealey, St. Johns University

Daniel K. Mroczek, Fordham University

Ronald Nowaczyk, Clemson University

Elaine Olaoye, Brookdale Community College

Robert Patterson, Washington State University

Sheryl S. Peterson, St. Petersburg Junior College

Joseph J. Plaud, University of North Dakota

David Reitman, Louisiana State University

Gerald Rubin, Central Virginia Community College

Brian Sanders, Drake University

Kim Scheuerman, Westmoreland Community College

Connie Schick, Bloomsburg University

Lauren Shapiro, Clemson University

Friedrich Stephan, Florida State University

Lorraine Sutton, University of Colorado-Boulder

Christopher Taylor, University of Arizona

David G. Thomas, Oklahoma State University

Rodney Triplet, Northern State University

Debra Valencia-Laver, California Polytechnic State University

Frans van Haaren, University of Florida

Peggy J. Wagner, Augusta College

Shawn L. Ward, Le Moyne College

Patrick S. Williams, University of Houston - Downtown

Cecelia K. Yoder, Oklahoma City Community College

Lorraine K. Youll, University of Central Oklahoma

Kathleen D. Zylan, Lynchburg College

Finally, my students, friends, and family have taken great interest in this text, from the start of the first edition to the completion of this revision. Lisa M. Bossio labored mightily on behalf of this text and helped me approach a difficult task with freshness and enthusiasm. Thanks, Lisa, as usual.

To the Student

Perhaps your introductory psychology course should come with a warning label:

> CAUTION: YOU MAY BECOME VERY INTERESTED IN THIS FIELD AND BE PERMANENTLY CHANGED AS A RESULT.

Years ago, as an engineering student, I took an introductory psychology course as an elective and found psychology so interesting that I changed my major and the rest of my life as well. Even if you do not become as smitten as I did, you probably already find psychology interesting. My challenge in writing this introductory text is to inform you about psychology while maintaining your interest. Here is some advice about how you might read each chapter so that you take away from it the major ideas and the important details:

- First, look at the outline that begins each chapter. It is organized in terms of the main headings of the chapter. These outlines provide a "big picture" into which you should be able to fit specific ideas.
- Next, read the summary at the end of each chapter; again, it is organized in terms of the chapter's main headings.
- Scan the list of key terms at the end of the chapter so that you will be alert to these important concepts when they are discussed.
- Next, read the chapter itself, taking time along the way to reflect on what you encounter. Each chapter begins with a vignette that I hope you find interesting. Nonetheless, the purpose of these vignettes is not entertainment. Rather, each has been chosen to be a vivid example of the topics discussed in the chapter, and so read the vignette with this purpose in mind.
- As you read the chapter, pay special attention to the terms that appear throughout in boldface print. These are important concepts that you need to master. They are defined in the margin right next to where they first appear, as well as in an alphabetized glossary at the end of the book.
- Try to answer the Stop and Think questions at the end of sections in the chapter. These cover some of the important concepts in the chapter and are similar to the questions you will be asked on actual exams. Answers are located at the end of the book.

Now do all of this again and again, until your understanding matches your interest.

You should also keep in mind that I introduce you to psychology by using a point of view called the biopsychosocial approach. In making sense of any given topic—from sensation to learning to intelligence to therapy to prejudice—one should specify the roles played by biological mechanisms, psychological processes, and social influences. Psychologists and people in general have often approached the explanation of behavior in either-or-terms, playing one type of explanation off against other types. In many if not all cases, the more reasonable strategy is to combine explanations, and a biopsychosocial approach does just this.

This text uses the biopsychosocial approach from start to finish. The very first chapter introduces the approach in detail, and every subsequent chapter explains how it illuminates specific topics. In particular, the biopsychosocial approach provides a way to think about two of the most interesting aspects of contemporary psychology: evolution and human diversity.

Another emphasis of this text is on research and how psychologists conduct it. Psychology is a science, which means that its explanations are checked against evidence. A variety of research methods are used by psychologists, and each chapter in *Psychology: A Biopsychosocial Approach* has a section titled *Doing Research* that discusses how psychologists actually investigate a given topic.

A final emphasis here is on how psychology applies to your everyday life. The applications detailed in the text help to explain why psychology is such an important field in today's world. Psychology has long been relevant, even before being relevant was considered relevant. I try to do justice to this critical feature of psychology.

There is a great deal of material that *Psychology: A Biopsychosocial Approach* covers, and your instructor will, of course, help you navigate it. I have tried to organize each chapter in a consistent way, starting with important definitions and a sketch of how the biopsychosocial approach is used in a specific area. As mentioned, each chapter contains a section devoted to research methods and a discussion of pertinent applications. Each chapter ends by discussing a given topic in biopsychosocial terms.

Welcome to psychology, and remember my warning.

—*Christopher Peterson*

About the Author

Christopher Peterson attended the University of Illinois as a National Merit Scholar, graduating with a major in psychology and a minor in mathematics. He then enrolled in the social/personality graduate program at the University of Colorado, where he received his Ph.D. in 1976. He next went to the University of Pennsylvania for postdoctoral respecialization in clinical psychology and experimental psychopathology.

Professor Peterson is an award-winning teacher, a three-time recipient of the LS&A Excellence in Education Award at the University of Michigan, Ann Arbor, where he is Professor of Psychology and Director of Clinical Training. Prior to teaching at the University of Michigan, he taught at Virginia Tech and at Kirkland and Hamilton Colleges. He has also been a visting faculty member at the University of Pennsylvania and at the University of Massachusetts, Amherst.

Dr. Peterson's research interests include cognitive influences on achievement, depression, and physical well-being. He is coauthor, with L. M. Bossio, of *Health and Optimism* and, with S. F. Maier and M. E. P. Seligman, of *Learned Helplessness: A Theory for the Age of Personal Control.* He has written other textbooks as well: *Personality*, Second Edition, and *The Psychology of Abnormality.* He has written numerous articles for professional journals, and he has been on the editorial boards of *Psychological Bulletin, Journal of Abnormal Psychology,* and *Journal of Personality* and *Social Psychology.* He is also a member of the American Psychological Associations Media Referral Service.

What Is Psychology?

On December 23, 1888, the artist Vincent Van Gogh cut off part of his left ear and took it to a prostitute named Rachel. He said, "Keep this object carefully."

For the past 100 years, many people—including psychologists—have tried to explain why Van Gogh cut off his ear. You might at first think that psychologists cannot explain what Van Gogh did because it is such a unique occurrence. But William M. Runyan (1981), in a provocative essay, tackled the dilemma by discussing how we might explain any specific action of a particular person. Van Gogh's behavior was unusual, to be sure, but the subject matter of psychology includes both the unusual and the commonplace.

Runyan cataloged possible explanations that have been suggested over the years to account for Van Gogh's action, including the following:

1. Van Gogh was frustrated with the engagement of his brother, to whom he was greatly attached, as well as with his inability to establish a personal and working relationship with the artist Paul Gauguin.

2. Rachel previously teased Van Gogh about having large ears.

3. Van Gogh was imitating the custom in bullfighting of a victorious matador severing the ear of a defeated bull and then giving it to the lady of his choice.

4. Van Gogh was imitating Jack the Ripper, who killed and mutilated prostitutes, in some cases cutting off their ears.

5. Van Gogh was trying to win attention and sympathy from any of a variety of people, including his brother, his mother, and/or his patrons.

6. Van Gogh experienced hallucinations—hearing voices that others did not—and thought his ears were diseased.

Runyan tried to sort through these alternative explanations, each of which proposes a possible cause for what the artist did. Can all of these explanations be true? Are some more reasonable than others? How might any given explanation be tested?

Consider these specific questions: Do we have evidence that Van Gogh experienced hallucinations? Do we have evidence that arguments with his brother, Gauguin, or anyone else occurred immediately before he cut off his ear? Do we know that Van Gogh had been teased about the size of his ears? Or that he was a fan of bullfights? Do we know that he had read about Jack the Ripper?

Runyan offered no absolute answer to the question of why Van Gogh cut off his ear. However, he did succeed in arguing—in light of available historical records—that some explanations are more likely than others. On the one hand, there is no evidence that the artist had ever been teased by Rachel about the size of his ears. On the other hand, there is ample evidence that he behaved poorly when his close relationship with his brother was threatened. Van Gogh cut off his ear shortly after his brother announced his engagement; he later experienced emotional problems both when his brother married and when his brother's first child was born.

Do not be disappointed that Runyan only narrowed the range of possible explanations. This narrowing is the best any scientist can do. A scientific explanation can never be absolute. Psychologists are always questioning and testing their explanations, looking for better ways to account for behavior and mental processes.

UNDERSTANDING PSYCHOLOGY: DEFINITION AND EXPLANATION

psychology
scientific study of behavior and mental processes

behavior
a person's (or animal's) actions and reactions that can be observed and measured by others

mental processes
occurrences within an individual's mind that cannot be directly observed by others

Psychology is the scientific study of behavior and mental processes. Psychology usually focuses on the thoughts, feelings, and actions of individual people (and sometimes animals), and this emphasis distinguishes it from related fields such as anthropology and sociology, whose focus is on groups of individuals.

Psychologists use the term **behavior** to refer to a person's (or animal's) actions and reactions that can be observed and measured by others. Examples of behavior include an infant babbling, a child working a puzzle, an adult voting in an election, and a rat running through a maze. **Mental processes** refer to occurrences within an individual's mind—hopes and dreams, thoughts and beliefs, wishes and fears—that cannot be directly observed by another person. Mental processes become legitimate topics for psychology when we specify how to draw conclusions about them from behaviors we can observe. For example, although a person's frustration cannot be directly observed, we can argue for its existence if the person acts in a characteristic way whenever his or her goals are thwarted.

To say psychology is a science means that its explanations are tentative and evaluated against observable evidence. This characterization captures the essence of the **scientific method.** The details of this process are covered in Chapter 2, as well as throughout this book. For the time being, though, the scientific method is presented in more general terms.

Hypotheses are specific predictions that are tested in studies. They are usually derived from more general explanations called **theories.** For example, the theory of evolution is a general explanation of our current psychological and physical characteristics: They helped our distant ancestors survive long enough to reproduce (Chapter 3). A specific hypothesis based on the theory of evolution might be this: When people offer help to others in emergencies, they are more likely to do so for blood relatives than for strangers (Chapter 15). If research results agree, then the evidence is consistent with the theory of evolution—and also with several other theories of social behavior—but it cannot prove the theory of evolution as a whole. General theories like evolution can be evaluated only in light of the results of many different studies investigating many specific hypotheses.

Scientific investigations are sometimes exploratory, aiming only to see what factors might influence behavior and mental processes. Specific hypotheses do not guide these investigations. Regardless, all investigations must eventually be related to a theory (see Figure 1.1). Why? Science is not the mere accumulation of facts. Rather, the scientific method is the systematic use of these facts to evaluate explanations.

Scientific facts, or **data,** refer to the information psychologists use to test hypotheses in an investigation. Data are observable. What was the person's score on that test? How fast did the monkey push the button? How close are those two children standing to one another? Scientific facts accumulate as science progresses. In contrast, scientific explanations are tentative attempts to understand the data. The defining feature of an explanation is that it can be tested against the evidence and thus proved right or wrong. Unlike scientific facts, explanations do not accumulate. Instead, they pass in and out of fashion, depending on how useful scientists find them. There is always an attempt to propose better explanations, but "better" reflects a relative judgment, made with respect to competing theories.

■ **scientific method**
process of evaluating tentative explanations against observable evidence

■ **hypothesis**
specific prediction tested in a scientific study

■ **theory**
general scientific explanation

■ **data**
scientific facts

Stop and Think

1 What makes psychology a science?

2 What is behavior?

3 What behaviors are you performing right now?

4 What is the scientific method?

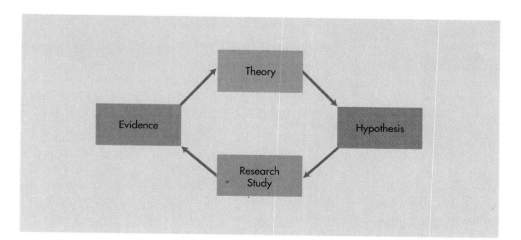

Figure 1.1
Scientific Method. What makes psychology a science is the use of evidence to evaluate explanations. A research study often tests a specific prediction—or hypothesis—based on a more general theory. But even if a study is exploratory and does not test a hypothesis, the evidence from the study is eventually used to evaluate a theory.

Everyday psychologists attempt to explain thoughts, feelings, or actions that are inconsistent with their experience, but the real miracles of human behavior are activities we may take for granted, like how and why we learn language, distinguish colors, or help others.

SCIENTIFIC PSYCHOLOGY VERSUS EVERYDAY PSYCHOLOGY

If we forget that science requires evidence, then we risk confusing the theories of psychology with opinion. Surely you have heard psychology criticized as being just common sense (or worse). But this criticism disregards the role that relevant evidence plays in psychology. We can understand scientific psychology better by contrasting it with a close relative that also tries to explain people's behavior: **everyday psychology,** the anecdotal explanations we use in the course of daily life to account for our own behavior or that of others (Heider, 1958; Kelley, 1992).

What Requires Explanation?

Although everyday psychology can provide insights into behavior, it differs from scientific psychology in several ways. First, scientific psychology attempts to explain everything that people do, whereas everyday psychology explains behavior that seems unique or fascinating. Scientific psychologists take the whole of human activity as their domain: the mundane and the exotic.

Everyday psychologists focus only on thoughts, feelings, or actions that are inconsistent with their experience. They have no interest in why we can recognize colors better during the day than at night, why we eat when we are hungry, or why infants crawl and children walk. Instead, they want to know why athletes overdose on drugs, why people poison medications in grocery stores, and why teenagers wear baggy clothes.

Sometimes psychology students are disappointed that scientific psychology does not focus on the bizarre things people do. Although psychology has something to say about the bizarre—remember our discussion of Van Gogh—its strategy is to say it in terms of theories about the whole of human behavior. The real miracles of human behavior are not the strange activities featured on daytime talk shows but rather the phenomena that most of us take for granted: How do we combine our sensations into coherent perceptions (Chapter 5)? How do we learn language (Chapter 9)? Why are some people happier than others (Chapter 13)?

■ **everyday psychology**
anecdotal explanations used in the course of everyday life to account for one's own behavior or that of others

How Does Behavior Originate?

Scientific psychology usually assumes **determinism:** All behaviors have causes. Everyday psychology usually assumes **free will:** A person's behavior is undertaken freely except in special cases, such as hypnosis, brainwashing, lust, and intoxication.

This difference between scientific psychology and everyday psychology comes into sharp contrast when psychologists are asked to testify in court concerning the merits of an insanity plea (Chapter 17). Was a defendant's behavior freely undertaken or caused by a psychological disorder? Onlookers may find psychologists' testimony in such cases to be somewhat strained. Indeed, there is an inherent difficulty in applying ideas from psychology, which assumes that all behaviors have causes, to the legal system, which—like everyday psychology—assumes that most behaviors reflect free will.

■ **determinism**
assumption that all behaviors have causes

■ **free will**
assumption that behavior is freely undertaken except in special cases

How Certain Are Explanations?

Tentativeness is one of the hallmarks of scientific explanation. All scientific explanations are subject to revision. Yet if we look at the way people in the street explain behavior, we find that they rarely regard their opinion as a hypothesis. Rather, once they decide upon an explanation, they rarely change it.

Explanations that cannot be revised are called **nonfalsifiable** because there is no way that they can ever be proved wrong. If they cannot be proved wrong, then any and all evidence becomes irrelevant, and the scientific method is not possible.

I remember a friend criticizing one of our mutual acquaintances as stupid and sneaky. "Wait a minute," I argued. "I think he is very intelligent. Look at his education, his vocabulary, his demanding job." My friend paused and then said with a smile, "I told you he was sneaky!"

■ **nonfalsifiable**
unable to be disproved by any observable evidence

How Are Explanations Evaluated?

Scientific psychology always checks its explanations against the facts, whereas everyday psychology may not do so. As pointed out earlier, scientific psychology evaluates its claims about the human condition against data (Chapter 2). If the available data support the explanation, the psychologist stays with his or her hypothesis but continues to evaluate the explanation against other information. If data contradict the explanation, then the psychologist concludes that it is wrong and tries to think of a better one. In contrast, the everyday psychologist is much less interested in evaluating explanations against evidence or continually revising them.

What About Exceptions to Explanations?

Scientific psychology offers explanations that refer to people in general, whereas everyday psychology focuses on specific examples. As a result, everyday psychology may seem richer. When scientific psychologists say "Supportive parents tend to have well-adjusted children" or "Learning a second language after adolescence is often difficult," some hear vague generalizations or altogether incorrect claims. The skeptic may retort, "My next-door neighbors are the nicest parents in the world, but their little Freddie terrorizes the entire block," or "My mother learned Japanese through a correspondence course at age 47 and had no trouble whatsoever." These are exceptions, but they do not disprove the more general statements that have been well established by research (Chapters 9 and 10).

All scientific hypotheses are generalizations, and one expects some exceptions to them. Meteorologists cannot predict every rainstorm, but they can predict yearly rainfall. Physicians cannot predict the course of every illness, but they can predict typical responses. Psychologists cannot predict every behavior of a given person, but they can predict typical thoughts, feelings, and actions.

In attempting to make sense of Van Gogh's behavior, for instance, a psychologist draws on explanations that apply to most people. The application of these theories to the artist may work well, but the psychologist must also consider that Van Gogh is an exception to what are otherwise reasonable accounts.

One of the goals of science is to reduce the number of exceptions to its claims. Scientific psychology has its share, even in well-researched areas, and such exceptions keep psychologists busy weighing the validity of any generalization. To this end, statistical procedures have been developed for making psychologists' judgments more precise (Chapter 2).

In contrast, everyday psychology focuses on the particular instance, not general trends. When the person in the street makes a pronouncement, we may find it more vivid, easier to grasp, and more believable than the qualified generalizations of a psychologist. However, everyday explanations may be so specific that they end up nonfalsifiable. Scientific psychology may give up vividness by offering generalizations, but it gains the ability to apply its claims to people in general, as well as the related ability to say whether or not the generalization is reasonable.

These points were brought home to me in my only television appearance, where I participated in a panel discussion on humor. I came prepared to talk about psychological theories and research concerning what people found to be funny. Among the other participants on the panel was a stand-up comedian who gave a short version of his routine. Before each joke, he said, "People usually like this one." Although I found the comedian's "explanations" to be circular at best, the panel moderator and the members of the studio audience were fascinated by what he had to say. They by and large ignored me.

Stop and Think

5   How does scientific psychology differ from everyday psychology?

6   Why is a nonfalsifiable explanation unscientific?

7   How does scientific psychology regard exceptions to its generalizations?

One of the topics of concern to social psychology is how groups affect individuals.

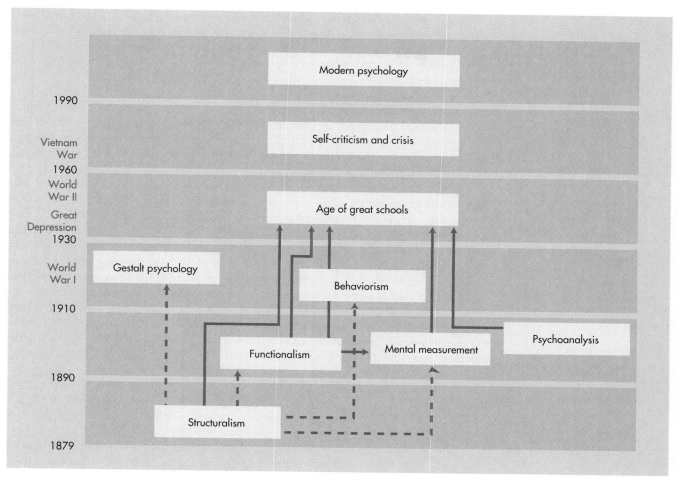

Figure 1.2
History of Psychology. Psychology began in 1879, when Wilhelm Wundt created the approach to psychology known as structuralism. Other approaches to psychology quickly appeared, sometimes in opposition to structuralism. These general approaches were dominant in the age of great schools, after which the field became more specialized. Psychology in the 1960s and 1970s underwent a period of self-criticism and crisis, from which modern psychology arose.

THE HISTORY OF PSYCHOLOGY

It has been said that psychology has a long past but a short history. Psychology as a separate science began little more than 100 years ago, but its stage was set by thousands of years of Western intellectual tradition (Boring, 1950). This section discusses the history of psychology as a formal discipline (see Figure 1.2). Over the years, the field has grown and become specialized. It has been marked by theoretical controversy, although psychologists today view different theories as complementary rather than opposing.

Setting the Stage for Psychology

We can assume that as long as there have been people, there has been the equivalent of everyday psychology. Indeed, we can suspect that the science of psychology began as everyday psychology thousands of years ago, when our ancestors started to examine their anecdotal explanations of behavior in terms of how these could be made more systematic and how they could best be evaluated as good or bad accounts.

Even today, the larger world raises questions about people and their behavior. For instance, clinical psychologists often find their topics of interest in problems surfacing within society that demand explanation and solution, such as sexual assault, crack babies, and mass suicides (Chapter 14). Social psychologists are similarly drawn to the study of why such terrible occurrences as ethnic prejudice, genocide, and state-sponsored torture are common across different cultures and how they can be prevented in the future (Chapter 15).

Minds and bodies in early Western thought.   Psychology as it exists in the Western world is usually traced to the joining of two intellectual traditions: concerns within philosophy about the nature of the mind and concerns within science about how the body works (Wertheimer, 1979). Psychology uses research strategies borrowed from physiology to answer questions about human nature that were first posed by philosophers.

The relationship between minds and bodies has long dominated Western thought and remains an enduring issue in modern psychology (Chapter 16). Are they the same thing, altogether different, or overlapping and interacting?

For example, the Greek philosopher Plato (ca. 428–348 B.C.) located the mind within the brain and regarded the two as distinct yet mutually influencing one another. Plato maintained, however, that the mind takes precedence over the body and that people come to know the world chiefly through their thinking as opposed to their sensory experiences, which, Plato argued, are highly imperfect as mirrors of reality.

In contrast, Plato's student and rival philosopher Aristotle (384–322 B.C.) regarded the mind and the body as one and the same. The only way to understand the mind, proposed Aristotle, is by studying the body. Aristotle's view did more to encourage the development of psychology as a science than Plato's view did because it legitimized the inductive use of observable evidence to arrive at generalizations about human nature. Plato's strategy, with its distrust of the information provided by our senses, encouraged a more deductive approach to understanding: We can better understand human nature by reasoning about it as opposed to going out in the world to examine people and how they behave.

The issues phrased by Plato, Aristotle, and countless thinkers who followed them set the stage for psychology by identifying basic questions about human nature. Often these questions asked about the relationship of the mind and the body. You will encounter the modern versions of these issues throughout this textbook—for instance, when we discuss how people come to know the world (Chapter 5), the meaning of consciousness (Chapter 6), the link between emotion and thought (Chapter 7), the way experience affects behavior (Chapter 8), how infants become children and children become adults (Chapter 10), and why people differ from one another (Chapter 12).

Philosophical trends resulting in psychology.   Psychology began as a discrete science in Europe in the late 1800s when long-standing philosophical and scientific trends came together. According to Wertheimer (1979), the important ingredients from philosophy included **critical empiricism:** the idea that all knowledge originates through our senses. Championed by philosophers such as John Locke (1632–1704), who proposed that people are born as blank slates upon which experience writes, critical empiricism leads us to ask just how this process takes place.

A second philosophical trend leading to the establishment of psychology as its own discipline was **associationism:** the notion that ideas are organized in the mind according to their original association in ongoing experience. Among the important supporters of associationism was James Mill (1773–1836), a British philosopher who was influenced by the earlier ideas of John Locke and others in the tradition of critical empiricism. A basic principle of association, as phrased by Mill and others, concerns the timing of our experiences. If we experience two events in close proximity to one another, we later think about them together. Associationism draws our attention to the links between thoughts and behaviors on the one hand and coinciding events in the world on the other hand. The psychology of learning, as discussed in Chapter 8, has long been dominated by a concern with associations, specifically between environmental events (stimuli) and behaviors (responses).

■ **critical empiricism**
assumption that all knowledge originates through the senses

■ **associationism**
assumption that ideas are organized in the mind according to their original association in ongoing experience

A final philosophical trend sparking the birth of psychology was **scientific materialism:** the idea that living things at their essence are part of the physical world and able to be understood in these terms. By this view, mind and body are the same. The techniques used to study the one are suitable for the study of the other. Scientific materialism provided the rationale for using scientific techniques devised for studying physiology to identify the workings of the mind.

■ **scientific materialism**
assumption that at their essence living things are part of the physical world and able to be understood in these terms

Not all Western philosophers agreed with empiricism, associationism, and materialism. As these ideas were carried over into the new discipline of psychology, not all psychologists agreed with them either. However, controversies often make a discipline more vigorous, as individuals take a stance on an issue and contrast the implications of their position with the implications of opposing perspectives. These discussions can lead to the growth of a discipline, sparking the interest and involvement of others.

As already discussed, the systematic use of observable evidence makes psychology a science. Scientific controversies therefore take place on a common ground. As you will learn throughout this book, the evidence suggests that broad philosophical questions like those being discussed can rarely if ever be answered in a simple way. Depending on many considerations, each position is sometimes reasonable and sometimes not. What results is a complex—yet coherent—view of human nature.

Scientific trends resulting in psychology. In the late 1800s, when psychology began, philosophers concerned with the mind built upon several important scientific trends. For example, the field of neurology had taken form, as physiologists began to learn about the details of the nervous system and in particular how our sensory organs work. Many of the questions that interested philosophers involved sensation and perception, so they saw in neurology and its research strategies a suitable way to test their notions about the mind.

Another influential scientific trend in the 1800s was the theory of evolution proposed by the English naturalist Charles Darwin (1809–1882). According to Darwin, species possess certain characteristics because they made the survival of their ancestors possible in their natural environments. In Chapter 3, we take a detailed look at evolution and its implications for psychology as the field currently exists. In the present context, appreciate that the theory of evolution fit with the assumption of scientific materialism to provide a rationale for the study of animals as a means of learning about people: Animals and people are products of the same process of evolution. Evolution as explained by Darwin stressed the importance of the characteristic environment inhabited by a species, so evolutionary theory further legitimized the examination of how individuals and their settings interact. Finally, evolutionary theory stressed the consequences of an organism's characteristics. Psychologically minded thinkers generalized this emphasis to a concern with the consequences of our mental and behavioral characteristics.

Yet one more scientific trend leading to psychology was the widespread assumption in nineteenth-century European science known as **atomism:** Complex objects in the physical world are composed of a finite number of basic elements (or atoms) that can combine in an infinite variety of ways. The periodic table of elements—a catalog of the building blocks of matter—had revolutionized the science of chemistry in the 1800s and inspired the very first psychologists to look for similar building blocks of conscious experience. If these could be identified, and the rules describing their combinations specified, then a presumably complete science of the mind would result.

■ **atomism**
assumption that complex objects are composed of a finite number of basic elements

Wilhelm Wundt: Structuralism

The first individual to identify himself as a psychologist was the German professor Wilhelm Wundt (1832–1920). In 1879, he founded the first psychology laboratory at the University of Leipzig. Wundt defined psychology as the science of consciousness and its subject matter as experience. The goal was to identify the basic building blocks

In 1879, Wilhelm Wundt founded the first psychology laboratory.

■ structuralism

approach to psychology that explains behavior in terms of how experience is structured from its simpler parts

■ introspection

attempt to identify the contents of thought by precisely describing one's mental experiences

of experience and how they are combined to create a person's complex sensations and perceptions. Today we refer to this approach to psychology as **structuralism,** which captures the concern with how consciousness is structured from simple parts.

Structuralism relied on the method of **introspection** to identify what is occurring in a person's mind. Using this method, an individual tries to look literally at the elements that compose his or her personal experience, examining mental contents and processes and attempting to discern what is fundamental about them. Introspection is not a casual report of what one is thinking. Rather, it is a disciplined description of immediate experience that avoids confusing experience with whatever external events are responsible for it.

Suppose you are watching television and are called upon to give an introspective account. You might describe the different sensations and feelings you are experiencing in basic terms like colors and shapes; that would be an acceptable introspection. But if you describe what you are doing as watching reruns of *Cheers,* that would be unacceptable. Norm and Cliff are not in your immediate experience but instead the result of your interpretations of your immediate experience.

The problem that early psychologists encountered with introspection was how to resolve disagreements. Theoretically, the immediate experience of all individuals should be composed of the same elements; theoretically, introspection by different individuals should yield the same results. What happened in practice, however, was disagreement, a result that called into question Wundt's favored means of conducting psychological research. Introspection as practiced by the very first psychologists could not be validated, and this method is remembered as unscientific.

Wundt should not be dismissed because his research method encountered difficulties. He is appropriately honored as the first psychologist. He phrased many of the important issues still addressed by those who study sensation and perception (Chapter 5), and showed the potential value of experimentation for answering questions about mental processes. Many of the important psychologists in the early twentieth century studied with Wundt at Leipzig, including Americans who returned home to establish the first psychology programs at such universities as California (Berkeley), Catholic, Clark, Columbia, Cornell, Iowa, Minnesota, Nebraska, Pennsylvania, Princeton, Stanford, and Yale (Benjamin, Durkin, Link, & Vestal, 1992).

Wundt's major contribution to psychology was his explicit statement about its purpose, agenda, and method. Subsequent psychologists disagreed with structuralism and championed their own ideas. Without structuralism as a point of departure, the history of psychology would certainly not have followed the same path.

■ Gestalt psychology

approach to psychology that explains behavior in terms of the relationships or patterns among mental events

Max Wertheimer: Gestalt Psychology

Gestalt is a German word that, roughly translated, means whole, pattern, or configuration. The notion of a gestalt lies at the center of one of the most important reactions to structuralism: **Gestalt psychology.** This approach took issue with Wundt's goal of first isolating the elements of consciousness and only later describing how those elements combine into complex mental events. Gestalt psychologists argued that conscious experience cannot be grasped by describing it in terms of its parts. Instead, experience is inherently whole and patterned. It is not the elements of consciousness that are important but the relationships among those elements.

A transposed melody is a good example of a gestalt. We can recognize a particular tune regardless of its key. The notes per se do not define it. Critical is the relationship among the notes. Another good example is the pattern of the pieces on a chessboard. Whether these pieces are made of ivory or plastic, whether they are big or small, or whatever their design, we can still recognize the same endgame.

The German psychologist Max Wertheimer (1880–1943) founded the Gestalt approach following his observation that a common visual illusion—apparent move-

Max Wertheimer created Gestalt psychology.

ment—contradicted the basic tenet of structuralism. Apparent movement is the phenomenon that makes us experience motion pictures as moving. Films are really a series of still pictures. Flashed in rapid enough succession, the pictures seem to move. The experience of movement cannot possibly be reduced to the elements that make up this experience because the elements are static, whereas the experience is not.

Wertheimer concluded that the whole of experience is not the same as the sum of its parts. This simple formula gave rise to a far-reaching approach to psychology that stresses relationships (gestalts) as fundamental. Gestalt psychologists studied sensation and perception and were particularly interested in how experience can be at odds with the physical world, as in visual illusions (Chapter 5). In these cases, our experiences tend toward simplicity. As we experience the world, we impose an organization upon it. Structuralism, according to the Gestalt psychologists, missed the most striking aspect of experience: its organization.

William James: Functionalism

William James made pioneering contributions to the approach to psychology known as functionalism.

■ **functionalism**
approach to psychology that emphasizes the consequences of mental processes

Another important reaction to structuralism was **functionalism,** which developed in the United States. Whereas the structuralists' approach was static, a classification of the elements of consciousness, the functionalists' interest centered on the consequences of mental processes. Wundt and his followers emphasized content; the functionalists emphasized process.

William James (1842–1910) looms as one of the giant figures in the history of functionalism. The brother of the novelist Henry James, William came from a prominent Boston family. He received his medical degree from Harvard, where he later taught physiology, then philosophy, and finally psychology. James was the first American psychologist. Indeed, James once said that the first psychology lecture he ever heard was one that he gave.

Historians of psychology point to his two-volume *Principles of Psychology,* first published in 1890, as the beginning of the functionalist point of view. In contrast to structuralism, which James reportedly found dull and nasty (Wertheimer, 1979), functionalism explored the everyday significance of consciousness—in short, how the mind is used.

Rather than looking at consciousness as a compound of elements, James likened it to a stream. James believed that consciousness is selective, flowing in one direction and not in another, as determined by personal significance. We think about food in the refrigerator if we have not eaten enough, about antacids in the medicine cabinet if we have eaten too much, and about other things if we have eaten just the right amount. Here we see the functionalist emphasis on the consequences of behavior. We think about different topics depending on our prevailing needs.

How different is functionalism from the psychology Wundt originally proposed? The major contrast is not so much in details—both approaches were concerned with consciousness and employed introspection as a research technique—as in spirit. Functionalism spoke to the practical and democratic temper of the United States in a way that structuralism did not.

In emphasizing consequences, the functionalists extended the scope of psychology. Psychology was brought into the real world, resulting in what we now refer to as applied psychology (Chapter 17). For example, functionalists such as John Dewey (1859–1952) were greatly interested in education. Their attempt to cultivate the optimal use of one's mind through instruction marks the beginnings of educational psychology (Dewey, 1913).

Psychology also came to include different types of people as legitimate subjects of investigation. Another functionalist, G. Stanley Hall (1844–1924), was interested in psychological development across the life span and was the first theorist to identify adolescence as a discrete psychological stage (Hall, 1904). American psychology is still

The behaviorist John Watson called on psychology to study only what could be observed.

■ **behaviorism**
approach to psychology that explains behavior in terms of observable actions

highly functional in its orientation, although psychologists today no longer identify themselves as functionalists.

John Watson: Behaviorism

The approach to psychology known as **behaviorism** was founded by John Watson (1878–1958), an American psychologist who was trained as a functionalist at the University of Chicago. Watson was originally interested in the behavior of animals. The tendency at this time was to explain animal behavior in terms of mental processes. Sometimes these interpretations became excessive, committing the error of anthropomorphism, attributing to animals the exact characteristics of people. We know pet owners who do this, talking about Spot or Tiger as fully functioning human beings, but the practice is hardly justified in light of the important differences between animals and people.

Watson preferred to interpret animal behavior in more objective terms. It is unnecessary to say that animals act in a certain way because they have intentions, if one can explain their actions by pointing to habits established through experience with the environment. Habits are observable and thus more plausible than intentions.

Watson's caution was understandable. Other students of animal behavior had raised the same objections concerning anthropomorphism, but Watson (1913) carried the objection one step further. If it makes no sense to talk about the mental life of animals, then why does it make sense to talk about the mental life of people?

Behaviorism became popular for at least three reasons. First, Watson's approach gave psychologists concrete methods for gathering data with which to test theories. All things being equal, research strategies that are simple to carry out are usually preferred.

Second, the research strategies favored by behaviorists not only were more straight forward than introspection as practiced by the structuralists but also produced more consistent results when used in studies. Reliable research findings are an obvious prerequisite for any science, and Watson proposed a point of view that made these possible for psychology (Chapter 2).

Third, Watson's approach was upbeat because it held that the human condition can be changed for the better. If what we do is the result of learning, then we can unlearn undesirable behaviors and relearn desirable ones. American psychologists were attracted to this rendering of the American dream in psychological language. Any individual, no matter how humble his or her original circumstances, can learn how to be a senator, a doctor, or a millionaire.

The rise of behaviorism is perhaps the most important chapter in the early history of American psychology. Its emphases on laboratory experimentation (often with animals), learning, the environment, and intervention to improve the human condition still characterize much of contemporary psychology.

Alfred Binet: Mental Measurement

The French psychologist Alfred Binet developed the first modern intelligence tests and helped to create the mental measurement tradition within psychology.

■ **mental measurement**
approach to psychology that regards differences among people as primary and tries to devise measures of those differences

Another strand in the early history of psychology was an interest in how to measure the ways people differ with respect to their psychological characteristics. The approaches so far discussed—structuralism, Gestalt psychology, functionalism, and behaviorism— usually aimed at making generalizations that applied to all individuals. The differences among people were not as important as their common characteristics. In contrast, those who pursued **mental measurement** regarded differences across people as primary, and they devoted themselves to devising research strategies for assessing these differences and relating them to other characteristics.

In the late 1800s, inspired by the theory of evolution, a number of researchers became interested in how people varied in their psychological fitness. Often these researchers' attention turned to intelligence, which they tried to measure by giving individuals simple tasks, such as counting the number of dots in a picture, and seeing how accurately and/or quickly they could complete them. The resulting scores were thought to reflect individual differences in intelligence. Notice the assumption of atomism behind this strategy: Intelligence is based in the efficiency of our sensory systems. However, these scores did not relate well to other characteristics of an individual that presumably reflect intelligence, such as how well he or she did at school.

The conclusion followed that these particular mental measurements were flawed, and here is where the French psychologist Alfred Binet (1857–1911) entered the scene to become the major figure in this tradition. With his colleague Theophile Simon, Binet in 1905 published a description of an intelligence test for schoolchildren that was based on complex tasks similar to those actually required in academic work. Children were asked to define words, interpret proverbs, recognize patterns, and memorize information. The better they did at such tasks, the more intelligent they were thought to be. Intelligence measured in this way successfully predicted how well or poorly a student did in school, and Binet's approach to mental measurement quickly replaced its predecessors.

Mental measurement began with tests of intelligence, which, as you well know, are still with us today (Chapter 11). However, the general intent of mental measurement, as well as its specific research strategies, has spread throughout all of psychology. Whether psychologists are interested in people's personalities, values, attitudes, abilities, or difficulties, they rely on Binet's tradition of individual differences and the sorts of measures he showed to be possible.

Sigmund Freud: Psychoanalysis

Our early history of psychology is incomplete without mention of the Viennese physician Sigmund Freud (1856–1939). He created **psychoanalysis,** a complex approach that rivals behaviorism in its influence on contemporary psychology. What is psychoanalysis? Fascination with sex, you may think, granted popular conceptions of the theory. There is a kernel of truth here, but this characterization does not fully capture the theory. Rather, psychoanalysis is an approach to psychology that explains human behavior in terms of unconscious conflicts and their resolutions.

The story of psychoanalysis begins with neurology, the study of the nervous system. As already noted, neurology became a medical specialty in the 1800s when knowledge of how the nervous system works made it possible to understand how it malfunctions. A whole new class of patients was recognized. People with mental and emotional difficulties were treated by neurologists, under the assumption that their problems stemmed from defects in their nervous systems.

Freud was among the first of these neurologists. His patients included people (mostly women) who experienced puzzling losses of physical functioning, with no clear physical cause. This disorder was termed hysteria. Although Freud approached these individuals as a neurologist, his achievement was proposing that psychological factors were responsible for their symptoms. He stressed the role of unconscious conflicts, many of them sexual. Freud regarded hysterical symptoms as a reaction to these conflicts. Treatment entailed bringing these unconscious conflicts into the patient's awareness, thus causing the symptoms to disappear.

Freud's original interest in hysteria led him to a general theory of abnormality, a strategy of treating emotional difficulties, a view of personality, and finally a comprehensive approach to the whole of psychology. Psychoanalytic theory regards people as complex energy systems. The energy is provided by instinctive drives, chiefly sexual and aggressive in nature. People seek to discharge energy, but the larger society typically opposes immediate gratification of sexual and aggressive instincts. People thus learn to channel their energy in other ways. Much of psychoanalytic theory catalogs these indirect means of discharging energy and what can go wrong if the process is thwarted.

■ **psychoanalysis**
approach to psychology that explains behavior in terms of unconscious conflicts and their resolutions

Sigmund Freud was a Viennese physician whose theory of psychoanalysis developed from his clinical practice.

Table 1.1   Great Schools of Psychology

Approach	Important event
Structuralism	Wilhelm Wundt established the first psychology laboratory in Germany.
Gestalt psychology	Max Wertheimer studied the illusion of apparent movement.
Functionalism	William James published *Principles of Psychology.*
Behaviorism	John Watson called on psychology to study only observable behavior.
Mental measurement	Alfred Binet created the modern intelligence test.
Psychoanalysis	Sigmund Freud described his first studies of hysteria.

Great Schools

Psychology in the 1920s and 1930s is often described as the age of great schools because of the central role played by the approaches just described (see Table 1.1). Theory and research centered on the issues that each approach deemed important.

Consider how advocates of these different approaches might have grappled with the puzzling behavior of Vincent Van Gogh. Structuralists would focus on the elements of his consciousness while he was behaving in self-destructive ways, whereas Gestalt psychologists would want to understand the overall pattern of his thoughts and actions. Of course, it would be impossible to ask Van Gogh to offer an introspective account at the moment he was slashing off his ear, but perhaps his paintings provide a more enduring record of how he saw himself and the world. Functionalists would focus on the consequences of what the artist did, whereas behaviorists would identify the environmental events that influenced his behavior. Those interested in mental measurement might compare and contrast Van Gogh with other artists of his era with respect to characteristics such as creativity, impulsiveness, and unhappiness; perhaps he fell at the extreme of all these tendencies and these factors explain why he parted company with his ear. Psychoanalysts would try to discern the unconscious conflicts that gave rise to his bizarre actions.

Following the 1930s, the importance of the great schools diminished, as psychologists became more tolerant of other points of view and more specialized in their own work. Structuralism, Gestalt psychology, and functionalism vanished as distinct approaches, whereas the strategies of mental measurement spread through so many fields of psychology that it soon became difficult to identify it as a discrete school. Behaviorism and psychoanalysis for the most part maintained their identities.

World War II

World War II played an important role in stimulating the growth of American psychology. The center of psychology moved from Europe to the United States. The Nazi persecution of Jews caused leading European scientists and intellectuals to immigrate to the United States, and both academic psychology and psychoanalysis in the United States were enriched as their ranks were expanded.

Further, the demands of the war spurred on applications of psychology to pressing social problems. Remember that psychology in the United States was always pragmatic. The war effort capitalized on this bent. What resulted were studies of prejudice, attitude change, group dynamics, and adjustment, first conducted in military settings and later generalized to civilian ones.

Psychologists who before the war had administered tests to aid in the diagnosis of psychiatric patients were pressed into service as therapists in their own right. Following the war, they created the field of clinical psychology, which uses the theories and findings of psychology to help people suffering with problems in their daily lives.

Postwar Trends

Psychology following World War II shows a number of clear trends (Boneau, 1992; Gilgen, 1982). Chief among them is the exponential growth of the field of psychology. By any and all criteria, psychology has become increasingly popular during the past few decades. The numbers of psychologists, psychology students, and psychology books increase every year.

Psychologists are even represented with some frequency in prime-time television culture. Consider Counselor Deanna Troy, Dr. Frasier Crane, and Agent Fox Mulder, all of whom—according to the story lines of their respective shows—have studied and now practice their own versions of psychology. To my great annoyance, many of the villains in the *Robocop* series not only live in Michigan (as I do) but are also psychologists (as I am).

Psychologists have also shown increasing specialization. In the era of great schools, somebody was simply a psychologist. Theorists attempted to offer general explanations. Today somebody working within psychology is a developmental psychologist, a clinical psychologist, or a social psychologist. Theorists usually present more narrow accounts. Researchers tend to study more specific questions.

Psychology has also moved toward increasing quantification. Many contemporary psychologists cannot do their work without using numbers. Theories in most fields of psychology have become so sophisticated that we cannot simply look at research evidence to evaluate them. Researchers instead use statistics to summarize the results of their studies and then to make inferences from them (Chapter 2).

A trend toward increasing application is also apparent in the recent history of psychology in the United States (Chapter 17). As already mentioned, clinical psychologists treat individuals with emotional or behavioral difficulties. Other applied psychologists work in such settings as hospitals (health psychologists), factories (industrial psychologists), advertising agencies (consumer psychologists), national parks (environmental psychologists), and locker rooms (sports psychologists). Some applied psychologists work in conjunction with lawyers in choosing jurors for trials, with politicians in mounting campaign strategies, and with architects in designing homes.

Psychology's Self-Criticism and Crisis

During the late 1960s and early 1970s, the United States as a whole underwent a period of turmoil and change. Much of this tumult centered on the unpopular Vietnam War, but every aspect of society was similarly scrutinized and criticized: politics, religion, morality. Psychology and psychologists underwent a period of self-criticism as well. Long-accepted practices and assumptions were called into question. Here is a sampling of the issues explored during this time:

■ The use of experiments to study complex human behavior is unethical.
■ Psychotherapy does not work.
■ Psychological testing is biased toward preserving the status quo.
■ Psychology in the United States is chauvinistic: Theories and findings have little relevance to people in other cultures.
■ Psychology tends to ignore women and ethnic minorities; when not ignored, they are depicted as deficient versions of white males.
■ Psychological theories have nothing to say about the good and noble side of human beings.
■ Results from laboratory studies do not apply to actual behavior in the real world.

These criticisms were not easy to dismiss. Indeed, some of them were raised by the most respected individuals within the profession.

Psychology Today

The United States survived the 1960s and 1970s, but ours is now a different nation. As citizens, many of us are more sophisticated, more skeptical, and more aware of the differences among us. The same holds true of scientific psychology. The criticisms raised in the 1960s and 1970s led psychologists to approach their science in a different way, expecting complexity and diversity.

In response to the view of people as puppets manipulated by internal or external causes, the perspective known as **humanistic psychology**—looking at people in terms of their freely-chosen choices (Chapter 12)—became increasingly popular. Further approaches to applied psychology appeared, trying to use psychological knowledge to solve concrete problems in the real world (Chapter 17). Psychotherapy became more pragmatic and—interestingly—more effective (Chapter 14). Alternative research methods were devised that allowed traditional questions to be explored more fully. Theorists and researchers became interested in the psychology of women and ethnic minorities, as well as the psychology of people in different cultures around the world (Bronstein & Quina, 1988).

Psychology in its earliest years was dominated by white males. Women and ethnic minorities were largely barred from the field. There were some notable exceptions, and the difficulties faced by these pioneering individuals were daunting (O'Connell & Russo, 1983, 1988).

For example, in 1890 Mary Calkins (1863–1930) wished to enroll in a graduate seminar in psychology taught by William James at Harvard University (Scarborough & Furumoto, 1987). The school's president told James not to admit her to the class, but James did anyway. The other students, all males, then dropped the class in protest. James continued the seminar, with Calkins as the only student. She later completed all of the requirements for a doctorate, yet Harvard would not award her a degree. Calkins nonetheless went on to a distinguished career as a professor at Wellesley College. Her work foreshadowed the interest of contemporary personality psychologists in cognitive views of the self (Chapter 12) because she believed that the self could be studied with

■ **humanistic psychology**
approach that looks at people in terms of their freely undertaken choices

Despite discrimination against her because of her sex, Mary Calkins had a distinguished career as a psychologist.

Since the 1970s, psychology has been keenly interested in people's diversity, especially across lines of ethnicity and gender.

introspection. Radcliffe College later offered to award Calkins a doctoral degree, but she refused (Hilgard, 1987).

Matters have since changed. A much more diverse group of people have embarked on careers in psychology and become leaders in the field. Indeed, one of the most striking features of psychology today is the large number of women in the field (American Psychological Association, 1995). In the 1990s, more than 70 percent of the bachelor's degrees in psychology were earned by women, as were more than 60 percent of the doctoral degrees.

Psychology is no longer a young science, full of naïveté and innocence. This conclusion is not cynical. Psychology matured during its stormy adolescence, and it is likely that the most exciting chapters in its history have yet to be written.

The cognitive revolution.   A principal occurrence in the recent history of psychology is that the field regained its concern with the mind. When the great schools of the 1930s waned, behaviorism was the exception that survived, ruling academic psychology into the 1960s. Learning theories dominated, and so too did learning theorists. But in the 1960s, theorists and researchers called for psychology to return to the study of **cognition:** the mental processes responsible for how we know the world. Ignoring the mind in any explanation of behavior had resulted in an incomplete view. New methods made it possible to study the mind without the pitfalls of introspection as practiced by the structuralists.

In 1967, Ulric Neisser published *Cognitive Psychology,* an influential book describing this new psychology of the mind. Since then, psychology has become increasingly cognitive in its approach. The so-called **cognitive revolution** affected not just the psychology of learning and memory but also social psychology, clinical psychology, and personality psychology.

Cognitive psychologists have often used the computer as a metaphor for the mind. The aptness of this comparison has stimulated a great deal of investigation (Gardner, 1985). Like any provocative metaphor, it is sometimes informative, sometimes not. Accordingly, as a backlash against the cognitive revolution, many psychologists have become increasingly interested in motivation and emotion (Chapter 7), aspects of people that are poorly explained in computer terms.

Neuroscience.   Another important occurrence in the recent history of psychology has been increased attention to the biological bases of behavior. Although some psychologists had long been interested in biological approaches, they tended to work in isolation from psychology as a whole. Under the influence of behaviorism, many theorists and researchers looked not within people for explanations but outside to their environments. Other than acknowledging that the nervous system somehow made learning possible, these psychologists ignored its details. Indeed, for the purposes of psychology, people and animals were regarded as largely interchangeable.

Matters have changed as technology provided more sophisticated ways of studying how the body works (Chapter 4). The ideas of biologists and neurologists are accorded more importance by psychologists. The complex role of the nervous system in all behavior has been recognized, as has the influence of behavior on biological functioning. Taken together, these changes resulted in **neuroscience,** a field that draws on a variety of disciplines to understand behavior in biological terms (Thompson, 1993).

The globalization of psychology.   The history of psychology discussed so far has focused on the development of the field in Europe and the United States. However, thinkers within African, Asian, Indian, Middle Eastern, and Native American cultures have been concerned with human nature as well. We can identify intellectual traditions within these cultures that parallel psychology and its predecessors in the Western world (Ansari, 1992; Duran & Duran, 1995; Myers, 1993; Paranjpe, Ho, & Rieber, 1988; Thomas, 1988; Wober, 1975). These traditions often vary greatly, in details as well as

■ **cognition**
mental processes responsible for how one knows the world

■ **cognitive revolution**
beginning in the 1960s, the increasingly cognitive approach of psychology

■ **neuroscience**
interdisciplinary field that attempts to understand behavior in biological terms

overall approach because every culture has its own way of thinking about human nature.

For example, as already explained, Western thinkers have often:

■ emphasized the individual over the group, leading to explanations of groups in terms of the individuals who compose them rather than vice versa (Chapter 15)
■ separated the individual and the world, leading to an interest in how they interact (Chapter 8)
■ distinguished between the mind and the body, also leading to an interest in how they interact (Chapter 16)
■ assumed that people are best understood as part of the material world, leading to an emphasis on our biological characteristics as opposed to our spiritual or religious aspects (Chapter 3)
■ believed that rationality is the most definitive and valued human attribute, leading to an emphasis on cognition as opposed to emotion (Chapter 9)
■ searched for simple cause → effect relationships, leading to an examination of people and their behavior out of context

Other cultures make different assumptions about people and their relationship to the world and one another, and so the resulting approaches to psychology differ.

Although Western psychology is obviously within our culture and throughout much of the world today, contemporary psychologists recognize that intellectual traditions other than their own provide unique insights into human behavior (Misumi & Peterson, 1990; Wang, 1993). Particularly as Western psychologists try to generalize their ideas to people in other cultures, it is important to adopt a global view of psychology and how best to carry it out (Shweder & Sullivan, 1993).

Stop and Think

8   What philosophical and scientific trends came together in the creation of psychology as a separate science?

9   Why is Wilhelm Wundt regarded as the first psychologist?

10 How was Gestalt psychology a reaction against structuralism? What other approaches to psychology were reactions against structuralism?

11 What trends characterize psychology after World War II?

12 What is the cognitive revolution?

BEHAVIOR IN A BIOPSYCHOSOCIAL CONTEXT

The final important event in the recent history of psychology is the recognition that behavior must be explained in terms of multiple contexts. This idea is so far-reaching in its implications for how to think about behavior that I use it as a way to organize this entire book. As has been explained, psychologists in the past tended to favor one type of explanation over all others. Many believed that people were nothing but unconscious drives and instincts, nothing but reactions to environmental rewards and punishments, or nothing but social puppets.

■ **biopsychosocial approach**
assumption that people and their behavior are best explained in terms of relevant biological mechanisms, psychological processes, and social influences

Most contemporary psychologists prefer to regard people as **biopsychosocial** beings, believing that people and their behavior are best explained in terms of relevant biological mechanisms, psychological processes, and social influences (Engel, 1980). Indeed, different perspectives must be used to explain the whole of behavior. Behavior exists in multiple contexts, and these provide the best way of understanding the diversity of people and their actions (see Figure 1.3).

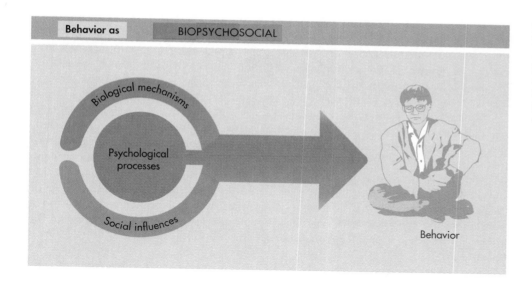

**Figure 1.3
Biopsychosocial Model.**
According to the biopsychosocial perspective, behavior must be explained in terms of biological mechanisms, psychological processes, and social influences.

The Biological Context

Behavior must be placed in a biological context. Behavior is made possible because of our bodies, which possess a characteristic structure and function. Thus, the attention of psychology is drawn to those parts of the body that shape and direct behavior: the nervous system, the endocrine system, and the immune system (Chapters 4 and 16).

At the same time, biology and behavior constantly interact. For example, among many animal species, increased amounts of the male hormone testosterone lead to aggressive behavior (Chapter 7). However, increased experience with fighting can also lead to higher testosterone levels (Rose, Gordon, & Bernstein, 1972). One of the tasks of psychology is to explain how this mutual influence between biology and behavior occurs (Dewsbury, 1991).

Is aggressiveness in males linked to the male hormone testosterone, or is it due to learning? Both possibilities could be true—which is why a biopsychosocial approach to psychology is so compelling.

When psychologists place behavior in its biological context, they become interested in the possible role of evolution (Chapter 3). Our characteristics, including behavior, exist and function as they do because they helped our distant ancestors live long enough to reproduce. For example, the sensitivity of people (and animals) to rewards like food and to punishments like pain makes evolutionary sense in that these typically involve events associated with survival (Chapter 8).

Related to this interest in evolution is a concern with genetics. Our genetic makeup is a blueprint for the characteristics we develop, and these may include specific behaviors. Although genes do not affect behavior in the absence of environmental influences, recent studies have shown that they do play a role in many forms of behavior, both normal and abnormal. Consider that the tendency to abuse alcohol runs through families. One reason is that some people—by virtue of their genetic makeup—are more likely than their sober counterparts to experience intoxication as pleasurable and hangovers as trivial. These people are more likely to drink, granted the presence of other influences on alcohol consumption, such as cultural norms (Chapter 6).

Psychology is not just the study of biology and behavior. A full account of why people think and behave as they do must include as well the psychological processes and the social influences that make our actions possible.

Psychological Processes in Context

Psychologists throughout the twentieth century have studied sensation, perception, consciousness, motivation, emotion, learning, memory, problem solving, language, and intelligence. These topics are still of central importance to psychology because people's actions reflect what they are thinking and feeling at the time they are behaving. These psychological processes explain how ongoing experiences are directly translated into behavior.

Much of this book examines psychological processes, explaining what is known about their determinants and consequences. However, psychology is not the study of isolated mechanisms. Even when we use a shorthand way of speaking about sensation, learning, or memory, we must remember that these processes do not operate independently of one another. For example, if we are interested in learning—that is, with how experience changes behavior—we also need to be concerned with how this experience registers in the first place (sensation) and with how it is later brought to bear on what we do (memory). Any given psychological process must be understood in terms of these other processes, as well as biological and social influences.

The Social Context

To place people's behavior in its social context, we describe how the social world influences behavior (Betancourt & Lopez, 1993; Graham, 1992; Yee, Fairchild, Weizmann, & Wyatt, 1993). All of us have a particular gender, a socially imparted role that provides our sense of masculinity or femininity. All of us are members of a particular family, which has a given structure and style that affect how we behave. All of us are citizens of a particular community and a particular nation. We find ourselves in a given socioeconomic class. We have a given ethnicity. We are participants in one or more cultures, sharing with others particular beliefs and values that have originated and developed over time (Cushman, 1990; Greenfield & Cocking, 1994).

These social contrasts among people are as fundamental as our biological and psychological characteristics. They are not a layer added to our human nature but instead critical aspects of it, influencing behavior by providing us with given goals, expectations, opportunities, and roles. All of these may differ markedly across social groups, and as a result, so does behavior.

Psychologists who study social contrasts risk political criticism (Scarr, 1988). The general public tends to interpret differences as deficiencies, even when no such implica-

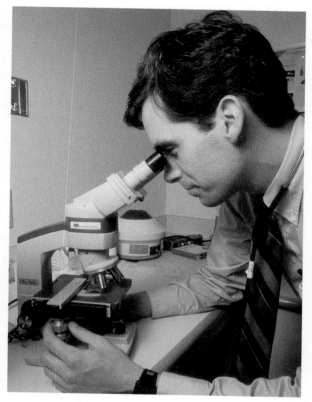

Behavior is influenced by biological, psychological, and social factors, and so psychologists study a great variety of topics.

tion is intended. To be sure, psychology throughout its early history can be faulted for treating white males as a standard against which other groups were measured (Gould, 1981; Tavris, 1992). Not surprisingly, these other groups were depicted as deficient versions of the standard.

After a transition period in the 1970s and 1980s when social contrasts were denied or minimized, psychology now tries to describe both what is the same and what is different about those from various social groups (Eagly, 1995). Psychologists are explicit that differences are not deficiencies. Indeed, social groups rarely differ across the board in their behavior. Research shows that a variety of behaviors are present in the repertoire of most individuals. When and where given behaviors are displayed usually depend on the social setting.

Despite the significance of such social contrasts, psychologists cannot focus exclusively on them. It is important to describe how men and women are different or the same, for example, but a psychologist's task is not complete until these differences or similarities are explained. Behavior is not the automatic consequence of given social attributes. Biological and psychological pathways lead from social characteristics to what we actually do. A full explanation needs to specify these routes.

Explaining Behavior in Biopsychosocial Terms

A mutual influence among the biological, psychological, and social contexts of behavior is probably the rule rather than the exception. Here is an extended example of how a biopsychosocial approach fleshes out explanation. Schizophrenia is a severe psychological problem characterized by symptoms such as hallucinations and delusions (Chapter 13). Schizophrenia is more likely to be diagnosed among those in lower socioeconomic classes, and social class is therefore likely to be an ingredient in any explanation of the disorder. However, the link between socioeconomic class and schizophrenia is far from perfect, for the vast majority of poor people are never diagnosed with the disorder and wealthy people are not always immune.

So, we need a further explanation. One possibility is in terms of stress: Poor people are more likely to experience difficult events, and these events may make schizophrenia more likely. This explanation is still incomplete, however because the disorder is not an automatic reaction to stress. Research suggests that those who develop schizophrenia may have a genetically based tendency to respond to stress with excess activity of a brain chemical called dopamine (Chapter 4). Among the psychological roles played by dopamine is the regulation of our attention (Chapter 5). Excess dopamine activity causes difficulty in separating relevant from irrelevant stimuli, and this difficulty may lead to the hallucinations and delusions that define schizophrenia.

Even this explanation is incomplete, however because some individuals develop schizophrenia by other routes (Heinrichs, 1993). Nonetheless, this account is satisfactory for many individuals with the disorder (see Figure 1.4). The important point is that the explanation includes biological mechanisms (genetic predisposition, excess dopamine activity), social factors (social class, stress), and psychological processes (difficulties with attention). Further, the influence among these factors is potentially complex. Consider that a problem with attention may produce stress and that stress may be an inherent part of an individual's attained social class.

We could make the account even more satisfactory by introducing further influences. For example, although schizophrenia is diagnosed at the same rate among men and women (about 1 percent), the average age at which it first appears is earlier for men than for women (about 20 years of age vs. 30). The reason for this difference is not agreed upon (Wyatt, Alexander, Egan, & Kirch, 1988), but researchers have shown that married individuals are less likely to develop schizophrenia than single persons are, perhaps because a supportive relationship protects against stress (Chapter 16). In our culture, women on average marry at an earlier age than men do, and this occurrence perhaps means that our cultural practices protect women against the early development of schizophrenia by providing them with a spouse. Thus, even a phenomenon

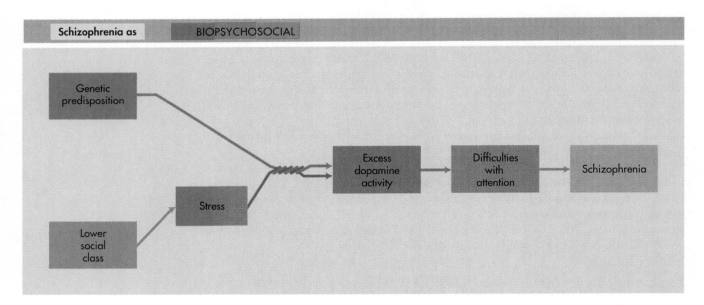

Figure 1.4
Schizophrenia as Biopsychosocial. Although regarded by many as a mental "illness," schizophrenia is clarified by approaching it in biopsychosocial terms. Influences on schizophrenia include both biological and social risk factors: a genetic predisposition and membership in the lower social class, respectively. When coupled with stress, these may lead to excess dopamine activity (a biological mechanism); such activity produces difficulty with attention (a psychological mechanism), which in turn leads to the symptoms that characterize schizophrenia.

regarded by many as an illness is clarified by considering the multiple contexts in which it arises.

Table 1.2 presents examples of phenomena that psychologists have examined in biopsychosocial terms, and you will encounter many others throughout this book. Because the biopsychosocial perspective was proposed for the first time with regard to people's problems, many of these examples involve physical or psychological disorders. However, explanations of normal functioning require contextualization just as much as explanations of abnormality do (Offer & Sabshin, 1991). The attempt to explain behavior in context now appears in all fields of the discipline (Cacioppo & Berntson, 1992; Sperry, 1993).

Stop and Think

13   What is a biopsychosocial approach to psychology?

THE FIELDS OF CONTEMPORARY PSYCHOLOGY

As explained in the section on the more recent history of psychology, the science has become specialized. Today, a given psychologist is usually most interested in one of the specific fields that have taken form around closely related issues and questions (see Table 1.3). A way to think about the fields of psychology is in terms of their respective emphases on the various contexts of behavior as just described. Although the focus of a psychologist is often on one context rather than others, all contexts matter. The ideas of one psychologist are supplemented and clarified by the ideas of other psychologists who work in different areas.

Fields That Emphasize the Biological Context

Biopsychologists emphasize the biological context of behavior: the anatomical structures and physiological functions that relate to our thoughts, feelings, and actions. They study the brain and nervous system (Chapter 4), how our senses work (Chapter 5), and the effects of hormones on our motives and emotions (Chapter 7). They may work on a microscopic level, investigating how a particular neuron operates, for instance, or they may tackle a broader question, such as whether psychological differences between males and females have a biological basis.

Fields That Emphasize Psychological Processes

Specific psychological processes are the major concern of many psychologists. They may study sensation and perception (Chapter 5), consciousness (Chapter 6), motivation and emotion (Chapter 7), learning (Chapter 8), memory, problem solving, and language (Chapter 9), and intelligence (Chapter 11). When psychologists take a cognitive approach to these topics, their field is called cognitive psychology.

Fields That Emphasize the Social Context

The social context of behavior is studied most explicitly by social psychologists (Chapter 15), who are concerned with how people's actions affect others. Seeking to understand the relationship between individuals and the social groups to which they belong, social psychologists investigate topics like conformity, obedience, discrimination, and altruism. Industrial-organizational psychologists study the behavior of individuals at work, often focusing on its interpersonal context (Chapter 17).

Table 1.2   Examples of Biopsychosocial Phenomena

Here are just some of the phenomena that psychologists have examined in biopsychosocial terms. Space does not permit a complete discussion, but stop and think about how each of these might involve biological mechanisms, social influences, and psychological processes.

Accident proneness (Millstein & Irwin, 1988)

Aggression, violence (Elliott, 1987; Lewis, Lovely, Yeager, & Ferguson, 1988)

Aging (Antonucci & Akiyama, 1993; Vaillant & Vaillant, 1990)

Bereavement (Hauser, 1983)

Child abuse (Teicher, Glod, Surrey, & Swett, 1993; Wartel, 1991)

Chronic pain (Katz, 1993; Pinsky, 1978; Whittington, 1985)

Compulsive shopping (Faber, 1992)

Consciousness (Wolf, 1985)

Deafness (Feinstein, 1983; Harvey & Dym, 1987)

Depression (Rosen, 1986)

Disability (Serrano, 1993)

Divorce (Oppawsky, 1991)

Emotional arousal (Blascovich, 1992)

Emotional communication (Lolas, 1989)

Empathy (Williams, 1990)

Exercise adherence (Clearing-Sky, 1988)

Fairy tales (Siegel & McDaniel, 1991)

Fear, anxiety (Nielsen, 1993; Perkins, 1982)

Hyperactivity (Maag & Reid, 1994)

Immigration (Hertz, 1993)

Infertility (Hertz, 1982; Williams, Bischoff, & Ludes, 1992)

Kissing (Morse, 1993)

Kleptomania (Goldman, 1991)

Language (Lenneberg, 1967)

Logical reasoning (Ciompi, 1994)

Marital discord (Sperry, 1989)

Mental retardation (Einfeld, 1992)

Nightmares (Blackwell, 1987)

Organ transplants (Pinard & Minde, 1991)

Parent-child attachment (Kolb, 1982)

Peer popularity (Miller, 1969)

Personality (Rothbart & Ahadi, 1994; Sperry, 1990; Wilson & Languis, 1990)

Pregnancy complications, birth defects (Smilkstein, 1984)

Premature birth (Tadmor & Brandes, 1994)

Retirement (Mattila, Joukamaa, & Salokangas, 1989)

Risk-taking (Irwin & Millstein, 1986)

Romantic love (Hajal, 1994)

Sensory acuity (Winogrond, 1984)

Sexual orientation (Friedman & Downey, 1993; Gladue, 1994)

Sibling relationships (Wood, Boyle, Watkins, & Nogueira, 1988)

Spatial orientation (Lugassy, 1986–1987)

Student stress (Vitaliano, Maiuro, Russo, & Mitchell, 1988)

Substance abuse (Wallace, 1985; Zucker & Gomberg, 1986)

Surrogate motherhood (Steadman & McCloskey, 1987)

Torture (Ortmann, Genefke, Jakobsen, & Lunde, 1987)

Unemployment (Schulman, 1994)

Voodoo death (Cohen, 1988)

Weight loss (Feuerstein, Papciak, Shapiro, & Tannenbaum, 1989)

Work stress (van der Pompe & de Heus, 1993)

Table 1.3 Representative Fields of Contemporary Psychology

Field	Emphasis
Biopsychology	Biological context of behavior
Cognitive psychology	Psychological processes like memory and problem solving
Social psychology	Social context of behavior
Industrial-organizational psychology	Behavior of people at work
Developmental psychology	Biological, psychological, and social changes across the life span
Personality psychology	Biological, psychological, and social differences among people
Abnormal psychology	Causes of psychological disorders
Clinical psychology	Prevention and treatment of psychological disorders
Health psychology	Psychological influences on health and illness

Biopsychosocial Fields

A simultaneous concern with multiple contexts of behavior marks other fields of psychology. For example, developmental psychologists study the physical, psychological, and social changes that take place throughout life, from conception to death (Chapter 10). They investigate how biological inheritance and particular experiences influence our behavior across the life span.

Personality psychologists study differences among people, often focusing on such traits as sociability, moodiness, and impulsivity (Chapter 12). These psychologists are interested in how an individual's thoughts, feelings, and actions are related. In short, they investigate the whole person in biopsychosocial terms.

Still other psychologists are concerned with describing and explaining psychological problems, such as anxiety, depression, and schizophrenia (Chapter 13). Their field is abnormal psychology, and it is closely related to the field of clinical psychology, which attempts to help people with psychological disorders (Chapter 14). Granted that people encounter problems in their daily lives, how can these be solved or even prevented? Health psychologists attempt to understand psychological influences on physical health and disease (Chapter 16).

Stop and Think

14 What fields of contemporary psychology focus on the biological context of behavior? On psychological processes? On the social context of behavior?

This chapter defined psychology and its subject matter. It also sketched the origins and development of psychology as a scientific field. Finally, it introduced you to the idea that people and their behavior are best understood in biopsychosocial terms. The next chapter focuses on research in psychology, after which we turn to detailed discussions of the various fields that constitute contemporary psychology.

SUMMARY

UNDERSTANDING PSYCHOLOGY: DEFINITION AND EXPLANATION

■ Psychology is the scientific field that describes and explains behavior and mental processes.
■ To say that psychology is a science means that its explanations are tentative hypotheses that must be checked against evidence.

SCIENTIFIC PSYCHOLOGY VERSUS EVERYDAY PSYCHOLOGY

■ People in everyday life offer explanations for behavior. This everyday psychology sometimes overlaps with scientific psychology, but it can differ critically by not being scientific.

THE HISTORY OF PSYCHOLOGY

■ Psychology began as a formal discipline just over 100 years ago, but its stage was set much earlier by Western philosophers and scientists who were concerned with the mind and how it works.
■ The German professor Wilhelm Wundt founded the first psychology laboratory in 1879 at the University of Leipzig. Wundt defined psychology as the science of consciousness and its subject matter as experience. The goal of psychology was to identify the basic building blocks of experience. Because of its interest in the structure of the mind, Wundt's psychology came to be known as structuralism.
■ The structuralists used introspection to identify the elements of consciousness. Introspection proved to be an unreliable research method, and rival approaches soon appeared.
■ Gestalt psychology, founded by Max Wertheimer, started with the premise that experience is inherently organized and not assembled from isolated elements.
■ William James was the leader of the American approach to psychology known as functionalism, which concerned itself with the consequences of mental processes. Functionalists believed that the proper focus of psychology was not on the mind's structure, but rather on its use.

■ Behaviorism began in 1913 when John Watson argued that psychology should study only observable behavior. Perhaps because of its emphasis on learning, behaviorism became extremely popular and influential in the United States.
■ By devising a useful way to measure intelligence, the French psychologist Alfred Binet helped found the field of mental measurement, which regards differences among people as primary.
■ The Viennese physician Sigmund Freud created psychoanalysis, a complex approach to psychology that stresses unconscious conflicts and how they are resolved.
■ The more recent history of psychology is characterized by great growth of the field, as well as increasing specialization, quantification, and application. The 1960s and 1970s were a time of self-criticism and doubt in psychology, mirroring larger societal trends, but psychology emerged from this period as a more mature field.
■ Among the important occurrences in the recent history of psychology are increased attention to the role of biology and the nervous system, the return of the field to the study of mental processes, and the globalization of psychology.

BEHAVIOR IN A BIOPSYCHOSOCIAL CONTEXT

■ Psychologists today believe that behavior is best understood in terms of the multiple contexts in which it occurs. The biopsychosocial approach to behavior stresses relevant biological mechanisms, psychological processes, and social influences.

THE FIELDS OF CONTEMPORARY PSYCHOLOGY

■ Contemporary psychology comprises a number of specialized fields. One way to organize these fields is in terms of their respective emphases on the biological, psychological, and/or social contexts of behavior.

KEY TERMS

psychology	4	free will	7	functionalism	13
behavior	4	nonfalsifiable	7	behaviorism	14
mental processes	4	critical empiricism	10	mental measurement	14
scientific method	5	associationism	10	psychoanalysis	15
hypothesis	5	scientific materialism	11	humanistic psychology	18
theory	5	atomism	11	cognition	19
data	5	structuralism	12	cognitive revolution	19
everyday psychology	6	introspection	12	neuroscience	19
determinism	7	Gestalt psychology	12	biopsychosocial approach	20

IOÁNES
STRATENSÍS
FLANDRVS
1570

Research in Psychology

In Chapter 1, the scientific method was defined as the systematic evaluation of tentative explanations against observable evidence. This strategy is so familiar to those of us in the modern world that it may be a bit startling to realize that science characterized in these terms is a relatively recent arrival on the historical scene. Although no single event or individual ushered in the scientific era, the contributions of the English statesman and philosopher Francis Bacon (1561–1626) are especially noteworthy.

Although he was born into a privileged family that had a strong presence in the court of Queen Elizabeth I, Bacon was the youngest son and found himself penniless at age 18 when his father died. He turned to the study of law and was appointed to a series of increasingly important positions in the court of King James I, who by then had succeeded Elizabeth. Bacon was eventually appointed Lord Chancellor, an office from which he was forced to resign at age 60 after being found guilty of accepting a bribe. He died several years later.

Throughout his life, Bacon wrote and published books, often on science, and these were not separate from his political life and concerns. He was the first person to believe that science would progress best if it were centrally organized and lavishly funded. Bacon's aim was to persuade the king to subsidize the scientific institutions he hoped to establish.

His rationale was that science could be useful to society as a whole, that it would provide people with a mastery over nature and allow them to

Francis Bacon's writings led to the modern scientific method, which uses evidence in a systematic way to evaluate explanations.

transform their quality of life. These ideas are taken for granted by many of us today and are exactly the sentiments that led the United States centuries after Bacon to create the National Science Foundation, the Centers for Disease Control, and the National Institute of Mental Health, among many other government-sponsored scientific institutions. But when Bacon proposed these ideas, they were unique.

Bacon's additional contributions to modern science included a detailed discussion of the scientific method. Previous thinkers had made use of observations to support their explanations, but Bacon was explicit about how a scientist might systematically make use of observations to understand the world. He specified three general principles.

The first was the principle of affirmation. An investigator should assemble all known instances of a given phenomenon to see what they had in common. For example, if scientists were interested in heat, they should study the sun, flames, blood from living animals, and so on.

The second principle proposed by Bacon was of negation. Here an investigator should assemble all known counterexamples of the phenomenon of interest to see what distinguished them from the positive examples. Thus, scientists interested in heat should study as well its absence in such examples as the moon's rays and blood from dead animals.

The third principle was one of comparison. Here an investigator should assemble instances of a phenomenon that differed in degree with respect to the property of interest. Thus, within the general category of instances possessing the quality of heat, scientists should try to understand why some were merely warm and others extremely hot.

Strictly speaking, Bacon himself was not a scientist. He had no laboratory and made no new discoveries, although he did flirt with how to make gold. Consistent with his principles, he argued that if a substance could be fashioned that had all the properties—density, softness, and color—that characterized gold and distinguished it from other substances, then none could dispute that it indeed was gold.

Bacon's contribution to modern science was the method and inspiration he provided. Both Isaac Newton and Charles Darwin wrote of their great debt to his ideas. One of Bacon's biographers commented, "When it was impossible to write a history of what [people] knew, [Bacon] drew up the map of what they had to learn" (Cranston, 1967, p. 235). As you read about psychology's contemporary research strategies in the present chapter, stop and reflect on how each embodies the principles of observation first spelled out by Francis Bacon.

UNDERSTANDING RESEARCH: DEFINITION AND EXPLANATION

To repeat, research is the process of checking hypotheses against evidence. All research involves making observations in a systematic way. The goal is to understand how different concepts relate to one another. Research makes psychology a science and distinct from everyday opinion (Chapter 1). This chapter takes a close look at the research methods used by psychologists. The focus is on four research strategies used across all fields of psychology: observations, case studies, correlational investigations, and experiments. In

Table 2.1   Examples of Specific Research Methods in Different Fields of Psychology

Field	Representative example
Biopsychology	Lesions: damaging a structure of the brain and determining the consequences
Sensation	Psychophysics: measuring the relationship between physical stimuli and a subject's psychological experience of them
Motivation	Thematic Apperception Test: assessing the strength of a specific motive, like achievement, by asking a subject to tell a story and then counting references to the motive
Emotion	Mood induction: having subjects read statements that produce happy or sad moods
Learning	Animal research: studying how rats and pigeons learn responses under highly controlled circumstances
Cognitive psychology	Nonsense syllables: showing subjects lists of meaningless syllables and later testing their memory for the list
Developmental psychology	Longitudinal strategy: following the same individuals across time
Personality psychology	Questionnaires: asking subjects to describe their own habits and traits
Abnormal psychology	Epidemiological surveys: studying the population as a whole to determine the frequency of specific psychological disorders and possible risk factors
Clinical psychology	Outcome research: investigating the effectiveness of psychotherapy by treating some subjects but not others
Social psychology	Deception: misleading subjects about the actual purpose of a study when it investigates value-laden topics, like prejudice or helping

subsequent chapters, more specific methods used within given fields are discussed as well (see Table 2.1). These specific methods can be classified as examples of the four general strategies.

Before discussing particular approaches, it is important to mention matters that concern all researchers: Investigators must devise measures of the concepts in which they are interested; they must show that these measures are consistent and credible; and they must evaluate the degree to which their research findings generally hold.

Operationalization

Devising a concrete and specific measure of a theoretical concept is called operationalization, and the resulting measure is termed an **operational definition.** An operational definition of hunger might be how quickly a person races through a cafeteria line. An operational definition of academic achievement might be a student's grade point average.

In everyday life, we are often quite careless in the operational definitions we use. It may be far from obvious to anyone listening to us talk just how we have gone about deciding that:

- Juan is a fun guy.
- Sarah is an intellectual.
- Professor Huong is demanding.

Our listeners know what these descriptions mean on an abstract level, but do they know the concrete rules we have used in identifying fun guys, intellectuals, or demanding instructors? Probably not. Could they go among the masses and find people that we would agree were fun, intellectual, or demanding? Again, probably not.

Everyday psychologists often fail to operationalize their concepts in an explicit and public way. Scientific psychologists, in contrast, start with clearly specified measures and an explicit description of how they are used. Researchers always study topics not in the abstract but in the concrete. To study aggression, a researcher may measure how many times a child punches a doll. To study memory, a researcher might investigate how many

■ **operational definition**
concrete and specific measure of a theoretical concept

A theoretical concept must be measured in a specific and concrete way called an operational definition. An operational definition of hunger, for instance, might be how many grams of food a person piles on a tray in a cafeteria.

words in a list a person can recall ten minutes after looking at it. Or to study intelligence, a researcher might ask subjects to interpret particular proverbs.

Confounds and Reactivity

There is no foolproof measure of anything, and so researchers must examine their operational definitions. In particular, they must be alert to **confounds:** irrelevant factors that distort results because they happen to be systematically associated with the factors of concern. Suppose a researcher operationalized love as the amount of money a person spends per week entertaining his or her steady date. Stop and think about the confounds that plague this particular measure, such as how much money the person has to spend and the activities the two of them prefer.

Let us examine the possible confounds in another operational definition, drawn from *Consumer Reports.* The editors of this magazine rely on operational definitions to judge the usefulness of products, and they try to make the basis of their judgments as public as possible. Nonetheless, confounds may exist. Here is one of their procedures for measuring "chocolate chip cookie goodness":

> First, the ultimate chocolate chip cookie is created to use as a standard. This is done by having two bakers modify the classic Nestlé recipe in all possible ways, creating a variety of different batches. "Sensory consultants" taste cookies from each batch and vote independently about which is the best. Second, store cookies are compared against the standard by different sensory consultants who rate how close each commercial brand is to the ultimate chocolate flavor, texture, and so on. (February, 1985)

This procedure involves an operational definition because it uses explicit measures that attempt to capture the abstract concept of concern.

■ **confound**
irrelevant factor that distorts results in an investigation because of its unintended association with the factors of concern

However, confounds that distort this measure may still exist. As a result of their expertise, the sensory consultants might have preferences for cookies that differ from the preferences of people in general, and this preference would bias their ratings. Or the oven in which the different batches of cookies are baked might become progressively more dirty, so that later batches would taste greasier than early batches when compared with the original cookies that were baked in a clean oven. If we did not know what was happening, we would conclude that the recipe, not the accumulating grime in the oven, made the critical difference.

One of the potential pitfalls of all measurement is **reactivity:** the alteration of a phenomenon by measuring it. Reactivity can be a particular problem for psychologists who measure what people think, feel, or do. Research subjects may act in a different way because they know someone is interested in their behavior.

■ **reactivity**
alteration of a phenomenon by measuring it

Reliability

We all know what **reliability** means in everyday life: consistency or stability. In research, reliability has the same meaning. Reliable measures yield the same result on different occasions. A standard step in psychology research involves checking whether or not measures are reliable. Perhaps you have completed a questionnaire and noted that some questions are repeated in different places. Whether the questionnaire aims at assessing an attitude, an opinion, or a trait, the repeated questions allow the researcher to estimate the measure's reliability. If the questionnaire is reliable, people should answer the same question in the same way.

■ **reliability**
consistency or stability of measures or findings

Reactivity can make measures seem either more or less reliable than they actually are. If you are asked the same question three times, you may feel obliged to answer consistently, even if your opinion fluctuates. Or a research subject may resent being asked the same question on repeated occasions. One reaction might well be to give a different answer, and doing so lowers reliability.

For reasons like these, researchers often calculate reliability in a subtler way than using the exact measures twice in a row. They devise alternative operationalizations of the same concept and see whether or not these different versions agree. If the different measures agree, the researchers will combine them into a composite (by averaging them together) that can be justifiably regarded as reliable. For example, in measuring the degree to which individuals experience a depressed mood, an investigator might ask people how frequently they feel sad, how frequently they feel gloomy, and how frequently they feel down in the dumps. These different questions presumably all get at the same factor, although in slightly different ways.

Validity

The **validity** of research means that it studies what it claims to study. This definition may sound strange. How could a researcher not be studying what he or she intends to study? Particular measures may be so confounded by unintended factors that they reflect only those factors and not what is intended.

■ **validity**
degree to which research studies what it claims to study

For instance, psychology researchers sometimes study competition and cooperation with a procedure called the Prisoners' Dilemma Game, based on a scenario like the following:

Two prisoners have plotted an escape a week from Thursday. The plans are set, but each realizes that he has two alternatives: (a) Proceed with escape as planned or (b) Speak to the warden and turn in his partner. Further, each realizes that the other has the same alternatives. A dilemma is produced because the cost versus the benefit of a particular alternative depends on what the other prisoner does.

Pretend that you are one of the prisoners in this dilemma. If you both opt for escape, you may or may not get away with it. If you try to escape and your partner tells on you, then you will be severely punished and he will be rewarded. On the other hand, if he tries to escape and you tell, then he will be punished and you will be rewarded. Finally, if you each turn in the other, the warden will have a good chuckle and punish you both.

On the face of it, the Prisoners' Dilemma Game provides an elegant operationalization of cooperation versus competition. It is highly suitable for research because it is simple to set up and to carry out. Once presented with the dilemma, research subjects can make dozens of choices in a short time. It is not even necessary to have a real partner. Instead, the researchers can give the subject phony choices attributed to a partner. In this way, they study how certain strategies, like consistent cooperation or consistent competition, affect the subject's own choice of strategy.

The Prisoners' Dilemma Game, for all its virtues as a research tool, has been criticized on the grounds of validity. Think of the differences between this laboratory procedure and real competition and cooperation, like that between Burger King and McDonald's, between South Korea and North Korea, or between you and your laboratory partner in organic chemistry. Are these differences critical in defining what we mean by competition and cooperation?

If the Prisoners' Dilemma Game operationalizes competition and cooperation by leaving out a necessary element, then it is not valid. The game usually allows no communication between a subject and his or her partner. In everyday life, those who cooperate or compete are usually in contact with each other. Is this feature critical? Also, this game often uses trivial stakes, like pennies or imaginary points. In everyday life, the stakes are high: money, fame, even the survival of humankind. Is this feature critical?

You can judge for yourself the validity of the Prisoners' Dilemma Game, but note that validity is not an all-or-nothing proposition. Particular procedures may be more or less valid than other procedures for given purposes, and they must be judged accordingly. Consider the use of animals in psychology experiments. Is this strategy a valid way to understand human beings? The answer depends on the aspect of human behavior in which you are interested. If you want to know how people learn simple habits, studies using animals may be quite informative. If you are interested in how people learn to play chess, studies using animals are probably not valid.

Generalization

■ **generalization**
how far and how well findings from a given study can be applied

■ **sample**
actual group of research subjects investigated in a study

■ **population**
larger group to which a researcher wishes to generalize from a study of a particular sample

Although researchers study particular animals or people, they usually intend to arrive at general conclusions. **Generalization,** how far and how well the findings from a given study can be applied, is therefore another concern to researchers. A useful distinction here is between samples and populations. A **sample** is the actual group of research subjects investigated in a study: 12 toddlers observed at a nursery school down the block, 96 college students attending a school in Florida, or 27 white rats running through a maze. In contrast, a **population** is the larger group to which a researcher wishes to generalize from a study of a particular sample: children, young adults, or mammals.

The more a given sample resembles the population of interest, the more widely the generalizations apply. The ideal way to achieve a sample that resembles the population of concern is to have equal access to all members of the population and then to select research subjects at random. All things being equal, the larger the sample, the more likely it is to resemble the population.

For example, researchers interested in the memory of older adults would probably not solicit volunteers for their study by explicitly advertising it as an investigation of memory. A sample of subjects obtained in this way might well be biased in the direction of those with excellent memories. Nor would researchers wish to study only two or

To allow generalization of their conclusions, researchers choose samples that represent the larger population of interest to them. To what population could one best generalize investigations of these particular individuals?

three individuals. Even if these subjects were chosen at random from a larger group of older adults, they might by chance alone differ from the typical individual.

For practical reasons, the ideal of a perfectly representative sample is virtually impossible to achieve. The best samples—at least in this sense—are usually public opinion polls (Chapter 15), wherein people are contacted by ringing doorbells, sending letters, or making phone calls on a random basis. But polls are costly and still end up not fully representing certain groups, such as those without permanent homes.

Recognizing the difficulties involved in broad generalization, some researchers opt for caution and phrase their conclusions in narrow ways. They protect themselves from criticism, but they sacrifice applicability of their findings. Deciding just how far to generalize results is a constant challenge.

Stop and Think

1 Suggest an operational definition of anger.

2 Can a measure be reliable but not valid, or vice versa?

3 Find a newspaper article describing the results of a psychology study. What is the sample, and what is the population?

OBSERVATIONS

With an appreciation of operationalization, reliability, validity, and generalization, let us now turn to some of the actual methods psychologists use. In one strategy of doing psychological research, behavior is observed as it naturally occurs. With this strategy, called **naturalistic observation,** the researcher tries to blend into the environment, disrupting behavior as little as possible in the attempt to describe what actually happens.

For example, Wachs and Desai (1993), studying how parents structure the environment for their children, observed 56 pairs of mothers and toddlers by visiting their homes and recording what ensued. In each case, the researchers visited on six different occasions and stayed for 45 minutes. They had a detailed and explicit list of the behaviors

■ **naturalistic observation**
research strategy in which behavior is observed as it naturally occurs

In natural observation, the researcher tries to blend into the environment and observe behavior as it actually occurs. One must always consider the possibility that a researcher's presence has some effect on others' behavior.

of interest to them, and they noted each occurrence. Did a mother specify to her child the names of objects? Did she demonstrate to the child how objects were used? The more frequently a mother structured the child's environment in these ways, the more likely the child was to turn to her when distressed, showing that a well-structured environment is associated with a secure attachment of the child to the parent (Chapter 10).

Sometimes researchers decide that the best way to study ongoing behavior is to enter into it. This approach is called **participant observation.** By participating carefully, researchers may be less obtrusive than if they sit on the sidelines. If an investigator is studying behavior in a bar or a shopping mall, it would make sense to order a beverage in the first case and to tote a shopping bag in the second.

■ **participant observation**
research strategy in which behavior is observed as it naturally occurs by joining into it

Weaknesses of Observations

In doing observational studies, researchers must not create or overly influence what they are attempting to study, although there is always a risk of this possibility. We have no guarantee, for example, that the presence of researchers taking notes in the corner of a living room does not affect how parents and children interact. Under the scrutiny of a psychologist, many children and most parents would be on their best behavior, which may or may not reflect their typical ways of acting. Similarly, the participant observer in a bar who buys repeated rounds of drinks for the other patrons, starts an argument about politics, or flirts with the bartender obviously weakens the study he or she is trying to conduct.

Researchers who use observational methods therefore try to minimize any disruptions their presence might cause. In their study of mothers and children, for instance, Wachs and Desai (1993) discarded their observations from the initial two visits, hoping that by then the families would have become accustomed to them. Participant observers often carry out their studies over months or even years, again with the hope that their presence will eventually be accepted.

Another potential weakness of observational methods is that researchers may bring unintentional biases to what they observe. Although their intent is to describe what happens in objective terms, such description can be distorted by expectations (Chapter 5). If an observer is testing a specific hypothesis, he or she may be more likely to notice confirming behaviors than disconfirming ones. Observational studies usually try to minimize such problems by making the rules of observation—the operationalizations—as explicit and concrete as possible. Studies using observation work best when they are meticulously planned.

Strengths of Observations

If the reactivity inherent in observational investigations can be minimized, researchers have a useful approach. The notable strength of observations is that they capture behavior as it occurs. Other research methods can be criticized as artificial, studying behavior under special conditions that may limit generalization. Observational studies, especially when carried out over a considerable period, provide rich information about what actually occurs when people behave. The social context of behavior, in particular, may be clarified by this approach.

To summarize, observational studies allow accurate descriptions of what people do, so long as reactivity does not overly distort observations and so long as biases based on expectations can be minimized. The goal of psychology is to explain behavior in general, not just behavior as it occurs in special circumstances. The results of observational studies can be critical in judging the generality of psychological explanations.

Stop and Think

4   Describe how observations might be used to investigate the effects of television on violence.

5   What are the strengths and weaknesses of observations as a research strategy?

CASE STUDIES

A second method of research is the **case study,** an intensive investigation of a single subject or group. Case studies are sometimes dismissed as unscientific, but this criticism is too harsh. When conducted correctly, a case study involves the testing of a hypothesis against evidence, the essence of the scientific method. At the same time, it is worth considering why case studies are open to criticism.

Sigmund Freud (1909a) reported one of psychology's best-known case studies: the case of Little Hans, a 5-year-old boy who was afraid of horses. According to Freud's interpretation, Hans was not afraid of horses per se. Rather, Hans was afraid of his father; in particular, he feared that his father planned to castrate him because of the unconscious sexual desires Hans harbored for his mother. Where do horses enter into this explanation? Freud believed that Little Hans did not consciously acknowledge his fear of castration at the hands of his father. Instead, the boy displaced his fear from Dad onto horses because his father was large and powerful.

Freud's explanation of Hans's fear may or may not strike you as plausible, but it is possible to test it against evidence. We can break his explanation down into its major components:

- Little Hans harbors sexual desires for his mother.
- Little Hans fears his father will retaliate.
- Little Hans transforms his fear of his father into fear of horses.

Freud provided evidence in support of each of these components. However, the evidence strikes some readers as tenuous (Wolpe & Rachman, 1960).

Freud used the following story, related by the boy's father, as evidence for Little Hans's sexual desires:

> This morning Hans was given his usual daily bath by his mother and afterwards dried and powdered. As his mother was powdering round his penis and taking care not to touch it, Hans said: "Why don't you put your finger there?"
>
> *Mother:* "Because that'd be piggish."
> *Hans:* "What's that? Piggish? Why?"
> *Mother:* "Because it's not proper."
> *Hans (laughing):* "But it's great fun." (p. 19)

■ **case study**
intensive investigation of a single subject or group

[handwritten margin note: Hans desired his mom, feared his dad would castrate him]

Is this incident good evidence for Freud's hypothesis that Little Hans sexually desired his mother? Not exactly. The incident shows that he wanted his mother to touch his penis and that he thought it would be fun. But it might well have been a spur-of-the-moment comment. Freud's hypothesis requires that this wish be a rather constant one, and so we would want to hear about repeated instances of Little Hans asking his mother to touch him. Instead, Freud gives evidence that Little Hans was preoccupied with his penis, as are many males. However, this evidence is not relevant to the hypothesis.

Weaknesses of Case Studies

The case study of Little Hans illustrates some of the weaknesses in this method of research. First, the reliability of information may be suspect. Freud obtained evidence secondhand (from Little Hans's father) as well as after the fact, and inaccuracy might have crept into the process.

Second, conclusions about links between potential causes and effects may not be valid. Freud presented the case of Little Hans in chronological order, trying to explain subsequent events as the result of earlier ones. So, Freud placed great emphasis on the birth of a little girl into the family and on Hans's observation that her genitals were different from his own. But how can we be certain that events would have happened differently had no little girl joined the family? We cannot, and thus the problem of inferring causality plagues all case studies that stress the critical role of singular events.

Third, how does one generalize from a case study? Even if everything Freud reported about Little Hans were perfectly reliable and valid, can we treat Little Hans as the prototypical little boy? Freud used this case study to argue for the universality of these impulses among young males, but obviously, that generalization is unwarranted without further studies.

Strengths of Case Studies

Freud's case study of Little Hans was flawed, but many of the difficulties enumerated are not inherent problems with this research strategy. They can be surmounted, leaving certain strengths. For example, case studies need not rely on the retrospective memory of the researcher or informants. Today, tape recorders or video cameras can be used to preserve information (Luborsky, 1970). Moreover, some researchers work from permanent documents like letters, diaries, or newspaper interviews (Allport, 1942).

A case study can be used to draw tentative conclusions about causes and effects if the investigator repeatedly tests the causal hypothesis with available information. For instance, Freud's interpretation of Little Hans's phobia leads to the following prediction:

increased worry about father's revenge → increased fear of horses

In other words, immediately following a rebuke by his father, the boy should be more afraid of horses than immediately following reassurance. A researcher might therefore pay attention to how Little Hans reacts to horses following rebukes versus reassurances. If Freud's hypothesis is correct, what pattern of behavior should be observed?

The researcher might even arrange rebukes or reassurances on the part of Hans's father and then expose the boy to a horse to see how frightened he becomes. How might you operationalize fear in this case? Perhaps the intensity and duration of shrieks by Little Hans could be used to measure his fear.

Finally, although a case study can never establish what is generally true about people, sometimes generalization is not the psychologist's purpose. One of the best reasons to use a case study is to provide a solid counterexample to a prevailing theory.

For instance, thinkers for centuries assumed that language was a uniquely human ability. All the evidence was certainly on their side because they had never encountered a talking animal. But in the 1960s and 1970s, several research groups reported success in teaching an ape to use language (Chapter 9). Although their conclusions continue to be controversial, no one dismisses them because they are based on studies of single subjects. The importance of these case studies is their challenge to conventional wisdom about animals' ability to master language.

Another reason for using a case study is that it may be the only way to investigate a rare phenomenon. Certain individuals or events are so singular that they are encountered only once or a few times in the life of a researcher. Are these individuals or events therefore off-limits for science? One would hope not.

In sum, investigations using the case study strategy have notable strengths: They provide rich detail about their subject matter; they demonstrate what may or may not be possible; and they may be the only way for researchers to study rare phenomena. On the other hand, case studies can encounter problems with accuracy of information, causal inference, and representativeness.

Stop and Think

6 Describe how a case study might be used to investigate the effects of television on violence.

7 What are the strengths and weaknesses of case studies as a research strategy?

CORRELATIONAL INVESTIGATIONS

What is the relationship between college grades and later income? Is good health associated with particular habits? Is divorce linked to emotional problems among children? Such questions can be investigated by gathering data pertaining to these factors and then seeing how those data are associated. A study that proceeds in this way is called a **correlational investigation.** The word *correlation* comes from *co-relation:* literally, the relation between two variables (Galton, 1888).

Two related questions concern researchers who conduct correlational investigations: Do two factors show any association at all? If so, how strong is this association? A strong relationship allows us to predict one factor from the other with great certainty. A weak relationship makes prediction much more tentative.

A positive correlation describes a relationship in which increases in one variable are associated with increases in the other variable, and vice versa (see Figure 2.1). For a simple example, hat size and shoe size are positively correlated. There may be exceptions—people with big feet and a small head, like Charlie Chaplin, or people with small feet and a big head, like Nancy Reagan. But most people who wear large hats also wear large shoes, and most people who wear small hats also wear small shoes.

In contrast, a negative correlation describes a relationship in which increases in one variable are associated with decreases in the other variable, and vice versa (again see Figure 2.1). Consider a group of parents. It is likely that the more children each set of parents has in college at the present time, the fewer expensive vacations each plans for the next year.

Finally, a zero correlation describes a relationship between two variables that have nothing to do with each other (once more see Figure 2.1). Increases or decreases in one variable tell you nothing about increases or decreases in the other. A student's college grade point average probably has a zero correlation with the length of his or her earlobes. The amount of spare change in a person's pocket probably has a zero correlation with his or her social security number.

Many of the hypotheses that concern psychologists can be answered with information about the correlations between variables. Accordingly, the correlational research strategy is widely used. Here is an example described by Friend (1994). Health psychologists have long suspected that people who are chronically angry put themselves at risk

■ **correlational investigation**
research strategy that ascertains how different factors are associated with one another

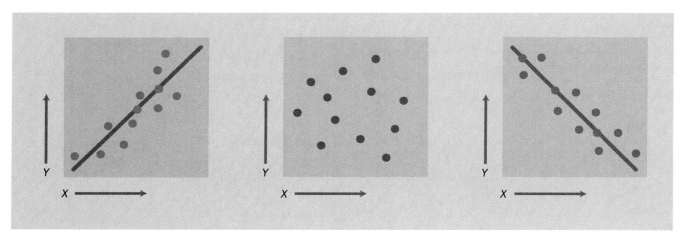

Figure 2.1
Examples of Correlations. What is the relationship between two variables? In the graph on the left, increases in one variable are associated with increases in the other. In the graph on the right, increases in one variable are associated with decreases in the other. In the middle graph, there is no relationship between the two variables.

for heart disease (Chapter 16). The Gallup Organization was asked to survey adults in ten American cities, asking them questions like:

1. You are in an express checkout line at the supermarket and a sign says "no more than ten items, please." Are you more likely to:

    a. Pick up a magazine to pass the time, or
    b. Glance ahead to see if anyone in front of you has more than ten items.

2. When you are stuck in a traffic jam:

    a. You usually are not particularly upset, or
    b. You quickly start to feel irritated and annoyed.

Each survey respondent was given a score based on the number of "angry" responses endorsed. These scores were then averaged for people in each city, thereby allowing the cities to be arranged from least hostile (Honolulu) to most hostile (Philadelphia).

These hostility scores were then correlated with information already available about the death rate in each city due to heart disease. The results are shown in Figure 2.2, and

According to correlational investigations, people in Philadelphia are relatively hostile and lead relatively short lives, whereas those in Honolulu are relatively less hostile and lead relatively longer lives. Is there a direct link between hostility and longevity, or does this correlation reflect some third variable?

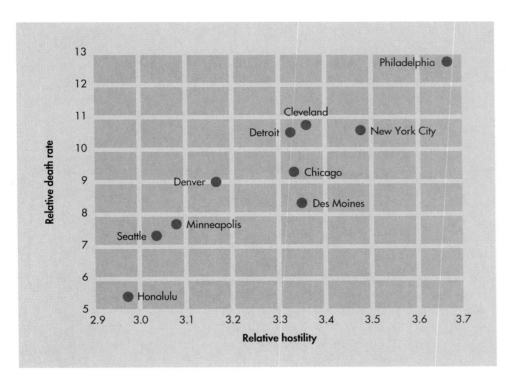

Figure 2.2
Does Hostility Lead to Death? Cities in the United States that have the highest levels of hostility also have the highest rates of death. Although we might be tempted to conclude that high levels of hostility in a city like Philadelphia directly cause the demise of its citizens, this may not be true, because the data here come from a correlational investigation. *Source: USA Today,* May 13, 1994, p. 5D.

as can be seen, there was a positive correlation between measured anger in a city and the death rate: Angrier cities had greater numbers of people dying of heart disease; less angry cities had fewer people dying of heart disease.

Weaknesses of Correlational Investigations

This survey is intriguing, and the immediate interpretation is that the expressed hostility in one's hometown leads to heart disease and eventually to death. But before we all move to Honolulu, stop and see that this "obvious" interpretation might be wrong. We cannot conclude with certainty that the hostility in given cities causes heart disease. Something else might be going on. Despite the correlation between residence and death rate, there may not be a direct link between the two. Another factor, called a third variable, may be producing both. Third variables are a particular type of confound, and researchers conducting correlational investigations must be alert for possible third variables that threaten their conclusions.

What are some possible third variables in this study? One possibility is that the people who originally settled in these cities differed in the first place in ways related to hostility and/or susceptibility to heart disease; the city itself might be irrelevant to the observed correlation. Another possibility is that the typical level of stress in each city—due, for example, to worries about crime, drugs, or unemployment—produces both hostility and heart disease. Yet another possibility is that pollution confounds the correlation between residence and death. The hostile cities tended to be older ones in the Northeast, with a greater accumulation of poisons in the air or water supply.

If a researcher can anticipate possible third variables, then these can be explicitly tested and ruled out. For example, in the study just described the results were adjusted for the ethnic makeup of the residents in the different cities. Honolulu has many more residents of Asian ancestry than the other cities, and Asian Americans tend to live longer than their African American or European American counterparts.

Strengths of Correlational Investigations

If correlational studies severely limit the researcher's ability to offer conclusions about causal links, why does anyone bother conducting these studies in the first place? Remember that all research strategies present a combination of strengths and weaknesses. Just because correlational data do not allow causal conclusions does not mean we should overlook the virtues of this approach.

Correlational investigations typically study a large number of individuals (or groups) with the goal of describing naturally occurring relationships among their characteristics. Results can be generalized with much more confidence than results from case studies. Even if the nature of the links is unclear, one can still say they exist.

Correlational research also makes it possible to grapple with topics impossible, unwieldy, and/or unethical to investigate with other strategies. Why are men more violent than women? A case study of a particularly violent man does not address the question of interest. Needed is a comparison of men and women with respect to violence—that is, a correlational study that looks at the relationship between gender and violence.

Researchers can and do draw cautious conclusions about causes and effects from information about correlations. When doing so, they tease out the role of possible third variables. Researchers can never rule out all third variables, but if the most plausible candidates are examined and shown to be irrelevant, then a causal conclusion can be offered as long as the researchers are careful to treat it as highly tentative.

In sum, correlational investigations can be quite useful to the researcher who wishes to describe the naturally occurring characteristics of large numbers of individuals or groups that are difficult or impossible to study otherwise. The drawback to the correlational strategy is the difficulty of offering firm conclusions about causes and effects.

Stop and Think

8 Describe how a correlational investigation might be used to investigate the effects of television on violence.

9 What are the strengths and weaknesses of correlational investigations as a research strategy?

EXPERIMENTS

Both scientists and the general public are impressed by experimental evidence, although their reasons for being impressed may differ. The general public may think of experiments as particularly reliable and valid—though by now, you know that reliability and

Suppose an experimenter finds that animals act listlessly following surgery in a specific part of the brain. Is this effect the result of the particular surgery? The only way to know with certainty is for the experimenter to add comparison groups, such as animals that have surgery in a different part of the brain.

Table 2.2   Summary: Comparison of Research Methods

Research method	Strengths	Weaknesses
Observations	Describe behavior as it naturally occurs	Can be biased by expectations; can be reactive
Case studies	Provide rich details; can demonstrate what is or is not possible; allow rare phenomena to be studied	May rely on secondhand information; cannot identify causes; do not allow generalization
Correlational investigations	Allow generalization; provide the only way to study certain topics	Cannot identify causes
Experiments	Identify causes	Cannot be used to study certain topics; can be reactive

validity do not automatically adhere to one research strategy more than another (see Table 2.2). Scientists like experimentation for a more specific reason: Experiments are the best way to identify causes. Because many hypotheses are phrased in terms of causes and effects, experiments are clearly valuable.

In an **experiment,** a researcher deliberately manipulates certain events and measures the effects of these manipulations on other events. An **independent variable** is the factor manipulated. It is the potential cause that the researcher wishes to investigate. It is called the independent variable because one hopes it is independent of extraneous factors. A **dependent variable** is the factor assessed by the researcher following the manipulation—the potential effect of concern. It is called the dependent variable because it presumably depends only on the manipulation. A dependent variable needs to be observable.

In their simplest form, experiments introduce the potential cause to one group of research subjects and withhold it from a second (see Figure 2.3). The former group is

■ **experiment**
research strategy in which a researcher deliberately manipulates certain events and measures the effects of those manipulations on other events

■ **independent variable**
in an experiment, the factor manipulated by the researcher

■ **dependent variable**
in an experiment, the factor assessed by the researcher following the manipulation—the potential effect

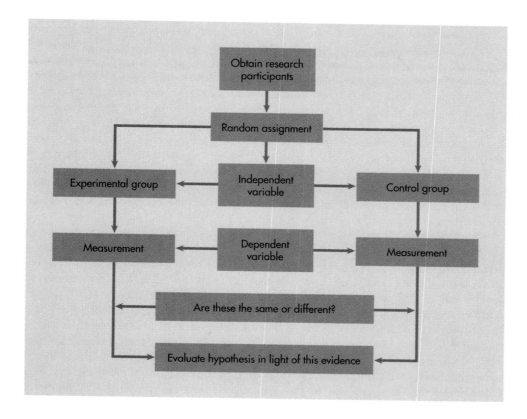

Figure 2.3
Design of an Experiment. In an experiment, research participants are randomly assigned to different conditions where the researcher controls what happens to them; these conditions are the independent variable. A common outcome is measured for all subjects; this measure is the dependent variable.

■ experimental group
in an experiment, the group of research subjects exposed to a potential cause

■ control group
in an experiment, the group of research subjects not exposed to a potential cause

termed the **experimental group,** and the latter the **control group.** In many studies using the experimental strategy, researchers use more than one control group because manipulations can affect more than just the intended cause. Additional control groups rule out the role of extraneous variables introduced by a manipulation.

For example, one of the ways psychologists study how the brain works is to destroy a particular part of it. They might perform surgery on a rat, opening its skull and making a wound in a given location in the brain. They let the animal recover and then observe its behavior. One obvious control group in this sort of research is animals whose brains were not destroyed by the experimenter. But in comparing the behavior of animals with and without damage to their brains, one is also making another comparison—that between animals with and without surgery. Suppose animals in the experimental group act listlessly, eat excessively, or fall ill. Is this effect due to the particular wound made by the researcher or to the invasive and traumatic surgery? One cannot tell. For this reason, another control group is a good idea: animals whose skulls are opened and then closed, without any damage to the brain. The researcher may also feel the need for yet another control group: animals receiving wounds in a different part of the brain.

The process of adding control groups to an experiment is analogous to the process of ruling out third variables in a correlational study. The extraneous variables that control groups try to eliminate are potential confounds that threaten validity. In both correlational and experimental studies, the researcher intends to sharpen conclusions, to have confidence that operational definitions are more, rather than less, valid.

The defining feature of an experiment is the explicit control researchers exercise over possible causes. Experimenters determine who will memorize information in a noisy environment and who will do so in utter silence. They choose the rats reared in crowded conditions as well as those living in solitude.

In an experiment, all research subjects must have an equal chance to be exposed to the different conditions created by the experimenter. In other words, subjects need to be assigned to the experimental and control groups on a random basis, in a process called **random assignment.** The goal here is to cancel possible third variables, so that the only difference between Group 1 and Group 2 is the factor manipulated by the researcher.

■ random assignment
in an experiment, the process of assigning subjects to experimental and control groups on a random basis

Sometimes a correlational study looks very much like an experiment in that a researcher wishes to regard one variable—like gender—as a cause of a second variable—like mood or achievement. Such studies are called quasi-experiments, but they differ critically from actual experiments because subjects are not randomly assigned to conditions.

Consider what happens if a researcher violates random assignment. Does aerobic exercise improve mood? An investigator might proceed by making up two types of recreational programs, with and without aerobic exercise. Aerobic exercise or not is the independent variable in this study; mood is the dependent variable. Then the researcher might recruit children in a junior high school as research subjects. They will be placed in one type of program or the other for one school period a day during the next school year. A questionnaire measuring mood will be given to everyone at the end of the year, and the researcher will see if the manipulated factor (aerobic exercise) has an effect on the children's reported mood.

Now suppose the researcher happens to assign the children to conditions according to their homerooms. Students with homerooms on the first floor are assigned to the aerobic exercise group, and students with homerooms on the second floor are assigned to the control group. But what happens if students in the first-floor homerooms tend to love school, whereas those in the second-floor homerooms tend to hate it? (Maybe the first-floor homerooms are more modern, closer to the playground, or whatever.) The experimenter has dramatically weakened the study because the exercise versus no exercise conditions are also "love school" versus "hate school" conditions. If exercise subjects have better moods, does this mean that aerobic exercise is the critical cause or does it mean that the students simply differed in the first place? One cannot tell—which is why random assignment of subjects to the manipulated conditions is critical. Otherwise, third variables are introduced and causal conclusions cannot be advanced.

People sometimes have trouble appreciating the importance of randomization in conducting an experiment. Perhaps the difficulty stems from common connotations of *random:* capriciousness and carelessness. In the context of experimentation, though, randomization accomplishes just the opposite. Rather than introducing unknown factors into research, randomization eliminates them, by spreading them across conditions so that they have no systematic effect.

Weaknesses of Experiments

Like the other research strategies, experiments have certain weaknesses. As noted in the discussion of the correlational method, researchers cannot manipulate all variables. They have no control over factors like sex, age, or race. In the case of certain complex behaviors, such as one's career, it may not even be evident what is a cause and what is an effect, and it is impossible to investigate these behaviors with an experiment.

Experiments have another drawback: They may be reactive with respect to some topics. Complex social behavior, in particular, may be altered when brought into a laboratory. For instance, it is difficult to study racial prejudice in an experiment nowadays, not because prejudice does not exist but rather because the typical research participant is unwilling to act in a prejudiced way under a psychologist's scrutiny. Along these lines, a subject in an experiment investigating the effectiveness of medication or psychotherapy may improve simply because of his or her expectation that the procedure will be helpful (Chapter 14).

Do not confuse this shortcoming with another common criticism—that experiments are invalid because they oversimplify what they are studying. Experiments are useful precisely because they make complex phenomena simple, holding constant all factors except one and systematically investigating the consequences of that one factor. This quality may make experiments seem artificial, but the trade-off between "artificiality" and experimental control is what allows causal conclusions.

The reactivity of experiments is a different matter, and the criticism here is more subtle. Psychology experiments can alter what they intend to study. The problem is not simplification but transformation. Remember the Prisoners' Dilemma Game from earlier in the chapter? Perhaps this research strategy captures not competition and cooperation but rather fun and games (Ring, 1967). Maybe the situation presented to subjects demands that they treat the Prisoners' Dilemma Game as something different from real competition or real cooperation.

Strengths of Experiments

If done correctly, experiments allow causal conclusions. They are particularly useful for investigating the possible mechanisms that give rise to behavior, and they thus see frequent use by researchers interested in such psychological processes as sensation, perception, motivation, emotion, learning, and cognition. If an experimental procedure proves valid, then researchers can use it repeatedly to study a given phenomenon, rather than waiting for the phenomenon to occur, as they must with other research strategies.

To conclude, the experimental research strategy allows researchers to exert intentional control over their topics of investigation and to support conclusions about causes and effects. However, not all phenomena lend themselves to experimentation.

Stop and Think

10 Describe how an experiment might be used to investigate the effects of television on violence.

11 What are the strengths and weaknesses of experiments as a research strategy?

STATISTICS

■ statistics
numerical representation of data

Remember the trend in psychology toward increasing quantification (Chapter 1). **Statistics** are the numerical representation of data. They are usually discussed without mentioning statisticians, the men and women who devised the means of this quantification in the first place. Statistics become a bit more human if we know why particular statisticians devised their approaches. For example, consider two central figures in the early history of statistics: Florence Nightingale (1820–1910) and William S. Gossett (1876–1938).

Florence Nightingale—the famous nurse of the Crimean War? You probably never thought of Florence Nightingale as a statistician, but her place in the history of statistics is as secure as her place in the history of medicine (Kennedy, 1984). Indeed, they are entwined. Nightingale was a tireless advocate of hospital reform. She believed the typical hospital of her day killed more people than it saved, due to bad food, poor hygiene, and other deficiencies. To buttress her arguments, Nightingale gathered and compared the facts about mortality rates in and out of hospitals, finding that hospitals were indeed hazardous to one's health. She appreciated the need for uniformity of records as no one had before.

The general public does not know William S. Gossett as well as it knows Florence Nightingale. Even statisticians might not recognize his name. He published his numerous contributions under a pseudonym—"Student"—because his employer did not want to publicize the fact that it hired scientifically trained researchers (Tankard, 1984). Gossett was a brewer for Arthur Guiness Sons & Co., Ltd., of Dublin.

The brewing of beer requires the combination of four ingredients: barley, hops, yeast, and water. Even subtle variations in their quantities and the manner in which they are combined produce beers with highly different tastes. Brewmasters over the centuries have tried to determine optimal combinations. Often their craft is regarded as an art—which is another way of saying that the right combinations often prove elusive.

The Guiness Company tried to make the brewing process less mysterious by hiring researchers to systematically investigate ways of combining the ingredients of beers. Gossett and the other scientific brewmasters carefully measured characteristics of the different ingredients and experimented with different combinations of them. Which approaches yielded the best-tasting beers? To answer this question objectively, Gossett devised formulas for making such inferences. Taste testers sampled different batches of beer and rated how each tasted. Average ratings were calculated and then compared. Student's t-test, which you will encounter if you ever take a statistics course, is a formula for judging whether average scores really are different from one another.

Statistics are tools. They have been used to save lives, and they have been used to make beer. Contemporary psychologists use statistics to better understand the human condition. One can neither conduct nor understand research without a grasp of basic statistics.

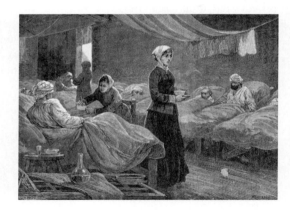

Florence Nightingale made important contributions to the field of statistics by showing the necessity of uniform hospital records.

Descriptive Statistics

Statistics describe one's data. Think back over the different investigations used as examples in this chapter. In no case did researchers look at every detail of their data. Rather, they offered an overview of the research results. **Descriptive statistics** are formulas that allow the researcher to simplify complex sets of data by describing their general characteristics and patterns. Consider the following statement:

> On average, people with a pessimistic view of the future live shorter lives.

This statement is easy to understand. But suppose you were presented instead with hundreds of unsummarized numbers pertaining to people's pessimism and longevity. Although such a list would be rich in detail, you might miss the straightforward generalization lurking within.

Central tendency.   For the vast majority of studies, researchers focus on just a few aspects of their data. First, they are often interested in describing the typical values of variables. How much do meals cost at that restaurant? What is the starting salary for someone with a college degree in this discipline? What kinds of grades does that teacher give? These questions ask about the **central tendency** of variables.

One way to understand the central tendency of a set of scores is simply to graph their distribution. However, when the number of scores is large this procedure can be unwieldy. Accordingly, researchers use one of several possible summary measures of central tendency. The mean of a variable is simply its arithmetic average. The median of a variable refers to the value that divides a set of scores in two, with half of the scores being larger than the median and the other half being smaller. Finally, the mode of a variable is the most frequently obtained value. Means, medians, and modes often agree, though not invariably. A researcher calculates one or another measure of central tendency depending on which yields the most useful estimate granted his or her purposes.

For example, suppose we are interested in the salary of workers in a small company (see Figure 2.4). There are ten workers; four of them earn $20,000 a year, two earn $22,000 a year, three earn $24,000 a year, and one earns $150,000. The mean income ($34,600) is probably a misleading way to describe the central tendency of their salaries. More meaningful is the median ($22,000) or mode ($20,000).

■ **descriptive statistics**
summaries of the general characteristics and patterns of data

■ **central tendency**
typical value of a variable

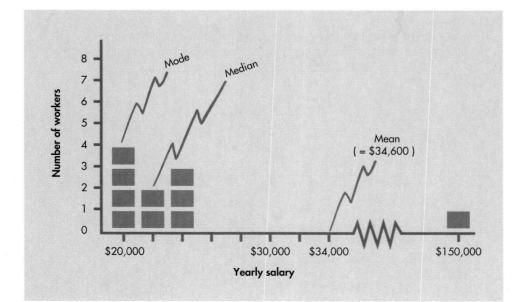

Figure 2.4
Examples of Measures of Central Tendency. This diagram shows the distribution of annual salaries in a small company. Different measures of the central tendency of this salary distribution can be calculated. The mode is the most common salary ($20,000), the median is the salary that divides the lower half of salaries from the upper half ($22,000), and the mean is the arithmetic average of all the salaries ($34,600). Which measure best captures the central tendency here?

Mean values are often used in describing the results of experiments. Imagine you are interested in the effects of psychotherapy on marital satisfaction. You might investigate this question in an experiment, assigning married subjects at random to two conditions: psychotherapy and no psychotherapy. You might operationalize marital satisfaction as the number of sappy notes each subject writes to his or her spouse in a seven-day period. Does psychotherapy lead to an increase in sappy notes? In other words, is the average number of notes greater for subjects in psychotherapy than for subjects not in psychotherapy?

■ variability
variation in a variable

Variability.   Researchers also focus on the **variability** of their measures. How much variation is there in a particular variable? If you are a sports fan, you know that some players or teams show a steady level of performance, whereas other players or teams can be either very good or very bad. The former show less variability than the latter. We can make the same observation about students. Two of your friends have identical C averages, let us say, but Constantly Consistent Charles achieves his GPA by getting a C in each and every course he takes, whereas Awesomely Fluctuating Annie-Flo gets only A's and F's.

The variability of data interests researchers for several reasons. In a correlational study, one must have a sufficient spread of scores to see which variables go together. For example, researchers have tried to investigate the correlates of depressed mood by soliciting volunteers and giving them a questionnaire that measures degree of depression. Sometimes other variables show no correlation whatsoever with depression scores. Why? Perhaps the subjects were exclusively cheerful individuals, as might be expected given that they volunteered for the study. One of the symptoms of depression is curtailment of activities, and, of course, voluntary participation in a psychology experiment is an activity. Insufficient variability works against the success of a correlational study.

Another reason for paying attention to variability is that one can best interpret central tendencies in light of variation among scores. Remember your C friends. If you were asked to characterize what kinds of students Charles and Annie-Flo are, you would have a lot of confidence in your description of Charles because his individual grades are so consistent. What could you say about Annie-Flo that would not require qualification? The variability of her grades precludes a confident answer.

The same reasoning applies to the interpretation of the results of experiments. Let us return to the wedded couples and their sappy notes. Table 2.3 presents two sets of

Table 2.3   Number of Notes Exchanged by Spouses Within a Seven-Day Period

Couples in psychotherapy		Couples not in psychotherapy	
Set 1			
Couple A	14	Couple F	10
Couple B	14	Couple G	11
Couple C	15	Couple H	10
Couple D	14	Couple I	12
Couple E	14	Couple J	10
	mean = 14.2		mean = 10.6
Set 2			
Couple K	21	Couple P	0
Couple L	7	Couple Q	21
Couple M	27	Couple R	2
Couple N	12	Couple S	3
Couple O	14	Couple T	27
	mean = 14.2		mean = 10.6

hypothetical data. In both cases, individuals in psychotherapy send more notes than people not in therapy. The data are arranged so that the means of the two conditions are identical in both versions of the data. But in the top set of scores, there is little variation within either group of subjects. In contrast, the bottom set of scores are highly variable. Which set of scores allows you to make the more confident conclusion about the effects of psychotherapy? The answer is clear—Set 1. This is why researchers pay attention to how much or how little scores vary.

Association.   Finally, researchers want to describe the degree to which two variables are associated with one another. Correlations are a common example of **association.** Earlier, they were described merely as positive, negative, or zero. Researchers in practice make finer distinctions by computing a numerical value called a **correlation coefficient.** Positive correlations range from 0.00 to 1.00, and negative correlations range from 0.00 to −1.00. The larger the magnitude of the coefficient (i.e., the farther the correlation coefficient is from 0.00), the greater the degree of correlation between the two variables.

What does it mean to say that two variables are highly correlated? Remember the graphs in Figure 2.1. Highly correlated variables yield a graph in which the data points come very close to being a straight line. Variables correlated to a lesser degree have data points that fall less tightly along a straight line.

Here is an example of variables correlated to different degrees. Consider the heights of you and your classmates. Suppose we find out the height of everybody's mother, as well as the height of everybody's grandmother. If we compute the correlation between children's height and mothers' height and the correlation between children's height and grandmothers' height, both will be positive because height (or its lack) runs in families. However, the former correlation will be stronger than the latter because whatever familial links exist are usually more direct between child and mother than between child and grandmother.

Inferential Statistics

Psychologists also use statistics to infer whether or not particular results came about by chance. When there is a decent possibility that the study's results represent random fluctuations, a researcher refrains from getting too excited. **Inferential statistics** are formulas that let the researcher calculate the likelihood that particular research results arose by chance. Thus, he or she can decide whether patterns in obtained data are reliable findings or simply flukes.

Suppose a teacher has two classes in the same subject, one in the morning and the other in the evening. She gives both classes the same multiple-choice examination. Let us further suppose that no students from the two classes discuss the examination in the afternoon. The morning class on average gets 77 percent of the questions correct, and the evening class gets 73 percent correct. Although 77 percent is obviously different from 73 percent, this difference might well be the result of chance. Maybe a few people in the morning class happened to guess well and a few people in the evening class happened to guess poorly. If it is just chance that produces this pattern, then we would not want to conclude that the time a class is offered has anything to do with grades. We must make a judgment about the possible role of chance. Inferential statistics provide an explicit way of making this judgment.

Researchers use formulas that take into account probabilities. These procedures usually start by assuming that all outcomes are equally likely. In the example just described, we assume that students in the morning class and those in the evening class are equally apt to do well or poorly on tests. We administer a test and calculate the average scores of students in the two classes, finding that those in the morning class do better. We find the same result for a second test and then for a third. The same pattern holds semester after semester. Chance could conceivably account for these results, but this possibility becomes increasingly remote as the pattern continues to occur.

■ **association**
relationship between two variables

■ **correlation coefficient**
number between −1.00 and 1.00 reflecting the degree to which two variables are correlated with one another

■ **inferential statistics**
probabilistic conclusions about data

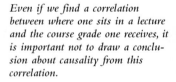

■ statistical significance
degree to which research results are unlikely to have occurred by chance

Results that are unlikely to have occurred by chance are termed **statistically significant.** Many psychologists use a 1 out of 20 (5 percent) criterion to designate results as statistically significant or not. If results could have arisen from chance no more than 1 time out of 20, then the researcher decides the results are worth taking seriously. The so-called .05 level is arbitrary (Cohen, 1994). Some researchers use a more (or less) stringent criterion.

Here is an example of how inferential statistics can be used to answer a question of interest to psychologists: Do people perform better when rewarded for their successes or when punished for their failures? Although there is no simple answer for all circumstances, imagine you are interested in the issue solely with respect to playing a video game. First you estimate the ability of your research subjects by having them play ten games, without rewards or punishments, and calculating each individual's average score. Then you begin the actual experiment. In one condition, when players exceed their past average they earn $1. In a second condition, when players fall short of their past average they lose $1. Fifty players are in each group, and you have each subject play 20 games with rewards or punishments, as the case may be. You operationalize performance as the score on the twenty-first game.

Which group does better? On a descriptive level, you answer this question by calculating the average scores in the two groups. Say you find that subjects in one group score 17 points higher on average than subjects in the other group. You are not done, however, until you decide what this difference really means. Maybe it does not matter whether you reward or punish video-game players. You would then expect average scores in the two groups to be about the same. Is 17 points higher "about the same"? Here is where inferential statistics are useful. Starting with the assumption of no difference, you calculate the probability that a 17-point discrepancy could occur by chance. The formula you use takes into account the variability of the scores. The more tightly bunched the scores are in each group, the less likely is the difference to have occurred by chance. All things being equal, results based on large as opposed to small samples are more likely to be judged statistically significant.

You do not need to understand the exact mathematics to see the point of inferential statistics. Rather, you should understand two important ideas: (a) Psychologists use inferential statistics to decide whether their results might have been produced by chance, and (b) Statistical significance should not be confused with theoretical signifi-

Even if we find a correlation between where one sits in a lecture and the course grade one receives, it is important not to draw a conclusion about causality from this correlation.

cance, practical significance, or validity; it means only that the results are probably not a fluke.

ETHICS

All researchers must confront the ethical implications of what they do. This confrontation usually occurs when research findings are applied in ways that may be harmful to individuals or to society. Sophisticated instruments of war are just one example of how science can enter the ethical arena. What starts out as basic science can end up as applied science that the world might be better off without. Psychologists face the same dilemma regarding the eventual use of their findings. However, unlike researchers in many other fields, psychologists additionally face an immediate dilemma when they use living beings—people or animals—in their research.

Research with People

Many of the requirements of sound research run the risk of infringing on the rights of the individual:

- To have representative research subjects, psychologists must (sometimes) persuade unenthusiastic people to participate.
- To have unbiased research subjects, psychologists must (sometimes) deceive people about the real purposes of the study.
- To investigate important behavior, psychologists must (sometimes) expose people to stress.
- To draw causal conclusions, psychologists must (sometimes) manipulate people.
- To evaluate the benefits of an intervention like psychotherapy, psychologists must (sometimes) withhold a potentially helpful treatment from people in need.

One of the most controversial studies in psychology is Stanley Milgram's (1963) investigation of obedience. That work is described in detail later in this book (Chapter 15), but let me focus here on the ethical issues involved. Milgram recruited adult research subjects through newspaper ads in New Haven, Connecticut, to participate in what was described as a study of learning. Upon arriving at the laboratory, each subject encountered another subject—a middle-aged man who in actuality was working with the experimenter. The real subject did not know this until the experiment was complete. The two subjects were told the procedure: One would play the role of a teacher, and the other the role of a student. When the student made a mistake, the teacher was to press a button that would shock him. Each mistake would result in an increasingly powerful shock.

Milgram designated the real subject as the teacher and the pretend subject as the student. The student went into a different room, and the teacher was seated at a console with buttons and dials controlling the shocks. As the experiment progressed, the student made errors, and the teacher delivered shocks. Actual shocks were not delivered, but again, the real subject did not know this. At one point, the student started banging on the wall and yelling about his heart condition. As you might imagine, the teacher became uncomfortable with this state of affairs and turned to the researcher for guidance. He was told, "The experiment requires that you continue."

Milgram's study of obedience raised important questions about the ethical treatment of subjects in experimental research. Should research subjects be deceived about the true purpose of a study? Should they be allowed to cease their participation in a study before it is over?

Two-thirds of the subjects continued to deliver shocks under these circumstances. Although many subjects were distressed, they nevertheless continued to obey the experimenter. When the research was completed, the subject met the student and saw that he was all right. The true purpose was then explained in detail to the subject.

The Milgram procedure raises a number of ethical questions (Baumrind, 1964). Were the research subjects treated fairly? They were misled about the nature of the experiment. They were exposed to something disquieting about themselves. Whether the information provided at the end of the study effectively dispelled anxiety is unclear.

On the other hand, one can argue that research benefits society as a whole and so is worth doing even if individual research subjects pay a price. Certainly, Milgram's investigation of disobedience makes an important contribution to knowledge. Prior to his study, Milgram surveyed other psychologists and asked them to predict the results. That very low levels of obedience were predicted means that Milgram's findings were far from obvious. The general conflict in doing psychology studies is therefore between the rights of the individual subject and the rights of the larger society. How can this conflict be resolved?

We can make after-the-fact judgments that a given study was or was not valuable, but hindsight is of no help in planning research. Accordingly, the American Psychological Association (1992) has published a code of ethical principles to help researchers with potential dilemmas. These ethical principles are not a cookbook of what thou shall and shall not do. Instead, the decision to undertake research is described as a judgment to be made by the individual psychologist about how best to contribute to psychological science and human welfare.

At the same time, psychologists try to avoid violating individual rights by following certain conventions. If you have ever participated as a subject in a psychology study, these conventions will be familiar to you. First, virtually all research settings, such as colleges, hospitals, and mental health centers, have an institutional review board composed of psychologists and nonpsychologists that reviews research proposals for possible ethical problems. These institutional review boards have complete control over whether a specific study will or will not be conducted. Second, researchers usually obtain informed consent from potential subjects before involving them in a study. They explain the general procedures to be followed ("You will complete questionnaires taking about 45 minutes") and any risks or discomforts the subjects may experience ("The noises you will hear are uncomfortably loud"). Then they ask the subjects to consent to participate under these conditions. Third, subjects are told explicitly that they have the right to withdraw from the study at any time they choose, without penalty. Finally, subjects are entitled to a full debriefing concerning the purpose of a study once it has been completed.

Not all psychologists are pleased with these conventions, arguing that important experiments like that of Milgram cannot be conducted if the ethical principles are strictly followed. The APA ethical principles allow exceptions to the guidelines but urge careful deliberation under these circumstances.

Research with Animals

Ethical dilemmas also face psychologists conducting research with animals, such as rats, mice, dogs, cats, and monkeys. In some of these studies, animals experience stress, pain, and eventually death. The use of animals in research is a subject of ongoing social and political controversy (Dewsbury, 1990). On the one hand, researchers point to the methodological benefits of animal research, including experimental control, objectivity, and efficiency, as well as the contributions animal research makes to human welfare, including the development of medical interventions that have saved countless human lives (Miller, 1985).

On the other hand, critics argue that whatever the benefits and contributions, these are outweighed by the suffering to which laboratory animals are exposed. Animals obviously have no voice in their participation in research; many of the safeguards that protect human beings as research subjects—such as informed consent and the right to withdraw—have no counterparts for animals.

There is no easy solution to this debate. Although psychologists who use animals in research submit their research proposals to an institutional review board that scrutinizes the procedures in terms of humane treatment (Baldwin, 1993), this check does not satisfy all critics. Federal laws specify how research animals should be housed and fed, but again, these laws do not satisfy all critics. Animal researchers are criticized for ignoring the rights of animals and for elevating human beings above other species (Tester, 1991). Critics charge that human welfare is not a sufficient justification for animal research (Shapiro, 1990).

A partial solution to the dilemma involves devising methodological alternatives to the traditional use of animals in laboratory studies (Bowd & Shapiro, 1993). Gallup and Suarez (1985) surveyed some of these alternatives. Although these may not always be fully adequate replacements when our interest is with complex behavior, some possibilities are intriguing:

- Naturalistic observation (studying animals in the wild)
- Case studies (studying animals one at a time)
- Use of lower animals (studying coldblooded animals)
- Plants as alternatives (studying the "behavior" of plants)
- Tissue cultures (studying parts of animals)
- Computer simulations (programming an animal on a computer)

Each alternative may be useful, depending on the question of interest.

But when our concern is with certain other topics, there is no reasonable alternative to the use of higher animals in research. Indeed, it is unlikely that animal research will cease in the foreseeable future, granted this work's past and future benefits to people. For example, if and when a means of curing individuals of AIDS or immunizing them against this disease is developed, it will be the result of research with monkeys that can be infected with viruses similar to HIV (Chapter 16). Society as a whole is no doubt reluctant to rule out such investigations.

Stop and Think

13 Think back to the different research approaches you considered for investigating the effects of television on violence. In each case, what ethical issues are raised and how might you best minimize or eliminate them?

PSYCHOLOGICAL RESEARCH IN A BIOPSYCHOSOCIAL CONTEXT

Chapter 1 stressed that behavior must be placed in its full context. The same is true of psychological theories and research. Individual psychologists are, after all, people. Their contributions to psychology are the result of their behavior. Biological mechanisms, psychological processes, and social influences are as relevant in explaining the behavior of psychologists as they are in explaining the behavior of everyone else (see Figure 2.5).

In biological terms, an individual must live long enough to make a contribution (Chapter 3). Although exceptions exist, psychology is not a field where the most notable contributions are made by young adults (Gardner, 1983). Think back to the pioneering psychologists discussed in Chapter 1. Wilhelm Wundt lived for almost 90 years; John Watson lived for almost 80 years; and Sigmund Freud lived for almost 85 years. They each were active throughout their lives and produced a huge amount of work for which they are remembered.

In psychological terms, an individual must possess sufficient motivation, intelligence, and creativity to make a contribution (Chapters 7 and 11). Notable psychologists are usually effective writers and charismatic enough to attract students who further their work (Simonton, 1994).

Figure 2.5
Psychological Research Contributions as Biopsychosocial. An individual scientist's contribution to psychology, like behavior in general, reflects biological, psychological, and social influences. The individual must live long enough to make a contribution (biological) and have sufficient motivation, intelligence, and creativity to do so (psychological). The potential contributor to psychology must also be free from discrimination that bars his or her participation in the field (social). In addition, prevailing cultural and historical factors shape the nature of the contribution and its impact on psychology (social).

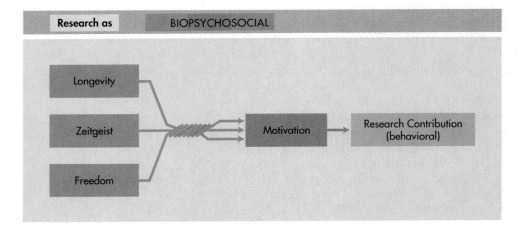

In social terms, an individual must be in the right time and place to make a contribution. Discrimination must not bar his or her potential participation in psychology. There were very few women among the first psychologists because most universities in Europe and the United States did not allow females to enroll in courses or to earn degrees (Chapter 1). The same was true for ethnic and religious minorities. As a Jew, Sigmund Freud was not allowed to be a university professor, and so he turned to a career in medicine, where greater opportunities were available (Gay, 1988).

Once an individual is in the field of psychology, his or her specific ideas are further shaped by social influences. Historians of science refer to the influence of a given historical era as the **Zeitgeist,** or "spirit of the times." The corresponding influence of a given culture is referred to as the **Ortgeist,** or "spirit of the place." The prevailing Zeitgeist and Ortgeist dictate what topics are of concern to a specific researcher, how he or she phrases questions and explanations concerning those topics, and what methods of investigation he or she uses.

For example, Freud's work was influenced by then prevailing ideas in physics about the conservation of energy (Chapter 12). More generally, the fact that Freud lived in Victorian Europe, a time and place characterized by a pervasive denial of sexuality, drew his attention to the importance of sexuality and the possible hazards involved in its expression (Gay, 1988). Most of his psychoanalytic patients were women, and women were more apt than men to encounter problems with the expression of their sexuality (Shorter, 1992).

As a practicing clinician, Freud was concerned with specific individuals and their problems, and his use of the case study approach readily followed. The less than objective nature of his case studies can be explained because he was inventing this research approach as he went along (Peterson, 1992). Some historians have argued that Freud's theories and methods are culturally and historically bounded, that they provide a good fit for his cultural era but not for other places and times (Ellenberger, 1970).

Another example is the popularity of functionalism in general and behaviorism in particular within the United States, where individual fulfillment and satisfaction are so greatly emphasized. Behaviorism appeals to the optimism inherent in the culture of the

■ **Zeitgeist**
influence of a given historical era on theories and research

■ **Ortgeist**
influence of a given culture on theories and research

Theory and research in psychology often stem from ongoing societal emphases. Sigmund Freud's psychoanalytic theory reflected Victorian Europe and its widespread repression of sexuality, and John Watson's behaviorism reflected the culture of possibility long popular in the United States.

United States (Peterson, Maier, & Seligman, 1993). One of the best-known declarations of the behaviorist John Watson (1925, p. 65) is the following:

> Give me a dozen healthy infants, well-formed, and my own specified world to bring them up in, and I'll guarantee to take any one at random and train him to become any type of specialist I might select—doctor, lawyer, artist, merchant-chief, and yes even beggar-man and thief, regardless of his talents, penchants, activities, vocations and race of his ancestors.

If people are products of their environments, then so too are their problems and, of course, the solutions to those problems.

In the United States, recent years have seen a great interest in the biological context of behavior. You will see in subsequent chapters that many of the newest discoveries about behavior concern its biological underpinnings. Whatever the biological bases of behavior might be, they have been there all along. Why the current interest?

The rise of conservatism during the 1980s influenced the way societal resources were used to support scientific research. Most scientists would agree that during the 1980s, biological investigations were more generously funded by the federal government than sociocultural ones. This reflects the political stance of Presidents Reagan and Bush (and the citizens who elected them). Political conservatives wish to preserve the societal status quo, not hold it responsible for creating psychological problems. As he left office, President Reagan signed a bill declaring the 1990s the Decade of the Brain (Goldstein, 1990; Judd, 1990).

We cannot know the degree to which the political pendulum will swing in the opposite direction, but there has been renewed interest in **cross-cultural psychology,** which compares and contrasts people's behavior in cultures around the world. Perhaps the recent explosion of ethnic conflicts between and within nations has contributed to this renewed interest.

The next chapter begins our discussion of the fields of psychology. It considers the theory of evolution and how it helps us to understand the biological context of behavior. Subsequent chapters move to other biological topics, then to important psychological processes such as sensation and perception, and finally to the social context of behavior. At the end of this book are two chapters devoted to applied psychology.

■ **cross-cultural psychology**
field of psychology that compares and contrasts people's behaviors across different cultures

SUMMARY

UNDERSTANDING RESEARCH: DEFINITION AND EXPLANATION

■ Regardless of the research method psychologists use, they must operationalize the concepts of interest—devise concrete measures of them.

■ Researchers must also make their measures reliable, so that they yield the same result on different occasions, and valid, so that they assess what the researchers intend to study.

■ Additionally, researchers must strive to make their methods generalizable.

■ Psychologists have several general research strategies available, each with its own strengths and weaknesses.

OBSERVATIONS

■ In observational studies, researchers attempt to describe behavior as it naturally occurs.

■ The strength of observations is their description of actual behavior, but this strategy can be biased by expectations on the part of the researcher. Observations can also disrupt behavior as it occurs.

CASE STUDIES

■ Case studies are intensive investigations of single individuals or groups.

■ A case study provides rich details and allows rare phenomena to be investigated, but it does not allow the researcher to identify causes or generalize conclusions.

CORRELATIONAL INVESTIGATIONS

■ Correlational investigations describe how variables are associated.

■ Correlational investigations allow results to be generalized, but they cannot identify causes.

EXPERIMENTS

■ Experiments manipulate possible causes and measure the effects of doing so.

■ The strength of an experiment is that it can identify causes; at the same time, an experiment may be reactive.

STATISTICS

■ Researchers use statistics to describe their data and to draw inferences, notably the conclusion that results did not arise by chance.

ETHICS

■ Whether psychologists study people or animals, they must address the ethical implications of their research. Every study represents a compromise between the rights of the individual and the potential benefits for the larger society.

PSYCHOLOGICAL RESEARCH IN A BIOPSYCHOSOCIAL CONTEXT

■ Psychologists do not work in a vacuum. The topics in which they are interested, the theories they propose, and the research methods they use are influenced by their own biological and psychological characteristics, as well as by historical and cultural forces.

KEY TERMS

Evolution and Behavior

Here is a demonstration you and your classmates might consider conducting for yourselves. You will need one baby, either male or female, and you will need several friends, both males and females. If you cannot find a baby, a doll will work. Ask each of your friends in turn to pick up the baby or doll and hold it for several minutes. Without telling your friends what you are doing, keep a record of how each of them holds the baby or doll: on the left side or on the right side of the body.

A pattern should emerge when you examine your record by males versus females. About two-thirds of the females will hold the baby or doll against the left sides of their bodies, whereas the males will show no consistent holding preference.

In point of fact, you probably will not want to conduct this demonstration, at least with a real infant because babies passed around like rugby balls will become frightened or fidgety and so too will you and your friends. So, be assured that research has shown the male-female difference in cradling infants to be well established.

Left-cradling of infants and dolls by females is evident as early as six years of age (Saling & Bonert, 1983), in a variety of cultures and ethnic groups (Saling, Abrams, & Chesler, 1983; Saling & Cooke, 1984). It is also evident in our primate cousins (Manning & Chamberlain, 1990). The phenomenon has existed for centuries, as shown by studies of paintings throughout the years of mothers and their infants (Finger, 1975; Grusser,

Left-cradling of infants by females appears as early as age six, and some psychologists interpret this behavior as the result of an evolved psychological mechanism.

1983). And by studying photographs in family albums, Manning and Denman (1994) concluded that left-cradling by females shows strong similarities across generations. Males do not show a comparable preference (Manning, 1991).

When psychologists encounter a behavioral phenomenon that seems to be true of people in general, across time and place, they start to wonder if it is an inherent characteristic of our species with a basis in our evolutionary history, having proved advantageous to our distant ancestors. When the behavioral phenomenon also characterizes our closest primate relatives, the possibility of an evolutionary explanation is strengthened. When the phenomenon runs through families in such a way as to suggest a genetic influence, an evolutionary explanation becomes even more viable.

Indeed, several different explanations in evolutionary terms have been proposed to make sense of left-cradling of infants by females (Calvin, 1983):

- It leaves the dominant right hand free to perform other activities.
- It allows the infant to hear the mother's heart beating.
- It results from the greater sensitivity to touch of the mother's left breast.

Left-cradling could also be due to the fact that the left side of the face is more emotionally expressive than the right side (Bruyer, 1981). We may think of our facial expressions as symmetrical, but left and right expressions differ, and it is easier to recognize emotions in a left expression than in a right expression (Manning & Chamberlain, 1991). If a mother holds her infant on her left side, the mother can better see the left side of the infant's face. If emotions are more likely to be displayed on this side, then the left-cradling tendency may have evolved to allow mothers to be most responsive to what their infants are feeling (Chapter 10).

UNDERSTANDING BIOLOGY AND BEHAVIOR: DEFINITION AND EXPLANATION

As stressed in Chapter 1, to understand fully the topics of psychology, you must appreciate the role played by biology. The present chapter discusses biological explanations of behavior, focusing on the theory of evolution and how psychologists use it to explain human behavior. **Evolution** refers to how species of animals and plants originate and change over time. Female left-cradling of infants is just one example of a complex behavior that seems to have a basis in evolution.

At the same time, evolutionary explanations of behavior can be controversial. They often rely on speculations about events occurring hundreds of thousands of years ago. Obtaining research evidence in the here and now can be difficult (Chapter 2), and such difficulties are compounded when the evidence needs to come from the there and then.

Another problem with evolutionary explanations of human behavior is that a theorist may be tempted to overlook alternative or additional explanations in terms of the environment. Perhaps females cradle infants on the left side of their bodies because they are imitating other females they have observed, who in turn have imitated still others. Evolution may have nothing to do with this phenomenon, despite its being so widespread across our species. After all, teenagers around the world wear blue jeans and Hard Rock Cafe T-shirts, but no one would conclude that these clothing preferences are based in evolution.

So, does an explanation referring only to evolution tell the whole story about people's behavior? Here we encounter the so-called **nature-versus-nurture debate.** Over the years, some psychologists have emphasized the role of our inherent biological characteristics (nature); others have stressed processes of learning and socialization (nurture). But explanations in terms of evolution and of the environment need not compete with one another. As noted in Chapter 1, many psychologists today attempt to move beyond this kind of debate to explain how nature and nurture interact to determine behavior.

Tinbergen (1968) recognized the need for contextualized explanations when he observed that biologists explain topics in one of four ways: by stressing cause, function, development, or evolution. These explanations are each different, but they are also compatible. These four modes of biological explanation, taken together, constitute a biopsychosocial account of behavior (Betzig, 1989; Dewsbury, 1992, 1994).

■ **evolution**
process by which species originate and change over time

■ **nature-versus-nurture debate**
controversy as to whether behavior is due to inherent biological characteristics (nature) or to learning and socialization (nurture)

For any human being, one of the most critical aspects of his or her environment is other people. We should therefore expect that human beings have tendencies encouraged by evolution that solidify social relationships.

Causes

Causes include the psychological and physiological mechanisms that produce behavior. Although Western thought has long split the mind and the body into separate spheres, regarding them as distinct and independent (Chapter 16), a more contemporary view sees psychological language and biological language as two ways of speaking about the same topics. Even if we do not wish to meld minds and bodies this completely, there is no reason to juxtapose them rigidly.

For example, the mechanisms responsible for left-cradling of infants may involve facial expressiveness on the part of the infant and an increased ability on the part of the mother to comfort her distressed child. An additional mechanism is discussed in Chapter 5: Even very young infants are more likely to look at faces in their immediate vicinity than they are to look at other things. This tendency means that the infant will be looking directly at the mother's face as opposed to looking away.

Functions

Functions refer to the adaptive significance of behavior: How does a species benefit from given behavioral styles and tendencies? Here we must take into account the typical environment where a species is found because adaptation means successfully meeting the demands of that environment: locating food, keeping safe, finding a mate, and having offspring.

For a human being, a critical aspect of the environment is other people (Caporael & Brewer, 1991). We should therefore expect that human beings have tendencies provided by evolution that solidify social relationships, between mates (Chapter 15), between parents and children (Chapter 10), between peers (Chapter 10), and between leaders and followers (Chapter 15). Left-cradling of infants may be one such tendency. As explained, this behavior on the part of mothers seems to accomplish several useful purposes while having no obvious drawbacks.

Development

Development includes the changes that occur over the individual's life span. Development includes not just the unfolding of an inherent nature but also the influences of the environment. Indeed, in development, the joint influence of nature and nurture is the rule rather than the exception. Researchers have shown, for instance, that moderate stimulation early in life is necessary for the nervous systems of many mammalian species to develop normally (Mohammed, Henriksson, Soderstrom, Ebendal, Olsson, & Seckl, 1993). Our biological characteristics are often affected by experience, and so we must not treat all biology-behavior correlations as if biology were always the cause and behavior always the effect. Matters are usually more complex—which is why the nature-nurture debate is misleading.

Remember the research finding that left-cradling of infants by females shows up as early as age six. It may be no coincidence that this age is when children—usually females in most cultures—first begin to help with the care of younger children. Appreciate that not everyone can always have other people to his or her left. Imagine if infants preferred to hold on to a caretaker against the left side of their own bodies. Unless child or caretaker is upside down, somebody must be to the right, so a left-cradling preference should develop only at a certain age.

Evolution

Evolution places behavior in the context of the long history of our species. How have given behaviors contributed to the survival of our ancestors? Whereas an explanation in terms of functions looks at the well-being of individuals, an explanation in terms of evolution looks at a group of individuals and how behavior helps the group perpetuate itself.

In many cases, such as the example of left-cradling of infants, no conflict exists between the well-being of the individual and the survival of the larger group. In other cases, these may oppose one another, and such instances are of great interest to evolutionary theorists. For example, some animals act altruistically toward each other, forgoing their own reproduction and sometimes even their own lives for others. Consider that the social insects (ants, termites, bees) have a large percentage of sterile members. How did this state of affairs come to be through evolution? One answer is that the survival of the group, which includes some members that do reproduce, is served by the sacrifice of the sterile individuals.

Conclusions About Biology and Behavior

Biological explanations of behavior can stress cause, function, development, or evolution, as the case may be. As already noted, the most satisfactory explanations do not force us to choose among these emphases, but rather try to account for how they all come together to make sense of a given behavior.

For example, the tendency to be optimistic (vs. pessimistic) runs through families in such a way as to suggest the existence of a genetic influence on this personality style. Identical twins resemble each other more than fraternal twins do with respect to their expectations that the future will be good (or bad) (Plomin, Scheier, Bergeman, & Pedersen, 1992; Schulman, Keith, & Seligman, 1993). It is unlikely that there is a specific optimism gene with a direct effect on an individual's expectations for the future, so what explains these results?

The more plausible explanation is complex (Seligman, 1994). We know that optimism is the result of success in life (Peterson, Maier, & Seligman, 1993). Success in life is in turn influenced by characteristics such as physical prowess, attractiveness, and intelligence. These characteristics are influenced by genetic factors. Optimism runs through families because some of its basic determinants do.

The important point is that nature and nurture do not compete in this explanation. The personality style is immediately determined by interaction with a given social setting, but this interaction is distantly determined by biological makeup. There are also examples of behaviors that are immediately determined by biological factors (e.g., physical illness or injury) that are distantly determined by environmental interactions (e.g., prior exposure to germs or toxins). When psychologists turn their attention to biology, they cannot ignore the role played by the social setting.

Another important point is that in making sense of how biology is related to behavior, we must distinguish between direct versus indirect effects. For instance, consider the link reported between steroid use and aggression (Gregg & Rejeski, 1990). While steroids may have a direct effect on aggression (Chapter 5), they also affect people's appearance by adding muscle mass. Muscular individuals are perceived differently by others, perhaps as threatening, and interactions may follow that result in aggression (Chapter 12). Here we see an indirect effect of biology on behavior.

Stop and Think

1 Describe how a specific behavior in Table 1.2 (Chapter 1, p. 26) might be explained in terms of its causes, functions, development, and evolution.

EVOLUTION

Evolution is discussed in this chapter because it is a critical aspect of biological explanations and hence of a biological perspective on behavior. To better explain the complex relationship between biology and behavior, I describe evolution and related concepts. Then I turn to how these ideas have been used to explain human behavior.

Evidence for Evolution

Charles Darwin (1809–1882) was an English naturalist with far-ranging interests. Like many scientists in the 1800s, he was intrigued with questions concerning evolution. He proposed his own theory of evolution in his 1859 book *Origin of Species.* In this book, he first argued that given species originate from other species, and eventually become distinct from these ancestors. Then he went on to explain why.

What reasons exist for believing that species evolve? *Origin of Species* mustered a great deal of evidence in support of the idea that evolution has indeed occurred. As you probably know, evolution was a highly controversial notion when Darwin and his contemporaries first became interested in the topic. Indeed, the very idea of evolution is still not accepted by some individuals today, but let us consider Darwin's evidence.

Domesticated plants and animals.   First, Darwin pointed to domesticated animals and plants to prove the fact of evolution. Cattle, pigs, dogs, sheep, goats, cats, chickens, and pigeons have wild and domesticated versions, as do wheat, corn, barley, cabbage, and peas. Darwin argued that each domesticated version evolved from a wild version.

In the case of domestic pigeons, such evolution occurred in the very recent past, under the watchful eye of scientists like Darwin. Pigeon fanciers create new breeds that differ strikingly from each other. By breeding increasingly extreme specimens with each other, pigeon breeders can produce fascinating variations in plumage, beak shape, and size. The end products of this breeding are completely different birds. The breeding history makes the fact of evolution clear. Similar examples come from intentionally breeding dogs, cats, roses, and corn.

Similar body parts.   As a second argument for the fact of evolution, Darwin pointed out that different species often have similar body parts. For example, the hands of people, the paws of dogs, the wings of bats, the hooves of horses, and the fins of dolphins all contain similar bones arranged in similar patterns. We can presume that different species were at some point related to each other, even though they have since changed.

Further support for this argument comes from research that has documented the recurrence across species of basic structures and forms. Consider the similarities of early development among species. The young often resemble each other more than the respective adults. Darwin (1859) discussed this resemblance in such species as crustaceans, insects, and cats.

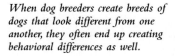

When dog breeders create breeds of dogs that look different from one another, they often end up creating behavioral differences as well.

For instance, both cougar kittens and lion cubs have spotted coats; as adults, neither cougars nor lions have spots, and the two look very different from one another. Embryos of different mammalian species also look very much alike, particularly in their earliest stages. All living creatures develop according to the blueprints found within their cells. Evidence like this points to links among species at earlier times, leading us to conclude that they have evolved from a common ancestor.

The fossil record. Another line of evidence in support of evolution comes from the fossil record. In the decades prior to Darwin's work, great strides were made in the field of geology. By Darwin's time, many scientists believed that the earth had existed for countless years.* Further, they recognized that aeons ago the earth was inhabited by plant and animal species no longer in existence. Putting these two ideas together, theorists in the 1800s accepted the notion that different species existed at different points in time. Fossils in earlier geologic periods resemble modern species less than more recent fossils, and so scientists had another reason for concluding that evolution had occurred.

Critics sometimes argue that the absence of missing links disproves the very idea of evolution. A missing link is an intermediate form of life between two different species. Critics feel that some number of these intermediate forms should exist if one species evolved from another. The problem is that critics ask for intermediates between contemporary species, like apes and people. But contemporary species are cousins, sharing a common ancestor. Think of the evolution of species as the branching of a tree, not as the addition of rungs to a ladder. By this view, there are no links, and so none is missing.

Natural Selection

Species change, but how do theorists explain these changes? Darwin's theory was inspired in part by the way pigeon breeders produce a new breed (Leakey, 1979). To create a pigeon with a long neck, let us say, pigeon fanciers choose those birds with longer than average necks and breed them together. Among the offspring are some number of long-necked birds. Now these birds are selected for breeding. After this process is repeated through numerous generations, what results (for the sake of our example) is a pigeon with an ostrichlike neck.

Darwin proposed that this process of selection can also occur naturally, without the intentional intervention of pigeon breeders. Hence, his theory of evolution emphasizes the role of **natural selection** in producing change. Nature plays the role of the pigeon breeder, although, of course, there is no final goal like a long neck. Necks become increasingly longer only if a longer neck aids the survival of a species every step of the way.

Here, then, are the main assumptions of Darwin's theory:

■ The members of particular species have characteristics that vary.
■ Some of these variable characteristics are passed on from parents to offspring.
■ Some of these variable characteristics aid survival.
■ Species produce more offspring than survive to become adults.

The conclusion follows that as one generation begets another generation, those characteristics that aid survival will become more common, whereas those that impede survival will become less common. Over time, new species can develop. By this view, members of nearby generations resemble each other to a great degree, but members of distant generations may resemble each other very little. Tiny differences multiplied over many years can become very large ones.

A contemporary example of how species change is the recent rise around the world in such infectious diseases as cholera, staph, strep, and tuberculosis (Lemonick, 1994). A

The English naturalist Charles Darwin revolutionized biology (and psychology) with his theory of evolution by natural selection.

■ **natural selection**
Darwin's explanation of evolution, holding that the natural environment of a species selects which individuals survive and reproduce, passing their characteristics on to offspring

---

*Christian doctrine, based on a literal reading of the Bible, estimated that the earth was created about 4000 B.C., whereas contemporary estimates by geologists suggest a starting point of at least 4 billion years ago.

few decades ago, many of these illnesses appeared to be all but erased by antibiotics, but certain strains of germs are immune to those drugs. With their competition—germs susceptible to antibiotics—out of the way, they have flourished.

According to the theory of evolution, any two species existing today at some point had a common ancestor. For some pairs of species, one need not trace them back too far to find their common ancestor. For other pairs of species, their common ancestor is lost in the dawn of time. When one speaks of human beings as related to the great apes (chimps, gorillas, and orangutans), one means that these species share a common ancestor in the relatively recent past, maybe 15 million years ago. One does not mean that people descended from the great apes, or vice versa.

Stop and Think

2   What evidence did Darwin cite in arguing that species had evolved?

3   What evidence supports Darwin's theory of evolution by natural selection?

4   What evidence would not support Darwin's theory of evolution by natural selection?

GENETICS

Darwin devised his theory of natural selection without knowing how the characteristics of parents are passed to their offspring. The mechanisms became clear only when studies conducted by an Austrian monk, Gregor Mendel (1822–1884), were later published. Mendel had investigated the inheritance of characteristics among pea plants, and his work eventually led to modern genetics.

The Gene

■ gene
microscopic mechanism of inheritance, composed of DNA molecules, passed from parents to offspring

Thanks to Mendel, evolutionary theorists of today regard the **gene** as the mechanism by which inheritance occurs. Genes are microscopic structures found within each cell of the body, composed of complex molecules called DNA (deoxyribonucleic acid). Think of genes as blueprints for biological development. Genes determine whether we are human beings, chimpanzees, or petunias. Genes determine whether we are males or females, tall or short, dark-haired or fair-haired.

■ chromosomes
sets of genes found in each cell of the body

Human beings have some 100,000 different genes. These are arranged along **chromosomes,** found in each cell of the body and inherited from one's parents. Each germ cell—egg and sperm—contains 23 chromosomes. When germ cells combine, the resulting

Because of genetic influences, heavy parents tend to have heavy children, and thin parents tend to have thin children. Weight is also determined by nutrition and by how the pituitary gland functions.

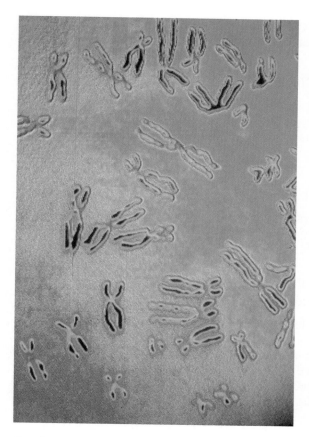 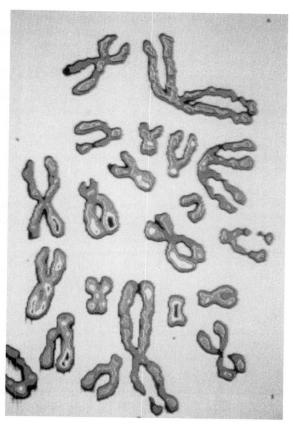

Our chromosomes exist in 23 pairs. A female's chromosomes are shown on the right, and a male's chromosomes on the left.

cell thus has 46 chromosomes—that is, 23 pairs. Reproduction takes half of the chromosomes from each parent and puts them together to form a unique offspring. The combination of parental chromosomes into unique patterns produces the variation upon which natural selection operates.

Variation across members of a species also occurs as a result of **mutations:** errors in the process of chromosome combination and/or replication. In many cases, mutations are so extreme that the resulting offspring cannot live. But in at least some cases, the mutation results in a viable organism and perhaps even one that survives better than others. For example, researchers fear that the AIDS virus might mutate into other forms; if and when a vaccine or cure is developed for existing strains of the virus, the new forms may be unaffected.

■ **mutation**
error in the process of chromosome combination and/or replication

Genotypes and Phenotypes

An individual's complete set of genes—from both parents—is called the **genotype.** The characteristics that the individual actually shows are called the **phenotype.** The phenotype reflects not only the plans contained in the genotype but also environmental events during development. So, an individual may have a genotype to be tall but, in the absence of adequate nourishment, not attain the height called for in the genetic plan. Or an individual may have a genotype to be short but then encounter problems with the pituitary gland so that great height results.

In other words, one's phenotype does not perfectly reflect one's genotype because innumerable events occurring during development, before and after birth, determine just how the plan contained in the genes is actually carried out. Indeed, some genes are

■ **genotype**
one's complete set of genes

■ **phenotype**
characteristics that one actually shows

activated only by appropriate input, which can include environmental influences. This is explicit recognition of a biopsychosocial influence.

Dominant and Recessive Genes

■ **dominant gene**
gene in a pair that influences the phenotype

■ **recessive gene**
gene in a pair that does not influence the phenotype

One member of each pair of genes is **dominant,** and the other is **recessive.** The dominant gene influences the phenotype, and the recessive gene does not. To use a familiar example, brown-eyed genes dominate blue-eyed genes. Hence, the gene for brown eyes is considered dominant and the gene for blue eyes is considered recessive. An individual's phenotype reflects a recessive gene only if both pairs of a gene are recessive. People with blue eyes have inherited a blue-eyed gene from both their mother and their father.

■ **polygenic inheritance**
determination of characteristics by more than one gene

Although the inheritance of eye color is a familiar example, it turns out to be oversimplified. Blue-eyed parents can have brown-eyed children because several genes are actually involved. This phenomenon is called **polygenic inheritance**—the determination of particular characteristics by more than one gene at a time—and it is the rule rather than the exception.

The Human Genome Project

■ **Human Genome Project**
ongoing scientific project to locate and describe all human genes

The **Human Genome Project** has attracted widespread scientific and popular attention (Cook-Degan, 1994; Wilkie, 1993). This international project, begun in the mid–1980s, aims at locating and describing all human genes. It will cost billions of dollars and should be completed by the early part of the twenty-first century. One of the hopes driving the Human Genome Project is that the specific genes that predispose poor health and early death can be identified and their negative effects neutralized (see Table 3.1). To do so will require a concrete understanding of the mechanisms leading from genetic instructions to complex human characteristics, such as susceptibility to disease. Thus, this project will contribute not just practical knowledge but also basic understanding of how a person comes to be.

Despite the promise of the Human Genome Project, it has been criticized. Some fear that the resources devoted to the project come at the expense of other scientific investigations. Geneticists believe that a large number of human genes are functionally irrelevant and that identifying them wastes time and money. Other critics worry about the possibility of genetic discrimination, denying people jobs, health insurance, and the like because their genetic inheritance puts them at risk for various illnesses. Critics also

---

Table 3.1   Examples of Genetically Influenced Illnesses

Many if not all diseases may eventually prove to be influenced by genetics. Here are some well-known examples of illnesses and conditions in which the contribution of genetics is already known to be significant.

Astigmatism	Infantile autism
Bipolar disorder	Klinefelter's syndrome
Color blindness	Male pattern baldness
Cystic fibrosis	Migraine headaches
Down's syndrome	Obsessive-compulsive disorder
Flat feet	Phenylketonuria
Fragile X syndrome	Polydactylism (extra digits)
Hemophilia	Schizophrenia
High cholesterol	Sickle-cell anemia
Huntington's chorea	Tay-Sachs disease
Hypertension	Turner's syndrome

worry that would-be parents will selectively terminate pregnancies until they conceive exactly the sort of child—in genetic terms—they wish to have.

Stop and Think

5   Explain how phenotypes are biopsychosocial.

6   What ethical concerns are raised by the Human Genome Project?

MODERN EVOLUTIONARY THEORY

Although Darwin's theory of evolution by natural selection has been highly influential and continues to be accepted as the general account of how species evolve, theorists after Darwin have elaborated and modified the theory. This section takes a look at some of the ideas that have emerged since Darwin first published *Origin of Species*. As you will see, these ideas improve the application of evolutionary concepts to human behavior.

Survival: Fitness Versus Inclusive Fitness

Herbert Spencer's (1864) catchphrase "survival of the fittest" is frequently used to summarize Darwin's theory of evolution. However, this slogan can be misleading. **Fitness** refers to successful reproduction, not staying power or longevity. To an evolutionary theorist, an organism is fit if it successfully passes its genes to the next generation. If we wish to be precise, we regard survival as referring to the continuation of genes, not individuals or species.

■ **fitness**
successful reproduction

Consider Pacific salmon. They use all their resources in a single spawning, after which they die (Daly & Wilson, 1983). The life history of this fish contradicts many usages of the term *survival,* but it exemplifies what biologists mean by the term. A pair of salmon produces from 3,000 to 5,000 eggs, a small number of which will become adults to repeat the process. To an evolutionary theorist, Pacific salmon are fit, not because they can swim upstream thousands of miles but because they can reproduce successfully.

Pacific salmon are fit, not because they can swim upstream thousands of miles but because they can reproduce successfully.

Some interpretations of evolution see the process as a competition among individual organisms. Yet the real competition occurs not among organisms but among their genes. Fitness transcends an individual to include all those organisms that share genes. Accordingly, there are circumstances in which laying down your life for the sake of another can be evolutionarily advantageous, as long as the two of you share common genes. If the sacrifice of your life enhances the reproductive success of your close relative, then your act enhances the survival of your own genes. So, **inclusive fitness** is the fitness of an individual plus the influence of the individual on the fitness of his or her kin (Hamilton, 1964).

Inclusive fitness extends the traditional interpretation of fitness, allowing evolutionary theory to be applied to topics that previously seemed outside its limits. Earlier we encountered the social insects and learned that most of them do not reproduce. The notion of inclusive fitness explains how this state of affairs evolved through natural selection. The sterile workers share genes with those few insects that do reproduce; hence, the success of the queen is the success of the workers as well.

Daly and Wilson (1983) described a striking example of inclusive fitness. Ground squirrels of one particular species stake out territories in close proximity to each other. When predators threaten, a squirrel gives a loud alarm call, alerting other squirrels while putting itself in danger. This behavior appears altruistic. But research also shows that sometimes a squirrel does not sound an alarm when a predator is near. The critical factor that determines if a squirrel gives an alarm is whether its neighbors happen to be close relatives.

Mechanisms and Functions: Proximate Causation Versus Ultimate Causation

The ground squirrel example might be misunderstood. A person hearing about these squirrels might conclude that these creatures know their relatives like human beings know their relatives, through frequent family reunions and long-distance calling circles, and that they apply this knowledge on a case-by-case basis when predators approach: "Here comes an eagle. Cousin Mildred is scuba diving off Florida, so I guess I'd best keep my mouth shut."

Facetiousness makes a point. We must distinguish between **proximate causation**—how a characteristic like sounding a distress call occurs in an individual— and **ultimate causation**—how this characteristic contributes to the fitness of a species. Although the alarm calls of ground squirrels seem to have evolved because they contributed to reproductive success (ultimate cause), one should not conclude that conscious considerations of inclusive fitness determine when a particular squirrel squeaks or not (proximate cause). These animals do not have an address book filled with the names of their close relatives. The direct cause is probably more mundane—like smells encountered during infancy. The ground squirrel will sound a warning call when in the presence of familiar smells because these will usually indicate that close relatives are in the immediate vicinity. In the absence of these smells, no warning call is made.

The distinction between proximate and ultimate causation corresponds to Tinbergen's (1968) distinction between explanation in terms of causes and explanation in terms of functions. The proximate causes of behavior are the mechanisms that produce it, and the ultimate causes are the survival functions served by the behavior. We need to specify both.

Development and Evolution: Ontogeny Versus Phylogeny

Ontogeny is the course of development of an individual organism within its lifetime, whereas **phylogeny** involves the evolution of a species or a genetically related group of organisms. Perhaps you have heard that "ontogeny recapitulates phylogeny." The phrase

■ **inclusive fitness**
fitness of an individual plus
fitness of the individual's relatives

■ **proximate causation**
how a characteristic occurs in an
individual

■ **ultimate causation**
how a characteristic contributes
to the fitness of a species

■ **ontogeny**
course of development of an
individual organism within its
lifetime

■ **phylogeny**
evolution of a species or genetically related group of organisms

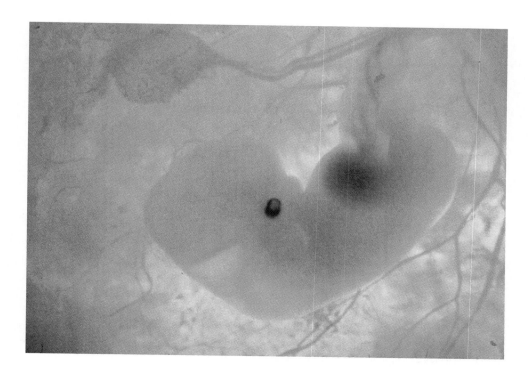

The phrase "ontogeny recapitulates phylogeny" means that during individual development, an organism undergoes changes similar to those its ancestors underwent as they evolved. This idea is not always true, but in this picture of a human embryo, note the presence of gill slits like those of a fish.

suggests that as an organism develops, it undergoes changes similar to those its ancestors underwent in evolution. This description is sometimes accurate. Consider human beings, who at the moment of conception are but a single cell; as embryos, we have gill slits that look like those of a fish.

But ontogeny does not recapitulate phylogeny in all cases. We cannot look to individual development for a foolproof notion of species development (Gould, 1977). For example, human beings develop language before they reproduce, but no one concludes that the capacity for language developed prior in evolution to the capacity for sexual reproduction.

The importance of the distinction between ontogeny and phylogeny is that the study of individual development cannot substitute for the study of evolution. Reconstructing the evolutionary history of our species is difficult, and previous generations of theorists attempted to describe our distant ancestors in terms of what they knew about contemporary infants and children. They depicted early human beings as childlike, a characterization that persists in popular portrayals of our ancestors in cartoons and movies. But because ontogeny does not always recapitulate phylogeny, there is no justification for generalizing from one to the other.

Constraints on Evolution

The forms of new species are constrained by the forms of old species. Evolution does not act on infinite variation in characteristics—only on variation that actually exists. As already noted, mutations often produce organisms that do not live, particularly when these are too different from the typical members of a species. Even when mutations prove viable, they still resemble their parents in most essential ways.

Why do human beings have only two eyes? Four eyes would help us as we traverse the city, the interstate highway, or the football field. However, we are constrained by our immediate ancestors. Their form was constrained by their immediate ancestors, and so on (Eldredge & Gould, 1972). At this point in evolution, it is virtually impossible for primates to develop four eyes, even through profound mutations or highly unusual selection pressures.

The process of evolution has no final destination and follows no preordained plan. Yet some thinkers have apparently had trouble grasping the idea that evolution need not imply progress. For instance, consider the phylogenetic scale, a familiar arrangement of living species in a presumed order from primitive to advanced:

$$\text{fish} \rightarrow \text{reptiles} \rightarrow \text{amphibians} \rightarrow \text{birds} \rightarrow \text{mammals}$$

Among mammals, there is a similar rank order, ending with primates. Among primates, the scale culminates in human beings. As a dimension of fitness, the phylogenetic scale makes no more sense than an attempt to arrange your cousins from primitive to advanced (Campbell & Hodos, 1991).

Environmental Change

Theorists tend to be drawn to the products of evolution—genes, individuals, and species. They may theorize about these products without sufficient attention to the environment in which evolution occurs. Evolution, however, is determined by the particular characteristics of the immediate surroundings. Once we remember that organisms live in a particular setting, we realize that we must describe fitness in relation to that setting. We cannot regard organisms as primitive or advanced. Are human beings more advanced than houseflies? Are guinea pigs more primitive than baboons? These are wrongheaded questions because these species live in different environments, or niches, to use the technical term.

Modern evolutionary theorists therefore pay more attention to the environment than was true of previous theorists in this tradition, recognizing that the course of evolution depends on how the environment changes. If an organism's niche stays the same, it becomes adapted to it as well as it can within imposed constraints, as just explained. Then the species no longer changes. Certain creatures, such as cockroaches, have apparently existed in much the same form for millions of years because the relevant features of their environments did not change.

Other creatures occupy niches that do change, sometimes rather rapidly. The climate may change, new predators may appear, or sources of food may disappear. Consider the fate of dinosaurs. There is a great deal of debate about why they vanished, and different theorists propose different accounts. All agree, however, that something drastic, to which they could not adapt, happened in the dinosaurs' environment. Either the climate changed too extremely, their sources of food disappeared, or newly evolved mammals appeared and wiped them out by eating the eggs they laid. The exact reason is not important in making the point that the environment of a species is critical in understanding its evolution.

When conditions change, what may have been a useful characteristic can become irrelevant or even harmful. Or the opposite may occur. A well-known example is the changes in coloration of the peppered moths that live in and around London (Bishop & Cook, 1975). Several hundred years ago, most of these moths were lightly colored, presumably an advantage to them because they could blend in with the lichen that covered the tree trunks where they were usually to be found. Birds that fed upon them could not readily see them. When occasionally a darkly colored moth was born, it did not survive too long.

However, with industrialization, the air around London became polluted and the lichen on the tree trunks died. Lightly colored moths were now easy prey for birds because they stood out against the dark trees. Darkly covered moths now had an advantage, and by 1950, 90 percent of the peppered moths in London were dark ones. More recently, with the advent of antipollution laws, the lichen are making a comeback and so

Although they are difficult to see, there is a lightly colored moth on the lichen-covered bark in the picture on the left and a darkly colored moth on the bark in the picture on the right. Because predators have the same difficulty detecting these moths, lightly colored moths are more likely to survive in the first situation and darkly colored moths in the second.

too are lightly colored moths. Although it is common to speak casually of evolution as something that occurred only in the past, it is ongoing for all species.

Stop and Think

7   What is the difference between fitness and inclusive fitness?

8   What is the difference between proximate causation and ultimate causation?

9   How is evolution a biopsychosocial phenomenon?

DOING *Evolution* RESEARCH

For a few species like the peppered moth, natural selection has had rapid and recent effects, and so we can actually glimpse evolution in progress. But for most species, including human beings, it is much more difficult to track the process. How, then, do researchers interested in applying evolutionary ideas to people go about their research? The best they can do is obtain indirect evidence that allows them to make inferences about evolution.

Relevant Evidence

When different sources of indirect evidence all point in the same direction, researchers have confidence in the conclusions. To argue that a specific behavior has a basis in evolution, a researcher usually tries to determine if:

- the behavior is (or at one time was) adaptive
- the behavior is apparent in most members of a species

- the behavior is apparent in most closely related species
- the behavior is influenced by genetics

In the example of left-cradling of infants by human females, all of these criteria are satisfied.

Perhaps the strongest evidence that a behavior has an evolutionary basis would be that the behavior is apparent in the ancestors of a species, but there is no fossil record of behavior. Rather, our ancestors left behind teeth and bones and on occasion tools and other artifacts. Inferences about behavior can be based on these relics but must be regarded as highly tentative.

Plausible Explanation

Evolutionary researchers need a theory that ties together the available evidence. They need to specify how the behavior of interest contributes to the fitness of a species in the niche the species occupies, keeping in mind that niches sometimes change. They need to specify the mechanisms that trigger the behavior.

Is their theory plausible? Is it more plausible than alternative explanations? For example, the behavior of left-cradling of infants can be plausibly explained in terms of evolution, but we additionally must decide that such an account makes more sense than one that emphasizes, for example, social imitation.

The Course of Human Evolution

Any evolutionary explanation of human behavior must be consistent with what is known about the course of human evolution. Although considerable disagreement exists about our distant ancestors and although fossil discoveries that demand new conceptualizations are ongoing, here is a sketch of what most researchers believe about human evolution (see Figure 3.1).

There is no fossil record of behavior. Psychologists interested in the evolution of human behavior must make inferences about behavior from what our distant ancestors did leave behind: teeth, bones, tools, and eight-track cassettes.

First, there is a consensus that human beings did evolve and that primates such as gorillas and chimpanzees are our closest living relatives. This conclusion is supported not only by the fossil record, but also by genetic analyses. People share more genetic material in common with primates than with other species. As already mentioned, human beings and the great apes probably shared a common ancestor some 15 million years ago.

Deciding at what point one of our ancestors was human is somewhat arbitrary, depending on the characteristic we use to define being human. Theorists often focus on an upright posture and the use of tools, if for no other reason than that these characteristics can be more readily inferred from the fossil record than other possible criteria.

Homo habilis was clearly human in these terms. This species lived in Africa 2 or 3 million years ago. Members of this species walked upright and had powerful hands. They were about 4 feet tall and weighed 80 to 90 pounds. In contrast to other primates living at this time, they had large heads.

About 1.6 million years ago, another humanlike species appeared: *Homo erectus.* Whether *Homo habilis* was the direct ancestor of *Homo erectus* or was displaced by this species is not known. *Homo erectus* had a larger head than *Homo habilis* did and apparently led a more complex life. Members of this species lived in small groups in semipermanent encampments where they prepared and consumed food. They hunted large animals and used fire. *Homo erectus* made a variety of tools that were more sophisticated than those used by *Homo habilis.* Presumably aided by their social nature and their hunting skills, members of *Homo erectus* spread not only throughout Africa, but also to Europe and Asia.

About 150,000 years ago, another group of human beings—*Homo sapiens neanderthalensis*—appeared in Europe and Central Asia. They constructed huts in which to live. They buried their dead in a ritualistic way, suggesting cultural practices not previously evident among human ancestors. Neanderthals were highly similar to modern human beings, differing chiefly by having thicker bones and larger teeth.

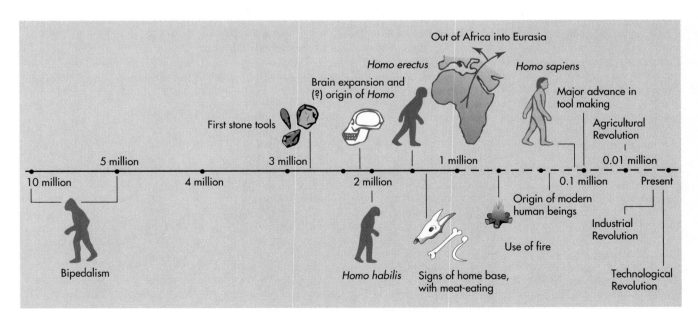

Figure 3.1
Course of Human Evolution. Here is one possible account of the origin and evolution of our species. Modern human beings (*Homo sapiens*) appeared about 100,000 years ago, although other humanlike species (e.g., *Homo habilis* and *Homo erectus*) long predated our own species. Whether these other species were the direct ancestors of modern human beings or were rivals displaced by our actual ancestors is not clear from the fossil record.

The relationship of Neanderthals to *Homo erectus* is not clear, nor do theorists agree about their relationship to modern human beings, *Homo sapiens,* who first appeared on the scene between 40,000 and 100,000 years ago. There is no agreement whether Neanderthals were the direct ancestors of modern human beings, a rival subspecies that was displaced by competition with modern human beings, or a group that interbred and merged with modern human beings. But Neanderthals and modern human beings coexisted for at least several thousand years.

One debate about the origins of modern human beings has apparently been resolved. Earlier in the twentieth century, there were two theoretical positions about the emergence of our species. The first theory proposed that modern human beings had several origins, arising independently from earlier human species in different parts of the world, and then interbreeding to result in the single species we are today. The second theory proposed that modern human beings had but a single origin.

Recent research with contemporary human beings points to the second theory (Cann, Stonekins, & Wilson, 1987; Dorit, Akashi, & Gilbert, 1995). By analyzing variability in genetic material from people around the world and taking the time line suggested by the fossil record into account, investigators have concluded that all contemporary people had to have descended from a single female ancestor who lived about 200,000 years ago and a single male ancestor who lived about 270,000 years ago. The variation in the genetic material is compatible with the idea of a single origin, as opposed to multiple origins.

Our distant predecessors have—predictably—been dubbed Eve and Adam, but let me be clear that they were not the only human beings present back then or the first ever to appear. They were certainly not each other's mates. Their bones have not been discovered. The point is that these individuals, whose existence has been inferred, were the direct ancestors of all 5 billion people who live today, an amazing enough conclusion.

In making sense of the course of human evolution, theorists variously emphasize our ancestors' ability to walk upright, their large brains, their social nature, and their skill at the use of tools as the most relevant characteristics in allowing adaptation to the world in which they found themselves. Also presumed to be critical are language, which allowed communication, and culture, which allowed knowledge to be passed from one generation to the next. All of these characteristics arguably made those who possessed them more fit than their contemporaries who did not.

We must be careful, however, not to assume that these characteristics were necessarily the ones on which natural selection operated during human evolution. It is just as

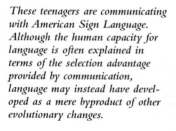

These teenagers are communicating with American Sign Language. Although the human capacity for language is often explained in terms of the selection advantage provided by communication, language may instead have developed as a mere byproduct of other evolutionary changes.

possible that these characteristics were the incidental byproducts of other evolutionary changes—for example, those that allowed our ancestors to live on the ground rather than in trees. These characteristics have since proved highly useful to our species, but their current function may not be why they evolved.

Stop and Think

10 Is the theory of evolution by natural selection nonfalsifiable?

11 Is human evolution still occurring? What evidence supports your answer?

EVOLUTIONARY EXPLANATIONS OF HUMAN BEHAVIOR

In his 1871 book *The Descent of Man,* Darwin applied his theory of evolution to human beings, concluding that our species evolved from an earlier one, that apes are our close cousins, and that the difference between human beings and apes is less than the difference between apes and other animals. These conclusions sparked criticism and controversy in some quarters (and still do). However, including human beings under the same evolutionary umbrella as other living creatures has also met with enthusiastic acceptance.

The theory of evolution, when applied to human beings, led to a new viewpoint within psychology. People's characteristics—including not just body parts but also thoughts, feelings, and actions—exist as they do because they have had survival value. Evolutionary theory was a particularly important influence on functionalism, which stressed the consequences of behavior (Chapter 1). This section discusses some of the theoretical attempts that have been made over the years to explain human behavior in evolutionary terms (see Table 3.2).

Social Darwinism

One of the earliest attempts to relate evolutionary ideas to human behavior was **social Darwinism,** the application of the theory of natural selection to human societies as a whole. Here is the logic: Cultures compete for scarce resources, and the more fit cultures survive, whereas the less fit do not. Social Darwinists in the 1800s pointed to the ascendance of European culture, Christian values, and the upper class. Here were clear instances of the survival of the fittest, or so, at least, the social Darwinists thought.

The social Darwinists ended up defending the status quo as the way it had to be. Those with power and privilege were fit and deserved their fate, just as the sick and feeble deserved their lot in life. The problem with this approach was that it used the theory of evolution to justify whatever happened to exist at the moment (Vining,

■ **social Darwinism**
application of the theory of natural selection to human societies as a whole

---

Table 3.2 Evolutionary Explanations of Human Behavior

Approach	Key emphasis
Social Darwinism	"Evolution" of societies as a whole
Comparative psychology	Comparisons and contrasts across species
Ethology	Behavior in the natural environments
Behavior genetics	Genetic influences on individual differences
Sociobiology	Complex social behavior
Evolutionary psychology	Evolved psychological mechanisms

1986). It was dragged into political, religious, and moral arenas, where it was used as a justification by those who wished to promote their particular beliefs. In fact, social Darwinism played a role in Nazi ideology about pure and impure races (Meyer, 1988). Nazism was so repugnant that few people after World War II were willing to identify themselves as social Darwinists (Bannister, 1979).

Comparative Psychology

■ **comparative psychology**
study of behavioral similarities and differences across animal species

Other approaches to psychology inspired by evolutionary thought have been more useful. **Comparative psychology** is the study of behavioral similarities and differences across animal species, usually with the goal of establishing evolutionary relationships among them. Comparative psychologists have often studied the performance of two or more vertebrate species at learning tasks requiring intelligence (Bitterman, 1965; Heim, 1954; Romanes, 1882; Thorndike, 1911). Similarities between human beings and other species can be illuminating in view of all the differences across species that would work against comparable behavior (Roitblat & von Fersen, 1992; Rumbaugh, 1990; Wasserman, 1993).

The following is a representative example (Hall, 1983). Suppose you present people with two stimuli—disks, buttons, levers, whatever—and arrange for a reward to follow when they choose the larger stimulus. This task requires a relative judgment and therefore demands a certain subtlety. Some theorists suggest that language allows people to respond appropriately, that we tag the stimuli as larger or smaller and answer accordingly. However, rats and pigeons are also capable of making these relative judgments. They can learn to choose the larger or smaller of two stimuli in order to earn a reward. These animals do not have language to assist them, and any psychologist interested in explaining human judgment must take into account the animal findings (Chapter 9). They suggest that judgments like these do not depend on having words to express concepts and, hence, that the ability to make complex judgments appeared early in evolutionary history.

Comparative psychologists are also interested in behavioral differences (Cosmides & Tooby, 1994; Tooby & Cosmides, 1989). As will be explained in detail in Chapter 8, psychologists who study learning have argued that different types of learning are apparent in different species. Animals that rely greatly on vision, for instance, such as birds, readily learn to associate visual stimuli with threat. Other species show comparable specificity of learning mechanisms.

Ethology

■ **ethology**
field that studies the behavior of animals in their natural environments

Ethology is the field that studies the behavior of animals in their natural environments as opposed to laboratories or other artificial settings. Ethologists bring a biological perspective to their investigations and look in particular at how patterns of behavior may have been inherited in different animal species (Eibl-Eibesfeldt, 1970; Lorenz, 1965; Tinbergen, 1951), including human beings (Morris, 1967).

■ **fixed-action patterns; instincts**
unlearned behaviors, common to an entire species, that occur in the presence of certain stimuli

Fixed-action patterns.   Ethologists often make use of the notion of **fixed-action patterns** (also known as **instincts**), unlearned behaviors, common to an entire species, that occur in the presence of certain stimuli. For instance, male stickleback fish will automatically attack other males, even if they have never before been exposed to them (Chapter 7). The trigger for this attack is the red belly characterizing males of this species (Tinbergen, 1951). These instincts presumably evolved, as their close link to reproduction implies.

As noted, fixed-action patterns are unlearned. This feature is shown by isolating an individual at birth from any environmental input that might influence the behavior. If the behavior later appears (the male stickleback attacks), the researcher can conclude that it is a fixed-action pattern. Similar demonstrations have been done with the behaviors of other animals, like the songs of certain bird species.

Human ethology.   Do people show instinctive behavior? Isolation experiments like those possible with fish or birds cannot ethically be conducted with human beings because one would need to keep an infant from all contact with other people. In some unfortunate cases, however, children grow up under such circumstances (see Chapter 10 for an example). These feral children (literally, wild children) show profound intellectual, emotional, and social poverty (Maclean, 1977). Very little of what we would call human behavior spontaneously occurs as they develop. Language typically does not exist, and the ability to form social relationships is gravely impaired. These facts argue against the possibility that complex human behavior is inherited as a whole.

For example, left-cradling of infants by human females would probably not be shown by someone who grew up in extreme isolation from others. This individual might not even recognize an infant as a human being, much less be led to cradle it. Indeed, many first-time parents need to be instructed about how best to hold newborns, supporting their heads and in general making them feel secure in their grasp. But granted the importance of this sort of learning, there is still room for an evolutionary influence (see Figure 3.2).

Consider the characteristics of faces that people regard as attractive. Human ethologists find considerable agreement across cultures. The width of an attractive female's eyes tend to be about 30 percent the width of her face, and her nose tends to occupy about 5 percent of the area of her face (Cunningham, 1986). Are these features deemed attractive because of inherent human tendencies or because of arbitrary social conventions?

It is impossible to know with certainty, but consider the results of further studies that superimpose facial photographs of many different individuals. The resulting composite, an average face if there was ever one, is usually rated as more attractive than the component faces, which belong to actual people (Langlois & Roggman, 1990). These findings also hold across different ethnic groups (Perrett, May, & Yoshikawa, 1994). We are drawn to prototypical faces, even though they rarely exist in the real world. Some ethologists therefore hypothesize that this tendency represents a fixed-action pattern. Attractiveness is an ingredient in our decisions to choose mates and friends, although love and friendship involve many additional considerations not shaped by evolution (Chapter 15).

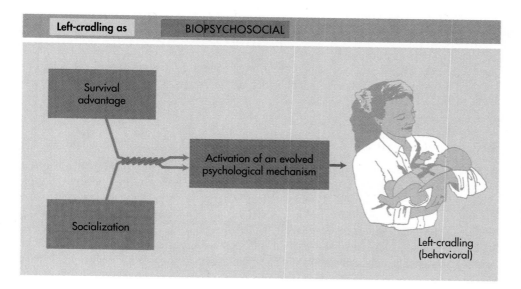

Figure 3.2
Left-Cradling of Infants as Biopsychosocial. Although the tendency of females to cradle infants on the left side of their bodies may have arisen in the course of evolution because it provided a survival advantage, this behavior also reflects psychological and social influences. For example, a person must learn to recognize an infant and its need to be cradled. Such socialization, coupled with the biological predisposition to cradle on the left side, leads to this behavior through several biological and psychological mechanisms.

Other examples of biologically based human tendencies include our smiles and laughs. Researchers have shown these to be highly stereotyped; their form and their function are the same across almost all people (Fridlund, 1991b; Provine & Yong, 1991). Infants born blind or deaf smile or laugh in the same circumstances as other infants do, a finding that argues against a role of imitation in producing these responses (McInnes & Treffry, 1982/1993). Even out of context, laughter triggers smiles and laughs by those who hear it (Provine, 1992). Further, parallels exist between human smiles and laughs and the facial and vocal expressions of other species. Barbary macaques, for example, smile to signal submission and appeasement to dominant monkeys, whereas they laugh to signal their willingness to play with their peers (Preuschoft, 1992).

In general because of the genetic similarity among primate species, the study of monkeys and apes as they live in their natural environments is a popular strategy by ethologists interested in human beings (Rodseth, Wrangham, Harrigan, & Smuts, 1991). Also informative are anthropological studies of particular human cultures, such as the !Kung of the Kalahari, the Aborigines of Australia, and the BaMbuti of the Congo, that still exist in much the same way they have for tens of thousands of years (Shostak, 1981; Turnbull, 1962). We can learn about behavior by studying it in the settings in which people presumably evolved.

Here is what such studies imply about the lives of the very first members of our species some 100,000 years ago, findings that supplement information available from the fossil record: They lived in small nomadic groups; they built temporary shelters and foraged for food; males hunted large animals; females gathered plants. Glantz and Pearce (1989, p. 15) reached the following conclusions regarding such groups:

> The social organization of a . . . hunting and gathering band is a miracle of dynamic balance. Freedom and conformity, self-reliance and cooperation, generosity and envy, sharing and greed, love and anger—all are bound together. . . . Every problematic impulse can be observed. . . . and yet it all works: the band swirls through desert and jungle in a tiny tornado of communication and support.
>
> There is no single explanation for this acrobatic triumph of sociality. The band is a product of long years of evolution, an integrated system. . . .
>
> The members of a band are closely related. Helping someone in the group means helping a relative or someone married to a relative. . . . As a result, self-interest and the good of the community are very difficult to separate.
>
> Order is achieved through tradition and conformity. No courts, judges, or prisons are necessary. No one wants to be ostracized from the circle.

As already emphasized, reconstructing the behavior of our ancestors thousands of generations removed is difficult, and firm answers will remain elusive. However, ethologists who concern themselves with human evolution argue that this strategy is among the best ways to understand people's behavior in the present. One conclusion that seems unassailable is that people have always been social in nature.

Behavior Genetics

behavior genetics
field that studies how genetic differences within a species are related to behavior differences

Yet another approach to psychology in evolutionary terms is **behavior genetics,** which studies how genetic differences within a species are related to behavior differences (Hirsch, 1967; Plomin & Rende, 1991; Wimer & Wimer, 1985). At first glance, this field seems to overlap with ethology, but there are two important differences. First, whereas ethologists are concerned with behaviors shown by all members of a species, behavior geneticists focus on behavioral differences within a species. Second, whereas ethologists usually study behaviors having an instinctive basis, behavior geneticists usually look at behaviors caused by complex interactions between genetic and environmental factors. So, ethologists study the nest building of stickleback fish, which is a

The Genain sisters are identical quadruplets who were all diagnosed with schizophrenia. However, the severity of this problem varied across the sisters, showing that genetics do not provide the whole explanation.

fixed-action pattern; behavior geneticists study topics like learning, intelligence, and personality, which reflect multiple determinants, biological and environmental.

Pioneers within behavior genetics showed that animals could be selectively bred to behave in one way or another. For example, Tryon (1940) produced good and bad maze learners among rats, just as the pigeon fanciers described earlier in this chapter produced animals that looked so different from each other. Similarly, dog breeders who intentionally create physical variations sometimes end up creating behavioral variations. You may know that cocker spaniels are placid and Irish setters are skittish—these are genetically based differences (Scott & Fuller, 1965).

Heritability.   A key concept in behavior genetics is **heritability,** the proportion of a trait's variation that is due to genetic factors. The more a trait's variation in a group of individuals is due to genetic factors, the greater is its heritability. For example, people's intelligence shows a fair degree of heritability, meaning that differences among people in intelligence in part reflect differences in their genes (Chapter 11).

Do not equate heritability with any simple notion of inherited. The preceding paragraph did not say that intelligence is inherited, passed directly from parents to children. Heritability is a more abstract concept, referring to a group of people, not to an individual. It refers to the variation in intelligence across these people, not to the intelligence of a given person. Behavior geneticists seek to link variation in traits or behaviors to variation in genes. This goal differs from that of ethology, which tries to show that entire behaviors are inherited.

The difference between heritability and inherited will become clearer when research on the heritability of intelligence (Chapter 11), personality characteristics (Chapter 12), and psychological disorders (Chapter 13) is discussed. In each case, evidence supports heritability, meaning that variation in these characteristics is influenced by genetic differences among people—but not that the characteristics themselves are inherited.

Although behavior genetics draws our attention to the biological bases of behavior, some theorists caution that evidence of a characteristic's heritability need not mean that the characteristic has a basis in our evolutionary history (Rowe & Osgood, 1984). Evolution usually minimizes variation within a species, so that members of a species come to resemble each other in ways that further survival. Behavior geneticists must therefore grapple with the question of why variability exists. A species as a whole may benefit because its members are different, but it is also possible that the characteristic of

■ **heritability**
proportion of a trait's variation across individuals that is due to genetic factors

interest is—in evolutionary terms—simply irrelevant. This debate is taken up in more detail in Chapter 12, which discusses the heritability of personality.

The role of the environment.   Granted the topics they study, behavior geneticists who study people expect the environment, in combination with genetic factors, to play a role in determining behavior (Loehlin, Willerman, & Horn, 1988). Behavior genetics is a young field, and much work remains to be done in specifying the concrete mechanisms by which genetic variation influences behavioral variation. In terms introduced earlier in the chapter, the weak point of behavior genetics research is its typical silence on the proximate causes of behavior. Intelligence is heritable, for example, but what specific biological and psychological mechanisms influenced by genetics make people more versus less intelligent (Chapter 11)?

Sociobiology

■ **sociobiology**
application of modern evolutionary theory to social behavior

Another recent attempt to explain human behavior using biological concepts, called **sociobiology,** is the application of modern evolutionary theory to social behavior (Wilson, 1975, 1978). Complex social interaction invariably proved a stumbling block to evolution theorists because any society requires cooperation, compromise, and occasional sacrifice on the part of its members (Shapiro & Gabbard, 1994). It was not clear to earlier generations of theorists how natural selection could encourage selfless behaviors like those by the ground squirrels described earlier.

Inclusive fitness and social behavior.   Sociobiology solves this problem by using the notion of inclusive fitness. As you recall, inclusive fitness allows altruism to be explained in biological terms by referring to genes shared by two organisms. Sociobiologists employ this concept to interpret social behavior just as they interpret individual characteristics—as adaptive. We follow certain social conventions because they helped our ancestors pass their genes on to subsequent generations. Sociobiologists have applied the concept of inclusive fitness to such topics as aggression, helping, sex roles, and morality (Beckstrom, 1993).

According to some sociobiologists, war is an inherent consequence of our evolutionary inheritance.

Many of these applications share a common problem: Explanations of behavior are offered after the fact. Predictions are derived, apparently from evolutionary considerations, about matters that are already well known. For instance, sociobiology explains why males are more aggressive than females by saying that this pattern has been adaptive for the human species. Males usually did the hunting, and so a tendency to be aggressive was adaptive. But the fact of male aggression hardly proves a sociobiological explanation because the sociobiologist started with knowledge of this fact.

Critics refer to such sociobiological explanations as just-so stories, after Rudyard Kipling's fanciful accounts of how animals developed their characteristics, like an elephant's baggy skin or a kangaroo's hop. Evolutionary theorists may be making up their own just-so stories, starting with some trait or behavior and working backward to explain how it developed. But such retrospective tales often leave the traits or behaviors in question as their only supporting evidence.

Controversy concerning sociobiology.   Sociobiology generates controversy for two related reasons. First, it argues that many of our species-typical activities, like male aggressiveness, are biologically based and, further, must somehow be adaptive. When a theorist suggests that the structures of the nervous system have functional significance, none would disagree. But eyebrows are raised when this same argument is applied to rape, infanticide, and war. Some sociobiologists have argued that these activities are the product of evolution, thus an adaptive part of a fixed human nature. Many others disagree, and the arguments color the entire field (Coe, 1981).

Second, sociobiology generates controversy when used to explain differences within the human species as biologically based. To say that men and women are fundamentally different because of evolutionary reasons is to undercut, at least by implication, social and political movements for equality between the sexes. To say that different ethnic groups are fundamentally different because of evolutionary reasons again implies that attempts to change current inequities are pointless and perhaps even wrong.

Consider male aggressiveness. If this is an inherent aspect of human nature, then perhaps women because they are not sufficiently violent, should not be allowed to serve in the military. Perhaps women should not be allowed to be police officers. Perhaps they should not be allowed to participate in competitive sports. Or we could reverse these ideas and argue that men because of their aggressive nature, should be the ones kept out of settings and circumstances where they might hurt others. Perhaps gun control should apply only to males. Needless to say, many people would find some or all of these prohibitions contrary to the ideals of our society.

One of the most heated debates about sociobiological ideas followed the publication of several papers by J. Philippe Rushton (1985, 1988), who argued that behavioral differences among individuals of European, Asian, and African ancestry are based in the different evolutionary histories of these groups. Among the particular behaviors Rushton discussed were sexual restraint, mental health, respect for the law, and marital stability. He offered broad conclusions that certain ethnic groups as a whole exhibit these behaviors in varying degrees relative to other ethnic groups and that the reason for these differences is biological.

Not surprisingly, these conclusions have been criticized (Zuckerman & Brody, 1988). Rushton ignored the role of cultural and economic factors in determining differences among groups. Further, he treated the so-called races as if they were defined solely on biological grounds. A different view treats races as essentially social categories, not biological ones (Chapter 11), and thus sees evolutionary theorizing about them to be meaningless.

Despite the controversial extrapolations by some theorists, sociobiology has many advocates within contemporary psychology. As you have seen, some previous attempts to explain human behavior in biological terms failed when they became too sweeping, assuming that biology requires no assistance from psychology (Parisi, 1987). If sociobiology can avoid the temptation to explain every aspect of the human condition, it will have greater fitness than its predecessors.

Evolutionary Psychology

■ **evolutionary psychology**
field that studies the evolved
psychological mechanisms that
give rise to behavior

The most recent attempt to apply evolutionary ideas to human behavior is **evolutionary psychology,** which can be distinguished by its explicit concern with the mechanisms that give rise to human behavior. Presumably, these proximate causes reflect the operation of evolution; they produced behaviors that were adaptive at some point in the history of our species. However, it cannot be assumed that they serve the survival of contemporary human beings. As Buss (1995, p. 10) observed:

> Humans are living fossils—collections of mechanisms produced by prior selection pressures operating on a long and unbroken line of ancestors. Today we activate and execute these specific mechanisms . . . whether or not they currently lead to fitness or reproductive success.

Evolved psychological mechanisms.   The task of the evolutionary psychologist is to identify these **evolved psychological mechanisms** by specifying the survival problem they once solved, the situations in which they are currently used, and the biological and/or psychological processes they entail. Buss (1995) proposed a number of evolved psychological mechanisms, and you will encounter many others throughout this book (see Table 3.3).

■ **evolved psychological mechanism**
biological and/or psychological
process that arose in the course of
evolution to solve a survival
problem of a species and still
influences behavior today

For example, human beings and many other primates tend to be afraid of snakes, even the first time they are encountered (Marks, 1987). Such a fear was probably advantageous to our distant ancestors, granted the environment in which they evolved. Fear of snakes is triggered by long, slithering stimuli in one's immediate vicinity; these stimuli speed up our hearts, change our breathing, and focus our attention; this arousal leads to freezing or fleeing. Similar arguments can be made about other common human fears: of spiders, heights, darkness, blood, and pointed objects (Chapter 13). Each of these common fears revolves around survival hazards faced by our ancestors.

Another possible example of an evolved psychological mechanism is the tendency of both men and women to prefer mates who are kind, intelligent, and dependable (Buss, 1989). The problem solved by this tendency is successful child rearing. In the course of evolution (as well as at the present time), a mate with these attributes is likely to be a good parent. Hence, an individual seeking a mate is attracted to someone like this, procreation takes its course, and, we would hope, everyone lives happily ever after.

In addition to these general preferences, Buss (1995) suggested that males and females show some specific differences in the types of mates they prefer, again because

---

Table 3.3   Evolved Psychological Mechanisms

According to evolutionary psychologists, people have numerous evolved psychological mechanisms. Here are some of the possibilities discussed in later chapters and the functions they presumably serve.

Mechanism	Function
Attachment	Solidify infant-caretaker bond (Chapter 10)
Conformity	Regularize behavior in a small group (Chapter 15)
Depression	Encourage cessation of frustrating activities (Chapter 13)
Fear of insects and snakes	Avoid poison (Chapter 13)
Female superiority in spatial-location memory	Increase success at foraging (Chapter 9)
Grasping reflex	Increase safety of infant (Chapter 10)
Language	Facilitate communication (Chapter 9)
Mechanisms of color vision	Improve visual perception (Chapter 5)
Modeling	Encourage imitation of high status individuals (Chapter 8)
Variation in personality traits	Increase flexibility of a group (Chapter 12)

Fear of heights is usually adaptive and may have a basis in evolution because it keeps us out of danger.

of evolved psychological mechanisms. He predicted that males are attracted to younger and good-looking women because these characteristics foreshadow the ability to bear children successfully. He predicted that females are attracted to older and industrious men because these characteristics signify the ability to provide resources for a family. These predictions were tested through questionnaire studies in 37 different countries, from Australia to Zambia, and were supported in the great majority of those cultures (Buss, 1994).

Studd and Gattiker (1991) used similar arguments to interpret sexual harassment in the workplace. Unwanted sexual advances are usually initiated by men and directed against younger women. Also, women react more negatively to such sexual advances than men do.

Evolutionary psychology is still in a fledgling state, and findings like the ones just discussed admit to other interpretations that make no reference to evolution. For example, sexual harassment may be more about harassment—a learned tendency to intimidate those in positions of less power—than about sex (Goodman, Koss, Fitzgerald, Russo, & Keita, 1993). The motive is power, not sexual desire (Chapter 7). In fact, men who sexually harass women also attempt to intimidate other men (Lee & Heppner, 1991).

Cautions concerning evolutionary psychology.   Evolutionary psychology promises to be an important addition to psychology as currently practiced because it can potentially shed light on so many different behaviors. Nonetheless, it is important to note some cautions about the use of this perspective.

First, let me repeat the defining feature of evolutionary psychology: It focuses on evolved psychological mechanisms. The closely allied approach of sociobiology is sometimes guilty of moving directly from evolutionary arguments to behaviors, without explaining how the behaviors are produced in individuals (Buss, 1995). It seems unlikely that people calculate considerations of inclusive fitness and act according to how closely related they are to people in their vicinity. In other words, inclusive fitness cannot be the proximate cause of our behavior.

A hazard in all forms of evolutionary explanation is the assumption that similar behaviors across species are produced by similar mechanisms. Only when mechanisms themselves are investigated can we offer informed conclusions about the resulting behaviors. Consider the existing computer programs that play chess well enough to defeat most human opponents (Simon & Chase, 1973). The observable "behavior" of these programs resembles that of chess masters, but the underlying mechanism is completely different (Chapter 9). Chess programs rely on brute force, rapidly calculating the immediate consequences of all possible moves and then choosing the best one according to simple rules. Human chess players, in contrast, have a more focused strategy, considering many fewer possibilities but at the same time taking a longer view.

Second, evolved psychological mechanisms may or may not be advantageous to people in the here and now. These mechanisms at one time served survival, but if the environment changes, their survival value may change as well. In the settings in which most of us now live, fear of snakes is almost never advantageous, particularly in its extreme. We rarely encounter snakes, and those we do encounter are rarely dangerous, yet our fear might lead us to curtail our everyday activities lest we encounter a snake (Chapter 13). It would make more sense in the modern world to have built-in tendencies to fear frayed wires, fast cars, and firearms, but these contemporary hazards posed no problems in the course of evolution.

Evolved psychological mechanisms that are currently advantageous to people may have arisen to solve a different problem (Gould, 1991). For instance, it has already been noted that the large brains of human beings make complex learning possible (Chapter 4). It is tempting to conclude that brain size increased throughout evolution because the capacity for complex learning was so adaptive. But perhaps human beings have large brains because this change was the way natural selection allowed our distant ancestors to add the neurological apparatus that made acute vision possible (Jerison, 1973). There was no room for these structures in the brains that then existed. The capacity for learning was irrelevant at the time, though human beings have since capitalized on this incidental function of large brains.

Third, the environmental context of behavior is critically important to evolutionary psychology. An evolved psychological mechanism is not an inflexible instinct. Evolution occurred in a given setting, and behavior is enacted in a given setting. Past environments shaped our psychological mechanisms, and current environments activate them. So, evolutionary psychologists cannot look at just biology in explaining behavior. Once again, the nature-nurture dichotomy should be dismissed as misleading. Culture provides one of the most important contexts in which evolved mechanisms arose and are deployed.

Fourth, evolutionary psychology is a theory and as such comprises tentative explanations that need to be tested against evidence (Chapter 2). Like any other broad theory of behavior, evolutionary psychology as a whole cannot be tested in a single investigation. Only specific hypotheses can be evaluated, and it is the sum of these findings on which we will base our eventual conclusions about the adequacy of this approach.

Stop and Think

12 Compare and contrast social Darwinism and sociobiology.

13 Compare and contrast ethology and comparative psychology.

14 Describe how behavior genetics is different from other biological approaches to human behavior.

15 Consider the evolved psychological mechanisms listed in Table 3.3. What evidence would be relevant to the conclusion that these are (or are not) the products of evolution?

EVOLUTION AND BEHAVIOR IN A BIOPSYCHOSOCIAL CONTEXT

As this chapter has made clear, evolutionary theory is contextual. The environment in which a species lives selects for or against given characteristics, including behavioral tendencies. Thus, evolutionary explanations are not just biological; they must also be phrased in terms of other contexts.

Let us consider a topic that illustrates the required complexity of evolutionary explanations: why people age and eventually die. (Chapter 10 discusses in detail the development of our physical characteristics.) Infants are not children, and children are not adults. Many of the changes that occur as we develop are part of our genetic inheritance, and they are easy to explain in evolutionary terms.

For example, the lengthy childhood of human beings, compared with other species, allows us adequate time to learn what we need to know to function in the world. It is advantageous to our species that young children are not capable of reproducing; children do not know enough to raise children themselves.

Less easy to explain, however, is why adults continue to change physically as they become older. Many of these changes can be described only as declines. The following are representative examples (Woodruff-Pak, 1988):

- Among the elderly, atrophy of the brain occurs, and brain function slows.
- The heart loses its capacity to compensate for stress.
- The respiratory system becomes less efficient.
- The gastrointestinal system loses strength, and the incidence of constipation increases.
- Bone mass decreases, particularly among women.
- The skin becomes less flexible: drying, wrinkling, and sagging.
- Muscles become smaller, weaker, and slower.

Our sensory and perceptual systems also age (Chapter 5). The documented changes that take place during middle and later adulthood include:

- loss of sensitivity of touch after age 50 or so
- loss of taste sensitivity
- hearing loss, particularly of higher-frequency sounds
- decline in visual acuity and speed of adaptation to the dark

Physical decline may be programmed into our genes, but the rate at which it occurs varies greatly across individuals and probably reflects psychological and social causes.

Also with age, people have a less efficient sense of balance, and this change produces dizziness and falls. Our bones also become more brittle, meaning that broken legs, arms, and hips can be quite common among the elderly.

Why do some people age more rapidly than others, leading to a shorter life? Indeed, why do people age at all? There are a number of theories to explain the process of aging, yet none has won general acceptance. Here are some of the theories proposed.

Biological and Environmental Influences on Aging

Physical decline may be programmed into our genes. Remember the notion of inclusive fitness: Organisms can sometimes further the survival of their own genes if they sacrifice themselves, so long as their death helps the survival of their close relatives. Perhaps it is adaptive for the elderly, who have already passed on their genes, to move out of the way and not use up resources that their offspring need. A maximum life expectancy might be inherited, with physical declines the mechanism that sets the limit.

Indeed, each species appears to have a characteristic maximum life expectancy. Even under the best of conditions, dogs do not live much past 25 years of age, and people do not live much past 110 years of age. Claims of extreme longevity among people, like yogurt eaters living in the Caucasus Mountains of the former Soviet Union, always prove exaggerated (Fry, 1985). Such claims persist, but 120 years is the oldest well-documented age of any person who has ever lived, achieved by a Japanese man named Shigechiyo Izumi (Woodruff-Pak, 1988) and a French woman named Jeanne Calment (Thomas, 1995). Some theorists believe that people's maximum life expectancy has not changed much for centuries (Fries & Crapo, 1981). Our average life expectancy has increased, but it appears to have an upper limit.

Another explanation of aging is that the processes responsible for it have never been selected against in the course of evolution. Perhaps our ancestors usually reproduced before the typical declines of aging began to occur, so that there was never any selection advantage for those who aged more slowly or even not at all. A related idea is that human life expectancy was quite short prior to the twentieth century. Our ancestors tended to die early while giving birth or because of injury or illness. That few if any died simply of old age means evolution could not encourage characteristics that slowed aging.

Although European Americans on average live longer than African Americans, research suggests that after age 75, African Americans may live longer. Any explanation of these findings needs to consider biological, psychological, and social influences on longevity.

Aging may also reflect accumulated mutations due to environment causes. Such mutations necessarily increase over time, and they eventually result in extremely abnormal chromosomes that cause the body to stop working because its cells can no longer replicate themselves.

Other explanations of aging focus on larger physical systems within the body, places in which the wear and tear of everyday life takes its toll. In particular, the cardiovascular system is quite vulnerable to the effects of aging (Chapter 16). Arteries become more brittle and less flexible as fatty acids (e.g., cholesterol) deposit themselves on vessel walls. As the blood vessels are compromised, so too is our circulation. And because circulation of blood is critical in maintaining our health, aging and death follow.

With age, the immune system becomes less able to recognize and fight off foreign organisms, such as viruses (Chapter 16). The body becomes increasingly confused and starts to treat its own cells as foreign material, fighting them and hence itself. This subversion of the immune system is the fundamental cause of diseases such as rheumatoid arthritis.

Psychological and Social Influences on Aging

Aging can be explained in terms of an interaction of biological and environmental factors. Recent work also suggests that psychological and social characteristics may influence physical well-being (Chapter 16). For example, personality traits such as optimism are associated with good health and long life, as is the number of close friends and confidants we have (Peterson & Bossio, 1991).

Figure 3.3 depicts just some of the factors found to be associated with longer life (Woodruff-Pak, 1988). Note that women tend to live longer than men and that European Americans and Asian Americans tend to live longer than African Americans and Hispanic Americans (Gibson, 1994; Markides, 1989). Although there is disagreement about what explains the gender difference in longevity (Kaplan, Anderson, & Wingard, 1991), the ethnic differences seem to be based in lifestyle. For example, African American males are much more likely to be the victims of violent death early in their lives, a factor that does, of course, reduce their average life expectancy (Blake & Darling, 1994).

An interesting aspect of longevity among people in the United States is evidence that once individuals reach age 75, African Americans end up living longer on average than European Americans do (Berkman, Singer, & Manton, 1989). The exact reasons for this reversal of ethnic differences in longevity prior to age 75 are not agreed upon, but we can expect that they are complex.

The factors presented in Figure 3.3 have been identified using correlational investigations; thus, they may not be direct causes of long life but instead be linked to other, as yet unknown factors responsible for longevity. So, total abstinence from drinking alcohol has been associated with shorter life than occasional drinking in small amounts has. Does this mean that drinking alcohol in small amounts is healthy? Perhaps, but more plausible is that abstaining is irrelevant and simply correlates with other characteristics of a person that are critical.

If you wish to increase the length of your life, you can try to match the profile of a long-lived person as best as you can. It is difficult to pick your gender or ethnicity, much less your grandparents, but some of these factors are under your control. For example, people who smoke live on average 12 years fewer than those who do not. That is a correlational result worth treating as a causal one.

This chapter has discussed evolution and how it can be used to understand human behavior. The next chapter continues this discussion of the biological context of behavior by focusing on the brain and nervous system. Like many of our other characteristics, these are the product of evolution and represent the important biological mechanisms responsible for behavior.

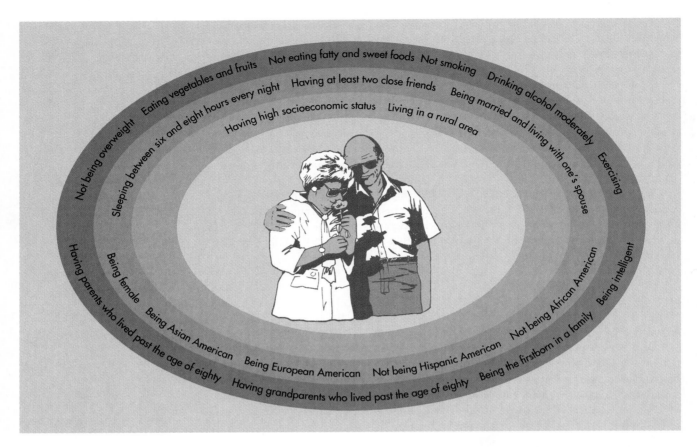

Figure 3.3
Predictors of Longevity in the Contemporary United States. Researchers have identified numerous factors associated with longer life for people in the United States. These predictors include biological, psychological, and social risk factors that interact in complex ways to produce longevity. Some of these factors—like one's habits—are able to be modified, perhaps with the result of increasing life expectancy.

SUMMARY

UNDERSTANDING BIOLOGY AND BEHAVIOR: DEFINITION AND EXPLANATION

■ Biology is important to psychology because we can think, feel, and act only in ways that are made possible by our bodies.

■ Biological explanations of behavior stress its cause, function, development, and/or evolution. Controversy arises when biological explanations are proposed to the exclusion of explanations phrased in terms of learning and the environment. However, these sorts of explanations need not compete with one another and—indeed—should be combined in a biopsychosocial approach.

EVOLUTION

■ Any biological explanation of behavior must take the ideas of evolution into account. More than 100 years ago, Charles Darwin proposed that species

change—evolve—in the direction of characteristics that allow survival and successful reproduction.

■ These adaptive characteristics come to predominate, and with sufficient time, new species may arise from old ones.

GENETICS

■ The characteristics of parents are passed on to their offspring through genes, microscopic structures that are found within each cell of the body and that provide plans for biological development.

■ The actual characteristics of any individual reflect the influence of genes on the events that occur during development.

MODERN EVOLUTIONARY THEORY

■ Since Darwin first proposed his theory of evolution by natural selection, new explanations of evolution have been introduced.

■ One of the important modern ideas is inclusive fitness, defined as the fitness of an individual organism plus the fitness of its close relatives, with whom the individual shares genes in common. Inclusive fitness allows complex social behavior to be explained in evolutionary terms. When individuals sacrifice their own life for the survival of their relatives, they in effect further the continuation of their own genes.

DOING *Evolution* RESEARCH

■ Evolution occurs over vast periods, so research must be indirect, relying in most cases on inferences from the fossil record.

■ Humanlike species first appeared about 2–3 million years ago, and the first modern human beings about 100,000 years ago. Researchers believe that all people alive today had the same female ancestor and the same male ancestor.

EVOLUTIONARY EXPLANATIONS OF HUMAN BEHAVIOR

■ Over the years, evolutionary theory has been applied in various ways to human behavior.

■ Social Darwinism is the largely discredited attempt to explain human societies in evolutionary terms.

■ Comparative psychology studies similarities and differences in behavior across animal species, with the goal of identifying evolutionary relationships.

■ Ethology studies the behavior of organisms—including people—as it occurs in a natural environment.

■ The field of behavior genetics investigates individual differences in behavior within a species, seeking to link behavioral variations to genetic variations.

■ Sociobiology relies on the idea of inclusive fitness to offer evolutionary explanations of complex social behavior.

■ The most recent attempt to explain human behavior in evolutionary terms is evolutionary psychology. This approach tries to specify evolved psychological mechanisms that arose in the course of evolution to solve problems of survival and that, when activated, still influence behavior today.

EVOLUTION AND BEHAVIOR IN A BIOPSYCHOSOCIAL CONTEXT

■ Why and how we age are good examples of the simultaneous influence of biopsychosocial factors.

KEY TERMS

The Brain and the Nervous System

We often take our bodies for granted, until injury or illness reminds us that we are physical beings. Something amiss with our bodies often translates into something amiss with our behavior: thoughts, feelings, and/or actions. Here are two cases that show the importance of the brain in everyday functioning.

In 1848, Phineas Gage was a young man working as a foreman on a construction project (Bigelow, 1850). Regarded as intelligent, energetic, and persistent, Gage was an expert in the use of dynamite for demolition. Still, one day a mistake occurred, and an explosion drove an iron bar through the front of his head. The bar, almost four feet in length, entered Gage's lower jaw and emerged from the top of his head. Miraculously, Gage did not die. Within two months, he was up and about and apparently recovered.

However, his behavior was changed, as if his entire personality had undergone an alteration. He was loud and profane, irresponsible, and unable to plan ahead. He was indecisive and got along poorly with others when their wishes conflicted with his own. All of this was in sharp contrast to Gage's behavior prior to the accident.

The change in Phineas Gage's personality can be traced to damage to his brain. Portions of the very front of his brain—the frontal lobes—were damaged by the iron bar. These control many of the functions of structures elsewhere in the brain, often inhibiting their influence on behavior. With

Here are a cast of the head of Phineas Gage and his actual skull. You can see where the iron bar passed through his head, seriously damaging his frontal lobes and permanently altering his personality.

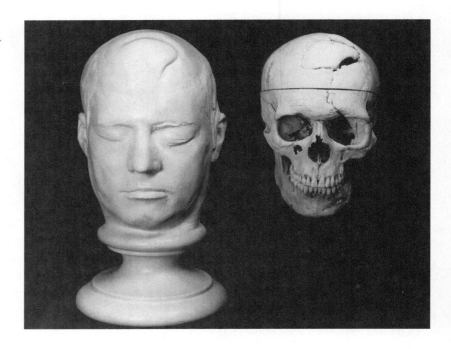

the destruction of his frontal lobes, Gage expressed his emotions directly and lost the ability to think through the consequences of his acts.

A contemporary example of the same sort of brain damage is a young American officer who was shot while serving in Vietnam (Blumer & Benson, 1975). A bullet entered his left temple and emerged above his right eye. An infection followed, requiring the surgical removal of most of his frontal lobes. Like Gage, Officer X recovered in many ways, but his personality was dramatically different. Prior to his wound and the surgery, he had been quiet and restrained. A West Point graduate, Officer X had been regarded by his men as a good commander. But now he was outspoken, brash, and disrespectful. He had trouble with simple tasks. Although he could speak, he did so imprecisely and often misused words.

UNDERSTANDING THE NERVOUS SYSTEM: DEFINITION AND EXPLANATION

This chapter continues the discussion of how biology influences behavior and mental processes by taking a detailed look at the structure and function of the nervous system and in particular the brain. The nervous system as a whole is responsible for gathering information from the environment, coordinating this information, and producing appropriate responses.

■ **neurons**

individual nerve cells that compose the nervous system

The nervous system is composed of microscopic cells called **neurons.** Neurons were discovered about 100 years ago. Though not impressive in size, they are impressive in sheer number. Estimates of the number of neurons in the brain vary, but it may exceed 100 billion (Hubel, 1979). Any given neuron may communicate with several thousand other neurons in its immediate area, meaning that there are trillions of potential neural interactions (Thompson, 1993). The complexity of these connections allows

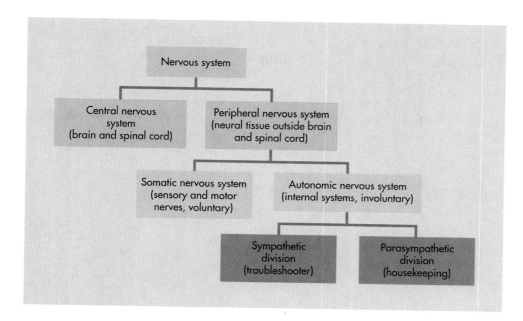

Figure 4.1
Major Parts of the Nervous System. The most general division of the nervous system is between the central nervous system (neurons in the brain and spinal cord) and the peripheral nervous system (neurons in all the other parts of the body). Further divisions are also shown in this diagram.

corresponding complexity of behavior, and so you can see why the psychology of human beings is so challenging to understand.

The Major Parts of the Nervous System

It is customary to make distinctions among the major parts of the nervous system (see Figure 4.1). First is the distinction between the **central nervous system,** which is composed of the neurons in the brain and spinal cord, and the **peripheral nervous system,** which is composed of the neurons in the rest of the body: legs, arms, face, and so on. The peripheral nervous system carries impulses from the central nervous system to our muscles and glands, as well as carrying impulses to the central nervous system from our various sense organs when they are stimulated.

The peripheral nervous system is divided into the **somatic nervous system,** which controls the skeletal muscles and sense organs, and the **autonomic nervous system,** which controls the heart, lungs, and digestive organs. The term *autonomic* is a synonym for *automatic*. The intended implication is that the autonomic nervous system operates for the most part automatically, with little conscious control.

Finally, the autonomic nervous system is made up of two parts. The **sympathetic nervous system** produces arousal. So, when you are threatened your pupils dilate, your heart rate accelerates, and your perspiration increases. The **parasympathetic nervous system** counteracts arousal once a threat has ceased, reversing the bodily processes set into operation by the sympathetic nervous system. These two systems usually work in opposition to one another, creating the appropriate balance between excitement and calm. Figure 4.2 shows the different organs respectively affected by these two divisions of the autonomic nervous system.

A topic of enduring interest to psychologists is how different parts of the nervous system are involved in our behaviors. The nervous system plays a role in every topic discussed in the rest of this book, from sensation and perception (Chapter 5) to personality (Chapter 12) and abnormality (Chapter 13). Linked to the nervous system is the **endocrine system,** which is composed of our glands. The endocrine system is involved in motivation and emotion (Chapter 7), reproduction, and development (Chapter 10).

■ **central nervous system**
neurons in the brain and spinal cord

■ **peripheral nervous system**
neurons that link the central nervous system to the senses, glands, and muscles

■ **somatic nervous system**
neurons that control the skeletal muscles and sense organs

■ **autonomic nervous system**
neurons that control the heart, lungs, and digestive organs

■ **sympathetic nervous system**
part of the autonomic nervous system that produces arousal

■ **parasympathetic nervous system**
part of the autonomic nervous system that counteracts arousal

■ **endocrine system**
set of glands that secrete hormones into the bloodstream

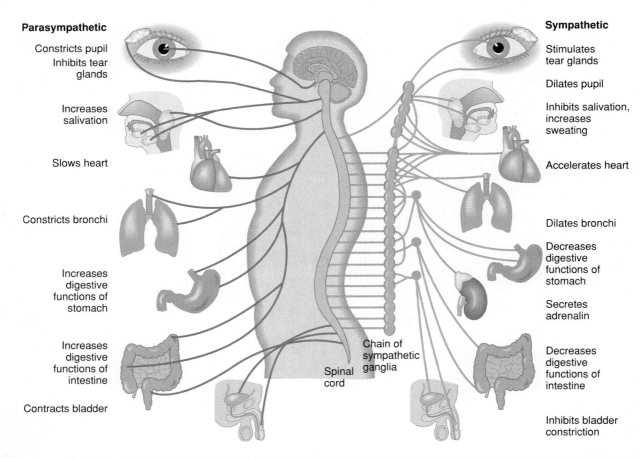

Parasympathetic

Constricts pupil
Inhibits tear
glands

Increases
salivation

Slows heart

Constricts bronchi

Increases
digestive
functions of
stomach

Increases
digestive
functions of
intestine

Contracts bladder

Sympathetic

Stimulates
tear glands

Dilates pupil

Inhibits salivation,
increases
sweating

Accelerates heart

Dilates bronchi

Decreases
digestive
functions of
stomach

Secretes
adrenalin

Decreases
digestive
functions of
intestine

Inhibits bladder
constriction

Chain of
sympathetic
ganglia

Spinal
cord

Figure 4.2
Sympathetic Nervous System and Parasympathetic Nervous System. The sympathetic nervous system is responsible for arousal, which expends energy, and the parasympathetic nervous system is responsible for relaxation, which conserves energy. These two parts of the autonomic nervous system work together to maintain a balance: Arousal is counteracted by relaxation, and vice versa.

A Biopsychosocial Perspective on the Nervous System and Behavior

Recall the four emphases of biological explanation, as discussed in Chapter 3:

■ Causes, which include the psychological and physiological mechanisms that give rise to behavior
■ Functions, which refer to the adaptive significance of behavior
■ Development, which encompasses the changes that occur across an individual's life span
■ Evolution, which places behavior in the context of the long history of our species

Each of these types of explanation proves useful in understanding the nervous system and its effects on behavior.

For example, when we map out links between injuries to specific parts of the brain and particular thoughts and behaviors, we have important information about the causes of those thoughts and behaviors. As will be described later in this chapter, studying the effects of brain injury is a popular research strategy of psychologists interested in the biological mechanisms of behavior.

Frontal lobe damage interferes with the ability to plan ahead. Psychologists are currently investigating how microcomputers can be used to help people with frontal lobe damage place behaviors, like those required for cooking, into the proper sequence.

When the effects of brain damage impair an individual's ability to get along in the world, we have important information about the functions of an intact brain. Consider that frontal lobe damage interferes with planning ahead and foreseeing the consequences of one's actions. Social relationships, in particular, are hampered by these difficulties (Chapter 15).

When we investigate the consequences of brain damage at different points in life, we have important information about the development of the brain (Rutter, 1993). For example, children often show better recovery from brain damage than adults do because intact parts of their nervous system can take over for damaged parts. This result implies that the organization of the nervous system is not fixed at birth but rather develops across the life span.

When we speculate about how our species benefits from its characteristic nervous system, we have important information about human evolution. It is obvious that the brain as a whole is advantageous, but it is perhaps more intriguing to ask why brain damage is often so selective in its effects. Phineas Gage and the American officer just described were profoundly affected by their injuries, but neither died from them. Our brains have certain redundancies built into them. The most resilient brain functions are the most crucial to survival.

Behavior is affected not only by biology but also by the environment. Even if full recovery from brain damage is not possible, alterations of the individual's world can aid rehabilitation. For example, psychologists are exploring the use of microcomputers to assist people with frontal lobe damage. An appropriately programmed microcomputer prompts them about the correct order in which to string together behaviors for different purposes, such as baking a cake or cleaning a floor (Kirsch, Levine, Fallon-Krueger, & Jaros, 1987). What their brains do not allow them to do, the microcomputer does. Such interventions might someday be as commonplace as eyeglasses, which similarly use technological means to compensate for a physical problem.

Stop and Think

1 What are the major divisions of the nervous system?

2 Explain the somatic nervous system in terms of causes, functions, development, and evolution.

3 How is brain damage a good example of biopsychosocial influences on behavior?

STRUCTURE AND FUNCTION OF THE NERVOUS SYSTEM

The brain and the nervous system provide the biological apparatus that makes all behaviors possible. In the language of evolutionary psychology, evolved psychological mechanisms produce behavior through physiological routes, chiefly neurological ones. Although some psychology students find the discussion of the brain and the nervous system to be a detour in their goal of understanding behavior, such a discussion is a necessary foundation for understanding biological mechanisms. What follows is an examination of the structure and function of the nervous system, starting with a close look at its most basic components, neurons.

Neurons

As noted, the brain and the nervous system are composed of microscopic cells called neurons. Also present in the brain are **glial cells,** which serve several functions. They literally hold the nervous system together, keeping neurons in their appropriate places. Glial cells provide nourishment to neurons and dispose of waste material. Throughout life and in particular during our early years, glial cells outnumber neurons ten to one.

Structure of the neuron.   Figure 4.3 shows a neuron and its major structures:

■ The **cell body,** which is the cell's largest concentration of mass and contains the nucleus of the cell
■ **Dendrites,** which receive messages from other neurons
■ **Axons,** which send messages to other neurons
■ **Terminal buttons,** which secrete chemicals that influence other neurons

■ **glial cells**
cells that hold neurons in place, provide nourishment to them, and dispose of waste material

■ **cell body**
the neuron's largest concentration of mass, containing the nucleus of the cell

■ **dendrites**
parts of the neuron that receive messages from other neurons

■ **axons**
parts of the neuron that send messages to other neurons

■ **terminal buttons**
end of the axon where chemicals are secreted that influence other neurons

Figure 4.3
A Representative Neuron.
Incoming neural messages are received by the dendrites of a neuron and transmitted to its cell body. Outgoing messages pass along the axon to the terminal buttons.

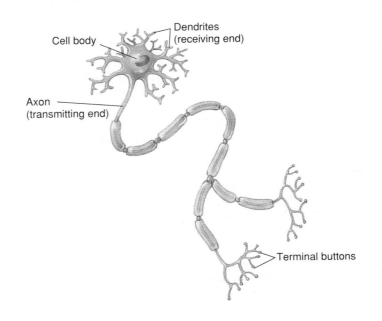

Cell body

Dendrites
(receiving end)

Axon
(transmitting end)

Terminal buttons

The neuron depicted here is a generalized one. Different neurons have markedly different shapes, depending on their specialized role. For example, the neurons responsible for our sensations differ according to the sensation in question: vision, hearing, taste, and so on (Chapter 5).

About half the neurons in an adult's body have their axons covered by a white, fatty substance called **myelin.** Myelin protects the axons and helps neurons send their messages more rapidly. Neurons with myelin may speed a communication along as rapidly as 120 meters per second, whereas neurons without myelin may communicate as slowly as 0.5 meters per second. For a context, consider that Olympic-class sprinters can cover about 10 meters in a second, which means that the most rapid neurons are more than ten times faster, whereas the least rapid are about twenty times slower. The neurons that send messages over a greater distance tend to be the ones covered with myelin.

At birth, an infant's neurons are not extensively covered with myelin. Myelination occurs over the first few years of life, and this aspect is one of the reasons why infants cannot move like children or adults. Their nervous systems do not allow highly skilled and coordinated movements (Chapter 10).

Although virtually all of the neurons in the human brain are present at birth (Schnell & Schwab, 1990), the connections between neurons change across the life span. During childhood, dendrites become more numerous, and the connections among neurons more complex. Indeed, in the first year of life the number of neural connections in parts of the human brain increases tenfold (Huttenlocher, 1979). Children have more dendrites than adults do, suggesting that the brain at first overproduces neural connections, then establishes which ones are most useful in terms of influencing behavior and its consequences, and eventually deletes the others (Cowan, 1979). The parallel between this hypothesized process and the theory of natural selection is intriguing; Edelman (1987) termed it neural Darwinism.

■ **myelin**
white, fatty substance that covers some neurons, protecting the axons and speeding neural messages

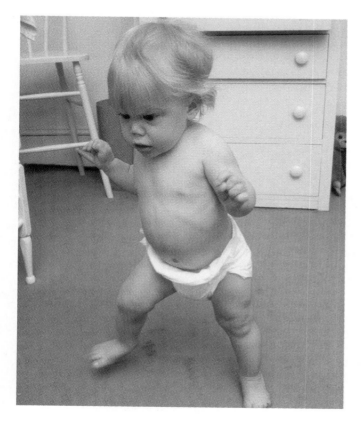

Young children move less skillfully than adults do because their neurons are not fully myelinated.

Function of the neuron.   Neurons are not directly connected to one another. Rather, they communicate by secreting chemicals that are responsible for transmitting neural impulses from one part of the nervous system to another. When a neuron transmits a neural impulse, we say that it has fired because an electrical signal has passed along its axon. Although these electrical signals can be triggered by external stimuli, as in the process of sensation, let me discuss the simple case of a neuron stimulated by another neuron.

A chemical called a **neurotransmitter** is secreted by the axon of one neuron into the space between it and a second neuron. This gap between two neurons is known as a **synapse,** and chemical communication usually occurs across the synapse from an axon to a dendrite. (You can keep this straight by telling yourself that an axon "acts on" a dendrite.) The dendrite of the second neuron detects the neurotransmitter. If the neurotransmitter is secreted in sufficient quantity, the second neuron fires. As different neurons fire, behavior eventually occurs.

When not transmitting a neural impulse, the inside and outside of a neuron have different electrical charges, called the **resting potential.** Relative to the outside, the inside is negative. Firing involves a series of electrical and chemical changes collectively termed the **action potential.** When a neuron is stimulated by an adjacent neuron, this stimulation produces a chemical change in the permeability of the cell surface, or membrane. The change in permeability leads to a temporary reversal of the inside and outside electrical charges. Relative to the outside, the inside becomes positive as electrically charged ions flow through the cell membrane.

This chemical/electrical flip-flop rapidly travels down the length of the axon, sometimes reaching speeds of several hundred miles per hour. Myelin, as already explained, speeds up the action potential. When a neural impulse reaches the axon, it leads to the secretion of a neurotransmitter, which in turn stimulates adjacent neurons, and the process is repeated (see Figure 4.4).

Communication between neurons is not continuous. It occurs in bursts, which is why we speak of neurons firing. Once a neuron has fired, it is unable to do so again until a brief time has passed, an interval typically a few thousandths of a second long. This pause is called the **refractory period,** during which time the resting potential of the neuron is restored.

The process just described is called **excitation** because the one neuron leads other neurons to fire. However, another process, called **inhibition,** also exists. With inhibition, a neuron affects other neurons by making them less likely to fire. The exact mechanism is again chemical. Inhibition occurs when the insides of these neurons become

---

■ **neurotransmitter**
chemical secreted by one neuron that influences a second neuron

■ **synapse**
the gap between two neurons into which a neurotransmitter is secreted

■ **resting potential**
the difference in electrical charge between the inside and outside of a neuron at rest

■ **action potential**
electrical and chemical changes that take place when a neuron fires

■ **refractory period**
period of time after a neuron fires when it cannot fire again until its resting potential is restored

■ **excitation**
process by which one neuron causes other neurons to fire

■ **inhibition**
process by which one neuron causes other neurons not to fire

Figure 4.4
Neurotransmitter Crossing a Synapse. Neurotransmitter molecules are released into the synapse between two neurons. After they cross the synaptic gap, the molecules bind to sites in the receptor neuron. Then the electrical state of the receiving neuron changes, and it becomes either more or less likely to fire. Remember that a given neuron may have synaptic connections with hundreds or even thousands of other neurons.

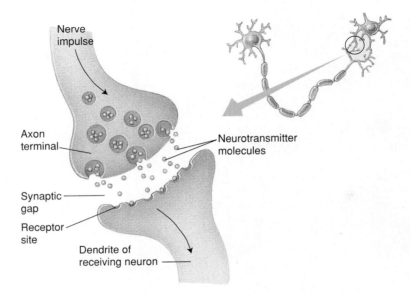

Nerve impulse

Axon terminal

Neurotransmitter molecules

Synaptic gap

Receptor site

Dendrite of receiving neuron

even more negative in charge relative to their outsides, thereby making excitation more difficult. A nervous system guided by checks and balances results. Given behaviors occur or do not occur depending on the relative mix of excitatory or inhibitory processes in the parts of the nervous system responsible for them.

Consider the example of strychnine, a highly toxic substance sometimes used as rat poison. Strychnine prevents inhibition from taking place at synapses. If an animal or person ingests strychnine, uncontrollable activity of the nervous system results: twitches, spasms, and eventually convulsions that may result in death. Strychnine is fatal because it upsets the nervous system's balance between excitation and inhibition.

A neuron either fires or does not, depending on whether enough neurotransmitter is present. Once the action potential is triggered, a neuron fires the same way each time. This phenomenon is called the **all-or-none principle.** It might seem a bit puzzling because it apparently contradicts our everyday experiences. Surely we perceive the world in degrees: the volume of a rock-and-roll band, the brightness of a light bulb, the spiciness of chili (Chapter 5). If neurons either fire or do not, how are these gradations introduced? There are two answers.

First, an intense stimulus such as a loud noise registers as intense not because it stimulates an individual neuron to respond more intensely but because it stimulates a greater number of neurons to fire. Second, an intense stimulus can also cause particular neurons to fire more frequently. Neural messages are combined, across time and across different neurons. So, when a given stimulus repeatedly stimulates multiple neurons, these messages are added together to produce a sensation of greater intensity than a stimulus that either stimulates fewer neurons or stimulates neurons less frequently.

■ **all-or-none principle**
idea that neurons fire either totally or not at all

Neurotransmitters

Excitation and inhibition are the only two processes possible when one neuron influences another. This fact might lead us to hypothesize that there are two transmitter substances, one excitatory and the other inhibitory (Carlson, 1986). This hypothesis is not the case. Instead, there are dozens of neurotransmitters (Panksepp, 1986). Some are exclusively excitatory, and some exclusively inhibitory, but many others both excite and inhibit, depending on the synapse into which they are secreted.

Major neurotransmitters.   Norepinephrine, acetylcholine, GABA, serotonin, and dopamine are among the major neurotransmitters (see Table 4.1). You will encounter some of these again in Chapter 13 on psychological abnormality. Biological theories link particular mental disorders to problems with these important neurotransmitters (Andreasen, 1984). Schizophrenia may be produced by too much dopamine activity, for instance, and depression may be the result of too little norepinephrine and serotonin activity. Medication for these disorders targets the implicated transmitter substances, decreasing or increasing their activity, as the case may be (Chapter 14).

Parkinson's disease is a disorder of the central nervous system that usually affects individuals after age 60. Among its symptoms are involuntary muscle contractions that

Table 4.1   Major Neurotransmitters

Neurotransmitter	Involved in
Norepinephrine	Stress; wakefulness; mood
Acetylcholine	Muscle action; memory; cognition
GABA (gamma-amino-butyric acid)	Relaxation
Serotonin	Sleep; appetite; mood
Dopamine	Voluntary movement; memory; cognition; mood
Endorphins	Pain suppression

Fluoxetine, more popularly known as Prozac, is a popular treatment for depression that selectively targets the neurotransmitter serotonin.

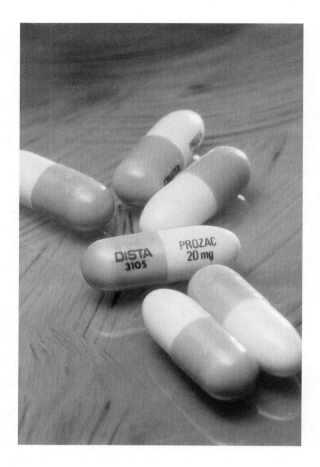

produce tremors. Although the cause of Parkinson's disease is at present unknown, the mechanism involves the degeneration of the substantia nigra, a region of the brain that produces the neurotransmitter dopamine. Tremors and other Parkinsonian symptoms result. One treatment of Parkinson's disease is therefore a drug that increases dopamine activity by providing to the brain one of the chemical precursors of this neurotransmitter.

When medications are given that increase or decrease neurotransmitter activity, they invariably have effects other than just alleviating psychological problems. Numerous parts of the brain are affected by each neurotransmitter, and so there may be unintended side effects. Tricyclics, for example, are drugs prescribed for depression that work by increasing norepinephrine and serotonin activity (Chapter 14). However, among the side effects of tricyclics are drowsiness, blurred vision, and low blood pressure; all of these are produced by increased neurotransmitter activity. Fluoxetine, more popularly known as Prozac, is a newer drug used to treat depression, and it is often preferred to tricyclics because it affects only serotonin activity. By being more selective in its effects on the brain, Prozac still alleviates depression but has fewer side effects.

Neurotransmitters also affect the efficiency with which the liver and kidneys break down and remove waste material from the body. Drugs used to treat psychological problems should never be combined with alcohol because they compromise kidney and liver functions. Alcohol therefore stays in the body longer and can have more damaging effects, including fatal ones.

As already explained, we can classify neurons as excitatory or inhibitory. Neurotransmitters allow a further classification in terms of the transmitter substance to which they are sensitive: There are dopamine neurons, serotonin neurons, and so on. One explanation of this specificity proposes that a neurotransmitter affects a neuron only if its molecular shape fits the appropriate sites in the membrane—like a key fits a lock (Cooper, Bloom, & Roth, 1986).

Endorphins.   People have long known that certain chemicals have analgesic properties—that is, they alleviate pain. Among these chemicals are opiates, the family of drugs that includes opium, morphine, and heroin (Chapter 6). These analgesics come from outside our bodies. But under some circumstances, the brain produces its own analgesic chemicals, called **endorphins.**

Endorphins are naturally secreted neurotransmitters and chemically similar to the opiates (Hughes, Smith, Kosterlitz, Fothergill, Morgan, & Morris, 1975). When secreted, they disrupt messages from pain receptors by inhibiting subsequent neurons that would otherwise carry those messages to the parts of the brain responsible for the experience of pain. Endorphins are secreted in response to pain and thereby allow people to endure stimulation that would otherwise be unbearable. Although the full picture of endorphins is still sketchy, they may be involved in childbirth, in the use of acupuncture, in the exhilaration sometimes experienced by those who habitually exercise (so-called runner's high), and even in people's acquired taste for spicy foods (Davis, 1984).

■ **endorphins**
pain-reducing chemicals produced in the brain that are similar to narcotics

Agonists and antagonists.   Certain chemicals are similar enough to neurotransmitters so that when they are introduced into the body, they occupy neural receptors. **Agonists** mimic actual neurotransmitters, causing neurons to fire. Narcotics, for example, trigger the part of the nervous system responsible for analgesia (Chapter 6).

Antagonists, in contrast, do not cause neurons to fire, but because they occupy receptor sites, they preclude the normal role of the actual neurotransmitters. For instance, botulism is a potentially fatal illness that results from bacteria found in improperly canned food. The bacteria produce a chemical that is an antagonist for acetylcholine; a person's muscle contractions are therefore weakened. In very small doses, though, this chemical is sometimes helpful in treating people with overly strong muscle contractions, as in crossed eyes or uncontrollable winking.

One of the biological treatments of heroin abuse is the administration of antagonists that prevent opiates from having an effect on the nervous system. As you might conclude, these antagonists also interfere with the effect of pain-inhibiting endorphins that work via the identical neurological routes (Kayser & Guilbaud, 1991).

■ **agonists**
chemicals that mimic actual neurotransmitters, causing neurons to fire

■ **antagonists**
chemicals that occupy receptor sites of neurons and prevent the normal role of actual neurotransmitters

Organization of the Nervous System

The nervous system involves a division of labor among its different cells. The simplest case is the **reflex,** whereby one neuron, the **receptor,** receives stimulation from the environment and automatically leads a second neuron, the **effector,** to initiate some response toward the environment. A hand touching a hot stove is immediately withdrawn. Receptors (signaling "It's hot") and effectors (signaling "Hand, get moving") are both involved here.

Among people, reflexes vary greatly in complexity. Spinal reflexes, for example, resemble the simple reflex just described. The pathway from stimulus to response goes directly to the spinal cord and back, without involving the brain. Many of our immediate reactions to pain are spinal reflexes. We may be aware that they have occurred, but consciousness has nothing to do with their mechanism.

Reflexes are but one example of how the nervous system is organized. The nervous system is characterized by multiple modes of organization (Rozin, 1984).

■ **reflex**
automatic response to an external event

■ **receptor**
neuron that receives stimulation from the environment

■ **effector**
neuron that initiates some response toward the environment

Spatial organization.   Take, for instance, the principle of spatial organization. Neurons located close to each other are likely to be involved in the same psychological functions. This mode of organization will be particularly obvious later in this chapter, when the different structures of the brain are discussed. Each structure is composed of adjacent neurons that perform similar functions, and thus we can identify a given structure, like the frontal lobes, as involved in a given behavior, such as planning ahead.

Biochemical organization.   The nervous system also shows a biochemical organization. As explained in the discussion of neurons, different sets of neurons are respectively sensitive to particular neurotransmitters, and their shared sensitivity creates one more basis of structure. We speak, therefore, of acetylcholine pathways and structures and link them to given behaviors. For example, the neurons sensitive to acetylcholine are involved in memory and are selectively destroyed in Alzheimer's disease (Chapter 6). Among the symptoms of this neurological condition are profound memory problems—which makes sense, granted the role of acetylcholine.

Hierarchical organization.   Finally, the nervous system shows hierarchical organization, meaning that its parts and functions are arranged in different levels. Higher levels regulate and control lower levels. The terms *higher* and *lower* have several related meanings. First, they refer to where in the nervous system these structures are located. Structures at the top of the brain usually direct those at the center and bottom of the brain; the brain itself often controls the rest of the nervous system. Next, the terms refer to the hypothesized evolutionary history of the brain. Lower centers presumably appeared prior to higher centers. Finally, the higher levels of the brain are involved in what we think of as characteristically human abilities: language, reasoning, and problem solving.

Redundancy in the nervous system.   Realizing that the nervous system has a multidimensional structure helps us to understand how and why it works as it does. Rozin (1984) offered these generalizations about the functioning of the nervous system:

■ *There is a balance between excitation and inhibition.* You encountered this idea already at the level of specific neurons. It also applies to the nervous system as a whole, a necessary consequence of its structural checks and balances.
■ *There is redundancy in the nervous system.* In other words, the nervous system can perform its functions in different ways. Although this quality makes it difficult to offer firm statements about the functioning of the nervous system, it certainly benefits the organism.

Lower structures of the brain are directed by higher structures, which are responsible for what we regard as characteristically human abilities: language, reasoning, and problem solving.

■ *There is recovery of function following damage to the nervous system.* The major benefit of redundancy is that people often recover from neurological injury or illness. Although neurons themselves do not usually regenerate after infancy, other parts of the nervous system can often take over following the loss of particular neurons.

■ *There is variation in the vulnerability of neurological functions.* As a rule, more redundancy occurs lower in the hierarchy.

These generalizations can be illustrated by considering one more time the example of brain damage. Consider the advantage to human beings and other species in having intact nervous systems that function in this way. We respond to the environment in appropriate ways, but our responses are usually not too extreme or too persistent because they are eventually counteracted. It is useful to experience fear when we are threatened, for example, but it would not be useful to remain fearful for the rest of our lives.

Following damage or insult to the nervous system, we are capable of reorganizing ourselves. As already mentioned, reorganization occurs more readily among infants and children than adults. So, the equivalent brain damage in an infant and a mature adult has different consequences. An infant can usually recover more fully than an adult.

These facts seem to make evolutionary sense. Younger organisms must survive long enough to pass on their characteristics to offspring. Recovery of neurological functioning enhances their ability to do so. A similar argument fails to hold for older organisms. They have already reproduced, and there is less need—biologically speaking—for them to be able to reorganize their nervous systems following injury.

Stop and Think

4 What is the difference between neural excitation and neural inhibition?

5 How is the nervous system organized?

6 Why is there redundancy in the nervous system?

THE BIOLOGY OF THE BRAIN

The human brain weighs about three pounds and is composed of perhaps 100 billion neurons. Ornstein and Thompson (1984) likened the overall structure to a ramshackle house originally built for a small family but then added to as subsequent generations needed accommodations. In the end, we have a layered structure, reflecting the presumed evolution of the brain. Ornstein and Thompson (1984, pp. 21–22) provided the following exercise to help one to visualize the brain:

> Place your fingers on both sides of your head beneath the earlobes. In the center of the space between your hands is the oldest part of the brain, the brain stem. Now, form your hands into fists. Each is about the size of one of the brain's hemispheres, and when both fists are joined at the heel of the hand they describe not only the approximate size and shape of the entire brain but also its symmetrical structure. Next, put on a pair of thick gloves—preferably light gray. They represent the cortex—the newest part of the brain and the area where functioning results in the most characteristically human creations, such as language and art.

Figure 4.5 depicts the three major layers of the brain. First is the **hindbrain,** consisting of most of the brain stem. The first part of the brain to appear during evolution, it controls breathing and heart rate. The **midbrain**—the upper part of the brain stem—is

■ **hindbrain**
lowest and oldest layer of the brain, consisting of most of the brain stem

■ **midbrain**
middle layer of the brain, consisting of the upper part of the brain stem

Figure 4.5
Layers of the Brain. It is customary to distinguish three layers of the brain: the hindbrain, the midbrain, and the forebrain. These layers correspond not only to the location of the structure but also to when it appeared in the course of evolution. The lowest level—the hindbrain—was the first to appear, and the highest level—the forebrain—was the most recent to appear.

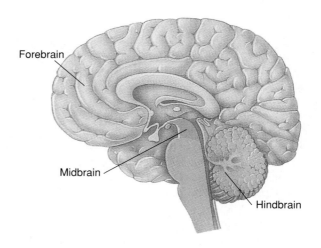

Forebrain

Midbrain

Hindbrain

■ **forebrain**
highest and newest layer of the brain

next. It plays a crucial role in coordinating other structures of the brain and handling communication among them. Then we have the **forebrain,** the most recent layer to evolve. Its purpose is to maintain such critical activities as movement, memory, and speech.

Evolution of the Brain

Before going into further details, let us consider some broad questions about the brain and the nervous system. These are phrased in terms of the theory of evolution.

Survival advantages.   If the brain and the nervous system are products of evolution, what survival value have they offered? Think how important it is for an organism to react in a unified way to its environment. An organism composed of connected but uncoordinated parts does not stand much of a chance in competition with one possessing an intact nervous system.

For instance, a consequence of diabetes in adults is the loss of sensation in one's extremities. The person so afflicted may be unaware of injuries because the brain does not receive a distress message from a finger or toe. Serious infection constantly threatens because a minor cut can easily be overlooked and neglected. Similar problems are faced by those with spinal cord injuries, who may be unaware of cuts, abrasions, and burns to parts of their bodies below the injury.

How the brain evolved.   How has the nervous system changed in the course of evolution? Although neurons and brains are not part of the fossil record, some consensus exists about the general process that occurred (Jerison, 1973; Kaas, 1987; Thompson, 1993). Virtually all multicelled animals have nervous systems that work according to similar principles, suggesting that communication between the parts of an animal appeared quite early in evolution, probably before the earliest multicelled creatures differentiated into their major types (e.g., mollusks, insects, and, eventually, vertebrates).

In the course of evolution, neurons began to clump together into groups called **ganglia.** Ganglia themselves became arranged in a hierarchy, so that some ganglia controlled others. As explained in Chapter 3, this process did not take place with the aim of evolving into the human brain. Instead, each step of the process conferred a survival advantage over the immediately preceding step, presumably a slowly but steadily increasing responsivity to the demands of the environment.

■ **ganglia**
clumps of neurons

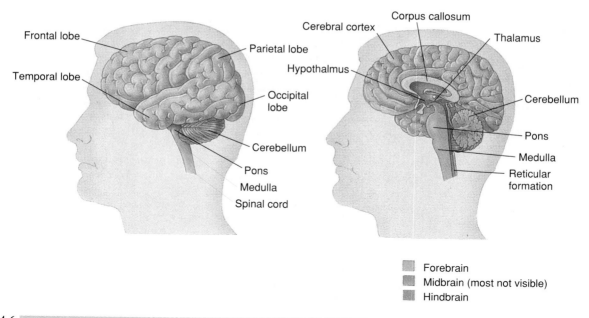

Figure 4.6
Major Structures of the Brain. The figure on the left shows the intact brain as it would appear from the left side. The figure on the right shows the brain as it would appear if cut in half through the middle. The hindbrain contains the pons, medulla, cerebellum, and the lower part of the reticular formation. The midbrain contains the upper part of the reticular formation. The forebrain contains still other structures, notably the thalamus, the hypothalamus, and the cerebral cortex.

For those animals that became elongated, the set of ganglia that ran their entire length took on increased importance. Just as a street running through the length of a town becomes Main Street, these ganglia became the central nervous system. The higher ganglia became the brain. What started out as several extra neurons at one end of a primitive animal evolved into the billions of interconnected neurons that compose the brain and make complex human behavior possible.

The brain presumably evolved through the addition of layers. It is tempting to view this process as the addition of new layers that left the original ones intact. For instance, the base of the human brain looks like the entire brain of a reptile and is sometimes called the reptilian brain. However, the layers of the human brain are integrated with each other. Each new layer adds a level to the hierarchy of the nervous system. Functions of the older parts of the brain necessarily changed as newer parts evolved because these newer parts typically coordinated the older parts. Human beings are not reptiles with fancy accessories.

The human brain acquired its distinctive structure and function over aeons. As discussed in Chapter 3, one can speculate about the selective advantage resulting from each of these characteristics, but at the same time, hypotheses need to be tempered by the realization that these ultimate explanations are often impossible to verify. Natural selection can work only on what exists, so that current structures were constrained by immediately preceding ones. Further, as also noted in Chapter 3, many if not most of the contemporary functions of the human brain may originally have developed to solve altogether different problems of adaptation:

> Natural selection built the brain; yet, by virtue of structural complexities so engendered, the same brain can perform a plethora of tasks that . . . [were not] the target of the original natural selection . . . [such as] singing . . . reading and writing. (Gould, 1991, p. 57)

Table 4.2	Major Structures of the Brain
Structure	**Function**
Medulla	Controls the heart, the lungs, and involuntary reflexes
Cerebellum	Coordinates intentional movements
Pons	Relays sensory messages to and from the spinal cord and other parts of the brain; plays a role in sleep and wakefulness
Reticular formation	Relays sensory information to the forebrain; controls general arousal and mode of consciousness
Limbic system	Controls expression of emotions; plays a role in memory
Hypothalamus	Controls and integrates activities of the autonomic nervous system; controls the pituitary gland
Thalamus	Organizes and sends messages to and from the very top of the brain; maintains awareness
Cerebral cortex	Exerts final control over other brain structures; initiates behavior

Without a clear picture of the earlier structures and their functions, we cannot offer a full evolutionary account of the present structures and their functions.

Let me now discuss the more specific parts of the brain. In each case, the types of functions attributed to each particular structure are described (see Table 4.2), but the nervous system is usually more complex. It is rarely so simple that one and only one brain structure controls a particular function.

The Medulla

The brain is connected to the spinal cord. In fact, there is no precise separation between the hindbrain and the spinal cord. The hindbrain itself is composed of several structures (see Figure 4.6). First is the **medulla,** the part of the brain stem directly connected to the spinal cord that controls respiration and cardiac function. Many of the functions of the medulla involve involuntary reflexes: vomiting, coughing, sneezing, and hiccupping. If a mosquito flies toward your eye, you blink without thinking about it. This automatic response is controlled by the medulla.

If you try, you can exert some conscious control over the functions of the medulla, but only within certain limits. The medulla controls breathing rate, for instance, and if you wish, you can hold your breath, thus overriding the medulla. You might even be able to hold your breath long enough to pass out, but you cannot refrain from breathing to the point of death. Once you lose consciousness, the medulla resumes its control of breathing.

A hard blow to the back of the head or upper neck can prove fatal if it damages the medulla and interferes with its control of vital functions. Loss of respiratory function, in particular, can lead to rapid death. Before vaccines for polio were developed, it was common for the polio virus to attack the part of the medulla responsible for breathing. Victims had to be placed on respirators.

The Cerebellum

A second structure of the hindbrain is the **cerebellum,** involved in coordination, posture, balance, and muscle tone. Our intentional movements do not originate in the cerebellum, but here is where they are coordinated and made into smooth movements (Ito, 1993). If a discrepancy exists between intended movements and actual movements, the cerebellum detects it and makes a correction by stimulating or inhibiting the appropriate muscles of the body.

■ **medulla**
part of the brain stem that is directly connected to the spinal cord and controls respiration and cardiac function

■ **cerebellum**
structure of the hindbrain involved in coordination, balance, and muscle tone

Take speaking, for example. In order to say what we intend to say, our lips, mouth, and tongue must be carefully orchestrated. Most people can speak flawlessly, at several hundred words per minute. If the cerebellum is damaged, however, speech may become slurred and the individual may stagger and tremble when moving. Among the types of brain injuries suffered by boxers, for example, damage to the cerebellum is common, and former fighters are sometimes described as punch-drunk because their behavior resembles the effects of acute intoxication (Boyle & Ames, 1983). However, in the case of brain-damaged fighters these impairments are permanent. The tremors that characterize Parkinson's disease also involve dysfunctions of the cerebellum (Jenkins & Frackowiak, 1993).

The Pons

A third structure of the hindbrain is the **pons,** a Latin term meaning bridge. In effect, the pons is a bulge in the brain stem; it links the hindbrain to the rest of the brain, playing the role of relay station. The pons sorts out and relays sensory messages from the spinal cord to other parts of the brain, and from these other parts of the brain back to the spinal cord. The pons also appears to play some role in sleep and wakefulness (Chapter 6). For example, research shows abnormal patterns of neural activity in the pons among people with narcolepsy, a disorder involving persistent attacks of uncontrollable sleep (Aldrich, Prokopowicz, Ockert, Hollingsworth, Penney, & Albin, 1994). Infants with highly irregular sleep patterns may have damage to the pons (Koyanagi et al., 1993).

■ **pons**
structure that links the hindbrain to the rest of the brain

The Reticular Formation

Occupying both the hindbrain and the midbrain is the **reticular formation** (see Figure 4.6), a complex network of neurons that reach into all parts of the brain, from bottom to top. The reticular formation is centrally located in the brain and richly

■ **reticular formation**
network of neurons centrally located in the brain and richly connected to other structures

The reticular formation controls people's general level of arousal and whether they are awake or asleep . . . or somewhere in between.

Figure 4.7
The Limbic System. The limbic system is a collection of structures in the forebrain.

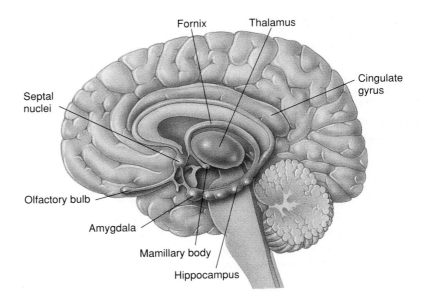

connected with other structures. It plays a coordinating role, linking parts of the hindbrain to parts of the forebrain; however, much has still to be learned about this structure.

We do know that the reticular formation receives sensory information that it then relays to structures in the forebrain. Most importantly, it also controls an individual's general level of arousal, as well as his or her mode of consciousness—awake or asleep (Chapter 6). When we awaken because of a loud sound or a bright light, we do so because the reticular formation has been stimulated.

In animals whose reticular formations have been destroyed, a constant state of sleep may occur, suggesting that the reticular system can turn off sensory information altogether, as well as turn it back on. Taking off from these implications, physicians have been able to rouse brain-damaged people from long-term comas by stimulating their reticular formation (Doman, Wilkinson, Dimancescu, & Pelligra, 1993).

The Limbic System

As already described, the forebrain controls our most characteristic human functions. It consists of a number of different structures, some of which are themselves composed of different structures. Let us consider the most important of these, starting with the **limbic system,** a collection of related structures (see Figure 4.7). These are particularly important in nonhuman animals, where they control behaviors we describe as instinctive (Chapter 3). In people, the limbic system is involved in the expression of emotions: pain, pleasure, anger, and sorrow (Chapter 7). The limbic system is also involved in turning off these emotions. Finally, it plays a significant role in memory, although the details of this function are not well understood.

One structure within the limbic system, the **amygdala,** seems to produce rage and aggression; another structure, the **septum,** seems to lessen those responses (Albert & Walsh, 1984). Again, the limbic system seems vulnerable to damage from boxing. One study comparing boxers and nonboxers found four times as many limbic system abnormalities among boxers (Boyle & Ames, 1983).

Another part of the limbic system is the **hippocampus,** involved in the processing of memories (Chapter 9). Animals and people with damage to the hippocampus are often unable to remember events for much longer than a few seconds (Matthies, 1989). Apparently, discrete substructures underly how memories are represented and how long

■ **limbic system**
structures in the forebrain involved in the expression of emotions

■ **amygdala**
part of the limbic system that produces rage and aggression

■ **septum**
part of the limbic system that reduces rage and aggression

■ **hippocampus**
part of the limbic system involved in the processing of memories

they persist (Eichenbaum, Otto, & Cohen, 1995). Accordingly, hippocampal damage can lead to impaired memory by one of two mechanisms: Either no record of an experience is made, or else the record does not last.

The Hypothalamus

The limbic system is linked to the **hypothalamus,** which is found at the top of the brain stem (see Figure 4.7). Among the most important functions of the hypothalamus are:

- controlling and integrating activities of the autonomic nervous system
- controlling the pituitary gland, which—as will be explained later in the chapter—affects the functioning of most of the body's endocrine glands
- along with the limbic system, regulating emotional expression
- controlling the temperature of the body
- regulating bodily rhythms responsible for sleep
- turning on (and off) sensations of hunger and thirst

The operation of the hypothalamus can be compared to that of a thermostat (Chapter 7). It monitors the state of our body—its fluid level, for example—and triggers reactions to restore balance as necessary. Too little fluid results in thirst, which motivates us to drink.

Depending on its specific location, damage to the hypothalamus can produce behavioral and emotional excesses or deficits (Simonov, 1989; Weddell, 1994). A case study of a 34-year-old woman with hypothalamic damage showed that both extremes can occur for the same person (Cohen & Albers, 1991). Across time, she displayed marked fluctuations in her body temperature, sleep-wake cycle, and intellectual functions.

The Thalamus

Close by the hypothalamus is the **thalamus.** (*Hypo* means under, and so the hypothalamus is underneath the thalamus; again see Figure 4.7). Like the pons, the thalamus is a principal relay center, sending messages to and from the structures located in the very top of the brain. But the thalamus does more than just relay messages. It also integrates and organizes them, ensuring that specific messages—for example, visual messages from our eyes or auditory messages from our ears—go to the appropriate part of the forebrain for these to be interpreted (Chapter 5). The thalamus is also thought to play a role in maintaining awareness (Chapter 6) and acquiring knowledge (Chapter 9).

Bhatnagar and Andy (1989) reported the results of a provocative case study: They alleviated the chronic stuttering of a 61-year-old man by stimulating his thalamus with an electric current. These researchers believed that stuttering is due to the failure of the thalamus to coordinate the different movements of the tongue and mouth that make speech possible. By stimulating their subject's thalamus, they synchronized his neural functioning so that he could speak fluently.

In a similar case study, researchers found that stimulation of the thalamus by electric current can suppress the tremors of an individual with Parkinson's disease (Caparros-Lefebvre, Ruchoux, Blond, Petit, & Percheron, 1994). The patient was a 60-year-old woman who had experienced a tremor for almost 15 years. The intervention was successful over a period of years, until the woman died. Further research is needed to identify the exact mechanism by which this procedure has its effects, although we can hypothesize that it might stimulate dopamine activity or somehow compensate for its low levels.

■ **hypothalamus**

structure at the top of the brain stem that controls much of the activity of the autonomic nervous system

■ **thalamus**

structure above the hypothalamus that integrates and organizes neural messages

The Cerebral Cortex

- **cerebral cortex**

  outer layer of the forebrain

- **cerebral hemispheres**

  symmetrical halves of the forebrain

- **corpus callosum**

  bundle of nerve fibers that is the major connection between the two cerebral hemispheres

- **occipital lobe**

  region of the cortex located at the rear of the brain and devoted to vision

- **temporal lobe**

  region of the cortex located near the temple and devoted to speech comprehension and memory

- **anterior commissure**

  bundle of nerve fibers that connects the two temporal lobes

- **frontal lobe**

  region of the cortex located right behind the forehead and involved in planning and decision making

- **parietal lobe**

  region of the brain found behind the frontal lobe and in front of the occipital lobe and involved in the integration of sensory information relayed from lower parts of the brain

The outer layer of the forebrain is called the **cerebral cortex.** The cerebral cortex is the most recent addition in the evolution of the brain, appearing perhaps 100 million years ago. As discussed, the brain and nervous system are arranged in a hierarchy, with higher structures controlling lower structures. In these terms, the cortex is the chief executive, having final say both in organizing information relayed by other structures and in initiating appropriate responses. The brain damage suffered by Phineas Gage and Officer X involved the cortex, with consequences for lower structures of the brain.

A view from the top shows that the forebrain comprises two structures, more or less symmetrical. These are the **cerebral hemispheres** (see Figure 4.8). They are connected by several bundles of nerve fibers, the most important of which is the **corpus callosum.**

Each cerebral hemisphere controls the opposite half of the body. The left arm is connected by neurons mainly to the right hemisphere, whereas the right arm is connected by neurons mainly to the left hemisphere. If a neurologist examines a patient who has recently lost strength or feeling on one side of the body following a blow to the head, there is good reason to suspect that damage has occurred to the opposite side of the brain. This left-right structure of the brain can be added to the previously discussed ways in which the nervous system is organized.

Looking at the brain from the side, we can divide the cortex into four regions, called lobes (again see Figure 4.8). These regions are separated by deep indentations in the brain, called fissures. The **occipital lobes** are at the rear of the brain. The **temporal lobes** are near the temples, and they are connected to one another by a bundle of nerve fibers called the **anterior commissure.** The **frontal lobes** are located right behind the forehead. The **parietal lobes** are found behind the frontal lobes and in front of the occipital lobes.

Each of these lobes has its own function. Thus, the occipital lobes are devoted mainly to vision. Researchers have discovered that occipital damage can produce blindness, even when no damage to the eyes has occurred. The temporal lobes control speech comprehension and memory. The frontal lobes are involved in planning and decision making; remember from the stories of Phineas Gage and Officer X that frontal lobe

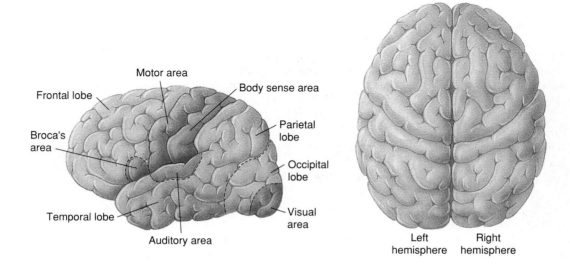

Figure 4.8
The Cerebral Cortex. The cortex is divided into the left hemisphere and the right hemisphere, each of which controls the opposite side of the body. Each of the hemispheres is divided into four lobes, each with characteristic functions.

damage makes it difficult to adapt to new situations. Finally, the parietal lobes integrate sensory information relayed from lower parts of the brain, in particular from the skin and muscles.

Stop and Think

7   How did the brain evolve?

8   What are the functions of the limbic system?

9   What are the functions of the cerebral cortex?

THE BRAIN AND BEHAVIOR

Let us move from our discussion of the brain's structure to an examination of its involvement in behavior. Researchers have made great strides in linking particular brain structures to particular behaviors, although details concerning the concrete mechanisms by which the behaviors arise remain elusive.

Localization of Function

As the surface of the brain, the cortex is more accessible to researchers than other structures. Accordingly, we know a fair amount about what the cortex does. Investigations of the cortex have clarified one of the long-standing debates within psychology about the nature of the brain and behavior: whether or not different human capacities are located within particular parts of the brain. This issue is called the debate over **localization of function** in the brain.

■ **localization of function**
position that specific parts of the brain are responsible for given behaviors

An extreme position in favor of localization can be found in the nineteenth-century practice known as phrenology. Phrenologists assumed that the mind was composed of different faculties (or abilities), that each faculty had a discrete location within the brain, and that dominant faculties could be discerned by inspecting a person's head for bumps, which presumably reflected the overdevelopment of the corresponding part of the brain (see Figure 4.9).

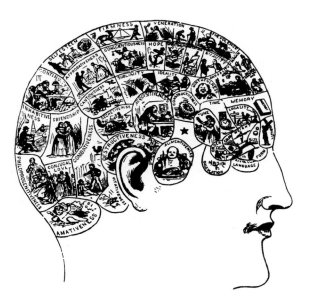

Figure 4.9
Phrenology Chart. In the 1800s, phrenologists believed they could determine people's particular abilities and traits by mapping the bumps on their heads. Each area of the skull was thought to correspond to a specific characteristic, as shown in this figure.

The point of view opposing phrenology proposes that the brain acts as an organized whole; its functions are performed not by its separate parts but rather by the brain as a single entity. Asking which part of the brain is responsible for memory, emotion, or motor coordination is like asking which part of a car is responsible for left turns or which player in the infield is responsible for a double play.

Years ago, Karl Lashley (1929) performed experiments with rats showing that their behavior was disrupted to the degree that large amounts of their brains were destroyed. The sheer amount of damage was more important than the particular location of the damage. Research like this swung psychological opinion away from the position of extreme localization of function toward an assumption of **mass action,** meaning that the brain acts as a whole.

But in recent years, the pendulum has swung back to a belief in at least some localization of function. For instance, as already explained, psychologists now believe that the four lobes of each hemisphere are involved to varying degrees in different functions. Studies of brain-damaged people clearly support this conclusion: Different functions are lost depending on the location of the damage.

Researchers, by stimulating different parts of the brain with electric current and seeing the results, have also mapped areas of the cortex where information is received or sent out (Penfield & Rasmussen, 1952). **Sensory projection areas** are parts of the cortex that receive information from the various senses—vision, hearing, taste, smell, and touch (Chapter 5). **Motor projection areas** send messages to the various muscles. A rule of thumb for understanding these areas is that the more complex and important a function is to an organism, the more cortical area is devoted to it (see Figure 4.10).

The cortex also contains **association areas,** so named because theorists once believed they linked the sensory and motor projection areas. Current opinion holds that the association areas are responsible for higher mental processes like memory, thought, and language.

In sum, localization of function is hardly as simple as the vision of the phrenologists. Although their general assumption has been vindicated—different parts of the brain do have characteristic functions—they lacked the technological means to identify these. The shape of your skull does not mirror the shape of your brain, and it does not provide a guide to your abilities.

Language

Let us next consider the relationship between the brain and language. In trying to understand what makes language possible, researchers have learned a great deal about the structure and function of the brain. Many questions about the brain and the nervous system are answered through animal studies. However, questions about the neurological basis of language can be answered only through studies with human beings, a factor that limits the researcher. Much of what we know comes from studies of people suffering damage to one or more parts of the brain. Researchers look for relationships between particular injuries and particular language deficits, hoping to infer what the process might be like in a neurologically intact individual.

Aphasia refers to a group of language problems that include the inabilities to express and/or comprehend speech or writing. More than a century ago, the French physician Paul Broca (1861) described the results of his autopsy of a patient who for years had suffered from an inability to produce words. Broca found that this man had damage in a small area of the left frontal lobe that has since been called **Broca's area.** Broca argued that this part of the brain translates ideas into words. (Interestingly, damage to Broca's area does not impair a person's ability to sing a familiar song—implying that the part of the brain involved in singing is different from that involved in speaking.)

Not long after, the German physician Carl Wernicke (1874) concluded from similar evidence that a part of the left temporal lobe is responsible for the comprehension of

■ mass action
idea that the brain acts as a whole

■ sensory projection areas
parts of the cortex that receive information from the various senses

■ motor projection areas
parts of the cortex that send messages to the various muscles

■ association areas
parts of the cortex where higher mental activities take place

■ Broca's area
brain structure involved in the production of speech

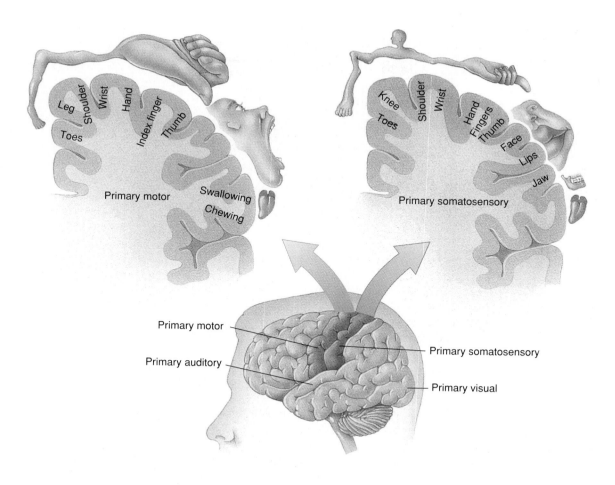

Figure 4.10
Projection Areas. These figures represent the motor and sensory projection areas of the cortex by showing the part of the body associated with each. The more cortical area devoted to a function, the more important it tends to be to our species. Note the size of the projection areas associated with the hands and the mouth.

speech. The patients he studied were able to produce words but were not able to comprehend them. Perhaps as a result, their speech was sometimes little more than a jumble of words. The part of the brain implicated in this form of aphasia is called **Wernicke's area.** Many people with damage to Wernicke's area do not seem to recognize that they have any difficulty with language. They follow social conventions while speaking to others, taking turns in conversation, even though what they say has no apparent meaning.

Findings like these show that many language functions are located in one part of the brain—for most individuals, the left hemisphere. The two halves of the brain are therefore not strictly symmetrical in function. People suffering a stroke in the left side of the brain, for instance, often have difficulty speaking or understanding speech. People suffering the identical damage in the right side of the brain usually encounter no such language difficulty, although they may have problems finding their way around or performing other tasks that require orienting themselves—a function of the right hemisphere.

There exist other ways to identify which hemisphere houses language functions. One simple strategy for determining the location of the speech areas is to inject a barbiturate into an artery that leads directly to the left hemisphere. If language is located there, speech is lost (temporarily) within a few seconds. If language is located in the right hemisphere, then a delay occurs in the loss of speech. This information is critical

■ **Wernicke's area**
brain structure involved in the comprehension of speech

In written Chinese, individual symbols are used to represent entire words. Brain damage has different effects on reading and writing for Chinese speakers than it does for speakers of Western languages.

when brain surgery is being considered; surgeons proceed much more cautiously when they know that their procedures may affect speech areas.

Brain damage affects the various aspects of language use in characteristic ways. Recent research sharpens this conclusion by showing that the details of these effects depend on the particular language (Tzeng, Chen, & Hung, 1991). For example, the Chinese language differs from Western languages in numerous ways (Bates, Chen, Tzeng, Li, & Opie, 1991). Verbs are not conjugated, as they are in English, and written Chinese uses individual symbols to represent entire words, as opposed to a small set of letters strung together in innumerable ways. When brain damage occurs in Chinese speakers, the effects on spoken and written language may be different from such effects when the identical damage occurs in speakers of Western languages (Hu, Qiuo, & Zhong, 1990). Chinese words are apparently processed in a part of the brain different from that used for Western words, in visual rather than phonetic terms; hence, the effects of brain damage on language use must be interpreted within a larger cultural context. A similar conclusion follows from studies of brain damage among speakers of American Sign Language (Bellugi, Poizner, & Klima, 1989).

Left and Right Brains

The various activities people perform (e.g., throwing, kicking, and writing) can often be performed more skillfully with one side of the body than with the other. Remember that the left side of the body is controlled by the right hemisphere, and vice versa. Thus, we refer to the corresponding brain hemisphere as dominant. The general phenomenon in which one hemisphere is more involved than the other in some behavior is termed **lateralization.**

Other animal species also show dominance (Bradshaw & Nettleton, 1989). Tufted capuchin monkeys, for example, can learn to crack open nuts with a stone and in doing so they display a consistent preference for using one hand rather than the other (Westergaard & Suomi, 1993). Parrots similarly prefer one foot over the other for grasping food (Harris, 1989). These findings with nonhuman species may provide hints about the evolutionary basis of lateralized behaviors.

The significance of lateralization is clarified by studies of **split-brain patients** (Thompson, 1993). Here, in an attempt to relieve individuals from severe epileptic seizures, neurosurgeons cut the corpus callosum that connects the two hemispheres. For

■ **lateralization**
greater involvement in some behavior of one hemisphere rather than the other

■ **split-brain patients**
individuals whose corpus callosum has been severed in order to relieve severe epileptic seizures

some patients, this surgery curbed their seizures. However, two important observations were made about the people who underwent this operation. First, in many ways their behavior was normal—a surprising finding, given the complexity of the brain and the severity of the surgery. Second, researchers discovered that, under certain laboratory conditions, the split-brain patients did behave in an unusual way.

Suppose visual information is made available to a patient in such a way that only one hemisphere of the brain receives this input. The other hemisphere behaves as if it were oblivious to this information:

> Split-brain patient N. G. sits in front of a screen with a small black dot at the center. She is asked to look directly at the dot. A picture of a cup is flashed briefly to the right of the dot. N. G. reports that she has seen a cup. Again, she is asked to look directly at the dot. This time, a picture of a spoon is flashed to the left of the dot. She is asked what she saw. She replies, "No, nothing." She is then asked to reach under the screen with her left hand and to select, by touch only, from among several objects the one that is the same as the one she has just seen. Her left hand palpates each object and then holds up the spoon. When asked what she is holding, she says, "Pencil." (Springer & Deutsch, 1985, pp. 29–30)

One conclusion is that we really have two brains, the left hemisphere and the right hemisphere. The split-brain operation separates the two hemispheres, which typically work together. But if separated, they act independently. When the picture of a spoon was flashed to the left of where this patient was looking, visual information went to her right hemisphere. Because her left hemisphere—the center of language functions—was unaware of the spoon, she reported that she saw nothing.

Another conclusion is that each brain half performs its functions in different ways. According to one version of this conclusion, the left brain is analytical and logical, whereas the right brain is intuitive and holistic (see Figure 4.11). These stereotypes are overstated, particularly in popular treatments that classify people as left-brained or right-brained (Williams & Stockmyer, 1987). This approach also obscures the important fact that the two hemispheres work together. Nevertheless, there is some basis to the distinction, and lateralization continues to be a hotly researched topic (Iaccino, 1993; Springer & Deutsch, 1993).

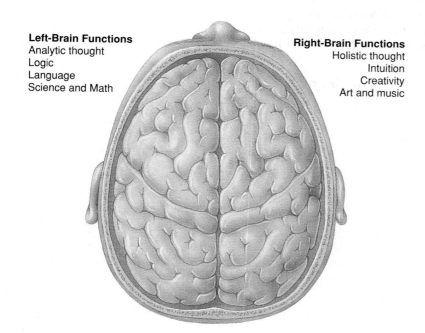

Left-Brain Functions
Analytic thought
Logic
Language
Science and Math

Right-Brain Functions
Holistic thought
Intuition
Creativity
Art and music

Figure 4.11
Functions of the Cerebral Hemispheres. The left hemisphere controls the right side of the body, and the right hemisphere controls the left side. More controversial and probably overstated is the idea that the two hemispheres process information in wholly different ways: the left hemisphere with logic, the right brain with intuition.

Experience and the Brain

One of the most central human characteristics is our ability to learn from experience. We have a far smaller number of fixed reflexes than our animal cousins, but the human capacity for learning leads to a further appreciation of biology's importance to human behavior. Experience presumably alters the brain and the nervous system, and thus our behavior (Chapter 8).

Psychologists have long speculated about how this alteration takes place (Thompson, 1986). One cannot simply open up people's skulls before and after they have learned how to write computer programs, for example, and observe where and how programming conventions have been added. It is not even clear just what one should look for when investigating how experience alters the brain.

Structural changes.   One might look at structural changes in the nervous system. In an intriguing research program, Rosenzweig (1984) followed this strategy. He started by raising rats in one of two environments: an enriched environment containing numerous objects the animals could manipulate and explore and an impoverished environment providing minimal variation and stimulation.

The brains of the rats reared in the enriched environment differed from those of the rats reared in the impoverished environment. Enriched brains were larger, better supplied with blood, and higher in protein content. The neurons in these brains were more complexly interconnected. It is tempting to explain the structural differences in terms of different experiences, but they may mirror mundane differences in health. Perhaps the rats raised in the enriched environment were healthy, whereas those raised in the impoverished environment were sickly because of the conditions in which they lived. Their brains therefore were different, but learning had nothing to do with the difference. Further, this line of research might show not so much the effects of an enriched environment as the effects of an impoverished one. Learning may not produce larger brains, but lack of learning may produce smaller ones.

Molecular changes.   Other researchers interested in the effects of experience on the brain look for changes at a molecular level. They have discovered that learning can influence the thresholds for secretion of a particular neurotransmitter and/or the amount of the chemical secreted (Farley & Alkon, 1985; Woody, 1986). In either case, certain actions become more or less likely. To date, researchers have investigated this process in extremely simple organisms, like mollusks, capable only of the rudiments of learning (Chapter 8). We need further research to see if results hold up for more complex learning by more complicated creatures.

Granted that experience can change both the structure and the function of the nervous system, we must be careful in how we interpret correlations between biology and behavior. When such correlations exist, an obvious interpretation is that the causal effect runs from biology to behavior. However, it may well be in given instances that this conclusion confuses cause and effect. For instance, highly anxious people have an overly active sympathetic nervous system (Chapter 13). Does this mean that biological responsivity, determined by genetics, makes anxiety disorders more likely, or does it mean that chronic anxiety in response to stressful events in the environment alters the nervous system? Both possibilities are probably true.

Stop and Think

10   Describe the debate over localization of function.

11   How are popular descriptions of left–right brain differences an oversimplification?

12   How does experience change the brain?

It is tempting to believe that a highly responsive nervous system causes anxious behavior, but causality may also run from anxious behavior to a responsive nervous system. The links between biology and behavior are often bidirectional.

SEX DIFFERENCES IN THE BRAIN

Let us conclude this discussion of the brain by considering whether the brains of men and women differ. Psychologists want to know if sex differences in the brain produce different ways of thinking and behaving. This issue needs to be approached in several ways, depending on the aspect of the brain in which we are interested.

Do Men and Women Show Structural Differences?

In terms of gross brain structure, there are no differences between human males and females, except that men's brains on average are bigger. This difference merely reflects the positive correlation between brain size and body size. Men tend to be larger than women, and so they tend to have larger brains. Within normal limits, brain size seems to have no particular psychological significance (Gould, 1981).

In terms of the microscopic features of individual neurons, there are few differences between men and women, except for the sex chromosomes in the cell nuclei. When differences do exist, such as in the number of dendrites in certain regions of the brain, these are not apparent until several years after birth (Breedlove, 1994). This finding might reflect postnatal effects of hormones or experience, but it might also mean that the genes responsible for these differences are not activated immediately.

In any event, one obvious brain difference between the sexes exists in those parts of the hypothalamus that regulate reproduction-related activities characteristic of only men or only women, such as menstruation (Allen, Hines, Shryne, & Gorski, 1989). However, these differences have not been shown to relate directly to other aspects of behavior or cognition.

A less obvious difference is that the corpus callosum and the anterior commissure, which connect the cerebral hemispheres, are sometimes larger in females than in males (Allen & Gorski, 1992; Hines, 1990). To be more exact, the absolute sizes are about the same

These are images of brains shown from below. On the left is a male's brain, and on the right is a female's brain. Both are engaged in the same task. Increased brain activity is shown in red, and as you can see, the female's brain shows activity on both sides, suggesting that skills are distributed more equally between the two hemispheres for females than for males.

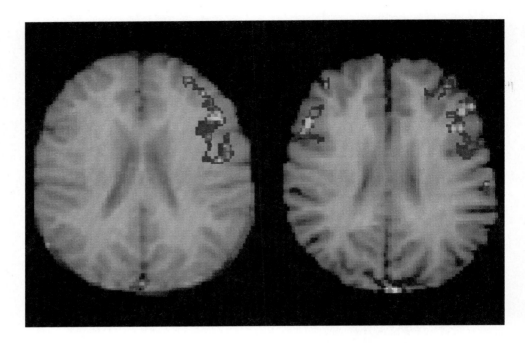

in the different sexes, but given the difference in brain size, they are proportionately larger in females than in males. One interpretation of this difference is that communication between the hemispheres is more efficient for women than men. The functions attributed to the left versus right hemispheres of the brain are more evenly distributed in women than men.

Do Men and Women Show Ability Differences?

One theory holds that spatial ability is enhanced when located mainly in one hemisphere, whereas language ability is enhanced when it is not so strictly localized (Levy, 1976; Levy & Heller, 1992). The predictions follow, therefore, that males on average should be superior at spatial tasks, such as mentally rotating objects or reading maps, and that females on average should be superior at verbal tasks, such as expressing ideas in words.

Some studies support these predictions, although it is important to note that other studies do not (Halpern, 1992). As will be described in Chapter 11, some of these sex differences in abilities have diminished in recent years, an occurrence that obviously is at odds with a simple explanation in terms of inherent brain differences. Certainly, learning and socialization influence the sorts of abilities people develop and display—meaning that a biopsychosocial explanation of these sex differences is demanded.

Conclusions About Sex Differences

We are best served by remembering the caution raised in Chapter 3 about the need to take a broad look at biology and behavior. To return to the four modes of biological explanation, we need to seek the cognitive or neural processes responsible for behavioral differences (cause) and not be content with the mere description of structural differences, like the size of the corpus callosum. We need to look for reasons why men benefit by spatial ability and women by verbal ability (function). We need to ask how these skills arise in little boys and little girls (development). We need to wonder about primates in the wild, seeking clues to human differences by examining the behavior of our cousins (evolution).

We must also consider the possibility that brain differences between men and women are the result of experience. Consider that studies with animals like mice show that the brains of males and females differ in size early in life and these differences are not limited to brain structures with reproductive functions (Juraska, 1991). However, at least part of the reason for these differences is environmental. Maternal stimulation (e.g., licking of infants) influences the number of neurons that survive, and this stimulation in turn is triggered by chemicals secreted by the infants (Moore, Dou, & Juraska, 1992). If male and female infants differ in the secretion of these chemicals and/or if mothers respond differently to the secretions of male versus female infants, then these infants will develop different brains.

If brain development in mice occurs in a social context, what does this imply about brain development in human males and females? If parents or teachers encourage different activities on the parts of boys and girls, these may well contribute to whatever brain differences exist between men and women. This idea means that the causal direction runs from nurture to nature as well as vice versa.

Stop and Think

13 Explain how male-female differences in the brain are biopsychosocial.

THE ENDOCRINE SYSTEM

The endocrine system is made up of the glands that secrete **hormones,** chemicals carried through the bloodstream that affect various bodily organs. Although technically not part of the nervous system, our glands are intimately linked to the brain and work in concert with it to affect behavior, as well as physical processes like reproduction and growth. Figure 4.12 shows where the major glands are located.

■ **hormones**

chemicals that are secreted by glands into the bloodstream and affect various bodily organs

Hypothalamus

Thyroid

Adrenal glands

Ovary (female)

Pituitary

Parathyroids

Pancreas

Testis (male)

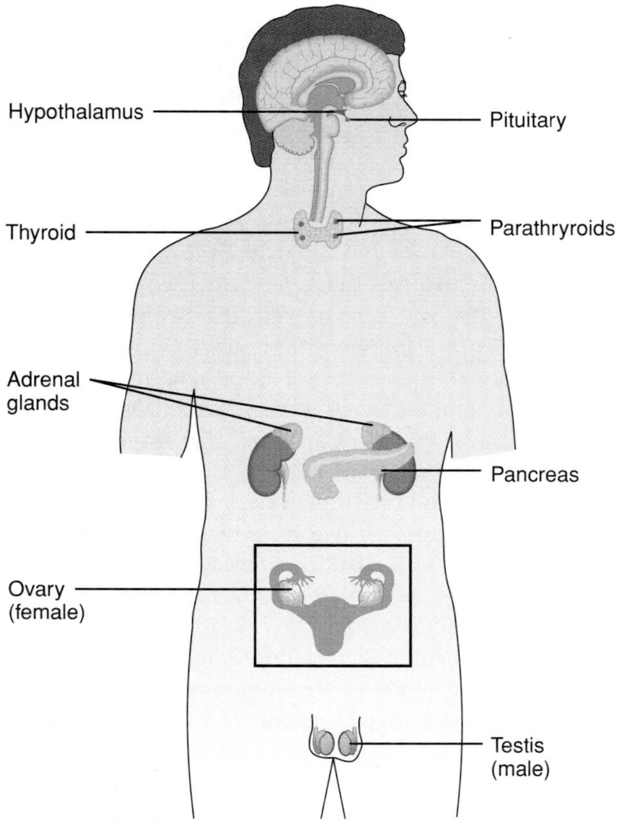

Figure 4.12
The Endocrine System. The endocrine system consists of glands that secrete hormones into the bloodstream, where they are carried to different parts of the body to affect physiology and behavior. The pituitary gland is particularly important because it is centrally linked to the rest of the endocrine system.

Hormones

Like the nervous system, the endocrine system communicates among its parts. This communication takes place by means of hormones released into the blood, meaning that the endocrine system is not nearly as speedy as the nervous system. So, some of our reactions to events take a while to occur and then linger long after the event is over.

Imagine merging onto a busy interstate highway. You put your turn signal on and find what looks like a reasonable space into which to ease your car. Suddenly, someone speeding along in the passing lane swerves right into your space. You slam on the brakes and avoid disaster in a quick and cool way. You did not hesitate in responding to the careless driver, and you did so skillfully enough that he may have been unaware that there was ever any danger. But as he weaves down the interstate blissfully unaware, your heart starts to pound, and your mouth goes dry. Your palms perspire so much that it is difficult to grasp your steering wheel. You stay in this state of emotional arousal for miles.

You avoided the careless driver because this is how your nervous system works—rapidly. You experienced a relatively slow and lingering emotional reaction because this is how your endocrine system works—slowly. To be specific, your emotional reaction to the driver was influenced by your **adrenal glands,** which are involved in responses to threat and danger.

For purposes of illustration, this discussion has contrasted the nervous system and the endocrine system. But as emphasized, the body operates as a whole. The nervous system and the endocrine system work together. Hormones affect the functioning of the brain. The brain affects the secretion of hormones. Indeed, the same chemical—such as norepinephrine, which the adrenals secrete—can function as both hormone and neurotransmitter. The example of your emotional response to the careless driver reflects an integrated response of the nervous system and the endocrine system.

Much of the endocrine system is controlled by hormones produced in the hypothalamus, which, you will recall, is part of the brain. Hormones from the hypothalamus, in particular, influence the **pituitary gland** (see Figure 4.12), which in turn controls the secretions of many of our other glands. For instance, the pituitary gland secretes a hormone that triggers the response of our adrenal glands to stress. Sometimes the pituitary is referred to as the master gland because it is so centrally linked to the rest of the endocrine system.

Pheromones

In some species, animals secrete hormone-like chemicals that serve communication between individuals. These are called **pheromones,** and they are used to mark out territories or to signal willingness to mate. When your cat rubs its cheek against your leg, you may interpret this as a friendly greeting, but Puff is actually leaving a chemical mark upon you.

Do human beings have pheromones? The answer is at present unclear. We know that perfumes are often made from animal pheromones and that advertisers and consumers make great claims about the social and sexual impact of perfumes. We know that people are sensitive to odors (Chapter 5) and that these often trigger vivid memories (Chapter 9). Very early in life, human infants learn to recognize the characteristic smell of their caretakers, and vice versa (Porter, 1991). But these facts do not capture the specificity of pheromones.

More informative is the demonstration by McClintock (1971) that the menstrual cycles of female college students tend to become synchronized with those of their roommates and close female friends. Follow-up studies have replicated this result among mother-daughter pairs, female soldiers serving together, female office workers, and lesbian couples (A. Weller & L. Weller, 1992, 1993, 1995). The critical factor is the amount of time women spend in each other's immediate company. Menstrual synchrony occurs among the females of other mammalian species as well, including

■ **adrenal glands**
endocrine glands that are located on top of the kidneys and control the body's response to threat and danger

■ **pituitary gland**
endocrine gland that is located at the base of the brain and controls the secretions of many other glands

■ **pheromones**
hormone-like chemicals involved in communication between individuals

primates, and in these cases pheromones appear to be responsible (Graham, 1991). Studies with human females have yet to implicate pheromones as a mechanism, and researchers must be alert to the possible roles played by shared experiences, common diets, and similar sleeping schedules (L. Weller & A. Weller, 1993).

Assuming that menstrual synchrony is an evolved psychological mechanism in at least some species, what is its function? Mennella, Blumberg, McClintock, and Moltz (1990) provided one answer in their study of Norway rats, a communal species in which females raise their offspring together and share nursing. In this species, menstrual synchrony leads to birth synchrony, which in turn is associated with increased survival of the rat pups.

Another hint concerning human pheromones comes from studies showing that very young infants who have never been breast-fed nonetheless prefer the smell of the breasts of lactating females (Makin & Porter, 1989). Presumably, some chemical is present that attracts the attention of newborns the first time they encounter it. Although the specific chemical has not been identified, it might be a human pheromone. More generally, we have another likely example of an evolved psychological mechanism (Chapter 3), in this case one that draws infants to a probable source of nourishment.

Androstenol is a steroid with a characteristic odor secreted in the sweat of human males and in the urine of both males and females (Brooksbank, Brown, & Gustafsson, 1974). According to some studies, exposure to androstenol affects mood, friendliness, and attraction to others (Kirk-Smith, Booth, Carroll, & Davies, 1978). These results suggest that this steroid may be a human pheromone, but the behavioral effects attributed to it are at best fragile and difficult to replicate (Benton & Wastell, 1986; Black & Biron, 1982). The search for human pheromones continues.

Stop and Think

14   Compare and contrast the endocrine system and the nervous system.

15   Why is the hypothalamus considered part of both the nervous system and the endocrine system?

16   How could the existence of human pheromones be definitively demonstrated?

Androstenol is a steroid with a characteristic odor that is secreted in the sweat of human males. Researchers have yet to decide if androstenol is a human pheromone, but it is a possible candidate.

Table 4.3   Neuropsychology Research Techniques

Technique	Strategy
Lesions and ablations	Damage or destroy parts of the nervous system and determine the consequences
Electrical stimulation	Stimulate the nervous system with electricity and determine the consequences
Chemical stimulation	Stimulate the nervous system with chemicals and determine the consequences
Electrical recording	Record electrical activity in the brain during different activities
Imaging	Take pictures of brain structures and/or functions during different activities
Computer modeling	Simulate functioning of the nervous system with a computer program and compare the consequences with what actually happens

DOING *Neuropsychology* RESEARCH

Neuropsychologists face a daunting task. As you have seen, the nervous system is incredibly complex, and the details of its functioning reside at a microscopic level. Research strategies are indirect, allowing inferences but rarely direct views. Investigators have devised various approaches to aid these inferences (see Table 4.3), and the results described in the previous sections of this chapter reflect their ingenuity.

Lesion and Ablation Techniques

■ **lesion**
wound or injury to a particular part of the brain or nervous system

■ **ablation**
complete destruction or removal of some part of the brain or nervous system

Lesion and ablation studies provide an important way to see how damage to the nervous system is linked to subsequent behavior. A **lesion** is a wound or injury to a particular part of the brain or nervous system; an **ablation** is the complete destruction or removal of some structure. Lesions and ablations may be deliberately created by researchers working with animals, or they may be studied as they naturally occur in accidents and illnesses.

In order to make a lesion in the intended part of the brain, a researcher places an animal in a device like this one that holds the animal's head still and allows a lesion to be made in a specific location.

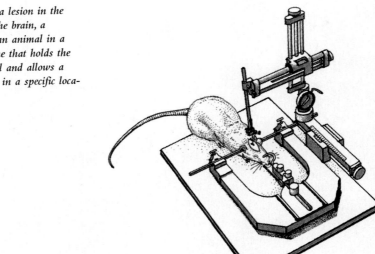

The vignettes that began this chapter are good examples, as are the autopsies conducted by Broca and Wernicke. In such cases, investigators attempt to correlate specific types of brain damage with given behavioral consequences. Although researchers who create lesions and ablations focus on damaged or destroyed neural tissue, they intend to offer conclusions about intact nervous systems. Quite often, when lesions and ablations and their effects are investigated, we obtain information that we could not get by observing an undamaged brain.

When lesions and ablations are deliberately created, great precision is needed so that researchers can say with certainty what structure has been affected by their procedure. The animal is held still in a special device; its skull is opened; and the lesion or ablation is made at a carefully measured location. Although the brains of different animals vary somewhat, they are similar enough that researchers following this procedure for different subjects can assume that an identical lesion or ablation was created.

Lesion and ablation studies provide some of the strongest support for the conclusion that brain structures are organized in a hierarchy. As noted, higher parts of the brain coordinate lower parts. Lesions at different points in the hierarchy disrupt the organism to varying degrees (Gallistel, 1980). Thus, an organism with damage to a very basic level of its brain can make miscellaneous motor movements but cannot coordinate them into action. An organism with damage at a somewhat higher level can string behaviors together but does so ineptly.

Electrical Stimulation Techniques

Neurons can be stimulated with electrical pulses, allowing researchers to identify neural connections: Pass a current through one part of the brain and see what happens in other parts. If the latter structures show an increase in activity, then they must be linked to the structure that was stimulated. Along these lines, electrical stimulation can also be used to map connections between brain structures and behaviors.

For example, with stimulation techniques researchers have located a pleasure center in the brain (Olds & Milner, 1954). Electrically stimulating the **medial forebrain bundle (MFB)**—a group of neurons connecting the middle of the brain to the top of the brain—produces pleasure. If an experimenter arranges matters so that a rat can stimulate its own MFB by pressing a lever, it will do so indefinitely at an extremely high

■ **medial forebrain bundle (MFB)** group of neurons that connects the middle of the brain to the top of the brain and is involved in pleasure

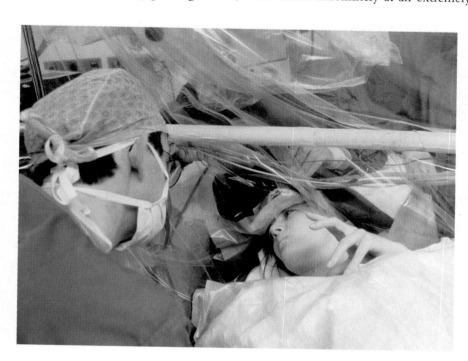

Brain surgery is sometimes undertaken when a patient is awake, and one of the ways psychologists have learned about the brain is from these patients' reports when different parts of their brains are stimulated.

rate. Reportedly, rats given the choice between self-stimulation of the pleasure center and food will starve to death. This phenomenon suggests that parts of the brain mediate reward, a potent determinant of how we behave (Chapter 8).

Another example of how electrical stimulation allows psychologists to study the brain comes from the work of Wilder Penfield. His original interest was in epilepsy and how brain surgery might alleviate the associated seizures. In some of the operations he performed, the patient was conscious. (This is not as strange as it sounds because the brain itself contains no pain receptors; Chapter 5.) Penfield found that when he stimulated parts of the brain surface, the patient reported vivid and detailed experiences.

Here is an example of what happened as a result of stimulation of a particular location called Point 23 in one patient:

> 12:30 P.M. . . . 23-repeated. The patient said, "I hear some music." 23-repeated without warning. The patient observed, "I hear the music."
>
> 12:45 P.M. 23-repeated again without warning. "I heard the music again; it is like the radio." When asked what tune it was, she said she did not know but that it was familiar. . . . When the electrode was held in place, the patient hummed the air, passing from chorus to verse while all in the operating room waited in silence. Then the operating nurse, Miss Stanley, interrupted. "I know it. It's 'Rolling Along Together.'" "Yes," the patient replied, "Those words are in it but I don't know whether that is the name of the song." (Penfield & Jasper, 1954, pp. 130–131)

Even though Penfield found such recollections in fewer than 10 percent of the patients whose brains he stimulated, his results imply that past experiences are somehow stored in their entirety somewhere in the brain, waiting to be elicited. As you will see in Chapter 9, this interpretation is at odds with most contemporary theories of memory, and some critics dismiss Penfield's results as hallucinations on the part of his patients, as opposed to memories of actual occurrences (Loftus & Loftus, 1980). In any event, Penfield's results must ultimately be explained.

Electrical stimulation techniques have been widely used to discover the functions of different parts of the brain. For instance, an electric current is applied to one part of the brain's surface and a particular feeling or sensation is reported: "I see a flash of light!" Another part is stimulated, with an altogether different effect: "My left arm is twitching!" The projection areas shown in Figure 4.10 were mapped out in this way.

Chemical Stimulation Techniques

Similar in spirit to electrical stimulation techniques is an approach that introduces different chemicals to various regions of the brain to determine the consequences. For example, neurons may be exposed to a given neurotransmitter. Do they fire? If so, we know they are sensitive to this particular neurotransmitter. Chemical stimulation techniques have also been used to identify agonists and antagonists.

Electrical Recording Techniques

When neurons generate and transmit impulses, electrical activity occurs, suggesting to researchers that records of this activity might provide another glimpse at how the brain and the nervous system work. Often such studies record electrical activity in response to a standard stimulus, such as a flashing light.

Several different recording techniques exist. For instance, a microelectrode monitors the electrical activity of a single neuron. Microelectrode studies have made possible our understanding of how individual neurons function.

In contrast to microelectrodes, a macroelectrode records the electrical activity of a much larger number of cells. A macroelectrode can be attached to the scalp and does

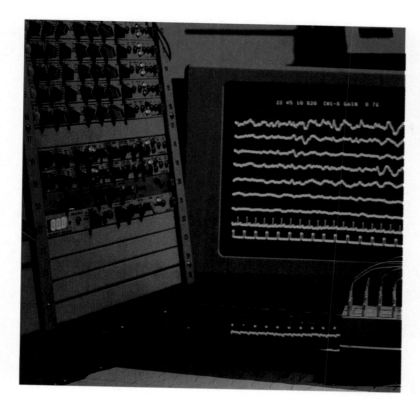

Figure 4.13
EEG Recordings. An EEG makes recordings of general electrical activity in the brain. This picture compares EEG recordings from a normal brain and from a brain during an epileptic seizure, which results from temporary electrical instability.

not require surgery to implant it. The **electroencephalogram (EEG)** is a record of overall brain activity. An EEG uses a device with macroelectrodes to detect general electrical patterns called brain waves (see Figure 4.13). Researchers have employed this method to examine what goes on in the brain during different states of consciousness (Chapter 6). For example, EEG recordings show that sleep consists of a series of stages, each with its own characteristic pattern of brain waves.

EEGs have also been recorded from individuals suffering from seizures. In an extreme form of seizure, which can last up to five minutes, the epileptic individual loses consciousness, falls to the floor, and experiences muscle spasms. Seizures apparently result from the brain's temporary electrical instability—a metaphorical short circuit. EEGs showing abnormal rhythms may warn of an impending seizure.

Imaging Techniques

Recent years have seen the introduction of another set of techniques for studying the brain that employ X-ray and related technology. The first of these techniques is called a **CAT scan,** an abbreviation for **computerized axial tomography.** Once a person's brain is X-rayed from various angles, a computer assembles the different pictures into a composite, helping a physician locate particular tumors or lesions in a way that a conventional X-ray cannot. Imaging techniques mean that neuropsychologists need not wait for brain-damaged patients to die in order to link specific lesions and ablations with alterations in behavior.

A second imaging technique is called a **PET scan,** short for **positron emission tomography.** This technique allows investigators to study metabolic activity in different parts of the brain by having an individual ingest a radioactive version of glucose. Then, as in the CAT scan procedure, the person's brain is X-rayed from various angles. The X-rays show which parts of the brain are metabolically active because the more active an area of the brain, the more it uses up the radioactive glucose. The resulting composite picture gives an overall view showing which parts of the brain are active and

■ **electroencephalogram (EEG)**
record of general electric patterns in the brain

■ **CAT scan; computerized axial tomography**
three-dimensional X-ray picture of the brain

■ **PET scan; positron emission tomography**
image of metabolic activity in the brain

These computerized axial tomography images (CAT Scan) are from a patient with a lesion in the area of the right occipital and parietal lobes. The lesion appears white in color because it is bleeding, and blood absorbs more radiation than the surrounding brain tissue.

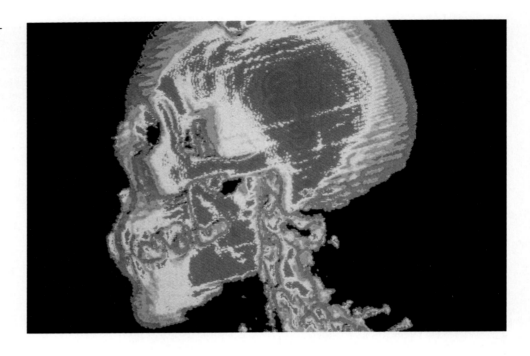

■ **MRI; magnetic resonance imaging** image of magnetic activity in the brain

which are not. Therefore, problems in the brain like tumors or lesions can be identified with a PET scan because they show abnormal patterns of metabolic activity.

A third imaging technique is **MRI,** or **magnetic resonance imaging.** It relies not on radiation but on magnetism to provide a glimpse at the structure and function of an intact brain. With MRI, the brain is exposed to a strong magnetic field that affects the activity of hydrogen atoms in water molecules. These patterns are then analyzed for unusual activity, too much or too little, as might occur in the case of a tumor. Although expensive, the MRI technique is particularly useful for studying soft tissue like the brain because bones and teeth—which contain little water—do not appear in the resulting images. Another advantage is that the MRI technique does not require exposure to radioactive substances.

This photo shows a series of positron emission tomography (PET Scan) images of the brain, formed while the individual was doing different activities. Portions of the brain in red are especially active metabolically.

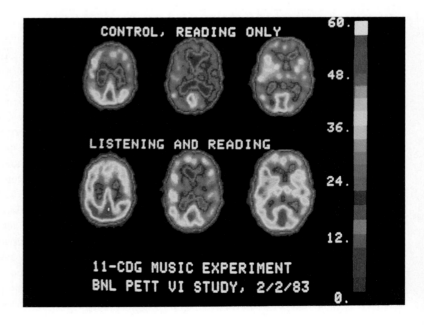

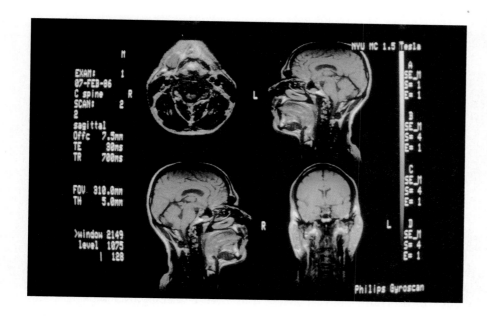

This magnetic resonance image (MRI) shows a human brain.

Imaging techniques have improved neuropsychologists' ability to draw conclusions about what parts of the brain are involved in what behaviors (Raichle, 1994). For example, a researcher might make brain images of individuals engaged in reading, writing, or arithmetic (Posner, Petersen, Fox, & Raichle, 1988). The researcher then compares these with the brain images of individuals not engaged in such activities. More or less involved brain regions are thereby indicated, suggesting where in the brain specific mental activities might occur. For example, visual imagery seems to involve the same parts of the brain as visual perception, suggesting that they share mechanisms in common (Chapters 5 and 9).

Computer Modeling Techniques

An altogether different strategy for studying the brain and its functions attempts to simulate the nervous system with a computer program (Wasserman, 1989). These simulations, called **neural networks,** consist of a set of hypothetical nodes (corresponding to neurons) connected to one another. Each connection is assigned a weight according to the strength of the association between the two nodes. The computer simulation is usually written in such a way that input (experience) changes these weights and hence the program's output (behavior). So, the more frequently two nodes communicate, the higher the weight of their connection becomes.

An early simulation attempted to model how children learn to form the past tenses of verbs (Rumelhart, McClelland, et al., 1986). The starting point of the neural network did not contain abstract grammatical rules. Rather, it formed past tenses simply by the accumulation of specific examples fed into it. The researchers introduced these specific examples in accordance with their frequency of usage in the English language and studied the output of the simulation over time. The past tenses of irregular verbs were initially formed as if they were regular verbs; for example, the past tense of *dig* was *digged* rather than *dug*. Over time, though, irregular verbs were learned correctly.

These changes follow the same progression that children show in their acquisition of language (Chapter 9). If a neural network "behaves" as actual people do, then one can argue that a similarity exists between its program and what happens in the brain. Neural networks are an obvious simplification, but therein lies their value to the researcher. Explicit theories of how the brain works can be investigated efficiently by creating a

■ **neural networks**
computer simulations of the nervous system

neural network, providing input, and comparing its output with actual behavior in analogous circumstances.

> **Stop and Think**
>
> **17** How could the various neuropsychological research techniques be used to investigate sex differences in the brain?
>
> **18** How could the various neuropsychological research techniques be used to investigate sexual orientation?

THE BRAIN AND THE NERVOUS SYSTEM IN A BIOPSYCHOSOCIAL CONTEXT

Biological explanations need to specify the concrete mechanisms by which biology influences behavior. In most cases, this goal is still to be achieved. Researchers know much more about which brain regions are involved in given behaviors than about how this involvement takes place. In specifying neurological mechanisms, psychologists must remember that these play themselves out in given environments, ranging from the immediate stimuli that trigger neural activity to the larger social settings in which people live.

One of the most important characteristics of the nervous system of human beings is that it can be modified by the environment: People can learn. This learning is passed from person to person in the process of socialization. Those in a given group learn the characteristic values and expectations of that group because their nervous system allows them to do so.

Let me consider a topic that illustrates the complexity involved in understanding how biology might influence behavior: the causes of **sexual orientation.** Why are some people straight and other people gay?

In recent years, findings have been reported that suggest some role of biology in determining sexual orientation. First, studies of twins show that male homosexuality is moderately heritable through the mother's side of the family (Hamer, Hu, Magnuson, Hu, & Pattatucci, 1993). Second, autopsies suggest that several brain differences exist between straight and gay men (LeVay, 1991). Although the relevant data have been criticized, certain regions of the hypothalamus may be smaller in gay men, whereas the anterior commissure and the corpus callosum are sometimes larger. These brain differences between straight and gay men correspond to brain differences between men and women, respectively.

LeVay (1993, p. 108) argued that these biological factors are important ingredients in any theory of sexual orientation:

> I do not know—nor does anyone else—what makes a person gay, bisexual, or straight. I do believe, however, that the answer to this question will be found by doing biological research in laboratories and not by simply talking about the topic, which is the way most people have studied it up to now.

At the same time, an explanation of sexual orientation must go beyond the specification of possible biological ingredients to identify pertinent mechanisms.

The Heritability of Sexual Orientation

The heritability of male homosexuality may seem puzzling. How could a homosexual orientation confer a survival advantage? The notion of inclusive fitness provides one answer. During times of scarce resources, a group of related individuals benefits only if

■ **sexual orientation**
type of person or activity that sexually arouses an individual, usually referring to people of the same or opposite sex

some of its members channel their sexual activity into reproduction. Fewer children result, but they will receive greater care and attention.

Like many sociobiology hypotheses, this explanation is difficult to test directly (Chapter 3). Perhaps we can predict that gay men tend to come from groups that have experienced great hardships over the aeons, necessitating a more cautious approach to reproduction than is the case among those who have always lived with abundance. Or perhaps we can predict that increased rates of homosexuality in a society have historically been associated with decreased rates of infant mortality. At the same time, it may simply be that the human capacity to develop a homosexual orientation is the result of evolved psychological mechanisms that originally arose for altogether different purposes.

The Neurological Basis of Sexual Orientation

Turning to the brain differences, what sense can we make of them? Studies with animals show that the regions of the hypothalamus that are different in gay versus straight men have something to do with sex-typical behaviors—males grasping females in order to mount them and females arching their backs in order to be mounted. There is a temptation to make much of this analogy, thinking it might explain human sexual orientation, until we realize that very little in human sexual behavior is sex-typical. That is, men and women, straight and gay, have diverse and overlapping sexual repertoires. There is no one way of engaging in sexual behavior that characterizes any large group of people or even most individuals. The importance of the hypothalamus to human sexual orientation remains unknown.

What about the differences in the size of the anterior commissure and corpus callosum? Recall from earlier in this chapter that such differences between men and women have been used to argue that women's cognitive skills are more evenly distributed between the hemispheres than men's are. Perhaps the same argument holds for the cognitive abilities of gay versus straight men. Perhaps homosexuality is associated with sex-atypical traits (LeVay, 1993).

Whatever these traits may be, they are not captured in stereotypes of gay men as feminine and lesbians as masculine because these are very poor generalizations. Rather, they are presumably more subtle psychological characteristics that lead people to behave in different ways and thus to elicit different responses from others (Chapter 12). Perhaps the interactions that ensue then determine sexual orientation. The details of this hypothesis have yet to be provided, and so this line of explanation is sketchy. The possibility must also be considered that brain differences between gay and straight men are the result of their given sexual experiences, not vice versa, meaning that the causal direction runs from behavior to biology.

Sexual Orientation as Biopsychosocial

One thing is clear: Biology cannot provide a complete explanation of sexual orientation (Bancroft, 1994). You may have heard about recent research with fruit flies in which deliberate genetic manipulations produced male flies that directed their sexual activity toward other males (Ferveur, Stortkuhl, Stocker, & Greenspan, 1995). Popular reports of these findings described the flies as gay (Thompson, 1995), a description that grabs our attention but is incredibly misleading.

The term *gay* is a social category that can be applied in a meaningful way only to human groups and lifestyles which, of course, reflect more than the operation of single genes. Even if we assume that these research findings have something to say about human beings and their sexual orientations, a less publicized result from the same investigation deserves attention: Male flies not subjected to the genetic manipulation came to behave sexually like the changed flies, if they spent sufficient time with them. So, even in this species, experience in a social context affects sexual behavior.

Variation in the numbers of people who are straight or gay exists across time and place, showing the importance of the social environment, even if we cannot specify just what aspects of the environment are critical (Ford & Beach, 1951). Most investigators agree that sexual orientation develops differently for men and women, and so the findings discussed here apply to gay men but not to lesbians. In any event, this kind of theorizing is speculative, and even the starting point—the data implicating biological differences between straight and gay men—is controversial (Fausto-Sterling, 1985; Friedman & Downey, 1993; Gooren, Fliers, & Courtney, 1990). Nevertheless, the potential power of a biopsychosocial approach to understanding behavior, in this case sexual orientation, is clear.

The next chapter discusses the processes by which we come to know the external world: sensation and perception. Our sensory organs consist of highly specialized neurons sensitive to different forms of energy. Perception refers to the ways we organize and interpret this neural input. The biological processes responsible for sensation and perception represent excellent examples of evolved psychological mechanisms.

SUMMARY

UNDERSTANDING THE NERVOUS SYSTEM: DEFINITION AND EXPLANATION

■ The brain and the nervous system are the center of mental activity. They receive information from the world, coordinate it, and then react.

■ The nervous system is an organized whole, with different divisions.

■ How best to understand the structure and function of the brain has long been of interest to psychologists, and a biopsychosocial perspective is probably the most promising approach to explanation.

STRUCTURE AND FUNCTION OF THE NERVOUS SYSTEM

■ The nervous system is composed of billions of cells called neurons, which communicate with each other by secreting neurotransmitters.

■ Neurotransmitters are chemicals that trigger electrical and chemical changes in other neurons.

■ The nervous system is simultaneously organized on a spatial basis, a biochemical basis, and a hierarchical basis. This multiple organization means that built into the nervous system is considerable redundancy, which can allow recovery of function following damage to a particular part.

THE BIOLOGY OF THE BRAIN

■ The brain evolved by adding layers to those that already existed. Higher levels came to control and coordinate lower levels, making possible complex behavior.

■ The brain has three major structures: the hindbrain, the midbrain, and the forebrain. These correspond to layers of the brain, from bottom to top, respectively.

■ Each of these layers contains its own structures, which may be more versus less involved in any particular behavior.

THE BRAIN AND BEHAVIOR

■ Many language functions are located in the left hemisphere.

■ According to research with split-brain patients, the two hemispheres can work independently and may process information in different ways. However, under most circumstances the brain acts as a whole.

■ People can and do learn from experience. Just how experience changes the brain is not well understood, although researchers have looked at structural changes as well as biochemical changes following particular experiences.

SEX DIFFERENCES IN THE BRAIN

■ Whether men and women show differences in their brains that correspond to sex differences in mental abilities is a topic of continuing research interest.

THE ENDOCRINE SYSTEM

■ The endocrine system is made up of glands that secrete hormones; chemicals carried through the bloodstream that affect bodily organs. Our glands are linked to the nervous system and work together with it to affect behavior as well as physical processes like reproduction and growth.

■ Pheromones are chemicals that allow communication between different animals of the same species. Whether people have pheromones is at present unclear.

DOING *Neuropsychology* RESEARCH

■ Researchers have at their disposal various techniques to study the brain and nervous system.

THE BRAIN AND THE NERVOUS SYSTEM IN A BIOPSYCHOSOCIAL CONTEXT

■ The determinants of sexual orientation seem to include biological, psychological, and social influences.

KEY TERMS

28
+ 7
35

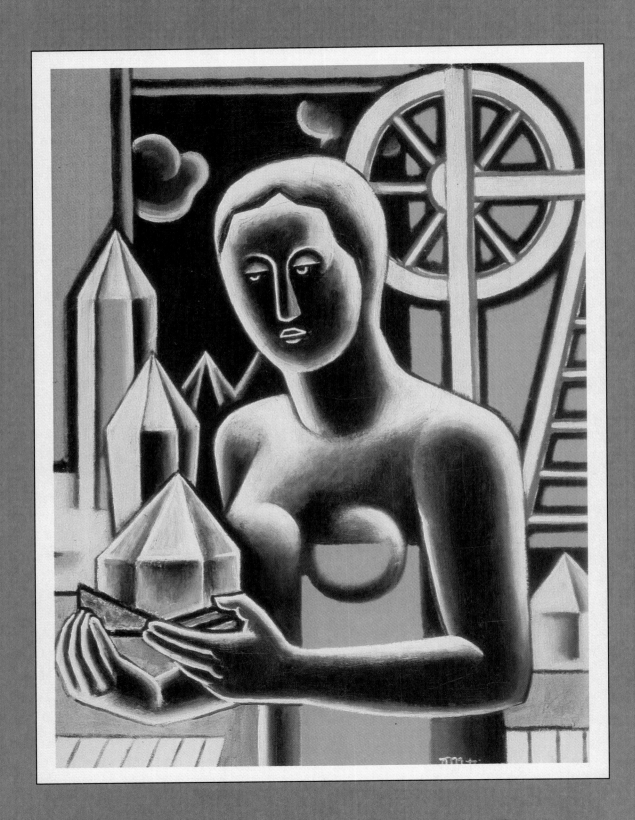

Sensation and Perception

Some people are born without sight but then as adults gain the ability to see. These individuals intrigue psychologists because they allow a unique glimpse at how people first come to see the world. Every infant goes through this process, but infants cannot tell us what they are seeing. Adults seeing for the first time are not identical to newborn infants, of course, but they can at least inform researchers whether the ability to see is present from the very first or whether it develops slowly.

S.B. was one such person (Gregory, 1966). Until age 52, S.B. was unable to see at all. He was, however, active and fearless in his approach to the world: He bicycled; he built things; he always tried to imagine how the objects he touched might look. At 52, S.B. underwent a corneal graft, an operation that enabled him to see for the first time in his life. Initially, he saw only blurs; objects did not take form. But in a few days, he was able to see objects as discrete shapes. Soon he had little difficulty recognizing objects by sight, as long as these were items he had previously touched. For example, he could readily tell time because while blind he had developed the habit of carrying a pocket watch with no crystal; he would feel where the hands were.

Other visual tasks proved more difficult. S.B. had considerable trouble perceiving distance—looking down from a window some 30 or 40 feet above the ground, he thought he could lower himself down by his hands. He never learned to read by sight, although he almost immediately recognized capital letters and numbers. Again, the crucial factor seemed to be his previous experience touching these symbols: In the school for the blind that he had attended, prior to learning Braille, he had learned to recognize by touch the shapes of capital letters and numbers.

You might think that S.B. was ecstatic about his new eyesight, but this was not the case. Shortly after the operation, he became depressed and less active, and he stayed this way until his death three years later. Depression can be a common reaction among those who gain sight as adults, perhaps because they realize what they have previously missed or perhaps because their new vision does not function optimally (Gazzaniga, 1992). In any event, following their operation some individuals—including S. B.— revert to living in the dark.

U NDERSTANDING SENSATION AND PERCEPTION: DEFINITION AND EXPLANATION

As you learned in the preceding chapter, the brain integrates and reacts to incoming information, including that of light, sound, and pressure. But how is this environmental stimulation translated into terms the brain can understand? Our sense organs evolved to be sensitive to various sources of environmental stimulation. The exact sources differ, but each **stimulus** is a form of energy. **Sensation** is the process by which this energy is transformed into neural activity (Chapter 4). Thus, our sense organs let the physical world speak to the nervous system in biological terms (Coren, Porac, & Ward, 1984). **Perception** is the process by which we organize and interpret sensory information in psychological terms.

When S. B. was born, his eyes were insensitive to light. An operation made this sensitivity possible. Initially, he had sensations, in that neural activity was stimulated by light. But he had no perceptions, in that this neural activity was not psychologically meaningful to him. Only with time did perceptions develop. Although the line between sensation and perception can sometimes be fuzzy, the sorts of questions asked by psychologists interested in these processes differ. Those interested in sensation ask, "How

■ **stimulus**
environmental energy that produces a response by an organism

■ **sensation**
process by which environmental energy is transformed into neural activity

■ **perception**
process by which sensory information is organized and interpreted in psychological terms

The physical properties of sound may be pleasant or unpleasant, depending on how individuals perceive their sensations.

bright is that object?" Those interested in perception ask, "What is that object?" (Coren, Porac, & Ward, 1984).

None of our sensations and perceptions is an exact reflection of the outside world. As just noted, they are the result of neural activity: electrochemical activity in the nervous system. Even so, we usually assume that the information available to us accurately renders external reality. Other people understand what we mean when we attribute our sensations to external objects:

- Lights are bright.
- Yogurt is sour.
- Blankets are soft.

Explaining how this external stimulation gives rise to rich psychological experience meaningful to ourselves and others is a fundamental task for psychologists.

How Do We Know the World?

For centuries, philosophers have debated whether particular ideas originate through experience or are born within us. Those who emphasize the role of experience in providing all knowledge are called **empiricists,** whereas those who support innate ideas like the notion of God or the principles of geometry are called **rationalists** (Chapter 1).

These two positions, which have been carried from philosophy into psychology, contrast in describing what an infant knows. The empiricists propose that babies know nothing because they have experienced nothing. Their world is a jumble of sights and sounds, tastes and smells, pleasures and pains. Only through experience can they begin to organize knowledge. The rationalists endorse a different view: By virtue of being people, we have knowledge at birth, including what to do with our sensations. Information does not arrive in a heap that we must learn to organize. Rather, automatically and without any learning, people organize their sensations.

This debate between the empiricists and the rationalists plays out the nature-nurture controversy discussed earlier (Chapter 3). Available evidence implies that both positions are to some degree correct. Contemporary psychologists believe sensation and perception each reflect a complex combination of innate and learned influences—which means that both are examples of biopsychosocial phenomena.

For example, in research that earned them a Nobel Prize, David Hubel and Torsten Wiesel (1962, 1979) identified in the cortex of mammals specialized cells that detect different patterns of visual stimuli. Some cells fired only in response to moving lines oriented in a given direction. Other cells fired only in response to stationary lines with a specific orientation. Cells that respond only to specific environmental characteristics like the orientation of lines are called **feature detectors,** and their function is innate (Koenderink, 1993).

However, learning is also critical in determining how we see the world. Consider again the example of S.B. In one instance, he was shown a woodworking tool in a glass case at a museum. He did not understand what he saw. Then it was taken out of the case. S.B. closed his eyes, touched it, and then exclaimed, "Now I can see!"

All of our senses share certain characteristics. Each is stimulated by external energy that produces neural impulses in receptor neurons, in a process known as **transduction.** These neural impulses give rise to different sensations that are coordinated into perception. Granted that all sensations arrive at the brain via a neural route, and granted that the neurons involved are anatomically identical, what explains the variety of sensations we eventually experience? One answer was proposed by Johannes Müller (1826, 1826b) in his **doctrine of specific nerve energies.** According to this view, neural messages register as different sensations because they move along specific nerves that terminate in given areas of the brain. The doctrine of specific nerve energies explains, for instance,

■ **empiricists**
philosophers who believe that particular ideas originate through experience

■ **rationalists**
philosophers who believe that particular ideas are innate

■ **feature detectors**
cells that respond only to highly specific environmental characteristics

■ **transduction**
process by which external energy produces neural impulses

■ **doctrine of specific nerve energies**
Müller's idea that neural messages register as different sensations because they move along nerves that terminate in different areas of the brain

Johannes Müller's doctrine of specific nerve energies is one explanation of the specificity of our sensations.

■ **synesthesia**
unusual sensory phenomenon in which stimulation of one type of sensory receptor gives rise to the experience of another sense

■ **information processing theory**
theory that explains the transformation of information

■ **bottom-up information processing**
information processing in which initial steps lead simply to subsequent steps

■ **top-down information processing**
information processing in which initial steps are influenced by subsequent and more general steps

why we can distinguish sound from odor: Nerves leading from the ears and the nose end in parts of the brain devoted respectively to hearing and smelling (Chapter 4).

This theory can also explain aspects of an unusual sensory phenomenon known as **synesthesia,** in which stimulation of one type of sensory receptor gives rise to the involuntary experience of another sense (Andrews, 1978; Cytowic & Wood, 1982; Marks, 1975). Here the individual tastes a sound, hears a color, or sees a smell. Synesthesia is not well understood, but some theorists suggest it is due to unusual connections among neurons (Motluk, 1994). Sensory receptors are in effect connected to the "wrong" nerves.

However, synesthesia can be temporarily produced by certain hallucinogenic drugs, and it is unlikely that brief intoxication rewires the brain (Chapter 6). Furthermore, Müller's theory fails to explain distinctions within a given sense. If all visual sensations use the same neural paths, then how can we tell that one stimulus is green and another red?

A further explanation is needed, and one popular hypothesis is that the overall pattern of neural excitation and inhibition in the brain produces the specificity of sensations (Kandel, 1981). Synesthesia, from this perspective, is the result of a complex integration of neural messages, perhaps in terms of their emotional associations (Cytowic, 1989). Just where in the brain this integration occurs is unknown, as is exactly how it takes place.

Information Processing Theory

Discussions of sensation tend to focus on the more biological characteristics of sensory systems, whereas discussions of perception tend to be phrased in more psychological terms. However, sensation and perception merge into one another, so much so that it is difficult to say where one ends and the other begins.

Psychologists have therefore been drawn to **information processing theory** in order to understand sensation and perception. The term *information* refers to whatever reduces uncertainty; many psychologists use the term as a synonym for *knowledge.* Information enters the body by way of the senses. To say that it is processed is to emphasize that people do something to the information—that is, they interpret it. According to this theory, sensation and perception represent different steps in the transformation of information, with sensation preceding perception.

Thus, we come to know the world in several ways. Sensory input is critical to this achievement, and so are general habits that influence how we process sensory information. Making sensation and perception even more complex is their link with such other psychological processes as consciousness (Chapter 6), motivation and emotion (Chapter 7), learning (Chapter 8), and cognition (Chapter 9). Sensation and perception may also reflect personality differences among people (Chapter 12). Finally, they are influenced by our culture and in turn influence our social context (Chapter 15).

In **bottom-up information processing,** initial steps lead simply to subsequent steps. For example, consider one possible process by which we recognize that certain visual stimuli spell out a word. We first discriminate between light and dark areas on a page where the word is contained. We next see the letters. We then identify the individual letters. We finally put the letters together to form the word.

Theorists fond of the bottom-up approach use a computer as their metaphor for information processing. A typical computer can proceed only in a bottom-up way. The common criticism of computers—garbage in, garbage out—reflects their reliance on bottom-up approaches. If the first step is flawed, nothing that follows can alter it.

The opposite approach is called **top-down information processing.** In this case, initial steps of information processing are influenced by subsequent steps. Expectations, goals, intentions, and general knowledge dominate and direct simpler psychological functions. Think again of word recognition and consider how frequently we overlook misspelled words. We know from the context of what we are reading that a specific word must be intended in a given place, and we recognize it accordingly, even though it

Top-down processes are responsible for our frequent tendency to overlook misspelled words found in a familiar context.

is misspelled. This phenomenon would be impossible if word recognition took place strictly by bottom-up processes.

Stop and Think

1 What is the biopsychosocial resolution of the debate between the rationalists and the empiricists?

2 According to information processing theory, what is the difference between sensation and perception?

DOING *Psychophysics* RESEARCH

Psychologists interested in sensation and perception want to know the relationship between physical stimuli (e.g., light or sound) and our psychological experience of them. They work within the field known as **psychophysics,** so named because it concerns itself with both mind (*psycho-*) and physical reality (*physics*).

Gustav Fechner (1801–1887) christened the field of psychophysics and developed many of its research methods (Gescheider, 1988). A professor of physics at the University of Leipzig (where Wundt later taught), Fechner had a strong interest in the workings of the mind, and psychophysics was born from his attempt to bridge the material world and the mental world. From its very beginnings, psychophysics has had three basic concerns. First, how do we detect stimuli in the environment? Second, how do we discriminate between two stimuli? Third, how do we ascertain how much of something is present?

■ **psychophysics**
field of psychology that studies the relationship between physical stimuli and psychological experience

Gustav Fechner gave the field of psychophysics its name and developed research strategies still used today.

Detection of Stimuli: Absolute Thresholds

Although we usually take the presence or absence of stimuli for granted, in some circumstances we are much less certain about what did or did not happen. Perhaps we heard our name called. Perhaps not. Perhaps the milk tasted sour. Perhaps not. These circumstances raise questions about the **absolute threshold** for a particular sensory system: the minimal amount of energy needed to create a sensation that we can detect.

To investigate absolute thresholds, Fechner and other psychophysicists devised several procedures (Gescheider, 1988). One is the method of constant stimuli. Here is how it might be used to identify the absolute threshold of a light's intensity. We need some device that can present light at various intensities. Some of these lights should be so dim that observers never see them; others, so bright that observers always see them; and still others, of intermediate intensity. Against a background of no other visible stimuli, we present these different intensities of light to our observers a number of times, in a random order. We ask them to say when they detect a particular light. After a number of trials, we can graph the likelihood of detecting the stimulus as a function of its intensity. The smallest intensity at which the light is detected 50 percent of the time is considered the absolute threshold.

Studies show that absolute thresholds are never perfectly constant because identified threshold values vary somewhat from test to test. To get around this variation, researchers measure the same threshold several times and average the results. Perhaps you are surprised that absolute values are not strictly absolute, but consider why. The stimulus an observer tries to detect is not the only source of stimulation in her environment. There may be a clock ticking away on her desk. During the day, with the competing noise provided by traffic, conversation, and television, she may be unable to hear the clock at all, even when she concentrates. At night, with no other sounds, the clock ticks loudly. The sound has stayed the same from day to night, but her absolute threshold for detecting it has changed. Also, the state of the nervous system varies across time, and such variation affects thresholds. Still, generalizations about these thresholds are possible. On average, each sensory system has a characteristic threshold (see Table 5.1).

For most senses, women tend to have lower absolute thresholds than men (Corso, 1959; Money, 1965; Weinstein & Sersen, 1961). Some theorists believe that the greater sensory sensitivity on the part of women is due to the presence of estrogen, which affects both sensory receptors and the central nervous system (Gandelman, 1983). Indeed, the absolute thresholds of women rise and fall during their menstrual cycle (Flaherty, Cowart-Steckler, & Pollack, 1988; Mair, Bouffard, Engen, & Morton, 1978). This phenomenon may reflect an evolved psychological mechanism that makes women most sensitive to the world when they are most fertile (Beach, 1983).

Absolute thresholds for many sensory systems change as we age (Ferrell, Crighton, & Sturrock, 1992; Peterka, Black, & Schoenhoff, 1990–1991). As newborns, infants have poor color vision, but at about 6 months of age, their ability to detect different colors approaches that of adults (Brown, 1990). Among the elderly, visual thresholds become

■ **absolute threshold**
minimal amount of energy needed to create a detectable sensation

Table 5.1   Absolute Thresholds for Some Familiar Events

Sensory system	Threshold
Vision	On a dark night, a candle flame at 30 miles
Sound	In quiet conditions, a ticking watch at 20 feet
Taste	A teaspoon of sugar in 2 gallons of water
Smell	In a 3-room apartment, one drop of perfume
Touch	From 1 centimeter, the falling of a bee's wing on the cheek

Source: Galanter (1962).

higher, as do those for touch. Sensitivity to taste also falls off as people age (Stevens, 1989; Weiffenbach, Tylenda, & Baum, 1990). Older adults may therefore have difficulty distinguishing among foods that look alike, such as blended or pureed dishes (Schiffman, 1977).

Introverted people have lower absolute thresholds than extraverted people (Eysenck, 1967). As will be discussed in Chapter 12, whether a person's characteristic style is inwardly or outwardly directed—that is, introverted or extraverted—is an important personality trait. These findings support the popular stereotype that introverts are sensitive to the world, in this case literally so.

Discrimination of Stimuli: Difference Thresholds

The second concern of psychophysics is the degree to which two stimuli must differ in order to be perceived as distinct. Stimuli can vary along numerous dimensions, like size, shape, or color, and this question is usually tackled in experiments that hold all dimensions constant except one. In such studies, subjects are asked to make comparisons between two stimuli that differ along only the varied dimension. Suppose you are sampling different types of chocolate, trying to select the one that is most sweet. You nibble different pieces, making sure that each is the same temperature and that each bite is the same size. You may treat one type of chocolate as a standard against which the others are evaluated as being more sweet or less sweet.

This procedure becomes formalized when researchers establish what is known as a **difference threshold,** the minimal distinction between two stimuli that can be discriminated. Like absolute thresholds, difference thresholds are not perfectly uniform, meaning that they need to be calculated several times and then averaged. The difference threshold for "greater than" is located at a point where stimuli greater than the standard are correctly discriminated half the time, and the difference threshold for "less than" at a point where stimuli less than the standard are correctly discriminated half the time.

A difference threshold is also referred to as a **just noticeable difference (jnd).** A small jnd is associated with good discrimination because two stimuli need not be too different in order to be recognized as distinct. A large jnd is associated with poor discrimination because different stimuli are not readily distinguished. Let me return to the chocolate-tasting example. If you cannot distinguish between the taste of two types of chocolate, then they fall within a jnd of each other. If they have different prices, then good for you—you can buy the less expensive one and never know the difference!

Weber's law.   Ernst Heinrich Weber (1795–1878) was among the first investigators of sensation. In some of his experiments, subjects were required to judge relative weights, comparing a series of weights in turn against a standard weight. Was a given weight different from the standard or not? In calculating various jnds, Weber discovered that the size of the jnd depends directly on the size of the standard. If we graph the jnd against the weight of the standard, the result is a straight line (see Figure 5.1).

Suppose you have a standard that weighs 10 pounds. For most people, the jnd for this standard is two-tenths of a pound (approximately 3 ounces), meaning that objects weighing less than 9.8 pounds or more than 10.2 pounds can be discriminated from the standard. Now suppose you have a standard that weighs 100 pounds. For most people, the jnd here is 2 pounds, meaning that objects weighing less than 98 pounds or more than 102 pounds can be discriminated from the standard. But objects weighing 99 pounds or 101 pounds cannot be discriminated from those that weigh 100 pounds.

This straight-line relationship between the jnd and the standard describes most sensory systems of most species reasonably well (Burkhardt, 1994), failing only at the extremes (Ward & Davidson, 1993). It is doubtful anyone could have predicted the simplicity and universality of this principle before conducting the relevant experiments. Psychologists have therefore called it **Weber's law** to emphasize that it reflects a basic property of the nervous system (Hess & Hayes, 1993; Wenxi, 1994).

■ **difference threshold; just noticeable difference (jnd)**
minimal distinction between two stimuli that can be discriminated

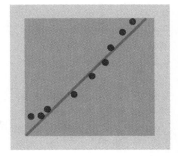

Figure 5.1
Weber's Law. As the standard becomes larger, so too does the jnd, and vice versa.

■ **Weber's law**
for most sensory systems, the straight-line relationship between the size of the standard and the jnd

Table 5.2   Weber Fractions

A Weber fraction is defined as the ratio, for a particular sensory dimension, of the jnd to the standard. The smaller this figure is, the more readily one can detect small changes. For instance, two lights must differ in brightness by at least 8 percent for the difference to be detected, whereas two electric shocks need differ in intensity by only 1 percent for the difference to be detected.

Sensory dimension	Fraction
Brightness	0.08
Taste (salt)	0.08
Loudness	0.05
Heaviness	0.02
Electric Shock	0.01

Weber fractions.   The ratio of the jnd to the standard is called a Weber fraction. We can compare the discrimination abilities of different senses in terms of their respective Weber fractions (see Table 5.2). Note that the Weber fraction for electric shock is small, meaning that we can readily detect slight changes. The Weber fraction for brightness is large, meaning that we cannot so easily detect changes. An evolutionary interpretation of these fractions makes sense: Variations in pain should grab our attention quickly.

Weber's law applies to more than just our sensory systems. Grewal and Marmorstein (1994), for example, showed that consumers' willingness to shop around for a less expensive product can be predicted by considering the typical price of the product (the standard) and the amount of money saved (the jnd). When products become more expensive, we are less willing to search for identical savings. So, we will drive several miles across town to save $1 on a pound of coffee but we will not drive the same distance to save $2 on a winter coat. These behaviors make no economic sense, but they are consistent with Weber's law.

Scaling of Stimuli: Fechner's Law

■ **scaling**
specification of the quantitative link between a physical dimension of a stimulus and the corresponding psychological dimension

Our sensations exist in varying degrees. Noises are more loud or less loud. Tastes are more bitter or less bitter. The intensity of a physical stimulus obviously has something to do with our psychological experience of it, but we can be more precise. Fechner was the first to investigate the exact relationship between stimulus intensity and sensation intensity, sometimes referred to as **scaling** because it specifies the quantitative link between a physical dimension and the corresponding psychological dimension.

Fechner turned to physics for scales to measure the intensity of stimuli, but he had to devise a way to scale the intensity of sensations. He decided to use Weber's law and the notion of the jnd to quantify subjective sensory intensity. Fechner assumed that all jnds have the same subjective size and that we can describe the intensity of any sensation as the number of jnds above the absolute threshold (McBride, 1983b).

■ **Fechner's law**
for most sensory systems, the straight-line relationship between changes in sensation intensity, measured by the number of jnds, and changes in stimulus intensity divided by the magnitude of the stimulus already present

What follows from this assumption is **Fechner's law,** which proposes that changes in sensation intensity, measured by the number of jnds, depend on changes in stimulus intensity divided by the magnitude of the stimulus already present. Although the exact relationship depends on the sensory system being considered, this principle is general, holding across most sensations (McBride, 1983a). Electric shock is a notable exception, in that the higher the initial shock intensity, the less it needs to be increased in order for people to detect a difference.

■ **adaptation-level theory**
idea that sensation is affected not only by a given stimulus but also by other stimuli present and stimuli that have been experienced in the past

Adaptation-Level Theory

Fechner addressed the relationship between stimulus intensity and sensation intensity without reference to context. His focus was only on the stimuli being judged. The stimulus being judged influences magnitude estimates, but **adaptation-level theory**

Because their peers are so tall, we tend to see basketball players like John Stockton (fourth from right) as short, when in actuality they are several inches taller than the average American male.

proposes that scaling is additionally affected by other stimuli surrounding the stimulus being judged. Also critical are residual stimuli, those that have been experienced in the past (Helson, 1964).

Background stimuli and residual stimuli create the context, or adaptation level, in which scaling occurs. Height is a typical example. We judge people as short or tall not only in terms of their actual heights but also in terms of other people in the vicinity and in terms of other people we have known. A common experience is to see National Basketball Association point guards like Kevin Johnson and John Stockton as short, even though they are both at least several inches taller than the average American male. They seem short because their peers are so tall.

Examples of adaptation level exist in other psychological domains. For example, one study found that judgments by homeless people about their own physical and social well-being depended on how long they had been homeless (Osborne, Karlin, Baumann, Osborne, & Nelms, 1993). Over time, with increasing exposure to others who were homeless, these people came to underestimate their actual problems. Similar effects of adaptation level have been reported for:

■ *preferences for physical distance from other people:* Individuals prefer greater distances if they work in solitary as opposed to crowded conditions (Gifford & Sacilotto, 1993).
■ *willingness to go along with requests:* Individuals are more willing if previous requests have been large as opposed to small (Dillard, 1991).
■ *complaints about symptoms by cancer patients:* Individuals complain less the longer they have suffered from the disease (Breetvelt & Van Dam, 1991).

In sum, there can never be a universal relationship between stimulus intensity and our responses. The processes involved in adaptation-level theory guarantee that Fechner's law and similar approaches will at best be generalizations. Sensation and perception are not isolated events. Eyes do not see—people see. Tongues do not taste—people taste. Ears do not hear—people hear. People are subject to innumerable influences, and so are their sensations and perceptions.

Stop and Think

3 What is the difference between an absolute threshold and a difference threshold?

4 What example of Weber's Law can you find in your everyday life?

5 How is adaptation-level theory a biopsychosocial approach?

SENSORY SYSTEMS

Aristotle enumerated five basic senses: vision, hearing, taste, smell, and touch (Kemp, 1990). For centuries, Aristotle's pronouncements were unquestioned, until the era of modern science ushered in a more skeptical attitude. When researchers looked for additional senses, they found them, as you will see later in this chapter.

Furthermore, the theory of evolution dispelled the notion that given senses are inherently basic. The importance of a particular sense depends on the species and the environmental niche it occupies. A species is best served by senses that allow sensitivity to the relevant information in its environment. Each sensory system is an evolved psychological mechanism. Perhaps when our distant ancestors began to walk upright and to be active during the day, visual information became more vital. Natural selection then produced the neurological apparatus that allows acute vision (Chapter 3).

Land and Fernald (1992) hypothesized that eyes developed many separate times in the course of evolution. However because the number of ways that visual images can be physically formed is limited, there are only a handful of different types of eyes across all species. This phenomenon is termed convergent evolution. It means that different species might resemble each other not because of a common ancestor but because natural selection independently produced the same result.

To say that species occupy different niches is more than the obvious observation that they occupy different physical settings. Their sensory systems vary, and thus they experience different worlds. Dogs, for example, evolved from creatures with their noses to the ground, and they developed the capacity to detect odors to which people are oblivious. Can you imagine the psychological perspective of a dog, in which the world is known more through smell than vision? Probably not. That the very question employs visual language (*imagine, perspective*) shows the importance of vision to human beings (Gallup & Cameron, 1992).

Another implication of the theory of evolution is that variation in sensory abilities exists within a given species. Differences in people's absolute thresholds have already been mentioned. And in some cases, people may lack a sense. They may be blind, like S.B., or insensitive to certain colors, or deaf. They may even be insensitive to pain, a condition that is not the blessing you might at first think it to be. Pain usually serves as

Dogs evolved from creatures with their noses to the ground, and the world they know is defined by its smells in a way we can barely imagine.

a warning signal that something is amiss, and without such signals the painless individual lives a hazardous and often short life.

What follows is a more detailed discussion of our senses, with a focus on the major human senses of vision and hearing. Also described are taste and smell. Finally, the cutaneous senses of touch and temperature are covered, along with senses that help us establish our physical position in the world.

Vision

Psychologists have studied vision for more than a century and have learned a great deal about it. Nevertheless, the complexities involved in how we see are dizzying, and so this section presents but an overview of the topic. Let me start by discussing light, the external energy that gives rise to vision.

Light. Physicists tell us that **light** is radiating energy that travels in an oscillating pattern of waves. We see objects that send out light themselves or reflect light from other sources. In either case, light waves have a number of physical characteristics that influence vision. Of particular importance are the amplitude, wavelength, and purity of light because they determine our different visual sensations.

The **amplitude** of light is the height of its wave (see Figure 5.2), and it represents the physical intensity of the light. We psychologically register the amplitude of light as its **brightness.** The difference between a dim light and a bright light is due to the difference in their amplitudes.

Radiant energy includes not only visible light but also X-rays, ultraviolet and infrared radiation, microwaves, and radio waves. What distinguishes one from another is their **wavelength,** the distance between the peaks of two successive waves (again see Figure 5.2). Wavelengths vary from distances almost too tiny to imagine, in the case of cosmic rays, to hundreds of feet, in the case of radio waves. Figure 5.3 arranges the types of radiant energy according to their wavelength. The length of a light wave is measured with a unit called a nanometer, equal to one-billionth of a meter. The wavelengths of the light we can see range from about 400 nanometers to about 700 nanometers. Nevertheless, variations in the wavelengths of visible light are psychologically important because they give rise to our experience of **hue,** or color. Wavelengths are why we see grass as green, bananas as yellow, and the sky as blue.

So far, I have sidestepped the fact that the actual light we see is almost always a mixture of different wavelengths. When we see an apple as red, it is because red wavelengths predominate, but other wavelengths are also mixed in. The degree to which light is dominated by a single wavelength of light is its **purity.** The psychological property to which purity gives rise is called **saturation,** which we more commonly call richness. The more different wavelengths are mixed into a light, the more pale and washed out it becomes. Pastel colors, for example, are extremely low in saturation.

■ **light**
radiating energy that travels in an oscillating pattern of waves

■ **amplitude**
height of a light wave

■ **brightness**
psychological experience of the physical intensity of light

■ **wavelength**
distance between the peaks of two successive light waves

■ **hue**
color; psychological experience of the wavelength of light

■ **purity**
degree to which light is dominated by a single wavelength

■ **saturation**
psychological experience of the purity of light

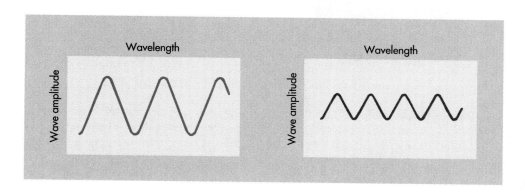

Figure 5.2
Light Waves. These representations of light waves differ in amplitude and wavelength. Amplitude determines the brightness of light, and wavelength determines its color. The light wave shown on the left is brighter than the light wave on the right, as well as closer in color to red (long wavelength) than to violet (short wavelength).

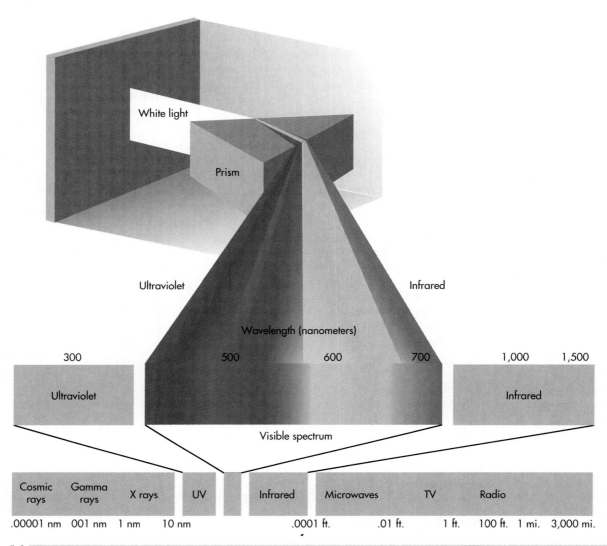

Figure 5.3
Radiant Energy. Each form of radiant energy—from cosmic rays to television and radio signals—comes in waves. What distinguishes them is their characteristic wavelengths. Visible light represents a small region of the spectrum of radiant energy.

Light of the lowest possible saturation is called white light. The light bulbs we use in our homes create only an approximation of white light. Fluorescent bulbs tend to produce too many short wavelengths (blues and violets), whereas incandescent bulbs tend to produce too many long wavelengths (reds and oranges). Sunlight comes closer to white light, not because it is pure but because it is impure—that is, of low saturation.

Our eyes respond to the amplitude, wavelength, and purity of light, changing light energy into neural impulses that we experience as intensity, hue, and saturation, respectively. The structures of the eye make this transduction possible for light that hits its receptors and also ensure that light gets to the receptors in the first place.

The eye.   The human eye is a sphere about one inch in diameter (see Figure 5.4). It keeps its shape because of internal pressure caused by a fluid called **vitreous humor.** Light enters the eye at its front through the **cornea,** a transparent membrane that protects the eye and refracts the light that hits it, bending it so that it goes through the **pupil.** The pupil is an opening in the colored part of the eye, which is called the **iris.**

■ **vitreous humor**
fluid within the eyeball

■ **cornea**
transparent membrane at the front of the eye

■ **pupil**
opening in the colored part of the eye

■ **iris**
colored part of the eye

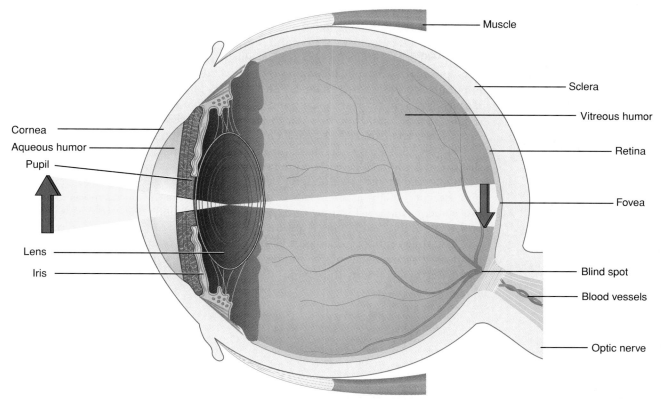

Muscle
Sclera
Vitreous humor
Retina
Fovea
Blind spot
Blood vessels
Optic nerve
Cornea
Aqueous humor
Pupil
Lens
Iris

Figure 5.4
Structure of the Human Eye. Light enters the eye through the pupil and is focused by the lens onto the retina at the back of the eye. The optic nerve carries neural impulses from the eye to the brain.

Whether green, blue, or brown, the iris controls the size of the pupil. The reflexive response of the iris to light levels changes the size of the pupil. In bright light, the iris contracts, making the pupil small and thus letting in little of the available light. In dim light, the iris dilates, opening the pupil wide and letting in much of the available light. The pupil also reacts to our psychological states, increasing in size when we experience fear, surprise, anger, or other heightened emotions (Chapter 7).

Once light passes through the pupil, it encounters the **lens.** The lens changes its shape in order to focus images, just like a zoom lens does on a camera. The lens becomes fatter when focusing on close objects and flatter when focusing on those far away. As

■ **lens**
structure of the eye that focuses images

Like the lens on a camera, the lens of the eye changes shape in order to focus images.

■ **retina**
structure at the back of the eye lined with nerve cells sensitive to light

■ **photoreceptors**
nerve cells sensitive to light

■ **rods**
photoreceptors shaped like cylinders that are responsible for vision in dim light

■ **cones**
photoreceptors with a tapered shape that are responsible for vision in bright light

■ **fovea**
central point in the retina where a visual image is focused

you may know from personal experience, sometimes the ability of the lens to accommodate is less than perfect, and we then suffer from either near- or farsightedness.

The lens focuses its image onto the **retina,** a structure at the back of the eye lined with nerve cells sensitive to light, called **photoreceptors.** As early as 1860, psychologists knew of two types of photoreceptors. **Rods** are shaped like cylinders and are responsible for vision in dim light. The sensations produced by rods are without color. **Cones** have a more tapered shape and are responsible for vision in bright light. Cones require more illumination in order to function, and they produce color sensations. In each eye are approximately 120 million rods and 6 million cones.

Figure 5.5 is a cross-section of the human retina that shows rods and cones. Notice that the rods and cones are not on the surface of the retina. Indeed, they face away from the pupil. Light must pass through several layers of other cells in order to stimulate the photoreceptors. This arrangement is due to the fact that photoreception is a neural process requiring a rich supply of oxygen. Hence, rods and cones are as close to blood vessels as possible, and blood vessels are not found on the surface of the retina.

The **fovea** is the central point in the retina where an image is focused. It contains the densest arrangement of the photoreceptors, most of which are cones. As a result of the density of cones in the fovea, our ability to discriminate among objects, called

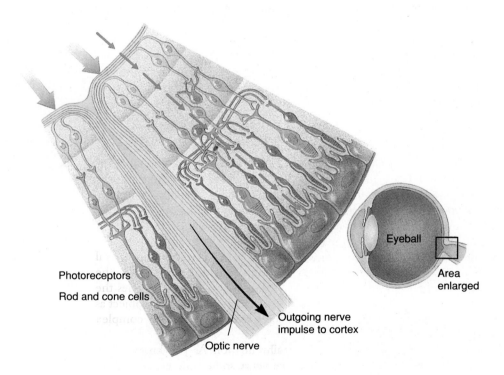

Photoreceptors

Rod and cone cells

Optic nerve

Outgoing nerve impulse to cortex

Eyeball

Area enlarged

Figure 5.5
Cross-Section of the Human Retina Showing Rods and Cones. The retina contains nerve cells that are sensitive to light and are called photoreceptors. Rods are photoreceptors responsible for vision in dim light, and they produce sensations without color. Cones are photoreceptors responsible for vision in bright light, and they produce sensations with color. Note that the photoreceptors face away from the pupil. This arrangement allows them access to the rich supply of oxygen they need in order to function.

Figure 5.6
Demonstration of Blind Spot. Close your right eye and stare at the cross on the top line. Holding the page about a foot from your eye, move the page slowly forward and backward until the star disappears. It has fallen on your blind spot. Similarly, close your right eye and stare at the cross on the bottom line. With the page about a foot from your eye, move the page slowly forward and backward until the break in the line disappears. Again, it has fallen on your blind spot, and you have filled in the missing information.

acuity, is greatest when light from these objects falls directly on the fovea, as when we look directly at them. In contrast, objects seen from the corner of our eyes appear less distinct because their images do not fall on the fovea. Instead, these images fall in an area peripheral to the fovea, where rods predominate. So-called peripheral vision is handled mainly by rods.

Photoreceptors contain **visual pigments,** chemicals sensitive to light. When exposed to light, these chemicals break down, causing photoreceptors to generate a neural impulse. Other neurons lead away from the photoreceptors and are bundled together in the **optic nerve** (again see Figure 5.5), which leads to the brain. The area where the optic nerve passes through the retina is without photoreceptors, creating a **blind spot.** Most of us are unaware that we have this blind spot because we fill in the missing information (see Figure 5.6).

Visual pigments can resynthesize by enzyme activity. They work over and over again. You may have heard that carrots are good for your night vision. Here is the rationale. Carrots contain vitamin A, one of the substances needed to resynthesize the visual pigments found in our rods. What would happen if you had a chronic deficiency of vitamin A? Your rods would not regain their photosensitivity after stimulation, and your ability to see in dim light would suffer.

Brightness and adaptation.   Let me now move to some of the important visual functions and how they occur. First is the sensation of brightness. In general terms, the experience of brightness is easy to explain; the more intense the light that reaches the retina, the more photoreceptors are stimulated and the more we experience an object as bright. But with closer analysis, the experience of brightness becomes more complex because other factors also prove influential.

One of these factors is the level of background illumination. As you know, when you move from a dark room to a well-lit one, or vice versa, some time elapses before you can see very well. In the one case, everything looks too bright and hence unclear. In the other, everything looks too dim and just as unclear. These familiar experiences are examples of **adaptation.** When we say that we must get used to the illumination in a room, what we really mean is that the visual pigments in our photoreceptors must adjust to background illumination. In the dark, our rods become more and more sensitive to light, and our cones less and less so. In the light, just the opposite happens.

This acclimation reflects chemical processes involving the pigments, as well as changes in the sensitivity of the nervous system (Green & Powers, 1982). Adaptation is

■ **acuity**
ability to make visual discriminations among objects

■ **visual pigments**
chemicals contained in photoreceptors that are sensitive to light

■ **optic nerve**
bundle of neurons that lead away from the photoreceptors to the brain

■ **blind spot**
area in the retina through which the optic nerve passes

■ **adaptation**
acclimation of photoreceptors to background illumination

not instantaneous. Our cones acclimate more rapidly than our rods, meaning that it takes less time for us to see clearly after entering a bright room from a dim room than vice versa. Adaptation to the light may take but a few seconds, whereas full adaptation to the dark may take 20 minutes. Adaptation allows us to be sensitive to a wide range of light intensities. For example, sunlight gives 1 million times the illumination of moonlight, yet we can see objects at both noon and midnight.

Earlier it was noted that cones are sensitive to the wavelengths of light. Psychologists now understand that cones work best at levels of high illumination. Rods are not sensitive to wavelength, but they respond better than cones at low illumination. So, images that fall chiefly on the rods—in other words, away from the fovea—are seen as brighter than those that fall chiefly on the cones. An interesting implication here is that we can more readily detect dim objects, like distant stars, if we do not look straight at them. If we look somewhat to the side, we bring into play the rods, which are more sensitive to the amplitude of light.

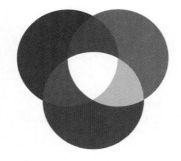

Figure 5.7
Color Mixture. The three primary colors can be combined to create all other colors.

■ primary colors
red, green, and blue

■ trichromatic color theory
theory that explains color vision in terms of the relative stimulation of red cones, green cones, and blue cones

Color vision.   Another important visual function is how we experience the sensation of color. Over the years, two different theories of color vision were popular: trichromatic theory and opponent-process theory. More recently, these two theories have been combined, and their integration is now accepted as the best available account (Abramov & Gordon, 1994; Hilgard, 1987; Schrodinger, 1994).

Remember that objects that reflect light of particular wavelengths are seen as having those particular colors. A first step toward explaining how we sense color might be to look for different types of cones sensitive to different wavelengths of light. The immediate objection to this kind of explanation is that there are an infinite number of wavelengths, but it is unlikely that we have an infinite variety of cones. So, we must look for a mechanism by which a finite number of visual elements can produce the thousands of shades of color that people can discriminate.

Following this reasoning, early theorists were interested in color mixture studies, which showed that any and all shades of colors could be produced by combining various amounts of red, green, and blue lights (see Figure 5.7). Red, green, and blue are therefore called **primary colors** because it is possible to construct all other colors from them.

Does the existence of primary colors mean that there are three types of cones? If so, then color vision can be explained readily in terms of the relative stimulation of red cones, green cones, and blue cones. Such an explanation—known as **trichromatic color theory**—was proposed almost two centuries ago by Thomas Young (1773–1829) and later popularized by Hermann von Helmholtz (1821–1894).

The most intriguing support for trichromatic theory comes from studies of colorblind individuals. Color blindness is an inherited problem that occurs almost exclusively in men. About 5 percent of men have one form or another of it. What does a colorblind person actually see? Psychophysics research suggests that color-blind people in effect fill in the colors they cannot see with those they can (Shepard & Cooper, 1992). Imagine watching a color television that does not show, for example, green images. What "should" be green is not absent or colorless but depicted in terms of other colors. Interestingly, color-blind adults understand the relationships between color words, even when they have never experienced the corresponding sensations. They have learned which words refer to similar or dissimilar colors. Just how this learning has occurred is not clear (Wilkinson, 1992).

Color blindness is not a single problem but rather a family of problems. Different types of color blindness involve different inabilities. Trichromatic theory correctly predicts that there should be five types of color blindness. Suppose there are three different types of cones. If people have none of these, they will be unable to make any distinctions among colors. The world will look black and white. Further, vision in bright light will be difficult because they have only rods. That is one form of color blindness. If individuals have one of these types of cones, regardless of which one, they will still be unable to make distinctions among colors. However, they will be able to see in bright light because cones are present. That is a second form of color blindness. Now suppose people have only two of these cones; they will therefore be insensitive to the third color—red or green or blue, as the case may be. That is a third, fourth, and fifth form of color blindness. No other types are found (Matlin, 1988).

Further support for trichromatic theory came from investigations of a human eye after it had been surgically removed (Bowmaker & Dartnall, 1980). Researchers aimed a narrow beam of pure light at particular cones and then measured how much of the light was absorbed. Any given cone was sensitive to light at one of three different wavelengths, corresponding exactly to red, green, and blue light.

Although the evidence for three types of cones is persuasive, trichromatic theory has problems explaining aspects of color vision. One difficulty is that psychologically there are not three primary colors but four. When people are given a large number of color samples and asked to sort them into pure types, they usually come up with the categories of red, green, and blue—as trichromatic theory predicts—but also yellow. Further, these four colors seem to fall into pairs that are psychological opposites—red versus green, blue versus yellow. Note that you cannot readily experience reddish green, for instance, or bluish yellow.

The second popular explanation of color vision was originally proposed by Ewald Hering (1834–1918) and is called **opponent-process color theory.** According to this theory, two systems are responsible for color vision. Each consists of a pair of colors that oppose each other. When neurons sensitive to one color in a pair are fired, those sensitive to the other pair are inhibited. The color we experience reflects a balance between red and green on the one hand and blue and yellow on the other.

Opponent-process theory explains the phenomenon of **negative afterimage** (see Figure 5.8). If you stare for a while at a green object and then look quickly away to a white surface, you will see a red spot; if you originally stare at a red object, you will then see a green afterimage. Blue and yellow objects respectively produce yellow or blue afterimages. In each instance, you see an image of the opposite color. Afterimages imply that our eyes are sensitive to four basic colors, arranged in pairs.

Opponent-process theory explains why there seem to be four primary colors. It accounts for negative afterimages. However, it does not handle the evidence that

■ **opponent-process color theory**
theory that explains color vision in terms of two systems, each composed of a pair of colors that oppose each other

■ **negative afterimage**
perceptual phenomenon in which one stares at an object of one color, quickly looks away, and sees an image of the "opposite" color

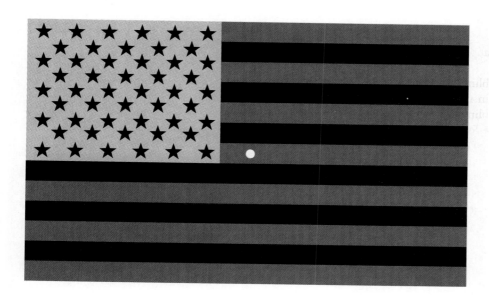

Figure 5.8
Demonstration of Negative Afterimage. Stare at the center of this green, black, and yellow flag for at least 30 seconds. Then look away and focus your eye on the center of a sheet of white paper. Please do not burn your negative afterimage!

most strongly supports trichromatic theory. Why are there five types of color blindness? And why do cones show sensitivity to light at one of three different wavelengths?

We do not have to end this discussion without a resolution because Leo Hurvich and Dorothea Jameson (1974) were able to combine trichromatic and opponent-process theories. Both theories are partially right, applying to different steps in the processing of visual information. In the retina, there are three types of cones that produce patterns of neural responses. In the brain, these patterns are integrated to produce the four (psychological) primary colors.

Color television works in much the same way that Hurvich and Jameson proposed our color vision works. A television camera first captures a scene in terms of red, green, and blue. The picture is then transformed into opponent processes for transmission. Engineers designed color television in this manner because it is the most efficient way to transmit information about color. Evolution hit upon the same strategy.

Hearing

Sound originates when an object vibrates and sets air molecules into motion against the ear. The object can be a tuning fork, vocal cords, a loudspeaker, or a fingernail on a blackboard. Like light, sound comes to us in waves, and psychologists distinguish several important properties of these waves that determine our different auditory sensations.

Sound.   First is **amplitude,** which you remember as the height of waves. In terms of sound, amplitude creates the psychological experience of **loudness.** The greater the amplitude of sound waves, the louder they are. Loudness is measured with units called decibels, as shown in Figure 5.9. Note that hearing loss occurs with prolonged exposure to sounds above a certain decibel level. These sounds need not be experienced as painful in order to do damage, and for certain workplaces—such as assembly lines or construction sites—loss of hearing sensitivity is a common hazard.

Second is **frequency,** the number of times waves repeat themselves in a given period. Frequency affects our psychological experience of **pitch,** whether a sound is experienced as high or low. High sounds have high frequencies, and low sounds have

■ **amplitude**
height of a sound wave

■ **loudness**
psychological experience of the amplitude of sound waves

■ **frequency**
number of times that sound waves repeat themselves in a given period

■ **pitch**
psychological experience of the frequency of sound waves

Researchers have found that, contrary to our stereotype of elephants as silent, these animals chatter among themselves constantly, making sounds too low for people to detect without special equipment.

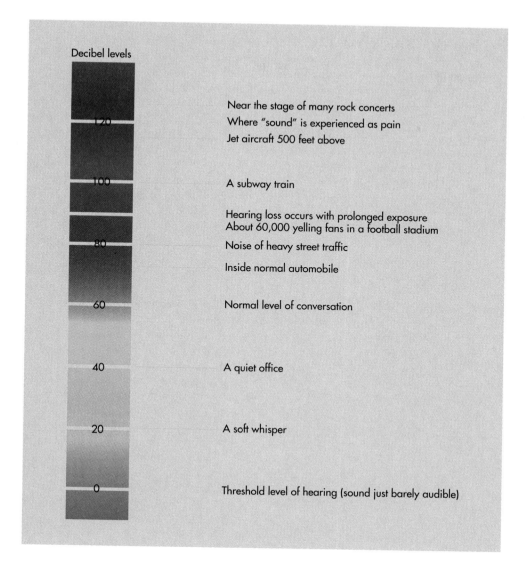

Decibel levels

120 — Near the stage of many rock concerts
Where "sound" is experienced as pain
Jet aircraft 500 feet above

100 — A subway train

Hearing loss occurs with prolonged exposure
About 60,000 yelling fans in a football stadium
80 — Noise of heavy street traffic

Inside normal automobile

60 — Normal level of conversation

40 — A quiet office

20 — A soft whisper

0 — Threshold level of hearing (sound just barely audible)

Figure 5.9
Loudness in Decibels of Various Sounds. Each 10-point increase on the decibel scale represents a tenfold increase in sound intensity. Long-term exposure to sounds at around 70 decibels can start to damage one's ears. At levels around 120 decibels, short-term exposure is immediately hazardous.

low frequencies. The hearing loss that occurs with old age or from repeated exposure to loud noise shows up chiefly in decreased ability to hear higher-frequency sounds.

The frequency of sounds is measured with a unit called a hertz, corresponding to one sound wave per second. People are sensitive to frequencies ranging from about 20 to 20,000 hertz. Some animals, like dogs, can hear sounds with higher frequencies than people can detect. Other animals, like elephants, are sensitive to sounds lower than those people can detect. Despite the stereotype that elephants are silent and stately creatures, researchers now know that they communicate with one another by making sounds too low for people to detect (Payne, 1989). When audio recordings of elephants are made with equipment sensitive to low-frequency sounds, they reveal a variety of vocalizations. When these are sped up, people hear them as barks, snorts, roars, grumbles, and growls.

A third property of sound is its **purity,** the degree to which a sound is dominated by waves of a single frequency. We experience the purity of sound waves as **timbre,** the sharpness or clarity of a tone. Some describe timbre as the quality of a sound. Every musical instrument is characterized by its own timbre, and we can thus distinguish between a violin and a trumpet, even when both are playing the same note at the same volume. Corresponding to white light is white noise, sound with a random mixture of frequencies. Radio static is a good example of white noise.

■ **purity**
degree to which a sound is dominated by waves of a single frequency

■ **timbre**
sharpness or clarity of sound

■ **pinna**
outer ear

■ **auditory canal**
connection between the outer
ear and the inner ear

■ **eardrum**
membrane at the end of the
eardrum

■ **malleus, incus, and stapes**
hammer, anvil, and stirrup; three
small bones in the inner ear that
transmit vibrations from the
eardrum to the oval window

■ **oval window**
membrane that focuses sound
waves and makes the fluid in the
cochlea move

■ **cochlea**
fluid-filled canals in the inner ear

■ **basilar membrane**
structure that runs the length of
the cochlea and has hair cells on
its surface

The ear.   The ears of all mammals have the same structure. Some theorists believe that ears evolved from the organs of touch found in primitive animals (Stebbins, 1980). This primitive organ, called the lateral line, is a series of nerve endings that stretches the length of a water-dwelling animal. Protruding from these nerves are sensory hairs stimulated by the movement of water. In the course of evolution, part of the lateral line sunk into the head of the animal, where it became the specialized organ we know as the ear. When animals moved from the water to the land, their ears came with them, and these organs proved useful in detecting sound waves traveling through the air.

Figure 5.10 presents a representative human ear. The outer ear, called the **pinna,** serves to channel sound waves into the **auditory canal.** At the end of the auditory canal is a membrane called the **eardrum.** Sound waves cause the eardrum to vibrate, and it in turn transmits the vibrations through three tiny bones that make up the middle ear: the **malleus** (or hammer), the **incus** (or anvil), and the **stapes** (or stirrup). These bones eventually pass the vibrations on to another membrane known as the **oval window.** The oval window is much smaller than the eardrum, meaning that the sound waves become more focused and thus amplified as they pass through the middle ear.

The oval window is part of the inner ear, which is composed chiefly of three spiral-shaped, fluid-filled canals known collectively as the **cochlea.** Movement of the oval window makes the fluid in these canals move, creating a wave in the cochlea that corresponds to the original sound wave. Inside the cochlea is the **basilar membrane,** which runs the length of the cochlea. The waves in the cochlea's fluid move the basilar

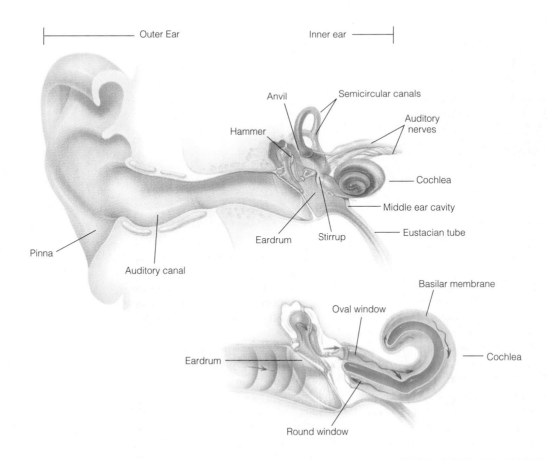

Figure 5.10
Structure of the Human Ear. Sound waves enter the outer ear (pinna) and are channeled into the auditory canal. At the end of the auditory canal is the eardrum, which sound waves cause to vibrate. These vibrations are transmitted into the middle ear and then the inner ear.

membrane, which in turn triggers movement of the **hair cells** on its surface. The hair cells are the receptors for hearing. Stimulation of the hair cells starts a neural impulse that travels through the **auditory nerve** and then to the brain.

How we hear.   How does stimulation of these auditory receptors produce what we hear? Loudness is reflected in the firing rate of individual nerve cells and also in the total neural activity. Pitch is more difficult to explain, and two theories seek to explain how we hear sounds of various frequencies. **Place theory** proposes that sound waves of different frequencies affect different locations along the basilar membrane (see again Figure 5.10; Bekesy, 1947). For example, high-frequency sounds tend to move the end of the basilar membrane closest to the oval window, as place theory proposes. But low-frequency sounds move the entire basilar membrane. **Frequency theory** suggests that the firing rate of neurons in the ear is determined by the frequency of a sound (Wever, 1949).

Both of these theories are correct, depending on the particular frequencies of sound. Lower frequencies are sensed, as frequency theory hypothesizes, by the rate at which neurons fire. Higher frequencies are sensed, as place theory predicts, by where the neurons are located. Intermediate frequencies are sensed by both place and frequency.

Hearing tells us more than simply the loudness and pitch of sounds; it also gives us information about the location of whatever object is producing the sounds (Phillips & Brugge, 1985). Both ears are essential to the task. Is the location to our left or right? Below us or above us? Far away or right in our face? We judge the location of a sound by attending to various sources of information concerning it. For instance, if a sound originates on one side of our head, it arrives at one ear somewhat sooner than the other, and it will be somewhat louder to that ear as well. It may produce different patterns of echoes depending on where it has originated. In localizing sounds, we often tilt our head one way or another, and these head movements provide further clues about the origin of sounds.

Taste

Life originated in the sea. The sense of taste is therefore the most widely represented across species because it allows the detection of chemicals dissolved in water. Accordingly, taste is called a **chemical sense,** and its adaptive functions are obvious. Taste provides clues about which foods are nutritious and which are harmful. For example, infants seem to have an inborn preference for sweet tastes (which signal foods high in calories) and an inborn aversion to bitter tastes (which signal poisons). Needless to say, taste is not a foolproof guide to the safety of substances, and for this reason, parents are careful to keep household cleaners out of the reach of children.

The tastes we come to prefer reflect our experiences with them. For example, early exposure to high-salt diets affects our later preference for salty foods (Hill & Mistretta, 1990). This preference may even be established before birth; if a pregnant woman is on a low-salt diet, her child later shows a reduced desire for salty foods. The larger culture is also critical in channeling our taste preferences in some directions rather than others. Every culture has its own cuisine: foods and styles of preparing them that are regarded as most desirable (Chapter 7).

Taste buds are the receptors sensitive to taste. They are mostly located on the tongue (see Figure 5.11) but also occur elsewhere in the mouth. Taste buds are not the bumps we can see on our tongue when we look in the mirror. These are called papillae, and taste buds are contained in and around them. Taste buds are much smaller than papillae; each papilla can contain several hundred taste buds. Taste buds are stimulated by water-soluble substances that come into contact with them. Cold foods usually have less taste than hot foods because they do not dissolve as readily in our saliva. Taste buds die off over time, and parts of them can be destroyed by foods that are too hot. However, taste buds regenerate constantly.

Considerable variation exists in the number of people's taste buds, with some individuals having as few as 500 and others as many as 10,000 (Bartoshuk, 1993). As a result,

■ **hair cells**
cells in the cochlea that send neural impulses to the brain

■ **auditory nerve**
bundle of nerves that runs from the inner ear to the brain

■ **place theory**
explanation of hearing proposing that sound waves of different frequencies affect different locations along the basilar membrane

■ **frequency theory**
explanation of hearing proposing that sound waves of different frequencies affect the firing rate of neurons in the ear

■ **chemical sense**
sense that detects chemicals dissolved in water: taste and odor

■ **taste buds**
receptors, mostly located on the tongue, that are sensitive to taste

Figure 5.11
**Structure of the Human
Tongue.** The tongue contains
taste buds sensitive to the taste of
chemicals dissolved in water. Also
shown here is an enlarged side
view of a taste bud for you.

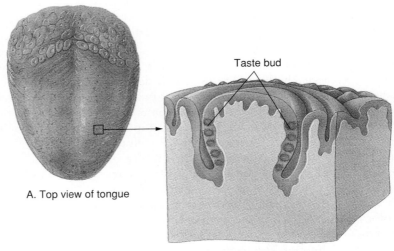

A. Top view of tongue

B. Enlarged cross-sectional
view of papilla

people differ in their sensitivity to taste. However, the variation in people's sensory
sensitivity is not nearly so great as the variation in the number of their taste buds.

There are four primary taste qualities: sweet, salty, sour, and bitter. We have different
taste buds that respond mainly to each of these different tastes, and the actual tastes we
experience result from the overall pattern of stimulation. At one time, it was believed
that the different taste buds were localized on different parts of the tongue, but recent
research shows that each is distributed throughout the entire tongue and mouth
(Bartoshuk & Beauchamp, 1994). Individuals who experience neural damage or anesthesia to one part of the tongue do not show selective impairment of their sensitivity to
different tastes. Indeed, they usually do not notice any change at all—which confirms
our subjective experience that taste arises from the entire mouth. When we are able to
localize a given taste, such as a spicy chili pepper under our tongue, we are relying on
our sense of touch—not taste—to tell where it originates.

Researchers have made some progress in understanding which substances are associated with which tastes. Organic compounds (those containing carbon, hydrogen, and
oxygen) often taste sweet. Substances containing nitrogen usually taste bitter. Salty
substances are those that form ions. Acidic substances taste sour. As investigators learn
more about the substances that give rise to different tastes, they can use this information
to create certain tastes on demand. Commercial sweeteners are a familiar example—
researchers intentionally design them to taste sweet without containing the calories that
characterize most other sweet-tasting substances.

Smell

Like taste, smell is a chemical sense. Taste and smell often work in concert, as you notice
every time your nose is congested: You cannot smell the food you eat, and it does not
taste like it otherwise would. We smell substances carried through the air to receptors
located at the top of our nasal cavity (see Figure 5.12). Odor detectors are also found in
the throat. Neurons leading from these receptors bundle together in the **olfactory
nerve,** which travels to the **olfactory bulb** at the base of the brain.

The sense of smell probably evolved from the sense of taste when our water-
dwelling ancestors long ago moved on to land. As mentioned earlier, smell is not as
important to human beings as it is to other animals (Goldberg & Wise, 1990). Consider
that dogs have about 100 million smell receptors, as opposed to the 10 million that
people have (Brown, 1975).

■ **olfactory nerve**
bundle of nerves leading from
odor detectors to the brain

■ **olfactory bulb**
structure at the base of the brain
to which the olfactory nerve
leads

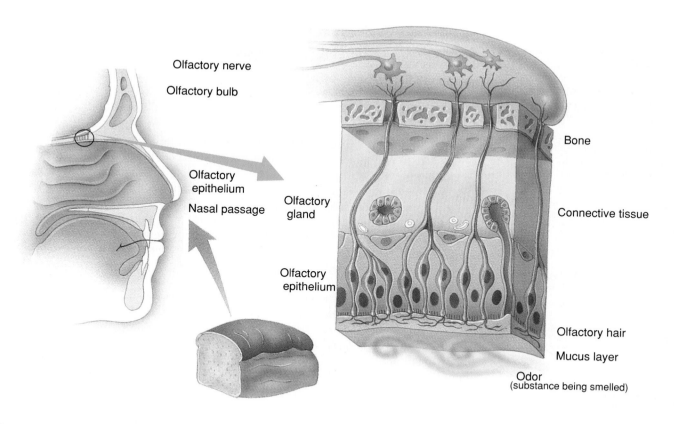

Figure 5.12
Human Nasal Cavity. Receptors at the top of the nasal cavity are sensitive to the smell of substances carried through the air. Neurons lead from these receptors to the olfactory nerve, which terminates in the olfactory bulb at the base of the brain.

Smell is poorly understood. Psychologists know that the neural pathways from smell receptors are directly connected to the brain, suggesting an important role early in evolution. But they do not know exactly how smell receptors are stimulated by the particular chemicals that reach them. Attempts to discover primary odors, analogous to the primary taste qualities just discussed, have been unsuccessful. According to some theorists, people may possess thousands of different types of odor receptors, each responsive to a specific odor molecule (Buck & Axel, 1991). Consistent with this view are studies showing that people cannot be readily characterized as generally sensitive or insensitive to odors (Koelega, 1994). Rather, sensitivity to one odor is largely independent of sensitivity to other odors.

If odor receptors are this specialized, then the information processing of odors is probably done more in the nose than in the brain. Indeed, the olfactory nerve and the olfactory bulb are directly connected. Other sensory receptors send messages to their final destinations in the brain through a greater number of intermediary structures. The olfactory bulb in turn is linked closely to the amygdala, which is responsible for our emotional experiences (Chapter 4). Observers have frequently commented on the ease with which given smells trigger emotion-laden memories (Engen, 1987; Paccosi, 1985), and perhaps this phenomenon has its basis in the architecture of the nervous system.

A popular account of smell is the **lock-and-key theory** (Amoore, 1964). According to this theory, different sites on smell receptors have different shapes, and only molecules with compatible shapes can fit into these sites, thereby stimulating the

■ **lock-and-key theory**
explanation of smell proposing that different sites on odor detectors have characteristic shapes that only certain molecules fit

appropriate smell. This theory is similar to the one discussed in Chapter 4 that explains why particular neurons are sensitive to given neurotransmitters. A further explanation of smell is the **vibration theory,** which proposes that once in place, molecules trigger odor detectors because they vibrate at a particular frequency and cause the receptor in question to fire (Wright, 1977, 1982).

Cutaneous Senses

All organisms have a surface (skin), and most also have capacities called **cutaneous senses.** These respond to touch (or pressure) and temperature. Pain is thought by some psychologists to be a cutaneous sense, but pain is sufficiently different and is discussed separately at the end of this chapter. The different cutaneous senses combine to produce other sensations like itching, tickling, and wetness (Tsirul'nikov, 1992).

Although different types of receptors are found in the skin, they tend not to match up one-to-one with the specific cutaneous senses. For instance, the cornea of the eye contains only one type of sensory receptor, yet it is sensitive to touch, cold, and pain. So far, researchers have discovered a specialized receptor only for touch: the **pacinian corpuscle** (see Figure 5.13). Perhaps information from the cutaneous senses is integrated in the brain in terms of the overall pattern of responses from receptors in the skin (Antonets, Zeveke, Malysheva, & Polevaya, 1992; O'Hare, 1991).

Touch.   The entire surface of our body responds to pressure against it, though sensitivity to touch varies, depending on the particular part of the body that is stimulated (see Figure 5.14). Pacinian corpuscles are found in a fatty layer of skin beneath the surface and are composed of onionlike layers. Each pacinian corpuscle contains dendrites connected to a single axon. When the layers of a pacinian corpuscle move, relative to the axon, the neuron fires. Pacinian corpuscles thus respond not to pressure but to changes in pressure. Then they fire, telling the brain how much force has been applied and where it has been applied (Horch, 1991).

■ **vibration theory**
explanation of smell proposing that once in place, molecules trigger odor detectors because they vibrate at a particular frequency

■ **cutaneous senses**
senses that respond to touch or temperature

■ **pacinian corpuscle**
specialized touch receptor

Figure 5.13
Pacinian Corpuscle. The pacinian corpuscle is a specialized receptor found in the skin that is sensitive to changes in pressure.

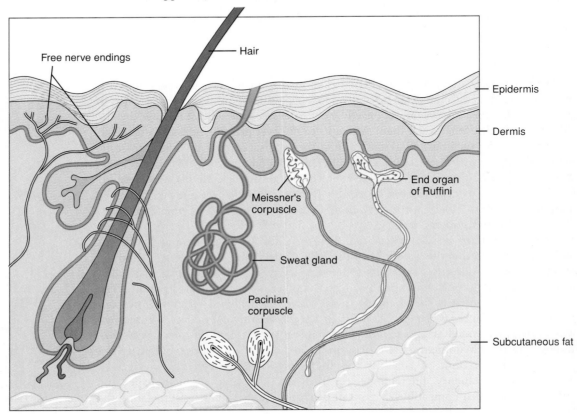

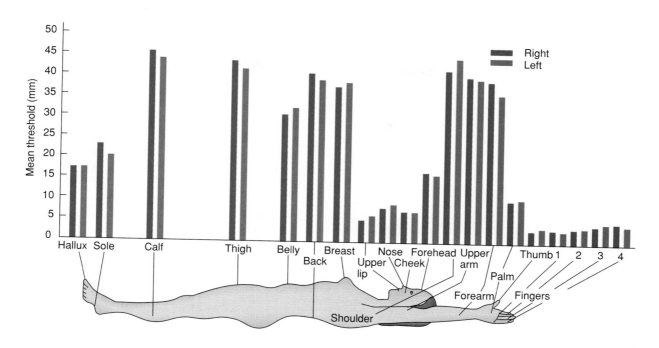

Figure 5.14
Two-Point Thresholds for Different Regions of the Skin. A two-point threshold refers to how far apart two stimuli touching the skin must be before they are felt as separate. This figure shows that considerable variation exists depending on the region of skin. Fingers show a low two-point threshold; they are highly sensitive. Calves and thighs show a high two-point theshold; they are much less sensitive. This diagram shows thresholds for an average female. Thresholds for males are similar but on the whole higher (Kenshalo, 1968).

Temperature. Researchers have long known that some areas of the skin are sensitive to warmth but not to cold, and vice versa (Dallenbach, 1927). This difference in sensitivity means that our sense of temperature is created by two different mechanisms (Casey, Zumberg, Heslep, & Morrow, 1993). Specific receptors sensitive to warmth or cold have not been located. When exclusively "warm" or exclusively "cold" parts of the skin are examined, the same sorts of receptors are found, suggesting that the pattern of stimulation across receptors is what is responsible for our sensation of temperature.

Consider the two entwined pipes shown in Figure 5.15. Through one we can send cold water, and through the other we can send warm water. People asked to take hold of these pipes give a yell and rapidly withdraw their hand. They experience a sensation of extreme heat, which, of course, is not the case. What is going on? The pipes simultaneously stimulate sections of the skin sensitive to warmth and to cold, with the net effect being a sensation of great heat as the sensory information is integrated (Craig & Bushnell, 1994).

Position Senses

When we move about the world, we need to know more than just the state of the environment. We also need to know what our own bodies are doing:

- Am I moving, or am I stationary?
- Where are my legs in relation to my body?
- Is my fist clenched or relaxed?

Answers to questions like these are provided by the **position senses,** of which there are two. The **kinesthetic sense** tells us about the movement or position of our muscles and

■ **position senses**
senses that detect the movement or position of the body or its parts

■ **kinesthetic sense**
sense that detects the movement or position of muscles and joints

Figure 5.15
Thermal Illusion. A sensation of extreme heat can be produced by the simultaneous sensations of warmth and cold. Even when you know that these pipes contain only warm and cold water, you will experience them as quite hot when you take hold of them at the same time. This illusion shows that our experience of temperature is due to the overall pattern of stimulation across receptors.

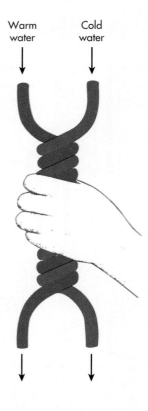

Warm water   Cold water

■ **vestibular sense**
sense responsible for balancing and for detecting the position of the body in relationship to gravity

joints, and the **vestibular sense** informs us about our balance and where we are in relationship to gravity (Leigh, 1994).

Consider the consequences of not having the information that the kinesthetic sense gives us. Oliver Sacks (1984, p. 75) described this state of affairs, following an injury to his leg:

> *I had lost my leg. . . .* I was now an amputee. And yet not an ordinary amputee. For the leg, objectively, externally, was still there; it had disappeared subjectively, internally. . . . I had lost the inner image, or representation, of the leg. There was a disturbance, an obliteration, of its representation in the brain—of this part of the "body image."

Sacks eventually regained his leg, but his account reminds us of the importance of the kinesthetic sense. We have all experienced less dramatic instances of its loss when our arm falls asleep or when we attempt to chew immediately after a shot of novocain.

According to Tseng and Cermak (1993), handwriting is guided more by the kinesthetic sense than by visual perception. Penmanship lessons that emphasize looking at good writing are apt to be of little effectiveness if they are not combined with exercises that involve kinesthetic instruction, such as how to grasp a pen or pencil.

Also taken for granted, except in its absence, is the vestibular sense, which allows us to stay oriented while we move (Grossman, Leigh, Bruce, Huebner, & Lanska, 1989). In people, the vestibular organs are contained in the semicircular canals and vestibular sacs of the inner ear (again see Figure 5.10). This location explains why ear infections are so disruptive to our balance. The vestibular organs consist of tiny hairs embedded in a jelly-like substance. As we begin to move, quickly or slowly, the hairs bend, causing the associated neurons to fire. Once we attain a particular speed, though, the hairs no longer bend and the neurons no longer fire. These organs are stimulated not by speed itself but by changes in speed or bodily orientation.

Children are less susceptible than adults to overstimulation of the vestibular sense and often seem to enjoy abrupt changes in their body's speed and orientation. Adults instead feel dizzy and nauseated, and many avoid roller coasters as a result.

When we spin about, we may overstimulate our vestibular organs, resulting in feelings of dizziness and nausea. Our susceptibility to such overstimulation varies with age, with children much less likely than adults to get sick from too much spinning. Indeed, many children seem to enjoy the sensations resulting from vestibular over-stimulation—which explains why children are more likely than adults to ride roller coasters.

The development of space travel has spurred additional investigations of the vestibular sense. Weightlessness removes the clues about bodily position and orientation provided by gravity (Lackner, 1993). The vestibular sense of astronauts is therefore disrupted when they first experience weightlessness; consequently, they become nauseated (Young et al., 1993). They eventually adapt by learning to rely on other senses to provide orienting information (Lackner & DiZio, 1993). The mechanisms that allow adaptation to weightlessness did not evolve for this purpose . . . unless you believe that our distant ancestors traveled to Earth from other planets by space-ships.

Stop and Think

6 How might you argue that vision—or any other sense, for that matter—is the most important one for people?

7 Compare and contrast taste and smell.

8 Describe how one or more other sensory systems might be used to compensate for the lack of the position senses.

PERCEPTION

How do we organize certain sensations so that we perceive the poster that hangs on our wall, or others so that we perceive a symphony? The term *perception* describes the process by which sensations are organized, as well as the product of this organization: an internal representation of some external stimulus. Research converges to characterize the process and product as selective, coherent, creative, personal, and cultural.

Perception Is Selective

To say that our perception is selective means that we do not simultaneously attend to all the stimuli occurring around us (Lavie & Tsal, 1994). In a crowded restaurant, you listen carefully to what your friend across the table is saying and not to conversations at other tables. On a bus, you look out the window to see how close you are to your intended stop; you do not notice the clothing or cologne of your fellow passengers. You accord some stimuli more weight than other stimuli. The ease with which you can do this depends on the competing stimuli. The selectiveness of perception is one of its fundamental characteristics, and the process by which we perceive some stimuli rather than others is called **attention** (Kinchla, 1992).

Orientation of attention.

■ **attention**
process by which some stimuli rather than others are perceived

■ **orientation**
positioning of sense organs to best receive environmental stimulation

Orientation refers to the positioning of our sense organs to best receive environmental stimulation. Intense stimuli demand our attention. Our prevailing needs and goals also direct our attention. We stare at objects we want to see; we stick our nose over objects we want to smell; we place our ears close to objects we want to hear. These are all examples of overt orientation. Psychologists are also concerned with covert orientation, which occurs when we direct our attention to stimuli without physically moving our sense organs (Posner, 1978): "Don't turn around and stare, but check out who just walked in the room." Covert orientation implies that attention does not just occur through our senses but also involves top-down processes.

Divided attention.

■ **divided attention**
ability to attend to different stimuli at the same time

Divided attention describes our ability to attend to different stimuli at the same time. As we learn to perform a task, we need to attend to its details less and less (Chapter 6). Performance becomes automatized, and our attention can be deployed elsewhere. Consider driving a car. When you first slid behind the wheel of an automobile, the amount of stimulation overwhelmed you. So many things competed for your attention: steering wheel, brakes, accelerator, turn signal, speedometer, pedestrians, school crossings, and other cars. With experience, you can do all sorts of things while driving, including listening to the radio, carrying on a conversation, and even watching the gas gauge.

Selective attention.

■ **selective attention**
ability to tune in some information while tuning out other information

Selective attention. Another topic of interest concerns **selective attention** (Johnston & Dark, 1986). You can tune in some information while tuning out other information. Tuned-in information is front and center in our conscious experience (Chapter 6), but what about tuned-out information? One way researchers answer this question is through studies of shadowing. They place headphones on a research subject and deliver one message to the right ear and another message to the left ear. The subject is asked to repeat one of the messages out loud (to shadow the message), under the assumption that he or she will therefore pay more attention to it. The typical finding is that subjects completely shut out the nonshadowed message. When asked later to recall its content, a subject can report nothing. He or she may not even know what language was spoken (Cherry, 1953). Other studies suggest that selective attention is more complex. If the nonshadowed message contains the subject's name, the subject notices it at least some of the time (Moray, 1959; Wood & Cowan, 1995).

As we learn to perform a task, we need to attend less to its details.

Theories of attention.   Currently, there are two different, yet equally popular, explanations of attention. First is the **bottleneck model,** so named because it hypothesizes a biological restriction on the amount of sensory stimulation we can attend to (Broadbent, 1958). Like cars in a traffic jam, sensory information piles up. Only a small amount can make it through the bottleneck at any one time. In paying attention to a conversation, then, you allow only words from your friend to come through the bottleneck. Unlike cars in a traffic jam, though, sensory information that does not get through the bottleneck quickly enough is lost, forgotten, or replaced. Theorists have more recently elaborated this model to propose that people's attention to complex tasks is limited by multiple bottlenecks (de Jong, 1993).

■ **bottleneck model**
theory of attention hypothesizing a biological restriction on the amount of sensory stimulation that can be attended to

Second is the **capacity model** of attention, which attributes the selectivity of perception not to biological restrictions but to psychological ones (Kahneman, 1973). According to this model, attention requires effort and we have only so much effort to give. Once this limit is reached, we can no longer attend to other stimuli. However, if we learn more efficient strategies for processing information, we can attend to an increasing number of stimuli (Chapter 9). To return to you and your friend in the restaurant, the capacity model implies that with practice, you will be able to attend both to what your friend is saying and to what is going on at adjacent tables. The bottleneck model, in contrast, argues for a necessary limitation on the amount of information to which you can attend.

■ **capacity model**
theory of attention proposing a psychological restriction on the amount of sensory stimulation that can be attended to

Variations in attention.   Investigations of orientation, divided attention, and selective attention suggest that neither the bottleneck model nor the capacity model fully accounts for all aspects of attention. Some combination of the two is needed, one that recognizes both structural limitations and processing limitations (Plude, Enns, & Brodeur, 1994). This conclusion is supported by explanations of how and why attention varies across as well as within people.

So, there is an upper limit to our attention determined by the nervous system (Colby, 1991; Hoptman & Davidson, 1994). For example, divided attention is often decreased among the elderly, presumably because of neurological decline (Madden, 1990; Rutman, 1990). Children may show attention deficit disorder, a problem characterized by the inability to sustain attention. Many theorists point to the relief provided by stimulants like Ritalin as evidence of the disorder's biological basis (Greenhill, 1992).

Among people in general, psychoactive drugs like nicotine and caffeine can temporarily enhance attention (Sherwood, 1993; Zwyghuizen-Doorenbos, Roehrs, Lipschutz, Timms, & Roth, 1990), whereas alcohol and marijuana decrease it (Marks & MacAvoy, 1989; Maylor, Rabbit, James, & Kerr, 1990).

People can also learn to improve their attention (Pashler, 1992). Specific instructions and practice are helpful, even among the elderly (Kramer, Larish, & Strayer, 1995; Trudeau, Overbury, & Conrod, 1990). Stoffregen and Becklen (1989) showed, for instance, that with practice, people can improve their ability to divide attention between two complex tasks. These researchers specifically studied subjects who were watching a baseball game and listening to another person speak. For those sports fans among you who might therefore be tempted to turn on ESPN the next time you are having an intimate conversation, please be aware that these results showed only that practice improves divided attention; they did not show that divided attention is as good as its undivided variety.

Perception Is Coherent

To say that our perception is coherent is to say that conscious experiences are psychologically meaningful wholes. Remember S.B., whose story began this chapter. When he first gained sight, all he saw were blurs. But he quickly came to see the world in terms of discrete (coherent) objects.

The exact means of achieving coherence of perception lay at the center of the debate between the structuralists and the Gestalt psychologists (Chapter 1). According to the structuralists, experience is composed of separate elements later combined into larger wholes. The Gestalt psychologists argued that experience as it occurs is inherently structured. Yet both the structuralists and the Gestalt psychologists agreed that everyday experience is coherent. Let me discuss several examples of the coherence of perception.

■ figure-ground relationship
tendency to organize perceptions in terms of a coherent object (the figure) within a context (the ground)

Form perception. To recognize an object, we use the principle of the **figure-ground relationship.** We group stimuli together into a unified form called a figure and distinguish the figure from surrounding stimuli, referred to as the ground. All perception of forms requires the organization of figures against backgrounds, a fact illustrated by ambiguous pictures like the one in Figure 5.16. You can see this either as an old woman or a young woman. Your perception may flip back and forth rapidly, but at any given moment you can see only one figure against one ground.

Psychologists have specified a number of principles that describe how we organize stimuli into coherent forms. These principles were first proposed by the Gestalt psychologists, and so they are called **gestalt organizational principles** of form perception. They include proximity, similarity, closure, and continuity. Examples are shown in Figure 5.17. Although these come from the realm of our visual perception, similar principles hold for other senses as well.

Proximity is our tendency to group together stimuli that are near each other. In the upper left of Figure 5.17, you see columns in the one case and rows in the other, organized by the principle of proximity. Similarity refers to our tendency to group together stimuli that are similar in size, shape, color, or form. Moving to the right, you see not vertical columns of varied shapes but horizontal rows of dots and dashes, organized by the principle of similarity. According to the principle of closure, when an object has gaps, like the one in the lower left of the figure, you fill them in. What results in this case is a tiger. The tendency to smooth out irregularities also shows continuity, as you can see in the lower right of the figure.

Current research into gestalt organizational principles attempts to locate just where they operate in the course of information processing. In contrast to the premise of the original Gestalt psychologists that perception of form takes place all at once and early in information processing, it now appears as if these principles result from several mechanisms operating at differing stages (Peterson & Gibson, 1994a, 1994b). Consistent with

Figure 5.16
Figure-Ground Reversal. You can see this picture either as an old woman or as a young woman, but at any given moment you see only one of them.

■ gestalt organizational principles
tendencies to organize stimuli into coherent forms

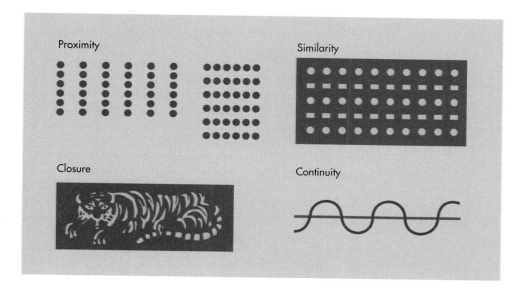

Figure 5.17
Gestalt Organizational Principles. We organize our stimuli into coherent forms according to several basic principles. These illustrations exemplify the principles of proximity, similarity, closure, and continuity.

this hypothesis is a case study of a 71-year-old woman with cortical degeneration (Kartsounis & Warrington, 1991). She could discriminate shapes when they were presented alone but not when they were overlapping. Her brain damage selectively affected her perception of forms.

Distance perception. In everyday life, we judge distances all the time, usually with great accuracy. How far away is that approaching truck? How close is that fork wrapped in spaghetti? Explaining how people go about perceiving distance has been a major concern of psychologists (Gibson, 1988).

Remember that vision involves the projection of images onto the retina, where they stimulate neurons leading to the brain. These images contain no information about distance or depth. The projections of objects at differing distances might look exactly the same, if the objects are of appropriately different sizes (see Figure 5.18). Why, then, do we have no trouble telling how far away an object is, whether it is under our nose, just beyond our reach, or somewhere over the rainbow?

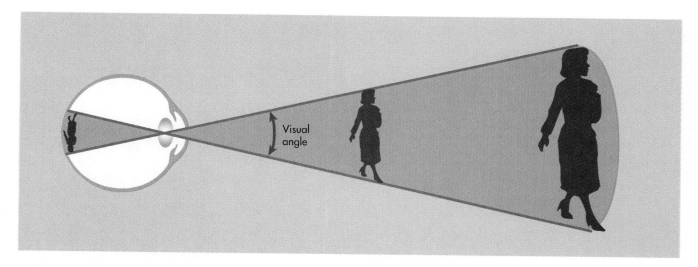

Figure 5.18
Retinal Size. Objects of different size may have the same retinal image, depending on their distance from the eye. Distance therefore cannot be perceived solely in terms of the size of retinal images.

■ **ecological approach**
Gibson's theory of perception
emphasizing the actual environment that people perceive and
the evolved psychological mechanisms that allow them to
perceive it

■ **texture gradient**
graduated changes in the grain of
an environment that provide
information about distance

James Gibson (1979) believed that the answer lies partly within our very makeup:
Depth perception is innate. His theory, called the **ecological approach,** emphasizes
the actual environment that people perceive and the evolved psychological mechanisms
that allow us to perceive it. We perceive not just an object but also its background,
which contains a wealth of information, including clues about depth. Backgrounds may
be composed of elements that produce a particular texture, which becomes denser with
distance. **Texture gradient** refers to the graduated changes in the grain of an environment and provides us with information about distance. The accompanying photo shows
sand in the desert. Notice how the ridges appear closer together as distance increases.
According to Gibson, people do not have to learn to perceive distance in the desert. The
relevant information is present all along, and our perceptual apparatus is sensitive to it.

Think one more time of the example of S.B., and remember his difficulty perceiving distances. Does this mean that Gibson was wrong? Not necessarily. Perhaps the
reason S.B. misjudged the distance to the ground when looking straight down from an
upstairs window is that he saw no texture gradient.

Supporting Gibson's view of distance perception are studies using what is known as
a visual cliff (Gibson & Walk, 1960). Here a transparent surface has underneath it two
patterns, one suggesting greater distance than the other. Very young infants and animals
show extreme reluctance to crawl from the "shallow" side to the "deep" side of the
surface, suggesting that depth perception has an innate component (Goldsmith &
Campos, 1990).

Gibson's approach to perception, with its emphasis on the structured environment,
stands in contrast to approaches that emphasize the role of experience. Perhaps depth
perception is a gradually acquired ability that results from learned associations. When we
see people, we see retinal images of various sizes. We learn that in some cases we can
reach out and touch them because they are close, whereas in other cases we cannot
because they are far away. For our visual world to make sense, we need to take into
account factors other than retinal images. In this example, the factor is touch. Obviously,

*Ridges of sand in the desert appear
closer together the farther away
they are from the viewer. This
gradation in texture is one of the
cues we use in perceiving distance.*

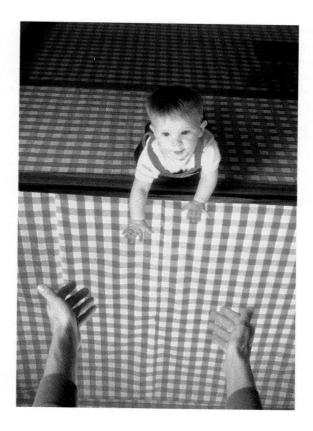

Under the transparent surface are two patterns, one suggesting greater distance than the other. Very young infants and animals are reluctant to crawl from the "shallow" to the "deep" side, suggesting the operation of an evolved psychological mechanism responsible for depth perception.

this example is simplified because our different senses can and do provide many possible clues that we can learn to associate with distance. Consider how sounds or smells associated with an object tell us how close or distant it might be.

Perception Is Creative

To say that our perception is creative means that it is not a literal version of reality but rather something we create. Among the raw ingredients of perception are, of course, our sensations, which are determined by external stimuli. However, perception is also determined by the habits, tendencies, and styles we bring to bear on our sensations (Wehner & Stadler, 1994).

Visual constancies.   Consider the following familiar experiences:

■ You see a friend at the top of a staircase. As he walks down the stairs, his size remains constant. This becomes intriguing when you appreciate that the light stimulating your retina is constantly changing. In particular, the size of the retinal image constantly changes. Why do you not experience a change in your friend's size?

■ You are reading this book while slouching in a chair. Although the book tilts away from you, it still maintains its rectangular shape. Again, this is intriguing. The retinal image changes from rectangular to trapezoidal as the book tilts. Why do you not experience a change in the book's shape?

■ You have switched to a new laundry detergent, and your pleasure knows no bounds because your clothes have never looked so bright. You walk down the street admiring the brightness of the sleeve of your favorite shirt. You pass beneath a large tree that shades the entire sidewalk, you, and your sleeve. You continue to admire how bright your clothes have become. Yet the intensity of light reflected by your shirt was greatly reduced when you walked under the tree. The amount of light stimulating your retina has changed. Why do you not experience a change in your shirt's brightness?

■ **visual constancies**
tendencies for visual perceptions to stay constant even as visual sensations change

These examples illustrate **visual constancies** of size, shape, and brightness: the tendencies for visual perceptions to stay constant even as visual sensations change.

As physical stimulation changes, our perceptual experiences remain constant. This phenomenon makes the world appear stable even though our moment-to-moment stimulation can fluctuate wildly. We somehow take into account factors besides the size, shape, or intensity of retinal stimulation, but what does "take into account" mean (Wallach, 1987)?

The answer depends on the particular type of constancy. For instance, brightness constancy appears built-in, produced by the physiological phenomenon of brightness contrast. Our eyes are particularly sensitive to the edges of objects, a feature that makes evolutionary sense. Edges mark the boundaries of things and thereby make it possible for us to detect them. Research with infants shows that they are particularly likely to examine the edges of objects, ignoring the interior (Maurer & Salapatek, 1976). Sensitivity to edges is produced by the fact that nerve cells in the retina, when stimulated, also inhibit adjacent nerve cells. Bright objects thus seem brighter than adjacent objects (because the nerve cells stimulated by the adjacent objects have been inhibited), whereas dim objects seem dimmer.

Do you see how brightness contrast explains brightness constancy? Remember the example of walking under a shady tree and seeing your bright shirtsleeve stay bright. The light reflected by your sleeve indeed decreased as you walked under the tree, but so did the light reflected by everything else, like your hand and the sidewalk. Absolute levels of retinal excitation and inhibition changed as you walked into the shade, but their particular balance stayed the same. As a result, brightness remained constant.

Size constancy and shape constancy are produced in part by learning (Slater, 1992). You saw in the previous section how people can learn to use the apparent size of objects to judge their distance. They can also learn to use the apparent distance of objects to judge their size.

Illusions.   Perception psychologists have long been interested in **illusions,** phenomena in which our perception of an object is at odds with its actual characteristics. The value of illusions is what they reveal about everyday perceptions, where the role of our creative tendencies may be much less obvious.

As you recall from Chapter 1, Gestalt psychology began with a particular illusion—apparent movement of objects that were in reality stationary—that was not readily accommodated within Wundt's system of psychology (Wertheimer, 1912). Apparent movement takes various forms. The phi phenomenon refers to the fact that stationary objects in different locations are seen to move if they flash at the appropriate interval (about four to five times per second). This phenomenon is responsible for our perception of "motion" pictures as moving, when in fact they are composed of a series of stationary images.

Another type of apparent movement is the autokinetic effect, the tendency of a single point of light in a darkened room to appear to move, even when it is stationary. The autokinetic effect is caused by slight movements of our eyes while we fixate on the point of light (Matin & MacKinnon, 1964). We lack a context in which to locate the light, and we are unaware that our eyes are moving. Instead, we attribute the movement to the light itself. Apparent movement illustrates the gestalt truism that the whole (perception) is not the same as its parts (sensations). That is, perception is creative.

Look at Figure 5.19. Which line is longer? Most people will say the one on the right, although in fact both lines are the same length. This is the Müller-Lyer illusion. One explanation for this illusion is that it is a carryover from our attempts in everyday life to perceive the size of objects while taking into account their distance from us (Gregory, 1966). Thus, the left line looks like the outside corner of a room, whereas the right line looks like the inside corner of a room. Inside corners tend to be farther away

■ **illusion**
phenomenon in which the perception of an object is at odds with its actual characteristics

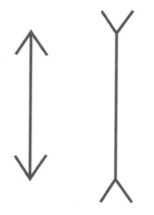

Figure 5.19
Müller-Lyer Illusion. The two lines above are actually the same length. One possible explanation of this illusion is that the left line looks like the outside corner of a room and that the right line looks like the inside corner. We treat the "outside" as closer than the "inside" and thus see it as shorter.

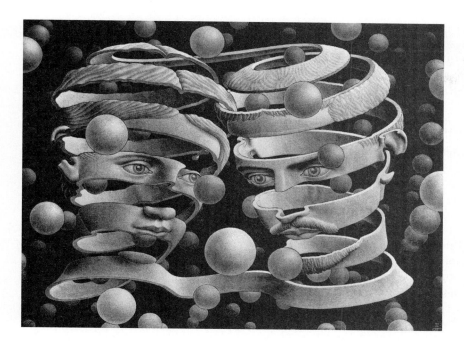

The prints of the popular artist M. C. Escher capitalize on principles of form perception to create compelling images that we nevertheless know cannot exist in the real world.

from us than outside corners, and we compensate by perceiving the right line as longer than it really is.

By the way, some researchers have challenged this particular explanation, and no fully accepted account of the Müller–Lyer illusion yet exists (DeLucia, 1993; Morgan, Hole, & Glennerster, 1990). As will be discussed shortly, researchers have investigated across different cultures people's susceptibility to the Müller–Lyer illusion.

Perception psychologists also study so-called impossible figures (see Figure 5.20). We at first perceive these illusions as coherent wholes, but when we trace out the patterns involved, we see that they defy reality. These illusions apparently stem from our habit of treating two-dimensional pictures as representations of three-dimensional objects, using what seem to be distance cues but really are not (Gregory, 1986). Our tendencies to do this are so ingrained that we persist even when we know our perceptions are impossible. That most people enjoy the discrepancy inherent in such illusions is shown by the continued popularity of artist M. C. Escher, whose prints abound with impossible figures.

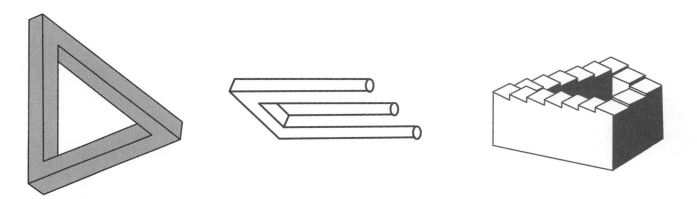

Figure 5.20

Impossible Figures. These drawings create illusions produced by our habit of treating two-dimensional pictures as representations of three-dimensional objects. Our use of apparent distance cues makes us perceive coherent figures that we know to be impossible.

The illusions just described are visual ones because they are well documented and easy to present in a book. However, we also experience illusions with our other senses (Gregory, 1986). Interestingly, the Müller-Lyer illusion also exists in the cutaneous realm; people display the same illusion shown in Figure 5.19 when handling objects, even if they do not see them (Suzuki & Arashida, 1992).

Perception Is Personal

To say that our perception is personal is to say that we see the world from our own point of view. In the obvious sense, this assertion is trivial; we see with our own eyes, hear with our own ears, and so on. But perception is personal in two less obvious ways, and these are worth discussing. They demonstrate the close link between perception and other psychological processes.

Perceptual learning.   Perceptual habits and styles develop over time, meaning that perception reflects the life history of the perceiver (Gibson, 1992). Certain ways of structuring sensations are built into our nervous system (Hubel & Wiesel, 1962, 1979). Infants apparently come into the world already equipped with certain feature detectors. In some cases, these are attuned to very simple stimulus properties, like the corners of objects, but in other cases, they respond to more complex features.

For instance, Johnson, Dziurawiec, Ellis, and Morton (1991) showed that in the first hour following birth, infants are more likely to track a moving stimulus that looks like a face than they are to track similar but non-facelike stimuli (see Figure 5.21). This tendency reflects the operation of an evolved psychological mechanism. The newborn is predisposed to attend to the most important aspect of the environment—the parent—and the parent's attention in turn is drawn to the responsiveness of the infant.

But feature detectors are merely components in perception. If these are not used, they lose their capacity. Blakemore and Cooper (1970) raised kittens in such a way that for the first five months of their lives, they saw only vertical (or horizontal) stripes. As adult cats, these animals were unable to perceive horizontal (or vertical) stimuli. They were unresponsive to a stick waved at them unless it was presented in the same orientation with which they had early experience: vertical or horizontal.

With age and experience, the individual learns to organize the basic components of perception in more sophisticated ways. Children become increasingly able to recognize patterns (Alberti & Witryol, 1990). Figure 5.22 is an arrangement of fruits and vegetables in the shape of a bird (Elkind, 1978a). Four-year-old children describe this figure only in terms of its parts: carrots, cherries, a pear, and a tomato. Seven-year-old children see both the parts and the whole: fruits and carrots and a bird. Nine-year-old children give the most integrated response: a bird made of fruits and vegetables. Stop and imagine, if you can, a world of parts but not wholes. We all once lived in such a world, where partridges and pear trees both exist yet have no relationship to one another.

That young children do not perceive patterns as readily as adults explains why lullabies across different cultures have simpler melodies than other songs from the same cultures do (Unyk, Trehub, Trainor, & Schellenberg, 1992). We sing lullabies to infants in order to soothe them. If the melody is too complex, they cannot grasp it, and they (and

Figure 5.21
Feature Detectors Among Infants. Newborn infants are more likely to pay attention to a stimulus that looks like a face, such as the one on the far left, than they are to similar but non-facelike stimuli. This finding implies that newborns have an evolved psychological mechanism that draws their attention to faces. *Source:* Johnson, M. A., Dziurawiec, S., Ellis, H., & Morton, J. (1991). Newborns' preferential tracking of face-like stimuli and its subsequent decline. *Cognition, 4,* 1–19.

we) will be sleepless. Speech directed to infants is similarly simple, in terms of not just words (Chapter 10) but also rhythm and pattern.

Perceptual sets.   The second way in which perception is personal is that psychological states and characteristics influence what and how we perceive. We often perceive what we expect to perceive. A **perceptual set** (or **mental set**) is a predisposition to perceive a particular stimulus in a particular context.

Perceptual sets can be created in different ways. Simple instructions are effective, for instance. If you are told to look at the young woman in Figure 5.16, you will be much more likely to see her instead of the old woman also present. Perceptual sets may result from habitual experiences, prevailing needs like hunger or thirst, emotions, personality characteristics, or social pressures (Beck, Neeper, Baskin, & Forehand, 1983; Logan & Goetsch, 1993; Palfai & Salovey, 1992; Toner & Gates, 1985).

Stereotypes may produce perceptual sets, leading us to see individuals in a stereotyped group only in terms consistent with the stereotype (Chapter 15). For example, Gibbons and Kassin (1987) presented artwork to research participants and described the artists as either retarded or nonretarded children. Although the paintings and drawings were identical, those attributed to retarded children were seen as less skilled.

A perceptual set is useful to the degree that it leads us to perceive stimulus characteristics that are relevant to the purpose at hand. In such cases, a perceptual set leads to more efficient processing of information (Auerbach & Leventhal, 1973; Macrae, Milne, & Bodenhausen, 1994). For instance, when I am grading a student's test, I attend to the content of what is written and not whether a pen or pencil was used. In other cases, a perceptual set channels information processing in the wrong direction (Dustman et al., 1984). Again, while grading a test, I may be looking only for the typical right answer and so may ignore an unusual but equally correct one.

Perception Is Cultural

Perception is also influenced by our larger social context. We can thus characterize perception as cultural. Our culture directs our attention to some stimuli rather than others, dictates how we group together configurations of stimuli and distinguish them from one another, and provides concepts with which we interpret stimuli. Accordingly, a round red light is seen as a signal to stop in cultures with automobiles but as something different in cultures without. As pointed out in the discussion of perceptual sets, we are greatly influenced by our expectations. One of the important sources of these expectations is cultural beliefs and practices. To the degree that these differ across cultures, then so too do perceptions (Deregowski, 1980; Tajfel, 1969).

Susceptibility to illusions.   Researchers have studied the susceptibility to illusions of people in different cultures. Differences exist, and these are interpretable in terms of the characteristic experiences provided by culture. A well-known investigation along these lines was conducted by Segall, Campbell, and Herskovitz (1963, 1966), who studied individuals from 15 different cultures, both European and non-European, in terms of their responses to the Müller-Lyer illusion (remember Figure 5.19). In general, Europeans were more susceptible to this visual illusion than non-Europeans, meaning that they tended—incorrectly—to perceive the right line as longer than the left line. In contrast, non-Europeans tended—correctly—to see the two lines as the same length.

Segall and his colleagues interpreted this difference in terms of the degree to which individuals were accustomed to a "carpentered" environment: a visual setting dominated by rectangularly shaped buildings. Recall one of the interpretations of the Müller-Lyer illusion: People see the lines as corresponding to outside corners of rooms versus inside corners. European individuals have more experience with rooms like these, and so they are more prone to the illusion.

As noted, other interpretations of this illusion are possible. Jahoda (1966), for instance, argued that the documented cultural differences are due to variations in expe-

Figure 5.22
Vegetable–Fruit–Bird. Four-year-old children see this picture only in terms of its parts. Seven-year-olds see the parts and the whole: fruits and vegetables and a bird. Nine-year-olds perceive an integrated whole: a bird made of fruits and vegetables.

■ **perceptual set; mental set**
predisposition to perceive a particular stimulus in a particular context

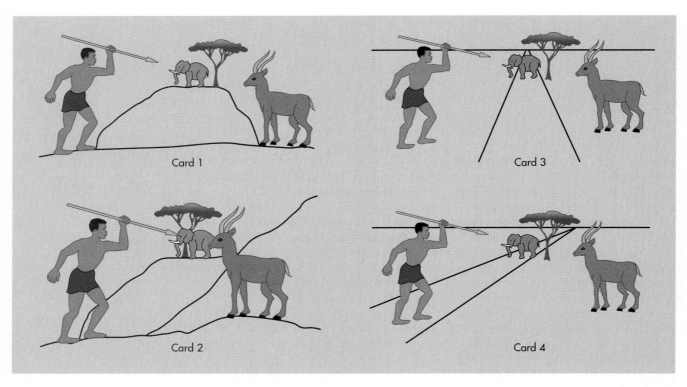

Figure 5.23
The Use of Distance Cues. Children in non-European cultures tend to interpret pictures like these in two-dimensional terms. They do not make use of Western artistic conventions used to signify distance, like the size of objects. *Source:* Hudson, W. (1960). Pictorial depth perception in sub-cultural groups in Africa. *Journal of Social Psychology, 52,* 183–208.

rience with two-dimensional representations of three-dimensional objects. Those in European cultures have a lifelong familiarity with such drawings and have learned to regard certain artistic conventions as distance cues. So, they perceive the Müller-Lyer illusion in these terms. Those without such familiarity do not bring these expectations to bear on the lines. Thus, they do not misinterpret what they see.

Look at the drawings in Figure 5.23. Mundy-Castle (1966) showed children from non-European cultures these pictures and asked them to answer such questions as:

- What do you see?
- What is the man doing?
- Can the deer see the man?
- Which is closer to the man: the elephant or the deer?

Research subjects correctly identified each item in the pictures, but they tended to interpret the pictures in two-dimensional terms, not making use of distance cues. This does not mean that these subjects were insensitive to distance in their everyday lives. Rather, they were unfamiliar with the conventions of European drawings used to signify distance.

Binocular rivalry.   Another demonstration of how culturally provided expectations influence perception is a study by Bagby (1957), who investigated the phenomenon of binocular rivalry. In binocular rivalry, different visual stimuli are shown separately to an individual's two eyes. Under appropriate circumstances, one image may dominate the other and be the only one the individual perceives.

Bagby's research subjects were from either Mexico or the United States; they were shown pairs of photographic slides for a few seconds, separately to each eye; and they were asked to describe what they saw. One slide depicted a characteristic Mexican scene (a bullfight), the other a characteristic United States scene (a baseball game). Results were clear-cut: The Mexican subjects selectively perceived the familiar Mexican scene, whereas the U.S. subjects selectively perceived the familar U.S. scene.

Culture and sensation.   Perception is the psychological interpretation of sensations, and so it is perhaps not surprising that culture can influence perception. The less obviously answered question is whether culture affects sensation. The answer seems to be that it does not. Other than the threshold differences mentioned earlier in this chapter, the biological characteristics of people's sensory systems are essentially the same. Culture influences attention, of course, but there is little reason to think that it influences sensation.

An intriguing line of research bears on this conclusion. It began with the argument by the linguist Benjamin Whorf (1956) that language (culture) shapes the way a person senses the world. The availability or not of different words to describe stimuli determines how these are experienced. Whorf's hypothesis has been intensively investigated with regard to the sensation and perception of color by people from different cultures (Simpson, 1991).

Different cultures provide their members with different sets of words to describe basic colors (Berlin & Kay, 1969; Korzh & Safuanova, 1993). The Dani of New Guinea have available only 2 words (*white* and *black*). People in the United States have 11 color words (*white, black, red, green, yellow, blue, brown, purple, pink, orange,* and *gray*). Those in Russia have the 11 English color words plus a twelfth: *goluboy,* which corresponds to a light blue.

If Whorf's hypothesis were true, then people from different cultures should be able to distinguish only among colors for which they have words. The Dani should make very few distinctions, whereas Russians should make many more. But people from all cultures make identical sensory discriminations among color classes (Heider, 1972). Culture dictates where they draw boundaries but not how they sense color. A similar conclusion follows from studies of taste in different cultures. Culture influences how different tastes are labeled and whether they are perceived as preferable but does not influence the ability to discriminate among their sensory characteristics (Laing et al., 1993).

Stop and Think

9   Do studies of perception support the position of the rationalists or the position of the empiricists?

10   Why do psychologists study illusions?

11   What example of a perceptual set can you offer from your everyday life?

12   Does culture influence sensation?

13   ESP (extrasensory perception) refers to perceptions without sensations. In terms of the ideas presented in this chapter, is ESP a possibility?

SENSATION AND PERCEPTION IN A BIOPSYCHOSOCIAL CONTEXT

Describing perception as selective, coherent, creative, personal, and cultural contextualizes the process by which we know the world, specifying both psychological and social influences on the process. Do not forget, as well, the important role of biological influences: Perception organizes our sensations, which arise when the nervous system is stimulated by external energy. Sensation and perception are best approached in biopsychosocial terms.

Pain as Biopsychosocial

Let me conclude by discussing pain, another example of a biopsychosocial phenomenon (see Figure 5.24). Pain is often described as a sensation and specifically as a cutaneous sense. However, this conceptualization is oversimplified. Stimuli that touch our skin may cause pain, but the sensation of pain is not limited to the stimulation of cutaneous receptors. Pain can and does occur through any sensory receptor. Deafening sounds, blinding lights, and overwhelming tastes produce pain just as readily as damaged skin. Pain from different sensory sources is readily combined in experience in a way that other sensations from different receptors are not (Algom, 1992). For instance, a moderately painful sound coupled with moderately painful pressure can produce a profoundly painful experience, yet it is the pain that is combined, not the sound and the touch.

Characterizing painful stimuli in terms of their simple physical properties proves difficult. Although pain usually results from intense stimuli, this generalization is not always true. Compare a pulsating shower with the prick of a pin. The water from the shower produces much more neural activity than the pin, but it is the pin that produces pain, not the shower.

In short, pain is a psychological puzzle. We can characterize it: Pain is unpleasant. We can describe its adaptive function: Pain serves as a warning signal that our well-being is threatened. We can note its powerful effect on behavior: Pain is something we try to avoid or escape. But we cannot—in a definitive way—say what pain is. Perhaps the puzzle results from the assumption that pain is just a sensation. Some psychologists argue that pain shares more in common with motives like hunger or thirst than it does with sensations like vision or taste (Price, 1988). Motives are experiences that impel us to behave in certain ways (Chapter 7). Pain fits this definition. It has a sensory component—so do hunger and thirst—but this component must be understood within its larger context.

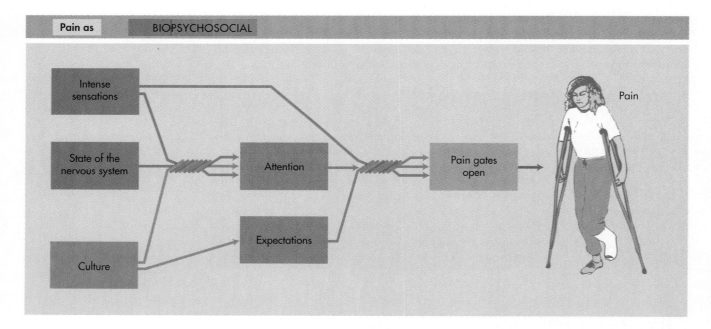

Figure 5.24
Pain as Biopsychosocial. According to gate-control theory, pain results from intense sensations that are allowed to pass through hypothesized gates in the spinal cord to the brain. Whether or not these pain gates are open is determined by biological, psychological, and social factors. So, the state of the nervous system—such as the presence or absence of endorphins—is important (biological), as are the individual's attention to and expectations concerning potentially painful stimuli (psychological) and how the individual's culture has encouraged him or her to respond to pain (social).

There are well-documented differences among cultural groups in their willingness and ability to tolerate intense stimuli (Fabrega, 1989; Ots, 1990; Pugh, 1991; Thomas & Rose, 1991; Villarruel & Ortiz de Montellano, 1992; Zborowski, 1969). For instance, in comparison to women from other ethnic groups, those from Asian cultures report more pain when having their ears pierced. The stereotype of Northern Europeans as stoic seems to have a basis in fact because many of these individuals can tolerate what would seem to be highly painful stimuli without complaint. Similarly, Northern Europeans are less likely than those from most other cultural groups to experience chronic pain disorders (Hes, 1958, 1968).

More than those from other cultural groups, European Americans expect to control how they feel (Bates & Rankin-Hill, 1994), whether or not they actually can (Peterson, Maier, & Seligman, 1993). These expectations in turn are associated with a decreased perception of pain (Averill, 1973; Miller, 1979; Thompson, 1981). Taken together, these findings again show how culture affects our experience of stimuli.

A contextualized view of pain is contained in **gate-control theory** (Melzack, 1973). According to this account, the nervous system is limited in the amount of sensory information it can handle at a given time. When too much information is present, cells in the spinal cord act as a gate, blocking some signals from going to the brain, while letting others pass. The brain may send messages to the spinal cord to open or close this hypothesized gate. Most of us have sustained an injury in the course of an engaging activity, like playing a sport, wherein we did not notice the gash in our leg or our chipped tooth until the activity ended. Presumably, the pain gate had been closed.

Perhaps people troubled by chronic pain have pain gates that stay open too long, for biological or psychological reasons. Accordingly, psychologists can help if they can devise a way to close the hypothesized gates. Endorphins, mentioned in Chapter 4, may be involved in the gating of pain (Basbaum & Fields, 1984). Some psychologists believe that the Chinese practice of acupuncture controls pain because it closes particular gates (Chapman, Wilson, & Gehrig, 1976). Other strategies for controlling pain include drugs, massage, hypnosis, relaxation, and distraction (Caillet, 1993; Hamill & Rowlingson, 1994). That pain can be combated in so many different ways underscores its biopsychosocial nature.

■ **gate-control theory**
explanation of pain proposing that cells in the spinal cord act as a gate, blocking some pain signals from going to the brain, while letting others pass

Pleasure as Biopsychosocial

It is noteworthy that psychologists have studied pain extensively while paying relatively little attention to pleasure (Glick & Bone, 1990). Regardless, the points just made about pain also clarify pleasure. Pleasure has a sensory component, but it is not limited to any given sensory receptor. We experience pleasure through touch, smell, taste, vision, and so on. Pleasure exerts a powerful influence on our behavior. Finally, it is difficult if not impossible to characterize a pleasurable stimulus in terms of its simple physical properties. For example, we may experience hot water as pleasurable when we are taking a shower but as painful when we are merely touching it, even though it is the same temperature (Herrmann, Candas, Hoeft, & Garreaud, 1994). Depending on what else is occurring, the identical sensory stimulation can produce pleasure, indifference, pain, or even revulsion.

Pleasure may best be regarded as a motive behind behavior (Chapter 7). It is influenced by a host of biological, psychological, and social factors. In the modern Western world, for instance, most of us find a kiss to be highly pleasurable. But kissing is not among the cultural practices of all groups. Those in traditional Chinese and Japanese societies did not kiss one another (Ford & Beach, 1951). Like pain, pleasure is best conceptualized in biopsychosocial terms.

Most if not all of the investigations described in the present chapter assume that people are aware of their sensations and perceptions. The techniques of psychophysics typically rely on what an individual reports concerning his or her experience of physical stimuli. This experience is presumably present in conscious awareness. However, not all psychologists take consciousness as a given. They try to explain consciousness in its own right, a task that proves daunting. Their efforts are the subject of the next chapter.

SUMMARY

UNDERSTANDING SENSATION AND PERCEPTION: DEFINITION AND EXPLANATION

■ Sensation is the process by which environmental energy is transformed into neural impulses sent to the brain. Perception is the process by which we organize and interpret this sensory information.

DOING *Psychophysics* RESEARCH

■ The field of psychophysics attempts to specify the relationship between physical stimuli and psychological experience.

■ The minimal amount of energy needed to create a psychological experience is called the absolute threshold of a sensory system.

■ The minimal physical distinction between two stimuli that can be discriminated is called the difference threshold.

■ In scaling, psychophysicists determine the mathematical relationship between the amount of a physical stimulus that is present and our psychological experience of it.

■ According to adaptation-level theory, sensation is affected not only by the stimuli on focus but also by those in the background and those experienced in the past.

SENSORY SYSTEMS

■ The sense of vision responds to the energy contained in light. Light is a wave of radiant energy, and we experience the various properties of such waves as brightness, hue, and saturation.

■ The human eye is a complex structure that gathers light and focuses it on nerve cells called photoreceptors. There are two types of photoreceptors: rods, responsible for vision in dim light, and cones, responsible for vision in bright light.

■ Brightness is obviously determined by the intensity of light but also by the level of background illumination and our adaptation to it.

■ The sensation of color has been explained over the years by two competing theories. The trichromatic color theory proposes that there are three different types of cones sensitive to red, green, and blue light. The opponent-process color theory proposes that color vision is created by two different systems that detect the balance between red and green light on the one hand and blue and yellow light on the other. Both theories have strong and weak points, and the currently accepted theory of color vision combines the two.

■ The sense of hearing responds to the energy contained in sound. Sound comes in waves, and the properties of sound waves produce our experience of loudness, pitch, and timbre.

■ Taste is called a chemical sense, because it responds to chemicals dissolved in water. Taste buds are the receptors sensitive to taste, and they are located mostly on the tongue. There are four basic tastes: sweet, salty, sour, and bitter. Different taste buds respond primarily to each of these different tastes.

■ Smell is also a chemical sense. We smell substances that are carried through the air to receptors located at the top of our nasal cavity. Psychologists have been unable to identify basic categories of odors.

■ The cutaneous senses allow us to detect pressure, warmth, and cold on our skin. A pacinian corpuscle is a specialized receptor that detects touch; however, other receptors in the skin do not match up one-to-one with specific sensations.

■ The kinesthetic sense tells us about the movement and position of our muscles and joints.

■ The vestibular sense informs us about our balance and our position relative to gravity.

PERCEPTION

■ Perception is selective, meaning that we cannot attend simultaneously to all the stimuli occurring around us.

■ Perception is coherent; our conscious experiences merge into a whole.

■ Perception is creative. We perceive not a literal version of reality but rather a creation that reflects external stimuli as well as the habits, tendencies, and styles we bring to bear on our sensations.

■ Perception is personal. We see the world from our own point of view, and we have our own perceptual styles that have developed over time. Also, our prevailing psychological states can influence what and how we perceive.

■ Finally, perception is cultural. Our larger social context draws our attention to some stimuli rather than others and provides us with ways of interpreting our sensations.

SENSATION AND PERCEPTION IN A BIOPSYCHOSOCIAL CONTEXT

■ Pain and pleasure are often described as sensations, but they are more complex and demand a biopsychosocial interpretation.

KEY TERMS

Consciousness

Theorists and researchers agree that consciousness exists in different forms: Contrast being asleep with being awake. However, the relationship among the different states of consciousness is unclear. An enduring issue is whether they can be arranged in a simple hierarchy. States of consciousness are often described as higher or lower, for example, but what is the basis for this description? Does higher consciousness mean more awareness? Is higher consciousness a property of its specific contents? Is there some single dimension along which all states of consciousness fall?

Several decades ago, enthusiasts claimed that drugs like mescaline and LSD, which dramatically alter sensation and perception, were mind-expanding or consciousness-raising (Weil, 1972). Let us examine this claim to see if it sheds any light on whether states of consciousness exist in a hierarchy.

Tom Wolfe's (1969) *The Electric Kool-Aid Acid Test* chronicled the LSD-based adventures of the novelist Ken Kesey and his friends. They called themselves the Merry Pranksters and found a source of continual amusement in LSD. Traveling up and down the West Coast in a bus, they mixed the drug with Kool-Aid and shared the beverage with unsuspecting people. At the same time that Kesey and his friends were playing their pranks, the Harvard University psychologist Timothy Leary (1964) was

States of consciousness are often described as higher or lower, but it is not clear that there exists a single dimension along which all such states can be arranged. Is the state of consciousness achieved by someone praying higher than, lower than, or equivalent to the state of consciousness experienced by whirling dervishes? How do these states of consciousness compare with sleep?

conducting well-publicized experiments with LSD and solemnly interpreting the results in terms of access to a higher state of religious experience.

The Merry Pranksters eventually drove to the East Coast to meet with Leary and his colleagues. As Wolfe told the story, the two groups had nothing to say to one another! Their conceptualizations of LSD and its alteration of consciousness were so profoundly at odds that they lacked a common vocabulary. Getting high on LSD involved altogether different experiences. The lesson seems to be that states of consciousness cannot be arranged along a single dimension with which everybody would agree. One's social group dictates which aspects of consciousness are experienced as higher or lower, expanded or compressed, profound or simply goofy.

UNDERSTANDING CONSCIOUSNESS: DEFINITION AND EXPLANATION

■ **consciousness**
awareness of one's current environment and mental life

■ **mind-body dualism**
philosophical position that people's minds and bodies are altogether different

Consciousness is often defined as awareness of our current environment and mental life. A precise definition is elusive because *awareness*, after all, is a synonym for *consciousness*. Most theorists nevertheless agree that consciousness includes our awareness of particular sensations, perceptions, needs, emotions, and cognitions.

Consciousness is a property of the brain and nervous system. There is no reason to believe that disembodied consciousness exists, but there is considerable debate about the relationship between the brain and consciousness. Centuries ago, the French philosopher René Descartes (1596–1650) proposed that people's minds and bodies were different, an idea referred to as **mind-body dualism.** The problem with this idea is that it leaves a fundamental question unanswered: How do the mind and the body interact? As you know from Chapter 4, this question remains unanswered except in the most approximate way.

The Role of Biology and Evolution

Many contemporary thinkers prefer to regard minds and bodies—that is, consciousness and the brain—as the same phenomenon described with radically different languages. Remember the philosophical position of **scientific materialism** introduced in Chapter 1: Living things are part of the physical world. Scientific materialism "solves" the problem of mind-body interaction by proposing that both are able to be understood in physical terms (Chapter 1). But materialism again leaves unanswered a fundamental question: How can we translate psychological concepts into physical ones (Gillett, 1988)?

Translations attempt to specify the biological mechanisms responsible for conscious experience, but so far theories are speculative. According to one view, for example, consciousness automatically appears when a sufficiently complex neural organization exists (Sperry, 1969, 1976, 1987, 1993). This hypothesis implies that animals have a form of consciousness (Blumberg & Wasserman, 1995; Dawkins, 1993; Radner, 1989; Rollin, 1986; Rushen, 1985).

Along these lines, Dennett (1991) sketched how consciousness might have evolved. Consider an animal that focused its sensory systems on predators, food, and potential mates and then mobilized its resources to deal optimally with these. Natural selection would presumably favor such orientation and mobilization, not just to specific stimuli but more generally. An animal that provided itself with occasional updates about its environment and internal state would have a survival advantage over an animal that did not. Periodic vigilance of this sort would eventually give rise to regular exploration of the outer and inner worlds, obtaining information for its own sake because it might someday be valuable.

Tooby and Cosmides (1990b) cautioned that the past functions of consciousness may not be its current functions. Like Dennett (1991), they suggested that consciousness evolved from tendencies by our distant ancestors to categorize situations according to their relevance for survival. As a result, different states of consciousness are accompanied by different feelings. Positive feelings (pleasure) led our ancestors to approach given situations, and negative feelings (pain) to avoid them (Chapter 7). Nowadays, states of consciousness are still marked by pleasure or pain, and we now approach or avoid these states in their own right.

This theory explains, in evolutionary terms, why people deliberately alter their consciousness with psychoactive drugs. The mechanisms responsible for intoxication produce pleasure that once upon a time drew our ancestors to food, water, or mates. Now we can tap into these mechanisms to experience pleasure that is separated from the survival advantages it once signaled. More generally, we are reminded that consciousness, when used in circumstances that differ from those in which it evolved, can produce problems for an individual (Sullivan, 1994). For instance, anxiety and depression involve the inability to turn off thoughts concerning vulnerability or loss, even when they are groundless (Chapter 13).

Another biologically based theory of consciousness looks at brain laterality (Ornstein, 1977). The right hemisphere presumably controls automatized—relatively nonconscious—processes; the left hemisphere, relatively conscious processes (Kurian & Santhakumari, 1990). These hypotheses are difficult to evaluate, however. We must be cautious in discussing the differences between left-brain and right-brain functions because the brain typically works as a whole (Chapter 4). Indeed, researchers to date have been unable to locate conscious experience in any single region of the brain (Toribio, 1993). This attempt may be futile if consciousness represents the integration of activities throughout the entire brain (Dennett, 1991).

The Role of Psychological Processes

Although consciousness involves brain activity, some theorists have concluded that any theory phrased only in neurological terms is incomplete (Gantt, 1994; Smith, 1993). Consciousness is a top-down activity (Chapter 5), meaning that regardless of its

■ **scientific materialism**
philosophical position that living things are part of the physical world

biological basis, it is influenced and directed by other psychological processes, such as motivation and emotion (Sommerhoff & MacDorman, 1994). According to this view, one of the defining characteristics of consciousness is that it reflects the goals and intentions of the individual (Munro, 1981).

The Role of Culture

Yet another theory regards consciousness as a cultural product. The psychologist Julian Jaynes (1976) argued that thousands of years ago, our ancestors had no concept of consciousness. Instead, they regarded their own conscious thoughts as visitations of gods and goddesses. It was not until about 3,000 years ago that people started to group their conscious thoughts together and label them as consciousness. In support of his argument, Jaynes pointed to historical evidence. He studied writings such as Homer's *Iliad* and *Odyssey* for mention of consciousness and found that older texts made no mention of the idea. Then all of a sudden, "consciousness" made its appearance.

A similar hypothesis is that the modern idea of a single self with unique characteristics dates only to the Middle Ages (Baumeister, 1987). Perhaps the self was invented as the idea of consciousness spread through the general population. Indeed, anthropologists have concluded that the concept of a single self still does not exist among Sri Lankan villagers (de Munck, 1992). These people instead regard themselves composed of a constellation of subselves displayed in different social settings. Sri Lankans do not view these subselves as directed by any single entity. Individual life is a series of transitions from one subself to another, all in accordance with situational demands and expectations. Try, if you can, to imagine experience in these terms. The very exercise—because it assumes you have a single self—is contradictory.

These different theoretical perspectives of consciousness are not incompatible. Taken together, they implicate both biological and cultural influences on consciousness,

According to some historians, the idea of the self arose in Western cultures as the notion of consciousness spread throughout the general population. Among Sri Lankan villagers, there is no single sense of self. Instead, these people regard themselves as composed of a constellation of independent subselves displayed in different settings.

which in turn are linked to critical psychological processes such as sensation, perception, motivation, emotion, learning, and cognition (Shvyrkov, 1988).

Stop and Think

1 What is consciousness?

2 How is consciousness biopsychosocial?

3 Criticize the evidence used by Jaynes to argue that consciousness is a cultural invention dating back only 3,000 years.

Doing *Consciousness* RESEARCH

There is no consensus about how to study consciousness (Banks, 1993). Introspection is one obvious strategy, and researchers have long relied on their own conscious experience as well as the reports of others to catalog different forms of consciousness. It is important, of course, to treat an individual's reports not as literally true but rather as a starting point for further investigation (Dennett, 1991). Even the most accurate description is not the same thing as explanation, and researchers attempt to go beyond description to place consciousness in its full context.

One research approach determines the biological, psychological, and/or social factors associated with introspective reports concerning different states of consciousness (Burns, 1990, 1991). If correlations exist, we have clues about the mechanisms responsible for consciousness and the roles it plays in our lives. Under what circumstances do we attend to stimuli in the environment? When are we inattentive? Are changes in brain functioning linked to different states of consciousness? What are the behavioral and mental consequences of these different states? You will see some of the answers to these questions throughout this chapter.

Another popular research strategy studies the ways in which people deliberately alter their consciousness: with daydreaming, hypnosis, meditation, and psychoactive drugs. These investigations give us information about the motivational significance of consciousness and—perhaps—relevant biological and psychological mechanisms.

Much of what we know about consciousness comes from investigations of people with physical and mental difficulties that affect their awareness. Abnormality is a window to the whole of psychology, but it provides special insight into consciousness. If we study people who cannot attend to their environments, for example, or those who experience unusual forms of sleeping and dreaming, then perhaps we can learn something important about everyday consciousness.

So long as psychologists lack a common way for making sense of consciousness, there is a limit to the utility of research (Dennett, 1991). This problem is different from saying that consciousness is poorly understood. Much about how the nervous system works is poorly understood, but psychologists at least agree to think about it in terms of its anatomical structure and electrochemical functioning (Chapter 4). But if we cannot define consciousness in the first place, then how can we study it? Consciousness is always described with metaphors—as a physical place or thing, as an ongoing process, as a narrative, even as a fiction—yet none of these metaphors is rich enough to explain the obvious complexity of consciousness. Psychologists have nonetheless attempted to study consciousness, and so let us next turn to what they have learned.

Stop and Think

4 Why is consciousness so difficult to study?

STATES OF CONSCIOUSNESS

As already mentioned, consciousness is experienced in qualitatively different forms. This section discusses several of the important states of consciousness, some familiar and others exotic. It starts with the state that characterizes our normal waking lives.

Normal Waking Consciousness

Ornstein (1988) called consciousness the front page of the mind. Like a newspaper, consciousness contains what is new, surprising, and important to us. In normal waking consciousness, each of us monitors ongoing experience. When something notable occurs, we bring it front and center into awareness.

Normal waking consciousness is characterized by selective attention (Chapter 5). Many of the tasks we perform during the day have become automatic, and so we perform them without full awareness. Consider driving a car down an interstate highway. You drive perfectly well, but you are not attending to everything going on about you. Oops—watch out! There is an abandoned car on the shoulder up ahead. Suddenly your consciousness is engaged. There is a problem to be solved. You check your rearview mirror, put on your turn signal, and swing into the passing lane.

Psychologists point out that there are two ways in which we go about our normal waking activities (Logan, 1980). In **automatic processing,** we initiate an activity and simply carry it out. Tying shoes, locking a car door, and dialing a telephone are typical examples of automatic processing. In **controlled processing,** we initiate an activity and then make a conscious effort to direct it. Activities that are unusual, difficult, or important involve controlled processing. The first time you used a typewriter or danced in public, you probably attended to every aspect of your behavior.

The distinction between automatic processing and controlled processing is not always clear because many of our activities combine them. When you drive your old car through a new neighborhood, your use of the gas pedal and the brake represents automatic processing; the route you plan represents controlled processing. In many cases, automatic processing begins as controlled processing. As behaviors become familiar, their performance is automatized, allowing us to pay attention to new demands.

Normal waking consciousness has obvious benefits (Ornstein, 1973, 1977). When we are aware of our activities, we can:

- select particularly useful information for our attention
- set priorities for our behavior
- guide our actions
- detect discrepancies in our experience
- resolve those discrepancies

These functions suggest why human beings (and perhaps animals) have evolved the capacity for awareness. Think of the selective advantage given to our ancestors who had more of this capacity than their contemporaries (Chapter 3).

At the same time, there are drawbacks to conscious attention. When we are aware of one aspect of our behavior, we may be oblivious to others. Also, consciousness can interrupt our ongoing behavior, meaning that as our capacity for consciousness evolved, so did a corresponding capacity to turn it off. According to one theory of schizophrenia (Chapter 13), the hallucinations that mark this disorder result from an individual's inability to shut out irrelevant stimuli; the schizophrenic individual is overly conscious and thereby impaired.

■ **automatic processing**
carrying out activities without conscious attention to them

■ **controlled processing**
carrying out activities with a conscious effort to direct them

Automatic processing often begins as controlled processing. As behaviors become familiar, we start to perform them automatically, leaving us free to pay attention elsewhere.

Lack of Awareness

In automatic processing, we are not aware of how we are carrying out activities because they have become routinized. No further explanation is needed. But sometimes our lack of awareness represents more than just the routinization of behavior. Other psychological mechanisms can lead to the lack of awareness. Clinical psychologists have been especially interested in these additional mechanisms because the absence of consciousness can accompany and be responsible for various psychological problems (Chapter 13).

The motivated unconscious.   Like other psychodynamic theorists, Sigmund Freud theorized extensively about the mind and distinguished among three types of awareness. The first has been identified already as normal waking consciousness, the experiences that are front and center in our minds. The second type of awareness is the **preconscious:** thoughts and memories not currently in awareness but readily available (Chapter 9). What is the name of your psychology instructor? When did you go to bed last night? Where is your car parked? You probably were not thinking about any of these questions as you read them, but you can answer each one. This material is in your preconscious.

    The third type of awareness about which Freud wrote is the **unconscious:** thoughts actively kept out of awareness because they are threatening to the conscious mind. Freud's key point was that the unconscious is motivated; we have a need to keep certain material out of our normal waking awareness because it is threatening.

    Perceptual defense.   If people protect themselves against thoughts that are unacceptable to their conscious minds, then the motivated unconscious should lead us to overlook nastiness in the world. Research shows that this possibility exists. In one experiment, for instance, research subjects were asked to identify words that were flashed for a fraction of a second on a screen (McGinnies, 1949). Some of the words

■ **preconscious**
thoughts and memories not currently in awareness but readily available to awareness

■ **unconscious**
thoughts actively kept from awareness because they are threatening

were of the four-letter variety. Subjects took longer to recognize these profane words than innocuous ones. This phenomenon, in which people protect themselves from offending stimuli, is called **perceptual defense** (Dixon, 1990; Erdelyi, 1974, 1985).

The motivated unconscious allows us to explain otherwise puzzling aspects of people's behavior. Perhaps you have friends who rant and rave about certain habits of people they detest, although they themselves have the exact same habits. This self-deception makes sense in view of the unconscious. In their conscious minds, your friends know they dislike people who are tardy, wasteful, or promiscuous; in their unconscious minds, they keep hidden from themselves the fact that they act in these ways as well. More generally, the unconscious plays a large role in psychodynamic theorizing about personality. According to Freud, our central needs and motives are maintained in our unconscious and actively kept from awareness (Chapter 12).

Defense mechanisms.   One of the most important aspects of Freud's psychoanalytic theory is the notion of **defense mechanisms,** unconscious strategies we use to defend ourselves against threat. Freud and other psychodynamic theorists described a variety of defense mechanisms people use, some familiar and some bizarre (see Table 6.1). In projection, for example, people attribute unacceptable characteristics of their own to other individuals. Some types of prejudice involve projection, as when sexually preoccupied individuals criticize the sexual behavior of other groups (Chapter 15). In repression, we actively keep an upsetting memory out of our conscious minds (Chapter 13).

Many of the defenses described in Table 6.1 have become part of our everyday vocabulary. These strategies were there all along, but it took Freud to recognize them

■ **perceptual defense**
process by which people protect themselves by not consciously perceiving threatening stimuli

■ **defense mechanisms**
unconscious strategies people use to defend against threat

Table 6.1   Defense Mechanisms

Defense mechanism	Characterization and example
Compensation	Investing one's energies in some activity to offset difficulties in another area; for example, working out or studying after a disappointing date
Denial	Acting as if something did not happen; for example, continuing to attend classes after flunking out of school
Displacement	Directing one's impulses toward a substitute object or person; for instance, kicking the dog or yelling at the children after a difficult day at work
Fantasy	Engaging in wishful thinking or daydreaming when feeling stress; for example, fantasizing about winning the lottery while studying for final examinations
Intellectualization	Discussing a traumatic event without experiencing any emotions, as when a patient with a serious illness calmly discusses the chances of survival
Projection	Attributing one's own unacceptable characteristics to others; for example, a hostile person who sees everyone else as angry
Rationalization	Rewriting history after a disappointment, like the fox in Aesop's fables who decided that the grapes he could not have were probably sour anyway
Reaction formation	Replacing one impulse with its opposite; for example, acting hatefully toward a person one finds attractive
Regression	Acting like an infant or child in stressful circumstances; for instance, throwing a tantrum during an argument
Repression	Forcing a threatening memory from awareness, as might happen when someone forgets the details of an assault
Sublimation	Channeling undesirable impulses into socially acceptable activities; for example, an aggressive individual might become a fire "fighter" or a police officer

and offer a single explanation. Subsequent theorists have debated how best to regard defense mechanisms. Some suggest that they can be ranked from relatively immature defenses such as denial to relatively mature defenses such as sublimation, depending on the degree to which the individual using the defense distorts reality (Vaillant, 1977). Also, defense mechanisms may not always be wholly unconscious, as Freud implied. They may not always be a reaction to threat; they can be undertaken in a show of initiative. Indeed, the term *coping mechanism* is favored over *defense mechanism* by some contemporary theorists because it has active—as opposed to reactive—connotations.

Subliminal perception. Sometimes people perceive stimuli without being consciously aware that they are doing so. This phenomenon is called **subliminal perception.** In the language of Chapter 5, it is the perception of stimuli at intensities below their absolute thresholds. Remember how an absolute threshold is determined: by asking the individual to report whether or not a given stimulus is present. If the individual cannot report the presence of a stimulus that still has an effect on his or her behavior, then subliminal perception has occurred.

■ **subliminal perception**
perception of stimuli without awareness

For example, Silverman, Bronstein, and Mendelsohn (1976) recruited male college students to participate in a dart-throwing tournament. Prior to throwing darts, they were exposed to one of several extremely brief messages flashed on a screen:

- BEATING DAD IS WRONG
- BEATING DAD IS OKAY
- PEOPLE ARE WALKING

From a psychodynamic perspective, these researchers expected the first message to stir up feelings of guilt and conflict, the second message to decrease those feelings, and the third message to be neutral. Although the subjects were arguably unaware of the message they had seen, those exposed to the guilt-inducing message scored worst in the dart contest, and those exposed to the guilt-reducing message scored best.

In a similar study, guilt-inducing messages presented subliminally increased physiological arousal, even though individuals were unaware of the effect (Masling, Bornstein, Poynton, Reed, & Katkin, 1991). The briefer the message, the more likely it was to affect their arousal, a finding which strengthens the argument that the process occurred outside of conscious awareness.

Subliminal perception is controversial, largely because of the methodological difficulties in demonstrating it (Balay & Shevrin, 1988, 1989; Hardaway, 1990; Weinberger & Hardaway, 1990; Weinberger & Silverman, 1990). Strictly speaking, a verbal report about the presence (or absence) of a stimulus is not equivalent to conscious experience (or lack of it), although most researchers treat the verbal report this way. If we inquire directly about the contents of consciousness, we can create awareness within an individual and invalidate our study. Many investigators therefore do not directly question their research subjects about what they have perceived. Instead, they present stimuli at thresholds well below what average people can detect, as determined in other studies. However, it is then conceivable that the subjects who seem to evidence subliminal perception simply have exceedingly low thresholds (Miller, 1991).

Even if subliminal perception does exist, it is doubtful that it strongly influences our behavior. Claims are sometimes made that advertisers use the phenomenon—flashing subliminal messages on television or movie screens, urging us to buy given products (Key, 1973; Packard, 1957)—but there is little reason to think that these messages, if indeed they are used, make much difference in consumer behavior (Ainsworth, 1989; Smith & Rogers, 1994).

Most psychologists agree that behavior changes most readily when people are aware of the process (Chapter 8). Claims that we can learn new information by playing audiotapes while sleeping are without support (Swets & Bjork, 1990; Wood, Bootzin, Kihlstrom, & Schacter, 1992). Perhaps you remember the fear expressed several years ago that heavy-metal rock-and-roll bands were corrupting their listeners by placing subliminal messages—backward—in their records, urging the young to worship the devil or kill themselves. Again, little evidence indicates that hidden messages influence the behavior of a listener (Begg, Needham, & Bookbinder, 1993; Staum & Brotons, 1992).

■ **dissociation**
splitting of consciousness into separate streams, with little or no communication between or among them

Dissociation.   Dissociation refers to the splitting of consciousness into separate streams, with little or no communication between or among them (Crabtree, 1992; Ellenberger, 1970). It is related to Freud's concept of the motivated unconscious because both explain why people have motives, thoughts, and feelings of which they are unaware. But whereas Freud's concept regards consciousness as unitary, dissociation is based on the assumption that consciousness can be split into different parts. The Freudian theory of the mind is often captured with the metaphor of an iceberg: The part below the surface is the unconscious mind, and the tip of the iceberg is the conscious mind. In contrast, the notion of dissociation sees the mind as a collection of icebergs.

Dissociative experiences are relatively common, according to a survey of adults in Winnipeg (Ross, Joshi, & Currie, 1990). Figure 6.1 presents the findings that a number of people report discontinuities in memory, consciousness, or identity. Psychological disorders characterized by dissociation, such as multiple personality disorder, are relatively rare (Chapter 13). Perhaps it is easier to understand these disorders if you think of them as dissociative experiences carried to an extreme.

Figure 6.1
Dissociative Experiences in the General Population. This chart shows the proportion of everyday adults who reported that each of these dissociative experiences occurred to them with at least occasional frequency (Ross, Joshi, & Currie, 1990).

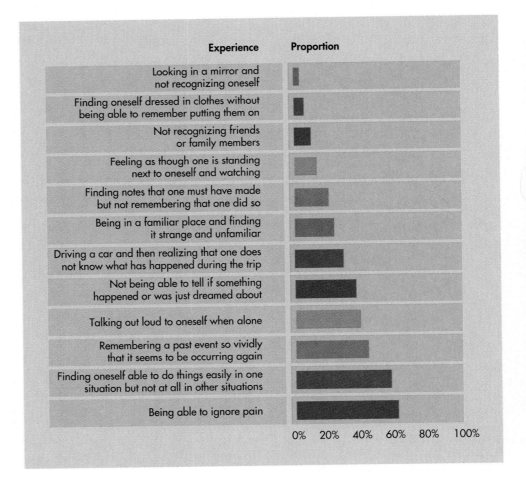

Sleep and Dreams

On average, we spend one-third of our lives in the state of consciousness known as sleep. When we sleep, we experience a reduction in our alertness, awareness, and perception of ongoing events. While sleeping, we are not conscious of being asleep. At the same time, we know that sleep is a state of consciousness with special characteristics that make it different from normal waking consciousness. Most notably, we dream while we sleep. As discussed in Chapter 4, the limbic system is responsible for sleep phenomena (Boral, 1986).

All of us sleep and dream. Psychologists have studied sleep and dreams extensively, yet answers to some of the most basic questions remain elusive. For example, the functions served by sleeping are not clear. Neither is the significance of dreams. Researchers have made some progress in describing the basic nature of sleep and dreams. This section first discusses the findings from this descriptive work, then considers theories about the function and significance of sleep and dreams, and finally covers sleep disorders.

Sleep research.   The scientific study of sleep became possible with the invention of the **electroencephalogram (EEG),** a recording device that measures electrical activity in the brain (Chapter 4). Electrodes are attached to a person's skull, and electrical patterns are recorded over time. The EEG was first available in the 1920s, and in the following decade it was used to measure brain activity during sleep (Loomis, Harvey, & Hobart, 1937). Researchers discovered that the sleeping individual's brain waves changed in regular ways throughout the night. From the very beginning of EEG research, investigators suspected that sleep could be described as a sequence of stages.

Other devices soon became available for investigating changes during sleep. The **electromyogram (EMG)** is a device similar to the EEG, except that its electrodes are attached underneath one's chin, where they record electrical activity of the muscles. So, the EMG provides information about one's muscular tension or relaxation.

The **electrooculogram (EOG)** is yet another recording device, with electrodes attached near the outer corners of the eyes. The EOG measures the movement of the eyes. As will be discussed shortly, eye movements during sleep are associated with a particular sleep stage.

Researchers typically study sleep in what is called a sleep laboratory, to which subjects report at the end of a day. The subjects prepare for bed just like you might,

■ **electroencephalogram (EEG)**
recording device that measures general patterns of electrical activity in the brain

■ **electromyogram (EMG)**
recording device that measures electrical activity of the muscles

■ **electrooculogram (EOG)**
recording device that measures eye movements

On average, we spend one-third of our lives in the state of consciousness known as sleep.

Researchers record eye movements during different stages of sleep with a device called the electrooculogram (EOG).

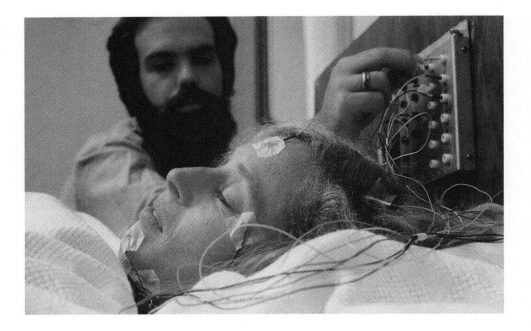

except that they allow electrodes to be attached to their scalp and face. Most individuals have no trouble relaxing and falling asleep. As a caution, though, many sleep researchers ask their subjects to sleep in the lab for several nights in a row, and use the first night simply to let them get used to the arrangements. On subsequent nights, various recordings are made over the duration of their sleep.

Stages of sleep.   From research in sleep laboratories, we have learned that sleep is characterized by a series of stages (see Figure 6.2). When we first lie down before falling asleep, we are in a state of consciousness described as relaxed wakefulness. In this state, the EEG pattern indicates a type of brain activity known as alpha waves, which are associated with relaxation. To the degree that a person in this presleep state begins to think about problems or tasks, these alpha waves are disrupted. In relaxed wakefulness, both the EMG and the EOG show considerable activity, indicating muscular tension and movements of the eyes.

If a person stays relaxed, eventually he or she will fall asleep. We speak about drifting off to sleep, but sleep researchers have found that people enter sleep suddenly. The first stage of sleep is called Stage 1 sleep and lasts only a few minutes. In Stage 1 sleep, a pattern of brain activity known as theta waves is detected by the EEG. Our sleeper in Stage 1 sleep is easily awakened.

Next, the sleeper enters Stage 2 sleep, which is deeper and marked by bursts of brain activity called sleep spindles. These bursts of activity vary but occur about every 15 seconds on average. Also present are K-complex waves: large, slow patterns of brain activity. Muscular tension is now greatly reduced. The eyes do not move.

After about 20 minutes of Stage 2 sleep, the sleeper passes through 30 minutes of Stage 3 sleep. Here the EEG detects the presence of yet another type of brain activity, known as delta waves. In Stage 3 sleep, other types of brain waves are present as well. A person's temperature, breathing, and pulse slow down. It is difficult to awaken someone from Stage 3 sleep.

Stage 4 sleep follows next, the deepest sleep we experience. The EEG shows mostly delta waves. The sleeper's muscles are completely relaxed. The eyes do not move. From the time our sleeper entered Stage 1 sleep and progressed to Stage 4 sleep, about one hour has passed. The sleeper will not stay in Stage 4 throughout the night but will pass back through Stage 3 and into Stage 2 sleep. Then the cycle repeats. In the course of a night, we go through the different stages of sleep four or five times.

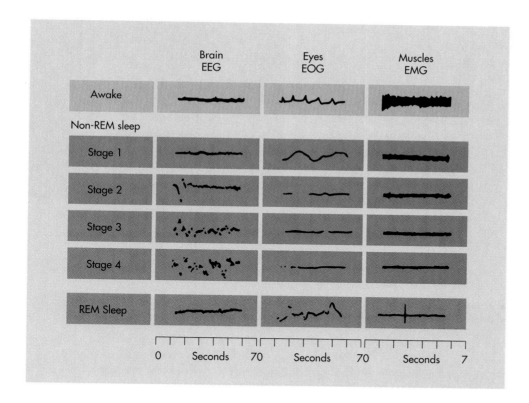

Figure 6.2
Stages of Sleep. Researchers
have discovered that sleep consists
of a series of stages, each with
characteristic patterns of brain
activity (measured by the EEG),
eye movements (measured by the
EOG), and muscular activity
(measured by the EMG).

There is one more important aspect of the sleep cycle. When an individual has passed through the first cycle of sleep stages and is back in Stage 2 sleep, yet another type of sleep becomes apparent. The sleeper's eyes begin to dart back and forth rapidly beneath closed eyelids. This phenomenon is appropriately called **REM (rapid eye movement) sleep.** REM sleep was first discovered in the 1950s (Aserinsky & Kleitman, 1953), and it has so intrigued sleep researchers that the other periods of sleep are collectively called **non-REM sleep.**

During REM sleep, brain waves again become active, heart rate and respiration speed up, and genitals are aroused. But our sleeper is also deeply asleep and quite difficult to awaken. Muscular movement below the neck is inhibited. Soon Stage 2 sleep is resumed, and then the individual passes into Stage 3 sleep, and the entire cycle is repeated. With each cycle, deep sleep becomes less likely and REM periods increase in length. The first REM period can be as brief as 30 seconds; later REM periods can last as long as one hour.

REM sleep originally attracted the interest of researchers because of the presence of dreams during this period (Hobson & Stickgold, 1994). A person awakened in the midst of REM sleep usually reports a vivid dream. Dreams can and do occur during all stages of sleep, but those in non-REM periods are less vivid and more jumbled.

The nature of dreams. The close association between vivid dreams and REM sleep gives researchers a convenient way of studying dreams. Subjects are asked to fall asleep, are monitored until the EOG detects eye movement, and then are awakened and questioned. Recall of dreams is very good in these circumstances. From research like this, psychologists know that everyone dreams every night. People who report that they do not dream really mean that they do not remember their dreams.

The experience of dreaming has five characteristic features (Hobson, 1988):

- Illogical content and organization
- Complex sensory impressions
- Uncritical acceptance of the dream as if it were part of everyday experience

■ **REM (rapid eye movement) sleep**
stage of sleep in which the eyes
dart back and forth rapidly

■ **non-REM sleep**
all stages of sleep other than
REM sleep

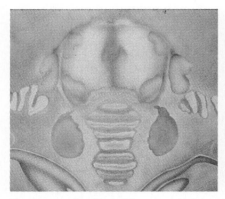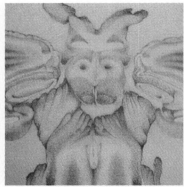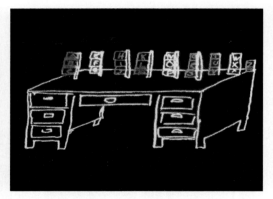

Dreams are often illogical in content and organization, but people try to understand what they mean. Shown here are the attempts by several artists to depict dream imagery.

■ Emotion so intense that it can terminate the dream
■ Difficulty in remembering a dream once it is over

Not all dreams have these five characteristics, but we are all familiar with these aspects.

Time in dreams corresponds fairly closely to time in waking life. In other words, when people are awakened early in a REM period, the dream they report is very brief, and when people are awakened late in a REM period, the dream they report is correspondingly longer. The particular movement of eyes during REM sleep bears no relationship to the content of dreams. When REM sleep was first described, theorists hypothesized that one's rapid eye movements corresponded to back-and-forth scanning of visual scenes in a dream (Dement, 1974), but subsequent research failed to support this intriguing possibility (Borbely, 1986).

Investigators have cataloged the types of dreams people report (Hall & Van de Castle, 1966). Many dreams are mundane, containing few bizarre or unusual elements. Strange dreams may be easier to remember, meaning that we overestimate their frequency (Chapter 9). Most dreams contain at least one person familiar to the dreamer. Physical activity and movements are usually effortless. Dreams with negative themes, like unhappiness and defeat, are somewhat more frequent than those with positive themes.

A **nightmare** is a dream with frightening content, and it should be distinguished from what is called a **sleep terror,** in which we wake up in a state of great fright and confusion. Nightmares usually occur during REM sleep, typically in one of the periods toward the end of the night. We awaken with a start and know instantly that we have had a bad dream.

In contrast, sleep terrors occur during a period of non-REM sleep, usually Stage 3 or Stage 4. Again, we abruptly awaken, but we are disoriented, perhaps for several minutes. During this time, we are in a panic, showing all the signs of the body's emergency reaction (Chapter 4). We do not know where we are or what we are doing. We have no memory of a dream. Sleep terrors seem to result from a blurring of states of consciousness (Cohen, 1979). Our mind suddenly becomes aware that our body is asleep and not moving, and the realization creates panic.

Sleep and dreams across the life span.   The nature of sleep and dreams changes as we grow older (see Figure 6.3). Infants sleep as many as 16 hours out of every 24, and half of this time is spent in REM sleep. Infants presumably dream but only gradually learn to distinguish dreaming as a special state (Maurer & Maurer, 1988). Young adults sleep 7 or 8 hours a night, of which 20 percent is REM sleep.

People in their sixties or seventies typically sleep only 6 hours a night, and only 15 percent of this is REM sleep (Bliwise, 1993). Further, at about age 60, a substantial

■ **nightmare**
dream with frightening content

■ **sleep terror**
awakening during non-REM sleep in a state of panic and disorientation

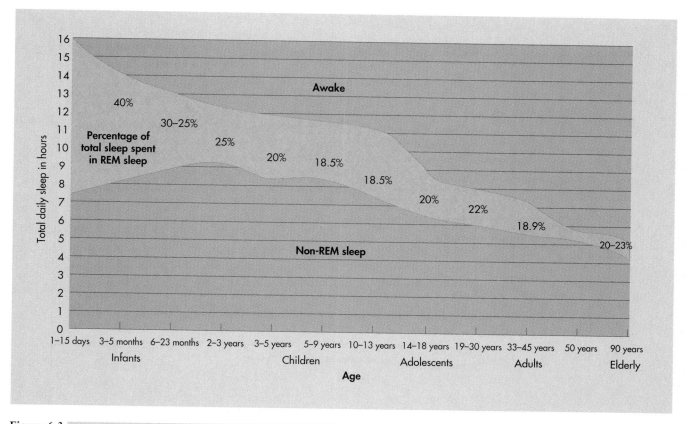

Figure 6.3
Sleep Across the Life Span. As people age, they spend less time sleeping and proportionately less time in REM sleep.

number of adults begin to complain that they do not get a good night's sleep. They sleep not only fewer hours but also more fitfully. The deepest stages of sleep shorten dramatically. These patterns provide clues about the functions of sleep and dreams (Cartwright, 1978), although theorists are still looking for answers.

Functions of sleep. People deprived of sleep become tired and irritable. Prolonged sleep deprivation can impair the performance of skilled tasks and increase hallucinations and delusions (Borbely, 1986). People who habitually sleep fewer than 7 hours per night do not live as long as people who get 7 or 8 hours of sleep (Kripke, Simons, Garfinkel, & Hammond, 1979). Interestingly, people who sleep more than 10 hours per night also tend to have a shortened life, although we must be careful not to interpret this correlation as a causal link; perhaps people who are unhealthy sleep longer and die sooner.

On the whole, sleep appears to be associated with psychological and physical well-being. Why? Different theories suggest different answers. One possibility is that we sleep in order to restore our bodies. Whatever wear and tear accumulates during our waking lives is repaired while we sleep.

The function of sleep is probably more complicated than this simple theory suggests. Individuals deprived of sleep for several days at a time require only a few extra hours of sleep to return to their normal cycle. In a celebrated case, a college student named Randy Gardner earned a place in the *Guiness Book of World Records* by staying awake for 264 hours and 11 minutes (Gulevich, Dement, & Johnson, 1966). He then slept for about 15 hours, woke up with no ill effects, and resumed his regular habit of sleeping 8 hours per night. If sleeping did nothing but restore wear and tear, you would expect Gardner to need more than a single extended period of sleep to feel rested.

Mancia (1981) proposed that sleep in adults is a holdover from the psychological life of the fetus in the womb. According to this theory, a sleeplike state characterizes fetal life and is an evolved psychological mechanism that allows the developing individual to be responsive to stimuli and integrate sensory experiences with bodily movements. Sleep continues throughout adulthood, but no specific function is served.

Other theorists take the provocative position that sleep has no inherent function at any point in development. Instead, sleeping is an evolutionary byproduct that no longer serves its original purpose, which was to keep our distant ancestors quiet and out of danger. Or perhaps sleep allows us to conserve our body's resources (Webb, 1975); studies of brain metabolism during sleep show that people use less energy while asleep than while awake (Madsen, 1993).

Support for an evolutionary view of sleep also comes from studies of the sleep patterns of different species. Mammals, birds, and reptiles all sleep, but they do so in characteristic ways, implying that sleep has become adapted to the niche of each type of creature (Borbely, 1986). For instance, rats sleep only 10 minutes at a time; then they awaken for an equally short period. Cows continue to chew their cud while asleep. Dolphins sleep with only one cerebral hemisphere at a time, an intriguing pattern perhaps related to living in the water and needing to be awake in order to remember to come to the surface and breathe.

Still another hypothesis about the function of sleep is that we consolidate newly acquired information during REM sleep (Li, Wu, Shao, & Liu, 1991; Valatx, 1989). If research subjects, by being awakened every time their EOG indicates eye movements, are deprived of REM sleep in a laboratory, they show deficits in retaining material they have recently learned (e.g., Dujardin, Guerrien, & Leconte, 1990). Similarly, if subjects are not allowed to sleep they do not as readily retain new information (Karni, Tanne, Rubenstein, Askenasy, & Sagi, 1994).

Individuals who have learned new skills or information increase the proportion of their REM sleep. For example, college students display an increase in REM sleep for several days following study for final exams (Smith & Lapp, 1991). Individuals who receive intensive training in a skill like Morse code before falling asleep show an increase in REM sleep (Mandai, Guerrien, Sockeel, Dujardin, & Leconte, 1989). Those who best learn their lessons show the greatest increase in REM sleep.

The details of what happens to memory during sleep are not yet known. Some theorists have proposed that learned associations are strenghtened during sleep, whereas other theorists have proposed that less relevant material is obliterated (Kudler, 1989). Still other theorists have hypothesized that information is integrated with emotion during sleep, thereby increasing its retention and later accessibility (Cai, 1991).

Dolphins sleep with one cerebral hemisphere at a time, a pattern perhaps related to living in water and needing to come to the surface to breathe.

Here are some further facts about sleep and memory. Information presented just prior to the onset of sleep is not remembered particularly well (Wyatt & Bootzin, 1994). This finding is probably familiar to you when you stop and realize that you cannot remember exactly when you do fall asleep. A form of amnesia characterizes the onset of sleep. Also, the beneficial effects of sleep on memory take several days to become evident, implying that the process is a complex one that unfolds over time (Nielsen & Powell, 1989). Given the amount of time needed for memory consolidation, the process may involve relatively slow-acting hormonal changes in addition to more rapidly-acting neurological ones (Severino, Bucci, & Creelman, 1989).

Functions of dreams.   Although dreams are as fascinating as sleep, psychologists do not have a complete understanding of their functions. Freud (1900) proposed that people dream in order to maintain the state of sleep. In our dreams, he hypothesized, we guard against threatening thoughts that might awaken us. If outside distractions like loud noises occur, we can sometimes incorporate them into our dreams and keep on sleeping (Dement & Wolpert, 1958). If reprehensible thoughts occur to us while dreaming, we disguise them. Freud's theory explains why dreams are incoherent—their confusing aspects constitute their disguise. He distinguished the **manifest content** of dreams—the images and events of which the dreamer is aware—from their **latent content**—the underlying significance of these images and events. The manifest content is not psychologically meaningful; rather, it is the latent content that reveals something important about the dreamer.

Here is an example from Freud (1916, p. 122):

> A lady who, though she was still young, had been married for many years, had the following dream: She was at the theatre with her husband. One side of the theatre was completely empty. Her husband told her that Elise L. and her fiancé had wanted to go too, but only had been able to get bad seats and of course they could not take those. She thought it would not really have done any harm if they had.

Using other information provided by this woman, Freud argued that the details in her dream all refer to being in a hurry. In actual life, she had recently attended a show and had bought her tickets so early that she had to pay a booking fee. However, there had been no need to pay extra for the tickets because the theater was half-empty for the show. Her friend Elise was the same age but had waited ten years longer than the dreamer to get married. Her fiancé was an attractive man, showing again that there is no need to be in such a hurry. Freud concluded that the manifest content of this dream disguised the dreamer's regret about marrying so early, as well as her jealousy of her friend Elise.

According to Freud, we can understand people's unconscious motives if we see through the disguise of their dreams. Indeed, Freud labeled dreams the "road to the unconscious" and incorporated dream interpretation into psychoanalytic therapy (Chapter 14).

Other theorists suggest that dreams represent an attempt to come to grips with unresolved challenges faced in waking life. In support of this idea is the fact that we often dream about ongoing matters in our lives. Whether these dreams actually help solve problems from our waking life is unclear (Dement, 1974).

There are isolated examples of dreams that solved problems faced by a dreamer (Krippner & Hughes, 1970). Elias Howe, who invented the sewing machine, had been working for some time on the idea of a sewing machine but could not figure out how to thread the needle. In a dream, he was taken captive by a savage tribe, and the tribe demanded that he create a workable sewing machine within 24 hours. He failed and was about to be put to death. As his captors approached him, they carried sharp spears with holes in their tips. This image provided the solution Howe needed—putting the

■ **manifest content**
dream images and events of which the dreamer is aware

■ **latent content**
underlying significance to the dreamer of a dream's manifest content

hole for the thread in the tip of the sewing machine needle. Cohen (1979) speculated that dreams best solve problems phrased in terms of visual imagery, as opposed to words or mathematics (Chapter 9).

Yet another explanation of dreams, the **activation-synthesis theory,** proposes that dreams are not themselves significant. Rather, a dream represents a person's interpretation of essentially random activity in the brain stem during sleep (Hobson & McCarley, 1977; Kahn & Hobson, 1993). By this view, dreaming is the same as any cognitive activity in which we use material stored in memory to make sense of incoming information (Chapter 9). The information interpreted in a dream is random, and so dreams make little sense. Dreamers do the best job they can in making their experiences coherent but are handicapped by the essentially random nature of dreams (Bulkley, 1991).

The psychoanalytic explanation of dreams and the activation-synthesis theory differ with respect to the presumed cause of dreams (Colace, Violani, & Solano, 1993). Psychoanalytic theory regards dreams as unconscious wishes; the activation-synthesis theory explains them as by-products of brain activity. Both theories agree that something is revealed about the dreamer by the nature of his or her dreams, but differ in the reasons why. Psychoanalytic theory looks beneath the manifest content of the dream to infer the dreamer's motives, whereas the activation-synthesis theory looks directly at how an individual interprets the dream (Foulkes, 1985).

Sleep disorders.   Among the most common psychological disorders are those involving problems with sleep (Kerr & Jowett, 1994). Two broad categories are distinguished: **Dyssomnias** refer to problems with the amount, quality, or timing of sleep, whereas **parasomnias** involve abnormal events during sleep (American Psychiatric Association, 1994). Sleep disorders also accompany a variety of other psychological disorders (Dealberto, 1992; Nofzinger, Buysse, Reynolds, & Kupfer, 1993; Vgontzas, Kales, Bixler, & Vela-Bueno, 1993).

Dyssomnias.   Like sleep itself, problems with sleep have a developmental path; different problems tend to occur at different points in life. These disorders are instructive as examples of a biopsychosocial perspective. For instance, there are more age changes for

■ activation-synthesis theory
theory proposing that dreams are not themselves significant but represent a person's interpretation of random activity in the brain stem during sleep

■ dyssomnias
problems with the amount, quality, or timing of sleep

■ parasomnias
abnormal events during sleep

Some theorists see dreams as expressing unconscious wishes; other theorists see them as the byproduct of brain activity. Both approaches agree that something is revealed about the dreamer by the nature of his or her dreams, but they differ in their views of what is revealed. Psychoanalytic theory regards the latent content of dreams as an expression of unconscious motives, whereas activation-synthesis theory looks at how the individual interprets the dream after it has occurred.

men than women. The nervous systems of men are more susceptible to problems, resulting in more sleep disorders.

The most common dyssomnia is **insomnia,** a problem in initiating sleep, maintaining sleep, or not feeling rested after sleep. Complaints of daytime fatigue or remarks by others that the individual is irritable or impaired are clues that insomnia is present. Insomnia occurs among 20 to 40 percent of adults in the contemporary United States, and its likelihood increases with age. Its most common form involves difficulty falling asleep. The insomniac is tense, anxious, and preoccupied upon retiring and may not fall asleep for hours.

Insomnia has diverse causes: stressful life events, jet lag, an irregular schedule of activity and rest, medical conditions marked by pain or discomfort, the use of various drugs, and psychological problems like anxiety or depression. A poor sleeping environment can also contribute to insomnia.

Treatment takes several forms. The insomniac is advised to increase daytime activities, to exercise, and to establish a regular sleep-wake routine. Naps should be avoided. The setting in which one sleeps should be made dark, quiet, and otherwise comfortable. Sleeping pills, although frequently prescribed, are not the treatment of choice because of the risk of abuse and further disruption of the sleep cycle (Allain, 1990; Dahl, 1992).

Hypersomnia refers to excessive daytime sleepiness or sleep attacks not accounted for by an inadequate amount of sleep. It also includes a prolonged transition to the fully awake state, a phenomenon known as sleep drunkenness. About 1 to 2 percent of individuals experience hypersomnia at some point in life. Most cases are caused by physical problems, substance abuse, or medication side effects, which are targeted for change in treatment (Dressler & Schönle, 1989).

A mismatch between a normal sleep-wake schedule for a person's environment and his or her natural sleep-wake pattern is called a **sleep-wake schedule disorder.** It can produce insomnia or hypersomnia. Lifestyle seems to be the overriding cause of sleep-wake schedule disorder. For example, an individual whose shifts at work constantly change is at risk for this disorder, which typically goes away when a regular sleep-wake schedule is established.

Parasomnias. The second class of sleep disorders includes abnormal events that occur during sleep. Nightmares and sleep terrors have already been mentioned. When these are frequent and/or particularly distressing to an individual, psychologists call it **dream anxiety disorder** and **sleep terror disorder,** respectively (Blanes, Burgess, Marks, & Gill, 1993; Taylor, 1993). Both are more common among children than adults. Dream anxiety disorder afflicts about 5 percent of the general population, whereas sleep terror disorder occurs in about 1 percent.

There are several possible causes of dream anxiety disorder: stressful life events, conflicts in everyday life, fevers, delirium, drug intoxication, and drug withdrawal. Treatment consists of providing reassurance on the one hand while minimizing stress on the other.

Sleep terror disorder has a biological basis. An immature nervous system is a risk factor, a fact which explains why this problem is usually outgrown. Treatment involves safety precautions so that the individual does not injure him- or herself upon awakening. Minor tranquilizers like Valium may also be prescribed.

In **sleepwalking disorder,** the individual arises from bed during sleep and walks about with a blank, staring face. The sleepwalker is unresponsive to others and is able to be awakened only with great difficulty. Upon awakening, the individual typically has no memory of the episode. Theorists believe that sleepwalking is related to sleep terrors, and the generalizations offered about sleep terrors apply to sleepwalking disorder as well.

Sleep apnea is a temporary failure of breathing during sleep. It afflicts mainly middle-age men who are overweight and have a history of high blood pressure and snoring. Sleep apnea is not fatal, but it is highly distressing to one's bed partner. Its mechanisms are unknown, although some have speculated that it is related to the phenomenon of **crib death** (or **sudden infant death syndrome),** in which an infant dies in his or her sleep for no apparent reason except that breathing stops.

■ **insomnia**
problem in initiating sleep, maintaining sleep, or not feeling rested after sleep

■ **hypersomnia**
excessive daytime sleepiness or sleep attacks not accounted for by an inadequate amount of sleep

■ **sleep-wake schedule disorder**
mismatch between a normal sleep-wake schedule for a person's environment and his or her natural sleep-wake pattern

■ **dream anxiety disorder**
sleep disorder characterized by frequent and/or particularly distressing nightmares

■ **sleep terror disorder**
sleep disorder characterized by frequent and/or particularly distressing sleep terrors

■ **sleepwalking disorder**
sleep disorder in which the individual arises from bed during sleep yet is unresponsive to others and able to be awakened only with difficulty

■ **sleep apnea**
temporary failure of breathing during sleep

■ **crib death; sudden infant death syndrome**
the death of an infant during sleep for no apparent reason except that breathing stops

Crib death is more likely to occur in cultures in which infants do not sleep with their parents (McKenna, 1990; McKenna & Mosko, 1991). The physical presence of an adult helps the infant regulate biological processes—in particular, breathing—during sleep. Sensory cues from adults, such as odor, presumably trigger an evolved psychological mechanism that helps infants overcome physiological crises during sleep, such as not breathing, that their immature systems cannot accomplish on their own.

Let me describe one more sleep disorder (see Table 6.2). **Enuresis** is repeated bedwetting after bladder control is achieved, which typically occurs between the ages of 2 and 3. This parasomnia is much more common among boys than girls. Perhaps 10 to 15 percent of children between the ages of 3 and 12 wet their beds, as do 1 to 3 percent of young adults. Several risk factors have been identified, including a family history of enuresis, a small bladder capacity, neurological immaturity, and the occurrence of stressful life events. Besides waiting for enuresis to resolve itself, psychologists can pursue more aggressive treatment. Education and reassurance that it will be outgrown should be provided to the individual and his or her family. Behavior therapy is sometimes helpful, as is the use of imipramine, an antidepressant medication that affects neurotransmitter activity (Chapter 14).

Disorders of Consciousness: Organic Syndromes

One of the best reasons for believing that consciousness has a biological basis is that neurological damage or dysfunction can produce profound changes in consciousness (Frith, 1992). Clinicians have described several different **organic syndromes,** constellations of psychological symptoms associated with neurological problems (American Psychiatric Association, 1987). The existence of organic syndromes like delirium and dementia underscores the importance of an intact nervous system to normal waking consciousness (Reber, 1992).

Delirium.   The syndrome of **delirium** refers to an overall impairment of thinking that has a biological cause. More specifically, delirious individuals show:

■ a reduced ability to pay attention to external stimuli
■ problems in shifting attention from one stimulus to another

■ **enuresis**
repeated bedwetting after bladder control is achieved

■ **organic syndromes**
constellations of psychological symptoms associated with neurological problems

■ **delirium**
overall impairment of thinking due to biological causes imposed on an otherwise intact nervous system

---

Table 6.2   Summary: Sleep Disorders

Dyssomnias refer to problems with the amount, quality, or timing of sleep, and parasomnias involve abnormal events during sleep.

Disorder	Characterization
Insomnia	Problem in initiating sleep, maintaining sleep, or not feeling rested after sleep
Hypersomnia	Excessive daytime sleepiness or sleep attacks not accounted for by an inadequate amount of sleep
Sleep-wake schedule disorder	Mismatch between a normal sleep-wake schedule for a person's environment and his or her natural sleep-wake pattern
Dream anxiety disorder	Frequent and/or particularly distressing nightmares
Sleep terror disorder	Frequent and/or particularly distressing sleep terrors
Sleepwalking disorder	Episodes of arising from bed during sleep yet being unresponsive to others and able to be awakened only with difficulty
Sleep apnea	Temporary failure of breathing during sleep
Crib death; sudden infant death syndrome	Death of an infant during sleep for no apparent reason except that breathing stops
Enuresis	Repeated bedwetting after bladder control is achieved

- disorganized thinking, as shown by rambling or incoherent speech
- a reduced level of consciousness, ranging from drowsiness to stupor
- sensory misperceptions, such as mistaking one stimulus for another, like hearing a door slamming as a pistol shot (or vice versa)
- hyperactivity or sluggishness, and rapid changes back and forth
- a disorientation with respect to time, place, and person; the individual may not know the time or date, where he or she happens to be, or even who he or she is
- impaired memory

Delirium usually has a sudden onset and a fluctuating course. It tends not to last very long, usually a few days and rarely more than a month. Children and the elderly are most at risk. Delirious people are incapacitated (Lipowski, 1992). Injuries are common as they blunder about the world. They are unable to cooperate with treatment or even to report exactly what is going on.

Delirium has a variety of causes (Sitzman, 1993). Infectious illnesses can bring it about; most of us have been a bit delirious when we have run a high fever for an extended period. Metabolic disorders frequently produce delirium, as do thiamine deficiency and diseases of the liver or kidneys. Cardiopulmonary insufficiency can make a person delirious, as can the side effects of some medications. Withdrawal from certain drugs, notably alcohol, can also result in delirium.

Studies suggest that delirium results not from any specifically located brain mechanism but rather from an overall slowing of function that is initally triggered by problems in a variety of brain regions (Trzepacz, 1994). For example, brain imaging studies show that delirious individuals evidence a reduction in brain metabolism, and EEG studies similarly show a reduction in brain wave activity (Lipowski, 1991). Also, delirious individuals often have reduced blood flow to the brain (Deutsch, 1992).

Dementia.   Like delirium, **dementia** refers to an overall impairment of cognitive functioning, including memory. There is an important distinction, however. In delirium, an imposition has been made on an otherwise intact nervous system. In dementia, the nervous system as a whole has been compromised, by illness or injury. Delirium is reversible, whereas dementia is not (Blass, Nolan, Black, & Kurita, 1991).

■ **dementia**
overall impairment of thinking due to the compromising of the nervous system as a whole by illness or injury

Delirium refers to an overall impairment of thinking and is reversible. Dementia is similar, except the impairment is due to a compromised nervous system and cannot be reversed.

In dementia, both short-term and long-term memory can be affected (Chapter 9). People with dementia also have difficulties with abstract thinking and judgment. Their personalities change. They may become apathetic or withdrawn. Sometimes personality changes may involve an exaggeration of previously existing traits. For example, people who were extraverted become impulsive, or those who were cautious become paranoid.

The course of dementia varies according to its specific cause (Chui, 1989; Perry & Perry, 1993). Though at one time the term *dementia* was reserved for conditions that worsened over time, today psychologists use the term more generally to refer to symptoms existing at a given time. However, generalizations can still be offered. Dementia is most likely to occur among the elderly, the result of a neurological illness or injury.

One such illness is Alzheimer's disease, characterized by the death of neurons throughout the brain but particularly in the hippocampus, which is involved in the processing of memories (Chapter 4). The most striking loss of neurons in this illness involve those that communicate with one another by secreting the neurotransmitter **acetylcholine.** At present, there is no cure or effective treatment for Alzheimer's disease, although drugs such as tacrine may slow its progression (Knapp, Knopman, Soloman, & Pendlebury, 1994).

In some cases, such as following a blow to the head, the onset of dementia is sudden. In other cases, as with a neurological disease, the onset is gradual, and people are aware of their loss of cognitive abilities. Depression is a common consequence, as individuals react to the loss of their intellect just as they would to the loss of a job or loved one (Chapter 13).

Interventions can help the person compensate for memory losses (Zencius, Wesolowski, & Burke, 1990). For example, people in the early stages of Alzheimer's disease may find it helpful if large signs are posted around their house reminding them of things to do and when to do them. Routines can be kept the same to avoid the confusions that arise from novel demands.

■ **acetylcholine**
neutrotransmitter involved in Alzheimer's disease

Amnestic syndrome.   **Amnestic syndrome** is memory impairment caused by a neurological problem. It is not associated with problems in attention or with general difficulties in thinking and judgment. Amnesia also results from psychological causes, such as a severe emotional trauma that leads a person to repress its occurrence and all other memories associated with it. The common causes of amnestic syndrome are head trauma, loss of oxygen to the brain, infections that occasionally occur with herpes simplex, and cerebral stroke. Other causes include thiamine deficiency and chronic alcohol use, which produces Korsakoff's syndrome.

Amnestic syndrome is often associated with specific lesions in the hippocampus and amygdala (Hommer, Weingartner, & Breier, 1993). The hippocampus is involved in the processing of memories, and the amygdala plays a role in the regulation of emotions (Chapter 4). Memories are often linked to feelings, and normal functioning of the amygdala may be necessary for full access to these memories.

■ **amnestic syndrome**
memory impairment caused by a neurological problem

Organic personality syndrome.   Sometimes the most striking consequence of neurological damage is a persistent change in the individual's personality. This change is referred to as **organic personality syndrome** and is shown by one or more of the following:

■ Instability of moods, including rapid shifts from a normal state to depression, anxiety, or irritability
■ Outbursts of aggression or rage that are disproportionate to whatever situations brought them about
■ Grossly impaired social judgment in such areas as spending money or engaging in sexual activity

■ **organic personality syndrome**
persistent change in one's personality due to neurological damage

■ Apathy and indifference
■ Suspicion and paranoia

Particular symptoms depend on the extent and location of the neurological damage.

The causes of organic personality syndrome include damage to the structure of the brain, such as a tumor pressing on neural tissue, head trauma, and circulatory disease. Some people with epilepsy develop organic personality syndrome. Less common causes include endocrine disorders and the ingestion of psychoactive substances.

People with organic personality disorder are usually unaware that their personalities are different (Prigatano & Schacter, 1991). They might be conscious of their environment and of their wants and needs, yet unaware that they now have trouble planning ahead and monitoring ongoing behavior. When these problems are pointed out, they seem to understand what is being said but are indifferent:

> To all outward appearances, Elliot is a perfectly normal middle-aged business-man. Despite an operation a decade ago for removal of a benign brain tumor the size of a small orange, he remains intelligent and seemingly rational, with a wry sense of humor. Yet his behavior makes it clear that there is something very wrong. After years of rock-solid competence, Elliot now has trouble keeping appointments and making decisions. He has squandered much of his life savings on a series of bad investments. And, strangest of all, the very fact that his behavior is self-destructive doesn't seem to bother him—and he keeps on making the same mistakes. (Lemonick, 1995a, p. 44)

Stuss and Benson (1986) made sense of such disturbed awareness by proposing that organic personality syndrome involves a specific disruption of self-awareness but not other forms of consciousness.

The previous discussion of dementia noted that personality changes could be part of the syndrome. The difference is one of relative emphasis: memory versus personality disturbance. Sometimes as a neurological disease progresses, the description must be changed from organic personality syndrome to dementia, as intellectual functions are increasingly compromised (see Table 6.3).

Individuals with organic personality syndrome may look completely normal. They can work and maintain social relationships. But outbursts of anger, mood fluctuations, and impaired judgment make it difficult for people around them, especially if those persons do not fully understand the organic basis of the syndrome (Lezak, 1978). Caretakers, chiefly parents or spouses, can become depressed. Marital problems are frequent. Children of a person with this syndrome are also vulnerable to the effects of

Table 6.3 Summary: Organic Disorders

Disorder	Characterization
Delirium	Overall impairment of thinking due to biological causes imposed on an otherwise intact nervous system
Dementia	Overall impairment of thinking due to the compromising of the nervous system as a whole by illness or injury
Amnestic syndrome	Memory impairment caused by a neurological problem
Organic personality syndrome	Persistent change in one's personality due to neurological damage

living with an unpredictable and uncontrollable parent, especially when they are too young to comprehend the notion of neurological damage.

DELIBERATE ALTERATION OF CONSCIOUSNESS

People have long found ways to deliberately alter consciousness, changing their perception, mood, and behaviors, leaving behind undesired states for those that promise to be pleasurable, exciting, interesting, or profound. This section discusses four ways to alter consciousness: daydreams, meditation, hypnosis, and psychoactive drugs.

Daydreams

■ **daydreaming**
fantasizing that one deliberately undertakes while awake

Daydreaming refers to the wishes and fantasies a person deliberately entertains while awake. In discussing daydreams, Freud (1908) proposed that only unhappy individuals shift their attention inward and away from the external world. But when Jerome L. Singer (1966, 1975, 1984) systematically investigated daydreaming, he found little evidence for equating daydreaming with unhappiness. Some daydreamers are happy, some unhappy—just like people in general. Indeed, Singer discovered that occasional daydreaming is almost universal. For most people, daydreaming begins in early childhood and lasts throughout their life. Considerable variation exists in the amount of time people devote to daydreaming (Lynn & Ruhe, 1986). Some individuals spend as many as half their waking hours engaged in daydreaming. Others spend much less time.

Daydreams can provide relief from stress or the opportunity to think through solutions to life's problems.

Contents of daydreams.   What specifically do people daydream about? According to Singer, the following categories capture most daydreams:

- Going back over what one should have said or done in actual situations
- Organizing and rehearsing future events
- Experiencing bizarre images like those in dreams
- Engaging in fantasy, imagining adventures and triumphs

People show consistent preferences for types of daydreaming and even for specific daydreams. Singer (1966) described several ongoing daydreams of his own that began in his childhood. In one, he is a great athlete. In another, he is a statesman. In a third, he imagines himself a composer.

Researchers have concluded that the content of daydreams is often consistent with other aspects of the person's life and psychological makeup. For example:

- Individuals who are unemotional and unexpressive in their everyday lives show reduced levels of daydreaming, as well as an absence of strong feelings in the daydreams they do have (Kirmayer & Robbins, 1993).
- The daydreams of those who are deaf often involve sign language (Anthony & Gibbins, 1992).
- People who perceive little control over important events in their lives daydream more about past events than future ones (Brannigan, Shahon, & Schaller, 1992).
- Those who are sexually active in their behavior are also sexually active in their daydreams (Purifoy, Grodsky, & Giambra, 1992).
- Self-centered individuals have self-centered daydreams (Raskin & Novacek, 1991).

Consequences of daydreams.   Those interested in daydreaming argue that it has several functions. It can provide an escape from stress or boredom. The person briefly turns off the external world in favor of an internal one, later returning to the task at hand, refreshed by the daydream. Daydreams can alter our moods or enhance our sexual excitement.

Daydreams can help us in everyday life. If we mentally rehearse what we might say during a conversation, or the route we will drive, or a different way to arrange our furniture, we may hit upon a useful course of action. Similarly, daydreaming can enhance our motivation. An example familiar to many of us starts out with "I'm going to show them" and ends with a plan we put into action. In contrast to Freud's (1908) negative view of daydreaming, research shows that it can be adaptive.

However, Freud was correct in concluding that there is an occasional downside because some individuals daydream about problems rather than attempting to solve them. Worried daydreams worsen anxiety and depression (Pruzinsky & Borkovec, 1990) and may increase passivity (Mattlar, Tarkkanen, Carlsson, Aaltonen, & Helenius, 1993; Stanford & Hynd, 1994; Valkenburg & van der Voort, 1994). Along these lines, Nyamathi and Vasquez (1989) interviewed homeless mothers and found that the frequency of their daydreaming was correlated with the neglect of their children's well-being. Lindstrom and Hurrell (1992) similarly found that frequent daydreaming was correlated with poor work performance by business managers. In both cases, daydreaming may be a problem because it takes time away from one's other tasks.

Meditation

A form of altering consciousness long practiced by many groups, **meditation** combines a refocusing of attention with relaxation. It sometimes involves repetitive activity, such as slow breathing or chanting. It can also involve reversing the routinization of thought through contemplation, becoming aware of stimuli we normally tune out, like the sound of our beating heart.

■ meditation
strategy of altering consciousness that combines a refocusing of attention with relaxation

Although there are different procedures for meditating, most meditators experience a common result. More than a century ago, William James (1890) described it as a **mystical experience,** combining these elements:

- A feeling of oneness with the universe
- A sense of truth
- An inability to express experience in mere words
- Vividness and clarity of sensations and perceptions

■ mystical experience
phenomenon characterized by a feeling of oneness with the universe and an inability to express experience in mere words

More recently, researchers have documented physiological changes during meditation (Deepak, Manchanda, & Maheshwari, 1994; Lebedeva & Dobronravova, 1990). Alpha waves predominate in the person's EEG (remember that this pattern is linked to relaxation); breathing becomes deeper and slower; and heart rate slows down. Patterns of brain metabolism may also change, increasing in the frontal lobes and decreasing in the occipital lobes (Herzog, Lele, Kuwert, Langen, Kops, & Feinendegen, 1990–1991).

Other researchers have claimed long-term benefits of meditation, concluding that meditators are happier and healthier than their nonmeditating counterparts (Bogart, 1991; Brown & Robinson, 1993; Chang & Hiebert, 1989; Kabat-Zinn, Massion, Kristekker, & Peterson, 1992). However, this conclusion has been challenged by critics who argue that meditation is beneficial because it leads to relaxation, and it is relaxation that produces the benefits (Holmes, 1984, 1985).

Hypnosis

■ hypnosis
psychological state characterized by heightened suggestibility

Hypnosis is a condition characterized by heightened suggestibility. The person appears relaxed but is not asleep. Hypnosis typically occurs when the subject is asked to narrow her attention to what the hypnotist is saying and then to follow his directions. The more suggestions she follows, the more hypnotized she is said to be. Some people are more susceptible to hypnosis than others. One characteristic shared by those who can be hypnotized easily is an ability to engage freely in fantasy (Kihlstrom, 1985).

Hypnotic induction.   In a representative induction of hypnosis, suggestions include the following (Hilgard, 1977):

- Swaying while standing
- Closing one's eyes
- Lowering one's outstretched arm

- Being unable to raise one's arm
- Being unable to say one's name
- Being unable to open one's eyes
- Following a command outside the hypnotized state (posthypnotic suggestion)
- Failing to remember events outside the hypnotized state (posthypnotic amnesia)

These are arranged in increasing order of difficulty. A person who follows all of these suggestions is a good candidate for some of the striking phenomena of hypnosis.

For example, a hypnotized individual might show age regression, following the suggestion to act like a child of a given age. She does not become a child or even re-create her own childhood behaviors. Rather, she acts in a childish way. Figure 6.4 illustrates what happens when a hypnotized individual is age-regressed and asked to write her name. What results is an immature style, but not the exact style of a child. Even so, this behavior is intriguing because regression occurs without self-consciousness.

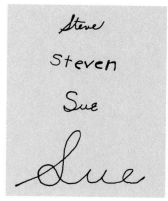

Figure 6.4
Age-Regressed Handwriting.
One of the interesting phenomena of hypnosis is age regression. An individual is hypnotized and given the suggestion that he or she is much younger. This picture shows what happens when age-regressed individuals are asked to write their names. What results is an immature style of writing but not the exact style of a child.

Consequences of hypnosis.   Over the years, many provocative claims have been made about hypnosis (Loftus, Garry, Brown, & Rader, 1994). Research has often qualified these claims, implying that the effects of hypnosis are complex. For instance, does hypnosis allow otherwise forgotten memories to be recovered? Most of us have read stories about how witnesses to a crime were hypnotized and able to recall obscure details like license plate numbers. This might tie up the loose ends of a crime story, but hypnosis provides no foolproof route to forgotten experiences (Chapter 9). Dywan and Bowers (1983) found that individuals could correctly remember more information when they were hypnotized. However, hypnotized subjects also had more false recollections. Correct and incorrect recall went together; as one increased, so did the other. False memories under hypnosis outnumbered true memories two to one.

Other studies indicate that the recall of hypnotized individuals is susceptible to bias by leading questions (Sheehan & Tilden, 1983). Further, false memories are reported with more confidence by subjects who are hypnotized (Krass, Kinoshita, & McConkey, 1989; Laurence & Perry, 1983). If hypnosis is used as an aid in criminal investigations, the potential for unintentional abuse must be kept in mind (McMaster, 1990; Scheflin, 1994).

No evidence indicates that hypnosis leads people to behave in harmful, immoral, or antisocial ways, unless such behaviors are already well established (Gibson, 1991). Hypnosis cannot be used to seduce an otherwise unwilling individual. In general, hypnosis rarely has negative effects, emotional or behavioral (Brentar & Lynn, 1989).

Hypnosis allows people to tolerate pain that they otherwise would find unbearable (Hilgard & Hilgard, 1983). In one common research strategy, subjects immerse their hand in a bucket of ice water. (This procedure hurts but is not dangerous.) When hypnotized and told that they are not feeling pain, they in fact do not. Hypnotism can rival morphine, tranquilizers, and acupuncture as a means of reducing pain (Jiranek, 1993). When endorphins were discovered (Chapter 4), some investigators wondered whether hypnosis reduces pain by stimulating the production of endorphins. These researchers administered to subjects a drug that blocks the effects of endorphins but found that hypnosis was still effective in reducing pain (Goldstein & Hilgard, 1975). How it works remains an open question.

Is hypnosis a special state of consciousness?   Considerable debate concerns whether hypnosis is a distinct state of consciousness (Kihlstrom, 1985). Most psychologists agree that hypnosis involves a state in which the hypnotized individual allows another person, the hypnotist, to take over certain functions, such as being aware and determining what is real. Hypnotism is associated with activation of those parts of the brain responsible for enhanced attention (Crawford, 1994). From this point, explanations diverge, particularly concerning the special status of the hypnotic state.

A hypnotized individual can withstand painful experiences that would otherwise be unbearable, such as holding one's hand in ice water.

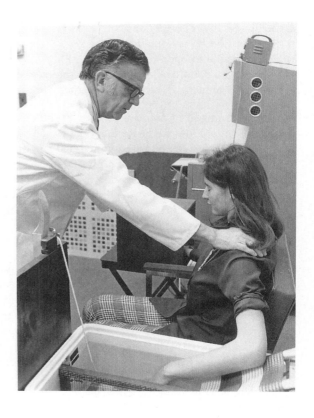

Some psychologists explain hypnosis simply as a way of acting that is characterized by heightened suggestibility (Sarbin & Coe, 1972). The hypnotized individual obeys the commands of the hypnotist, but this is no different from what happens when a motorist obeys the commands of a traffic cop. Hypnotized individuals cannot be induced to do something they would not ordinarily do.

Other psychologists explain hypnosis as a special state of consciousness marked by dissociation (Hilgard, 1973, 1977). As discussed earlier, dissociation is characterized by two streams of consciousness, with little communication between them. By this view, the hypnotized individual has a divided awareness. In the hypnotized state, one part of the subject yields to the suggestions of the hypnotist. The other part, sometimes called the **hidden observer,** is concealed from the hypnotized consciousness and yet remains aware of what is going on.

One way to reveal the hidden observer is to give the hypnotized individual paper and pencil and ask him to write but not be aware that he is doing so. Some people follow this instruction, showing a consciousness of which they are unaware; under the direction of the hidden observer, they write messages about which their hypnotized consciousness knows nothing.

Whether hypnosis is a special state of consciousness is a continuing debate (Silverstein, 1993). Regardless, it has practical applications. Therapists attempt to remove the symptoms of their patients through hypnotic suggestion. Its use in the relief of pain has already been discussed. It has also been used to reduce cravings for addictive substances like nicotine, to combat fear and anxiety, and to undo amnesia (Frankel, 1976). In reviewing these applications, Kihlstrom (1985) urged caution, noting that carefully controlled investigations of the benefits claimed for hypnotherapy still need to be conducted. Further, the actual mechanisms responsible for hypnotic phenomena are as yet unidentified (Otto-Salaj, Nadon, Hoyt, Register, & Kihlstrom, 1992; Rape & Bush, 1994).

■ **hidden observer**
in hypnosis, the part of the mind that does not yield to the suggestions of the hypnotist and is concealed from the part of the mind that does

Psychoactive Drugs

The most common way of deliberately altering consciousness is through **psychoactive drugs,** chemicals that affect brain activity and consciousness. The more desirable the changed state of consciousness, the more likely an individual is to use a given drug for this purpose. Abuse can follow.

We live in a drug-using and drug-abusing society. Indeed, we are a drug-using and drug-abusing species. People have long used psychoactive drugs to alter their thoughts, feelings, and actions (Brecher et al., 1972). For example:

- When the Bible tells us that ointment and perfume rejoice the heart (Proverbs 27:9), the reference is probably to psychoactive drugs.
- Ashes recovered from altars abandoned 2,500 years ago on islands in the Mediterranean have been identified as marijuana.
- Native Americans used peyote and mescal (hallucinogens extracted from cactus).
- More than 3,500 years ago, the Aztecs consumed magic mushrooms (psilocybin).
- The Incas chewed coca leaves (the source of contemporary cocaine and crack).
- In 1885, coca leaves were added to John Pemberton's sovereign remedy—a product marketed under the name of Coca-Cola.
- The Victorians in Europe were great fans of nitrous oxide, camphor, ether, and chloroform.
- People in various cultures sniff, snort, smoke, and/or swallow substances like fungus, nutmeg, morning glory seeds, glue, oven spray, Sterno, Aqua Velva, and gasoline.

There appears to be a taboo in the popular media about acknowledging that drugs alter consciousness (Weil, 1972). Think of the countless advertisements we see every year, urging us to drink beer because it tastes good and/or is less filling. But we all know that neither the taste of beer nor its caloric content has much to do with why people drink it. We consume alcohol because it produces an enjoyable alteration of our consciousness. Similarly, why do people use narcotics? One of heroin's famous casualties, comedian John Belushi, proclaimed that using it was "like kissing God" (Woodward, 1985, p. 321).

The same is true for the other drugs we use and abuse. We call the alteration in consciousness following the use of a psychoactive drug **intoxication.** Depending on the specific drug, the effects of intoxication range from euphoria to depression. Another alteration in consciousness follows the cessation or reduction of drug use; this is called **withdrawal.** Again, the specific nature of withdrawal depends on the drug in question, but withdrawal typically has the opposite effects of intoxication and is unpleasant. Both intoxication and withdrawal are self-limiting. As the substance clears the body, these syndromes cease. In some cases, drug use damages or destroys brain tissue and thus has lasting effects. Such enduring effects may result in organic syndromes like delirium, dementia, or amnesia. Common to psychoactive drugs is the phenomenon of **tolerance** with increased use—the need to take more and more of a drug in order to produce the same effect.

Psychoactive drugs produce highly pleasurable states, prompting theorists to examine the brain structures that are responsible for our ability to experience any form of pleasure. Drugs seem to affect the same parts of the brain that are responsible for pleasure brought about by food or sex (Koob & Bloom, 1988). Specifically, psychoactive drugs activate areas in the forebrain that receive from the limbic system input pertaining to mood and emotion. Cocaine, for example, increases activity of the neurotransmitter **dopamine,** which produces intense pleasure (Wise & Bozarth, 1987). Other drugs give rise to different subjective experiences but produce pleasure by the same mechanism. Conversely, the craving for drugs that characterizes withdrawal is presumably the result of a reduction in dopamine activity in a brain that is accustomed to a higher level (Modell, Mountz, & Beresford, 1990).

■ **psychoactive drugs**
chemicals that affect brain activity and consciousness

■ **intoxication**
alteration in brain function brought about by drug use

■ **withdrawal**
alteration in brain function brought about by the cessation of drug use

■ **tolerance**
need to take more of a psychoactive drug in order to produce the same effect

■ **dopamine**
neurotransmitter involved in the experience of pleasure

■ **stimulants**

psychoactive drugs that increase arousal and speed up mental and physical activity

■ **depressants**

psychoactive drugs that reduce awareness of external stimuli and slow down bodily functions

Types of drugs.   Let me start with thumbnail sketches of the major types of psychoactive drugs, focusing on how they affect consciousness. **Stimulants** increase arousal and speed up mental and physical activity. These drugs also increase alertness and elevate mood. Sometimes stimulants produce agitation and insomnia. The most widely used stimulant is caffeine, found in coffee, tea, chocolate, and many soft drinks. Another familiar stimulant is nicotine, the active ingredient in tobacco. Amphetamine and cocaine are other familiar stimulants.

In terms of their effects on consciousness, **depressants** are the opposite of stimulants. Depressants reduce awareness of external stimuli and slow down bodily functions. In small amounts, they create a relaxed state and banish anxiety and inhibition. In large amounts, they lead to sedation and sleep, even coma and death.

Alcohol is the most widely used depressant. At least in our culture, it is the most frequently used of all the psychoactive drugs. Americans spend tens of billions of dollars every year on alcohol, even though it takes an incredible toll on physical health. Alcohol is also the psychoactive drug about which psychologists know the most. It is legal in most places in the United States, relatively inexpensive compared with the cost of other drugs, and widely accepted.

As we drink alcohol, it is absorbed mainly through the small intestine. Once in the blood, it is metabolized: broken down into water and carbon dioxide. The rate of alcohol metabolism is fixed and can be exceeded by one's rate of ingestion, meaning that alcohol circulates in the blood until it can be broken down. Hence, one's blood alcohol content (BAC) is a more exact index of intoxication than the amount of alcohol consumed. Most states define legal intoxication as a BAC of 0.10 percent, roughly three or four drinks in an hour, although body size determines the precise number. There is essentially the same amount of alcohol in a can of beer, a glass of wine, and a cocktail. If you drink them at the same rate, all will have the exact same effect on you.

Alcohol depresses the functioning of the nervous system, but because it initially affects brain centers that are inhibitory, people may experience alcohol intoxication as stimulating (Chapter 4). As time passes and more alcohol is consumed and metabolized, the person begins to have difficulty thinking, speaking, walking, and/or seeing. He or she might become withdrawn and sullen. In larger amounts, alcohol induces sleep.

Around the world and certainly in the United States, the depressant alcohol is one of the most widely used psychoactive drugs.

The long-term effects of alcohol are numerous. A person comes to tolerate alcohol and to depend on it. Lesions in the brain develop, producing dementia and amnesia. Risk of heart failure increases. Hypertension is common, as is capillary rupture (which explains why chronic alcohol abusers have red noses). Alcohol contains calories but no nutrients, and so an abuser is malnourished because he or she does not want food. Liver tissue is destroyed as cirrhosis develops. Curtailing alcohol use may bring on seizures.

Depressants also include the **opiates** (or **narcotics**): opium, morphine, heroin, and methadone, to name a few. Opium is derived from juice in the seeds of the poppy plant. The other opiates are either made from opium or synthesized in laboratories. All are effective painkillers.

Minor tranquilizers like Valium are also classified as depressants. They are frequently prescribed for anxiety disorders because they counteract arousal of the sympathetic nervous system (Chapter 14). However, minor tranquilizers are also subject to abuse, something users may overlook when they obtain them through legal channels.

Barbiturates like phenobarbital are yet another type of depressant. They work by slowing down activity in our entire nervous system. Barbiturates have been used to aid sleep and to combat anxiety and seizures. Despite these benefits, they are dangerous. If people overdose, it can be fatal, particularly if they have mixed them with alcohol. Finally, withdrawing from barbiturates is not merely unpleasant but potentially life-threatening. Chronic users can experience convulsions when these drugs are suddenly stopped.

Hallucinogens produce hallucinations, usually visual. The user sees things that are not present, or sees things in ways that other people do not. Other types of sensations and perceptions can be influenced as well, notably a person's sense of time. Hallucinogens have varying effects on mood. In some cases, euphoria results; in other cases, the consequence is extreme fear. Hallucinogens may exaggerate the user's present mood, for better or for worse.

One well-known hallucinogen is LSD (lysergic acid diethylamide). Its consciousness-altering effects were first discovered when a Swiss researcher named Albert Hofmann (1968) accidentally swallowed a small amount. He described the experience as follows:

> I had a great difficulty in speaking coherently, my field of vision swayed before me, and objects appeared distorted like images in curved mirrors. I had the impression of being unable to move from the spot. The faces of those around me appeared as grotesque, colored masks. Everything seemed to sway and the proportions were distorted like the reflections in the surface of moving water. Moreover, all objects appeared in unpleasant, constantly changing colors, the predominant shades being sickly green and blue. When I closed my eyes, an unending series of colorful, very realistic and fantastic images surged in on me. (pp. 185–186)

Other hallucinogens include mescaline, psilocybin, and PCP (phencyclidine).

Marijuana is a drug produced from the leaves and flowers of the hemp plant, long used as a source of rope. It can be classified as a hallucinogen, although some disagree because marijuana distorts perception only in extremely high doses. The more typical effects of marijuana are mild euphoria and increased appetite.

Like many other psychoactive drugs, marijuana is illegal in the United States. It is, however, the most widely used illegal drug in this country. Vigorous debate concerns the consequences of its long-term use. Marijuana is usually smoked, and a user is at risk for bronchitis and lung ailments. Other negative effects, such as depression and sexual difficulties, are suspected but not agreed upon by all researchers. Part of the problem with evaluating the effects of this drug is that people who use it differ from those who do not (Shedler & Block, 1990). Is a supposed consequence due to the marijuana or to a prior characteristic of the user? A similar point can be made about research into the consequences of any psychoactive drug (see Table 6.4).

■ **opiates; narcotics**
depressants derived from poppy plants or synthesized in laboratories to be chemically similar

■ **minor tranquilizers**
depressants like Valium that counteract arousal of the sympathetic nervous system

■ **barbiturates**
depressants like phenobarbital that slow down activity in the entire nervous system

■ **hallucinogens**
psychoactive drugs that produce hallucinations

Table 6.4   Summary: Psychoactive Drugs

Type of drug	Examples
Stimulants	Caffeine, nicotine, amphetamine, cocaine
Depressants	Alcohol, opiates, minor tranquilizers, barbiturates
Hallucinogens	LSD, mescaline, psilocybin, PCP, marijuana

■ **substance dependence**
cluster of cognitive, behavioral, and physiological symptoms that indicate severe impairment and distress due to drug use

■ **substance abuse**
difficulties or distress due to drug use

Drug use, abuse, and dependence.   When does drug use become abuse? Substance use falls along a continuum. Whether the drug is alcohol, tobacco, cocaine, or PCP, people cannot be classified simply as completely abstinent or hopelessly addicted. Some people use none, some use a lot, and many fall in between. Mental health professionals regard substance use as problematic when it begins to interfere with an individual's life (American Psychiatric Association, 1994). Problems can occur in a variety of areas—physical, psychological, and interpersonal—and so the best definition of problematic drug use is one that places it in a biopsychosocial context.

There are two types of drug problems. The more severe problem is termed **substance dependence:** a cluster of cognitive, behavioral, and physiological symptoms that indicate severe impairment and distress due to drug use (see Table 6.5). Diagnosticians note whether substance dependence includes tolerance or withdrawal. If so, the drug-dependent person is deemed physiologically dependent. However, physiological dependence is not necessary for the diagnosis of substance dependence. For example, only minimal withdrawal characterizes drugs such as LSD or marijuana, but a person is still regarded as dependent if other symptoms are present.

When drug-using individuals do not fully meet the criteria for a diagnosis of dependence but still encounter difficulties or distress due to drug use, psychologists refer to their problem as **substance abuse.** Abusers encounter problems at work, school, or home; they find themselves in hazardous situations; they get in trouble with the law; they continue to use drugs despite the problems produced or exacerbated by doing so. Consider people who repeatedly drive when intoxicated, drink alcohol despite an ulcer, or buy cocaine rather than pay back loans.

Estimates of the frequency of drug dependence and abuse depend on the criteria employed. When the popular media report statistics about the prevalence of drug problems, the quoted numbers are rarely based on the full meanings of dependence and abuse (Kandel, 1991; Kozel, 1990). They usually reflect responses to brief surveys that ask people about the frequency and amount of their substance use. A decision is then

Table 6.5   Criteria of Substance Dependence

Substance dependence is shown by the following:

Need for increased amounts of the drug to achieve the desired effect and/or decreased effect with continued use of the same amount (tolerance)

Characteristic symptoms when drug use is stopped and/or the drug is used to prevent or relieve these symptoms (withdrawal)

Drug use in larger amounts or over a longer period than intended

Persistent desire to use the drug or unsuccessful attempts to decrease or stop drug use

Great deal of time devoted to obtaining or using the drug

Cessation of other activities in order to use the drug

Continued drug use despite recognition of its harmfulness

Source: American Psychiatric Association (1994).

Substance abusers often find themselves in hazardous situations; they get in trouble with the law; they encounter problems at work, school, and home.

made about where to place a cutoff between use and abuse, and the number of people who fall on the abuse side of the line is reported. This information has value by allowing comparisons across time and place about drug use, but it does not permit firm conclusions about the extent of drug dependence or abuse.

What is clear is that problems with alcohol are common among those in the contemporary United States. A survey by Kessler and colleagues (1994) estimated that 10 percent of American adults have an alcohol problem currently, and that almost 25 percent have had such a problem at one time in life.

Here are some other generalizations about drug use and abuse in the United States. First, many drug abusers are quite broad in their tastes, using a variety of substances—successively or simultaneously. The psychology of substance abuse has traditionally focused on a given drug—for example, alcohol or heroin—and this approach may have to change.

Complicating matters is the fact that street drugs are often identified incorrectly. Users believing they are buying one drug might be buying one or more other drugs. It is virtually impossible to obtain heroin or cocaine not mixed with other psychoactive drugs (Gomez & Rodriguez, 1989). Relatedly, new drugs subject to abuse are being developed all the time. By intent, designer drugs have chemical structures that are not illegal at the time of their creation.

Also, although drug abuse in recent history has been primarily an activity of males, this fact is changing, as women in increasing numbers join men in the tendency to use and abuse drugs (Harrison, 1989). Whether theories and treatments developed mainly with respect to males will generalize to females remains to be seen (Toneatto, Sobell, & Sobell, 1992).

Finally, although we seem to be seeing an overall decrease in the use of many drugs, those individuals who do begin to use them are starting earlier in life (Harrison, 1992). Again, whether theories and treatments developed for adults will apply to children or adolescents is unclear.

How do psychologists explain substance dependence and abuse? Various causes interact to produce these problems. Vaillant (1983) called for an integrated model, citing a Japanese proverb about drinking:

> First the man takes a drink;
> Then the drink takes a drink;
> And finally the drink takes the man.

At different stages in drug use/abuse, different factors intervene.

Obviously, drug abuse involves the body, and so biological factors help explain it. There may be a genetic predisposition to abuse drugs; the mechanism presumably is the inherent tendency to experience the effects of intoxication as pleasurable and the effects of withdrawal as minimal. Regardless, drug use changes the way the brain functions, both in the short term and in the long term. Intoxication becomes the typical—and often the most comfortable—mode of operation. Tolerance and withdrawal make sense in terms of a biologically based vicious circle that strives to maintain homeostasis.

Drug abuse is frequently described as an illness, but this characterization is dubious if it means that drug abuse can be explained solely in biological terms. Like other complex human activities, drug abuse is biopsychosocial. It is like an illness insofar as there are biological causes and consequences, but it is not a disease like chicken pox that plays itself out largely in isolation from nonbiological processes (Chapter 16).

Psychological factors are also part of the explanation. People who use and abuse drugs have motives for their actions, and these are entwined with positive expectations about the effects of drugs. Alcohol users, for example, believe that several drinks make them more socially skilled, despite objective evidence to the contrary. Drug use can—however temporarily—dampen anxiety or depression. Unpleasant memories are blotted out. Inhibitions are removed.

The person who drinks is affected by the immediate environment, including friends and family members, and so reward and imitation also play a role in explanation. A strong predictor of whether individuals use drugs is the degree to which their peers approve of such behavior. Any parent whose child says "My friends get high, but I just say no" should be skeptical.

Finally, a person's larger social environment plays a role in legitimizing (or not) the use and abuse of drugs. Ethnicity is perhaps the single most important influence on an individual's drug use. For instance, one generalization that none would challenge is that alcohol use in the contemporary United States is more frequent among those of Western European descent than those of Asian descent. Why?

Most discussions address why Asian Americans drink so little, instead of asking why European Americans drink so much! Be that as it may, theoretical speculation often centers on cultural and religious values that stress moderation for Asian Americans (Cahalan, 1978). Some role may be played by the body's inherent response to alcohol ingestion; those of Asian descent are more likely to experience flushing of the skin and other unpleasant reactions to intoxication.

Drug treatment.   Therapists currently know very little about what helps alcohol abusers and why. Some good news is that a number of abusers improve without intervention (Vaillant, 1983). People taper drug use when they have a good reason for doing so, such as continuing a relationship with someone who disapproves. Some more good news is that a variety of treatments, such as behavior therapy (Chapters 8 and 14), are effective, at least in the short run (Miller & Hester, 1986). But researchers cannot say that any given approach is better than any other (Marlatt, Baer, Donovan, & Kivlahan, 1988). And other than knowing that social stability predicts a good outcome, we cannot say with certainty who is most likely to benefit from treatment. Relapse is a possibility for anyone who appears to have been successfully treated for drug abuse (Riley, Sobell, Leo, Sobell, & Klajner, 1987). This fact is unsurprising given the multiplicity of influences on drug consumption.

Drug-abusing individuals can also find help outside the traditional mental health system. **Alcoholics Anonymous (AA)** is a self-help group founded more than 50 years ago by recovering alcohol abusers. AA chapters exist in most cities in the United States and in 100 other countries. They hold frequent meetings, at which members tell their stories and hear the stories of others. AA's official stance is that members remain alcoholics for life, even if they have not had a drink in years. Its goal is to prevent a relapse, and so members seek out meetings and each other when they are tempted to drink.

■ **Alcoholics Anonymous (AA)**
self-help group for recovering alcohol abusers

Alcoholics Anonymous (AA) is a self-help group that offers an explicit belief system to its members. AA members meet regularly to tell their stories and to receive support for their sobriety.

AA requires a lifetime commitment and thus a lifestyle change. It provides its members with an explicit belief system (see Table 6.6) and a social group with which to relate. AA is not for everyone, and early dropout rates can be as high as 80 percent (Edwards, Hensman, Hawker, & Williamson, 1967). Still, for those who stay with the AA program, alcohol abuse tends to stop (Vaillant, 1983).

Table 6.6   The Twelve Steps of Alcoholics Anonymous

The members of Alcoholics Anonymous are given an explicit set of beliefs about alcohol and its abuse. The Twelve Steps shown here are a well-known example of this belief system.

1. We admitted that we were powerless over alcohol . . . that our lives had become unmanageable.

2. Came to believe that a Power greater than ourselves could restore us to sanity.

3. Made a decision to turn our will and our lives over to the care of God as we understood Him.

4. Made a searching and fearless moral inventory of ourselves.

5. Admitted to God, to ourselves, and to another human being the exact nature of our wrongs.

6. Were entirely ready to have God remove all these defects of character.

7. Humbly asked Him to remove our shortcomings.

8. Made a list of all persons we had harmed and became willing to make amends to them all.

9. Made direct amends to such people wherever possible, except when to do so would injure them or others.

10. Continued to take personal inventory and when we were wrong, promptly admitted it.

11. Sought through prayer and meditation to improve our conscious contact with God as we understood him, praying only for a knowledge of His will for us and the power to carry that out.

12. Having had a spiritual awakening as the result of these steps, we tried to carry this message to alcoholics, and to practice these principles in all of our affairs.

Source: Alcoholics Anonymous. The Twelve Steps are reprinted with permission of Alcoholics Anonymous World Services, Inc. Permission to reprint this material does not mean that AA has reviewed or approved the contents of this publication, nor that AA agrees with the views expressed herein. AA is a program of recovery from alcoholism only. Use of the Twelve Steps in connection with programs and activities which are patterned after AA, but which address other problems, does not imply otherwise.

■ **relapse prevention**
strategies for preventing return of
drug or alcohol problems after
successful treatment for abuse or
dependence

Treatment of drug abuse should not end simply because a person has returned to a sober state. **Relapse prevention** is based on the assumption that a person successfully treated for drug problems is at risk for relapse whenever she encounters the circumstances associated with abuse in the first place (Marlatt & Gordon, 1985). The focus of relapse prevention is on helping the person identify these circumstances and devise responses to them other than drug use. The greater the range of possible risk factors with which the person can cope, the less likely a relapse.

> **Stop and Think**
>
> **9**   According to research, who daydreams, and why?
>
> **10** What is the mystical experience?
>
> **11** Is hypnosis a special state of consciousness?
>
> **12** Are the Twelve Steps of Alcoholics Anonymous a religious belief system?
>
> **13** What is relapse prevention?
>
> **14** How are drug use and drug abuse biopsychosocial?

CONSCIOUSNESS IN A BIOPSYCHOSOCIAL CONTEXT

This chapter introduced psychology's approach to consciousness by noting the elusiveness of its definition and the consequent difficulty of investigating it. Research nonetheless suggests that different forms of consciousness are linked to brain processes; that it plays numerous psychological roles and is entwined with emotion, motivation, memory, cognition, and behavior; and that it is shaped and directed by social influences, including the individual's culture (Grob & Dobkin de Rios, 1992; Hughes, 1991; Janus, 1991). In short, consciousness is biopsychosocial.

The Living Dead

I can make this point one more time by considering a phenomenon you may think exists only in bad movies: zombies. But there is a basis in reality to zombie movies that illustrates how biological, psychological, and social factors come together to create the special state of consciousness experienced by the so-called living dead.

My discussion is based on research in Haiti by Wade Davis (1988), an ethnobiologist. Ethnobiology is a field that bridges anthropology and biology, focusing on how people in different social groups use animals and plants in their lives. Davis originally became interested in zombies because of widespread reports in Haiti of a powder used for centuries to separate an individual's soul from his or her body. Once this separation occurred, the individual's body—called a zombie—could be made to do the bidding of whoever administered the powder.

The existence of zombies is widely accepted in Haiti. Contrary to movie portrayals, Haitians do not fear zombies. Rather, they fear becoming one. This may all sound very fanciful, but Davis was able to document at least one case in Haiti in which a man was pronounced dead (by Western-trained physicians who issued a death certificate) and then buried. Years later, he reappeared, and was identified by his relatives and hundreds of his former neighbors. The man reported that he had indeed died after exposure to zombie powder. He had been taken from his grave shortly after burial by a powerful voodoo priest who enslaved him. When the priest died, the man regained his soul and was able to return home.

Zombies as Biopsychosocial

Davis accepted much of what the recovered zombie said, although he preferred to interpret it in terms of Western science. Davis reasoned that the zombie powder had to be a powerful toxin derived from plants or animals native to Haiti. It had to produce a state that was difficult to distinguish from death, lasting long enough for an afflicted person to be buried. Finally, it had to wear off when the person was removed from the grave several days later.

So, Davis set out to find the powder. You might think that voodoo practitioners would be reluctant to give such a powder to a visiting American, but Davis easily obtained a number of samples, simply by paying for them. The voodoo priests explained that the powder itself was not all that potent; it was their magic that made it so. Nevertheless, the different samples of zombie powder, from several regions of Haiti, all shared two ingredients. One was a hallucinogen made from botanical material; the other was a poison found in the livers and ovaries of puffer fish.

As it turns out, ethnobiologists already knew a great deal about the effects of this poison because puffer fish are considered great delicacies in Japan. If the parts of the fish containing the poison are not properly removed, people consuming the fish become completely paralyzed. Heart rate and respiration slow to such an extent that these persons seem dead. In most cases, they indeed die, but in some instances, they recover in a few days. Of particular interest is that the paralyzed individuals who recover have at no point lost consciousness. They describe the terror they experienced as physicians tried to revive them but then gave up and pronounced them dead. In some parts of Japan, local law requires that victims of puffer fish poisoning not be buried for at least three days.

Davis concluded that this poison probably produces part of what Haitians identify as the zombie phenomenon. However, the poison cannot provide the entire explanation. When Japanese diners ingest the poison, they are regarded as sick, not as zombies. But when Haitians ingest it, they are seen as zombies, by themselves and by others because their culture legitimizes this interpretation.

Remember that their paralysis is accompanied as well by hallucinations, producing an overwhelming experience. They believe that they have died and that their soul has

When people eat the poisonous liver or ovaries of the puffer fish, they may become paralyzed but not lose consciousness. This experience, in the cultural context of Haiti, may give rise to the phenomenon of zombies.

Figure 6.5
Zombies as Biopsychosocial.
Haitian zombies result from a combination of biological causes (zombie powder), psychological causes (paralysis, hallucinations, and expectations), and social causes (cultural beliefs).

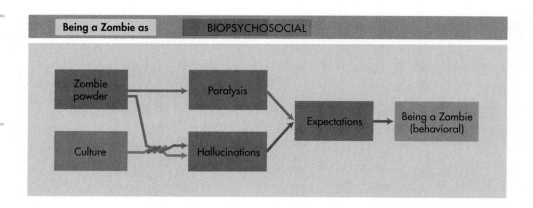

been separated from their body. Even when the poison clears their system, they remain affected by their own expectations and a society that regards them as dead.

It is unlikely that there have ever been more than a handful of zombies in Haiti. Davis argued that the mere threat of becoming a zombie serves a widespread role of social control in Haiti. Those most at risk are individuals who refuse to share property with their family members. This is a grievous crime in a country created in the aftermath of the only successful slave revolt in history: In the late 1700s, the African slaves in Haiti battled their French owners to become free and to take control of the land they were once forced to work.

The Haitian religion of voodoo provides one interpretation of zombies, and the science of psychology provides another. Psychology points to the biological, psychological, and social forces that can come together to shape an individual's conscious experience following ingestion of zombie powder (see Figure 6.5).

As remarked upon several times in this chapter, consciousness is closely linked to other psychological processes. The next chapter takes an explicit look at two of the most important of these: motivation and emotion. At times, we are quite aware of our motives and our emotions; at other times, much less so—meaning that continued attention to what psychologists know about consciousness is required to understand these processes.

SUMMARY

UNDERSTANDING CONSCIOUSNESS: DEFINITION AND EXPLANATION

■ Consciousness is difficult to define precisely, but it usually refers to our awareness of the environment and our own mental contents and processes.
■ Explanations of consciousness are usually phrased in biological, psychological, and/or cultural terms.

DOING *Consciousness* RESEARCH

■ Introspection is the obvious place to start in studying consciousness, but we must be careful not to treat people's verbal reports of mental states as identical to these states.
■ Further strategies for investigating consciousness involve determining the factors that correlate with different conscious experiences.
■ Psychologists have found that the study of how people deliberately alter their consciousness is espe-

cially informative. Also of interest to researchers are abnormal forms of consciousness.

STATES OF CONSCIOUSNESS

■ We experience consciousness in different forms known as states of consciousness.
■ Normal waking consciousness switches between automatic processing, in which we initiate an activity and simply carry it out, and controlled processing, in which we initiate an activity and then make a conscious effort to direct it.
■ There exist several psychological states characterized by a lack of awareness. Sigmund Freud argued that people possess a motivated unconscious, material actively kept out of awareness because it is threatening. Subliminal perception refers to the perception of stimuli at levels below their absolute thresholds. Dissociation describes the splitting of consciousness into separate streams with little or no communication between them.

■ We spend about one-third of our lives in the state of consciousness known as sleep. Researchers have discovered that when we sleep, we cycle several times through various discrete stages characterized by differing amounts and patterns of brain activity, muscular tension, and eye movements. Although sleep is apparently associated with physical and psychological well-being, its exact functions have not been determined.

■ Similarly, psychologists do not agree on the significance of dreams. Freud proposed that they represent disguised wishes and motives. The activation-synthesis theory proposes that dreams are the interpretation of random brain activity.

■ There exist several disorders that involve sleeping and dreaming. Dyssomnias are problems with sleep itself, whereas parasomnias are abnormal events occurring during sleep.

■ Damage to the nervous system can produce alterations in consciousness known as organic syndromes, which include delirium, dementia, amnestic syndrome, and organic personality disorder.

DELIBERATE ALTERATION OF CONSCIOUSNESS

■ People deliberately alter their state of consciousness, using various techniques.

■ Daydreaming occurs when we shift attention inward and away from the external world. Research shows daydreaming to be an almost universal occurrence. Various useful functions have been suggested for daydreaming, including tension relief, problem solution, and enhancement of motivation.

■ Meditation combines a refocusing of attention with relaxation. During meditation, characteristic physiological changes occur. Some psychologists claim meditation offers long-term emotional and physical benefits, although this claim is disputed.

■ Hypnosis is a state characterized by heightened suggestibility. Although some claims about the special nature of hypnosis have proved to be exaggerations, other claims are supported by research. For example, hypnosis allows individuals to tolerate pain they would otherwise find unbearable.

■ Perhaps the most common way of altering consciousness is through the ingestion of psychoactive drugs, those affecting brain activity. Among the common categories of psychoactive drugs are stimulants like amphetamine and cocaine; depressants like alcohol, narcotics, and barbiturates; and hallucinogens like LSD, mescaline, and marijuana. Each produces characteristic alterations in consciousness, during intoxication and during withdrawal.

■ The abuse of psychoactive drugs represents a huge societal problem, and psychologists have developed various strategies to help people curtail abuse. Much, however, remains to be learned.

CONSCIOUSNESS IN A BIOPSYCHOSOCIAL CONTEXT

■ The biopsychosocial nature of consciousness is illustrated by the phenomenon of the Haitian zombie, a special state of awareness produced by a combination of chemicals and societal expectations.

KEY TERMS

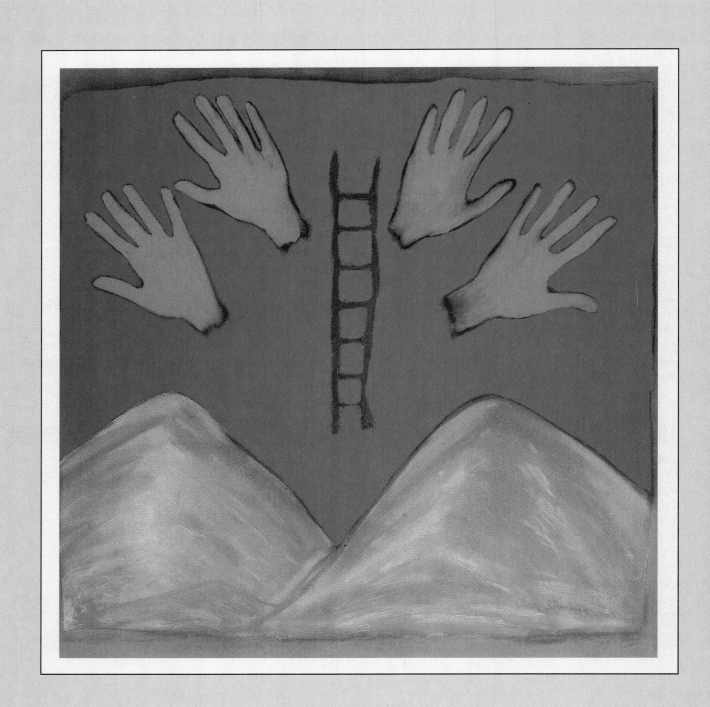

Motivation and Emotion

The Russian actor and producer Konstantin Stanislavsky (1863–1938) created method acting. Stanislavsky wanted to teach actors to be more convincing. Classical teaching focused only on the technical talents of actors—enunciation, song, and dance—and did not allow them to be imaginative in character portrayal. Audience members were always aware that they were watching people playing parts. So, Stanislavsky tried to develop the internal resources of actors. He taught them to create psychological states appropriate to the roles being played (Lundrigan, 1991).

In particular, actors were taught to devise states of motivation and emotion like those involved in actual behavior. Strategies such as improvisation, physical exercises, and relaxation accomplish this goal of allowing an actor to become the part that is played.

Here are some representative exercises used in method acting:

Sense Memory. Actors try to remember their sensations so that they can bring them alive on stage. An exercise might involve an actor imagining a cup of hot coffee on a table next to him. He can smell the coffee's rich aroma. He imagines picking up the cup and feeling the warmth on his fingers. He then tastes the coffee and feels it slide down his throat. The smell tickles his nostrils. The exercise ends with the actor putting the empty cup back on the table.

When actors prepare for a role, they focus on the psychological states of their characters, including motives and emotions.

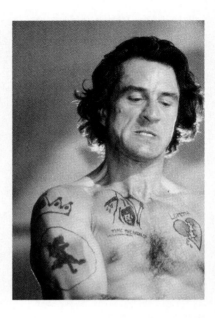

Affective Memory. Actors try to remember key events from their pasts and the emotions that accompanied them. Then they apply those feelings to the characters they are portraying. The premise here is that a compelling character must have depth, including thoughts and feelings. The best way for an actor to add such depth to a character is to borrow it from his or her own past.

Concentration. Actors must relax on stage, but they must also concentrate. So, a typical exercise to aid concentration might involve the actor sitting in a chair with her eyes closed. Calling forth mental images, she starts to create a sensory circle around herself. She tries to keep her concentration within the boundaries of the circle, just thinking about the chair and the floor. Once comfortable, the actor expands her circle of concentration to include a stage.

By the 1920s, Stanislavsky's acting technique found its way to the United States, where it became the basis of good acting (O'Malley, 1979). Among those who studied method acting are Jane Fonda, Dustin Hoffman, Marlon Brando, Robert DeNiro, and Marilyn Monroe.

UNDERSTANDING MOTIVES AND EMOTIONS: DEFINITION AND EXPLANATION

■ **motivation**
processes that arouse, direct, and maintain behavior

■ **emotion**
subjective feelings in response to situations, as well as associated patterns of physiological arousal, thought, and behavior

The terms *motivation* and *emotion* both come from the same word—*motion*. **Motivation** includes processes like hunger and thirst that arouse, direct, and maintain behavior. **Emotion** includes not only subjective feelings like anger and fear that move through us in response to situations but also patterns of physiological arousal, thought, and behavior.

Motivation and Emotion as Biopsychosocial

Motivation and emotion are best approached in biopsychosocial terms. Let us start by considering the evolutionary significance of motives and emotions. Individuals obviously benefit if they can direct their activities toward some goals rather than others, depending on what they need at the moment and what their environment allows (Liotti, Ceccarelli, & Chouhy, 1993; MacDonald, 1991). Contrast them with individuals who are always hungry, angry, or sexually aroused. If behavior never varies, adaptation to a complex world is all but impossible.

Although they may have a basis in biology, people's motives and emotions are not inflexible reflexes. They are linked to other psychological processes, especially thoughts and beliefs about how to behave in given situations. The cognitive influences on motivation and emotion are the result of learning, and depending on an individual's culture, different motives and emotions may arise in the course of socialization.

Classifying Motives and Emotions

Although motivation and emotion reflect biological, psychological, and social influences, theorists have long attempted to classify specific motives and emotions in terms of the relative importance of their determinants. For instance, motives are typically described as either primary or acquired. **Primary motives** are biological in nature: hunger, thirst, and sex. **Acquired motives** have been learned: achievement, power, and mastery, to name a few.

Similarly, emotions have been described as either basic or complex. **Basic emotions** are experienced by people in a variety of cultures: anger, fear, sadness, disgust, surprise, curiosity, acceptance, and joy (Ekman, 1984). Because of the universality of these basic emotions, some theorists regard them as inherent in our biological makeup. **Complex emotions,** like guilt, love, shyness, or humor, combine these basic emotions in ways shaped by socialization within a specific culture.

From a biopsychosocial perspective, any rigid distinction between primary and acquired motives or basic and complex emotions is an oversimplification. Thus, although hunger involves tissue needs and stomach contractions, these cannot account for why some hungry people seek out a Pepsi and a cheeseburger but others look for tofu and sprouts. And when somebody steps on our foot, we feel angry because crushed toes hurt, but biology alone does not explain why our anger vanishes if the person who stepped on our foot is apologetic yet increases if we are told to watch where we place our feet.

Like other psychological processes, motivation and emotion must be examined within multiple contexts (O'Connor, 1991). If we wish to describe motives as primary or acquired and emotions as basic or complex, we need to recognize these labels as end points of a continuum that reflects the relative importance of biological versus social factors in theorizing about them.

The Interaction of Motivation and Emotion

Many theorists stress that motivation and emotion work together. For example, Silvan Tomkins (1962, 1963, 1982) proposed that emotions make one's needs obvious to oneself. The psychological urgency that accompanies motives is the product of emotions. Consider oxygen deprivation. If someone covers our nose and mouth so that we cannot breathe, we thrash about to try to breathe. It is tempting to explain our behavior in these terms:

$$\text{no oxygen} \rightarrow \text{thrashing} \rightarrow \text{breathing oxygen}$$

But if a person is very slowly deprived of oxygen, panic does not occur. Instead, euphoria results, and there is no attempt to obtain more oxygen. So, Tomkins argued that emotions amplify our drives and immediately cause behavior. The emotion of panic, not the physiological requirement of oxygen, makes us struggle to breathe when our nose

■ **primary motives**
motives that are biological in nature: hunger, thirst, and sex

■ **acquired motives**
motives that have been learned: achievement, power, and mastery

■ **basic emotions**
emotions that are experienced by people in a variety of cultures: anger, fear, sadness, disgust, surprise, curiosity, acceptance, and joy

■ **complex emotions**
combinations of basic emotions in ways shaped by socialization within a specific culture

and mouth are obstructed. Motives are important because they provide information, but emotions take over to ensure that our bodies act on this information.

In this chapter, motivation and emotion are discussed separately but in similar ways. I first discuss theoretical approaches that have been popular, then examine research strategies, and finally address variations across gender and culture. These separate presentations make it easier for you not only to understand what psychologists have learned about motives and emotions but also to appreciate that in actual behavior, motivation and emotion constantly interact with each other.

Stop and Think

1   What is the difference between motivation and emotion?

2   What is a primary motive?

3   According to Tomkins, how are motives and emotions related?

APPROACHES TO MOTIVATION

Past explanations of motives focused on either biological or social determinants. As noted, it is more plausible to acknowledge multiple determinants of motives. However, previous approaches alert us to the likely ingredients of a biopsychosocial explanation of motivation.

Motives as Instincts

■ **instinct**
complex behavior that appears without having been explicitly learned

When we explain the behavior of animals, the concept of **instinct** is popular. In many species, complex behaviors appear without having been explicitly learned. Consider sex and aggression in the stickleback fish, a popular research subject for ethologists (Chapter 3). During the spring, the male undergoes hormonal changes that prepare him for reproduction. His belly turns red and he builds a nest. He begins to patrol the territory around the nest. If he encounters another male, recognizable by its red belly, he attacks him. If he encounters a female, recognizable by a swollen belly filled with eggs, he courts her. Then she follows him to his nest, where she releases her eggs. He fertilizes the eggs and watches over them until they hatch.

The courting behavior of the male stickleback fish, shown on the left, is instinctive, the result of hormonal changes.

Several aspects of this scenario deserve attention. First is the connection between sex and aggression. In many species, including mammals, the male hormone testosterone increases aggressiveness. Second, the stickleback's behaviors (attack or courtship) are complex, unlearned sequences. Third, these sequences occur in response to specific environmental events. These are called releasing stimuli. Red bellies lead to attack; swollen bellies lead to courtship.

Let us move from stickleback fish to people. Does complex behavior on the part of people ever appear without being learned? In the nineteenth century and early in the twentieth century, explanations of human behavior in terms of instincts were popular (McDougall, 1908). Theorists proposed numerous human instincts, like sympathy, secretiveness, cleanliness, and modesty. In each case, they started with a behavior that needed an explanation, such as male aggression. Then they suggested an instinctive motive for the behavior. Finally, they concluded that this motive proved adaptive in the course of evolution, and hence natural selection led to its current form.

As pointed out in Chapter 3, evolutionary explanations can be circular:

> If a man seeks his fellows, it is the instinct of gregariousness; if he walks alone, it is the solitary instinct; if he twiddles his thumbs, it is the thumb-twiddling instinct; if he does not twiddle his thumbs, it is the thumb-not-twiddling instinct. Thus everything is explained with the facility of magic—word magic. (Holt, 1931, p.4)

Contemporary psychologists refrain from circular explanations like these. The prevailing view is that our motives are less rigidly wired into the nervous system than those of the stickleback. The ways that we satisfy our motives are a function of learning and culture.

At the same time, there probably is a basis in evolution for certain human motives. For example, people are attracted to creatures with a youthful appearance, those with large eyes and heads, from kittens and puppies to Brad Pitt and Whitney Houston. Cuteness of this sort may be a releasing stimulus for nurturant behavior (Lorenz, 1966). Other mammals, like cats and dogs, show the same response, and one could argue that such tendencies evolved because they contribute to the survival of the young and helpless.

Very few parents physically attack their own children, perhaps because the appearance of a young child inhibits attack (Southwick, Pal, & Siddiqui, 1972). But those parents who do abuse their children tend to have poor impulse control, suggesting that they are oblivious to the inhibiting effects of an infant's appearance (Parke & Collmer, 1978). Furthermore, premature children are particularly apt to be abused, perhaps because they neither look nor sound like normal infants (Gill, 1970).

Motives as Needs and Drives

In the 1940s, theorists began to think of motives as internal states that set behavior in motion (Hull, 1943). Two related concepts are central in this viewpoint: needs and drives. A **need** is the lack of a biological essential, like food or water. A **drive** is the state of tension or arousal that a need produces. When a person experiences a drive, he or she tries to reduce the tension by satisfying the need in question. Suppose someone is thirsty. She may ask for a glass of water, stick her head under a faucet, or melt an ice cube in her mouth. If one or more of these behaviors reduces thirst, she is no longer motivated to seek out and drink liquid.

To need-and-drive theorists, all motives work in the same way, as diagrammed in Figure 7.1. This approach to motivation includes a crucial role for biology because the drive is stimulated by physiological needs. However, the actual behaviors that reduce the drives are typically learned, a fact which distinguishes need-and-drive theories from instinct theories.

The process of **homeostasis**—the maintenance of a stable or balanced state of physiological conditions—is important in need-and-drive accounts of motivation.

■ **need**
lack of a biological essential

■ **drive**
state of tension or arousal produced by a need

■ **homeostasis**
maintenance of a stable or balanced state of physiological conditions

Figure 7.1
Need–and–Drive Theory of Motivation. According to need-and-drive theory, our motives are based in biological needs that give rise to states of tension, called drives. Drives lead us to behave in ways to reduce the tension. The specific ways in which we behave in order to satisfy our needs are learned.

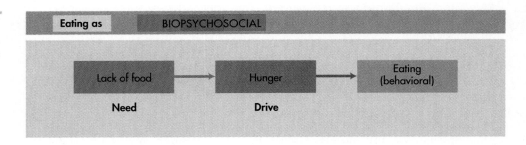

Drives are aroused when our internal state gets out of balance—for instance, when we are too hungry or too thirsty. The goal of behavior caused by a drive is to return our system to a balanced state.

A common means of maintaining homeostasis is by a feedback system. Such a system produces changes that are then "fed back" to the system where they influence its subsequent operation. Most of us live in houses or apartments with thermostats that turn the furnace on when the temperature falls too low and turn it off when the temperature rises too high. Thermostats keep the temperature within certain limits, just as needs and drives maintain the homeostasis of our bodies.

So far, the focus has been on motives based in physiological needs. However, motives can be learned; psychologists speak of these motives as acquired drives (Dickinson & Balleine, 1994). For example, in Chapter 8 you will learn that previously neutral stimuli can take on rewarding or punishing properties through learning.

Suppose a rat is placed in a cage with an electrified floor. A buzzer sounds, and a shock is administered a few seconds later. If the animal scrambles from one side of the cage to the other within these few seconds, the shock does not occur. The first several times this procedure is played out, the rat gets shocked. But after a while, it starts moving when the buzzer sounds. Learning has occurred because the rat now avoids shock. We can say that the rat has learned to fear the buzzer. Fear then leads to avoidance (Mowrer, 1950). Fear of the buzzer is an acquired drive that motivates attempts to reduce it.

The idea of acquired drives greatly extends the scope of need-and-drive theories. Nonetheless, not all of our motives conform to this script. Take the sexual behavior of human beings, as opposed to stickleback fish. Sex functions like a drive in that orgasms lead to a temporary waning of sexual activity, but people may act in ways to increase rather than decrease their sexual drive. This familiar scenario is contrary to how needs and drives operate among animals.

Motives as Cognitions

Theories that explain human motivation in terms of instincts or in terms of needs and drives neglect the role played by interpretations. Even a biologically based motive such as hunger reflects thoughts and beliefs about how best to satisfy our desires. These cognitions are the result of socialization and therefore reflect the norms and values of our prevailing culture.

Food preference is a good example of how biologically based motives take on social significance (Murphy, 1947). Infants are generally hungry or not. But as we grow older, hunger becomes specific and symbolic. We hunger not for generic food but for baked potatoes, eggplant parmigiana, stir-fried vegetables, or borscht (Harris, 1985). Many of us would rather go hungry than eat certain foods.

Other human motives—like thirst, sex, or aggression—have similar social significance (Tuorila, Pangborn, & Schutz, 1990). Within a given culture, we learn how to satisfy each of these motives in a socially acceptable way. If our behavior is at odds with what others around us believe, we may be judged harshly as incompetent, abnormal, criminal, or immoral (Chapter 13).

Food preference is a good example of how biologically based motives take on social significance. Here is a meal of alligator, insects, and crawfish. Any takers?

Recent decades have seen an explosion of cognitive theories of motivation (Weiner, 1985). These theories all assume that cognitions distinguish one motive from another. Beliefs may even determine whether a goal is pursued at all. Consider religious or moral belief systems that forbid satisfying sexual or aggressive motives. Many people live according to these beliefs, and the examples of their celibacy or nonviolence show the importance of beliefs. Instinct theories and need-and-drive theories of motivation make no room for cognitions as determinants of behavior. But once cognitions are added to the equation, we have a much fuller theoretical account (see Table 7.1).

Table 7.1   Summary: Approaches to Motivation

Approach	Key emphasis
Instincts	Biologically driven motives to perform complex yet unlearned behaviors
Needs and drives	Physiological needs giving rise to motives (drives) to perform behaviors that reduce the needs
Cognitions	Thoughts and beliefs about the behaviors that best satisfy motives

Stop and Think

4 How can a researcher demonstrate an instinct?

5 Are there motives that do not have a corresponding physiological need?

6 Think of an example from your everyday life of a motive that is well explained in cognitive terms.

DOING *Motivation* RESEARCH

Psychologists study the motivation of both animals and people. With animals, the focus is usually on motives that can be explained as instincts or drives; with people, the focus is often on motives that involve goals toward which we consciously strive. In either case, motives are conceived as states—physiological, cognitive, or both—that channel behavior in certain directions rather than others.

Animal Motivation

When a researcher wants to investigate the physiological underpinnings of motivation, he or she relies on strategies like those described in Chapter 4 for studying the brain and nervous system (Whalen & Simon, 1984). Interest often centers on the hypothalamus, which links the autonomic nervous system with the endocrine system (Sudakov, 1994). The autonomic nervous system and our glands work together to maintain homeostasis, and the hypothalamus serves as the thermostat for many of our motives. This function of the hypothalamus has been repeatedly demonstrated in lesion studies of animals.

Depending on the exact part of the hypothalamus that is destroyed, motives such as eating, drinking, sex, or aggression are affected. In each case, either too much or too little of the motivated behavior is produced. Figure 7.2 shows an example: A rat with a lesion in one part of its hypothalamus eats enthusiastically and endlessly, tripling its normal weight in a matter of weeks. A lesion in a different area of the hypothalamus will cause a rat to stop eating. Similar results have been obtained in studies that stimulate the hypothalamus with electrical current (Gafurov & Batuev, 1993), drugs (Gasanov & Kuliev, 1992), or neurotransmitters (Batuev & Gafurov, 1991).

As these results imply, the hypothalamus contains two parts, one that excites behavior and one that inhibits it (Stellar, 1954). **Dual-center theory** proposes that these two

■ **dual-center theory**
theory proposing that two parts (or centers) of the hypothalamus that work together to maintain the body's homeostasis

Figure 7.2
Rat with Lesion in Hypothalamus. The surgical destruction of a specific part of a rat's hypothalamus leads the rat to eat and eat and eat. Its weight may triple in a matter of weeks. This demonstration underscores the role of the hypothalamus in turning on and turning off motivated behavior.

parts (or centers) each respond to information—neural or hormonal—and work together to maintain the body's homeostasis. If one center is destroyed, as by a lesion, the system is disrupted. Dual-center theory is today considered an oversimplification (Mook, 1987). For example, both the fat rat and the skinny rat previously mentioned may return to their normal feeding patterns, even though the hypothalamus remains damaged. Other systems take over for the damaged areas. Still, dual-center theory is useful for perspective, reminding us that motivation involves not just turning behavior on but also turning it off.

More recent research into the brain mechanisms of motivation has identified some of the physiological underpinnings. For example, activity of different neurotransmitters is involved in different motives or even various aspects of the same motive. Zabik, Sprague, and Odio (1993) studied rats and found that drinking was initiated by dopamine neurons, whereas it was ended by norepinephrine neurons. So, initial thirst and eventual satisfaction of thirst are controlled by different mechanisms.

In another study, rats had an electrode implanted in their pleasure centers (Chapter 4) and were allowed for ten days to press a lever that stimulated them (Rao, Disraju, & Raju, 1993). When their brains were later compared with those of rats without this experience, increases in the branching of dendrites in the hypothalamus were found. Not only do brain mechanisms influence motives, but the satisfying of motives also influences brain mechanisms.

Human Motivation

One of the major figures in human motivation was Henry Murray (1893–1988), who proposed what he intended as a complete catalog of human needs. Murray (1938) believed we can recognize a need by several criteria:

- Attention to certain aspects of the environment rather than others
- Reports of particular feelings
- Repeated patterns of behavior
- Typical consequences of these behaviors
- Satisfaction with attaining these consequences
- Dissatisfaction with failure to attain these consequences

Using these guidelines, Murray identified approximately 20 human needs (see Table 7.2).

When people tell stories about ambiguous pictures, they may project their own motives onto what they see.

Table 7.2   Murray's Catalog of Needs

Here is Henry Murray's (1938) suggested list of important human needs.

Need	Characterization
Abasement	Need to submit to external forces, to comply, to accept punishment
Achievement	Need to accomplish, to overcome obstacles, to do something difficult
Affiliation	Need to form and maintain friendships, to live with others, to cooperate, to love
Aggression	Need to overcome opposition, to assault or injure, to belittle or accuse another person
Autonomy	Need to be free of restraint, to resist influence, to defy authority
Counteraction	Need to make up for failure, to refuse defeat, to defend one's honor
Defendance	Need to defend self against criticism, to justify one's actions, to offer explanations and excuses
Deference	Need to admire a superior, to cooperate with a leader, to serve another
Dominance	Need to control one's environment, to persuade, to lead and direct
Exhibition	Need to make an impression, to attract attention to oneself, to excite others
Harmavoidance	Need to avoid physical harm, to escape danger, to take precautions
Infavoidance	Need to avoid humiliation, to avoid failure, to hide shame
Nurturance	Need to assist the helpless, to express sympathy, to nourish another
Order	Need to put things in order, to be tidy, to act precisely
Play	Need to have fun, to seek diversion, to laugh
Power	Need to have an impact on others, to be in charge of people and situations
Rejection	Need to snub, to reject, to be aloof
Sentience	Need to seek and enjoy sensuous feelings
Sex	Need to form and maintain an erotic relationship, to have sexual intercourse
Succorance	Need to have one's need gratified by another, to seek aid, to be dependent
Understanding	Need to ask and answer questions, to analyze experiences, to discriminate among ideas

For instance, the need for order might show itself as knowledge of specific dates and deadlines (selective attention), as pride and purpose while doing errands (particular feelings), as persistent emptying of garbage cans (repeated patterns of behavior), as checkmarks on a list of things to do (typical consequences), as pleasure from an alphabetized spice rack (satisfaction with the attainment of order), and/or as misery with a cluttered desk (dissatisfaction with the failure to achieve order). Murray organized needs along several dimensions, such as more versus less biological and direct versus indirect expression.

People differ in the characteristic strength of their needs. For example, some individuals have a strong need for achievement and a weak need for play, whereas others show the opposite pattern. Advertisers use Murray's analysis of human needs (McNeal, 1982), sometimes making a product appeal to people who score high in need for achievement ("When you deserve the very best") and sometimes making a product appeal to people who score high in need for play ("It's a good time for the great taste"). Some advertisers work both sides of the street ("Oh yes, you can have it all").

Murray is remembered not only for cataloging human motives but also for creating a means to measure the strength of motives. Along with Christiana Morgan, he devised the **Thematic Apperception Test (TAT)** (Morgan & Murray, 1935), still used today (Keiser & Prather, 1990). With this test, subjects are first shown ambiguous pictures, like the one in Figure 7.3, and then asked to tell a story about what is going on.

■ **Thematic Apperception Test (TAT)** series of ambiguous pictures about which stories are told, used to infer the strength of one's needs

The TAT is called a projective technique because subjects project their own motives onto the characters in the story (Chapter 12). The picture itself provides no clues about what is occurring. If a subject mentions achievement, play, or power, the researcher has good reason to believe that these themes are coming from the subject and reflect the particular strength of his or her motives. The TAT is scored by counting the number of times a theme pertaining to a particular motive is mentioned; the more references to that motive, the higher the subject's score for it (Smith, 1992).

Stop and Think

7 What is dual-center theory?

8 What are some possible confounds in the use of the TAT to measure motives?

9 Use Murray's list of motives (Table 7.2) to describe the apparent needs of some particular figure in the public eye.

GENDER, CULTURE, AND MOTIVATION

How do motives differ across social contrasts like gender and ethnicity? As will be discussed in Chapter 12, men and women, on average, differ in two broad classes of motives that are usually described as agency versus communion (Helgeson, 1994). Men are more likely than women to behave in ways that focus on themselves and form separations from others (agency), whereas women are more likely to behave in ways that focus on others and form connections (communion). For example, among NCAA college athletes, males prefer the competitive aspects of sports, and females prefer the social aspects (Flood & Hellstedt, 1991). The mechanism giving rise to these differences is the gender role an individual adopts (Levit, 1991). Also important are the social settings in which men and women typically find themselves and what they demand or allow an individual to do (Shaffer, Pegalis, & Cornell, 1992).

Figure 7.3
TAT-Like Picture. One way to measure an individual's motives is to ask him or her to respond to an ambiguous picture like the one shown here. The picture itself has no fixed significance, and so a person's response to it is thought to reveal his or her important motives.

These generalizations about gender differences are broad. The types and strengths of motives possessed by men and women overlap considerably. Psychological well-being is usually best served by a balance between motives reflecting agency and those reflecting communion (Helgeson, 1993).

We can also ask whether people in different cultures show different motives. Again, there is considerable overlap. People in all times and places experience thirst, hunger, sexual arousal, and the need to affiliate with others. Nevertheless, researchers have documented differences in the relative importance of such motives as achievement and affiliation (Brandon, 1991; Fung, 1992; Keith & Benson, 1992; Rubin, Fernandez-Collado, & Hernandez-Sampieri, 1992). In the contemporary United States, for instance, European Americans place a higher emphasis on achievement than those in most other ethnic groups do, whereas Hispanic Americans place a higher emphasis on affiliation than those in most other ethnic groups do (Bernstein, 1991–1992).

> **Stop and Think**
>
> **10** Contrast communion and agency. Are there behaviors that can satisfy both of these motives?

PARTICULAR MOTIVES

Let us now take a close look at several particular motives. These are arranged from primary motives to acquired motives, but remember that most if not all motives reflect biopsychosocial influences.

Thirst

When our bodies are low on water, we experience thirst. We seek liquid and drink. Once we fill up, we stop drinking. Thirst is thus a feedback system, and researchers have mapped out how this system works. Current opinion holds that two different biological mechanisms produce thirst. First, if the volume of fluid inside the cells of our body becomes too low, thirst occurs. Second, if the volume of fluid outside our cells becomes too low, thirst also occurs. So, the theory used to explain the causes of thirst is called the **double-depletion hypothesis** because it specifies two routes—intracellular depletion of fluid and extracellular depletion of fluid—to thirst.

Another influence on drinking is the type of food we have recently eaten. For example, we become thirsty if we have consumed food high in protein or carbohydrates (de Castro, 1991). This phenomenon is an example of how one motive—thirst—can be influenced by another motive—hunger—and how the second motive has or has not been recently satisfied.

What happens in our bodies to signal that we have had enough to drink? The fluid volume inside and outside our cells is, of course, one type of signal, but there are others as well. Feedback from our mouth (no longer feeling dry) and our stomach (no longer feeling empty) can inhibit thirst. In addition, we learn to keep track of the amount of fluid we drink. If you have been exercising on a hot day, you become quite thirsty, but when you find a water fountain, you sip slowly. Finally, as water begins to enter the cells of our body, our feelings of thirst are inhibited (Blass & Hall, 1976).

Hunger

The Hungry Fly sounds like a B-grade horror movie, but it is a book by Vincent Dethier (1976) describing how flies respond when hungry. Flies are skilled at finding stray spills containing sugar because they have nerve cells in their feet that detect sugar. Suppose a

---

■ **double-depletion hypothesis**
theory of thirst proposing two causes of thirst: depletion of fluid within the cells of the body and depletion of fluid outside the cells

fly is taking a stroll one day and steps with its right foot into a puddle of something sweet. The sugar detectors are stimulated, and a message is sent to the brain. The brain then inhibits movement on the right side of the body.

The fly keeps on walking with its left legs. As it circles, its left foot encounters the sugar solution. Again the nerve cells fire, and now movement on the left side is inhibited. What happens when movement on both sides of the fly's body stops? The fly automatically extends its proboscis and starts to eat. As the sugar is ingested, the fly eventually fills up, and nerve cells in its digestive tract are stimulated. This process cancels feeding and disinhibits movement. The fly is now free to leave.

Hunger in flies involves a simple yet elegant biological reaction. Flies never eat and run, and they certainly thrive. Notice how the mechanism of a motive—in this case, hunger—can be wired into the nervous system of an organism. Notice also the process of homeostasis. The fly eats when it encounters sugar but only if its stomach is empty. The fly is protected from starvation on the one hand and overeating on the other. The various parts of the fly (sugar receptors, brain, legs, and digestive system) are coordinated to maintain homeostasis through a feedback system.

Hunger resembles thirst in that it too is a feedback system that can be both stimulated and inhibited. For human beings, the details are not well understood, but we have several likely candidates as stimuli to hunger, including:

- stomach contractions signifying the stomach is empty
- a low concentration of glucose in the blood
- a low level of fat stored in the body

None of these factors by itself is critical. For instance, people who have had their stomachs surgically removed still experience hunger, showing that stomach contractions do not tell the whole story. People with diabetes—which leads to a high concentration of blood sugar—still experience hunger, showing that a low glucose level is not the sole stimulus for hunger. Finally, people with high levels of fat stored in the body still experience hunger, showing that fat level alone does not cause hunger.

The cautious conclusion is that all of these internal states influence hunger, in some yet-to-be-specified combination. Also to be considered are external influences on hunger. The aroma, taste, or appearance of food can stimulate our desire to eat. Some restaurants bring a tray of desserts to their customers after a meal instead of referring to them on the menu, perhaps to capitalize on this influence. We also may eat when the clock on the wall tells us it is time for lunch or dinner, or simply because other people in our vicinity happen to be eating. In sum, events inside and outside our bodies trigger hunger. The same is true of hunger's inhibition: Many possible factors work in combination with one another, such as feedback from the mouth, stomach, intestines, and blood.

More general influences exist as well, including a person's sense of how his or her body should look. The scales onto which many of us hop each morning are part of a feedback system that regulates hunger, at least to the degree that we act according to the provided information.

Specific hungers. The well-being of animals and people requires that they eat foods containing fats, proteins, vitamins, and minerals. How do organisms manage to eat the correct foods? In some cases, Mother and Father tell us what to eat, but in other cases, there are **specific hungers:** motives to consume food containing particular substances. If organisms lack sodium, for instance, they experience a desire for salty foods. Research suggests that some species, like rats, might have specific hungers for protein and for carbohydrates (Rozin, 1968). It is not clear how many specific hungers people have, but we may have one only for sodium.

Instead, we possess a general reflex that accomplishes the same thing as a host of specific hungers. When we feel sick to our stomach, we avoid the particular foods we had been eating (Rozin & Kalat, 1971). Given this aversion to recent tastes, we end up seeking new foods. This makes sense because a diet deficient in a necessary substance

■ **specific hungers**
motives to consume food containing particular substances

Hunger can be stimulated by external stimuli. The sight of desserts in a bakery window or on a restaurant's pastry cart is likely to arouse a desire to eat sweets, even if our stomachs are full.

usually makes us feel ill. As we try new foods in the wake of our illness, we might encounter the substance we needed in the first place. Of course, sometimes gastric upset has nothing to do with our diet, as when a bout with the flu coincides with guacamole. We might develop an aversion to avocados, an unfortunate consequence of a generally helpful reflex. However, we are mostly protected from such coincidences because taste aversion occurs most readily with new foods. We tend not to avoid familiar foods, no matter how sick we may feel.

Obesity.   The physiological mechanisms responsible for hunger and thirst show considerable redundancy. Problems nonetheless occur with these motives. So, **obesity** is commonly defined as 20 percent or more in excess of what is considered a normal and healthy weight; millions of people in the United States can be described as obese. What causes this?

One theory attributes obesity to homeostasis (Keesey & Powley, 1986). Specifically, **set-point theory** proposes that our bodies work to maintain a certain level of body fat, called the set point. As we depart from our set point, higher or lower, processes take place to counteract the change. If our body fat increases, we eat less frequently and increase our activity. And if our body fat decreases, we eat more frequently and decrease our activity.

The problem for obese individuals may be that their set point is too high; they are predisposed to be heavy. If they eat less food, their bodies simply use the calories more efficiently. Studies indicate that, contrary to our stereotypes, many obese people do not eat much more than people of normal weight (Spitzer & Rodin, 1981). Their bodies resist the loss of fat, and so it takes very few calories to keep them overweight. The question remains as to why the set point is too high in the first place (Stallone & Stunkard, 1991). The debate continues, but genetic influences and/or early eating habits may be responsible. It is also unclear whether set point can be changed, but habits like exercising or smoking might alter it (Rodin & Wack, 1984).

Whether or not set point can be changed, set-point theory does not imply that weight loss is impossible. However, the theory does have two implications that would-be dieters must follow. First, it is difficult to lose weight; the body resists weight loss, even when that is a healthy goal (Garner & Wooley, 1991). Second, dieting is not a

■ **obesity**
condition of being 20 percent or more in excess of what is considered a normal and healthy weight

■ **set-point theory**
idea that one's body is set to maintain a certain level of fat

once-in-a-lifetime experience (Perpina & Baños, 1989). For people with a high set point, the struggle to stay thin is ongoing (Westover & Lanyon, 1990).

There are many causes of obesity, and set-point theory focuses on only one of them (Brownell & Wadden, 1992). Generally, people become obese because they take in more calories than they use. Overeating is one obvious cause of obesity, and so too is a sedentary lifestyle (Shah & Jeffery, 1991). Also contributing to obesity are genetic factors, eating habits established early in life, and the tendency to eat when anxious or depressed (Stunkard, Harris, Pedersen, & McClearn, 1990).

Anorexia and bulimia. Two other problems that involve eating deserve our attention because they show that primary motives can be overridden by psychological and social factors. **Anorexia nervosa** occurs when a deliberate restriction of calories results in extreme weight loss (American Psychiatric Association, 1994). People with anorexia have a distorted image of their own body size and shape. They believe they look fat, even as they are starving. Anorexia leads to serious physical problems associated with malnutrition and proves fatal in as many as 18 percent of cases (Sharp & Freeman, 1993).

■ **anorexia nervosa**
deliberate restriction of calories resulting in extreme weight loss

The onset of anorexia is usually during adolescence, and in the overwhelming majority of cases—about 95 percent—its victims are females. It is more common among individuals in the middle and upper socioeconomic classes than among individuals in the lower class. Anorexia also appears to be most common among those of European ancestry, although it occurs in all ethnic groups (Davis & Yager, 1992; Dolan, 1991). Estimates of its frequency among teenage females in the United States range from 0.1 to 15.0 percent.

No agreement exists as to the causes of anorexia (Braun & Chouinard, 1992). Biologically oriented theorists speculate about dysfunctions of the hypothalamus. Psychodynamic theorists speculate that the anorexic individual is afraid of sexuality and alters her body so that she looks prepubescent. Cognitive-behavioral theorists wonder about the role played by the family; perhaps anorexia involves a struggle for control between the parents and their child, one with life-and-death consequences. All of these possibilities must be considered in conjunction with our cultural preoccupation with being thin.

Treating the disorder is difficult because anorexia involves the insistence that nothing is wrong (Rastam, 1994). In cases of extreme weight loss, aggressive medical intervention is necessary to restore the person's nutritional state to normal. Involuntary hospitalization and forced feeding may follow. Behavior therapy is thought to be helpful in the treatment of anorexia, as is family therapy.

Another eating disorder is **bulimia nervosa:** the alternation between bingeing (ingesting thousands of calories of food in a short period) and purging (ridding oneself of those calories through vomiting, taking laxatives, fasting, or exercising) (American Psychiatric Association, 1994). The person with bulimia is often of normal weight but is preoccupied with the fear of becoming fat. Although not as dangerous as anorexia, bulimia has a variety of negative consequences. People who frequently vomit may erode their teeth (because digestive juices from their stomachs attack tooth enamel), suffer dehydration, and create electrolyte imbalance. The problem is often accompanied by depression, and the sheer amount of time needed to binge and purge means that the person has limited time for other activities.

■ **bulimia nervosa**
alternation between bingeing (ingesting thousands of calories of food in a short time) and purging (ridding oneself of those calories)

The typical individual with bulimia is a female of European ancestry from the middle or upper class, as with anorexia (Vandereycken, 1994). Onset is often in the early twenties. Estimates of its frequency vary greatly, depending on the particular criteria used to define its presence (Schotte & Stunkard, 1987). Consequently, some studies report that almost 20 percent of U.S. college women are bulimic, whereas others give a figure as low as 1 percent. Regardless, bulimia is probably more common than anorexia, and is on the rise in our society (Tury & Szabo, 1991).

There is no generally agreed upon cause of bulimia or treatments for it (Martin, 1990; Mitchell, Raymond, & Specker, 1993). Given its association with depression,

Cultural factors, such as the body type a society regards as attractive, can derail even basic motives like hunger. People with the eating disorder anorexia have a distorted sense of the size and shape of their bodies. Even as they are starving, they believe that they are fat.

many therapists treat bulimia with the strategies available for helping people with depressive disorder (Chapter 14). Also, tentative support for behavior therapy and family therapy has been reported (Mitchell, 1991).

Sexuality

Sex differs from the motives so far discussed. First, sexual activity is not necessary for individual survival in the way that drinking and eating are. Second, as noted, our sex drive often leads us not to reduce tension and arousal but rather to increase these. Stated another way, homeostasis is not always the goal of sexual activity. Third, unlike thirst and hunger, present in full force at birth, our sex drive develops over time.

What lies behind people's sexual activity? At a biological level, this question has several answers. One is that we behave sexually in order to reproduce. Sex is a deeply rooted human characteristic. We are driven to engage in sexual activity because it is our nature, and our nature has been shaped by evolution (Chapter 3). If any of us had but a single ancestor who did not pursue sexual activity, then we would not be here. Another answer is that we engage in sexual activity because it makes us feel good. Only a fraction of this activity is channeled into reproduction. Clearly, the desire for pleasure is behind the rest of it. These two biological motives for sex—reproduction and pleasure—are not incompatible. In evolutionary terms, we can say that natural selection conspired to make sex feel good precisely so that we would do it for the purpose of reproduction.

But there are other motives driving human sexuality. Sexuality, at least in our culture, is a way of expressing love for another person. Part of the identity we form during our teenage years is sexual, and so sexuality also serves the motive of self-expression. For most of us, it is tied into our self-esteem. Note how we have moved from biologically based motives (reproduction and pleasure) to psychological ones shaped by the larger culture (expression and identity). Sexual activity requires a biopsychosocial explanation.

Hormones.   Sexual activity involves our bodies—specifically, our genitals, reproductive organs, and various erogenous zones. Almost all of the body's hormones influence our sexuality, but those with the most obvious effects—testosterone and estrogen—are produced by our sex organs. To complicate matters, although testosterone is produced mainly in the testes of men, it is also produced in the adrenal cortex, meaning that women's bodies contain male and female sex hormones. When we are tempted to explain the behavior of males in terms of testosterone, we must remember that small quantities of this hormone also exist in females.

What role do our sex hormones play in human sexual response? Common sense suggests that hormones have something to do with our sex drive, but the influence is more complicated than a one-to-one relationship between people's hormones and their behavior. The sex hormones are critical in ensuring physical development and creating anatomical differences between males and females. They trigger the onset of puberty, which turns children into adults capable of having their own children. Among women, menstruation, pregnancy, and childbirth follow a course influenced by complex interactions among circulating hormones. Among men, such cycles do not occur, but the amount of testosterone in their bodies influences the level of their sex drive.

However, hormones do not tell the whole story of human sexuality. Research has not found that levels of estrogen influence a female's sex drive (Persky, 1983). And males who as adults have been castrated (had their testes removed) often experience no loss of sexual interest, despite a drastic decrease in the level of testosterone in their bodies. Something else must be going on: Psychological factors influence our sex drive, sometimes overriding more biological influences. Compared to sexuality in other species, human sexuality depends less on hormones and more on experiences.

Sexual behavior.   Sexual behavior is a broad topic that is difficult to organize. One common distinction psychologists make is between the sheer frequency of sexual activity and the specific direction of this activity. Inasmuch as the more interesting aspect of sexuality is its direction, let me briefly discuss frequency before taking a detailed look at direction.

Surveys of sexuality have often placed particular emphasis on orgasms (Kinsey, Pomeroy, & Martin, 1948; Kinsey, Pomeroy, Martin, & Gebhard, 1953). The total sexual outlet of a person is determined by counting orgasms within a given period. Needless to say, an orgasm as an operational definition of sexual behavior is hardly perfect. No one would wish to argue that an orgasm, or even behavior that culminates in one, is the whole of human sexual behavior. At the least, a more adequate operational definition of sexual behavior would include its personal and social significance.

Still, research using this operationalization allows us to offer general statements about the frequency of sexual behavior among people in our society (Katchadourian, 1985):

■ Over their lifetime, men have more orgasms than women; however, women as a group show a greater range than men in the frequency of total sexual outlet.
■ For men, the frequency of orgasm is at its highest point during adolescence; it declines thereafter, particularly after age 30.
■ For women, the frequency of orgasm increases from adolescence until age 30, stays constant for the next ten years, and then declines.

Let us move on to where sexual activity is directed.

Sexual orientation.   Freud distinguished between the concepts of sexual object, a person or thing one finds sexually attractive, and sexual aim, what one wishes to do with a sexual object. The use of the term *object* to include people may seem strange, but the intent is to encompass the entire range of what a person might find sexually attractive.

Many theorists divide people into four categories, based on their orientation to sexual objects: Autosexuals direct the sex drive toward themselves, as in masturbation; heterosexuals direct the sex drive toward members of the opposite sex; homosexuals direct the sex drive toward members of the same sex; and bisexuals direct the sex drive toward members of the same sex and those of the opposite sex.

These categories might be at the wrong level of abstraction because many people—perhaps all people—define the object of their sexual drive in more specific, elaborate, and personal ways (Stoller, 1985). A heterosexual male, for instance, is usually not attracted equally to all women; he may prefer only those who are slender, or those with freckles, or those with long black hair, or those with tattoos, or those who laugh at his bad jokes.

■ **sexual orientation**
sexual object and aim of a particular person

The term **sexual orientation** is used to indicate the sexual object and aim of a particular person—whatever turns one on. Why does someone respond sexually to one object as opposed to another? There is no widely accepted explanation. All would agree that this process involves some interaction between biological and social factors, but controversy enters when we try to place greater emphasis on one influence over the other (Chapter 4).

Psychologists have frequently proposed theories to explain homosexuality, many dating to the time when homosexuality was assumed to represent a discrete category of people. Psychology has undoubtedly seen many more theories of homosexuality than heterosexuality. According to traditional Christian belief, heterosexuality is the way it is "supposed to be" and so needs no further explanation. As this idea was carried into science, it made heterosexuality the inherent consequence of normal development.

People define the object of their attraction in specific and highly personal ways. Why does someone respond sexually to one object as opposed to another? There is no generally agreed upon explanation, but it probably includes biological, psychological, and social factors.

Psychologists therefore focused their explanations on departures from what was considered normal: homosexuality.

However, surveys today show that people cannot be neatly divided into groups of exclusive heterosexuals and exclusive homosexuals. A number of individuals occupy a middle ground. Psychology needs not so much a theory of specific sexual orientations as a theory of sexual orientation in general: heterosexual, homosexual, bisexual, and autosexual.

Sexual development.   A sound theory needs to explain the following aspects about sexual development. For starters, the capacity to be sexually aroused is present at birth. Newborn baby boys have erections, sometimes as many as 40 per day (Conn & Kanner, 1940). Vaginal lubrication has been observed in newborn baby girls. Ultrasound studies show erections by male fetuses (Masters, 1980). These signs of sexual responsiveness have the nature of reflexes because they are triggered by external events, such as feeding or defecation. However, they also have a sensual component because even newborns smile and coo during genital stimulation.

The capacity to display a physical response to sexual stimulation is built into us, and a link to pleasure is part of its character. Nonetheless, infant and child sexuality differs from that of adults because it is more general and diffuse. In the course of development, a sexual orientation is created: The sexual drive and response become attached to certain objects and aims but not others.

Both infants and children masturbate, meaning that autoeroticism is the earliest form of sexual behavior for many people. Some preadolescent children engage in sex play with siblings or peers. One hesitates to specify exact percentages here because there is great variation. At least in the United States, boys seem more likely to masturbate and to engage in sex play than their female counterparts.

Cross-cultural and cross-historical studies document vast differences in the frequency of homosexual and heterosexual orientations, so socialization must play an important role in determining sexual orientation.

While this is going on, the child is becoming a truly social being (Chapter 10). The attitudes of parents and society are communicated to him or her. Children are provided with diverse models of how a sexual being acts, thinks, and feels. Our sexual identity becomes entwined with other aspects of our identity, and great variations can be introduced by the specifics of our histories.

In the United States, very little sexual socialization takes place overtly. Rather, parents give children brief messages without explanations ("That's not a nice thing to do"), or the wrong explanations ("If you keep touching yourself there, it will fall off"), or a host of nonverbal messages that associate sexual behavior with guilt or shame.

Those in other cultures socialize their children differently with respect to sexuality. At least prior to extensive Western contact, the following practices were common (Ford & Beach, 1950):

■ Children among the Siriono (in Bolivia) were manually masturbated by their parents in order to soothe them.
■ Infant boys among the Mangaia Islanders (in the South Pacific) were orally stimulated by their mothers.
■ Boys and girls among the Chewa (in Africa) were encouraged to play with one another sexually in order to be fertile as adults.
■ Prepubescent girls among the Lepcha (in the Himalayas) were encouraged to have intercourse with adult males in order to grow up at all.
■ Children among the Trobriand Islanders (in the South Pacific) were taught by adults how to have intercourse.

I chose these examples because they are permissive (indeed, abusive) by Western standards, but there are also examples that we would regard as extremely restrictive (and again, abusive). For instance, if a boy among the Kwoma (in New Guinea) had an erection, an adult woman would beat his penis with a stick. Kwoma boys learned quickly never to touch their penises, even when urinating.

In all cultures, sexual orientation becomes more specialized and elaborate at the onset of adolescence. The influx of sexual hormones at puberty accompanies an upsurge in a teenager's sexual drive, although we should note again that no essential link exists between the two. Sex drive is not just hormone levels because interest in sex need not wane with age, despite decreases in hormone levels (von Sydow, 1992).

Theorist John Money (1986) proposed that sexual orientation emerges from an interaction of biological predispositions and specific experiences. Simple learning is probably not responsible. That is, one might argue that sexual orientation is produced by the repeated pairing of given objects and aims with sexual pleasure (Chapter 8), but this account does not square with the evidence. Sexual orientation almost always appears before explicit sexual activity of the type embodied in the orientation.

Money suggested instead that individuals abstract the gist of a sexual orientation from early observations and experiences, just as people abstract the gist of a language— its grammar (Chapter 9). He called the gist of sexual orientation a **lovemap** and hypothesized that people use it to direct their subsequent sexual activity, just as we use grammar to direct our use of language.

Money's theory can be criticized for not providing details about the origins of given lovemaps. There is presumably a biological predisposition to abstract some sort of lovemap; very few people have no sexual orientation whatsoever. Does biology play a more specific role? Few studies find physiological differences between people with different sexual orientations. Two exceptions were discussed in Chapter 4: (a) the study by LeVay (1991) showing differences between gay and straight men in the size of particular brain structures and (b) the study by Hamer and colleagues (1993) finding that a homosexual orientation among men was heritable through the mother's side.

The significance of these studies is not yet clear. Further investigations need to discover the mechanisms—biological and psychological—leading to actual behavior (Ernulf & Innala, 1991). How does socialization figure into the process, as it surely must?

■ **lovemap**
Money's term for the gist of one's sexual orientation

Cross-cultural and cross-historical studies document vast differences in the frequency of homosexual (and heterosexual) orientation. Furthermore, surveys suggest that male homosexuals are more likely than heterosexuals to be born later in a family and to have a larger number of brothers (Blanchard, Zucker, Bradley, & Hume, 1995).

Aggression

Psychologists define **aggression** as intentionally destructive acts directed against individuals or groups. Over the years, a controversy has developed over whether human aggression is a primary or an acquired motive. Many now believe that aggression in people is largely acquired (Laub & Lauritsen, 1993), but let us consider the evidence on both sides, starting with the view that aggression is biologically based.

First, aggression can be influenced by physiological states. We saw, for instance, how male sticklebacks are predisposed by hormonal changes to attack other males. Among most mammalian species is a similar link between male hormones and aggression. The hormones do not directly cause aggression, but they make the animal much more likely to respond aggressively when the appropriate provocations are present.

Second, among some species, aggression is inhibited by built-in reflexes, indicating again that biological factors can regulate aggression. When two males confront each other, the fight ends abruptly when the loser makes a submissive display, like lowering the head or baring the neck. Then the winner no longer presses his advantage. Both live to fight another day.

What about people? One argument, advanced by ethologist Konrad Lorenz (1966), is that the impulse to act aggressively is inherent in human beings just as it is in animals. But because human technology makes it possible for people to aggress at a distance, with sticks and stones, bullets and bombs, we never developed submissive displays that were effective. So, human aggression has escalated throughout history.

You might wonder whether male sex hormones affect aggression in human beings as they do in lower animals. Males throughout the world are more likely than females to commit violent crimes. Some studies find a positive correlation between males' testosterone levels and their tendencies to act in hostile ways (Kreuz & Rose, 1972). Recent publicity about the psychological effects of steroids, which contain male sex hormones, further supports this argument. Excessive rage and violence apparently occur among some who abuse these drugs (Marti-Carbonell, Darbra, Garau, & Balada, 1992).

Let us now consider the arguments in favor of regarding human aggression as an acquired motive. Unlike thirst and hunger, aggression does not work according to a feedback system. There is no homeostatic level of aggression that an individual needs to maintain. Indeed, human aggression occurs in response to some external event, such as frustration or pain, and it continues to occur if it leads to a desired consequence. It is therefore instrumental or learned (Chapter 8). Furthermore, people's interpretations are critical in determining how we act in a particular situation (Chapter 15). If someone trips us, for example, we may respond with aggression if playing hockey and with amusement if dancing.

Relevant to this discussion is an influential theory of aggression—the **frustration-aggression hypothesis**—which attributes all aggression to frustration: the failure to attain a desired goal (Dollard, Doob, Miller, Mowrer, & Sears, 1939). Aggression is regarded as a reflex, and without the trigger of frustration, no one would ever lash out at another person.

Descriptively, the frustration-aggression hypothesis accounts for many instances of aggression. Do we curse a vending machine or kick at it when it delivers the product we want? Of course not. Historical research finds that riots and revolutions are most likely to occur when people's hopes have been raised but then dashed. However, when the frustration-aggression hypothesis is examined more closely, qualifications are needed. For example, perhaps only frustrations that threaten one's sense of self trigger aggression. Perhaps aggression follows only when behavior directed toward a goal is

■ **aggression**
intentionally destructive acts directed against individuals or groups

■ **frustration-aggression hypothesis**
theory that all aggression is due to the failure to attain a desired goal

interrupted. We also know that under some circumstances, frustration leads not to aggression but rather to renewed efforts to achieve one's goals (Brehm, 1966). Under still other circumstances, frustration leads to passivity (Seligman, 1975). Even when the frustration-aggression link exists, it may represent not so much a reflex as expectations and interpretations. We kick uncooperative vending machines more frequently than we kick personal computers that do not do what we want. Vending machines sometimes deliver when threatened. Computers just break.

Acknowledging these qualifications, Berkowitz (1981) proposed a modified version of the frustration-aggression hypothesis. According to his revised account, frustration results in a readiness to act aggressively; however, we follow through on this readiness only when we encounter environmental circumstances previously associated with aggression, such as hockey games or saloons. This theory gives us two ways to head off aggression: either prevent frustration or remove cues to violence.

What about the evidence that aggression is more common in men than in women? The role of socialization must be taken into account (Bjorkqvist, 1994). Boys might be encouraged to be aggressive, whereas girls are not. With sufficient incentives, girls are just as capable as boys of performing the aggressive responses that a model has displayed (Fishbein, 1992).

Perhaps the apparent correlation between testosterone and hostility reflects the operation of some third factor, like physical appearance, that in turn influences hostility and violence. A young male with bulging muscles may lead others to treat him in an aggressive way; when he responds in turn, he establishes a link that appears to be biological but is in fact interpersonal (Chapter 3). Another possibility is that aggressive behavior increases the level of a male's testosterone rather than vice versa, as most biological theorists propose (Archer, 1991). Until the answer is known, we should remember what psychologists already do know: Whatever the cause of aggression, people can learn not to act this way (Stern & Fodor, 1989).

Achievement Motivation

■ **achievement motivation**
need to accomplish something difficult in situations characterized by a standard of excellence

Some people throw themselves into their schoolwork or their job, wanting to do the best they can. Others are indifferent. We can explain these different approaches as due to variation in one's underlying motive to achieve. **Achievement motivation** is the need to accomplish something difficult in situations that are characterized by a standard of excellence (Murray, 1938). Psychologists typically measure it by looking at TAT responses. Achievement motivation is apparently produced by parents who encourage their children to be independent and successful (McClelland, 1985).

In a well-known study, Atkinson and Litwin (1960) used the TAT to measure achievement motivation among research subjects who attempted a task requiring them to toss rings over a peg. The subjects chose the distance they stood from the peg. Subjects high in the need to achieve chose an intermediate distance neither too close nor too far more frequently than subjects low in the need to achieve. Do you see why? Standing too close makes success automatic and hence a poor way to satisfy the need to achieve. Standing too far away turns the task into a game of chance, again a poor way to satisfy achievement needs.

Studies like this one generalize to more important behaviors. For instance, longitudinal investigations have shown that those high in achievement motivation earn better grades in school (Dwinell & Higbee, 1991) and more money in their careers (McClelland & Franz, 1992).

In an intriguing line of research, David McClelland (1961) investigated societal differences in achievement motivation. With the TAT as a model, he devised ways of scoring an entire society for its level of achievement motivation. He scored grade school primers from different countries for themes of achievement. In other words, he treated each story like a response to a TAT picture and counted references to achievement. Did the characters strive to do well at work or school, or were they portrayed as doing other things?

Achievement motivation is produced by parents who encourage their children to be independent and successful. Michael Jordan has had more success as a basketball player than as a baseball player, but his strong motivation to achieve was apparent at both sports.

The more achievement themes that were present in a nation's schoolbooks, the greater its economic growth a generation later! These findings do not prove a cause-and-effect relationship because they are based on correlations. However, McClelland tentatively concluded that achievement motivation was increased in children who read stories containing achievement themes and decreased in children who did not. Several decades later, achievement motivation apparently translated itself into actual behavior as measured by dollars and cents.

One approach to understanding the achievement motive has been to break it up into smaller components (Atkinson, 1958). It is possible, for example, to distinguish between a desire for success versus a fear of failure. For many, these are linked, but imagine the person who wishes very much to be successful but cares little about failures along the way. We would expect her to be a risk taker: "Nothing ventured, nothing gained." Conversely, the person whose achievement motivation is dominated by a fear of failure follows a cautious path: "Better safe than sorry." Another distinction here is between those who are driven to achieve goals defined in terms of performance versus those who pursue goals defined in terms of increased skills (Dweck, 1990).

In recent years, psychologists interested in achievement motivation have investigated the role played by an individual's beliefs (Graham, 1991). Regardless of how motivated someone may be to achieve, this motive is not translated into action if the goal is perceived as unattainable. For example, individuals who believe that they lack the required skills to achieve or that the task in question is extremely difficult tend not to exert the same effort as those who believe otherwise (Weiner, 1978, 1986).

Power Motivation

Power motivation is the need to have an impact on others, to be in charge of people and situations (Murray, 1938). Again, the strength of this motive can be gauged by looking at TAT stories and counting the number of times social impact is mentioned.

Researchers have examined the need for power and leadership (Winter, 1988, 1991). Both men and women who are high in power motivation are more likely than those low in this motivation to hold elective office. They also are more likely to pursue careers in which they can influence others, such as teaching, psychotherapy, journalism, and business management.

Winter (1973, 1993) scored the need for power among political leaders, treating their speeches as if they were TAT stories. Power motivation among presidents of the United States has varied greatly during the twentieth century. High scorers include Theodore

■ **power motivation**
need to have an impact on others

Roosevelt, Franklin Roosevelt, Woodrow Wilson, John Kennedy, and Lyndon Johnson, and low scorers include Robert Taft, Herbert Hoover, and Dwight Eisenhower. Note the tendency for Democrats to be higher on the need for power than Republicans; note also that presidents in office when the country entered a war tended as well to score high.

Another line of research looks at the relationship between power motivation and physical health. In his research, David McClelland (1975) found that a high level of this motive, when coupled with excessive self-restraint, puts someone at risk for poor health. Although the physiological mechanisms are not agreed upon, perhaps the conflict between power motivation and its restraint stresses the sympathetic nervous system, which in turn takes a toll on health (McClelland, 1982). Another possible mechanism involves the immune system (Jemmott et al., 1990).

These findings are provocative, but we must be cautious in interpreting them. All are correlational results. Although Winter, McClelland, and other researchers wish to conclude that this motive leads to certain occupational and health outcomes, other possibilities exist. Perhaps health determines how an individual responds to a measure of power motivation. Perhaps occupation determines a person's power motivation. Perhaps a third variable, such as economic status, influences both motivation and its supposed consequences. Researchers are not oblivious to these possibilities, and they try their best to rule them out (Chapter 2).

Mastery

■ **mastery**
need to behave in a competent way

The need for **mastery** is the motivation to behave in a competent way, regardless of what one is doing. Mastery has been variously described as:

> capability, capacity, efficiency, proficiency, and skill. It is therefore . . . suitable . . . to describe such things as grasping and exploring, crawling and walking, attention and perception, language and thinking, manipulating and changing the surroundings, all of which promote an effective—a competent—interaction with the environment. (White, 1959, p. 317)

In short, people experience pleasure in doing things well (Meier, 1993; Pittman & Heller, 1987). The need for mastery seems similar to the need for young creatures of many species to play—a tendency that helps them rehearse behaviors that will prove useful when they become adults (Huizinga, 1950).

Remember the first time you mastered a bicycle, a typewriter, or a video game. You felt good because you had satisfied your need for mastery. Some theorists extend this need to include the world of ideas, proposing that people are motivated to understand what they encounter (Antonovsky, 1979). When faced with puzzling occurrences, we try to make sense of them, not stopping until we find a satisfactory explanation. The need for mastery may be why crossword puzzles, soap operas, and riddles intrigue us. Similarly, Kusyszyn (1990) suggested that mastery is one of the motives for gambling.

Table 7.3   Summary: Important Human Motives

People's motives can be described as primary versus acquired.

Motive	Description
Thirst	Primary
Hunger	Primary
Sexuality	Primary
Aggression	Acquired
Achievement motivation	Acquired
Power motivation	Acquired
Mastery	Acquired

Mastery is not simply getting what one wants. Rather, mastery involves doing things in a skilled manner. Chess players need not win in order to satisfy their need for mastery.

We suspect that most gamblers do not consistently win, but perhaps the desire to make money is not the motivational point.

Being able to control the environment is obviously an advantage because we can attain what is desirable and avoid what is not (Peterson, Maier, & Seligman, 1993). But the need for mastery is not the same as getting what one wants. Rather, the need for mastery is satisfied when one acts in a skillful manner, whether or not desired goals are attained. For people high in this need, what matters is how they play the game.

Thomas and Kaplan (1994) discussed the way in which this need can be highly relevant for those with physical disabilities, particularly when these have been acquired later in life. When physical skills are compromised, individuals become upset. Their distress has two sources: Certain outcomes have become less attainable, and they feel incompetent.

Stop and Think

11 What is a specific hunger?

12 How does sex differ from other primary motives?

13 Why do most psychologists believe that aggression is an acquired human motive?

14 Describe an example from your everyday life of how you satisfy your need for mastery.

MOTIVATION IN A BIOPSYCHOSOCIAL CONTEXT

One lesson from psychology's study of motivation is that a single person marches to different drummers (see Table 7.3). How can we make sense of all the motives that arouse and direct our actions? One important attempt to systematize human motives was made by Abraham Maslow (1970), who suggested that our motives are arranged according to a **hierarchy of needs** (see Figure 7.4).

At the bottom are biologically based needs, such as hunger and thirst. We cannot leave these needs unsatisfied for too long because our lives are at stake. Only when these needs are met does the need to be free from threatened danger arise. Maslow called this need one of safety—both physical and psychological. We need to believe the world is stable and coherent.

Next in the hierarchy is attachment, which leads us to seek out other people, to love and be loved. If we successfully satisfy this need for attachment, then we need to feel

■ **hierarchy of needs**
Maslow's idea that motives are arranged in a hierarchy reflecting the order in which they are satisfied

Figure 7.4
Maslow's Hierarchy of Needs.
Abraham Maslow proposed that people have a variety of needs and that these can be arranged in a hierarchy according to the order in which they are satisfied. Needs at the bottom of the hierarchy (biological and safety needs) must be satisfied before higher needs become relevant. Although its details can be criticized, Maslow's theory serves as an important reminder that needs are biopsychosocial.

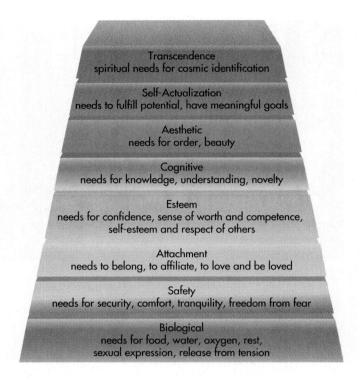

Transcendence
spiritual needs for cosmic identification

Self-Actualization
needs to fulfill potential, have meaningful goals

Aesthetic
needs for order, beauty

Cognitive
needs for knowledge, understanding, novelty

Esteem
needs for confidence, sense of worth and competence, self-esteem and respect of others

Attachment
needs to belong, to affiliate, to love and be loved

Safety
needs for security, comfort, tranquility, freedom from fear

Biological
needs for food, water, oxygen, rest, sexual expression, release from tension

■ **self-actualization**
full use and exploitation of one's talents, capacities, and potentialities

esteemed, by ourselves and others. Maslow grouped our needs for knowledge, understanding, and novelty together as cognitive needs and proposed that they are next in his hierarchy (Chapter 9). Then we find aesthetic needs: the desire for order and beauty.

Near the top of his hierarchy is **self-actualization:** "the full use and exploitation of talents, capacities, potentialities" (Maslow, 1970, p. 150). Maslow argued that we must satisfy lower needs before we seek satisfaction of higher needs. The need for self-actualization is difficult to achieve because it becomes relevant only when the needs that fall below it have been successfully addressed. Maslow was particularly interested in the self-actualized individual, to whom he attributed such characteristics as spontaneity, autonomy, sense of humor, and a capacity for deep interpersonal relations. Finally, at the very top of the hierarchy is the need for transcendence, which refers to spiritual and religious needs.

The particular order in which Maslow arranged the different needs can be criticized (Neher, 1991). A parent might run into a burning building to save a stranded child or forgo all manner of personal satisfactions to pay for the child's music lessons. Along these lines, a study comparing homeless individuals and college students in terms of their need for self-actualization found no differences (Sumerlin & Norman, 1992).

Another complexity is introduced by the recognition that higher needs may dictate the manner in which lower needs are satisfied (Heylighen, 1992). For instance, an individual's religious beliefs might prescribe acceptable and unacceptable foods. And according to some theorists, people often pursue goals simultaneously from different levels of the hierarchy (Umoren, 1992).

Nonetheless, Maslow's general idea is sensible. His hierarchy approximates the order in which most people attend to their various needs (Aram & Piraino, 1978; Wicker, Brown, Wiehe, Hagen, & Reed, 1993). Hungry people tend not to pursue their aesthetic needs until their stomachs are full (Seeley, 1992). Hungry people are not as concerned in their political lives with issues of equality and equity as individuals whose more basic needs have been satisfied (cf. Davies, 1991). One reason why social security and military defense are treated by many as untouchable expenditures when budget cuts are discussed in the United States is that these are typically cast in terms of safety, next to the bottom line in Maslow's scheme.

Keep in mind a basic idea inherent in Maslow's suggested hierarchy of needs: People's motives are interconnected and organized. Whether or not we try to satisfy a particular motive depends on the current state of our other motives. Said another way, we need to understand a given motive in the context of other motives, and this context is a biopsychosocial one.

APPROACHES TO EMOTION

What are the basic types of emotions? What are their causes? What are their consequences? Psychologists interested in emotion want to know how and why we experience the particular emotions we do: fear or loathing, love or hate, passion or apathy. Over the years, several approaches to understanding emotions have appeared. As with motivation, these approaches to emotion often focus on either the biological or the social aspects. These perspectives are different, but they complement one another. Each takes one particular aspect of our emotional life as its special concern, and when we integrate these approaches, we have a biopsychosocial explanation.

Evolutionary Approach: Focus on Functions

The first theoretical viewpoint to be discussed is the evolutionary approach begun by Charles Darwin. In his 1872 book, *The Expression of Emotions in Man and Animals*, Darwin drew parallels between animals and people in their emotional reactions to events. For example, dogs, cats, gorillas, and human beings all bare their teeth when threatened (Brothers, 1990). Darwin suggested that emotions increase chances for survival because they are appropriate responses in the situations where they are experienced. This approach leads one to seek the survival function of emotions (Nesse, 1990).

Basic emotions.   Robert Plutchik (1962, 1980, 1984) is a modern theorist in the evolutionary tradition. He proposed that we experience eight basic emotions: acceptance, disgust, fear, anger, joy, sadness, surprise, and anticipation. Plutchik linked each to an adaptive pattern of behavior (see Table 7.4). For example, fear accompanies the avoidance of danger. It is obviously adaptive to be afraid, as opposed to indifferent, when we feel threatened, and so fear is experienced in threatening situations.

Many species, including human beings and their primate cousins, bare their teeth when threatened. Darwin proposed that such basic emotions increase the chances for survival because they prepare the organism for appropriate action.

Table 7.4   Patterns of Survival and Associated Emotions

Plutchik theorized about the ways in which basic human emotions increase fitness. He proposed eight patterns of behavior necessary for survival and identified a basic emotion corresponding to each.

Pattern of survival	Emotion
Incorporation: ingestion of food or acceptance of beneficial stimuli from the environment	Acceptance
Rejection: expulsion of material that has previously been incorporated	Disgust
Protection: avoidance of danger	Fear
Destruction: removal of a barrier that prevents an important need from being satisfied	Anger
Reproduction: passing on genetic material to offspring	Joy
Reintegration: reaction to the loss of something important that aims at regaining contact	Sadness
Orientation: reaction to novel situations	Surprise
Exploration: mapping of a given environment	Anticipation

Plutchik's model is based on the work of perception psychologists who study color vision (Chapter 5). In his scheme of things, the basic emotions are like primary colors because both can be combined to produce innumerable variations. We experience love when joy and acceptance are combined; we experience contempt from a combination of anger and disgust; and so on. Plutchik arranged emotions in a circle reflecting their relative similarity and dissimilarity (see Figure 7.5). The closer together two emotions, the more they are alike; the farther apart, the more they are different.

Similar to brightness is the intensity of an emotion, which Plutchik interpreted as the degree of arousal that accompanies the emotion. Apprehension is a mild version of fear; boredom, a mild version of disgust; distraction, a mild version of surprise. Plutchik

Figure 7.5
Basic Emotions. According to Robert Plutchik, there are eight basic emotions, shown here in the inner circle. Complex emotions, shown in the outer circle, result from different combinations of the basic emotions.

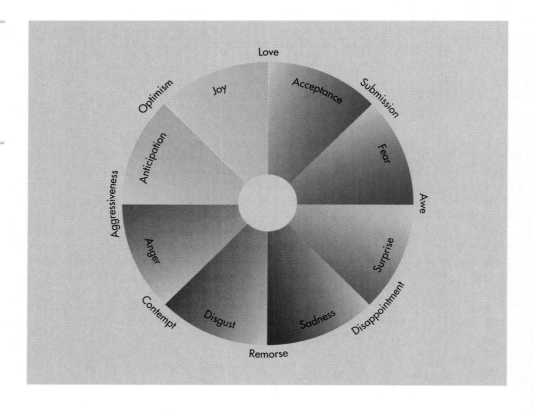

argued that emotions become more difficult to distinguish at lower intensities, so that people turn to their environment for clues about what they must be feeling. In the case of extreme anger, joy, or grief, people know exactly what they are experiencing. In less extreme cases, people are genuinely confused, and so they consider the circumstances that prompt these emotions.

Heritability of emotions.   Viewing emotions in evolutionary terms leads us to consider their possible heritability. Research supports the conclusion that individual differences in the intensity of basic emotions are due in part to genetics. As will be discussed in Chapter 10, for instance, twin studies suggest that one's overall level of emotionality is heritable (Buss & Plomin, 1975, 1984). Even newborns show consistent tendencies to be either placid or emotional. Studies similarly suggest that emotional disorders involving excessive anxiety or depression are heritable, as are personality disorders characterized by a lack of emotion (Chapter 13).

Facial expression.   Most theorists in the evolutionary tradition give importance to how people display emotions in their facial expressions (Whissell, 1985). Human beings are social creatures, and there is a survival advantage to being able to communicate our feelings to others (Fridlund, 1991a). Indeed, evolved psychological mechanisms draw our attention specifically to faces (Chapter 5). Research finds that people around the world recognize basic emotions expressed in facial photographs of persons from cultures other than their own (see the photos in Figure 7.6) (Izard, 1994; Russell, 1994).

To evolutionary theorists, these expressions are innate evolved psychological mechanisms. Even though cultures differ greatly in the words they use to describe emotions (Mumford, 1993), facial expressions across cultures are similar (Ekman, 1993). Basic emotions occur rapidly, automatically, briefly, and in response to characteristic circumstances (Ekman, 1992; Izard, 1992).

Some theorists propose that each emotion has its own neurological underpinning, further strengthening the argument that emotions are based in evolution (Levenson, Ekman, Heider, & Friesen, 1992). For example, Tomkins (1984) interpreted basic emotions in terms of whether the associated neural activity is increasing, decreasing, or

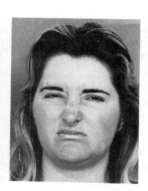
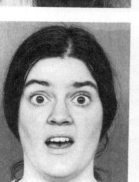

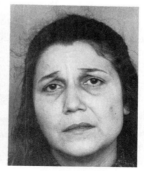

Figure 7.6
Facial Expression of Universal Emotions. People in different cultures have little difficulty agreeing that facial expressions like these express particular emotions. This evidence supports the idea of basic emotions.

constant. For example, anticipation, fear, and surprise are all characterized by increased patterns of neural firing. Surprise shows the most rapid increase, whereas anticipation shows the least.

Psychophysiological Approach: Focus on Bodily Mechanisms

Theorists interested in the biological mechanisms responsible for emotions join with another tradition of theorizing: the psychophysiological approach. These theories explain emotion as a psychological reaction to physiological occurrences.

James-Lange theory of emotion.   William James (1884, 1890) observed that the typical way of thinking about emotion is to assign it an intermediate position in the following sequence:

$$event \rightarrow emotion \rightarrow physiological\ response$$

To use a famous example from James, common sense proposes that we see a bear, experience fear, and then run. But James took issue with this view and proposed a different sequence:

$$event \rightarrow physiological\ response \rightarrow emotion$$

■ **James-Lange theory of emotion**
theory that emotions are the perception of the body's physiological responses

We see a bear, run, and only then experience fear. To James, the perception of our body's physiological responses is the emotion. A Danish physiologist named Carl Lange independently proposed the same idea, and so this account is now known as the **James-Lange theory of emotion.** It is an important theory because it encourages researchers to look at the relationship between what our body does and what we feel as a result.

Facial feedback.   As already described, evolutionary theorists often hypothesize that the face reflects emotions. Other theorists reverse this argument, proposing that our facial expressions determine the emotions we experience. This position is a version of the James-Lange theory because it holds that our bodily responses—specifically, our facial expressions—dictate the emotions we experience (Cappella, 1993).

Consistent with this theory, researchers have shown that when people are asked to smile or frown, they report emotions appropriate to their expressions (Hess, Kappas, McHugo, Lanzetta, & Kleck, 1992; Ohira & Kurono, 1993; Sun & Meng, 1993). An elegant demonstration was devised by Larsen, Kasimatis, and Frey (1992), who subtly altered the facial expressions of their research subjects. They glued golf tees on the foreheads of subjects and asked them to move them while also holding a pen in their mouths. In effect, they were asking subjects to make a sad face without asking them to do so. When subjects reported their emotions, they described greater sadness than subjects in a comparison group did.

According to Zajonc (1985), facial expressions influence blood flow to the brain, altering brain temperature, and determining emotions (Berridge & Zajonc, 1991; Zajonc, Murphy, & Ingelhart, 1989). This hypothesis supports the old adage that smiles and laughs help one survive difficult times. Facial expressions are only one determinant of emotion, of course, but their role illustrates the psychophysiological approach.

Arousal.   Many psychologists in the psychophysiological tradition today focus on the overall activity of the nervous system and the endocrine system. As you remember from Chapter 4, the autonomic nervous system is divided into two parts. The parasympathetic nervous system maintains a relaxed and unemotional state. It controls digestion, keeps the heart rate steady, and directs breathing. The sympathetic nervous system, in contrast, produces arousal. Digestion is inhibited, the pupils dilate, the heart beats faster, the face becomes flushed, breathing speeds up, and the palms sweat. These physiological

According to Robert Zajonc, smiling increases blood flow to the brain, thereby elevating mood. If this theory is correct, then smiling indeed helps one get through hard times.

responses are the body's emergency reaction, which readies us to respond to threat. We are prepared to fight off whatever threatens us and/or to run away from it. Critical here are the adrenal glands. In response to threat, the adrenals secrete hormones that stimulate physiological arousal.

Considerable debate exists as to whether different emotions are associated with characteristic patterns of sympathetic arousal (Levenson, 1992). If there are differences in arousal across emotions, they are probably quite small. It is therefore fair to say that all emotions somehow involve the emergency reaction. This observation helps explain why a lie detection device, or **polygraph,** cannot directly sense falsehood. Rather, it measures arousal, which presumably accompanies the intent to deceive (Ekman, 1986). Although we do not need a polygraph to detect obvious signs of arousal such as sweating or blushing, this device helps to detect more subtle signs of arousal: changes in blood pressure and skin temperature.

All of these can be recorded and measured with sensors attached to the body. These read changes in the nervous system when an examiner asks the subject questions. Did you steal $50 from Aunt Jessie yesterday? Suppose the person says no, but the sensors on his fingers show a sharp increase in perspiration and those on his chest indicate that his heart rate just shot up. These dramatic increases in arousal indicate that he may be lying.

Or they may not. Too many problems surround polygraphs, as well as the way the tests are administered, to feel confident about their results. Consider their use in a criminal investigation. Police officers might be biased against one of the subjects, making him or her anxious. Indeed, any strong emotion, such as a subject's hostility, can make it difficult for the polygraph operator to interpret reactions.

■ **polygraph**
so-called lie detector device that actually measures physiological arousal, which may or may not accompany the intent to deceive

Neurological Approach: Focus on Neurological Mechanisms

Yet another theoretical tradition in the psychology of emotions is the neurological approach introduced by Walter Cannon (1929, 1939). Theorists in this tradition also seek to explain the biological causes of emotions. However, Cannon disagreed with James and Lange, arguing that the process hypothesized in their theory is implausible.

Cannon instead believed that the physiological changes occurring during the body's emergency reaction do not differ greatly from emotion to emotion (Alcaraz-García, 1993). All emotions have the same bodily underpinnings. Whether the emotion in question is fear, anger, love, disgust, or joy, your physiology is the same—aroused. If these changes are the basis of emotions, as James and Lange suggested, then where do distinctions come into play? Furthermore, even if physiological differences exist, there is no reason to believe that people are particularly sensitive to them.

Cannon–Bard theory of emotion.   To explain our experience of emotions, Cannon looked specifically at the brain (Borod, 1993). He proposed that in response to given stimuli, the brain produces both bodily changes and emotions. The emergency reaction and the experience of emotions occur not one after the other but instead simultaneously. Another physiologist, named Philip Bard (1928), proposed much the same theory, and this approach is today called the **Cannon–Bard theory of emotion:** Emotions are the product of brain activity.

■ **Cannon-Bard theory of emotion**
theory that emotions are
produced by brain activity

Researchers have conducted numerous lesion and stimulation studies to map the neurological basis of emotions. Results usually point to the importance of the limbic system, located in the center of the brain (Joseph, 1992). A consistent conclusion is that higher parts of the brain can inhibit emotional expression. Here is Cannon's (1929, p. 246) description of a cat after its cerebral hemispheres were surgically removed:

> As soon as recovery from anesthesia was complete a remarkable group of activities appeared, such as usually seen in an infuriated animal a sort of sham rage . . . lashing of the tail, arching of the trunk, thrusting and jerking of the restrained limbs, display of the claws and clawing motions, snarling and attempts to bite. Besides these . . . were erection of the tail hairs, sweating of the toe pads, dilation of the pupils, micturition, a high blood pressure, a very rapid heart beat, an abundant outpouring of adrenalin, and an increase in blood sugar up to five times the normal concentration.

Remember the point made in Chapter 4 that higher parts of the brain often control lower parts. In this example, when the cerebral hemispheres of the cat were removed, they no longer controlled its limbic system, and emotions occurred automatically.

Laterality.   Research has identified emotion-specific brain mechanisms (Bermudez-Sarguera & Infante-Ochoa, 1988; Leventhal & Tomarken, 1986). For example, Davidson (1984) proposed that the left hemisphere of the brain is responsible for positive emotions, whereas the right hemisphere is responsible for negative emotions. Accordingly, left-brain damage results in depression, fear, and pessimism, and right-brain damage produces indifference or even euphoria (Derryberry & Tucker, 1992).

Hatta, Nakaseko, and Yamamoto (1992) asked research subjects to handle identical objects with their right and left hands and report the emotional tone of the resulting sensations. Objects in the right hand (the nerves from which lead to the left hemisphere) were described in more positive terms than those in the left hand.

Other researchers favor a different view of brain laterality and emotions, suggesting that the right hemisphere is in general more involved in processing all emotions, positive and negative, than the left hemisphere is (Bryden & MacRae, 1988). So, when individuals see pictures of faces only with their left visual fields—and hence receive this information only in their right hemispheres—they more successfully recognize depicted emotions than when the presentations are reversed (Alvarez & Fuentes, 1994; Hahdahl, Iversen, & Jonsen, 1993). Similarly, subjects better recognize the emotional tone of words presented to their left ears than to their right ears; interestingly, correct recognition of the meaning of the word is associated with the opposite pattern (Bulman-Fleming & Bryden, 1994).

Another line of research finds that the left side of the face is more emotionally expressive (Bruyer, 1981). We may think of our facial expressions as symmetrical, but left and right expressions differ. It is easier to read emotions in a left expression, a finding that again points to a greater role of the right hemisphere. You may remember the discussion in Chapter 3 of how mothers cradle infants on the left side of the body, a practice that may allow them to be most responsive to their infants.

Cognitive Approach: Focus on Psychological Mechanisms

A final tradition of theorizing stresses the role played by the individual's thoughts and beliefs (see Table 7.5). In general, all theories of emotion acknowledge that situations can trigger emotional reactions only when they are given a psychological representation (Ellsworth, 1994)—that is, when people perceive these situations (Chapter 5). However, the premise of the cognitive approach to emotions is that one's conscious identification of an emotion dictates its specific experience (Chapter 6). Other theorists disagree, arguing that emotions can occur automatically, without awareness (Murphy & Zajonc, 1993; Zajonc, 1980).

Two-factor theory of emotion. Stanley Schachter and Jerome Singer (1962) proposed the **two-factor theory of emotion,** which suggests that emotions result from the joint presence of two factors: physiological arousal and a cognitive label that is placed on this arousal. Schachter and Singer agreed with the Cannon-Bard position that all emotions have the same physiological underpinnings. What distinguishes among different emotions is how arousal is interpreted. In some cases, you tag your arousal as anger; in other cases, as euphoria, fear, or love. According to this theory, an infinite variety of emotions exist, limited only by available labels.

■ **two-factor theory of emotion**
theory that emotions result from physiological arousal and a cognitive label placed on this arousal

Schachter and Singer conducted an ingenious experiment that supported their two-factor theory. Subjects were injected with adrenalin, creating a state of arousal. Some subjects were told what effects the injection would have. Other subjects were misled, told instead that the injection was a special vitamin; no reference was made to its arousing effects.

All subjects were put in a situation that would produce an emotional reaction. One experimental condition was designed to create anger in the subjects. For instance, they were asked to complete a questionnaire regarding their mother's sexual activity outside of her marriage. Another experimental condition was designed to create euphoria. The subjects here were joined by other people (who were actually working in conjunction with the researchers) who acted in a silly fashion, folding questionnaires into airplanes and zooming them about the room.

Schachter and Singer then asked their subjects to report any emotions they were experiencing. The subjects in the anger condition reported feeling angry, whereas the subjects in the euphoria condition reported feeling happy. These results occurred most strongly for those who believed they had been injected with a vitamin. Those given accurate information about the arousing effects of the injection did not report the same strong emotions.

Table 7.5	Summary: Approaches to Emotion

Approach	Key emphasis
Evolutionary	Functions of emotions
Psychophysiological	Bodily mechanisms of emotions
Neurological	Neurological mechanisms of emotions
Cognitive	Psychological (cognitive) mechanisms of emotions

To explain these results, Schachter and Singer proposed that people who experience physiological arousal search for its source. In some cases, the cause is readily apparent: "Oh, this must be the effect of the injection." In other cases, the cause may not be obvious, and the person turns to her immediate environment for an answer. If something insulting is taking place, she attributes the arousal to anger. If something silly is going on, she instead attributes the arousal to euphoria.

This study by Schachter and Singer has proved difficult to replicate (Sinclair, Hoffman, Mark, & Martin, 1994), and critics point out that not all people in all situations are easily misled about the actual source of their emotional reactions. As Plutchik suggested, two-factor theory applies best when there is ambiguity about the causes of people's reactions. Perhaps children, who are in the process of learning how to label their emotions, are particularly well described by two-factor theory.

Appraisal.   If people identify their emotions at least in part by attending to the situations in which they find themselves, just how does this process take place? Phoebe Ellsworth and Craig Smith attempted to catalog the characteristics of situations that produce different emotions, positive and negative (Ellsworth & Smith, 1988a, 1988b; Smith & Ellsworth, 1985, 1987). Bernard Weiner (1986) presented a similar theory of emotions in terms of what people believe about the causes of situations that trigger emotions (Chapter 15).

According to the research of Ellsworth and Smith, each emotion is associated with a characteristic appraisal—interpretation—of situations (see Figure 7.7). Appraisals can be described along various dimensions, such as the degree to which a situation:

- is pleasant
- is effortful
- requires attention
- is under the person's control

Knowing how an individual appraises a situation allows his or her emotion to be predicted with good accuracy; knowing the emotion that is experienced allows appraisal to be predicted with good accuracy. A study of appraisal and emotion among individuals in the United States, Japan, Hong Kong, and China found considerable generality in the specific links (Mauro, Sato, & Tucker, 1992).

Ellsworth and Smith's work does not demand that conscious appraisals precede emotional experiences, but their research attests to the important role cognitions play. Psychologists interested in emotion are reminded to integrate their studies with investigations of cognitive processes (Chapter 9).

Two-factor theory applies best when there is ambiguity about the causes of people's emotions. Each individual here may be using the laughter by others as a clue about his or her own emotions.

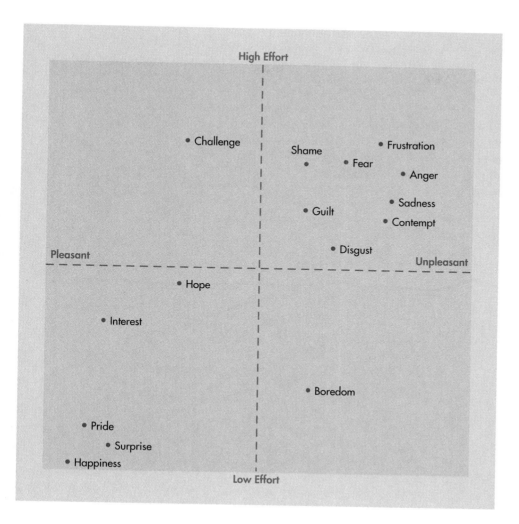

Figure 7.7
Appraisals and Emotions.
Phoebe Ellsworth and Craig
Smith have described the links
between specific ways of
thinking about events (appraisals)
and the emotions experienced
in response to them. This graph
shows the way in which
different emotions are related
to two dimensions of appraisal:
pleasantness and effort.
Source: C. A. Smith and P. C.
Ellsworth (1988). Patterns of
cognitive appraisal in emotion.
*Journal of Personality and Social
Psychology, 48,* p. 826.

Stop and Think

15 What is the James–Lange theory of emotions?

16 What is the Cannon–Bard theory of emotions?

17 What is the Schachter–Singer (two-factor) theory of emotions?

18 How does each of the theoretical approaches to emotion assign an important role to faces?

DOING *Emotion* RESEARCH

Emotions have different components, and researchers choose strategies appropriate to the aspect in which they are interested: subjective feelings, physiological bases, cognitions, and so on. Perhaps the most widely used strategy because it is so simple, is to ascertain the presence and intensity of different emotions by asking research subjects to use checklists or rating scales to describe how they feel.

For instance, the Multiple Affect Adjective Check List (MAACL) (Zuckerman & Lubin, 1965) presents individuals with a list of words referring to different emotions and asks them to indicate which ones apply to their current emotional state. The more anger words on the MAACL that someone chooses, the angrier he or she is said to be. This strategy is valid to the degree that people are aware of their emotions and can articulate them upon request.

Researchers might not always want to make these assumptions (Friedmann & Goldstein, 1993; Russell, 1993; Tischer, 1988). They then turn to other strategies, including:

- scoring facial expressions and other nonverbal behaviors, such as posture and gaze, for various emotions (McClenney & Neiss, 1989)
- interviewing subjects about emotionally charged topics and judging the emotions they express (Kazarian, 1992)
- judging the emotions evident in stories that subjects tell (Parkinson & Manstead, 1993)

The last approach is similar to the use of the TAT to operationalize different motives, and indeed, responses to projective tests are often scored for the presence of given emotions.

As discussed, researchers sometimes study emotions experimentally. One strategy, used by Schachter and Singer (1968) in their experiment investigating the two-factor theory of emotion, is to create an actual situation that makes a person angry, anxious, or happy. Some critics question the validity of this procedure, as well as its ethics (Bertilson, 1990). Thus, an alternative strategy is to ask subjects to read self-referring statements that are pertinent to the emotion of interest: "This is great—I really do feel good—I *am* elated about things" (Velten, 1968, p. 475). This approach is effective in temporarily producing different emotions (Larsen & Sinnett, 1991; Seibert & Ellis, 1991; Sinclair, Mark, Enzle, & Borkovec, 1994).

Related approaches that are more subtle ask research participants to listen to happy or sad passages of music or to watch film excerpts with the appropriate emotional content (Gerrards-Hesse, Spies, & Hesse, 1994; Kelly, 1993). Also, researchers may hypnotize subjects and suggest to them that they are experiencing different emotions (Hesse, Spies, Hänze, & Gerrards-Hesse, 1992). All of these approaches are effective, but none is superior to just asking subjects to "get into" the target mood (Slyker & McNally, 1991).

Perhaps most people have their own techniques, like those of method acting, for producing emotions. In fact, the ability to regulate one's own feelings is a skill that develops early in life for most individuals (Campos, Campos, & Barrett, 1989). Those who do not develop this skill are at increased risk for psychological problems because anxious or depressed moods can escalate into chronic emotional disorders (Gross & Munoz, 1995).

Stop and Think

19 What are some possible confounds in the use of questionnaires like the MAACL to measure emotions?

GENDER, CULTURE, AND EMOTION

Do males and females differ in how emotional they are? Stereotypes hold that women are more emotional than men (Fabes & Martin, 1991), but a more analytic view is needed that considers the specific emotion in question (Barbera & Martínez-Benlloch, 1989). So, women often report more anxiety and depression than do men, who often report more anger (Littlewood, Cramer, Hoekstra, & Humphrey, 1991; Wright, Newman, Meyer, & May, 1993).

Complicating matters is research showing that men, at least in the Western world, are encouraged by their socialization to inhibit emotional expression (Eisler & Blalock, 1991). For example, studies of how males and females react to the death of a loved one find that men are more likely to control their expression of grief (Lister, 1991). These findings do not mean that males and females differ in their emotional experience, only in what they reveal to others (Gross & Levenson, 1993). Indeed, males and females learn early in life to express emotions considered appropriate to their gender and to inhibit those considered inappropriate (Fivush, 1991; Karbon, Fabes, Carlo, & Martin, 1992).

Similar points can be made about emotional expression and experience across cultures. Cultures differ in what emotions people commonly experience and how these typically are expressed (Ekman & Friesen, 1975; Russell, 1991; Scherer & Wallbott, 1994). Those from some cultures are highly expressive; those from others, much less so. For example, contrary to stereotypes, American subjects inhibit their expression more than British subjects (McConatha, Lightner, & Deaner, 1994). And Japanese inhibit their expression even more than Americans (Frymier, Klopf, & Ishii, 1990).

It follows, therefore, that we need to be cautious in how we interpret the emotional expression of those from different cultures. Americans smile more than Germans, and Japanese smile even more than Americans (Hall & Hall, 1990). Does this reflect a dimension of experienced happiness? Probably not. Instead, these differences follow from the American norm that cheerfulness in almost any circumstance is a desirable characteristic and the Japanese norm that negative emotions, such as embarrassment and anger, should be disguised in public (Matsumoto, 1990).

In some cultures, emotions are displayed chiefly through facial expressions; in other cultures, hand gestures and bodily postures are critical (Sogon & Masutani, 1989). Indeed, there exist complex emotions in some cultures that have no counterparts elsewhere. For example, although jealousy appears to be nearly universal, specifically sexual jealousy occurs only in some cultures (Hupka, 1981). And many Americans seem not to experience the emotion of shame, which figures prominently in the lives of people elsewhere, particularly in Asian cultures that stress the importance of the larger group (Bierbrauer, 1992; Crites, 1991; Imahori & Cupach, 1994).

People in various cultures also differ in the ease with which they recognize basic emotions (Gallois, 1993; Mehta, Ward, & Strongman, 1992; Russell, 1994). In a study of bilingual Indian college students, Matsumoto and Assar (1992) found that recognition of facial expressions varied with the language in which the experiment was conducted, Hindi or English, suggesting that language affects the interpretation of emotions, even for the same individual. Mesquita and Frijda (1992) concluded that emotional experience and expression are both universal and culturally specific, depending on what aspects of emotion are on focus (Mauro, Sato, & Tucker, 1992).

Even though the basic emotions identified by theorists in the evolutionary tradition have counterparts around the world, socialization plays an important role in dictating the circumstances in which they are elicited. Consider disgust. Evolutionary theorists attribute the origins of this basic emotion to how we respond to aversive smells or tastes. So, we wrinkle our noses and stick out our tongues when they are irritated

Japanese usually inhibit their facial expression of emotions more than Americans, and it is clear—as this photo shows—that this is a learned tendency.

(Rozin, Lowery, & Ebert, 1994). But disgust is generalized beyond the circumstances that originally activate it. Think about the following (Rozin & Fallon, 1987):

- Take a perfectly clean glass.
- Drool or spit into it.
- Swirl your saliva about.
- Then drink it.

Most people cannot bring themselves to do the last step, and they experience an involuntary sense of disgust.

When you are done shuddering, appreciate that this phenomenon is paradoxical granted that it is your own saliva that disgusts you. Something else must be occurring other than oral irritation. Nemeroff and Rozin (1994) interpreted demonstrations like these as the generalization of disgust to stimuli associated with contamination—typically, body products such as saliva, urine, feces, and blood (Page, 1994). We learn these associations because infants are remarkably oblivious to the presence of body products except when these are physically irritating. Note that you suspend your disgust in response to saliva when you are kissing someone, although you probably would not drink your lover's saliva from a glass.

Disgust can also be generalized into moral domains, with culture dictating the details (Rachman, 1994). For example, urban residents may find much about nature disgusting and hence not enjoy being in the wilderness; rural residents have a different reaction (Bixler, Carlisle, Hammitt, & Floyd, 1994). In the United States, nudity may produce a response of disgust (and, of course, sexual arousal), but in Japan, nudity may trigger sentimental feelings about the family (Downs, 1990). Dishonesty and other moral transgressions by others may lead us to feel disgust (Jendrek, 1992). People even regard themselves as disgusting (Satoh, 1994).

Generalization of disgust has far-reaching social consequences. Demb (1990) interviewed adolescent females in the United States and found that they often regarded condoms as disgusting and were reluctant to use them. Sexual activity itself was not regarded with much disgust; thus, we have a clue about why unwanted pregnancy and sexually transmitted diseases are so common in our society. Vonderheide and Mosher (1988) reported similar reactions to the use of diaphragms.

Some cultures encourage their members to regard all sexual activity as disgusting. This norm does not, of course, result in the elimination of sexual behavior, but it leads men and women to segregate their sexuality from other aspects of their lives. Minces (1991) attributed the oppressed status of women in traditional Muslim societies in part to the disgust men feel toward female sexuality. Women become necessary evils, to be used by men for purposes of reproduction and sensual gratification but not otherwise to be approached.

How different are the cultural norms in the contemporary United States? King and Lococo (1990) surveyed American college students about their feelings concerning textbooks for sex education courses. About 15 percent said they would not take such a course if the book contained sexually explicit pictures, and the majority reported they would not show the book to their parents.

Stop and Think

20 Why is it important to distinguish between the experience of an emotion and the expression of it?

21 How is the emotion of disgust biopsychosocial?

EMOTION IN A BIOPSYCHOSOCIAL CONTEXT

Can the insights of these different theories of emotions be integrated? Carroll Izard (1993) made such an attempt. He started with the premise that emotions are critical in our lives and can be activated in numerous ways. According to Izard, given emotions can be brought about by:

- neural mechanisms (the neurological tradition)
- sensorimotor feedback (the psychophysiological tradition)
- drives and other emotions
- thoughts and beliefs (the cognitive tradition)

He further suggested that the four systems that activate emotion can be placed in a loose hierarchy, in terms of when they produce emotions and the complexity of the stimuli that set them into operation. Neural mechanisms are the only activator necessary for emotions to occur. The other activators may or may not be involved in given emotions, although in many cases all come together to produce an emotion (see Figure 7.8).

Izard cited the example of a typically happy man who suddenly felt a sharp pain following a sudden blow to his lower back. He spun around in anger to see that a woman in a wheelchair had accidentally crashed into him. She was embarrassed, and his reaction immediately became one of sadness and sympathy. He helped her recover from the accident.

This example, although commonplace, becomes complex when we start to account for the man's various emotional reactions. His typical mood—happiness—was the product of a characteristic neural state. The pain caused by the sudden blow to his back stimulated the emotion of anger, which immediately ceased when he understood the reason for his pain. With these cognitions in mind, he then experienced different emotions: sadness and sympathy.

All of the mechanisms specified by Izard have a basis in evolution, presumably arising to solve different survival problems. Neural systems maintain an individual's stable level of emotional experience, which can be considered part of his or her characteristic personality (Chapter 12). Sensorimotor systems facilitate social communication and strengthen emotional bonds with others (Chapters 10 and 15). Drive systems trigger emotions when homeostasis is disturbed. Finally, cognitive systems activate emotions in situations that require comparison, categorization, inference, or judgment (Chapter 9). Izard further argued that two-way influences can occur between all of these determinants, and so his theory is a fully contextualized one.

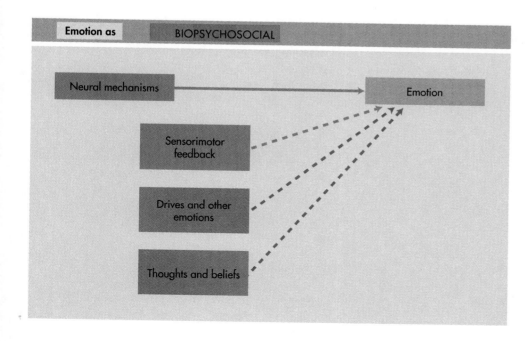

Figure 7.8
Emotions as Biopsychosocial.
Carroll Izard proposed that each emotion reflects biological and psychological mechanisms. These in turn may also be influenced by an individual's culture.

The emotions that this photograph suggests depends on how it is interpreted. Is the man's hand on the woman's shoulder seen as paternalistic or friendly, as harrassing or tender?

In this and previous chapters, the importance of learning has been emphasized frequently. Through our experience with the environment, we acquire perceptual styles (Chapter 5), preferred ways of altering states of consciousness (Chapter 6), and habitual motives and emotions. The next chapter takes a detailed look at how such learning takes place.

SUMMARY

UNDERSTANDING MOTIVES AND EMOTIONS: DEFINITION AND EXPLANATION

■ Motivation refers to the basic causes of behavior, and emotion refers to the feelings we experience as we behave.

■ Psychologistts have often proposed classifications of human motives and emotions. One common distinction with regard to motives is between primary motives—those that are biological in nature—and acquired motives—those that are learned. Emotions are similarly classified into basic ones—evident in people from all cultures—and complex ones—resulting from a combination of basic emotions and reflecting socialization.

■ Despite the popularity of these classifications, all motives and emotions are best approached in biopsychosocial terms.

APPROACHES TO MOTIVATION

■ At the turn of the century, explanations of motivation in terms of unlearned instincts were popular. These proved problematic, however, when applied to human beings.

■ Instinct explanations gave way in the 1940s to theories examining motives in terms of physiological needs and drives. A need is a lack of some biological essential, whereas a drive is a state of tension or arousal that a need produces in someone, moving him or her to reduce the need.

■ Most recently, theorizing about motivation has stressed the individual's thoughts and beliefs. These theories stress the role played by someone's interpretation in defining particular motives.

DOING *Motivation* RESEARCH

■ Psychologists use a variety of research methods to study motivation. When animals are the research subjects, techniques for investigating the brain and nervous system are often employed.

■ When human beings are the research subjects, projective tests like the Thematic Apperception Test (TAT) may be used to gauge the presence and strength of particular motives. In these tests, people are asked to respond to ambiguous stimuli, thereby projecting their own needs onto what they see.

GENDER, CULTURE, AND MOTIVATION

■ Although various motives are present in all social groups, differences exist in their degrees of importance.

■ Women, for example, on average are more likely to be motivated by interpersonal considerations, whereas men, on average, are more likely to be motivated by individualistic considerations.

■ Individuals in different cultures emphasize motives that are consistent with their culture's values.

PARTICULAR MOTIVES

■ Among the important motives with a clear biological basis are thirst, hunger, and sex.

■ These motives are reasonably described in terms of needs and drives, and researchers have mapped out the biological processes that underlie them. However, when we compare these motives 'in animals and human beings, we find that learning and experience play a much greater role for people.

■ Among the important motives that clearly reflect socialization are aggression, achievement motivation, power motivation, and mastery.

MOTIVATION IN A BIOPSYCHOSOCIAL CONTEXT

■ Abraham Maslow has proposed an integrative theory of motivation, arguing that human needs exist in a hierarchy. Needs at the bottom, such as hunger and thirst, must be satisfied before needs at the top, such as love and self-esteem. One of the highest needs Maslow identified is self-actualization: the need to use one's talents and potentialities to the fullest.

APPROACHES TO EMOTION

■ Several perspectives on emotion have been popular. First is the evolutionary approach begun by Darwin and followed today by Plutchik. This approach looks at emotions in terms of their survival value.

■ Another perspective on emotion is the neuropsychological approach of James and Lange. This view regards emotions as one's psychological reaction to bodily sensations, particularly to the emergency reaction—the set of physiological responses that readies one to respond to threat.

■ A third approach to emotions is neurological and tries to link emotions to activity in the brain and nervous system. Cannon and Bard made important contributions to this neurological approach. The limbic system is regarded as critically important to emotion. Furthermore, higher parts of the brain serve to inhibit emotional expression.

■ Cognitive theories of emotion suggest that the emotions we experience are due to the way we interpret our experience. By this view, it is our interpretations that distinguish among different emotions.

DOING *Emotion* RESEARCH

■ The most straightforward way of investigating emotions is to ask people to report in words the emotions they experience.

■ Because verbal reports are not always the most valid way to assess emotions, researchers have developed additional ways of inferring emotions from other aspects of a person's behavior, such as judging emotions from an individual's facial expression.

GENDER, CULTURE, AND EMOTION

■ People in different social groups tend to experience different emotions, although broad generalizations are difficult. We must take into account the specific emotion in which we are interested and be careful to distinguish between the experience of an emotion and the expression of it.

EMOTION IN A BIOPSYCHOSOCIAL CONTEXT

■ Carroll Izard proposed an integrative explanation of emotions, suggesting that each emotion reflects biological, psychological, and social influences.

KEY TERMS

Pierre

Learning

I used to be a letter carrier for the postal service. You know, sleet, rain, snow, and all that stuff that never got in the way of mail delivery. But dogs often did, particularly ferocious ones, and to a letter carrier all dogs are ferocious. When I delivered the mail to a home with a dog, the dog would dash out of the backyard and run at me, its collar jingling as the creature launched itself at my jugular. After this occurred a number of times, just the sound of the collar would make me cringe.

I had learned something. My behavior had changed because of what had happened to me. Before my experience as a letter carrier, jingling sounds had no emotional impact on me. After my experience, they produced fear. To this very day, I catch my breath and feel my heart accelerate when a key chain is tossed on a table and produces a sound like that of a dog's collar.

Now take the perspective of the dog. What did it learn when the mail was delivered? One obvious lesson is that when it barked and growled, the letter carrier ran. The next time the mail was delivered, it attacked again with even more vigor. It too showed a change in behavior, and for all we know it may still be attacking letter carriers today.

UNDERSTANDING LEARNING: DEFINITION AND EXPLANATION

When I first took introductory psychology, I looked forward to the section of the course devoted to learning. I assumed we would focus on the details of a student's everyday life, like taking notes, reading a textbook, mastering a subject, choosing a career, and making distinctions between all of the above and none of the above on multiple-choice examinations. However, as you must by now be suspecting, none of these activities was specifically addressed. Why not? I entertained too restricted a definition of learning: what took place in college courses.

Psychologists opt for a much broader definition of **learning:** any relatively permanent change in behavior resulting from experience. The qualification "relatively permanent" excludes temporary states like fatigue, illness, or injury. In this chapter, the term *learning* is used in this deliberately general sense to refer to changes brought about by experience.

Examples of learning in your everyday life are numerous. You used to hunt and peck at a computer keyboard. Now you type without looking. You used to be indifferent to soccer games. Now your heart pounds during corner kicks. You used to get lost on the way across town. Now you take ever more efficient shortcuts. These changes in your behavior came about not through physical growth or maturation but through your interactions with the world.

Most psychologists distinguish between learning and performance. Learning is what occurs as a result of experience, but it may or may not show itself in ways we can immediately observe. You may have passed your cooking class with flying crullers, learning how to make gooey delicacies, but if you or your friends are not hungry, you probably will not display what you have learned. Performance refers to a person's observable behavior. Although some changes in performance can be attributed to learning—like the desserts you can make now that you could not make before—not all changes in performance reflect learning. Suppose you improve your grade in a course from the first exam to the second, but only because the teacher made the second test extremely easy. Your performance changed, but not because of learning.

Types of Learning

At one time, psychologists debated whether there was a basic form of learning. In the 1920s and 1930s, during psychology's era of great schools (Chapter 1), there was controversy over which was the basic type of learning. Most psychologists today acknowledge several types of learning, and none is considered more primary than others.

Habituation, for example, is a form of learning in which we stop paying attention to an environmental stimulus that never changes, like the clock that ticks in our living room or the faucet that drips in our bathroom (Chapter 6). Habituation is shown by

■ **learning**
any relatively permanent change in behavior resulting from experience

■ **habituation**
form of learning in which we stop paying attention to an environmental stimulus that never changes

Most psychologists distinguish between learning and performance because learning is not always evident in performance.

many animal species, even invertebrates (Rankin & Broster, 1992). It is an instance of learning because behavior changes as a result of experience. In effect, it involves learning to ignore stimuli that do not change.

Another form of learning is **sensitization,** in which we become more responsive to a stimulus we encounter repeatedly. For example, a rush–hour driver who has a close call every few minutes may show escalating fear in response to swerving cars. Like habituation, sensitization occurs in many animal species and satisfies the definition of learning: behavior change as a result of experience.

A more complex form of learning is **conditioning,** which refers to the acquisition of particular behaviors in the presence of particular environmental stimuli. Conditioning is sometimes called associative learning because at its essence it involves the learning of associations (Chapter 1). Habituation and sensitization, in contrast, exemplify nonassociative learning because they occur independently of other stimuli.

Two types of conditioning are discussed in detail in this chapter: classical conditioning and operant conditioning. Classical conditioning refers to the learning of associations between particular stimuli; operant conditioning refers to the learning of associations between responses and stimuli that follow them. My learning to fear jingling sounds is an example of classical conditioning, whereas Fido's learning to make letter carriers flee is an example of operant conditioning.

As explained in Chapter 1, when John Watson (1913) called on psychologists to abandon their study of mental processes, he founded **behaviorism,** an approach that regards observable behavior as the only proper subject matter of psychology. Behaviorism has shaped psychology as a whole, particularly in the United States, where its claims about the importance of the environment in determining behavior resonate with this country's ideology of equality (Rakos, 1992).

To behaviorists, behavior is caused by environmental stimuli, and under the influence of Watson's message, psychology lost its mind. The study of unobservables became a taboo subject. Certainly, Watson was correct when he branded Wundt's method of

■ **sensitization**
form of learning in which we become more responsive to a stimulus we encounter repeatedly

■ **conditioning**
form of learning involving the acquisition of particular behaviors in the presence of particular environmental stimuli

■ **behaviorism**
approach to psychology that stresses observable behavior

introspection an unreliable research strategy. But in arguing that thoughts and beliefs are an inappropriate subject matter for science, the behaviorists went too far.

Their argument confuses data with explanations. Data need to be public and observable. But science is not just data. It includes explanations with concepts that may be unobservable. Consider gravity, atoms, natural selection, magnetism, or any number of other perfectly respectable scientific notions. We have never seen any of these things, but we still accept them as good explanations because they have many observable consequences.

Similarly, you cannot see thoughts, hopes, dreams, intentions, attitudes, memories, skills, or interests, but you can see the consequences of these mental states and processes. If these unobservable notions help to explain the consequences, then they have a role in psychology. This idea is now accepted by many behaviorists. Although the explanation of observable behavior remains their goal, one of the best ways to accomplish this goal is to make thoughts and beliefs part of the explanation (Staddon, 1993).

■ **cognitive learning**

form of learning in which an individual behaves differently as a result of acquiring new information about the relationships between responses and stimuli

In **cognitive learning,** a person or animal behaves differently as a result of acquiring new information about the relationships between behaviors and their consequences. An example of cognitive learning is when someone explains to you how to use a word-processing program. You have acquired a new way of thinking about the link between keystrokes (format, search, delete) and the appearance of your paper, and your behavior of writing has changed.

Learning as Biopsychosocial

Traditionally, the psychology of learning has been at odds with the biopsychosocial approach described in Chapter 1. Although learning was thought to depend on stimuli in the immediate environment and to serve survival purposes, no further contextualization of the process was deemed necessary. Indeed, learning theorists assumed that all learning occurs in the same manner, regardless of the behavior in question or even the species.

Like psychologists in other fields, those interested in learning have come to appreciate that their subject matter demands a biopsychosocial approach. Explanations need to take into account the biological mechanisms involved in learning, the social influences on the process, and the relevance of other psychological processes such as consciousness. The present chapter begins with a discussion of the traditional approaches to learning and concludes with a look at its current conceptualization in biopsychosocial terms.

Stop and Think

1   Give examples of the difference between learning and performance.

2   Give examples of habituation and sensitization.

3   How is learning biopsychosocial?

DOING *Learning* RESEARCH

Most psychologists seek to explain complex behavior in the simplest possible way. In keeping with this goal, researchers have often approached learning in stark terms. For example, common operational definitions (measures) have included seeing how a pigeon learns to peck a key when doing so produces a pellet of grain, and seeing how a rat learns to run a maze when doing so turns off an electrical shock delivered through the floor. To the uninitiated, these strategies may seem unusual, but they make sense granted the goal of simple explanations.

Studies of learning are usually experiments. Remember that the strength of the experimental method is its ability to identify causes—events in the environment—that have effects on behavior (Chapter 2). Experiments are perfectly suited to studying conditioning because they allow stimuli to be manipulated explicitly.

In learning experiments, both human beings and animals are used as subjects. Some psychologists are interested in animal behavior in its own right. But why do learning researchers interested in people use animals in their experiments? As just mentioned, many early theorists assumed that learning occurs in the same way among all species. If this is so, one might as well study forms of learning that are particularly simple. Pigeons readily learn to peck at an object in order to acquire food. And rats readily learn to run through a maze in order to escape shock. These forms of learning are assumed to be equivalent to those that prove more difficult to study. "Pigeon, rat, monkey, which is which? It doesn't matter. Behavior shows astonishingly similar properties" (Skinner, 1956, pp. 230–231).

Also, animals allow the researcher to minimize extraneous variation among subjects while maximizing the impact of experimental manipulations. Learning researchers use animals specially bred to have minimal genetic differences. These animals are kept under uniform conditions in special colonies. If researchers are interested in how an animal learns responses for food, for instance, they deprive it of food until it is at 80 percent of its normal weight. If researchers are interested in punishment, they can use strong electric shocks.

Finally, researchers implement their experiments using specially constructed mechanical devices: A rat may be placed in a maze with food at its end, or a pigeon may be placed in a box with a button that can be pushed to produce a pellet of grain. These devices are far removed from the natural environment of rats and pigeons, not to mention people.

What is the rationale for the use of such apparatuses? The theoretical emphasis on the environment inspires researchers to create experimental situations in which relevant stimuli can be manipulated, while leaving out irrelevant stimuli. These situations represent simple worlds, but this simplification is deliberate, paring the environment down to the simplest possible characteristics. Furthermore, these devices are easy for the experimenter to manipulate. Stimuli such as food or electric shock can be presented automatically, and the response of the animal can be recorded as it occurs.

How simple can explanations of learning become while still doing justice to their subject matter? Do we really learn nothing more than simple associations? Is learning so

Psychologists interested in learning often study animals in highly simplified situations that lend themselves to experimental manipulations.

simple that the same set of principles applies to worms, pigeons, cats, dogs, and people? Can a research strategy that deliberately makes learning as simple as possible produce results that apply to the seemingly complex accomplishments of people? There are no generally agreed-upon answers to these questions. Hence, just keep in mind that these are legitimate concerns.

Stop and Think

4 Why do psychologists interested in learning often study animals?

5 Why do psychologists interested in learning often use experiments?

CLASSICAL CONDITIONING

■ **classical conditioning**
learning that takes places when we associate two environmental stimuli that occur together in time

Classical conditioning is learning that takes place when we associate two environmental stimuli that occur together in time. One of these stimuli triggers a reflexive response. The second stimulus is originally neutral with respect to that response, but after it has been associated in time with the first stimulus, it comes to trigger the response in its own right. Remember the earlier example from my career as a letter carrier. The dog automatically elicited fear from me, and at first the sound of the dog's collar had no effect. Eventually, however, I began to associate the jingling sound with my fear of the dog. Just the sound of the collar scared me as much as the dog itself.

Pavlov's Discovery

The Russian physiologist Ivan Pavlov discovered classical conditioning while studying digestion among dogs.

Classical conditioning was first described by the Russian scientist Ivan Pavlov (1849–1936) and thus is sometimes called Pavlovian conditioning. Although Pavlov's place in the history of psychology is secure, he was not a psychologist. He had a medical degree and was particularly interested in the physiology of digestion. In fact, his work in physiology earned him a Nobel Prize in 1904.

Pavlov's research on digestion led him to discover the principles of classical conditioning. Using dogs as research subjects, he studied their salivation. If you know dogs, you know their forté is salivating. In particular, dogs salivate when food is placed in their mouths. This response is a **reflex,** an involuntary behavior requiring no learning (Chapter 4). However, dogs also start to salivate when presented with objects that have been associated with food, such as a dish in which the food is served or even a person who fills the dish with food. This observation could have been made by anyone who had ever been around dogs, but it was Pavlov who first recognized that the phenomenon was interesting. Stimuli originally neutral with regard to eliciting salivation come to elicit salivation on their own. The crucial factor is that the neutral stimulus be paired with food. As this association is encountered repeatedly, the animal begins to make a new response to the neutral stimulus; its behavior changes, and we conclude that learning has occurred.

Pavlov called the food presented to the dogs the **unconditioned stimulus (UCS)** because it produced a response as a reflex, without learning (see Figure 8.1). The dog's salivation in response to the food he called the **unconditioned response (UCR).** Note that when a UCS elicits a UCR, no learning has taken place; the UCR is simply an innate reflex. The originally neutral stimulus that is paired with the unconditioned stimulus is called the **conditioned stimulus (CS).** The food dish and Pavlov's research assistant are both conditioned stimuli. Finally, the response that the conditioned stimulus produces after being paired with the unconditioned stimulus is the **conditioned response (CR)** because it is learned. When the dog salivated to the food dish or the research assistant, it was showing a conditioned response.

■ **reflex**
involuntary and unlearned response to a stimulus

■ **unconditioned stimulus (UCS)**
in classical conditioning, a stimulus that produces a response as a reflex, without learning

■ **unconditioned response (UCR)**
in classical conditioning, the response produced by an unconditioned stimulus

■ **conditioned stimulus (CS)**
in classical conditioning, a stimulus paired with the unconditioned stimulus

■ **conditioned response (CR)**
in classical conditioning, the response produced by the conditioned stimulus after pairing with the unconditioned stimulus

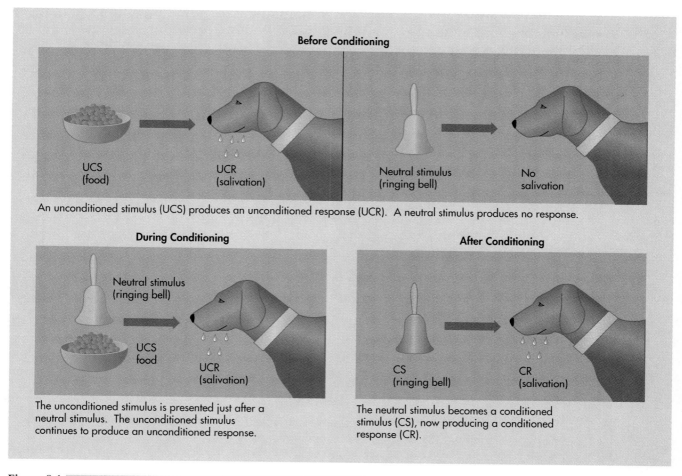

Before Conditioning

UCS
(food) → UCR
(salivation)

Neutral stimulus
(ringing bell) → No
salivation

An unconditioned stimulus (UCS) produces an unconditioned response (UCR). A neutral stimulus produces no response.

During Conditioning

Neutral stimulus
(ringing bell)
UCS
food → UCR
(salivation)

The unconditioned stimulus is presented just after a neutral stimulus. The unconditioned stimulus continues to produce an unconditioned response.

After Conditioning

CS
(ringing bell) → CR
(salivation)

The neutral stimulus becomes a conditioned stimulus (CS), now producing a conditioned response (CR).

Figure 8.1
Example of Classical Conditioning. In Pavlov's famous experiment, a ringing bell (the CS) came to elicit salivation (the CR) after it had been paired with food (the UCS), which produces salivation as a reflex (the UCR).

Processes in Classical Conditioning

Pavlov soon developed a more controlled way of studying classical conditioning (see Figure 8.2). Continuing to use dogs as his subjects, he held them immobile in a harness. He fed them meat powder at precise times. A tube in their mouths collected saliva, allowing its quantity and rate of secretion to be measured exactly. Before giving the dogs food, Pavlov would sound a tone—a buzzer or bell. As this procedure was repeated, the dog became conditioned, salivating in response to the tone itself. Using this experimental strategy, Pavlov and other researchers identified several important processes involved in classical conditioning.

Acquisition. The process in which the conditioned response becomes stronger through repeated pairings of the conditioned stimulus (CS—the tone) with the unconditioned stimulus (UCS—the food) is known as **acquisition.** As the number of pairings (or conditioning trials) increases, the dog begins to associate the CS and UCS. Soon the conditioned response (CR—salivation) will appear when the CS is presented alone. With more trials, the CR grows in magnitude (the dog produces greater amounts of saliva) and decreases in latency (the dog salivates more quickly following the appearance of the CS). Eventually, as the number of pairings increases, the magnitude and latency of

■ **acquisition**
in classical conditioning, the process in which the conditioned response becomes stronger through repeated pairings of the conditioned stimulus with the unconditioned stimulus

**Figure 8.2
Studying Pavlovian
Conditioning.** With this apparatus, classical conditioning can
be studied precisely. The dog is
held immobile in a harness, and
its saliva is collected in a tube.

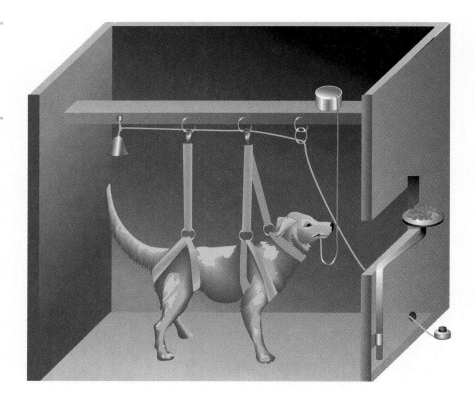

the CR reach leveling-off points, meaning that there is a limit to how much behavior
can be changed by classical conditioning (see Figure 8.3).

Researchers have investigated the factors in the classical conditioning procedure
that affect its magnitude and latency, as well as the rate at which it occurs. The relationship in time between the UCS and the CS is usually important. We now know that classical conditioning occurs most readily when the CS precedes the UCS. This
arrangement is known as **forward conditioning.** The exact time interval for optimal
learning varies from response to response, but usually the briefer the interval, the more
rapidly conditioning occurs.

■ **forward conditioning**

classical conditioning in which
the conditioned stimulus
precedes the unconditioned stimulus

**Figure 8.3
Processes in Classical
Conditioning.** During acquisition, the strength of a classically
conditioned response grows.
During extinction, it weakens.
However, the response may
appear again at a later time,
showing spontaneous recovery.

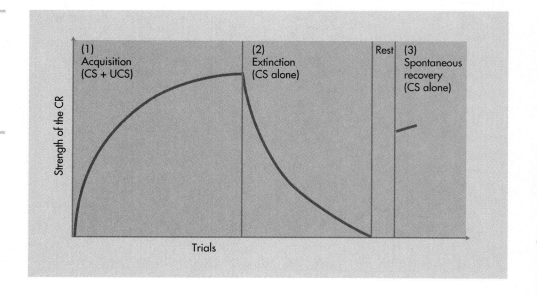

What happens if the CS and UCS are presented at the same time, in a procedure called **simultaneous conditioning?** Conditioning is not as likely to occur as in forward conditioning. And what happens if the UCS precedes the CS, in what is referred to as **backward conditioning?** Conditioning takes place with great difficulty, if at all. Note that the difficulty of conditioning responses with the simultaneous or backward procedure gives us reason to question that mere association in time is critical in classical conditioning. In all cases—forward, simultaneous, and backward conditioning—the CS and the UCS are equally associated in time, but only in the case of forward conditioning does the occurrence of the CS provide new information.

Forward conditioning is an example of what learning theorists call a **contingency,** meaning that the conditioned stimulus predicts the subsequent occurrence of the unconditioned stimulus (Rescorla, 1988). The efficiency of forward conditioning, compared with simultaneous or backward conditioning, implies that learning is more than the mindless formation of associations. Classical conditioning may at its essence involve the learning of expectations about what stimuli predict what other stimuli, thus making it an example of cognitive learning.

Despite the examples so far provided, the CR is not always the same response as the UCR. In many cases, the two resemble each other, as in the example of Pavlov's dogs, where both the CR and the UCR involve salivation. But in other cases, the CR and UCR are altogether different responses. For instance, suppose a rat hears a tone for several seconds and then the experimenter provides a pellet of food. Here we have the ingredients for classical conditioning: a CS (tone) and a UCS (food). How does the animal's behavior change in this situation? It becomes more active when the tone sounds—moving about and jerking its head (Holland, 1977, 1980). Note that this increased activity, the CR, does not resemble the UCR, the inherent response to food.

Classical conditioning is presumably an evolved psychological mechanism that aids survival (Chapter 3). We can make evolutionary sense of examples in which the CR resembles the UCR as well as those in which it does not. Salivation facilitates digestion, and so an organism that salivates when encountering stimuli that signal the presence of food is given a head start. Increased activity in response to such stimuli is also adaptive because it helps the organism locate where food might be.

Extinction and spontaneous recovery. After an association between a conditioned stimulus and an unconditioned stimulus has been learned, the conditioned stimulus alone will elicit a response. However, if the conditioned stimulus is repeatedly

■ **simultaneous conditioning**
classical conditioning in which the conditioned stimulus and the unconditioned stimulus occur at the same time

■ **backward conditioning**
classical conditioning in which the conditioned stimulus follows the unconditioned stimulus

■ **contingency**
in classical conditioning, the prediction of the subsequent occurrence of the unconditioned stimulus by the conditioned stimulus

Classical conditioning at its essence may involve learning which stimuli predict other stimuli.

■ **extinction**
in classical conditioning, the loss of the power of the conditioned stimulus to elicit the conditioned response after it no longer is paired with the unconditioned stimulus

presented to the person or animal but is no longer paired with the unconditioned stimulus, the CS eventually loses its power to elicit a response. This process is known as **extinction** (see again Figure 8.3). Extinction leads the organism to change its behavior when the associations in the environment change. The organism stops responding when responses are no longer appropriate. Had Pavlov begun to present the tone alone to his dogs, no longer pairing it with meat powder, they would eventually have stopped salivating at the tone.

One interpretation of extinction sees it simply as the erasure of the learned association between CS and UCS. But Pavlov thought extinction involved new learning, in this case learning that the CS and the UCS did not go together. The CS now inhibits the response that the UCS reflexively elicits. So, in Pavlov's original experiment, extinction occurs when the dog learns not to salivate in the presence of the CS. Remember that the nervous system involves both excitation and inhibition (Chapter 4). Learning can reflect both processes as well.

■ **spontaneous recovery**
in classical conditioning, reappearance of a conditioned response after extinction

These ideas explain the phenomenon of **spontaneous recovery,** in which a classically conditioned response that has become extinct will sometimes reappear (see again Figure 8.3). For example, spontaneous recovery occurs when the new learning (not salivating to the CS) is weakened and the old learning (salivating to the CS) resurfaces. If extinction involves the erasure of old learning, then spontaneous recovery should not exist.

Generalization and discrimination.   After I learned to associate the jingling sound of a dog collar with a ferocious attack, I responded with a start to the sound of a jingling key chain. The sounds were similar but not identical. This example illustrates another important phenomenon, known as **generalization:** The more similar a new stimulus is to the conditioned stimulus, the more likely that stimulus is to elicit the conditioned response.

■ **generalization**
in classical conditioning, the ability of stimuli similar to the conditioned stimulus to elicit the conditioned response

Generalization does not always occur, however. If a stimulus is too dissimilar, it will not elicit a response. The more dissimilar a new stimulus is to the conditioned stimulus, the less likely that new stimulus is to elicit the conditioned response. This phenomenon is called **discrimination.** Suppose you develop an allergy to shrimp, and every time you eat shrimp you become ill. You find yourself nauseated by just the taste of shrimp, and at first you have the same reaction to the taste of clams, oysters, and fish as well. But you eventually learn that you can eat these types of seafood with no problem. Your aversion to shrimp remains, and you have thus learned to discriminate.

■ **discrimination**
in classical conditioning, the failure of stimuli dissimilar to the conditioned stimulus to elicit the conditioned response

Classical conditioning helps both people and animals live in the real world. Generalization is useful because we can apply our learning as stimuli change, without having to start all over again in every new situation. Discrimination is useful as well because when situations change too much, we can refrain from performing what we have learned in other settings.

Second-order conditioning.   We know that a conditioned stimulus, after pairing with an unconditioned stimulus, can elicit a response by itself. Now suppose we pair a third stimulus with the conditioned stimulus. Does further conditioning take place? In some cases, yes. This process of pairing a neutral stimulus with a conditioned stimulus is called **second-order** (or **higher-order**) **conditioning.** Second-order conditioning is not the same as generalization because it depends on the pairing of stimuli with one another, not simply on their similarity.

■ **second-order conditioning; higher-order conditioning**
classical conditioning in which a stimulus comes to elicit a conditioned response after pairing with a conditioned stimulus

Consider a person who starts out afraid of thunder, who then comes to fear lightning (because of its association with thunder), and then rain (because of its association with lightning), and finally the entire outdoors (because of its association with rain). The significance of second-order conditioning is that it gives classical conditioning the potential to provide a much broader explanation of learning, encompassing not just various conditioned stimuli but also stimuli associated with them.

Applications of Classical Conditioning

When Pavlov first described classical conditioning, psychologists saw it as an explanation for all behavior, human and animal (Watson, 1913). Most psychologists today recognize limits to the applicability of classical conditioning to people's behavior, although in many areas classical conditioning still fares well as an explanation.

For example, you may have noticed that many of the examples so far involve stimuli that make the organism feel either good (e.g., meat powder in the mouth of a hungry dog) or bad (e.g., a ferocious animal or a booming thunderstorm). Psychologists call the former instances appetitive conditioning because they involve pleasant stimuli, and the latter instances aversive conditioning because they involve unpleasant stimuli. An emotional reaction is common to both.

Conditioned emotional responses.　We have now arrived at the area where classical conditioning most readily applies to human behavior: in the acquisition of emotional associations. Why do we like or dislike certain objects, events, or situations? Perhaps because they have been associated with pleasant or unpleasant stimuli. When in elementary school, I would sometimes get the flu and stay home. I would sit on the couch and watch daytime television, all the time feeling dizzy and nauseated. Eventually, I was unable to watch these shows anymore because they made me feel sick.

Researchers have shown that the emotional aspects of substance abuse can be classically conditioned (Siegel, 1983). Originally neutral stimuli associated with intoxication come to elicit these feelings in their own right, and this occurrence may explain why heroin addicts who cannot obtain this drug may inject water into their veins and experience a version of the heroin high. Similar conditioning occurs with respect to originally neutral stimuli repeatedly associated with feelings of withdrawal. If you formerly smoked cigarettes, you know that the possibility of resuming this habit is greatest when you find yourself in situations similar to those in which you once smoked.

Anyone who has tried to quit smoking knows that the craving for a cigarette is strongest in situations where one has frequently smoked in the past.

More complex emotions can also reflect classical conditioning. For example, attitudes toward a social group or political issue entail an evaluation and hence an emotional response (Chapter 15). At least part of this emotional response is determined by classical conditioning (Staats & Staats, 1958). Did you ever notice that political candidates are frequently tall, handsome men with full heads of hair? Are we swayed to their platform because their good looks make us feel good?

In several experiments, Scott (1957, 1959) showed that people are more likely to agree with a message if they hear it while eating. Do you see the Pavlovian point? The message is paired with food, and food makes us feel good. The message comes to make us feel good as well, regardless of its content.

Advertisers are well aware of the power of classical conditioning, and it is common to see the most mundane products accompanied in advertisements by stimuli that are clever, impressive, or sexy (Chapter 17). Presumably, the consumer comes to associate lawn mowers, office furniture, or fast food with these other stimuli and ends up enthralled.

Classical conditioning can also be responsible for emotional disorders (Chapter 13). In a famous example, John Watson, in collaboration with Rosalie Rayner (1920), showed that fear could be established through classical conditioning. Their research subject was an infant named Little Albert. When initially presented with a white rat, he showed no negative reaction. Then Watson and Rayner again showed Albert the rat. Behind him, the researchers made an extremely loud noise by striking a metal bar, which they knew from previous testing would upset the infant. CLANG! Albert jumped violently. The experience was repeated: first the rat, then the loud noise. CLANG! Albert started to whimper. After repeated pairings of the rat and the noise, what happened when the rat alone was shown to the child?

> The instant the rat was shown the baby began to cry. Almost instantly he turned sharply to the left, fell over on his left side, raised himself on all fours and began to crawl away so rapidly that he was caught with difficulty before reaching the edge of the table. (p. 5)

Watson and Rayner's study of Little Albert is an important demonstration of how human fears can be established by classical conditioning. (Photo courtesy of Benjamin Harris)

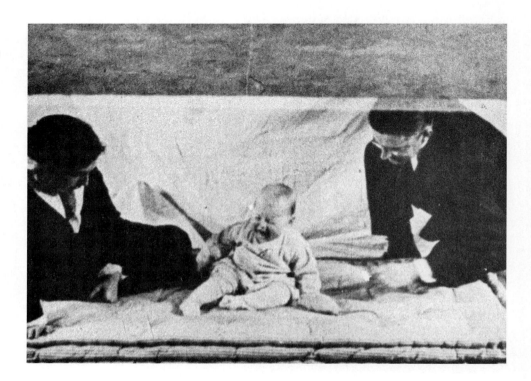

You can see that classical conditioning occurred. The white rat (CS) was initially paired with a loud noise (UCS) that reflexively produced a fear response (UCR). After just a few pairings of the rat and the noise, the rat elicited a fear response (CR) all by itself.

Several days later, Watson and Rayner demonstrated that Little Albert's fear of the rat had generalized to other furry white things. He was presented with a dog, a rabbit, and even Watson wearing a Santa Claus mask. In each case, the infant whimpered and cried.

Subsequent researchers have not always been able to replicate the results of Watson and Rayner, and ethical objections to scaring an infant can be raised (Harris, 1979). Nonetheless, the Albert study remains a provocative demonstration of how classical conditioning can be involved in emotional disorders. The child's fear response resembles a phobia: fear and avoidance of some object, event, or activity where no danger is actually posed (Chapter 13). This experiment gives us one way to think about phobias—as the result of classical conditioning. It also raises an important question: If fears can be acquired through learning, can they be removed in the same way? The answer is yes, through **counterconditioning,** which employs behavior therapy techniques based on classical conditioning principles to replace undesirable responses to stimuli with desirable ones (Chapter 14).

Suppose we wish to cure Albert of his fear of furry white things. We might engage him in some pleasurable activity, such as eating cookies or playing with blocks. Then we would introduce the white rat. If this is done gradually, starting at a distance and slowly moving the rat closer, Albert will not be overcome with fear. Instead, he will feel good and eventually start to like rats because he has learned to associate them with something pleasurable.

An alternative procedure, again derived from classical conditioning, would be to expose Albert to the rat without letting him crawl away. At first, Albert will not be happy, but eventually he will stop whimpering and crying. We are extinguishing his association between the rat and the noise. When this procedure is used in behavior therapy, it is called flooding, a colorful metaphor that captures the strategy of allowing fear to flood over (and out of) the phobic individual. Spontaneous recovery of the fear response may occur, in which case flooding is repeated.

■ **counterconditioning**
behavior therapy techniques based on classical conditioning that replace undesirable responses to stimuli with desirable ones

Conditioning and disease.   Classical conditioning may be involved in susceptibility to illness (Chapter 16). In a classic experiment, Ader and Cohen (1981) found that they could condition the immune system of rats. In conjunction with a particular taste, they administered drugs that suppress the body's ability to fight disease. Learning occurred because the animals formed a link between the taste and poor immune functioning. When the animals later encountered the taste alone, their bodies less readily produced antibodies in response to foreign material.

Ader and Cohen's demonstration extends even further the types of responses that can be classically conditioned. Their research suggests that certain stimuli can become associated with poor health and thus contribute to illness in their own right (Ader & Cohen, 1993). Although rainy weather does not directly cause the flu, perhaps a repeated association of dampness with illness means that raindrops and puddles can eventually be hazardous to your health, just like Mother told you all along. Conversely, if healthy immune functioning can be conditioned, perhaps disease can be countered not just by physicians but also by psychologists (Chapter 16).

In his book *Anatomy of an Illness,* Norman Cousins (1981) offered a now famous account of how he mustered his body's psychological resources to combat a potentially fatal disease. One of his tactics was to check out of his hospital room and into a plush hotel (which proved less expensive than the hospital), where he watched funny movies. It is impossible to tell from this case study what was responsible for Cousins's successful battle with his disease, but perhaps classical conditioning was part of his journey to good health. He avoided stimuli that were associated with illness (the hospital) and sought out stimuli that were associated with health and feelings of well-being (fancy

Is it possible that past associations between hospitals and illness make a hospital a less than ideal situation in which to recover from an illness?

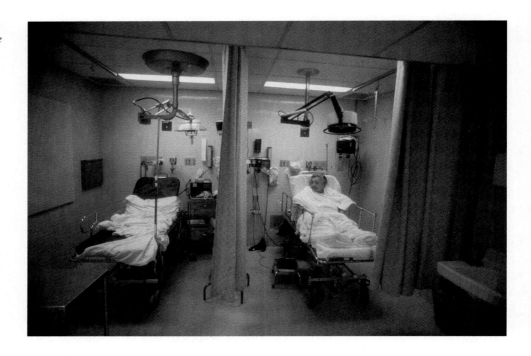

surroundings and humor). Perhaps he elicited good health from his body (Kiecolt–Glaser & Glaser, 1992). Pavlov the physician would have been pleased with this turn of events.

> **Stop and Think**
>
> **6** Think of an example from your everyday life of classical conditioning, and describe it with the terminology introduced in this section.

O PERANT CONDITIONING

■ operant conditioning
learning that takes place when we come to associate a behavior with its consequences

The student who becomes the class clown because of the attention it brings to him has learned to associate a behavior with its consequences. This form of learning is **operant conditioning.** Depending on the consequences, this behavior will become more or less likely to occur in the future. What happens when a child tells jokes in the classroom? If he makes his classmates laugh, he will tell even more jokes. Other consequences might reduce his tendency. Suppose he is ignored by his classmates? This consequence might lead him to be quiet.

■ operant
behavior that is emitted spontaneously

Psychologists use the term **operant** to describe any behavior that the person or animal emits spontaneously (Glenn, Ellis, & Greenspoon, 1992). Such behaviors are termed operants because they operate on the environment, producing consequences for the person or animal. Examples of operants include animals pressing bars or levers to produce food and/or avoid electric shock, basketball players shooting free throws, children playing tag, and scientists designing experiments. Unlike the sorts of behaviors explained by classical conditioning, operants are not reflexively triggered by particular stimuli. Instead, they are influenced by what follows from them, rather than by what precedes them.

Thorndike's Discovery

An American psychologist, Edward L. Thorndike (1874–1949), is usually credited with the first formal theory of operant conditioning, which he called **instrumental conditioning** to underscore his interest in responses that proved instrumental (useful) to the individual. Thorndike studied how cats solve problems, placing them in puzzle boxes like the one in Figure 8.4 and observing their attempts to escape. The puzzle box was built so that its door would spring open if the cat pushed against a lever.

When a cat is thus confined, it becomes very active. It claws and bites and struggles. After some time, it eventually moves the lever that opens the door, and it bounds from its prison. The researcher then puts the cat back in the box. Again, the cat does all sorts of things, and eventually it again moves the lever and wins its freedom. Back in the box. More frantic movements. Back out of the box. Over time, the cat becomes more efficient at escaping. Irrelevant behaviors are no longer made. Instead, the cat in the box immediately moves the lever and escapes. Through trial and error, it has learned that moving the lever opens the door and allows escape.

Thorndike was struck by the way in which useful responses remained while futile responses fell away. He concluded that reward stamped in these useful responses and that lack of reward stamped out the useless ones. Thorndike (1911) named this process the **law of effect** and proposed it as a basic principle of learning. The law of effect became the foundation for what would later be called operant conditioning. If the effect of a

■ **instrumental conditioning**
Thorndike's term for describing operant conditioning, to emphasize his interest in responses that prove instrumental (useful) to the individual

■ **law of effect**
Thorndike's proposal that reward stamps in responses, whereas lack of reward stamps out responses

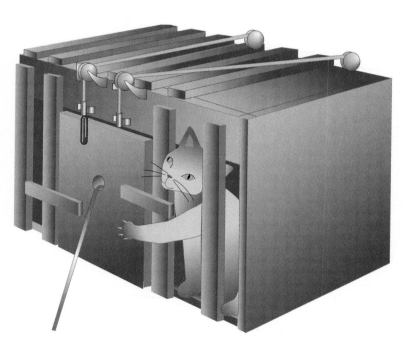

Figure 8.4
Thorndike's Puzzle Box. To study learning, Thorndike placed cats in boxes like this one. To get out of the box, the cat has to move the lever, a response that occurs more and more rapidly over time.

B.F. Skinner (left) was the most important behaviorist of his generation. His favorite research was the pigeon.

behavior is to bring reward (pressing a lever → escape), then the behavior is more likely to occur (lever pressing increases). If the effect of a behavior is not to bring reward, then the behavior is less likely to occur.

Theorists over the years have noted the parallel between the law of effect and the theory of evolution by natural selection (Chapter 3). In both cases, the environment determines what survives—behaviors or species, as the case may be (Alessi, 1992; Schull, 1990). Both are examples of functional explanations because they stress the importance of consequences (Chapter 1). Again, we are reminded that nature and nurture need not compete as explanations because the mechanisms by which they affect behavior may be similar.

Like Pavlov's discovery of classical conditioning, Thorndike's law of effect describes a form of learning, and his experiments provided researchers with a concrete procedure for investigating it. Subsequent studies of operant conditioning use much the same methods as Thorndike did. Various animal species continue to be used as research subjects, with rats and pigeons overtaking cats in popularity.

Skinner's Approach

Watson, Pavlov, and Thorndike were the pioneers of learning theory. Burrhus Frederick (B. F.) Skinner (1904–1990) was the most influential individual among the next generation of learning theorists (Chiesa, 1992; Lattal, 1992). Skinner's work continued that of Thorndike in that he was particularly interested in how the consequences of behaviors affect their subsequent occurrence. It was Skinner who introduced the term *operant* to describe any behavior that the person or animal makes spontaneously. Remember that an operant is not a specific reflex but rather a behavior that appears in the absence of specific triggers.

Skinner also gave the field the so-called Skinner box, or **operant chamber** (see Figure 8.5), which provides a simple way to study operant conditioning. In one of its typical forms, an operant chamber consists of an enclosed box with a lever that can be pushed and a place where food pellets are delivered. The chamber might be equipped with various lights or buzzers as well.

■ **operant chamber**
Skinner box; mechanized device for studying operant conditioning

Lever Food Pellet
cup dispenser

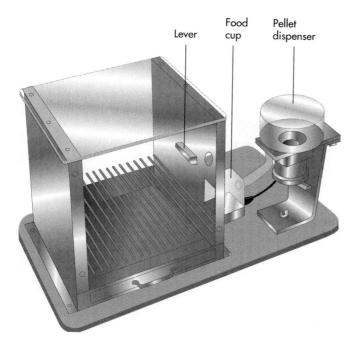

Figure 8.5
Operant Chamber. In an operant chamber, a response like
pressing a lever produces reinforcement like a food pellet.

All of the components of an operant chamber are under the control of the researcher. The chamber might be programmed so that a food pellet appears whenever the lever is pushed once, or twice, or in whatever manner is of interest to the researcher. Things can be arranged so that lever pressing produces food only when a given light is turned on, or only when another light is turned off. Favorite research subjects include pigeons or rats, but operant chambers have been designed for all sorts of creatures, from lizards to human beings to elephants.

Common to all operant chambers is that they allow a particular operant—pressing the lever, for instance—to be studied under controlled conditions. Usually operant chambers are equipped with mechanical devices that automatically record how often the operant occurs in a given period (see Figure 8.6). Then when the researcher manip-ulates the consequences of the operant, it becomes possible to gauge the effects. Is the frequency of the operant increased, decreased, or unaffected?

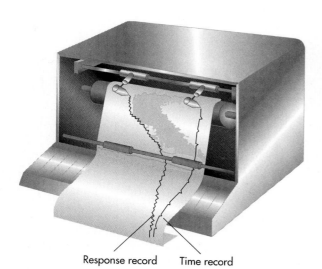

Response record   Time record

Figure 8.6
Cumulative Recorder. This
device records the frequency of
operants—like pressing a lever—
in a given period. The pen moves
every time a response is made,
making a mark on the moving
sheet of paper. The steeper the
line, the more rapidly the operant
is occurring.

■ **reinforcer**
change in the environment that follows a behavior and increases the probability that it will recur

■ **reinforcement**
process by which reinforcers affect behavior

■ **positive reinforcement**
reinforcement in which a stimulus is presented after a response

■ **negative reinforcement**
reinforcement in which a stimulus is removed after a response

■ **punishment**
process by which a stimulus that follows a response reduces the probability that the response will recur

Defining reinforcement and punishment.   As a behaviorist, Skinner did not use the term *reward* because it refers to something that makes a person or animal feel good and feeling good is an unobservable state. Skinner therefore spoke of reinforcers, defining them only in terms of their effects on behavior. **Reinforcers** are changes in the environment that follow some behavior and increase the probability that the behavior will recur. **Reinforcement** is the process by which this occurs. We have no idea if a reinforcer makes an individual feel good, bad, or indifferent, and for Skinner, these feelings do not help us explain behavior.

Skinner further distinguished between **positive reinforcement,** which involves a stimulus presented after a response, and **negative reinforcement,** which involves a stimulus removed after a response. A positive reinforcer might be money given to a child for cleaning his or her room. A negative reinforcer might be the annoying buzz of an alarm clock which one learns rapidly to turn off once it sounds. A reinforcer reinforces, whether positively or negatively, meaning that it increases the probability of a behavior.

Punishment is the process by which a stimulus follows a response and reduces the frequency of that response. The man who loses his license for drunk driving is less likely—we would hope—to drive after drinking. Punishers are not the same thing as negative reinforcers (see Table 8.1), for punishment reduces the frequency of behavior, whereas reinforcement increases it.

In positive punishment, a stimulus that reduces the frequency of some response is presented. Getting yelled at by your boss when you are late, for instance, exemplifies positive punishment because it reduces tardiness on your part in the future. In negative punishment, a reinforcer is removed, again with the effect of reducing the frequency of some response. Losing your salary bonus because you file reports late will lead you to decrease this behavior. From Skinner's perspective, we go too far when we ask if punishment is painful or unpleasant because we cannot observe the inner states to which these words refer. All we can see is the effect of stimuli on an animal's or a person's behavior.

Functional analysis of behavior.   To identify reinforcers and punishers, we must consider the individual case and look at how particular stimuli affect the behaviors of a given organism. We can make some good bets that food will reinforce and electric shock will punish, but this will not always be true. Identifying reinforcers and punishers

A punisher is any stimulus—like a ticket—that reduces the frequency of a behavior—like speeding.

Table 8.1   Summary: Important Operant Conditioning Processes

Process	Effect on frequency of behavior
Positive reinforcement	**Increases** frequency by presenting a stimulus
Negative reinforcement	**Increases** frequency by removing a stimulus
Punishment	**Decreases** frequency by presenting or removing a stimulus

by observing actual behavior and its consequences is what matters. Skinner called this process a **functional analysis** of behavior.

Functional analyses show that we can be mistaken in our guesses about which stimuli will prove reinforcing or punishing. We might think, for instance, that a parent who spanks and scolds a child following some action is punishing the child—that is, reducing the frequency of that action. But in some cases, the child becomes more likely to behave in a way that leads to spankings and scoldings. We then conclude that these consequences are reinforcing for this child. If the parent wishes to reduce the frequency of the child's behavior, perhaps the wise course is to withhold the spankings and scoldings. Reinforcement and punishment are not always as simple as they first seem, and they are discussed in greater detail later in this chapter.

Processes in Operant Conditioning

When Skinner and other researchers studied operant conditioning, they discovered a number of processes that help explain how this type of learning occurs. Many of these processes are analogous to those described with respect to classical conditioning, and they are similarly labeled.

Acquisition. As with classical conditioning, psychologists want to know the factors that determine the rate of acquiring new responses. **Acquisition** describes the process by which operants increase in frequency. Three factors influence acquisition. First is the degree to which reinforcement consistently follows that response and no other response. Second is the immediacy of the reinforcement. All other things being equal, a reinforcer that follows a response quickly is more likely to affect learning than one that follows with some delay. Third is repetition. The more frequently a given consequence follows a particular behavior, the more likely the two are to become associated and the more likely behavior is to be affected by that consequence.

How can you increase the rate at which you study for a particular course, like introductory psychology? Start with a reinforcer—perhaps a favorite snack or television program. Then arrange your life so that you eat the snack or watch the show only when you have studied your textbook for at least two hours. No exceptions. You do not eat the snack or watch the show under any other circumstances. Next be sure that after you study this book for two hours, you toss it aside and quickly get your reward. Finally, do this again and again.

Shaping and chaining. Operant conditioning begins with a spontaneous behavior occurring at some frequency. How, then, can it explain complicated behaviors such as making a cheese soufflé? Most of us do not spontaneously perform this behavior. Instead, we gradually learn to perform complex behaviors by starting with simpler versions of them. When an approximate version of the behavior is first performed, it is reinforced. Over time, closer versions of the behavior are reinforced. If the standard for reinforcement changes gradually over successive occasions, simple responses can eventually become complex ones. This process is called **shaping**.

If you have ever trained a dog to do a trick like rolling over, you know that you cannot usually wait for Rover to do this on his own. Instead, you first wait for him to

■ functional analysis

identification of reinforcers and punishers by observing actual behavior and its consequences

■ acquisition

in operant conditioning, process by which the frequency of an operant increases

■ shaping

process by which simple responses become complex ones through changing the standard for reinforcement on successive occasions

With the operant conditioning procedures of shaping and chaining, complex and novel behaviors can be acquired. Perhaps this water-skier is now working on his bare-footing technique.

crouch on the ground. Then you give him a food treat. Then you wait for him to roll onto his side. Another treat. Then you wait for him to roll onto his back. Yet another treat. Finally, you wait for him to roll over completely. Shaping explains how seemingly new responses can be acquired through operant conditioning.

Another apparent limitation of operant conditioning is that people or animals perform complicated sequences of behaviors over long periods with no reinforcement until the very end. For example, people buy airplane tickets, drive to the airport, check their luggage, get a boarding pass, find their seat, fly across the country, get off the plane, push through a crowd of people, report their lost luggage, push through another crowd of people, and only then receive reinforcement—hugs and kisses from family or friends.

How do examples like these square with the notion that immediate reinforcement is a crucial factor in learning? Again, theorists have an answer: People or animals will learn a response that allows them to perform another response that brings a reward. A third response will be learned, and so on, in a process known appropriately as **chaining.** Reinforcement need not occur following each response in a long series, so long as it follows the last behavior in the sequence.

For example, Simek, O'Brien, and Figlerski (1994) described the successful use of a chaining procedure in improving the golf scores of college players. Driving and putting were broken into their component steps and taught one at a time, with the eventual reinforcement being a place on the starting team. Similar chaining procedures have been used to teach mentally retarded individuals how to make corsages (Hur & Osborne, 1993), to teach students how to use computers (McGregor & Axelrod, 1988), and to teach beginners how to play the piano (Ash & Holding, 1990).

Extinction and spontaneous recovery.   Suppose you have learned a response that produces a reinforcing consequence. The rate at which you perform that behavior will increase. But suppose the world changes so that the response you have learned no longer produces a reinforcement. Obviously, you perform the behavior less frequently. Its rate will eventually fall to whatever it was before reinforcement was initiated. **Extinction** has occurred—a decrease in the frequency of an operant behavior when reinforcers are withheld.

Clinical psychologists who work with children use extinction procedures to eliminate tantrums, profanity, or disobedience. First, they identify the reinforcers that maintain these behaviors, let us say attention from parents, teachers, or peers. Then they ensure that when the child throws a tantrum, says a nasty word, or disobeys a request,

■ **chaining**

process by which a sequence of responses is learned through operant conditioning: first the last response, then the next-to-last response, and so on

■ **extinction**

in operant conditioning, decrease in the frequency of an operant when reinforcers are withheld reinforcers do not follow. In plain English, the child is ignored. If extinction can be done consistently, then the undesirable behavior will decrease.

Extinction procedures are easier to recommend in the abstract than to carry through in reality. One problem with carrying out extinction is that it is slow. Another problem is that behaviors may show a temporary increase in their rate before they start to decrease. For instance, you call a friend on the telephone. When there is no answer, you at first call back more frequently, and only eventually less often.

There is still another problem with using extinction to decrease undesired behaviors. The child whose profanity has been consistently ignored and who now seems to have lost this nasty habit may start cursing again, at an even greater rate than previously. Parents and teachers might despair, believing extinction has been a failure, but the reappearance of an extinguished operant is not unusual. This phenomenon is called **spontaneous recovery.** Extinction must again be undertaken. Indeed, many operant responses require several periods of extinction before they finally cease.

Generalization and discrimination.   Imagine that your dog has now learned to roll over because you gave him a treat every time he did so. When he sees you, he rolls over and opens his mouth. But when he is out cruising the streets alone, he never stops, rolls over, and opens his mouth. Why not? Because you are not present. He has learned not only what responses lead to what consequences but also in what circumstances these associations hold true. To use a technical phrase, you have become a **discriminative stimulus,** a signal that reinforcement is (or is not) available.

Discriminative stimuli affect the degree to which people or animals generalize responses learned through operant conditioning. If stimuli in a new situation are similar enough to those in a previous situation where responses led to reinforcers, then **generalization** takes place. If the new stimuli are dissimilar, then learning is not generalized; rather, **discrimination** takes place. Back to Rover. He has learned to roll over when you bend down and say "Please." When you say "Fleas," he may also roll over. This is generalization because the words sound the same. But if you say "Yuck, bugs," he does not roll over. This is discrimination.

Reinforcement

Let us now take a closer look at two of the important phenomena of operant conditioning: first reinforcement, then punishment. Psychologists have investigated a number of basic questions about both. What is their nature? What are their basic types? How do they influence behavior?

Conditioned reinforcement.   Some stimuli are reinforcing because of their inherent biological properties. These are **primary reinforcers** and include both positive and negative reinforcers. Obvious examples include food, water, and relief from pain. But as you go about your everyday life, few of the stimuli that affect your behavior are primary reinforcers. Instead, what reinforce you are stimuli like smiles, money, good grades, and pats on the back. Why do these stimuli function as reinforcers?

A neutral stimulus can become a reinforcer if it is repeatedly paired with a primary reinforcer. Stimuli that derive their reinforcing nature from prior association with primary reinforcers are called **secondary** (or **conditioned**) **reinforcers.** A host of stimuli can become conditioned reinforcers. Note how these reinforcers greatly extend the ability of operant conditioning to explain complex behavior. Even in situations where no primary reinforcers are present, we can use operant conditioning to explain behavior if we are able to specify conditioned reinforcers such as praise.

In several studies, chimpanzees were taught to perform particular responses for a food reward (Cowles, 1937; Wolfe, 1936). Along with the food, they were given tokens (e.g., poker chips) that had no inherent meaning to them. However, the tokens could later be exchanged for food. After the link between tokens and food was established, the

■ **spontaneous recovery**
in operant conditioning, the reappearance of an extinguished operant

■ **discriminative stimulus**
stimulus indicating that reinforcement is (or is not) available

■ **generalization**
in operant conditioning, the process by which an organism behaves in a new situation as it did in an old situation because the discriminative stimuli in them are similar

■ **discrimination**
in operant conditioning, the process by which an organism does not behave in a new situation as it did in an old situation because the discriminative stimuli in them are dissimilar

■ **primary reinforcer**
stimulus that is reinforcing because of its inherent biological properties

■ **secondary reinforcer; conditioned reinforcer**
stimulus that is reinforcing because of its prior association with a primary reinforcer

Because of their inherent biological properties, primary reinforcers increase the frequency of behaviors.

tokens themselves functioned as reinforcers. The chimps would learn a response in order to earn a token. Learning occurred even with a one-hour delay between getting the token and exchanging it for food, as long as the chimp was allowed to hold on to the token. If more than one chimp became involved in the process, they began to beg or steal each other's tokens. The parallels between the chimps' approach to poker chips and people's approach to money are obvious and intriguing.

Explanations of reinforcement.   What actually makes certain stimuli reinforcing? One possibility is that reinforcers work because they reduce biological needs (Bolles, 1967). In some cases, this hypothesis is reasonable. Food reinforces a hungry person because the hunger drive is reduced. Water reinforces a thirsty person because the thirst drive is reduced. In other cases, though, this drive reduction hypothesis does not explain what is going on (Chapter 7). For instance, many animals will learn a response that does nothing other than turn on a light. Here there is reinforcement, but where is the drive reduction?

A different account of reinforcement was suggested by White and Milner (1992), who argued that reinforcers do not affect the learning of associations. Instead, they increase the likelihood of behavior through their effect on two other psychological processes. First, reinforcers enhance what people or animals recall from their experience with the environment (Chapter 9). Second, reinforcers enhance their motivation to respond in a given setting (Chapter 7). According to White and Milner (1992), these two processes by which reinforcers influence behavior occur by distinct physiological mechanisms. This theory links learning to other aspects of psychological and biological functioning, in this case memory, motivation, and their physiological bases.

Yet another explanation of what makes stimuli reinforcing is known as the **Premack principle** because it was proposed by the psychologist David Premack

■ **Premack principle**
Premack's hypothesis that preferred activities act as reinforcers for less preferred activities

(1965). He suggested that more preferred activities can act as reinforcers for less preferred activities. Think of an activity you prefer, like watching television, and one you do not prefer, like dusting. If you arrange matters so that you will gain access to television if you first dust, then you will have a clean apartment. Television watching reinforces dusting. But now reverse the link between these activities. Obviously, dusting will not reinforce television watching.

Applied psychologists have used the Premack principle to improve the performance of workers (Timberlake & Farmer-Dougan, 1991). For example, researchers arranged the tasks required of engineers from less preferred to more preferred (Makin & Hoyle, 1993). When the opportunity to perform more preferable tasks was used to reinforce the performance of less preferable tasks, employee performance improved. A similar strategy improved work performance at a fast-food restaurant (Welsh, Bernstein, & Luthans, 1992).

The Premack principle has considerable generality. For a hungry person, eating is a highly preferred activity that will reinforce almost any other activity. Further, the Premack principle helps the psychologist identify possible reinforcers without having to rely on trial and error. It also explains what is punishing: being forced to engage in a less preferred activity following performance of a more preferred one. Suppose you had to dust your apartment after each instance in which you watched television. According to Premack, your television watching would decrease.

The Premack principle has been challenged by some researchers, who argue that rigorous evidence in support of its predictions is scant (Knapp, 1974). A revision has been suggested: Access to activities is reinforcing when the person or animal has not been allowed to engage freely in these activities, but not otherwise (Timberlake & Allison, 1974). Regardless, an important implication of the Premack principle and its more recent modification is that reinforcement and punishment are not inherent properties of stimuli. No firm line divides reinforcers and punishers from other stimuli. What is reinforcing or punishing depends on the activity we wish to increase or decrease. Again, the learning of given responses must be placed in a larger context—in this case, the context provided by other possible responses and their relative likelihoods.

Schedules of reinforcement.   In the discussion so far, reinforcement usually follows every response. But the world does not always work this way. Often reinforcement follows a particular behavior only some of the time. An individual who sells products over the telephone may have to make 101 phone calls before she makes a single sale.

People persist at behaviors that are reinforced only intermittently, a principle well known to those who program slot machines.

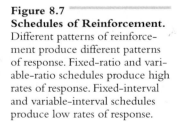

■ continuous reinforcement
operant conditioning in which
reinforcement occurs after every
response

■ intermittent reinforcement
operant conditioning in which
reinforcement does not occur
after every response

■ partial reinforcement effect
resistance to extinction of
responses acquired with intermittent as opposed to continuous
reinforcement

■ schedules of reinforcement
different patterns of providing
reinforcement following a
response

Let us take a look at learning under circumstances where reinforcement does not always follow a response. In the process of acquiring some response, **continuous reinforcement** after every response speeds learning. But after a response has been learned, **intermittent reinforcement** has an important effect on its performance: The person or animal reinforced only once in a while keeps on responding vigorously in the absence of reinforcement. The response that has been learned resists extinction. This phenomenon is known as the **partial reinforcement effect,** and it helps to explain what might otherwise seem like unusual persistence at a mostly futile endeavor.

Why does a person keep betting on football games? Because he wins every once in a while. Why does a person keep fishing? Because she catches a fish every once in a while. Why do adolescents keep playing a video game? Because they win every once in a while. Consider these activities—betting, fishing, and playing a video game—and the unlikely case where a person is reinforced every time he or she engages in them. What happens, then, if reinforcement suddenly stops? Betting, fishing, and dropping quarters soon stop as well. These behaviors are extinguished. But take the more likely case where reinforcement is intermittent. Now what happens when there is a long dry spell, a period of no reinforcement? People keep responding.

Psychologists study intermittent reinforcement by manipulating **schedules of reinforcement:** different patterns of delivering a reward following the desired response. Several different schedules have been identified, each with characteristic effects on performance.

When in high school, I had a summer job cleaning carpets in people's homes. I worked with the owner of the business, and his rule was that we would take a break only after we had cleaned three rooms. Once the carpet in the third room was cleaned, we stopped working and relaxed. This sort of schedule is called a fixed-ratio schedule because reinforcement (the break) came after a fixed number of responses (cleaning three carpets). When fixed-ratio schedules are instituted in a Skinner box, their effect is to produce high rates of responding, with brief pauses following the reinforcement (see Figure 8.7).

The use of fixed-ratio schedules in the workplace is called piecework. One is paid only for what one produces. These schedules lead to high rates of productivity. They are popular with management but at the same time unpopular with workers because salary from day to day and from week to week is inconsistent. Workers become reluctant to rest, go to the bathroom, or take a sick day. Union contracts over the years have eliminated piecework in favor of hourly wages (Schwartz, 1984). Animals show the same

Figure 8.7
Schedules of Reinforcement.
Different patterns of reinforcement produce different patterns of response. Fixed-ratio and variable-ratio schedules produce high rates of response. Fixed-interval and variable-interval schedules produce low rates of response.

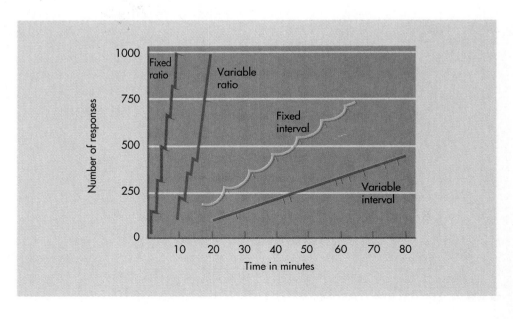

aversion to fixed-ratio schedules. Even though these schedules lead to high rates of responding, if given the opportunity to escape this schedule (i.e., to turn it off momentarily), a pigeon will do so (Appel, 1963).

What happens when reinforcement is delivered only after a number of responses have been made but this number varies? Here we have a variable-ratio schedule. This schedule leads to the highest rate of responding of all the schedules psychologists have studied (see Figure 8.7). There are no pauses following the reinforcement. Gambling is a frequently cited example of a variable-ratio schedule because slot machines and other games of chance pay off on a variable-ratio schedule. If you have visited Atlantic City, Las Vegas, or similar places, you have seen the effect these variable-ratio schedules have on the patrons of casinos. They respond and respond and respond.

In a fixed-interval schedule, reinforcement occurs for the first response a person or animal makes, granted that a given interval of time has passed since the last reinforcement. Once the subject is reinforced, further responses have no effect until the interval of time passes again. Then the first response once more produces reinforcement. Suppose you have a newspaper delivered every day at the crack of dawn. When you go out in the morning, you find the paper and take it inside to read it. If you go out again in the afternoon, however, you will not find a newspaper. You have to wait until the next morning.

Fixed-interval schedules produce a characteristic rate of performance termed a scallop (see Figure 8.7). Immediately after reinforcement occurs, the response rate is very low. It increases slowly as the required time interval passes, though, so that when the interval is over, the response rate is high. Then it falls off again.

You should be able to puzzle out what a variable-interval schedule involves. Basically, reinforcement occurs for the first response a person or animal makes, following some interval of time since the last reinforcer was given. The specific interval varies—sometimes one length, sometimes another. Think of when you have called a friend on the telephone, only to find that the line is busy. You call back, knowing that eventually your friend will be off the phone. But you do not know when your friend will hang up. It might be seconds. It might be hours. What is the effect of this variable-interval schedule on your redialing? You call back at a low yet stable rate (see Figure 8.7). Responses reinforced on a variable-interval schedule prove resistant to extinction.

Learning to be helpless.   Sometimes responses and outcomes are completely independent of one another. Consider the weather, which takes its course despite what we may do or not do. You can think of this situation as a reinforcement schedule with no relationship between what the organism does and the delivery of rewards or punishments. But something is learned: There is no link between what one does and what happens. What is interesting and important about this form of learning is that it may be generalized to a new situation. Even if consequences follow responses in the new situation, the person or animal may not learn this association because it has already learned to be helpless. We therefore call this phenomenon **learned helplessness** (Peterson, Maier, & Seligman, 1993).

Learned helplessness was first observed in studies with dogs who were immobilized and given electric shocks (Overmier & Seligman, 1967; Seligman & Maier, 1967). Regardless of what the dogs did or did not do, the shocks went on and off. Twenty-four hours later, these animals were placed in a long box with a barrier in the middle. Shocks were periodically delivered through the floor of the box, and the dogs could escape them by jumping over the barrier and running to the other end of the box. Researchers found that animals previously exposed to uncontrollable shocks acted passively when placed in a shuttle box. They simply sat there and endured the shocks. In contrast, animals without prior experience with uncontrollable shocks had no difficulty learning to escape the shocks.

Learned helplessness may help explain certain examples of human passivity. For instance, Seligman (1974, 1975) suggested that learned helplessness lies at the root of

■ **learned helplessness**
passivity following learning that responses and outcomes are unrelated

Learned helplessness theory proposes that people learn when responses and outcomes are unrelated. One consequence of this learning can be depression.

depression (Chapter 13). Other theorists have proposed that people may fail in school, at work, or in interpersonal relationships because they have learned in one situation that responses and outcomes are unrelated and then have generalized this learning to a second situation (Peterson, Maier, & Seligman, 1993). Consider children who have been abused by their parents, severely beaten regardless of what they did or did not do. Outside their home and away from their parents, these children may act listlessly. Although new situations include those in which behaviors indeed produce reward, these abused children are passive. They never learn that responses can be instrumental. Their passivity, so puzzling to an observer who does not know their prior history, makes sense if we know the original situation where helplessness was learned.

Punishment

As we have seen, punishment, like extinction, decreases the frequency of some behavior. However, extinction and punishment differ. We can make the difference clear by returning to our example of the child who throws tantrums, curses, and/or disobeys. This undesirable behavior can be decreased through extinction, but it can also be decreased through punishment. We have to identify a stimulus that functions as a punisher. For our purposes, perhaps a loud "No!" will suffice. Perhaps not. Regardless, if punishment is to be effective it must be intense, consistent, and immediate. Then it will decrease the undesired behavior.

Many psychologists recommend against the use of punishment as a means of decreasing behavior. They sometimes argue that it suppresses not just the targeted behavior but all operants by producing a host of disruptive emotional reactions. While it is true that punishment may temporarily disrupt a person's overall behavior, only the response that is specifically punished decreases in the long run (Schwartz, 1984). The profane child may first respond to punishment for cursing by not talking at all but will eventually show a specific decrease in swearing.

Other critics of punishment argue that it does not add to one's repertoire of available responses. Undesired behaviors are presumably performed in the first place because they produce reinforcement. If these are suppressed by punishment, then the person is left with nothing. This argument is obviously correct. It is reasonable to reinforce an alternative behavior, rather than simply punish the target behavior. In the example of the child who uses nasty words to get attention, we might consider rewarding the child for talking politely.

Punishment is justified in circumstances where we cannot afford delay in eliminating undesirable behavior. Here is a compelling example. Autism is a profound disturbance occasionally seen in young children. Autistic children show marked impairment in language and social relationships. These children may also perform self-damaging acts, like repeatedly pounding their heads against the wall, even to the point of fracturing their skulls and creating brain damage. One might deal with this behavior by ignoring it or by reinforcing alternative behaviors. Needless to say, such strategies may take too long, resulting in a seriously injured child.

To prevent self-damaging acts, some therapists use punishment, like spankings or electric shock. These procedures are effective (Lovaas, 1977) but have been controversial because they seem cruel. In a well-publicized case some years ago, Massachusetts barred such punishment procedures in a school for autistic children. The children at the school went back to hurting themselves, and their parents went to court to get the ban overturned.

Applications of Operant Conditioning

Operant conditioning encompasses not just Thorndike's law of effect but concepts like shaping, chaining, conditioned reinforcement, discriminative stimuli, and schedules of reinforcement as well. Taken together, these concepts provide a powerful explanation of behavior. In this section, where I discuss applications of operant conditioning, it would be easier for me to list those behaviors not influenced by this form of learning because almost everything we do (or do not do) is sensitive to the consequences.

Criteria for good applications.   At the same time, I can specify particularly good applications. These involve situations where behavior is (a) discrete, (b) observable, and (c) sensibly described in terms of the rate at which it occurs. When what we do departs from these criteria, operant conditioning becomes a less satisfactory explanation.

A discrete action is a behavior that has a specific beginning and ending, such as a rat pressing a lever or a student working a math problem. Although it is possible to talk about a person's job, identity, college career, or personality as behavior, these designations are fuzzy because there are no particular responses to which these abstract notions refer.

An observable action is an overt response in the fashion of Watson and Skinner. Some theorists have tried to explain thinking in operant terms, rephrasing thoughts and beliefs as covert behavior, but again this seems fuzzy; behavior, by definition, has to be seen.

Finally, not everything a person does is best described at the rate at which it occurs. Consider language. Some behaviorists have tried to include language within their general formula, but as you will see in Chapter 9, this effort has not been successful. Although reinforcers and punishers influence how language is used, language itself is not learned through the trial-and-error process hypothesized by operant conditioning. The essence of language—its meaning—is not explained at all by a theory that stresses the rate at which behaviors occur.

Operant techniques in therapy.   We can turn to behavior therapy for good examples of operant conditioning. Operant techniques systematically manipulate the consequences of behaviors in order to reduce the frequency of undesired behaviors and increase the frequency of desired ones. For example, time out is an operant procedure recommended for decreasing disruptive behavior in children. When a child acts up, he or she is removed from the situation and placed in a quiet room where reinforcement is unavailable for a fixed period, say five or ten minutes. This reduces the likelihood of future misconduct.

Social skills training involves learning how to do the things that produce reinforcement when one is interacting with others, like making eye contact, listening attentively, and paying compliments. These may seem like obvious strategies for social interaction,

*Time out is an operant condition-
ing procedure that can be used with
disruptive children. When they act
up, they are removed to a quiet
room where reinforcement is
unavailable for a fixed period.*

but many people seem not to know how to make others take an interest in them. Once
these skills are imparted, reinforcement becomes more plentiful (Lewinsohn, 1974).

Behavioral contracting is a technique sometimes used in marital therapy. Here a
couple first make explicit their expectations for each other's behavior; they then agree
on how each will respond to particular behaviors by their partner. Behavioral contracting in effect makes schedules of reinforcement clear and consistent.

A clinical psychologist is not needed to implement these techniques. You can carry
them out yourself. Indeed, you can even do them with yourself—which puts you in the
position of being your own behavior therapist. You can use your knowledge of operant
conditioning in a deliberate way to modify the world so that you end up acting in ways
you desire. For example, I make use of the Premack principle in getting myself to do
household chores. My example of dusting (yech!) and television viewing (yeah!) was
not chosen at random.

Stop and Think

7   Think of an example from your everyday life of operant conditioning, and describe it
with the terminology introduced in this section.

8   Describe Skinner's contributions to the study of psychology.

9   When is punishment justified? When is it not?

EXTENSIONS OF TRADITIONAL THEORIES

Classical conditioning and operant conditioning are simple forms of learning. In each
case, the organism learns associations, and such conditioning has considerable generality.
Animals from aardvarks to zebras show classical conditioning and operant conditioning.

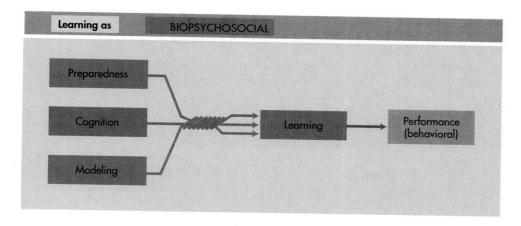

Figure 8.8
Learning as Biopsychosocial.
Learning has traditionally been explained only in terms of associations between stimuli and responses. Recent extensions approach learning in biopsychosocial terms. The evolutionary history of a species prepares individuals to learn certain behaviors more readily than others (biological). People can learn from watching models perform behavior (social). Finally, cognition is intrinsically involved in most if not all forms of learning (psychological).

So too do people, and there is no reason to believe that these forms of learning differ across social contrasts such as ethnicity or gender (Frisby, 1993).

Conditioning seems to occur less readily among elderly individuals (Woodruff-Pak, Logan, & Thompson, 1990). This result may be due to age-related changes in sensory acuity that make older individuals less sensitive to stimuli (Chapter 5). In extreme cases, it may also reflect organic disorders such as Alzheimer's disease (Chapter 6) that attack the parts of the central nervous system that make learning possible (Chapter 4). The point remains, however, that when conditioning is observed among the elderly, it still follows the same principles as among the young.

Recall from Chapter 4 the discussion of neural networks, computer models of how the brain works. Virtually all of these models assume that associations are the basic components of neural and mental activity. Many of these models learn in ways that fit the conditioning principles derived from studies of living organisms (Klopf, Morgan, & Weaver, 1993). Yet is learning nothing but associations? Traditional learning theorists answer yes and see no need for any further explanation. But many contemporary psychologists believe that theories need to be contextualized by specifying other influences on learning: biological, psychological, and social (see Figure 8.8). The remainder of this chapter presents several lines of work that extend the concepts and findings of traditional approaches to learning.

Distinguishing Classical and Operant Conditioning

Psychologists originally believed that classical conditioning applied only to involuntary responses (reflexes or bodily processes), whereas operant conditioning applied only to voluntary responses. Subsequent research has shown this distinction to be false. Involuntary responses can be modified by operant conditioning (Schwartz, 1972, 1975). Biofeedback, for example, is a procedure for measuring and amplifying changes in bodily processes, such as heart rate or blood pressure, so that people can be aware of them (Dienstfrey, 1991). Once information about their biology is fed back to them, people know when their efforts to modify these processes are succeeding (Miller, 1978).

It is also possible for apparently voluntary responses to be elicited. Consider a common response studied by those interested in operant conditioning: a pigeon pecking at an object in order to get a kernel of grain. Pecking is usually regarded as an excellent example of operant learning because its rate is strongly determined by the reward that follows. However, pecking is also influenced by classical conditioning. Pigeons tend to peck at stimuli associated with feeding, even when pecking has never produced food (Brown & Jenkins, 1968). This phenomenon is called autoshaping. It illustrates the difficulty in distinguishing between classically conditioned responses and operantly conditioned ones because the same response of pecking reflects both types of learning.

Classical conditioning and operant conditioning are jointly involved in many types of behavior. One more time, think of the example of me as a letter carrier. Although used to illustrate classical conditioning, that example illustrates operant conditioning as well. I learned that the faster I delivered the mail to certain houses, the sooner I would be away from a situation that scared me. The more general phenomenon here is called avoidance learning. First, through classical conditioning one learns that certain situations are frightening. Second, through operant conditioning one learns to reduce this fear by getting out of those situations.

Phenomena like biofeedback, autoshaping, and avoidance learning extend traditional theories of learning by showing that the distinction between classical conditioning and operant conditioning can be difficult to make. In theory, these two types of learning are quite different. But in reality, a particular example of learning often and perhaps always reflects both types of conditioning. The processes involved in these two basic forms of learning mutually influence one another.

Modeling: Social Influences on Learning

In classical or operant conditioning, the person or animal must do something for learning to occur. However, not all learning requires that we first go through the motions. Suppose you visit a new restaurant for the first time. You walk in and see a sign that invites you to seat yourself. You do so. But no one comes for your order, and this surprises you. You have heard this is a great place, and so how could service be so bad? Then you look around, and you see that the other customers are walking back and forth from a counter at the back of the restaurant. Aha! They place orders with a person working there, and a few minutes later they pick up their food and drinks at the same counter.

What do you do? You get up and place your order. No big deal. However, from the viewpoint of traditional learning theory, this is a very big deal. You have demonstrated observational learning, or **modeling.** The fact that you have learned something simply through observing the behavior of others cannot be accommodated within the framework of either classical conditioning or operant conditioning.

Many of the apparent instances of shaping and chaining cited by operant theorists can be explained much more simply as the result of modeling. Remember the example offered earlier of learning the different steps involved in taking an airplane flight? Most fliers have probably acquired these behaviors not one at a time but rather all at once, by flying with an experienced traveler or merely talking to one.

■ **modeling**
type of learning that takes place by observing the behavior of others

We can learn behaviors by watching other people perform them and seeing the consequences.

Albert Bandura (1974) argued that modeling is the most typical way human beings learn. We acquire many of our values, attitudes, and characteristic patterns of behavior not in small parts through trial and error but in whole pieces by observing others as they behave.

In a classic experiment, children viewed a film in which an adult actor punched and kicked an inflatable plastic Bobo Doll (Bandura, Ross, & Ross, 1963). When the children later found themselves face to face with a Bobo Doll, they pummeled it as had the adult in the film. Children who had not previously seen the film were less likely to act aggressively toward the doll.

Research has identified a number of factors that influence the degree of observational learning (Bandura, 1986). Among these are characteristics of the models, those who are observed. If they are liked, then an individual is more likely to follow their example—for instance, you may dress or talk like a friend you admire. The consequences of the actions by models also matter. If they are rewarded, then observational learning is encouraged; if they are punished, then observational learning is less likely to occur. Consider the taunting and bragging so common among today's professional athletes. When youngsters see these behaviors and note that they apparently lead to lucrative endorsement contracts, is it any wonder that they too may start to display poor sportsmanship? Finally, similarity between models and the observer, along such lines as gender, age, or ethnicity, facilitates modeling. Women are more likely to model themselves after women, and men after men. Think of your own role models. Do your choices reflect Bandura's ideas?

The phenomenon of modeling draws our attention to the various psychological processes that influence learning and performance. Modeling is obviously cognitive in nature; our thoughts and beliefs are intrinsically part of the process of modeling. Furthermore, modeling can take place only when the individual:

- pays attention to a model's behavior
- retains in memory what has been observed
- possesses the necessary physical and/or cognitive abilities to enact the behavior that has been modeled
- has sufficient motivation to perform this behavior

As the Bobo Doll experiment implies, modeling may play a role in aggression (Chapter 7). People may act violently to the degree that they see others act violently. Models can come from a person's family, his or her peer group, or the mass media. The

Albert Bandura's studies of observational learning extend traditional approaches to learning to include the social context.

After watching an adult model beat a plastic Bobo Doll, children may do the same.

more attractive a model and the more his or her violent actions result in reward rather than punishment, the more we expect an observer to follow suit.

If aggression can be learned through modeling, society must make some decisions about how violence is portrayed on television or in movies. Consider these facts:

■ More American homes have a television set than have a telephone or a bathtub.
■ The average television set in the United States is turned on 7 hours per day.
■ Among prime-time shows, 8 out of 10 contain violence, at rates ranging from 5 to 20 violent acts per hour.
■ The highest rates are found on Saturday-morning cartoons.

What effects do these numerous models have on people's behavior?

In surveys of the population at large, researchers found that the extent of television viewing was positively correlated with later aggression. Although confounds threaten this strategy, evidence further suggested that children who watch violent television shows while growing up are more likely to be convicted of serious crimes when adults than children whose television diet does not contain violence (Wood, Wong, & Chachere, 1991).

Modeling provides a powerful explanation for a wide variety of behaviors, from using drugs (Presti, Ary, & Lichtenstein, 1992) to adopting gender roles (Katz & Walsh, 1991) to forming racial attitudes (Nunns & Bluen, 1992). Observational learning can also be used deliberately to decrease undesired behaviors such as aggression (Vidyasagar & Mishra, 1993). Modeling represents a compelling example of how learning is embedded in a larger social context.

Biological and Evolutionary Influences on Learning

In both classical conditioning and operant conditioning, we find the assumption that learning obeys general laws regardless of the response or the species. From this assumption follows the position that all responses are equally able to be learned. This position is termed **equipotentiality.** The problem with equipotentiality, and hence with the assumption on which it is based, is that not all responses are equally easy to learn. Research shows that an organism's biology determines what it can learn. Some responses are learned only with great difficulty. Others are learned readily.

Taste aversion.   For instance, if you drink too much alcohol and then become violently ill, you might later avoid the type of drink in which you overindulged because just the taste and smell of it make you queasy. This phenomenon is called **taste aversion,** on the face of it a simple example of classical conditioning. But examine this example carefully and it makes no sense given the assumption of equipotentiality. Why did you learn to associate illness with the taste of alcohol rather than with ice cubes, shot glasses, or the loud music that played while you drank on and on?

You might say that you formed an aversion to the taste of alcohol, of course because that is what made you sick. But that is too easy a way out of the puzzle. Suppose that after a meal of lasagna, asparagus, and chocolate chip cookies, you come down with the flu. Although they were not the real culprits, you later avoid these foods because they were paired with being ill. Apparently, we are predisposed to form certain associations rather than others. We readily form an association between tastes and gastric upset. This bias has been confirmed in animal studies, as has a similar bias in which research subjects link external pain more readily to visual stimuli than to tastes (Garcia & Koelling, 1966).

A persuasive way to account for these biases is to place them in an evolutionary context (Chapter 3). Think about our distant ancestors and the selection pressures to which they were exposed. The ability to learn—to modify behavior based on experience—is a tremendous advantage. Organisms capable of learning possess much greater fitness than those lacking this ability. So, how about being able to learn, in an especially

■ **equipotentiality**
assumption that all responses are equally able to be learned

■ **taste aversion**
avoidance of a stimulus with a particular taste after that taste has been associated with illness

efficient fashion, those associations that exist in the world? Whereas upset stomachs often result when we eat or drink something foul, an organism predisposed to form this link will survive better than one that has to learn it by trial and error. Similarly, whereas pain is often due to external stimuli that we can see, an organism predisposed to make this link will have increased fitness because its predisposition leads it to form the accurate association quickly.

Preparedness.   Such examples imply that there are three types of learning, each reflecting different influences of evolution (Seligman, 1970). **Prepared learning** is learning that is predisposed by our evolutionary history. We can recognize it by several criteria:

■ **prepared learning**
learning predisposed by our evolutionary history

- It occurs rapidly, requiring few trials.
- It involves associations over considerable periods.
- It is relatively permanent.

Think of how taste aversion satisfies these criteria. Some theorists speculate that people's phobias (irrational fears, e.g., fear of insects) and fetishes (inanimate sexual turn-ons, e.g., shoes or underwear) represent the operation of prepared learning. What is striking about phobias and fetishes is that they encompass a narrow range of objects, those that typically are linked to fear or desire, respectively.

Contraprepared learning is learning that evolution has made difficult to acquire, if it can be acquired at all. For example, although teaching cats to move toward something in order to be fed is easy, teaching them that if they move away from something they will be fed is difficult. There is little evolutionary advantage in learning that one can get what one wants by backing away from it.

■ **contraprepared learning**
learning that our evolutionary history has made difficult

Finally, **unprepared learning** is learning that is neither favored nor disfavored by evolutionary considerations. The instances of classical and operant conditioning typically studied in experiments by learning psychologists probably represent unprepared learning.

■ **unprepared learning**
leaning neither predisposed nor precluded by evolution

These distinctions are not the only possible way to relate evolution to learning. They maintain some universality in the principles that describe learning, in effect saying that there are three sets of learning principles: those governing prepared, contraprepared, and unprepared learning. But one can push this idea to the extreme, concluding that many laws of learning apply only to a particular species and, further, only to a given type of response.

Instinctive drift.   Breland and Breland (1961) described their difficulties in using operant conditioning techniques to teach tricks to animals. Although successful in teaching their animals tricks, the Brelands found that with time, the animals approached these tricks in ways characteristic of their particular species. For example, a raccoon can be taught to pick up a coin and deposit it in a bank, but it does not do this without first handling and rubbing the coin. A pig can be taught the same trick, but it first throws the coin in the air and then, when the coin falls to the ground, pokes at it with its snout. If you know something about raccoons and pigs in their natural worlds, this misbehavior (as the Brelands labeled it) is not at all strange. It is exactly how these creatures treat their food. The term for these tendencies is **instinctive drift** because the new learning becomes blended with the instinctive (unlearned) tendencies of the species (Chapter 3).

■ **instinctive drift**
blending of learning with instinctive (unlearned) tendencies

In order to understand learning, we must also appreciate the biological nature of the organism that is doing the learning. If we regard evolution as a process that produces solutions to specific survival problems (Chapter 3), then it should not be surprising that many different forms of learning exist, varying with the species and response in question. Learning needs to be interpreted in terms of the characteristic niche of a species (Alexander, 1990).

With operant conditioning, animals can be taught a variety of behaviors. However, these behaviors are often colored by the way an animal behaves in its natural environment. This phenomenon is called instinctive drift. Before executing a flying 360-degree slam dunk, for example, the raccoon pictured here might be tempted to wash the basketball.

For example, in contrast to birds and mammals, amphibians and reptiles do not readily learn new responses. Why? Warm-blooded animals are more mobile than cold-blooded animals, and hence their characteristic environments are less constant. The ability to acquire new ways of behaving as the environment changes is clearly more advantageous to warm-blooded animals.

The biological basis of learning.   Biology affects not only what we learn but how we learn it. Experience with the world presumably alters the biology of the organism in some way so that behavior is changed. One of the enduring puzzles in this line of inquiry is the fact that learning can be highly enduring, lasting decades, whereas our biological characteristics are constantly changing (Rose, 1993). Many different possibilities have been proposed, ranging from neural function to brain structure (Chapter 4).

Studies of a mollusk known as *Aplysia* (or sea slug) have been especially important for understanding the neurological basis of learning (Kandel, Schwartz, & Jessell, 1991). This creature has an extremely simple central nervous system, consisting of only 20,000 neurons (vs. more than 100 billion in a human being). The connections among the different neurons in *Aplysia* are simple and well described, and they are constant across different animals. Finally, some of *Aplysia*'s neurons are large enough—up to a full millimeter in diameter—to be easily monitored.

Despite its simplicity, *Aplysia* shows different forms of learning, including habituation, sensitization, and conditioning. Researchers have begun to describe exactly what happens within a given neuron when this creature learns: Enduring chemical changes take place, affecting the firing of adjacent neurons (Chapter 4). Depending on the type of learning, different biochemical processes are involved, before and after the synapse, suggesting that even for a simple creature, the mechanism is multiple. In more complex animals, it appears that coordinated changes involving large classes of neurons occur during learning.

Of course, not all psychologists believe that conclusions about learning in sea slugs generalize to learning in people. First, the generalization involves extreme reductionism. Second, those interested in learning do not move casually from one species to another, particularly when the starting point is an invertebrate, for the biological basis of learning may differ profoundly across species. The studies of *Aplysia* merit attention because they show how the biochemical basis of learning can be studied; nevertheless, further research using other species is needed.

The sea slug has an extremely simple and well-understood nervous system. As a result, it has been a favorite research subject of psychologists interested in the neurological basis of learning.

A different line of research studies people or animals with brain damage in order to identify the larger parts of the brain associated with learning (Macphail, 1993). Particularly important is the hippocampus, located in the limbic system (Chapter 4). People with damage to the hippocampus are often unable to acquire new information, suggesting that no permanent record of their experience has been made. Similarly, rats with hippocampal damage cannot easily learn to run a maze to receive a food reward.

Other attempts to understand the biological basis of learning are more specific. The term **engram** has been coined to refer to the microscopic physical changes in the body that correspond to learning (Lashley, 1950). The engram has yet to be fully identified, although psychologists believe that several candidates are promising, such as changes in the likelihood of given neurons firing or not, changes in connections between and among neurons, and/or alterations in hormones and complex peptides like RNA (Thompson, 1976).

■ **engram**
as-yet-undiscovered physical changes in the body that correspond to learning

The Role of Cognition in Learning

Many statements of classical conditioning and operant conditioning imply that these forms of learning are independent of our thoughts and beliefs. But research suggests that learning involves a variety of cognitive mechanisms, and these must be addressed if we are fully to explain learning.

Consciousness.   Indeed, among human beings one of the most important determinants of even simple conditioning is whether individuals are aware of the relevant associations. Once established, learning often becomes automatic, meaning that individuals become unaware of what maintains it (Chapter 6). But some theorists argue that awareness is necessary for conditioning to occur in the first place (Brewer, 1974; Marinkovic, Schell, & Dawson, 1989). Considerable irony exists in this conclusion, given that psychology's interest in conditioning began with Watson's dissatisfaction with mentalistic accounts of behavior.

Given the theoretical significance of this contention, researchers have devoted effort to seeing whether conditioning among people can occur without awareness. As you remember from Chapter 6, the very definition of consciousness is elusive, and research that tries to rule out its role in learning is often open to methodological criticisms (Davey, 1994). For example, asking people if they were aware of the associations in place during learning may make them aware after the fact and thereby distort their retrospective report. Perhaps the best evidence for learning without awareness comes from studies that demonstrate conditioning to stimuli presented at intensities so low that people cannot identify their presence or absence (De Houwer, Baeyens, & Eelen, 1994; Krosnick, Betz, Jussim, & Lynn, 1992).

Whatever the eventual resolution of this debate, none would argue with the conclusion that awareness facilitates learning. Telling research subjects about the associations in place during conditioning produces acquisition or extinction much more readily than trial-and-error experience does (Boakes, 1989).

Further, as these results imply, the human capacity for language makes associative learning among people different from associative learning among animals (Hayes & Hayes, 1992). People often represent the associations they learn verbally, meaning that when they generalize and discriminate their learning, they do so along semantic lines. The meanings of stimuli and responses, as opposed to just their physical properties, become important.

For instance, years ago I was mugged in daylight while walking along a street in a residential section of a small town. My behavior changed as a result; I became afraid while walking at night along downtown streets in large cities. I was not afraid in situations similar to the one in which I was actually attacked. Instead, my fear appeared only in situations I regarded as potentially dangerous.

Cognitive maps.   Edward C. Tolman (1948, 1959) was one of the first behaviorists to argue that cognition is important in learning. He studied rats that learned to traverse a maze in order to gain food at the end. Tolman's animals had no difficulty learning to get through the maze, but then he changed the maze by placing barriers along the once successful route. The food was still in the same location, but the old path would not get the animal to it. If learning is only a series of particular responses, then the rats should have been stymied because their previous responses no longer worked. But the rats still found the food by taking a different path, and Tolman concluded that they had learned a **cognitive map,** a mental representation of the maze as a whole.

■ **cognitive map**
mental representation of a physical place

People too form cognitive maps of physical places, not only real locales but imaginary ones (Kitchin, 1994). These mental representations shape and direct behavior. They can facilitate recall. Moreover, they can improve problem solving and the learning of complex skills (Chapter 9). For example, individuals who use personal computers often create in their minds a cognitive map that depicts in metaphorical terms how information is stored as it moves in and out of the computer's memory. If you use a personal computer, stop and think about the metaphor you entertain. Even if your cognitive map does not conform to what actually happens in the computer hardware—and it invariably will not—you can still use a computer more readily to the degree that your map helps you traverse the computer environment in order to accomplish your goals. To this end, software designers create programs that facilitate useful cognitive maps.

Insight.   Another example of cognitive factors in learning comes from the Gestalt psychologist Wolfgang Kohler's (1924) studies of problem solving among chimpanzees. Kohler was marooned during World War I on one of the Canary Islands. Lacking access to human subjects, he did research with the chimp colony on the island. In one of the problems Kohler posed, a chimp was placed in a cage in which Kohler had suspended a banana on a string hanging from the ceiling, out of reach. Kohler had also placed a box and a stick in the cage. Successful chimps moved the box under the banana, climbed onto the box, and used the stick to knock down the banana. Kohler called this form of learning **insight,** a sudden understanding of the relationship among the parts of a problem that leads to a solution.

■ **insight**
form of learning marked by a sudden understanding of the relationship among the parts of a problem that leads to a solution

An interesting follow-up to Kohler's studies is an experiment by Epstein, Kirshnit, Lanza, and Rubin (1984), using pigeons as research subjects. These investigators showed

Animals from chimpanzees to pigeons can solve the banana-and-box problem. Cognitively oriented psychologists conclude that this accomplishment shows insight.

that pigeons could learn to solve the banana-and-box problem devised by Kohler, as long as the pigeons first learned the component behaviors: moving a box to a particular spot on the floor of the operant chamber, climbing on top of the box, and pecking at a button otherwise out of reach to produce a food pellet. This study shows how insight is made possible by previous learning that may be much more mundane.

Information.   Yet one more demonstration of the role cognition plays in simple learning is the following example showing how the information provided by the CS is critical in producing conditioning. Suppose you can control the stimuli presented to a person. First, you sound a brief tone. Then, just a moment later, you turn on a brief light. And just another moment later, you deliver an electric shock to your subject's foot. You repeat this procedure a number of times.

   What happens? You might expect that your research subject will learn to associate the light with the shock and thus show some response when the light alone is turned on. Conditioning might take place with the tone, but this association will not be as strong as the link between the light and the shock because it is not as close in time. However, when experiments like this are conducted (see Figure 8.9), exactly the opposite occurs (Kamin, 1969): The subject flinches in response to the tone but not at all to the light. Conditioning does not occur to the light because it is redundant with the tone and thus provides no new information to the subject. Once we start talking about

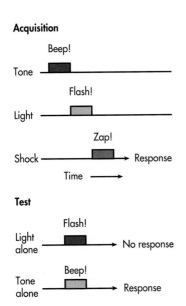

Acquisition

Tone — Beep! ⬛———

Light — Flash! ⬜———

Shock — Zap! ⬛—→ Response

Time ——→

Test

Light alone — Flash! ⬛—→ No response

Tone alone — Beep! ⬜—→ Response

Figure 8.9
Information and Classical Conditioning. During acquisition, a tone is sounded, then a light is turned on, and finally a shock occurs. Later, when the light alone is turned on, no conditioned response occurs; when the tone alone is sounded, conditioning is evident. This result shows that conditioning occurs to stimuli that provide information about the unconditioned stimulus. No conditioning occurs to the light because it is redundant with the tone.

classical conditioning in terms of the information the CS provides, the processes under-lying this apparently simple form of learning must be regarded as sophisticated and complex.

Rules.   As you are seeing, psychologists today increasingly hold that learning involves cognition. In fact, one currently popular way to describe learning is to say that people and animals learn rules in contrast to associations, which are the simplest of links. A **rule** is an abstract guideline about how to act in certain situations: Under these circum-stances, a particular action leads to a particular outcome. If a person can phrase such a rule in words, then learning is made even more efficient. However, we need not require that a rule be verbally represented to conclude that it is cognitive (Chapter 9).

■ **rule**
abstract guideline about how to
act in a certain situation

For instance, animals can master the following task without benefit of words. First, the animal is shown two shapes: squares, circles, triangles, whatever. Each shape has a lever underneath it. If the animal pushes the lever beneath the larger stimulus, it is given a food reward. Then the animal is shown another pair of shapes. Again, pressing the lever beneath the larger of the pair results in reinforcement. After repeated trials, the animal consistently chooses the larger shape, showing that it has acquired the rule governing reward. We can say that the animal shows a grasp of the "larger than" concept.

Other studies show that pigeons can learn to select slides based on whether or not they contain pictures of trees, vehicles, or even a specific person (Herrnstein, Loveland, & Cable, 1976). And the pigeons do more than learn particular responses to particular slides because once a pigeon learns to make a distinction in one set of slides, it can apply this rule perfectly with an altogether different set of slides. In a similar study, Porter and Neuringer (1984) showed that pigeons can learn to distinguish the music of Bach and Stravinsky. Pigeons apparently understand abstract concepts. The importance of these studies is not what they tell us about pigeons but what they imply about learning in people. If simple creatures like pigeons learn rules and acquire concepts, then we should not hesitate in attributing this mode of learning to people.

Stop and Think

10 Compare and contrast classical conditioning and operant conditioning.

11 How does the phenomenon of modeling draw psychology's attention to the role of cognition in learning?

12 How is taste aversion an example of preparedness?

13 Is cognition involved in all forms of learning? If not, can you describe an example of learning in which cognition is not involved?

LEARNING IN A BIOPSYCHOSOCIAL CONTEXT

Throughout this chapter, and especially in the discussion of the extensions of traditional theories, I have pointed out how learning must be located in its biopsychosocial context. Biology influences what and how learning takes place. Animals and people arguably evolved in such a way that some types of learning occur readily, some types only with difficulty, and still other types not at all. Psychological processes, beyond those explicitly implicated in theories of classical and operant conditioning, influence learn-ing. And the larger social setting influences learning through modeling because we can and do learn complex actions simply by watching other people perform them.

In the beginning of this chapter, I explained my confusion as an introductory psychology student when I discovered that discussions of learning focused on simple processes involved in behavior change, rather than what occurred in classrooms. However, recognition of the full context of learning allows us to examine classroom

In Asian countries, formal academic instruction does not begin until the child leaves the "age of innocence" and enters the "age of reason."

learning. To provide an example, I draw on studies by Stevenson and Stigler (1992) comparing elementary school education in the United States, Japan, and China.

It is widely recognized that Asian students outperform their American counterparts on standard measures of educational achievement, particularly in mathematics and science (Chapter 11). Why is this so? Speculation abounds in the popular media of the United States, usually drawing on stereotypes depicting Asian students as docile and passive drudges, overworked at home and school. But Stevenson and Stigler found little evidence for these stereotypes. Instead, their research identified numerous differences in the specific way learning occurs in contemporary Asian versus American cultures. These differences make good sense in terms of what psychology has discovered about optimal learning. The real question, as you will see, might be why American elementary school students learn as well as they actually do.

Let me enumerate some of these differences. First, Asian students do not receive academic instruction until they enter school, at about age 6. Many American parents teach their toddlers the alphabet, and preschools and kindergartens similarly try to give an academic head start to quite young children. According to Stevenson and Stigler, there is no evidence that extremely early learning of this sort is beneficial to children who are not developmentally able to understand its point (Chapter 10). To be sure, American toddlers can learn to identify letters, but they do so by rote, ending up baffled and perhaps helpless.

By contrast, the prevailing belief in Asian cultures is that young children exist in an "age of innocence" until they are about 6. They presumably lack the biologically based cognitive competence to acquire academic skills. Instead, Asian children are indulged by their parents, given great freedom and encouragement to explore their immediate social world. Only when children attain the "age of reason" does formal academic instruction begin.

As emphasized several times in this chapter, learning represents the influence of biology. The development of the brain and nervous system needs to reach a point where abstract knowledge can be grasped. The Asian approach seems more biologically realistic than the American approach.

Asian toddlers do learn while they are young. Learning to count, calculate, and read may take place in the course of other activities that are of interest to the child. Most importantly, Asian children learn to be outgoing social beings who can adapt to a group. This skill pays dividends later on when academic instruction actually begins.

Second, when Asian children begin elementary school, the focus of their entire lives is on being a student. Their parents believe that studying and doing well in school are their children's primary responsibilities, and they arrange home life to reinforce this expectation. Workbooks containing academic activities see frequent use at home. Most Asian cities publish newspapers just for children. Teachers and parents communicate daily via notes. In the United States, parents are much more likely to see learning as the domain of school, segregating it from home life once formal education begins.

Virtually all Asian children are provided with a desk or place to study at home. Even though American homes tend to be much more spacious, elementary school children are much less likely to be provided with desks by their parents. Asian children are also not as apt as their American counterparts to be given chores around the home. While still in school, Asian adolescents almost never hold outside jobs for pay (Chapter 17). Their focus is on school learning. American students are encouraged instead to be well rounded—which may or may not include excelling at their studies.

The Asian emphasis on academic learning makes it more central to the lives of young people, hence more likely to occur because it is consistently and broadly reinforced. At the same time, American students and their parents express greater satisfaction with the academic achievement that does occur. Most American parents regard their child's work as above average, but, of course, not everyone can be above average. Asian students and parents hold higher standards and are more realistic in evaluating achievement. So, American students need not perform particularly well in order to earn reinforcement.

Third, Asian children are much more likely than American children to be taught basic skills that make more abstract learning possible. For example, Asian children are explicitly taught in school how to organize their desks, use the bathroom, change their clothing, and move from one academic task to another. They are taught how to answer questions loudly and clearly, take notes, and organize their work. As we saw in the discussion of chaining and shaping, complex behaviors are readily acquired in this way. American teachers rarely teach these constituent behaviors. As a result, even American college students can find study skills mysterious.

Fourth, Asian and American cultures differ in terms of what is believed to make learning possible. Influenced by Confucian thought, Asians believe effort is paramount. Americans are much more likely to endorse innate ability as the major determinant of eventual achievement. Interestingly, students in Asian classrooms are never tracked by ability as they are in American classrooms. Special education classes are rare in Asia, reserved exclusively for students with severe physical challenges. All Asian students are expected to learn if they exert sufficient effort.

One important consequence of these varying beliefs about effort versus ability is that failure is regarded differently in Asian and American classrooms. Asian students do not become embarrassed or helpless when they do not solve a mathematics problem; they assume the solution will eventually be achieved. Indeed, a great deal of class time in Asian elementary schools is spent discussing mistakes and what can be learned from them. In contrast, American teachers try to minimize failures, under the assumption that the child will be stigmatized by apparent proof of his or her inability.

An important ingredient of learning is a consistent association between behaviors and outcomes, and both success and failure are needed for learning to occur. Indeed, a student can learn to persevere when frustrated in initial attempts (Eisenberger, 1992). Furthermore, the discussion of failures facilitates the conscious learning of abstract rules that can be broadly applied.

Fifth, Asian students spend more time in school than American students, and they spend their time differently. Asian students are given a recess every 45 minutes, and lunch breaks may last as long as 90 minutes. Time for extracurricular activities is an explicit part of the school day. These activities facilitate academic learning, which best occurs through repetition spread over time (Zimmer & Hocevar, 1994).

During lessons, Asian teachers spend less time lecturing students and disciplining them. Instead, they usually work interactively with students. Less emphasis is placed on getting single right answers and more on identifying a variety of approaches and evaluating their strengths and weaknesses. When Asian teachers do lecture, they thoroughly introduce activities and then summarize them when they are completed. Information placed in a sensible overall context is better remembered (Chapter 9).

The proportion of class time spent on actual teaching and learning is higher in Asia than in the United States. American students spend twice as much time moving from one task to another as Asian students. American students spend four times as much time inappropriately out of their seats. Again, the general point from the psychology of learning is clear: One learns better when one spends time learning.

A final difference between Asian and American education is the greater use of models in Japan and China as opposed to the United States. Asian children are much more likely to work together in groups, a practice that allows them to learn from one another. They also respect their teachers more, and this aspect facilitates modeling.

Every Japanese child knows of Ninomiya Kinjiro, and every Chinese child of Lai Ning. If you do not know of these storied figures, find out, and then ponder how your elementary school years would have been different had these young heroes been constant models for your own behavior. Who are the models of American students? Madonna, Shaquille O'Neal, and Beavis and Butt-Head?

Before you decide to send your children abroad to study, remember the caution made in Chapter 1 that differences do not necessarily mean deficiencies. American education has certain strengths in comparison to Asian education. Asian high schools are stressful, and the suicide rate for Japanese high school students is among the highest in the world (Iga, 1981; Kitamura, 1982; La Vecchia, Lucchini, & Levi, 1994). In China and Japan, it is widely believed that American universities are much more beneficial than their Asian counterparts. American schools, particularly at the elementary level, are called upon to do many more things than Asian schools, which focus almost exclusively on academic instruction. These multiple demands may well reflect the values of those in the United States, and so we need to place the documented differences in the context of varying societal priorities. But if those of us here want to see academic learning improved in our elementary schools, the Japanese and Chinese provide some important lessons. Their approach is more consistent with a biopsychosocial view of learning (see Table 8.2).

In this chapter, you have seen how psychologists approach the study of learning. Among the basic forms of learning are classical conditioning and operant conditioning. A great deal of theory and research has been concerned with explaining the processes involved in such learning. Recent extensions of traditional views show learning to be more complicated than it at first seems. Learning must be placed in a biopsychosocial context. It is a critically important psychological phenomenon, and you will see numerous applications of learning throughout the rest of this book.

Table 8.2   Why Asian Elementary Education Facilitates Learning

Compared with typical classroom practices in the United States, features of Asian elementary education facilitate learning by approaching the process in appropriate biopsychosocial terms.

Feature	Reason for benefit
1. Academic instruction starts only at age 6.	Biological: This is the age at which the child is developmentally able to learn abstract skills.
2. Focus of a child's life is on being a student.	Psychological: Academic learning is more central to the child, thus more likely to be reinforced.
3. Basic social and academic skills are explicitly taught.	Psychological: Complex skills are more readily acquired when component skills have been learned.
4. Effort is regarded as more important than ability.	Psychological: Motivation to persevere despite failure is sustained.
5. More time in school is spent on academic instruction.	Psychological: Learning is enhanced with repetition.
6. Models are used to demonstrate desired behaviors.	Social: Modeling is an efficient way to learn.

SUMMARY

UNDERSTANDING LEARNING: DEFINITION AND EXPLANATION

■ Learning refers to relatively permanent changes in behavior that result from interactions with the environment.
■ Psychologists interested in learning have long been concerned with describing its basic types.
■ When John Watson founded behaviorism in 1913, he directed psychology's attention to processes of learning as an explanation of overt behavior.
■ Current explanations of learning stress its biopsychosocial nature.

DOING *Learning* RESEARCH

■ To study learning, researchers often employ animals as research subjects, conduct experiments, and use specially constructed mechanical devices that greatly simplify their subjects' environment.

CLASSICAL CONDITIONING

■ One important type of learning is classical conditioning, in which organisms learn to associate two environmental stimuli.
■ Researchers have described in detail how associations formed by classical conditioning are acquired, generalized, discriminated, and extinguished.
■ Classical conditioning provides a good explanation of how people come to link various emotions—both positive and negative—to particular events and situations.

OPERANT CONDITIONING

■ Another important type of learning is operant conditioning, in which organisms learn the consequences of their responses—either reinforcers or punishers.
■ B. F. Skinner, the best-known behaviorist and learning theorist of his generation, defined reinforcers as any stimuli that increase the likelihood of some response and punishers as any stimuli that decrease its likelihood.
■ Researchers have studied various processes involved in operant conditioning, especially how it is acquired, how complex behaviors can be built up from simple ones, and how it is generalized, discriminated, and extinguished.

■ Previously neutral stimuli can become reinforcers or punishers in their own right if they are associated with other reinforcers or punishers.
■ Some theorists have tried to understand what makes a stimulus reinforcing or punishing. According to David Premack, more preferred activities serve as reinforcers for less preferred activities, and vice versa for punishers.
■ The particular pattern of reinforcement following a response can vary, and psychologists have studied these so-called schedules of reinforcement. One important conclusion is that responses reinforced intermittently—not on every occasion—resist extinction.
■ Some psychologists argue that punishment is not a good way to change behavior because it adds nothing to an individual's repertoire of responses. However, punishment probably is justified in circumstances where no delay can be tolerated in eliminating undesirable behavior.
■ Operant conditioning has wide applicability because so much of our behavior is sensitive to its consequences.

EXTENSIONS OF TRADITIONAL THEORIES

■ Recent years have seen extensions of the traditional psychology of learning in a biopsychosocial direction.
■ For example, classical conditioning and operant conditioning prove far more difficult to distinguish in practice than in theory. Perhaps both types of learning are involved in most instances of behavior.
■ People need not actually perform responses in order to learn. Sometimes observation of others suffices to change behavior. This phenomenon is called modeling, and it may be the way in which we acquire most of our complex behaviors.
■ Although traditional theories of learning assume that all associations are formed in the same way, research suggests that our biology influences the relative ease or difficulty with which we learn particular associations.
■ One's thoughts and beliefs may be involved in even the simplest instances of learning, implying that all human learning involves cognitive processes.

LEARNING IN A BIOPSYCHOSOCIAL CONTEXT

■ A biopsychosocial approach to learning helps explain why students in Asian elementary schools learn more than their counterparts in the United States.

KEY TERMS

Cognition

Psychologists are sometimes asked to help make sense of allegations of abuse, especially those that occurred years ago yet were remembered only recently. How does one decide if these memories are accurate? If they are, then the abuser should be prosecuted and punished. If they are not, then the charges should be dismissed.

Sometimes it is all but impossible to decide what is the right thing to do, as the following case shows (Loftus & Ketcham, 1994; Wright, 1994). Paul Ingram was a middle-aged man from Washington State. He had a wife and four children. He was a fundamentalist Christian and a leading citizen in his small town. In 1988, his 22-year-old daughter, Erika, began to remember incidents of sexual abuse from her early childhood. She named her father and older brothers as the perpetrators. The circumstances that first triggered her memories are unclear; they were variously described as returning spontaneously or in response to a direct suggestion during a religious retreat.

In any event, Ingram was greatly shaken and proclaimed his innocence to the police when they first interrogated him. He did not believe, however, that his daughter would lie, and so he considered the possibility that he had repressed his own memories. He prayed repeatedly and tried to remember the crimes with which he was charged. Ingram eventually remembered some of them and confessed.

Erika remembered more and more horrible incidents from her childhood:

> She claimed that her father had forced her to have sex with goats and dogs. Her mother also had sex with the animals, while her father took pictures. . . . She described satanic orgies, infant sacrifices, and gruesome abortions. She said she personally witnessed the sacrifice of 25 or more babies, whose tiny, mutilated bodies were buried in the woods behind the Ingram house. And once . . . cult members aborted her baby with a coat hanger and rubbed the fetus's bloody, dismembered body all over her naked torso. (Loftus & Ketcham, 1994, p. 250)

It is difficult to evaluate the accuracy of the memories of abuse reported by Paul and Erika Ingram.

Erika also implicated other town members, including several who worked for the police department. When confronted with these new accusations, her father continued to confirm and even add to them.

Investigators could find no trace of discarded bodies on the Ingram property. Nor could they find any scars on Erika's body that corresponded to the tortures she remembered. For example, she remembered that her father had once nailed her arm to the floor, but her arm was unblemished.

The investigators became skeptical of the most gruesome incidents. As it turned out, only Ingram was charged, with several counts of third-degree rape. He entered a guilty plea and was sentenced to 20 years in prison. Once behind bars, he renounced his confession and returned to his original statement that he never sexually abused his daughter. Appeals of his sentence to date have been refused because Ingram signed a confession and pleaded guilty.

What are we to make of the memories of Erika and Paul Ingram? Any discussion of repressed memories occurs in a highly charged political and moral context (Lindsay, 1994). Skeptics may be criticized as excusing child abuse; believers may be criticized as witch-hunters. Unfortunately, it is impossible at present to make general sense of long-repressed memories (Loftus, 1993). Research-based arguments can be made for and against their reality.

Here are findings that support the existence of long-repressed memories:

■ Abuse during childhood is alarmingly common. For example, Briere and Runtz (1988) estimated that 15 percent of college-age women had sexual contact with a significantly older individual prior to age 15.
■ Abuse during childhood has a host of negative consequences, including symptoms of anxiety, depression, and dissociation (Sandberg & Lynn, 1992). In other words, incidents of abuse can be highly upsetting and, as a result, kept out of the conscious mind (Chapter 6).
■ Trauma may permanently affect the nervous system, including the mechanisms responsible for memory (Koss, Tromp, & Tharan, 1995).
■ Long-forgotten memories may return granted appropriate clues—in particular, reminders of the original events and the emotional state that accompanied them.

But there are also findings that argue against the existence of long-repressed memories:

■ The typical response in the wake of sexual or physical trauma is for the person to put the abuse out of his or her mind, not to remember it.

■ When trauma produces dissociative problems that involve amnesia, the person nonetheless knows there are gaps in memory (Chapter 13). In contrast, many individuals who report long-repressed memories had no sense of gaps in their lives until these memories returned. Indeed, they often regarded their childhoods as uneventful and even happy.

■ Very few people remember any events at all from early in life—that is, before age 3—perhaps because linguistic labels were not attached to them. Long-repressed "memories" often predate this time.

■ When long-forgotten memories are eventually retrieved, they usually lack detail and clarity.

■ Subjectively plausible "memories" of events that never occurred can be created in the course of hypnosis or other forms of heightened suggestion (Brenneis, 1994).

Psychologists are able to conclude only that some long-repressed memories are probably accurate, whereas others are probably not (Denton, 1994). Part of the difficulty is the lack of a theory about the mechanisms involved in the recall of distant and/or traumatic occurrences. As this chapter explains, psychologists have usually studied memory and forgetting by using abstract stimuli under carefully controlled—and hence short-term—conditions. Perhaps the conclusions emerging from this decontextualized research do not generalize to memories of early abuse (Herman, 1992).

UNDERSTANDING COGNITION: DEFINITION AND EXPLANATION

Cognition refers to the processes that acquire, retain, transform, and use knowledge (Sternberg & Smith, 1988). This chapter focuses on four important topics within the field of psychology that studies cognition. First is how we mentally represent knowledge. Second is **memory:** how we initially acquire and then gain access to these mental representations of knowledge. Third is **problem solving,** referring to how we reduce the discrepancy between what we know and what we want to know. And fourth is **language,** which can be defined as a systematic way of communicating ideas or feelings using signs, sounds, gestures, or marks having symbolic significance.

A Brief History of Cognitive Psychology

Over the years, psychology has flip-flopped with respect to the importance of mental representations and processes. As explained in Chapter 1, the first psychologists defined psychology as the study of the mind. But as you saw in Chapter 8, the influential approach of behaviorism dismissed the importance of cognition and attempted to rid psychology of the mind.

Why is cognitive psychology alive and well today? Psychologists could not escape the importance of cognition. It is virtually impossible to speak about human beings without referring to their capacity for knowledge. Even the simplest habits have mentalistic aspects. Cognition underlies much of what we regard as uniquely human: language, learning, memory, personal identity, and culture. These processes help us cope with the demands of the world in the ways that we do.

Cognition regained a prominent place within psychology during the 1960s (Gardner, 1985; Hilgard, 1987). From different traditions came methods that improved upon the flawed practice of introspection. These methods, which will be discussed shortly, led to modern cognitive psychology, and the field grew in popularity. Many date the resurgence of interest in the field as 1967, when Ulric Neisser pulled together the ingredients in his appropriately titled book *Cognitive Psychology.*

The major concern of cognitive psychologists is how to capture the essence of the mind. The mind—its contents and processes—cannot be seen. Although introspection-

■ **cognition**
psychological processes that acquire, retain, transform, and use knowledge

■ **memory**
initial acquisition and subsequent access to mental representations of knowledge

■ **problem solving**
reduction of the discrepancy between what one knows and what one wants to know

■ **language**
systematic way of communicating ideas or feelings using signs, sounds, gestures, or marks having symbolic significance

Many date the resurgence of psychology's interest in cognition to 1967, when Ulric Neisser published his influential book on the topic.

ists thought they were glimpsing the mind when they identified the elements of consciousness, the mind is not a thing at which we can look (Ryle, 1949). Theoretical metaphors (or models) are used to clarify the nature of cognition. Over the years, theorists have likened the mind to a wax tablet, a piece of paper, a library, a railroad terminal, a telephone switchboard, and a computer. More than most fields, cognitive psychology has seen a rich succession of metaphors (Gentner & Stevens, 1983; Giere, 1992; Gopnik & Gopnik, 1986; Gorman, 1992).

Indeed, we can think about the mind only in metaphorical terms. These metaphors often come from prevailing technology, probably because theorists believe the mind is so complicated that they need to have a complicated comparison in order to do it justice. Cognitive psychologists propose so many different metaphors that their sheer number can be overwhelming. However, all acknowledge that cognition consists of both representations and processes. All assume that knowledge has an organization of some kind. And all try to be consistent with what we know about the brain and nervous system (McGaugh, Weinberger, & Lynch, 1995), under the assumption that cognition has a biological underpinning (Chapter 4).

Cognition as Biopsychosocial

Cognition involves all of the psychological processes discussed so far in this book and the social influences on these processes. Language, for example, can be learned only from other people. As just mentioned, psychologists today are greatly interested in the biological basis of cognition. Rounding out a biopsychosocial perspective on cognition are recent attempts to place the topic in the context of our evolutionary history (Corballis, 1992; Cosmides & Tooby, 1994; Donald, 1993; Hurford, 1991; Ulbaek, 1990). We can think of cognitive processes as evolved psychological mechanisms that arose to solve specific survival problems.

Psychologists often speak about cognitive processes as if they were highly general, independent of their content. From the standpoint of evolution, this assumption is probably an oversimplification. Natural selection led to a variety of cognitive mechanisms, each linked to a specific content (Tooby & Cosmides, 1989). For example, the mechanisms responsible for memory differ depending on the type of information— faces, odors, or narrative sequences—and on when the information to be remembered was initially encountered. We should also keep in mind the caution raised in earlier chapters about not confusing the current function of an evolved psychological mechanism with its original function (Geary, 1995).

Information Processing

As explained in Chapter 5, psychologists are drawn to information theory as one possible way to understand cognition (Massaro & Cowan, 1993). With the popularity of computers, we are all familiar with the term *bit*, short for *binary digit* (0 or 1) and defined as the amount of information that reduces the possible alternatives by half. Remember the game Twenty Questions? The number of yes-no questions you must pose in order to zero in on the answer is the number of bits of information it contains. Information is whatever reduces uncertainty; many cognitive psychologists use the term as a synonym for knowledge. To say that information is processed is to emphasize that people do something to it. Cognition regarded as information processing is necessarily dynamic— it moves and changes.

Cognition involves various stages of information processing that are defined by the different transformations taking place. First, the information is organized. Then it is represented in terms that are psychologically meaningful. Next, it is variously transformed or acted upon. Finally, it directs a person's subsequent actions.

Serial versus parallel processing.   In its simplest form, information processing that follows a particular stimulus moves in one direction. This phenomenon is called **serial processing.** Suppose you are cooking dinner. If you prepare one dish at a time, this is

■ **serial processing**
information processing of one stimulus at a time

similar to serial processing. However, information processing is often more complex, just like actual cooking. One stimulus can give rise simultaneously to different processes: **parallel processing.** Reading is a good example because it requires that we move our eyes, recognize words, and understand meanings. These actions are done simultaneously, not one after another. Actual cognition usually represents a mix of serial and parallel processes (Dehaene & Cohen, 1994; Egeth & Dagenbach, 1991; Zohary & Hochstein, 1989).

Bottom-up versus top-down processing.   In **bottom-up information processing,** simple aspects of thinking are not influenced by more complex ones. For instance, consider how we might recognize that certain visual stimuli represent the letters that spell out a word (Glass & Holyoak, 1986). We first distinguish between light and dark areas on a page where the word is contained. We next see the letters as figures and the page as a background (Chapter 5). We then identify the individual letters. We finally put the letters together to form the word.

Theorists fond of the bottom-up approach often use a computer as their metaphor for information processing. A typical computer cannot proceed other than bottom-up. The common criticism of computers—garbage in, garbage out—reflects the reliance of most computers on a bottom-up approach to processing information. Granted the first step, no matter how silly or flawed, the subsequent steps follow.

Information-processing approaches became popular as computers became well known. Computers provide a fertile vocabulary for describing cognition. The central characteristics of cognition—representation and task solution—are what computers do. The problem with the computer metaphor is that it cannot readily capture processes where later considerations affect earlier ones. Computers have no controlling executive that modifies early stages in light of later ones.

The opposite of a bottom-up approach is, of course, called **top-down information processing.** In this case, the simple aspects of information processing are influenced by the complex ones. Our higher mental functions, such as goals, intentions, and general knowledge, dominate and direct lower functions. Critical in supporting the top-down approach to cognition were a series of studies by John Bransford and his colleagues, finding that general knowledge affects even the simplest cognitive task. In one experiment, for instance, subjects were instructed to listen to sentences that included the following:

- The ants ate the jelly.
- The ants were in the kitchen.

When later questioned about sentences they did or did not hear, subjects reported that they had heard sentences like "The ants in the kitchen ate the jelly" (Bransford & Franks, 1971). This is a reasonable inference, you might say, but it argues against bottom-up processing because it is an inference. Computers do not make inferences; they do not bring to bear other information on their programmed tasks, reasonable or otherwise (Bransford, 1979).

Davis and Bistodeau (1993) studied how bilingual college students read and made sense of passages written in either their first or their second language. According to the subjects, reading one's first language involves top-down information processing, whereas reading one's second language involves bottom-up information processing. For example, in the first language the overall gist of a passage is used to make sense of the meaning of individual words, whereas in the second language the meaning of individual words is used to make sense of the overall gist.

Depth of processing.   Yet another way to regard information processing, **depth of processing** (Craik & Lockhart, 1972), developed as the result of research like Bransford conducted. The essence of this approach is the assumption that people can encode

Margin glossary

■ **parallel processing**
information processing of several stimuli at the same time

■ **bottom-up information processing**
information processing in which simple aspects of thinking are not influenced by complex ones

■ **top-down information processing**
information processing in which simple aspects of thinking are influenced by complex ones

■ **depth of processing**
degree to which information is encoded or transformed

To understand a familiar language, we use top-down processes, but with an unfamiliar language, we are more likely to use bottom-up processes.

incoming information in various ways, some simple, or shallow, and some elaborate, or deep (see Table 9.1).

Suppose you have written a short story and have named your central character Bob. Then you decide to change the name to Herbert. You read over your pages, on the lookout for *Bob* so that you can change it. This approach is a rather superficial way of accessing information because you focus only on what the words in your story look like. In contrast, let us say you decide to change your characterization of Bob/Herbert from friendly to aloof. Again, you read over your pages, but now you look for synonyms of *friendly*. This approach is a deeper way of accessing information because you must focus on the meaning of words. When we learn material, the more deeply we process it, the easier it is to recall it later (Venneri, Stucci, Cubelli, & Nichelli, 1993).

So, we remember advertisements better to the degree that they contain unusual elements (Hunt, Kernan, & Bonfield, 1992). Even one unusual feature can trigger deeper processing of the entire message, thus improving recall. Perhaps advertisers have long been aware of this phenomenon—which explains, for example, the frequent use of talking animals and babies in many advertisements. They grab our attention, set off deep information processing, and register the desired message. Along these lines, messages with personal relevance are processed more deeply and thus remembered better than those without it (Forsyth & Wibberly, 1993). Simply including a listener's name in a

Table 9.1   Summary: Types of Information Processing

Information processing theory provides a way of describing different ways of acquiring, representing, and using knowledge.

Type of processing	Characterization
Serial	Processing of one stimulus at a time
Parallel	Processing of several stimuli at the same time
Bottom–up	Processing in which simple aspects of thinking are not influenced by complex ones
Top–down	Processing in which simple aspects of thinking are influenced by complex ones, such as general knowledge
Shallow	Processing that involves few transformations
Deep	Processing that involves many transformations

message can prompt deeper processing. Have you noticed that telephone solicitors often use your name in every sentence as they pitch their product? This strategy is not only ingratiating but is also a stimulus for deeper processing of their message.

Stop and Think

1 What is cognition, and why do psychologists usually describe it with metaphors?

2 What are some of the social influences on memory?

3 How might the effect of emotion on thinking be explained in terms of information processing?

DOING *Cognition* RESEARCH

Cognitive psychologists have devised several methods that allow them to infer from overt behavior what and how a person is thinking (Schwartz & Reisberg, 1991). Let me briefly discuss some of them.

Reaction Times

Cognitive activity occurs over time. This assumption is plausible because cognition must be grounded in brain activity that does not take place instantaneously. From this assumption comes the strategy of studying mental events by seeing how long it takes people to perform tasks we present to them. The longer a person's reaction time, the longer he or she needs to carry out the mental activity underlying the task performance.

For example, researchers have studied how people use mental imagery to solve problems in their heads. What is the nature of these images? One answer is that they are much like perceptions of actual objects; the amount of time it takes to solve a problem in one's head should correspond to the amount of time it takes to solve the problem using external aids. Consider the abacus, a device for arithmetic calculations used in Asian cultures. Expert users of the abacus do not bother to actually move the beads. Instead, they visualize the abacus and perform the calculations with the image they have formed. When these persons are asked to report on the intermediate steps involved,

Expert users of the abacus, a device for arithmetic calculation used in Asian cultures, do not actually move the beads. Instead, they visualize the abacus and perform the calculations with the image they have formed.

their response times parallel the respective steps that would occur were they actually moving the beads (Stigler, 1984).

Errors

When researchers ask subjects to do things, performance is rarely perfect. Errors need not always be a problem, at least for investigators because the analysis of errors can be a powerful technique for making inferences about cognition (Kalechofsky, 1987). Indeed, errors sometimes tell us more than correct answers. Incorrect additions or deletions— that is, errors of commission and omission—can be particularly informative.

Imagine we show a person some words and ask him to memorize them. We later test his memory and find that his recall is systematically flawed. This finding implies that the original material must have been represented in a way so as to produce the observed pattern of mistakes. If errors involve confusing the way words sound (remembering *sappy* as *happy*), this finding tells us that the words were represented in auditory terms. If errors involve the confusion of what words mean (remembering *rich* as *wealthy*), this finding tells us that their representation was in semantic terms.

Development

Researchers have found the study of development useful for understanding the very beginnings of cognitive activity (Levy, 1994). For example, when children begin to utter words and sentences, they overgeneralize what they know and make language more consistent than it actually is. All four-legged creatures are dogs. All past tense verbs end in -*ed*: "I throwed the ball." Findings like these suggest that when we learn language, we learn more than particular words and sentences. We also learn rules. The exceptions to the rules can be acquired only when the rules are mastered.

Cognitive Disorders

Every field of psychology finds in examples of abnormality a useful perspective on what is normal. Cognitive psychology is no exception. Some researchers pose tasks for subjects who have suffered various brain pathologies: illnesses and injuries. Their observed performance provides clues about how knowledge is represented and transformed (Caramazza, 1990).

Consider memory loss following a blow to the head. Lynch and Yarnell (1973) watched football practices, on the lookout for collisions that dazed a player. When such collisions occurred, the investigators quickly interviewed the players: "What play was being run when the collision happened?" The answer was generally correct. But when the same players were asked the same question some minutes later, they often could not answer it. These results imply that experiences must be transformed before they are committed to permanent memory. Although the players at first knew what had happened, their dazed condition interfered with its transformation into a long-term representation.

Thinking-Aloud Protocols

Contemporary psychologists have discovered that a version of introspection can reveal something about the workings of the mind, so long as they do not ask people to report on what they do not know (Nisbett & Wilson, 1977). If you ask people to think out loud while solving a problem, their comments provide valuable information about what and how they think (Ericsson & Simon, 1984). One finding from studies using this approach of thinking-aloud protocols is that people jump around a lot in solving problems. They try and discard many possibilities before settling on a solution.

For example, Swanson (1988) used a thinking-aloud procedure to compare the way learning-disabled children differed from other children in terms of solving problems

Table 9.2 Summary: Research Methods in Cognitive Psychology

The research strategies used by cognitive psychologists allow inferences about the content or process of thinking.

Method	Inference allowed
Reaction times	How long do cognitive activities take?
Errors	How is cognition represented?
Development	How do cognitive processes originate and change?
Cognitive disorders	What is the biological basis of cognition?
Thinking-aloud protocols	What steps are followed in cognitive activities?
Modeling	How do people solve problems?

that involved the arrangement of pictures in a sequence (Chapter 11). Learning-disabled children had difficulty framing the problem to be solved and then deciding what aspects of the task material were irrelevant. These results imply that learning disability can be described in more precise psychological terms. Interventions with learning-disabled children should specify not just how to solve a problem but also how not to do so.

Modeling

Cognitive science is a field that developed through the combination of several more established disciplines, including cognitive psychology, linguistics, computer science, anthropology, and neuroscience (Gardner, 1985). It shares with cognitive psychology the goal of understanding the what and how of human knowledge but draws on a broader set of methods than those of psychology alone. One of the chief techniques of cognitive science is to create explicit models of cognitive processes. In particular, cognitive science lays great stock on the use of the computer to shed light on cognition in general and problem solving in particular (see Table 9.2).

Here we find **artificial intelligence:** deliberately created computer programs that perform tasks similar to those that people perform. There are two types of such programs. The first is intended as a simulation of the end product of human cognition, as well as the intermediate steps. The second makes no attempt to mimic the process; it aims only to achieve the end product. In either case, though, the results provide us with information concerning how human cognition occurs and how we might improve it because the steps of a computer program are explicitly known.

Programs exist that can diagnose diseases, recognize writing and speaking, forecast weather, offer tax advice, give airplane pilots directions for landing, play chess, and judge wines (Mebel & Dreschler-Fischer, 1994). Programs that function at the level of human specialists in a particular domain are called expert systems (Karagiannis, 1994). Needless to say, experts create computer models, usually based on thinking-aloud protocols and programmed in the form of if-then statements (if X occurs, then ask about Y) (Krol, de Bruyn, & Van den Bercken, 1992; Memmi & Nguyen-Xuan, 1988).

■ **cognitive science**
interdisciplinary field concerned with knowledge

■ **artificial intelligence**
deliberately created computer programs that perform tasks similar to those that people perform

Stop and Think

4 What are some possible confounds in the use of reaction times to study cognition?

5 Are thinking-aloud protocols different from introspection as practiced by the structuralists (Chapter 1)?

6 Think of a science fiction portrayal of an intelligent computer, like Data in *Star Trek*. Does your example imply any limitations in studying artificial intelligence to shed light on cognition?

COGNITIVE REPRESENTATIONS

How is information represented in the mind? The difficulties encountered years ago by the structuralists imply that we cannot identify the basic mental elements, probably because there are none (Chapter 1). Psychologists today have proposed a variety of cognitive representations, and the number of these makes it seem that the mind is crowded. But remember that the mind is not a physical place but a metaphorical one. We can arrange cognitive representations in order, from the most concrete to the most abstract.

Images

■ **image**
cognitive representation much like perception except without an external stimulus

An **image** is a mental representation much like perception except that it is not triggered by an external stimulus (Chapter 5). When we speak of images, we usually mean visual ones, but they exist for most senses. For example, we can imagine the warm sun on our face and fine sand between our toes. We can imagine someone calling our name.

Researchers have found that the resemblance between imagery and perception goes beyond superficial similarity. For instance, images interfere with perception in the same sensory mode (Segal & Fusella, 1970). Someone with a visual image in mind is less likely to detect a visual stimulus, whereas someone with an auditory image is less likely to detect an auditory stimulus. This pattern implies that imagery and perception use common mental operations. Research with brain imaging techniques suggests that similar parts of the brain are active during imagery and the corresponding sensory experience (Kosslyn et al., 1993; Tippett, 1992).

Stephen Kosslyn (1980) and his colleagues have conducted studies on visual imagery that further support the similarity between imagery and perception. Research subjects are asked first to form a visual image and then to perform some task using the image such as answering the question, "How far is it between Points A and B?" on an imagined map. Reaction times are the same as if subjects were looking at an actual picture (see Figure 9.1).

Subjects skilled at visual imagery are susceptible to visual illusions in their images, like those described in Chapter 5 (Wallace, 1984). Subjects not skilled at visual imagery do not experience illusions in their images. Again, these results point to the similarity between imagery and perception.

Still, many theorists are reluctant to propose that images are simply pictures in the head (Anderson, 1985; Dennett, 1991; Pylyshyn, 1984). They point to differences between mental images and actual perceptions. Specifically, images are more able to be manipulated than perceptions are and can be distorted by general knowledge in a way that perceptions cannot be (Carmichael, Hogan, & Walter, 1932). Another difference between images and perceptions is that images are arranged in a hierarchy, whereas perceptions are not.

■ **mental map; cognitive map**
cognitive representation of a physical place

Both of these differences can be illustrated with geographic images, so-called **mental maps** (also called **cognitive maps;** see Chapter 8). Form an image of the United States in your mind. Now answer the following questions about this image (Stevens & Coupe, 1978):

■ Which is farther east: San Diego or Reno?
■ Which is farther north: Seattle or Montreal?
■ Which is farther west: the Atlantic or the Pacific entrance to the Panama Canal?

In each case, the first answer is the correct one, but most people choose the second one because of the distorting effects of their general knowledge. They think of California as west of Nevada, Canada as north of the United States, and the Atlantic Ocean as east of the Pacific Ocean. Mental images are an example of top-down processing. They are

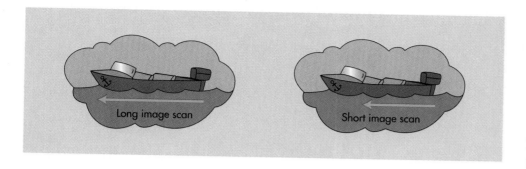

Long image scan

Short image scan

Figure 9.1
Reaction Times to Visual Images. Subjects were shown a picture of a motorboat. They were then asked to look away and form a mental image of the boat and to look in particular at its motor. When asked whether the boat had a windshield, subjects answered more quickly than when asked whether the boat had an anchor (Kosslyn, 1980). Note that the windshield is closer to the motor than the anchor is, implying that the quicker reaction time was due to scanning of the visual image.

represented at different levels (states vs. cities), and the higher representation affects the lower one (Lautrey & Chartier, 1987).

Linear Orderings

Somewhat more abstract than a mental image is a **linear ordering:** a representation of elements structured in some order. For example, we might remember the order in which we met three people: Tom, Dick, and Harry. We might represent the steps to go through in readying a personal computer for use or in arranging clothes on a clothesline (Sowden & Blades, 1994). We might recall the relative heights or weights of a group of individuals. Or we might remember the relative authority of people in a social group (A. Fiske, 1992).

> ■ **linear ordering**
> cognitive representation of elements in some order

Here are some generalizations about linear orderings (Anderson, 1985). We can readily recall those items on either end of the order (Ebbinghaus, 1885). When we are asked to make judgments about two items in a linear ordering, we respond quickly when the items are far apart on the scale. "Which president served the earlier term: Adams or Jefferson?" "Monroe or Nixon?" Most people answer the second question more quickly than the first.

When the number of elements increases, we tend to group them into a hierarchy, forming small linear orderings among subsets of elements. These orderings in turn are placed in their own order. Consider the alphabet, which many of us have memorized to the tune "Twinkle, Twinkle, Little Star." Pauses in the song correspond to breaks among the subgroupings of letters: ABCD EFG HIJK LMNOP QRS TUV WXYZ (Anderson, 1985).

Klahr, Chase, and Lovelace (1983) gave subjects a letter in the alphabet and asked them to come up with the next one as quickly as possible. The fastest reaction times occurred when subjects were given the first letter of a subgrouping, like E, H, or L. Reaction times slowed toward the end of subgroupings.

Concepts

An even more abstract cognitive representation is the **concept,** any mental categorization of elements into a group. Categorization is a central cognitive process because no others would be possible if we did not make distinctions. When we consider all of the elements that people categorize, we should expect concepts to take many different forms (Glass & Holyoak, 1986; Schwartz & Reisberg, 1991; Wilhite & Payne, 1992).

> ■ **concept**
> cognitive representation of a category of elements

One way to represent a concept is simply by listing all of the elements that belong to it. For instance, think of the concept American car, which we can represent by listing Ford, Chevrolet, Chrysler, and so on.

When the number of elements in a concept is large, we are unable to recall all of them and so rely on a rule to generate them. These generative rules are an efficient way of representing what may be an infinite number of elements. Consider the rules for

A concept is any mental representation of elements in a group. What comes to your mind when you think of the concept "American car"?

producing Roman numerals. These rules allow us to create all possible Roman numerals by memorizing only a handful of them in the first place (e.g., I, V, X, L, C, and M).

Another way to represent a concept is by the characteristics that its elements share. We can group together everything that contains DNA and call this the concept of living things. We can group together everything on which we can sit and call this the concept of seats. We can group together everyone to whom we speak when meeting and call this the concept of acquaintances.

Propositional networks.   Many concepts come with a verbal tag attached, and psychologists have attempted to understand how the meaning of these verbal tags is cognitively represented. It is currently believed that meanings are represented in a network of associations. This approach is similar to how traditional learning theorists view the essence of learning (Chapter 8), except that the links in the network represent not temporal associations between stimuli and responses but instead logical relationships among words (Rumelhart, Lindsay, & Norman, 1972). These associations are termed a **propositional network:** propositions arranged in a hierarchy (see Figure 9.2).

In commenting on propositional networks, Anderson (1985, p. 116) compared them to "a tangle of marbles connected by strings." More technically, the marbles are called nodes, and the strings that connect them are called relations. Mental activity occurs when part of the network is activated. In other words, we think about an idea when the part of the network corresponding to it is metaphorically stimulated. For example, in Figure 9.2 we think about candy when the upper part of the network is activated, and about Russia when the bottom part is activated. Network models explain how one thought can lead to another and still another by proposing that activation spreads throughout the network (Collins & Loftus, 1975).

One important type of propositional network is called a **schema,** defined as an organized set of information about some concept. A schema is not a heap of miscellaneous beliefs; it is a representation of how these beliefs are related to one another. Anderson (1985, p. 124) used house as an example of a schema. Here are some of the things many of us believe about a house:

■ It belongs to the larger category of: building.
■ It is made of: wood, stucco, and/or brick.

■ **propositional network**
cognitive representation of the meaning of a concept in terms of a network of associations

■ **schema**
organized set of information about some concept

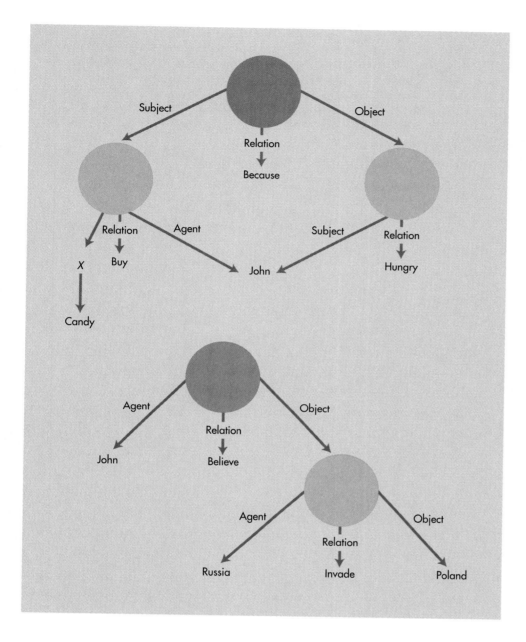

Figure 9.2
Propositional Network. Here
are examples of how information
is represented in a propositional
network. In the top, the information is that "John bought some
candy because he was hungry." In
the bottom, the information is
that "John believed that Russia
would invade Poland."

- It contains: rooms.
- It functions as: human dwelling.
- It is shaped like: rectangle.

Certainly, not all people have exactly the same schema for a house, but this one is representative.

   A schema is not tied to a particular instance. Our schema for a house refers not to
our house or to the house next door but rather to a generic house. A schema allows us
to go beyond the immediate information we have available to make plausible inferences. Suppose a friend says, "I'm so excited! I just bought a house!" You are probably
safe in assuming that her house is a building, that it is made of wood or brick, that it has
rooms, that she plans to live in it, and so forth. Of course, you can be wrong. She may
have bought a dollhouse, a doghouse, a teepee, or a grass hut. But regardless, your
schema of house is packed with a great deal of information, including how to recognize
exceptions to it.

Schemas affect a variety of cognitive processes. Many of us have schemas for people with given personality traits, for instance. If someone is introduced to us as an extravert, we interact with him as if he were extraverted, whether or not he actually is (Cantor & Mischel, 1977, 1979). We notice his extraverted behaviors, and we recall them later. Social psychologists have borrowed the notion of a schema to help explain stereotypes and their persistence (Chapter 15).

Artificial and natural concepts.   Traditionally, psychologists carried out research using concepts that were specially devised for their experiments (Bourne, 1966). Researchers created abstract stimuli that varied along different dimensions (see Figure 9.3). Subjects were asked to identify which stimuli were examples of a concept and which were not. They would choose one stimulus and were told if they were right or wrong. Over time, the subjects would acquire the concept by learning which characteristics of the stimuli were associated with right answers (all green circles).

Two decades ago, the assumption that every concept was defined by necessary and sufficient characteristics was unquestioned. That is, psychologists assumed that for any concept there were critical properties that all examples of the given concept possess (necessary characteristics) and that only examples of that concept possess (sufficient characteristics). For instance, three-sidedness is a necessary and sufficient condition for the concept triangle. Concepts like these are now termed **artificial concepts,** to emphasize that not all concepts are so defined. In particular, many of the concepts people use in their everyday life (e.g., normality or illness) do not have necessary and sufficient conditions. These are therefore called **natural concepts.**

The philosopher Ludwig Wittgenstein (1953) asked how we might define a game. We start by thinking of properties that all games possess. But for each supposed property, we can cite a counterexample. Games require two people—but then there is solitaire. Games have winners and losers—but then there is Frisbee. Games are for fun—but then there is professional football. The concept of game is not characterized by necessary and sufficient conditions.

Conclusions from research on artificial concepts do not apply to natural concepts (Peng, Kandel, & Wang, 1991; Shiina, 1991; Sholomii, Chuprikova, & Zakharova, 1989). So, a great deal of current theorizing and research has looked specifically at natural concepts. If these are not defined by critical elements, then what does define them?

One possibility is that natural concepts are marked by a family resemblance among their elements (Rosch & Mervis, 1975). Just as members of a family tend to have characteristics in common, so too do natural concepts. But none of these characteristics in and of itself is critical. That is why you can recognize the child playing in the street as a member of the Smith family even though he does not have red hair like most of his relatives. His other characteristics—skinny legs and a long nose—identify him as a Smith.

A related possibility is that natural concepts are defined by a prototype or typical member of the category in question (Attneave, 1957). By this view, people acquire natural concepts by abstracting from repeated instances of the concept an average member. The concept is mentally represented as this average. Then this prototype is used to categorize subsequent instances in terms of their resemblance to it. Our familiar social stereotypes are good examples of prototypes. Is someone a jock, a sorority member, or a movie star?

There is yet another answer to what defines natural concepts: remembered instances (Medin & Schaffer, 1978). Is he a basketball player? He must be because he moves like Herman, and Herman was certainly a basketball player. Remembered instances are particular members of a concept, whereas a prototype is an average of particular members. The distinction can be a bit ambiguous, and at present cognitive psychologists are not certain how best to characterize natural concepts.

The notion of natural concepts has broad implications. Most generally, these concepts do not have fixed boundaries. Particular instances can "kind of" belong to a category, prompting some theorists to describe natural concepts as fuzzy sets. Traditional

■ **artificial concept**
concept defined by necessary and sufficient conditions

■ **natural concept**
concept without necessary or sufficient conditions

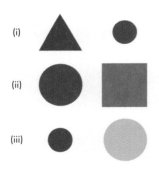

(i)

(ii)

(iii)

Figure 9.3
Concept Identification Stimuli. Subjects are presented with pairs of abstract stimuli that vary along dimensions like color, size, and shape. They choose one member of each pair and are told "right" or "wrong." Over a series of trials, their task is to determine which characteristics of the stimuli define the concept.

Natural concepts, like fruit, have both good and bad examples. Apples are prototypic instances, and hence are "good" fruits. Kiwis, no matter how tasty, are "bad" fruits.

logic assumes that things either are or are not, and hence proves unwieldy in dealing with certain natural concepts.

Another point is that instances of a concept vary from good to bad. This conclusion should not surprise you because we all know that there are good examples and bad examples of almost all abstract notions. Research shows that people agree as to which examples of natural concepts are good and which are bad (Rosch, 1975). So, an apple is a good example of the concept of fruit, just as a collie is a good dog and a robin is a good bird. We can call these examples prototypes and say that they possess many of the characteristics that define the family resemblance of the concept in question. (A kiwi is a bad example of a fruit, as well as a bad example of a bird. And a basenji is a bad dog, however well behaved it might be.) The relevance for cognition in general is that good examples are more readily recognized by individuals as belonging to a concept, more easily distinguished from members of different categories, and more frequently recalled when committed to memory.

Eleanor Rosch and her colleagues (1976) suggested that people categorize the world at a level that maximizes the perceptual similarity among objects within a category and the perceptual dissimilarity between these objects and those in other categories. Consider this hierarchy:

- Kitchen table
- Table
- Furniture

These researchers' argument is that table represents the basic level at which people most easily categorize objects. Kitchen table is too concrete, whereas furniture is too abstract. Studies support this idea, showing that cognitive processes such as recognition proceed most efficiently when content is at the basic level. Also, when children start to name objects, they first use terms from the basic level. This notion assumes a bottom–up approach because perception dominates abstract meaning, not vice versa.

Rules

Rules are the most abstract cognitive representation. You have just encountered generative rules as one way of representing a concept, but rules have relevance throughout all of psychology. Indeed, theorists frequently describe memory, problem solving, and

■ **rules**

cognitive representations that allow examples of a concept to be generated language as rule-based, arguing that generative rules as a basic mechanism of cognition appeared early in the course of evolution (Bloom, 1994; Corballis, 1992, 1994).

What happens when we say a sentence? Perhaps we search through the mental category of all possible sentences until we find the one we want, and then we say it. But this possibility is not reasonable. Many sentences we say are creative—we have never said them before (Chomsky, 1957, 1959). Sentences themselves cannot have a cognitive representation. Instead, theorists propose, we cognitively represent rules that allow us to generate sentences. These are collectively termed the **grammar** of a language. For example, one familiar rule is that we can usually create the plural of a word by adding an *s* at its end. With grammar available, we can say an infinite number of creative sentences. Similarly, these rules allow us to understand sentences, including those we have never heard before. The grammar that underlies language is not something people are aware of while speaking or listening. Rather, we know about grammar only indirectly, by observing how people use language.

According to some theorists, the disorder of infantile autism reflects the absence of generative rules (Nagase, 1993). In autism, the individual shows a profound disturbance in communication and little evidence for a sense of self. If the autistic individual develops language, his or her speech includes a striking feature: *You* and *I* are frequently interchanged. This phenomenon implies that the generative rules responsible for the use of personal pronouns are amiss, perhaps because of brain dysfunction (DeLong, 1992).

Cognitive theorists use the term *grammar* not just for language but also for the rules that underlie any complex behavior for which the particulars cannot possibly be represented in the mind. Consider the content of the small talk you make while waiting with some friends for the elevator. How is this possible, this medley of questions and jokes and postures and facial expressions, exchanged and coordinated with those of one or more other people? Small talk is infinite. One of its guiding principles is to avoid repetition.

Small talk can be described, therefore, as having a grammar because underlying rules are used to generate and understand it. You certainly do not walk around with a store of witty comments represented in final form waiting to be unleashed on the world. A similar argument can be made for improvisational jazz, fast-break basketball, or gourmet cooking (see Table 9.3).

■ **grammar**
rules that allow language to be generated and understood

Stop and Think

7 What is a linear ordering?

8 In evolutionary terms, why do people find it easier to create images for some senses (e.g., vision) rather than others (e.g., smell)?

9 Drawing on your everyday life, think of an example of an artificial concept. What are its necessary and sufficient conditions?

Table 9.3   Summary: Cognitive Representations

Different cognitive representations vary in their concreteness.

Representation	Example
Image	Memory of a song by a favorite performer
Linear ordering	Memory of one's class schedule for Tuesday
Concept	Organized knowledge about the Bill of Rights
Rule	Grammar of a langauge

Encoding, storage, and retrieval are concepts that can be applied not only to our memory but to other information systems as well, like library catalogs and computers.

MEMORY

The process by which we put information into memory in one or more possible ways is called **encoding.** We speak of its representation once in memory as the **storage** of information. The process by which information is located in memory and then used is called **retrieval.** Keeping in mind the metaphor implicit in these terms can help you grasp them: The terms liken memories to things that can be put away at one time and taken out at another. This metaphor can be misleading, however because it leads us to treat memories as essentially accurate accounts of an individual's actual experiences. Think back to the memories of sexual abuse with which this chapter began. One can be highly skeptical about the accuracy of their details; indeed, one can even be skeptical that events like these happened at all to the people who "remembered" them.

We can also look at encoding, storage, and retrieval in terms of information processing, seeing them as aspects of the same basic process. These terms can be applied not only to human memory but also to other systems concerned with information, including computers, libraries, or your list of things to do during the day. In each case, there are ways of acquiring information, retaining it, and then making it available for use.

Psychologists recently have distinguished between **explicit memory,** which refers to the deliberate attempt to remember information, and **implicit memory,** which involves the operation of unintentional processes (Nelson, Schreiber, & McEvoy, 1992). Subliminal perception, discussed in Chapter 6, is an example of implicit memory because information is acquired without the individual being aware of it.

Failure of memory—or **forgetting**—has several sources. We may be unable to remember a particular item of information because we never encoded it in the first place because we are unable to retrieve it from storage, or because the memory has literally been lost.

■ **encoding**
process by which information is placed in memory

■ **storage**
representation of information in memory

■ **retrieval**
process by which information is located in memory and then used

■ **explicit memory**
deliberate attempt to remember information

■ **implicit memory**
unintentional recall or recognition of information

■ **forgetting**
failure of memory

Using himself as a research subject, Herman Ebbinghaus carried out the first systematic experiments on memory.

■ **nonsense syllables**

sets of letters with no inherent meaning, used in memory research

■ **serial position effect**

better memory for items at the beginning or end of a linear ordering

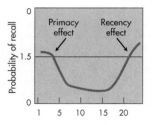

Figure 9.4
Serial Position Effect. When people are shown a list of words and then asked to recall them, they best recall the first few words—the primacy effect—and the last few words—the recency effect.

The Contributions of Herman Ebbinghaus

Herman Ebbinghaus (1850–1909), a German philosopher and psychologist, is credited with the first systematic studies of memory. His procedures were simple, yet they produced reliable results with important implications for how the mind works. Even today, his work continues to be influential, if only as a point of departure (Caparros & Anguera, 1986).

To gain some appreciation of the significance of Ebbinghaus's (1885) pioneering investigations, consider that he worked when there were no other researchers to provide him with theoretical or methodological strategies to follow. He had to make a number of important decisions about how to proceed with his investigations, not least of which was deciding what kind of material should be memorized. He created what have come to be known as **nonsense syllables,** sets of letters with no inherent meaning, such as ZPS, CER, and EEQ.

Why use a nonsense syllable? This technique allows the researcher to study memory without having to worry about the meaning of the material being memorized. Meaningfulness influences memorization, and by eliminating it, Ebbinghaus simplified matters. You have seen in previous discussions, like Chapter 8 on learning, how simple versions of phenomena can sometimes be enlightening. In particular, simplifications lend themselves to experimentation, and Ebbinghaus studied memory experimentally. He used himself as his own research subject. He would study a list of nonsense syllables until he had memorized it. Then sometime later he would test himself for recall.

A number of reliable principles emerged from his studies, findings that are still accepted today. He showed that the more times a person rehearsed a list of syllables, the better it was committed to memory. He also showed that when we commit more than one list of syllables to memory, we will experience interference with our recall of each, especially when the syllables are similar.

The **serial position effect** refers to the fact that in a series of nonsense syllables, those at the beginning or ending of the series are better remembered than those in the middle (see Figure 9.4). Ebbinghaus was the first researcher to demonstrate this effect, which proves quite common, even among animals (Crystal & Shettleworth, 1994). It is an example of a linear ordering, and most of us encounter it whenever we meet a series of people at a party. We remember the faces and names of the first and last people more readily than those of people in the middle.

The serial position effect describes what we remember from baseball games, dances, movies, lectures, and textbooks. It even describes what we remember from complex material that is organized into a hierarchy (Pohl, 1990). So, across a college course, we remember material better from the first and last lectures, and within these lectures, from the beginnings and endings.

Damage to an individual's frontal lobes, discussed in Chapters 4 and 6, interferes with the serial position effect (Eslinger & Grattan, 1994). People with lesions in their frontal lobes no longer have enhanced memory for information presented at the beginning and ending of sequences. Remember that one of the striking behavioral deficits of frontal lobe damage is the inability to carry out complex sequences of acts, and so perhaps the serial position effect reflects an evolved psychological mechanism that allows us to organize what we do across time.

Ebbinghaus's approach fits with a particular view of the way the mind works—specifically, the idea that learning consists of associations between items. Accordingly, the associations we make with particular items determines our recall. Some associations help our recall because they lead to the item in question, whereas others inhibit it because they mislead us. Remember that we encountered associations in Chapter 8 as a common ingredient in traditional theories of learning. The Ebbinghaus tradition of memory and the behavioral tradition of animal learning are therefore compatible, a fact which explains why studies of memory did not stop during the reign of behaviorism (Chapter 1).

Memory Systems

Following the example of Ebbinghaus, psychologists studied memory extensively. One important discovery was that we can distinguish among three types of memory: sensory memory, short-term memory, and long-term memory (Schacter & Tulving, 1994), corresponding to the steps through which incoming information is processed as it is remembered (see Figure 9.5).

At one time, these types of memory were regarded as discrete stages in the encoding → storage process (Atkinson & Shiffrin, 1968; Waugh & Norman, 1965). This view is called the **multistore model of memory** because it assumes that memories are represented (stored) in several different ways. Today there is skepticism about our ability to determine when one type of memory ends and another type begins. An alternative view thus holds that there is only one type of memory (Craik & Lockhart, 1972). The supposed stages of memory represent different depths of information processing, and this approach is called the **levels of processing model of memory.** By this view, memory stages constantly interact with one another (Massaro & Cowan, 1993). In any event, different aspects of memory—whether we regard them as stages or levels—involve different processes.

Sensory memory. In Chapter 5, it was pointed out that sensation and perception blur into one another. A similar observation can be made about perception and cognition, for it is difficult to know when perception stops and cognition begins. This is particularly so with our **sensory memory,** which briefly holds a relatively faithful version of our sensory experiences, such as a sight, a sound, or a touch. A synonym for *sensory memory* is **sensory register** because it registers what we have perceived. The sensory memory is limited both in the amount of information it can hold and in how long it

■ **multistore model of memory**
theory that memories are represented in several different ways

■ **levels of processing model of memory**
theory that the supposed stages of memory represent different depths of information processing

■ **sensory memory; sensory register**
brief but relatively faithful memory of sensory experiences

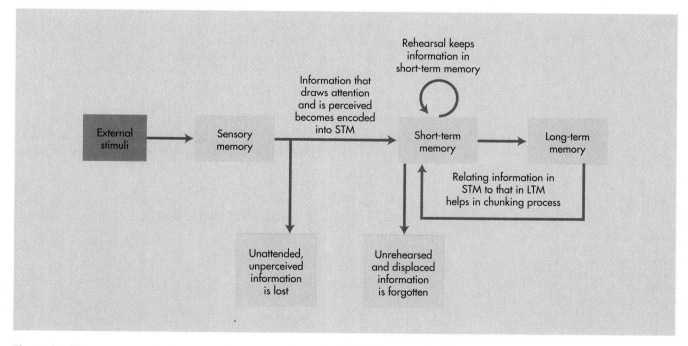

Figure 9.5
Memory Systems. One popular view of memory proposes that information passes through discrete stages: sensory memory, short-term memory (STM), and long-term memory (LTM). Information can be lost or forgotten at every step in the process.

The sensory memory is limited in both the amount of information it can hold and in how long it can hold this information. The more intense the original stimulus, the longer it is represented in a sensory memory.

can do so. The more intense the original stimulus, the longer it lingers. A scream stays in the sensory memory longer than a whisper.

A visual image that briefly lingers in sensory memory following the presentation of a stimulus is called an **icon.** A classic experiment by George Sperling (1960) helped to establish the existence of icons and to provide some clues about how they function. He showed research subjects an array of letters for a fraction of a second (see Figure 9.6). The array had three rows. When the letter display was turned off, a tone was sounded that was high, medium, or low in pitch. If the tone was high, subjects were to recall the top row of letters. If it was medium, they were to report the middle row. And so on.

Sperling's subjects could recall the letters in the indicated row with no difficulty, even when each row contained four or five letters. At some point, they must have represented to themselves all the letters in the array. However, these representations proved

■ **icon**
visual image in sensory memory

Figure 9.6
Sperling's (1960) Experiment.
Subjects were presented with an array of letters for just a fraction of a second. A tone was then sounded telling them which row of letters to recall: top, middle, or bottom. Subjects correctly reported the requested letters. However, they could not remember the entire array. These results show that information is kept in sensory memory for only a brief period.

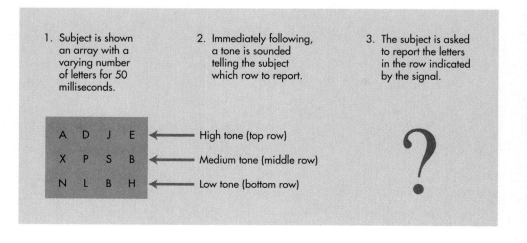

fleeting, lasting no more than one-quarter of a second. When asked to recall all the letters, subjects failed, invariably coming up with only four or five.

Other research suggests that icons are minimally transformed from the original sensation (Neisser, 1967). They lie somewhere between perception and cognition. They are important because they make our visual experience continuous. Our eyes work by making little jumps. From instant to instant, there are breaks in the flow of sensory information. Icons smooth out these breaks.

Other sensations—like touch—have the equivalent of icons, although these have not been studied as frequently as icons (Bliss, Crane, Mansfield, & Townsend, 1966). Sensory memory has also been shown for hearing, where the briefly lingering image is called an **echo.** It behaves much like an icon, except that it does not go away quite as rapidly. Echoes typically last several seconds and sometimes as long as ten seconds (Lu, Williamson, & Kaufman, 1992; Samms, Hari, Rif, & Knuutila, 1993).

Short-term memory.   The next stage, or level, is called **short-term memory,** where a limited amount of information is held for a brief period, usually 15 to 20 seconds. Only some of the information from the sensory memory passes into short-term memory. Which aspects move on? Obviously, selective attention is involved (Chapter 5). Information that is bizarre often grabs our attention. To the degree that particular information is familiar and/or meaningful, it passes into short-term memory as well. However, if the information is too familiar, we might tune it out. Finally, the amount of information that we can represent at any given time in short-term memory is severely limited.

George Miller (1956) wrote a well-known paper on "the magic number seven, plus or minus two," in which he argued that the capacity of short-term memory is between five and nine items (bits) of information. In other words, the number of discrete items that we can represent at any one time is about seven. Some of you may be skeptical because you know you can hold on to more information than this. If you get a long-distance number from directory assistance, you usually do not need to write it down before you dial even though the area code and number together comprise ten digits.

This phenomenon does not contradict Miller's argument because we have grouped the digits into meaningful wholes in a process known as **chunking** (Allen & Crozier, 1992; Baddeley, 1994). Some of us know that the area code for San Francisco is 415, for example, or that the area code for Chicago is 312. We thus can turn three items of information into one.

Or suppose your roommate asks you to pick up the following items at the grocery store: flour, baking powder, salt, butter, sugar, bananas, and walnuts. Will you remember all of these? Maybe, maybe not. But suppose you say to yourself, "Those are the ingredients for banana bread." Then you will have no trouble remembering the specific items because you have been able to chunk them into a meaningful and tasty whole. By consolidating information, we increase the capacity of short-term memory (Ericsson & Chase, 1982).

What happens to information when it passes into short-term memory? It tends not to be represented deeply. Words are often stored in terms of how they sound rather than what they mean. Studies show that recall errors for information that is in short-term memory usually stem from our confusion between the sounds of letters and words, not their meanings (Conrad, 1963, 1964). If subjects are visually presented with single letters and then asked to recall what they have just seen, they confuse E with G or V or B. Interestingly, E's and F's are not confused in short-term memory, even though they look alike. One conclusion from such studies is that short-term memory is a way of talking to ourselves.

As noted, information does not stay long in short-term memory; most of it is lost after about 20 seconds (Peterson & Peterson, 1959). The amount of information stored and the length of time it stays there can be increased in several ways. You can rehearse the information. When I get a phone number from directory assistance, for instance, I

■ **echo**
auditory image in sensory memory

■ **short-term memory**
stage of memory into which information passes from sensory memory and is held for about 15 to 20 seconds

■ **chunking**
process in which cognitive elements are grouped into larger wholes

repeat it aloud several times, and this practice usually helps me hold on to it long enough to dial it.

You can also elaborate the information and make it more meaningful. Where I live, the first three digits of a telephone number reflect the approximate date that the telephone service began. I can remember a telephone number better if I stop and realize, "Yes, he has lived in Ann Arbor for a decade" or "She recently moved and has a new phone number."

Finally, you can chunk the material, grouping it into meaningful wholes. As already discussed, chunking allows us to deal with the well-documented limits on short-term memory. We may be able to entertain only seven discrete items in our mind at any one time, but if these are chunks we nonetheless can consider a great deal of information simultaneously.

■ **long-term memory**
stage of memory into which information passes from short-term memory and is held for an extremely long time

Long-term memory.   The next and final stage in the memory process is **long-term memory,** so named because information can be retained for an extremely long time. Its capacity is virtually unlimited. Information moves into long-term memory from short-term memory, and here we have our entire storehouse of past experiences: thoughts, feelings, and events. Our skills and abilities are also represented in long-term memory, as are our identity and personality. As in short-term memory, there is selectivity as to what information passes into it. For instance, I know that yesterday I answered questions in class, but today I do not remember the specific questions or the specific students who asked them.

A popular research strategy for investigating long-term memory involves asking subjects to memorize stories and later recall them. This tradition can be traced to Frederick Bartlett (1932), who had subjects read and later recall complex stories. He found that recall was not literal. Instead, subjects abstracted the major points of the story (as they saw them) and represented the essence of the story in their memory. When later asked to recall what they had read, they elaborated on the gist of the story, sometimes departing considerably from the original material.

Findings like these imply that long-term memory is an active process (Bransford, 1979; Kintsch, 1974; Neisser, 1967). Theorists sometimes say that memory is constructive. Memories are not reproductions of experiences stored somewhere in the mind; rather, they are created anew each time they are remembered. As noted earlier, the terms *storage* and *retrieval* are highly misleading here because they tempt us to treat memories as fixed things rather than constructions. Memories of events from long ago can be quite different from the events themselves because often they have been reconstructed numerous times.

Verify this conclusion for yourself by thinking back to your childhood. What important events do you recall? Then talk to your family members or old friends about these events and you will probably find considerable disagreement about what actually happened. It should not be surprising that the accuracy of supposedly long-repressed memories proves so difficult to evaluate.

Typically, representation occurs deeply in long-term memory. The critical characteristic of most long-term memories is that the represented information is meaningful to the individual. Representations are therefore abstract, elaborate, and organized. Cognitive psychologists propose the following divisions (Tulving, 1985, 1986):

■ *Procedural memory*—knowledge of how to do something: bake bread, change a tire, or build a charcoal fire
■ *Semantic memory*—knowledge of particular facts about the world, like the name of the president, the location of the post office in town, and the meanings of words
■ *Episodic memory*—knowledge of events that one has experienced, for example, where one grew up, went to school, and worked during summers, one's autobiography, so to speak

One way of describing long-term memories distinguishes between procedural memories (knowing how) and declarative memories (knowing that). Declarative memories are divided into semantic memories (general knowledge) and episodic memories (personal recollections). You might draw on procedural memories to ride a bike, semantic memories to identify a bird, and episodic memories to recall your graduation or wedding.

Although the distinctions among these types of long-term memory can be difficult to draw, the important point is that all contain information that is meaningful and organized.

Remembering

How do we retrieve information from our memory? The answer is straightforward with respect to sensory memory and short-term memory. Information is simply there in a person's awareness. Retrieval from long-term memory is a different matter. Granted all the information we have represented in long-term memory, it is remarkable that we can get as much out of it as rapidly as we do.

Psychologists speak of two types of retrieval: recognition and recall. **Recognition** is the realization that certain information looks familiar: "Do I need to turn left or right at Green Street to get to Fred's house?" In **recall,** we retrieve information from memory without being provided with explicit clues. "How do I get to Fred's house?" Recognition corresponds to examinations with multiple-choice questions, whereas recall corresponds to exams with fill-in-the blank questions.

■ recognition
realization that presented information is familiar

■ recall
retrieval of information from memory without explicit clues

Recognition.   In recognition, the person faces the task of deciding whether a presented stimulus matches a representation in memory. According to one explanation, the process is simple. Given the stimulus to be recognized, the individual takes into account its central characteristics and compares these to her mental representations that have similar characteristics. So, there's a dog playing in your front yard. Do you recognize it? It's a golden retriever. How many golden retrievers do you know? There's the one that your cousin just bought. This one's bigger. There's the one that your college roommate has. This one's smaller. There's the one that your neighbor is taking care of for her parents. Yes, that's a match. These comparisons take place within a fraction of a second (Intraub, 1980).

The critical factor in recognition is the similarity between the stimulus in question and an individual's mental representations. Encoded representations might not exactly match the object to be identified, and recognition is thereby hampered. An interesting example of this comes from research asking subjects to recognize extremely familiar objects: U.S. coins (Nickerson & Adams, 1979). Most of us have considerable difficulty distinguishing actual coins from those that are similar because our mental representations of the coins are not particularly detailed (see Figure 9.7).

Sometimes a person's expectations influence his memory. Elizabeth Loftus (1979) studied how eyewitnesses to a crime testify about what happened. Although eyewitness testimony is accorded great weight in our judicial system, Loftus's research consistently showed that it is subject to the same influences as any memory task. Consider a lineup where you have to pick out the suspect. This is a recognition task, and it can be distorted by your expectations. For instance, suppose you believe that the criminal was a certain sex, race, or age. These beliefs may lead you to focus only on this characteristic, perhaps resulting in a misidentification.

Figure 9.7
Actual Versus False Coins.
The coins on the left in each pair are actual U.S. coins. People frequently confuse these with the coins on the right in each pair, which you can verify as false by checking the change in your pocket. *Source:* Rubin & Kontis (1983).

Recall.   Recall is a more complicated process than recognition. Here the person must undertake the first step of generating possible answers to the memory task and then undergo the comparison process already described for recognition. This process is called the **generate-and-recognize model of recall** (Glass & Holyoak, 1986). Researchers have extensively studied how the first step of generation takes place. The person uses various cues to generate possible responses. The effectiveness of a given cue depends on how the person's long-term memory is organized. Let us say you have to name all 50 states. You might generate the names by going through the states alphabetically. Or you might do it geographically. If for some reason you know area codes or zip codes, you might generate the names of states by running through these in numerical order.

■ **generate-and-recognize model of recall**
theory of recall proposing that a person generates possible answers to a memory task and then attempts to recognize one as the correct answer

With repeated use, a single cue loses its effectiveness in suggesting potential responses. A person who uses several strategies for generating cues will therefore do better than someone who uses just one. The more ways in which a person's long-term memory is organized, the better the recall.

What else do we know about recall? The more recently you have thought of an item of information, the easier it is to recall: "What did the last batter do?" Another important factor influencing recall is practice. If you have frequently generated a response in the past, you can readily generate it in the present. In college, for example, the identification number we placed on tests was our social security number. I wrote mine on so many tests that my social security number is still easy for me to recall.

Tip-of-the-tongue phenomenon.   Researchers investigating recall have documented several interesting aspects of it. One of these is the **tip-of-the-tongue phenomenon** (Brown & McNeill, 1966). We have all had the experience of knowing that we have a given memory but being unable to come up with it: "Where did I put that library book that's now overdue? I know it must be here in my bedroom, but where?"

■ **tip-of-the-tongue phenomenon**
experience of knowing that one has a given memory but being unable to retrieve it

Psychologists have studied this experience by giving their subjects dictionary definitions of somewhat obscure words (see Table 9.4). Some of the subjects "know" the word being defined but are unable to produce it. However, they can correctly specify the letter with which the word starts, the number of syllables it contains, and other words it sounds like. The information on the tip of someone's tongue is often a proper name, and about half the time it is eventually remembered.

Research suggests that the tip-of-the-tongue phenomenon is nearly universal, occurring to people on average once a week, more frequently for older adults than younger adults (Brown, 1991). The phenomenon shows the importance of active

Table 9.4 Words on the Tip of One's Tongue

Brown and McNeill (1966) showed subjects definitions such as those below. When subjects could not think of the exact word but reported that it was on the tip of their tongue, they were asked to specify the word's first letter, how many syllables it had, and other words that sounded like it. Often, the subjects could answer these questions.

1. Favoritism shown to a relative, such as giving him or her a job
2. A projecting part of a church that is usually semicircular in shape and vaulted
3. A waxy substance believed to originate in the intestines of whales and used in making perfumes
4. A flat-bottomed Chinese boat
5. A staff with two entwined snakes and two wings at the top

(1. nepotism 2. apse 3. ambergris 4. sampan 5. caduceus)

processes in recall because a person can deliberately use information that is known about the word to remember it.

Context-dependent and state-dependent recall. Another interesting phenomenon is that we can more readily recall memories in the same setting in which we encoded them than in different settings. A dramatic demonstration of such **context-dependent recall** comes from an experiment that used divers as research subjects (Godden & Baddeley, 1975). Divers learned a list of words either on shore or 20 feet below the surface. Recall for words learned on dry land was better when tested on shore than underwater, whereas recall for words learned underwater showed the opposite pattern.

Related to context-dependent recall is **state-dependent recall.** If we initially encode information when in a given physiological state like drunkenness or exhaustion, then we can more readily recall this information when in the same state (Eich, 1980). Extensions of this idea have examined how moods influence recall (Blaney, 1986;

■ **context-dependent recall**
better recall of a memory in the same setting in which it was encoded than in different settings

■ **state-dependent recall**
better recall of a memory in the same physiological or emotional state in which it was encoded than in different states

The idea of state-dependent recall suggests that the student with his head down will be unable to recall the information being discussed unless in a similarly drowsy state. The idea of context-dependent recall implies that recall will be best in the same classroom.

Bower, 1981; Bower & Mayer, 1989). Information learned when a person is happy, sad, or anxious is better recalled when the person is in the same mood (Ellis & Ashbrook, 1989; Ucros, 1989). For both context-dependent and state-dependent recall, the interpretation is straightforward: The context or state of the individual provides yet another cue for recall. These phenomena make evolutionary sense because they tie the recall of information to situations and circumstances in which it is most likely to be useful.

Both context-dependent recall and state-dependent recall can be used to explain why long-forgotten memories can suddenly return. Environmental or emotional cues for recall, unencountered for years, may appear and allow access to the memories associated with them. Perhaps you have had the experience of a specific smell or song triggering a recollection of an event you had not thought about for decades. These types of recall suggest possible mechanisms for how long-repressed memories—if they exist—may surface after long periods.

■ **flashbulb memories**
highly vivid recollections of
emotionally charged events

Flashbulb memories.   Related to state-dependent recall are so-called **flashbulb memories,** highly vivid recollections of emotionally charged events (Brown & Kulik, 1977). A classic example is the circumstances in which one first heard that President John Kennedy was shot. Most people can describe in detail where they were and what they were doing when they head the news from Dallas. A less dated example is the circumstances in which one first heard that O. J. Simpson was acquitted of the murder charges against him.

Flashbulb memories were initially given special status and regarded by some theorists as an exception to the view that memories are constructed. Flashbulb memories seemed to be literal representations of actual experiences; their vividness and accuracy presumably derived from their unique emotional quality. Subsequent researchers are more skeptical, having shown that these memories change over time (Cohen, Conway, & Maylor, 1994). Also, the fact that they are often recounted to others needs to be considered in making sense of them: They may be remembered because they are frequently retrieved. The term *flashbulb* is probably misleading, and such memories, although vivid, obey the same principles as memories of more mundane events (Weaver, 1993).

Forgetting

Forgetting has many determinants. Three prominent theories of forgetting emphasize the roles played by decay of the memory over time, by interference from other memories, and by inadequate retrieval cues.

■ **decay**
forgetting due to the passage of
time

Decay of memories over time.   The term **decay** describes forgetting due to the passage of time. Strictly speaking, any information that fails to move from sensory memory to short-term memory can be described as having decayed, as can any information that fails to move from short-term memory to long-term memory. But decay is typically used to describe storage loss in long-term memory. Showing decay from long-term memory can be difficult because one must show that the memory is truly gone and not just unable to be retrieved. Still, decay from long-term memory is plausible, particularly when the memory has been retrieved infrequently and when a great deal of time has passed (Loftus & Loftus, 1980).

Interference from other memories.   The second explanation of forgetting proposes that our recall for material we have learned is affected by the presence of other material in memory. As already mentioned, Ebbinghaus (1885) first documented the role of interference in the recall of word lists. It can occur for other types of information as well, particularly in short-term memory. We have all had the experience of being introduced to a roomful of people and then being unable to remember a single name.

When previously acquired material gets in the way of remembering subsequent material, it is called **proactive interference.** Suppose you learn List A, then List B, and finally are tested for memory of List B. If the fact that you first memorized List A impairs your recall, this is due to proactive interference. When learning a new list makes it difficult to remember an old list, it is called **retroactive interference.** Here you learn List A, then List B, and finally are tested on List A. If your recall for List A is poor, then retroactive interference has occurred.

We can interpret interference in terms of competing associations among items in the lists. Interference is not an exotic phenomenon. Everyday life gives us plenty of examples, anytime we have a series of things to remember, like errands or phone messages. As students, you dread having several examinations on the same day, at least partly because interference hampers your performance. Or consider learning to drive cars with different types of manual transmissions. Proactive and retroactive interference can readily take place, as you shift (so to speak) from a four-speed to a five-speed model.

Retrieval failure.   Sometimes we fail to remember because we do not have the means to retrieve memories. Our cues are inadequate. This is called **retrieval failure.** For instance, several years ago I attended the twentieth-year reunion of my high school class. I had seen very few of my classmates over the years, and on my way to the reunion I tried to remember different friends and acquaintances who might attend. I was unsuccessful. However, once at the reunion, seeing my classmates with their name tags, I not only remembered everybody, but a number of other memories seemingly lost readily came to mind.

Chapter 13 will discuss a dramatic example of retrieval failure: psychogenic amnesia, in which extensive memory loss follows a traumatic event. A common interpretation of this form of amnesia is that memories are repressed to the degree that someone finds them painful. Psychogenic amnesia represents a problem with retrieval because the memories are stored but inaccessible. With time, most individuals recover their memory. Hypnosis, free association, and/or tranquilizing drugs can aid the process. When amnesia occurs due to physical damage or an injury to the brain, it is called organic amnesia (Chapter 6). Although some information lost in organic amnesia is due to the actual destruction of memories, other lost information represents a retrieval failure because memories are regained with the passage of time.

The Biological Basis of Memory

Studies of people with brain damage provide clues about where memory might be stored in the brain. As described in Chapter 4, researchers have noted relationships between lesions and memory deficits. The initial encoding of knowledge seems to take place in the limbic system, and long-term memories appear to be stored in the cortex (Murray & Mishkin, 1985; Squire & Ojemann, 1992). Researchers have begun to specify the actual changes that occur in the nervous system when something is learned (Chapter 8). We can suspect that there is no single biological basis for memory. Depending on the type of memory, the biological details probably differ (Krauz, Drosdov, Malyshev, & Tverdokhleb, 1988).

Currently of interest is the neurotransmitter **acetylcholine** (Hasselmo & Bower, 1993). Deficits in acetylcholine are related to memory problems of those suffering from Alzheimer's disease (Chapter 6). This fact implies that the forgetfulness of Alzheimer patients could be reduced if acetylcholine were increased (Coyle, Price, & Delong, 1983). Drugs that increase brain levels of this neurotransmitter have been developed and are being tested with these patients. Other researchers are looking at how these drugs

■ **proactive interference**
forgetting due to interference from previously acquired information

■ **retroactive interference**
forgetting due to interference from subsequently acquired information

■ **retrieval failure**
forgetting due to inadequate cues for retrieval

■ **acetylcholine**
neurotransmitter related to the memory problems of those suffering from Alzheimer's disease

"YOU SIMPLY ASSOCIATE EACH NUMBER WITH A WORD, SUCH AS 'TABLE' AND 3,476,029."

affect memory in laboratory animals, and the day may come when people can routinely strengthen their memories with similar drugs (McGuire, 1990; Olton & Raffaele, 1990).

Improving Memory

■ mnemonics
strategies and techniques used to improve memory

Until memory can be boosted with drugs, we must rely on psychological strategies and techniques to improve memory (Cook, 1989). These are sometimes called **mnemonics,** and a number of them have been described over the centuries (Patten, 1990). One type of mnemonic associates new information with something familiar. For example, the method of loci (*loci* means "places") dates to the ancient Greeks. Here the person thinks of a familiar scene, like the street on which he or she lives, and remembers items of information by placing them in the scene. A grocery list might result in a loaf of bread being placed on the corner, a gallon of milk being placed in the vacant lot, and a dozen eggs being placed on top of your neighbor's car.

More generally, people can use visual imagery to improve their memory. Let us say you have a list of words in a foreign language that you need to remember for an examination or for a trip abroad. Atkinson (1975) suggested that you come up with a visual association between the foreign word and its English equivalent. For instance, the French word for *sea* is *mer,* which sounds somewhat like our word *mare.* You might create a visual image of a horse galloping through the surf.

Those who use mnemonics show better recall than those who do not (Hill, Schwob, & Ottman, 1993), partly because interference is reduced or eliminated altogether (Patten, 1990). Mnemonics based on the first letters of the items are quite popular. ROY G BIV is a well-known acronym for remembering the order of colors in the visual spectrum: red, orange, yellow, green, blue, indigo, and violet (Chapter 5).

One of the rationales for advertising jingles is that a message set to music is better remembered than a message that is not, whether or not the listener wants to remember the message. Here we have an example of an imposed mnemonic. Jingles do not invariably improve recall (Yalch, 1991). It is important, for example, that the music be entwined with the message, not simply played in the background, where it can be distracting.

Let us not overlook the numerous external strategies that can serve as memory aids: lists, notes, timers, calendars, and so on (Harris, 1978). These approaches tend to be used more often than internal strategies, such as the method of loci. Though psychologists have not investigated external strategies nearly as much as internal strategies, the former serve the same purpose as the latter (Neisser, 1982).

Some researchers have compiled the findings of cognitive psychologists to suggest the optimal way of studying material so that recall is served. A representative approach is called the PQ4R method (Thomas & Robinson, 1972). The acronym comes from the suggested stages:

1. Preview the material to be remembered.
2. Make up questions about the material.
3. Read the material carefully.
4. Reflect on the material.
5. Recite the important points in the material.
6. Review the material in your mind.

This method and similar ones help students remember course material (Anderson, 1985). You might try using this method to study the chapters in this book. Can you see why the method works so well? It structures material in your memory and gives you multiple cues for its access.

Stop and Think

10 From the viewpoint of evolutionary psychology, why do echoes linger longer in sensory memory than icons?

11 What is a flashbulb memory?

12 Think of a mnemonic to help you remember the three stages of memory.

PROBLEM SOLVING

One important way in which people use knowledge is to solve problems. A **problem** is a discrepancy between what we know and what we want to know. When we solve a problem, we reduce this discrepancy. Many of life's demands can be thought of as problems to be solved (Cantor & Kihlstrom, 1987), although we may not typically think about them in these terms. Given that we know a great deal about most of the tasks we perform, we often solve the problems they pose quite readily. Thus, we overlook the fact that a problem confronted us in the first place.

Suppose we wake up and want coffee. The problem is how to get coffee, but we usually stumble along without difficulty to its solution. In the jargon of cognitive psychology, we have **strong methods** available for many problems; we know exactly how to proceed. When we do not know exactly how to proceed, we have only **weak methods** available. What happens if we find that our coffee maker is not working? We do not know exactly how to get coffee, but we have a few hunches. Maybe the next-door neighbor has brewed a pot. Maybe the convenience store down the street is open. These hunches represent weak methods for solving our problem because we cannot be certain they will provide a solution.

■ **problem**
discrepancy between what one knows and what one wants to know

■ **strong method**
approach to solving a problem that is obvious and explicit

■ **weak method**
approach to solving a problem that is neither obvious nor explicit

■ **problem-space**

cognitive representation of a problem: its initial state, its desired goal state, and the admissible operations or transformations that allow one to get from the one to the other

In solving a problem, a person must first represent it cognitively. This representation is called a **problem-space,** and it consists of an initial state (our broken coffee maker), a desired goal state (a cup of coffee), and the admissible operations or transformations that allow a person to get from the one to the other (visit our neighbor and/or drive to the corner 7-Eleven). The problem is solved when the initial state is transformed into the goal state.

Some problems are well defined, meaning that their initial states and goal states are clearly specified. How much money did you spend today? This question involves a well-defined problem because you know how to proceed: Add up your credit card receipts and check stubs. Other problems are ill defined because their problem-space is vague. Is your college major right for you? This question poses an ill-defined problem. It may not even be clear how you would recognize a solution. You have to decide what "right for you" means and then proceed to evaluate your major against this criterion.

Important in solving problems is our awareness of what we are doing. More formally, this is known as **metacognition:** awareness of oneself as a cognitive being. Someone skilled at metacognition knows what she knows and what she does not and can monitor ongoing cognitive processes (Flavell, 1979, 1981). Metacognition greatly aids in people's solutions of problems because they can direct their activities rather than just rely on trial and error.

■ **metacognition**

awareness of oneself as a cognitive being

Some of you may experience test anxiety, which means that you get worked up during a test, your mind goes blank, and you cannot think of answers that you know. Anxiety interferes with your metacognition. Your mind is not blank but, rather, filled with thoughts and feelings that keep you from monitoring your performance (Sarason, 1980). You may be worrying about your summer job, your date that evening, or whether your friend in the class will get a better grade than you; none of this helps you perform your best. There exist interventions that reduce test anxiety by instruction in appropriate metacognitive skills, such as how to devote attention to relevant tasks (Redding, 1990).

Metacognition refers to our awareness of our own cognitive processes. Metacognition can greatly aid the solution of problems because individuals can direct their thoughts in presumably profitable directions.

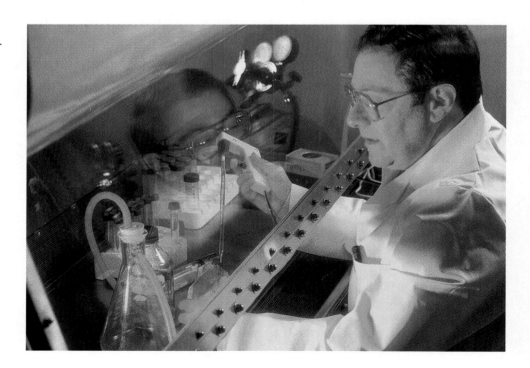

Problem Representation

The initial representation of a problem is critical in determining its solution. Pitfalls abound. For instance, a person might be distracted by irrelevant information. Consider the following problem:

> A man buys a horse for $10, then sells it for $20. The next day, he realizes that he wanted the horse after all, and so he buys it back for $30. After a while, he decides to sell it and does so for $40. What is the net profit or loss from this series of transactions?

Many people say that the man comes out even (Glucksberg, 1988). This answer is wrong, though, as you can see if you consider this problem:

> A man buys a horse for $10, then sells it for $20. The next day, he buys a cow for $30, and after a while, he sells it for $40. What is the net profit or loss from this series of transactions?

Here most people say correctly that the man comes out $20 ahead. Do you see that the two problems are identical in form? Those who answer the first incorrectly may have become distracted by the irrelevant fact that the same horse has gone back and forth several times. They have framed the problem wrongly, failing to separate the two transactions.

Functional fixedness refers to our persistence in representing problems in only one way, perhaps preventing an appropriate solution (Duncker, 1945). A well-known example is provided by the two-string problem (see Figure 9.8). Two strings hang from the ceiling of a room, far enough apart that a person cannot grasp both at once. However, the task of the research subject is to tie the two strings together. In the room are various objects, including a pair of pliers. One good solution is to tie the pliers to one string and then start to swing it like a pendulum. The subject holds on to the other string and grasps the swinging string when it comes within reach. Not all subjects arrive

■ **functional fixedness**
tendency to persist in representing problems in a particular way, perhaps preventing their solution

Figure 9.8
Two-String Problem. How can the person tie together the two strings hanging from the ceiling when he cannot grasp them both at the same time?

at this solution because they do not see that the pliers can be used to set the string in motion. Instead, they have fixed upon the typical function of the pliers, which is irrelevant to the problem at hand.

The narrative format frequently used to pose mathematical or scientific problems to beginning students creates functional fixedness because there are so many irrelevant aspects that the students might consider (Solomon, 1994). Students should be instructed to ignore certain features of these problems—it does not matter if the moving bodies in a physics exercise are baseballs, locomotives, or rockets—and to see the problem in terms of space, time, and motion. Or problems can be presented first in more abstract terms, without the distracting details, and only later generalized to baseballs, locomotives, and so on.

Problem Solution

In representing a problem, we have already begun to solve it. If a strong method is available, we use it and are done. Otherwise, we use one or more weak methods (Lesgold, 1988):

- Means-end analysis procedures that narrow the distance between the initial state of the problem and the desired goal state
- Working-forward procedures that begin with the initial state and transform it, in the hope of approaching the goal state
- Working-backward procedures that begin with the goal state and transform it, in the hope of approaching the initial state
- Generate-and-test procedures that create many possible transformations of the initial state, checking each in turn against the desired goal state

Remember your first day at college. You peered at a map, needing to get from the point marked "You are here" to the other side of campus. How could you solve the problem of getting across campus by each of these weak methods?

With means-end analysis, you might break the problem into parts and first get halfway across campus. Working forward, you trace a walkway on the map from where you stand to where you want to go. Working backward, you trace a path that begins with where you want to go. With the generate-and-test method, you walk in ever widening circles, hoping eventually to arrive at your intended destination.

Sometimes the transformations that are available to you guarantee a solution to the problem at hand. In this case, they are called **algorithms.** Suppose you are looking for a book of poetry on your shelf. If you start at one side of the shelf and deliberately read each title, you are bound to come across the volume you seek (so long as it is there).

Other times, though, we do not use transformations that guarantee a solution. Instead, we employ **heuristics,** cognitive shortcuts that often prove efficient and effective, though not always (Kahneman, Slovic, & Tversky, 1982). When I look for a book on my shelf, I usually start by remembering its color. I rapidly scan the volumes with that color, and I check those that pass the test. This strategy is a heuristic rather than an algorithm because it sometimes fails, even if the book I seek is on the shelf. Why? Because over the years, the colors of some of my books have faded. If the red book I want has turned into a pink one, then I cannot find it with this strategy. I must resort to the algorithm of reading each title.

In a series of intriguing studies, Daniel Kahneman and Amos Tversky (1973) showed that people frequently use heuristics to solve problems. Such basic cognitive processes as prediction, judgment, and categorization are based largely on cognitive shortcuts. These shortcuts frequently work, which is why our use of heuristics may go undetected. But Kahneman and Tversky devised problems that reveal their use.

Let us say you meet a fellow student. He is soft-spoken and wears glasses. He remarks that he does not like to be outdoors. Here is your task: Decide if this student is majoring in classics or psychology. You will probably choose classics, but if your college

■ algorithm
approach to solving a problem that guarantees a solution

■ heuristic
approach to solving a problem that is efficient but may or may not lead to a solution

Is this individual more likely to be a cheerleader, an athlete, an art student, or a psychology major? If you use the representativeness heuristic to answer this question, you will overlook the fact that these college "types" differ greatly in their frequency on campus.

is like most, you are likely to have made a mistake. You have not taken into account the fact that there are many more psychology majors than classics majors. In predicting what any given student is studying, you should take into account the relevant numbers in the student body as a whole. There are more soft-spoken, spectacled psychology majors who like to stay indoors than there are classics majors with these characteristics, simply because there are many more psychology majors.

People often ignore the numbers and base judgments only on the degree to which the particular case resembles a general class. In doing so, they are using what Kahneman and Tversky call the representativeness heuristic. Let us take a second look at our soft-spoken student. He resembles our prototype of a classics major. So, that is what we think him to be, despite the odds.

Another cognitive shortcut we may use in making judgments is the availability heuristic. People often judge the frequency of events in terms of the ease with which they can be brought to mind. Actual frequency determines ease of recall, and so this heuristic can prove accurate. But consider this question: Which type of word is more common in the English language, those that start with the letter *R* or those that have *R* as their third letter? Most people choose the first answer, even though the second one is correct. It is easier to think of words that begin with a particular letter than words that have that letter embedded within them. Here the availability heuristic leads us astray.

You know that a host of factors influence our recall, and all of them can influence judgments based on availability. For example, unusual occurrences often come readily to mind, and this phenomenon can bias people's judgments about the likelihood of those occurrences. Consider that people overestimate the chances of dying in a flood or tornado because these events tend to receive prominent coverage in the media; conversely, people underestimate the chances of dying from less memorable causes like diabetes and asthma (Fischhoff, 1988).

Improving Problem Solving

The ability to find successful solutions to life's tasks underlies productive thinking and is at the very heart of intelligence (Cantor & Kihlstrom, 1987). Is there something that we can do to improve our ability to solve problems? This question can be posed on two levels: specific and general. First, can we improve thinking with regard to given tasks? Here there is no doubt that practice leads to improvement. Experts differ from novices because they have spent thousands of hours performing the task of concern. Their experience leads to task-specific skills that let them better represent and solve problems (Lesgold, 1988).

People differ not only in terms of the content of their cognition but also in the ways they structure and use it (Chi, Feltovich, & Glaser, 1981). For instance, chess experts have been extensively investigated (Simon & Gilmartin, 1973). Relative to novices, masters look at chessboards in much more sophisticated ways. They do not see just a bunch of pieces. They see structured patterns and the moves these allow. Indeed, a master can recognize as many as 50,000 different configurations of pieces, and he or she can recall what should be done in response to each. Chess masters respond to the whole of the chessboard, whereas novices respond to parts.

Second, can we improve our general ability to solve problems of all types? Here there is disagreement. One of the traditional rationales for education is that it improves thinking. Although classes have a particular content, whether history or algebra, many educators hope that the skills developed from the study of one topic will generalize to other areas of life.

As far back as the ancient Greeks, people have believed that the "formal discipline" learned in the study of logic or mathematics has broad generality. Training in a specific field presumably makes us think more logically, and this enhanced thinking presumably pays dividends elsewhere. But there is reason for doubt. People taught to solve a specific type of problem may still be unable to solve a similar problem phrased in different terms.

Along these lines, individuals have great difficulty in seeing how the abstract rules of formal logic apply in concrete situations (Wason, 1966). People who can solve logic problems using abstract symbols might be unable to solve the identical problems phrased in terms of everyday life. If most people cannot apply the rules of logic, we cannot argue that formal discipline provides these rules.

Stop and Think

13 In problem-solving terms, describe the task of finding a summer job.

14 What is functional fixedness?

LANGUAGE

At one time, psychologists assumed that people's use of language was just another example of behavior. The behaviorist John Watson (1925) argued that we should study language in terms of how movements of the tongue and larynx produce it. B. F. Skinner (1957) continued this tradition in his book *Verbal Behavior,* in which he generalized from studies of animal learning to human language to conclude that people speak as they do because they have been reinforced for doing so. Here is how he explained someone learning to read:

> If a child responds cat in the presence of the marks CAT and not otherwise, he receives approval; if he responds dog in the presence of the marks DOG and not otherwise, he also receives approval, and so on. (p. 66)

This explanation seems reasonable as far as it goes, but it is in the "and so on" that a behaviorist interpretation of language falls apart. Let me explain the problems with this approach.

Chomsky's Linguistic Theory

In 1959, the linguist (and social activist) Noam Chomsky published a highly critical review of Skinner's book, in which he showed that language cannot be learned one word at a time, as operant conditioning theories propose. His major argument was that language is creative: Many of the sentences we speak and hear are completely novel, yet we have no trouble understanding what they convey. Skinner's approach, and others like his, cannot explain this important aspect of language (Andresen, 1991; Epstein, 1991; Pinker, 1994; Stemmer, 1990).

Chomsky (1957) proposed that language instead has a structure that must be acknowledged if we are to explain it. The surface structure of language refers to someone's actual utterances. In contrast, the deep structure of language refers to the underlying rules one possesses that generate language. By this view, we miss what is important about language if we focus only on the surface structure. Consider these two sentences:

1. Andrew threw the ball in the air.
2. The ball was thrown in the air by Andrew.

At the level of surface structure, these two sentences represent different utterances. But at the level of deep structure, they convey the same meaning. Sentences like these two are frequently confused in recall, implying that their cognitive representations are the same.

Most psychologists now generally accept Chomsky's belief that language has a structure and that its cognitive representation involves rules (Pinker, 1994). But they find several of his other claims controversial (Hacker, 1990; Schnitzer, 1990), including his theory of **transformational grammar.** This theory proposes that people create sentences by performing operations, called transformations, on underlying meanings represented in deep structure. The number of transformations is finite, and one or more is performed every time a sentence is uttered and every time an uttered sentence is comprehended.

For instance, the two sentences just described concerning Andrew and the thrown ball both have the same meaning and thus the same representation in deep structure. Each sentence comes about when the speaker transforms it from the underlying meaning; each sentence is comprehended when the listener transforms it back to the underlying meaning. Transformational grammar has had its share of criticism, not least of which is that theorists cannot agree on what the basic transformations might be.

Chomsky further believed that much of our capacity to acquire language is innate. He posited a neural mechanism dubbed a language acquisition device (LAD). It allows children to process the particular language to which they are exposed, abstract its rules, and then use them. Perhaps we should regard the hypothesized LAD not so much as an explanation of how language is acquired as a suggestion that the eventual explanation must take into account the nervous system as well as the environment.

■ **transformational grammar**
Chomsky's linguistic theory proposing that people create sentences by performing operations (transformations) on underlying meanings

Stages of Language Development

Chomsky's arguments are in principle statements about what language can and cannot be, not theories to be tested against research evidence (Lea, 1992). Developmental psychologists have studied children and how their capacity for language actually develops (Chapter 10). Observational studies have given us a chronology (see Table 9.5).

At about 4 months of age, infants begin babbling, repeating the same sounds over and over. Some of these syllables will later be used in the language the child learns to

Table 9.5 Stages of Language Development

Children pass through the following stages in learning to use language.

Approximate age	Accomplishment
4 months	Babbling: repeating the same sound over and over
9 months	Dropping sounds out of babbling repertoire not heard in the spoken language of others; using particular sounds in the same context
12 to 18 months	Using single words
18 to 24 months	Using two-word sentences
30 months	Using more complex sentences; rapidly expanding vocabulary

speak, but not all. Indeed, infants around the world babble in exactly the same way, implying that they are all born with the capacity to speak any language (Jakobson, 1968; Pinker, 1994; Rice, 1989). At about 9 months of age, the sounds that the child does not hear in the language spoken around her start to fall out of her babbling repertoire.

Also at 9 months, the child starts to use particular sounds in the same context. So, a child uses one expression (like *ooo*) to indicate pleasure and another expression (like *uhh*) to indicate displeasure. Some of these expressions are addressed to adults (like *dah*) when the child wants something done.

Infants around the world babble in exactly the same way. At 9 months of age, however, infants stop making sounds that they do not hear around them.

Actual words begin to appear between the ages of 12 and 18 months. Single words come first, usually accompanying some action. These tend to be words that are easy to pronounce, which is why children say *Dada* and *Mama* before they say *Father* or *Mother*. The child starts to comment on changes in the immediate environment, including the appearance of another person on the scene.

Language use consists of one word at a time until the child's vocabulary contains about 50 words, typically by the time she is between 18 and 24 months. Then 2-word sentences start to appear (Clark, 1978). These brief sentences, consisting of a noun and a verb, are called telegraphic speech because they are so compressed, but their meanings are usually clear to an adult listener:

- Daddy look.
- Want cookie.
- Kitty wet.

Language development is off and running for most children at 30 months of age. They add new words and longer sentences to their vocabulary daily. The word parents come to dread—*NO!*—becomes popular. The general trend is that the child's language becomes less tied to her immediate surroundings. The social uses of language are increasingly exploited.

A Critical Period for Language Development?

How does this remarkable transformation from a babbling baby into a fully verbal person take place? You already know Chomsky's answer to this question: human nature. So long as a young child is exposed to some form of language, her language ability will develop. Only in an extremely unusual case does this not take place.

In light of the information gleaned from unfortunate individuals raised in circumstances in which they are not exposed to language (Chapter 10), many psychologists believe that language acquisition occurs most readily during a critical period sometime between infancy and puberty, when the brain is ready to perform this function (Hurford, 1991; Johnson, Fabian, & Pascual-Leone, 1989; Lenneberg, 1967). As discussed in Chapter 4, specific areas of the brain are involved in language. Damage to these areas prior to puberty is not nearly as disruptive to one's use of language as is damage after puberty, suggesting that during the critical period of language development, one part of the brain can take over for another.

Additional evidence for a critical period is the fact that most adults find it more difficult to learn a foreign language than children do (Johnson & Newport, 1991; Wuillemin, Richardson, & Lynch, 1994). This latter finding is not limited to spoken languages; speakers of American Sign Language are more fluent when they have learned it during childhood as opposed to adulthood (Mayberry & Eichen, 1991).

Social Influences on Language Acquisition

Most parents spend a great deal of time talking to and with their children (Klink & Klink, 1990; Kuhl, Williams, Lacerda, Stevens, & Lindblom, 1992). One interesting result from studies of this process is that the typical parents do not give their children explicit instruction in grammar (Hirsch-Pasek, Treiman, & Schneiderman, 1984). When parents correct speech, it is often the content that is criticized, not the grammar (Brown & Hanlon, 1970). If a child says, "I eated the cookie," his father says, "No, that was a cracker." If the child then says, "I eated the cracker," then his father says, "Good!" Parents will provide the grammatically correct sentence for the child, but if the child is very young, he is not criticized for his poor grammar. These findings support Chomsky's argument that reinforcement cannot explain the whole of language use. Without ever being explicitly shaped, grammar eventually develops.

Children often imitate the speech of those around them. But they imitate only the grammatical forms they have already mastered. If the sentence to be mimicked is complicated, the child says it more simply (McNeill, 1966, p. 69):

> Mother: Say "nobody likes me."
> Child: Nobody don't like me.
> . . . [after eight repetitions of the above exchange]
> Mother: Listen carefully. . . "nobody likes me."
> Child: Oh! Nobody don't likes me.

Imitation is used by children to practice language that they have already acquired (Slobin, 1979).

Language Use by Apes

Although language is a cherished human ability, debate exists as to whether language is unique to human beings. Evolutionary theorists have attempted to specify the precursors of human language in the systems of communications used by animal species, such as facial expressions, gestures, songs, and other vocalizations (Burling, 1993; Gibson, 1994; Richman, 1993; Savage-Rumbaugh, 1990, 1993). Although agreement exists within this theoretical tradition that human language has evolutionary precursors, considerable debate surrounds what these might be and how they arose (Hewes, 1992).

As mentioned in Chapter 2, in the 1960s and 1970s, several independent research groups reported some success in teaching a small number of female apes to use language. Their reports make for fascinating reading and imply that the mechanisms responsible for language might exist across species.

For example, in June 1966, Allen and Beatrice Gardner began to teach the infant chimp Washoe how to use American Sign Language. Although she was wild-born, Washoe quickly adjusted to her many human companions, playmates, and instructors. She was exposed to a wide variety of objects together with their appropriate signs. Eventually, Washoe started to sign for the objects. After 4 years of instruction, she could make 132 signs: asking for objects, posing questions about them, and answering others (Gardner & Gardner, 1969).

As she grew older, Washoe began to talk about her likes and dislikes, just as human children do. She loved to be tickled, to pick flowers, to play with dolls, and to go for rides in a car. She hated to brush her teeth, and she found barking dogs frightening.

At about the same time, David Premack taught a 5-year-old chimp named Sarah to communicate. Instead of learning to sign, Sarah learned to read and write, using variously shaped and variously colored pieces of plastic, each representing a word. Beginning with the word *banana*, Premack rewarded Sarah with a real banana whenever she placed the plastic symbol on a large board. She was then introduced to new fruits and new plastic words. Before long, Sarah could carry on conversations using the symbols for 130 words, including *apple, dish, green, give,* and *take* (Premack & Premack, 1972).

Finally there is Koko, the first gorilla to be instructed in sign language. After 6 years of instruction, Francine Patterson (1978) reported that Koko had a working vocabulary of about 375 signs, including those for *belly button, airplane,* and *stethoscope*. With this many words at her fingertips, so to speak, Koko expressed a variety of likes and dislikes. For example, she preferred men to women, and corn on the cob to olives or radishes. Arguing, trading insults, and relaxing with a book were some of her favorite pastimes.

Skeptics argue that true language use by apes has not been demonstrated because Washoe, Sarah, Koko, and others do not show the spontaneity and creativity that human beings do when speaking. Perhaps the appropriate conclusion is simply that these special

Kanzai is a "talking" pygmy chimp who answers questions and makes requests by punching symbols on a computer keyboard.

animals learned to produce something like language that allows communication between them and us (Shanker, 1994; Terrace, 1985).

Stop and Think

15 Summarize Chomsky's criticism of behaviorist explanations of language.

16 How is language biopsychosocial?

COGNITION IN A BIOPSYCHOSOCIAL CONTEXT

Cognitive psychologists have often studied how people think by posing to them simple yet abstract tasks. However, some theorists worry that this sort of research may not generalize to everyday cognition. Much research in cognitive psychology depicts people as highly rational: logical, orderly, and unemotional processors of information (Gardner, 1985). As you well know, human cognition as it usually occurs is a mixture of rational and irrational processes (Epstein, 1992, 1994).

The term *quasi-rational* has been used to describe the mixture of rationality and irrationality that characterizes most cognition. We use cognition to adapt to situations, and it cannot be too far removed from the way things are. But because cognition is used in the service of our adaptation, it is carried out from our own point of view. It necessarily reflects our personal concerns, and it is entwined with our motives and emotions (Chapter 7). When cognition is studied in isolation from its context, researchers may end up with little to say about cognition as people actually use it. Some researchers have begun to contextualize cognition by asking how it differs across such social contrasts as gender. Here is what they have so far learned.

Gender and the Content of Thought

Research shows that the content of thinking by males and females varies. For example:

■ Males recall the details of a stereotypically masculine task, like how to follow directions to a place, better than females, who in turn better recall the details of a stereotypically feminine task, like what to buy at a store (Herrmann, Crawford, & Holdsworth, 1992).

■ Males are superior to females in remembering pictures of automobiles, and females are superior to males in remembering pictures of children (McKelvie, Standing, St. Jean, & Law, 1993).

■ After reading a story about a heterosexual encounter, males better recall the erotic details, and females better recall the romantic details (Geer & McGlone, 1990).

Results like these reflect more about socialization than about inherent differences in how information is represented and transformed (Kleinfeld & Nelson, 1991). Males and females are encouraged to think about certain topics rather than others, and so these results occur.

Gender and the Process of Thought

Mental retardation and learning disorders are much more likely to occur among males than females (American Psychiatric Association, 1994), perhaps because the nervous systems of males are more prone to injury. Also, men on average are superior to women in terms of spatial thinking. This difference may reflect an evolved psychological mechanism that arose to help men in their role as hunters (Eals & Silverman, 1994). Women on average are superior to men in terms of language skills and memory for the locations of objects. Again, this difference may be due to an evolved psychological mechanism that arose to help women in their roles as raisers of children and gatherers of food (Eals & Silverman, 1994).

Females are superior to males in recognizing odors (Lehrner, 1993). Remember from Chapter 5 that women on average have a more acute sense of smell than men do, and so their superiority in smell memory might derive from their greater sensory ability. Memory for odors appears to result from different biological and psychological mechanisms more than memory for other sorts of information does (Schab, 1991). It is nearly impossible for you to rehearse in your mind different smells, as you can readily do for words, faces, or physical movements. We usually remember smells only when we confront a particular odor and try to identify it. Smell memory, therefore, seems to have a here-and-now function—which makes evolutionary sense, for what is the survival advantage of being able to rehearse a smell?

Gender and Language

Researchers have also examined how males and females differ in their everyday use of language (Coates, 1992; Graddol & Swann, 1989). Their studies do not show that the underlying mechanisms of language are different, but they do reveal considerable variation in how men and women converse. One of the ways to make sense of this line of research is by remembering that women tend to occupy low-status roles in our society and thus need to act in more proper and self-effacing ways.

For example, women use a more grammatically correct version of language than men do. Women are more polite in their utterances, and men are more likely to use profanity. Women pay more compliments than men do, and they ask more questions. Men tend to phrase requests as direct commands ("Move over!"), whereas women tend to phrase them as suggestions ("Would you consider moving over?"). Women more frequently use phrases like "You know" or "Isn't it?" Linguists call these hedges and tag questions, respectively, and suggest that they convey tentativeness (Lakoff, 1975). Women more than men tend to raise their voices at the ends of sentences, turning them into questions even when they are not.

These sorts of differences are even more apparent when we focus on conversations between a male and a female. In contrast to stereotypes that women are more talkative, studies find that men usually talk more in these circumstances than women do. When women are speaking, men frequently interrupt them; women almost never interrupt men (Zimmerman & West, 1975). If conversations lag, women tend to get them going again, asking questions that the men then answer (Fishman, 1980). These conversational differences apparently appear early in life. For instance, observational studies of classroom discussions by schoolchildren have found that girls move them along, in particular enabling boys to participate; the reverse almost never occurs (Cheshire & Jenkins, 1991; Jenkins & Cheshire, 1990).

In this and previous chapters, discussion has focused on psychological processes such as sensation, perception, motivation, emotion, learning, and cognition. The next chapter describes the field of developmental psychology. Developmentalists maintain an interest in these sorts of psychological processes, but they also try to understand how they arise and change across the individual's life span.

SUMMARY

UNDERSTANDING COGNITION: DEFINITION AND EXPLANATION

- Memory is our mental representation of knowledge. Cognition encompasses the psychological processes that transform and retain this knowledge.
- With the rise of behaviorism, cognition ceased to be of central interest to many psychologists. However, the importance of cognition for a full explanation of human activity is undeniable, and by the 1960s cognition returned to a legitimate place within psychology.
- Many cognitive psychologists today conceive cognition in terms of information processing.

DOING *Cognition* RESEARCH

- Cognitive psychologists have available a host of research strategies that allow them to infer what and how a person is thinking. They assess the reaction times of subjects to tasks, the errors that are made, the course of development, the consequences of brain illness and injury, and what people say aloud while thinking. Researchers also simulate cognitive processes with computer programs.

COGNITIVE REPRESENTATIONS

- Various cognitive representations can be distinguished, and they differ in their degree of concreteness or abstractness.
- An image is a cognitive representation that resembles perception in some but not all ways.
- A linear ordering is a cognitive representation of elements that are structured in some order.
- One of the most important cognitive representations is the concept, the categorization of elements into a group. Concepts are represented in several ways: by simple enumeration, rules, properties, and propositional networks.
- A propositional network is a set of logical associations among words. One type of propositional network is called a schema, an organized set of beliefs about some concept.
- Artificial concepts are defined by necessary and sufficient characteristics. Many of the concepts people use in everyday life are not so defined and are called natural categories. These tend to be fuzzily defined, in terms of so-called family resemblances among their elements, prototypes (typical members), and/or remembered instances.
- Another way of representing the particulars of congition is with rules that allow these particulars to be generated as necessary. Such rules are collectively called a grammar, and language is one familiar example of a cognitive activity possible only because people have a representation of its underlying grammar.

MEMORY

- The process by which we put information into memory is called encoding. Once information is in memory, we speak of its storage. The process by which information is located in our memory and then used is called retrieval. Failure of memory is termed forgetting.
- Memory researchers distinguish among three different types of memory, although they disagree regarding whether these correspond to discrete stages in the encoding of information or simply to the degree to which information is transformed as it is remembered.
- Sensory memory briefly holds a relatively faithful version of our sensory experiences. Icons are visual

images that persist in the sensory memory after we see something; echoes are auditory images that persist after we hear something. Sensory memory is limited both in the amount of information it can hold and in how long it can hold this information.

■ From sensory memory, some information passes into short-term memory, where it is held for up to 20 seconds. Short-term memory is limited in the amount of information it can contain—about seven discrete items of information. However, the capacity of short-term memory can be greatly increased if we group disparate information into meaningful wholes, in a process known as chunking.

■ From short-term memory, some information passes into long-term memory. In long-term memory resides our entire storehouse of past experiences, our skills and abilities, and our identity and personality. Long-term memory can be divided into memory of episodes, meanings, and procedures. Regardless, information in long-term memory is abstract, elaborate, and organized.

■ There are two types of retrieval from long-term memory: recognition and recall.

■ In recognition, we decide if certain information presented to us looks familiar. Recognition memory is explained by proposing that we compare stimuli with our mental representations.

■ In recall, we retrieve information from memory without being provided with explicit clues. Recall memory is explained by the generate-and-recognize model, which proposes that we create possible answers to the memory task and then compare these answers with what is in our memory, as in recognition. The more ways we have to generate possible responses, the better our recall.

■ Forgetting has several explanations. One explanation stresses decay, the loss of memories over time. Another explanation emphasizes interference due to the presence of other material in memory. A third explanation points to inadequate retrieval clues.

■ Psychologists want to know how memory is stored in the brain. The as-yet-unidentified physical basis of memory has proved elusive. One current candidate is the particular chemical makeup of individual nerve cells and their tendencies to fire or not.

■ Memory can be improved through internal strategies, like the method of loci, or through external strategies, like lists or notes.

PROBLEM SOLVING

■ One of the important uses to which we put cognition is to solve problems. Most generally, a problem is a discrepancy between what we know and what we want to know.

■ To solve a problem, one must first represent it in terms of a starting point, a desired end state, and the admissible operations for getting from the beginning to the end. This representation is called a problem-space.

■ The initial representation of a problem is critical in determining its solution. Functional fixedness refers to our tendency to persist in representing problems in a particular way, perhaps precluding an appropriate solution.

■ Algorithms are procedures that guarantee a solution to a problem. Heuristics are procedures that sometimes lead to a solution to a problem and sometimes do not.

LANGUAGE

■ Although psychologists at one time treated language as verbal behavior controlled by reinforcement, Noam Chomsky's approach to language as having an underlying structure of meaning proved more compelling.

■ Language develops in regular patterns, from babbling to single words to sentences, under the influence of both biological and social factors.

COGNITION IN A BIOPSYCHOSOCIAL CONTEXT

■ Cognition is best approached in biopsychosocial terms, a conclusion supported by comparing the contents and processes of thought and language across the contrast of gender.

KEY TERMS

Development

The thought that anyone would treat a child as less than a precious gift is horrifying, yet cases of profound abuse directed against children by their own parents are reported with some frequency. Here is the story of a girl whom psychologists named Genie, after the creatures of myth who spend years cooped up in small bottles until called forth (Curtiss, 1977; Rymer, 1993). Although chilling, the case highlights important ideas about how people develop over their lives.

For the first 20 months of her life, Genie was fed poorly and mostly ignored. Then her father locked her in a room, where she stayed for more than a dozen years. During the day, she was strapped naked onto a potty-chair. At night, she was strapped into a crib. She saw almost no one. She never heard language. She was beaten for making the slightest noise.

At age 13, Genie was rescued and taken from her family. She was physically and psychologically retarded. She did not speak at all. She had never eaten solid food, and so she did not know how to chew. She swallowed only with great difficulty. She could not stand up straight. She could not run or jump. She salivated constantly. At the time of her rescue, Genie was described as "primitive, hardly human" (Curtiss, 1977, p. 9).

With extensive rehabilitation over a period of years, Genie became more socialized. She learned some language, self-control, and the basics of forming social relationships. She was never what the rest of the world considers normal, but her development—granted the cruelty of her early life—was miraculous.

It is difficult to hear Genie's story without puzzling over the motives of her father. He eventually committed suicide, leaving a note reading, "The world will never understand." We may also wonder why the rest of the family stood by while this outrage took place. Genie's mother was blind and in many ways a captive herself, although it was she who eventually fled with her child from the father.

UNDERSTANDING DEVELOPMENT: DEFINITION AND EXPLANATION

■ **development**
physical and psychological changes that take place throughout life

■ **maturation**
unfolding of biologically based processes of growth

Development includes all the physical, psychological, and social changes that take place throughout life, from conception to death. Development encompasses numerous influences above and beyond **maturation**—the unfolding of biologically based processes of growth. Also critical are learning and socialization. Nature and nurture

Development encompasses all the biological, psychological, and social changes that take place throughout life, from conception to death. Developmental psychologists seek to understand the roles played by maturation, learning, and socialization in the process of an infant becoming a child, a child an adolescent, and an adolescent an adult.

constantly interact in the course of development, as you saw in the case of Genie. The severe traumas she experienced early in life affected her physical development, which affected her psychological development, which affected how others treated her.

Ages and Stages: Describing the Times of One's Life

The end of adolescence was once considered the end of development. Adulthood was regarded as a period of great stability. Today, psychologists believe that people develop throughout adulthood, and so developmental psychology studies the entire life span.

In describing development, psychologists have found it useful to distinguish different periods of life. Table 10.1 specifies one way to describe these periods. Each is identified with an approximate age range. However, a person's chronological age measured in months or years—although convenient because of its objectivity—may not match his or her developmental age, when a particular characteristic is first demonstrated. For example, if most children walk at 1 year of age, a child of 9 months who walks has a developmental age of 1 year (with respect to walking).

Many developmental theorists have approached these distinctions as if they were discrete stages of life. The principles describing how people behave at each stage are thought to differ greatly. For example, infants think in altogether different ways from how children do, and children think in altogether different ways from how adolescents or adults do. Other theorists are not so convinced that development is best described in terms of discrete stages. Of course, changes occur throughout life, but in many cases they are gradual—quantitative rather than qualitative.

More generally, stage theories can be criticized because they ignore the larger settings that dictate the details of development. Even when the environment is on focus, theorists' and researchers' attention is often on rather immediate factors influencing development, such as the way in which parents encourage or discourage particular behaviors by their children. Many developmental psychologists prefer this close look, and it is appropriate granted their goals. However, we should not lose track of the larger context in which development occurs.

Development as Biopsychosocial

One of the assumptions made by most stage theorists is that changes in one area, such as physical development, are paralleled by changes in other areas, such as cognitive development and social development. These changes occur together because each reflects the specific stage in which the individual happens to be. Critics of stage theories propose instead that changes in one area of development directly influence changes in all of the other areas (see Figure 10.1).

Table 10.1 The Times of One's Life	
Here is one way that psychologists divide an individual's life.	
Period	**Important domain(s) of development**
Prenatal period (conception to birth)	Physical growth
Infancy (birth to 18 months)	Motor development; attachment
Early childhood (18 months to 6 years)	Language; gender identity
Late childhood (6 years to 13 years)	Cognitive development
Adolescence (13 years to 20 years)	Identity; independence; sexuality
Young adulthood (20 years to 40 years)	Career; family
Middle adulthood (40 years to 60 years)	Self-assessment
Later adulthood (60 years to death)	Retirement

Figure 10.1
Development as
Biopsychosocial.
Developmental psychologists
distinguish between areas of
development—such as physical
development, cognitive development, and social development—
but changes in one area mutually
influence changes in the other
areas throughout life.

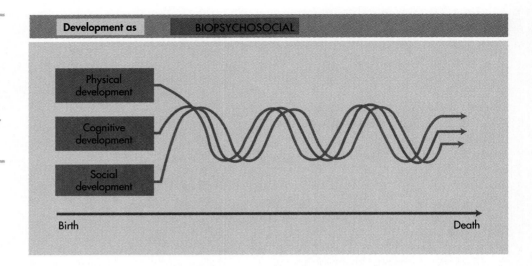

For example, consider that the mothers of attractive babies interact more with their infants than the mothers of unattractive babies do (Langlois, Ritter, Casey, & Sawin, 1995). From the moment of birth, attractive infants live in a different world from that of their less attractive peers. They will be given different opportunities and experiences. They will become different sorts of children, adolescents, and adults. What began as a simple physical difference among newborns ends up having widespread consequences for the psychological and social characteristics they eventually develop. This example illustrates the biopsychosocial nature of development and the constant interaction among its different influences.

Similar cascades can be set into motion by virtually any biological, psychological, or social contrast among individuals early in life, such as gender, ethnicity, socioeconomic class, physical skills, temperament, or intelligence (Berkowitz & Keller, 1994). None of these starting points is necessarily more basic than any other, and we must accord people's various characteristics equal weight in directing their subsequent development (Lerner & von Eye, 1992). See how this view of development goes beyond stage theories to capture the complex biopsychosocial mechanisms responsible for change.

It is impossible to discuss development without addressing the cultural and historical context in which it occurs. Consider these phenomena that profoundly shape who and what we are today:

- Single mothers
- Effective birth control
- Television and the mass culture it creates
- Universally required schooling
- Working mothers
- Mandatory retirement
- High divorce rate
- Life expectancy in excess of 70 years

Each is a relatively recent arrival on the historical scene yet exerts an enormous impact on the development of individuals.

For example, the availability of effective birth control means that people can delay being parents if they choose. Among some segments of our population, typical mothers and fathers are now older than they once were. They have greater economic resources available to them as they raise their children, but they also may have less energy. In any event, their children differ from those of younger parents. When the children of older parents themselves become adults, they can be faced with the prospect of caring for their now elderly parents at the same time as they are raising their own young children. These children in turn are less likely to be influenced by their grandparents.

Another example of how development must be placed in its historical context starts again with the availability of birth control and how it has led—in some segments of our population—to smaller families. Children today are less likely to grow up with brothers and sisters than children in generations past. This difference exerts an influence throughout life on their development.

Finally, consider that technology now makes it possible to know long before it is born whether a baby will be a male or a female. In contemporary China, where family size is strictly limited by law, parents often elect abortion when a baby will be a female. The inevitable effect of this decision, multiplied over many parents, is a generation in the making in which males outnumber females by at least 1 million per year (Tuljapurkar, Li, & Feldman, 1995). We can assume that most of the excess Chinese males will never have a spouse or a child of their own. What will the consequences be for China and for the entire world?

Critical in understanding the larger context of development are the societal institutions and practices that exist during an individual's life. These include marriage, school, and work, among many others. The effects of these institutions are widespread and ongoing throughout life. For instance, school-age children are affected by the particular educational practices of their society not just while attending school but before and after. And the effects of schooling are not narrowly academic and intellectual: All domains of development are affected by educational practices. This influence extends as well to the parents of students and indeed to everyone in society.

Stop and Think

1 What is the difference between developmental age and chronological age?

2 How is development biopsychosocial?

DOING *Developmental* RESEARCH

Studies of development are studies of change—which means that time is a more critical variable in developmental research than in most other areas of psychology. How do developmental researchers incorporate this variable into their studies? Two general strategies exist. The first involves **cross-sectional studies.** In these, individuals of different ages are simultaneously studied and then compared. The second strategy uses **longitudinal studies,** which follow the same individuals over a long period. Each strategy has its pros and cons.

Cross-Sectional Research

Suppose you are interested in the development of friendships among children. With a cross-sectional research strategy, you obtain subjects of differing ages and see how they make friends. You can plausibly argue that any differences you find across the age groups reflect development.

The chief virtue of cross-sectional research is its efficiency. The investigator does not have to wait for time to pass in order to draw conclusions about development. Furthermore, the investigator can often choose subjects of different ages who are highly comparable except, of course, for how old they are.

Nonetheless, cross-sectional research presents challenges. Confounds need to be avoided when recruiting subjects of various ages. Six-year-old children should not be chosen from a parochial school when 8-year-olds are chosen from a public school.

■ **cross-sectional study**
investigation that simultaneously compares individuals of different ages

■ **longitudinal study**
investigation that follows the same individuals over a considerable period of time

A cohort effect means that people born at different points in time may differ from each other by virtue of prevailing historical and social conditions. For example, think of the first Presidential election in which you were able to vote. The issues raised during this campaign may shape the way you regard politics for the rest of your life, and these of course often differ across elections.

■ **cohort effects**
differences among people that are due to prevailing historical and social conditions when they were born

Another concern in cross-sectional studies is that they might not reveal the full process underlying development but instead provide only snapshots of moments in time. Age comparisons might suggest processes, but they cannot prove them.

So, consider what developmental researchers refer to as **cohort effects,** the fact that people born at different points in time may differ from each other by virtue of historical and social conditions (Chapter 1). For example, in the contemporary United States, younger and older adults are less likely to have a substance abuse problem than middle-age adults are (Golub & Johnson, 1994). One might conclude that as people enter middle age, they are at increased risk for substance abuse, and that as they leave middle age, their risk is reduced. But these conclusions may not be correct. Middle-age adults today came of age during the 1960s, when drug use was at a peak in the United States. Their problems with substance abuse in middle age might be due to historical influences rather than developmental ones (Chapter 6). Their increased risk for substance abuse may be a cohort effect, and they may carry it with them throughout their lives.

Longitudinal Research

Longitudinal studies provide a more valid view of the process of development because they map out changes for an individual over time. Although only a handful of studies have lasted for decades, they give us invaluable information about development. Longitudinal studies help researchers distinguish developmental effects from cohort effects.

But like any research strategy, longitudinal studies have their own limitations. Chief among them is attrition: Research participants drop out for many reasons—losing interest, moving away, falling ill, or dying. Attrition in a longitudinal study cannot be fixed after the fact.

Longitudinal research is also constrained by the original choice of subjects, techniques, and questions. For example, the Harvard Study of Adult Development is an ongoing investigation that began in the late 1930s of several hundred Harvard students (Vaillant, 1993). There were no women students at Harvard in the 1930s, and so this study tells us about men only.

Finally, longitudinal studies are expensive and demanding to conduct. Often the major limiting resource for researchers is time. Even if they have the other means with which to conduct a longitudinal study, many investigators are reluctant to wait 20 or 30 years to see its outcome. Indeed, they might not be confident that they will even be alive at the end of the study they have begun (Chapter 2).

Developmental research therefore relies on both cross-sectional and longitudinal strategies. When findings from each approach agree, then psychologists have confidence in the conclusions that are suggested.

The rest of this chapter discusses development as it occurs in several areas of life: biological, psychological, and social. For convenience, developmental psychologists often focus on one specific area of development, but remember the earlier point that changes in one area are entwined with changes in others. Do not be misled by the separate discussions that follow.

Stop and Think

3 Why would a researcher use a cross-sectional strategy rather than a longitudinal strategy to study development?

4 What is a cohort effect?

PHYSICAL DEVELOPMENT

Physical development refers to processes of bodily change and growth throughout life. These changes are tremendous and obvious: Contrast infants, children, adolescents, and adults in terms of their physical characteristics and abilities. Although physical development clearly shows the role of biological mechanisms in development, keep in mind the bidirectional influence between biology and experience (Chapter 4). At least some aspects of physical development are the result of input from the environment. The case of Genie at the beginning of this chapter is an extreme but excellent example of how physical development can be influenced—in her case, for the worse—by what is going on in the environment.

■ **physical development**
processes of bodily change and growth in the developing individual

Prenatal Physical Development

Physical development begins at the moment of conception, when a male's sperm cell fertilizes a female's ovum, combining chromosomes from each parent into the particular genetic mix that serves as the individual's biological blueprint (Chapter 3). The drama of conception takes place on a microscopic stage. The ovum is smaller than the period that ends this sentence, yet it is much larger than the sperm, which is only 1/500 of an inch long.

A typical pregnancy, from conception to birth, lasts about nine months (see Figure 10.2). Following conception, the newly fertilized cell, called a **zygote,** rapidly divides and increases in size. The zygote attaches itself to the wall of the mother's uterus and from that point is referred to as an **embryo.** Further growth occurs. At the beginning of the third month following conception, the developing embryo, although not yet an inch long, has a recognizable face, arms, and legs—even fingers and toes. From this point until birth, it is termed a **fetus.**

At about 4 months, the fetus begins to move in ways that the mother can feel, as it kicks against her abdominal wall. These movements become smoother with further development. The fetus can make a fist, bend its wrist, open its mouth, and swallow. Male or female genitals take form. Characteristic fingerprints appear.

At about 6 months, the fetus develops the ability to breathe. So, a baby born as early as 23 or 24 weeks following conception has some chance of surviving. However, such

■ **zygote**
newly fertilized cell

■ **embryo**
developing unborn organism from about two weeks to two months after conception

■ **fetus**
developing unborn child from about the third month after conception until birth

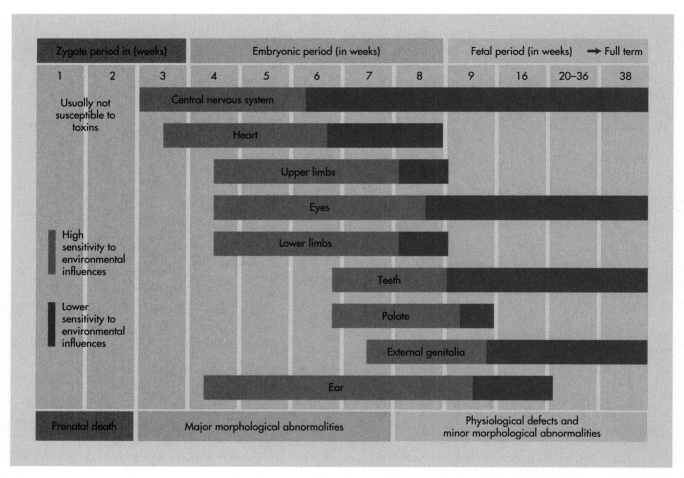

Figure 10.2
Prenatal Development. This graph shows the progression from zygote to embryo to fetus during the first 38 weeks following conception.

extremely premature infants weigh little more than one pound and often have immature lungs and digestive systems, all of which work against their survival.

The mother's uterus is quite literally the environment for the developing embryo/fetus. Changes in the uterus therefore affect its development. Although the uterus protects the fetus from harm, a variety of factors can be disruptive. Depending on the particular factor and when it occurs during pregnancy, different consequences may follow.

Maternal malnutrition, for example, can result in a child that is small, weak, and susceptible to disease (Pollitt, 1994; Ricciuti, 1993). So too can smoking. Maternal drug use or alcohol consumption greatly increases the chances of a stillborn child or one with serious physical deformities. Fetal alcohol syndrome refers to a complex of characteristics seen in the children of alcoholic mothers: small size, mental retardation, distinctive facial features, and a variety of heart and limb defects (Hankin, 1994; Streissguth, 1994). Even occasional drinking during pregnancy can cause damage because the liver of the fetus is not effective at breaking down alcohol.

Sex Differences

In the sixth week following conception, males and females start to follow different biological courses because of the effects of sex hormones on the developing embryo. The basic model of the human embryo is a female, and only when testosterone is added does the embryo develop the physical characteristics of a male. So, a chromosomally male individual will develop as a female in the absence of testosterone (Money & Ehrhardt, 1972).

Although the distinctions between males and females seem simple, they are quite complicated. Male and female are fuzzy categories (Chapter 9), and these terms are used to encompass a number of specific contrasts: physical, psychological, and social. Physical differences between males and females are often called **sex differences.** So, chromosomes determine a person's sex. All eggs have an X chromosome. Biological sex is determined by whether the egg is fertilized by a sperm cell carrying an X chromosome or one carrying a Y chromosome. Males have one X chromosome and one Y chromosome (XY). Females have two X chromosomes (XX). Another contrast involves sex glands. Males have testes, which produce sperm cells. Females have ovaries, which produce eggs. Yet one more contrast concerns sex organs. Males have penises. Females have vaginas.

■ **sex differences**
physical differences between males and females

Throughout much of childhood, girls and boys are about the same height and weight. With adolescence, this similarity changes, so that males on average are larger than females. Males and females enter adulthood with marked physical differences in size, shape, and strength. They have different endocrine systems, and any behavior influenced by their hormones may reflect a biological difference between males and females (Chapter 4).

Not all of the differences between males and females have an inherent biological basis. Parents respond differently to sons and daughters, from birth on (Berk, 1989). For instance, parents perceive their sons as alert, strong, and hardy and their daughters as soft, weak, and delicate even when there are no objective differences (Condry & Condry, 1976; Rubin, Provenzano, & Luria, 1974; Stern & Karraker, 1989; Vogel, Lake, Evans, & Karraker, 1991). Parents also play more roughly with sons than daughters (Yogman, 1981). They interrupt their daughters but let their sons finish sentences (Greif, 1979). Accordingly, males and females develop within different social environments, and they learn to be different types of people.

The Newborn's Reflexes

Newborns enter the world with a considerable range of **reflexes:** automatic, coordinated responses to external stimuli (Chapters 4 and 8). These reflexes aid survival and can be regarded as evolved psychological mechanisms. Consider the following examples, just some of the reflexes present early in life.

■ **reflex**
automatic, coordinated response to an external stimulus

Throughout childhood, girls and boys are about the same height and weight. With puberty, this similarity changes, so that males on the average become larger than females.

The rooting reflex is the tendency of the newborn to turn his mouth toward whatever touches his cheek. This reflex helps the newborn find his mother's breast to be fed. When something touches the infant's lips, the sucking reflex is triggered. So, once mother's breast is found, the infant automatically begins to nurse.

The grasping reflex leads the child to grab onto anything that touches his palm. This reflex is so strong that the infant can literally suspend his own weight for a brief time. Some speculate that this reflex can be traced to the time when our distant ancestors lived in trees and the ability to hang on for dear life proved useful.

The Moro reflex refers to the child's reaction to loud noises or the sudden loss of physical support. She throws her arms and legs outward. She spreads her fingers. Then she clenches her fists and pulls her arms and legs back together. Again, the survival value of this reflex is clear: It leads the child, when threatened, to grab a nearby parent.

Infants make use of these reflexes early in their lives, and then they disappear. The ones just described go away after three or four months. If a newborn lacks one or more of them, there may be something wrong with his or her neurological development, and pediatricians routinely test for them (Majnemer, Brownstein, Kadanoff, & Shevell, 1992). In some cases of injury or illness among adults, these basic reflexes can reappear, again indicating neurological problems, such as Alzheimer's disease (Franssen, Kluger, Torossian, & Reisberg, 1993; Gasquoine, 1993).

Growth and Motor Development

"My, haven't you grown!" Every child gets sick of hearing this from relatives because they say it so often. But growing is one of the most obvious things children do. Here are a few generalizations about physical growth:

■ Growth occurs at a greater rate earlier in life, although there is a spurt in adolescence.
■ The proportions of the body change as well as its overall size; after the first year of life, the head becomes proportionately smaller, whereas the limbs become longer (see Figure 10.3).
■ Growth is influenced by genetic factors, but such environmental influences as poor nutrition, disease, and neglect can reduce both the rate of growth and its overall attainment.

■ **motor development**
processes of change in the skill with which the body is used

Not only does the child's body become bigger, but he or she becomes more skilled at using it. This process is called **motor development** and reflects the interplay of environ-

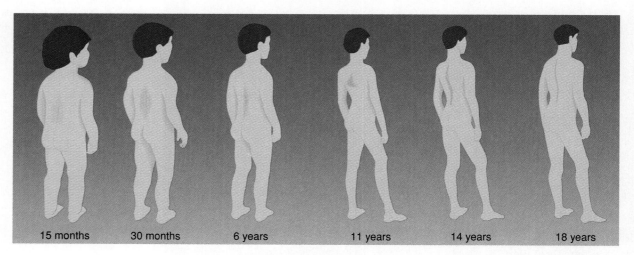

| 15 months | 30 months | 6 years | 11 years | 14 years | 18 years |

Figure 10.3
Body Proportions across the Life Span. Note that as the child grows, the head becomes relatively smaller and the legs become relatively longer.

mental and biological factors. The child's nervous system must mature, and practice is needed to perfect movements. The overall process of motor development can be described as the ongoing differentiation of physical skills followed by their reorganization.

At birth, the nervous system is not fully formed. Not all nerve fibers are covered by myelin, and so infants cannot yet move all parts of their bodies skillfully (Chapter 4). With myelination, children show a progression of movements they can control: first movement of the head and neck, then the shoulders, then the elbows and knees, and finally the fingers and toes. Motor development also proceeds from large actions like waving to small actions like picking up Cheerios.

At what ages do babies show particular motor skills? Research documents striking variability, perhaps as a result of differences in nutrition and stimulation, which can vary across cohorts. Less controversial is the sequence in which different skills are mastered, and Figure 10.4 shows when some important abilities—on average—first appear.

Adolescent Physical Development

The word **puberty** comes from a Latin word meaning "to grow hair" and refers to the physical changes that accompany adolescence. These changes are of several types. Primary sexual characteristics are those related to reproduction: Testes and ovaries mature, so that males can father children and females can bear them.

In females, the first menstruation is called the menarche. Menarche is treated as a special event in many cultures, but in our society we often surround it with secrecy, so that a young female may be taken by surprise when she first begins to menstruate. Males do not have so dramatic a transition into physical adulthood, although the first ejaculation is a notable event.

With the onset of puberty, secondary sexual characteristics also start to develop—for example, facial hair for males, breasts for females. As already mentioned, there occurs a growth spurt and increased height and weight. Body composition changes—an adolescent fills out. Strength and endurance increase. The voice changes, more so for males than females. It is not just the absolute magnitude of these changes that makes puberty a striking process. It is also the rate at which these changes take place. For instance, adolescent males on average grow three to five inches in height during the first year of their growth spurt.

At present, the physical changes that mark puberty start to occur around age ten or eleven for females and around age eleven or twelve for males. These ages are lower than 100 years ago, and we can attribute this cohort effect to improved nutrition (Gilger, Geary, & Eisele, 1991). What you should note about the earlier onset of puberty is that it is not necessarily matched by a speeding up of development in psychological and social areas. Young teenagers are capable of having their own children—and sometimes do—but may be poorly equipped in a psychological or social sense to raise them.

I was told a story by a friend who was involved in a charitable program that gave holiday presents to the children of poor mothers, some of whom were barely in their teens. The program was not a great success because a few of the mothers wanted toys and dolls for themselves. They were jealous of the attention given to their own infants. Here we have a striking example of how development in different areas does not always occur in synchrony.

Adult Physical Development

Physical development does not end with the beginning of adulthood. Our physical body continues to develop, eventually changing over time for the worse. People vary greatly in the rate at which they show these declines, but as described in Chapter 3, they eventually occur for everyone. One of the most pervasive changes with age is the speed with which we do things (Gottsdanker, 1982). On average, older people take longer to perform most behaviors: walking, talking, and making decisions. We do not know at

■ **puberty**
physical changes that accompany adolescence

Milestones of Motor Development in the First Two Years

Age	Locomotor skills	Nonlocomotor skills	Manipulative skills
1 month	stepping reflex	lifts head slightly; follows slowly moving objects with eyes	holds object if placed in hand
2–3 months		Lifts head up to 90 degrees when lying on stomach	begins to swipe at objects in sight
4–6 months	rolls over; sits with some support; moves on hands and knees ("creeps")	holds head erect in sitting position	reaches for and grasps objects
7–9 months	sits without support; crawls		transfers objects from one hand to the other
10–12 months	pulls himself to standing; walks grasping furniture ("cruising"); then walks without help	squats and stoops	some signs of hand preference; grasps a spoon across palm but has poor aim of food to mouth
13–18 months	walks backward and sideways; runs (14–20 months)	rolls ball to adult	stacks two blocks; puts objects into small containers and dumps them

Source: Frankenburg & Dodds (1967).

Figure 10.4

Sequence of Motor Development. Although there is considerable variation in the ages at which different children can perform various behaviors, the sequence in which these behaviors occur is the same.

During puberty, secondary sexual characteristics develop. In addition to growing facial hair, adolescent males often show a pronounced growth spurt.

present the mechanisms responsible for the slowing down of behavior. Changes in sensory acuity or the speed of neural conduction have been ruled out as explanations.

Biological, psychological, and social factors all play a role in determining the rate and extent of physical changes in adulthood, just as they do at earlier points in life. Life expectancy has increased for those in the United States throughout the twentieth century (see Figure 10.5), meaning that the population as a whole is older than it once was. This phenomenon in turn affects the development of everyone, not just older individuals. Consider that parents, teachers, and government officials are—on average—older than was once typical. Even rock-and-roll performers are older! Younger adults may have to wait longer than they once did to take on valued occupational roles (Chapter 17). Ponder the implications of this lengthy waiting period. The point made

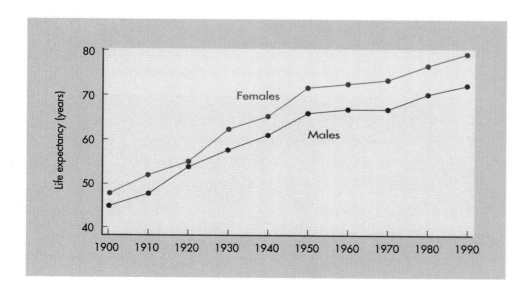

Figure 10.5
Life Expectancy in the United States. Throughout the twentieth century, the life expectancy of Americans has increased, with implications for all areas of development.
Source: U.S. Department of Commerce (1995).

**Figure 10.6
Temperament as
Biopsychosocial.** Temperament
is a biologically based style that is
heritable, but its effect on behavior depends on how those in the
social environment, such as caretakers, respond to this style.

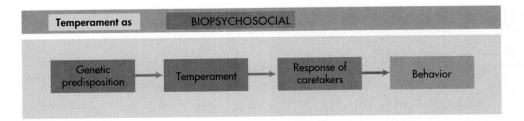

earlier about cascades of influences set into motion by changes in one area of development is underscored by the example of our aging population.

Physical Development as Biopsychosocial: The Example of Temperament

Let me close this section by discussing one more aspect of physical development that shows the importance of a biopsychosocial approach. **Temperament** is an infant's style of interacting with the world. The key word is *style*, which refers not to what an infant does but to the way he or she goes about it. Psychologists have distinguished several dimensions of temperament, including emotionality, activity, and sociability (Buss & Plomin, 1975, 1984). These dimensions are reflected in the frequency of relevant behaviors, their intensity, and/or their duration. Consider emotionality. One child cries frequently, loudly, and endlessly. Another child cries rarely, softly, and briefly. The former child would be regarded as emotional, and the latter as placid.

The components of temperament are heritable, a conclusion that follows from twin studies comparing the resemblance of identical and fraternal twins (McCall, 1990; Prior, 1992; Segal, 1990). On a theoretical level, this means that temperament is based in biology and thus an aspect of physical development. On a practical level, this finding helps us understand why newborns differ. So-called difficult babies may be predisposed to be emotional.

In any event, an infant's temperament affects how caretakers respond, and their response in turn affects subsequent development (Bezirganian & Cohen, 1992; Kagan, Reznick, & Gibbons, 1989; Pridham, Chang, & Chiu, 1994). Consider a child who is temperamentally active (Thomas & Chess, 1977). In an urban environment, her high activity level leads her into danger, as she darts among cars on busy streets. Here her parents worry about her and respond with severe prohibitions and punishments, which in turn affect the woman she will be. Perhaps she will end up cautious and resentful. But suppose this same child and her boundless energy are placed in a rural environment. Her temperament does not court danger, and her parents encourage her to explore the world. She becomes a bold and confident adult. The eventual effect of temperament on an individual's behavior can be understood only in terms of the larger context of this person's life, including the temperaments of his or her parents (see Figure 10.6).

■ **temperament**
biologically based style of behaving

Stop and Think

5 At what point after conception can we speak of behavior first appearing?

6 What is meant by "The basic model of the human embryo is a female"?

7 How is the Moro reflex an evolved psychological mechanism?

8 What role does myelin play in motor development?

9 What are the developmental implications of increasing life expectancy in the United States during the twentieth century?

10 What is temperament?

COGNITIVE DEVELOPMENT

One of the most important areas of psychological development is how the processes of gaining knowledge change across the life span. These changes are described as **cognitive development,** and they include changes in sensation, perception, learning, memory, problem solving, language, and intelligence. Many of these changes have been described already, in previous chapters.

■ **cognitive development**
processes of change in how knowledge is gained and used

At the basis of cognitive development are evolved psychological mechanisms that allow the individual to attain optimal ways of thinking. Human beings differ markedly from other creatures in terms of how long it takes them to become adults. Some theorists have speculated that people's lengthy childhood was favored by natural selection as a way to allow cognitive complexity to develop (Slama-Cazacu, 1992). In general, species with a relatively long versus relatively short childhood differ in terms of their cognitive capacity (Chapter 8).

The major theorist in cognitive development has been Jean Piaget (1896–1980), a native of Switzerland. Originally trained as a biologist, Piaget turned to the study of how children think about the world. Through observation and questioning of children, Piaget (1926, 1928, 1929, 1932, 1950) devised a theory of cognitive development, proposing that thinking develops in an orderly way through stages that build upon one another. The principles underlying thought develop, and so younger children think differently from the way in which older children or adults do. This section discusses first Piaget's theory and then criticisms of it, and finally cognitive changes during adulthood.

Piaget's Theory

Like the cognitive theorists discussed in Chapter 9, Piaget was concerned with both mental representations and mental processes. He provided careful descriptions of how these change over time and proposed an influential theory to make sense of these changes. In his theory, Piaget introduced several important concepts now employed by all theorists in this area.

Piaget used the term **scheme** to refer to any mental structure that represents knowledge. A scheme can be as simple as the sucking reflex or as complex as language. Another important Piagetian concept is the **operation:** one or more mental processes used to transform and manipulate information. For example, addition and subtraction are operations that make arithmetic possible. According to Piaget, the key changes in cognitive development involve the child's available operations. These operations become more complex, more adaptive, and more independent of immediate stimuli. Cognitive development moves toward increasing abstractness. Earlier operations provide the foundation on which later operations are built.

■ **scheme**
mental structure that represents knowledge

■ **operation**
mental process used to transform and manipulate information

Although cognitive development is predisposed by our biology and reflects the maturation of the nervous system, changes can take place only through interaction with the world and the organization of information. Piaget distinguished two general processes for handling new information. In **assimilation,** people modify or change new information to fit what they already know. In **accommodation,** people change what they know in order to fit the information. Suppose a young child goes to a zoo and sees a camel for the first time (Berk, 1989). She might call it a horse, assimilating the camel to a scheme she already has—that of a horse. Or she might call the camel a lumpy horse and accommodate her scheme to what she sees, recognizing that horses come in two varieties—regular and lumpy. Assimilation and accommodation continually interact in the course of cognitive development.

■ **assimilation**
modification of new information to fit what is already known

■ **accommodation**
modification of what is already known to fit new information

According to Piaget, cognitive structures develop through four separate stages. Although the exact times at which children enter or leave a given stage differ, the sequence is thought to be the same for everyone. A problem at one stage prevents the child from moving to the next stage. Genie, for example, when first rescued from her home, was as cognitively advanced as a typical infant of 15 months. She made rapid progress in learning language until she attained the level of a typical child of 6 years, at which point her cognitive development simply stopped. In Piaget's terms, the necessary schemes for further development did not develop. Genie's vocabulary was more advanced than her grammar, implying that different operations are involved for each and that those responsible for vocabulary were able to develop more than those responsible for grammar.

Sensorimotor stage.

■ **sensorimotor stage**
Piaget's first stage of cognitive development, from birth to about age 2, characterized by advances in motor development and object permanence

The **sensorimotor stage** occurs from birth to about age 2. Advances in the child's motor development allow him to explore his environment. He hits, shakes, touches, and tastes whatever he encounters. These sensory and motor activities create a scheme. They exemplify accommodation because the child thereby learns which of his actions are under his willful control and which are not (Mandler, 1992).

■ **object permanence**
knowledge that objects exist even when out of sight

During the sensorimotor stage, the notion of **object permanence** develops: the knowledge that objects exist even when out of sight (Soubbotskiy, 1987). Suppose an infant is propped up so that she can see an interesting object in the researcher's hand. The researcher moves her hand, and the child's eyes follow along. What happens if the researcher's hand moves behind a screen, so that the infant can no longer see the object? In the first few months of life, once the hand and the object it holds are out of sight, the child does not look for its reappearance. She acts as if the object does not exist anymore. An older infant continues to turn her head, expecting the object to appear on the other side of the screen. Piaget argued from such findings that the child must develop the idea that things continue to exist when they cannot be seen.

Preoperational stage.

■ **preoperational stage**
Piaget's second stage of cognitive development, from ages 2 to 6, characterized by symbolic thinking and egocentrism

The cognitive skills acquired during the sensorimotor stage make possible further development. The **preoperational stage** takes place between ages 2 and 6. The paramount cognitive achievement during this stage is the beginning of symbolic thinking. Consider these behaviors, which appear at this time:

- Making believe that one object is another
- Pretending to be Mother or Father
- Starting to draw, intentionally representing objects on paper
- Reporting the occurrence of dreams
- Using language

With the ability to represent the world in symbolic terms, the child has at her disposal a host of new cognitive skills.

Object permanence is an achievement of cognitive development that allows the child to understand that objects exist when out of sight.

At the same time, the child at this stage does not think exactly like an adult. Children are **egocentric,** meaning that they see things only from their own point of view. Consider a classic demonstration devised by Piaget. Children are shown a model of a mountain on a table, and are asked to walk around and inspect it from all sides. Then the children are seated on one side of the mountain, and a doll is placed on the opposite side. They are asked how the mountain looks to the doll. Early on, they do not appreciate that the doll would see things differently; they believe that the doll sees the mountain as if from their own perspective. Toward the end of this stage, children understand that the doll would see the mountain differently, but they remain unable to specify how (Suzuki, 1993).

Egocentrism occurs in other ways (Matthys, Cohen-Kettenis, & Berkhout, 1994). If a child is asked what his mother or father might like for a present, the child will probably suggest something he himself would like, such as a toy or a cookie. The child is not being selfish; he simply cannot grasp a perspective that is not his own.

Piaget characterized the child's thinking during the preoperational stage as prelogical. Children do not recognize cause-and-effect links between events, or they misunderstand them (Piaget & Inhelder, 1969). Children also display **animism,** believing that inanimate objects are living beings with intentions, consciousness, and feelings (Poulin-Dubois & Heroux, 1994). Why do clouds drift slowly through the air? A child in the preoperational stage might explain that clouds do not have legs and thus must move ever so slowly, like a worm. Animism is an example of egocentrism because the child assumes that everything in the world must be alive like she is.

Concrete operations stage. During the **concrete operations stage,** which begins at about age 7 and lasts until about age 11, the child's thinking becomes more logical and integrated. He can now think of objects along more than one dimension at a time. He learns that they can be transformed or manipulated in one way without being changed in other ways.

Piaget studied a variety of examples of what is called **conservation:** the recognition that characteristics of objects or substances, such as number, length, mass, area, and volume, stay the same even if their appearance changes (Markovits, 1993). For instance, a child can be shown a tall thin glass filled with milk. The same milk is then poured into a short wide glass. Which glass holds more milk? "The tall one," says the preoperational child because the level of milk is higher. Or a child might be shown a plate on which five cookies are bunched closely together. The researcher then spreads them out. Which plate has more cookies? "The second," because here the cookies occupy more space.

The ability to conserve means that the child can undertake mental operations that are reversible. Therefore, the child in the concrete operations stage recognizes that the milk poured into different glasses is the same and that cookies spread around a plate remain the same. Logic becomes possible, and so does complex problem solving (Chapter 9).

Formal operations stage. The final stage of cognitive development appears about age 12 and is called the **formal operations stage** (see Table 10.2); the child's mental processes can now operate in the abstract (Díaz-Barriga, 1987). The adolescent can pose and answer hypothetical questions. Weighty topics such as the self, love, art, friendship, justice, and the meaning of life occupy the adolescent, able to think about these matters for the first time. The world is viewed not just as it is but as it might be . . . or should be . . . or cannot be. The young adolescent brings these cognitive skills to bear on other domains of development. To return to the earlier example of young teenagers having children, consider what happens when someone has the physical ability to becomes a parent before the stage of formal operations begins. The person may be unable to make decisions based on likely long-term consequences (Holmbeck, Crossman, Wandrei, & Gasiewski, 1994).

■ **egocentrism**
ability to see things only from one's own point of view

■ **animism**
belief that inanimate objects are living beings

■ **concrete operations stage**
Piaget's third stage of cognitive development, from ages 7 to about 11, characterized by an understanding of conservation

■ **conservation**
recognition that characteristics of objects or substances can stay the same even if their appearance changes

■ **formal operations stage**
Piaget's final stage of cognitive development, from age 11 through adulthood, characterized by the ability to think abstractly

Table 10.2   Summary: Piaget's Stages of Cognitive Development

According to Piaget, children's thinking can be described in terms of four separate stages through which they pass in a fixed order.

Stage	Characterization
Sensorimotor (birth to age 2)	Children explore the environment and build up schemes; they develop the concept of object permanence.
Preoperational (ages 2 to 6)	Children think symbolically; they show egocentrism.
Concrete operations (ages 7 to 11)	Children think logically and coherently; they develop the ability to think of objects along more than one dimension at a time.
Formal operations (ages 12 and older)	Children think abstractly; they can pose and answer hypothetical questions.

Criticisms of Piaget's Approach

Although Piaget's writings on cognitive development stimulated a great deal of interest, many challenges have appeared that question his approach (Halford, 1989; Siegel, 1993). One criticism is that he relied too much on verbal inquiries. Not everything that someone knows can be put into words, and this is particularly true for young children. Schemes may exist that go undetected in verbal inquiry.

It has also been charged that Piaget's theory hinges on the particular tasks he posed for the children in his studies (Bryant, 1989), and it places great emphasis on what children at a given age cannot do (Strauss, 1989). It is hazardous to say "never" in science, for there is always the chance that another researcher can devise a procedure showing that a given accomplishment by a child is possible earlier than thought. Indeed, if the appropriate task is used, achievements like object permanence or conservation can be demonstrated much earlier than Piaget thought (Bruner, 1964). Specific training helps children acquire skills earlier than he believed possible (Brainerd, 1978; Larivee, Longeot, & Normandeau, 1989). Gelman (1969), for instance, demonstrated that children could be taught conservation if they were instructed that certain cues were irrelevant to the task posed to them.

According to some researchers, only about half of adults tested appear to have achieved Piaget's final stage of formal operations in which one is interested in abstract topics such as the meaning of life, love, and art.

Such studies lead to another criticism—namely, the stages do not separate themselves as neatly as Piaget proposed (Bidell & Fischer, 1989; Brainerd, 1978). If the skills reflecting concrete operations are apparent for a particular child on some tasks but not others, we cannot argue that these skills represent discrete stages (Gelman & Baillargeon, 1983).

There is one more problem with Piaget's theorizing. According to some researchers, only about half the adults tested appear to have achieved Piaget's final stage of formal operations (Neimark, 1982). This finding is, of course, problematic because common sense tells us that most adults can think in abstract and hypothetical terms. That adults sometimes show formal operations thinking and sometimes do not again demonstrates that Piaget's stages are not as rigidly defined as he implied. Some topics are easier to think about abstractly than others (Chapter 9)—which means that an individual's "stage" of cognitive development needs to be described in terms of the specific contents of thought.

Where does this leave us? Piaget remains an important figure because he first drew psychology's attention to the fact that the ways and means of an individual's cognition can and do change. Research suggests that changes in children's brains during development roughly parallel changes in their level of cognitive development (Fischer, 1987). None of the contemporary criticisms of Piaget's work questions the general trend from concrete thinking to increasing complexity and abstractness. However, the details of his approach, particularly regarding stages, need to be revised.

Cognitive Changes in Adulthood

Piaget's theorizing stopped with adolescence, but cognitive development continues throughout adulthood. Many of these changes are for the better because adults continue not only to acquire new information but also to learn new skills for transforming and applying it. For example, thinking becomes more integrative throughout one's adult life, subsuming larger chunks of information within typical categories of thought (Devolder & Pressley, 1989; Kramer & Woodruff, 1984).

People fear that senility—the widespread loss of cognitive abilities—is an inevitable consequence of aging, but only a small number of the elderly, perhaps 5 percent, become senile. Among this group, the most common cause of senility is Alzheimer's disease (Chapter 6). Cognitive declines less dramatic than those brought about by Alzheimer's disease do occur over the adult years. Classical conditioning decreases (Chapter 8). The ability to assimilate new information rapidly falls off. Recall memory becomes less accurate, although this finding might reflect differences in initial acquisition (Chapter 9). Because metacognitive abilities stay the same throughout adulthood, the individual can often compensate for these other losses.

When intelligence tests were first made available (Chapter 11), researchers using cross-sectional designs found massive declines in intelligence with age. Later data from longitudinal studies contradicted these initial findings. Intelligence apparently does not decline with age once cohort effects are taken into account. Throughout the twentieth century, each successive generation has had more education; cross-sectional comparisons by age end up comparing people with differing amounts of schooling (Baltes, 1968; Schaie, 1965).

Stop and Think

11 Drawing from your everyday life, think of examples of assimilation and accommodation.

12 What is object permanence?

13 What are the major criticisms of Piaget's theory of cognitive development?

MORAL DEVELOPMENT

■ moral development
processes of change in judgments of the rightness or wrongness of acts

Our moral sense also develops as we age. Morality is a system of judgments about the rightness or wrongness of the acts performed by ourselves and others. **Moral development** therefore refers to the changes that take place in these judgments across a person's life span. Piaget (1932) proposed that moral development is tied to cognitive development, following the same progression from concrete to abstract. Lawrence Kohlberg (1927–1987) elaborated Piaget's ideas to become the best-known theorist in this area.

Kohlberg's Theory

Kohlberg (1981, 1984) studied the development of moral reasoning by posing to research subjects of different ages a moral dilemma such as the following:

> In Europe, a woman was near death from a special kind of cancer. There was one drug that the doctors thought might save her. It was a form of radium that a druggist in the same town had recently discovered. The drug was expensive to make, but the druggist was charging ten times what the drug cost him to make. He paid $200 for the radium and charged $2000 for a small dose of the drug. The sick woman's husband, Heinz, went to everybody he knew to borrow the money, but could only get together about $1000, which was half of what it cost. He told the druggist that his wife was dying and asked him to sell it cheaper or let him pay later. But the druggist said, "No, I discovered the drug and I'm going to make money from it." So Heinz got desperate and considered breaking into the man's store to steal the drug for his wife. Should Heinz steal the radium? (Kohlberg & Gilligan, 1971, pp. 1072–1073)

The subject is asked to decide if it would be right or wrong for Heinz to steal, and then to justify this decision. To Kohlberg, how one justifies the course of moral action is more important than the actual decision.

Kohlberg's theory of moral development, like Piaget's, embodies a stage approach. A particular individual either is at a given level of reasoning or is not, and people pass through these levels in the proposed sequence only. Kohlberg proposed three general levels of development, each divided into two stages, resulting in six different stages of moral development (see Table 10.3). Less advanced moral judgments are tied to particular situations. More advanced moral judgments transcend the particular and use general standards of justice, equality, and respect.

■ preconventional reasoning
Kohlberg's first stage of moral development, in which the individual justifies moral action in terms of rewards and punishments

According to Kohlberg, **preconventional reasoning** takes into account only rewards and punishments. Morality is placed outside the individual. A child at the level of preconventional morality would say that Heinz should not steal the drug because he would be punished if he did.

■ conventional reasoning
Kohlberg's second stage of moral development, in which the individual justifies moral action in terms of society's rules and conventions

Those exhibiting **conventional reasoning** justify moral action in terms of society's rules and conventions. Most adolescents and adults think in these terms. Their concern is with conforming to social standards, rules, or laws. Someone at the level of conventional morality would say that Heinz should not steal the drug because it is against the law to do so.

■ postconventional reasoning
Kohlberg's final stage of moral development, in which the individual justifies moral action in terms of his or her own abstract standards

Postconventional reasoning, shown by only 20 percent of the adult population, involves the application of one's own abstract standards. Those at this level recognize that laws and rules are useful but sometimes in conflict. In resolving moral conflicts, people at this stage try to judge the relative importance and intentions of different laws. Therefore, an answer to Heinz's dilemma might be that he should steal the drug because respect for another's property must give way to respect for human life.

Table 10.3   Summary: Kohlberg's Levels and Stages of Moral Development

According to Kohlberg, people pass through these stages in how they justify moral action.

Stage	Level	Characterization
Preconventional	1. Obedience and punishment orientation	Rules are obeyed to avoid punishment.
	2. Instrumental orientation	Rules are obeyed to earn rewards.
Conventional	3. Good boy/good girl orientation	Rules are obeyed to earn approval and avoid disapproval.
	4. Authority-maintaining orientation	Rules are obeyed to show respect for authority.
Postconventional	5. Contractual orientation	Morality reflects a social agreement to act in ways intended to serve the common good and to protect the rights of individuals.
	6. Conscience orientation	Morality reflects internalized standards.

A child at the preconventional level of moral development believes that morality exists outside the individual and is based solely on rewards and punishments. If you get punished for doing something, it is wrong, but if you are not punished, it is OK.

Criticisms of Kohlberg's Approach

Although highly influential, Kohlberg's approach has been criticized, on both theoretical and research grounds (Hayes, 1994). His overall scheme may reflect his own value judgments. Specifically, according to the way he measured moral development, a political liberal would often score higher in moral reasoning than a political conservative would. The law-and-order emphasis of many conservatives would come across as preconventional morality (Rich, 1993). This phenomenon makes it difficult to argue that Kohlberg's stages reflect something intrinsic about development. Along these lines, individuals in high-prestige occupations—who can often afford to break the rules—evidence a higher level of moral reasoning than those in low-prestige occupations do (Gibson, 1990). This finding might also reflect how socialization into different careers encourages people to talk about dilemmas.

Kohlberg's levels do not apply equally well in all cultures, particularly those without the formal institutions such as courts and schools that dominate our particular world (Simpson, 1974). Kohlberg took issue with this charge and to his credit studied moral development in different cultures (Nisan & Kohlberg, 1982). Although some evidence for cross-cultural generality in the sequencing of stages has emerged (Cortese, 1989; Heubner & Garrod, 1993; Lei, 1994; Snarey, 1985), people from different cultures also show characteristic moral reasoning in keeping with their ideologies (Blum, 1990). For example, Americans phrase their moral judgments in terms of individual considerations, whereas Indians speak in terms of interpersonal ones (Miller, 1994).

Furthermore, some critics argue that the types of dilemmas Kohlberg posed in his research are unrealistic and hence his results lack generality. Other critics observe that the scoring of responses to the dilemmas is not always reliable. Finally, the specific dilemma posed to research subjects can affect the level of observed moral reasoning, arguing against the assumption that Kohlberg's stages are global (Carpendale & Krebs, 1992).

The highest stage of moral reasoning is rarely encountered using Kohlberg's research technique (Colby, Kohlberg, Gibbs, & Lieberman, 1983; Mwamwenda, 1992). But surely most adults understand morality in abstract terms. They may not always show postconventional morality in their judgments, but they do at least some of the time. Witness the societal dismay at the influence of special interest groups on the legislation that Congress passes. Although this influence does not involve any technical illegality (conventional morality), it seems to flaunt higher principles (postconventional morality). The concern of citizens reflects postconventional moral reasoning.

As with Piaget's stages, researchers find that instructing children in moral reasoning can accelerate their passage through Kohlberg's hierarchy (Geiger, 1994). The relevant studies expose children to examples of moral reasoning at levels higher than their own, assessing the effect on moral development sometime later. Findings are mixed (Rest, 1983), but the occasional finding that short-term training affects someone's measured stage is inconsistent with Kohlberg's theory.

The relationship between moral reasoning and moral behavior is not clear. Research in the Kohlberg tradition often assumes that the former leads to the latter without explicitly showing that it does. Some studies find that people at the level of postconventional reasoning are less likely than others to lie or cheat, but other investigations do not find the expected link (Clarke-Stewart, Friedman, & Koch, 1985). Researchers interested in moral development have tended to neglect the emotional and motivational aspects of morality, which doubtlessly influence whether thought is translated into action (Blasi, 1990; Nunn & Hazler, 1990). So, believing that someone faced with Heinz's dilemma should steal the drug is not the same thing as actually doing so if the situation were indeed to present itself.

Gilligan's Theory

Kohlberg's approach has also been criticized for embracing a masculine view of morality; in fact, his original studies used only male research subjects. Carol Gilligan (1982) argued that there are two general approaches to moral reasoning. The first orientation concerns itself with rules and principles, taking justice as its bottom line. This approach is the morality studied by most developmental psychologists, from Piaget to Kohlberg. The second orientation reflects human relationships; it is a morality of caring.

By and large, Gilligan hypothesized, men and women respectively speak in these different moral voices. In resolving moral dilemmas, men will speak of rights and obligations, phrasing them as costs and benefits: Heinz should steal the drug because the sentence will not be severe. Women speak of the need to preserve human relationships: Heinz should talk to the druggist and work out a way to buy the drug on installment. If the male morality of justice is taken as the standard, those who think primarily in terms of human relationships are necessarily placed at a lower level.

Some of Gilligan's arguments draw criticism. Her initial premise—that women score lower than men on Kohlberg's dilemmas when his scoring system is employed— is not always true. Some studies find that women and men score about the same (Galotti, 1989; Silberman & Snarey, 1993; Walker, 1984), whereas other studies support Gilligan's hypothesis about gender differences (Mennuti & Creamer, 1991; Stander & Jensen, 1993; Yacker & Weinberg, 1990). Regardless, her general point is valid: There are different types of morality, and psychology should take a broad approach in studying their development (Tavris, 1994).

Stop and Think

14 How is Kohlberg's theory of moral development similar to Piaget's theory of cognitive development?

15 What are some possible confounds in the use of moral dilemmas to study moral development?

16 What is Gilligan's criticism of Kohlberg's theory of moral development?

SOCIAL DEVELOPMENT

Socialization is the process by which an individual acquires the knowledge appropriate to a given society. The child becomes not a generic social being but a particular type of social being. A specific personality emerges from the infinite number possible. He or she develops certain attitudes and values and adopts certain roles, creating a unique identity.

Social development refers to the development of our characteristic attitudes, values, and roles, all of which affect the way we relate to other people (Chapter 15). People can be described as social from the moment of birth, but the nature of social relationships changes across the life course. This section begins with a general discussion of social development and then takes a close look at how infants, children, adolescents, and adults come to relate to other people.

Erikson's Theory

Freud's follower Erik Erikson (1902–1994) is the most influential theorist of social development. Erikson (1963, 1968, 1982) both built upon and modified Freud's theory of development (Chapter 12). Erikson proposed that throughout their lives, people pass through stages. At each stage, a particular conflict is central and a satisfactory resolution must be reached if the individual is to progress through subsequent stages. Erikson called his approach a theory of **psychosocial stages** because each stage revolves around a specific social milestone with far-reaching psychological implications (see Table 10.4).

Trust versus mistrust.   The newborn infant must first achieve a sense of safety, trusting that his environment (in the form of caretakers) will provide for his well-being. If a

Influential theorist Erik Erikson proposed that social development is ongoing throughout life.

■ **social development**
processes of change in attitudes, values, and roles

■ **psychosocial stages**
according to Erikson, the stages people pass through during life, each characterized by a social challenge to be resolved

Table 10.4 Summary: Erikson's Stages of Psychosocial Development	
According to Erikson, all people pass through the following stages.	
Stage	**Characterization**
Trust versus mistrust (birth to age 1)	Infants must learn to achieve a sense of safety, trusting caretakers to provide for their well-being.
Autonomy versus self-doubt (age 1 to age 2)	Children must learn to make things happen, to choose, to exercise will.
Initiative versus guilt (age 3 to age 6)	Children must learn to initiate their own activities, thereby gaining self-confidence.
Competence versus inferiority (age 6 to puberty)	Children must learn to explore systematically their skills and abilities.
Identity versus role confusion (puberty to age 18)	Adolescents must create a set of personal values and goals by which to live, represented as a coherent identity.
Intimacy versus isolation (age 18 to age 25)	Young adults must learn to merge their identity with that of another person.
Generativity versus stagnation (age 25 to age 50)	Middle adults must learn to concern themselves with the world and the next generation.
Ego integrity versus despair (age 50 to death)	Later adults must come to terms with how they have resolved previous issues.

child's needs for food, warmth, and physical contacts are met, then the child develops trust. If not, the child develops mistrust, which is shown as anxiety and insecurity.

Autonomy versus self-doubt.   At about 18 months, when the child's physical development allows movement and exploration, she begins to confront the notion of her own self. She is somebody who can make things happen or prevent them from happening. Central to this task is the control of her own body, and here is the social significance of toilet training. Toilet training can be an area of conflict between children and their parents. Who will prevail? If the child successfully resolves this stage, he or she achieves a sense of autonomy. Otherwise, children doubt their own ability to make things happen.

Initiative versus guilt.   The next stage takes place from about ages 3 to 6, when the child starts to initiate his own activities, intellectual and physical. Erikson regarded this stage as critical in allowing the child to gain self-confidence. If thwarted by parents in these self-initiated activities, the child is likely to experience guilt and a lack of self-worth.

Competence versus inferiority.   From age 6 to the onset of puberty, the child begins to explore systematically her skills and abilities. School begins, and she starts to interact with peers. A number of possible skills can be developed: physical, intellectual, and social. Children take lessons in ballet or gymnastics, or throw themselves into art classes or swimming pools or the intense study of dinosaurs. Successful resolution of this stage produces feelings of competence. Children who experience failure in mastering skills during this stage may suffer feelings of inferiority.

Identity versus role confusion.   For Erikson, the central issue of adolescence is the creation of an ideology: a set of personal values and goals by which to live. An ideology translates itself into an occupational identity, a gender identity, a sexual identity, a politi-

Activist Ralph Nader appears to be resolving the psychosocial issue of generativity by working to improve the world for future generations.

cal identity, a religious identity, a social identity, and so on. These identities orient adolescents to the future, determining not just who they are but who they will be. An identity can be chosen only after one has the cognitive skills to do so—in particular, the ability to think in hypothetical terms.

Intimacy versus isolation.   For those who leave adolescence with an identity, the next task is to merge this identity with that of another individual to achieve intimacy. By Erikson's view, people cannot find out who they are in a relationship. Just the contrary— identity is a prerequisite for a relationship characterized by shared feelings and closeness. Those who fail to achieve an intimate relationship with another person feel isolated.

Generativity versus stagnation.   When identity and intimacy are achieved, men and women enter Erikson's next psychosocial stage. Here the concern is with matters outside oneself, with the world and the next generation. Erikson termed this concern **generativity.** An obvious way to resolve this issue is by raising one's own children. There are other ways as well, through an occupation such as teaching or through one's support for causes like environmentalism or the elimination of nuclear weapons. According to Erikson, those who do not achieve generativity will feel stagnant and self-absorbed.

■ **generativity**
concern with the world outside oneself and in particular the next generation

Ego integrity versus despair.   The final Eriksonian stage comes at the end of life, as a person looks back over the issues he or she faced. If they have been resolved successfully, the person feels content, having achieved the state of **ego integrity.** One leads but a single life, and integrity results from the conviction that one has led it well (Wong, 1989). If not, the person feels despair. Life has been too short, too unfair, too filled with failure.

■ **ego integrity**
according to Erikson, the focus of later adulthood: acceptance of one's choices in life and a sense that one's dilemmas have been resolved

Criticisms of Erikson's approach.   We can regard Erikson's theory with varying degrees of skepticism. Little evidence supports his strict stage approach to social development. His theory is probably a better description for men than women (Sanguiliano, 1978). For instance, women's identities might be forged from their relationships, rather than vice versa. Note the similarity between this argument and that of Gilligan, mentioned earlier in this chapter: Women are oriented toward other people throughout their lives. Accordingly, women's identities are defined by other people, suggesting that their developmental sequence leads from intimacy to identity (Levene, 1990; Peterson & Stewart, 1993).

Erikson's stage theory explicitly proposes a right way to pass through adulthood. Many developmental psychologists, however, have become wary of such a notion, arguing that various routes pass through adulthood. Development can be compared to a mountain down which numerous crisscrossing gullies run (Bee, 1987). As children, we stand atop the mountain. We come down the mountain in the course of development. At each point, we face numerous choices, although our previous path constrains us at each point. There are easier or harder ways to come down the mountain, and we might end up in more or less desirable locations. But there is no one best way to make the trip.

Think about the implications of this metaphor. The initial reaction of many people upon reading about theories of social development like Erikson's—and certainly my own—is to feel out of step. Why are the stages, crises, or accomplishments proposed not occurring on schedule, in the right order, or even at all?

A more general look at Erikson's approach reveals much to recommend it (Kishton, 1994; Zuschlag & Whitbourne, 1994). First, his work reminds us that development is a continual process throughout one's life span. Second, his work supports the notion that development is biopsychosocial. Third, the theory specifies the changing issues that confront a person throughout life. Fourth, Erikson argued that the tasks confronting us are social ones—we do not develop in isolation from one another.

Cultures seem to recognize the social nature of people's conflicts and provide their members with help to accomplish the tasks confronting them at different periods of life (Cote, 1993). For instance, consider the dating rituals institutionalized within our own society. These rituals help young people achieve intimacy by bringing them together precisely when intimacy is their prevailing concern.

Infant and Child Social Development

One of the intriguing things that infants do is to imitate adult facial expressions (Abravanel & Sigafoos, 1984). Six-month-old infants who look at an adult opening and closing his mouth with a popping sound repeat this sequence, including the sound (Kaye & Marcus, 1978). Even infants as young as several weeks will imitate adult expressions like sticking out the tongue (Meltzoff & Moore, 1977, 1994). An infant who imitates adult expressions ends up responding appropriately to the emotional state of the parent. This phenomenon can be interpreted in evolutionary terms. Infants who are socially responsive have a selective advantage because their parents are drawn to interact with them (Meltzoff, 1985, 1988).

Is there a critical period for attachment?   The child's first social relationship is an emotional attachment to his or her caregiver (Bowlby, 1969). Some developmental theorists believe that this first relationship sets the tone for subsequent relationships throughout life (Chapter 15). This speculation leads to the question of whether there exists a critical period for the development of an attachment to others.

Animals have such periods. For example, shortly after hatching, ducklings follow whatever moving object they first encounter, in a process called **imprinting** (Lorenz, 1937). Usually this object is their mother, but ducklings can also imprint on other animals or even people if they encounter them during the critical period. In most cases,

■ **imprinting**
attachment formed by the young of some species to whatever moving object they first encounter

imprinting keeps the vulnerable ducklings out of danger. The process can be disrupted, though, if there is no moving object for them to follow.

Human infants do not start out life by following their mothers around. But some theorists suggest that a newborn must form an attachment to a caretaker during a critical period within the first few years of life. If an attachment is not formed, or is formed poorly, then later social development is, by this view, thwarted. Genie, for example, was socially isolated for much of her early life and never became fully responsive to people, despite a great deal of exposure to others following her rescue. Perhaps the necessary foundations for social relationships were never established.

Although it is clear that extreme deprivation like that experienced by Genie interferes with social development, this fact does not prove that attachment by infants involves a critical period. Perhaps Genie's problems relating to others resulted from her physical or intellectual retardation. To disentangle these possibilities, we would need to show that social isolation has irreparable consequences even for otherwise healthy individuals.

Needless to say, no researcher would ever experiment with infants in this way. For this reason, some researchers have studied the development of attachment among our primate cousins. Harry Harlow's (1958) experiments with rhesus monkeys are a well-known example. Harlow wanted to know if the attachment of infants to their mothers was due just to the fact that infants need to be fed. Or is social attachment significant in its own right?

Harlow separated monkeys at birth from their mothers and raised them individually in cages with two stationary models. One figure was made of wire and the other of terry cloth (see Figure 10.7). The wire mother had a nipple that provided milk, whereas the cloth mother provided no food but had a pleasing texture. If attachment is the result of being fed, then the infant monkey should form an attachment to the model associated with food.

The infant monkeys preferred the cloth models. They sought out the wire models when hungry but otherwise stayed closer to the cloth ones. When the infants were frightened by an unfamiliar sight or sound, they ran to the cloth mothers and clung to them. Harlow concluded that infants are predisposed to form attachments with objects

A child's attachment to a caregiver provides the basis for subsequent social relationships.

Figure 10.7
Cloth Mother. In his investigations of attachment, Harry Harlow showed that infant monkeys, even when fed by a wire model, preferred to spend their time with a cloth model.

that are easy to cuddle, like the terry-cloth models. Blankets and teddy bears may be popular among human children for exactly the same reason. Harlow's research is important for showing that even among animals, social bonds reflect more than the satisfaction of physiological needs.

In a related line of research, Harlow (1965) raised rhesus monkeys in complete isolation. After a year without contact with other monkeys, these animals were fearful and withdrawn. Some of their common behaviors, like biting themselves, can only be described as bizarre. The isolated monkeys did not interact normally with other monkeys, and they could not interact with infants. They were not malnourished or physically traumatized, but because they did not have social contact with their kind, their social development was impaired.

Other studies show that such problems can be corrected if deprived monkeys are placed together with normally raised monkeys (Novak & Harlow, 1975). Eventually, the isolated monkeys learn to interact normally and display few effects of their earlier isolation. Similarly, studies with human children also find that many of the effects of early deprivation can be reversed if the child subsequently finds herself in a supportive environment (White, 1967). However, if the deprivation occurs for too long a time, it cannot be easily reversed, suggesting that there is some merit to the idea of critical periods for social development. The case of Genie is consistent with this possibility.

Stages of attachment.   Let us turn from this discussion of critical periods to consider how attachment changes throughout the early life of infants and children. Observational studies show that a newborn's attachment goes through several stages

(Goldberg, 1991; Schneider, 1991). During the first few months of life, the infant is socially responsive but makes no distinctions among people. He or she looks at everyone and can be comforted by anyone.

This period comes to an end when the child discriminates her primary caretakers from others. She responds differently to familiar people, smiling and vocalizing in their presence and being more easily comforted by them.

At about age 6 or 7 months, a third period is entered, where the child shows a strong attachment to a single individual. This stage is marked by the infant actively seeking contact with this person. She crawls after the person and calls out to him or her. Strangers cause fear. This pattern may continue for the next several years of the child's life.

This third stage of attachment has been studied by observing how infants react when separated from their mothers. A popular way to study attachment among infants between 12 and 18 months of age is with the Strange Situation Test (Ainsworth & Wittig, 1969). The child, accompanied by his mother, comes to the researchers' laboratory, which is equipped with its own playroom. The playroom is filled with toys. A carefully scripted series of encounters take place, observed by researchers behind a one-way mirror:

- The mother puts the baby on the floor, some distance from the toys, and then takes a seat.
- A stranger enters the playroom and also sits down.
- The stranger talks to the mother, and then the stranger attempts to play with the baby.
- Next the mother leaves her baby alone with the stranger for a few minutes; she returns shortly to be reunited with her infant.
- Then both the mother and the stranger leave, again for a few minutes.
- The stranger returns first and attempts to play with the baby.
- Finally, the mother returns and picks up her baby.

This procedure provides rich information about how the child reacts to separation. When the mother first leaves the room, about half the children cry before she comes back. More than three-quarters respond to her return by reaching to her in some way: smiling, touching, speaking. When the mother leaves the room again, the typical child becomes upset again. The stranger proves unsuccessful in soothing the child. When the mother returns, half the children keep on crying, and three-quarters of them climb into her arms.

Children respond to the Strange Situation Test in various ways. Ainsworth (1973) described three different patterns of behavior in these circumstances. Avoidant children (about 20 percent of those tested) do not cry when their mother leaves and either ignore her or turn away upon her return. Securely attached children (about 70 percent) show the pattern of seeking and maintaining contact with their mother. The third pattern, shown by only about 10 percent of children, is termed ambivalent. These kids cry when the mother leaves but take no comfort from her return.

The Strange Situation Test can be used to assess the effect of other factors on attachment. Children whose mothers are supportive and affectionate in dealing with them show the securely attached pattern—they are sad to see their mothers leave and glad to see them return; mothers who are critical and rejecting produce avoidant or ambivalent infants (Ainsworth, 1973). If a mother is depressed, she may be emotionally unavailable to her child, an aspect that can result in an avoidant pattern on the part of the child (Lowenstein & Field, 1993). Whatever pattern is established has lasting effects on how the child relates to others. For example, insecurely attached children are less sociable with peers at age 2, less flexible and persistent at age 4, and more likely to be depressed and withdrawn at age 6 (Clarke-Stewart, Friedman, & Koch, 1985).

Attachment in the modern world.   The bond between a child and her parent is obviously strong, and some people therefore worry that the changes we see in modern society, such as single mothers, divorce, two-career families, day care, and nontraditional gender roles, may adversely affect a child's social development. These issues have been hotly debated (Mardell, 1992; McKim, 1993; Roggman, Langlois, Hubbs-Tait, & Rieser-Danner, 1994; Schachere, 1990; Zigler & Frank, 1988).

For instance, do parents who allow another person to care for their young child undercut the child's attachment to them? Do they prevent any sort of attachment? What are the long-term effects of a generation of children raised in day care? A review of the relevant research, by Clarke-Stewart and Fein (1983), found no cause for alarm. Indeed, day care struck these reviewers as beneficial for a child. When compared with children reared at home, day-care children still showed attachment to their mothers, going to them in distress. At the same time, children in day care displayed increased social competence and independence. They also scored higher on tests of cognitive and intellectual development.

On the other hand, some studies suggest that day-care children may be less securely attached to their mothers, in that they are less disturbed by their absence and do not stand as close to them in the Strange Situation Test (Belsky, 1988). These findings seem to imply an insecure relationship, or they might just mean that the day-care child is more independent and familiar with brief separations (Clarke-Stewart, 1989). These findings also might mean that the child has formed attachments to individuals in addition to the mother.

These conclusions are clarified by a cross-cultural examination of how children are successfully raised (McGurk, Caplan, Hennessy, & Moss, 1993). Considerable variation is found around the world, and children being raised only by their parents is far from the norm. For example, among the Efe, an ethnic group in Zaire, the child from birth interacts simultaneously and successively with a variety of individuals in the community, not just his or her parents (Tronick, Morelli, & Ivey, 1992). More generally, the form of child raising represented by day care in the United States has long-standing equivalents in other cultures, and there is no evidence that they harm social development (Mott, 1991).

The origin of gender roles.   As explained earlier, the terms *male* and *female* include not only biological characteristics but also psychological and social characteristics. Psychological and social differences between men and women are often termed **gender differences.** One important gender difference is a person's gender identity: whether he or she experiences the self as a male or female (Chapter 1). Another important difference is a person's gender role: societal standards about how males or females should behave.

Most people with XY chromosomes have testes and penises, experience themselves as males, and fulfill male roles in society. Most people with XX chromosomes have ovaries and vaginas, experience themselves as females, and fulfill female roles in society. However, there are exceptions: People's chromosomes, genitals, gender identities, and gender roles can combine in all possible ways (Money & Ehrhardt, 1972). Thus, when we talk about males and females, their similarities and their differences, we must be specific about our level of discussion. Sex differences—which by definition are biological in nature—are apt to be the same across time and place. Gender differences vary greatly throughout history and from culture to culture.

Societies differ in terms of how distinctly gender roles are specified (Whiting & Child, 1953). For example, societies characterized by nuclear families (mother, father, and children under one roof) have less distinction between gender roles than those characterized by extended families (several families under one roof). Why? In a nuclear family, the absence of one adult means that the other adult, of the opposite sex, must be able to perform the relevant tasks. In an extended family, there are almost always other adults of the same sex to do the tasks of an absent individual; no one needs to be familiar with the role of the other gender.

Research into the psychological differences between males and females has been thoroughly summarized by Maccoby and Jacklin (1974) and more recently by Eagly

■ **gender differences**
psychological and social differences between men and women

(1994, 1995; Eagly & Johnson, 1990; Eagly & Wood, 1991). On the whole, males and females are quite similar with respect to most characteristics. However, some differences do emerge (see Table 10.5). Note that these gender differences are mostly consistent with societal stereotypes.

Where do the differences originate? Biology may well play a role, particularly in aggression (Plomin, 1994). Males are more aggressive than females in nearly all human cultures as well as most nonhuman species (Chapter 7). This phenomenon is perhaps due to testosterone levels, which have been linked to aggression. But a longitudinal study by Halpern, Udry, Campbell, and Suchindran (1993) that followed young males through the onset of puberty found no correlation between testosterone level and aggressive behavior. Research here continues.

Socialization is clearly implicated in many male-female differences (Bjorkqvist, 1994). As they grow, boys and girls learn to become men and women. They imitate adults and are reinforced for showing behavior deemed suitable for their gender. For instance, as early as the second year of life, children are rewarded by their parents for gender-appropriate behavior and discouraged from gender-inappropriate behavior (Fagot, 1978). Girls end up playing with dolls and helping around the house. Boys end up playing baseball and hollering.

Parents' tendency to see their sons and daughters differently reflects widely held stereotypes about the ways males and females ought to be (Stern & Karraker, 1989). School teachers are not immune to gender stereotypes. For example, boys are given more attention by teachers when they are assertive, whereas girls are rewarded for being gentle (Fagot, Hagan, Leinbach, & Kronsberg, 1985). Stereotypes like these create gender differences in actual behavior when they are translated into our reactions to boys and girls.

Adolescent Social Development

As you may remember from your own life, adolescents often feel as if the whole world is an audience for their coming-of-age. Their heightened self-consciousness can make the most trivial event—such as a facial blemish or a poorly fitting pair of jeans—painful (Elkind, 1978b). Here we see the cognitive characteristics of adolescence (heightened self-awareness) combining with the physical characteristics (the changes that mark

Table 10.5   Gender Differences

According to Maccoby and Jacklin (1974), here is what research shows about psychological differences between males and females.

Well-established gender differences

1. Females have greater verbal ability than males.
2. Males have greater visual-spatial ability than females.
3. Males have greater mathematical ability than females.
4. Males are more aggressive than females.

Open question about gender differences

1. Fear and anxiety?
2. Activity level?
3. Competitiveness?
4. Dominance?
5. Compliance?
6. Nurturance and "maternal" behavior?

Unfounded beliefs about gender differences

1. Females are more social than males.
2. Females are more suggestible than males.
3. Males are more analytic than females.
4. Females lack the motive to achieve.

puberty) to affect the individual's self-esteem and social behavior. In this section, we take a look at some of the social changes and influences that occur during adolescence. These are organized in terms of the societal institutions that provide the context of adolescent development: the family, school, and friends. I close with a discussion of sexual development during adolescence, a good example of a biopsychosocial phenomenon.

The family.   Although some social critics speak of the death of the American family in the late 20th century and the dire consequences for social development, there is no reason to think the family will disappear. What is clear is that the family has changed drastically over the last few decades. Consider the stereotype of the ideal American family: father as wage earner, mother as housewife, and children. Only 25 percent of adolescents now live in such a family. Just as common for an adolescent is a single-parent household, headed usually by a working mother. Another common pattern in the modern world is a two-parent household in which only one parent is biologically related to the child.

Such changes in the family result from societal trends in work (women entering the labor force in unprecedented numbers), housing (people changing dwelling places more frequently), values (growing importance of self-fulfillment rather than social obligation), and family composition (decreasing family size). The net effect of these changes is a different American family.

How has the social development of adolescents been affected? Researchers have focused their efforts particularly on the effects of divorce, absent fathers, and working mothers. Note the assumption here that deviations from the traditional family structure are potentially disruptive and worthy of investigation.

It is difficult to offer generalizations about the effects of these variations (Free, 1991; Furstenberg, 1990; Kelly, 1993; Tasker & Richards, 1994; Zuk, 1991). How an event like parental divorce affects an adolescent depends on such factors as what age and sex the individual is and how the parents respond. Further, one must distinguish between short-term and long-term consequences. Finally, note that factors such as

Parental divorce can threaten an adolescent's sense of identity as it is in the process of being formed.

divorce, an absent father, and a working mother are not independent of one another. A researcher faces great difficulties in trying to understand the specific consequences of one factor in isolation from the others.

These qualifications aside, here is what psychologists have learned from this type of research when their focus was on the impact of divorce on adolescents. As common sense suggests, the period immediately surrounding divorce is marked by heightened family conflict (Hamilton, 1993). Disputes over personal possessions, family finances, and child custody occur. These disputes take a toll on the well-being of all family members (Johnson, Wilkinson, & McNeil, 1995). To these difficulties are added potentially stressful life events that can follow in the wake of separation and divorce: moving from a familiar home and neighborhood, changing friends and schools, having less income. Household routines might fall apart (Wallerstein & Kelley, 1974). Disciplining of the children can become inconsistent (Hetherington, Cox, & Cox, 1978, 1982).

Given these disruptions and losses, then, the adolescent may respond to the divorce of his or her parents with anger, fear, depression, guilt, and a sense of divided loyalty (Hetherington, 1979). School performance may suffer. The adolescent may turn increasingly to the peer group to escape the unpleasantness of home life, with truancy, drug use, and delinquency among the possible consequences (Dornbusch et al., 1985; Fergusson, Horwood, & Lynskey, 1994; Lamminpaa, 1995). Female adolescents may show an increase in their sexual activity.

Not all adolescents respond to divorce in negative ways. Some—particularly those who are the oldest in a family—show enhanced maturity in the wake of divorce. The better an adolescent understands the reasons behind divorce, the less damage is done (Neal, 1983). In other words, the ability to think abstractly about other people helps an adolescent deal with the aftermath of his or her parents' divorce.

Because research is more difficult to conduct over greater periods of time, the immediate response of adolescents to divorce is better understood than the eventual response. However, several longitudinal investigations of the long-term impact of divorce on children have been completed. Perhaps the most striking result is that the impact can be enduring, and contrary to earlier suggestions by researchers, adolescents may be particularly vulnerable (Wallerstein, 1991; Wallerstein & Kelley, 1974).

Wallerstein and Blakeslee (1989) followed the members of 60 different families for ten years after divorce. Here is what they concluded:

- Adolescents are frightened by divorce because they end up without guidance through adolescence.
- They fear they will repeat the failures of their parents.
- They feel rejected by their parents following the divorce because the parents appear preoccupied with their own issues.
- They are disturbed to see their parents develop new sexual relationships, at precisely the time when they as adolescents are grappling with their own sexuality.

These conclusions make sense in light of the primary task of adolescence: forming an identity. Divorce can be harmful to adolescents if its lessons are harsh ones. An adolescent may become distrustful of others and pessimistic about long-term relationships. However, other studies caution us that effects can be positive as well as negative, depending on a host of conditions, such as the civility of the parents to one another (Dunne & Hedrick, 1994; Ellwood & Stolberg, 1993; Emery, 1982; Grossman & Rowat, 1995; Hetherington & Arasteh, 1988).

School.   It is impossible to speak about adolescent social development without placing it in the context of schools. Universal school attendance by adolescents in the United States has occurred only during the last 70 or so years (Tanner, 1972). The school year has steadily lengthened since that time, from 162 days in 1920 to 180 days today. European and Asian school years can be as long as 220 days (Chapter 8).

Compulsory education was brought about by a combination of several societal factors: industrialization, urbanization, and immigration. Schools were seen by the larger society as a way of socializing adolescents—Americanizing them and preparing them for life and work in a complex world. What did your high school present to you: traditional academic education, vocational training, or innovative electives? My high school, 30 years ago, offered choices among all of these programs, and most students were tracked into one to the exclusion of the others. Your course of studies determined the cliques you joined.

Schools have been seen by many as a vehicle for social change. Desegregation, for instance, has been carried out mainly in the schools—not in the workplace, not in the housing market, and not in leisure activities. More recently, schools have been the place where students formally learn about sexuality. Some people also want schools to be the place where adolescents learn to affirm their patriotism and/or their belief in God.

Friends.   Becoming an adolescent marks the beginning of personal friendships (Chapter 15). Adolescents want to know how their friends think and feel about things (Youniss & Smollar, 1985). They are more responsive to others, trying to anticipate and interpret their desires. They worry for the first time that others are not returning their effort. Personal friendships require that individuals be able to take another's point of view, something young children cannot do because their level of cognitive development does not allow it (Youniss & Haynie, 1992).

For the teenager struggling with identity issues, peer groups provide many answers about who and what one can be. From these possibilities, the adolescent eventually chooses an identity that feels comfortable. The technical term for the group that provides one's identity is the **reference group** because the individual refers to this group to define and evaluate the self. In our society, a person's peer group, especially during adolescence, is composed of individuals of the same age (Csikszentmihalyi, Larson, & Prescott, 1977; Greenberger & Steinberg, 1981).

▪ reference group
group that provides one's identity

Once a peer group exists, it has a powerful influence on adolescents' social development. One of our societal signs that a child has become an adolescent is the development of these groups. If you were raised in the United States, your high school was probably much like mine. Students gathered into groups that dressed alike, acted alike, and thought alike. We had slang names for each group, no doubt still common. Whatever the specific labels, there is a group that pursues sports, another that pursues academics, and still another that pursues alcohol or drugs.

What determines the reference group that we choose during adolescence? Such groups cohere around similarities—adolescents within a group are usually the same age, social class, and ethnicity. Similarities in attitudes, such as orientation to school, also affect the choice of reference groups. Once adolescents take a reference group as their own, they seek further similarity with their peers. Thus, the reference group's influence on an adolescent both precedes and follows his or her decision to join the group.

These ideas place so-called **peer pressure** in perspective. Peer pressure has become a favorite explanation for the problems that plague adolescents today, from drug and alcohol abuse to dropping out of school to unplanned pregnancies. However, a person's peers do not literally force him or her to engage in any of these activities (May, 1993). Indeed, adolescents who experience such difficulties tend not to have any sort of peer group (Ennett & Bauman, 1994). A literal interpretation of peer pressure is wrong. Rather, peer pressure legitimizes activities, so that an adolescent who is interested will then try them. Legitimization is different from coercion. Peers may be more influential in an adolescent's continuation of a given activity such as drug use than in its actual beginning (Griffiths, 1990; Morgan & Grube, 1991).

The practical implication is clear. Parents who want their adolescent children to resist going along with the crowd have to do more than limit contact with the peer group. Parents must additionally make the activities that they favor seem attractive (Denton & Kampfe, 1994; White & DeBlassie, 1992).

Sexual awakening as biopsychosocial.   The physical changes of puberty, discussed earlier, combine with societal expectations to place sexuality in the forefront among the issues that concern adolescents. Sexual development during adolescence is best approached in biopsychosocial terms (see Figure 10.8).

■ **peer pressure**
legitimization of activities by one's peer group

Peer pressure is often used to explain everything wrong with adolescents. However, peer pressure does not force an unwilling individual to do anything. Peer pressure instead legitimizes behaviors and actions, for better or for worse.

**Figure 10.8
Adolescent Sexual
Development as
Biopsychosocial.** The biological changes of puberty combine with societal expectations about sexuality, as well as peer and family influences, to forge an adolescent's sexual identity, which determines how the individual behaves sexually. Also critical are the thoughts and emotions an adolescent brings to bear on sexuality.

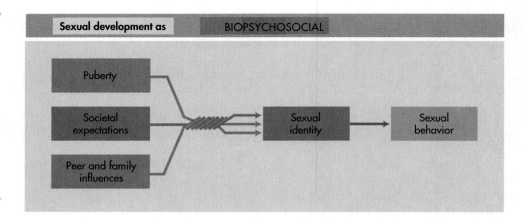

In recent decades, young people's attitudes toward sex have become more liberal, following the larger social trends collectively called the sexual revolution. The majority of American teenagers today believe that sex before marriage is appropriate if the partners are in love. Intercourse among adolescents has also become more common (de Gaston, Jensen, & Weed, 1995). Surveys estimate that more than 50 percent of contemporary high school students have had intercourse by the time they graduate (Friedman, 1992). Many sexually active adolescents do not regularly use contraception, resulting in an alarming number of unplanned teenage pregnancies. Indeed, the United States has double the rate of teenage pregnancies found in other industrialized countries. Sexually transmitted diseases like AIDS are spreading at a high rate among young people who do not follow guidelines for safer sex (Chapter 16).

At first glance, these generalizations seem contradictory. If young people are becoming more liberal in their sexual attitudes and activities, why is there no corresponding increase in caution? The answer, at least in part, is that sexuality is still regarded with ambivalence by many adolescents (Flores-Ortiz, 1994; Silbereisen & Noack, 1988). To take the steps necessary for contraception is to acknowledge that one is planning to have intercourse, a difficult admission for many youngsters to make to themselves, to their partners, or to the person from whom they obtain the means of contraception (Cvetkovich, Grote, Bjorseth, & Sarkissian, 1975; Moore & Rosenthal, 1992).

Adult Social Development

Although we may think of adulthood as defined by the stable periods, such as an ongoing marriage or job, just as important psychologically are the transitions between these stable periods. People make transitions with the resources available to them: biological, psychological, and social. Individuals can better raise a child if they are healthy and vigorous. They can better cope with the death of a spouse if they have established solid relationships with other people. They can retire with more satisfaction if they have developed leisure interests. For many people, the most important tasks of adult social development include marriage and parenthood. Also important is the work people do throughout their adult years; Chapter 17 discusses in detail work and the development of careers.

Marriage.   One of the most profound transitions that most adults make is from the status of single person to that of married person. The vast majority make this transition during young adulthood. Marriage is one of the socially sanctioned ways of declaring that the psychosocial issue of intimacy has been resolved. But there is much more to marriage: Marriage involves a drastic change in the roles people play.

How does the transition into marriage take place? Developmental psychologists describe the process as a series of steps (Karney & Bradbury, 1995). The most superficial step involves judging a prospective mate on such characteristics as appearance, social class, and behavior. The next involves looking a bit deeper at his or her beliefs and attitudes. Agreement here is important. Finally, prospective mates choose each other on the basis of how well their needs mesh. Two individuals with a need to dominate an interaction do not get along as well as a leader and a follower (Winch, 1958).

In the United States, about 95 percent of the population marries at some point. This overall figure has stayed much the same over recent decades, although the average age of first marriage has increased, particularly among women with careers. This is yet another example of how larger social trends influence the cascade of development. More women have professions today, which means they marry later . . . which means they have children later . . . which means their children have older parents.

Marital satisfaction.   Researchers have extensively studied marital satisfaction and find, not surprisingly, that satisfaction is high early in the marriage (O'Leary & Smith, 1991). It reaches a low point when a couple has adolescent children. Among those who stay married for decades, marital satisfaction starts to rise again once the children have left home.

These are descriptive trends, and we should not assume that time is the critical factor. Many other factors are linked with marital satisfaction—for example, emotional security, respect, communication, sexual intimacy, and loyalty—and the way in which these factors combine to influence satisfaction depends on how long a couple has been together (Kirchler, 1989; Levenson, Carstensen, & Gottman, 1993; Swensen, Eskew, & Kohlhepp, 1981). On the whole, men report greater satisfaction with marriage than women do. Women tend to value their marriage more if they have children or if they work outside the home (Baruch, Barnett, & Rivers, 1983; Russell & Wells, 1994).

Many women today have both a family and a career, but those committed to both their children and their work tend to experience decreased satisfaction with their marriage (Philliber & Hiller, 1983). The likely explanation is that their husbands more often than not fail to share equally in raising the children, and the women become overextended.

An interesting fact is that married adults are physically and emotionally healthier than their single counterparts (Chapter 16). There are various explanations for this phenomenon. Perhaps the less healthy do not get married in the first place. Perhaps the companionship that marriage provides protects a person against poor health (Cobb, 1976). Whatever the reasons, the benefits of marriage on health are greater for men than for women.

Cohabitation.   In years past, a person was either married or single. But more recently, living together, or cohabitation, has become common in the United States. Perhaps as many as 2.3 million couples live together without being married, implying that cohabitation is a significant social phenomenon. Some debate exists as to whether cohabitation represents a true alternative to marriage or a step in the process of courtship (Bower & Christopherson, 1977).

Among those couples who lived together before getting married, marital satisfaction is lower than among couples who did not live together prior to marriage (Nock, 1995). Divorce may be more likely (Browder, 1988). In thinking about these results, keep in mind the possibility of confounds. People who live together before marrying are different in the first place from those who do not (Axinn & Thornton, 1993; Cunningham & Antill, 1994; Huffman, Chang, Rausch, & Schaffer, 1994). For instance,

Women who work and have children tend to report less satisfaction with their marriages than do women who either have no children or do not work. The explanation for this finding is probably that husbands in the United States often do not share equally with wives in raising their children.

men and women who live together before marriage tend to have slightly less education and are somewhat more likely to be employed than those who marry without first living together (Watson, 1983). Perhaps these differences and not cohabitation produce later variations in marital satisfaction and stability.

Parenthood.   Another major adult transition is taking on the role of parent. Several recent trends are important. First, except for the post–World War II burst between 1947 and 1957 that gave us the baby boom generation, the birthrate in the United States has steadily decreased throughout the twentieth century. Families are becoming smaller. Second because of effective birth control, most adults become parents later in life. Although most children are still born to women younger than 30, the birthrate among women older than 30 has increased. Third, the rise in divorce results in an increasingly large number of single-parent families. Fourth, remarriage following divorce is leading to a growing number of families that include stepparents.

Psychologists have been greatly interested in styles of parenting—how parents encourage behaviors they like in their children and discourage others. Research has identified three major styles of parenting in the United States (Baumrind, 1971, 1978). **Authoritarian parenting** is firm, punitive, and emotionally cold. Such parents value obedience from their children and do not encourage their independence or involve them in decision making. **Permissive parenting** is loving but lax. Such parents exert little control over their children. Indeed, these children are given freedom and are allowed to make decisions, but they have little guidance. **Authoritative parenting** involves negotiating with children. Such parents set limits for a child but explain why,

■ **authoritarian parenting**
style of raising children that is firm, punitive, and emotionally cold

■ **permissive parenting**
style of raising children that is loving but lax

■ **authoritative parenting**
style of raising children that involves negotiating, setting limits but explaining why, and encouraging independence

and they encourage independence. As the child demonstrates responsibility, the parents provide more freedom. Decisions are arrived at through give-and-take.

These different styles of parenting affect the subsequent social development of children (Becker, 1964; Durbin, Darling, Steinberg, & Brown, 1993; Parish & McCluskey, 1994). Authoritarian parents tend to produce children who are unhappy, dependent, and submissive. Permissive parents raise children who are likely to be outgoing and sociable but also immature, impatient, and aggressive. The best approach appears to be that of authoritative parents, whose children tend to be friendly, cooperative, socially responsible, and self-reliant. Regardless of the style of parenting that children experience, they tend to raise their own children as they were raised (Van Ijzendoorn, 1992).

Mothers and fathers sometimes differ in their parenting styles, and these differences introduce further complexities into any description of how their children are affected (Bentley & Fox, 1991; Forehand & Nousiainen, 1993; Fox, Kimmerly, & Schafer, 1991). Even so, parenting style is only one influence on children's social development. Just as important as the type of discipline is the affection shown by parents. It is also important to consider a two-way influence between parent and child. Because children differ with respect to their temperaments, parents may use the method of discipline that their children allow them to.

Researchers find that being a parent is both a rewarding and a stressful aspect of adult social development (Mowbray, Oyserman, & Ross, 1995). The vast majority of parents report that if given the chance to start their life over, they would choose again to have babies (Yankelovich, 1981). Nonetheless, the presence of children in a household profoundly changes the relationship between husbands and wives. Child-rearing responsibilities often fall to mothers, perhaps contributing to the increased depression found among them (Brown & Harris, 1978). Following the birth of a child, the typical mother takes on more household chores, regardless of how she and her mate previously divided the tasks (Cowan, Cowan, Coie, & Coie, 1978).

When children grow up and leave home, the roles of parents change. At one time, psychologists thought that parents, particularly mothers, were vulnerable to the so-called empty nest syndrome—a loss of purpose experienced when all the children have left home. But research fails to bear out this notion. If anything, just the opposite occurs: Mothers report the most satisfaction and the highest morale once their children leave home (Neugarten, 1970). And why not? On the one hand, life becomes less demanding. And on the other hand, the successful development of offspring from dependent children to autonomous adults means that a parent has done well.

Divorce. In the middle 1800s, only about 4 percent of marriages ended in divorce. By the 1970s and therafter, this figure had grown to more than 40 percent. At first glance, this seems an incredible crisis for the American family. But if we take a closer look that places these figures in a historical context, we gain another perspective. There is the same proportion of intact marriages today as there was more than a century ago because people on average live much longer today. Once upon a time, marriages ended with the untimely death of one partner or the other. Today the same proportion of marriages end with divorce. Of course, the end of a marriage by death is different from the end of a marriage by divorce, but the fact remains that the proportion of intact American families has not changed at all throughout the twentieth century.

The average divorce, if we can speak of such a thing, occurs after six or seven years of marriage (Norton, 1983). But divorce can occur at any point during marriage. Surprisingly, marital dissatisfaction is not a strong predictor of divorce. Considerations like alternative mates, career decisions, and financial crises combine to create a divorce. The degree to which divorce is regarded as legitimate within a person's cultural group is another crucial factor. For an obvious example, among those whose religion prohibits it, divorce is less likely than among the general population.

The empty nest syndrome refers to the sense of loss that parents—particularly mothers—presumably experience when their last child leaves home. Research suggests that for the most part, the empty nest syndrome is a myth; parents usually feel highly satisfied when their children grow up and live on their own.

Regardless of what causes divorce, it is a painful experience. We have already noted the impact of divorce on adolescents specifically and children generally. Negative consequences exist for adults as well. During the immediate aftermath of a divorce, depression or alcohol abuse may occur. There is also a greater risk of physical illness (Chapter 16). These problems are increased when the couple has children. In the majority of cases, mothers receive custody following a divorce, causing single mothers to be especially burdened (Pledge, 1992). None of these findings suggests that divorce is always harmful for individuals (Masheter, 1990). Most people make a satisfactory adjustment within two years following a divorce (Hetherington, Cox, & Cox, 1979).

The majority of those who divorce remarry, particularly if they have divorced early in adulthood. A second marriage is necessarily different from a first marriage, but on average it is as satisfying (Huyck, 1982). Whether second marriages are more or less likely to end in divorce is unclear because the comparison is confounded by age and hence the increased possibility of the death of one partner.

Death and dying.   Current thinking conceives death not as a discrete event but rather as a process that unfolds over time. Some theorists therefore prefer to describe what happens to us at the end of our life as dying; it too is a developmental process (Smith & Maher, 1991; Sweeting & Gilhooly, 1990).

Elisabeth Kübler-Ross (1969) conducted interviews with terminally ill individuals, both children and adults. She proposed that the process of dying takes places in five stages, through which people pass in order:

■ *Denial*—the first reaction is to refuse to believe that death is going to happen: "There must be a mistake here."
■ *Anger*—the second stage is resentment: against those who remain healthy, against those taking care of the individual, against whatever circumstances put the person in this position.
■ *Bargaining*—in the third stage, the individual tries to "make a deal" with doctors, nurses, or God: "If I get better, I'll devote my life to good deeds."

■ *Depression*—bargaining then gives way to depression, which Kübler-Ross saw as a form of mourning for oneself and for all the losses that death will bring.

■ *Acceptance*—finally, the dying individual comes to accept and understand death as inevitable, and dies quietly, even serenely.

Like other stage theories of development, this one assumes that each step is necessary for the subsequent ones to occur. For instance, the initial stage of denial allows the individual to gather his defenses to cope with his pending death. The bargaining stage allows him to keep going long enough to finish the important business in his life.

Although Kübler-Ross legitimized the study of a long-neglected period of life, her particular theory has not been generally accepted. When other researchers looked for her stages, they did not find them among all dying individuals; even when present, the five stages do not always appear in the order she proposed (Schulz & Aderman, 1974). A dying person's attitude toward death can change continuously. Though acceptance might come after periods of denial, anger, bargaining, and depression, any of these responses might reappear (Butler & Lewis, 1981). Dying is no more simple than living, and we should expect that there are various ways to go about it.

Nevertheless, Kübler-Ross is an important theorist, the first to call our attention to the psychological process of dying. As you know, social attitudes toward death in the United States can be described as repressive. We do not witness death. We do not discuss death. We do not even acknowledge it: People pass away rather than die. We are often ill equipped to deal with death, our own or others. Kübler-Ross helped to change these attitudes, and death is now more openly discussed than it once was.

For instance, psychologists have studied people's attitudes toward death and dying, with a focus on the fears people express about their own mortality (Tomer, 1991). Where in the life span is an individual most likely to fear death? Surprisingly, perhaps, middle adulthood is when people are most likely to voice explicit fear (Bengston, Cuellar, & Ragan, 1977). With increasing age, adults become less frightened about death. At the same time, they are more likely to think and talk about death.

Researchers have also found that older adults who have achieved their goals in life fear death less than those who believe they have fallen short (Neimeyer & Chapman, 1980/1981). This finding is consistent with Erikson's hypothesis that the satisfactory resolution of one's major life tasks results in a sense of integrity in later adulthood. A belief in the significance of the life one has led makes the end of life less frightening.

Widowhood.   When people die, they leave others behind—notably, their spouses. One more issue of adult social development that deserves mention is widowhood. Because women tend to marry men several years older than they are and on average live about seven years longer than men, the loss of a spouse to death is much more common among women than men. By some estimates, there are more than ten times as many widows in the United States as widowers.

The transition to widowhood is stressful, particularly when this change is unexpectedly early in life (Ball, 1976/1977). When an individual loses a spouse, she loses not only a relationship with a loved one but also that person's support and assistance. Also gone is her own role as a spouse. Both physical and psychological difficulties can follow in the wake of widowhood (Balkwell, 1981; Stroebe & Stroebe, 1983). Close and supportive relationships with other people help to buffer her against the resulting stress. Interestingly, her friends are of more help in this regard than her children are, perhaps because friends are more likely to have had firsthand experience with widowhood themselves (Ferraro, 1984).

Stop and Think

17 Which of Erikson's psychosocial stages seem to have the greatest cross-cultural generality?

18 What is generativity?

19 What are some possible confounds in the use of the Strange Situation Test to study attachment?

20 What are gender differences, and what is the distinction between gender differences and sex differences?

21 Does peer pressure force adolescents to behave in certain ways?

22 When is marital satisfaction highest?

23 Some psychologists have argued that typical studies of parenting style and child behavior are confounded by genetics. How could this confound be removed?

24 Does research support the existence of stages of dying?

DEVELOPMENT IN A BIOPSYCHOSOCIAL CONTEXT

Although the different domains of development—physical, cognitive, moral, and social—have been discussed separately, their mutual influences on one another are obvious. As stressed at the beginning of this chapter, the study of development requires recognition that the influences on behavior cascade over time.

Development as "Inside Out" and as "Outside In"

The multiple determinants of development must be located in several social contexts. The immediate social environment of each individual is closely linked to larger social settings, each nested within one another: the community, the nation, and the world. Each of these contexts must be located in history. Urie Bronfenbrenner (1970), an influential developmental psychologist, stressed how each larger setting shapes the smaller settings within it.

Leo Vygotsky (1962, 1978), another influential developmental psychologist, made a similar point when discussing theories like those proposed by Piaget or Kohlberg that explain development from the inside out. These "inside out" theories usually stress the role of maturation in development: the unfolding of an inner—presumably biological—nature. Vygotsky proposed that development additionally occurs from the "outside in." Development represents the incorporation of knowledge from the larger social context and occurs through a constant give-and-take between the individual and the world. By this view, we should expect considerable variety in the psychological characteristics developed by people across different social settings (Barbarin, 1993).

Cross-Generational Effects of the Japanese-American Internment

An example of how development can be approached from an outside-in direction is Donna Nagata's (1993) research into the long-term consequences of the internment of Japanese American individuals during World War II. By government order, more than 110,000 U.S. citizens of Japanese ancestry were relocated to concentration camps in isolated parts of the United States. Relocation began in early 1942, and most individuals were kept in the camps for several years.

It is important to know that there was no reason to believe that Japanese Americans threatened national security, that Americans of German and Italian ancestry were not relocated, and that many Japanese Americans served with distinction in the U.S. armed forces. The vast majority of relocated individuals went along with the orders, however unhappily—which leads one to question further why the government ever thought Japanese Americans posed a threat.

Nagata specifically studied the psychological effects of internment on the *Sansei,* third-generation Japanese Americans born after the war and thus after internment. Although relocation directly involved the previous generation of Japanese Americans, she found that the *Sansei* were also greatly affected by this event.

For example, the children of individuals in the camps were less likely to be knowledgeable about their Japanese heritage and more likely to have doubts about their rights as citizens. At the same time, many of these children became politically active as adults, particularly in the arena of civil liberties. *Sansei* whose parents were interned earned less money as adults than other *Sansei* did. Individuals whose parents were interned were more likely to marry outside their ethnic group.

These effects were greater for *Sansei* whose parents originally lived in the continental United States as opposed to Hawaii. More than 90 percent of the Japanese American population in the continental United States were sent to the camps, versus only 1 percent of the Japanese American population in Hawaii. The reason is that Japanese Americans in Hawaii had a different history and higher status; they were not nearly so likely to be singled out for discrimination. Research like Nagata's shows not only how

The influence of historical conditions on individual development is an example of an outside-in perspective. During World War II, Japanese Americans were placed in internment camps, an experience that affected not only them but their children born after the war.

development is affected by outside-in influences but also that these influences can persist across generations.

Psychology's study of development often focuses our attention on how people differ from one another and the factors responsible for these differences. Complex influences seem to be the rule. The next chapter takes a look at an important human characteristic—intelligence—that shows similar variety and complexity. The general points raised about the importance of viewing development in biopsychosocial terms apply as well to the specific characteristic of intelligence.

SUMMARY

UNDERSTANDING DEVELOPMENT: DEFINITION AND EXPLANATION

■ Developmental psychologists study changes in people's biological, psychological, and social characteristics across time. Changes in different domains of development mutually influence one another.

DOING *Developmental* RESEARCH

■ Two general research strategies are used in developmental psychology: cross-sectional approaches, which simultaneously study people of different ages, and longitudinal approaches, which study the same people over time.

PHYSICAL DEVELOPMENT

■ Physical development reflects the interaction of biological and environmental factors. It includes prenatal development, as well as the physical changes occurring during infancy, childhood, adolescence, and adulthood.
■ Sex differences in development begin at the moment of conception and continue throughout life.
■ Temperament is a biologically based style of behaving, but its influence on behavior provides a good example of how development is biopsychosocial.

COGNITIVE DEVELOPMENT

■ Jean Piaget theorized extensively about cognitive development and proposed that children's thinking progresses through several stages, becoming less concrete and more symbolic with each stage.
■ Although the details of Piaget's theory of cognitive development have been criticized in recent years, his general approach has made the entire field possible.
■ Cognitive development continues throughout adulthood and is characterized by both declines and gains.

MORAL DEVELOPMENT

■ Lawrence Kohlberg followed Piaget's example in studying moral development in terms of how people reason about moral dilemmas.
■ Kohlberg proposed that people's moral reasoning is originally tied to external considerations but progresses to abstract principles such as justice and equality.

■ Critics such as Carol Gilligan have taken issue with Kohlberg's approach, most notably by observing that Kohlberg assumed a moral system based on rules rather than one based on the preservation of human relationships.

SOCIAL DEVELOPMENT

■ Social development refers to a person's development as a social being.
■ Erik Erikson's psychosocial theory has been the most influential account of social development during adolescence and adulthood. According to Erikson, the stages of development are defined by particular psychosocial conflicts that people must confront. Only when a conflict is successfully resolved can the person go on to satisfactorily resolve subsequent conflicts.
■ The first social relationship is the infant's attachment to his or her mother, and this process has been extensively investigated by seeing how the young child reacts to brief separations from the mother.
■ From the very beginning of life, individuals are socialized to act in accordance with societal norms describing behavior appropriate for males and females.
■ Adolescent development occurs within the contexts provided by the family, school, and friends.
■ Developmental psychologists who study adults are interested in how people approach such major issues in life as marriage, parenthood, death, and widowhood.

DEVELOPMENT IN A BIOPSYCHOSOCIAL CONTEXT

■ Theories have often explained development from the "inside out" by focusing on biological and psychological mechanisms within the individual.
■ In contrast, an "outside in" perspective on development focuses on the social and historical contexts in which the individual is found.
■ An example of an outside-in approach is provided by research into the effects across generations of the internment of Japanese Americans by the U.S. government during World War II.

KEY TERMS

Intelligence

Enrique Ramos is a high school senior who wants to attend the state university and study engineering. But Enrique's family does not have enough money to pay for his college tuition. And Enrique's situation is even more complex because his high school has abolished course grades in favor of pass/fail designations, making it difficult for the university admissions committee to evaluate his academic ability. As it turns out, Enrique is able to go to the college of his choice when he is awarded a National Merit Scholarship following his strong performance on the qualifying exam.

Stephanie Johnson is also a high school senior who wants to attend the state university. An excellent student, Stephanie has received all As in her high school courses and upon graduation will be class valedictorian. But Stephanie is turned down from the university because her Scholastic Aptitude Test (SAT) scores are below average.

Fred Payton is yet another high school senior. Although he plans to attend a university, at present he does not know which one. A highly acclaimed basketball player, Fred has already been offered more than 50 college scholarships. He will make his choice based on how well he believes the college team will fare over the next few years. However, a potential pitfall looms for Fred and whatever school he chooses: He has yet to take the SAT. Although his high school grades have for the most part been satisfactory, Fred needs to attain a particular SAT score in order to be eligible to play intercollegiate sports during his first year in college.

One more high school senior is Eva Chin, who has devoted much of her life to playing the viola, is quite talented, and wants to study music performance in college. So, Eva has applied to the state university, which has a strong music department and a well-known student orchestra that tours Europe every spring. She is asked to audition. She plays well and on the spot is promised admission to the university and a place in the traveling orchestra. "But I haven't sent you my transcript or my SAT scores," she says to the music professors. "That doesn't matter," they tell her. "We've heard you play."

UNDERSTANDING INTELLIGENCE: DEFINITION AND EXPLANATION

■ **intelligence**
adaptive and purposive behavior

We show our **intelligence** when we act in adaptive ways, confronting and surmounting the challenges that face us, and in purposeful ways, pursuing a goal (Sternberg & Salter, 1982). There is no question that intelligence allows us flexibility, both individually and collectively. It gives us a great selection advantage.

Consider how people have spread to all corners of the world and learned to live in settings as diverse as the Arctic and the Sahara. Consider the accomplishment that agriculture represents. Consider enormous cities like Tokyo and Rio de Janeiro. Consider technological miracles from the telephone to the Space Shuttle. Consider art, music, and literature. Consider dance and gymnastics. Consider our deliberate eradication of disease and promotion of health. That all of these achievements can be attributed to intelligence is why intelligence is one of the most valued human characteristics.

The definition of intelligence as adaptive and purposeful behavior is abstract, and psychologists have therefore searched for concrete measures. One popular approach has been standardized tests like the SAT or GRE, but these tests have long been controversial.

Defining and Measuring Intelligence

Although we can agree that striking behaviors like those just described reflect intelligence in the extreme, much less agreement exists about everyday examples of intelligence. Unfortunately, as psychologists have studied intelligence throughout the twentieth century, they settled on operational definitions without fully examining the meaning of this complex psychological characteristic.

So, the most popular operationalization of intelligence has been standardized tests like the SAT. These presumably allow psychologists to predict who will or will not show intelligent behavior, but the tests have long been controversial (Lawson, 1944/1992). In retrospect, we can see that this controversy was all but inevitable given that measures of intelligence were devised before its meaning was agreed upon.

The example of Stephanie Johnson illustrates the controversy. She is an excellent student but a poor test taker. It seems unreasonable to treat her as unintelligent, but that is how the state university has dealt with her, regarding the test as more significant than her actual behavior as a student. The fate of Enrique Ramos seems more satisfactory. Because of a standardized test, he has been given an opportunity otherwise denied to him.

Though we hope Enrique will make the most of his opportunity, we all know at least a few people whose sole accomplishment in life seems to be high test scores attained once upon a time when they were children. These supposedly gifted individuals were given special attention, awards, and scholarships but never did anything that benefited themselves or others. Why do we persist in regarding them as intelligent in the absence of behavior that reflects intelligence?

Another controversy revolves around the fact that a test taker is often given but one score, implying that intelligence is a single continuum along which all people can be placed (Davidson, 1990; Hunt, 1990). Is this practice reasonable? It assumes that people who are intelligent in one area of life must be intelligent in all other areas. It ignores the setting in which a person does or does not display intelligent behavior.

What about individuals like Fred and Eva? One could argue that athletic talent and musical talent are forms of intelligent behavior because they are adaptive and purposive. Such talents are readily determined by observing an individual's performance as opposed to asking him or her to take a test like the SAT. Along these lines, why do our colleges require athletes but not musicians to attain a minimal SAT score?

Intelligence as Biopsychosocial

Throughout this book, you have seen the nature-nurture issue raised. This chapter is no exception. At one extreme is the view that intelligence is largely a matter of genetic inheritance; at the other extreme is the argument that intelligence is a product of particular experiences—notably, education.

This issue heats up when it is extended to address race differences in intelligence. On tests like the SAT, African Americans on average score lower than European Americans, and Asian Americans on average score highest. Some suggest that these facts reflect inherent differences in intelligence among these ethnic groups. Others disagree, pointing out first that intelligence tests tend to have an unintended bias against members of certain groups, and second that people in these groups tend not to have access to the experiences that allow those in other groups to score well.

Related to the nature-nurture issue is another controversy: whether intelligence can be changed. Those who favor a biological view of the basis of intelligence regard it as fixed, whereas those who favor an environmental view are more optimistic that things can be done to boost intelligence. An evenhanded conclusion is that intelligence is a biopsychosocial phenomenon (Ceci, Ramey, & Ramey, 1990); nonetheless, much of

Can intelligence be changed? Those who believe that intelligence is largely based on genetics are not optimistic, whereas those who believe that intelligence is largely due to social influences believe that educational interventions can raise intelligence.

what is known about intelligence has come from investigations treating it in stark terms of nature versus nurture.

Stop and Think

1   What is intelligence?

2   How have psychologists usually measured intelligence?

DOING *Intelligence* RESEARCH

Psychologists who study intelligence are aware of the problems with how it has typically been measured, and they have tried to overcome them. One long-standing attempt is the search for measures of intelligence that are not influenced by a person's particular background. These measures are described as being **culture-fair intelligence tests** (Carroll, 1982).

However, it has proved difficult if not impossible to devise a test that does not in some way rely on a particular culture for its grounding. Consider the questions in Table 11.1. When these questions were administered to children in both urban and rural settings, children from cities did better on Test A, whereas children from farms did better on Test B (Shimberg, 1929). Intelligence tests reflect what one knows because of where one lives.

Or consider this item from a popular intelligence test: Washington is to Adams as first is to _____. This analogy is a reasonable question if one has studied American history and recognizes Washington and Adams as the names of the first two presidents. But all sorts of perfectly intelligent people might not know this. It seems unreasonable to regard correct answers to this particular question as indicating innate intelligence, but that is exactly how advocates of this test interpret them.

It is not only the content of test items that may favor one group over another but also the way items are phrased. Not everyone in the United States speaks the same version of the English language. Many intelligence tests are phrased in the dialect of the white middle class, and those from other backgrounds might be at a disadvantage.

■ **culture-fair intelligence tests**
intelligence tests designed to measure abilities that are unaffected by an individual's particular background

Table 11.1   Intelligence Test Questions

Test A

1. What are the colors in the American flag?
2. Who is president of the United States?
3. What is the largest river in the United States?
4. How can banks afford to pay interest on the money you deposit?
5. What is the freezing point of water?
6. What is a referendum in government?

Test B

1. Of what is butter made?
2. Name a vegetable that grows above ground.
3. Why does seasoned wood burn more easily than green wood?
4. About how often do we have a full moon?
5. Who was president of the United States during the [First] World War?
6. How can you locate the pole star?

Source: Shimberg (1929).

One test often cited as culture fair is the Raven (1948) Standard Progressive Matrices Test, consisting of 60 designs, each with a missing part (see Figure 11.1). The individual taking the test must choose the missing part from several possibilities. This test is thought by some psychologists to measure logical abilities and powers of discrimination independently of cultural background, although this claim has been disputed by other researchers.

Perhaps the problem with culture-fair intelligence tests is that they do not question the initial premise that we can speak of intelligence apart from a particular environment. Let us return to the definition of intelligence as adaptive and purposeful behavior. Is there such a thing as behavior out of context? Is there such a thing as adaptation out of context?

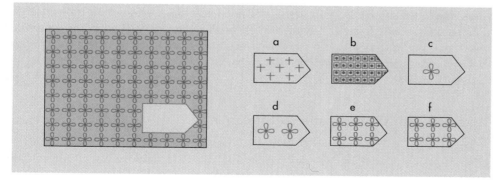

Figure 11.1

Raven Standard Progressive Matrices Example. Which lettered block best completes this pattern? Some psychologists believe that the Raven Matrices Test, which presents an individual with many such problems, is a culture-fair measure of intelligence. Other psychologists disagree, believing that intelligence must be specified with respect to a given environment or culture. For instance, the Raven Matrices Test seems to be a highly appropriate measure of one of the skills needed by people who hang wallpaper or lay tiles but is probably less useful for determining who will excel in other occupations.

Although intelligence is sensibly located in given times and places, only recently have psychologists taken this idea seriously and moved beyond the study of test scores. At the end of this chapter, I describe some recent approaches to intelligence that approach it in biopsychosocial terms. Until then, I detail how psychologists arrived at this perspective. Important lessons about intelligence and how to study it were learned along the way, but appreciate the controversies that have accompanied past investigations. Many stemmed from the premature choice of an operational definition of intelligence.

Stop and Think

3   What are the benefits of measuring intelligence with tests instead of other operationalizations?

4   Can intelligence tests ever be culture fair?

A HISTORY OF INTELLIGENCE TESTING

As already noted, the most common operationalization of intelligence has held that you are intelligent if you score high on an intelligence test and unintelligent if you score low. These labels, placed on people by their test performance, profoundly affect the lives people lead. What schools are open to them? What jobs? What promotions?

Psychologists sometimes divide intelligence tests into aptitude tests, which attempt to measure one's capacity for learning, and achievement tests, which attempt to measure what one has already learned. The SAT, for instance, is an aptitude test because it is used to predict how a student will do in college. A midterm exam in art history, on the other hand, is an achievement test because it is used to determine how much a student has already learned.

The distinction between aptitude tests and achievement tests is easier to make in theory than in practice. Aptitude tests necessarily reflect some learning on the part of the test taker (if only how to follow the test's instructions). Some prefer to describe only aptitude tests as true measures of intelligence. In any event, the practical distinction between aptitude and achievement can be murky, and so I will use the term *intelligence test* to refer to both aptitude tests and achievement tests.

The notions of reliability and validity introduced in Chapter 2 need to be kept in mind. Intelligence tests are quite reliable, yielding the same score for an individual on different occasions. However, the validity of intelligence tests—whether they measure what they purport to measure—is not so easily decided. Much of the controversy surrounding these tests represents disagreement about their validity (Bagnato & Neisworth, 1994).

Francis Galton's Approach to Intelligence

A pivotal event in the history of intelligence testing was the 1869 publication of the book *Hereditary Genius*, by Sir Francis Galton (1822–1911). Galton was an upper-class Englishman, a half-cousin of Charles Darwin. Like other men of his class at this time, Galton did not work. Rather, he pursued various interests, which included science in general and human abilities in particular. The theory of evolution captivated science during his era, and so he applied evolutionary ideas to his study of human abilities.

Galton was interested in how people differed from each other with respect to their abilities.

The psychological investigation of intelligence began with the work of Sir Francis Galton.

I have no patience with the hypothesis occasionally expressed, and often implied, especially in tales written to teach children to be good, that babies are born pretty much alike, and that the sole agencies in creating differences between boy and boy, and man and man, are steady application and moral effort. It is in the most unqualified manner that I object to pretensions of natural equality. The experiences of the nursery, the school, the University, and of professional careers, are a chain of proofs to the contrary. (Galton, 1869, p. 12)

Note the contrast between Galton's ideas and those of John Watson, the American behaviorist (Chapter 8). Watson was concerned with what people have in common—their capacity to learn—whereas Galton was concerned with how people differ from each other—in this case, the limits of their capacities.

Galton believed that a person's intellectual capacity is not linked to specific domains. Rather, intelligence is a general characteristic brought to bear in a variety of ways. Hence, he used the term *genius* to describe individuals and not their feats.

People lay too much stress on apparent specialties, thinking over-rashly because a man is devoted to some particular pursuit, he could not possibly have succeeded in anything else. After a man of genius has selected his hobby, and adapted himself to it as to seem unfitted for any other occupation in life, and to be possessed of but one special aptitude, I often notice, with admiration, how well he bears himself when circumstances suddenly thrust him into a strange position. (pp. 20–21)

Galton further believed that the differences in people's intelligence could be quantified. Not only do people differ, but they differ in degrees. He also suggested that these differences fall along a bell-shaped curve, with most people clustered in the middle. Moving farther toward one extreme or the other (toward the more intelligent or the less intelligent), ever fewer people were represented.

I propose . . . to range men according to their natural abilities, putting them in classes separated by equal degrees of merit, and to show the relative number of individuals included in the several classes. Perhaps some person might be inclined to make an offhand guess that the number of men included in the dif-

---

Table 11.2 Francis Galton's Frequency Distribution of Intelligence

According to Francis Galton, people differ in their intelligence, and these differences fall along a bell-shaped curve. The more extreme someone's degree of intelligence, either below or above average, the more infrequently that degree is encountered in the population.

Grades of natural ability		Proportion of people in the grade of mental ability
Below Average	**Above Average**	**Proportion: One in**
a	A	4
b	B	6
c	C	16
d	D	64
e	E	413
f	F	4,300
g	G	79,000
x	X	1,000,000

Source: Adapted from Galton (1869).

ferent classes would be pretty equal. If he thinks so, I can assure him he is most
. . . mistaken. (p. 22)

He gave people letter grades that reflected their relative intelligence and hence their
relative frequency in the population. "A" people were one in four, "B" were one in six,
and so on (see Table 11.2).

Galton argued that differences in genius were inherited. As the title suggests,
Hereditary Genius documented how talents and achievements run in families. Galton
showed that accomplished men (like himself) had accomplished relatives (like his half-
cousin Darwin). In retrospect, we can see that a society like Galton's England almost
guarantees the conclusion that genius runs in families. Property and titles and influence
and opportunities passed from grandfather to father to son.

Galton's data just as readily imply that accomplishments are a result of privilege, not
biology. He was aware of this alternative view and was one of the first to explicitly
phrase the nature-nurture issue. How many of a person's characteristics can be attributed to biology (nature) and how many to learning and socialization (nurture)? Galton
argued that with respect to intelligence, the role of nurture was negligible. As already
mentioned, this debate is still alive today.

Galton also believed that people's potential for genius could be measured prior to
any actual accomplishment. Starting with the assumption that information comes from
our senses, he proposed that people with superior sensory and motor abilities must be
more able. Hence, his intelligence tests measured individual differences in the strength
of people's grip, the rate at which they could tap their finger, the speed with which they
reacted to a sound, the accuracy with which they could divide a line in two, and so on.

Darwin's theory of evolution affected Galton's approach to intelligence. Galton
founded the movement known as **eugenics,** which held that the human species could
be improved through systematic application of the theory of evolution (Chapter 3).
Biologically superior people should be encouraged to interbreed, and the less superior
should be dealt out of the process altogether.

This controversial position was espoused by the Nazis, who used the language of
biological superiority and inferiority to express their hatred of other groups. Eugenics
has been associated with intelligence testing from the start, and its negative connotations
often taint the testing movement. Still, eugenics has not entirely disappeared. It is still
apparent, for example, in the commonly held opinion that mentally retarded individuals
should not be allowed to have children.

Because of Galton, the meaning of intelligence became entwined with Darwinian
ideas of fitness (Gould, 1981). When Galton proposed that some people had more
genius than others, he seemed to be saying that these people were more fit. A further
leap was sometimes made from fitness to moral worth. This unfortunate equivalence still
holds in the minds of some people today, who think the results of an intelligence test say
it all about a person. But remember that fitness refers to the capacity for survival and
reproduction (Chapter 3), not intelligence, genius, worth, or any of the other notions
with which we mistakenly associate it.

Despite the racism they have been used to rationalize, Francis Galton's views are
important for two reasons. First, modern approaches to intelligence stem directly from
his work. Even when contemporary psychologists disagree with him, they tend to use
his terminology and take positions on the issues that he first phrased. Second, his work
shows that science is never undertaken in a vacuum. Theory and research reflect the
larger social and historical setting in which scientists work (Chapter 2).

Alfred Binet's Approach to Intelligence

As explained in Chapter 1, the earliest intelligence tests relied on simple sensory and
motor tests. These proved unrelated to presumably relevant behavior, like grades in

■ **eugenics**
attempt to improve the human
species through the systematic
application of the theory of
evolution

school (Cattell & Farrand, 1896; Wissler, 1901). So, they were quickly abandoned, replaced by tests that used more complex tasks.

The central figure behind this innovation was the French psychologist Alfred Binet (1857–1911), who was interested not only in educational issues such as testing but also in states of consciousness (Chapter 6) and psychopathology (Chapter 13). Binet's contributions to the measurement of intelligence were sparked when the French minister of public instruction asked him to solve a problem confronted by the schools (Schneider, 1992). How could a teacher distinguish students unable to learn (the mentally retarded) from those unwilling to learn? If this distinction were possible, so went the reasoning, then those unable to profit from typical instruction could be sent to special schools where they might be helped. Perhaps a test might be devised to measure one's ability to learn. Binet came up with a way to make this distinction. His first intelligence test was published in 1905, and it proved so popular that it was repeatedly revised (e.g., Binet & Simon, 1913).

Binet instituted a number of procedures that still characterize intelligence testing today. First, his tests posed complex tasks for subjects (see Table 11.3). He compiled many test activities for students, trying to represent the range of activities actually involved in schoolwork. The test was administered to one student at a time, by an examiner who posed tasks and questions. The process usually took several hours. Initial items on the test were easy, and subsequent items became more difficult. The testing continued until the student failed to give correct answers.

Second, Binet administered test items to large numbers of students to determine the distribution of typical scores. A given student's scores could then be compared with these standards, which are called **norms,** and interpreted as above, below, or at the average.

Third, Binet showed that his tests accomplished their intended purpose of identifying students unable to profit from typical instruction. He assembled a variety of possible items and administered these to numerous children. He then determined which items allowed the prediction of good and poor school performance. Only those items that successfully made this distinction were kept for the test's final version.

As you know, the validity of an operational definition refers to whether it captures what it intends to measure. There are various ways to judge validity. Binet established

■ **norms**

average scores for test performance, based on research with large samples

---

Table 11.3   Examples from Binet's Intelligence Tests

Alfred Binet's approach to the measurement of intelligence posed complex tasks to children and recognized that individuals of different ages are best tested with different tasks.

Year 3

1. Point to eyes, nose, and mouth.
2. Repeat two digits.
3. Identify objects in a picture.
4. Repeat a sentence of six syllables.

Year 7

1. Show right hand and left ear.
2. Describe a picture.
3. Carry out three commands given simultaneously.
4. Count the value of six coins.

Year 15

1. Repeat seven digits.
2. Find three rhymes for a given word in one minute.
3. Repeat a sentence of 26 syllables.
4. Interpret a set of given facts.

what is known as criterion validity for his test, judging it by how well it predicted the particular criterion of doing well in academic classes (good grades on tests and papers). This approach remains a popular strategy for demonstrating the validity of an intelligence test.

One of the rules of thumb concerning criterion validity is that when scores on the criterion variable are closely bunched, it is difficult for a test to make sharp distinctions among them. Binet was concerned with the gross distinction between the mentally retarded and the mentally normal, and his test indeed achieved its intended function. But as intelligence tests have become popular, they have been called upon to make finer discriminations among highly capable students, and they have become less dependable and useful (Sicoly, 1992).

Remember Stephanie Johnson, who had below-average SAT scores. In her case, the average is based on those individuals who wish to attend college, certainly a select group. Being in the lower half of this group is hardly proof that one is unintelligent; after all, 50 percent of those who take the SAT must be below average.

A fourth innovation by Binet was the recognition that whatever they were measuring should reflect the student's chronological age, and so they created different norms for individuals at each age. A student's score could then be described by referring to the average score of children at that particular age. This was the student's **mental age.** Suppose your test score matches the way an average 8-year-old child scores. Your mental age, regardless of your chronological age, is therefore 8.

Today you might hear people saying that sixth-grade classes are reading at an eighth-grade level (or vice versa). This comment reflects the Binet innovation of describing a test score in terms of the age-group for which it is typical. If your mental age is higher than your chronological age, then you have above-average intelligence. If your mental age is lower than your chronological age, then you have below-average intelligence. If the two are the same, then you have average intelligence.

The most important implication of this view is that intelligence as measured with a test is relative, in several ways. It is obviously relative to one's chronological age. Equal performance by two children of different ages means that they have different degrees of intelligence. Also, as just described, intelligence is relative to the group on whom the scores have been normed. Depending on the people in that group, one's mental age can vary. Intelligence is also relative to the particular questions posed on the test. Tests such as Binet's must be periodically updated. For example, one place where revisions have to be made is in the section concerned with vocabulary. Words pass in and out of common use, and if we are to measure intelligence by assessing vocabulary, we have to recognize the changes that occur in language over time.

Another implication is that rigid distinctions among people of different levels of intelligence are arbitrary. Although cutoffs are often used to identify the mentally retarded on the one hand and the geniuses on the other, the cutoff values are arbitrary. The population does not fall into three discrete clumps of people: the retarded, the geniuses, and the rest of us.

Lewis Terman's Contribution

Binet's tests were successful in that they distinguished between students who could and could not profit from traditional instruction. Their tests were soon translated into other languages and imported to other countries, including the United States. Several individuals undertook the English translation, but the best known was originally done in 1916 at Stanford University by Lewis M. Terman (1877–1956). Today we call this test the **Stanford-Binet Intelligence Scale** to reflect its origins in Binet's work and its translation at Stanford.

■ **mental age**
average intelligence test score of children of a given chronological age

■ **Stanford-Binet Intelligence Scale**
intelligence test based on Binet's original measure and its translation into English by Terman at Stanford University

The Stanford–Binet reflects an important innovation: dividing one's mental age by one's chronological age, then multiplying by 100 to avoid decimal places (Stern, 1914). This quotient is called the **intelligence quotient,** abbreviated as **IQ:**

$$IQ = \frac{\text{mental age}}{\text{chronological age}} \times 100$$

■ **intelligence quotient (IQ)**
ratio of one's mental age and chronological age, multiplied by 100

The qualifications discussed earlier about the relativity of measured intelligence apply to IQ scores as well.

IQ is no longer defined as the quotient of mental age and chronological age. Today we compare someone's score on the Stanford–Binet to the scores of the larger population of those the same age who have taken the test. An IQ of 100 is average, by definition. An IQ of 115 means that you score higher than 84 percent of people your age who have taken the test, whereas an IQ of 85 means that your score exceeds that of 16 percent of people your age (see Figure 11.2).

The original Binet test was intended to make distinctions only within the group of students not doing well in school. Presumably, students who were performing satisfactorily in their schoolwork never needed to be tested because their performance was proof that they had the ability to perform. Indeed, Binet was reportedly reluctant to regard his measure as a test of mental ability for all students. He feared that test results would be used to restrict opportunities, not enhance them.

Terman disagreed with this restricted use of intelligence tests and advocated instead the testing of all students:

What pupils should be tested? The answer is, all. If only selected children are tested, many of the cases most in need of adjustment will be overlooked. The purpose of the tests is to tell us what we do not already know, and it would be a mistake to test only those students who are recognized as obviously below or above average. Some of the biggest surprises are encountered in testing those who have been looked upon as close to average in ability. Universal testing is fully warranted. (Terman, Dickson, Sutherland, Franzen, Tupper, & Fernald, 1923, p. 22)

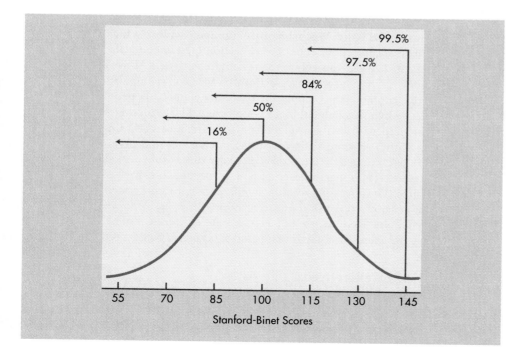

Figure 11.2
Distribution of IQ Scores. If a large number of people took an intelligence test, like the Stanford–Binet, here is how their scores would look. Most scores would cluster in the middle. Extreme scores, in either direction, would be less likely. The numbers at the top of the curve show the percentage of people who would score below the indicated score.

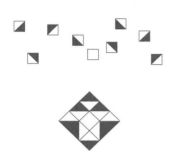

Figure 11.3
Wechsler Block Design. One of the items in the Wechsler Intelligence Scales gives a person plastic blocks and asks him or her to arrange them to reproduce a specific design.

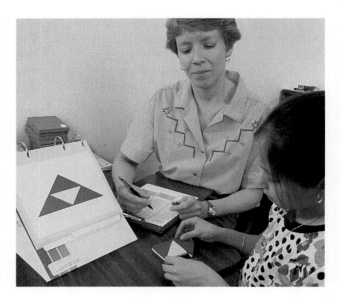

Both the child and adult versions of the Wechsler Intelligence Scales have separate verbal and performance sections. Here, a school psychologist administers an intelligence test to an elementary school student.

■ **Wechsler Intelligence Scales**
intelligence tests that were devised by David Wechsler and yield separate verbal and performance scores

Figure 11.4
Wechsler Picture Arrangement. Another item in the Wechsler Intelligence Scales asks an individual to arrange several pictures in the correct order so as to tell a coherent story, from beginning to end.

Terman's call was heeded, particularly in the United States, where mass intelligence testing is now the rule (Neisworth & Bagnato, 1992).

Terman agreed with Galton that intelligence is largely a matter of biological inheritance. This view spread throughout the mass testing movement, resulting in the use of intelligence testing to decide who need not be given opportunities for further schooling, as well as to support pronouncements that different racial and ethnic groups varied in terms of their biological makeup (Vialle, 1994).

The Wechsler Intelligence Scales

In 1939, the psychologist David Wechsler developed his own test of intelligence, and it improved on the Stanford-Binet in several ways. Wechsler wanted a test that could be used with adults, not just children. He also believed that people who came from non-English-speaking homes were at a disadvantage taking tests phrased exclusively in English. He thus devised the **Wechsler Intelligence Scales,** which have separate verbal and performance sections. The verbal sections test individuals' knowledge of general information ("What is a ruby?") and comprehension ("Why do people keep money in a bank?"). The performance sections require the manipulation of material without any verbal content. For example, the block design task asks people to reproduce the designs they see by using colored blocks (see Figure 11.3). Another task asks people to put pictures together to form a coherent story (see Figure 11.4). Once tested, each person ends up with a separate score for verbal intelligence and performance intelligence. Wechsler's tests are widely used today and have undergone periodic revisions.

A parallel test for school-age children provides separate scores for verbal and performance intelligence. The idea of breaking intelligence into components has become popular, and the most recent version of the Stanford-Binet has been modified to yield not only an overall intelligence score but also separate estimates of one's verbal, quantitative, reasoning, and memory abilities (Thorndike, Hagan, & Sattler, 1986).

Group Tests of Intelligence

The Stanford-Binet and the Wechsler Intelligence Scales require individual administration. The next chapter in the history of intelligence testing involved the development of group tests that did not need to be administered individually. World War I gave group testing its first big boost.

Whether Army Alpha and Army Beta helped to win the war, as some believed, they did help to legitimize the idea of group intelligence testing.

Army Alpha and Army Beta. Robert M. Yerkes (1876–1956) and other psychologists, including Terman, created an intelligence test that could be administered in written form to large groups. The U.S. Army cooperated by giving this test to 1.75 million army recruits between 1917 and 1919. There were two versions of the test. Army Alpha was a test for literate individuals; Army Beta was a test for illiterate individuals, relying on pictures rather than words (see Figure 11.5). The tests had two purposes: eliminating the unfit (those scoring low) and choosing candidates for officers (those scoring high).

Whether Army Alpha and Army Beta helped to win the war, as Yerkes believed, is unclear (Gould, 1981). What is clear is that intelligence testing was legitimized by the existence of norms based on almost 2 million individuals. Once the results of the army testing became available, commercial testing businesses and educational institutions showed great interest in them (Chapter 17).

Strictly speaking, Army Alpha and Army Beta did not yield IQ scores. Rather, these tests assigned grades ranging from A, the highest grade, to E, the lowest. However, these letter grades could be translated into IQ scores, leading to the conclusion that the average mental age of European American army recruits was 13. The general public was dismayed because this conclusion suggested that we were a nation of adolescents. Those who favored eugenics pointed to these results as proof of the impending doom of the United States.

Another result of the army testing was that the recruits were compared in terms of their country of origin. Recruits from Southern and Eastern European backgrounds typically scored lower than those from Western and Northern Europe. Citing these results, some lobbied for restrictions on immigration by certain groups and for screening of would-be immigrants by testing, arguing that large numbers of individuals with low intelligence would be detrimental to the country. Administration of intelligence tests to European immigrants at Ellis Island followed. Imagine these people, newly arrived from a crowded and tiring boat trip, speaking little or no English, being asked to do something they did not understand. It is hardly surprising that their test scores made them appear unintelligent (Goddard, 1917).

From the Alpha Test

Disarranged Sentence: property floods life and destroy
(True or False)

If you save $7 a month for 4 months, how much will you save?

Revolvers are made by: Smith & Wesson   Armour & Co.
Ingersol   Anheuser-Busch

Why is tennis good exercise?

The Battle of Gettysburg was fought in: 1863   1813
1778   1812

From the Beta Test

What is missing from the picture below?

From the Beta Test

Rearrange the three pictures below in the correct order.

Figure 11.5

Examples from Army Alpha and Army Beta Intelligence Tests. Army Alpha was a test for those who could read and thus respond to written material. Army Beta was a test for those who could not read and thus relied on pictures.

Finally, when African Americans and other ethnic minorities were compared with European Americans, they tended to score lower on the army intelligence tests, once again reinforcing stereotyped beliefs about the innate superiority of some groups over others. Here is what Terman (1916, pp. 91–92) said about racial minorities in the United States:

> Their dullness seems to be racial. There is no possibility at present of convincing society that they should not be allowed to reproduce, although from a eugenic point of view, they constitute a grave problem because of their unusually prolific breeding.

Note the irony in complaining about the biological fitness of a group of people judged intellectually unfit.

Modern group tests. Today the best-known descendant of Army Alpha is the Scholastic Aptitude Test (SAT), which you probably took as part of your application for college. It is a group-administered test that presumably measures one's aptitude for college work. There are other group tests that are used to select students for medical school, law school, business school, and graduate school. Most of these tests are designed to measure aptitude, not achievement. Remember the point made earlier that aptitude tests and achievement tests can be difficult to distinguish. Considerable controversy exists as to what tests like the SAT actually measure and whether this is best regarded as aptitude.

Many of you are aware of the private businesses that prepare students to score higher on these group tests than they might on their own. These businesses sometimes make extreme claims about the effectiveness of such coaching, but those claims are difficult to evaluate (Owen, 1985). Crash courses that teach test-taking strategies can result in slight gains on the SAT, perhaps enough to make a difference for a college applicant on the border between admission and rejection, or for a college athlete whose career is threatened by NCAA guidelines about eligibility (Kulik, Bangert-Drowns, & Kulik, 1984). These results—although modest—should give pause to any who interpret the SAT as a valid measure of inherent aptitude. Theoretically, crash courses should have no effect on intelligence.

Intelligence tests deserve their share of criticism. But there are benefits to intelligence testing that deserve acknowledgment. Remember Binet's original purpose. The use of intelligence tests to match educational approaches to particular students remains a good use of such tests. If an intelligence test identifies a promising student otherwise overlooked, this use too can be praised.

Stop and Think

5   Why is Binet considered the originator of modern intelligence testing?

6   What is an intelligence quotient?

DETERMINANTS OF INTELLIGENCE

By the 1930s, criticisms of cultural bias in intelligence tests first raised with regard to Army Alpha and Army Beta were taken seriously by most psychologists (Hilgard, 1987). Throughout much of the 1940s and 1950s, intelligence testing continued, but it ceased being a focus of societal debate. However, in the 1960s a new round of the nature-nurture debate, with all of its social policy implications, raged anew.

The debate began in 1969 with the publication of an article entitled "How Much Can We Boost IQ and Scholastic Achievement?" by the educational psychologist Arthur Jensen. Social events immediately prior to 1969 help explain the impact of his work. The 1950s and 1960s had seen a number of landmarks in the civil rights movement:

■ In 1954, the Supreme Court outlawed segregation in public schools.
■ In 1956, Martin Luther King, Jr., started to campaign against segregation in public transportation.
■ In 1957, Congress passed the Equal Rights Act.
■ In 1963, King led his March on Washington and gave his famous "I Have a Dream" speech.
■ In 1964, Congress strengthened the Equal Rights Act.
■ In 1965, President Johnson declared "war on poverty," and funds were made available for the Head Start program, which provided learning experiences for underprivileged children prior to their entering school, in an attempt to give them a head start on school.

These were times of growing hope and promise for blacks and whites alike, and then Jensen's article appeared, with implications to the contrary.

Jensen started with a well-established fact: African Americans on average score about 15 IQ points below European Americans. This fact was not itself controversial. What was controversial was Jensen's conclusion that blacks score lower than whites because of biological differences.

Thus, according to Jensen, compensatory education (e.g., Head Start) could do little to boost IQ and scholastic achievement because a person would have to push against inherent limitations. Although Jensen considered the possibility that this racial difference resulted from environmental factors—namely, that African Americans tend to have less access to the experiences and educational benefits that lead to good performance on conventional intelligence tests—he disagreed with that explanation and championed the nature view. Other psychologists jumped into the fray and took issue with Jensen's conclusions (Kamin, 1974).

The debate about the relative roles of nature and nurture in intelligence was highlighted by the desegregation of schools in the United States. This photo shows a segregated classroom in Tennessee, and it seems difficult to argue from group comparisons that intelligence is mainly biological when the schools attended by those in one group are markedly inferior to the schools attended by those in another group.

The most recent chapter in the ongoing controversy about ethnic differences in intelligence occurred in 1994 with the publication of Richard Herrnstein and Charles Murray's book *The Bell Curve*. This book argued for the validity of general intelligence tests and reported evidence that scores on these tests predict not only academic performance but also occupational attainment, socioeconomic status, marital stability, parenting, citizenship, and law-abidingness.

The Bell Curve was discussed most frequently in the popular media in terms of its thesis that black-white differences in intelligence are based in biology, a conclusion the authors themselves regarded as unresolved. Some other important points were raised in the book that have not received nearly as much popular attention.

One of these ideas is the argument that intelligence as measured by typical tests has become increasingly important in our modern society because of the demands made in almost all quarters for acquiring and using complex information, skills made possible only by intelligence (Hunt, 1995). According to Herrnstein and Murray, an ever smaller number of people can succeed in the modern world. These authors described this group as a cognitive elite: individuals—of all ethnic groups—who by virtue of their intelligence win admission to the best schools and thus receive the best jobs, make the most money, have the best marriages, and assert the most societal influence.

The topic of race differences will be discussed again later in this section (see also Fraser, 1995). But first we need to cover what psychologists have learned in recent years about the roles of genetics and the environment in determining intelligence (as measured by IQ tests).

Genetic Influences on Intelligence

When researchers study the role of heredity, they must rely on correlational methods. In fact, Francis Galton invented the notion of correlation (which he called *co-relation,* meaning "relation with") precisely to quantify the degree to which the genius of fathers corresponded to the genius of their sons.

If, for instance, intelligence reflects genetic influence, then we would expect that the IQ scores of relatives would show a positive correlation with each other. The closer the relation, the higher this positive correlation should be. So, a parent and his or her children have in common 50 percent of their genes. A grandparent and his or her grandchildren have in common 25 percent of their genes. The results of numerous studies show the pattern expected by hereditarians: The closer the biological relatedness, the higher the correlation between intelligence test scores. On the other hand, these correlations might also reflect similarity among people's environments.

An especially useful type of such family studies is the study of twins. These studies compare the IQs of identical twins (who have in common 100 percent of their genes) and fraternal twins (who are no more similar genetically than ordinary siblings—i.e., 50 percent overlap). A further refinement is made when these twins are divided into those raised together (presumably in a similar environment) and those raised apart (presumably in dissimilar environments).

A true experiment to determine the relative influences of genetics and the environment is impossible because a researcher cannot manipulate these factors. However, a researcher can make use of the special characteristics of twins to carry out a study that is similar to an experiment (Chapter 2). The effects of nature and nurture can be separated by looking at the correlations between the IQs of identical and fraternal twins, raised together and raised apart.

This strategy has some flaws. Certain assumptions must be made that are not strictly true. For example, we must assume that identical twins raised together experience the same environment, as do fraternal twins raised together. We know that each twin has a slightly different relationship with his or her parents. Also, how does the fact of being an identical twin affect the way parents, teachers, and peers treat someone? How about the way the twin views him- or herself? We must also assume that those twins raised separately are placed randomly in orphanages or foster homes, so that their environments are not similar. Again, this assumption is not strictly true. In locating foster homes, agencies try to match the background of the biological family. If this matching is done for both members of a set of twins, then "raised apart" might not be all that different from "raised together."

Researchers are mindful of these possible confounds and try their best to control them. The results of many studies suggest that genetic factors contribute to intelligence (Plomin, 1987). In other words, as the data in Figure 11.6 show, the correlations between intelligence test scores of twins fall in the order we would expect from a hereditarian perspective.

Such findings do not mean that intelligence is inherited. They show only that intelligence is heritable: influenced by genetics. As explained earlier, *heritable* is a technical term meaning the degree to which variation in a characteristic (e.g., intelligence) reflects variation in genes (Chapter 3). *Heritable* does not mean that the characteristic is

Studies of identical twins raised together and apart provide one way to disentangle the effects of nature and nurture. However, this strategy is not foolproof because it is not a true experiment under the control of a researcher.

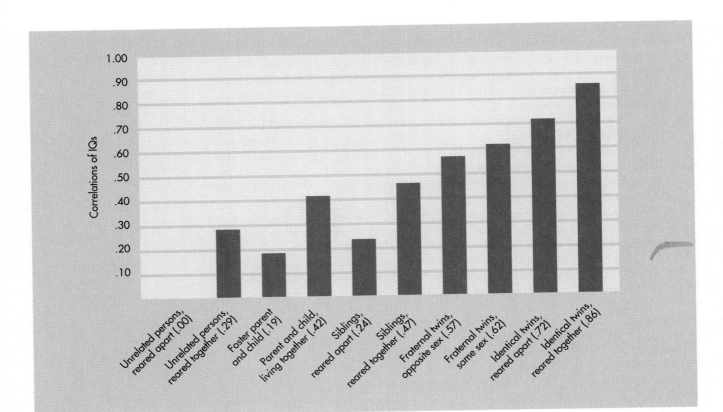

Figure 11.6
Correlations of IQ Scores from Family Studies. The closer the biological relatedness of two individuals, the higher the correlation between their IQ scores. This pattern is consistent with the conclusion that measured intelligence is heritable.
Sources: Bouchard & McGue (1981); Erlenmeyer-Kimling & Jarvik (1963); Rowe & Plomin (1981).

inherited as a whole; it means that a certain proportion of the differences in intelligence within a group of people has a genetic basis.

We do not know what genes produce this variation in intelligence. Nor do we know the mechanisms that produce the variation in intelligence. Studies imply that the speed and consistency with which the nervous system works are contributing factors (Reed & Jensen, 1992; Vernon, 1990a, 1990b; Vernon & Mori, 1992; Vernon & Weese, 1993). There is some evidence that neurological efficiency is a heritable characteristic (Baker, Vernon, & Ho, 1991), but biological characteristics can reflect the role of experience as well as genetics. More work is needed to explain how microscopic features of the nervous system give rise to the complex achievements we identify as intelligence (Ceci, 1990; Vernon, 1991).

Finally, the heritability estimates are not so high that we can conclude that genetics are all that matter. If something other than heredity influences intelligence test scores, then it must be the environment.

Environmental Influences on Intelligence

To investigate possible environmental influences on intelligence, researchers have looked at how intelligence changes over the life span, trying to determine what is associated with these changes. Results document a number of influences. For example, prenatal events are important. Injury or illness to the mother while she is pregnant can adversely affect the child's intelligence (Chapter 10). Pregnant mothers should avoid smoking, drinking, physical trauma, poor nutrition, and illnesses like German measles.

On the positive side, studies that intervene with pregnant women to improve their medical care and diet demonstrate improvements in their children's IQs (Harrell, Woodyard, & Gates, 1956).

Difficulties in the process of birth itself can also lower intelligence. A baby deprived of oxygen during birth, or suffering some trauma to the head, can be affected for the worse. Once a child is born, other experiences can raise or lower intelligence (Loehlin, Lindzey, & Spuhler, 1975; Vernon, 1979). Good nutrition and a stimulating environment are vital.

A positive correlation exists between intelligence and socioeconomic status, particularly as children become older, suggesting that all of the experiences made available by money and status affect intelligence for the better. Research has also shown that intelligence decreases as the number of children in a family increases, perhaps because parents cannot give as much attention to each child (Zajonc, 1976).

In the 1960s, Head Start programs were begun to help prepare poor children for school. Remember that Arthur Jensen criticized these programs for trying to overcome deficits rooted in biology. Attempts to evaluate the success of these compensatory attempts have been complicated and controversial (Hunt, 1982; Zigler & Berman, 1983). Head Start programs are difficult to evaluate because they have been conducted in drastically different ways, some more successfully than others. Nevertheless, early studies indicated that IQ was boosted for those preschoolers who participated in Head Start. Later studies suggested that these gains in measured intelligence were not maintained as the children continued in school.

Note, though, that the goal of Head Start programs was to boost not IQ scores but rather the academic performance of participants once they got to school. The evidence shows that this happened and, further, that these gains were maintained throughout school (Jordan, Grallo, Deutsch, & Deutsch, 1985). Judged on these grounds, Head Start programs have been successful.

In evaluating the success or failure of these programs in terms of IQ scores, researchers sometimes betray a curious bias. The appropriate use of IQ scores is to predict academic performance. If it turns out that IQ scores and academic performance do not rise in lockstep for children in Head Start programs, this means that the intelligence tests do not work here. But many critics of Head Start programs end up treating the test as more real than the criterion against which it is validated.

Imagine taking a medical test that predicts from your cholesterol level your risk of heart disease. On the whole, there is a positive correlation, but one that is less than perfect. Suppose the doctor says to you:

> You have a very high cholesterol level. Your heart and circulatory system seem completely healthy, but I'm a believer in the test. I've filled out your death certificate and called the coroner. We'll arrange your burial as soon as you tell me how you plan to pay for it.

This example sounds silly, but it is exactly what happens when we treat IQ scores as more real than academic performance.

Labels based on IQ scores have considerable power in our society. Consider, for example, one of the most sobering studies ever conducted: Robert Rosenthal's investigation of teacher expectations about intelligence (Rosenthal & Jacobson, 1968). At the beginning of a school year, Rosenthal received permission from grade school teachers to administer a special IQ test to their students. Unlike typical tests, these new tests would predict IQ in the future. There are, of course, no such tests; indeed, there probably never will be such tests. But the teachers believed Rosenthal's story. Then he instituted a specific intervention. "Don't let this influence you," he said, "but I thought you'd like to know that in your classroom, John and Susan scored particularly high on the test. Their intellects will bloom in the coming year."

One important influence on the performance of students is the expectations of their teachers. If teachers believe students are intelligent, then these students perform better.

There was nothing special about John and Susan because Rosenthal chose them at random. But their teachers expected them to show some sort of intellectual leap in the future. By the end of the year, their grades had greatly improved. Their performance on conventional intelligence tests improved as well, sometimes dramatically.

Presumably, the teachers treated the Johns and Susans differently, perhaps taking more time with them, perhaps encouraging them, perhaps challenging them to do better. Whatever transpired as a result of the expectation planted by Rosenthal affected these students' academic performance. Intelligence as measured by typical tests was affected as well. Faced with these results, it is hard to maintain that IQ reflects a biological inheritance. Note the insidious implication here as well: If teacher expectations can affect academic performance and intelligence tests for the better, can they not affect them for the worse? Teachers who expect that given students because of their ethnicity or social class, are unintelligent may end up treating them in such a way that they become unintelligent.

So, first, we can conclude that the environment matters (although we already knew this from the less than perfect role played by biology). Second, we do not know the exact mechanism that leads from particular experiences to intelligent behavior.

Investigations of the determinants of intelligence demand a biopsychosocial approach because intelligence is influenced by both biology and the social environment. However, studies of these two general influences have often been conducted in isolation from one another, leaving unanswered the question of how genetics and the environment interact to determine intelligence. Furthermore, both sorts of investigations tend to neglect the psychological processes—cognitive, motivational, and emotional—that link biological and social influences to actual behavior. Instead, they calculate what can be termed distant correlations between biological or social factors on the one hand and measured IQ on the other, neglecting the intervening processes and mechanisms.

Stop and Think

7   How is intelligence biopsychosocial?

8   How is intelligence research not biopsychosocial?

INTELLIGENCE ACROSS SOCIAL CONTRASTS

The debate over how to interpret race differences in intelligence test scores has been mentioned several times. This section begins with a more detailed discussion of the topic in light of the information just provided about the influences on intelligence. The section ends with a discussion of gender differences in intelligence test scores.

Race and Intelligence

The debate about racial differences in intelligence has expanded in recent years beyond black-white comparisons to include other social groups (Darou, 1992). Research suggests that those of East Asian ancestry (Chinese, Japanese, and Korean individuals) score on average between 3 and 10 IQ points higher than European Americans (Lynn, 1991; Lynn & Song, 1992; Vernon, 1982). Some theorists interpret this difference in terms of inherent biological factors, whereas others point to environmental determinants (Sue & Okazaki, 1990).

Is heredity responsible for the documented differences in IQ among blacks and whites and Asians? The answer is no. Race is an important category in our society, one of the ways in which we think about ourselves and others. However, race is a social category, not a biological one (Chapter 1).

In biology, the term *race* refers to a subgroup of a species that is geographically separated from other subgroups and hence not interbreeding with them. This definition has little to do with the so-called human races, particularly in the United States, where races are defined by a murky combination of superficial physical characteristics like skin color and hair texture and bureaucratic designations like the nation from which one's ancestors emigrated. If one wanted to describe biologically based variations across human beings that are linked to the geographic origins of their immediate ancestors, the currently popular groupings of African, European, and Asian would not result (Cavalli-Sforza, Menozi, & Piazza, 1994). Instead, one would focus on characteristics such as liver enzymes and blood type, which to the best of our knowledge are psychologically irrelevant.

In the United States, different racial groups live in the same place, and marriage among these groups occurs frequently. For example, a large number of American blacks have immediate ancestors of European origin, and many American whites have immediate ancestors of African origin. Similarly, among many contemporary Asian American groups—particularly Japanese Americans—marriage outside one's ethnic group is more typical than marriage within the group (Kitano, Yeung, Chai, & Hatanaka, 1984). In general, it does not make sense to force people into racial categories and then to compound the awkward fit by saying that these fuzzy categories are actually biological ones.

Several lines of research suggest that ethnic differences in measured intelligence do not reflect biological differences. For example, one study looked at the IQs of children born to German mothers and American fathers following the U.S. occupation of Germany after World War II (Eyferth, 1961). There was no difference between the IQs of children with white fathers and the IQs of those with black fathers.

Another study looked at the IQs of African American children in terms of the mix of their African versus European ancestry (Loehlin, Lindzey, & Spuhler, 1975). Again, the proportion of European genes bore no relationship to measured intelligence among African American children.

Yet more evidence is provided by a study of black children adopted by white families (Scarr & Weinberg, 1976). These adopted children raised in a white environment had IQs that averaged 106, exceeding the national average for African Americans and for European Americans.

Another fact to consider is the suggestion in the research literature that Asian American intellectual superiority declines the longer one's family has lived in the United States (Sue & Okazaki, 1990), even when marriage outside the ethnic group does not occur. Presumably, acculturation results in a different approach to intellectual pursuits and achievements (remember the discussion in Chapter 8 of elementary education in Asian countries versus the United States).

There is one more consideration in our discussion of race and intelligence. Ethnic minorities in the United States, particularly African Americans, tend to be poor. Even if they are not economically disadvantaged, many members of ethnic minority groups experience discrimination, which limits opportunities and attainments (Jaynes & Williams, 1989). Discrimination affects not just how members of different groups perform on intelligence tests but also the criteria used to validate those tests, like grades in school. Comparing ethnic groups means comparing people with dramatically different histories and experiences that obviously affect measured intelligence and its apparent consequences.

Sue and Okazaki (1990) used this line of reasoning to explain why Asian Americans on average excel in academics, particularly mathematics and the natural sciences. School—unlike, for instance, sports, entertainment, or politics—is a domain where Asian Americans do not usually encounter prejudicial treatment. Hence, they have often channeled their efforts and energy into scholastic achievement, with good results. In the case of African Americans, patterns of prejudice across domains are different, and African Americans focus their efforts within domains such as sports and entertainment, where barriers are least likely to be found.

Taken together, these results make a case against the hereditarian hypothesis insofar as it applies to ethnic differences in measured intelligence. Appreciate that there is no inconsistency in arguing that intelligence has a biological basis but that ethnic differences do not. Herrnstein and Murray (1994) suggested the metaphor of planting the identical strains of corn in Iowa versus the Mojave Desert. Genetic factors dictate in general how well the corn grows, but differences between the Iowa and Mojave Desert crops have nothing to do with these genetic factors. Evidence for heritability of a characteristic within a group is not the same thing as evidence for heritability of that characteristic between groups.

Asian Americans on average excel in mathematics and the natural sciences. One explanation is that they do not encounter discrimination in these academic fields and thus channel their energy into them.

Gender and Intelligence

On average, men and women do not differ in terms of their overall IQ scores. Why? Simply put, when intelligence tests were first developed, particular items that favored men over women or women over men were discarded. This strategy is still followed, and many intelligence tests are periodically revised to remove any gender differences that might appear. As a result, the debates over ethnic differences in IQ have no real counterpart in the realm of gender differences.

However, when researchers have looked at gender differences in terms of more specific types of intelligence, they have often found differences (Lim, 1994). In 1974, Maccoby and Jacklin published an important review of the state of knowledge at that time concerning the similarities and differences between men and women (Chapter 10). Here is what they reported:

- Females have greater verbal ability than males.
- Males excel in visual–spatial ability.
- Males have greater mathematical ability than females.

These differences correspond to common stereotypes about men and women in society: Women talk, and men tinker.

A more subtle gender difference is the finding that even when men and women do not differ in mean scores on intelligence subtests, men have more variable performance than women (Feingold, 1992a, 1992b, 1993b). That is, males are more likely than females to be represented at both ends of the intelligence continuum, especially in terms of visual–spatial and mathematical abilities.

As discussed earlier, in Chapters 4 and 9, theorists have speculated about these differences. Some have proposed that they are neurologically based (Lynn, 1994; Wickett, Vernon, & Lee, 1994), presumably making sense in terms of evolved psychological mechanisms. Men with spatial and mathematical ability were better able to hunt, and women with verbal abilities were better able to raise children.

In evolutionary terms, why should men show greater variability? Perhaps the neurological mechanisms responsible for superior spatial and mathematical abilities are necessarily fragile. A few men with extremely poor abilities might be the price our species has paid to have a few other men with superior abilities. These arguments are difficult to evaluate, and other theorists have disagreed with their thrust, pointing out that socialization might be the reason for gender differences (Deaux, 1985; Eccles, 1985). Perhaps males and females are encouraged by parents and teachers to develop different skills and so, on average, they do.

For example, some studies suggest that these differences are more evident among adults than adolescents and, further, that they do not exist at all among young children (Feingold, 1993a). This pattern is consistent with the idea that socialization occurring during the school years produces the gender differences. Other studies find that these particular gender differences are more likely to be found in the United States than in other countries, again supporting the role of socialization (Feingold, 1994b).

But something interesting has happened since Maccoby and Jacklin's review. In 1988, Alan Feingold presented data showing that in recent decades, many of the previously documented gender differences in specific intellectual abilities have disappeared. The only exception is male superiority at the upper end of mathematical ability.

Feingold's data explain neither why most of the differences have vanished nor why the mathematics difference remains. We can only speculate about the impact of social movements like feminism, the new popularity of women's sports, the availability of different role models for youngsters, or changes in the elementary school curriculum. In any event, Feingold's data are intriguing. Consider the implications for psychology's approach to intelligence. The differences that have vanished cannot reflect an inherent biological basis if they vanish in two decades (Humphreys, 1988). That is not how evolution works. Perhaps evidence bearing on other nature-nurture debates will be forthcoming if we continue to study changes in psychological characteristics over time.

Stop and Think

9 Describe race differences in measured intelligence.

10 Describe gender differences in measured intelligence.

EXTREMES OF INTELLIGENCE

This section discusses the extremes of intelligent behavior, from mentally retarded individuals to prodigies, geniuses, savants, and the highly creative. We do not leave intelligence tests and IQ scores behind because they are one aspect of the definition of these extremes. But as you will see, there is more to intelligence than IQ.

Mentally Retarded Individuals

■ **mental retardation**
below-average general intellectual functioning existing along with deficits in adaptive behavior

According to the definition proposed by the American Association on Mental Retardation (Grossman, 1977), **mental retardation** is below-average general intellectual functioning existing concurrently with deficits in adaptive behavior and evident before age 18. Earlier definitions relied solely on IQ scores, and cutoffs based on IQ are still used to distinguish degrees of retardation (see Table 11.4). The modern definition of mental retardation adds to low intelligence the inability to meet the demands of everyday life: achieving personal independence and social responsibility (American Psychiatric Association, 1994).

Mental retardation spans a range of difficulties, both physical and psychological:

Retarded individuals vary widely in intellectual ability, from the profoundly retarded who may possess no speech and no testable IQ, and who must live vegetative lives under continual medical supervision, to the mildly retarded, many of whom appear to have perfectly normal intellectual ability until confronted by tasks of mathematics or reading. Some retarded individuals also have disabling physical handicaps, but many have none. Some have severe emotional problems, but others are remarkably well adjusted. Some will require protective

Table 11.4   Levels and Characteristics of Mental Retardation

Level	Percentage of retarded individuals	IQ score	Characterization
Mild	75.0	55–69	Can develop social and communication skills; can do sixth-grade work without special help; can perform semiskilled jobs
Moderate	20.0	40–54	Can talk; have difficulty learning social conventions; can do second-grade work; can work in protected settings
Severe	3.5	25–39	Have difficulty learning to speak; show poor motor development
Profound	1.5	< 25	Unable to learn any but simple motor tasks; severe physical problems common; require custodial care

Mental retardation refers to below-average intelligence that occurs along with deficits in adaptive behavior. It includes a wide range of abilities and difficulties, both psychological and physical.

care throughout their lives, but others will learn to live independently as adults. (Edgerton, 1979, pp. 2–3)

In the United States, about 3 out of 100 children are retarded. Of these, about 2 out of every 3 are boys, perhaps because their nervous systems are more vulnerable to damage (Chapter 4). Pathological physical conditions or environmental influences can cause mental retardation.

Organic retardation.   When mental retardation can be traced to specific illness, injury, or physiological dysfunction, it is called **organic retardation.** Different factors may be responsible, including the following:

■ **organic retardation**
mental retardation due to specific illness, injury, or physiological dysfunction

- Infections of a mother while carrying her baby (e.g., rubella)
- Infections of the young child (e.g., meningitis, mumps, or chicken pox)
- Intoxication or poisoning (due to lead, alcohol, or other harmful substances)
- Trauma to the head
- Anoxia (lack of oxygen)
- Malnutrition (of the pregnant mother or the young child)
- Metabolic disorders (e.g., Tay–Sachs disease or phenylketonuria)
- Gross brain disease
- Premature birth
- Cranial malformation

Genetic problems can also produce organic retardation (Chapter 3). Here the best-known example is **Down syndrome,** which stems from the presence of an extra chromosome. Approximately 25 percent of the organically retarded have Down syndrome, which is usually recognizable at birth. Characteristic signs include poor muscle tone, a small head, a small nose, slanting eyes, small ears, a protruding and fissured tongue, a short neck, small hands with short fingers, dry skin, and sparse, fine hair.

■ **Down syndrome**
type of organic retardation caused by an extra chromosome

Most children with Down syndrome have IQs that place them in the severely to moderately retarded range. Many have difficulty using language in complex and abstract ways. As adults, few live completely independently, but many carry on well with some supervision from a parent, friend, or other caregiver. Children with Down syndrome who are raised in institutions tend to be less competent than those raised by their parents, presumably because a family provides a more stimulating environment. This in turn triggers the child's intellectual and social growth. Down syndrome cannot be cured in the sense of making it go away; however, with the appropriate education and experiences, individuals can live outside institutions, hold jobs, and maintain social relationships. Again, both nature and nurture are important in determining what happens.

Sociocultural retardation.   When mental retardation cannot be linked to specific physical causes, it is instead attributed to social disadvantages and called **sociocultural retardation.** Children so labeled often come from social groups that are educationally and economically below average. Many come from broken homes. About 75 percent of the retarded are socioculturally retarded, and poor children are ten times more likely to be represented than those from the population at large.

A number of factors contribute to sociocultural retardation. Even if demonstrable physical injury does not take place, lead poisoning, poor nutrition, or lingering child-hood disease (all more likely among the lower class) can chip away at a child's intellectual ability. An environment that provides no intellectual stimulation, such as that offered by books or conversations around the dinner table, can also negatively affect intelligence.

One of the striking facts concerning sociocultural retardation is that psychologists know little about what happens, once they leave school, to individuals given this label. Most are never again identified as retarded. Following school, they presumably get along in satisfactory fashion, meeting the subsequent demands of life. Contrast this fact with Herrnstein and Murray's (1994) discussion of people whose IQ scores keep them out of the cognitive elite. According to Herrnstein and Murray, individuals with low IQs are not equipped for life in the modern world, but the fate of the socioculturally retarded suggests otherwise.

The expression *six-hour retardation* is sometimes used to describe children with low IQs whose only difficulty in adaptation shows up in school. The great majority of sociocultur-ally retarded children are from culturally different backgrounds, and so the possibility remains that "they are simply unprepared in terms of language, culture, or motivation to cope effectively with the academic demands that schools place on them" (Edgerton, 1979, p. 73). Here is an irony in how mental retardation is defined. Although there have been attempts to broaden the definition beyond IQ scores to include failure at the demands of life, for school-age children the most significant demands placed on them are by school. We already know that a low IQ foreshadows poor school performance, and so the broadened definition adds nothing to their IQ scores, which predict that they do not do well in school.

Children referred to special classes for the mentally retarded are disproportionately ethnic minorities. Even when their tested IQs are the same, the minority child is more likely to be regarded as retarded than the majority child (Mercer, 1973). When European American children have problems in school, they are thought to have a learning disability; African American children who encounter problems in school are thought to be retarded (Franks, 1971). Learning disability and mental retardation are quite different: The former is a specific problem with reading, writing, or speaking, whereas the latter is a general difficulty.

Opinions differ as to how retarded children are best served in school. One point of view, which harks all the way back to Binet, is that mentally retarded children should be separated from normal children and given special education tailored to their needs. The other point of view holds that retarded children should be educated with normal chil-dren, in a practice called **mainstreaming.** Whenever possible, mainstreaming is now required by law, but the issue is not resolved because definitive research on the value of mainstreaming is difficult to do. In comparing special education classes with main-streaming, we might end up comparing not just alternative ways of educating our chil-dren but also third variables like social class, stigma, or level of school funding.

■ **sociocultural retardation**
mental retardation due to social disadvantage

■ **mainstreaming**
education of mentally retarded individuals with normal children

Prodigies in fields like music, mathematics, and athletics are more common than in other fields because—perhaps—these fields require skills inherent in our species. In any event, prodigies do not achieve their skills without extensive instruction and practice.

Prodigies

A **prodigy** is a child who shows a special skill or talent advanced far beyond what is considered normal for his or her age. There are many well-documented cases of such children (Barlow, 1952):

> Zerah Colburn (b. 1804)—At age 6, Colburn gave public exhibitions in which he calculated the products of three-digit numbers as rapidly as problems were posed to him.
>
> Jean Louis Cardiac (b. 1719)—When 3 months old, he could recite the alphabet; at age 3, he could read Latin; at age 6, he could read French, English, Greek, and Hebrew.
>
> Christian Friedrich Heinecken (b. 1721)—At age 2, Heinecken was well acquainted with the major events described in the Bible.
>
> John Stuart Mill (b. 1806)—By age 3, he knew Greek, and by age 10, he had studied all of Plato.
>
> Wolfgang Amadeus Mozart (b. 1756)— An accomplished composer and performer by age 6, Mozart at that age began a European tour that lasted several years.

Granted the interest generated by early displays of talents, popular newspapers and magazines regularly feature stories on prodigies in such areas as music, chess, mathematics, and language.

Prodigies by definition are so rare that psychologists know little about them. One psychologist who has studied prodigies is David Feldman (1980, 1993). He was attracted to these individuals because they seem at odds with one of the principles of developmental psychology: Psychological development proceeds in an orderly sequence (Chapter 10). You have to crawl before you walk, and you have to walk before you run. Prodigies challenge this truism, seeming to run from the start.

Feldman's (1980) investigations of six prodigies—two chess players, one violinist, a natural scientist, a writer, and a child not yet 3 years of age who could read adult-level books—suggest that prodigies are not as bizarre as they at first seem. One of his conclusions is that prodigies appear only in some fields of endeavor. Musical, mathe-

■ prodigy
child with a special skill or talent advanced far beyond what is considered normal for his or her age

matical, or athletic prodigies are relatively common. Feldman called these fields universal ones because they tap perceptual and physiologically based abilities inherent in the human species. In other fields, prodigies do not exist. There are no reports of prodigious achievement within the social sciences, for instance. Feldman called these fields cultural ones because achievement within them less directly reflects inherent skills.

Another conclusion is that prodigious achievements are not spontaneous. Rather, they develop through stages (Goldsmith, 1992). The individual passes through these stages more quickly than others but nevertheless starts from the beginning. For instance, Bobby Fisher, the former world champion of chess, could beat strong players when he was 6 years old, but not until he was a teenager could he compete with Grand Masters.

Feldman further found that prodigies do not achieve their advanced levels without extensive instruction, usually of a formal nature. Without guidance through the stages involved in mastering a skill, their expert achievement does not occur (Korzenik, 1992). To use another chess example: 50 percent of the top players under age 13 in the United States come from New York or California, where instruction in chess is readily available.

Also, aside from their particular skill, prodigies are otherwise normal children. Feldman administered to his subjects the sorts of tests that developmental psychologists use to gauge physical and cognitive development (Chapter 10), and the children invariably fell within the normal ranges. Our stereotype of a child prodigy as a miniature adult is incorrect.

Finally, prodigies may or may not grow up to make noted contributions within their fields as adults. History shows that only some prodigies become accomplished adults. Remember Mozart and Mill in the list that began this section? They were hailed as geniuses when adults. It is much more common, however, for a child prodigy not to win such renown as an adult.

Why do some prodigies become accomplished adults, whereas others do not? Feldman proposed that prodigies' early achievements are a coincidence: a coming together of a specialized individual and a specialized environment. We are tempted to look solely within the child for a clue to his or her skill, but the environment is just as important. "Early prodigious achievement is a joint effort among dedicated individuals, of whom the prodigy is but one participant" (Feldman, 1980, p. 148). Parents are important; instructors are important; someone to pay the bill for special instruction is important too. So, a continuing combination of individual promise and nurturance is crucial in determining whether a prodigy grows up to be a successful adult (Tannenbaum, 1992).

The advent of intelligence tests made possible another type of prodigy: a child with an extremely high IQ. The accomplishment of the high-IQ child is simply his or her performance on an intelligence test, not a remarkable feat in music, mathematics, or language. However, granted the significance placed on IQ, there is considerable interest in these children.

Lewis Terman (1925) conducted an extensive study of children with high IQs. In the early 1920s, he located some 1,500 children in the state of California with high scores on the Stanford-Binet (135 or above). These children were thoroughly studied through their teenage years, their early adulthood, and finally their late adulthood (Cravens, 1992; Tomlinson-Keasey & Little, 1990).

When Terman began his research, the prevailing belief was that gifted children were tainted, both physically and emotionally. They were thought to be uncoordinated, sickly, and poorly adjusted. It was also thought that they would not as adults fulfill their potential. However, Terman showed that children with high IQs were not spindly neurotics. On average, they exceeded their normal classmates in physical prowess, health, social adjustment, and emotional stability. A similar study by Leta Hollingworth (1942), which focused on children with Stanford-Binet IQ scores in excess of 180, yielded the same conclusions. Children with high IQs are usually physically and emotionally superior to their less gifted counterparts. These results have been replicated even more recently by Subotnik, Karp, and Morgan (1989).

There is one exception, though, in the substantial minority of these children who had difficulty adjusting to school. In the early part of this century, a student was placed in the grade where he or she could do the work. High-IQ children were placed several years ahead of where they would ordinarily find themselves. They were the youngest and smallest in their classes. Imagine the problems for these children when they were thrown in with adolescents. Interestingly, school systems today are more reluctant to allow children to skip grades, precisely because of the problems associated with being a child among teenagers.

One more note about Terman's study before we move on. What happened to those children with high IQs? On the whole, Terman's subjects grew up to be successful adults, as evidenced by their various occupational and educational attainments (Pyryt, 1993). But they were not uniformly the best and brightest members of their generation—showing once again that IQ is not the only psychological characteristic that foreshadows a person's accomplishments in life.

Geniuses

Psychologists are also interested in adults who are geniuses. This term is generally used to describe individuals with high IQs, but we can define a **genius** as someone whose accomplishments exert a profound influence on contemporary and subsequent generations (Simonton, 1984). Researchers try to determine the factors that contribute to these profound accomplishments. What are the possible causes of genius?

Catherine Cox (1926), an associate of Terman, conducted one of the first studies of genius. Cox began with a sample of 300 famous historical figures and then worked backward through biographical material to find evidence for their intellectual precociousness. From this evidence, she could calculate IQ. One of her subjects was John Stuart Mill, whose early accomplishments we previously noted. She determined the age at which he could read Greek, understand Plato, and master calculus, as well as the age at which the average person could do these things. Dividing the latter (mental age) by the former (chronological age) yields Mill's intelligence quotient—about 190. See Table 11.5 for other examples.

Cox also arranged her sample from more to less eminent (although, of course, all were eminent) and reported that her intelligence estimates positively correlated with

■ **genius**
someone whose accomplishments exert a profound influence on contemporary and subsequent generations

Table 11.5

Geniuses Identified by Catherine Cox (1926)

Individual	Precocious behavior	Estimated IQ
Jean Jacques Rousseau	"At age 6 the boy was so carried away by his reading that he shed tears in sympathy with the misfortunes of his romantic heroes."	130
Johannes Kepler	"In the elementary schools the teachers praised Kepler for his fortunate gifts . . . [including] remarkable proficiency at Latin."	140
René Descartes	"Before he was 8 years old, René was called by his father 'the little philosopher' because of his questions about reasons and causes."	150
William Pitt	"At age 7 he was writing letters to his father . . . even at this early age he had political aspirations."	160
Samuel Taylor Coleridge	"Coleridge talked for the first time before he was 2 years old, saying 'Nasty Doctor Young' while his hand was being dressed for a burn. . . . [A]t 3 he could read a chapter in the Bible."	175

rankings of eminence. This conclusion has been challenged because Cox did not take into account possible confounds (e.g., reliability of the historical material) that might affect both ratings of intelligence and ratings of eminence. Nevertheless, her study shows how one might use historical material to investigate genius.

Dean Simonton (1984, 1993, 1994) is a contemporary psychologist who followed this example in a more rigorous way, devising methods of reliably coding variables of interest from historical material. He studied several samples of historically eminent individuals: political leaders, writers, artists, generals, composers, even famous psychologists. What did he conclude? Genius does not have a single determinant but, rather, reflects a complex of psychological, social, and historical factors. Being the firstborn in a family is positively correlated with later attainment, as is intelligence, cognitive flexibility, and the personality traits of dominance and extraversion. Also important are formal instruction and the presence of a role model.

Finally, one must be in the right place at the right time for accomplishments to have an impact. For instance, Simonton (1992) studied female writers in Japan over the last 1,500 years. Within any given era, the impact of these women depended on societal ideologies about male superiority. We can make a similar point about the achievements of women in the United States (Mowrer-Popiel, Pollard, & Pollard, 1993).

Savants

■ **savant**
individual with mediocre or even deficient skills in most domains who possesses one extraordinarily developed ability

Savants (once called *idiot savants*, meaning "learned fools") are individuals who, despite mediocre or even deficient skills in most domains, possess one extraordinarily developed ability (Treffert, 1989). They challenge psychologists to think more creatively about intelligence because both extremes are contained in the same person. Savants are found in the same domains as those in which prodigies exist: music, art, and mathematics (Gardner, 1976, 1983). For example, some savants can perform lightning-quick calculations. They can rapidly add up long lists of numbers, tell the day of the week on which any date in history happened to fall, and perform other similar feats (Smith, 1983).

In the 1960s, a set of identical twins came to the attention of the world because of their uncanny ability to tell on what day of the week various dates fell. Although they had IQs that placed them in the retarded range, their calculating abilities were phenom-

In the film "The Rainman," Dustin Hoffman played a character who had an uncanny ability with numbers.

enal. One twin in particular was accurate with any date between 4100 B.C. and 40,400 A.D. (Horwitz, Kestenbaum, Person, & Jarvik, 1965).

Or consider Nadia, a young girl who suffered from autism, a profound psychological disturbance. She had an incredible talent for drawing (Selfe, 1977). Her sketches are remarkable for their skill and accuracy (see Figure 11.7). At the same time, Nadia was greatly impaired in what we would consider general intelligence. Her behavior was often counterproductive; sometimes she drew right off the edge of a paper without noticing.

Then there is the memory expert that Luria (1987) described. This individual, S., could not forget anything. He made his living on stage, displaying his abilities. In the 1920s, S. came to the attention of Luria, who would give him long lists of words, numbers, or mathematical formulas to remember. S. could always remember, even when retested decades later.

The abilities of savants are difficult if not impossible for us to explain (Gardner, 1983). Typically, these persons have not been given formal instruction in their skill, although they do practice extensively. What else is responsible? In the case of S., he perceived the world differently from the way the rest of us do, showing synesthesia: the tendency of one type of sensory impression to call up other types (Chapter 5). To S., a word had not only a sound but also a taste, a feel, and a smell. When he remembered words, he remembered all the sensory impressions associated with them.

Luria likened S.'s memory not to a cognitive process but to a perceptual one. One of the strategies S. used in remembering a list of words involved taking a mental walk and placing the items to be remembered along a familiar street. When called upon to remember, he would simply walk down the street again and see (and smell and hear) what was stored.

Most of us simply do not think in this way (Casey, Gordon, Mannheim, & Rumsey, 1993; Hermelin, Pring, & Heavey, 1994). Perhaps we should be grateful. S. suffered because of the imagery that made his phenomenal memory possible. He could not readily grasp abstractions, as in a poem because he was so overwhelmed by particular associations to the individual words. He confused inner and outer reality. Before he did something, he would imagine how it would be, and if his imaginary scene departed from reality, he became perplexed. For instance, he once described going to court to press a minor case. He had rehearsed the case in his mind, but upon arriving in court, he found that the judge did not look exactly as he had imagined. S. became so disoriented that he lost the case.

In sum, however puzzling they are, savants interest psychologists because of what they imply about intelligence in general (Wehmeyer, 1992). One important implication is that intelligence is plural, not a unitary characteristic that allows us to place all people along the same line according to how much of it they possess (Howe, 1989). Our modern society likes to rank everything and everybody. Witness the Top 40 countdown of records, Emmy Awards, Golden Globes, Pulitzer Prizes, David Letterman's Top Ten, grade point averages, batting averages, the Fortune 500 list, and Miss America contests. Some of these rankings are fun, and some are valid. However, ranking people solely by intelligence is neither.

Creative Individuals

Most psychologists distinguish creativity from intelligence, holding that **creativity** characterizes behavior that is adaptive and purposeful (intelligent) as well as novel. Creativity represents not only an appropriate solution to some problem of life but a new one as well.

The story of psychology's approach to creativity is much the same as the story of its efforts to study intelligence. Many theorists and researchers regard creativity as a general characteristic that people possess to varying degrees. A common explanation of creativity is that it involves a cognitive style called divergent thinking, the ability to think along many alternative paths (Runco, 1992). Attempts to measure creativity embody this definition and are exemplified by the so-called Unusual Uses Test, in which people are asked to think of all the things they can do with an ice cube and a screwdriver (or any

■ **creativity**
behavior that is adaptive and purposeful as well as novel

Figure 11.7
Drawing by Nadia. Although suffering from autism, this young girl could make highly skilled drawings like this one, done when she was only 5 years old.

such objects). The more uses a person can think of in a given period, and the more unusual, the more creative he or she is said to be.

These tests, however, do not relate to actual creativity (Wallach, 1985). The problem is not so much with the tests as with the conception that creativity is a characteristic of a person, as opposed to a product of that person. In forgetting this, psychologists take creative behavior out of its context. Indeed, Robert Weisberg (1986) pursued this analysis a step further and has written extensively on what he calls the myths of creativity. Here are some of the myths he attacked:

- Creativity reflects the unconscious incubation of ideas.
- Creativity involves sudden leaps ("Aha" experiences).
- Creativity results from special types of thinking.
- Creative individuals possess psychological characteristics that set them apart from other people.

Weisberg preferred what he called an incremental approach to creativity. The person who does something creative is not different in kind from those who do not, but simply different in degree. Creative works, whether scientific, literary, or artistic, reflect a gradual process. Training is important, practice is important, and the help of other people is important.

Are creative individuals exactly like everyone else? There are skills that perhaps are necessary for someone to be creative, like a degree of intelligence, the ability to concentrate, and the ability to be productive (Anastasi, 1971; Contreas Ortiz & Romo Santos,

1989). But these are not sufficient to explain creativity; the skills that make for a creative artist are not the same as those that make for a creative scientist.

In an often cited study, MacKinnon (1962) investigated the personality characteristics of the most highly creative architects in the United States, as judged by a panel of experts. When compared with a randomly chosen sample of architects, matched only by age, the creative architects differed in numerous ways. They were open to experience, unconventional, spontaneous, and flexible. (These results are usually the ones reported in textbooks.) However, MacKinnon also included a second comparison group, one composed of architects who worked side by side with those judged creative. They shared many things in common with the creative group, except that they had not been judged creative. MacKinnon found that there were essentially no personality differences between these two groups. In short, no special traits are uniquely associated with creative accomplishment in architecture.

Where does this leave us? Weisberg suggested that our judgments of creativity are best left to posterity. If we are to understand creativity, we should recognize that it exists in the eye of the beholder. Perhaps psychologists who study creativity should look less at the person who produces creative work and more at the people who will later be impressed by what he or she did (Gardner, 1988; Lubart, 1990). The social context of behavior dictates whether it is regarded as creative.

Stop and Think

11 Why is the distinction between organic and sociocultural retardation not always clear?

12 What is a prodigy?

13 What is a genius?

14 How does the existence of savants challenge traditional views of intelligence?

IS INTELLIGENCE SINGULAR OR PLURAL?

Throughout this chapter, I have mentioned the difficulty psychologists have faced in defining intelligence. One issue in particular has attracted a great deal of attention by theorists and researchers: whether intelligence is one, several, or many things. The present section discusses this debate and its implications for what intelligence means.

Intelligence as Singular

One point of view holds that intelligence is singular: a highly general characteristic widely exhibited across different areas. Francis Galton championed this idea, as we already saw, and so did Charles Spearman (1863–1945), another early investigator of intelligence. Spearman was struck by the finding that when a group of people were given tests measuring different abilities and aptitudes (e.g., tests of classics, mathematics, or French), test scores often correlated with each other. In other words, people who scored high on one test tended to score high on others, and people who scored low on one test tended to score low on others as well.

From findings like these, Spearman (1904) argued for the existence of what he called **general intelligence,** abbreviated as **g.** For Spearman, g is whatever underlies the fact that tests tend to correlate with each other; g is the factor common to all cases of intelligent performance.

However, different tests do not show perfect consistency. Spearman therefore concluded that besides g, there are also specific intelligences that influence performance on particular tests. A **specific intelligence** is abbreviated as **s.** So, people's performance

■ **general intelligence (g)**
type of intelligence reflected in many or all types of performance

■ **specific intelligence (s)**
type of intelligence reflected in only one type of performance

on any given test reflects a combination of their general intelligence and their specific intelligence for whatever that test measures.

Spearman proposed that if two different tests correlated, it was because they both reflected g. By definition, they could not reflect the same s. But this is not the only way to make sense of these data, and indeed, many disagree with Spearman. Two tests might correlate because they both reflect the same s. It is a matter of judgment whether a test of French and a test of classics do or do not reflect anything in common except general intelligence. Spearman's tests were not an infinite sampling of areas in which people perform—there is no way they could be—and so we should not be surprised that he was unable to convince everyone that intelligence is singular.

Intelligence as Plural

In contrast to Spearman, other psychologists emphasize s over g, suggesting that intelligence is composed of a set of abilities and capacities largely independent of one another (Thorndike, 1990). For instance, in 1938 L. L. Thurstone (1887–1955) proposed that intelligence spans a number of distinct abilities (see Table 11.6).

Raymond B. Cattell made a distinction between two different types of intelligence. **Crystallized intelligence** refers to skills or knowledge that has been formed through education or practice, whereas **fluid intelligence** means the ability to adapt to new situations (Cattell, 1971; Horn, 1968). Cattell believed that crystallized intelligence reflects life experience and that fluid intelligence reflects inherent ability. This distinction allowed him to argue that intelligence reflects either nature or nurture, depending on the aspect observed.

Yet one more view of intelligence as plural was proposed by J. P. Guilford (1967), who argued that the number of separate abilities and skills typically subsumed under intelligence exceeds 100. His scheme is more than just a list of different abilities because he explained them in terms of information processing (Chapter 9). Each ability is a mental operation performed on some informational input and resulting in some behavioral output:

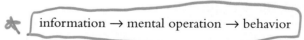

information → mental operation → behavior

Guilford distinguished among types of contents (e.g., symbols or words), types of mental operations that can be applied to these contents (e.g., cognition, memory, or evaluation), and types of products resulting from these mental operations (e.g., transforming one product into another or drawing implications). The possible combinations multiply into a large number of separate abilities.

■ crystallized intelligence
skills or knowledge formed through education or practice

■ fluid intelligence
ability to adapt to new situations

Table 11.6   Thurstone's Abilities

Ability	Characterization
Numerical	Ability to perform arithmetic operations
Word fluency	Ability to think of words rapidly
Verbal comprehension	Ability to define words
Spatial	Ability to recognize objects rotated in space
Memory	Ability to recall information
Inductive reasoning	Ability to derive general principles
Perceptual speed	Ability to rapidly compare visual patterns

Source: Adapted from Thurstone & Thurstone (1941).

More recently, the Harvard psychologist Howard Gardner (1983, 1993) proposed another pluralistic view of intelligence. Here are the types of intelligence he distinguished:

- Linguistic—sensitivity to the meanings and functions of language
- Logical-mathematical—competence at organizing ideas in abstract ways
- Spatial—capacity for visual or spatial imagery, including the ability to transform images
- Musical—ability to produce and organize sounds according to prescribed pitch and rhythm
- Bodily—kinesthetic mastery over body movements
- Personal—ability to access one's own feelings and those of others

The first three types of intelligence are those measured with traditional tests, but Gardner felt that the others are just as important, despite their neglect by psychologists (Kornhaber, Krechevsky, & Gardner, 1990).

To Gardner, intelligence is a set of problem-solving skills that allow the individual to resolve difficulties he or she encounters. Each skill can be regarded as an evolved psychological mechanism, hence based in biology and activated in appropriate circumstances. These skills are presumably independent of each other. A person can be high or low in one type of intelligence yet low or high in another type.

How did Gardner go about identifying these six types of intelligence from the many possible candidates? He employed several criteria, including whether or not a particular set of skills is selectively isolated by brain damage. If damage to nervous tissue selectively attacks or spares a given competence, then one can argue that it has a biological basis (Chapter 4). Gardner also looked for a distinctive developmental history for a set of skills, an associated set of symbols people use in exercising these particular skills, and the existence of prodigies who excel at them. When all these criteria point to the same ability, Gardner labeled it a basic intelligence.

Gardner's theoretical approach is exciting. It started with a conception of intelligence and specified how one would know intelligence when one encountered it in the real world. Only when the criteria are met did Gardner suggest that a type of intelligence is present. Contrast this with the approaches described earlier in this chapter, where intelligence tests preceded conceptions of intelligence, and subsequent work debated just what was meant by intelligence. On the downside, Gardner's approach is speculative, something he admitted by calling his approach the "idea" of **multiple intelligences.** Psychologists need to devise measures of these intelligences and explore them further (Kornhaber, Krechevsky, & Gardner, 1990).

How has the conception of intelligence as plural fared? Though many psychologists endorse the view that intelligence is plural, intelligence as singular is alive and well today (Modgil & Modgil, 1987). As you have seen throughout this chapter, intelligence is still regarded by many as a characteristic that transcends our background and leaps from our genes onto tests. Even when intelligence tests yield several scores, we often lump them together into an overall score.

Perhaps we need to start over, putting tests aside and looking to intelligent behavior, focusing on actions that show adaptation and purpose (Goleman, 1995; Keating, 1990). The biggest problem with the conception of intelligence as plural has been investigators' failure to develop useful measures of the separate factors. The dilemma may be the same as the earlier debate between g and s, and how different two skills need to be before they can be measured or predicted independently of one another.

■ **multiple intelligences**
Gardner's idea that there are several independent types of intelligence, each a biologically-based set of problem-solving skills

Stop and Think

15 What is the difference between g and s?

16 What are the survival problems solved by each of Gardner's multiple intelligences?

Those who view intelligence as plural point to the variety of ways in which people can be intelligent. Maya Lin can visualize and transform physical space; Toni Morrison can express ideas and images in words; Morris Dees can sway other people; Carl Lewis can control and coordinate his body.

INTELLIGENCE IN A BIOPSYCHOSOCIAL CONTEXT

Intelligence is a complex human characteristic that has both biological and social determinants. Although virtually all psychologists acknowledge the biopsychosocial nature of intelligence, theory and research have been cast starkly in terms of the nature-nurture issue. In previous chapters, you saw that the nature-nurture issue itself is an oversimplification. The goal for investigators is to explain how biology and the environment work together to give rise to adaptive and purposeful behavior.

A contemporary approach to intelligent behavior that attempts to place it in a fuller context is that of the Yale psychologist Robert Sternberg (1985, 1986, 1988). Sternberg argued that intelligence is best approached simultaneously from three different directions. He therefore called his approach a **triarchic theory** ("ruled by three") and presented his ideas in terms of three separate subtheories. Taken as a whole, Sternberg's triarchic theory addresses the biological, psychological, and social aspects of intelligence (see Figure 11.8).

■ **triarchic theory**
Sternberg's theory of intelligence in terms of its context, tasks, and mechanisms

Focus on the Environment

Sternberg's first subtheory focuses on the environment in which one functions because intelligence must be specified relative to a particular setting. What is considered intelligent in one setting may be irrelevant in a second setting or even stupid in a third:

> The intelligence of an African pygmy could not legitimately be assessed by placing the pygmy into a North American culture and using North American tests, unless it were relevant to test the pygmy for survival in a North American culture. Similarly, a North American's intelligence could not be assessed in terms of his or her adaptation to a pygmy society unless adaptation to that society were relevant or potentially relevant to the person's life. (Sternberg, 1985, pp. 47–48)

Intelligent behavior necessarily changes across time, place, and culture. Sternberg offered the intriguing observation that the advent of pocket calculators might make arithmetic

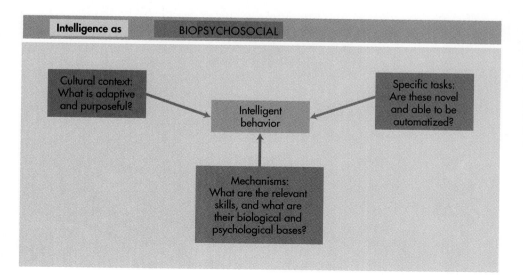

Figure 11.8
Intelligence as Biopsychosocial. A complete theory of intelligence needs to acknowledge biological and social influences as well as the psychological mechanisms that are responsible for intelligent behavior in a given environment.

ability considered so important by Binet, Thurstone, and other theorists virtually irrelevant in the modern world.

This view of intelligence implies that adaptation to the environment can take place in a variety of ways. Consider someone who has rented an apartment, sight unseen, and has just moved into it. Adaptation consists of finding a place for everything and putting everything in its place. Some people can readily do this, adapting themselves to their new environment. Other people might adapt their new environment to themselves, asking the landlord, say, to knock down a wall. Still others might choose an alternative environment: As they are moving in, perhaps they see that the apartment across the hall, which is vacant, is a better place for them and arrange to rent that one. All of these people are intelligent, but intelligence takes a different form in each case.

Focus on Tasks

Sternberg's second subtheory focuses on the specific tasks that best reveal someone's intelligence. Such tasks have to be somewhat novel, and they must lend themselves to becoming automatized. Both are involved in what is meant by adaptation—encountering some new demand in the environment (novelty) and learning to deal efficiently with it (automatization).

For many Americans, the task of driving a car through rush-hour traffic in a strange city would be a reasonable way to assess intelligence. For most college students, intelligence is reflected not just in what grades they earn in their classes but in how they go about choosing courses that result in a degree, balance their work load in a given term, prepare them for their future careers, and allow them to sleep until noon on Fridays.

This particular subtheory tells the psychologist to measure intelligence by finding tasks relevant to a person's life that are somewhat novel and can become automatized.

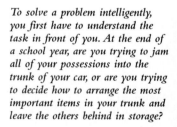

To solve a problem intelligently, you first have to understand the task in front of you. At the end of a school year, are you trying to jam all of your possessions into the trunk of your car, or are you trying to decide how to arrange the most important items in your trunk and leave the others behind in storage?

This strategy avoids the circular definition that intelligence is whatever intelligence tests measure, and it reminds us of the need to look at a person's characteristic environment. Furthermore, a variety of tasks can be used to measure intelligence. Finally, someone can do well on a given task because he possesses skill at confronting novelty, skill at automatizing, or both. Indeed, at different stages in performing a task, a person's skills come into play in various ways.

Focus on Mechanisms

Sternberg's third subtheory concerns itself with the actual psychological mechanisms that underlie intelligent behavior. How does a person go about deciding which problems need to be solved? What strategy does she use once she chooses a problem? How does she judge potential solutions? How does she use external feedback? These mental steps can be given a more precise description, thereby wedding intelligent behavior to underlying information processing and demystifying what intelligence means (Chapter 9).

Suppose you are given an analogy to solve: Lawyer is to client as doctor is to _____. A typical approach to intelligence might be to look at your answer, score it right or wrong, and move on. But Sternberg studied the process that leads up to your answer: You first have to understand the task that has been posed and you then solve the problem. Sternberg (1985) found, for example, that when you take your time with the first step, you do well with the second step. Among the cognitive processes associated with intelligence are the speed with which people process information (which may have a biological basis), short-term memory capacity, and skill at metacognition.

This subtheory also makes room for the role of motivation and emotion in producing intelligent behavior (Goleman, 1995). We have to feel that a task is worth solving in the first place, and we must be able to sustain our efforts once we take on this task. When we include motives and emotion in what we mean by intelligence, people who seem "intelligent" because they have high IQs yet never accomplish much cease to be a puzzle. Cognitive skills result in intelligent behavior only when coupled with motivational and emotional skills.

What emerges from Sternberg's work and that of others who opt for a close look at the multiple processes underlying intelligent behavior is the conclusion that people can be intelligent in different ways (Hunt, 1983; Vernon, 1983). Different routes lead to intelligent action. People can excel in various ways.

Some individuals are skilled at selecting and shaping real-world environments that are relevant to their lives. We colloquially call this being street-smart. Sternberg (1986) cited an example of a retarded man who could not tell time but did not want to tell anyone that he could not. He solved his problem by wearing a watch that did not work. Then he could stop people and ask them what time it was.

Some people are skilled at adapting themselves to novel situations. They can meet demands the first time they encounter them, and they can readily add behaviors to their repertoire. This is what we call creativity.

Finally, some people are skilled at processing standardized information. They can readily acquire vocabulary and facts. Sternberg's triarchic theory does not so much dismiss what traditional intelligence tests measure as suggest that they be supplemented by considering other forms of intelligence.

This chapter has described how psychologists have studied intelligence, one of the important ways in which people differ. The next chapter is concerned with the psychology of personality, again a topic that focuses attention on how people differ. Measures of personality differences have often used intelligence tests as a model. As you might expect granted the controversy surrounding intelligence tests, measures of personality have been the subject of debate as well.

SUMMARY

UNDERSTANDING INTELLIGENCE: DEFINITION AND EXPLANATION

■ Intelligent behavior is adaptive and purposive, and intelligence is one of the most valued human characteristics.

■ Psychological investigations of intelligence can be criticized for settling on concrete measures of intelligence—intelligence tests—before the meaning of intelligence was fully examined and agreed upon.

■ Even though measures of intelligence need to be improved, contemporary psychologists agree that intelligence should be explained in biopsychosocial terms.

DOING *Intelligence* RESEARCH

■ Psychologists have long searched for measures of intelligence that are not influenced by an individual's culture.

■ Such culture-fair tests may not exist because intelligence needs to be defined and measured with respect to a given setting.

A HISTORY OF INTELLIGENCE TESTING

■ Modern intelligence testing began with the work of Francis Galton, a cousin and contemporary of Darwin. Galton approached intelligence in evolutionary terms, regarding it as a biologically based capacity. Galton thought that intelligence could be measured with extremely simple tests of reaction time and sensory acuity, but this proved incorrect.

■ Now it is recognized that intelligence is best measured with complex tasks, an approach pioneered in the early 1900s by the French psychologist Alfred Binet, who developed tests still used today.

■ At Stanford University, Lewis Terman popularized intelligence testing in the United States.

■ World War I saw the development of tests that could be administered to groups of people, not just individuals. Various intelligence tests are currently available and see frequent use.

DETERMINANTS OF INTELLIGENCE

■ What causes intelligence? One extreme view argues that intelligence is largely a matter of genetic inheritance. Another extreme view proposes instead that intelligence is determined mainly by particular experiences in a given environment.

■ Intelligence reflects both genetic and environmental influences, and future research needs to investigate how these interact, as well as the mechanisms that lead from these influences to actual behavior.

INTELLIGENCE ACROSS SOCIAL CONTRASTS

■ The debate about the causes of intelligence takes on social significance because Americans from various ethnic groups (African American, European American, and Asian American) on average score differently on intelligence tests.

■ Some psychologists have concluded that the racial difference has a biological basis. This view is disputed by several lines of evidence and argument, not the least of which is that the so-called "races" represent social categories, not biological ones.

■ Relevant to the debate about ethnic differences in intelligence is research showing that previously documented gender differences in aspects of intelligence have vanished altogether in recent decades, presumably as society has changed in its treatment of males and females.

EXTREMES OF INTELLIGENCE

■ Several groups of individuals have attracted the attention of psychologists interested in intelligence.

■ Mentally retarded individuals show below-average intelligence and deficits in adaptive behavior.

■ Prodigies are children with special skills or talents far in advance of what we consider normal for their age.

■ Geniuses are people whose intellectual capacity allows them to exert a profound influence on contemporary and subsequent generations.

■ Savants have mediocre or even deficient skills in most domains, yet possess one extraordinarily developed ability. Those at the extremes of intelligence show us that there exist a variety of ways to be intelligent.

■ Finally, creative individuals are people who devise appropriate and novel solutions to some problem in life.

IS INTELLIGENCE SINGULAR OR PLURAL?

■ Psychologists have long debated whether intelligence is a single capacity or a group of relatively distinct abilities.

INTELLIGENCE IN A BIOPSYCHOSOCIAL CONTEXT

■ Robert Sternberg proposed that intelligence is plural and best explained in biopsychosocial terms. His triarchic theory emphasizes the environments in which behavior occurs, the tasks that best reveal intelligence, and the psychological mechanisms that lead to intelligent behavior.

KEY TERMS

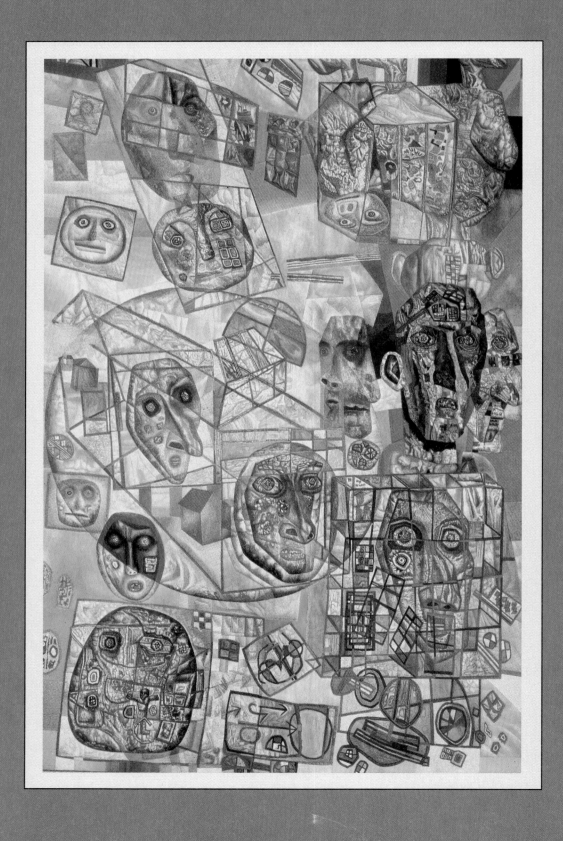

Personality

Speculation about human nature is as old as human nature itself. One early view was presented by Theophrastus (372–287 B.C.), a student of Aristotle. Theophrastus viewed his fellow men and women as falling into categories. This personality approach is called a **typology.** Here are paraphrased versions of some of his types (based on Jebb's 1870 translation):

- *The greedy man.* The greedy individual is one who, when he entertains, will not set enough bread on the table. He will borrow from a guest staying in his house. He will take his children to a play only when the theater has free admittance. If a friend is to be married, he will travel abroad in order to avoid giving a wedding present.

- *The gossip.* This person will sit down beside an individual she does not know and proceed to criticize her husband, then relate her dream of last night, then go through in detail what she had for dinner. Then she will remark that the men of the present day are greatly inferior to those of the past, and how cheap wheat has become in the market, and what a number of foreign visitors are in town, and how hard it is to live, and that yesterday she felt sick.

- *The patron of rascals.* She throws herself into the company of those who have been found guilty in criminal cases, believing she will thereby become worldly. She champions worthless persons and forms conspiracies.

■ *The slacker.* He is found in a torn T-shirt and baggy trousers, driving an old car filled with Styrofoam cups. He has finished college and works as a dishwasher. What little money he makes he spends on concert tickets. He is a heavy drinker and a vegetarian. Although he intends someday to decide upon a career, he believes ambition is wrong. He complains all the time about his life yet cannot imagine living any other way, unless he can do so in Seattle.

These descriptions are easily recognized as individuals we might know today, and show the long-standing appeal of classifying people.

UNDERSTANDING PERSONALITY: DEFINITION AND EXPLANATION

Do categories like those of Theophrastus capture the essence of a person, or do they seem compelling only because they reflect social stereotypes? Indeed, what is a person's essence? What differences exist among people? What is the origin of these differences? The answers to such questions are of concern to the field of **personality** psychology, which studies entire people as opposed to processes within them. Personality is a natural concept, as discussed in Chapter 9, and the features that capture its meaning can be specified. Usually, personality refers to those psychological characteristics of an individual that are general, enduring, distinctive, integrated, and functional.

The Meaning of Personality

Let us examine each of these features. A person's thoughts, deeds, and feelings are general when they are apparent across different settings. Consider a thrifty individual. She acts thrifty whenever the opportunity presents itself: in delicatessens and department stores, in locker rooms and libraries, at gas stations and garbage dumps. If she does not, then thrift is not part of her personality.

Some of the things people do are fleeting, whereas others are stable over time. Contrast a bad mood with chronic depression. Personality usually refers to enduring behaviors, those that generalize beyond the immediate circumstances. Granted, personality can and does change throughout an individual's life, but change occurs gradually or in response to profound events.

To say a quality is characteristic of someone's personality is to stress how it distinguishes him or her from others. Perhaps you are more outgoing than most other people; being outgoing is thus a part of your personality. Sometimes a particular combination of qualities best characterizes an individual's personality: wild and crazy, young and restless, dazed and confused.

Everyday people and psychologists alike often regard personality as a characteristic of the entire person—meaning that personality refers to the integration of more specific characteristics that may on the surface look inconsistent. Reggie White is a ferocious football player who is also an ordained minister. These characteristics seem to clash, but when we understand that White is a passionate and committed man, their combination makes sense.

Finally, personality usually refers to how we meet the demands of the world. Therefore, it is either functional or not. Why do some people earn straight As while others go straight to jail? The answer might be found in personality. Most of the major personality theorists have also been clinicians working with troubled individuals who have adapted poorly to the world. Their theories of psychopathology have become as well theories of personality.

Personality includes psychological characteristics that are general, enduring, distinctive, integrated, and functional. The diverse roles of Reggie White—ferocious football player and devout minister—make sense when we think of his personality as marked by passion and commitment.

Personality as Biopsychosocial

Given this definition of personality, it follows that its full explanation must be biopsychosocial. Thus, evolutionary psychology helps us to specify the biological context of personality in terms of evolved psychological mechanisms that arose to solve survival problems (Buss, 1991). That some of our behavioral characteristics are general, enduring, and integrated allows us to approach life and its demands in a coherent way. An individual who behaves as a single entity is apt to be more functional than one who is a mere collection of independent parts.

For example, individuals who have borderline personality disorder show marked fluctuations in identity, mood, and behavior (Chapter 13). Such people may have a large psychological repertoire, but their lives are not happy. Strained relationships are common, as are substance abuse and suicide attempts. It is as if those with this disorder do not have a personality, and they thus fail to meet many of the demands of the world.

As explained, personality refers to the unique mix of psychological processes within an individual, but personality also resides within a social context. The social context includes immediate interpersonal influences on personality, such as the family, as well as the larger culture.

At one time, personality psychologists theorized extensively about national character: personality traits shared by individuals of a given nationality (Barker, 1927; Duijker, 1960; Lynn, 1971). For several reasons, interest in this line of work died out. Many of the studies examined value-laden traits, such as punctuality or perseverance, and their findings seemed to extend prejudicial stereotypes (Chapter 15). Further, variations within a group were ignored. Perhaps most critically, little attempt was made to explain why a given national group had its particular characteristics. Researchers were content just to describe personality.

Nonetheless, people do differ by virtue of their cultural setting. Culture legitimizes certain forms of social interaction rather than others. These then influence the personality of those in that culture. For example, competitiveness is valued more in some

Culture shapes what we mean by personality. In the United States, many people are as concerned with being a personality as they are with having a personality.

cultures than in others, and not surprisingly, individuals in those cultures tend to have competitive personalities (Lynn, 1993).

Culture can even shape what is meant by personality. In the United States, personality typically includes an individual's distinctive traits: how he or she differs from others. But in Japan, individuals assume a fundamental interdependence between themselves and others (Markus & Kitayama, 1991). Standing out is not a socially sanctioned goal and may meet with disapproval. In contrast, many individuals in the United States strive to maintain their independence from other people by cultivating and expressing unique characteristics, not only having a personality but being one.

To understand personality in cultural terms while avoiding the pitfalls of previous investigations of national character, a researcher must look not only at people's traits but also at how those traits function within a setting. People from different cultures may show differences in personality (Dana & Whatley, 1991; Timbrook & Graham, 1994), but these need to be explained in terms of culturally provided roles and expectations.

For example, if ethnicity is more central to the self-concept of an African American than it is to that of a European American (White & Burke, 1987), the reason is that the former individual is a member of a visible minority with a history of prejudicial treatment by the dominant culture (Kambon & Hopkins, 1993). This factor leads the African American individual to be much more aware of his or her ethnicity.

Theories of Personality

Over the years, numerous personality theories have been proposed, and they can be classified within several major approaches, each assuming its own model of human nature. Personality psychologists within each approach emphasize different aspects of personality, favor different research methods, and use different standards to evaluate sufficient explanations (see Table 12.1).

Traditional personality theories variously emphasize biological influences on behavior, social influences, or psychological processes such as emotion, motivation, learning, and cognition. Sometimes personality psychology is called **personology,** to stress that it concerns itself with the person as a whole, as opposed to parts of people

■ **personology**
term for personality psychology that stresses the study of the person as a whole

Table 12.1   Summary: Theories of Personality

Theory	Key emphases
Psychodynamic	Motivation and emotion; unconscious conflicts
Trait	Biology; individual differences
Phenomenological	Cognition
Social learning	Social environment; learning

considered in isolation from one another. Although this term has existed for years (Murray, 1938), personology is particularly apt today as psychologists search for an integrated perspective (see Figure 12.1).

The history of theorizing about personality parallels the more general history of psychology (Chapter 1). The major theoretical approaches are akin to the great schools that dominated psychology throughout the early part of the twentieth century. Although these grand personality theories are alive and well today in the sense that they dictate research activities and applications, also present is a call to integrate the insights of different perspectives.

Let us examine several historically important perspectives on personality. Each provides the details of one component of an overall perspective on personality. We will then look at several of the research issues in which personality psychologists have been most interested.

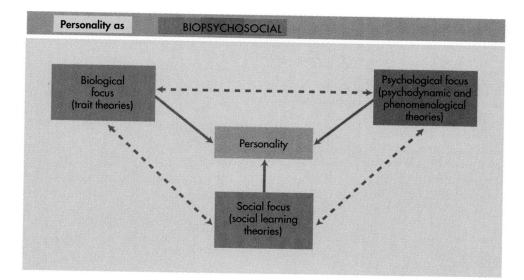

Figure 12.1
Personality as Biopsychosocial. Although most theories of personality acknowledge its biopsychosocial nature, these theories have traditionally emphasized one particular aspect of personality and its determinants. Trait theories focus on biological aspects of personality; psychodynamic theories and phenomenological theories focus on psychological aspects (motivation and emotion in the first case and cognition in the second case); and social learning theories focus on social aspects.

Stop and Think

1   Is a person's height part of his or her personality? How about his or her social class?

2   From a biopsychosocial perspective, how does personality include all other topics within psychology?

THE PSYCHODYNAMIC APPROACH: EMPHASIS ON MOTIVATION AND EMOTION

The first of the modern personality theories to take form grew out of Sigmund Freud's attempts to understand the psychological disorder known in his time as hysteria (Chapter 1). Freud believed that sexual conflicts from childhood caused this condition. When he proposed his theory at the turn of the century, he attracted numerous followers as well as critics. Many of his followers ended up as critics, disagreeing with aspects of Freud's theory and proposing new theories. These new theories nonetheless preserved many of Freud's major ideas. Therefore, the **psychodynamic approach** refers to the whole family of theories by Freud and others. These theories make the following assumptions about human nature:

■ **psychodynamic approach**
family of theories by Freud and others that stress psychological forces and conflicts

■ **libido**
psychological energy that drives behavior

■ People possess psychological energy called **libido.** Our behavior is driven by this energy.
■ Drives and instincts provide this energy and are thus part of people's biological inheritance. We are motivated to satisfy instinctive needs.
■ Often conflict exists between the individual and society because a person's biological instincts do not always conform to social rules.
■ Unconscious motives, forcibly kept from awareness because they offend and threaten the conscious mind, are among the most important determinants of behavior.
■ Past events shape subsequent behavior. In particular, struggles and conflicts during childhood affect an adult's thoughts, feelings, and actions.
■ Like Piaget's theory of cognitive development, psychodynamic views of personality development assume that people must pass satisfactorily through early stages in order to negotiate later stages with success.

Not every psychodynamic theory embraces all of these positions, but together they represent a generic version of this approach to human nature.

According to the psychodynamic approach to personality, events during early childhood shape who we are as adults.

Sigmund Freud: Unconscious Conflicts

The best place to start our discussion of the psychodynamic approach is with its creator, Sigmund Freud (1856–1939). Freud was a Viennese physician trained in neurology. While treating patients suffering from hysteria, he began to develop his theory of psychoanalysis (Chapter 1). Freud first worked with another physician, Joseph Breuer, from whom he learned the technique of catharsis, the so-called talking cure. Hysterical patients were hypnotized and encouraged to talk about earlier events; as they touched upon areas of conflict, they sometimes experienced an outpouring of emotion and an end to their symptoms (Jackson, 1994; Straton, 1990).

Breuer and Freud (1895) interpreted hysteria and catharsis in terms of energy (libido). Hysterical symptoms represented a restraining of this energy, and catharsis represented its freeing. Freud did not like hypnosis, however, and soon abandoned it in favor of another means of achieving catharsis: free association. Patients were encouraged to say anything and everything that came into their minds, without censoring. Their train of associations often led back to a hidden conflict, and catharsis followed. Remember from Chapter 9 how memories can be interwoven with feelings; Freud's technique of free association capitalizes on this characteristic of memory (Epstein, 1990).

At first, Freud believed that the conflicts he discovered referred to his patients' childhood experiences. Accordingly, he suggested that childhood sexual abuse produced adult hysteria. He later modified this belief, suggesting instead his patients' memories represented sexual wishes on their part.* These wishes had undergone **repression,** or removal to the unconscious (Chapter 6), but continued to influence the patients.

Freud was a prolific writer who frequently revised his theories. His *Collected Works* occupy more than 20 volumes, and it is difficult to present a brief overview. The following sections cover some of Freud's major ideas, notably the structure of personality, the role of instincts, and the way in which personality develops.

The structure of personality. Freud proposed that the mind has three parts: the conscious, the preconscious, and the unconscious. The **conscious** is what we are aware of at a particular moment ("My favorite television show is about to start"). The **preconscious** is whatever we can voluntarily call into awareness, such as telephone numbers, birthdays, and definitions of psychodynamic terms. The **unconscious** contains thoughts, feelings, and desires of which we are not aware.

The psychodynamic unconscious is motivated, meaning that its content is not the result of simple forgetfulness (Chapter 6). Rather, ideas become unconscious because they upset us. For instance, one of Freud's (1918) case histories concerns a troubled young man whose psychological difficulties seemed to start when he witnessed his parents making love. Although this man did not consciously remember what he had seen years before, Freud concluded that the memory remained in his unconscious and affected his later behavior. The man was specifically afraid of wolves and other animals, presumably because they reminded him of how his father looked while making love to his mother long ago.

Later in Freud's career, he revised his view of the mind. He described mental functioning with a new set of distinctions (see Figure 12.2). The **id** is where our instincts are located and where the so-called pleasure principle rules. Under the influence of the id, our thinking is dominated by wishes and impulses. We see the world as we would like it

■ **repression**
removal to the unconscious

■ **conscious**
what one is aware of at a particular moment

■ **preconscious**
whatever one can voluntarily call into awareness

■ **unconscious**
thoughts, feelings, and desires of which one is not aware

■ **id**
mental structure in which one's instincts are located

---

*Recent surveys show that the sexual abuse of children has been much more widespread than originally believed (Browne & Finkelhor, 1986). Many of Freud's original patients might well have been accurately reporting what happened to them (Masson, 1983). If so, important revisions of psychodynamic theory may be needed. Contemporary psychodynamic scholars are debating what to make of this new evidence (Kupfersmid, 1993).

Figure 12.2
The Structure of Personality.
Freud described personality in
two important ways: (a) in terms
of the conscious, preconscious,
and unconscious and (b) in terms
of the id, ego, and superego.
These are distinct descriptions. As
this drawing shows, the id is
completely unconscious, but the
ego and superego each contain
conscious, preconscious, and
unconscious aspects.

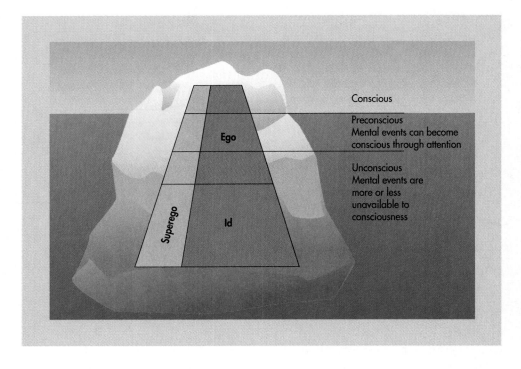

■ ego
mental structure that allows one
to satisfy needs and desires in
socially acceptable ways

■ superego
mental stucture that contains
one's internalization of parental
and societal values

■ life instinct; Eros
motive for pleasure

to be. The id alone is present at birth; the newborn is just a bundle of instincts seeking immediate gratification.

As we develop, we gradually become aware of external reality, and a second mental structure develops: the **ego.** The ego is practical; it allows us to adapt to the world and to satisfy our needs and desires in socially acceptable ways. The ego operates according to the reality principle, which makes our thinking rational and logical.

Because the id is present prior to the ego, the pleasure principle is more basic to our functioning than the reality principle. Freud termed thinking dominated by wishes and impulses primary process, whereas he called rational and logical thinking secondary process, to emphasize its derived nature. Primary process is the language of dreams, fevers, drunken stupors, and lust. According to Freud, children think exclusively in terms of primary process. Only through socialization do logic and order—secondary process—enter the mental scene. Note the parallel between Freud's ideas and Piaget's regarding cognitive development (Chapter 10).

The last mental structure to develop is a person's moral sense, which Freud called the **superego.** The superego emerges at about age 3 or 4 and represents the child's internalization of parental and societal values. Freud regarded the id, ego, and superego as constantly interacting in a given situation. How they blend together for an individual explains his or her particular personality.

The ego mediates between the impulses of the id and the prohibitions of the superego. Suppose your boss infuriates you. You want to punch him out (id), but doing so would create trouble (superego). So, you tell a joke at his expense to your fellow workers (Zelvys, 1990). It may not give you the same satisfaction as hitting him, but it does not get you fired. In general, the ego uses the defense mechanisms discussed in Chapter 6 to strike suitable compromises between the id and superego.

Life and death instincts.   Freud explained behavior with instincts, although he used the idea of an instinct much more broadly than contemporary ethologists do (Chapter 3). According to Freud, people are primarily motivated by pleasure. He called this motive the **life instinct,** or **Eros** (after the Greek god of love), and proposed that it was behind much of what we do, including but not limited to sexual behavior. Toward the end of his life, however, Freud became convinced that Eros did not explain the whole of

Freud proposed that the id is present at birth and responsible for our pursuit of immediate pleasure and gratification.

human motivation. He was struck by the tendency of some individuals to act out, again and again, painful episodes from their past.

This compulsion to repeat horrible experiences cannot be explained if our only instinct is a desire for pleasure (Himmelstein, 1979). So, Freud proposed a **death instinct,** or **Thanatos** (after the Greek god of death). The death instinct motivates violence and aggression, against others as well as ourselves. It explains warfare and hatred, drug and alcohol abuse, murder and suicide. Contemporary psychologists, however, usually do not explain human aggression in terms of instincts (Chapter 7). Not surprisingly, Freud's death instinct has been the least accepted aspect of his theory (Lind, 1991; Maratos, 1994).

■ death instinct; Thanatos
motive for violence and aggression

The development of personality.   One of Freud's best-known assumptions is that children are inherently sexual. Freud's (1905) pronouncements on the universality of childhood sexuality created controversy, as you might imagine. Let us examine what he meant. When Freud said that children are sexual, he did not mean in the same way that adults are sexual. Rather, he proposed that children and adults possess the same sexual instinct, desiring and seeking out physical pleasure as the id impels them to do. But the means by which their sexual instincts are satisfied changes throughout development. One key to understanding personality is therefore in terms of **psychosexual stages,** defined by the part of our body that gives us pleasure (see Table 12.2).

During the oral stage, from birth to age 1, the child's mouth is the source of gratification: sucking, biting, chewing, and crying. With weaning, the child enters the anal stage, from about 1 to 3 years, and elimination becomes the source of pleasure. Retaining or expelling feces provides pleasure to the youngster (and aggravation to his or her parents). The child encounters external restraints during this stage, in the form of toilet training. The manner in which weaning and toilet training occur—harshly or permissively—is thought to affect adult personality.

■ psychosexual stages
periods of development defined by the part of the body that provides pleasure to an individual

Table 12.2 Summary: Freud's Psychosexual Stages	
According to Freud, all people must pass in sequence through the following stages.	
Stage	**Characterization**
Oral (birth to age 1)	The child satisfies his or her needs through activities involving the mouth: nursing, chewing, and biting.
Anal (ages 1 to 3)	Gratification centers on elimination, either retaining or expelling feces.
Phallic (ages 3 to 5)	Satisfaction is achieved through self-stimulation of the genitals (masturbation).
Latency period (ages 6 to puberty)	Gratification has no particular focus.
Genital (from puberty on)	Satisfaction is achieved through sexual contact with others.

■ **Oedipus complex**

according to Freud, events during the phallic stage in which children feel sexual desire for the opposite-sex parent and treat the same-sex parent as a rival

Next comes the phallic stage, from about 3 to 5 years, when the source of pleasure first centers on the sexual organs. Playing doctor is popular. Children become interested in masturbation and curious about the origin of babies. Some critical events occur during the phallic stage, and Freud used the Greek myth of Oedipus as a metaphor for these events. Oedipus was the tragic character who unknowingly killed his father and married his mother. Freud suggested that this myth taps a universal desire, what he called the **Oedipus complex.** During the phallic stage, children feel unconscious sexual desire for the opposite-sex parent. The same-sex parent becomes the rival. Once in this triangle, children sense that the same-sex parent will not bow out, gracefully or otherwise. They begin to fear that the same-sex parent will retaliate against them.

The Oedipus complex is resolved when children realize that they will not win the opposite-sex parent for themselves. They therefore settle for the next best thing—to possess Mom or Dad indirectly and symbolically, by taking on the characteristics of the other parent. By this process, children acquire the personalities they will have as adults.

Freud believed that women do not resolve the Oedipal complex as fully as men do (Krausz, 1994). The fear of retaliation from the opposite-sex parent takes a sexual form; specifically, the child fears castration. Little girls, who obviously lack a penis, believe that they have already been castrated, meaning that they have anxieties that little boys do not. These are presumably carried into adulthood. Freud regarded women as not only fundamentally different from men but also inferior (Temperley, 1993).

After the phallic stage, at about 6 years, children enter what Freud called a latency period, where sexual impulses are curbed. Development in other domains—cognitive, moral, and social—becomes more important (Chapter 10).

The genital stage, which coincides with the onset of puberty, is the last step in psychosexual development. During this stage, sexual impulses again emerge, only now pleasure is obtained through the genitals in the course of sexual activity with others.

Like other stage theories of development, Freud's theory proposes that we must pass through the stages in a particular order (Chapter 10). If we do not pass successfully through a stage because we are either frustrated by not enough satisfaction or indulged by too much, a **fixation** results. Psychic energy is left behind, and the concerns of that particular stage continue to dominate in adult personality. The behavior of a person fixated at the oral stage, for example, will center on oral gratification, through excessive eating, drinking, smoking, or talking (Lewis, 1993). Such individuals are also thought to be highly dependent on others, seeking nurturance from them. A person fixated at the anal stage might symbolically express either the retention of feces, by relentlessly pursuing neatness and order, or the expulsion of them, by being unbelievably sloppy and wasteful. Finally, a person fixated at the phallic stage shows an exaggerated concern with sexuality, a concern that may be expressed in excessive vanity. The contemporary macho

■ **fixation**

failure to resolve a particular psychosexual stage, so that the concerns of that stage continue to dominate one's adult personality

The Oedipal complex is resolved when a child begins to take on the characteristics of the same-sex parent.

man, draped in gold chains and drenched in cologne, presumably acquired his excess baggage while passing through the phallic stage (Kalfus, 1994).

Many of Freud's specific claims about psychosexual development are not supported by research (Peterson, 1992). His theorizing about women, in particular, does not square with the facts. Freud assumed the ideological biases of his era, not appreciating the influence of cultural practices that assigned to women an inferior status. Indeed, the validity of Freud's psychoanalytic theory for individuals in times and places other than his own has been questioned (Littlewood, 1990; Slote, 1992). Nonetheless, his ideas about psychosexual development have become theoretical cornerstones.

Psychodynamic Approaches After Freud

Psychodynamic theory began with a focus on abnormality, but Freud went on to apply it broadly: to dreams, humor, creativity, religion, and even the origin and function of society. Consequently, psychodynamic theory became an influential approach to the study of normal personality. As noted earlier, other theorists followed Freud's lead and proposed their own versions of psychodynamic theory (see Table 12.3). These theorists often disagreed with Freud's emphasis on sexuality; most preferred a more social explanation. So, we again encounter the nature–nurture debate.

Carl Jung: The collective unconscious.   An early follower of Freud was Carl Jung (1875–1961), a Swiss physician who first worked with schizophrenic patients. Jung (1907) believed that the bizarre hallucinations and delusions marking schizophrenia paralleled Freud's descriptions of the dreams of less troubled individuals. In both cases, primary process thinking dominates (Chapter 13).

Jung broke with Freud over the importance of sexual motivation. In going his own way, Jung became interested in symbols, studying mythology and anthropology. He was struck by the degree to which the same images appeared in different times and places.

One of Freud's early followers was the Swiss psychiatrist Carl Jung, who later broke with Freud to propose his own version of psychodynamic theory.

Table 12.3   Summary: Psychodynamic Approaches After Freud

Most of the psychodynamic theorists who followed Freud placed less emphasis on people's instincts and sexuality. Each theorist instead emphasized other determinants of personality.

Theorist	Key emphasis
Carl Jung	Collective unconscious
Alfred Adler	Compensation for perceived inferiority
Neo-Freudians	Social relationships
Erik Erikson	Psychosocial development
Object relations theorists	Mental representations of self and others

■ **archetypes**
according to Jung, universal symbols

■ **collective unconscious**
repository of ancestral experiences and memories that all people share

Jung called these presumably universal symbols **archetypes** and proposed that they are located in a **collective unconscious:** a repository of ancestral experiences and memories that all people share. For example, Jung identified one archetype as the shadow, which represents evil and malice. People fill in the details of an archetype in accordance with their time and place—the shadow might be Lucifer, Dracula, Mr. Hyde, Darth Vader, or Hannibal Lechter—but its meaning is universal (Blennerhassett, 1993).

Jung proposed that the collective unconscious represents tried-and-true ways of thinking about life and that when people tap into it, they receive the wisdom of the ages. He further believed the collective unconscious to be a more important aspect of personality than Freud's unconscious, which includes only an individual's personal history (Nyborg, 1992). Jung's ideas are intriguing, but they are virtually impossible to verify. He did not specify the mechanisms by which the collective unconscious is passed across generations or the way in which archetypes take form for an individual (Lewis, 1989).

■ **inferiority complex**
Adler's idea that all people feel inadequate with respect to some aspect of the self and try to compensate

Alfred Adler: Compensating for inferiority.   Also among Freud's early followers was another Viennese physician, Alfred Adler (1870–1937). At first enthusiastic about Freud's ideas, Adler came to disagree with the primacy Freud had assigned to sexuality. The disagreement resulted in a complete break between them, personally and professionally. Adler (1910) believed that conflict plays an important role in shaping our personality but that its nature is social rather than sexual. He introduced the concept of the **inferiority complex,** suggesting that all people feel inadequate with respect to some aspect of their being, physical or psychological. Our development can be understood as our attempt to compensate for this perceived inferiority with respect to others. For instance, Theodore Roosevelt was a sickly child who developed himself into a robust adult.

Another example of Adler's (1927) interest in the social determinants of personality is his theorizing about the child's position in the family. He believed that birth order dictates the way children are treated and how their personalities develop (Leman, 1985). Thus, the eldest child is the original center of attention in a family, acquiring a need for power and authority; the second child continually strives to overcome the older rival; and the youngest may be spoiled and pampered on the one hand or flexible on the other. Birth order is a social phenomenon, not a biological one. Research bears out some of Adler's ideas about birth order (Watkins, 1992). For instance, firstborn individuals are more likely to become famous (Simonton, 1994). Among those who have run for president, firstborns have won more frequently than later-borns.

Karen Horney argued that people are motivated to feel safe and secure with others. The social emphasis of her theory stands in contrast to Freud's concern with biologically based instincts.

■ **neo-Freudians**
theorists influenced by Freud who stress people's social character rather than their sexual instincts

Neo-Freudians: Social relationships.   A second generation of psychodynamic theorists followed Adler's lead by stressing the social character of people over their instinctive, sexually motivated nature. The theorists who adopted this point of view became known as **neo-Freudians.** So, Karen Horney (1885–1952) discarded the Oedipus myth to argue that people are motivated by feelings of isolation from other people (Olfman, 1994;

Shafter, 1992). According to Horney (1937, 1945), the primary human need is to feel safe and secure with others. If people do not feel secure, they experience what Horney called basic anxiety. Fellow neo-Freudians proposed similar theories that elevated people's social relationships to primary status in determining personality (Fromm, 1947; Sullivan, 1947). Often these theories de-emphasized the conflict between id and superego, instead regarding the ego as an active—not reactive—agent that does much more than mediate between our instincts and our conscience (Hartmann, 1939; White, 1959).

Erik Erikson: Psychosocial development.   You encountered the theory of Erik Erikson (1902–1994) in Chapter 10, where his ideas about life-span development were discussed. Unlike many other psychodynamic theorists, Erikson never formally broke with Freud. Erikson called himself a post-Freudian, one who follows Freud and builds on his earlier ideas. But Erikson could quite easily be classified with the neo-Freudians because his developmental theory has an explicit social emphasis. Social dilemmas, such as trust versus mistrust and intimacy versus isolation, define the stages of life in Erikson's psychosocial theory of development, and they are resolved with the help of culturally provided institutions (Cote, 1993).

Erikson also contributed to psychohistory, a field that uses psychological theories to shed light on historical figures and events. Erikson published studies of Adolf Hitler, Martin Luther, George Bernard Shaw, Gandhi, and Thomas Jefferson, among others. More recent examples of psychohistory include analyses by other researchers of the personalities of David Koresh (Adityanjee, 1994), Bill Clinton (Elovitz, 1994), Anne Sexton (Long, 1993), Saddam Hussein (Mayer, 1993), and François Mitterand (Guiton, 1992). For instance, Bill Clinton's early childhood was marked by frequent fighting between his mother and stepfather, and his lifelong attempt to be evenhanded and pragmatic presumably resulted.

An important goal of psychohistory is to understand a person in the context of his or her particular era. To grasp someone's motives, we have to locate their meaning within a given time and place. This principle underscores the neo-Freudian attempt to view personality in social terms.

Object relations: Mental representations.   Many contemporary psychodynamic theorists are interested in the mental representations people have of themselves and others. These representations are called **object relations** (Greenberg & Mitchell, 1983; Stricker & Healey, 1990). *Object* was Freud's term for people or things, and *relations* refer to the perceived link between these objects and the individual. For example, one person may think of his relationships with others as friendly and supportive, whereas a second person may see these as hostile. Or remember borderline personality disorder, as discussed earlier in this chapter—individuals with this problematic style of behaving are unable to integrate their different object relations.

■ **object relations**
mental representations people have of themselves and others

In one sense, this emphasis on object relations reflects the trend in recent decades for psychologists to be more interested in cognition (Westen, 1991). However, object relations theories maintain the traditional psychodynamic emphases on unconscious, irrational, and emotional processes (Ingram & Lerner, 1992).

Evaluating the Psychodynamic Approach

The psychodynamic approach represents the earliest attempt by psychologists to explain the whole of personality. The accounts of Freud, Adler, Jung, Horney, Erikson, and others continue to be influential, although more recent personality theories challenge them. Many critics find psychodynamic theories to be so complex that they cannot readily be tested by research. Nonetheless, two aspects of the psychodynamic approach have strongly shaped modern thinking about personality. First is the idea that many of our important motives are unconscious. Second is the idea that early childhood events can affect our characteristic behavior as adults.

> ### Stop and Think
>
> **3**   Compare and contrast the psychodynamic theories of Freud and Jung.
>
> **4**   Compare and contrast the psychodynamic theories of Freud and Adler.
>
> **5**   How is the approach of the neo-Freudians similar to that of Freud?
>
> **6**   To which other psychodynamic theorist is Erik Erikson most similar?

THE TRAIT APPROACH: EMPHASIS ON BIOLOGY

■ **trait approach**
group of personality theories that classifies people in terms of their stable and general individual differences

Like the psychodynamic approach, the **trait approach** consists of a group of related theories united by common emphases. Most trait theories concern themselves with the following questions:

■ What are the fundamental ways in which people differ?
■ How can these differences best be measured?
■ How do individual differences relate to adaptation?
■ What is the origin of a particular individual difference?

Trait theories sometimes describe personalities as falling into a few separate categories, or types; you saw an example in the character sketches that began this chapter. More commonly, trait theories describe personality in terms of a few quantitative (more vs. less) dimensions, or traits. For example, people can be placed along a dimension reflecting the degree to which they are emotional versus unemotional.

A personality typology attempts to describe people in terms of a small number of separate categories or types—for example, "wild and crazy" versus "sober and somber."

The trait approach can be traced to Darwin's theory of evolution. Remember Darwin's emphasis on individual variation within a species and how it determines functioning in a given setting (Chapter 3). Also, trait theorists are often interested in whether personality characteristics are heritable, which leads them to consider further the biological basis of types and traits.

Gordon Allport: Setting the Trait Agenda

The Harvard psychologist Gordon Allport (1897–1967) set the agenda for contemporary trait strategies. His importance within the trait approach corresponds to that of Freud within the psychodynamic tradition. Allport taught the first personality psychology course in the United States, and in 1937 he wrote one of the first personality textbooks. Even theorists who disagree with Allport's particular ideas use his terms and take positions on the issues he stated (Funder, 1991).

Gordon Allport set the agenda for the trait approach to personality.

Allport's approach can be contrasted with the psychodynamic approach. Whereas psychoanalysts began with an emphasis on abnormality and then generalized to normality, Allport focused on normal individuals. He felt that Freud's theories applied only to troubled individuals. Instead of understanding people in terms of unconscious conflicts from their past, Allport believed the key to personality lay in the individual's conscious and rational striving toward future goals (DeCarvalho, 1991).

Allport regarded traits as the most appropriate units with which to understand personality. He defined a **trait** as:

> a neuropsychic structure having the capacity to render many stimuli functionally equivalent, and to initiate and guide equivalent (meaningfully consistent) forms of adaptive and expressive behavior. (1961, p. 347)

■ **trait**
stable and pervasive individual difference that initiates and guides diverse behavior

In calling a trait neuropsychic, Allport meant that it has a biological as well as a psychological basis. By saying that a trait renders different stimuli functionally equivalent, he meant that traits are associated with a consistent pattern of response across different situations. In proposing that a trait initiates and guides behavior, he meant that traits cause us to think, feel, and act in certain ways. Finally, in defining traits as adaptive (meaning they aid survival) and expressive (meaning they show up in a person's style of behaving), Allport came very close to the modern definition of an evolved psychological mechanism (Chapter 3).

In one of Allport's well-known endeavors, he and a colleague read an entire dictionary and located 17,953 words describing personality traits, everything from abashed to zestful (Allport & Odbert, 1936). Not all of these traits sensibly apply to everyone, and Allport (1961) believed each of us possesses only seven to ten traits. These particular qualities, termed **personal traits,** differ from person to person. So, for example, my personality might be described as cautious and humorous because I consistently act in these ways. However, your personality might be poorly described with these traits. Perhaps sometimes you are cautious and sometimes you are bold. You might occasionally crack a joke but otherwise be somber.

■ **personal traits**
traits that describe only some people

In contrast to personal traits are **common traits,** so named by Allport because they can be used to describe everyone. Consider the strength of one's needs, like those described in Chapter 7 (Murray, 1938): We can arrange all people from low to moderate to high on achievement motivation. Allport believed that common traits have limited usefulness in capturing individuality, and so he urged a focus on personal traits. This recommendation is appealing but makes conventional research difficult if not impossible. If different people require different traits to describe their personalities, a psychologist cannot offer generalizations about people.

■ **common traits**
traits that describe all people

However, Allport argued that generalizations should not be the goal of personality psychology. According to him, psychology per se is a nomothetic science, striving to make statements about all people (Chapter 1). Personality should be studied by recognizing that each person is a unique individual who needs his or her own explanation (DeCarvalho, 1990). Most trait theorists disagree with Allport's call for an idiographic science because the methods required do not exist. Indeed, were we to take Allport's recommendation for an idiographic science seriously, we would need a distinct research approach for every individual.

Traits and Biology

A major concern of trait theorists is whether individual differences in personality are influenced by genetics or created solely through experience. Certainly we can see resemblances within many families, but we know from our previous discussions that these can reflect common nurture as well as common nature. Several approaches to this issue are well known.

Body build and personality.   One strategy for distinguishing nature and nurture with respect to personality is to find an actual biological basis for individual differences. An early example of this approach is William Sheldon's (1899–1977) investigations of a person's physique (or body build) and how physique corresponds to personality. Sheldon (1940, 1942) started with the observation that physiques could be described along three dimensions:

- Endomorphy—degree of roundness
- Mesomorphy—degree of muscularity
- Ectomorphy—degree of linearity

He devised ways of rating each of these dimensions with 7-point scales, from low (1) to high (7). An individual's profile of scores is called a somatotype. A chubby person would be rated 7–1–1, whereas a skinny person would be rated 1–1–7. Most of us, being average, would have a 4–4–4 somatotype.

Sheldon's theory became an account of personality when he hypothesized that different physiques are associated with different styles of behaving. Endomorphs are easygoing and affectionate, mesomorphs are action-oriented, and ectomorphs are sensitive and inhibited. Sheldon's original investigations have been criticized because he rated both the somatotypes and the personality characteristics of research subjects; unintended bias due to his expectations may have confounded the results. However, more recent research in which ratings of physique are made independently of ratings of traits tends to support Sheldon's hypothesized links between physique and personality (Quinn & Wilson, 1989). The reasons for these links are unclear. Whereas Sheldon believed that the links are directly biological, other psychologists have pointed to social stereotyping.

Heritability of personality.   A more contemporary approach in the spirit of Sheldon's biological theorizing investigates the genetic basis of individual differences. The twin method is used for separating nature and nurture to show that many personality traits are heritable. Tellegen, Lykken, Bouchard, Wilcox, Segal, and Rich (1988) studied identical twins and fraternal twins, those raised together and those raised apart. The twins completed questionnaires measuring such traits as extraversion versus introversion. On average, 50 percent of the variation in personality test scores was due to genetic variation. Heritability estimates like these do not mean that complex characteristics are inherited as a whole but rather that their variation across individuals has a genetic basis (Chapters 3 and 11). The next step in this line of research is to specify the mechanisms that translate genetic influence into actual behavior (Eysenck, 1990a; Plomin & Nesselroade, 1990).

Factor Analytic Theories of Personality

Trait theorists are often more concerned with the measurement of individual differences than most other personality psychologists are (Chapter 1). Let us consider the work of researchers who use a statistical technique called **factor analysis** to identify the basic dimensions of personality. Factor analysis is a procedure for detecting patterns in a large set of correlations (Chapter 2). Suppose research subjects complete dozens of personality questionnaires, each measuring a different trait. Factor analysis allows the researcher to summarize which measures go together and which do not. Sets of characteristics found together in most people are thought to reflect an underlying dimension, or factor, of personality.

Factor analytic theorists of personality make a useful distinction between surface traits and source traits (Cattell, 1950). Surface traits are the characteristics of people that meet the eye, any of the thousands of individual differences people display. In contrast, source traits are the underlying differences that give rise to these surface traits. There are many more surface traits than source traits; the latter are necessarily abstract and general. Surface traits such as moodiness, restlessness, and irritability may reflect a single underlying source trait—unhappiness, for example.

Factor analytic research proceeds by assessing numerous surface traits and then looking for basic patterns: The factors identified are thought to be source traits. The two most influential factor analytic theorists are Raymond Cattell (1905–) and Hans Eysenck (1916–). Cattell (1950) identified 16 basic factors of personality, presented in Figure 12.3.

Eysenck (1947), in contrast, identified but two factors (see Figure 12.4). The first is **introversion-extraversion,** referring to the degree to which people are inwardly or outwardly oriented. The second is **neuroticism,** referring to the degree to which people are moody and nervous. Eysenck proposed a physiological interpretation for these factors, arguing that introversion-extraversion reflects the chronic level of cortical excitation and that neuroticism stems from the reactivity of the autonomic nervous system (Chapter 4). In some of his writings, Eysenck (1976) identified a third factor, **psychoticism,** defined as the degree to which people are insensitive, odd, and detached. He hypothesized that increased psychoticism is linked to increased levels of testosterone.

At first glance, Cattell and Eysenck seem to disagree. But Eysenck's scheme is compatible with Cattell's, differing chiefly at its level of abstraction (Guilford, 1975). In other words, if you factor analyze Cattell's 16 factors, Eysenck's 3 factors emerge (Heaven, Connors, & Stones, 1994).

Both Eysenck and Cattell believed that the basic personality traits are heritable, and so they join with other trait theorists in regarding personality as having a genetic basis. Missing in their work to date is any detailed investigation of the biological mechanisms by which information on one's chromosomes is translated into complex behavior. However, Eysenck's physiological interpretations of the personality factors he identified provide a starting point.

Basic Traits: The Big Five

Are some traits more basic than others? Within physics, the consensus is that time, mass, and space are the fundamental units of our physical universe. Which of the 17,000-plus trait words found by Allport and Odbert are the fundamental ones? At present, there is no agreement, but there is no lack of candidates either. As just described, Cattell and Eysenck are just two of the many personality theorists who have proposed a set of basic traits.

A particularly popular suggestion is the so-called **Big Five,** originally described by psychologist Warren Norman (1963). According to Norman, the five personality traits that capture the important ways in which people differ from each other are:

- Neuroticism (worried, nervous, emotional)
- Extraversion (sociable, fun loving, active)

■ **factor analysis**
statistical procedure for detecting patterns in a large set of correlations

Although their work differs in details, both Raymond Cattell and Hans Eysenck pioneered the factor analytic approach to personality.

■ **introversion-extraversion**
degree to which people are inwardly or outwardly oriented

■ **neuroticism**
degree to which people are moody and nervous

■ **psychoticism**
degree to which people are insensitive, odd, and detached

■ **Big Five**
five personality traits thought to describe the important ways in which people differ: neuroticism, extraversion, openness, agreeableness, and conscientiousness

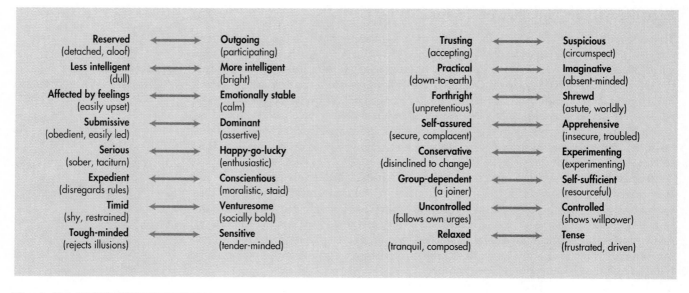

Reserved (detached, aloof)	← →	**Outgoing** (participating)	**Trusting** (accepting)	← →	**Suspicious** (circumspect)
Less intelligent (dull)	← →	**More intelligent** (bright)	**Practical** (down-to-earth)	← →	**Imaginative** (absent-minded)
Affected by feelings (easily upset)	← →	**Emotionally stable** (calm)	**Forthright** (unpretentious)	← →	**Shrewd** (astute, worldly)
Submissive (obedient, easily led)	← →	**Dominant** (assertive)	**Self-assured** (secure, complacent)	← →	**Apprehensive** (insecure, troubled)
Serious (sober, taciturn)	← →	**Happy-go-lucky** (enthusiastic)	**Conservative** (disinclined to change)	← →	**Experimenting** (experimenting)
Expedient (disregards rules)	← →	**Conscientious** (moralistic, staid)	**Group-dependent** (a joiner)	← →	**Self-sufficient** (resourceful)
Timid (shy, restrained)	← →	**Venturesome** (socially bold)	**Uncontrolled** (follows own urges)	← →	**Controlled** (shows willpower)
Tough-minded (rejects illusions)	← →	**Sensitive** (tender-minded)	**Relaxed** (tranquil, composed)	← →	**Tense** (frustrated, driven)

Figure 12.3
Cattell's 16 Personality Factors. Through factor analysis, Raymond Cattell identified 16 basic dimensions along which people differ. These are called source traits, and are at the root of countless surface traits that meet the eye.

- Openness (imaginative, creative, artistic)
- Agreeableness (good-natured, softhearted, sympathetic)
- Conscientiousness (reliable, hardworking, neat, punctual)

These are presumably dimensions of personality along which all people fall.

At first glance, the Big Five seems limited, but Norman's scheme actually predicts a fair degree of variation across people. Suppose we make just three distinctions with respect to each of the basic dimensions: high, medium, and low. These traits are inde-

Figure 12.4
Eysenck's Personality Dimensions. Through factor analysis, Hans Eysenck identified two basic dimensions along which people differ. Shown in this figure are some of the surface traits related to these two source traits.

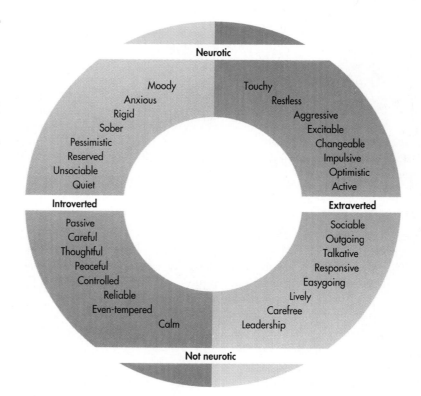

The Big Five is an attempt to specify the major ways in which people's personalities differ. Pablo Picasso, for instance, might be described as high on neuroticism, low on extraversion, high on openness, low on agreeableness, and medium on conscientiousness. Even if this description is accurate, does it fully capture the essence of Picasso's personality?

pendent, meaning that many different combinations are possible. One person may be high on the first trait, low on the second trait, medium on the third, high on the fourth, and high on the fifth. A second person may show a different pattern. With three distinctions for each trait, we have 243 possible combinations (that is, $3 \times 3 \times 3 \times 3 \times 3$). Suppose we make five distinctions. That gives us 3,125 combinations. Seven distinctions allow 16,807 combinations.

Support for the Big Five comes from research that uses factor analysis (Goldberg, 1990, 1992, 1993). McCrae and Costa (1987), for example, asked research subjects to describe themselves or other people either by choosing appropriate adjectives or by rating the degree to which the different adjectives applied. In all cases, factor analysis revealed the same five factors. In fact, identical results have been obtained in different cultures, implying that the Big Five may be universal dimensions of personality (Church & Katigbak, 1989; de Raad & Szirmak, 1994; John, Goldberg, & Angleitner, 1984; Rolland, 1993).

Evaluating the Trait Approach

The trait approach to personality has made its greatest contribution to the field by identifying the ways in which people differ and by creating research procedures for assessing those differences. All personality researchers use the tests and measures devised by trait psychologists. The trait approach can also be praised for drawing attention to the biological and genetic basis of personality, although a great deal of work is still needed to identify the relevant mechanisms. Along these lines, trait theory often neglects to specify how a trait leads to behavior. Critics regard the Big Five as a useful classification but not a full explanation of individual differences (Eysenck, 1993; Hough, 1992; Mischel & Shoda, 1994; Pervin, 1994).

Many of the important individual differences among people are heritable, but why should they be? This question does not ask about the evolutionary significance of species-typical characteristics such as a large brain, upright posture, social responsiveness, or the capacity for language (Chapter 3). Rather, it concerns the variability of characteristics within our species. Evolution usually minimizes variation, and so why are some people extraverted and others introverted?

Several answers are possible (Tooby & Cosmides, 1990a). One is that the well-being of a group as a whole is served by variation in traits across individuals. Variation guarantees maximum flexibility in adapting to different environments and promotes the fitness of our entire species (Buss, 1991). Another possible explanation is that personality traits, at least within normal ranges, are irrelevant for survival and so have never been selected against. A third possibility is that variation in personality is a consequence of other biological characteristics of people, such as the structure or function of the nervous system; natural selection produced these other characteristics, and what we mean by personality merely came along for the evolutionary ride (Gould, 1991).

Finally, the trait approach to personality can be criticized for neglecting the influence of the social environment on behavior (Van Heck, Perugini, Caprara, & Froger, 1994). Many trait theorists assume that people act in much the same way—that is, consistent with their traits—regardless of where they find themselves. This assumption has been hotly debated, and the issue is covered in detail in the section titled "The Consistency Controversy," at the end of this chapter.

Stop and Think

7 Find an example from the popular media that proposes a typology of personality.

8 For a specific trait, like extraversion, speculate about the mechanisms that might lead from its genetic predisposition to actual behavior.

9 Describe your own personality in terms of the Big Five.

THE PHENOMENOLOGICAL APPROACH: EMPHASIS ON COGNITION

■ **phenomenological approach; cognitive approach**
group of personality theories that stress what and how people think

The **phenomenological** (or **cognitive**) **approach** to personality defines personality by what and how we think. Although other personality theories discussed so far acknowledge the importance of a person's mental life, phenomenological theories see conscious thoughts and beliefs as the primary aspect of personality. How we feel and how we act are determined by how we think, not vice versa.

Phenomenological theories share the following assumptions:

■ Behavior can be understood only in terms of how an individual perceives the world. This psychological reality may overlap perfectly, somewhat, or not at all with physical reality.
■ People are like scientists in that they entertain theories about themselves and the world and then try to test those theories.
■ People attempt to make their thoughts more accurate, precise, and/or consistent.
■ What people say about their own thoughts and beliefs is taken seriously. To study personality, a researcher can start by asking research subjects what they think.

The phenomenological approach applies ideas from Gestalt psychology to complex behavior (Lewin, 1951). The two are united by a concern with how people structure their experiences (Chapter 1). The most influential phenomenological theories today are George Kelly's personal construct theory and Carl Rogers's self-theory, and so we now turn to their work.

George Kelly: Personal Constructs

A clinical psychologist, George Kelly (1905–1967) developed a therapy focusing on how a client interprets events. Kelly (1955) believed that a variety of interpretations are always possible, with some more useful to an individual than others. From this notion, he developed **personal construct theory.** Personal constructs are the categories with which we interpret our experiences (Brown & Chiesa, 1990), and Kelly regarded these categories as the basic units of personality. Thus, one individual may think of other people chiefly in terms of their physical appearance, whereas another individual may think of others in terms of their power and prestige.

Kelly used the term *personal* because cognitive activity belongs to the individual. The term *construct* means that people build (or construct) their personality with the ideas they entertain. His theory assumes that people can revise or replace any of their interpretations. Our interpretations are literally our personality, and so personality need not be fixed. Contrast this notion with psychodynamic or trait conceptions, which assume that personality, once established, is unchanging.

Kelly was interested in not only the specific contents of personal constructs but also their more abstract properties. For example, constructs vary in their range of convenience: the set of events for which they work best. Remember your first day on a new job, where nothing made sense to you? Kelly would say that the constructs you brought with you through the door were inadequate. Their range of convenience did not include the demands placed on you by this new job. You devised new constructs, expanded the ones already at your disposal, or quit the job.

In a study of police officers, Winter (1993) found that those who reacted to stress with violence or lawbreaking brought fewer constructs to bear on their feelings than was true of officers who did not act out in response to stress. Presumably, the complexity of the construct system devoted to emotions allows flexibility in how one responds to them.

Kelly also proposed that personal constructs are organized in a hierarchy. Some—superordinate constructs—are more important and are used to organize other constructs. These overarching constructs differ from person to person. For some, the superordinate construct may be religion. For others, it may be politics. For still others, it may be family. Think of all the people you know. What distinguishes your friends from your mere acquaintances? Perhaps the most critical contrast (to you) is that your friends are sports fans and your acquaintances are not. Or perhaps you divide friends from

personal construct theory
Kelly's explanation of personality in terms of the categories with which people interpret their experiences

According to personal construct theory, people's behavior reflects their interpretations of the world.

acquaintances based on their academic major, their membership in a fraternity, or their ethnicity. In each case, the central contrast is your superordinate construct.

People also use personal constructs to anticipate future events (Pfenninger & Klion, 1994). Sometimes these anticipations prove useful. When constructs allow new experiences to be readily understood, people keep using them. At other times, construct-based anticipations are not useful, and people accordingly revise their constructs. For example, most of you have constructs that allow you to make sense of what happens in a fast-food restaurant. Once established, these constructs rarely need to be changed, even if you opt for a Whopper rather than your typical Big Mac. But now consider the constructs about classes that you brought with you from high school to college. At least some of these constructs did not help you make sense of your college courses and how to study for them, and so you needed to change how you thought.

Carl Rogers: Self-Actualization

Like Kelly, Carl Rogers (1902–1987) was a clinical psychologist whose personality theory grew out of his experiences in working with clients. Rogers (1942) first worked within a Freudian framework but eventually concluded that a therapist's insights rarely had beneficial effects on his or her clients. If anything, the clients seemed to know better than a therapist what ailed them and what needed to be done. Rogers developed this notion into **self-theory,** an approach that defines personality in terms of how people view themselves in relationship to their worlds.

Central to Rogers's (1951) theory is a drive toward **self-actualization,** familiar to us from Maslow's work (discussed in Chapter 7). Both Rogers and Maslow assumed that people strive to achieve their full potential, increasing their complexity, independence, and social responsibility (Bozarth & Brodley, 1991). Further, people know what is good for them and how to achieve it. This is an upbeat and optimistic view of human nature, and both Rogers and Maslow were prominent figures in humanistic psychology, the approach emphasizing that human beings are essentially good and motivated toward personal growth (Chapter 1).

But not all individuals actualize themselves. Rogers blamed the social environment for the failure of self-actualization, particularly when other people give individuals distorted views of themselves. He made a distinction between experience and awareness: Experience refers to everything that happens to a person, and awareness to the part of experience a person thinks about in symbolic terms. If a person is to become self-actualized, awareness and experience must come together. When a discrepancy occurs between awareness and experience, self-actualization is thwarted and problems follow.

According to Rogers, discrepancies result when we encounter **conditional regard:** acceptance that depends on particular ways of behaving. A parent, for instance, might say, "I love you, but if you marry that person, I never want to see you again." Conditional regard leads us to use other people's rules to define our own desires and needs. We no longer define ourselves, and we do not know what to make of our experience.

Rogers believed that the casualties of conditional regard can be reclaimed by reversing this process. We should be given **unconditional regard:** acceptance regardless of what we think, feel, or do. A parent might say, "I don't approve of you marrying that person, but I support your right to make that decision and will always love you." Under these circumstances, we can again come to rely on personal definitions and interpretations. Awareness and experience come together, and self-actualization takes over as a motive.

Rogers's system of psychotherapy is called client-centered therapy because it centers on the client. The therapist creates a social setting characterized by unconditional regard, which allows clients to devise their own solutions to problems (Bohart, 1991). Psychologists agree that the most successful therapy is conducted by clinicians who are warm, sincere, and accepting (Finke, 1990). In the course of client-centered therapy, one's perceived self and one's ideal self converge. The client-centered emphasis

Carl Rogers was an influential theorist in the phenomenological tradition.

■ **self-theory**
Rogers's explanation of personality in terms of how people view themselves in relationship to their worlds

■ **self-actualization**
tendency of people to strive to achieve their full potential, increasing their complexity, independence, and social responsibility

■ **conditional regard**
acceptance from others that depends on particular ways of behaving

■ **unconditional regard**
acceptance from others that occurs regardless of what one thinks, feels, or does

on acceptance makes this approach to therapy broadly applicable (Freeman, 1993; Hayashi, Kuno, Osawa, Shimizu, & Suetake, 1992) because therapists can be helpful only once they accept the characteristics that clients bring to therapy (Chapter 14).

Evaluating the Phenomenological Approach

The phenomenological approach to personality has grown in popularity during recent years, in part because it makes clear contact with the influential cognitive revolution that has swept through psychology as a whole. Phenomenological theories allow personality psychologists and cognitive psychologists to speak readily to one another (Cantor & Kihlstrom, 1987). These theories have also led to effective psychotherapies that target thoughts and beliefs for change (Chapter 14).

The shortcoming of the phenomenological approach is the drawback of cognitive psychology in general: an overemphasis on how people process information and an underemphasis on people's emotional sides. Kelly, Rogers, and other cognitive theorists trace our feelings to our thoughts but fail to do justice to our emotions (Chapter 7). Emotions influence thoughts, not just vice versa (Frey & Adams-Webber, 1992), and motives impel us to act on some thoughts but not others (Henry & Maze, 1989). Cognitive theories of personality are often silent on these matters.

Stop and Think

10 What is a personal construct?

11 What is unconditional regard?

12 Compare and contrast the phenomenological theories of Kelly and Rogers.

THE SOCIAL LEARNING APPROACH: EMPHASIS ON THE SOCIAL ENVIRONMENT

The last perspective on personality is the **social learning approach:** a group of related theories that explain our complex behavior using principles of learning. The roots of this approach are in behaviorism (Chapter 8). Social learning theorists believe that the environment determines behavior and that the most important aspect of the environment is other people. Hence, the term *social* is used for emphasis. The following assumptions are common to these theories:

■ social learning approach
group of personality theories that stress principles of learning

■ Learning is the most important psychological process.
■ The most basic explanations of personality are phrased in terms of the social environment.
■ Behavioral change is possible through interventions that are guided by learning theory.

Most social learning theories introduce unobservable factors in their explanations, including drives and expectations. Modern social learning theories are similar to the theories of Kelly and Rogers; however, in contrast to the phenomenological approach, the social learning approach ties cognitions to particular settings, thereby preserving a learning emphasis.

John Dollard and Neal Miller: Drive Reduction

The first social learning theorists were John Dollard (1900–1980) and Neal Miller (1909–). Their influential book *Personality and Psychotherapy*, published in 1950, assumed people learn behaviors that reduce their physiological drives (Chapter 7). They noted

According to Dollard and Miller, approach-avoidance conflicts are difficult to resolve. The outcome these conflicts promise seems to be attractive at a distance but becomes unattractive as we get closer to achieving it. So, a clean and orderly room seems a good idea, but . . .

the similarity between the drive reduction concept and the psychodynamic hypothesis that people strive to satisfy their instincts. They therefore attempted to integrate learning theory and psychoanalysis, discussing in detail how Freudian phenomena could be explained in terms of learning.

Dollard and Miller suggested that repression results from reinforcement for not thinking about particular topics. Suppose a sexual encounter has left you feeling anxious. If and when you stop thinking about it, the anxiety stops. That is reinforcing, and so you are likely to continue not thinking about it. The difference between the psychodynamic unconscious and the social learning unconscious is that the former is a place to which thoughts are banished, whereas the latter is a "behavior" (thinking) you are not performing.

Also like Freud, Dollard and Miller viewed development in terms of the interplay between biological drives and the social environment. Conflicts surface when parents punish their children for attempting to satisfy drives like hunger, elimination, sex, and aggression. Dollard and Miller introduced the idea of an **approach–avoidance conflict** to describe a course of activity both attractive (because it reduces drives) and unattractive (because it produces punishment). By this view, the issue at the center of each of Freud's psychosexual stages is an approach-avoidance conflict. For example, it is pleasurable for a child to masturbate, but it is not pleasurable to be punished for doing so.

Approach-avoidance conflicts are difficult to resolve, and they can become part of our personality. When the goal is distant, in time or space, it looks attractive and so we pursue it. When the goal becomes closer, it looks unattractive and so we avoid it. What results is oscillation, a back-and-forth movement in the vicinity of the goal. Think of goals like cleaning out your closet, organizing your desk, or starting your term paper. These all seem attractive until you begin to do something about them. Then their unattractive features become evident and you stop. Approach-avoidance conflicts may figure prominently in procrastination.

■ **approach-avoidance conflict**
course of activity both attractive (because it reduces drives) and unattractive (because it produces punishment)

Albert Bandura: Modeling

Chapter 8 described the approach Albert Bandura (1925–) took to learning. He believed that people acquire complex behavior through modeling. We watch other people behave, and then we act accordingly. If we see people act aggressively and get exactly what they want, then we are likely to act the same way. Bandura used modeling as the cornerstone of his version of social learning theory.

Another key concept in Bandura's (1977) view of personality is **self-efficacy,** an individual's belief that a given behavior can be enacted. According to Bandura, self-efficacy is the immediate mechanism by which any and all behavior changes. Only if people believe they can perform a behavior will they do so. Modeling is effective because it strengthens self-efficacy, showing an individual that a behavior can be performed.

■ **self-efficacy**
belief that one can perform a given behavior

Studies find that an individual's self-efficacy for a given response ("I am certain I can give this speech") is a better predictor of performance than past success or failure in performance (Bandura, 1989, 1993). One of psychology's truisms is that past behavior predicts future behavior, but the notion of self-efficacy improves on this truism.

Bandura (1986) stressed that behavior, cognition, and the environment mutually influence each other. This mutual influence, called **reciprocal determinism,** is one more key concept for understanding personality in social learning terms (Baranowski, 1989–1990; Kihlstrom & Harackiewicz, 1990). Consider the example of watching television. Your interests (cognition) determine the channel you select (behavior). If your television set is hooked to a Nielsen box, then your channel selection influences subsequent programming (environment). What is available on television shapes your interests. All possible directions of influence can occur.

■ **reciprocal determinism**
idea that behavior, cognition, and the environment mutually influence each other

Evaluating the Social Learning Approach

The social learning approach to personality explicitly incorporates processes of learning and an emphasis on the social environment. Social learning theories direct our attention away from factors within the person (motives, traits, and thoughts) to the context in which he or she behaves (Cantor, 1990).

However, a focus solely on the social environment yields an incomplete view of personality. Even if the environment is of critical importance, the social learning approach often fails to address central issues. How do people decide which of several simultaneous drives to reduce by their actions? How do people decide which of several simultaneous models to emulate in their behavior? Why are most people some of the time and some people all of the time unresponsive to social influence? Answers to these questions must be sought in other theoretical traditions, and so again we see the need to integrate the different approaches to personality.

Stop and Think

13   Describe an example from your everyday life of an approach–avoidance conflict.

14   What is reciprocal determinism?

15   Compare and contrast the social learning theory of Dollard and Miller with the theory of Bandura.

DOING *Personality* RESEARCH

Personality psychology did not become a science until researchers began to measure individual differences among people. Although intelligence testing served as a model for personality assessment, intelligence testing and personality assessment are not the same thing. First, intelligence testing tries to assess maximum performance, whereas personality assessment aims to measure typical performance. Second, intelligence tests have right answers, whereas personality measures do not. Third, intelligence tests often have an explicit criterion against which they can be validated. We saw in Chapter 11 how researchers can check intelligence test results against academic performance. Most measures of personality do not have such a criterion available because personality refers to diverse aspects of a person's behavior.

This difficulty with validating personality testing is another example of the familiar refrain that no measure is foolproof. All operationalizations, including those of individual differences in personality, are subject to confounds. The best a researcher can do is be on the lookout for these threats and then try to eliminate the most obvious ones.

Assessment Strategies

Once researchers decide what types of individual differences they wish to study—motives, traits, personal constructs, whatever—they must settle on a strategy for doing so. Their decision concerning the basic units of personality usually dictates the investigative strategy (see Table 12.4). Psychodynamic notions are readily investigated with in-depth case studies (Alexander, 1990) and traits with brief questionnaires asking about typical behaviors (Angleitner & Wiggins, 1986; Robinson, Shaver, & Wrightsman, 1991). These assessment strategies were the first to appear (Megargee & Spielberger, 1992), although additional approaches now exist.

Clinical assessment.   Clinical assessment attempts "to describe the particular person in as full, multifaceted, and multilevel a way as possible" (Korchin & Schuldberg, 1981, p. 1147). Researchers first ask subjects to respond to ambiguous tasks and open-ended questions, and they then rely strongly on their own intuition to make sense of subjects' responses. Clinical assessment is highly compatible with the psychodynamic goal of providing a complex view of our behavior.

Statistical assessment.   In contrast, statistical assessment places people along carefully defined personality dimensions by using their responses to questionnaires. The goal of statistical assessment is to maximize objectivity while minimizing judgment and inference on the part of the researcher. Test reliability and validity take on central importance. This approach to assessment serves the goals of personality psychologists who favor the trait approach.

Those who use clinical assessment have frequently disagreed with those who use statistical assessment concerning which strategy allows better predictions of behavior (Meehl, 1954, 1957). If you are called upon to say how a particular individual will think, act, or feel, are you better off knowing rich details about the person's life (as provided by clinical assessment) or knowing his or her scores on objective personality tests (as provided by statistical assessment)? Perhaps surprisingly, research consistently shows that statistical assessment yields more accurate predictions (Garb, 1994).

Ponder the implications. Personality psychologists work in a variety of settings where they must make predictions about individuals: the clinic, the classroom, the armed forces, and the government (Chapter 17). Relying on hunches will lead to poor predictions. We would be better off if we used objective tests to make predictions.

Table 12.4   Summary: Personality Assessment Strategies

Strategy	Theoretical basis
Clinical assessment	Psychodynamic theories
Statistical assessment	Trait theories
Cognitive assessment	Phenomenological theories
Behavioral assessment	Social learning theories

The goal of personality assessment is to describe people's characteristic individual differences in an objective way, but what we mean by personality often does not have a single or simple criterion.

Prediction is, after all, a statistical matter, an attempt to determine the most likely course of action granted certain conditions. Statistical assessment is engineered to allow the researcher to predict the most likely behavior by an individual. The value of clinical assessment lies elsewhere. Clinical assessment suggests to the researcher factors worthy of attention in the first place, and thus these two approaches might best be used in tandem (Kleinmuntz, 1990).

Shedler, Mayman, and Manis (1993) conducted several studies that combined clinical and statistical assessment to determine the degree to which individuals were troubled. Research participants described some of their earliest memories, which were evaluated by clinical psychologists as psychologically healthy or not (clinical assessment). Participants also completed a questionnaire asking them to report the extent to which they experienced symptoms of anxiety and depression; according to their questionnaire responses, they were divided into two groups: psychologically healthy or not (statistical assessment). Shedler and colleagues were interested in the discrepancies between the clinicians' judgments and the research participants' self-reports. Individuals who described themselves as psychologically healthier than the clinicians judged them to be showed elevated levels of physiological arousal as measured by the appropriate recording device.

The researchers concluded that these people consciously denied their own distress but that the stress was physiologically evident. This research provides an important caution about relying on self-report questionnaires to measure personality: There are things that people do not know or will not reveal about themselves.

In a follow-up study of individuals in psychotherapy, researchers showed that the degree of discrepancy between clinicians' judgments and clients' self-ratings predicted the eventual success of therapy (Reynolds, Mayman, & Peterson, 1995). Here, however, it was the individuals who saw themselves as healthier than the clinicians did who fared better in treatment. Perhaps these individuals were more optimistic about the outcome of therapy. Even if they were not initially accurate, their expectations translated themselves into a positive result. This research provides a caution about relying on clinician judgments to measure personality: There are things that observers, no matter how expert, do not know or cannot infer about people.

Cognitive assessment.   Derived from the phenomenological approach to personality, cognitive assessment aims to determine a person's characteristic ways of thinking (Merluzzi, Glass, & Genest, 1981). Sometimes cognitive assessment relies on questionnaires, asking research subjects to indicate which of several beliefs they usually hold. At other times, cognitive assessment uses a technique called thought monitoring, in which subjects are asked to keep track of the thoughts that occur to them in particular situations. For example, an individual who experiences negative emotions is asked to write down the thoughts accompanying them. The resulting "Daily Record of Dysfunctional Thoughts" is used in cognitive therapy for depression (Beck, Rush, Shaw, & Emery, 1979), a topic examined in Chapter 14.

Cognitive assessment is most useful when we are concerned with thoughts and beliefs that are available to an individual's awareness and able to be expressed with words. However, not all of our cognitions fit this formula. Personal constructs, for example, are not the same thing as our vocabulary. Not all constructs have a verbal label attached to them, and so constructs can be difficult to measure with the typical strategies of cognitive assessment.

Behavioral assessment.   More recently, behavioral assessment has been developed. Its goal is to describe a person's actual behavior in particular circumstances (Ciminero, Calhoun, & Adams, 1986). Here is an example from a psychological clinic where I once worked. An 8-year-old girl was brought in by her father because her elementary school teacher said she had disciplinary problems. The situation was quite complicated. The family had recently moved to the United States from Eastern Europe so that the father could attend graduate school. After just a few weeks, the mother returned to their home country to care for an ill relative, taking with her the two younger children in the family. The girl then began to have problems at school.

We could have spoken at length with the girl about her feelings of rejection and abandonment (clinical assessment). We could have administered objective tests to see how she compared with her American peers with respect to intelligence, self-control, and social skills (statistical assessment). We could have talked to her concerning her beliefs about her classmates (cognitive assessment). But instead, we followed her to school, observing how she behaved and the consequences that followed her actions (behavioral assessment).

We discovered that the little girl was excluded from games during recess because she did not know how to play them. She rarely talked to the other students because they made fun of her accent. The only time anyone took her seriously was when the teacher noticed her fidgeting. In light of this information, we recommended that the school give her remedial instruction in school-yard games as well as special help with her pronunciation. The teacher caught the spirit of our suggestions and went one step further, devoting a week of class to life in other countries, an event that made our client the center of positive attention.

You should recognize behavioral assessment as an example of the method of functional analysis as recommended by Skinner (Chapter 8). Behavioral assessment provides a description not only of an individual's behavior but also of the reinforcements and punishments that influence behavior. This assessment strategy can be difficult to carry out, and the researcher must be aware that his or her presence might influence how an individual behaves (Chapter 2). Also because of its focus on what can be observed, the method necessarily overlooks other aspects of personality.

Specific Measures of Individual Differences

This section surveys some of the popular measures that personality psychologists use as they go about their research. Most of these procedures can be placed within one of the four assessment traditions just discussed: clinical, statistical, behavioral, or cognitive (see Table 12.5).

Table 12.5 Summary: Specific Measures of Individual Differences	
Measure	**Assessment tradition(s)**
Projective techniques	Clinical
Objective tests	Statistical
Personality inventories	Statistical
Observations and ratings by judges	Statistical; behavioral
Experience sampling	Phenomenological; behavioral

Projective techniques.   Personality researchers in the clinical assessment tradition often use **projective techniques:** procedures that ask research subjects to respond to ambiguous stimuli (Rabin, 1968). The stimuli themselves do not demand particular reactions, and so theoretically, anything the subjects say in response to them reveals the workings of their personality.

Chapter 7 discussed Morgan and Murray's (1935) Thematic Apperception Test (TAT), used to gauge individual differences in needs. You can now see why the TAT is considered a projective technique and why it is favored by researchers who attempt clinical assessment (Bellak, 1986; Teglasi, 1993). Here is an example of a TAT story told in response to a picture of a boy sitting at a desk with a book in front of him:

> A boy in a classroom. . . is daydreaming about something. He is recalling a previously experienced incident that struck his mind to be more appealing than being in the classroom. He is thinking about the experience and is now imagining himself in the situation. He hopes to be there. He will probably get called on by the instructor to recite and will be embarrassed. (McClelland, 1961, p. 41)

What does this story suggest about the subject's need for achievement? About his attitude toward education? About his fears concerning books and teachers? We can assume that his need to achieve is low, at least in traditional academic domains.

Hermann Rorschach's (1942) inkblots, known as the Rorschach Inkblot Test, represent another well-known projective procedure. This test presents subjects with a series of symmetrical inkblots, asking them what each blot looks like and why. Their responses are scored in terms of what they see, as well as their explanations (Exner, 1974–1982). Some of the inkblots are printed in brilliant colors. A person's response to the color cards is usually interpreted in terms of his or her characteristic response to emotion. For instance, a person who ignores the colors may also ignore the feelings that color everyday experience.

Projective techniques are frequently criticized on the grounds of reliability and validity. Two psychologists interpreting the same set of responses may arrive at different conclusions, and test scores may not relate well to other aspects of the subject's behavior. To some degree, this criticism is to be expected, for it uses criteria from the statistical tradition of assessment to evaluate methods within the clinical tradition. Projective techniques continue to be used, however because they can reveal information of which subjects are unaware (Murstein, 1963).

Objective tests.   If a personality psychologist wants to make predictions, objective tests are the appropriate procedure. **Objective tests** are measures in which scores are assigned according to explicit rules (Butcher, 1995). Consider a questionnaire measure of a trait such as introversion-extraversion. Subjects agree or disagree with various statements, some reflecting introversion ("I like to spend time alone") and others reflecting extraversion ("I like to go to crowded parties"). People receive a high score on introversion or extraversion to the degree that they agree with the appropriate statements;

■ **projective techniques**
procedures that ask research subjects to respond to ambiguous stimuli

■ **objective tests**
measures in which scores are assigned according to explicit rules

In the Rorschach inkblot test, people are shown ambiguous stimuli like this one and asked to report what they see. This procedure is called a projective technique because people are thought to project their own needs and issues onto the objectively meaningless picture.

they receive a low score to the degree that they disagree with such statements. There is no ambiguity here, and so this is an objective test.

The term *objective* refers only to the method by which the psychologist uses these tests to describe personality. It does not imply that they are perfect measures. An objective test can be flawed. First, it may fail to be reliable (Chapter 2). **Test-retest reliability** refers to whether the test gives the same scores to an individual on repeated occasions; **internal reliability** refers to whether different items on the same test give the same scores to an individual at the same point in time. No test is perfectly reliable, in either the test–retest sense or the internal sense, but researchers continually strive to increase the reliability of their measures. Poor reliability limits predictability and thus the usefulness of a measure.

Second, objective tests may fail because they lack validity, not measuring what they intend to measure. As noted in Chapter 2, validity is not as simple a notion as reliability. There are different criteria by which the validity of tests is evaluated; these criteria and examples of them are shown in Table 12.6.

■ **test-retest reliability**
degree to which a test gives the same scores to an individual on repeated occasions

■ **internal reliability**
degree to which different items on the same test give the same scores to an individual at the same point in time

■ **personality inventory**
set of objective tests that attempts to measure the range of individual differences

Personality inventories.   A **personality inventory** is a set of objective tests that attempts to measure the range of individual differences. Two important qualifications concern personality inventories. First, they do not reveal every way in which people differ from each other. Rather, their goal is to measure major individual differences. Second, as we have seen, opinion is divided as to what constitutes the major individual differences. For example, Raymond Cattell believed there were 16 factors of personality (see again Figure 12.3); his Sixteen Personality Factor Inventory measures all of these factors (Cattell, Eber, & Tatsuoka, 1970). In contrast, Hans Eysenck opted for a smaller number of major individual differences, and the personality inventory he devised includes a smaller number of measures (Eysenck & Eysenck, 1975).

The best-known personality inventory is the Minnesota Multiphasic Personality Inventory (MMPI), created in the 1940s at the University of Minnesota (Hathaway & McKinley, 1943) and revised in the late 1980s (Butcher, Dahlstrom, Graham, Tellegen, & Kaemmer, 1989). The original intent of the MMPI was to aid psychiatric diagnoses.

Table 12.6   Types of Validity

Type	Example
Face validity	
Does the test look like it measures what it is supposed to measure?	Exit interviews outside voting booths that ask about political preferences (Chapter 15)
Content validity	
Does the test contain a sample of the behavior of interest?	Typing test to measure secretarial skills (Chapter 17)
Criterion validity	
Does the test predict some behavior of interest?	Questionnaire measure of introversion that correlates with the pursuit of solitary hobbies
Known-groups validity	
Does the test distinguish between groups of people known to differ on the characteristic of interest?	Behavioral measure of helplessness that distinguishes between trauma victims (helpless) and other people (not helpless) (Chapter 13)
Construct validity	
Does the test relate to other tests as theory predicts?	Self-rating of creativity that correlates with a measure of divergent thinking (Chapter 11)

Hundreds of items were assembled, all of them to be answered true or false. Here are some examples:

- Evil spirits possess me at times.
- I go to church almost every week.
- I sweat very easily even on cool days.
- I think Lincoln was greater than Washington.

Numerous individuals with known psychiatric diagnoses (determined by clinicians) answered these questions, and researchers calculated which responses were consistently correlated with a particular diagnosis.

Over the decades, hundreds of thousands of individuals have taken the MMPI, and it has proved successful in identifying patients' problems. Many diagnosticians therefore routinely administer the MMPI to their clients. Although one does not make a diagnosis solely on the basis of MMPI scores, a diagnostician takes these scores quite seriously.

The MMPI was developed by the known-groups method of determining validity (remember Table 12.6). That is, items were identified that successfully distinguished between respondents in two groups known to differ with respect to a characteristic of interest, such as depression or anxiety. The items have no necessary face validity, meaning that it is difficult to look at a particular question and decide what it is measuring. Scoring of the MMPI continually changes as researchers identify ways to predict characteristics not envisioned by those who originally devised the MMPI. However, by convention, one set of characteristics—shown in Table 12.7—is typically scored from MMPI responses. The MMPI has also been used to study normal individuals. An individual's personality can be described in terms of where he or she falls along the dimensions listed in Table 12.7. Consider the view of human nature embedded here: The basic individual differences are ones that distinguish among different forms of abnormality.

Observations and ratings by judges.   Questionnaires requiring people to describe their own characteristics or behaviors may give too restricted a view of personality. Respondents often present themselves in the best possible light, meaning that their descriptions can be skewed toward self-flattery. The majority of people in the United States, for instance, regard themselves as above average in characteristics like sense of humor, intelligence, and popularity (Lewinsohn, Mischel, Chaplin, & Barton, 1980).

Table 12.7   MMPI Subscales

Subscale	Characterization
Hypochondriasis	Exaggerated concerns about physical well-being
Depression	Sadness, worthlessness, and pessimism
Hysteria	Bodily complaints due to psychological causes
Psychopathic deviance	Disregard for social and moral standards
Masculinity/femininity	Adherence to traditional gender-role values
Paranoia	Suspiciousness and feelings of persecution
Psychasthenia	Irrational fears and nervous compulsions
Schizophrenia	Bizarre thoughts or actions
Hypomania	Emotional excitability and excess activity
Social introversion	Social withdrawal

Another drawback to self-report is that people may be unable to report on individual characteristics of interest. An obvious example is research subjects composed of young children who cannot readily describe themselves. A less obvious example is a characteristic of concern that falls outside of awareness, such as defense mechanisms like repression or projection.

So, personality researchers may study people by asking those who know them to make judgments (Funder & West, 1993). In some cases, these judges provide direct ratings of traits: "Is this person thrifty, reverent, courteous, and brave?" In other cases, they offer judgments concerning particular behaviors: "How many times in the last week did this person help elderly women across the street?" Studies of temperament among children often ask parents to rate the activity, emotionality, and sociability of their offspring (Plomin, 1986). Similarly, studies of emotional disturbance among children often rely on teacher ratings of such characteristics as aggression and withdrawal (Achenbach, 1986).

Like other research techniques, ratings by judges are not perfect. One problem in particular plagues them: Judges might let their opinion on one aspect of a subject's personality color their opinion elsewhere. For example, these so-called halo effects introduce a confound when employers try to rate the performance of their employees (Chapter 17). Because it is difficult for judges to make finer distinctions, employees usually get rated high or low on all characteristics. A partial solution to this problem is to define the characteristics of concern narrowly and explicitly, typically in terms of overt behaviors. "The employee arrives at work on time every Monday" is less susceptible to rating bias than "This employee is conscientious."

Experience sampling.   The newest way to study personality is thoroughly high-tech. Popularly called the beeper method, this procedure is more formally known as **experience sampling** (Alliger & Williams, 1993; Larson, 1989). Research subjects are given an electronic device not much larger than a pack of cigarettes. They carry it around with them, and at randomly determined intervals it gives off a signal (Beep!). Subjects then complete a questionnaire, describing where they are, what they are doing, how they are feeling, and what they are thinking. The most high tech version of experience sampling allows subjects to enter their responses on a tiny keyboard; however, a pencil and paper usually suffice.

For instance, Hillbrand and Waite (1994) used experience sampling to study the naturally occurring moods and thoughts of a 39-year-old male rapist. Compared with men who had no history of sex crimes, he frequently reported thoughts with sexual content, often when he was distressed and feeling inadequate. Both he and his therapists used the information to devise better responses to stress than thinking along sexual lines.

■ **experience sampling**
procedure in which research subjects are contacted at random intervals and asked to describe where they are, what they are doing, how they are feeling, and what they are thinking

For another example, Harlow and Cantor (1994) used experience sampling to map out how female college students' concern with academic activities could spill over into their social activities. This phenomenon usually took the form of a student asking her friends for reassurance about academic pursuits. If such reassurance seeking was done too frequently, the women reported lower social satisfaction because not all of their friends provided the desired reassurance.

Assuming that subjects indeed answer questions on the spot, experience sampling avoids problems with memory. Subjects need not think about what they usually do; they need only report what is going on at the present time. The immediacy of the procedure allows the researcher to draw conclusions about subjects' everyday thoughts, feelings, and actions. Moreover, experience sampling allows the researcher to take the subject's immediate surroundings into account, a decided benefit given current attention to the setting in which our behavior occurs. Beepers give the researcher a glimpse at the subject's environment—although they do not work too well in swimming pools, nightclubs, or churches (Hormuth, 1986).

Stop and Think

16 Describe your own personality in terms of the MMPI subscales.

17 What is experience sampling?

18 How might the different assessment strategies be combined into an overall approach to the measurement of personality? What is left out?

THE CONSISTENCY CONTROVERSY

Do people act consistently in different situations? For most personality theories (particularly psychodynamic and trait accounts), cross-situational consistency is a basic assumption. The language we use to describe individual characteristics presupposes consistency. Somebody who is gregarious should seek out others in a variety of circumstances. That is what gregarious means.

Walter Mischel (1968) challenged the assumption of personality consistency in *Personality and Assessment*. He surveyed research dealing with consistency and found little evidence to support this widespread assumption. He then suggested that psychodynamic and trait approaches were wrong and should be replaced with social learning theory, which expects little consistency across various situations because people respond to the rewards and punishments present in each setting. Mischel proposed that personality is to be found in particular situations. Behavior remains sensible and orderly, but its coherence stems not from psychological states and traits but from the environment and how people think about it. The most radical interpretation of Mischel's conclusion is that there is no such thing as personality.

Mischel's Argument: People Are Not Consistent

Personality and Assessment started out as a textbook, a survey of different approaches to personality. But when Walter Mischel studied the available research literature, the textbook took a backseat. To his surprise, he found little evidence that people acted consistently. A representative investigation was Hartshorne and May's (1928) study of children's moral conduct. These investigators wanted to know if a general trait of honesty or dishonesty exists. Concretely, when schoolchildren are given different opportunities to transgress, do the same children always step over the line? Hartshorne and May thought of many situations in which a young person might lie, cheat, or steal. Settings included the home, the classroom, and the playground. Findings showed that moral conduct is not particularly consistent. Although correlations across situations were usually positive, they were not of great magnitude, suggesting that honesty is not the general trait that most theories (and most people) believe it to be.

Personality and Assessment similarly described investigations of dependency, aggression, rigidity, avoidance, and conditionability. This list is not arbitrary; these characteristics occupy central places in the major personality theories. In addition, the principal approaches to psychopathology (Chapter 13) and clinical psychology (Chapter 14) presuppose consistency in these characteristics. But in no case was evidence strong that these were general characteristics.

Needless to say, in attacking the idea of consistency, Mischel attacked the very field of personality as it had existed for decades. Some read his book as claiming that people have no personality, at least as the word is typically used. Further, a profound statement about human nature lurks in Mischel's message. Psychologists and everyday people make a mistake by looking within people to understand them. Mischel felt that it was better to look at the situations in which behavior occurs.

To complete his argument, Mischel needed to tie up two loose ends. First, if there is little consistency in how people behave, why do so many of us believe in pervasive traits? Mischel suggested that people construct consistency out of very little raw material, relying on cognitive biases (Chapter 9). Traits exist not so much in the person we observe as in our ways of looking at that person. For example, stereotypes lead us to see consistencies even when they do not exist (Chapter 15).

Second, if traits do not sensibly describe how people behave, then what have personality psychologists been investigating over the years? Mischel contended that personality research all too rarely looks at people's actual behavior. Instead, investigators concern themselves with how people respond to personality tests. This kind of research is subject to a host of confounds, yielding a false view of consistency.

Mischel's criticisms stimulated research more sophisticated than prior investigations. Taken collectively, this research gives us a better understanding of consistency and hence of personality. Let us take a look at several of the important reactions.

Aggregation of Behaviors over Time

Seymour Epstein (1979, 1990) observed that personality researchers tend not to be careful when they measure behaviors reflecting a particular trait. Within a given setting, researchers usually assess a single behavior on a single occasion. How much confidence would we place in an intelligence test that consisted of just one question? Suppose a college transcript had only one grade recorded? Could we judge a football team that ran only one play?

Needless to say, we recognize these as inadequate measures, and we know that the way to improve matters is to include more questions, more grades, or more plays. Epstein advised researchers interested in cross-situational consistency to look at behaviors in a particular setting on repeated occasions. He called this strategy multiple assessment aggregation, and he showed that measures of behavior aggregated over time are much more consistent than single measures (see also Overholser, 1992).

Trait-Environment Interactions

Another research reaction to Mischel's critique of consistency integrates trait and situational approaches. Does it make sense to talk of people independently of particular situations? Does it make sense to talk of situations independently of people? The answer to both of these questions is clearly no. The more reasonable position is that the interaction between a person's traits and his or her world best explains that individual's personality (Bowers, 1973; Ekehammar, 1974; Endler & Magnusson, 1976).

The term **interaction** has a particular meaning here: We can understand the effects of one factor (trait or environment) only by knowing the other factor. Suppose we have

■ **interaction**
joint effect on behavior of traits and the environment

Although personality psychologists often look within a person for explanations of his or her behavior, situations can be just as important in explaining behavior.

two people, an introvert and an extravert, as well as two settings, a raucous rock concert and an isolated art museum. Let us concern ourselves with happiness. Who is happier—the introvert or the extravert? We cannot say unless we know where these people are. And where is a person happier—at the rock concert or at the art museum? Again, we cannot say unless we know who is in these places. Psychologists now recognize that we should take into account trait–environment interactions like these in order to understand consistency (Endler & Parker, 1992; Ross & Nisbett, 1991).

Interactionism is more complex than the example just cited because personality can shape the environment. One attempt to flesh out this idea was made by Buss (1987), who described three kinds of interactions between personality and the social environment. In evocation, the person unintentionally elicits a particular response from the environment. Suspicious individuals, for instance, constantly test others, conveying their profound mistrust. The consequence? People forever tested and questioned eventually tire of the process and become angry with the individuals who question them. A suspicious style maintains itself not because there is a trait within the person but because there is a vicious circle that involves behavior.

In manipulation, people intentionally alter the world. The tactics they choose are influenced by their traits, to be sure, but the consequences of the tactics change the person. Consider an individual's style of dress, which is often chosen to make a statement to other people about how one wishes to be regarded (Roach-Higgins & Eicher, 1992). When clothing has an effect, the individual's social setting is changed and so too is his or her behavior. When I see people who wear T-shirts that say "I'm with Stupid," I cannot help but wonder how their partners react to them.

In manipulation, people act in a deliberate way to alter the world. One of the most common types of manipulation is choosing to dress in one way or another, thereby creating reactions on the part of other people that in turn influence the individual.

Finally, in selection, a person chooses to enter particular situations or avoid them. Extraverted individuals, for example, might be drawn to the fast lane because it promises stimulation. Once there, they are shaped in such a way that their lifestyle becomes faster and faster. Or consider shy individuals who do not seek out the company of other people. They fail to develop social skills, and this lack further keeps them from social settings.

Predicting Some of the People Some of the Time

Do you remember Gordon Allport's proposal that different people possess different traits? This idea implies that personality consistency should not be investigated by measuring the same characteristics for all people. For any particular trait, some people are consistent and others are inconsistent. If these people are lumped together in a study of trait consistency, we will see a modest degree of consistency at most, but it will not mean that all people are always inconsistent.

Daryl Bem and Andrea Allen (1974) tested this line of reasoning in an investigation of 64 college students, who were asked, "How much do you vary from one situation to another in terms of how friendly and outgoing you are?" The same subjects were also asked to rate their consistency with respect to conscientiousness. The researchers then determined friendly (or unfriendly) behavior in several settings, as well as conscientious (or unconscientious) behavior. When they combined the results for all subjects, Bem and Allen found only a moderate degree of consistency. But when they split subjects into consistent and inconsistent groups (by dividing them according to their own ratings), the researchers found high consistency among those in the consistent group and low consistency among those in the inconsistent group, for both friendliness and conscientiousness.

Other researchers have replicated Bem and Allen's findings (Kenrick & Stringfield, 1980) but not always (Mischel & Peake, 1982). Part of the problem in replicating these results may be that few people have a good sense of how variable their behavior is (Herringer, 1993). This approach asks research participants to assign themselves to consistent and inconsistent groups, and in doing so participants may be inaccurate. A better research strategy would be to supplement or replace self-reports about consistency with other measures, like what participants' friends say about them (Chaplin, 1991). In any event, Bem and Allen's conclusion remains reasonable: Sometimes the best a personality psychologist can do with personality traits is to predict some of the people some of the time.

Self-Monitoring

One more perspective on the consistency controversy comes from research into an individual difference known as self-monitoring (Snyder, 1983). People high in self-monitoring pay close attention to situations and guide their behavior according to the feedback they receive. High self-monitors are socially adept, able to modify their actions to fit particular circumstances. Low self-monitors attend little to situational demands and more to their own inner states and feelings. When we describe people as oblivious, we probably mean oblivious to us; these individuals may be low self-monitors and thus highly attentive to their own experiences.

We should not be surprised that high self-monitors act differently across different situations and that low self-monitors act the same (Lippa & Donaldson, 1990; Snyder & Gangestad, 1982). The high self-monitors are not inconsistent; they show consistency in their responsivity. Their consistency resides at a different level from that of the low self-monitors.

A Resolution to the Consistency Controversy

Do people act consistently across different situations or not? Walter Mischel was for the most part correct when he concluded that little evidence existed in 1968 to support the assumption of personality consistency. However, in the decades since *Personality and Assessment* appeared, the evidence has been gathered. The consistency controversy has been resolved with a specification of necessary qualifications. Personality researchers can demonstrate consistency by aggregating observations of behavior over time, by taking into account interactions between traits and environments, by distinguishing consistent from inconsistent individuals, and/or by looking for consistency at different levels of personality. No single research project has simultaneously included all of these refinements, but if one did, the researchers would be likely to find striking consistency (Schmitt, 1992).

Stop and Think

19 What is the consistency controversy?

20 Describe an example from your everyday life of a trait-environment interaction.

PERSONALITY IN A BIOPSYCHOSOCIAL CONTEXT

To study people in their entirety, personality psychologists have drawn on broad perspectives—specifically, psychodynamic, trait, phenomenological, and social learning approaches. Each approach emphasizes different components of personality, and all are in principle compatible.

Indeed, recent theoretical extensions of each approach usually acknowledge the importance of other approaches. For example:

■ Biologically minded theorists have attempted to specify the neurological basis for Freudian concepts (Gaillard, 1992; Katz, 1991; Thompson, Baxter, & Schwartz, 1992; Zuelzer & Maas, 1994).

■ Contemporary object relations theorists stress the importance of people's thoughts and beliefs about the social environment (Westen, 1991).

■ Trait theorists are interested in the specific settings where traits are (or are not) displayed (Van Heck, Perugini, Caprara, & Froger, 1994).

■ Phenomenological theorists recognize that at least some of the cognitive processes giving rise to personality exist outside conscious awareness (Kihlstrom, 1990).

■ Social learning theorists now attempt to describe the idiosyncratic ways in which a person interprets situations (Shoda, Mischel, & Wright, 1993, 1994).

As these integrative attempts continue, a biopsychosocial perspective on personality will result.

Gender and Personality: Theory and Evidence

Let me conclude by examining a question of scientific and popular interest: Do men and women have different personalities? Psychodynamic theories, particularly Freud's original account, usually posit broad gender differences because men and women take different routes through the stages of psychosexual development. Trait theories expect to find gender differences in characteristics reflecting evolved psychological mechanisms related to reproduction. Phenomenological and social learning theories are neutral with regard to gender differences: Men and women may or may not have different personalities, depending on the circumstances they have encountered that lead to characteristic thoughts and habits (Bussey & Bandura, 1992).

But what does the evidence show? It depends on how personality is defined. In our society, if we regard an interest in competitive sports like football as a personality characteristic, we will find a pronounced gender difference. If we treat an interest in sewing as a personality characteristic, we will find another pronounced gender difference. Such differences in surface traits and behaviors reflect prevailing gender roles and are hardly surprising.

Of greater interest to personality psychology are gender differences in more general personality characteristics—source traits—like those measured by popular personality inventories. Feingold (1994a) undertook an extensive review of the relevant research literature, surveying studies conducted from the 1940s through the 1990s, mostly in the United States but also in other countries, such as Finland and China. When possible, he took the age and amount of education of research participants into account.

Feingold's review was based on hundreds of studies using more than 150,000 research participants. Gender differences were indeed apparent for several personality characteristics. Men, on average, were more assertive and had somewhat higher self-esteem than women. Women, on average, were more extraverted, anxious, trusting, and nurturant than men. These differences held up across nations, time, age, and education. It should be emphasized, however, that despite these differences in mean scores, there was overlap between men and women in these characteristics.

Gender and Personality: Conclusions

One way to summarize the gender differences documented by Feingold (1994a) is to say that men and women tend to treat other people (and themselves) differently. Men assert themselves over others and feel good about themselves, whereas women accom-

Do men and women have different personality traits? Research shows some differences as well as considerable overlap.

modate themselves to others and feel less good about themselves. Theorists have sometimes described this contrast as one between agency (a focus on the self and on forming separations from others) versus communion (a focus on others and on forming connections with them), agreeing that men tend to display agency whereas women tend to display communion (Helgeson, 1994).

What are we to make of the personality differences that exist? Perhaps they are the result of evolved psychological mechanisms that solved the respective survival problems encountered by men and women in the course of evolution. For example, according to this line of reasoning, males attempt to father as many children as possible, meaning that evolution has encouraged assertiveness and selfishness, and females attempt to raise the children they bear as well as possible, meaning that evolution has encouraged nurturance and interpersonal skills. These hypotheses remain speculative, however, unless we can specify the actual mechanisms that influence behavior.

Although many personality traits are heritable, we cannot leap from this fact to the conclusion that genetics account for the gender difference. Remember the point made in Chapter 11 about ethnic differences and intelligence: Just because a characteristic is heritable within a group does not mean that a difference in this characteristic between groups has a genetic basis.

We might also interpret these gender differences in personality as the result of socialization. Men and women learn to treat others and themselves differently. That these differences occur across a number of presumably critical contrasts such as age, education, and culture weakens this interpretation, but not completely. The socialization of men versus women might be similar across time and place.

The best explanation will result from research that goes beyond the mere description of differences and looks at the processes that give rise to them. As stressed in Chapter 1, differences in behavior across contrasts like gender are impossible to understand as long as mechanisms are neglected.

Psychologists interested in gender differences in personality have recognized this point. For example, Krampen, Effertz, Jostock, and Muller (1990) studied gender differences in personality and included a measure of gender role as well. Although males and females differed along the lines shown by Feingold (1994a), they did so in large part because they tended to endorse masculine and feminine gender roles, respectively.

Gender role was a better predictor of personality than biological sex: Men with feminine roles and women with masculine roles had personality characteristics congruent with those roles. This study does not answer all the questions we would want to pose, of course, such as why people adopt one gender role over the other. But it does show how the mechanisms responsible for personality differences might be identified.

We are not finished with personality psychology. In the next two chapters, you will see how the major personality theories influence the way psychologists explain and treat people's psychological problems.

SUMMARY

UNDERSTANDING PERSONALITY: DEFINITION AND EXPLANATION

■ Personality psychologists are interested in people in their biopsychosocial entirety.
■ Personality theories over the years can be placed into several groups that share in common assumptions and approaches.

THE PSYCHODYNAMIC APPROACH: EMPHASIS ON MOTIVATION AND EMOTION

■ Psychodynamic theories stress motivation and emotion as the keys to understanding personality.
■ The central theorist in this tradition is Sigmund Freud. Other influential theorists who followed Freud and placed less emphasis on biology and sexuality include Carl Jung, Alfred Adler, the neo-Freudians, Erik Erikson, and object relations theorists.

THE TRAIT APPROACH: EMPHASIS ON BIOLOGY

■ Trait theories approach personality by describing people, placing them in basic categories or along dimensions that reflect how much of a particular characteristic they possess. Trait theorists are interested in the biological basis of these individual differences.
■ Gordon Allport first stated the issues that still concern trait theorists. Raymond Cattell and Hans Eysenck are two contemporary theorists who use the statistical technique of factor analysis to identify people's traits.

THE PHENOMENOLOGICAL APPROACH: EMPHASIS ON COGNITION

■ Phenomenological theorists focus on the way people think about themselves and the world.
■ George Kelly's personal construct theory and Carl Rogers's self-theory are two important statements within this tradition.

THE SOCIAL LEARNING APPROACH: EMPHASIS ON THE SOCIAL ENVIRONMENT

■ Social learning theorists approach personality in terms of situations and emphasize processes of learning. Central importance is given to the role of other people in one's environment, hence the use of the term *social* to describe these theories.
■ Social learning theories of note have been proposed by John Dollard and Neal Miller and by Albert Bandura.

DOING *Personality* RESEARCH

■ Personality assessment refers to the measurement of individual differences.
■ Several traditions of personality assessment can be distinguished, each corresponding to one of the major theoretical approaches to personality.
■ Personality researchers may use projective tests, objective tests, personality inventories, judgments by others, and/or experience sampling.

THE CONSISTENCY CONTROVERSY

■ In recent decades, the most significant controversy in personality research stemmed from Walter Mischel's argument that people do not act consistently across situations.
■ Research reactions to Mischel's proposal successfully demonstrated consistency under some circumstances, but these required a much greater sophistication than past research into the issue.

PERSONALITY IN A BIOPSYCHOSOCIAL CONTEXT

■ Males and females differ in some ways in their personalities, and an explanation of why they do so needs to be phrased in biopsychosocial terms.

Key Terms

Psychological Disorders

In his article "On Being Sane in Insane Places," David Rosenhan (1973) described one of the most famous studies in psychology. Rosenhan and seven other researchers each arranged to be admitted to mental hospitals, by telling the examining physician that they heard voices saying "empty, dull, and thud." Based on this one symptom, they were given the diagnosis of schizophrenia. Length of hospitalization varied from 7 to 52 days, with an average stay of 19 days. Only in one case was the presence of one of these pseudopatients known in advance to hospital administrators. In the other cases, the pseudopatients were on their own.

Once admitted, these pseudopatients acted in a perfectly normal fashion, yet hospital staff members never suspected they were anything other than what the initial diagnosis said. In fact, the label was used to interpret what the pseudopatients did. For example, Rosenhan and the others took notes while on the ward. At first, they disguised what they were doing. Then they realized that they could take notes openly because the nurses and doctors just saw it as another manifestation of their presumed illness. One nurse duly recorded in a chart, "Patient engages in writing behavior."

This description strips away the meaning of what the person was actually doing. When you take notes in class, are you "engaged in writing behavior"? A better description is that you are taking notes, a meaningful activity chosen by a healthy individual. But if you are described as schizophrenic, then the same activity becomes a sign or symptom of the disorder.

UNDERSTANDING PSYCHOLOGICAL DISORDERS: DEFINITION AND EXPLANATION

■ abnormal psychology
field that studies people's emotional, cognitive, and/or behavioral problems

Rosenhan's pseudopatient study can be criticized for putting staff members of mental hospitals in an impossible position (Spitzer, 1975). Just because psychological normality is sometimes misidentified does not mean that such mistakes are common in the mental health system. Nonetheless, this study is provocative, and it serves to introduce the subject matter of the present chapter. **Abnormal psychology** is the field that studies people's emotional, cognitive, and/or behavioral problems (see Table 13.1). Such problems are sometimes called psychopathology, to stress their psychological nature. Psychologists who study psychopathology have two paramount concerns: defining psychological abnormality and explaining it.

Table 13.1   Types of Psychological Disorders

Here are some of the psychological problems people can experience.

Type of Problem	Characterization
Disorders usually first diagnosed in infancy, childhood, or adolescence	Problems that usually show themselves before adulthood, such as conduct disorder and mental retardation (Chapter 11)
Delirium, dementia, amnestic syndrome, and other cognitive disorders	Problems associated with impairment of the brain by illness or injury, such as difficulties in thinking brought on by chronic exposure to toxic substances (Chapter 6)
Substance-related disorders	Psychological and social problems resulting from the ingestion of substances like alcohol, narcotics, and cocaine (Chapter 6)
Schizophrenia	Problems involving deterioration of self-care, work, and social relations, as well as profound disturbances in thought, language, and communication
Mood disorders	Problems characterized by extreme and inappropriate sadness and/or elation, such as depression and bipolar disorder
Anxiety disorders	Problems characterized by excessive worry and apprehension, like phobia and panic disorder
Somatoform disorders	Problems with physical symptoms that have no biological cause, such as hysteria and hypochondriasis
Factitious disorders	Physical or psychological "problems" that are deliberately produced or faked
Dissociative disorders	Problems marked by a splitting of consciousness, memory, and/or identity, such as dissociative amnesia and multiple personality disorder
Sexual and gender-identity disorders	Problems involving sexuality, either the orientation toward inappropriate sexual objects or the inability to perform sexually, or cross-gender identification
Eating disorders	Problems involving unusual patterns of food consumption, such as anorexia and bulimia (Chapter 7)
Sleep disorders	Problems in which the normal process of sleep is disturbed or unusual events like nightmares or sleepwalking take place (Chapter 6)
Impulse-control disorders	Problems characterized by an inability to refrain from performing acts harmful to the self or others, such as kleptomania (stealing), pyromania (fire-starting), and compulsive gambling
Adjustment disorders	Problems involving a maladaptive reaction to an identifiable stressor, like divorce or unemployment
Psychological factors affecting physical condition	Problems in which physical illnesses are caused or exacerbated by psychological factors, such as tension headaches and gastric ulcers (Chapter 16)

Source: American Psychiatric Association (1994).

The Meaning of Psychological Abnormality

When was the last time you said, "What? That's awful! Something ought to be done about it." Maybe those were not your exact words, but we commonly make statements like these. Perhaps it was when you heard about a parent abusing a child, a woman attempting suicide, or a man standing in the middle of traffic, cursing. Statements about abnormality, by you or by a professional, usually include three related judgments (Peterson, 1996): an assertion that something is wrong with a person's thoughts, feelings, or actions ("What?"); a label placed on this state of affairs ("awful"); and a recommendation that matters be made right ("Something ought to be done about it").

As the concept is typically used, abnormality has no necessary or sufficient conditions (Cantor, Smith, French, & Mezzich, 1980). Rather, **abnormality** is fuzzily captured by a set of features that include suffering, maladaptiveness, loss of control, unconventionality, and the production of discomfort among observers (Rosenhan & Seligman, 1989). None of these criteria by itself defines abnormality, but the more of them that are present and the more intense they are, the more likely we are to say that psychopathology exists.

People in all cultures recognize psychological suffering. Despite the difficulty in offering a precise definition, extreme examples of abnormality are easily recognized and agreed upon. The particular instances of abnormality discussed in this chapter are for the most part extreme examples. Although there is often disagreement about the best way to explain them, there is little question that they are problems.

Over the years, different explanations of abnormality have been popular—in particular, a biological approach, a psychodynamic approach, and a cognitive-behavioral approach. Each of these perspectives comprises a set of interrelated assumptions about human nature, the way problems develop, and how problems can be resolved or prevented. As noted in Chapter 1, the biopsychosocial approach to behavior first emerged in the attempt to explain abnormality, and so at present there is wide agreement that the best way to understand disorders is by simultaneously considering the relevant biological mechanisms, psychological processes, and social influences.

■ **abnormality**
behavior with features that include suffering, maladaptiveness, loss of control, unconventionality, and the production of discomfort among observers

Although unconventionality is usually part of a description of abnormality, it is not sufficient. Such factors as suffering, loss of control, and maladaptiveness must also be considered.

Biological Perspectives on Psychological Disorders

A biological approach to psychological disorders regards people as physical systems (Lloyd, 1990). Abnormal behavior is seen as a disease—as mental illness. According to the biological approach, people are susceptible to injury, breakdown, or malfunction (Guze, 1989). A great deal of research has explored the specific biological mechanisms that underlie psychological abnormality. As will be explained, these mechanisms usually involve the central nervous system and specifically neurotransmitter activity (Chapter 4). Therapy from a biological perspective involves physical interventions such as drugs or surgery that attempt to correct or compensate for whatever is wrong with an individual's biology.

Like biological approaches in general, a biological perspective on abnormality often examines disorders in terms of evolution and genetics (Chapter 3). Although the specific genes that influence abnormality have yet to be identified, research has consistently shown that many psychological disorders are heritable. The question thus arises as to why genes should predispose abnormality. Biological theorists do not claim that problems are adaptive. Quite clearly, they are not. A satisfactory explanation needs to be more subtle.

One possibility is that psychological disorders are exaggerated forms of typically adaptive mechanisms. For example, our social responsiveness is usually a good tendency, for ourselves and others, and we can argue that it is part of our evolutionary heritage (Chapter 15). If taken to an extreme, however, our sensitivity to others can produce casualties—social anxiety, insecurity, and dependency. Because biologically based characteristics vary across individuals, some people must fall at the extremes (Chapter 3). Perhaps they are the ones most likely to develop disorders.

Another possibility is that abnormality results from mechanisms that originally appeared for adaptive purposes but now produce only distress because our worlds have changed (Cuzzillo, 1991; Smith, 1993). For instance, we may be predisposed by our evolutionary history to fear snakes (Chapters 3 and 8), but in the modern world this predisposition is usually counterproductive.

Yet another possible explanation of the heritability of disorders starts with the observation that psychologically troubled individuals have more than their share of eminent relatives (Simonton, 1994). The same genes that predispose problems for some individuals may influence achievement among their relatives—which answers the otherwise puzzling question as to why genes associated with abnormality have persisted. The idea of inclusive fitness suggests that madness is the price our species pays for genius (Chapter 3).

Psychodynamic Perspectives on Psychological Disorders

Theorists have long tried to specify the psychological processes that produce abnormal thoughts, feelings, and actions. One influential perspective is provided by psychodynamic theories. As discussed in Chapter 12, Freud and other psychodynamic thinkers have regarded people as energy systems. Problems result when psychic energy is tied up in a particular problem and not available for more productive activities.

Why is the energy of some people so poorly invested? The psychodynamic approach proposes that the person who behaves abnormally suffers from unconscious conflicts rooted in childhood experiences. These conflicts are too threatening to acknowledge, and only through an active expenditure of energy can the conflict be kept out of consciousness.

A typical means of ignoring conflicts is by using defense mechanisms (Chapter 6). Within normal ranges, defense mechanisms are useful, but when taken to an extreme, they can result in abnormality. In repression, for instance, we put troubling thoughts out of our minds, and doing so can be beneficial. However, if we repress too many of our memories, what can result is the loss of our personal identity.

Cognitive-Behavioral Perspectives on Psychological Disorders

The cognitive-behavioral approach views people as information processing systems and their problems as the result of faulty learning. Depressed people, for instance, may have learned to regard themselves in inappropriately harsh terms because of constant criticism by their parents. Their depression makes sense once their habitual thoughts are revealed. Therapy involves unlearning problematic habits and replacing them with more useful ones.

Modeling can produce psychological problems, and an important emphasis of the cognitive-behavioral approach is thus on the troubled individual's larger social and cultural setting (Draguns, 1989; Good, 1992; Littlewood, 1990). Society provides roles and expectations, some of which are easier to carry out than others. For instance, those of us in the contemporary United States are often told that we can "have it all," but in point of fact, combining a career and a family can be very difficult. Stress can be the result when someone tries to perform too many social roles at the same time (Duxbury, Higgins, & Lee, 1994).

A way of behaving that is sensible in one social context can produce difficulties when generalized to another (Lewis-Fernandez & Kleinman, 1994). An example occurs when people migrate from one country to another. The likelihood of a variety of psychological disorders increases in the wake (Roth & Ekblad, 1993). At least part of the reason is that a person's habitual ways of interacting with others may not work well in the new culture. For instance, what in the United States is considered being direct and honest in communication is often regarded in Japan as being rude and selfish (Cocroft & Ting-Toomey, 1994). Individuals who have emigrated from the one country to the other may find themselves socially isolated and thus at risk for depression.

Psychological Disorders as Biopsychosocial

Taken separately, each of these perspectives on abnormality is open to criticism. The biological approach, for example, has been criticized for promoting the notion that the problems of everyday life are diseases. Thomas Szasz (1961) called this the myth of mental illness and argued that psychological problems such as depression, anxiety, and schizophrenia are not illnesses in the sense that pneumonia, chicken pox, and malaria are illnesses. Szasz believed that when we mistakenly regard these problems as illnesses, we absolve the person from any responsibility in trying to solve them. The counterargument is that when we hold people responsible for solving their problems, we come close to blaming them for having problems in the first place, and that is neither reasonable nor productive.

Psychodynamic theories and cognitive-behavioral theories may neglect biological considerations. In view of recent research showing genetic links and neurological bases for many different disorders, this neglect is a serious oversight (Kety, 1974). Another problem with both the psychodynamic approach and the cognitive-behavioral perspective is that they assume people basically strive to feel good, whether through discharging their drives or through gaining reinforcement. But abnormality often involves suffering. How can self-destruction be explained?

Granted that each traditional approach has shortcomings, attempts have been made to weave together their respective strengths. What results is a biopsychosocial perspective on disorders. One popular example of a biopsychosocial approach is called the **diathesis-stress model** of abnormality. It proposes that people develop disorders if they have a biological or psychological weakness (diathesis) that leads to a problem when certain situational conditions (stress) are encountered (Monroe & Simons, 1991).

You may be familiar with the diathesis-stress approach because it is often used to explain some forms of cancer in terms of a biological predisposition coupled with certain environmental occurrences like exposure to toxins. As discussed later, this

■ **diathesis-stress model**
integrative approach that explains abnormality as due to a biological weakness (diathesis) coupled with certain environmental conditions (stress)

perspective may be equally useful in helping us understand the various psychological disorders, which usually include biological, psychological, and environmental factors.

Stop and Think

1 If we regard abnormality as a natural (fuzzy) concept (Chapter 9), what is the implication for operational definitions of abnormality?

2 What standard of psychological health is assumed by each of the traditional perspectives on abnormality?

3 How is the diathesis-stress model of abnormality a biopsychosocial approach?

HISTORICAL PERSPECTIVES ON ABNORMALITY

A historical view of how abnormality has been explained sheds light on the complexity of the subject, so let me describe this history for you. Psychologists usually distinguish three major eras with regard to how abnormality has been conceived: the supernatural era, the illness era, and the psychological era (see Figure 13.1).

The Supernatural Era

Thousands of years ago, abnormal behavior was viewed in terms of prevailing beliefs about magic, including the following (Frazer, 1922):

1. There exist forces in nature that can be directed by divine intervention or liberated by special arts.
2. These forces determine what people think, feel, and do.
3. The techniques of magic include certain words (or spells), substances, and symbols.
4. People and their environments are inseparable.

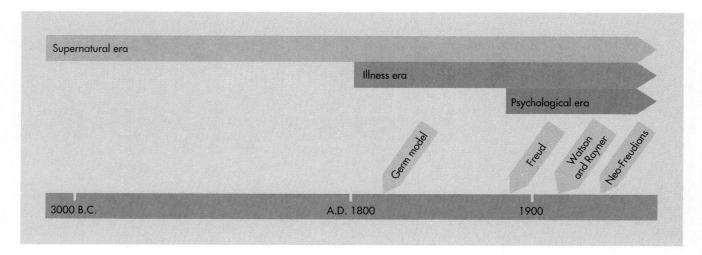

Figure 13.1
History of Abnormality. A historical view shows that psychological disorders have been interpreted in different ways. These interpretations give rise to characteristic strategies of prevention and treatment.

5. People can influence each other through telepathy.
6. The future can be predicted.

Such beliefs led people to explain unusual behavior as due to possession by a spirit, the casting of a spell, or the influence of some unseen force (Ward, 1989).

The ancient Greeks and Romans attributed abnormal behavior to the influence of various gods and goddesses: "Those whom the Gods would destroy they first make mad." In Homer's *Iliad*, for example, heroes on the battlefield show dramatic changes in behavior, due to the influence of a god or goddess. Similar notions can be found in the Bible. When King Saul did not follow the commandment of God, "an evil spirit from the Lord tormented him" until he repented (1 Samuel 16:14).

In the Middle Ages, when Christianity dominated much of life in Europe, people equated abnormality with being possessed by the Devil. Afflicted people were often tortured to drive the Devil out of their bodies and, failing this, were burned at the stake to make their bodies inhospitable for Satan. Driving away the Devil saved the person's soul.

We may be tempted to dismiss these practices as ignorant or inhumane, but that misses an important point. People confronted with abnormality are impelled to explain it and to do something about it. In their efforts, they draw on the beliefs they hold. When these beliefs involve the supernatural, then abnormality is viewed in those terms. In cultures that still endorse aspects of a magical view, we see continued use of these ideas to explain and treat psychological problems (Hohmann, Richeport, Mariott, Canino, Rubio-Stipec, & Bird, 1990).

The Illness Era

As modern science developed in the 1800s, the next stage in conceiving abnormality appeared: Abnormality began to be explained in terms of defects within the body. Particularly important was the realization that illness could be caused by tiny organisms called germs (Chapter 16).

The first psychological disorder to be explained in these terms was general paresis. At one time, this was a common disorder, responsible for as many as 20 percent of all admissions to mental hospitals in the United States (Dale, 1980). General paresis involves progressive paralysis and loss of intellectual ability:

> Individuals tend to be unmannerly, tactless, unconcerned with their appearance, and unethical in their behavior. Memory defects . . . become more obvious. Afflicted individuals may be unable to remember what they did just a short time ago. . . . They may ask when dinner will be served only a few minutes after they have finished eating it. This memory impairment extends to less immediate events, and memory losses are made up for by various fabrications. (Carson, Butcher, & Coleman, 1988, p. 457)

German neurologist Richard von Krafft-Ebing established the link between untreated syphilis and the psychological disorder general paresis.

During the late 1800s, the German neurologist Richard von Krafft-Ebing established a link between syphilis and general paresis by injecting several patients who suffered from general paresis with pus from syphilitic sores. None of the patients developed syphilis. According to the logic of the germ theory of illness, they had already been exposed to the infection. The study is considered a landmark because it showed that a physical illness (syphilis) can produce psychological abnormality (general paresis) decades later.

The success of Krafft-Ebing's demonstration inspired subsequent researchers to continue the search for the causes of abnormality within a person's body: in hormones, genes, brain function, biorhythms, and nutrition. Collectively, this approach is the biological perspective discussed earlier.

You may recall that Sigmund Freud was originally trained as a neurologist. During the early 1800s, neurology developed as a separate specialty within medicine (Chapter 1). Researchers soon learned enough about the nervous system to speculate about how damage to it might produce abnormal behavior. Freud's emphasis on energy, on processes of inhibition and excitation, and on the far-reaching effects of early trauma all stem directly from nineteenth-century neurology (Chapter 4). Although psychodynamic theory is phrased in psychological language, its roots are in the illness era (Sulloway, 1979).

The Psychological Era

In the third era of interpreting psychological disorders, abnormality and normality began to be regarded as subject to the same psychological laws and principles. This view has dominated during the twentieth century, and we can identify it as the psychological era. Psychodynamic theories and cognitive-behavioral theories have been particularly influential within this era.

We can contrast the psychological era with its predecessors. In the supernatural era, it was assumed that abnormal behavior is imposed on a person by an outside force. In the illness era, it was assumed that abnormal behavior results from a malfunction within the body. In the psychological era, abnormal behavior is considered something that a person does because of the operation of psychological processes like motivation, emotion, learning, and cognition.

Although no single event brought about the psychological era, several noteworthy occurrences transpired. Freud's interpretation of hysteria in terms of unconscious conflicts legitimized psychological explanations of abnormality. When Freud's theories were expanded by the neo-Freudians to include the individual's social setting, there was further reason to examine the psychological basis of abnormality.

Another significant event in the psychological era was the study, described in Chapter 8, in which John Watson and Rosalie Rayner (1920) conditioned a fear response in the infant Little Albert. This investigation is important because it demonstrates how abnormality (a phobia, in this case) can result from learning. Just as Krafft-Ebing's study encouraged researchers to seek further examples of abnormality as an illness, Watson and Rayner's study encouraged researchers to search for further examples of abnormality as a learned phenomenon.

Although the different eras of explaining abnormality have been presented in the order in which they first appeared, the theories that characterize each still exist today. A supernatural perspective still prevails in parts of the world. Many mental health professionals in the United States endorse an illness perspective, viewing psychological disorders as diseases and treating them with hospitalization and drugs. And still other mental health professionals embrace a psychological perspective, treating problems with techniques suggested by psychodynamic, cognitive-behavioral, and other psychological theories (Chapter 14). All these points of view have support, depending on the specific aspect of abnormality of interest. An overall view is necessarily a biopsychosocial one.

Stop and Think

4 Find examples from the popular media of magical beliefs.

5 Why is Krafft-Ebing's research historically important?

6 Is Freud's approach to abnormality biological or psychological?

7 Why is Watson and Rayner's research historically important?

DOING *Psychopathology* RESEARCH

To study psychological disorders, researchers use observations, case studies, correlational studies, and experiments (Chapter 2). However, psychopathology research has certain special requirements, discussed in this section.

Samples

In an ideal investigation, the sample is representative of the larger population of interest. Investigations of psychological abnormality typically fall short of this ideal. As explained in Chapter 2, researchers rarely have the resources to choose a truly random sample. This becomes a particular problem when the goal of a study is to estimate the frequency of disorders in the general population or to learn how best to help people with those disorders (Mezzich, Jorge, & Salloum, 1994).

A recent survey of American adults attempted to estimate the frequency of different psychological disorders and the utilization of mental health services (Kessler et al., 1994). This study attempted to choose a random sample of all American adults. Even so, the sample was not perfectly representative. The researchers interviewed individuals on the telephone, and not everyone had a phone or was willing or able to talk on it. Those with unlisted numbers escaped the sample, and the homeless were excluded. Those hospitalized because of psychological or medical problems, those in prison, and those serving in the armed forces were also excluded. To take these limitations into account, the researchers adjusted their estimates based on other information available about excluded groups. The point remains that it is all but impossible to obtain a completely representative sample in psychopathology research.

More often, abnormality is studied using convenience samples, research participants who are studied simply because they are available to the researcher. Often these are individuals in treatment at a clinic or hospital to which the researcher has access. The hope is that a convenience sample is also a representative one, but we should always be skeptical. We know that many people with disorders are not in treatment. We also know that medical facilities have biases about who is admitted and treated. For instance, people's insurance policies may be a more important determinant of where and how they are treated than their actual disorders (Chapter 14).

Measures

A psychologist must also define and measure the type of abnormality that is of concern. Suppose researchers are interested in depression (Marsella, 1987); they must decide how to identify its presence and its degree. Over the years, psychologists have used a variety of measures. Some are not particularly rigorous, such as identifying "depressed" research participants solely on the basis of responses to a self-report questionnaire. The reliability and validity of such questionnaires can be quite low because single measures of any psychological concept are problematic (Campbell & Fiske, 1959). In recent years, researchers have become more careful about choosing measures of abnormality.

One procedure now popular with those who use questionnaire measures of abnormality is to administer them at two different points in time. Research participants must have extreme scores on both occasions before they are considered abnormal. That a person may score in the anxious range of a questionnaire one day but in the nonanxious range the following week shows the wisdom of this approach.

Another popular procedure is the use of **research diagnostic criteria:** assigning research participants to particular diagnostic categories only if they show unambiguous signs of schizophrenia, depression, or whatever (Feighner, Robins, Guze, Woodruff,

■ **research diagnostic criteria** stringent rules for including subjects in a psychopathology study

Self-report questionnaires can be of limited value in measuring abnormality.

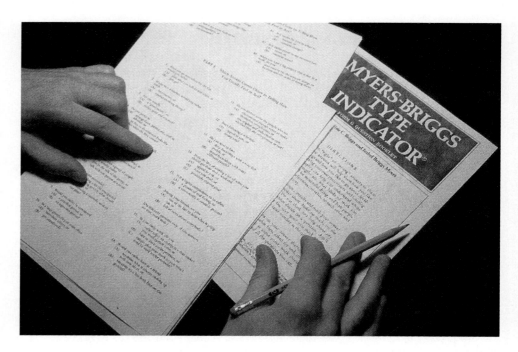

Winokur, & Munoz, 1972). Because a researcher can throw out less clear cases, research diagnoses are stricter than diagnoses given to patients in therapy. Conclusions thus become crisper.

Research Designs

An investigation is not simply a heap of research participants and measures. Rather, the elements of a study are assembled in a deliberate way to give the researcher the information that is of interest. The overall structure of a study and its elements is referred to as its research design. A researcher's hypotheses, logic, common sense, and lessons from prior investigations determine the details of a given research design. Will the study as structured answer the questions of interest while minimizing alternative explanations?

Suppose you conduct an investigation of people with the eating disorder of anorexia (Chapter 7), and you proceed by comparing them with individuals without a disorder of any kind. You find that the people with anorexia were more likely to have been sexually abused during childhood than those without anorexia (Kearney-Cooke & Striegel-Moore, 1994). You are tempted to conclude that inconsistent punishment during childhood puts a person at risk for anorexia.

But keep in mind that you studied only two groups of people: those with anorexia and those without anorexia or any other problem. You may have discovered only that abused children grow up to have problems, including but not necessarily limited to anorexia. Before you offer a specific conclusion, you need to study people with a variety of psychological disorders.

The more general point is that a research design must allow conclusions about relevant mechanisms. Throughout this book, studies have been criticized that simply document behavioral differences between, for example, men versus women. Gender does not have an automatic effect on behavior; it only influences what we do through the intermediary of psychological mechanisms. The same applies to studies of abnormality. It is not enough to show that people with a given diagnosis versus people without differ; we must additionally try to uncover the process by which problems result in characteristic thoughts, feelings, and actions (Persons, 1986).

Stop and Think

8   What is a convenience sample?

9   What are research diagnostic criteria?

DIAGNOSIS

Mental health professionals interested in abnormal behavior devote much time and effort to describing the various types of psychological difficulties. Careful descriptions of psychological disorders are needed to make valid diagnoses. These, in turn, allow the planning of successful treatments.

To diagnose means to distinguish or differentiate. As applied to psychological disorders, **diagnosis** usually means the placement of people's problems in categories according to the particular signs or symptoms of these difficulties. If we can describe an individual as depressed, for instance, instead of anxious, we then know a great deal about his or her problem.

Diagnosis requires a set of diagnostic categories and rules for assigning people to those categories. Ideally, the categories available to the diagnostician should not overlap. Dementia, for example, is distinct and separate from intoxication (Chapter 6). The diagnostic categories should also include the range of problems people actually experience, with few or no disorders left over.

No diagnostic scheme used to describe psychological abnormality measures up perfectly to these ideals. For instance, the same symptoms can sometimes characterize more than one disorder. You will see an example of symptom overlap later in this chapter, when personality disorders are discussed. Or consider that sets of diagnostic categories developed in one culture may not have appropriate places for disorders that are common in another culture.

> ■ **diagnosis**
> placement of people in categories according to the particular signs or symptoms of their difficulties

DSM-IV

The system of classifying mental disorders that is most widely used in the United States today is one proposed by the American Psychiatric Association (1994) and contained in a book with a long title: *Diagnostic and Statistical Manual of Mental Disorders—Fourth Edition,* usually referred to as **DSM-IV.** DSM-IV describes disorders in five different domains, called axes (see Table 13.2). A full DSM-IV diagnosis contains information on each axis. Clinicians typically gather information by interviewing patients or administering various tests, as described in Chapter 12.

> ■ **DSM-IV—*Diagnostic and Statistical Manual of Mental Disorders—Fourth Edition***
> American Psychiatric Association's manual that contains diagnostic criteria for psychological disorders

Table 13.2   DSM-IV Axes

I. Clinical syndromes
II. Personality disorders
III. Physical illnesses or conditions
IV. Existing stressors
V. Global level of functioning

■ **clinical syndromes**
problems with identifiable beginnings that bring a person into therapy

■ **personality disorders**
long-standing personality styles that can make a clinical syndrome worse as well as create difficulties in their own right

Axis I describes **clinical syndromes:** problems with identifiable beginnings that bring a person into therapy. Clinical syndromes include such difficulties as alcohol abuse, depression, phobia, and schizophrenia.

Two types of diagnoses are made on Axis II. First, global problems that occur in the context of development—like mental retardation (Chapter 11)—are noted. Second, **personality disorders**—long-standing personality styles that can make a clinical syndrome worse as well as create difficulties in their own right—are also included.

On Axis III, the diagnostician notes any physical illnesses or conditions relevant to the individual's clinical syndrome. Suppose a person has thyroid disease. Among its possible consequences are mood changes, and one would certainly want to take this into account when judging whether or not the person should be given an Axis I diagnosis of depression.

As cognitive-behavioral theories propose, abnormal behavior should be explained by considering the setting where it occurs. Axis IV of DSM-IV captures one important situational characteristic: the presence of existing stressors, such as unemployment or divorce.

Finally, Axis V is a global assessment of how well or how poorly a person functions in social and occupational realms, both at present and during the prior year. It is important to know how a person got along before his or her clinical syndrome developed because this provides a plausible goal for therapy. A person's level of optimal functioning in the past provides a reasonable clue about his or her optimal level in the future.

Pros and Cons of Diagnosis

Diagnosing psychological abnormality can be controversial. On the positive side, diagnoses improve communication. Professionals know the types of problems that fall within various diagnostic categories, and hence diagnoses serve as a convenient shorthand. If one clinician says to another, "Mr. Smith experiences panic disorder, without agoraphobia," they both know that Mr. Smith suffers intense attacks of anxiety but does not avoid situations from which he cannot readily flee. They both know that Mr. Smith's problems probably began in his late twenties, that he is apt to be depressed, and that he frequently broods about the possibility of future panic attacks.

A second advantage is that diagnoses can provide clues about the presumed cause of a disorder—its **etiology**—based on previous research with other individuals who have

■ **etiology**
presumed cause of a disorder

Among the benefits of diagnosis is improved communication among professionals, who are provided a common vocabulary.

the same diagnosis. Bipolar disorder, for instance, in which periods of extreme depression alternate with periods of extreme mania, has a strong genetic basis.

Third, diagnoses allow predictions about the likely outcome of a disorder—its **prognosis.** It has been established, for example, that individuals with the type of schizophrenia characterized by paranoid beliefs usually fare better than individuals with other types of schizophrenia.

Fourth, diagnoses can suggest effective forms of treatment. Mr. Smith's panic disorder will probably respond favorably to antidepressant medication. A therapist will recommend this treatment if a patient warrants Mr. Smith's particular diagnosis. Without the particular diagnosis, there would be no reason to explore this form of therapy.

Diagnostic schemes, however, have some drawbacks. First, they are not theoretically neutral. DSM-IV in many ways embodies the biological approach because it tends to focus on severe problems necessitating hospitalization. This emphasis presents difficulties for psychologists who advocate other approaches and work with clients who have less severe problems.

Second, diagnosis assumes a clear line between abnormality and normality. By the logic of DSM-IV and similar diagnostic schemes, people either are given a diagnosis or are not given one. Although many disorders exist in degrees of severity, DSM-IV treats problems as simply present or absent.

Third, although DSM-IV is more reliable than its previous versions, reliability is still a problem, at least for some disorders. Two diagnosticians assessing the same individual may arrive at altogether different diagnoses. Diagnoses of personality disorders, for example, have very low reliabilities. All the virtues of diagnoses vanish if they fail to be reliable.

Finally, diagnostic labels can take on a life of their own and create problems for patients above and beyond the difficulties they originally faced. People who were "once treated for depression" might find this description following them around for the rest of their lives. Remember what happened to Rosenhan and the other pseudopatients in his study. After diagnosis, the label of schizophrenia adhered to them and altered how others viewed them.

The difficulties surrounding the diagnosis of psychological disorders are not likely to be resolved in the near future. Regardless, DSM-IV is widely used to describe people's psychological problems, and it will continue to be popular. Attempts to improve diagnostic systems will also be ongoing.

■ **prognosis**
likely outcome of a disorder

Stop and Think

10 What are the five axes of DSM-IV?

11 What are the benefits of diagnosis?

12 What are the drawbacks of diagnosis?

TYPES OF DISORDERS

The remainder of this chapter discusses some of the psychological disorders listed in DSM-IV (remember Table 13.1). Recall that organic syndromes like delirium and dementia were mentioned in Chapter 6, along with substance abuse and dependence and sleep disorders. Chapter 7 discussed eating disorders, and Chapter 11 looked at mental retardation. Chapter 16 will discuss psychosomatic disorders.

Here are some general points to consider as you read about psychological disorders. First, the study of psychopathology is a subset of general psychology and should be approached with a scientific attitude. Psychological disorders are so interesting in their own right that we can lose track of psychology's goals of explaining how they come about and of devising means to prevent and treat them.

Second, many of us have a tendency to distance ourselves from people with problems. We can sometimes see ourselves in them and their problems, and this makes us uncomfortable. When you are tempted to think of people with problems as "those kinds of people," keep in mind that all people, with and without psychological difficulties, share much in common.

Third, we may also tend to romanticize abnormality, to think that people with strange problems are charismatic and creative, that they march to a different drummer somehow more true than our own. Not exactly. Different drummers exist, and they should be followed by those who hear them. But choice has little to do with the major disorders. The people described in this chapter are not to be envied. They have problems with life, and most are socially isolated.

Fourth, many of our problems exist in degrees, meaning that you should not panic simply because part of what you experience in your life is similar to striking cases of abnormality. Sadness and worry, stubbornness and error, confusion and hurt are all part of the human experience. If you occasionally experience a symptom of some disorder, that itself is normal. Do not waste time diagnosing yourself or your friends, wondering if a problem exists. Real disorders make themselves known in an unmistakable fashion.

In the sections that follow, the symptoms of different disorders are described, along with what is known about each disorder's causes and consequences. Effective treatments are also mentioned, although a detailed view of therapy is postponed until Chapter 14.

Anxiety Disorders

Anxiety shares much in common with fear—the same feelings of apprehension and uneasiness, the same emergency reaction, and the same fight-or-flight behavioral response, as we discussed in Chapter 7 (Marks, 1987). Anxiety differs from fear in that the anxious individual feels threatened, but the sense of danger is usually not specific.

Although anxiety is part of everyday experience, when it is global or severe, it becomes a problem. There are several related difficulties in which anxiety predominates. DSM-IV calls these **anxiety disorders.** People feel uneasy, show the bodily emergency reaction, and expect harm to befall them. They feel inadequate and avoid problems instead of trying to solve them. DSM-IV describes several specific anxiety disorders, to which we now turn our attention.

Phobia.   An individual who shows persistent fear and avoidance of some specific object or situation has a **phobia.** We can distinguish two types of phobias. First are specific phobias, in which a person is excessively afraid of a particular object or event. The most common of the specific phobias include fear of animals (spiders, other insects, snakes, rats, or mice), blood, enclosed spaces, heights, and air travel.

The second type of phobia is called a social phobia because individuals are afraid of particular situations where they might be observed by others. Fears revolve around the presumed humiliation that will occur if they somehow fail to perform some act adequately. Consider:

- becoming tongue-tied while speaking in public
- choking on food while eating in public
- blushing while in public
- not being able to urinate in a public bathroom

These fears, of course, interfere with the performance of these behaviors.

The social phobic avoids situations in which embarrassment might occur, often going to great lengths to do so. Note that this phobia is not simply a concern with what other people think. Rather, social phobia qualifies as an instance of abnormality to the

---

■ **anxiety**

emotion similar to fear except that one's sense of danger is usually not specific

■ **anxiety disorders**

disorders in which anxiety predominates

■ **phobia**

anxiety disorder in which an individual shows persistent fear and avoidance of some specific object or situation

degree that it interferes with an individual's life. Alcohol and drug abuse may accompany social phobias, as people try to medicate their worries.

Phobias are often very specific, and people who experience them do not necessarily seek treatment. It is therefore difficult to specify their frequency with accuracy, although estimates suggest that 1 to 3 percent of our population has one or more of them (Boyd et al., 1990; Marks, 1986; Reich, 1986). African Americans and European Americans show the same prevalence of phobias (Paradis, Hatch, & Friedman, 1994). Women are more likely than men to have these problems, and this sex difference becomes apparent only with the onset of puberty (Marks, 1987). The greater likelihood of phobias among adult women might reflect the operation of an evolved psychological mechanism predisposing certain types of emotional learning (Chapter 8), or it might mean that women are more vulnerable to physical danger and hence have learned to be more cautious.

Over the years, there has been no shortage of possible explanations of phobias. Each of the traditional approaches to abnormality attempts to explain them. For example, biological theorists point to physiological predispositions to be fearful that presumably interact with specific experiences to produce phobias.

Psychodynamic theorists see a phobia as an expression of an underlying conflict. It can be a sexual conflict, but other types of conflicts can also be implicated. Consider the case of a woman's fear of church bells (Prince, 1924). Years earlier, her mother had gone through a lengthy illness before dying. The woman frequently went to a church to pray for her mother's health, an experience always accompanied by the ringing of the church bells. On one occasion, she did not pray because she was tired of doing so, and her mother died shortly thereafter. The subsequent phobia symbolized the guilt she experienced because she had on that occasion put her own needs over those of her dying mother.

Learning theories view traumatic events as the cause of phobias. Weighing against this explanation is the fact that many phobics cannot recall a particular event involving the phobic object or situation (Ollendick & King, 1991). Indeed, some phobias involve objects never encountered by a person, such as giant snakes. Perhaps modeling is a better explanation than classical conditioning because it can explain how a phobia might be acquired without direct experience with the object or situation.

Although explaining phobias is complicated, treating them is not. Behavior therapy can effectively eliminate many phobias. Regardless of the cause of a phobia, the person can be taught not to fear the object or situation, by being exposed repeatedly to it (Marks, 1990).

Post-traumatic stress disorder.   Phobias involve fear out of proportion to the objective circumstances. The next disorder follows a threatening event sufficient to upset anyone, such as:

■ military combat
■ civilian disaster
■ imprisonment in a concentration camp
■ rape or assault
■ torture

After terrible events like these, anyone will have an immediate reaction, but some people will also show a long-term reaction called **post-traumatic stress disorder (PTSD).** One of its defining characteristics is that the person reexperiences the original traumatic event, through dreams, vivid memories, or flashbacks: acting and feeling as if it is literally recurring.

For instance, a Vietnam veteran I knew experienced flashbacks every few days, believing himself in the jungle and leading his group into an ambush. He would crouch in the middle of a room and scan its corners with such apprehension that every onlooker followed his gaze.

A variety of anxiety symptoms mark this disorder: sleep difficulty, irritability, concentration problems, and an exaggerated startle response. People with PTSD try to avoid reminders of the trauma. At the same time, they show social estrangement, diminished interest in other activities, and a sense of hopelessness about the future.

What causes PTSD? By definition, a trauma must be present, but it cannot bear the entire load of explanation because not all who experience a trauma have a long-term negative reaction. A host of additional factors seem to bring about post-traumatic stress in some individuals while precluding it in others (Norris, 1992). Among the factors that make it more likely to occur are physical disability caused by the original event (Strom, 1980), lack of immediate counseling (Ludwig & Ranson, 1947), and a prior history of problems (Andreasen, 1984).

Another risk factor is the person's inability to find any meaning in the traumatic experience. This idea might explain why the Vietnam War appears to have produced

■ **post-traumatic stress disorder (PTSD)**

anxiety disorder that can follow a traumatic event and is characterized by anxiety and reexperiencing of the traumatic event

The war in Vietnam produced more than its share of post-traumatic stress disorders, perhaps because it was conducted in such a way that made it difficult for soldiers to see the significance of what they were doing.

more than its share of post-traumatic stress disorders (Breslau & Davis, 1992). The war was not conducted in a way that made it easy for the participating soldiers to make sense of what they witnessed. It was not a war over territory, which is tangible, but a war over body counts, which are abstract numbers. GIs were shipped over not with friends from their hometown but with strangers chosen randomly by a computer.

Even though PTSD can persist for decades, treatment is possible (Murray, 1992). Talking about the trauma in a supportive context is a common ingredient in successful therapies. Perhaps when people talk about traumatic events, they release deep conflicts and experience emotional relief. Perhaps they extinguish their fear. Or perhaps as they talk about the traumatic events, they come to think about them differently and experience a sense of mastery.

Generalized anxiety disorder.   Sometimes people are anxious almost all of the time, and no specific event or situation is attached to their feelings. This difficulty is called **generalized anxiety disorder (GAD).** Remember Chicken Little, the storybook character who was afraid that the sky would fall on her head? She serves as an apt example of GAD because the sky is everywhere and so too, then, is anxiety about its pending fall.

According to DSM-IV, the diagnostician should look for a person worrying excessively and inappropriately about several domains of life, like family, job, and health. People with GAD show the full range of anxiety responses. They tremble and twitch. They feel tired and tense. They are chronically aroused, with rapid breathing, racing pulse, clammy hands, recurrent diarrhea, frequent urination, and a lump in their throats. They have difficulty concentrating because they are so easily distracted.

GAD occurs in about 3 to 4 percent of adults in the United States. Blacks and whites are equally likely to be given the diagnosis, and women outnumber men (Whitaker et al., 1990). When we turn our attention away from the United States, cross-cultural comparisons unfortunately prove less informative than we would like. According to some studies, generalized anxiety disorder is more common in modern, Western societies than in less technological cultures, but others disagree (Hollifield, Katon, Spain, & Pule, 1990). Hampering these comparisons is that while most cultures recognize a state akin to generalized anxiety, its particular manifestations differ—in some cases, with bodily symptoms predominating; in other cases, emotional symptoms; and in still other cases, cognitive ones (Guthrie & Tanco, 1980).

What causes GAD? Again, different causes intermingle. Generalized anxiety involves the body, of course, particularly the autonomic nervous system. Individual differences in its reactivity are heritable and may predispose GAD (Sandín, 1990). Another possibility is that experience with traumatic events alters the sensitivity of the nervous system so that the person more readily experiences fear and anxiety (Pitman, Van der Kolk, Orr, & Greenberg, 1990).

Psychodynamic theorists use the term free-floating anxiety to refer to highly general symptoms of anxiety that the person is unable to connect to a particular context because to do so would be too threatening. By this view, a generalized anxiety disorder defends against a more specific fear. For example, one man reported increasing anxiety several days before he had to go away on a trip:

> A sense of uneasy tension was constantly present in his stomach, and he often felt mildly flushed and unable to think as clearly as he wished. These [symptoms] . . . totally destroyed any pleasurable anticipations about his journey. (Nemiah, 1980, p. 1487)

Other details suggest that our unhappy traveler was really afraid of being separated from his loved ones because as an infant he had felt abandoned by his mother. He repressed these particular feelings because they were linked to the hostility he felt toward his mother. In place of the hostility with which he felt so uncomfortable, he substituted a general state of uneasiness.

■ **generalized anxiety disorder (GAD)**
disorder characterized by pervasive and chronic anxiety

Cognitive-behavioral theorists trace anxiety to particular learning that is generalized in the way that any learning can be generalized (Chapter 8). Cognitive psychologists stress the role of exaggerated beliefs in bringing about generalization (Beck, 1976). Suppose you encounter difficulties in one sphere of life and become anxious. If you say to yourself, "I'm the sort of person who always has these disasters happen," then you are apt to feel anxious in other areas of your life as well.

Treatment of this disorder takes different forms. Tranquilizing medicine can be used to control the person's bodily symptoms (Cassano, Perugi, Musetti, & Savino, 1990). Psychotherapy is another avenue; it allows a person to talk about the anxiety, achieving insight, reassurance, or both. Behavior therapists teach anxious clients how to relax.

Panic disorder and agoraphobia.   We have all experienced momentary panic: periods of intense anxiety. Usually panic accompanies a life-threatening situation, such as merging onto a busy highway or walking down a dark alley. But some of us experience panic attacks in the absence of any objective danger, with sufficient frequency and disruption to constitute a major problem.

■ **panic disorder**
anxiety disorder characterized by recurrent panic attacks

In these cases, the diagnosis is one of **panic disorder.** Attacks occur suddenly and without warning. They usually last several minutes and are highly unpleasant, arousing intense discomfort and fear. Victims of panic attacks feel like they are choking or smothering. They are dizzy, nauseated, and shaky; they fear losing their minds; they might think they are about to die. After several panic attacks, people start to fear the onset of another one and so become generally apprehensive.

■ **agoraphobia**
fear of being in a situation from which escape is difficult or embarrassing

Agoraphobia, fear of being in a situation from which escape is difficult or embarrassing, frequently accompanies panic disorder. It manifests itself as avoidance of activities such as traveling, shopping, standing in line, and attending movies. In extreme cases, a person with agoraphobia can become completely housebound, not going outside for years or even decades. The link between panic disorder and agoraphobia is probably direct: An individual who has panic attacks might be afraid of having one in public and

Agoraphobia, the fear of being in a situation from which escape is difficult, can lead a person to become housebound. It is diagnosed more frequently among women than men.

will avoid going out. However, people can have panic attacks without agoraphobia or agoraphobia without panic attacks.

Taken together, agoraphobia and panic disorder affect as many as 5 percent of the population (Kessler et al., 1994). African Americans and European Americans show the same likelihood of having these problems, and women are more likely than men to have them (Friedman, Paradis, & Hatch, 1994). Onset is usually in the late twenties. Without treatment, these disorders can be chronic (Pollack et al., 1990).

Research suggests that both biological and psychological mechanisms are at work in panic disorder. Evidence for a biological basis comes from twin studies that show panic disorder to be highly heritable (Torgersen, 1983). Also, panic attacks can be created chemically, with doses of sodium lactate, a chemical that naturally builds up in the body during exercise (Liebowitz et al., 1985). In individuals with a history of panic attacks, a smaller dose of sodium lactate can produce a panic attack, suggesting that such persons have an excess of sodium lactate in the first place. Finally, these disorders often respond well to medication that directly targets panic symptoms (Mavissakalian, 1990).

However, the physiological aspects of agoraphobia and panic disorder may become problems for people only if they interpret them catastrophically (Beck & Emery, 1985). To understand these problems, we must look not just at a person's biology but also at that person's thoughts and beliefs. An interesting therapy emerges from this cognitive approach: encouraging people with these problems to reinterpret the disorder in other terms—say, as a harmless consequence of hyperventilation. This strategy reduces the frequency of panic attacks, as well as the other anxiety symptoms that accompany them (Beck, Sokol, Clark, Berchick, & Wright, 1992).

Obsessive-compulsive disorder. Some people are plagued by recurring thoughts. Attempts to ignore or suppress them are unsuccessful. These thoughts are called **obsessions,** and several themes are common:

- *Violence*—losing control and striking one's child
- *Contamination*—getting AIDS from shaking hands
- *Blasphemy*—having sexual fantasies while praying
- *Doubt*—wondering if an already mailed check was signed

Compulsions are the behavioral counterpart of obsessions: repetitive actions carried out to prevent some dreaded event. People know their behavior is excessive and unreasonable but cannot resist performing it in order to alleviate their anxiety.

Obsessions and compulsions often accompany each other, and so the term **obsessive-compulsive disorder (OCD)** describes both. As many as 2 to 3 percent of our population suffers with this disorder, with blacks and whites and men and women equally likely to have it (Friedman, Hatch, & Paradis, 1993; Rasmussen & Eisen, 1992). If extreme, OCD can disrupt life (Rapoport, 1989). Imagine what you would not be doing if you washed your hands 350 times a day, if you recited the Lord's Prayer every 25 seconds, or if you peered into every passing car on the lookout for a terrorist.

Freud's (1909b) explanation of OCD is still influential. He proposed that obsessive-compulsive disorder represents ambivalence surrounding events during the anal stage (Chapter 12). In short, obsessions and compulsions symbolize the struggles of toilet training—which is why they frequently revolve around themes of contamination and violence.

Cognitive-behavioral mechanisms readily explain the persistence of obsessions and compulsions. Repetitive thoughts and actions reduce anxiety because they distract people from whatever is distressing them (Rachman & Hodgson, 1980). Accordingly, these thoughts and deeds are reinforced. Whatever created the initial distress is left unchanged, meaning that the obsessions and compulsions persist.

OCD is difficult to treat (Stern, 1978). Psychodynamic therapy and tranquilizing medication do not appear to help. Antidepressant medication proves more successful (Marks & O'Sullivan, 1988), as does behavior therapy (Foa, Kozak, Steketee, &

■ **obsession**
recurring unpleasant thought

■ **compulsion**
repetitive action carried out to prevent some dreaded event

■ **obsessive-compulsive disorder (OCD)**
anxiety disorder characterized by obsessions and compulsions

Figure 13.2
Anxiety Disorders as Biopsychosocial. Anxiety disorders are the result of such biological causes as insufficient GABA activity, such psychological causes as unconscious conflicts and learning, and such social causes as an individual's culture.

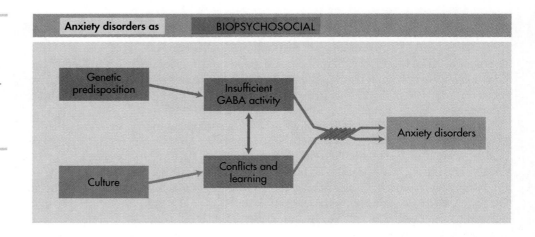

■ **GABA**
neurotransmitter necessary for the parasympathetic nervous system to counteract arousal

McCarthy, 1992). Some therapists try to combine strategies with obsessive-compulsive clients, under the assumption that the benefits will be cumulative (Chapter 14).

Anxiety disorders as biopsychosocial.   As you have seen, anxiety disorders have a variety of contributing causes: biological, psychological, and social (see Figure 13.2). This section discusses how each of these types of causes influences anxiety disorders.

Let us first consider biological predispositions and mechanisms. The tendency of people to experience anxiety in the face of threat is an individual difference with a genetic basis. We would thus expect these disorders to be heritable, and indeed they are (Wang, Crowe, & Noyes, 1992). Another biological ingredient in most of these disorders is insufficient activity of **GABA,** a neurotransmitter necessary for the parasympathetic nervous system to counteract arousal (Haefely, 1990). Tranquilizers—like Valium—work by stimulating GABA activity (Chapter 14).

A possible psychological predisposition to anxiety disorders involves unconscious conflicts. Freud theorized extensively about anxiety (Zerbe, 1990), distinguishing three types:

- *Realistic anxiety*—legitimate fear of things in the world
- *Neurotic anxiety*—fear of one's own impulses
- *Moral anxiety*—fear of one's own conscience

By the psychodynamic view, anxiety is not a disorder in its own right but a process that can produce a variety of disorders, depending on how the individual defends against it. Anxiety disorders can reflect any or all of the three types of fear Freud specified.

Learning also plays a role in many anxiety disorders (Mineka, 1985). For example, anxiety can be classically conditioned. Fear is viewed as an unlearned response to a threat. If other stimuli are paired with whatever arouses fear, then the originally neutral stimulus comes to arouse fear (anxiety) in its own right. We saw this process, for instance, in the case of Little Albert.

Why does anxiety as a conditioned response not extinguish itself? You know from Chapter 8 that conditioned responses can be readily extinguished by exposing the person to the conditioned stimulus without the accompanying unconditioned stimulus. This fact seems at odds with the persistence of many anxiety disorders. Outside the laboratory, however, people with anxiety do not stand still long enough for extinction to take place. Indeed, a person fleeing an anxiety-provoking situation is reinforced because his or her flight decreases the fear.

Cognitive influences on anxiety disorders exist. Anxiety has been interpreted as the result of people's beliefs that they cannot control or understand situations (Kelly, 1955). Similarly, anxiety can be seen as the result of people's exaggerated beliefs about their own fragility (Beck & Emery, 1985). The anxious individual assumes a catastrophe waits around every corner. If you believe you are vulnerable and inadequate, you may end up behaving that way. Thus, fear and anxiety disorders can be a vicious circle: Anxious thoughts lead to anxious behavior, which leads to more anxious thoughts.

Finally, the social influences on anxiety disorders include events in the social environment that can trigger these difficulties, as well as other people from whom we may learn beliefs that arouse and maintain anxiety. Other people can also prevent or reduce anxiety. For instance, social support in the wake of a trauma helps a person cope with what has happened and thereby reduce the likelihood of later PTSD (Chapter 16).

Somatoform Disorders

Some cases of psychological abnormality involve physical symptoms that have no actual basis in physiology. These are called **somatoform disorders,** and they are the result of psychological conflicts.

Somatoform disorders often begin when people are in their teens or twenties. These disorders can persist for decades, and they impair everyday life to varying degrees. On the whole, somatoform disorders appear to be more common among women than men, but accurate estimates are difficult because these disorders are often confused with actual physical illnesses (Goodwin & Guze, 1989).

Treatment of somatoform disorders does not directly address physical symptoms (Morrison, 1990). Instead, the therapist identifies a person's conflicts and helps resolve them and/or encourages the person to find less extreme means of gaining what he or she wants.

Conversion disorder.   The best-known of these difficulties is **conversion disorder,** familiar from previous chapters by its former name, hysteria. This disorder involves a loss of physical functioning without a physical cause—for example, hysterical blindness, deafness, or paralysis. The term *conversion* implies that a psychological issue has been converted into physical symptoms. Any of a number of symptoms are possible, from dramatic ones such as a false pregnancy to more mundane ones such as nausea or constipation. At present, the mundane symptoms are the ones that are typically encountered (Lakosina, Kostiunina, Kal'ke, & Shashkova, 1987).

When I worked as a psychologist in a hospital, I observed a striking example of conversion disorder. A man woke up one morning, suddenly unable to see. His family rushed him to the hospital, where he was examined by eye specialists. They could find nothing wrong with his eyes, and so they called in neurology experts, thinking that his blindness stemmed from damage to his brain. The neurologists could find nothing wrong with his brain, and so they called in psychiatrists and psychologists, who diagnosed his difficulty as a conversion disorder. His blindness had developed shortly after a fight he had had with his wife, during which he screamed, "I never want to see you again!"

DSM-IV provides several criteria for diagnosing conversion disorder. The individual must show a loss or alteration of physical functioning; a biological basis for the physical symptoms must be ruled out; and the symptoms cannot be under the individual's voluntary control. There is a temptation, perhaps, when considering cases of conversion disorder, to think that the symptoms are somehow not real or that the individual is faking them. Both suspicions are wrong. Those with this disorder truly cannot see or hear or move, and they are quite sincere about it (Krull & Schifferdecker, 1990). Finally, the onset of symptoms must bear some psychological relationship to conflicts or needs, as just described for the patient who became blind.

Hypochondriasis.   Another well-known somatoform disorder is **hypochondriasis:** a preoccupation with having one or more serious illnesses, when all medical evidence is to the contrary (Kellner, 1986, 1990). An individual with hypochondriasis is overly concerned with particular bodily functions, such as sweating or the beating of the heart.

■ **somatoform disorder**
disorder characterized by physical symptoms that have no actual basis in physiology

■ **conversion disorder**
hysteria; a loss of physical functioning without a physical cause

■ **hypochondriasis**
preoccupation with having one or more serious illnesses, when all medical evidence is to the contrary

Hypochondriasis is a preoccupation with illness, despite all medical evidence to the contrary. Hypochondriacs are not faking, however, because they are sincerely convinced that they have an illness no one has yet been able to diagnose.

Small injuries or illnesses are interpreted as signs of impending physical doom. As in conversion disorder, hypochondriacal individuals are not deliberately faking. They often visit numerous doctors, never believing that they receive adequate medical care (Barsky, Wyshak, Klerman, & Latham, 1990).

Somatoform disorders as biopsychosocial. Somatoform disorders can be explained in biopsychosocial terms (see Figure 13.3). By definition, these disorders have no direct biological causes, but their symptoms appear as physical ones. According to psychodynamic theorists, a given physical symptom is thought to symbolize an under-

Figure 13.3
Somatoform Disorders as Biopsychosocial. The physical symptoms of somatoform disorders are brought about by a combination of psychological and social causes.

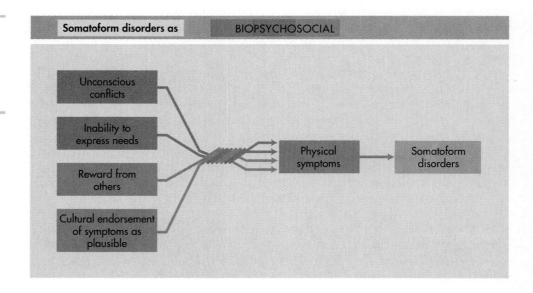

lying conflict that the person keeps from consciousness by metaphorically converting it into a physical difficulty (Mace, 1992a, 1992b). Let us return to the blind patient. He was strongly ambivalent about his wife, and he resolved his conflict by becoming blind and not having to look at her.

Cognitive-behavioral theorists believe that physical symptoms allow the individual to gain some reward, such as the attention of others, and/or to avoid unwanted responsibilities. Studies suggest that those with conversion disorder are often unable to articulate their wants and needs, and so they may use physical symptoms as a means of communication (Ots, 1990; Parsons & Wakeley, 1991).

This explains why the particular forms of somatoform disorders have changed over the years. The symptoms have to be meaningful within a given time and place and consistent with prevailing scientific theories (Shorter, 1992). In Freud's era—Victorian Europe—bizarre physical symptoms were more credible as cries for help than they are today. Nowadays people in general know more about how the body works, and they thus turn to vaguer complaints. This idea may also explain why women are more likely than men to experience conversion disorder: They may be denied other ways of expressing themselves.

Dissociative Disorders

Remember from Chapter 6 the discussion of dissociation, which refers to discontinuities in an individual's consciousness. Dissociative experiences are relatively common in cultures around the world (McClenon, 1994). In some cases, though, individuals experience dissociation so frequently and so intensely that they develop severe problems termed **dissociative disorders.** Though relatively rare, these disorders are of great interest to psychologists because of the insights they provide into the nature of consciousness and abnormality.

Dissociative amnesia.

Dissociative amnesia is the sudden inability to recall personally important information, such as one's name or address. Memory loss is more extensive than can be accounted for by ordinary forgetfulness. Dissociative amnesia cannot have an immediate biological cause, meaning that we must distinguish it from cases of amnesia caused by a head injury. Instead, psychological factors prove relevant.

This disorder is typically observed in the immediate aftermath of severe stress, usually when life is threatened but occasionally when identity is at risk (Brna & Wilson, 1990). During an episode of amnesia, the person is perplexed and disoriented. When memory loss surrounds past events, the person is aware of his or her amnesia, which makes dissociative amnesia different from cases of amnesia with a biological cause (Chapter 6).

For example, I once worked with a man who showed up at the front door of a hospital with absolutely no prior memories. When a physical examination detected no injuries or illnesses that would explain his memory loss, he was referred to psychiatrists and psychologists. By contacting local police departments for reports of missing people who met his description, we eventually discovered who he was and learned that he had disappeared shortly after a terrible day in which he had lost both his job and his wife. His amnesia was a way not to confront what had happened to him.

Dissociative amnesia almost always follows in the wake of a trauma. Information about its frequency in specific times and places is therefore somewhat arbitrary. During times of military combat, dissociative amnesia is more frequent than during times of peace. The annual incidence of amnesia during times of peace is estimated at between 5 and 10 cases per 100,000 adults, and it occurs more frequently among females than males (Koski & Marttila, 1990; Miller, Petersen, Metter, Millikan, & Yanagihara, 1987).

Rapid recovery is the rule, usually within a few days. Often nothing need be done in order for people's memory to return. At other times, people's memory can be jogged by confrontation, or they can be given tranquilizing medication, such as sodium amytal (similar to truth serum), which liberates memory by stifling the anxiety that serves to

■ **dissociative disorder**
disorder characterized by discontinuities in an individual's consciousness

■ **dissociative amnesia**
sudden inability to recall personally important information because of psychological trauma

keep it repressed. Hypnotism can sometimes speed recall as well. In any case, memory returns all at once, and recurrence is rare.

Dissociative identity disorder.   Yet another dissociative disorder is **dissociative identity disorder**, more commonly known as **multiple personality disorder (MPD).** It is defined by the following criteria:

- The presence within the same person of two or more distinct identities or personalities, each with its own enduring and characteristic style
- At least two of these identities or personalities recurrently taking control of the person's behavior
- The inability to recall important personal information, above and beyond ordinary forgetfulness

Each personality has its own set of memories, social relationships, and behaviors. Different personalities can evidence different allergies, body temperatures, eyeglass prescriptions, IQ scores, and sexual orientations (Miller, Blackburn, Scholes, White, & Mamalis, 1991; Miller & Triggiano, 1992; Putnam, Zahn, & Post, 1990).

In many cases of MPD, one personality does not know what happened to another personality when it was in control. In other cases, however, degrees of overlap occur in memories and styles; that is, some personalities may be aware of the existence of others. Regardless, the individual with MPD is aware of the presence of gaps in his or her life that occur when different personalities are in control. Transition from one personality to another usually takes place within seconds or minutes. Stress can trigger these transitions. With hypnosis or tranquilizing medication, different personalities can be brought forth by an examining psychiatrist or psychologist.

The personalities often have different relationships with each other (Putnam, 1989). Some are allies; others are rivals, trying to sabotage one another. At times, one personality may appear more mature and stable than the others. Suicide attempts, self-mutilation, and violence frequently occur with this disorder. Transitions between identities often take place precisely at moments of danger. One personality may put herself in a dangerous situation and then leave to let another personality handle it.

Some psychologists are skeptical that multiple personality disorder really exists, but others estimate that there are several thousand cases of MPD in the United States today (Putnam, 1989). Women with this problem apparently outnumber men by at least three to one. The disorder's onset is usually in childhood, most often following severe sexual abuse. This factor probably accounts for the marked sex difference in prevalence (Ross, Miller, Bjornson, Reagor, Fraser, & Anderson, 1991; Ross, Miller, Reagor, Bjornson, Fraser, & Anderson, 1990). Although boys and girls are both subject to abuse, females are more often the victims.

Although childhood abuse is a risk factor, the disorder may not be evident until years later, usually surfacing during the late twenties. MPD rarely goes away by itself, but with age, the disorder becomes less disruptive. There are some hints that MPD runs through families, although the significance of this is not clear, granted the small number of reported cases.

At present, the most promising treatment is one in which the different personalities are introduced to one another and metaphorically fused into a single entity (Kluft, 1984, 1988). The mere introduction of dissociated selves is a critical first step toward integration. When barriers of amnesia are removed, it becomes difficult to think of the person as having segregated streams of consciousness.

Dissociative disorders as biopsychosocial.   Like other psychological difficulties, the dissociative disorders are best explained by noting that several risk factors combine in their development. Remember that dissociative experiences are relatively common, whereas dissociative disorders are not, implying that the various causes must be present in unusual degrees in order for a full-blown problem to occur. Again, a biopsychosocial conception proves useful (see Figure 13.4).

■ dissociative identity disorder; multiple personality disorder (MPD) presence within the same person of two or more distinct identities or personalities

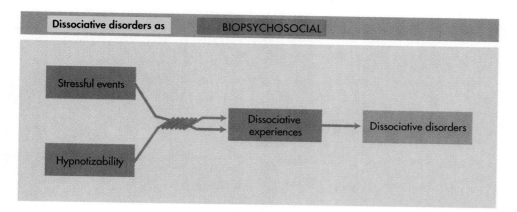

Figure 13.4
Dissociative Disorders as Biopsychosocial. Dissociative disorders can be regarded as dissociative experiences taken to an extreme. Whether people have dissociative experiences is a function of stressful events coupled with hypnotizability.

Stressful events contribute to most cases of dissociative disorder among both men and women of diverse ethnicities (Roesler & McKenzie, 1994; Zatzick, Marmar, Weiss, & Metzler, 1994). In the case of amnesia, the link between trauma and disorder is obvious because amnesia almost always develops in immediate response to a troubling occurrence. In MPD, the association between trauma and disorder might not be quite so obvious because a great deal of time often passes between the original abuse and the appearance of the disorder. What predicts the development of MPD following abuse? One answer is in terms of the extent of the trauma. Individuals with MPD are typically subject to numerous assaults, sexual and physical, over an extended period (Putnam, Guroff, Silberman, Barban, & Post, 1986).

Trauma is a necessary but not sufficient condition for dissociative disorders to develop. We can infer that a diathesis must also be present. Perhaps the relevant diathesis is a tendency to have dissociative experiences when exposed to stress. A related candidate is a personality dimension that we can identify as susceptibility to hypnosis; by implication, hypnotizability predisposes dissociative disorders (Frischholz et al., 1992). So, people create a trance in response to stressful circumstances (Bliss, 1980). They dissociate themselves from the worst aspects of a trauma. The greater the trauma, the more elaborate the self-hypnotism, reaching its height in the case of MPD, where different identities are created out of this state of dissociation in order to bear the brunt of abuse.

Mood Disorders

Mood disorders are problems characterized by extreme sadness and/or elation. These are among the most common psychological difficulties in the late twentieth century. Indeed, depression appears to be on the increase in contemporary society, an ironic trend given the societal emphasis on feeling good. But maybe this state of affairs is not so paradoxical after all. If it were easy to feel good, we would not have so many pop psychology books and bumper stickers urging us to be happy.

There are two major types of mood disorder: depressive disorder and bipolar disorder. In **depressive disorder,** or **major depression,** the person experiences excessively negative moods. In **bipolar disorder** (formerly called manic-depression), periods of depression alternate with periods of excessive agitation and elation (mania). Cases of pure mania also occur, but they are rare (Goodwin & Guze, 1989).

Depressive disorder.   There are few better examples of the difficulty in drawing a line between normality and abnormality than depression. It refers to a transient mood—an appropriate reaction to disappointment—as well as a chronic disorder. When does "normal" depression become minor depression, and when does minor depression become major depression? There are no clear boundaries. There are a number of signs and symptoms of depression, and the more that are present, the more severe the disorder.

■ **mood disorders**
disorders characterized by extreme sadness and/or elation

■ **depressive disorder; major depression**
mood disorder in which one experiences excessively negative moods

■ **bipolar disorder**
manic-depression; mood disorder in which periods of depression alternate with periods of excessive agitation and elation

Depression is largely independent of social class and ethnicity, and is more likely among younger as opposed to older adults.

People display depression in a variety of ways, as shown in Table 13.3. A depressed mood is obviously present in depressive disorder, but note that symptoms can involve all psychological spheres.

Here are some facts about the occurrence of depression. First, your chance of becoming depressed enough to be given a diagnosis at some period in your lifetime is estimated as somewhere between 8 and 23 percent (Kessler et al., 1994). Second, depression occurs much more frequently among women than men, at least twice as often and maybe eight times as often; this gender difference is found worldwide (Weissman, Bland, Joyce, Newman, Wells, & Wittchen, 1993). Numerous explanations of the gender difference have been proposed, but none seems fully adequate (Nolen-Hoeksema, 1987). We can suspect that the gender difference is due to multiple causes: biological, psychological, and social. Third, the prevalence of depression among adults is largely independent of social class and race (Fellin, 1989; Somervell, Leaf, Weissman, Blazer, & Bruce, 1989). Fourth, this disorder is more common among younger adults as opposed to older adults (Robins et al., 1984).

Table 13.3 Symptoms of Depression	
Type of symptom	**Example**
Emotional	Depressed mood
Motivational	Loss of interest or pleasure in activities
Physiological	Weight loss or gain; sleep disturbance
Behavioral	Restlessness or sluggishness
Cognitive	Feelings of worthlessness; excessive guilt; decreased ability to concentrate; recurrent thoughts of death

Suicide and depressive disorder.   Suicide as a depressive symptom deserves special mention (Holinger, 1987; Klerman, 1987). Although not all suicidal individuals are depressed and not all depressed people are suicidal, a strong link exists between depression and suicide in the United States. Of the 200,000 or more known suicide attempts each year in the United States, perhaps 80 percent are carried out by seriously depressed individuals. Depression is a potentially lethal disorder that should be taken seriously.

Despite the strong link between depression and suicide, some differences exist in the social profiles associated with each. In the United States, the typical depressive is a young adult female, whereas the typical suicide victim is a male over 50 years of age. Usually the suicide victim has a serious physical illness and is familiar with firearms. Alcohol abuse contributes to many completed suicides (Adams & Overholser, 1992; Merrill, Milner, Owens, & Vale, 1992). By the way, females attempt suicide more than males do, but because men choose more lethal means (e.g., guns rather than pills), they "succeed" more frequently (Marzuk, Leon, Tardiff, Morgan, Stajic, & Mann, 1992).

Depressive disorders as biopsychosocial.   Like the other psychological disorders discussed so far, depression is best explained in terms of several mechanisms (see Figure 13.5). Let me start by discussing the biological influences. Family studies show that individuals with a depressed biological relative are much more likely to become depressed than those without such a relative (Downey & Coyne, 1990). Also, the bodily symptoms of depression imply that the disorder is biological because they can take opposite forms. We would expect this particular pattern if a person's physiology were somehow out of balance: agitation or lethargy, too much sleep or too little sleep, weight loss or weight gain. Further support for a biological role is that some physical illnesses cause depression. Similarly, some medications produce depression as a side effect. Finally, the disorder can be successfully treated by a variety of biological interventions: drugs, electroconvulsive shock, and aerobic exercise (Chapter 14).

Biological theorists point to low levels of neurotransmitter activity, particularly **norepinephrine** and **serotonin,** as the cause of the disorder (Fritze, Deckert, Lanczik, Strik, Struck, & Wodarz, 1992; Rothschild, 1988; Schildkraut, 1965). Among their other roles, these neurotransmitters are involved in the functioning of the hypothalamus, which helps to regulate sleep, appetite, sexuality, and physical movement—exactly the domains in which several depressive symptoms are found (Grahame-Smith, 1992; Jacobs, 1991). The other symptoms of depression follow as a result.

According to biological theories, interventions such as antidepressant medications and electroconvulsive shock succeed to the degree that they increase the activity of

■ **norepinephrine**
neurotransmitter involved in depressive disorder

■ **serotonin**
neurotransmitter involved in depressive disorder

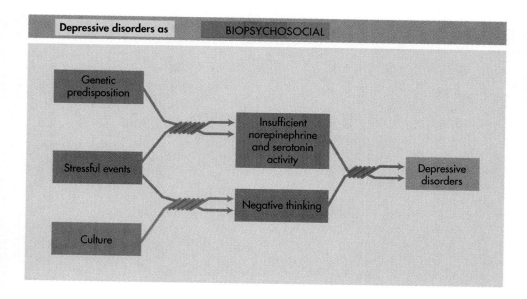

Depressive disorders as   BIOPSYCHOSOCIAL

Genetic predisposition

Stressful events

Culture

Insufficient norepinephrine and serotonin activity

Negative thinking

Depressive disorders

Figure 13.5
Depressive Disorders as Biopsychosocial. Among the causes of depressive disorders are a genetic predisposition, stressful life events, and a culture that encourages negative thinking.

norepinephrine and serotonin (Conte & Karasu, 1992; Couvreur, Ansseau, & Franck, 1989). Research methods are not yet sophisticated enough to directly measure these neurotransmitters in the brains of depressives, but the indirect evidence is strong.

Psychodynamic theorists identify unconscious processes as the most important psychological mechanisms in depression (Mendelson, 1974). Freud (1917) introduced an influential formulation in his paper "Mourning and Melancholia," in which he contrasted mourning (grief) with melancholia (depression). In grief, people are simply sad, whereas in depression, people are sad and believe they are worthless. Why do people have negative beliefs about themselves? Freud suggested that we consider the reason why we have negative beliefs about anyone: because we are angry at them. So, Freud proposed that depression is anger turned against the self. This view explains why suicide frequently accompanies the disorder—suicide is murder perpetrated against the self.

The depressive's anger stems from childhood, argued Freud; the period when the child's sense of self is created by how his or her parents behave. If the parents frequently disappoint the child by acting inconsistently, then the child develops a readiness to be depressed (angry) in the face of disappointment. Not all of these dynamics are easy to investigate, but some studies show that adult depressives have suffered losses in childhood, such as the death of a parent, and further, that current disappointments and failures can trigger depressive episodes (Lloyd, 1980).

The cognitive-behavioral approach suggests further mechanisms involved in cases of depressive disorder. Reinforcement theories attribute depression to low levels of reward in an individual's environment (Lewinsohn, 1974). This account appears simplistic, but there are two ways people can find themselves in an impoverished world. One is to be somewhere that is objectively boring (Lewinsohn & Libet, 1972). The other is to lack the skills needed to gain rewards that do exist in a particular setting (Libet & Lewinsohn, 1973). If you do not know how to start or maintain friendships, you are unlikely to have friends and all the rewards they make possible. So, therapy from the reinforcement point of view takes two forms as well: Either change the person's world so that reinforcement is more plentiful or impart skills to the person so that he or she can win reinforcement (Weissman, 1984).

Seligman's (1974, 1975) learned helplessness theory proposes that depression is a person's inevitable reaction to uncontrollable events. Just as dogs and rats exposed to uncontrollable shocks become listless, so too do people who cannot influence important events in their lives (Chapter 8). Studies show that uncontrollable events often precede depressive episodes (Paykel, 1974).

Learned helplessness theory has been revised to emphasize interpretations of the cause of the original events (Abramson, Seligman, & Teasdale, 1978). According to this reformulated theory, depression follows uncontrollability when a person explains an uncontrollable event with causes that are internal ("It's me"), stable ("It's going to last forever"), and global ("It's going to undermine everything I do"). Explanatory style refers to the causal explanations that people habitually offer for negative events (Buchanan & Seligman, 1995; Peterson & Seligman, 1984). Research shows that causal explanations and explanatory style relate to depression as proposed by learned helplessness theory (Peterson, Maier, & Seligman, 1993).

Further psychological influences on depression are specified by Aaron Beck's (1967, 1976) cognitive theory. Beck contended that depression is not so much a disorder of mood as one of thought: Depressed people think about themselves, their world, and their future in highly negative terms. Everything is bleak and grim. These negative thoughts then create the negative mood of the depressive.

Presumably, the depressive sees things as worse than they are. Why is this worldview maintained? Why do events to the contrary not challenge depressive beliefs? Beck provided two answers.

First, depressed people are prone to automatic thoughts: unbidden and habitual ways of thinking that continually put themselves down. Suppose you are at a party and you see an attractive person you met a few weeks before. You might walk across the

According to psychiatrist Aaron Beck, depressed people experience automatic thoughts that put themselves down. A slow checkout line at the grocery store is proof that one is a loser: "I always pick the slow line; I'm a dope!"

room to strike up a conversation. Then again, automatic thoughts might freeze you midstep:

- She won't remember who I am.
- She's probably waiting for her boyfriend.
- I'll say something stupid.
- I look ugly!
- I have nothing to say to her anyway.
- I should have known—she's ignoring me already.
- I hate parties!
- I'm the only one not having fun.
- I'm going to die old and lonely.

If automatic thoughts are not depressing enough, Beck argued, then depression is further maintained by errors in logic, slipshod ways of thinking that keep self-deprecating beliefs immune to reality (Cook & Peterson, 1986). For example, a depressed person selectively attends to negative events while overlooking positive ones. On the way to pick up an honorary degree, let us suppose, you get a traffic ticket, and the ticket is all you can think about for the rest of the week. Or a depressed person may turn the petty hassles of everyday life into personal misfortunes. Waiting in a slow checkout line at the grocery store is proof positive that you are a loser, for picking this time to go shopping, for choosing that particular line, for offending the cashier, for living and breathing and needing to eat.

Some critics of Beck's cognitive theory suggest that negative cognitions are the result of depression, not the cause (Peterson, 1996). In all likelihood, a two-way influence exists. Nonetheless, Beck's approach is influential because it captures the way depressed people think and because it gives rise to an effective treatment of depression (Stravynski & Greenberg, 1992). In **cognitive therapy,** the therapist works with depressed clients to challenge their negative beliefs. These beliefs must first be made explicit because automatic thoughts can be so ingrained that clients pay little attention to them, only to their depressing consequences. Once they become aware of their negative beliefs, clients are taught to evaluate them against the evidence and presumably find little justification.

Not that many decades ago, the outlook for depression was as bleak as the disorder itself. Little could be done except to keep depressives from killing themselves until their

■ **cognitive therapy**
treatment of depression that challenges negative beliefs

Table 13.4   Symptoms of Mania

Type of symptom	Example
Emotional	Elated mood
Motivational	Excessive involvement in pleasurable yet foolish pursuits
Physiological	Decreased need for sleep
Behavioral	Increased activity; increased talkativeness
Cognitive	Racing thoughts; increased distractability

depression passed, usually (but not always) in three to six months. But now there is good news. There are many successful treatments: antidepressant medication, electroconvulsive shock, social skills training, and talking therapies—notably, Beck's approach (Chapter 14).

Bipolar disorder.   In bipolar disorder, depressed episodes alternate with manic episodes. We already know the signs of depression. **Mania** in many ways is its opposite (see Table 13.4). Although mania might at first glance seem a desirable state, it is highly disruptive to the individual and leads to all sorts of interpersonal difficulties. Bipolar disorder affects about 1 percent of the population worldwide, with its onset usually between the ages of 20 and 30 (Goodwin & Jamison, 1990). Women and men are equally likely to have bipolar disorder, and it is equally apt to occur across lines of ethnicity and social class.

Bipolar disorder is highly heritable (McGuffin & Katz, 1989). At the same time, genetics are not the whole picture. Additional factors—presumably, environmental conditions—must combine with genetic inheritance to produce the disorder. Along these lines, stressful life events such as unemployment may precipitate particular depressive or manic episodes (Ellicott, Hammen, Gitlin, Brown, & Jamison, 1990; Hunt, Bruce-Jones, & Silverstone, 1992). The diathesis for bipolar disorder presumably involves imbalances among neurotransmitters responsible for synchronizing mood.

The typical treatment for bipolar disorder is **lithium,** a naturally occurring salt that reduces a person's mood swings. The physical mechanism by which lithium works is unclear (Jefferson, 1989, 1990), but its effects are not. It stabilizes the bipolar individual, preventing manic and depressive episodes (O'Connell, Mayo, Flatow, Cuthbertson, & O'Brien, 1991). It does not cure bipolar disorder in the sense that penicillin cures pneumonia. Rather, lithium is more like high blood pressure medication: A person must stay on the drug even when feeling and acting normally. Encouraging people to comply with lithium treatment can be a problem, though. The drug has undesirable side effects, including kidney and liver damage, dry mouth, and skin irritation (Gitlin, Cochran, & Jamison, 1989).

Schizophrenia

Schizophrenia refers to a group of psychological disorders characterized by disturbed thinking and deteriorated functioning. Schizophrenia is regarded by many people as the epitome of abnormality because it involves so many of its pertinent features. The individual with schizophrenia may stop eating or bathing. He may hear voices that accuse him of terrible crimes. He may believe that he is from another planet or that the CIA is persecuting him.

Schizophrenia shows itself in different forms, and DSM-IV makes several distinctions within the general diagnostic category. A schizophrenic person who shows bizarre motor movements is described as catatonic. A schizophrenic patient who has complicated delusions of persecution or grandiosity is said to be paranoid. If a person with

■ mania
state of excessive elation and agitation

■ lithium
naturally occurring salt used to treat bipolar disorder

■ schizophrenia
group of psychological disorders characterized by disturbed thinking and deteriorated functioning

schizophrenia is frequently incoherent and shows inappropriate emotions such as constant giggling, he or she is classified as disorganized. A schizophrenic individual who fits none of these categories is described as undifferentiated. Finally, the term *residual schizophrenia* is used to describe individuals who once warranted a diagnosis of schizophrenia, do not do so at the present time, yet still show peculiarities in their behavior.

Schizophrenia occurs in about 1 percent of people in virtually all cultures (Jablensky, 1989). Men and women are equally likely to be diagnosed with schizophrenia, although the average age of onset is earlier for men (before age 25) than for women (after age 25) (Andia & Zisook, 1991; Tien & Eaton, 1992). Also, as discussed in Chapter 1, the prognosis for females seems better than for males (Munk-Jorgensen & Mortensen, 1992). In the United States, schizophrenia is diagnosed most frequently among those from the lower class. This finding may reflect differences in vulnerability or differences in seeking (and receiving) effective help (Adebimpe, 1994).

Symptoms of thought disorder.
Disturbances in thinking are common in schizophrenia. Here are some of the possible ways these can be evident. **Delusions** are not eccentric beliefs but bizarre and unsettling ideas that are completely implausible to anyone else in the individual's social group. A schizophrenic individual might believe that her thoughts are being stolen from her head, that the government has hidden a nuclear device in her backyard, or that she is 6 million years old.

Hallucinations are sensations and perceptions with no basis in reality. They are frequently auditory—voices conveying insults and threats. For instance, a patient with whom I worked had been a cook in the army and was tormented by a voice that urged him to jump into the 50-gallon vat of scalding soup he prepared every evening. When he finally attempted to follow these directions, he was hospitalized.

Sometimes seen in schizophrenia is flat affect: The person shows no signs of emotion, speaks in a monotone, and has an immobile face. Sometimes he reports that he has no feelings. Sometimes emotions are expressed but in a completely inappropriate manner. Another patient I knew was told that his mother died, and hearing that, he gave a hearty laugh.

Also common in schizophrenia are abrupt shifts from one topic to another, with only the wispiest of transitions. A person's speech may be impoverished, conveying no information despite many words. The schizophrenic individual might also make up her own words, called neologisms:

> A schizophrenic woman who had been hospitalized for several years kept repeating, in an otherwise quite rational conversation, the word *polamolalittersjitterstittersleelitla*. Her psychiatrist asked her to spell it out, and she then proceeded to explain to him the meaning of the various components, which she insisted were to be used as one word. "Polamolalitters" was intended to recall the disease poliomyelitis . . . The component "litters" stood for untidiness and messiness, the way she felt inside . . . [and so on]. (Lehmann, 1980, p. 1161)

By the way, this example contains another sign of schizophrenic thought disorder—clang associations, or the stringing together of words that sound alike (*litters, jitters, titters*). Still another characteristic of schizophrenic speech is described as word salad: sentences composed of words in no discernible order, tossed together like the ingredients in a salad.

Schizophrenia as biopsychosocial.
Few would contest that schizophrenia is a severe psychological disorder, but over the years, there has been heated debate about how to explain schizophrenia. Biological theorists regarded it as a discrete disease, a lit-

Colin Ferguson, who killed a number of commuters on a train, represented himself in court, where his delusions of persecution were evident to most onlookers.

■ **delusions**
patently false beliefs

■ **hallucinations**
sensations and perceptions with no basis in reality

eral mental illness that could be explained and treated in medical terms. Other theorists strongly disagreed, arguing variously that schizophrenia was:

- a myth (Szasz, 1961)
- a moral verdict (Sarbin & Mancuso, 1980)
- a product of society (Scheff, 1966)
- a role forced upon an individual (Goffman, 1961)
- a sane reaction to an insane world (Laing, 1967)
- a scientific delusion (Boyle, 1990)

According to these theorists, schizophrenia must be understood in terms of the social context and in terms of the psychological meaning of its defining symptoms. Ronald Laing (1965), in particular, stressed that even the most bizarre symptoms mean something to the schizophrenic individual. In contrast, sore throats and runny noses do not contain levels of meaning for individuals with a cold.

Current explanations of schizophrenia move beyond such either-or debates and regard schizophrenia in biopsychosocial terms. Biological, psychological, and social mechanisms come together to produce schizophrenia. Let me mention some of the mechanisms that have been identified.

Biological mechanisms include genetics. Family and twin studies show that schizophrenia is heritable (Gottesman, 1991). For instance, if one identical twin is diagnosed schizophrenic, the odds are almost fifty-fifty that the other twin will also have the diagnosis. Among fraternal twins, the odds are one in ten.

Researchers have also identified some of the neurological mechanisms involved in schizophrenia. Consider these findings:

- PET scans (discussed in Chapter 4) comparing the brains of schizophrenic individuals with the brains of normal individuals show differences in activity (see Figure 13.6).
- Chronic amphetamine use can produce a syndrome indistinguishable from (naturally occurring) schizophrenia.
- Schizophrenic symptoms can be treated with drugs such as Thorazine and Haldol.
- An interesting relationship exists between Parkinson's disease (Chapter 4) and schizophrenia: The drugs respectively used to treat each disorder produce as side effects symptoms like those of the other disorder.

■ dopamine hypothesis
theory that schizophrenia results from excess activity of the neurotransmitter dopamine

A popular explanation of these findings is the **dopamine hypothesis:** Schizophrenia results from excess activity of the neurotransmitter dopamine (Goldstein & Deutsch, 1992; Matthysse, 1977). Several lines of evidence support this hypothesis. For example, chronic amphetamine use increases dopamine activity in the brain. Thorazine and Haldol work by decreasing levels of dopamine activity. Also, Parkinson's disease is known to be characterized by insufficient dopamine, implying that schizophrenia is marked by excessive dopamine. Finally, studies that examined the brains of schizophrenic patients following death found an increased number of dopamine receptors, again supporting the dopamine hypothesis (Pearce, Seeman, Jellinger, & Tourtellotte, 1990).

Researchers have also identified social influences on schizophrenia. For example, traumatic events may precipitate a schizophrenic episode (Nuechterlein et al., 1992). As already mentioned, schizophrenia is most common among members of the lower class, perhaps because their lives are more stressful. Finally, family dynamics influence the course of schizophrenia.

■ expressed emotion
degree to which families are critical and emotionally confrontive

For example, consider a characteristic of families called **expressed emotion:** the degree to which families are critical and emotionally confrontive (Leff & Vaughn, 1985). After individuals with schizophrenia have been discharged from a hospital, presumably on their way to recovery, their prognosis can be predicted from the expressed emotion of their families and how much time is spent with them. Prolonged contact with highly critical family members results in rehospitalization.

A diathesis-stress model can accommodate the evidence that schizophrenia is a biological disorder as well as the evidence that it is a social disorder (Fowles, 1992).

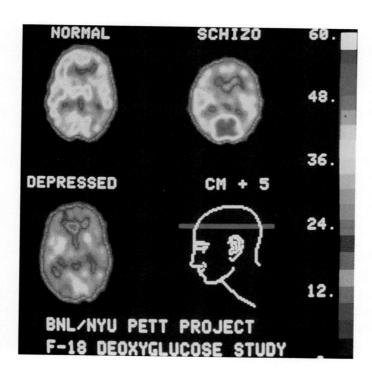

Figure 13.6
PET-Scan of Schizophrenic Brain. Different colors indicate different degrees of brain activity. The schizophrenic individual's brain—on the right—shows a different pattern of activity from the normal individual's brain—on the left. This difference supports a biological basis to schizophrenia.

Suppose that an individual inherits a tendency for excess dopamine activity. Suppose that under social stress, this tendency becomes an actuality. The excess dopamine activity affects the person's perceptual experience, particularly his or her selective attention (Chapter 5), producing great anxiety (Erlenmeyer-Kimling & Cornblatt, 1992). In response to unsettling experiences, the person develops bizarre beliefs, unusual emotions, and idiosyncratic ways of thinking. While all of these processes play themselves out, the demands of everyday life are necessarily neglected. No one has mapped out the natural history of schizophrenia in this (or any other) specific way, but the point remains that a diathesis-stress conception is a potentially powerful way of integrating what we know about the disorder.

The treatment of schizophrenia underscores the biopsychosocial nature of this disorder. In the 1950s, it was discovered that drugs called **neuroleptics** effectively curtail many of the symptoms of schizophrenia. These drugs created a major revolution in treatment. By controlling their most disruptive symptoms, these drugs allowed schizophrenic patients to leave the hospitals to which they had been committed. Indeed, the number of hospitalized schizophrenics was reduced by almost 75 percent in the two decades following the introduction of neuroleptics (Witkin, 1981). Despite this success in reducing the number and length of psychiatric hospitalizations, neuroleptics leave much to be desired.

First, typical neuroleptics treat only positive symptoms of schizophrenia: the delusions and hallucinations that DSM-IV explicitly lists as hallmarks of this disorder. These drugs do not affect negative symptoms, the psychological deficiencies such as social withdrawal that also play a part. When we examine this disorder from the inside, from the viewpoint of the schizophrenic individual, we find a person who feels unreal, uncommitted, empty, depressed, and even evil (Bernheim & Lewine, 1979). Neuroleptics do not change these feelings and experiences. Many theorists today believe that the distinction between positive symptoms and negative symptoms is a more useful way to classify types of schizophrenia than the subcategories contained in DSM-IV (Peterson, 1996). The usefulness of newly developed drugs like clozapine, which seems to target both positive and negative symptoms, is currently being explored (Peterson, 1996).

■ **neuroleptics**
drugs that control many of the symptoms of schizophrenia

Second, in the meantime, most of the drugs available produce unpleasant side effects, including oversedation, decreased spontaneity, motor restlessness, involuntary movements of the head and mouth, susceptibility to sunburn, constipation, low blood pressure, jaundice, and impotence. As you can imagine, compliance with the medication is a continual problem.

Most therapists agree that medication is an important part of the treatment of schizophrenia but must be supplemented (Falloon, 1992). Individual therapy, family therapy, and group therapy are all used in conjunction with neuroleptics. At one time, it was believed that a person who experienced an episode of schizophrenia always worsened. This conclusion is no longer justified, and we can be cautiously optimistic. Some individuals continue to be troubled throughout their lives, but others get along quite satisfactorily, putting schizophrenia behind them (Bleuler, 1978).

Personality Disorders

Personality disorders are pervasive styles of behaving that exacerbate other disorders while also creating difficulties in their own right (Nestadt, Romanoski, Samuels, Folstein, & McHugh, 1992). As mentioned earlier, personality disorders are described on Axis II of DSM-IV, distinguished from the clinical syndromes discussed so far because they are long-standing styles of behaving as opposed to discrete disorders.

DSM-IV distinguishes ten different personality disorders, described briefly in Table 13.5. A personality disorder is not simply an eccentric style, which can be innocuous or even charming (Weeks, 1988). Rather, personality disorders are considered examples of abnormality because they are linked to personal and social maladjustment. These disorders are notoriously difficult to treat, and they hamper the successful treatment of clinical syndromes such as anxiety disorders or depression (Reich & Green, 1991; Shea et al., 1990).

The ten disorders in Table 13.5 are sometimes classified into three larger groups or clusters (American Psychiatric Association, 1994). Cluster 1 consists of paranoid, schizoid, and schizotypal disorders—styles of behaving that are odd or eccentric. Interest in these disorders stems in part from their presumed relationship with schizophrenia (Rado, 1956). Persons with schizophrenia have more than their share of close relatives with odd personality disorders, and vice versa, suggesting that common factors underlie both sorts of difficulties (Meehl, 1962, 1989, 1990).

Table 13.5   DSM-IV Personality Disorders

Type of disorder	Characterization
Paranoid	Pervasive yet unwarranted belief that others intend harm
Schizoid	Indifference to others and a restricted range of emotional expression
Schizotypal	Peculiarities in thoughts, actions, and appearance
Antisocial	Irresponsible behavior toward others
Borderline	Instability in mood, relationships, and self-image
Histrionic	Excessive emotionality and attention seeking
Narcissistic	Grandiosity about the self, hypersensitivity to what others think, and lack of empathy
Avoidant	Social discomfort, fear of evaluation, and timidity
Dependent	Dependence on and submissiveness to others
Obsessive-compulsive	Perfectionism and inflexibility

Cluster 2 includes antisocial, borderline, histrionic, and narcissistic disorders. People with these personality disorders are excessively dramatic, erratic, and/or emotional, and their problems play themselves out interpersonally. Theoretical speculation about these disorders focuses on what went wrong with an individual to produce the deficiency that marks his or her personality style. In each case, some combination of biological processes and social influences conspires to produce the particular style of behaving (Cadoret, Troughton, Bagford, & Woodworth, 1990).

For example, why are individuals diagnosed with antisocial personality disorder unmoved by the suffering of others? The disorder may be predisposed by an inability to experience anxiety while thinking about a risky course of action. If you are indifferent to the negative consequences of what you do, at least some of your behaviors will end up hurting others.

Finally, Cluster 3 includes disorders involving anxiety and timidity: avoidant, dependent, and obsessive-compulsive personality disorders. These disorders are related to the anxiety disorders discussed earlier in this chapter because similar mechanisms appear to be involved. Along these lines, interventions effective for anxiety disorders have been used with some success to treat the timid personality disorders (Beck, Freeman, et al., 1990).

Personality disorders stir debate, particularly among those psychologists who question the very notion of personality types (Chapter 12). If people's characteristic behavior is determined at least in part by the situations in which they find themselves, then it is highly misleading to regard their personalities as disordered. Instead, their problems stem from their social environments (Leary, 1957; Millon, 1990).

Most of the personality disorders cannot be reliably diagnosed (Ferguson & Tyrer, 1988; Reich, 1989; Standage, 1989). Part of the diagnostic problem is the neglect of the social setting in which personality disorders are displayed. Another contributing factor is that the defining symptoms for different disorders show considerable overlap, especially within a given cluster.

Critics further charge that the diagnostic criteria themselves are biased, often in ways congruent with social stereotypes and roles (Kaplan, 1983a, 1983b). Almost all of the personality disorders are diagnosed at different rates among men and women (Reich, 1987). Women, for instance, are much more likely than men to be diagnosed as histrionic or dependent, and men are much more likely than women to be diagnosed as narcissistic or antisocial.

Looked at in this way, these personality disorders seem very much like exaggerated gender roles for women and men, respectively (Landrine, 1989; Rienzi & Scrams, 1991). Again, we are reminded not to locate the disorder solely within the individual but to consider as well the part played by societal expectations about how women and men should behave (Nuckolls, 1992).

The general concept of personality disorders can nonetheless be useful, reminding us that people's problems can result from their lifestyle. However, in explaining—and treating—such problems, a psychologist must look at the social context in which they are found.

Those with antisocial personality disorder are unmoved by the suffering of others. Although those with antisocial personality disorder are not always criminals, senseless crimes—like those of murderer Gary Gilmore—exemplify the disorder.

Stop and Think

13 How are anxiety disorders biopsychosocial?

14 What is hypochondriasis?

15 Why is multiple personality disorder more likely to occur among females than males?

16 Contrast the symptoms of depression with those of mania.

17 What is the dopamine hypothesis?

18 Why are personality disorders difficult to diagnose reliably?

PSYCHOLOGICAL DISORDERS IN A BIOPSYCHOSOCIAL CONTEXT

Much of this chapter has focused on the biological and psychological aspects of abnormality. This section completes the contextualization of psychological disorders by examining the influence of the larger culture.

Cross-Cultural Psychopathology

■ **cross-cultural psychopathology**
field that attempts to explain cultural influences on disorders

Cross-cultural psychopathology is the field that attempts to explain cultural influences on disorders. Over the years, cross-cultural psychopathology has moved back and forth between two extremes (Marsella, 1988). Some theorists have expressed the opinion that culture does not much matter: Disorders are essentially the same regardless of the culture in which they occur. Other theorists have argued for an extreme cultural relativism: All disorders are unique to a particular time and place.

Today, a middle ground is occupied by most cross-cultural psychologists. Many of the broad categories of abnormality—anxiety, depression, schizophrenia, and substance abuse—have a certain universality, perhaps because they have a basis in biology and/or common environmental demands. But culture nonetheless shapes many of these disorders, how they manifest themselves, and to whom they are most likely to occur: males versus females, younger versus older individuals, poor people versus rich people.

For example, cross-cultural studies of depression show that virtually every culture recognizes behaviors reflecting despondency, fatigue, and diminished sexual interest (Kleinman & Good, 1985). These are central depressive symptoms in the contemporary United States. At the same time, a closer look reveals important differences. In Nigeria, depression as a syndrome is not recognized, although its component symptoms are. In many East Asian cultures, the core symptoms of depression tend not to be accompanied by guilt and self-deprecation as they are in Western cultures.

Culture-Bound Syndromes

■ **culture-bound syndromes**
psychological disorders that occur only within specific cultures

Some psychological disorders occur only within specific cultures. Such problems are called **culture-bound syndromes** because they are not found elsewhere. A number of these have attracted the attention of theorists and researchers.

Seen chiefly among Asians, *taijinkyofusho* (sometimes called *anthropophobia* in English) involves heightened anxiety over face-to-face contact with another person. It is marked as well by easy blushing and fear of rejection. The individual with *taijinkyofusho* imagines he or she suffers a variety of shortcomings and deficiencies, such as an offensive facial expression or unpleasant body odor.

When we speak of a person running *amok,* we are using a Malaysian word that refers to a widely recognized syndrome among young males in the Malay culture (and elsewhere around the world). *Amok* consists of a sudden mass assault on others, usually with a sword or ax, sometimes resulting in numerous deaths. The *amok* individual may then kill himself as well. If he does not die, he typically has no memory of the episode.

Koro is observed among males in a variety of Asian cultures and occasionally in Europe and the United States. *Koro* is the fear that the penis is retracting into the abdomen and will eventually cause death. Occasionally *koro* epidemics—in which hundreds of men in the same region experience its symptoms—have been reported.

Bulimia occurs among middle- and upper-class young women in the United States and Western Europe. It has not been described in other parts of the world. As you recall from Chapter 7, bulimia is characterized by episodes of food bingeing, in which large

Not all disorders are found in every culture. For instance, bulimia occurs chiefly among upper middle class young women in the United States and Western Europe. Princess Diana's problem with bulimia has been frequently discussed in the media.

amounts of high-calorie food are consumed, followed by self-induced purging, such as vomiting. Feelings of depression often accompany bulimia.

Many more culture-bound syndromes could be described (Peterson, 1996), but let me draw some conclusions from those already delineated. First, culture-bound syndromes must be interpreted in terms of the particular culture in which they occur. Given syndromes have shared meanings within a cultural group. *Taijinkyofusho* can be interpreted in terms of Asian cultural concerns about maintaining harmonious personal interactions. Despite looking like a random behavioral explosion, *amok* conforms to a societal script in Malaysia that recognizes the syndrome as a possible reaction to insult or jealousy (Carr & Tan, 1976; Tan & Carr, 1977). *Koro* occurs in a culture that uses the metaphor of a tree to describe the penis; a tree has a root that is vulnerable to invisible attacks (Chowdhury, 1991). *Bulimia* follows from the contemporary Western idealization of female thinness (McCarthy, 1990).

Second, were the symptoms of these syndromes to occur in other cultures, most would still be considered problematic ways of behaving. Senseless violence against others, excessive fear and anxiety, and inaccurate somatic complaints would be considered abnormal in virtually any setting. The particular constellations of symptoms vary dramatically across cultures, yet the symptoms themselves have greater universality, perhaps because they are produced by biological and psychological mechanisms that are present in all people.

Third, when Western researchers study culture-bound syndromes, they are usually drawn to faraway places. It is doubtless easier to recognize a contextualized form of abnormality in another culture. Bulimia was deliberately included in the list of culture-bound syndromes to provoke your thinking. It is rarely described as a culture-bound syndrome, although it fits the definition perfectly. Western researchers are probably guilty of looking too much within the bulimic individual for the causes of her problem and not enough at the larger cultural context that makes eating disorders so common in the contemporary United States and Europe. We should move beyond the intrinsic interest of culture-bound syndromes and see that all psychological problems, even those found widely around the world, occur in a cultural context.

The next chapter takes a look at what psychologists do to help people who suffer from psychological disorders. Keep in mind how methods of treatment are based on views of human nature such as those presented in Chapter 12. It is not coincidental that so many of the influential personality theorists were also clinicians: Freud, Adler, Jung, Horney, Kelly, and Rogers, to name just a few.

SUMMARY

UNDERSTANDING PSYCHOLOGICAL DISORDERS: DEFINITION AND EXPLANATION

■ Psychological abnormality is difficult to define precisely. One possible definition regards abnormality as a fuzzy category, characterized by such attributes as suffering, maladaptiveness, loss of control, and unconventionality.

■ At present, abnormality is explained with three competing sets of theories: the biomedical model, which sees people as physical systems susceptible to breakdown or malfunction; the psychodynamic model, which sees people as energy systems at risk for overload or short circuit; and the cognitive-behavioral model, which sees people as information processing systems prone to ignorance or error. Together, these theories provide a biopsychosocial perspective on psychological disorders.

HISTORICAL PERSPECTIVES ON ABNORMALITY

■ Throughout history, abnormality has been viewed from three different vantage points, in terms of supernatural, illness, and psychological considerations. Each of these perspectives makes certain assumptions about the causes of and treatments for particular problems.

DOING *Psychopathology* RESEARCH

■ Researchers interested in psychological abnormality attempt to identify the risk factors and mechanisms of different disorders.

■ Researchers must pay special attention to how well their samples resemble the larger populations to which they wish to generalize. Unambiguous diagnoses are essential in psychopathology research, and an investigator must be sure that his or her research design allows valid inferences.

DIAGNOSIS

■ Diagnosis is the placement of a person into a category according to his or her problems. The American Psychiatric Association's DSM-IV is currently popular as a diagnostic scheme. It describes people's prob-

lems in terms of five areas: acute disorders, underlying personality styles that exacerbate these disorders or create problems in their own right, physical disorders, severity of stressors in the environment, and level of highest functioning in the past.

■ Diagnosis is controversial, and reasons for and against it can be cited.

■ On the positive side, diagnosis can facilitate communication, provide clues about the presumed cause of a disorder, allow educated predictions about the likely outcomes of a disorder, and suggest effective forms of treatment.

■ On the negative side, diagnosis is never theoretically neutral; it presupposes a particular model of abnormality, and this can be limiting. Also, traditional diagnosis assumes discontinuity between abnormality and normality. The reliability of diagnosis is a continuing problem, particularly because diagnostic labels may take on a life of their own and create problems for individuals above and beyond any actual difficulties they had prior to receiving a label.

TYPES OF DISORDERS

■ Anxiety disorders are problems characterized by excessive apprehension and avoidance: phobia, post-traumatic stress disorder, generalized anxiety disorder, panic disorder, and obsessive-compulsive disorder.

■ Somatoform disorders are physical symptoms with no physical cause, such as conversion disorder and hypochondriasis.

■ Dissociative disorders include psychogenic amnesia and multiple personality disorder.

■ Mood disorders are marked by excessive and inappropriate emotions. In depressive disorder, sadness predominates, whereas in bipolar disorder, periods of sadness alternate with periods of elation.

■ Schizophrenia is a thought disorder characterized by delusions, hallucinations, unusual styles of thinking, and deteriorated functioning.

■ Finally, personality disorders are pervasive styles of behaving that exacerbate other types of disorders while creating problems in their own right.

■ In each case, a biopsychosocial perspective provides the most useful explanation.

Psychological Disorders in a Biopsychosocial Context

■ This chapter focused on biological and psychological influences on disorders, but abnormality must be located as well in its cultural context.

■ Cross-cultural psychopathology is the field that compares and contrasts disorders across cultures.

■ Some psychological problems, called culture-bound syndromes, exist only in specific cultural settings.

Key Terms

Therapy

Among the most familiar roles of a psychologist is helping individuals to solve their problems. Within this role, however, we find considerable diversity. Indeed, there is no such thing as generic psychological help. When psychologists work as therapists, they draw on specific theories like those discussed in the preceding chapters. These theories influence therapists by determining goals for therapy, techniques to be used to reach those goals, and judgments as to whether those goals have been met (Peterson, 1996).

In the preceding chapter, you encountered several approaches to explaining abnormality. These approaches provide the most popular strategies for treating psychological problems. Consider a hypothetical individual, Mr. Johnson, a 31-year-old man with an exceedingly strong interest in betting on horse races. According to DSM-IV, Mr. Johnson has an impulse control disorder (American Psychiatric Association, 1994). He embezzled thousands of dollars from his employer in order to pay gambling debts. He was caught, charged, and convicted. However, the judge has agreed to suspend his sentence if he will repay his employer and seek therapy.

Mr. Johnson has come to a clinic that allows potential clients to walk in without a prior appointment. He stands in the lobby. There are three doors on which he might knock. Behind each is a therapist.

If Mr. Johnson knocks on the first door, he will find a mental health professional who advocates a biomedical approach to psychopathology.

Although no antigambling drug is available, this does not mean that biomedical treatment has nothing to offer. Mr. Johnson's difficulties may stem from an undiagnosed problem, such as bipolar disorder, that is biologically predisposed (Chapter 13). Gambling might be one of the reckless activities characterizing a manic episode. Assuming that other signs of bipolar disorder are present, perhaps lithium will be prescribed.

Or maybe Mr. Johnson has an underlying anxiety disorder. Gambling allows him to feel better because it distracts him. The problem is that he runs up large debts in these attempts, and he gives himself even more cause to feel anxious. The therapist might be able to help Mr. Johnson by giving him medications that reduce his anxiety, thus removing his impulse to gamble.

Some of you might not be satisfied that Mr. Johnson's problem can be solved so simply. Biomedical treatments help in the short run, but can we assume he will not gamble in the future? What else is going on in his life that has made gambling attractive? What about his job and his family? These are all legitimate questions, and they illustrate how theories define the goal of therapy.

Suppose Mr. Johnson knocks on the second door. Behind this door is a therapist with a psychodynamic point of view. Her treatment plan and goal are different: Mr. Johnson would benefit from a long-term alteration of his personality. Personality from this perspective means the unique combination of the processes and structures stressed by Freud and his followers (Chapter 12). People like Mr. Johnson have problems because their psychic energy is tied up in symptoms. To cure an individual, therefore, is to free up this energy for better use.

How would the psychodynamic therapist react to Mr. Johnson? She would want to understand the conflicts that led him to gamble in the first place. She would use free association and dream interpretation. Then she would try to remove these conflicts. This process might take years.

How reasonable is such an approach to treatment? Mr. Johnson is ruining his life, gambling away money he does not have, and the therapist wants to talk about his dreams and early memories? What if incarceration takes place before insight? These questions stem from a different theoretical view of psychological problems and their best solutions.

Let us suppose that Mr. Johnson knocks instead on the door of the third therapist, who takes a cognitive-behavioral approach and thus believes abnormality is the result of faulty learning. This therapist would want to know exactly what Mr. Johnson does when he gambles. He would try to specify the prevailing rewards and punishments that make these behaviors more likely than others—reading a book, planting a garden, or baking cookies. Perhaps Mr. Johnson learned long ago that gambling is exciting. Perhaps the local racetrack is the only place where he feels happy. At home and at work, perhaps everybody criticizes him. Given the rest of Mr. Johnson's life, gambling is an attractive alternative, despite the grief it brings in its wake.

The cognitive-behavioral therapist might arrange matters so that Mr. Johnson's betting is punished and his nonbetting rewarded. He might ask his client to put up a $100 deposit. If he bets more than $2 per race, the deposit will be donated to some local organization that Mr. Johnson dislikes. That is punishing. At the same time, he tells Mr. Johnson to join a backpacking club that stays away from racetracks and instead takes vigorous hikes every weekend. That is rewarding—I think.

Some of you might find this form of therapy superficial, treating the symptoms of a problem but not its source. Maybe betting on horses is, for Mr. Johnson, a relatively harmless reaction to his real problems. If this outlet is closed, who knows what will happen to him?

UNDERSTANDING THERAPY: DEFINITION AND EXPLANATION

The subject of this chapter is **therapy:** the treatment by mental health professionals of psychological disorders. People in a variety of roles work as therapists (see Table 14.1). So, clinical and counseling psychologists are trained in psychology and undertake therapy from a psychological perspective. Psychiatrists are trained in medicine and often take a biomedical approach. In the contemporary United States, clinical social workers, who are broadly trained in social sciences, including psychology, provide more hours of therapy than any other type of professional. Although many therapists fit the common stereotype—carrying out therapy as one-on-one interaction between an expert and a person with a problem—this approach is just one of the forms that therapy takes.

■ **therapy**
treatment of psychological disorders by mental health professionals

General Approaches to Therapy

Therapy is colored by theory, as we saw in the hypothetical case of Mr. Johnson. Depending on their view of the nature of problems, therapists take different approaches to treatment. **Biomedical therapies** treat problems by intervening biologically—for example, with drugs or surgery. **Psychological therapies,** also known as **psychotherapies,** treat problems with psychological means. Examples, as you just saw, include

■ **biomedical therapies**
treatment of problems with biological interventions

■ **psychological therapies; psychotherapies**
treatment of problems with psychological interventions

Table 14.1 Mental Health Professionals	
Professional	**Characterization**
Clinical psychologist	Individual with advanced graduate work in psychology, usually leading to a Ph.D. (Doctor of Philosophy) or Psy.D. (Doctor of Psychology) degree, who provides therapy to people suffering from psychological difficulties
Counseling psychologist	Individual with advanced graduate work in psychology, usually leading to a Ph.D. (Doctor of Philosophy) or Psy.D. (Doctor of Psychology) degree, who helps clients achieve academic, vocational, or personal goals
Psychiatrist	Individual with a medical degree who has completed a residency in a mental health setting
Clinical social worker	Individual with an M.S.W. (Master of Social Work) degree who provides therapy to individuals or groups
Psychoanalyst	Individual with training in a mental health profession (e.g., psychology, psychiatry, or social work) who has additionally received instruction in performing psychoanalytic therapy

There are a variety of approaches to therapy. If you decide to see a therapist, it will be helpful to think about the type of therapy you prefer and to talk to different therapists before making a decision.

psychodynamic therapy and cognitive-behavior therapy. Talking is often an important ingredient in psychotherapy because it can lead to insight into one's problems. Psychological therapies may also involve changing a person's environment or how he or she interacts with others.

Talking therapy is more than just having conversations with people about their problems. Otherwise, bartenders, tax lawyers, cab drivers, and hair stylists would be considered therapists. Unlike others who listen to people talk about their problems, psychotherapists use the facts and theories of general psychology to help individuals with their difficulties. Their approach may involve talking, but the talking has a special character. It follows a deliberate strategy, one the therapist believes will benefit the client.

Few therapists are as single-minded as those in the hypothetical case of Mr. Johnson, but all mental health professionals have rationales for why people have difficulties and for how these problems can best be solved. Many practice what is called **eclectic therapy,** meaning that they draw on a variety of techniques in their work. But eclectic does not mean they have no theories. Indeed, eclectic therapists rely on numerous theories, choosing different approaches and combining them in various ways for different problems (Castonguay & Goldfried, 1994; Fay & Lazarus, 1993; Omer, 1993).

■ **eclectic therapy**
approach to treatment that draws on a variety of techniques

Therapy as Biopsychosocial

When strategies from different therapy traditions are combined, they are often more effective than when used individually, suggesting that the best approach to therapy is biopsychosocial (Klerman et al., 1994). A depressed or anxious individual might be prescribed antidepressant medication and asked to start psychotherapy. A person diagnosed with schizophrenia might receive both drugs and family therapy. The rationale for these therapeutic combinations follows from a biopsychosocial conceptualization of problems. If psychological difficulties result from multiple influences, then their solution should try to target as many of these influences as possible. In an ideal world, our hypothetical Mr. Johnson should consider walking through the doors of all three therapists.

The practical problem in combination treatments is that not all therapists are able to provide every form of treatment. The historical distinctions among mental health professionals explain why. At present, only psychiatrists can prescribe medication, although some clinical psychologists have argued recently that they too should be allowed to do so (Chafetz & Buelow, 1994). In any event, training within a given mental health profession tends to focus on one treatment approach to the relative exclusion of others (Mayne, Norcross, & Sayette, 1994). One way around these problems is for therapists to work within multidisciplinary teams wherein each team member contributes his or her particular expertise.

Why are combined treatments more effective than individual treatments? Klerman and colleagues (1994) suggested several possible mechanisms for the effectiveness of combination therapies:

1. By reducing distress, medications allow the individual to communicate more readily with a psychotherapist.
2. By improving cognitive abilities such as attention, medications allow the individual to make better sense of what transpires in psychotherapy.
3. By uncovering forgotten memories and breaking down defenses, medications encourage insights on the part of the individual that are then used in psychotherapy.
4. By capitalizing on positive expectations about medical interventions, medications promote optimism and perseverance in psychotherapy.
5. There may be less social stigma associated with having a "mental illness" than a "psychological problem," meaning that, for many individuals, medications allow an easier route into psychotherapy.
6. Psychotherapy explains to people why they should comply with medication.
7. Medications bring short-term relief of symptoms, whereas psychotherapy prevents recurrence of problems by imparting new skills and abilities.

Perhaps the most obvious explanation is that different therapies treat different symptoms, and so the more therapies brought to bear, the greater the change in a person's problem. As changes are made in one area of life, these lead to changes elsewhere.

More than one of these explanations can be correct, and their particular mix probably differs from problem to problem, or even from person to person with what looks like the same disorder. Regardless, they suggest the range of possibilities that we need to consider in explaining therapy effectiveness.

This chapter first discusses specific strategies of treatment. Remember that the current trend is to use these strategies in conjunction with one another, and so do not be misled by their separate discussions. The chapter next looks at how researchers have attacked the central question concerning therapy: Does it work? The answer is yes, but this conclusion is relatively recent. Finally, the chapter covers what is known about therapists and clients and the outcome of treatment.

Stop and Think

1 Compare and contrast biomedical therapies and psychotherapies with respect to assumptions about human nature, psychological difficulties, and their solutions.

2 Why would anyone ever have believed that therapy need not be approached in biopsychosocial terms?

SPECIFIC TYPES OF THERAPY

There are many different types of therapy, with the number growing all the time. It is impossible to describe all of the existing therapies in a chapter such as this. What this section does instead is look at the major types of therapy. It starts with biomedical approaches to the treatment of abnormality, particularly the use of drugs. Technically speaking, these are not psychological treatments because they must be administered by a medical doctor, usually a psychiatrist. But psychologists can work in conjunction with psychiatrists in treating clients. Then the section considers psychological therapies: psychoanalysis, cognitive therapy, behavior therapy, family therapy, group therapy, and others.

cathy®   **by Cathy Guisewite**

Biomedical Therapies

Biomedical treatments of abnormality focus on the body, under the assumption that people's problems reflect physical malfunctioning. The most popular biomedical therapies involve the use of drugs, but surgery and shock treatments are also used. These treatments all change physical functioning, presumably in a beneficial way.

Psychosurgery.   Surgery undertaken on the brain in an attempt to treat psychological disorders is called **psychosurgery**. A **lobotomy** is a well-known example. In this operation, fibers connecting parts of the brain are severed, with the goal of helping patients with depression or schizophrenia. In 1935, a Portuguese neurologist named Eges Moniz cut through the top of a mental patient's skull. Moniz then severed the nerve fibers linking the frontal lobes of the brain to the thalamus (Chapter 4). He believed that by destroying the pathway between these two areas, presumably the respective centers of thought and emotion, he would lessen the negative effects of feelings on thinking. The patient not only lived but seemed better off as a result of the operation.

The medical community was greatly excited about this work. For years, psychopathologies such as depression and schizophrenia had resisted treatment. The lobotomy was considered a major medical breakthrough, for which Moniz was awarded the Nobel Prize in 1949 (Valenstein, 1986).

Soon, different physicians devised their own versions of Moniz's brain operation, looking for a better method. Two American doctors, Walter Freeman and James Watts, came up with an alternative in which the surgeon entered the patient's brain not through the top of the skull but through its sides. They administered only local anesthesia for this procedure.

At first, there was little organized criticism of lobotomies in the United States. Skepticism was occasionally expressed, but Freeman and Watts kept positive media attention focused on the operation. They toured the country, giving lectures and performing hundreds of lobotomies at mental hospitals. They also wrote a popular book on the procedure. In 1942, only 300 lobotomies had been performed in the United States. By 1951, the number exceeded 18,000, many performed personally by Freeman or Watts.

In the late 1940s, Freeman broke away from Watts and introduced another refinement: entering the brain through the eye socket, pushing the eyeball aside and using an ice pick to sever brain tissue because standard surgical scalpels proved too fragile and kept breaking off in a patient's brain. He toured the country, demonstrating how to perform his version of a lobotomy.

Widespread criticism of lobotomies began to surface by the mid–1950s, when the medical community realized that there was really no evidence that these operations benefited patients. A close look showed that lobotomies left most patients worse off. Among the serious consequences were apathy, withdrawal, seizures, hyperactivity, impaired learning, and death.

■ **psychosurgery**
treatment of problems with brain surgery

■ **lobotomy**
type of psychosurgery in which fibers connecting parts of the brain are severed; once used to treat depression and schizophrenia

By the 1960s, the operation was no longer performed, and a rather unusual episode in the treatment of psychological abnormality came to an end. However, psychosurgery as a treatment of abnormality is still reasonable in cases where a specific problem in the brain, such as a tumor, produces difficulties (Rappaport, 1992). Psychosurgery is also used for otherwise untreatable epilepsy and severe obsessive-compulsive disorders. The objection to lobotomies is not that they involve surgery but that they were undertaken in cases where no demonstrable problems with brain tissue existed.

Electroconvulsive therapy.   Another biomedical therapy involves briefly passing electric current through the brain of a patient, thereby causing a seizure. This procedure, known as **electroconvulsive therapy (ECT),** effectively treats severe cases of depressive disorder (Benbow, 1991; Sestoft, 1991). ECT is not as barbaric as it sounds. The patient is given a general anesthetic before receiving any shock and a muscle relaxant to prevent injury during the seizure. No pain is experienced. Fatalities are rare, occurring in perhaps 0.003 percent of patients. For comparison, the mortality rate due to antidepressant drugs is several times higher (Henry, Alexander, & Sener, 1995).

■ **electroconvulsive therapy (ECT)** treatment of depression by passing a brief electric current through the brain of a patient and causing a seizure

Why did therapists ever consider ECT as a treatment for depression? It had been observed that patients with schizophrenia who also had epilepsy showed less psychotic behavior following a seizure (Kalinowsky, 1980). This observation suggested that convulsions were beneficial, and so therapists deliberately created them, first with drugs and later with electric current. Through trial and error, researchers learned that people with depression were most likely to be helped by convulsions. Granted this history, it is misleading to refer to ECT as shock therapy because the critical ingredient is the convulsion, not the shock that produces it.

Despite its usefulness for depression, ECT does have drawbacks (Shukla, 1989). Memory loss for events surrounding the course of treatment (usually a dozen shocks over a two-week period) is common. Some researchers also suspect loss of distant memories, although studies are contradictory on this point. What is clear is that when ECT succeeds, it relieves severe depression much more quickly than drugs or talking therapies. For this reason, ECT is often recommended for individuals at immediate risk for suicide, for whom any delay in improvement might prove fatal. Similarly, people in the public eye who become depressed may opt for ECT because it rapidly gets them back into the swing.

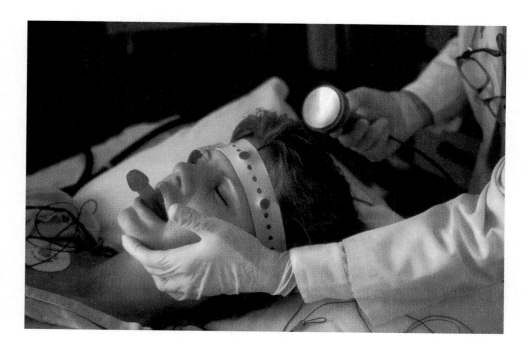

The mechanisms by which electroconvulsive therapy works are unknown, but this treatment is effective for depression.

Why ECT works is unclear. Psychologists have proposed various theories, but none has been widely accepted. Psychodynamic theorists suggested, for instance, that ECT satisfies a depressed patient's wish for punishment. Or perhaps ECT wipes out unpleasant memories. Biomedical theorists have more promising explanations in terms of chemical changes in the brain, but because the effects of shock on the brain are numerous and diffuse, it has so far been impossible to pinpoint just why ECT works (King & Liston, 1990).

Drug therapy.   Chapter 13, which presented the major disorders, mentioned various drugs prescribed by psychiatrists. There are several main categories of drugs that combat psychological problems, each targeting one of the principal types of disorders—for example, anxiety, depression, bipolar disorder, and schizophrenia. Table 14.2 lists the most important of these drugs and the problems they are used to treat. Also noted are the side effects and dangers of each medication.

■ minor tranquilizers
drugs, such as Valium and Librium, used to treat generalized anxiety

Minor tranquilizers include such drugs as Valium and Librium (Hollister, Muller-Oerlinghausen, Rickels, & Shader, 1993; Miller & Gold, 1990). These are among the most frequently prescribed medications in the United States, with more than 70 million prescriptions written each year (Rickels, 1981). The minor tranquilizers reduce anxiety and are particularly effective for people with generalized anxiety disorders who do not also experience panic attacks or have severe phobias (Willerman & Cohen, 1990). The minor tranquilizers work by stimulating GABA activity, which counteracts sympathetic arousal (Chapter 4).

■ antidepressants
drugs, such as tricyclics, MAO-inhibitors, and Prozac, used to treat depression and certain anxiety disorders

Antidepressants are of three types: tricyclics, MAO-inhibitors, and selective serotonin reuptake inhibitors (of which Prozac is the best-known example) (Solomon & Bauer, 1993). All three effectively treat depressive disorder and may prevent or delay subsequent depressive episodes. Antidepressants are also used with success to treat certain cases of panic disorder and obsessive-compulsive disorder. Although the mode of action is somewhat different for each drug, all increase the availability of norepinephrine and/or serotonin (Briley & Moret, 1993). The overall effectiveness of these classes of antidepressant medication is much the same, and MAO-inhibitors are least preferred because they have more side effects.

■ lithium
drug used to treat bipolar disorder

As mentioned in Chapter 13, **lithium** is the typical treatment for bipolar disorder (Thau, Meszaros, & Simhandl, 1993), but it does not constitute a literal cure. Rather, lithium dampens the mood swings that characterize bipolar disorder only as long as the individual continues to take the medication. The mechanism by which lithium works is not known, but it presumably affects the neurotransmitters responsible for mood swings.

■ major tranquilizers; neuroleptics
drugs, such as Thorazine and Haldol, used to treat schizophrenia

Major tranquilizers (also called **neuroleptics**) constitute a family of drugs used to treat schizophrenia (Blanchard & Neale, 1992; Marder, Wirshing, & Van Putten, 1991). Examples include Thorazine and Haldol. Like lithium, the major tranquilizers are not a cure. They help control the flagrant symptoms of schizophrenia as long as the individual takes them. Neuroleptics work by affecting the availability of the neurotransmit-

Table 14.2   Summary: Psychiatric Medications

Drug	Disorder(s) used to treat	Side effects
Minor tranquilizers	Generalized anxiety disorder	Drowsiness; lightheadedness; depression; abuse
Antidepressants	Unipolar disorder; obsessive-compulsive disorder; panic disorder	Drowsiness; dizziness; low blood pressure
Lithium	Bipolar disorder	Thirst; skin irritation; liver and kidney damage
Major tranquilizers	Schizophrenia	Movement disorders; dry mouth; weight gain; depression; constipation

Neuroleptics are used to help control the symptoms of schizophrenia. These photos show a young man with this disorder. On the left, he is unmedicated and appears highly agitated. On the right, he has taken antipsychotic medication.

ter dopamine in the brain. They have severe side effects, and compliance on the part of patients can be a constant problem.

The use of drugs to treat psychological problems has aroused sharp debate both in and out of the mental health professions. The evidence for the effectiveness of the drugs listed in Table 14.2 cannot be denied. Medications can and do help people with psychological disorders, and it is shortsighted to categorically dismiss the use of drugs in the treatment of abnormality. However, these drugs rarely hold the entire answer to an individual's problem. They invariably treat symptoms as opposed to curing problems. Although sometimes symptom relief is all one desires, at other times these antidotes encourage people to turn their backs on the real source of their difficulties. Some people become addicted to psychiatric medication, particularly the minor tranquilizers. They start with one problem and end up with two or more.

Drug therapy has undesirable side effects, but high blood pressure medicine, cold tablets, and antibiotics can also create undesirable consequences. In this sense, there are no miracle drugs, and a physician's decision to prescribe medication is always a compromise, in which it is hoped that the benefits will outweigh the costs.

Other biomedical treatments.   Our bodies can be affected by more than just drugs, ECT, and surgery. Biomedically oriented therapists have left few procedures untried in their attempt to bring relief to people with problems. In the 1800s, patients were spun around, blindfolded, hosed with water, and physically immobilized. These therapies were thought to correct whatever was wrong with the body, and hence they qualify as biomedical treatments.

More contemporary treatments with the same rationale include quite a variety of procedures:

- The induction of comas
- Forced sleep via drugs, such as barbiturates
- Sleep deprivation
- Deep muscle massage
- Purification of blood by hemodialysis
- Inhalation of carbon dioxide
- Acupuncture
- Macrobiotic diets
- Vitamin supplements

Two contemporary biomedical treatments are intriguing. The first is aerobic exercise. Researchers have found that a program of running or dancing decreases depression (McCann & Holmes, 1984). Physical exertion increases norepinephrine and serotonin activity, which in turn elevates mood. However, research may eventually show that this apparently biological treatment also works through psychological mechanisms. For example, perhaps people who exercise develop a sense of mastery by sticking to a program (Chapter 7). They might experience an enhanced sense of self-efficacy that then decreases their depression (Chapter 13).

A second contemporary biomedical treatment uses light. Seasonal affective disorder refers to recurrent episodes of depression that worsen in the fall and improve in the spring. In a pioneering study, Rosenthal and colleagues (1984) advertised in the *Washington Post* for people whose mood swings showed this pattern and found 29 individuals who consented to be studied. The amount of sunlight experienced was important because if these persons traveled north or south (from Washington), their moods respectively became more or less depressed.

Rosenthal and his colleagues then treated 11 of these individuals by exposing them to bright white light (three hours in the morning and three hours in the afternoon). The individuals improved in most cases, experiencing a relapse when the lights were removed. Theorists explain the effectiveness of this treatment by proposing that light stimulates melatonin (a hormone) that in turn affects biological rhythms that in turn elevate mood (Hill, 1992; Kasper, 1994).

Individual Talking Therapies

As mentioned earlier, many psychotherapies involve talking to an individual about his or her problems. The goal of such talking is to encourage insight into the causes of one's behavior and/or how it can be changed. Psychoanalysis is the grandparent of all psychotherapies that depend on talking. Even when subsequent therapies have embraced a drastically different rationale from that of psychoanalysis, many of their specific procedures have evolved from the strategies that Sigmund Freud and his followers developed. This section therefore begins with **psychoanalytic therapy.**

Psychoanalysis.   Psychoanalysts define successful therapy as treatment that frees a person's psychic energy from symptoms so that it can be used more productively elsewhere. The goal of psychoanalytic therapy is to identify repressed conflicts that tie up this energy, using several techniques.

One such technique is free association, which involves the patient saying whatever comes to mind, without attempting to censor it. The train of associations can lead to areas of unconscious conflict (Chapter 12). The client must observe the "fundamental rule" of free association and report everything that comes to mind. During free association, the client may recline on a couch while the therapist sits out of direct sight so as not to interfere with the process. The client talks, and the analyst interjects interpretive comments only occasionally. Interpretations are valid to the degree that they trigger a change in the client.

For example, an anxious client might enter psychoanalysis believing that his problems revolve around stress at work. But all of his free associations lead back to conflicts with his family. When the psychoanalyst eventually points this out to the client, the individual may experience a sudden realization that he has displaced what really upsets him. Because his parents were frequently absent during his childhood, he unconsciously fears that his wife and children will similarly abandon him. This fear takes the form of worrying about his performance at work, where in actuality things are fine. With his new insight, the client can perhaps start to confront his fears of abandonment.

Another technique is dream interpretation, in which the patient describes dreams, free associates to their surface content, and works with the therapist to interpret their underlying meaning and significance. Remember the discussion of Freud's interpreta-

■ **psychoanalytic therapy**
approach to psychotherapy developed by Freud that attempts to free a person's psychic energy from symptoms

tion of a dream in Chapter 6. How might this interpretation be used in psychoanalytic therapy with the dreamer?

The psychoanalyst also uses analysis of transference. With this technique, the therapist interprets the thoughts and feelings the client has about therapy as similar to thoughts and feelings about previous relationships, often from childhood. For example, the client might expect the therapist to be harsh and judgmental, just as her father was. Again, the goal for the client is to gain insight, this time by seeing how feelings about a past relationship have been transferred to the present relationship with the therapist.

Accompanying all of these techniques is **resistance** on the part of the client, an unwillingness to accept what the techniques reveal about areas of conflict. Patients do not easily relinquish their problems, especially those that involve impulses to use drugs, to overeat, and to gamble.

■ **resistance**
unwillingness on the part of a client to accept what therapy reveals about areas of conflict

What actually happens in psychoanalysis? The popular stereotype involves a bearded fellow tossing out interpretations to a dazzled client. The truth is that the psychoanalyst listens more than he or she talks. The only way that unconscious material can be made conscious is if clients unearth it for themselves. Accordingly, the major task of the analyst is to encourage this process.

Luborsky (1984) identified three active ingredients in psychoanalytic therapy, all of which have been incorporated into the other talking therapies. First is self-understanding. Different therapists define understanding in various ways, but all agree that clients must come to see the reasons for their actions. Next is the establishment of a good working relationship between the therapist and the client. Third is a recognition that backsliding can occur following successful therapy. Psychoanalysts try to combat this problem by explicitly discussing with their clients the significance of therapy termination and the anxiety it arouses.

When Freud developed psychoanalytic therapy, he recommended it for intelligent people at least 50 years of age who functioned relatively well in the world. Therapy sessions lasted one hour each and occurred six days a week, for at least six months and perhaps for several years. Freud likened psychoanalysis to a chess game. Both have stages: a beginning, a middle, and an end. There is an ultimate goal throughout, but the means to this end differ across the stages.

This photo shows Freud's office where he saw his patients. Note the famous couch.

In its contemporary versions, psychoanalysis is used with a wider range of clients, although it is still far from suitable for all. Therapy takes place from two to four times a week; the psychoanalytic hour has now shrunk to 45 minutes. The process continues to take a long time, usually two to five years.

Who benefits most from psychoanalysis? Although research does not provide a good answer, Luborsky and Spence (1978) tentatively concluded that psychoanalysis is best indicated for well-educated people who experience strong anxiety but no severe problems in living. Circumscribed anxiety disorders, such as specific phobia, can be treated effectively in ways other than with psychoanalytic therapy, and so psychoanalysis is probably best reserved for people with diffuse fears or worries, who can afford the time and money psychoanalysis requires.

Psychoanalysis has a secure place in the history of clinical psychology, but an ever decreasing number of individuals undertake training to be psychoanalysts. Fewer people with problems seek out this form of treatment, and insurance companies are less willing to pay for it. What has been responsible for this waning of interest? For one thing, the effectiveness of psychoanalysis has not been firmly established, particularly in comparison with more contemporary therapies. In addition, these newer therapies are almost always quicker and less expensive than psychoanalysis.

Psychodynamic therapy.   Although classic psychoanalysis as created and practiced by Freud has declined in popularity, so-called **psychodynamic therapy** is still popular (Henry, Strupp, Schacht, & Gaston, 1994). Psychodynamic therapy refers to a grouping of approaches that share with psychoanalysis the premise that a client's problems are caused by unconscious conflicts and distortions in thinking about the self and others. Many psychodynamic therapists follow the lead of the neo-Freudians and other theorists who downplay Freud's emphases on psychic energy and libido and emphasize instead the social nature of disorders (Chapter 12).

Psychodynamic therapy takes various forms, but in general it is briefer than classic psychoanalysis. Clients meet with therapists once or twice a week for several months. There is a more pragmatic, here-and-now emphasis. Different techniques might be used, including those of classic psychoanalysis but not limited to them (Eagle & Wolitzky, 1994). So, therapists may be more directive; they may assign tasks to clients to be completed outside of the therapy session; and they may meet with couples or families. Psychodynamic therapy maintains the psychoanalytic concerns with insight and transference.

The effectiveness of brief psychodynamic treatment has been more extensively investigated than the effectiveness of psychoanalysis, although not always with clients whose problems seem best suited for psychodynamic therapy (Henry et al., 1994). Regardless, the evidence points to at least modest success of these approaches for individuals with a variety of disorders (Crits-Christoph, 1992; Svartberg & Stiles, 1992).

Client-centered therapy.   One of the first alternatives to psychoanalytic therapy was developed by Carl Rogers (1942, 1951), whose personality theory was discussed in Chapter 12. Rogers believed that people develop problems when their experience is at odds with their awareness. Conditional regard from other people produces these discrepancies, which in turn produce psychological problems. According to Rogers, the solution is to reverse the process and create a benign environment for the person: a place where her inherent drive toward self-actualization can operate without restriction.

This assumption is the premise of **client-centered therapy** (also called **person-centered therapy**). The therapist creates a therapeutic atmosphere with several techniques (Prochaska, 1984; Rowan, 1992), including:

■ a nondirective stance, which allows the client to devise her own solutions to problems

■ a good therapeutic relationship characterized by sincerity and concern

---

■ **psychodynamic therapy**
approach to psychotherapy based on the assumption that problems are caused by unconscious conflicts and distortions in thinking

■ **client-centered therapy; person-centered therapy**
approach to psychotherapy developed by Rogers that provides clients with unconditional positive regard

Client-centered therapists attempt to create a therapeutic atmosphere that is nonjudgmental and characterized by unconditional positive regard.

■ accurate empathic understanding of the client's inner world
■ unconditional positive regard: acceptance of the client as a person with worth and dignity

Under these circumstances, clients come to think more highly of themselves, and their problems are resolved.

Therapists often reflect back to the client's thoughts and feelings:

Client: I feel discouraged about life these days.
Therapist: It sounds like things have been rough.
Client: Yeah . . . work is a drag, and all my wife and I do is fight. When I wake up in the morning, the only thing I look forward to during the whole day is going to sleep again that night.
Therapist: And that's the way you feel now.

It is easy to caricature client-centered therapy as simple agreement with whatever a client says, but to do so is unfair. All of us know the difference between people who actively listen and try to understand our experience and those who nod their heads while their thoughts are elsewhere.

Client-centered therapy may take the form of one-on-one therapy, conducted once a week for months, or it may be a single marathon session with a large number of people. Rogers (1970) pioneered encounter groups, which bring together groups of people in conflict, such as labor and management, blacks and whites, students and teachers, or Protestants and Catholics, under conditions where they can understand each other better. These groups sometimes lead to confrontation, but they are thought to be worthwhile because interchanges between participants are open and honest.

Client-centered therapy effectively promotes change for many people with problems (Freeman, 1993; Greenberg, Elliott, & Lietar, 1994; Owen, 1990). However, this kind of treatment is probably not helpful for those whose problems are solidly based in a grim reality rather than in their perceptions. A person without a job or a home has a problem that involves more than just a discrepancy between experience and awareness. In such a case, we would be better off trying to change the person's reality. Also, client-centered therapy is probably not helpful for those who would benefit from specific suggestions about how to behave (Shilling, 1984). Mr. Johnson, for example, whose story introduced this chapter, might best be helped by an approach that is more directive than client-centered therapy.

Rational-emotive therapy.   Another alternative to psychoanalysis is **rational-emotive therapy,** created by the psychologist Albert Ellis (1962). Rational-emotive therapy is a thoroughly cognitive approach to people and their problems. According to Ellis, the manner in which people think about things can be the source of their problems. People who entertain irrational beliefs often become anxious or depressed. Consider the following:

■ I *must* do well at everything I try.
■ I *must* be loved and respected by everyone I know.
■ I *must* be completely happy all the time.
■ I *must* get my way with other people.

Ellis called this tendency "musturbation" and argued that rigid beliefs provide a poor road map for navigating the world.

In rational-emotive therapy, the therapist helps the client identify irrational beliefs and then actively disputes them. Therapy is therefore quite directive. On the face of it, the therapist seems argumentative when he or she challenges the client, but the arguments occur in the context of an accepting relationship. The therapist disputes beliefs, not the client:

> Client: I feel discouraged about life these days.
> Therapist: It sounds like you think no one should be discouraged.
> Client: Well, being discouraged is a drag. I can't stand it.
> Therapist: I'd agree that discouragement is no fun, but don't confuse your wants with your needs. Why do you say you can't stand discouragement? You've survived pretty well so far.
> Client: But when I wake up in the morning, the only thing I look forward to during the whole day is going to sleep that night!
> Therapist: Do you really mean that?

Rational-emotive therapy helps people with anxiety disorders (Engels, Garnefski, & Diekstra, 1993), although disagreement exists as to whether disputation is the critical ingredient of this treatment (Shilling, 1984). Rational-emotive therapy might work because therapists care about their clients—not because they disagree with their beliefs (Patterson, 1986).

Cognitive therapy.   A final individual therapy, **cognitive therapy,** was developed by the psychiatrist Aaron Beck (1976; Beck & Emery, 1985; Beck, Rush, Shaw, & Emery, 1979). Cognitive therapy is highly similar to rational-emotive therapy, as just described. The cognitive therapist tries to change particular thoughts, under the assumption that if one can modify people's thinking, it will reduce their depression and anxiety. Beck described cognitive therapy as collaborative empiricism to emphasize that the therapist and client work together (collaborate) to check the client's beliefs against the facts of the matter (empiricism).

■ **rational-emotive therapy**
approach to psychotherapy developed by Ellis that is based on the assumption that problems are caused by irrational beliefs

■ **cognitive therapy**
approach to psychotherapy developed by Beck that attempts to change the cognitions that cause and maintain anxiety and depression

The first step in cognitive therapy is to identify the client's automatic thoughts, habitual put-downs that flash through the mind in the course of everyday activity. The client begins to pay attention to these thoughts, and not just to the emotional damage they do. He writes them down, along with the feelings they produce. Then he challenges these automatic thoughts by asking what evidence is available for believing them, as in the following example:

I got depressed at work when the boss walked by me without saying hello. My thoughts were that I did a lousy job on my last project, that he was mad at me, and that I was probably going to be fired.

But when I think further about that incident, I guess I can see that my boss was probably preoccupied. His son has been ill. Plus, I've done projects like that before, with good results. And I got a good raise just two months ago.

Cognitive therapy is more complex than this example. Automatic thoughts are not mere errors, like mistaken telephone numbers, that can be readily corrected once you attend to them. Rather, these thoughts are deeply ingrained, and clients therefore challenge them only reluctantly. Cognitive therapists often devise experiments to aid belief change:

You think you're a social loser? Maybe yes, maybe no. Why don't you find out by asking ten different people to have a cup of coffee with you?

Keep track of how many people say yes. And tell me before you start how many people would have to accept your invitation for you not to be a loser.

The therapist must use some common sense in these assignments and not send an accountant off to party with the Hell's Angels. But maladaptive beliefs can be effectively challenged by appropriately chosen experiences.

Cognitive therapy usually involves 10 to 15 weekly sessions. It alleviates depression and anxiety (Hollon & Beck, 1994). It also holds promise for people who suffer from chronic pain, obesity, marital strife, and eating disorders. To date, studies have not identified critical ingredients. According to Beck's explanation of his therapy, therapeutic change should occur in lockstep with cognitive changes, but this hypothesis awaits confirmation (Whisman, 1993).

Behavior Therapy

If people can learn to behave in an abnormal way, then they can learn to behave in a normal way. This rationale underlies the approach known as **behavior therapy**: techniques for helping a client rid himself of undesired habits and replace them with desired ones (Franks, 1984). The psychology of learning suggests specific strategies (Chapter 8).

Classical conditioning procedures are used to change emotional associations to particular stimuli. In systematic desensitization, a person is taught to relax and then to imagine feared objects or situations, starting with mildly upsetting images and moving gradually to images that are quite frightening. Joseph Wolpe developed this classical conditioning therapy in 1958, and since then it has become the treatment of choice for circumscribed fears and phobias, effective 80 percent of the time (Rachman & Wilson, 1980).

Learning theory suggests that phobias persist because people flee from the objects they fear, thereby reducing anxiety and reinforcing their avoidance (Chapter 8). What happens if people do not flee? Presumably, they learn that the snake, the bug, or the social interaction does not bring them harm. Their fear extinguishes.

Another classical conditioning treatment for anxiety disorders is called flooding. An individual with agoraphobia, for instance, may be taken to a shopping center and not allowed to leave. The first hour is frightening, sometimes unpleasantly so, but eventually the individual's fear subsides. Flooding brings relief to as many as 75 percent of individuals with phobias, and the benefits remain years later (Emmelkamp & Kuipers, 1979).

■ **behavior therapy**
therapy techniques based on the psychology of learning

In systematic desensitization, a fearful individual is taught to relax while imagining the feared object or situation. In some versions of this behavior therapy, the individual actually confronts what is feared, but usually systematic desensitization is done in thought alone.

However, flooding involves a potential hazard. If a client flees from the anxiety-provoking situation before anxiety has had time to dissipate, his or her escape response will be reinforced. Then, the individual will be even less likely to confront the situation in the future.

Operant conditioning procedures that change a person's behavior by manipulating its consequences also fall within behavior therapy. Bad habits can be eliminated by punishing particular behaviors. Good habits can be increased by reinforcement. This approach intervenes in the person's environment. The therapist changes the rules of the game (the prevailing pattern of punishments and rewards), thereby modifying the client's behavior.

Consider aversion therapy, in which an aversive stimulus is associated with an undesirable behavior, in the hope that the client will learn to link the behavior with its new consequences and thereby stop doing it. For example, alcohol might be mixed with a drug that produces nausea. Or someone with an objectionable sexual impulse—such as one that involves children—might have an inappropriate sexual response followed by shock.

For another example of an operant approach to therapy, consider a child who never shares with other children, never follows his or her parent's suggestions, never does homework, and never walks the dog. For an explanation of these actions, a behavior therapist would look not to the child but to the child's environment. Perhaps the parents unintentionally reward those behaviors that so upset them by paying attention to their child when he or she acts negatively. When the child happens to behave, once in a blue moon, the parents ignore the child, or even worse, heap on unpleasant demands.

One solution is parent training: teaching the parents how to respond to their child (Kazdin, 1994). Parents learn to reward the child for behaviors they wish to increase and not to reward the child for behaviors they wish to decrease. This may strike you as obvious. Are there really any parents out there who do not know they can catch more flies with honey than with vinegar? There are thousands if not millions of such parents. Just go to a crowded shopping mall some weekend and watch how parents respond to their children.

Behavior therapists also use techniques derived from Albert Bandura's (1986) notion of observational learning. Problems can be solved by having clients watch models, either on film or in person, who successfully cope with whatever overwhelms them. Fears and phobias can be effectively eliminated this way. For example, consider people's fears about surgery. If shown a film of a patient who goes through a surgical procedure without fear, a person experiences less apprehension about doing so him- or herself (King, Hamilton, & Murphy, 1983).

A considerable mythology surrounds behavior therapy. First, some believe that behavior therapy is an all-powerful strategy for making anyone do anything the behavior therapist wishes. This view is inaccurate. Behavior therapy has its share of failures, particularly as a treatment for substance abuse (Miller, 1983). Second, some believe that behavior therapy does not work at all. This conclusion too is inaccurate (Emmelkamp, 1994; Sweet & Loizeaux, 1991). Third, some believe that behavior therapy is dehumanizing. Perhaps the brief descriptions of the procedures in books like this one are responsible for this misconception. Out of context, the techniques might seem cold and mechanical. But behavior therapists are not technicians. They are first and foremost therapists—which means that they use their strategies within a therapeutic relationship.

Couples, Family, and Group Therapies

DSM-IV assumes that problems exist within a person. But this assumption is not always reasonable. Some problems are found in the relationships between and among people. In these cases, therapy cannot proceed simply by treating the parts of the relationship. Instead, the relationship itself must become the client (Alexander, Holtzworth-Munroe, & Jameson, 1994).

In **couples therapy,** the client is the cohabiting couple (Dunn & Schwebel, 1995; Lebow & Gurman, 1995). One of the goals of couples therapy is for partners to learn how to solve their problems together. Deciding who is right or wrong in squabbles is often counterproductive, and so one common strategy is to teach the couple how to fight fairly. Rather than each telling the other what a wretched human being he or she is, the emphasis is on learning to specify what about the other person's behavior is so annoying and how it can be changed.

There are three types of couples therapy (Sundberg, Taplin, & Tyler, 1983). With developmental approaches, partners are urged to see that their relationship evolves. What was comfortable at one stage in a relationship may be awkward at another. For example, many marriages break up soon after the honeymoon ends because the couple does not appreciate that honeymoons do end. With communications approaches to couples therapy, partners are helped both to send and to receive messages more skillfully. Too many couples believe they can read each other's minds, but they never test this assumption by asking each other about things. Finally, with behavioral approaches, the therapist has the partners make their contract with each other explicit and specific. What does each want from the other, and what is each willing to give in return? This strategy may sound crass, but it is preferable to strife and an eventual breakup. Still,

■ **couples therapy**
approach to psychotherapy that treats the cohabiting couple

The premise of couples therapy and family therapy is that individual problems are regarded and treated as an expression of interpersonal difficulties.

couples therapy does not always save relationships. Sometimes the explicit goal is to dissolve a relationship in the least damaging way.

In **family therapy,** the client is the entire family: parents, children, and anyone else sharing the same roof with them (Avis & Sprenkle, 1990). The rationale underlying family therapy is that what look like individual problems are really manifestations of disturbed family relationships. One member of a family, often a child, is frequently called the identified patient because he or she shows psychopathology most obviously, but the cause is not within this individual.

Suppose a child becomes a problem at school after several years of model behavior. A family therapist would look for recent changes within the family. Maybe Mom and Dad are contemplating divorce. Maybe a grandparent has moved into the house, and the child now has to share a bedroom with a younger sibling. Family therapy is usually explained from the vantage point of **systems theory,** which regards families as complex wholes. Changes in one part affect all other parts.

The goal of family therapy is to encourage healthier interactions among family members. To this end, family therapists use exercises to reveal to the family their modes of relating. For instance, a therapist might ask family members to switch places and act out each other's roles. Or family members might be encouraged to exaggerate the things they do to annoy each other. Once insights are gained, the therapist can try to bring about change.

Group therapy shares the same rationale as couples therapy and family therapy: Problems are best conceived and treated in a social context (Ferencik, 1992; VanderVoort & Fuhriman, 1991). However, in this form of treatment, the therapy group is composed of individuals who do not know each other prior to treatment. Usually the members of a group have similar problems (e.g., schizophrenia) or life transitions (e.g., divorce).

Group therapy helps people in a number of ways (Yalom, 1995):

- By instilling hope in the members
- By letting them know they are not the only ones with problems
- By allowing members to help one another
- By developing social skills
- By seeing the impact one has on others
- By creating bonds with a group

The group therapist tries to facilitate changes by leading group discussions. Comments on the group process (the patterns of interaction rather than its content) are important: "Does everyone notice how you gang up on James?" The hope in group therapy is that participants will gain insights into how they relate to one another and will then use these insights in other areas of life to create better relationships.

Community Psychology

As a rule, therapy is conservative: It tries to fit the person to the world, not vice versa. There is an exception to this generalization: **community psychology.** Some therapists do not wait for people to develop problems before trying to help. Instead, they try to avoid problems by changing the larger community (Bloom, 1984). If they can eliminate or minimize the preconditions for disorders, then they can reduce the prevalence of psychological problems (Blair, 1992).

Community psychology takes as its role model the field of public health, which combats disease with prevention instead of antibiotics. What is the psychological equivalent of draining swamps? We can identify several. In prevention, community psychologists try to undo or minimize possible causes of problems before they can have an impact. For example, Head Start programs give youngsters from low-income families an educational boost prior to first grade, in the hope of staving off the problems that occur later in life when schooling goes wrong (Chapter 11). Public service announcements about how AIDS can be spread is another example of prevention (Chapter 16).

■ family therapy
approach to psychotherapy that treats the entire family

■ systems theory
theoretical approach of many family therapists, who assume that families are complex wholes in which changes in one part affect all other parts

■ group therapy
approach to psychotherapy that treats groups of people with similar problems or challenges

■ community psychology
approach that attempts to change social conditions in order to eliminate or minimize the causes of disorders

Community psychologists do not wait for problems to develop before trying to help. They try to head off problems in the first place—for instance, by providing information about substance abuse to the general public.

In consultation, community psychologists make their expertise available to community groups. For instance, they may give lectures on depression and suicide to community groups; they may be interviewed for magazines or newspapers; or they may be hired by businesses to give advice on the treatment or prevention of problems, such as drug and alcohol use among workers.

In rehabilitation, community psychologists help people who have been institutionalized make a smooth transition back to everyday life. This is a particular problem for individuals leaving psychiatric hospitals. Many homeless individuals in our large cities are former psychiatric patients who have not fared well since leaving hospitals.

In social advocacy, community psychologists enter into the political process, urging passage of legislation that will benefit the psychological well-being of citizens. Psychologists throughout the years have taken stances in support of desegregation, gun control, aid to dependent children, and mandatory seat belts in automobiles. The line between psychology and society is nowhere more fuzzy than in the work of community psychologists.

The effectiveness of community psychology is not clear. It is fair to say that there is less enthusiasm about community psychology today than several decades ago (Peterson, 1996). There are two possible reasons. Perhaps too few of society's resources have so far been invested in community psychology projects, thereby decreasing the chance for their success. Or perhaps certain problems are inevitable and cannot be prevented or minimized, regardless of the effort made.

Feminist Therapy

New approaches to treatment and prevention appear with regularity, and one of the most notable in recent decades is **feminist therapy,** an intervention informed by feminist philosophy (Enns, 1993). According to this perspective, the psychological problems women experience can be understood only in terms of the positions women occupy in society. Women do not have the same political and economic power that men do, and our society is structured in such a way that this gender-based hierarchy maintains itself.

Feminist therapists believe that traditional mental health approaches contribute to the societal status quo. Women's problems are often regarded as characteristics of individual women and not of the social and historical forces that have shaped them. Physical and sexual abuse of women is not seen as a societal issue. Women who conform too

■ **feminist therapy**
approach to psychotherapy informed by feminist philosophy

much or too little to society's gender-role prescriptions run the risk of being diagnosed as abnormal. According to many theories, women are to blame for the psychological problems of their children (Surrey, 1990).

Feminist therapy arose in the 1970s out of the experience of women in consciousness-raising groups. As women gave voice to their criticisms of societal institutions, psychotherapy became an easy target. In an influential critique, Chesler (1972) argued that psychotherapy involved the bending of the client's will to that of the therapist. The majority of clients were women, and the majority of therapists were men, and so psychotherapy was one more example of women's subordination to men. Some believed women should not participate at all in traditional psychotherapy but instead rely on self-help groups (Tennov, 1973). Others argued that therapy could be refashioned to benefit women, and from their efforts came feminist therapy (Enns, 1993). What changes were needed? Most importantly, therapy should not place the therapist above the client in status or privilege (Gilbert, 1980). Its goal should be to empower the client, not bring her into line.

A feminist approach has often been incorporated into existing strategies of psychotherapy (Enns, 1993). Although many of Freud's pronouncements are at odds with feminist thought, some feminist therapists have been able to work within the psychodynamic tradition (Chodorow, 1989). Feminist therapists have also been attracted to family systems approaches (Goldner, 1985), expanding the basic premises to apply to families in which abuse occurs, as well as to nontraditional families (Goodrich, Rampage, Ellman, & Halstead, 1988).

Feminist therapy has been influential in challenging long-held assumptions in the mental health professions. The possibility of gender bias in diagnosis is now recognized by many. More profoundly, the possibility that our very conceptions of normality and abnormality involve assumptions based on gender is also being considered. For example, Brown (1992) has suggested that the post-traumatic stress disorder that follows assault or abuse be relabeled as a normal reaction to these events and treated accordingly (Chapter 13).

Although feminist therapy can be criticized for being political in nature (Lazerson, 1992), this criticism seems unfair. A political underpinning guides its practitioners, but the same is true for any approach to treatment. Indeed, feminist therapy can be praised for making its political assumptions explicit.

Stop and Think

3   What is psychosurgery?

4   What is meant by "Drugs can treat but not cure bipolar disorder and schizophrenia"?

5   Compare and contrast client-centered therapy and psychoanalysis.

6   Compare and contrast cognitive therapy and psychoanalysis.

7   What is behavior therapy?

8   Feminist therapy often uses strategies from other approaches to therapy. Which other approaches are most sensibly combined with feminist therapy?

DOING *Therapy Outcome* RESEARCH

■ **outcome research**
investigation of the effectiveness of therapy

As you learned about the different approaches to treatment, you might have wondered what therapies work best. If you are a skeptic, you might even have wondered if therapies work at all. The attempt to study the effectiveness of therapy is called **outcome research.** This section covers the history of outcome research (see Figure 14.1).

When Freud and others first began using psychological methods to treat problems, it was obvious when therapy was effective. The first psychotherapy patients were hyster-

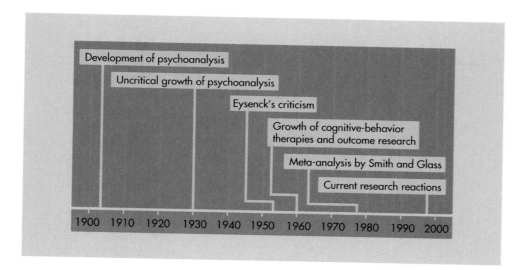

Figure 14.1
History of Therapy Outcome Research. The effectiveness of psychotherapy was at first unquestioned. Skepticism surfaced in the 1950s but has since been laid to rest by the results of outcome research. We now know that therapy is effective, and researchers have turned their attention to more specific questions.

ics, with bizarre alterations in physical functioning. Many were women who experienced sudden paralysis or losses of vision or hearing. Following a psychological intervention such as hypnosis or free association, their symptoms often vanished. There was little ambiguity about the cure because both the therapist and the patient observed a change that was sudden, dramatic, and unlikely to have occurred without the intervention. The evidence was too compelling to question whether therapy worked.

As psychoanalysts began to treat an ever greater number and variety of patients, and as other forms of psychotherapy appeared, the issue of effectiveness still did not arise. Therapists and patients continued to believe that beneficial change took place. Note, though, that the factors originally compelling a belief in therapy effectiveness fell away with the rise and spread of psychotherapy. Patients were typically "neurotic"—defined not by overt symptoms but by presumed underlying processes (Chapter 12). How can we tell that change occurs if symptoms are not critical? Further, change for most patients is gradual. And therapy may take years, during which many events could happen that might better explain any change that occurs, such as marriage, the birth of a child, or a new job.

Eysenck: Therapy Is Ineffective

The popularity of psychotherapy combined with the lack of hard evidence of its effectiveness almost demanded that somebody stick a pin into the therapy balloon. The psychologist Hans Eysenck wielded the pin. In 1952, he published a criticism of the entire business of psychotherapy. Does therapy work? Typically, the question was answered by pointing to an improvement in the patient's condition over the course of therapy. Eysenck argued, reasonably, that the results of particular case studies do not fully answer the question because a person may well have improved without the therapist's intervention—so-called spontaneous remission.

The more useful comparison is therefore between those who receive therapy and those who do not. You will recognize this as the simplest form of an experiment, where therapy (or not) is the independent variable and patient improvement is the dependent variable.

Eysenck did not conduct his own study. Instead, he assembled data from different investigations. From five studies of the effect of psychoanalytic therapy, he calculated an average figure of 44 percent of neurotic patients showing improvement (as judged by their therapist). Nineteen studies of eclectic therapy yielded a 64 percent average of neurotic patients showing improvement (again, as judged by their therapist). Next Eysenck needed to know how many people with problems similar to those of therapy

"OF COURSE I'VE BECOME MORE MATURE SINCE YOU STARTED TREATING ME. YOU'VE BEEN AT IT SINCE I WAS FOURTEEN YEARS OLD."

clients improved without therapy. He chose two such comparison groups: (a) the proportion of patients with anxiety or depressive disorders discharged from state mental hospitals because they improved (even though they received only minimal care and no therapy) and (b) the proportion of individuals who filed disability claims for psychological reasons with insurance companies and then returned to work within a two-year period. In both cases, the figure was 72 percent, exceeding the improvement rate for psychotherapy.

Although he pointed out that further research would be a good idea, Eysenck (1952, pp. 322–323) drew some strong conclusions from his comparisons:

These data . . . fail to prove that psychotherapy, Freudian or otherwise, facilitates the recovery of neurotic patients. They show that roughly two-thirds of a group of neurotic patients will recover or improve to a marked extent within about two years of the onset of their illness, whether they are treated by means of psychotherapy or not. . . . These results and conclusions will no doubt contradict the strong feeling of usefulness and therapeutic success which many psychiatrists and clinical psychologists hold. While it is true that subjective feelings of this type have no place in science, they are likely to prevent an easy acceptance of the general argument presented here.

These are very strong words for a professional article.

Eysenck's challenge demanded attention. It failed to convince all readers because his data were not as compelling as he thought them to be. Patients were not randomly assigned to receive therapy or not, and unknown factors may have confounded his comparisons. Further, different criteria were used to determine improvement: therapist judgment on the one hand and hospital discharge or returning to work on the other. Nevertheless, his conclusions reminded psychologists that proof of their work was not readily available.

Difficulties in Evaluating Therapy

Eysenck highlighted the problem of spontaneous remission (benefit without intervention), but other problems also make it difficult to decide whether therapy works. For instance, what criterion of improvement should be used? As you saw earlier in this chapter, psychologists with allegiance to the different models think of therapeutic change in different ways, making it difficult to compare across types of therapy.

A related issue is the operationalization of improvement that the researcher chooses. Early studies of therapy effectiveness relied almost exclusively on the therapist's judgment about the matter. You can see why this operationalization is less than ideal. Therapists are not immune to the human tendency to present oneself in a positive light.

Asking the client about the effectiveness of therapy may be somewhat more objective than asking the therapist, but again the skeptic would be unconvinced that this is a rigorous measure. Clients, just like therapists, strongly wish to believe that treatment has been worthwhile.

Outcome research is plagued by heterogeneity of clients. To the degree that clients receiving therapy are different from one another, extraneous variables cloud conclusions. The same can be said about heterogeneity of therapists. To the degree that therapists take drastically different approaches with their clients, still other confounds enter the picture. Indeed, not all therapists who endorse a given approach deliver that form of therapy (Fiedler, 1950, 1951).

Next is the problem posed by placebo cures. In medicine, a placebo is a drug that benefits a person not because of its inherent chemical properties but because the individual expects to feel better. In psychotherapy, therefore, a placebo cure is one brought about by expectations on the part of the client, and not because the therapist did anything that was specifically helpful. Presumably, such benefits in therapy are short-lived, but they confound any attempt to evaluate the effectiveness of therapy.

A large number of individuals who start out in therapy drop out before it is finished. This attrition also makes research difficult. Imagine 60 percent of the white rats in a learning experiment deciding that running a maze is a poor use of their time. How much confidence would we have in the data yielded by those who remain? Those who drop out of therapy are not a random group of clients. Perhaps the clients who stay in therapy are those who are improving the most. All we gain by studying these people is the ability to offer the circular conclusion that therapy is beneficial for clients who improve. Or perhaps the clients who stay in therapy have enough money to afford treatment and hence also have access to other means of solving their difficulties.

Yet another problem in doing research on the effects of psychotherapy is relapse: problems returning after a period of time. For instance, people with substance use disorders, anxiety, or depression may solve their problems in the course of therapy, only to encounter the same difficulty some months or years later. Was therapy a success or a failure for these individuals? A simple answer eludes us because we need to know the time period involved and the circumstances surrounding the return of the problem. Regardless, many researchers try to follow therapy clients not only through therapy but for months or even years beyond.

One last problem worth noting is that of the appropriate comparison group in therapy research. You can easily imagine the ideal comparison. We start with individuals, each having the exact same problem. We randomly divide them into two groups. One group receives therapy, and the other group does not. But it is hard to get people to stand still and stay in such a comparison group, particularly if they have a serious problem and particularly if therapy (for the other research subjects) takes months or years. Random assignment also raises ethical questions about withholding treatment. One cannot imagine, for instance, telling suicidal individuals that they cannot be treated because they need to be in a control group.

By now, you may be thinking that the effectiveness of therapy is impossible to determine. But that conclusion is far from the consensus. In the decades since Eysenck's

(1952) attack on therapy effectiveness, researchers have devised reasonable solutions to these difficulties (Lambert & Bergin, 1994). The solutions are not foolproof, but as sophisticated consumers of psychology research, you know that no field of psychology has perfect research methods.

Trends Making Outcome Research Possible

Here are some recent trends that made it possible to have better studies of therapy effectiveness:

■ Behavioral therapies became increasingly popular and so did their reliance on observable behaviors as a criterion for change. For example, a person with agoraphobia is improved to the degree that he or she goes to crowded stores. This trend made the dependent variable in outcome research easier to measure.

■ Similarly, there was a trend to use hard measures of improvement, such as observation of actual behaviors, as opposed to soft measures, such as therapist or client opinions. For example, the effectiveness of therapy for specific phobias is measured by asking the client to touch a snake, a lizard, or whatever. This trend made the dependent variable in outcome research more valid.

■ Time limits were set on therapy—often, 10 or 15 weekly sessions. This trend made it easier to conclude that therapy—as opposed to intervening events occurring over years—is critical in producing change.

■ Individuals on a waiting list to receive therapy were used as the comparison group: "Well, Mrs. Jones, your child will start therapy in two months; in the meantime, we'd like to ask her some questions." This trend allowed a more satisfactory control group than those used by Eysenck.

■ Particularly stringent criteria for including subjects in studies, called research diagnoses, were used, ensuring that subjects receiving therapy were homogeneous with respect to their problem (Chapter 13). For instance, subjects included in a study of therapy for depression should unambiguously be depressed and also have no other disorder.

■ There was growing use of therapy manuals, explicit descriptions of what a therapist should do in given sessions (Luborsky & DeRubeis, 1984). This trend meant that all clients receive the same intervention.

■ Attention comparison groups were used, made up of individuals who meet with a professional to discuss problems but are not given active therapy. This trend began to control for placebo effects by creating a comparison group of individuals who are provided with positive expectations yet no therapy.

■ There was greater acceptance of analogue research: studying people with circumscribed and specific problems (e.g., test anxiety). It is recognized that these problems are not as profound as those of most individuals in therapy, but they are thought to resemble them in relevant ways (Chapter 13). This trend allowed outcome research to be conducted more efficiently because therapy need not last as long as it would for individuals with severe problems, and because similar subjects not in therapy are easier to obtain for a comparison group.

An exemplary investigation of the effectiveness of therapy was Gordon Paul's (1966) study of the treatment of public speaking anxiety. Paul used an analogue approach, obtaining research subjects from public speaking classes at the University of Illinois, classes that at the time were required of all new students. Anxiety about giving speeches in front of others is not by itself a DSM-IV disorder, although it is a possible symptom of several disorders—notably, social phobia.

Of the 710 students enrolled in these classes, Paul chose the 96 who were most anxious about speaking in public (and were willing to participate and were not in therapy elsewhere). Anxiety was ascertained by responses to a questionnaire that all public speaking students completed. The questionnaire posed questions such as the following (pp. 107–108):

Gordon Paul's exemplary investigation of therapy outcome used college students who were afraid of public speaking.

true false   1.   I am in constant fear of forgetting my speech.

true false   2.   My thoughts become confused and jumbled when I speak before an audience.

true false   3.   I always avoid speaking in public if possible.

Once chosen for the research, and prior to therapy, the subjects completed a practice speech that allowed Paul to obtain a number of objective measures of their anxiety about speaking, including their pulse rate and degree of perspiration right before they began speaking. During the speech, four observers independently tallied the presence or absence of such behavioral manifestations of anxiety as pacing, swaying, grimacing, knees trembling, throat clearing, voice quivering, and stammering.

Then the subjects were randomly assigned to one of five conditions (see Figure 14.2). Group 1 received insight-oriented psychotherapy, meaning that it encouraged individuals to understand why they experienced anxiety about speaking in public.

Group 2 was treated with systematic desensitization. They were taught to relax, and while in a relaxed state, they were encouraged to imagine speaking in public. Classical conditioning provides the rationale for this technique because the person learns to associate speaking not with anxiety but with relaxation (Chapter 8).

Group 3 received an attention placebo. They met with a therapist who gave them a "fast-acting tranquilizer" (really made of baking soda) that supposedly would build their tolerance for stress. To prove the effectiveness of this tranquilizer, these subjects participated in the supposedly stressful task of detecting sonar signals from an audiotape. The task was actually not at all stressful. It usually produces drowsiness. So, Paul encouraged subjects to expect some kind of benefit.

Five experienced therapists administered the respective treatments to individual subjects in these three groups. Having the same therapists deliver different therapies cancels out confounds otherwise introduced if the given therapists are assigned to only one condition. In each case, the therapists were told that a reduction in anxiety symptoms was their goal. They spent five hours with each client over a six-week period. The therapy sessions were tape-recorded to ensure that the required form of therapy was undertaken.

The two other groups in Paul's experiment were a no-treatment classroom control, made up of individuals who were just like the subjects in the therapy conditions but did

Figure 14.2
Design of Paul's Experiment.
Gordon Paul's investigation of
how public speaking anxiety
could be effectively treated was a
pioneering demonstration of
outcome research.

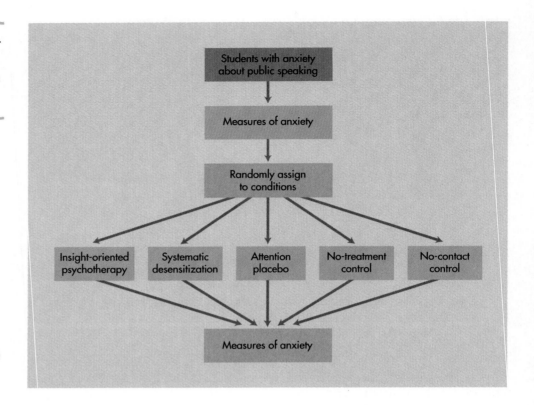

not receive individual therapy, and a no-contact classroom control, made up of individuals who scored anxious on the original questionnaire but were never contacted about participating in the research. These subjects did not give the practice speech. Paul needed these comparison groups to see if subjects experienced a reduction in anxiety without therapy or anything resembling it.

Once the therapy sessions were over, all subjects completed questionnaires measuring their speaking anxiety. Subjects in the treatment groups gave another practice speech, as did those in the no-treatment classroom control. The physiological measures were again taken, and observers again tallied manifestations of anxiety during speeches.

Paul's results were clear and impressive. In terms of the questionnaire measures as well as the behavioral observations, subjects in all the treatment groups improved relative to the control subjects. Anxiety was reduced, and the conclusion follows that therapy works. Those in the systematic desensitization group improved most of all and were the only subjects who showed a reduction in the physiological measures. Ratings by therapists and clients corroborated these findings. Perhaps soft measures of therapy effectiveness are useful after all. Finally, the benefits of therapy were still present when the subjects were tested two years later (Paul, 1967).

Smith and Glass: Therapy Is Effective

Paul's study showed how therapy effectiveness can be investigated. Researchers followed this example, and in the subsequent decades hundreds of similar investigations were conducted. In 1977, a crucial review of this literature was reported by Mary Smith and Gene Glass. They surveyed 375 separate studies of therapy outcome, representing 25,000-plus subjects. The sheer magnitude of the research summarized is not why this literature review is noteworthy. Instead, Smith and Glass (1977) solved a problem faced by all who try to summarize separate investigations: What do you say when some studies point to one conclusion, other studies to the opposite conclusion, and still other studies to no conclusion at all?

Smith and Glass provided an answer by using the statistical technique of **meta-analysis.** This procedure takes the results of separate experimental studies and combines them to yield an overall estimate of the magnitude of an experimental effect (in this case, therapy). Specifically, they used meta-analysis to answer two questions. First, is therapy more effective than no therapy? Second, are some forms of therapy more effective than others?

> The results . . . demonstrate the beneficial effects of counseling and psychotherapy. Despite volumes devoted to the theoretical differences among different schools of psychotherapy, the results of research demonstrate negligible differences in the effects produced by different therapy types. Unconditional judgments of superiority of one type of therapy or another, and all that these claims imply about treatment and training policy, are unjustified. (Smith & Glass, 1977, p. 760)

In other words, therapy works—but all forms work with the same effectiveness. The typical person who is in therapy has a better outcome than 80 percent of individuals with the same problem who are not in therapy (see Figure 14.3).

This conclusion is good news to the consumer looking for therapy but is confusing to therapists committed to a given approach. Researchers are currently taking a more detailed look at psychotherapy (Peterson, 1996). Granted that skepticism concerning therapy effectiveness has been laid to rest (Lipsey & Wilson, 1993), investigators are asking more specific questions:

- What is common to different forms of successful therapy?
- Can specific ingredients that are responsible for change be isolated?
- Is it possible to match particular therapies to particular problems (see Table 14.3)?
- How can long-term relapse be prevented?

Therapists hope that answers to these questions will allow them to devise and conduct forms of psychotherapy that are even more effective.

■ **meta-analysis**
statistical technique that takes the results of separate experimental studies and combines them to yield an overall estimate of an experimental effect

Stop and Think

9 What is a placebo effect?

10 Why is meta-analysis important in the history of outcome research?

11 What treatments are best used with what psychological problems?

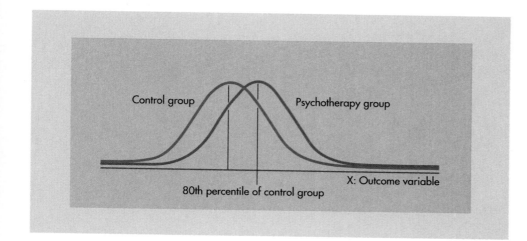

Control group   Psychotherapy group

X: Outcome variable

80th percentile of control group

**Figure 14.3
Effectiveness of
Psychotherapy.** The typical individual who is in psychotherapy has a better outcome than 80 percent of individuals who have the same problem but are not in psychotherapy. *Source:*Smith, M. L., Glass, G. V., & Miller, T. I. (1980). *The benefits of psychotherapy.* Baltimore: Johns Hopkins University Press, p. 88.

Table 14.3   Matching Treatments and Psychological Disorders

Here are treatments believed to be effective for various psychological disorders discussed in Chapter 13 and elsewhere.

Psychological disorder	Effective treatment
Phobia	Behavior therapy (exposure)
Post-traumatic stress disorder	Behavior therapy (exposure); social support
Generalized anxiety disorder	Minor tranquilizers; rational-emotive therapy; cognitive therapy
Panic disorder	Behavior therapy (exposure); cognitive therapy
Obsessive-compulsive disorder	Behavior therapy (exposure); antidepressants
Obesity	Behavior therapy
Anorexia	Behavior therapy; family therapy
Bulimia	Behavior therapy; treatments for depressive disorder (see below)
Depressive disorder	Antidepressants; psychodynamic therapy; cognitive therapy; behavior therapy (social skills training)
Bipolar disorder	Lithium
Schizophrenia	Major tranquilizers
Mental retardation	Specific educational interventions

THERAPISTS AND CLIENTS

The effectiveness of therapy is clear, but this is a generalization. Therapy works better in some cases than in others. Can we explain why? A great deal of research has attempted to identify the ingredients that make for successful therapy. This section describes what is required of the therapist, the client, and the relationship between the two for therapy to be most effective.

The Therapist

All who comment on therapy remark that part of its effectiveness stems from the therapist's role. Mental health professionals are not simply friends to those with problems. They have a socially sanctioned role as experts on thoughts, feelings, actions, and relationships, and the general public is understandably impressed.

Education versus training.   An important question is how best to prepare somebody to be a therapist. A significant distinction here is between training and education (Eaton, 1980). Training emphasizes imitation, repetition, and discipline, whereas education stresses creativity, initiative, and freedom. Training provides particular skills; education gives the person the ability to acquire new skills. Sketched this way, education is necessarily more valuable than training. The issue becomes controversial, however, when we focus on specifics. Perhaps an educational program is too permissive, and what passes for creativity is just a lack of uniform standards. Emphasis on education overlooks the fact that therapists need to know particular things.

Paul Meehl (1977, pp. 278–280), a noted clinical psychologist, related the following story, a conversation between himself and a student therapist:

Meehl: You look kind of low today.
Student: Well, I should be—one of my therapy cases blew his brains out over the weekend. . . .
Meehl: Did you see this man when he first came into the hospital?

Student: Yes . . . he was very depressed at that time.

Meehl: Well, was he psychotically depressed?

Student: I don't know. . . .

Meehl: Tell me some of the ways he was "very depressed" at the time he came into the hospital.

Student: He was mute.

Meehl: If he was literally mute . . . then you have the diagnosis right away . . . psychotic depression.

Student: I guess I didn't know that.

Meehl: Why was he sent out on pass?

Student: Well . . . his depression was lifting considerably.

Meehl: . . . When does a patient with psychotic depression have the greatest risk of suicide?

Student: I don't know.

Meehl: Well, what do the textbooks of psychiatry and abnormal psychology say about the time of greatest suicide risk for a patient with psychotic depression?

Student: I don't know.

Meehl: You mean you have never read, or heard in a lecture, or been told by your supervisors, that the time when a psychotically depressed patient is most likely to kill himself is when his depression is lifting?

Student: No, I never heard that.

Meehl: Well you have heard it now. You better read a couple of old books, and maybe next time you will be able to save somebody's life.

This exchange illustrates the importance of the training/education issue. The student therapist was no doubt educated, at least in some sense, but he had not been trained. A therapist must know specifics, and thus training should not be dismissed.

Boards and agencies that give approval to graduate programs in clinical psychology are currently focusing on this issue. So, the American Psychological Association certifies some graduate programs but not others. In recent years, it has certified programs only if they require specific courses: statistics, assessment, psychopathology, therapy, and ethics (Robiner, Arbisi, & Edwall, 1994). Required courses have steadily become more numerous, so much so that little time is left for other graduate school activities. A backlash has therefore occurred at some universities, where faculty members feel that mandated training is smothering education.

Mystique. Considerable mystique surrounds the role of the therapist. Therapists are sometimes seen as possessing mysterious power, able to analyze people with a single glance and devise solutions to all of their problems. In fact, some writers suggest that therapists play the role of shaman or priest in our modern society (Torrey, 1986). We nowadays may hesitate in using words such as *good* and *bad* to describe a person's lifestyle, but we freely substitute terms such as *adjusted* and *maladjusted* or *normal* and *abnormal*—thus giving therapists final judgment on these matters (Chapter 13). Consider that a therapist is a staple guest on a daytime talk show when people talk about how terrible their lives are.

Certainly, therapists have special skills. But is therapy entirely a matter of mystique? One opinion is that the role of the therapist is the most important tool he or she has. To diminish the role would be to diminish the effectiveness of therapy. Some therapists, for instance, deliberately remove all clues of their personal life from their office: no family pictures, no knickknacks, no books. They become quite unlike their clients, and all the more impressive as a result.

Another opinion is that therapists are effective to the degree that they know given strategies for bringing about change. Here the role itself is de-emphasized, with stress falling on a particular medication, technique for resolving disputes, or way to effect an environmental change. The therapist wants to be thought of as an expert in his domain, of course, but he really is like the rest of us in other ways.

Individual therapists place themselves somewhere along the dimension emphasizing mystique on the one hand and technique on the other. Students are drawn to the study of therapy for one of two reasons, either because it allows them to be seen as skilled at human relations—mystique—or because it allows them to apply psychological science—techniques (Kimble, 1984).

Characteristics of the good therapist.   When students are admitted into graduate school in clinical psychology, they are expected to be good students, but no program goes strictly by numerical criteria like grades. Admissions committees additionally try to choose a certain type of person.

Carl Rogers (1951), the humanistic psychologist and founder of client-centered therapy (discussed earlier in this chapter), theorized extensively on the type of person who makes the best therapist: somebody well adjusted, empathic, warm, and supportive. Although these attributes have particular meaning within Rogers's system (Chapter 12), most therapists accept that these characteristics lead to effective therapy. The problem is how to assess them (Chinsky & Rappaport, 1970; Kachele, 1992; Knobel, 1990). Researchers have not been able to map general personality characteristics into the more specific attributes of the effective therapist (Beutler, Machado, & Neufeldt, 1994).

More promising are investigations that directly study specific therapist characteristics chosen on theoretical grounds to be relevant to outcome. For example, Hall and Malony (1983) showed that dominant therapists tended to be ineffective with clients from cultural backgrounds different from their own. Less dominant therapists were effective in these cases, perhaps because they regarded cultural differences with more respect. For another example, Beutler and Consoli (1993) argued that a therapist's flexibility is more important than any static personality trait because the flexible therapist can tailor his or her approach to the specific needs of the client.

Therapist age, gender, experience, and theoretical orientation are not consistently related to the outcome of therapy.

Studies have also looked at how such therapist characteristics as age, experience, gender, ethnicity, and theoretical orientation affect therapy. Ambiguity is invited because these attributes are not handed out randomly in our society. Investigations of age, gender, or race end up as investigations of everything correlated with them—including education and income. Disentangling the confounds is difficult. Most therapists are white and from the middle or upper class, meaning that the full range of people is not well represented among the ranks of therapists.

Nevertheless, consider the conclusions offered by Beutler and colleagues (1994) following their review of the relevant research. Therapist age shows little relation to successful treatment. Therapist experience also shows little relationship to the outcome of therapy, although more experienced therapists are more adept when dealing with severe or complex problems.

What about gender? According to Beutler and colleagues (1994), neither women nor men on average are more effective as therapists. Little evidence indicates that therapy proceeds better when therapists and clients are of the same gender, although the popularity of feminist therapy might lead us to expect this to be the case. However, researchers should continue to look at the role played by therapist gender in light of other studies that suggest male and female therapists receive different training (Nelson & Holloway, 1990). Male therapists, for instance, are taught to be more direct and controlling than female therapists are. How this training plays itself out in psychotherapy is unclear, but remember the study just described, showing that dominant therapists are less effective with certain types of clients.

The effect of therapist ethnicity is also unclear. Abramowitz and Murray (1983) surveyed different summaries of relevant research by different reviewers and concluded that a given reviewer tends to interpret results according to his or her own race. White reviewers minimize the differences in outcome as a function of therapist ethnicity that are sometimes found, whereas nonwhite reviewers place great weight on them. A tentative conclusion is that ethnic similarity is beneficial in the earliest stages of therapy because it can prevent premature termination (Beutler et al., 1994). When a therapist and client are from different ethnic groups and therapy gets off on the wrong foot, the problem is not because of skin color itself but because of insensitivity to differences. Therapists (and clients) must try to be aware of what it means to stand in another's shoes—what Rogers means by empathy (Bernal & Castro, 1994).

Finally, as already mentioned, the theoretical orientation of a therapist (the approach he or she uses) does not relate to therapy outcome across the board. In other

Ethnic similarity between therapist and client is most important early in therapy, where it helps to prevent premature termination due to misunderstandings.

words, there is no best therapy. This conclusion is well accepted by now, and therapists are thus taking a more refined view of their profession, wondering if particular therapies are best suited for particular problems.

Whom does the therapist serve?   Therapists have a complex relationship with society at large. Although many therapists attribute the problems their clients experience to social conditions such as poverty and blocked opportunities, therapy is usually conservative. In many ways, it is the business of helping the individual fit into the world, even if the world is crazy, cruel, or contradictory. Remember the disorders described in Chapter 13: most of them can be located within the individual. Societal problems such as genocide, unemployment, and homelessness are not usually considered psychopathological, despite the suffering and maladaptiveness they involve.

Whom does the therapist serve? On one level, the answer is the client, who should perhaps regard therapy as a consumer product (Seligman, 1995). But few clients directly pay their therapist. Instead, the therapist is reimbursed by an institution (a school or business), a government agency, or an insurance company. So, on another level, the therapist serves society. Recent legislation requires that therapists report suspected cases of child abuse, even if the information is obtained in an apparently confidential conversation between therapist and client (Levine, Anderson, Ferretti, & Steinberg, 1993). Similarly, therapists are required to report specific threats by their clients to harm another individual (Kagle & Kopels, 1994). The therapist must perform a balancing act.

The Client

There are several routes into therapy. People can refer themselves. A teacher, friend, relative, or employer can suggest that they seek help. Or they can be required by a court order to see a therapist (Chapter 17). Different problems dictate the route an individual takes into therapy, or even whether the journey is begun.

One out of every five Americans will seek out therapy at some point in life, but not everyone with a problem turns to a therapist (Kessler and colleagues, 1994). One factor pushing an individual into therapy seems to be demoralization (Garfield, 1994). In other words, a person seeks out therapy because he or she feels helpless in the wake of some problem. Common sense suggests, however, that demoralization in the extreme will keep a person out of therapy.

Another issue is the kind of therapy administered to different clients. Individuals from the lower socioeconomic class tend to receive biomedical treatment, whereas those from the middle and upper classes tend to receive psychological treatment (Garfield, 1994). This pattern has been evident for decades (Hollingshead & Redlich, 1958) and may reflect the different problems experienced by people of different socioeconomic classes. Poverty is associated with increased rates of certain disorders, including schizophrenia (Dohrenwend & Dohrenwend, 1981). Perhaps the disorders of those from the lower class on the one hand and the middle and upper classes on the other differ so that drugs and psychotherapy are, respectively, appropriate treatments. However, social-class differences in disorders are not as pronounced as social-class differences in treatments. Further, we do not always know enough to say whether biomedical or psychological therapy is the preferred approach in a particular case. As already pointed out, biomedical treatment and psychological treatment can be profitably combined.

The data on the relationship between social class and type of treatment might instead show bias in the delivery of services. This finding does not mean intentional prejudice on the part of the individual therapist. Rather, considerations such as the cost of different forms of therapy play an important role. Granted the time required of the therapist, psychological therapy is often much more expensive than biomedical therapy. Combination treatments are even more costly. Therapists do not work for free, and the client's ability to pay for therapy determines what type of treatment is offered.

Ideally, clients continue in therapy until their original problems are solved or at least reduced. In practice, clients dropping out of treatment before satisfactory change is common: Dropout estimates greater than 60 percent are often cited (Taube, Burns, & Kessler, 1984). Who stays in therapy until the end? Again, social class is a strong predictor: Clients from the lower class leave therapy earlier than those from the middle and upper classes (Christensen, Valbak, & Weeke, 1991). Education also predicts continuation: The more educated a client, the longer he or she stays in therapy (Wickizer et al., 1994). Not consistently related to continuation are client sex, age, race, or type of problem.

One factor determining continuation is whether a client's expectations for therapy are being met. A conflict here provides a simple rationale for why lower-class and/or less educated people do not stay in therapy. Their expectations about the procedures and goals of therapy are at odds with those of their therapists, who are typically from the middle or upper class and highly educated. A useful strategy is to precede therapy with a training interview in which a potential client is told exactly what to expect (Orne & Wender, 1968).

Psychologists have also been interested in who improves the most in therapy. Researchers have not isolated specific personality characteristics associated with success, but the acronym YAVIS captures what many believe to be an ideal candidate for therapy: the young, attractive, verbal, intelligent, and successful (Schofield, 1964). People with these attributes have abundant resources, and their problems are apt to be less severe in the first place.

Chapter 13 discussed the importance of placing abnormality in its social context. The same is true of therapy, and the conclusions summarized here reveal as much about our society as they do about the people who seek help for psychological problems. One of the thorny matters in clinical psychology is how best to serve the psychological needs of people from different backgrounds (Sue, Zane, & Young, 1994). Therapists cannot change their social attributes; the best they can do is to become aware of what is typical and valued within different groups (Lopez et al., 1989). This awareness provides a starting point for treatment. At the same time, the therapist must take into account the individual differences that exist within groups.

For instance, Sue and Zane (1987) described the sincere but misguided attempt by a European American therapist to interpret the problems of his Chinese American client in terms of traditional Chinese culture. But neither the client nor any of his relatives in four generations had ever set foot in China. It is necessary to understand the specific client and how he or she sees matters. Ethnicity is a relevant factor but is rarely the whole picture concerning treatment goals and effective strategies for achieving those goals.

The Therapist–Client Relationship

Whatever else therapy might be, it is always a human interaction. Such interactions are not simply the sum of the two (or more) persons involved. Freud was among the first to direct explicit attention to the relationship between the therapist and client. As discussed earlier, **transference** is his term for the tendency of a client to relate to his therapist as he relates to other important individuals in his life, such as a parent or spouse. Working through the transference is an important aspect of psychoanalytic therapy: The person must separate current styles of behaving from past styles. Although occurring within the client, transference reflects the relationship between the client and the therapist.

■ **transference**
tendency of clients to relate to therapists as they have related to other important individuals in their lives

Freud and other psychoanalytic therapists recommended that therapists behave in a neutral way so that transference would readily occur and hence be easy to recognize and resolve (Bornstein, 1993). This recommendation usually means that therapists should set aside their reactions to clients. Therapists allow their clients to project attitudes and feelings from prior relationships. Research shows that successful therapy is accompanied by a resolution of transference issues (Luborsky, Crits-Christoph, & Mellon, 1986).

Another approach to the therapist-client relationship assumes that different therapists excel in different situations. As suggested by interactionist approaches to personality (Chapter 12), therapists with certain personalities might do best when matched

Psychoanalysts attempt to remain unexpressive as their patients speak. This strategy is believed to make transference easier to recognize and resolve.

with certain clients. Research has been guided by the matching model hypothesis: Therapists and clients work best together when they possess the same personality characteristics.

In a relevant study, basic dimensions of personality were determined by factor analysis at the beginning of therapy, for both therapists and their clients (Berzins, 1977). According to the matching model hypothesis, the therapists and clients who were most similar with respect to their underlying factors of personality would embark on the most successful treatment. But at the end of therapy, little evidence was found for the matching hypothesis. If anything, the results suggested that complementary personalities were important. For example, dependent clients fared best with autonomous therapists, whereas autonomous clients improved most with dependent therapists.

Yet another view concerning the relationship between therapist and client focuses on their shared expectations for therapy (Frank, 1978). To the degree that both parties believe therapy will be helpful, it is likely to continue and indeed be helpful (Priebe & Gruyters, 1993; Tryon & Kane, 1990). This **helping alliance** between therapist and client is so important that some theorists propose it as a necessary condition for successful therapy. Regardless of the particular techniques and strategies of a therapist, nothing happens if these are not carried out within an empathic, warm, and genuine relationship between therapist and client (Patterson, 1986).

■ **helping alliance**
expectations shared by a client and a therapist that treatment will be helpful

Stop and Think

12 Think of an example from your education of the distinction between education and training.

13 What is the helping alliance?

14 Why do people in therapy who have the least severe problems often improve the most?

THERAPY IN A BIOPSYCHOSOCIAL CONTEXT

Therapies obviously are diverse. One way to see what they have in common is provided by Jerome Frank (1974), in his book *Persuasion and Healing*. He conducted a cross-cultural and cross-historical survey of different strategies for relieving distress and suffering. He identified four common factors:

- A particular relationship between the healer and the client, in which the client has faith in the healer's competence and desire to help
- A locale for treatment that is designated by society as a place of healing
- A rationale for treatment that includes an explanation of illness and health
- A task or procedure that is prescribed by the rationale

According to Frank's analysis, healing strategies, including psychotherapy, are successful to the degree that they enhance the individual's sense of mastery and reduce his or her alienation from others.

Said another way, the biological and psychological tasks of therapy must be placed in their interpersonal and societal contexts in order to solve problems (see Figure 14.4). We can imagine that some tasks might be more suitable than others for particular problems—although this is not in general what research to date has shown—but no tasks are effective unless used in this larger social context. Change can be brought about by a cascade of different influences, and the more of these that are used, the more likely change is to occur.

Whatever its form, therapy involves a social relationship, and the effectiveness of diverse treatments is strong evidence of the power of social influence. The next chapter begins a discussion of social psychology, which is concerned with how the behavior of people in general is affected by the presence of others. The explicit focus of social psychology is, of course, on the social context in which behavior occurs.

POSTSCRIPT: WHAT CAN A FRIEND DO?

Whenever I teach a psychology course, I am approached by at least one student, who waits after class until just the two of us remain. He or she always starts with "I have a friend . . ." and proceeds to describe a person who is really hurting. Maybe it is a problem with depression or bulimia or alcohol or sexuality. Regardless, the person may or

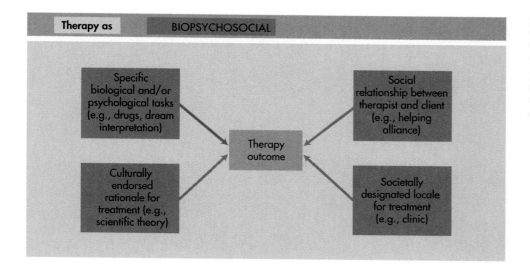

Figure 14.4
Therapy as Biopsychosocial.
The tasks of therapy, whether biological or psychological, are played out within interpersonal and cultural contexts that facilitate a good outcome.

may not acknowledge that anything is wrong, even though the friend who is talking to me is convinced the person needs help.

"What can a friend do?" is ultimately what my students want to know. There are several answers here, and perhaps they will be useful to you if you are ever close to an individual experiencing a serious problem. On the "somebody ought to do something" level (Chapter 13), there is nothing you can legally undertake unless your friend poses an immediate danger to self or others (Chapter 17). No one can be forced to start therapy, and no magic formula makes a person want to be helped.

On the "I want to tell his or her family" level, I urge you to think this through carefully. There may be little that family members can do except get angry or worried. And then your friend will have another problem.

On the "is it OK to talk directly to my friend?" level, I say yes, so long as you talk as a friend does. Say you are worried; say you would like to help; say you are a friend. Do not play diagnostician or therapist. The best thing a friend can do is to be a friend, and that is quite significant.

SUMMARY

UNDERSTANDING THERAPY: DEFINITION AND EXPLANATION

■ Psychotherapists use the facts and theories of psychology to help solve someone's problems in living.

■ Several strategies of therapy exist—for instance, biomedical, psychoanalytic, and cognitive-behavioral—but treatments that combine these strategies are often the most effective.

SPECIFIC TYPES OF THERAPY

■ Biomedical therapies include drugs, electroconvulsive therapy, and psychosurgery.

■ Individual talking therapies include psychoanalysis (developed by Freud) and psychodynamic therapy, client-centered therapy (Rogers), rational-emotive therapy (Ellis), and cognitive therapy (Beck).

■ Behavior therapy uses principles of learning to change an individual's behavior. Particular techniques are based on classical conditioning, operant conditioning, or modeling.

■ Couples therapy, family therapy, and group therapy embody the assumption that problems reside not in the individual but between and among people. Treatment must therefore be social as well.

■ Community psychology tries to change societal conditions to make problems less likely.

■ Feminist therapy approaches treatment by recognizing that power and privilege are often distributed in society according to gender. People's problems must be understood in these terms, and so too must therapy.

DOING *Therapy Outcome* RESEARCH

■ Whether or not therapy works has been the most hotly contested issue in the entire field of clinical psychology. Numerous difficulties confront the researcher who wishes to investigate the effectiveness of therapy.

■ When these difficulties are surmounted, however, the conclusion from research is that therapy is effective.

■ At present, no one form of therapy seems more effective than any other form.

THERAPISTS AND CLIENTS

■ Although a variety of therapies exist, all have in common a person who has a problem (the client) working with another person who is an expert in change (the therapist) to solve that problem.

■ Psychologists have extensively studied therapists, clients, and their working relationships in an attempt to specify the factors that contribute to successful therapy.

■ Therapist characteristics, such as age, experience, gender, ethnicity, and theoretical orientation, for example, bear no consistent relationship to the success of therapy. More important are characteristics such as warmth, empathy, and supportiveness on the part of the therapist; these facilitate effective therapy regardless of the particular approach that is followed.

■ Therapists have a sometimes complex relationship with society as a whole because it is not always clear just who they serve: the individual client or the larger social group.

■ Demoralization in the face of a problem seems to determine who seeks out therapy and who does not. Many people who begin therapy drop out before it is over because their expectations are not being met. Clients who stay in therapy and improve the most tend to be those who have abundant resources and less severe problems in the first place.

■ The relationship between client and therapist is obviously important to the success of therapy. To the degree that client and therapist can form a successful working relationship, therapy is successful.

THERAPY IN A BIOPSYCHOSOCIAL CONTEXT

■ Specific therapies, whether biomedical or psychological, are carried out in a cultural context that recognizes and legitimizes the therapist as healer.

POSTSCRIPT: WHAT CAN A FRIEND DO?

■ If a friend appears to have a psychological problem, the way you can be most helpful is to be a friend.

KEY TERMS

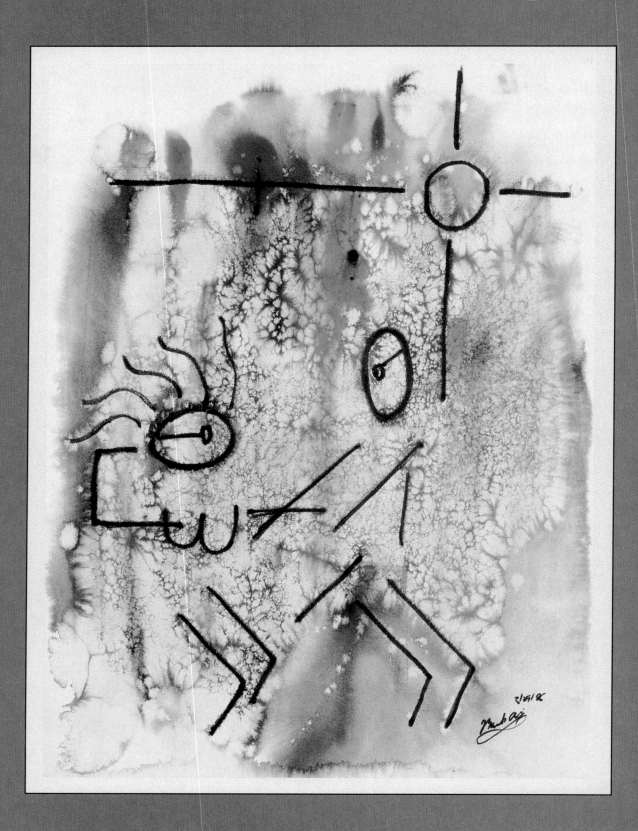

Social Cognition and Social Influence

On March 3, 1991, Rodney King unwillingly participated in one of the most frequently viewed incidents ever captured on film. On that day, King, a black male, was stopped for a traffic violation by Los Angeles police officers. A passerby with a video camera captured the beating to which King was then subjected. Two officers, who were white, repeatedly hit King with their nightsticks for more than two minutes, even after he had fallen to the ground. Another officer, also white, kicked him several times. According to King's testimony later, the officers made racial slurs while beating him. King suffered numerous injuries, among them a broken leg, a shattered cheekbone, and a ruptured eye socket.

The police officers were subsequently charged with using excessive force, and when on April 29, 1992, a jury found them innocent, widescale rioting erupted in Los Angeles, resulting in $1 billion in property damages. Businesses owned by Korean Americans were frequent targets of the mostly black rioters. The riots also produced numerous injuries. For example, Reginald Denny, a white truck driver, was dragged from his vehicle and severely beaten by several black men.

UNDERSTANDING SOCIAL COGNITION AND SOCIAL INFLUENCE: DEFINITION AND EXPLANATION

The field of psychology that is concerned with people as social beings is **social psychology:** "an attempt to understand and explain how the thought, feeling, and behavior of individuals are influenced by the actual,

■ social psychology

field that explains how individuals are influenced by the presence of others

imagined or implied presence of others" (Allport, 1968, p. 3). Social psychology assumes behavior is shaped by a person's relationships with others.

The Rodney King beating and the Los Angeles riots that followed raise many questions about social influence (Fiske, 1994; Lester & Arcuri, 1994). Why were first the police officers and then the rioters so violent? Why did the violence occur across racial lines? Is it significant that both King's beating and the rioting were done by groups of individuals? Why were so many onlookers passive? One notable exception was Gregory Williams, a black man who rescued Reginald Denny from his attackers.

Subsequent interviews with the police officers and those who rioted revealed that their explanations of their actions differed from those of people who simply observed on film what had happened. The police officers, for instance, said that Rodney King appeared to be intoxicated with PCP, and their treatment of him was dictated by the likelihood of violence on his part. Many people who saw the videotape, in contrast, regarded the officers as frightening and aggressive. The rioters explained that their actions were provoked by a miscarriage of justice, whereas people who observed the riots on television saw the rioters as irresponsible. What role do such interpretations play in making sense of social behavior?

Social psychologists describe the Los Angeles riots as behavioral contagion: a particular action sweeping over a group of people. It shows how immediately susceptible individuals can be to the actions of others. Once several people began looting, others followed, until a riot was under way.

Social Cognition Determines Social Influence

■ social cognition

cognitive representations and processes that people use to make sense of the social world

At the same time, social situations do not have an automatic effect on an individual. It is only when the person perceives and interprets social situations that social influence takes place. So, social psychology is a cognitive endeavor (Manis, 1977). **Social cognition** describes people's thoughts and beliefs about others, as well as the processes responsible for those thoughts and beliefs. Social cognition is not of interest to social psychologists in its own right. Rather, our thoughts and beliefs are important because they are critical determinants of how we behave.

■ social influence

ways that people affect the social behavior of one another

Social cognition flows naturally into **social influence:** all the ways people may affect the social behavior of one another. The psychological processes discussed earlier in this book—attention, perception, learning, memory, motivation, and emotion—shape the nature of social cognition and hence social influence. These processes in turn reflect

Although much about the Rodney King beating and its aftermath revealed an ugly side of social influence, Gregory Williams provided an inspiration when he rescued Reginald Denny from rioters who were attacking him.

the biological characteristics of people, meaning that a full explanation of social influence must acknowledge the possible role of the nervous system and evolution in determining what we do and how we do it.

Evolutionary Explanations of Social Behavior

As described in Chapter 3, sociobiology is an attempt to view social influence in evolutionary terms, by pointing to the selection advantage given to our ancestors by certain ways of behaving toward one another. As you will see, many of the topics discussed in this chapter have been given sociobiological interpretations. The best evolutionary explanations of social behavior are those specifying the evolved psychological mechanisms that give rise to behavior in social settings (Buss, 1995). We might propose, for instance, that by virtue of evolution, males are more likely than females to be aggressive. The male hormone testosterone is linked to male aggression in many species (Chapter 7). Although the role of testosterone in human aggression is less clear, there is no escaping the fact that the police officers who beat Rodney King and the vast majority of the Los Angeles rioters were males.

An evolutionary psychologist might propose that violence is apt to be directed against those regarded as belonging to a different social group. The earliest human beings lived in small bands of closely related individuals (Chapter 3). Perhaps evolved psychological mechanisms predispose us to like those in our own group and to dislike those in other groups, to such an extent that violence against them follows (Reynolds, Falger, & Vine, 1987).

The Diversity of Social Settings

In terms of the biopsychosocial perspective used to organize the ideas in this book, social psychology most obviously provides ways of thinking about the interpersonal context of behavior. Social settings include not only the immediate presence of other human beings but also the more general context provided by communities, cultures, and historical eras. These provide people with values and expectations concerning social behavior: the rules of the prevailing social game.

These rules may differ dramatically across time and place. We must be careful not to treat the theories and findings of social psychology—as the field exists in the contemporary United States—as if they were universal (Gergen, 1973). The least controversial social fact across time and place is that people are responsive to others. However, the details of social responsiveness are often dictated by the larger culture.

Stop and Think

1 How is social psychology a cognitive approach to behavior?

2 Assume that social behavior is the result of evolved psychological mechanisms. Are there few or many of these mechanisms?

HISTORY OF SOCIAL PSYCHOLOGY

No introduction to social psychology would be complete without mention of Kurt Lewin (1890–1947), the father of the modern discipline (Marrow, 1977). Lewin was a German Jew who fled to the United States during the rise of Hitler. He brought with him the orientation of a Gestalt psychologist and a keen interest in social problems. Remember from Chapter 1 the emphases that define the Gestalt approach:

■ The idea that psychological phenomena are best described in terms of relationships among elements; these relationships are termed gestalts (meaning in German: whole, pattern, configuration)

Kurt Lewin gave modern social psychology its character by stressing a Gestalt approach and emphasizing the importance of practical research.

■ The assumption that some relationships are more psychologically fundamental than others; these are called good gestalts

■ **field theory**
Lewin's idea that people are self-regulating, dynamic systems

Lewin (1951) phrased his ideas in terms of **field theory:** the notion that people are self-regulating, dynamic systems that seek out balance and harmony within themselves as well as between themselves and the world. In other words, people tend toward good gestalts.

Lewin's theorizing began with the stance that behavior is best understood in terms of the psychological field in which it takes place. He called this field the lifespace, the total of all forces acting on a person at a given time. These forces include internal biological needs as well as external social pressures. Lewin regarded the lifespace as the individual's construction of his or her relationship with the environment. The key term here is *construction,* which means that the lifespace is a psychological reality phrased in cognitive terms. The physical world bears on the psychological world because many of our constructions have a basis in reality. Nevertheless, Lewin urged social psychologists to concern themselves not with stimuli but with people's interpretations of them. Lewin believed that people behave only in terms of how they perceive the world.

Two other aspects of Lewin's approach to social psychology are important. First, he believed that complex social behavior could be brought into the laboratory and studied experimentally (Lewin, Lippett, & White, 1939). Second, Lewin was strongly committed to the use of psychology to address social problems. Science is divided by many into pure and applied research. Pure research addresses questions that are interesting or intriguing to the individual scientist; applied research is practical, concerned with providing useful solutions to pressing needs. Lewin disagreed with this distinction, feeling instead that a particular investigation could serve both theoretical and practical purposes. **Action research** is the explicit attempt to make scientific investigations pertinent to larger social matters, like leadership style, group process, prejudice, aggression, and physical health.

■ **action research**
attempt to make scientific investigations relevant to social issues

Lewin's call for social psychologists to pursue action research has been widely answered in the United States. Many research programs explicitly address current societal needs. Indeed, some of these programs have cohered into discrete fields of applied psychology (Chapter 17).

Stop and Think

3 How would social psychology in the United States be different were its roots in behaviorism? In psychoanalysis?

D OING *Social Psychology* RESEARCH

Like other researchers, social psychologists employ a variety of tactics, many of them already familiar to you from previous chapters. However, two of the major research methods social psychologists use are sufficiently unique that an explicit discussion of them is appropriate: deception experiments and surveys.

Deception Experiments

■ **deception experiment**
experiment in which subjects are misled about its actual purpose

When experimenters mislead their research subjects about the true purpose of their investigation, they are conducting a **deception experiment.** Although many of the experiments done by social psychologists do not use deception, this strategy has nonetheless proved invaluable over the years. Why? The particular topics they study often make it impossible for social psychologists to tell subjects exactly what is going

Social psychologists sometimes deceive research participants about the actual purpose of a study. The intent is to provide more valid results.

on. Consider the phenomena that interest social psychologists: prejudice, altruism, conformity, and obedience. These are obviously value-laden.

Imagine telling a research subject, "This study is concerned with prejudice toward the elderly. We will ask you to observe older people or younger people performing a task. Their performance will be identical, but we will ask you to evaluate how well they do, to see if their age affects your evaluation." Think how this approach would influence the behavior of subjects and limit the generality of conclusions.

So, deception experiments may often be undertaken in social psychology. In active deceptions, subjects are told something incorrect concerning the experiment's purpose or procedures. In passive deceptions, they are told nothing. Regardless, the social psychologist uses deception to avoid influencing the subjects' spontaneous behavior. Deception presumably prevents research participants from being overly mindful while they are being studied.

Deception may also be used for another reason: experimental realism, which exists if the experimental "situation is realistic to the subject, if it involves him, if he is forced to take it seriously, if it has impact on him" (Aronson & Carlsmith, 1969, p. 22). Experimental realism is a virtue of social psychology investigations because it allows a researcher to capture how people behave in everyday social interactions. Paradoxically, deception furthers the goal of experimental realism. Suppose social psychologists want to study how people respond to an emergency. They could ask their research subjects to imagine an emergency and to check off on a questionnaire the responses they would make were it to occur. Or the researchers could arrange things so that smoke pours under the door of the laboratory, alarms and buzzers begin to sound, and people scream. Then they could see what the research subjects do. The first strategy uses no deception, whereas the second strategy is thoroughly misleading. But which is more realistic?

No research approach is foolproof—including deception experiments. This strategy has been debated, on ethical and scientific grounds (Oliansky, 1991). Deception experiments represent an exception to the American Psychological Association's (1992) ethical principle stating that researcher subjects should be informed about what a study requires of them. Institutional review boards carefully scrutinize deception experiments to ensure that deception is not damaging; a full explanation and justification of the deception must be provided to the subject once the experiment is complete (Chapter 2).

Some critics believe that a deception experiment creates a credibility gap between the researcher and the subject (Forward, Canter, & Kirsch, 1976). Although research participants may be deceived about the specific purpose of the study in which they are participating, they are often not deceived that it is a deception experiment. Subjects may be suspicious, perhaps anxious, and even hostile (Weber & Cook, 1972). All of these possibilities complicate and confound the interpretation of results, perhaps to a considerable degree. On the other hand, the vast majority of research subjects who participate in deception experiments do not seem to resent the experience. Indeed, they seem to find it more interesting than participating in nondeception experiments (Smith & Richardson, 1983).

Surveys

■ **survey**
research strategy in which subjects are selected at random from some larger group and asked questions, the answers to which are treated as representative of the larger group

A different approach to social psychology research is a **survey,** in which research subjects are selected at random from some larger group and asked questions—sometimes face to face, sometimes over the phone, sometimes using a written questionnaire (Dillman, 1978). Of interest are the particular answers people give (43 percent of Americans hate to fly) and how these answers relate to other characteristics of the respondents (the more frequently Americans fly, the more they hate to do so). These answers are treated as representations of the sentiments of the larger group.

You are familiar with the famous polls conducted by George Gallup (1972) and others about political preferences. Such polls are strikingly accurate, almost always predicting the outcome of elections. The reason for their accuracy is the care with which respondents are sampled. If people are selected randomly from the larger population—that is, if every person has an equal chance of being selected in the final sample—no more than 1500 individuals are needed to estimate within 3 percent the opinions of the more than 250 million people who live in the United States. Randomization guarantees this. If you stir the soup before you sample it, you can be pretty confident that the spoonful you taste represents the whole pot. Ditto for surveys.

Investigators have used survey methods to understand such topics as marriage, income, sexual behavior, unemployment, and politics. The strength of the survey approach is that researchers can offer conclusions about the thoughts and feelings of people in general, as opposed to those of college students who happen to participate in psychology experiments.

But surveys also have several drawbacks. These include the generic problems with correlational research, notably the inability to discern causes and effects (Chapter 2). Other problems are unique to surveys. Questions can be phrased, intentionally or unintentionally, in ways that influence the resulting answers. This probably explains why surveys undertaken by advocates versus opponents of a social issue, such as gun control, often yield discrepant results.

If representative sampling does not occur, then the whole survey is flawed. The most famous error in survey history occurred in 1948 when Thomas Dewey, the Republican candidate for president, was projected as the winner over Democrat Harry Truman. The problem was that people were polled over the phone and not everyone had a phone. Those who did tended to be well-to-do and to prefer Dewey. The mistake was not with polling, as some may conclude from this example, but with the way the polling was done. Nevertheless, a perfectly representative sample is an ideal that can only be approached. For instance, stop and think about how a sample drawn at random from voter registration lists, street addresses, or telephone books might not accurately represent the larger population of interest (Chapter 2).

Survey researchers are usually limited in the sorts of questions they can ask subjects (Cannell & Kahn, 1969). Time poses one constraint. Respondents will not sit still for an infinite number of questions. Complicated queries cannot be posed, particularly over the telephone. Intimate topics must be avoided. Also, the researcher must remember the tendency for people to present themselves in a desirable light (Chapter 12). This means survey researchers cannot ask loaded questions. If one were to go only by the results of contemporary polls, prejudice has been erased in the United States because so few will admit to it when asked. Needless to say, researchers nowadays need more subtle means than a survey to study prejudice (Sears & Kinder, 1985). Surveys remain valuable, however, for the investigation of topics that subjects are more willing to describe without distortion.

Stop and Think

4   Many of the important studies described in this chapter are deception experiments. How could their topics have been investigated with surveys?

SOCIAL COGNITION

Social psychologists describe the way we come to know about people as **social perception.** Because we also pose the same questions about ourselves, social perception also includes the process of self-knowledge. Social perception is an important aspect of social cognition, and theorists have described it in detail (S. Fiske, 1993; Jones, 1990; Schneider, 1991; Zebrowitz, 1990).

> ■ **social perception**
> process by which people come to know about themselves and others

Remember that social psychologists are concerned with social cognition because it helps explain how people interact with one another. As Susan Fiske (1992) put it, "thinking is for doing," and social cognition can thus be placed in the long-standing American tradition of functionalism (Chapter 1).

For example, men who are sexually aggressive tend to interpret friendliness on the part of women as flirtation even when this was not intended (Malamuth & Brown, 1994). Associated with this interpretive tendency is a suspiciousness of women and a consequent discounting of what women say. To a sexually aggressive man, a woman's no might mean maybe or even yes. You can imagine how this interpretive tendency influences subsequent behavior; the way a man thinks might lead him to harass or assault a woman.

Contents Versus Processes of Social Cognition

Like psychologists who study general cognition, those interested in social cognition often distinguish between the contents and the processes of thought (Chapter 9). Although the contents of social cognition are provided by socialization, some theorists argue that the principles describing its process are inherently part of the nervous system and how it organizes information (Kenrick, Neuberg, Zierk, & Krones, 1994).

For example, consider that social errors like calling a person by the wrong name are similar in Western and Eastern cultures (A. Fiske, 1993). These errors are most common when the misidentified person is of the same gender as the intended individual and when the basic social relationship (e.g., friend, child, or employer) is the same. Errors tend not to occur along lines of age, race, or name similarity. These findings suggest that gender and social role are highly general categories used in thinking about other people, and perhaps they reflect the operation of evolved psychological mechanisms.

General Principles of Social Cognition

Social cognition is usually described as obeying some mixture of three general principles: accuracy, balance, and self-aggrandizement (Krebs & Van Hesteren, 1994). Social cognition can be highly sensitive to the actual characteristics of self and others (accuracy). Sometimes it takes a simplified form, tending toward consistency (balance). And all other things being equal, social thinkers often regard themselves in the most flattering terms (self-aggrandizement). These principles compete with one another in dictating the contents of thought, just as Piaget's notions of assimilation and accommodation do in the course of cognitive development (Chapter 10).

Although accuracy, balance, and self-aggrandizement are critical determinants of social cognition, they are not the sole influences. Social psychology's study of cognition can be criticized for neglecting the emotional aspects of thought (Westen, 1991). This neglect is currently being corrected, as researchers show that an individual's emotional state is an important influence on both the contents and processes of social cognition (Bodenhausen, Sheppard, & Kramer, 1994). For example, angry people are likely to remember the hostile details of social interactions (Allred & Smith, 1991). If they bring these memories to bear on future interactions, they are apt to elicit further hostility on the part of others, setting into operation an ever escalating cycle of anger and hostility. Does this help explain why a veteran police officer might overreact to a potentially threatening individual?

Social Description

We do not think about people in a vacuum. As we learn about an individual's characteristics, we often relate this new information to beliefs we already have. Social psychologists find the notion of a schema useful in explaining how we assimilate new information. Remember that a **schema** is an organized set of beliefs about the world (Chapters 9 and 10). People use the knowledge contained in a schema to go beyond given information.

So, a schema helps us to fill in the blanks of social interaction. Suppose you are told that someone's new friend is a young man who belongs to a fraternity. All at once, you know a great deal about him, as you draw on your fraternity schema to make sense of him. A schema may be accurate or inaccurate in any particular case. Think of the fraternity member and how your schema could be correct in some ways and totally incorrect in other ways. Perhaps we should regard a schema as a theory about the social world (Markus & Zajonc, 1985). Like any theory, it works well in some cases and poorly in others.

Prototypes. Many schemas take the form of typical members of a social group (Cantor, 1980). As you may recall from Chapter 9, these typical examples are called **prototypes.** Consider college professors. What are the central features of this group of people? Many answer this question by listing characteristics like old, tweedy, and male. Now consider the following scenario (Fiske & Taylor, 1984, p. 139):

> A young woman, casually dressed, walked over to the campus bookstore's requisition desk. "I'd like to order the books for a course," she said. The older woman behind the desk said, "The books aren't in for the fall semester." "I know," the first woman replied. "I'd like to *order* the books for the course." "Oh, certainly. Well, what books does the professor want?" asked the other, helpfully. "I *am* the professor," was the frustrated reply.

Accurate or inaccurate, prototypes provide assumptions that we use to navigate the social world.

Stereotypes. A special case of a prototype is a **stereotype,** usually defined as a rigid and overly simple set of beliefs about members of a social group (Lippmann, 1922). We are all familiar with consensual beliefs about Arabs, Jews, lawyers, Presbyterians, feminists, jocks, and so on. Although prototypes can often be useful because of their efficiency (Macrae, Stangor, & Milne, 1994), social psychologists often reserve the term *stereotype* for beliefs that are unjustified and harmful. Like all prototypes, stereotypes

■ **schema**
organized set of beliefs

■ **prototype**
typical example of a concept

■ **stereotype**
rigid and overly simple set of beliefs about members of a social group

affect how we think, feel, and act toward members of social groups. Stereotypes often go hand in hand with prejudice because these beliefs tend to accompany strong feelings (Grant, 1991). By allowing people to fend off contrary evidence, stereotypes provide a ready rationale for prejudiced attitudes: "That's just the way they are, those types of people."

Social Explanation

Social perception also includes social explanation. People's concern with explaining why social events happen is probably universal. Consider this quote from Miyamoto Musashi, a samurai warrior who wrote in 1645:

> When I reached thirty I looked back on my past. The previous victories were not due to my having mastered strategy. Perhaps it was natural ability, or the order of heaven, or that other schools' strategy was inferior. (Weiner, 1986, p. 1)

Now consider this quote from a *Los Angeles Times* sports commentator in 1982:

> Here it is Thanksgiving week, and the Los Angeles Rams are looking like the biggest turkeys in town. Coach Ray Malavasi has eliminated bad luck, biorhythms, and sunspots as the reasons why his football team has lost 9 of its last 10 games. Now he's considering the unthinkable possibilities that: a) he has lousy players or b) they aren't really trying. (Weiner, 1986, p. 1)

We might as well have considered quotes from stories about political campaigns, crimes, accidents, or Hollywood premieres because all of these contain causal explanations. If people separated by thousands of miles, hundreds of years, and myriad cultural differences are equally concerned with the causes of events, then we can suspect that causal explanations are important aspects of social cognition.

■ **causal attribution**
belief about the cause of some
event

■ **attribution theory**
explanation of the role played by
causal attributions in social
behavior

Causal attributions.   A **causal attribution** is a belief about the cause of some event. The term *attribution* makes it clear that a particular explanation may or may not be correct. What matters is that the person regards his or her causal attributions as true and then acts accordingly. The study of attributions has become extremely popular in contemporary social psychology. The attempt to explain the role played by causal attributions in social behavior is called **attribution theory,** of which several versions exist (Shaver, 1975).

The first attribution theory emerged from Fritz Heider's (1958) descriptions of how people explain events—particularly actions by others—in their everyday lives. The judgment that a given action was intentional or not is critical and is often made by deciding whether people's behavior reflects their inner characteristics or the situational demands (Jones & Davis, 1965). In the former case, we speak of internal attributions and regard the behavior as intentional; in the latter case, we speak of external attributions and regard the behavior as unintentional.

Some social psychologists have observed that the internal-external distinction makes most sense in Western cultures that exalt individuality and juxtapose the person and the world (Peterson, 1991). In cultures that emphasize groups—for example, India—causal attributions tend to be phrased in terms of the relationships between people, which include both internal and external factors (Miller, 1984).

A more recent version of attribution theory is Harold Kelley's (1973) account of how people arrive at a particular causal attribution for some event (see Figure 15.1). Kelley's attribution theory prescribes how a reasonable person interested in the truth should think. Kelley suggested that people proceed exactly as a scientist would, by gathering information about how different factors relate to the event in question. To the degree that the presence or absence of a factor is associated with the subsequent occurrence or nonoccurrence of the event, then it is a likely cause.

If you are trying to explain why you performed poorly on a midterm exam, you think of all the factors that might have influenced your performance. You decide that

Attribution theory is concerned with how people answer questions that begin with why. Why did I miss this putt? Why did I bet so much money on this match? And why don't I just throw my golf club into the water and walk away?

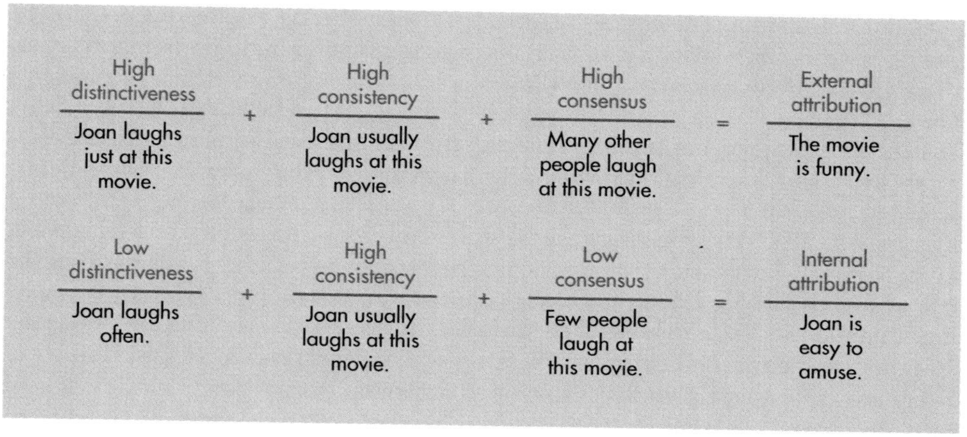

High distinctiveness		High consistency		High consensus		External attribution
Joan laughs just at this movie.	+	Joan usually laughs at this movie.	+	Many other people laugh at this movie.	=	The movie is funny.
Low distinctiveness		High consistency		Low consensus		Internal attribution
Joan laughs often.	+	Joan usually laughs at this movie.	+	Few people laugh at this movie.	=	Joan is easy to amuse.

Figure 15.1
Kelley's Attribution Theory. To explain how we arrive at particular attributions, Harold Kelley suggested that we pay attention to three criteria: distinctiveness, consistency, and consensus. Suppose our friend Joan laughs uproariously at a movie. Is this because of something about Joan (internal attribution) or because of something about the movie (external attribution)? We ask ourselves how distinctive Joan's response is; we ask how consistent it is; and we ask about the consensus shown in other people's responses to the movie. Depending on our answers to these questions, we arrive at the explanation of Joan's laughter that makes the most sense. As this figure shows, a response high in distinctiveness, consistency, and consensus leads us to make an external attribution, and a response low in distinctiveness and consensus but high in consistency leads us to make an internal attribution.

the only factor consistently distinguishing your good performances from your bad performances is the amount of time you devote to reviewing course material. That becomes your causal attribution, and the process is clearly a rational one.

Consequences of attributions.   Causal attributions affect how individuals respond to events. For instance, motivation is influenced by how one explains events (Weiner, 1986). Suppose you get a D− on your midterm examination in Spanish. You might attribute this outcome to a stable characteristic within yourself: "I have no ability at language." Or you might explain your poor grade with an unstable cause: "I didn't study enough." In the latter case, you expect to do better on the final exam and hence prepare for it. In the former case, you expect no change in your performance and you do not bother studying at all.

Our emotional reaction to events is also influenced by how we explain them (Chapter 7). In general, successes make us glad, whereas failures make us sad. But within these overall emotional reactions, attributions shape our particular feelings (Weiner, 1986). To the degree that we explain a success in terms of ability and effort, we feel pride. To the degree that we explain a failure in terms of task difficulty or bad luck, we preserve our self-esteem.

Attributional tendencies.   The tendency to take credit for success but not failure is termed the **self-serving bias.** To call this tendency self-serving is to imply that people are motivated to enhance their self-esteem, but it is possible to explain this bias solely in terms of the information available to a person. When people undertake an activity at which they believe themselves competent, they expect to succeed. When they do succeed, explaining it in terms of their own characteristics makes sense. In contrast, when they fail, they look outside themselves and explain it in terms of external factors. Motivation is not responsible for the difference in how we explain our successes and failures—just the different information to which we pay attention.

■ **self-serving bias**
tendency to take credit for one's success but not failure

Other attributional tendencies exist as well. One pervasive phenomenon in the United States is our tendency to explain other people's actions in terms of their internal characteristics: needs, drives, and traits. "Look at him carrying on over there! *He must not have any inhibitions.*" We overlook the possibility that situational forces may be influencing his behavior. This tendency is called the **fundamental attribution error** (Ross, 1977).

When asked to explain our own behaviors, we more readily refer to environmental demands and influences. "I really carried on! *The music was so loud that it put everyone in a great mood.*" The difference between how we explain our own behaviors versus how we explain the behaviors of other people we observe is called the **actor-observer effect.** It is also widespread in the United States (Jones & Nisbett, 1972). For example, attributions made by employees and managers for employee absenteeism show the expected actor-observer differences (Johns, 1994). Employees excuse their own absences by citing extenuating circumstances, whereas employers interpret the same absences in terms of employee characteristics like laziness. Another example is provided by how the Los Angeles police officers and rioters versus onlookers explained the violent actions that took place.

Social Evaluation

Social perception also includes the evaluation of social behavior. Like other aspects of social cognition, social evaluations influence how we subsequently behave. In making judgments about events in the social world, we base our evaluations on several sets of criteria.

Norms.   One important evaluation recognizes that people enact different roles in their social lives. Each role serves a certain function within some larger group, and part of every role is a set of expectations about appropriate and inappropriate behavior. These expectations are called **norms,** and people typically conform to them. When norms are violated, people find themselves the object of social scorn or worse (DeRidder & Tripathi, 1992).

Norms exist at different levels. Purely local norms are those that describe how you and your roommates believe food in the common refrigerator should be treated. Butter and bread can be used by any and all, regardless of who purchased them. Hot dogs and eggs can mostly be used by everyone, except only the purchaser can take the last one. And so on.

Norms are also held by larger groups. For instance, among psychologists it is almost a universally held belief that clinicians and their clients should not be friends during the course of therapy (Chapter 14). Lawyers, doctors, and tax accountants have different norms about mixing professional and personal relationships; these individuals often do not think twice about befriending those to whom they offer professional services.

Finally, societies as a whole have certain norms. In different nations, for instance, we find different ways of forging business agreements. What is considered direct negotiation in one country may be regarded as rudeness in another. More generally, at least one reason nations come into conflict is that their citizens hold different beliefs about what is appropriate versus inappropriate behavior.

Scripts.   We also judge people according to how they go about acting in social settings. Most social events unfold over time, and usually an accepted sequence of events is to be followed. Schank and Abelson (1977) introduced the term **script** to capture this aspect of social cognition. People believe that there is a right way to order a meal, catch a plane, or ask a favor. For instance, if in a fancy restaurant you begin a meal with dessert, you will attract attention. Indeed, when an individual departs from an accepted script people take special notice (Bower, Black, & Turner, 1979). Those who do not follow scripts run the risk of being judged socially inept, morally wrong, or psychologically abnormal (Chapter 13).

■ **fundamental attribution error**
tendency to overlook the possibility that situational forces influence behavior

■ **actor-observer effect**
tendency to explain one's own behavior in terms of situational forces but others' behavior in terms of internal causes

■ **norms**
expectations about appropriate and inappropriate behavior

■ **script**
accepted sequence of social events that unfold over time

Values. We evaluate not only other people but ourselves. A **value** is an enduring belief that certain personal goals are preferable to others (Rokeach, 1973, 1979). People, of course, differ in their values, with important consequences for their behavior. Social psychologists have found that if they attend to values, it helps them explain how and why people pursue their lives as they do.

■ **value**
belief that certain personal goals are preferable to others

Gordon Allport (1937) proposed one influential catalog of values:

- Religious (seeking to understand the universe as a whole)
- Aesthetic (finding fulfillment in beauty and harmony)
- Theoretical (trying to discover truth)
- Economic (emphasizing those things that are useful and practical)
- Social (treating other people as ends in themselves)
- Political (seeking power, influence, and renown)

Allport also developed a questionnaire to assess the relative importance of these values to a person (Allport, Vernon, & Lindzey, 1960). With this questionnaire, respondents are shown statements that express these different values and are asked to indicate how much they endorse each. Scores on this questionnaire prove to be related to how people choose to pursue their lives. For instance, values assessed in this way predict the course of studies one elects at college and the sorts of jobs one decides to take (Judge & Bretz, 1992).

Although a variety of values is apparent in any given culture, we can still characterize different cultural groups in terms of those that are most widely endorsed (Ellis & Petersen, 1992). For example, fundamentalist Christians in the United States value obedience in their children (Ellison & Sherkat, 1993). They favor more authoritarian approaches to child rearing (Chapter 10), in keeping with their beliefs that human nature is sinful and that sinfulness should be punished.

Members of religious groups that believe in people's inherent sinfulness are more likely to endorse strict obedience by their children.

Is Social Cognition Special?

Critical to understanding social influence is knowing how the social players think about themselves, others, and their relationships. It is worth emphasizing that social cognition is often mindless—that is, automatized and taking place outside of conscious awareness (Chapter 6). When people become mindful of social influence, its impact is often blunted (Langer, 1989).

Is social cognition an example of the more generic phenomena studied by cognitive psychologists (Chapter 9)? Many social psychologists disagree, arguing that social cognition is special because its contents are people and not things (Heider, 1944, 1958):

- People intentionally influence the environment; things do not.
- People think about us; that is, a critical aspect of what we think about others is what they think about us.
- Social stimuli change under our scrutiny.
- Social cognition cannot be judged as accurate (or inaccurate) as readily as we can judge generic cognition.
- People are usually much more complex than things.
- Accordingly, social cognition involves a greater need not just to describe but to explain; both people and teacups may be fragile, but we feel more impelled to explain the fragility of the former than the latter.

At the same time, social cognition cannot be altogether different from cognition in general. Constraints on information processing do not vanish simply because we are thinking about human beings. Regardless of what we think about, we structure our thoughts in certain ways that maximize accuracy, balance, and/or self-aggrandizement. Our attention continues to be drawn to topics that are personally relevant.

Stop and Think

5 What aspects of social cognition would you expect to be the same across different cultures?

6 What is the difference between a prototype and a stereotype?

7 What is attribution theory?

INDIVIDUAL BEHAVIOR IN A GROUP CONTEXT

In light of this discussion of social cognition, let us consider some of the ways in which social influence occurs. In each case, notice the critical role played by the thoughts and beliefs of the people involved. We start with a series of investigations by social psychologists into how and why people in groups often come to think, feel, and act in similar ways. All show the powerful influence of the group on the individual. These studies also raise some disturbing questions about what it means to be so responsive to social influence.

Conformity

■ **conformity**
the changing of one's behavior to be consistent with that of others

Conformity describes people changing their behavior to be consistent with the behavior of others. Conformity was first studied in the laboratory by the social psychologist Muzafer Sherif (1937). He capitalized on the autokinetic effect: a perceptual phenomenon in which a point of light in an otherwise dark room appears to jump around. It is actually our eyeballs that move, but against the black background the light seems to move (Chapter 5).

Sherif recruited several subjects to sit in a dark room and watch a light appear. The subjects were instructed to call out the distance and direction they saw it move. Two inches to the left. Eight inches up. And so on. As this process was repeated, the subjects started to agree with each other about the movement of the light, which in fact was not moving at all. In other words, a norm had been formed. This norm had no basis in reality, yet when subjects came together a year later they still followed it.

The generality of Sherif's findings can be questioned because the experimental situation was genuinely ambiguous. Maybe studies of the autokinetic effect tell us little about conformity in other domains of life. Let us therefore consider a second investigation.

In Solomon Asch's (1956) study, about a half-dozen subjects were seated around a table, all facing one another. The experimenter explained that the study concerned itself with people's ability to make perceptual judgments. The task of each subject, therefore, was to choose the one line from a group of several that matched a standard line. The experimenter showed each set of lines to the group and then asked each subject to say which line matched.

Unlike the task faced by Sherif's subjects, this one had an unambiguously right answer. Now suppose you were one of the subjects in the experiment. All of you were asked to make your judgment aloud. You go in order, and you just happen to be the last subject. You hear each of the other people before you give the same answer: one that seems quite wrong to you.

In actuality, the subjects who preceded the last subject were working with Asch. You do not know that, of course, and when it becomes your turn, what are you going to do? Almost 40 percent of the time, you will go along with what the other people said. This result is striking. But things get even more intriguing. When later interviewed, some of you who conformed seem unaware that you had gone against the evidence provided by your senses.

Subsequent research by Asch showed that conformity increased with the number of preceding people giving incorrect judgments, although a leveling-off point was reached. If at least one person in the group dissented from the majority, conformity on the part of the real research subject decreased dramatically. In other words, although conformity is quite obviously an example of social influence, so too is resistance to conformity.

Social psychologists are not interested in lights and lines for their own sake. Rather, the point of the Sherif and Asch studies is that other people profoundly influence what we do. If we go along with others in situations like these, where there is no explicit pressure to conform, we are no doubt more likely to be swayed in the murkier arenas of life.

Is conformity good or bad? This is too simple a question because conformity can have either negative or positive effects. Obviously, conformity threatens individuality in a society that values independent thinking. But conformity can also be good and useful, as when automobile drivers stay on the same side of the road at the same speed. Regardless of the value we place on conformity, it is a pervasive social process (Larsen, 1990).

Obedience to Authority

■ **obedience**

doing what a person in authority tells one to do

Although conformity and obedience are both examples of social influence, we can readily distinguish between the two. Conformity is behaving like one's peers are behaving, and people typically deny that conformity is behind their actions. In contrast, **obedience** is doing what a person in authority tells one to do. People who obey readily acknowledge the influence that has led to their particular actions: "I just work here." "I'm just following orders." "Those are the rules."

Stanley Milgram's (1963) study of obedience is the epitome of social psychological work. Milgram addressed a pressing social concern—obedience—with a compelling deception experiment. He made it abundantly clear that he intended to shed light on events like the Holocaust:

> It has been reliably estimated that from 1933 to 1945 millions of innocent people were systematically slaughtered on command. Gas chambers were built, death camps were guarded, daily quotas of corpses were produced with the same efficiency as the manufacture of appliances. These inhumane policies may have originated in the mind of a single person, but they could only have been carried out on a massive scale if a very large number of people obeyed orders. (Milgram, 1974, p. 1)

As described in Chapter 2, the major finding of Milgram's study was that when instructed by a researcher to deliver electric shocks to another person, two-thirds of the research subjects obeyed, even when their victim banged on the wall and complained about his heart condition. What makes the study so intriguing is that the two-thirds figure defies common sense. We must conclude that obedience to authority is a much more potent and widespread phenomenon than we might at first believe.

In subsequent investigations, Milgram (1974) systematically varied aspects of the situation to see how the rate of obedience would be affected. These studies flesh out our understanding of obedience and its determinants. Table 15.1 summarizes some of the findings.

In understanding Milgram's results, we must avoid the fundamental attribution error discussed earlier and understand that obedience as he studied it is determined by the social situation, not the personality characteristics of those who obeyed (Drout & Vander, 1993).

But why does obedience occur? Milgram (1974) observed that obedience is a fundamental element of social life. Whenever people come together in an organized group, a chain of command is forged. In many ways, obedience is beneficial. We are relieved, for instance, that restaurants obey laws about cleanliness and that airplane pilots obey commands from the control tower.

Like conformity, obedience is so ingrained that it can readily be harnessed to evil purposes (Mixon, 1989). People who obey enter a psychological state in which they allow an authority figure to define reality for them. They let this figure accept ultimate responsibility for what is occurring. "A substantial proportion of people do what they are told to do, irrespective of the content of the act and without limitations of conscience, so long as they perceive that the command comes from a legitimate authority" (Milgram, 1974, p. 189). Milgram termed the embracing of this psychological state

Table 15.1   Result of Obedience Experiments

Manipulated factor	Effect on obedience
Physical closeness of victim to subject	Reduced
Physical closeness of authority figure to subject	Increased
Salience of injury to victim	No effect
Prestige of university where research was conducted	No effect
Tidiness of laboratory	No effect
Subject being allowed to choose shock levels	Painful shocks not given
Two authority figures in conflict	Reduced
Victim having peer who rebels	Reduced
Subject designated "assistant" to authority figure	Increased

Source: Milgram (1974).

during obedience the agentic shift, meaning that the person ceases to be an agent in charge of initiating his or her own actions. The authority figure is accorded the power to do so.

The Loss of Self: Deindividuation and Person–Role Merger

Yet another way in which other people influence how we behave is shown in the phenomenon of **deindividuation:** when a person finds himself submerged in a group and feels anonymous (Diener, 1977). As a result of deindividuation, inner restraints are relaxed (Festinger, Pepitone, & Newcomb, 1952). People become alienated from one another and may perpetrate outrages. Cross-cultural investigations find that warriors who costume themselves for battle, thereby achieving anonymity, are more aggressive than those who do not do so (Watson, 1973). Further, research in the United States finds that Halloween trick-or-treaters are more likely to "trick" when wearing a thorough disguise than when not doing so (Diener, Fraser, Beaman, & Kelem, 1976).

The Los Angeles riots following the acquittal of the police officers who beat Rodney King provide a good example of deindividuation. Participants in the riots were

■ **deindividuation**
feelings of anonymity resulting from submersion in a group

When individuals are anonymous, they may be more likely to act aggressively against others.

swept into activities at odds with their typical behavior (Aguirre, Quarantelli, & Mendoza, 1988). Left unanswered by this analysis is why crowds seem to bring out the worst in people's behavior. Anonymity usually produces violence, not altruism. Is it possible that violence is such a part of most people's nature that only accountability holds it in check?

■ **person-role merger**
identification with a social role to such a degree that the person becomes the role

Related to deindividuation is a phenomenon known as **person-role merger,** in which people identify so strongly with their assigned roles in some group that they become those roles. Whereas in deindividuation an individual's personal identity is lost in the anonymity provided by a group, in person-role merger personal identity is lost in the requirements of a specific role. Roles influence how people regard themselves as well as how others react to them. You saw an example in Chapter 13's discussion of Rosenhan's (1973) study of individuals playing the role of mental patients.

Person-role merger is most apt to occur when the number of people who play a role is limited, when the role is powerful and highly conspicuous, and when particular people play that role well (Turner, 1978). Consider such roles as professional football coach, military commander, or wife of the U.S. president. People who once filled these roles may still be addressed as Coach, Colonel, or First Lady long after they have moved on to other roles. Perhaps the Los Angeles police officers who beat Rodney King were so immersed in their roles as law enforcers that no other considerations influenced their behavior while they subdued him.

A much more noble example of person-role merger comes from the 1995 outbreak of the *Ebola* virus in Zaire (Lemonick, 1995b). Health care workers did not hesitate in tending to the ill, even though they knew that contact with the blood of infected individuals would be fatal within a matter of weeks. Indeed, many of the early victims of this epidemic were doctors and nurses who put aside their personal well-being to fulfill their roles.

People in general may experience person-role merger, and the merger can take place rather quickly if the role is sufficiently engaging. A well-known demonstration is Philip Zimbardo's (1972) investigation of a mock prison that he constructed in the basement of the psychology department at Stanford University. Zimbardo recruited students to play the role of either a prison guard or a prisoner. The given role each played was determined by a flip of a coin.

The subjects were given uniforms appropriate to their role and encouraged to act out their parts. Guards were given billy clubs and whistles and the task of enforcing rules. Prisoners were locked in barren cells. In less than a day of playing out their respective roles, the guards and the prisoners became lost in the anonymity provided by their respective uniforms and the roles. They ceased playing at their respective parts and began to take them seriously. The guards humiliated the prisoners; the prisoners rebelled against the guards. After six days, the study was stopped—leaving us with a powerful example of social influence.

The subjects in this study were apparently influenced profoundly by roles they played for less than one week. However, Zimbardo's prison study has been criticized as simply a matter of students behaving as the researcher expected. But this criticism may miss the point (DeJong, 1975; Thayer & Saarni, 1975). Role playing in real life involves meeting expectations just as much as role playing in simulations does. The difference may be one of degree. Imagine the impact of social roles that are followed for years or a lifetime. In Zimbardo's own words, here are the important implications of this study:

> We preselected normal people, people we felt were similar to intelligent citizens, lawmakers, law enforcers, and prison staff members. When such people were randomly assigned as prisoners or guards, the power of the situation overwhelmed their prior socialization, values, and personality traits. And that's the message—the corrupting power of the prison situation—that we've taken to prison officials, judges, lawyers, and committees of the U.S. Senate and House. (Myers, 1987, p. 197)

Social Influence as Biopsychosocial

This section has discussed several well-known studies by social psychologists interested in social influence: conformity, obedience to authority, deindividuation, and person-role merger. These studies were for the most part done in the United States, but their general conclusion—that people in groups often come to behave in similar ways—applies to other cultures as well (Meeus & Raaijmakers, 1989; Neuliep & Crandall, 1993) (see Figure 15.2).

Biological context.   Sociobiologists interpret the universality of social influence in terms of evolved psychological mechanisms that facilitate adaptation to life in small groups (Brewer & Caporael, 1990). Conformity and obedience maintain the coherence of a group, an aspect that is obviously necessary for the group and its members to survive. Similarly, deindividuation and person-role merger lead group members to suspend their personal inclinations and direct their activities in ways dictated by the group.

Psychological context.   The psychological mechanisms by which these sorts of social influence take place involve social cognition. Although researchers like Sherif, Asch, and Milgram did not delve deeply into what their subjects were thinking, subsequent investigators have questioned subjects about their thoughts and beliefs concerning social influence (Nissani, 1990). For effects within a group to occur, individuals must perceive the group and its demands as legitimately applying to them (Rainey, Santilli, & Fallon, 1992).

Participation in a group affects social cognition in ways that further increase group influence (Mullen, 1991; Mullen, Johnson, & Anthony, 1994). So, a two-way effect exists between group influence and ways of thinking. Also relevant to understanding social influence are the emotions experienced by the group members. Emotional arousal often increases group influence (Taylor, O'Neal, Langley, & Butcher, 1991), in part because people's consideration of alternative ways of acting is narrowed (Paulhus & Lim, 1994).

For instance, a study of police patrol records found that the likelihood of violence on the part of individual officers was a function of the anxiety that accompanied given activities, such as stopping motorists who might be concealing weapons (Wilson & Brewer, 1993). Also making violence more likely were the presence of bystanders and the presence of other officers. Both of these factors arguably increase the relevance of group membership as well as emotional arousal.

Cultural context.   Despite the universality of social influence, its degree varies systematically with other factors, notably an individual's culture. As the group becomes more salient to its members, social influence becomes stronger. In cultures that value collectivity more than the individual, such as China, Japan, and Vietnam, we find greater endorsement of conformity and obedience than in the United States (Ho, 1994; Kurosawa, 1993; Ma, 1989; Nguyen & Williams, 1989; Ying & Zhang, 1992).

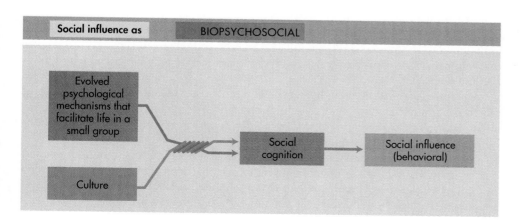

**Figure 15.2
Social Influence as Biopsychosocial.** One of the human universals is that people are influenced by one another. Social influence occurs because of biological, psychological, and social factors.

In Asian cultures, where the group is greatly valued, conformity and obedience are especially likely to occur. But even in the United States, where the individual is greatly valued, social influence remains powerful.

These findings make the experiments discussed in this section all the more striking because they were conducted in the United States yet still showed a strong impact of the group on the individual.

Stop and Think

8   Compare and contrast conformity and obedience.

9   Drawing from your everyday life, describe an example of deindividuation.

10   How is social influence biopsychosocial?

PREJUDICE AND DISCRIMINATION

■ **prejudice**
prejudgment of people based solely on the group to which they belong

■ **discrimination**
behavior resulting from prejudice

Prejudice refers to the prejudgment of a person based solely on the group to which he or she belongs. **Discrimination** describes what happens when a person acts on this prejudgment. In other words, prejudice involves thoughts, whereas discrimination involves behaviors. Contemporary society gives us all too many examples of both (Perlmutter, 1992).

Racism encompasses prejudice and discrimination directed at people because of the ethnic group to which they belong. A racist may be prejudiced against blacks, for instance, or people of Asian ancestry, or Native Americans. Recent events in Eastern Europe attest to the pervasiveness of racism.

Sexism is prejudice and discrimination directed at people because of their gender. A sexist may believe that women should not work, that men should never be awarded custody of a child following divorce, or that restaurants and clubs should be allowed to bar men or women from entering.

Ageism is prejudice and discrimination directed at people because of their age. An ageist may harbor negative feelings about older people: "We only want youthful employees around here." Or an ageist may be prejudiced against younger individuals: "Never trust anyone under 30."

Social psychologists have traditionally explained prejudice and discrimination in terms of attitudes (Duckitt, 1992b). An **attitude** is a stable and general disposition toward some object, usually defined as an evaluation of the object (Tesser & Shaffer, 1991). As studied by social psychologists, the object of an attitude is often a social group or social issue. Attitudes can be complex, influencing beliefs, feelings, and behaviors. Your attitude toward young children, for instance, is linked to characteristic beliefs about them (you believe they represent the future of the world), characteristic emotions concerning them (you find them adorable), and characteristic behaviors (you bend over and talk to them in shopping malls).

■ **attitude**
stable and general disposition toward an object, usually a social group

Of all the characteristics of social cognition, attitudes have been the most extensively investigated. The particular attitudes about which we know the most are racial attitudes, those held by white Americans about black Americans. Social psychology in this country experienced great growth as a field in the 1950s and 1960s, coinciding with the integration of public schools and intense societal scrutiny of race relations. Social psychologists turned their attention to racial prejudice and discrimination, and found the notion of attitudes useful in explaining what they discovered.

Many Americans would like to believe that discrimination is a thing of the past, that civil rights legislation, affirmative action, and black political involvement have led to an integrated society. These hopes are not mirrored in reality. Discrimination against blacks (and other minority groups) persists, and prejudiced attitudes held by whites are in large part responsible (Jaynes & Williams, 1989). Social psychologists will probably be busy for the foreseeable future with studies of racial attitudes. Needless to say, attitudes can be held about any social group, and discrimination can be discerned in many quarters. We would hope that what is known about racial attitudes applies to attitudes about other social groups as well.

Origin of Attitudes

Sociobiologists argue that the tendency to make a strong distinction between the group to which one belongs versus other groups is part of our evolutionary heritage. Our distant ancestors lived in small groups of closely related individuals, and prejudice and discrimination directed against others might have served the purpose of inclusive fitness (Chapter 3). In the modern world, distinctions between in-groups and out-groups are made along numerous lines. Evolved psychological mechanisms that lead people to value their own group while devaluing others' can lead to the various -isms just described.

According to this view, racism is not an inevitable aspect of human nature; it is predisposed by evolved mechanisms only because our culture regards race as a critical distinction among groups of people. Accordingly, racial prejudice and discrimination are likely to occur, particularly when additional factors, such as learning, socialization, and the various types of social influence already discussed, encourage them (Duckitt, 1992a).

Consider that our modern society is structured so that blacks and whites often come into contact with one another only in limited ways: directly through occupational roles and symbolically through the media. To the degree that these interactions are associated with unpleasant feelings, we form negative attitudes through classical conditioning. To the degree that these interactions produce aversive consequences, we form negative attitudes through operant conditioning. To the degree that we see others express prejudiced attitudes, we form negative attitudes through modeling. To the degree that we hear others express prejudicial stereotypes, we adopt these as our own through cognitive learning.

Attitudes and Behavior

The chief reason social psychologists have been interested in attitudes is that they presumably influence actual behavior; people act in discriminatory ways because they have prejudiced attitudes. But just how well does this presumption square with the facts? For several decades, a controversy raged in social psychology over whether such attitudes really do predict overt behavior. The issue was whether or not thoughts and actions are consistent with each other.

Evidence for inconsistency between attitudes and behavior. Richard LaPiere (1934) reported a famous demonstration of attitude-behavior inconsistency. For three months, LaPiere, a white male, took an automobile trip with a Chinese American couple, twice across the United States and up and down the West Coast. The three of them stopped at 251 different hotels and restaurants and were only once refused service. Later, LaPiere wrote every one of these 251 establishments and asked if they would accept Chinese patrons. About 50 percent wrote back, and of these, 90 percent indicated that they would not.

So, we have evidence of prejudiced attitudes on the parts of people who ran hotels and restaurants in the United States during the 1930s. But we also know that these attitudes did not translate themselves into behavior because these establishments were precisely the ones that had recently rendered service to LaPiere and his traveling companions. One conclusion suggested by this discrepancy is that attitudes and behaviors are unrelated.

Findings like these continued to accumulate until a crisis occurred with regard to the issue. Some of the leading social psychologists despaired:

> Studies suggest that it is considerably more likely that attitudes will be unrelated to or only slightly related to overt behaviors than that attitudes will be closely related to actions. (Wicker, 1969, p. 65)

Theorists even suggested that the entire idea of attitudes be abandoned (Abelson, 1972; Wicker, 1971).

Evidence for consistency between attitudes and behavior. At the same time that some social psychologists were showing that attitudes and behaviors are inconsistent, other researchers were documenting instances where attitudes and behaviors proved to be highly consistent. For instance:

■ Among voters, attitudes toward political candidates predict actual voting for or against them.
■ Among soldiers, attitudes toward combat predict actual performance under fire.
■ Among whites, attitudes toward blacks predict participation in civil rights activities.
■ Attitudes toward organ transplants predict the granting of permission to remove one's organs after death.
■ Attitudes toward movies predict one's attendance at them.

The real task of the social psychologist is to explain when attitudes and behaviors are consistent and when they are not.

Resolution. Several factors not taken into account in earlier studies of attitudes and behavior proved important in explaining the relationship between them (see Figure 15.3). Each in turn clarifies LaPiere's findings.

First are the circumstances under which a person originally acquires an attitude. Attitudes stemming from direct experience are more consistent with our behavior than those acquired secondhand. Perhaps in the 1930s, few of the hotel or restaurant proprietors had ever met a Chinese American.

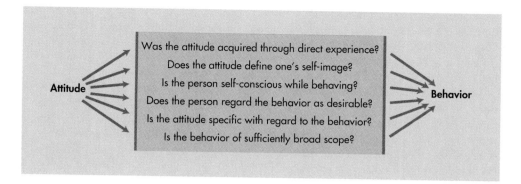

Attitude → Behavior

Was the attitude acquired through direct experience?
Does the attitude define one's self-image?
Is the person self-conscious while behaving?
Does the person regard the behavior as desirable?
Is the attitude specific with regard to the behavior?
Is the behavior of sufficiently broad scope?

Figure 15.3
Factors Influencing Attitude-Behavior Consistency. A number of factors determine whether attitudes are consistent with overt behavior. To the degree that the questions shown here can be answered yes, we would expect attitudes and behaviors to be consistent with one another.

Second is the degree to which an attitude helps define a person's self-image. If who you are is tied up in your evaluations of a particular group or object, then you act quite consistently. Again, perhaps the subjects studied by LaPiere had little investment in their feelings about Chinese Americans.

Third is whether people are self-conscious while they are behaving. Sometimes people need to reflect on their attitudes before they behave consistently with them. People who are not thinking about the meaning of their actions—those who are mindlessly enacting social scripts—tend to behave inconsistently. Saying no in a letter is a more automatic (and much easier) task than doing so face to face.

Fourth is a person's evaluation of the particular behavior that supposedly reflects the attitude in question. If a strong norm exists for or against acting in a particular way, the person's attitude exerts little influence on behavior. Here the individual is not so much inconsistent (with attitudes) as consistent (with the expectations of others). Perhaps the hotel and restaurant proprietors felt obliged to serve those who showed up at their door in the company of a white person.

Fifth is the generality of the attitude with regard to the behavior that is being predicted. Highly general attitudes toward the environment, for instance, do not predict given behaviors like returning aluminum cans as well as more specific attitudes toward

People behave consistently with their attitudes to the degree that their attitudes reflect their self-concepts.

recycling do. One's attitude toward Chinese people in general may have little bearing on how one treats particular individuals. Have we not all been in a group when an individual expressed a negative attitude about some social category (whites, Catholics, males, New Yorkers) to which one of the group members belonged, oblivious to the fact that his or her good friend was one of those wretched individuals?

Sixth is the scope of the behavior relevant to the attitude. The correlations between how one feels and how one acts can be boosted considerably if one's behavior is measured in various ways on various occasions. In LaPiere's study, only a single behavior was ascertained (serving the Chinese American couple). Perhaps a wider range of observations would have revealed behaviors consistent with the expressed attitudes of the hotel and restaurant proprietors.

Do our evaluations of social groups predict our behavior toward them? The answer is yes, although the relationship is hardly as simple as social psychologists originally hoped. A host of factors above and beyond our evaluations determine how we act. These factors may be constrained by norms and prevailing situational demands.

Attitude Change

Granted that our attitudes bear a relationship to our behavior, when and how might they change? Social psychologists have devised several strategies for changing attitudes (Olson & Zanna, 1993; Suedfeld, 1971; Zimbardo, 1991).

Persuasive communications. Attitude change through messages explicitly designed for this purpose is called **persuasive communications.** Hundreds of studies have examined the process by which a person is (or is not) persuaded to change her attitude by hearing a message urging this change (Bettinghaus, 1980). Researchers typically break the process of persuasion into three parts: the source of the persuasive message, the message itself, and the audience.

■ **persuasive communications**
messages designed to change attitudes

The source of the message. Change takes place to the degree that the source is credible, and credibility is served by expertise and trustworthiness (Brigham, 1986). You can look at advertisements as persuasive communications. Popular in ads today are celebrities who are regarded by the general public as experts with respect to the product they advocate. When a talented basketball star urges the general public to buy athletic shoes, we are duly impressed, if not by his expertise then at least by his fame and fortune.

Public service announcements can be seen as persuasive communications because they attempt to change people's attitudes about dangerous habits like drug use. Popular in such announcements, again, are celebrities. They are presumably regarded by the general public as experts with respect to the hazards of the fast lane. When a rock-and-roll star or a raucous comedian urges us to just say no to drugs, we are inclined to listen.

The message. Next is the message itself. Should you advocate an extreme position to produce maximum attitude change? The answer here is yes up to a point, after which extremity boomerangs and works against attitude change (Sherif & Hovland, 1961). Imagine that you want to create an effective message urging people to engage in safer sex so as to halt the spread of the AIDS epidemic. The safest sex of all is complete abstinence, but many individuals are likely to hear this as an extreme recommendation. Accordingly, a message urging abstinence would probably be ineffective in changing the attitudes and behaviors of the typical person hearing it.

Should you present arguments for and against the suggestion? Here the answer is no when the audience is already in general agreement but yes when the audience is initially skeptical (Lumsdaine & Janis, 1953). In the 1960s, we saw the consequences of a failure to heed this advice about how to create a persuasive communication. Public service announcements about the hazards of marijuana use were extremely one-sided,

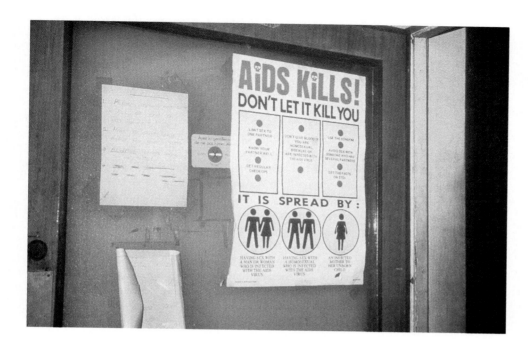

Attitudes can be changed by frightening individuals as long as the message they receive includes a recommendation about how to reduce their fear.

although many people in the general public knew from their own observations that mental breakdowns were far from a common reaction to this drug. What resulted was a tendency on the part of some to dismiss subsequent messages about drug use, even when these were on target.

Should you appeal to people's fears if you are trying to change their attitudes? At one time, social psychologists believed that the arousal of moderate fear was more effective in changing an attitude than the arousal of strong fear. But subsequent research suggested that attitude change can indeed be brought about most effectively by a strong fear appeal if specific recommendations are provided for how one can then go about reducing this fear (Sutton, 1982). A message about AIDS should stress that this is a deadly disease with no current cure; it should also explain that AIDS is readily preventable by simple changes in one's sexual behavior (Chapter 16).

The audience.   Finally, we have the audience of the message: the person or persons to be persuaded. The persuader can exert the least control over the target because people exercise considerable choice in the messages to which they expose themselves. People usually pay attention only to messages with which they already agree. Take campaign speeches by politicians. They obviously intend to change attitudes (and hence voting), but speeches by given candidates attract the attention mostly of voters already committed to them.

Social psychology researchers have investigated how audience members' self-esteem and intelligence predispose attitude change following a persuasive communication. High self-esteem apparently works against easy attitude change (Cook, 1970). The effect of intelligence appears to be more complicated. Although a degree of intelligence is needed to comprehend a message, after a point intelligence makes a person less likely to be persuaded (McGuire, 1968).

The effects of persuasive communications are numerous and complicated. One of my social psychologist friends calls this area of work "it depends" research because this phrase captures the prevailing wisdom with regard to most lines of investigation. Nevertheless, some theorists have attempted a larger view of persuasive communications.

Two routes to persuasion.   Petty and Cacioppo (1986) theorized that persuasive communications change our attitudes through two means. What they called the central route is change that results from people thinking actively about an issue. The peripheral route is change through conceptually irrelevant means—for example because the source of a message is funny or cute. Petty and Cacioppo further proposed that attitude change through the central route is usually more enduring. In contrast, attitude change through the peripheral route is usually easier to accomplish, at least in the short run. Does this idea explain recent trends in advertisements that dwell on trivial details of whatever is being pushed upon the public, whether hamburgers, beer, or political candidates?

One of the implications of the approach taken by Petty and Cacioppo is that the type of persuasive message we choose should take into account whether individuals will be thinking deeply when they hear the message. If we suspect that they will be listening intently to our message, we should concentrate on bolstering its arguments because any attitude change it produces will be through the central route. In contrast, if we suspect that our audience will be uninterested or distracted, we should embellish its form.

■ cognitive dissonance theory
Festinger's idea that when people perceive an inconsistency between their attitudes and their behaviors, they attempt to reduce it, perhaps by changing their attitudes

Cognitive dissonance.   A different approach to attitude change comes from Leon Festinger's (1957) **cognitive dissonance theory.** This theory concerns itself with the situation where a person perceives an inconsistency between her attitude toward some object and her behavior toward it. In such an event, an unpleasant feeling called dissonance results, and the person casts about for a way to reduce it. One way to reduce dissonance is to attribute her inconsistency to external pressure, but if this fails another strategy is to change her original attitude.

Suppose you dislike country music but find yourself humming along to a country song that plays on your car radio. Your behavior is inconsistent with your attitude, and when you recognize this inconsistency you feel uncomfortable. You might say to yourself, "My radio does not receive any other stations, so I have to listen to this song," but you might also decide that you actually like country music. In either case, your dissonance is eliminated.

Cognitive dissonance suggests a strategy of attitude change: Encourage a person with a particular attitude to behave contrary to it. Dissonance should arise that might be reduced through attitude change. In a classic experiment testing this hypothesized process, Festinger and Carlsmith (1959) recruited college students as subjects to perform

People who favor vegetarianism will experience cognitive dissonance when they consume meat. They can reduce this unpleasant feeling by changing their original attitude.

an incredibly boring task: to stack spools on a tray, take them off, restack them, and so on for an hour. Each subject was then dismissed, but on his way out, the experimenter said, "Whoops, it looks like my assistant didn't show up. I need some help. I need someone to tell the next subject what an interesting task this will be. Will you help me out? I'll be able to pay you."

The subject said yes, unaware that he was still participating in the experiment. The researcher then told the subject either that the payment would be $1 (small) or that it would be $20 (large). The subject then spoke to the next person, after which he again was dismissed. But there was one more step. The subject, still an unaware participant in the experiment, was interviewed by another researcher, who asked him to rate how interesting the original task had been.

In essence, subjects were paid either a small amount or a large amount for telling a lie about how interesting the task was. Then they were given the opportunity to change their minds. According to dissonance theory, which type of subject should subsequently have reported a more favorable evaluation of the task (an attitude change)? Puzzle this through by remembering that attitude change is proportional to the dissonance aroused. Would you feel greater inconsistency if paid $1 to say a boring task was interesting, or if paid $20? Most people experience greater dissonance with the smaller reward because it provides no decent rationale for the lie. And this is what Festinger and Carlsmith found: a more positive attitude for subjects paid $1 as opposed to those paid $20.

The practical implication is that we can change attitudes by inducing people to display counter-attitudinal behaviors (Leippe & Eisenstadt, 1994). They will then bring attitudes into line with the behaviors already performed. The smaller the inducement, so long as it is successful, the more attitude change should be produced. Have you noticed that individuals who solicit for religious groups in airports and on street corners often press a book or flower into your hand before they begin their pitch? You have accepted something from them, and you stand and listen to what they say; not to do so would clash with your belief that you should be polite to people who give you gifts.

Group contact.   Yet another approach to attitude change arranges matters so that people of different races interact in ways that produce positive thoughts and feelings. This work stemmed from an earlier notion called the **contact hypothesis,** which proposed that mere contact between different groups would suffice to decrease prejudice. Subsequent research showed this to be an oversimplification. However, if the contact takes a particular form, then prejudice can be combated.

In a series of studies of actual work groups composed of whites and blacks, Stuart Cook (1970) delineated a number of the critical factors:

- Getting to know people as individuals (not simply as people who fill roles)
- Equal status
- A norm of friendliness toward people in general
- A cooperative reward structure (rather than a competitive one)
- Personal characteristics of group members being at odds with stereotypes

More recent research has confirmed these findings (Gaertner, Rust, Dovidio, & Bachman, 1994).

In their 1954 *Brown v. Board of Education of Topeka* decision, the Supreme Court ruled against deliberately segregated public schools, and a profound social change began in our country. Part of the evidence considered by the Court was a statement from prominent social scientists detailing the negative consequences of segregation, including racial prejudice (Cook, 1984). The suggestion was further made that integration would decrease prejudice so long as it was carried out in a way that created the sorts of conditions just described (Desforges, Lord, Ramsey, & Mason, 1991).

You have seen that social psychologists know a great deal about the circumstances in which attitudes pertain to overt behavior, as well as how to go about changing them. Perhaps this knowledge can be used more systematically than it has been to improve the

■ **contact hypothesis**
idea that mere contact between different groups decreases prejudice

When people of different races come into contact with one another in circumstances that are friendly and cooperative, racial prejudice can be decreased.

status of African Americans and other minority groups by removing the very real barriers represented by prejudiced attitudes.

Common goals.   If prejudice and discrimination are likely to occur when people make a distinction between their own group and others', then the most general intervention is to dissolve this distinction. When people start to think of themselves as members of one large group, then there is no out-group against which negative feelings and behaviors can be directed. Consider the implications of a study done decades ago: Muzafer Sherif's (1966) investigation of cooperation and competition among boys at a summer camp.

Twenty 11-year-old boys from Oklahoma arrived at a 3-week summer camp. None of them knew each other previously. They were divided into two groups and kept apart for a week. During that week, each group cooperated in the various activities of summer camp: building fires, camping out, and telling tall tales. Each group became unified, and the boys even came up with names for their groups: the Rattlers and the Eagles.

During the second week of camp, the two groups were brought together in a tournament featuring competition between Rattlers and Eagles. In no time, the boys in each group became openly hostile to those in the other group. They called each other names, pelted each other with garbage, ransacked each other's cabins, and started fistfights. The boys had been randomly assigned to the groups. No historical precedent existed for their mutual antagonism. Merely placing an individual into one group was enough to cause him to devalue a second group. Ostensibly friendly competition only made things worse. Even when Sherif called off the competition, the boys remained hostile.

But the story does not end here. Sherif knew that a particular arrangement of social circumstances had created the difficulties. Perhaps a different arrangement might solve them. He set up a supposed emergency: "Boys, I've got some bad news. Our truck broke down. All of you have to pull together to get it started." By creating this and other common goals, Sherif reduced the fighting. The more the Rattlers and the Eagles worked together, the better they got along. The creation of a common goal encourages people to think of themselves as members of a single group. Is it naive to think that the future of the world might be served by finding the same goal for people in all social groups? "Can't we all just get along?"

Stop and Think

11 Describe how the different strategies of attitude change might be combined in a comprehensive program to change the prejudiced attitudes two social groups hold toward one another.

12 According to historians, one of the important determinants of prejudice is economic competition between two groups. How does economic competition affect prejudice through biopsychosocial routes?

13 Leon Festinger, who proposed cognitive dissonance theory, studied with Kurt Lewin. How is dissonance theory consistent with the approach of Gestalt psychology?

HELPING

Although the previous discussions may imply that social behavior is invariably ugly, people do help each other out. Social psychologists place helping within the general category of **prosocial behavior:** acts that benefit other people while having no obvious benefits for the person who carries them out (Spacapan & Oskamp, 1992).

■ **prosocial behavior**
acts that benefit other people while having no obvious benefits for the person who carries them out

Determinants of Prosocial Behavior

What causes us to help others? Theorists suggest various answers. Sociobiologists provide an evolutionary perspective with their notion of inclusive fitness. Chapter 3 discussed examples of how an animal that lays down its life for close relatives in effect passes on its own genes. Helping among people may thus have a similar basis (Rushton, 1989).

In support of the sociobiological explanation of helping is ample evidence that we help our relatives more readily than we help individuals unrelated to us. When a natural disaster strikes, for instance, family members are given help first, followed by friends and neighbors, and strangers last of all (Form & Nosow, 1958).

But evolutionary explanations do not rule out the importance of psychological factors. A dramatic example was the Christians in Europe who rescued Jews during World War II (Oliner & Oliner, 1988). If and when their assistance was discovered by the Nazis, these rescuers were sent to concentration camps, often to perish. Even so, some people helped, just as Gregory Williams helped Reginald Denny when he was attacked during the Los Angeles riots.

Psychologists interested in helping provide a long list of its psychological determinants, such as:

- guilt
- empathy
- good moods
- a personal value in favor of helping
- a prevailing social norm that encourages helping

The more of these factors that are present and the stronger they are, the more likely a person is to help others (Batson et al., 1988). Naturally, the absence of these factors works against helping. These findings have been replicated in different cultures (Hedge & Yousif, 1992; R. Johnson et al., 1989), showing that the psychological determinants of helping (or not) have considerable generality.

The Unresponsive Bystander

Research interest in the psychological determinants of helping received a boost some years ago by a well-publicized failure of individuals to help those in need. In 1964, a young woman named Kitty Genovese was murdered in New York City . . . over a 35-minute period. Thirty-eight of her neighbors overheard her screams. Some even watched the assault through their windows. No one intervened. No one even called the police.

When this horrible incident was reported in the news, two social psychologists, John Darley and Bibb Latané (1968), were stimulated to look more generally at conditions that make bystanders unresponsive to an emergency. As Darley recounted:

> Because we were social psychologists, we thought about not how people are different nor about the personality flaws of the "apathetic" individuals who failed to act that night, but rather about how people are the same and how anyone in that situation might react as did these people. (Myers, 1987, p. 456)

According to Darley and Latané, her neighbors did not help the struggling Kitty Genovese precisely because they knew others were present. They assumed someone else was getting involved. Ironically, had only one individual heard her screams—as opposed to the 38 people who actually did—the outcome might have been different.

Darley and Latané (1968) began to study the phenomenon of bystander intervention: individuals helping out in an emergency they happen to observe. These researchers systematically created their own emergencies. They dropped coins in an elevator; they blew smoke under the door of a room; they simulated injuries and seizures. Regardless of the particular emergency that was staged, they noted the number of people present and how long it took anyone to offer help. They found that the more people present, the greater the hesitation of any given individual to get involved.

Their explanation points to decisions a would-be helper must make:

- Is this really an emergency?
- Am I responsible for helping?
- What are the costs of helping?
- Do I know what to do?

To the degree ambiguity enters into any of these questions, the individual looks at what other people are doing. They, of course, are looking at him or her as well.

Failure to intervene can result from two processes. In pluralistic ignorance, everyone uses each other's inaction as a clue that no emergency exists. In diffusion of responsibil-

The tragic murder of Kitty Genovese in 1964 led social psychologists to investigate why people do not intervene in emergencies.

ity, the nature of the emergency is recognized, as in the murder of Kitty Genovese, but the presence of others suggests to each individual that someone else will assume responsibility and help. In either case, we see that social influence can prevent helping.

The good news is that social influence can also lead one to help others. When we observe a person acting in a helpful way, we become more likely to act this way ourselves when given the opportunity. Researchers conducted a study along a Los Angeles highway (Bryan & Test, 1967). There they staged automobile breakdowns at two points along the road, a quarter-mile apart. If they arranged matters so that someone could be seen helping the driver of the first car change a flat tire, then drivers were more likely to stop a minute later to help the driver of the second car.

Research also shows that the failure of bystanders to intervene in an emergency occurs mainly when the victim is a stranger. Darley and Latané's original investigations have been repeated, with one important modification (Rutkowski, Gruder, & Romer, 1983): Before an emergency occurred, some of the previously unacquainted subjects briefly interacted in small groups. They discussed their likes and dislikes with one another and tried to discover ways in which they were similar. As you might imagine, these exercises increased group cohesiveness.

After this exercise, an emergency was staged. One of the subjects—actually a confederate working with the experimenters—went into another room. A crash and a scream were then heard. Subjects who had participated in the group discussion were more likely to help than subjects without this experience. Further, the larger the group size, the more likely subjects were to help, an outcome reversing the findings of Darley and Latané that group size inhibits bystander intervention. Group exercises created a norm for social responsibility among group members; the larger the group, the better this norm was established.

So far, we have focused on relationships between groups and individuals. We turn next to a discussion of relationships between two people.

Stop and Think

14 How is helping biopsychosocial?

ATTRACTION

Human beings are drawn to one another, and this tendency may have its basis in our evolutionary history (Buss, 1990). Nonetheless, a relationship between two people can take many different forms (Berscheid, 1994; Rubin, 1973). Norms prescribe innumerable types of relationships, both formal and informal, and relationships in different historical eras and cultures vary according to dominant values (Lee, 1988; Murstein, Merighi, & Vyse, 1991). Hatfield and Rapson (1993) made the provocative observation that personal relationships around the world are becoming more similar as Western culture is spread through the global media. The pursuit of pleasure and the avoidance of pain, traditionally goals in Western relationships, are increasingly relevant to understanding relationships in Eastern cultures.

Consider some of the relationships individuals may have with others. In affiliation, the people involved simply want to be associated with some other person. In liking, the people involved have a positive attitude toward each other. When liking is coupled with a mutual perception of similarity, we call it friendship. When a relationship is characterized by exclusiveness, absorption, predispositions to help one another, and interdependence, we call it—at least in our culture—love.

Theorists disagree as to whether or not these types of relationships fall along a single dimension. If we focus just on the intensity of feelings, we can create a hierarchy from least to most intense:

affiliation→liking→friendship→love

But love involves more than just intense friendship, friendship more than just intense liking, and so on. Most social psychologists have therefore concluded that each of these relationships should be studied in its own right.

Affiliation

■ **affiliation**
tendency to seek out other people

Affiliation refers to our tendency to seek out other people. This tendency is so natural for most of us that we may never question just why we place ourselves in the company of others. Once we ask this question, though, we can turn to social psychologists for several answers.

■ **social comparison**
tendency to compare one's skills, aptitudes, attitudes, and values with those of others

Social comparison.   Leon Festinger's (1954) notion of **social comparison** provides a motive for affiliation. In order to evaluate our skills, aptitudes, attitudes, and values, we compare them with those of others. We cannot do this without associating with other people. In short, affiliation helps us evaluate ourselves (Buunk, Van Yperen, Taylor, & Collins, 1991; Kulik & Mahler, 1989).

Shelley Taylor (1985) documented the use of social comparison in her study of how women coped with the aftermath of breast cancer. Her original intent was to discern factors predicting positive or negative adjustment, but she found that all of the patients she studied were doing well psychologically. Although their physical conditions varied widely, each woman engaged in what can be termed downward social comparison. All were able to think of somebody else who had things worse, and thus coped well. Interestingly, if a patient's condition deteriorated, she simply changed the target of her social comparison.

Does misery love company?   Another line of work that investigated affiliation was Stanley Schachter's (1959) investigations of the maxim that misery loves company. Schachter recruited psychology students as research subjects and told them they were to receive a series of electric shocks, painful but not harmful. A control group of subjects was not told this. For both groups, there was a ten-minute delay while a researcher set up the experimental equipment. The subjects could wait alone or with others. Which did they choose? Compared with the subjects not expecting to be shocked, those in the experimental group preferred to pass the ten minutes in the company of others. We thus seek out others when we are anxious, presumably because other people decrease our worries. Again, social comparison processes may be at work. Other people may provide clues about how we should act and feel in an ambiguous situation. Further research by

In order to evaluate ourselves, we compare our attitudes, values, and behaviors with those of others. This need for social comparison provides one of our motives for affiliation.

Schachter clarified this phenomenon. When given a further choice, anxious people prefer to associate with other anxious individuals: Misery loves miserable company.

Liking

Psychologists who study relationships have tried to identify factors responsible for the initiation and maintenance of satisfying friendships. To the degree that these factors can be identified, friendships can be made more likely. Here is a list of research findings about the factors that predict our liking for people (Byrne, 1971):

- Proximity—other things being equal, we like those who live close to us.
- Similarity—other things being equal, we like those whose personality traits, values, and beliefs are similar to our own.
- Complementarity of needs—other things being equal, we like those who satisfy our needs.
- High ability—other things being equal, we like those who are competent.
- Attractiveness—other things being equal, we like those who are physically pleasing.
- Reciprocity—other things being equal, we like those who like us.

None of these findings is earth-shattering. But think about how they might be used by enlightened social engineers. Suppose you were put in charge of creating a dormitory where friendships would abound. What would you do?

That we find ourselves attracted to people with good looks deserves further mention because attractiveness is a potent aspect of social influence. Research shows widely held stereotypes concerning physically attractive people; they are seen as happier, more intelligent, more successful, and better adjusted than their less attractive counterparts (Hatfield & Sprecher, 1986). Needless to say, these stereotypes do not always reflect the facts of the matter. We can see them instead as one more example of the tendency to create balance among our thoughts—in this case, equating what is beautiful with what is good (Dion, Berscheid, & Walster, 1972).

This stereotype has widespread consequences (Cialdini, 1985). Consider that attractive individuals are more likely to win elections, to be offered help when in distress, and to receive favorable treatment from the judicial system. In an intriguing experiment suggested by these findings, prisoners were given plastic surgery to correct facial disfigurement (Kurtzburg, Safar, & Cavior, 1968). When compared with a group of prisoners whose appearance had not been improved, they were less likely to return to jail following release. Do these findings mean that they had been rehabilitated by their surgery and thus were less likely to commit crimes, or do they merely show that good-looking criminals avoid subsequent punishment?

Friendship and Love

The determinants of initial attraction may not be the same as the determinants of lasting attraction. Social psychologists have explored several perspectives on enduring relationships. One influential approach emphasizes social exchange, explaining relationships in terms of what the people involved give to each other (Kelley & Thibaut, 1978). Another important approach generalizes theories of emotional attachment, originally introduced to explain the bonds between parents and infants (Chapter 10), to personal relationships between adults.

Equity theory.   One example of a social exchange approach is **equity theory:** Relationships persist to the degree that both people involved believe that what they are getting out of the relationship is proportional to what they are putting into it (Walster, Walster, & Berscheid, 1978). Equitable relationships last, and inequitable ones break up (Winn, Crawford, & Fischer, 1991). Surely we have all been friends with people who

■ **equity theory**
idea that relationships persist to the degree that both people involved believe that what they are receiving from a relationship is proportional to what they are investing

never remember our birthday, return our phone calls, or defend us against gossip, although we do all these things for them. This is an unstable relationship—a bad gestalt. Something has to change. Our friends need to do more, or we need to do less, or there is no future.

Equity theory assumes that people calculate the costs and benefits involved in interacting with others. A number of studies support its general predictions. For instance, equity theory suggests that people in a romance bring with them comparable degrees of physical attractiveness. Good looks in a romantic partner are highly desirable and thus constitute a considerable benefit in a relationship. One of the simplest ways of achieving equity with a person who is good-looking is to be good-looking yourself. This is exactly what happens: Lovers often pair up according to looks (McKillip & Riedel, 1983; Murstein, 1976).

Equity theory also predicts that when people in a relationship are mismatched on one dimension, like physical attractiveness, then a compensating mismatch needs to be present on another dimension, like occupational success. For example, highly attractive women are more likely to marry rich men, whose wealth can compensate for other shortcomings (Elder, 1969). We can lament that physical attractiveness is a commodity in our social world, but it is a fact that social psychologists repeatedly discover.

According to evolutionary psychologists, males and females differ in how they evaluate the desirability of a potential opposite-sex mate (Buss & Schmitt, 1993). Chapter 3 described cross-cultural research showing that men place more emphasis on youth and physical attractiveness, whereas women tend to value industriousness. These preferences may be the result of evolved psychological mechanisms solving the different survival problems faced by our male and female ancestors in choosing the best mates.

This evolutionary interpretation is compatible with equity theory, although it proposes that men and women calculate the perceived benefits of a romantic partner differently. Consider that young men and women in the United States experience romantic jealousy for different reasons (Buss, Larsen, Westen, & Semmelroth, 1992). Men become more jealous at the prospect of their (female) partner's sexual infidelity; women become more jealous at the prospect of their (male) partner's emotional infidelity. Buss and colleagues (1992) advanced an evolutionary interpretation of these results, proposing that men value sexual fidelity because they want to be certain they have fathered their partner's child, whereas women value emotional fidelity because

According to evolutionary theorists, men value sexual fidelity, whereas women value emotional fidelity.

they want to be certain of the continued presence and support of their partner once a child has been born to them.

Equity in the here and now is not the only influence on whether long-term relationships continue. Psychologists have documented other factors that determine who stays together and who parts company. For example, a couple is less likely to break up if the partners are satisfied with their relationship, if no suitable alternatives are present, and if each has invested a great deal of time and effort in their relationship (Rusbult, 1980; Rusbult, Zembrodt, & Gunn, 1982).

Equity theory has limits in its ability to explain friendships and romances. Here is why. Interpersonal relationships exist on two levels (Kelley & Thibaut, 1978). First are the specific actions and characteristics of the people involved. These more or less line up in terms of equity. But second are the various ways in which people interpret their relationships. People's interpretations cannot be greatly at odds with their specific behaviors. However, a relationship that is strictly a mutual exchange can be thought of only as a business deal. To prevent this crass interpretation on their own parts, individuals in a friendship or romance must sacrifice some of their own rewards for the good of their partner. Then the relationship can be interpreted as a genuine one. What is the point? A purely equitable relationship cannot work because no one wishes to think of his or her friendship or romance in these terms.

Attachment theory.   Social exchange is not the only social psychological perspective on relationships. Another theory started with research into the attachment between a child and her caregiver. This is a deep emotional bond that appears early in life. Attachment develops through stages, and it shows itself in different patterns.

Applied to romantic relationships between adults, these ideas are known as **attachment theory** (Hazan & Shaver, 1987). According to attachment theory, adults approach romantic relationships in accordance with their attachment history. If they were secure in their attachments as infants, they will be secure in their romances. If they were avoidant or ambivalent infants, they will be avoidant or ambivalent lovers.

In an initial attempt to test this theory, Hazan and Shaver (1987) placed a love quiz in a newspaper. Within one week, they received more than 1,000 replies. Their quiz was actually a questionnaire containing several parts. First, they asked respondents to characterize their attachment style by choosing the one description from the following that best described their approach to relationships:

■ **attachment theory**
idea that adults approach romantic relationships in accordance with their attachment history as infants

> *Secure:* I find it relatively easy to get close to others and I am comfortable depending on them and having them depend on me. I don't often worry about being abandoned or about someone getting too close to me.
> *Avoidant:* I am somewhat uncomfortable being close to others; I find it difficult to trust them completely, difficult to allow myself to depend on them. I am nervous when anyone gets too close, and often, love partners want me to be more intimate than I feel comfortable being.
> *Ambivalent:* I find that others are reluctant to get as close as I would like. I often worry that my partner doesn't really love me or won't want to stay with me. I want to merge completely with another person, and this desire sometimes scares people away.

The proportions of people endorsing these descriptions were 56 percent, 25 percent, and 19 percent, respectively, which are approximately the same proportions of secure, avoidant, and ambivalent infants. These findings are consistent with the hypothesis that infant attachment styles are carried into adulthood because the proportions stay the same (Feeney & Noller, 1990; Mikulincer & Erev, 1991).

Also supporting this hypothesis were retrospective reports of subjects about their parents. Secure subjects reported warmer relationships between themselves and each parent as well as between their parents. Avoidant subjects were more likely to describe their parents as cold and rejecting. Finally, ambivalent subjects saw their fathers—but not their mothers—as unfair.

Respondents were also asked to describe their most important romance. Secure lovers used terms like *happy, friendly,* and *loving,* whereas avoidant lovers expressed fear of intimacy and a great deal of jealousy. Ambivalent lovers described love as an obsession and reported great highs and great lows in their romances. Although respondents in the three groups were on average 36 years of age, the individuals with a secure attachment style reported that their most significant romance had lasted ten years, about twice as long as the romances reported by those with avoidant or ambivalent styles.

Integrating equity theory and attachment theory.   In equity theory, we see an emphasis on the calculation of perceived costs and benefits. Equity theory is a thoroughly cognitive approach to friendship and love. In contrast, attachment theory emphasizes feelings. The tension between thoughts and feelings is an enduring issue in psychology, but it seems possible to integrate these perspectives, to view relationships as due to how we think about one another as well as how we feel.

Useful along these lines is a distinction between exchange relationships and communal relationships (Clark & Mills, 1979). In exchange relationships, people give benefits to one another with the expectation that comparable benefits will soon be repaid. These relationships are well explained by equity theory, and they tend to occur between people who do not know each other very well or who have strictly business as their reason for relating. In contrast, communal relationships are those in which people feel a special responsibility for one another's needs. Benefits are provided because there is a need for them and a desire to show concern. However, specific debts are not incurred, meaning that communal relationships are poorly explained by equity theory. Attachment theory may account for communal relationships, which we tend to have with our family members, friends, and romantic partners.

Stop and Think

15   What are the motives for affiliation?

16   What are the determinants of liking?

17   How might one's calculation of costs and benefits as proposed in equity theory be biased by the use of judgment heuristics (Chapter 9)?

GROUP PROCESSES

Obviously, social interactions take place between and among specific people. But can we explain the characteristics of social interaction simply in terms of the characteristics of the individual participants? In the language of Gestalt psychology, when is the whole equal to the sum of its parts and when is it different? Almost all social psychologists acknowledge that social interactions have an organization not readily derived from the characteristics of individual participants.

Social psychologists use the term **aggregation** to describe an assembly of individuals physically in the same place. They may have nothing more to do with each other than the fact that they are in the same place at the same time, like Christmas shoppers in Kmart, pedestrians hurrying along Fifth Avenue at lunchtime, or joggers on a high school track.

A **collectivity** is simply a social category: two or more individuals who can be discussed as a whole (Brown, 1954). All aggregations are collectivities, by definition, but not all collectivities are aggregations because people in a collectivity do not have to be gathered in the same place at the same time: voters over 65 years of age, Elvis imper-

■ **aggregation**
assembly of individuals physically in the same place

■ **collectivity**
any social category: two or more individuals who can be discussed as a whole

A collectivity is any social category: two or more people who can be discussed as a whole.

sonators, people with unlisted telephone numbers, basketball players with green eyes, jugglers, and employees of the United States Postal Service.

A **group** is a set of interacting individuals who mutually influence each other (Shaw, 1981). The group in group therapy (Chapter 14) is a good example, as are families, athletic teams, dance bands, and juries.

Finally, an **organization** is an enduring and organized group (Chapter 17). Usually an organization has a body of traditions and customs. Its members think of the organization as a whole, and their roles are differentiated and specialized. By this definition, many work groups qualify as organizations. Consider IBM or the lunch shift at the local McDonalds. Social groups like the Boy Scouts, political groups like the Democratic National Committee, and special interest groups like the National Rifle Association are also examples of organizations. One way to distinguish organizations from other groups is to ask whether particular members are dispensable. Regardless of who is coaching, playing, or ailing, National Football League teams go on. Thus, they are organizations. In contrast, most families would not have much of an existence without Mom and Dad and the kids. They are not organizations.

Social Loafing

Social loafing refers to the fact that people in a group may not work as hard as people alone (Latané, Williams, & Harkins, 1979). Social loafing has been shown for physical tasks, like clapping, as well as intellectual tasks, like problem solving. It is most likely to occur when an individual's contributions to the group's outcome cannot be easily identified. Some theorists see broad applicability of this concept, using it to explain failures of typing pools, unions, athletic teams, and collective farms in the former Soviet Union (Geen, 1991). Arguing against such generality are findings that social loafing vanishes when the task is attractive, when the group is highly cohesive, or when individuals are accountable (Atoum & Farah, 1993; Everett, Smith, & Williams, 1992; George, 1992;

■ **group**
set of interacting individuals who mutually influence each other

■ **organization**
enduring and organized group

■ **social loafing**
tendency of people in a group not to work as hard as when alone

Hardy, 1990). Also important is the cultural context of the group (Karau & Williams, 1993). Individuals from cultures that value the group, such as China, are less likely to display social loafing than those from cultures that value the individual, such as the United States (Earley, 1989).

Groupthink

In reviewing U.S. history, the social psychologist Irving Janis (1982) was struck that certain events could be described only as colossal blunders. Consider, for example, the failure to prepare for Japan's attack on Pearl Harbor in 1941, the decision to mount the Bay of Pigs invasion of Cuba in 1961, and the escalation of the Vietnam War from 1964 to 1967. Noteworthy about these blunders is that they were all products of supposedly careful group consideration by the brightest political and military leaders.

To account for such disastrous group decisions, Janis proposed that in certain groups, processes are set into motion that suppress criticism and preclude the consideration of alternatives. Collectively, these processes are termed **groupthink;** its symptoms are:

- an illusion that the group is invulnerable to any harm
- rationalization of past errors ("It wasn't our fault")
- unquestioned belief in the group's moral correctness ("We are good")
- stereotyped view of the opponent ("They are bad . . . and stupid")
- pressure to conform
- self-censorship
- the mistaken belief that all the group members are in agreement
- mindguards (members who protect leaders from criticism)

These factors conspire to produce a group where dissent never takes place. Furthermore, the members are not even aware that their group suppresses open discussion, thus leaving themselves at risk for bad decisions. What they see is a harmonious and confident group.

Groupthink shows one more time how social cognition and social influence mutually affect one another. Researchers have applied it to such events as strikes by professional athletes, the Iran-Contra affair, and the fatal decision to launch the Space Shuttle *Challenger* (Moorhead, Ference, & Neck, 1991; Walker & Watson, 1994). The phenomenon appears to have considerable generality (Aldag & Fuller, 1993; Mullen, Anthony, Salas, & Driskell, 1994; Park, 1990). Applied psychologists use findings about groupthink to guide interventions in business organizations (Miranda, 1994). For example, if a norm is established within an organization that legitimizes disagreement, then groupthink is reduced and better decisions are made.

Group Polarization

Conventional wisdom tells us that the best way to make an important decision is to discuss it with others. This is why companies have boards of directors, why the legal system has juries, why the president has a cabinet, and why universities have trustees. Groups are said to deliberate over their decisions, presumably arriving at a more careful conclusion than individuals would. But social psychologists have shown that under some circumstances, groups make more extreme decisions than individuals, a phenomenon called **group polarization.**

Group polarization has been demonstrated in numerous experiments. In a typical study, individuals are given brief descriptions of somebody facing a dilemma (Stoner, 1961). One choice might bring great happiness and reward, but it has a risk involved; it could lead to disaster. The other choice promises fewer benefits but carries no risk. What are the minimal odds of success for the first choice that should impel a person to opt for it? Individual subjects make an estimate: 10 percent, 35 percent, 90 percent, whatever.

■ groupthink
processes within a group that suppress criticism and preclude the consideration of alternatives, thereby resulting in disastrous decisions

■ group polarization
tendency of groups to make more extreme decisions than individuals

Then they come together in a small group to discuss the same dilemmas and again arrive at estimates of the minimal odds. As you would expect, their estimates converge, but typically around a value more extreme than the average of the individual estimates. This result captures what is meant by group polarization.

Sometimes the group decision is riskier than individual decisions, and sometimes it is more cautious. The explanation is that groups polarize the initial inclinations of group members (Myers & Lamm, 1976). For example, in one study, psychologists interviewed burglars about their perceptions of the vulnerability of given sites (Cromwell, Marks, Olson, & Avary, 1991). When interviewed in small peer groups, burglars were more cautious than when interviewed individually. Like groupthink, group polarization is robust, and it occurs in Western and Eastern cultures (Williams & Taormina, 1992, 1993).

What exactly produces group polarization? One explanation is that dilemmas—by definition—have no obvious solution. Individuals are uncertain about the course of action to take. When exposed to the opinions of other people, they compare their own opinions. People want to have the right opinion or attitude, and so they shift in accordance with the general thrust of others, sometimes doing them one better in the process.

Group polarization might represent people's conformity to the prototypical group member, a hypothetical individual who may have no actual counterpart (McGarty, Turner, Hogg, David, & Wetherell, 1992). Group polarization is most likely to occur when the group is important to its members and when the individuals are relatively anonymous (Spears, Lea, & Lee, 1990). On the other hand, the tendency toward group polarization is reduced when one or more group members dissent from the majority decision (Williams & Taormina, 1993). So, we see again an example of how social cognition and social influence come together to affect behavior in a group context.

Leadership

One of the most common ways in which groups are structured is in terms of leaders and followers. Consider the sorts of questions psychologists wish to answer: What is a leader? What kind of person is the most effective leader? What kind of leadership style produces the best results?

The most general question of all is why groups so frequently have a leader-follower organization. As you might imagine, sociobiologists point to the widespread tendency across many animal species for a hierarchy of dominance within a group to occur. Such a hierarchy minimizes conflicts because the less dominant animals consistently defer to the more dominant animals with respect to food, mates, and the direction of group activities. For example, in herds of domestic goats, most likely to be followed by others are those animals with the most direct relatives in the group (Escos, Alados, & Boza, 1993).

Perhaps human beings have a similar evolved tendency to follow dominant leaders. Inclusive fitness is obviously not the proximal cause of this tendency, for most human groups in the modern world are not composed of closely related individuals. Nonetheless, it may be more than a coincidence that the language of kinship is often used metaphorically to describe leaders and followers in human groups (Johnson, Ratwik, & Sawyer, 1987). Members are referred to as brothers or sisters; leaders, as fathers or mothers. Think of the hierarchy of the Roman Catholic Church, for instance, presided over by the Holy Father (the pope).

Great men and women.   Although questions about leadership have remained central within social psychology for years, we can see drastic changes in the ways they have been pursued (House & Singh, 1987). Early attempts to understand leadership focused on great men or great women who put their stamp on others and on history. This view suggests that some people are leaders and some are not, with particular personality traits characterizing each group (Chapter 12). For instance, we can set Abraham Lincoln,

According to the great person view of leadership, certain individuals become leaders regardless of what they happen to be doing, whether governing nations or managing fast-food franchises.

Indira Gandhi, Margaret Thatcher, and Boris Yeltsin apart from others because of their personalities. They would have been leaders in any situation. They happen to have made their mark as heads of state, but they could just as easily have led universities, armies, fast-food franchises, or labor unions.

This is a commonsense view of leadership. However, early researchers were not able to identify leadership traits. Literally hundreds of studies compared the personality traits of leaders and followers, and reviews concluded that the yield of this research was meager (Bass, 1960; Bird, 1940; Gibb, 1969; Mann, 1959; Stodgill, 1948).

The leader and the group.   By the 1950s, the great man or woman theory of leadership was abandoned in favor of a view examining the functions of leadership (Bales, 1950; Hemphill, 1950; Stodgill, 1969). In other words, what is it that leaders do? One effect of this sort of scrutiny was an emphasis on how leaders differ from each other.

Two dimensions are critical (Bales, 1953). First is task orientation: the degree to which a leader is concerned with achieving her group's goals. Second is group maintenance: the degree to which the leader tries to boost morale and cohesiveness among her group's members. Research showed that these dimensions are largely independent, meaning that a particular leader can be high on one but not on the other. Further, talking about leadership as unitary proved to be difficult—precisely because leaders are not necessarily talented at both aspects of leadership.

In judging leadership effectiveness, one must also know the goals of the group. A group like a bridge club, whose only purpose is to have fun every other Thursday evening, is not well served by a task-oriented leader who neglects group maintenance. The converse would be true for a crew of mechanics whose only job is to change the tires of race cars as rapidly as possible. Of course, many groups are more complex than these examples and need attention to both task performance and group harmony. In such cases, leaders who excel at both functions are obviously most effective (Hemphill, 1955).

Attention to the functions of leadership in terms of the goals of the group allows us to make sense of cross-cultural differences in styles of preferred leadership (Gerstner & Day, 1994). As noted, leadership is a near-universal phenomenon, but different styles of leadership occur in various cultures in accordance with dominant values. For example, leaders in Asian cultures are more attentive to maintaining harmonious group relations than their counterparts in Western cultures (Chen, Rubin, & Sun, 1992; Smith, Peterson, Misumi, & Bond, 1992).

In recent decades, social psychology's view of leadership has expanded to include both the leader and the group. A popular theory that embraces this expanded conception is Fred Fiedler's (1971) **contingency theory.** The term *contingency* captures the central premise: The best leader for a group depends on the nature of the group to be led. Like previous theorists, Fiedler distinguished leaders as task-oriented or maintenance-oriented. These characteristics interact with such attributes of the group as:

■ **contingency theory**
Fiedler's idea that the best leader for a group depends on the nature of the group

- the degree to which the members trust the leader
- the explicitness with which group goals and tasks are specified
- the power that the leader has over the followers

Studies support the claim that effective leadership is jointly determined by characteristics of the leader and the group (Strube & Garcia, 1981). A group's characteristics are influenced by the needs and goals of the larger organization in which the group is located (Chapter 17).

Great men and women again.   In recent years, there has been a renewed interest in individual characteristics associated with leadership. When research subjects have participated in a variety of small groups, the same people have tended to emerge as leaders, presumably because they have certain qualities that set them apart from others (Kenny & Zaccaro, 1983).

What might these be? You saw that previous reviews of the research literature were unsuccessful in identifying leadership traits, and so we face a dilemma. Two resolutions are likely. First, the previous literature reviews were wrong in their conclusions; there are indeed characteristics that leaders share. When the studies previously reviewed are summarized quantitatively with the statistical technique of meta-analysis (Chapter 14), relationships between leadership on the one hand and intelligence, dominance, and masculinity on the other indeed emerge (Lord, De Vader, & Alliger, 1986). These relationships are modest in magnitude but consistent.

Second, new studies show that leaders tend to be more flexible than followers (Cronshaw & Ellis, 1991; Ellis & Cronshaw, 1992). Stated another way, leaders show more varied behavior than their followers because they are able to adapt themselves to the particular needs of the group at the moment. When past studies tried to characterize leaders in terms of invariant traits, researchers looked right past the important fact that their behavior varies.

The renewed interest in leader characteristics does not invalidate Fiedler's contingency theory and related formulations. Although qualities of leaders set them apart from followers, it remains an open question whether these are in turn related to effectiveness. Here we would do well to remember the premise of contingency theory that a leader's effectiveness depends not only on his or her characteristics but also on the purpose of the group being led.

Stop and Think

18 Drawing on your everyday life, describe an example of social loafing.

19 Using current history, describe an example of groupthink.

20 How do leaders in the contemporary United States reflect our specific culture?

SOCIAL PROCESSES IN A BIOPSYCHOSOCIAL CONTEXT

This chapter has described numerous examples of social influence, beginning with the Rodney King incident and its aftermath. Critically important to social influence is the operation of various psychological processes, in particular how the social players think about themselves, others, and their relationships. I conclude this chapter by discussing an extreme instance of social influence: the process by which people are trained by the state to inflict pain.

The fundamental attribution error might lead us to regard as profoundly disturbed those who fill the role of professional torturers in different countries, but the facts suggest otherwise. Most torturers do their job in order to achieve the mundane goals of their everyday lives (Lifton, 1986). Like less dramatic instances of social influence, the process by which their behaviors are encouraged is a biopsychosocial phenomenon (see Table 15.2).

Torture has been widely used for political purposes. But who fills the institutionalized role of torturer? On the basis of her historical and cross-cultural studies of torturers, Gibson (1991) suggested several generalizations. Taken together, they implicate biological, psychological, and social influences on how someone becomes a torturer.

Those initially recruited for this role usually meet certain requirements. They must possess the physical prowess and endurance to perform their job. They must have the capacity to experience strong fear of those who direct their activities. They must be intelligent enough to understand what is required of them (knowledge of the structure and function of the nervous system is regarded as an asset). Potential torturers must value obedience. Interestingly, they must not be antisocial in the typical sense of this term (Chapter 13). Rather, they must be highly sensitive to tradition and authority. Many torturers come from religious backgrounds.

Once recruited, professional torturers embark on their careers only after extended training that uses the social influence processes discussed in this chapter. They are isolated from their friends and families and spend time only with fellow recruits. They are taught to regard themselves as elite and morally superior. They are encouraged to blame and dehumanize their victims. Torturing is modeled for them. They are harassed and intimidated, and sometimes themselves tortured. Obedience is rewarded and disobedience punished. An unwilling recruit might be told that his family members will be killed unless he displays more enthusiasm.

To a considerable degree, military or police training involves the similar use of social influence to produce obedient individuals. In the modern world, therefore, torturers are often recruited from among the ranks of soldiers or police officers because

Table 15.2 Training People to Inflict Pain

According to Gibson (1991), a variety of influences—biological, psychological, and social—are brought to bear in recruiting and training individuals to fill the role of professional torturer.

Torturers are recruited on the basis of:
  Biological characteristics
    Physical prowess
    Endurance
    Capacity to experience fear
  Psychological characteristics
    Intelligence
    Obedience to authority and tradition
  Social characteristics
    Strict religious background
    Police or military experience

Torturers are trained by:
  Biological interventions
    Harassing and intimidating them
  Psychological interventions
    Teaching them they are elite and morally superior
    Dehumanizing their victims
    Rewarding obedience
    Punishing disobedience
  Social interventions
    Isolating them from friends and families
    Having them associate only with other torturers
    Modeling

they have been given a head start on the process that can turn them into individuals willing to inflict pain.

This example was deliberately chosen because it is disquieting, and it makes a powerful point about the potential impact of social influence. Let me repeat that all of us are similarly responsive to other people. If we never find ourselves making other people suffer needlessly, it is because we have not been subjected to the social influences that make this possible.

Our introduction to psychology is almost complete. The final two chapters discuss applications of psychology. Because many of these applications take place within a social setting, the theories and findings discussed in the present chapter will be mentioned again shortly. So too will many of the ideas from earlier chapters.

SUMMARY

UNDERSTANDING SOCIAL COGNITION AND SOCIAL INFLUENCE: DEFINITION AND EXPLANATION

■ Social psychology studies people as social beings—in particular, how individuals are influenced by the presence of others.
■ Social influence reflects how the individual perceives and interprets social situations.
■ The term social cognition is used to describe the cognitive representations and processes people use in making sense of the social world.

HISTORY OF SOCIAL PSYCHOLOGY

■ The founder of modern social psychology was Kurt Lewin, who brought to the study of social problems the perspectives of a Gestalt psychologist.

DOING *Social Psychology* RESEARCH

■ Deception experiments are studies in which the researcher deliberately conceals the purposes of the investigation from the research participants, under the assumption that knowledge of a study's goal might lead subjects to behave differently from how they would otherwise behave.

■ Surveys, in contrast, are investigations in which the researcher chooses a sample of individuals representative of some larger group and asks them about their thoughts and feelings concerning any of a number of topics.

SOCIAL COGNITION

■ Among the important processes of social cognition are those responsible for social description, explanation, and evaluation.

■ When we learn about someone's characteristics, we relate this new information to beliefs we already have. Social psychologists use the term schema to describe the organized set of beliefs to which we assimilate new information. A schema may be represented as a prototype—a typical member of a social group.

■ Attribution theory concerns itself with how we arrive at causal explanations for others' behavior as well as our own. The particular explanations we choose exert considerable influence on our subsequent motives and emotions.

■ When we evaluate the appropriateness of social behavior, we use several sets of criteria: Norms are expectations about the behaviors that should be displayed by those filling specific social roles; scripts refer to accepted sequences of action for a social event; and values are enduring beliefs that certain goals are preferable to others.

INDIVIDUAL BEHAVIOR IN A GROUP CONTEXT

■ When people conform, they change their behavior to be consistent with the behavior of those around them.

■ Obedience, in contrast to conformity, is doing what a person in authority tells one to do.

■ Deindividuation occurs when people find themselves submerged in a group and feel anonymous. Deindividuated people may perpetrate outrages against others.

■ In person-role merger, an individual identifies so strongly with an assigned social role that he or she becomes that role.

PREJUDICE AND DISCRIMINATION

■ An attitude is defined as a stable and general disposition toward some object, usually a social group. Discrimination is often explained by social psychologists as the result of prejudiced attitudes.

■ To what degree do our attitudes toward social groups predict our behavior? For several decades, there was an ongoing controversy about the corre-

spondence between attitudes and behavior. This controversy has been resolved with the realization that the attitude-behavior link is not simple; rather, it depends on many factors not originally considered by researchers.

■ Attitudes can be changed in several ways. A person might hear a persuasive communication and change how he or she thinks about an issue; an individual might perceive an inconsistency between attitudes and behaviors and then change the original attitudes so as to reduce this inconsistency; or a person might change his or her attitude by having contact with members of the relevant social group, especially when this contact involves the pursuit of common goals.

HELPING

■ Helping is one example of what social psychologists call prosocial behavior: acts that benefit other people while having no obvious benefits for the person who carries them out.

■ Helping is best explained in biopsychosocial terms.

ATTRACTION

■ Affiliation refers to our tendency to seek out others. People have various motives for affiliation, including social comparison and the reduction of anxiety.

■ Most of the factors that lead to initial attraction between people are commonsensical, such as similarity and attractiveness.

■ Lasting relationships can be explained by equity theory. Relationships persist to the degree that both people involved feel that what they are getting out of the relationship is proportional to what they are putting into it.

■ Another explanation of lasting relationships is attachment theory, which suggests that relationships between adults are similar to and derived from the types of relationships infants have with their caretakers.

GROUP PROCESSES

■ Social loafing describes the tendency of people in groups not to work as hard as they do when they are alone.

■ In groupthink, processes of social influence may suppress criticism and prevent the consideration of alternatives, resulting in disastrous group decisions.

■ Group polarization is the tendency of group discussion to polarize group members' initial inclinations. This means that groups may make more extreme decisions than individuals alone.

■ Early studies of leadership attempted to discover traits that set leaders apart from followers. These attempts proved unsuccessful, and leadership is now seen as more complex. The best leader for a group often depends on the nature of the group to be led. Nevertheless, recent studies have shown that some characteristics do distinguish leaders from followers.

SOCIAL PROCESSES IN A BIOPSYCHOSOCIAL CONTEXT

■ Social influence is best explained in biopsychosocial terms, as shown by the example of the processes involved in training people to be professional torturers.

KEY TERMS

social psychology	560	fundamental attribution error	570	contact hypothesis	585
social cognition	560	actor-observer effect	570	prosocial behavior	587
social influence	560	norm	570	affiliation	590
field theory	562	script	570	social comparison	590
action research	562	value	571	equity theory	591
deception experiment	562	conformity	572	attachment theory	593
survey	564	obedience	574	aggregation	594
social perception	565	deindividuation	575	collectivity	594
schema	566	person-role merger	576	group	595
prototype	566	prejudice	578	organization	595
stereotype	566	discrimination	578	social loafing	595
causal attribution	568	attitude	579	groupthink	596
attribution theory	568	persuasive communications	582	group polarization	596
self-serving bias	569	cognitive dissonance theory	584	contingency theory	599

Health Psychology

It may not qualify as a flashbulb memory (Chapter 9), but I am sure many of us vividly remember the announcement on November 7, 1991, by the basketball player Earvin "Magic" Johnson that he was retiring from his professional career because he had tested positive for HIV, the virus that causes AIDS. Though AIDS had already claimed tens of thousands of lives by the time Magic Johnson made his announcement, many people had been able to distance themselves from the disease. Johnson's celebrity and his candor about his sexual habits brought the message to the general public that AIDS is everyone's problem.

Magic Johnson retired because it was believed that the physical demands made on a professional athlete would weaken his body and hasten the appearance of full-blown AIDS. Also figuring into his retirement was the fear on the part of other basketball players that they might contract the virus through physical contact with him. The immediate reaction of many people was that Johnson had received a death sentence. Although Magic seemed upbeat about his condition, many of us probably thought he was fooling himself. Stories written about him at that time read like obituaries.

More than four years later, on January 30, 1996, Magic Johnson was not only alive and well but returning to play in the National Basketball Association. He was bigger and stronger and as skilled as ever. Again, he attracted a great deal of attention, but discussion in the sports media centered not on how long he would live but on how much his presence would improve the record of his Lakers team.

There was some grumbling by a few players about his HIV-positive status; nonetheless, most players hailed his return. As Charles Barkley remarked, "It's not like we're going to have unprotected sex with Magic . . . we're just going to play basketball." Speaking louder than any sound bites was the way Dennis Rodman of the Chicago Bulls guarded Magic in the second game of his resumed career. Rodman bumped, shoved, and fouled him with as much vigor as Rodman bumps, shoves, and fouls any player—which is to say with considerable vigor.

We, of course, have no way of knowing the rest of the Magic Johnson story. Perhaps by the time you read these paragraphs, he will be ill or even dead. But perhaps he will be celebrating another championship. The important point for our purposes is that we need to think about illness and health in ways that go beyond the presence or absence of a virus.

We should consider people's behavior and how it can make disease more likely versus less likely. We should consider people's emotions and motives in the face of illness. We should consider how people think about health and disease. Finally, we should consider the social context of illness, whether people with an illness are stigmatized or supported by others. This chapter takes a broad look at physical well-being, focusing on psychological and social influences.

UNDERSTANDING PSYCHOLOGY AND HEALTH: DEFINITION AND EXPLANATION`

One of the important discoveries in recent years is that psychological factors contribute to health, both good and bad. Two new disciplines—health psychology and behavioral medicine—approach health and illness in psychological terms. **Health psychology** applies psychological theories and research to the topic of physical well-being. Behavioral medicine expands traditional medical approaches to illness to include the psychological context of health and illness. They meet in the middle to give us a biopsychological conception of what it means to be healthy or ill.

Physical Well-Being as Biopsychosocial

The role of the body in physical well-being is obvious, but so too are the roles of psychological and social factors, once we look for them. Indeed, one of the goals of both health psychology and behavioral medicine is to encourage good health by psychological means (Chapter 14). We know that behavioral risk factors for poor health, such as smoking or not exercising, can be changed and that such changes can have positive effects. Emotional styles and ways of relating to others, when changed by therapy, may also provide health benefits.

Psychologists have long been interested in mental disorders that present themselves in terms of physical symptoms. Remember the discussion in Chapter 1 of hysteria, which sparked Freud's theorizing about psychological abnormality. Hysteria involves puzzling physical inabilities—blindness, paralysis, and the like—and Freud pointed out that these symptoms had no actual physical basis but instead resulted from emotional conflicts (Chapter 13). In contrast, **psychosomatic disorders** are real physical disor-

■ **health psychology**
field of psychology concerned with physical well-being

■ **psychosomatic disorders**
physical illnesses influenced by psychological factors

One of the goals of health psychology is to encourage good health by psychological means. We know that behavioral risk factors for poor health, such as smoking or not exercising, can be changed with beneficial effects. And research is unanimous in showing that people with rich and supportive social relationships live longer and better lives.

ders, with a demonstrable pathology of the body. Like hysteria, though, these disorders can also result from emotional conflicts.

Over the years, the field of psychosomatic medicine concerned itself with just a handful of disorders—for example, ulcers, asthma, and hypertension. Early psychosomatic theorists identified these diseases as caused by emotional conflicts. Now psychologists believe that a number of diseases are influenced by psychological factors. In fact, all diseases may have psychological components.

Theorizing About Psychology and Health

Several basic points can be made concerning how best to explain the influence of psychological factors on health and illness. First, medical professions have for centuries made too strict a distinction between what is categorized as mind and what is categorized as body. As will be discussed shortly, there are historical reasons for this rigid distinction, which is now seen as limited. As explained in previous chapters, psychological factors and biological factors mutually influence one another. Recent research shows that this mutual influence is particularly important when our focus is on health and illness.

Second, despite the possible relevance of psychological factors to illness, we must not conclude that these are the only or even the most important influences. We all carry with us vulnerabilities and resiliencies as part of our genetic inheritance (Chapter 3). One of the best predictors of longevity, for example, is how long our ancestors lived.

Third, to identify a psychological influence on illness is not to blame the person for falling ill, although we can easily slip into this way of thinking (Sontag, 1979, 1988). The psychological risk factors for illness are not freely chosen (Chapter 1), and so it makes no sense to criticize people because their psychological characteristics put them at risk for illness.

Fourth, although most psychologists believe that psychological factors influence physical health and illness, considerable disagreement exists about the specificity of this influence. Do certain psychological states or traits make given illnesses more or less likely, or do they simply exert a general influence on well-being? As discussed later in this chapter, theorists over the years have proposed that angry people are at risk for heart disease, hopeless people for cancer, and so on. However, research suggests that such highly specific links rarely exist (Friedman & Booth-Kewley, 1987).

> **Stop and Think**
>
> **1** Think back to Chapter 1's discussion of everyday psychology. How do everyday psychologists explain health and illness?
>
> **2** Today many health psychologists are trained as clinical psychologists. What are the pros and cons of this trend?
>
> **3** Why is the life expectancy in the United States not the highest in the world?

THE MIND-BODY RELATIONSHIP IN HISTORICAL PERSPECTIVE

Conceptions of the relationship between the mind and the body have changed drastically over the years (see Figure 16.1). Early Western thinkers such as Aristotle (384–322 B.C.) made no firm distinction between minds and bodies and believed that the well-being of one implied the well-being of the other. Greek standards of beauty referred not merely to good looks but also to intellectual and moral superiority.

■ **humours**
bodily fluids long thought to influence physical and emotional health

For centuries, the dominant Western account of physical health was the theory of humours, holding that physical health and emotional health were not appreciably different. When people's bodily fluids—called **humours**—were imbalanced, they became ill, mentally and physically. Four humours were identified: blood, phlegm, yellow bile, and black bile. Too much black bile, for example, was thought to result in physical symptoms like seizures as well as psychological symptoms like depression (Jackson, 1986). Various treatments that increased or decreased humours were used to restore the balance.

The view that humours affected the well-being of bodies and minds meant that the mind-body relationship needed no further explanation. Minds and bodies were not seen as separate. Humoural theory further implied that there was only one cause of all disease: humoural imbalance.

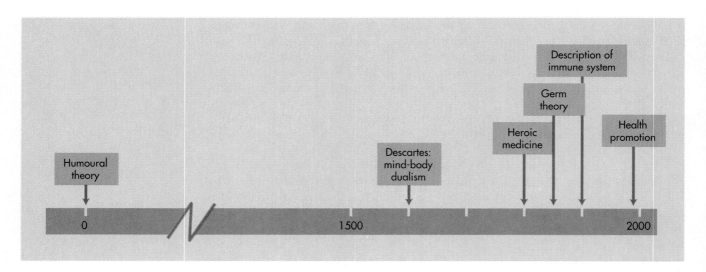

Figure 16.1
The Mind–Body Relationship in Historical Perspective. Over the centuries, different conceptions of how the mind and the body are related with respect to physical health have been popular.

Mind–Body Dualism

Humoural theory was dramatically altered by the theorizing of the French philosopher René Descartes (1596–1650), who viewed mind and body as largely separate. This position is known as **mind-body dualism.** Contrast this notion with that of the Greek thinkers before Descartes. Mind-body dualism poses a problem in explaining (or even allowing for) mind-body disorders. If minds and bodies are separate, then by definition there can be no disorders brought about by the influence of the one on the other.

Descartes was one of the first theorists to propose an account of how the body moved. His was a thoroughly mechanistic view of people and their behavior. In saying that our behavior had causes, Descartes implied that people did not have free will. This implication was a direct assault on Christian doctrine and its assumption of free will. The Catholic Church saw Descartes's views as heresy and punishable by death. To solve this dilemma, Descartes proposed that the body works in a mechanical fashion, subject to causes and effects. The soul (mind) is free.

By the 1800s, theorists found that scientific concepts—including causality—could be applied to the mind (Chapter 1). This development in effect dismissed the basis of Descartes's distinction. But by this time, different disciplines had sprung up to explain bodies (neurology, biology) and minds (psychology, psychiatry). The mind-body dualism originally proposed by Descartes had become the mind-body problem: a puzzle to be explained without the conceptual means for doing so (Chapter 6).

■ **mind-body dualism**
idea that minds and bodies are separate and independent

Heroic Medicine and Its Alternatives

Medical practice in the early 1800s was guided by humoural theory, with no acknowledgment of psychological influences on health and illness. This practice is sometimes referred to as **heroic medicine,** to reflect the aggressive approach taken by orthodox physicians to restore humoural imbalance (Weil, 1988). Like earlier healers, heroic doctors believed that an imbalance of bodily fluids was responsible for illness. But they added a new twist. With the growing popularity of scientific materialism—the philosophical doctrine that all living things should be explained only with reference to physical and chemical forces (Chapter 1)—nineteenth-century physicians thought that illness was not self-limiting. In other words, people who fell ill could not get better on their own. To believe otherwise was to assume that the body had powers that nonliving things did not have. This was unacceptable.

If a person fell ill, the physician had to do something or else death would result. The more extreme the illness, the more heroic the strategy used to treat the patient. Bleeding was a popular practice. Physicians assumed that the removal of bad blood from a patient would restore his or her system to an appropriate balance. They removed a pint of blood, then another, then another, and so on. Draining pints of blood from those already ill is, of course, absurd granted our current knowledge. But to the nineteenth-century physician, bleeding was often the chosen treatment.

Other interventions to restore humoural balance were also popular:

■ **heroic medicine**
medical approach in the 1800s that treated illness by aggressive interventions such as bleeding

> Intestinal purging was held in high esteem, and the drug most often used to produce it was calomel (mercurous chloride). Heroic doctors gave their patients huge doses of calomel . . . until the patient began to salivate freely, a sign that the drug was working. Toxicology tests today list salivation as an early sign of mercury poisoning, one of the most dangerous forms of heavy metal poisoning. (Weil, 1988, p. 13)

Criticism of orthodox medical practice was common in the 1800s. People suspected that going to a physician was actually bad for one's health, and so alternative healing traditions flourished (Fuller, 1988). Some advocated the use of traditional herbs. Others counseled individuals to improve their diets. Homeopathy developed as an alternative to traditional medicine. Here the physician treated illness by administering minute amounts of drugs, the smaller the better. Homeopathic cures were more effective than those of heroic medicine, if only because they had no particular effect on the ill individual. At the same time, chiropractic medicine developed, based on the manipulation of a patient's bones and joints. The popular health movement also took form, urging people to take responsibility for their own health by learning more about their bodies and how to treat them.

At the same time, an approach appeared called the mind cure, holding that people's health and illness were solely products of the mind. Even death was caused by incorrect thinking. If a person thought correctly, he or she need never die. Among the advocates of the mind cure was Mary Baker Eddy (1821–1910), who founded Christian Science in 1879. To this day, Christian Scientists regard medical care as unnecessary for the right-thinking person.

The American Medical Association (AMA) was founded in 1846 to combat rival medical traditions, particularly homeopathy (Coulter, 1982). The AMA gained control of medical schools and state licensing boards. It decreed that licensed physicians should not work with other sorts of healers and, indeed, should not treat patients who had previously consulted alternative healers. The growth of alternative healing practices slowed as a result, and with it the belief that psychological factors influence health and illness.

Perhaps as important as the AMA's political strong-arming was a change in the way medicine was practiced. Bleeding and purging were phased out and replaced with treatments involving small doses of drugs, as the homeopaths advocated. Part of this new medical practice was the growing use of sedating drugs—notably, alcohol and opiates—to combat illness. There is no reason to think that these drugs actually cured anyone, but patients left a doctor's office with few complaints.

Germ Theory

■ **germ theory**
idea that illnesses are caused by microorganisms (germs)

In the 1800s, germ theory emerged from research by scientists such as Louis Pasteur (1822–1895) and eventually replaced humoural theory as an account of illness. In its simplest form, **germ theory** proposed that illnesses were caused by microorganisms

Germ theory provided the rationale for immunization. Countless lives have been saved by immunization, yet germ theory does not tell the whole story about health and illness. Many diseases, such as heart disease and most forms of cancer, are not caused by microorganisms.

known as germs. Germs were regarded as necessary and sufficient conditions for illness. Every disease had its own germ, recognizable by a careful description of a patient's symptoms. Germs created problems for an individual because they interfered at the cellular level with his or her bodily functioning. Treatments that removed germs were effective because they ended this interference. It also followed that illness could be prevented if germs were kept from entering the body.

As germ theory became popular, medicine was reshaped (Magner, 1992). Diagnosis became more important because each disease had its own germ. Drugs to eradicate different germs were discovered, and the power to prescribe them was eventually limited by legislative action to licensed physicians. At this time, there was the beginning of immunization—exposing a person to a tiny amount of a germ in order to build up his or her resistance. Additionally, the field of public health began, guided by the realization that one way to combat illness was to prevent it in the first place by removing environmental sources of germs. Hygiene became a matter of health, as well as etiquette.

Interventions based on germ theory enhanced the health of the average citizen. Yet despite its practical benefits, germ theory is not strictly true. We now know that germs are an important ingredient in many illnesses, but germs by themselves are rarely the whole story. There are diseases—such as heart disease and many forms of cancer—for which no microorganism is responsible.

Even if we look only at infectious diseases, germ theory is still not strictly true. Most of the time, many of us are host to germs without falling ill. Other influences must conspire as well for germs to create disease—the germ has to be present in a sufficient amount; the person's body must be vulnerable to the germ. Furthermore, germ theory disregards psychological factors, viewing patients as little more than the battleground on which physicians and germs fight. What patients think, feel, or do is irrelevant, so long as they take the medicine prescribed to them.

However, as will be explained in the rest of this chapter, the most modern view of how minds and bodies are related returns to Aristotle's insights. Minds and bodies are again believed to have a mutual influence on one another (Chapter 4). Not only do contemporary theories allow for minds and bodies to interact, but numerous studies have shown that such interaction takes place constantly. Particularly important in modern conceptions is the role behavior plays in health and illness. Once behavior is assigned a central role in our physical well-being, health and illness can be seen only as influenced by psychological processes and social conditions.

The Immune System

The **immune system** is a collection of cells that recognizes and attacks foreign material that can cause illness. The immune system was discovered much later than the other major systems of the body because it is not located in a single organ. It is not a single entity but, rather, present throughout the body. The discovery of the immune system made it possible for theorists of a materialistic bent to explain, without positing a mystical will to live, how people could recover from illness.

■ **immune system**
bodily system that identifies and combats foreign material invading the body, including germs

The description and explanation of the immune system helped lead to health psychology because the immune system is an important meeting point of mind and body with regard to health and illness. Immunity to disease was familiar to people throughout the world for centuries (Silverstein, 1989). They knew, for instance, that if a person contracted smallpox during a particular epidemic, he or she would be spared during a subsequent one. In different parts of the world, inoculation was part of folk medicine. Someone was deliberately exposed to material from the body of an infected individual to develop a mild case of the given disease. The inoculated person would later be free from the disease.

The immune system allows our body to make a biological distinction between what belongs in our systems versus what does not. When it recognizes material that does not belong, it attacks it, using several strategies (see Figure 16.2). Over the years,

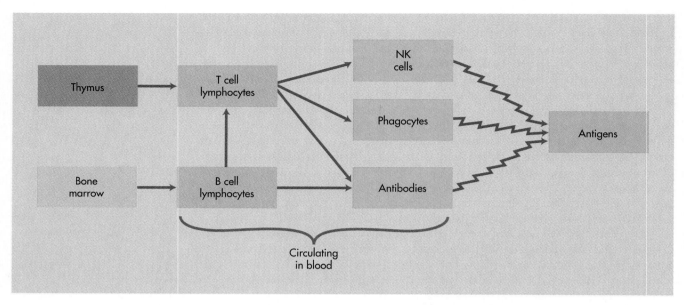

Figure 16.2
The Immune System. The immune system is not a single organ but rather cells distributed throughout the entire body. These cells work together to identify and combat in several ways foreign material called antigens.

immunologists have disagreed about the specific mechanisms of immunological defense. The current belief is that many ways exist to mount the defense and that the particular strategy differs from disease to disease.

The foreign material that has invaded the body is called an antigen. Antigens include germs, of course, which we can subdivide into bacteria, viruses, and parasites. Antigens also include cells from other individuals or species, drugs, and cancer cells that form within our own body. In autoimmunological diseases, such as rheumatoid arthritis, the immune system mistakenly treats its own healthy cells as antigens.

Antigens stimulate various immunological responses. One is the production of an antibody by white blood cells called B cell lymphocytes, which originate in bone marrow (hence the *B*) and are then carried to the lymph nodes, spleen, and tonsils. Simply put, antibodies destroy or deactivate antigens. B cell lymphocytes can produce a great variety of antibodies, and each attacks a specific type of antigen.

Another mode of fighting off an invasion is by T cell lymphocytes, white blood cells that are produced in the thymus (hence the *T*). T cell lymphocytes directly kill foreign cells as well as stimulate the activity of phagocytes, cells that engulf foreign material. T cells also interact with B cells, activating or deactivating them as needed. It is believed that the AIDS virus disables T cells, leaving the body without the ability to mount an immunological defense.

Yet another means by which the immune system fights off antigens is with natural killer (NK) cells, which directly attack cancerous cells and those infected with viruses. Cancerous cells are thought to be killed via the secretion of a chemical called interferon, which you might recognize as the name of an experimental drug for the treatment of cancer. In administering interferon, physicians are trying to mimic the operation of NK cells.

In some cases, the body can fight off an invasion the first time an attack is mounted. In other cases, the immune system learns how to do this only through experience—by the person falling ill. Children therefore have more colds than adults do because children's immune systems are not as experienced. Lymphocytes become increasingly adept at recognizing an antigen and triggering the appropriate response, meaning that the immune system is self-regulating. The immune system recognizes particular antigens,

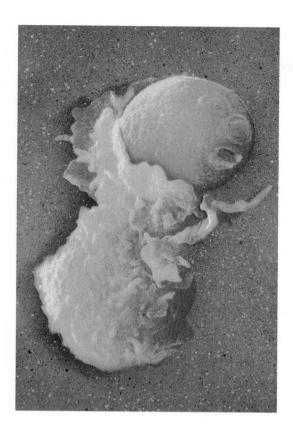

This photograph shows a lympho-cyte attacking an antigen. Lymphocytes are just one of several ways in which the immune system protects us from foreign material.

designs a defense against them, and then remembers this information for future attacks. The process is nothing short of miraculous. One of the enduring concerns of immunol-ogy is detailing exactly how this recognition and memory take place.

The players on the immunological team circulate in the blood, and so they are often studied by researchers via blood samples. (Sometimes saliva samples are used.) A strong immune response is marked by an increase in the number of these players follow-ing the introduction of a foreign material. When the response to an antigen is sluggish, the immune system is said to be suppressed. We thus talk of **immunosuppression:** a reduced or nonexistent immunological response to an antigen.

In our discussion so far, the function of the immune system has been described in rather mechanical terms, and this in fact is how it was first understood, as a reflexive response to the invasion of foreign material. In the last decade, researchers have learned that the immune system is much more complex than a simple reflex (Pelletier & Herzing, 1989). It communicates with both the endocrine system and the nervous system, resulting in a constant give-and-take among all of them. Remember, psycholog-ical factors are unambiguously involved in the nervous system and the endocrine system (Chapter 4). If the immune system is intimately linked to these systems, then it is neces-sarily influenced by psychological factors as well (Vollhardt, 1991).

■ **immunosuppression**
suppression of the immune system

Health Promotion

A broad look at history reveals three major eras of how people have approached illness and health (Taylor, Denham, & Ureda, 1982). In the first era, up to the time when germ theory appeared, the focus was solely on disease treatment. People went about their lives until they fell ill; then physicians attempted to combat the illness. In the second era, starting with germ theory, the focus expanded to disease prevention. Public health workers tried to prevent germs from entering the body. Swamps that hosted malaria-carrying mosquitoes were drained. Surgeons began to wash their hands before and after they operated. And food was inspected and dated for freshness.

What these two eras share in common is that the individual who is supposed to benefit is passive. He or she need do nothing except to follow the advice of the physician or the public health expert. But in the third era, which took form in the last few decades, the individual is called upon to behave in a health-promoting way.

Health psychologists are interested in how to encourage people to behave in healthy ways. They have adapted a variety of therapy techniques, particularly from the cognitive-behavioral arena, to promote health (Chapter 14). Strategies involving relaxation, stress management, and biofeedback have been especially popular (Goleman & Gurin, 1993).

Sometimes these techniques are merged with mass communication strategies to give us broad, media-based programs to promote health (Winett, King, & Altman, 1989). For example, in one project, health psychologists undertook a community-based health promotion program that targeted more than 100,000 California residents (Farquhar, Maccoby, & Solomon, 1984). The goal of the program was to increase knowledge about health and illness, encourage healthier habits, and decrease mortality rates. Various strategies were employed, including informational messages about healthy behaviors delivered through television, radio, and newspapers; classes and lectures concerning psychological influences on health; and environmental changes such as identifying calories, fat, and cholesterol in food served in restaurants. These interventions continued for six years and were successful in meeting their goals. When the residents in these communities were compared with those of otherwise similar towns, they showed increased knowledge of the risk factors for disease, decreased blood pressure and heart rate, decreased smoking, and reduced risk for cardiovascular disease.

A critical difference between health promotion and psychotherapy is that the typical client in therapy is hurting and has an immediate motivation to do something in order to feel better. In contrast, the ordinary citizen who is asked to promote his or her own health might feel perfectly fine. Health promotion messages suggest that if people make changes in the short run, forgoing such immediate pleasures as drinking and smoking, they will benefit in the long run.

Health promotion campaigns are not always successful. People might believe there is a link between behavior and health but then think they are immune to these principles. For example, Weinstein (1989) has documented a widespread tendency on the part of most people to see themselves as below average in risk for different illnesses; this unrealistic optimism undercuts efforts at health promotion. Even if people believe they are at risk, they may regard themselves as incapable of a lifestyle change or unwilling to make the necessary sacrifices. Further, people often desire unrealistically immediate results from their efforts.

If they are to be useful, health-promoting programs must do more than provide simple information and occasional encouragement (Peterson & Stunkard, 1989). Health promotion campaigns that are successful—like the California project just described—are deliberately broad-based, changing people's abstract knowledge as well as their personal beliefs and attitudes, their habits, and their social environments.

Stop and Think

4 Find an article on health and illness that has appeared in the popular media and ignores the biological basis of disease, interpreting it only in psychological terms.

5 Why is contemporary medicine so biological in its approach?

6 According to surveys, only one-third of patients take medication as prescribed to them. From a biopsychosocial perspective, why might this be?

DOING *Health Psychology* RESEARCH

In order to identify psychological risk factors for illness, a researcher simply determines what correlates with good versus bad health. Surveys of the general population have shown that a variety of behaviors are linked to the likelihood of particular illnesses. Hardly a day goes by without an announcement that eating one sort of food or another is associated with an increased risk of death from cardiovascular disease and/or cancer. These are correlational findings, and so causality remains ambiguous (Chapter 2). However, these correlations should at least give us pause as we plan tonight's dinner.

In other cases, we can experimentally manipulate certain factors and see what leads to health or illness. For instance, in experiments with animals, researchers have investigated the way in which stressful events like electric shock affect the likelihood of cancer developing. In these cases, causality is demonstrated, though we can always be skeptical about the degree to which studies of animals exposed to extreme stress generalize to the lives of people.

Potential risk factors—behavioral and environmental—for illness are much better understood than they once were. What still challenges researchers is the need to specify the mechanisms that translate these risk factors into actual illnesses. Angry people are at increased risk for heart disease, but exactly what does anger do that weakens the heart? Despite the complexity involved in specifying mechanisms leading from risk factors to poor health, in recent years a great deal of progress has been made with respect to our understanding of these mechanisms.

Throughout this book, the difficulties involved in conceptualizing and operationalizing psychological concepts have been mentioned. Physical health and illness are also difficult to define and thus to measure and research. The current belief is that no single and simple definition is adequate. Rather, a number of factors are considered in our judgment of illness, but most of these factors are neither necessary nor sufficient:

- General complaints about feeling ill
- Specific symptoms such as shortness of breath

Many people believe there is a connection between behavior and health, but at the same time they act as if they personally are exempt from such principles.

- Identifiable damage to the body
- Presence of germs
- Impairment of daily activities
- A short life as opposed to a long one

These factors may contradict one another. Someone might feel fine but harbor all sorts of germs. Someone else might be free of germs but feel poorly. Or someone might live a long but impaired life, or a short but vigorous one. One of the intriguing puzzles of modern epidemiology is why women have more illnesses than men do but also live longer (Verbrugge, 1989).

In making sense of health psychology research, we must be careful to understand just how physical health and illness are measured. There is a tendency, perhaps, to regard "hard" measures of health and illness—those based on physical tests—as more valid, but from a biopsychosocial perspective this bias is not warranted. Biological measures of illness, such as bodily damage or the presence of germs, are no more fundamental than psychological measures, such as a person's general sense of well-being or the degree to which he or she can lead an active life.

Many health psychologists tend to focus on the quantity of life: how long people live and the degree to which they are free from disease. But there is "more" to life than its quantity. The quality of life—how people live for as long or as short as they do—is surely as important. Living well is sometimes referred to as wellness, a concept that cannot be operationalized by longevity or freedom from disease (Barsky, 1988). Wellness captures health in biopsychosocial terms because it involves a zest for ongoing life, a fulfilling career, and satisfactory relationships with family members and friends. So, Magic Johnson can be considered ill in the specific sense that he is HIV positive, but he can also be considered quite healthy in the broader sense of wellness.

A person need not choose between quantity and quality of life because the influences on the one are often the same for the other. But when we think about psychological influences in health, we should not make the absence of disorders our sole criterion of well-being. We need also to consider how psychology can add to the quality of life (Seeman, 1989).

Stop and Think

7 Find an article in the popular media that describes a study identifying behavioral risk factors for illness. Is the research a case study, a correlational investigation, or an experiment? How is illness operationalized? Are any confounds apparent in the research?

BIOLOGICAL INFLUENCES ON HEALTH AND ILLNESS

At the turn of the century, almost half of Americans died from infectious diseases caused by germs (Purtilo & Purtilo, 1989). But with the strides made in their treatment and prevention, these diseases are now much less likely to cause death. More common today is death from cardiovascular disease or cancer (see Figure 16.3).

Nonetheless, infectious diseases have not been wiped out, and some—such as AIDS—are on the increase. At least two factors are relevant (Lemonick, 1994). First, people from different parts of the globe are increasingly likely to come into contact with one another and the germs each may carry. Second, many germs show a remarkable capacity for mutation into forms that resist conventional medical treatments (Chapter 3).

This section sketches the biological features of several illnesses of great contemporary concern. Cardiovascular diseases and cancer are on focus because these are the leading causes of death in the United States. Also on focus is AIDS because of the societal

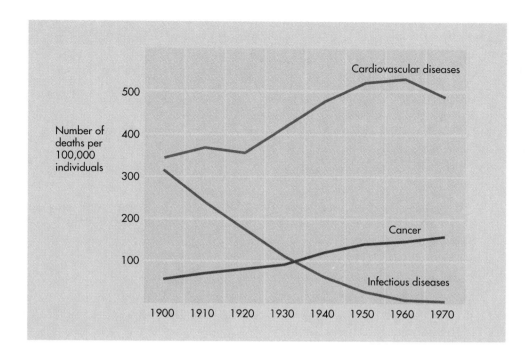

Figure 16.3
Causes of Death in the United States. Throughout the twentieth century, infectious diseases like diphtheria and measles have become much less likely as causes of death, while cardiovascular diseases and cancer have become more likely. *Source:* U.S. Department of Commerce (1995).

issues this illness raises. Subsequent sections of this chapter discuss the psychological and social influences on illness, again focusing on these specific diseases. Taken together, what results is a biopsychosocial approach to health and illness (see Figure 16.4).

Cardiovascular Diseases

The circulatory system is so named because it circulates blood throughout the entire body, carries oxygen and nutrients to our cells, and transports waste material away from them. The heart is a muscle that rhythmically contracts, sending blood away from it through the arteries and then getting it back through the veins. This system is usually quite efficient. In a lifetime of 70-plus years, a person's heart will beat more than 25 billion times, pumping the equivalent of 100 million gallons of blood through its vessels.

But things can go wrong. **Cardiovascular diseases** include several difficulties with the heart and circulatory system:

- *Coronary heart disease*—blockage of the arteries that supply blood to the heart muscle
- *Myocardial infarction* (MI)—heart attack; death of part of the heart muscle due to deprivation of oxygen or nutrients
- *Arteriosclerosis*—reduction in blood supply or decreased flexibility of blood, due, for instance, to the blockage of arteries by deposits of cholesterol
- *Hypertension*—high blood pressure
- *Cerebrovascular accident*—stroke; abnormality in the blood supply to the brain, resulting in brain damage

These problems frequently occur together because each can worsen all of the others. The chain of influence might start with high blood pressure, for example, which increases the likelihood of coronary heart disease as much as fourfold. Or it might start with arteriosclerosis. Once the arteries are clogged, blood pressure increases because the same amount of blood must now be pumped through a smaller opening.

Cardiovascular diseases are currently the leading cause of death in the United States, for both men and women. Epidemiologists describe the fatality of a disease in terms of its annual mortality incidence: how many people per 100,000 in the general population die from a disease in a given year. In 1970, cardiovascular diseases were associated with 496 deaths per 100,000, more than half of all deaths in the United States. By 1980, this figure

■ **cardiovascular diseases**
diseases involving the heart and circulatory system

Figure 16.4
Health and Illness as Biopsychosocial. An individual's physical well-being is the result of biological influences, such as genetic predispositions and immunological functioning; psychological influences, such as behavior, emotion, and cognition; and social influences, such as social support and the larger culture.

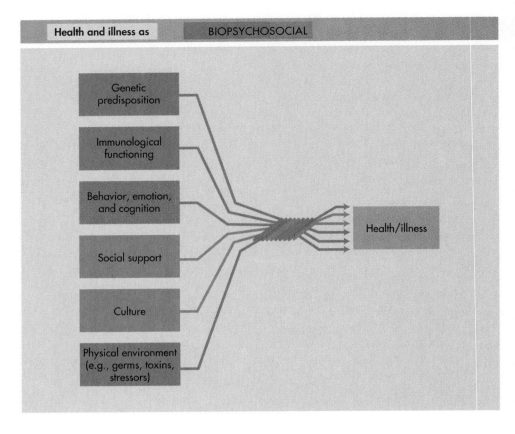

had fallen to 436 deaths per 100,000. By 1990, the annual mortality incidence was 368 (U.S. Department of Commerce, 1995). The reduction in the annual mortality index for cardiovascular diseases can be explained in terms of people's greater awareness of the risk factors for these illnesses and their deliberate attempts to reduce them.

Cancer

■ **cancer**
group of diseases characterized by the uncontrollable growth of cells

Cancer is not a single disease but rather a group of several hundred diseases all characterized by the uncontrollable growth of cells. The body's cells are always in the process of growing, and in the normal individual, this process simply keeps pace with the loss of

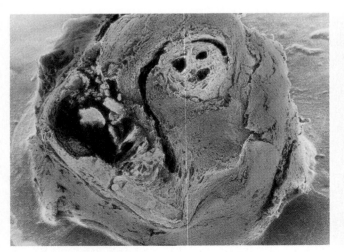

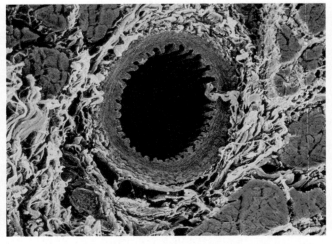

Arteriosclerosis is an impairment in the blood supply and can be brought about by deposits of cholesterol, as shown in the photograph on the left. For comparison, a healthy artery is shown on the right.

cells, with no net gain. In cancer, certain cells keep multiplying, eventually leading to the death of normal cells. If unchecked, it leads to the death of the afflicted individual. Cancer is currently second only to cardiovascular diseases as the cause of death among citizens in the United States, accounting for more than 200 deaths per 100,000 individuals every year (U.S. Department of Commerce, 1995). Almost 1 million new cases of cancer are diagnosed every year. As things now stand, about 75 million Americans will develop cancer at some point in their lives.

Different cancers are usually identified by the types of cells involved. For example, leukemia refers to cancer of the blood cells or the blood-forming organs, whereas sarcoma is cancer of the bone, muscle, or connective tissue. Carcinoma is cancer of the epithelial cells (cells on the inner or outer surface of the body, e.g., lung or skin cancer, respectively), and lymphoma is cancer of the lymph system, which is critical in fighting infection.

Usually, the body is successful in detecting and disabling its own abnormal cells. But in cancer, this defense is inadequate. A cell mutates in such a way that it multiplies beyond the needs of the body. The reason why this happens is unclear, and there may be as many specific causes as there are types of cancer.

Each new abnormal cell continues to divide. A **tumor** is eventually formed, a mass of cells. Not all tumors are cancerous. What makes a tumor malignant (cancerous) as opposed to benign (noncancerous) is the degree to which it is self-contained. Benign tumors are not necessarily innocuous because they can obstruct or press into normal tissue. Still, benign tumors obey the bodily edict not to spread unchecked. Malignant tumors are always dangerous because they are not self-contained. Cells from a malignant tumor can spread throughout the body, forming new tumors. The spread of cancer cells is called **metastasis.** Metastasis itself is a variable process, affecting one part of the body or many.

■ **tumor**
mass of cells

■ **metastasis**
spread of cancer cells

AIDS

AIDS, or **acquired immunodeficiency syndrome,** was first diagnosed in the United States in 1981. AIDS is a fatal disease caused by a virus that enters the body through contact with the bodily fluids from an individual infected with the virus. AIDS can thus be transmitted by having sex with someone carrying the virus. AIDS can also be transmitted by sharing needles and syringes with an infected individual. In a few cases, people have developed AIDS following a transfusion of infected blood. Babies born to mothers who carry the virus are at risk as well.

■ **AIDS; acquired immunodeficiency syndrome**
disease characterized by pervasive immunosuppression

The good news, if there is any, is that AIDS is not easily transmitted (U.S. Department of Health and Human Services, 1988). Despite stories that have appeared in the sensationalistic media, someone cannot get AIDS from kissing, from casual contact with infected individuals, from mosquito bites, from swimming pools, from telephones, or from toilet seats. AIDS is passed on only through certain bodily fluids. Blood, semen, and vaginal secretions can be dangerous; under virtually all circumstances, tears, sweat, saliva, urine, and feces pose no danger because the AIDS virus is present in such minute quantities.

AIDS is a particularly dangerous disease because it destroys a person's ability to fight off other diseases. Illnesses rare in the general population become much more likely among those with AIDS because their bodies never start to defend against them in the first place. AIDS also creates symptoms in its own right, and some of these include psychological difficulties. The AIDS virus can attack the central nervous system (Chapter 4), resulting in cognitive impairment ranging from forgetfulness to profound dementia (Chapter 6).

At present, there is neither an immunization against AIDS nor a cure for an infected individual. The virus can stay inactive within someone's body for a long period. Exact estimates vary greatly, but if and when AIDS develops, the majority of people die within several years. Drugs that slow the progress of AIDS, such as AZT, are now available.

The vast majority of adults with AIDS are between ages 20 and 49, a period of life when people are not prepared to deal psychologically with death.

However, they are expensive and have side effects that make them unsuitable for some individuals. AIDS was first diagnosed in this country among homosexual males, but we now know that AIDS honors no barriers. It threatens to become a worldwide scourge of a magnitude not seen since the plagues of the Middle Ages. In 1994, the annual mortality index due to AIDS was 12 per 100,000 individuals (U.S. Department of Commerce, 1995). It is among the leading causes of death among young adults in the United States, and its incidence continues on the rise.

For many reasons, AIDS has attracted the attention of psychologists. Consider the psychological consequences of AIDS. As noted, the majority of those with full-blown AIDS die within several years. Most people who develop AIDS are young adults who are unprepared to deal with imminent death. To date, many of the people who have died from AIDS in the United States were homosexual men or intravenous drug users, individuals already stigmatized and subject to discrimination. Their problems obviously multiply with a diagnosis of AIDS. AIDS can disfigure and disable the body, interfering with someone's ability to cope with stress. Available treatments for AIDS can cause such psychological symptoms as listlessness, depression, and anxiety.

> Few other diseases produce as many losses . . . of physical strength, mental acuity, ability to work, self-sufficiency, social roles, income and savings, housing, and the emotional support of loved ones. Often, self-esteem also fades in the wake of catastrophic losses. (U.S. Department of Health and Human Services, 1986, p.1)

Psychologists try to help infected individuals cope and also to change society's attitudes in order to reduce prejudice and discrimination against those with AIDS (Backer, Batchelor, Jones, & Mays, 1988). Psychologists also try to halt the spread of AIDS by encouraging people to alter behaviors that put them at increased risk for becoming infected with HIV.

PSYCHOLOGICAL INFLUENCES ON HEALTH AND ILLNESS

As explained earlier, it has been difficult for previous theorists to explain the relationship between bodies and minds. This task has become much easier with the development of a new field known as **psychoneuroimmunology,** which studies the mutual influences among psychological, neurological, and immunological factors.

■ **psychoneuroimmunology**
interdisciplinary field concerned with the mutual influences among psychological, neurological, and immunological factors

Psychoneuroimmunology

Psychoneuroimmunology was sparked by the discovery that the body's immune response can be conditioned. Chapter 8 described a classic experiment with rats (Ader & Cohen, 1981). To repeat: Researchers paired a saccharine taste with a drug that suppresses immune functioning. This pairing was done several times. Eventually, the saccharine was presented alone, and antigens were introduced into the rats' bodies. Their immune systems responded sluggishly to the invasion. Without the presentation of saccharine, their immune systems responded effectively to antigens.

Do you see the significance of this demonstration? On a theoretical level, it shows that psychological factors—in this case, learning—can directly influence the operation of the immune system. On a practical level, it implies that certain environmental stimuli can become associated with poor immune functioning. If and when these stimuli are encountered, the individual is at increased risk for poor health. The other side of the coin, perhaps, is that resilience of the immune system can also be conditioned (Kiecolt-Glaser & Glaser, 1992), meaning that health can be boosted through an association with healthy stimuli.

Another important discovery legitimizing psychoneuroimmunology is that a depressed mood is associated with poor functioning of the immune system (Schleifer, Keller, Siris, Davis, & Stein, 1985). While epidemiologists had long documented that illness and death are more likely to occur among the depressed, the mechanism bringing this about was not understood (Kaplan & Reynolds, 1988; Parmelee, Katz, & Lawton, 1992; Silverstone, 1990). Biochemical research now suggests that among the physiological changes accompanying depression is an interference with immune functioning, perhaps brought about by an increase in cortisol, a hormone secreted by the adrenal glands when we are stressed (Friedman & DiMatteo, 1989).

Researchers are currently working to understand the biochemical pathways that link the nervous system, the endocrine system, and the immune system. In Chapter 4, it was pointed out that the nervous system and the endocrine system each communicate within themselves, by neurotransmitters and hormones, respectively. Discoveries in psychoneuroimmunology blur this distinction because the immune system is sensitive to both neurotransmitters and hormones.

The conceptual relationship between the mind and body has had a long and often controversial history. Perhaps with the advent of psychoneuroimmunology, we have a resolution. We know that the mind and the body are in constant communication with one another along several different channels. The possibility that psychological factors can influence physical health, often doubted or theoretically precluded, has now been conclusively shown.

Stress and Coping

Stress is an important concept in health psychology and behavioral medicine, but it proves somewhat difficult to define. Although there is general agreement that stress is what occurs when demands are made on someone, there is much less agreement when we try to be more precise. Sometimes we talk as if stress were a property of the environment: "That place was a pressure cooker; I couldn't wait to leave." Sometimes stress is attributed to a particular societal role, like being an emergency room nurse, a police officer, or an air traffic controller. Other times stress refers to the bodily changes that result from environmental demands: "My back is tied up in knots, just like my life!" Sometimes stress means one's psychological response: "I'm all stressed out."

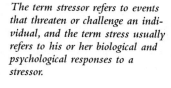

■ **stress**
complex response to environmental demands

So, **stress** can be defined as a complex transaction between a particular individual and a particular environment that takes place when the person is threatened or challenged. These demands can be experienced as positive, as when someone poses to us a challenge that we enjoy meeting: "Would you like to go out with me?" Positive stress—also called eustress—gives us the opportunity to satisfy our need for mastery, as well as many other motives (Chapter 7).

Demands can also be experienced as negative. Negative stress—that is, distress—disrupts our life, leading to anxiety and depression, poor health, and even death. Psychologists often use the term *stressor* to refer to the events that threaten or challenge an individual. They reserve *stress* for the biological and psychological consequences of exposing an individual to a stressor.

People are not usually passive victims of the stressors they happen to encounter. They will typically try to decrease stress by thinking, feeling, or acting in particular ways. That is, they cope. What makes coping an interesting topic for psychologists is that people cope in a variety of ways, some successful and some not. Being able to predict which coping style someone will choose, as well as the success of his or her choice, has long been a goal of psychologists working in this area.

The term stressor refers to events that threaten or challenge an individual, and the term stress usually refers to his or her biological and psychological responses to a stressor.

Researchers have linked stress to psychological problems as well as to physical illnesses, and psychologists seek to understand the exact details of this link. Further, psychologists are interested in helping people respond better to stress, thus reducing the damage that might otherwise be caused. Several conceptualizations of stress and coping exist, and they differ in terms of an emphasis on biological versus psychological aspects. These need not be seen as competing, though, because stress involves both.

General adaptation syndrome.   The Canadian physiologist Hans Selye (1956) offered an influential description of how the body responds to stress. He proposed that regardless of the given type of environmental stressor, its continued presence leads to the same set of physiological reactions, which he called the **general adaptation syndrome** (see Figure 16.5). It has three stages:

- *Alarm reaction*—internal resources are mobilized to restore homeostasis.
- *Resistance*—resources are used to fight off the effects of the stressor.
- *Exhaustion*—if resistance is unsuccessful or the stressor persists, resources are eventually depleted and resistance to new stressors is reduced.

The strength of Selye's general adaptation syndrome is that it is indeed general. The stressor can be a physical stimulus, such as extreme cold. It can be a psychological stressor, such as difficult demands at work or an unhappy romance. Or it can be a germ.

Stress taxes the individual's overall resilience, and any stressor makes one more vulnerable to the effects of any other stressor (Numan, Barklind, & Lubin, 1981). For example, staying up late to study for exams can make a student more vulnerable to colds or other illnesses. There is no specificity here concerning particular problems or illnesses. Various psychological problems, such as depression, are risk factors for most physical illnesses. Various physical illnesses are risk factors for many psychological problems, such as anxiety.

Stressful life events and hassles.   One of the best-known lines of research into stress and its effects is that of Thomas Holmes and Richard Rahe (1967), who specified a number of life events that require adjustment on the part of the individual to whom they occur (see Figure 16.6). The death of one's spouse, divorce, and the loss of one's job are stressful life events that require considerable adjustment. Even good events, such as marriage, retirement, and a new job, are stressful because they involve readjustment.

■ **general adaptation syndrome**
sequence of physiological reactions to an environmental stressor: alarm reaction, resistance, and exhaustion

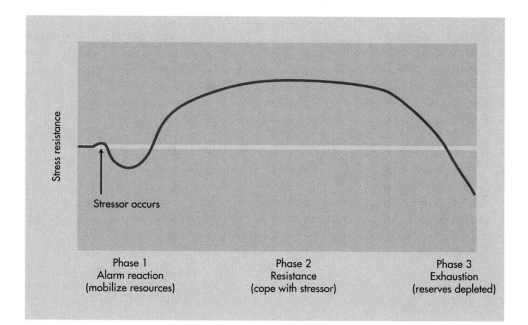

**Figure 16.5
General Adaptation Syndrome.** Hans Selye's (1956) general adaptation syndrome describes the stages of response to any stressor: alarm reaction, resistance, and exhaustion.

Stress resistance

Stressor occurs

Phase 1
Alarm reaction
(mobilize resources)

Phase 2
Resistance
(cope with stressor)

Phase 3
Exhaustion
(reserves depleted)

Figure 16.6
Stressful Life Events. This
chart shows some of the stressful
life events that make physical and
psychological difficulties more
likely to occur. The "life change
units" associated with each event
reflect the amount of adjustment
it requires on the part of an individual. The higher the rating, the
more likely an event is to damage
someone's well-being. *Source:*
Holmes & Rahe (1967).

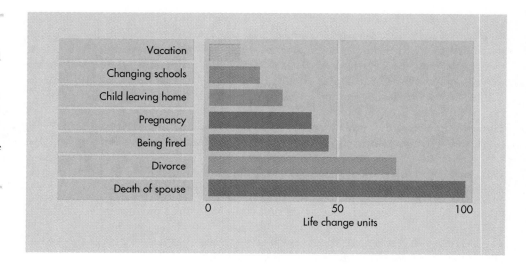

When we determine, in a 6- or 12-month period, the number and severity of
stressful events that occur to people, we find a positive correlation with the likelihood
that they will develop emotional or physical problems. In other words, the greater the
stress, the more likely people are to become psychologically or physically impaired. One
of the most stressful events identified by Holmes and Rahe is physical illness, meaning
that one illness can create a vicious circle in which other illnesses become more likely
to occur.

More specifically, researchers have found that stress interferes with the functioning
of the immune system, thus making illness more likely to occur (Cohen & Williamson,
1991). Individuals experiencing stressful events, such as final examinations, show more
immunosuppression than their nonstressed counterparts do (Glaser, Kiecolt-Glaser,
Bonneau, Malarkey, Kennedy, & Hughes, 1992; Glaser, Kiecolt-Glaser, Stout, Tarr,
Speicher, & Holliday, 1985; Kiecolt-Glaser, Garner, Speicher, Penn, Holliday, & Glaser,
1984; Kiecolt-Glaser et al., 1986). They are also more likely to develop colds when
exposed to respiratory viruses (Cohen, Tyrrell, & Smith, 1991).

It is not simply major life events that take a toll on well-being. Following the lead
of the Holmes and Rahe (1967) approach, Kanner, Coyne, Schaefer, and Lazarus (1981)
devised a measure of what they called **hassles:** minor annoyances of everyday life, such
as broken zippers, parking tickets, and the need to feed a neighbor's pet. As these hassles
accumulate, so too does the likelihood of emotional and physical problems. Because of
their sheer number, hassles may prove more important influences on well-being than
major life events (Weinberger, Hiner, & Tierney, 1987).

Stress and cognition.   The initial studies of stressful life events and illness were done
in the early 1960s by epidemiologists like Holmes and Rahe. Their research procedure
was simple: Determine the number of stressful events people experienced, determine
their physical health, and then calculate the correlation between the two. When psychologists became interested in this type of research, they looked not just at the occurrence or nonoccurrence of stressful events but also at what people thought about them.
This inquiry began in earnest in the middle to late 1960s, exactly as cognitive theorizing swept through psychology as a whole (Chapter 1).

As research progressed, it became clear that taking into account particular ways of
thinking about stressful events improved the ability to predict which events would or
would not make illness more likely to occur. Exits such as getting a divorce bring more
problems in their wake than entrances such as beginning college. Events seen as unpredictable, uncontrollable, and/or meaningless are more likely to lead to illness and even

■ **hassles**
minor annoyances of everyday
life

death (Mineka & Henderson, 1985). Furthermore, events associated with emotional conflict are particularly harmful. In some cases, these ways of thinking reflect the grim reality of the events, but in other cases, they go beyond the facts of the matter.

The best-known cognitive treatment of stress was introduced by Richard Lazarus (1966, 1982, 1991; Lazarus & Folkman, 1984). He argued that stressful events and their impact must be understood in terms of how the individual perceives them. In **primary appraisal,** the individual asks what is at stake in the event. Events take on altogether different significance depending on their implications for the individual. A speeding ticket, for example, means one thing if a person is driving on a suspended driver's license, and something else if she is not. In **secondary appraisal,** the individual takes stock of the resources at her disposal for meeting the demands of the event. Again, events vary drastically according to whether the person believes she can handle it and how. So, the impact of a speeding ticket varies depending on whether a person has enough money to pay for it and the increased cost of car insurance that follows.

Problem-focused coping refers to attempts to meet the stressful event head-on and remove its effects. **Emotion-focused coping** is more indirect, referring to attempts to moderate one's own emotional response to an event that itself cannot be altered. Lazarus pointed out that no strategy of coping is always preferred. Different events demand different coping styles. Broken radiators tend to require problem-focused coping, whereas broken hearts usually respond better to emotion-focused coping. But the point is that the impact of a stressful event depends on how the individual appraises it.

Some researchers interested in stress and coping from a cognitive perspective have investigated the role of habitual ways of thinking about stressful events and have discovered links between certain styles of thinking and subsequent illness. Suzanne Kobasa (1979), for instance, studied a personality dimension labeled **hardiness:** the ability to find meaning and challenge in the demands of life. In a series of studies, she found that hardy individuals were less likely than others to fall ill when confronted with stressful events (Kobasa, 1982; Kobasa, Maddi, & Courington, 1981; Kobasa, Maddi, & Kahn, 1982). We can assume that Magic Johnson would fall at the extreme of the hardiness dimension. After learning of his HIV-positive status, he went on living: marrying, having

■ **primary appraisal**
judgment about what is at stake in a stressful event

■ **secondary appraisal**
judgment about the resources available to cope with a stressful event

■ **problem-focused coping**
attempt to remove the effects of a stressful event

■ **emotion-focused coping**
attempt to moderate one's emotional response to a stressful event

■ **hardiness**
personality dimension reflecting the ability to find meaning and challenge in the demands of life

Problem-focused coping refers to someone's attempts to undo a stressful event. Emotion-focused coping, in contrast, is more indirect, involving the attempt to moderate one's own emotional response to a stressful event. A broken automobile usually responds to problem-focused coping, whereas a broken heart often requires emotion-focused coping.

a child, adopting another, coauthoring a book, traveling, maintaining friendships, and exploring different business opportunities.

Michael Scheier and Charles Carver (1985, 1987) have investigated a personality dimension they identified as **dispositional optimism,** defined as the expectation that good events will be plentiful in the future. They have found that optimistic individuals are less likely to fall ill and that they rehabilitate themselves more quickly from illnesses (Scheier et al., 1989).

Much of my own research falls within this line of work. With my colleagues, I have investigated how an individual's **explanatory style** is associated with illness (Peterson & Bossio, 1991). Explanatory style reflects how people generally explain the causes of bad events that happen to them. Some people favor an upbeat style of explanation ("It was just one of those days"), whereas others favor pessimistic explanations that are sweeping and self-blaming ("I'm not good at anything I do"). As noted in Chapter 13, a pessimistic explanatory style is correlated with depression.

In a series of studies, we have found that a pessimistic explanatory style is also associated with poor health, measured in a variety of ways. Granted the association between explanatory style and depression, we have tried to show that these links between explanatory style and poor health are not simply a byproduct of the association of both with depression. In other words, we calculated the correlation between explanatory style and health above and beyond any effects of depression. There is still a link between explanatory style and poor health.

Mostly untouched in this research is what the biological and psychological mechanisms might be that lead from ways of thinking to poor health. One possibility is that those who think in negative ways experience the world as a stressful place and so are at risk for any and all illnesses (Dykema, Bergbower, & Peterson, 1995). Other possibilities include direct consequences of negative thinking on the immune system, depression, and passivity (Lin & Peterson, 1990; Peterson, 1988; Peterson, Colvin & Lin, 1992).

Stress and cancer.   As described, stress has been linked to various illnesses, but let me focus here on its particular relationship with cancer. Epidemiological studies have correlated the occurrence of stressful life events with the onset of various forms of cancer, although the statistical relationships involved are modest in size. Many people get cancer without any unusual experience with stress; conversely, many people experience stress and do not get cancer.

To identify more concretely when and why stressful events might be linked to cancer, many researchers have studied the process experimentally with animal subjects. The typical procedure starts with animals bred to be susceptible to cancer. The researcher then injects them with malignant cells and finally exposes them to some experience or not. Does the experience trigger the growth of cancerous tumors in these animals? This procedure is not ethically possible with people. It is also not strictly parallel to the development of cancer among people because the manipulated variables are so extreme that the research is in effect done with sledgehammers.

Some studies like these show that stress (exposure to repeated electric shocks) results in the growth of cancerous tumors (Sklar & Anisman, 1979). At the same time, not all such studies support this conclusion. Stress sometimes results in a decreased likelihood of cancer, presumably because the immune system has been stimulated into greater activity (Sklar & Anisman, 1981). Perhaps the effect of stress on the development of cancer depends on whether the stress is acute or chronic, on the type of cancer involved, and finally on when the stress occurs in the process of tumor development (Justice, 1985). Remember the point made earlier that stress is not necessarily harmful. If nothing else, these results imply that it is hazardous to offer broad generalizations about the operation of the immune system (O'Leary, 1990).

Animal studies suggest that uncontrollability is among the critical factors explaining why stress can affect cancer. Visintainer, Volpicelli, and Seligman (1982) exposed cancer-susceptible rats to uncontrollable versus controllable shock, finding that the former

---

■ **dispositional optimism**
personality dimension reflecting the expectation that good events will be plentiful in the future

■ **explanatory style**
personality dimension reflecting how people explain the causes of bad events that befall them

stimulated the growth of tumors. Other studies with this same basic design have found that uncontrollability adversely affects the immune system—which may explain why cancer becomes more likely to occur (Peterson & Bossio, 1991).

These studies show that the physical properties of shock do not cause cancer. Rather, it is the cognitive representation of shock—as uncontrollable—that proves critical. Studies like these are among the strongest support for the role of psychological influences on physical well-being.

Stress management and inoculation. Health psychologists can help people manage stress by instructing them in strategies that reduce the negative impact of life events and hassles. Here are some of the approaches they suggest:

- Relax in the face of stress; breathe deeply and regularly.
- Get in good physical condition.
- Think about things differently; remember past triumphs.
- Give yourself occasional pats on the back.
- Take breaks and vacations.
- Turn to other people for support.

None of these suggestions is profound advice unless you decide to follow it. These stress management techniques are designed to make you feel better. Each seeks to change a particular influence on distress: biological, psychological, or social.

One need not wait for stressors to occur in order to cope with them. It is possible to anticipate stress and head it off. Psychologists have developed programs of stress inoculation that impart to a person skills and strategies for coping with stress before it occurs (Kendall & Turk, 1984). These programs usually have three parts.

In the first part, the person is instructed in the basics of the cognitive approach to stress and coping. He is helped to become aware of the relationship between how he thinks about events and how he then reacts to them. Then he is invited to try out different ways of thinking about potentially stressful events. Suppose he is about to undergo surgery, and the goal of stress inoculation is to help him reduce his anxiety and increase

One way to cope with stress is to take time away from demands and relax. Stress management techniques like relaxation protect a person from the damaging consequences of stress.

his sense of control. He is encouraged to regard the surgery not as something that may end his life but instead as something that will soon allow him to do new things. Where before he felt helpless in the face of surgery, he now feels he can exert some control over its outcome by following recommended procedures before and after the operation.

In the second part, the person is shown specifically how to cope. It is silly to tell someone "Just don't worry" if he does not know how to limit his concerns. There are a variety of behavioral and cognitive techniques that successfully reduce negative emotions by removing their antecedents (Chapter 14). The person is instructed in how to use these.

In the third part of stress inoculation, the person practices his newly acquired skills. In our example of the man about to undergo surgery, he might visit the hospital prior to his surgery. As he tours the ward where he will stay, he will probably experience some anxiety, which he can then combat with the strategies he has learned, such as breathing deeply or distracting himself. If he is unsuccessful, then it is back to the second part of stress inoculation for more instruction. Stress inoculation programs such as the one just described help people meet challenges (Kendall, Williams, Pechacek, Graham, Shisslak, & Herzoff, 1979; Langer, Janis, & Wolfer, 1975).

Behavior

The idea that behavior has something to do with physical health is relatively new. With the background provided in this chapter, you can see why. Past conceptions of illness left no room for behavioral factors. People could make injuries more or less likely to occur, depending on how they behaved, but illnesses were caused by invading germs that overwhelmed the immune system. These are microscopic events that take place largely in isolation from behavior.

However, as epidemiological data became increasingly available in recent decades, researchers were struck by the nonrandom distribution of particular illnesses across the population as a whole. Some groups of people were more likely to develop certain illnesses than others. Part of this variation could be explained by differences in exposure to germs or toxins. Syphilis was long recognized as something more likely to be experienced by sailors than other people, and so was scurvy. Theorists eventually realized that both illnesses were the result of the lifestyle of sailors: sexual activity with those carrying the syphilis germ and a diet deficient in vitamin C, respectively.

Behavior and general health.   Throughout the twentieth century, as researchers took a closer look at who fell ill and who did not, they discovered a set of behaviors that were related to people's general health. Belloc (1973; Belloc & Breslow, 1972), for example, focused on such healthy behaviors as:

- eating breakfast
- not eating between meals
- keeping weight within normal limits
- sleeping eight hours a night
- exercising
- not smoking
- not drinking to excess

Those who engaged in such habits were on average healthier than those who did not. They also lived longer. All of these risk factors are behavioral in nature, suggesting that if people can be encouraged to change their behaviors, they should live longer and better lives.

Behavior and specific illnesses.   At the same time, certain behaviors dramatically increase the likelihood that people will fall ill. The behavioral risk factors for cardiovascular disease are well documented: cigarette smoking, obesity, lack of exercise, and a diet

Among the behaviors linked to specific illnesses are smoking, eating a diet rich in fat, drinking to excess, having unprotected sex, and exposing oneself to the sun for prolonged periods.

high in saturated fats (and thus cholesterol). The risk associated with each habit multiplies when others are present.

Among the influences on cancer are such behavioral factors as smoking, drinking, eating a diet rich in fat, sunbathing, and engaging in certain sexual practices (Levy, 1985). Obviously, any behavior that puts a person in contact with cancer-triggering substances such as asbestos, coal dust, or paint fumes is also a risk factor. It is unlikely that these behaviors alone are sufficient causes of cancer. Rather, they become important contributors granted that other influences are present.

AIDS is particularly relevant to our discussion of health and behavior because the spread of this disease can be largely halted if people eliminate the practices that put themselves and others at risk for infection. These behaviors are well understood and have been well publicized (see Table 16.1).

According to surveys, people's sexual activity has changed—somewhat—because of the threat of AIDS and other sexually transmitted diseases (Lau et al., 1992; Mays, Albee, & Schneider, 1989; Murstein, Chalpin, Heard, & Vyse, 1989). Many people in the

---

Table 16.1   What Behaviors Put You at Risk for AIDS?

You are at risk for being infected with the AIDS virus if you have sex with someone who is infected or if you share needles and syringes with someone who is infected.

Since you can't be sure who is infected, your chances of coming into contact with the virus increase with the number of sex partners you have. Any exchange of infected blood, semen, or vaginal fluid can spread the virus and place you at great risk.

The following behaviors are risky when performed with an infected person. You can't tell by looking whether a person is infected.

Sharing drug needles and syringes.

Anal sex, with or without a condom.

Vaginal or oral sex with someone who shoots drugs or engages in anal sex.

Sex with someone you don't know well (a pickup or prostitute) or with someone you know has several sex partners.

Unprotected sex (without a condom) with an infected person.

Source: U.S. Department of Health and Human Services (1988, p. 3).

United States are more cautious in their practices, but behavior has not changed so drastically that the sexual transmission of AIDS has ceased (Roffman, Gillmore, Gilchrist, Mathias, & Krueger, 1990).

Why do people find it difficult to engage in safer sex? From a purely rational point of view, it seems inexplicable that someone would behave in a way that would make infection from the AIDS virus more likely to occur. However, those of us in the United States have long equated sexuality with sin and guilt, and we are often highly anxious when thinking about the topic. Sex is too basic an impulse to expect most people to refrain from it altogether (Chapter 7), and so what we see is great ambivalence about sexual activity. We have sex only when we are drunk. We have sex without taking precautions to avoid disease. We have sex without talking to our partners.

Many people in the United States at first managed to ignore or shrug off AIDS because the vast majority of those suffering from the disease were gay men. Initial attempts to inform the public—especially teenagers—about the disease were resisted. The tide has since turned, and a great deal of information has been made available (U.S. Department of Health and Human Services, 1988). But even now, there are signs of a heterosexual backlash: People continue to believe that heterosexuals cannot get AIDS.

Emotions

Let us turn from the role of behavior in health to consider emotions. One of the most important figures in this line of inquiry was the physician Franz Alexander (1939, 1950). He theorized within the psychodynamic tradition about the relationship between unconscious emotional conflicts and physical illnesses.

Emotional conflicts and illness.   Following Freud's example, Alexander proposed that symptoms have a symbolic relationship to conflict (Chapter 12). For instance, people with acne presumably experience ambivalence about being at the center of attention by others. They want both to be noticed and not to be noticed. Facial blemishes symbolize this conflict because they attract attention as well as turn it away.

Alexander also proposed that particular biological pathways link the symptoms to the conflict. Freud did not have to specify such mechanisms when he explained hysteria; after all, hysterical symptoms have no physical basis, and so there is no damage to explain. But if psychological factors have actual physical effects, these must be explained.

Alexander wrote in particular about several diseases, including hypertension, ulcers, asthma, and arthritis. He specified the underlying conflict and hypothesized how it gave rise to biological processes that produced the illness in question. For instance, a hostile and competitive person experiences chronic excitation of the body's emergency response. The effect is high blood pressure, which puts him at risk for cardiac disease.

Alexander's pronouncements proved highly influential, satisfying those who advocated psychological influences on illness (because he specified the symbolism of symptoms) and those who focused on biological influences (because he specified physiological mechanisms). The only problem with his theorizing is that it proved to be mostly wrong (Weiner, 1977). His best evidence was striking case studies in which a person with a given physical symptom clearly had the conflict in question.

For instance, Alexander described a young woman with colitis who experienced frequent bouts of diarrhea. These attacks occurred whenever her financial debts were brought to her attention. A long-standing tradition of psychodynamic theorizing equates feces with money (consider the expression *filthy rich*), and so the interpretation follows that this woman was repaying her debts in a symbolic way, with diarrhea because she could not repay them in a literal way (Brown, 1959). At the same time, she conveyed her annoyance that the matter had been brought up.

Case studies like these seem to confirm Alexander's theory. But they might be isolated coincidences, or they might identify the right ingredients but misplace the cause (Chapter 2). An inability to fulfill obligations might be a result of colitis, which—after all—keeps a person close to home.

Also, Alexander posited specific links between psychological factors and particular illnesses, and again this claim has not fared well in the ensuing years. As noted, many theorists believe that psychological factors, including emotional conflicts, are nonspecific risk factors, making any and all illnesses more likely to occur (Friedman & Booth-Kewley, 1987). Others admit some specificity, making broad distinctions between cardiovascular disease, for example, and cancer, but certainly not the fine distinctions Alexander proposed.

A version of Alexander's hypothesis proposes that emotional conflicts produce physical illness for individuals in characteristic ways. Because of physically based vulnerabilities, some people may be most susceptible to respiratory infections, others to gastrointestinal difficulties, and still others to lower back problems. The idea that stress and conflict affect one system of a person's body rather than another is supported by research, but an important qualification needs to be made: The system in question varies across the person's life (Vaillant, 1978). At any given time, somatic symptoms in one sphere might dominate, but these spheres change. Again, this finding argues against the fine detail of Alexander's theorizing because we would expect more stability in symptoms than is actually observed.

Still, Alexander is justifiably honored as the founder of the modern psychosomatic perspective (Weiner, 1977). He was correct in his general thrust that emotional conflicts take a toll on physical well-being. He relegitimized looking for the psychological basis of symptoms. And he elevated this theorizing to a new level, by searching for the actual mechanisms that lead from psychological factors to physical symptoms.

Type A behavior pattern. The **Type A behavior pattern** is a set of behaviors marked by excessive time urgency, competitiveness, and hostility. The Type A personality is "aggressively involved in a chronic, incessant struggle to achieve more and more in less and less time, and if required to do so, against the opposing efforts of other things or other persons" (Friedman & Rosenman, 1974, p. 67). The opposite style of behavior is called Type B, and people of this sort are easygoing and cooperative. Compared with Type B personalities, Type As are thought to be at increased risk for heart disease (Matthews, 1982).

■ **Type A behavior pattern**
set of behaviors marked by excessive time urgency, competitiveness, and hostility and thought to increase one's risk for heart disease

According to some theorists, emotional conflicts produce physical illness in characteristic ways: One person may develop stomach problems, and another headaches.

The Type A behavior pattern is a mixed blessing. Although it can contribute to illness, it is also associated with perseverance, academic achievement, career advancement, and high salaries (Glass, 1977). The Type A style therefore raises a point about what we should consider normal or abnormal (Chapter 13). What are the relative merits of a successful life versus one free of cardiovascular disease?

The link between the Type A behavior pattern and heart disease is complex. Although many studies have supported the hypothesized association, some more recent research finds no correlation between such behavior and heart disease (Wright, 1988). Other studies imply that not the entire behavior pattern but only the element of hostility is what puts one at risk (Barefoot, Dahlstrom, & Williams, 1983).

When this style was first described, the results seemed more uniform in linking it to cardiovascular diseases. In recent years, there have been more failures to find the link (Ragland & Brand, 1988b). This trend could mean several things (Miller, Turner, Tinsdale, Posavac, & Dugoni, 1991). One possibility is that researchers and/or journal editors early on may not have been interested in reporting studies with "no results" and hence focused only on investigations that showed increased risk. Another possibility is more intriguing: that people have made use of the widespread publicity about the Type A style to assess their own risk for heart disease and make compensatory changes elsewhere, as in their diet or frequency of exercise.

Some studies suggest that whereas the Type A style is a risk factor for initial heart attacks, it might also be beneficial in recovering from them. If a Type A individual has a heart attack, he is more likely to make a good recovery than the Type B individual who has had a heart attack (Ragland & Brand, 1988a). However, there are other interpretations. Perhaps Type As have more severe heart attacks than Type Bs; those few who do survive are more robust than the Type Bs who survive. Or perhaps Type As can muster their resources better than Type Bs in order to recover from heart attacks.

What is the mechanism linking the Type A style to cardiovascular diseases? The critical ingredient appears to be anger at a world that thwarts what an individual wants to do, and so imagine what happens when he is always angry. His bodily emergency reaction, which includes an increase in heart rate and blood pressure, is constantly engaged. Eventually the cardiovascular system is weakened, particularly when its chronic activation is coupled with other risk factors for heart disease. This hypothesis linking anger to cardiovascular diseases through the intermediary of the body's emergency reaction is not that different from Franz Alexander's proposition decades earlier. At least this aspect of his work survived the test of time.

Granted that Type A is a risk factor for cardiovascular diseases, what is a person to do? Some Type As can compensate in other areas of their lives, trying to reduce their overall likelihood of a cardiovascular disease. The more direct approach, assuming a person is willing, is to try to change the style itself. Strategies for changing Type A behavior have been developed. They rely first on information about the components of the style (time urgency, competitiveness, and hostility) and second on cognitive-behavioral interventions that address these components. For instance, circumstances can be arranged so that a person who is excessively concerned with time is rewarded if he shows up for appointments a few minutes late and punished if he interrupts other people as they speak or work at tasks.

Studies find that these strategies reduce the Type A style (Nakano, 1990; Nunes, Frank, & Kornfeld, 1987; Roskies et al., 1986). These changes in turn map into reduced risk for cardiovascular diseases (Friedman, 1989; Johnston, 1989; Thoreson & Powell, 1992). We know from one study that reductions in Type A style have led to reductions in cholesterol (Gill et al., 1985). We know from another study that reductions in Type A style have led to decreased blood pressure (Bennett, Wallace, Carroll, & Smith, 1991). And we know from yet other studies that the risk of recurrent cardiovascular diseases has decreased among those who received Type A counseling (Friedman et al., 1986; Mendes de Leon, Powell, & Kaplan, 1991; Powell & Thoreson, 1988).

Racism and cardiovascular diseases.   The likelihood of cardiovascular disease varies across different groups. African Americans, for example, are at much greater risk than European Americans, males by 33 percent and females by 60 percent (U.S. Department of Health and Human Services, 1992). Examination of why this might be underscores the multiplicity of influences on physical well-being (James, 1984a, 1984b).

Some theorists have pointed to physical differences between blacks and whites as responsible for the differences in risk of heart disease, and others to dietary differences (Eisner, 1990; Francis, 1990; Klag, Whelton, Coresh, Grim, & Kuller, 1991). But in addition to any roles played by biology or diet, psychological factors figure prominently.

Remember Franz Alexander's theorizing about how chronic anger leads to hypertension, which in turn leads to a cardiovascular disease. On average, African Americans show elevated blood pressure, perhaps as the result of accumulated anger at a world filled with prejudice and discrimination. A study by Krieger (1990) supports this hypothesis. She interviewed black and white women in California, determining their health status—specifically, their blood pressure—as well as how they responded to instances of unfair treatment based on race or gender. Among African Americans, those who reacted to unfair treatment by keeping quiet and accepting the discrimination were four times more likely to be hypertensive than those who reacted by speaking out and taking some action. Among European Americans was found no such association, perhaps because few of them reacted to unfair treatment by quietly accepting the discrimination.

Another psychological influence on hypertension that helps explain why African Americans are at increased risk for cardiovascular diseases is a personality variable dubbed **John Henryism.** John Henry is a figure in American folklore, a black railroad worker whose job of laying track by hand was threatened when a steam hammer that could do the same work was introduced. According to legend, a contest between John Henry and the steam hammer took place. John Henry won the contest, laying more track, but he died thereafter of a heart attack.

■ **John Henryism**
personality dimension reflecting the belief that all events can be controlled solely through hard work and determination

Among African Americans, those who reacted to unfair treatment by keeping quiet and accepting the discrimination were four times more likely to have hypertension than those who reacted by speaking out and taking action.

Sherman James, a researcher, saw in this legend a metaphor for African Americans who believe they can control all events in their lives solely through hard work and determination (James, Hartnett, & Kalsbeek, 1983; James, LaCroix, Kleinbaum, & Strogatz, 1984). He created a questionnaire asking respondents the degree to which they believed in such values and then investigated the relationship of John Henryism to blood pressure among black males. Those who scored high on the John Henryism measure but were low in socioeconomic status were most likely to be hypertensive (James, Strogatz, Wing, & Ramsey, 1987). Constant striving for control over events without the resources to achieve it can take a toll on health, although third variables might confound this conclusion.

Assuming the validity of this finding, it seems to apply to all groups (Duijkers, Drijver, Kromhout, & James, 1988). However, it fits particularly well for contemporary African Americans (James, Keenan, Strogatz, Browning, & Garrett, 1992), who often face a very real limit to what they can attain regardless of how hard they work. Disorders such as hypertension, no less than psychological difficulties, must be located in their societal context.

Hopelessness and cancer.   Let us now move to the role of emotions in cancer. It has long been believed that certain emotional styles are associated with the eventual onset of cancer (Sontag, 1979). In the second century, for example, the Greek physician Galen proposed that melancholic (depressed) individuals were most likely to develop cancer. This opinion has been echoed throughout history: Cancer is most likely to occur among those who are emotionally nonexpressive, depressed, helpless, and/or hopeless (Gross, 1989; Jensen, 1991).

Longitudinal studies have been conducted that measure these hypothesized predispositions and then follow subjects over time to see who develops cancer (Hahn & Petitti, 1988; Persky, Kempthorne-Rawson, & Shekelle, 1987). Numerous factors threaten the validity of such studies (Levenson & Bemis, 1991). Obviously, a large number of research subjects must be included because cancer itself is a relatively rare event. An adequate time period must be employed, so that enough people have a chance of developing the disease. Yet another threat is the possible existence of confounds. Emotional styles might bear a statistical relationship to the subsequent development of cancer simply because they are somehow linked to environmental or occupational factors that themselves produce cancer.

Suppose a researcher finds that pessimistic people are at increased risk for cancer. It is important to show that this correlation is not due to the fact that people who work as coal miners, for instance, are more likely to be pessimistic than other people and also more likely to develop cancer. In this example, there is no direct link between pessimism and cancer. The critical factor is a person's occupation.

Eysenck (1988, 1990b, 1991) discussed in detail two studies conducted by researchers in Yugoslavia. Each study followed hundreds of men and women for a full decade. At the beginning of the studies, the participants filled out questionnaires measuring such dispositions as helplessness, hopelessness, and emotional repression. These factors showed a surprisingly strong correlation with whether the individuals developed cancer at some point in the following years. Indeed, these personality styles showed a stronger relationship to the development of cancer than habits like smoking and drinking did. This result is not the typical finding (Amelang, 1991; Derogatis, 1991; Fox, 1991).

Other studies have been unsuccessful in finding any link between emotional styles and cancer (Zonderman, Costa, & McCrae, 1989), whereas still others support the conclusions of the Yugoslavian studies but at much more modest levels (Schmale & Iker, 1971). Perhaps the best conclusion right now is that results are mixed but encouraging enough to warrant further research. Future studies should do more than just establish (or fail to establish) correlations across decades between traits and cancer. They should attempt to understand the mechanisms involved because emotion cannot instantly translate itself into cancerous cells (Gil, 1989; Linkins & Comstock, 1990). Is the pathway, if one exists, solely immunological, or does it also loop outside the body through unhealthy habits made more likely by a person's characteristic emotional style?

Stop and Think

11 What is psychoneuroimmunology?

12 How is stress biopsychosocial?

13 What is John Henryism?

SOCIAL INFLUENCES ON HEALTH AND ILLNESS

A final set of influences on health and illness includes social relationships with other people. These influences exist, at least in part, because of their link to cognitive, behavioral, and emotional risk factors for poor health. Indeed, a mutual influence is probably the rule in understanding the biological, psychological, and social mechanisms of well-being.

Social Support

A well established finding in epidemiology is that people with a rich and supportive network of family and friends enjoy better health and longer lives than their counterparts who are socially estranged (Cobb, 1976). Being with other people is healthy for us, psychologically and physically.

How is it that other people work their magic upon us? Theorists have attacked this question by asking just what people provide for one another. They use the term **social support** to describe the benefits involved. Social support includes offering a person in distress such things as:

■ **social support**
benefits provided by people to
one another

- emotional reassurance or comfort
- tangible resources, such as food, money, or shelter
- suggestions about how to tackle problems
- perspective, such as giving a person another way of seeing things

Any of a number of interpersonal exchanges can be classified as social support. Some are obviously relevant to our physical health—other people can, for instance, be quite helpful in our campaigns to lose weight or exercise more. But the effects of social support go beyond health-specific advice and lead us back to where we started: Other people are simply good for us.

The routes between social support and physical well-being appear to be several. For example, people in supportive relationships tend to have more resilient immune systems, to be in better moods, and to experience fewer stressful events (Cohen, 1988). The other side of the coin is that ruptured social relationships can take a toll on our health. Studies suggest that unhappy marriages can tax the physiology of both husbands and wives (Gottman & Levenson, 1992; Levenson & Gottman, 1983, 1985), including their immune functioning (Kiecolt-Glaser, Fisher, Ogrocki, Stout, Speicher, & Glaser, 1987; Kiecolt-Glaser, Kennedy, Malkoff, Fisher, Speicher, & Glaser, 1988).

Social Support and AIDS

Although AIDS is at present an inevitably fatal disease, the amount of time that infected individuals survive following diagnosis varies greatly. One of the solid generalizations about survival time with AIDS is that gay men who have contracted the disease outlive intravenous drug users with the disease (Melnick et al., 1994). An obvious explanation for this difference is that drug users—by virtue of the stressful lives they have led—are less resilient.

But another possibility is that gay men garner for themselves more social support and that this support leads to increased longevity. AIDS victims experience stigma, and so too do homosexuals in our society, yet at least within the gay community, AIDS victims often receive considerable assistance. This support may translate itself into increased survival time, probably through a variety of routes. There might be a direct effect on the immune system, but it is also clear that social support helps a person adopt a healthier lifestyle, reducing the risk of contracting the various diseases that AIDS makes more likely (Stoddard, Zapka, & McCuskar, 1992). Remember that people with AIDS die not of AIDS itself but rather of diseases they contract by virtue of their suppressed immune response.

Another finding of note is that women with AIDS often do not live as long as men with AIDS (Melnick et al., 1994). Again, one obvious possibility is that women are less resilient than men in the face of AIDS, although we know that women in general live longer than men. Another explanation is that women with AIDS are not diagnosed as quickly as men because AIDS is less common among women. Hence, the reduced survival time of women might be an artifact of late diagnosis and/or delayed treatment. But consider one more possibility: Women with AIDS do not receive social support so readily from friends and family members because they do not know how to react.

Researchers have explored psychosocial factors associated with survival time among gay men with AIDS. In these studies, the degree to which the immune system is compromised is typically measured by an appropriate immunological test and statistically equated across research participants. This strategy disentangles—to some extent—ambiguities about causes and effects.

A consistent predictor of increased survival time is social support (Reillo, 1990; Turner, Hays, & Coates, 1993; Willoughby et al., 1994). Also important are the degree to which an individual is actively involved in the gay rights movement, the absence of psychological problems, an early life relatively free of trauma, and membership in the middle or upper social classes (Bofinger, Marguth, Pankofer, Seidl, & Ermann, 1993; Caumartin, Joseph, & Chmiel, 1991; Craib et al., 1994; Hogg, Strathdee, Craib, O'Shaughnessy, Montaner, & Schechter, 1994). Although the data are somewhat contradictory, the degree to which an individual with AIDS passively accepts the diagnosis and its grim prognosis may be associated with early death (Reed, Kemeny, Taylor, Wang, & Visscher, 1994). This latter finding—if it proves valid—is compatible with the research previously described that links pessimism to poor health. One way to bolster optimism is to have a rich and supportive network of friends (Peterson & Bossio, 1991).

Loss of a Loved One

For centuries, poets have written about lovers dying of a broken heart. Interestingly, studies support this romantic assertion by finding that people are at increased risk for death themselves following the death of someone especially close to them, particularly a spouse (Stroebe & Stroebe, 1987). For example, Richard Nixon died in 1994, ten months after the death of his wife, Pat. According to Holmes and Rahe's scheme of life events, the death of a spouse is the single most stressful occurrence a person can experience, and former President Nixon's grief was well documented.

However, the widower or widow is not at continual risk. Vulnerability is increased for only about 6 to 12 months after his or her loss. During this time, the person is likely to be depressed and listless and to have a sluggish immune response (Bartrop, Luckhurst, Lazarus, Kiloh, & Penny, 1977). But if the person does not die during this period—and he or she usually does not—then health eventually rebounds.

James Pennebaker and his colleagues studied individuals whose spouses had recently died (Pennebaker, Hughes, & O'Heeron, 1987; Pennebaker & O'Heeron, 1984). They asked these research subjects if they had talked to another person about

When people lose a spouse, they are at increased risk for illness for 6 to 12 months after the loss. If they do not talk to others about their feelings, they tend to have more physical complaints.

their grief. Some had and some had not, and among those who had not spoken to another person, the extent of their physical complaints during the subsequent year were markedly increased. This research leads to the conclusion that when people are experiencing some strong emotion and lack the opportunity or ability to talk about it, they may end up with physical problems. This pathway might reflect an increased susceptibility to actual illnesses, but it also might mean that symptoms function as a way of communicating when other channels—like direct requests for sympathy—are unavailable. Remember the earlier point that health psychology needs a broad conception of illness (and health)—in particular, one recognizing that physical complaints have interpersonal significance.

Along these lines, Stroebe and Stroebe (1987) suggested that various factors can moderate the relationship between a social loss and poor health. Although death is never a pleasant event, it is easier to find meaning in some deaths than others. For example, when someone dies as a hero or after a painful illness, his or her death is often easier to understand than when death results from a bizarre household accident or a random act of violence. In the former case, the surviving spouse is not so apt to fall ill, and thus we return to research linking cognitive factors to health.

Group Therapy for Cancer

A final illustration of social influences on health and illness is the attempt to directly change the course of cancer by psychological therapy. In an important study, David Spiegel and colleagues (1989) discovered that group therapy increased the longevity of women with severe cases of breast cancer. Subjects were randomly assigned to one of two conditions: supportive group sessions meeting once a week versus a control condition that did not receive group therapy. Women in both groups received comparable medical treatment. The women were followed for a ten-year period, until almost all of them had died. Those in the treatment group lived, on average, 18 months longer than those in the comparison group. This is a meaningful difference. The Spiegel study is the first methodologically sound demonstration of a link between a psychological intervention and the life expectancy of cancer patients.

But the study raises questions. First, was it something about the experimental group that increased life, or something about the comparison group that decreased life? The study's design does not allow these possibilities to be distinguished, and in fact the life expectancy of those in the comparison group seems to have been lower than typical, meaning that something unknown may have happened to those in the control group to reduce their life expectancy. Second, the study does not tell us why therapy was beneficial, if indeed it was. As part of the research, a battery of personality measures were administered to the subjects, but these proved unrelated to life expectancy. The mechanism linking group therapy and survival time therefore remains a mystery. Third, the study does not show that group therapy cures cancer, only that it might extend the life expectancy of those who have the disease.

Other researchers are following the example of Spiegel and colleagues and conducting their own investigations of therapy for cancer patients (Greer, Moorey, & Baruch, 1991; Grossarth-Maticek & Eysenck, 1991). Though it is too early to say what the outcome will be, all agree that we are entering an exciting era, not only for cancer treatment but also for clinical psychology.

Stop and Think

14   What is social support?

15   From a biopsychosocial perspective, why do women in the contemporary United States live longer than men (Chapter 3)?

16   How should an individual diagnosed with cancer think, feel, and behave in order to live longer and better?

HEALTH AND ILLNESS IN A BIOPSYCHOSOCIAL CONTEXT

Once the relationship between the mind and the body was established, psychological and social influences on physical well-being began to be accepted as plausible and then studied. This chapter has described the way in which psychological and social factors, along with biological influences, affect health. To conclude, let me add to the list of influences on health by addressing the role of the larger society, which provide norms for the appropriate experience of illness and its possible treatment.

Shamanism

The approach to healing represented by contemporary medical professions in the United States is but one of many that exist around the world. In a large number of cultures, including some in the United States, shamans—or spiritual healers—are frequently consulted by people with physical illnesses. A shaman has a drastically different conception of illness from that assumed by germ theory. Problems are attributed to spiritual difficulties or to malevolent external forces (Chapter 13). In any event, shamans can often bring relief to individuals, restoring health by various rituals and procedures.

Consider the informal health system represented by the *curanderas* found in some Mexican American communities (Torrey, 1986). These people fill several overlapping roles, diagnosing and treating physical complaints. The *curanderas* are specialized. Some rely on herbs for cures; others combine herbs with spiritual treatment. Some use only holy water; others treat only certain illnesses.

Most of the *curanderas* are females. They learn their profession through an apprenticeship, and all have a pronounced religious manner. Most accept only a small fee for their services, regarding their gift of healing as coming directly from God (Martinez & Martin, 1966).

Shamans view physical problems as stemming from spiritual difficulties. Here is a Mexican-American curandera.

One of the problems for which a person might seek out a *curandera* is called *susto*, known as the fright disease because it is presumably caused by a traumatic experience, either natural (e.g., an auto accident) or supernatural (e.g., a ghost). Its symptoms include fatigue, restlessness, decreased appetite, weakness, loss of interest in everyday activities, social withdrawal, and sadness. Note that a worldview ends up affecting the very nature of problems. Believing that fatigue is due to an encounter with a ghost gives a different significance to your symptom from believing that it is due to poor diet, overwork, or mononucleosis.

How should we regard shamanism? We should be as skeptical as we are of conventional medical procedures but not necessarily more so (Danesi & Adetunji, 1994). Many of those who seek out conventional medical treatment also rely on shamans, meaning that healers of all stripes should be aware of the practices of the others and the assumptions on which these are based (Jackson, 1993).

Alternative Medicine

A related point concerns the growing popularity of so-called alternative medicine among patients in the United States. Alternative medicine includes techniques such as homeopathy, developed more than a century ago in the wake of heroic medicine; treatments such as acupuncture and herbs, borrowed from other cultures; and strategies such as crystals, associated with the New Age movement. Many of these techniques are based on a biopsychosocial conception of well-being.

A general survey of adults in the United States, conducted in 1990, found that 34 percent of respondents had used at least one form of alternative medicine during the past year (Eisenberg, Kessler, Foster, Norlock, Calkins, & Delbanco, 1993). Individuals with more education and higher incomes were more likely than others to have sought alternative treatment. Visits to alternative healers, such as acupuncturists or chiropractors, were as common as those to primary care physicians. The amount of money spent out-of-pocket for alternative medicine exceeded that spent for hospitalizations.

According to this survey, the majority of those receiving alternative treatment also saw conventional physicians for the same illnesses. Some commentators therefore call these alternative approaches complementary medicine because patients do not see them as incompatible with conventional treatments. However, patients usually do not inform their physicians about their use of alternative approaches, a fact suggesting that they fear criticism or rejection.

Shamanism and alternative medicine deserve greater attention from the scientific establishment than they have received in the past. Our understanding of health and illness can only be increased by studying different approaches to healing: when they work, when they do not, and why. In 1991, the U.S. Congress established the Office of Alternative Medicine as part of the National Institutes of Health—which means that this scrutiny is beginning in earnest.

This chapter described the application of psychological theories and results to physical health and illness. Health psychology is just one of a number of applied psychologies. The next chapter discusses some other important fields of application.

SUMMARY

UNDERSTANDING PSYCHOLOGY AND HEALTH: DEFINITION AND EXPLANATION

■ Health psychology is the field that studies psychological influences on health and illness.
■ Psychologists today approach physical well-being from a biopsychosocial perspective.

THE MIND-BODY RELATIONSHIP IN HISTORICAL PERSPECTIVE

■ Throughout history, different ideas about the relationship between the mind and the body have been popular. Depending on the specific idea, the possibility of psychological influences on health has been considered obvious, impossible, or problematic.
■ Early Greek thinkers believed that the mind and the body were not altogether separate.
■ In contrast, the French philosopher Descartes separated the mind and the body.
■ Medical practice in the early 1800s focused entirely on the body, treating illness with aggressive strategies, such as bleeding, in an attempt to restore bodily fluids to a healthy balance. This approach left little room for psychological influences on health, although also existing at this time were alternative approaches to healing that took a biopsychosocial approach.
■ Germ theory was proposed in the 1800s and revolutionized medicine. According to germ theory, microorganisms are necessary and sufficient causes of all illnesses. Germ theory left little room for psychological influences.
■ In the early part of the twentieth century, the immune system was described. This bodily system identifies and attacks foreign material, such as germs.

■ In recent decades, the influence on health of psychological factors—especially behavior—has again been recognized, leading to a concern with what people can do to promote their own well-being.

DOING *Health Psychology* RESEARCH

■ Health psychology researchers identify psychological risk factors for illness by determining what correlates with various operationalizations of good versus bad health or by manipulating factors in experiments and seeing the consequence for health.
■ More challenging is the specification of the mechanisms that translate risk factors into physical well-being or its absence.

BIOLOGICAL INFLUENCES ON HEALTH AND ILLNESS

■ Cardiovascular diseases include several difficulties with the heart and circulatory system and are the leading cause of death in the United States.
■ Cancer is a group of diseases characterized by the uncontrollable growth of cells and is the second leading cause of death in the United States.
■ Although death due to infectious diseases has decreased throughout the twentieth century, these diseases still pose a danger. For example, AIDS, or acquired immunosufficiency disease, is caused by a virus. It is a particularly dangerous disease because it destroys a person's ability to fight off other diseases.

PSYCHOLOGICAL INFLUENCES ON HEALTH AND ILLNESS

■ The new field of psychoneuroimmunology studies the mutual influences among psychological, neurological, and immunological factors, especially as they affect health and illness. Psychoneuroimmunology explicitly recognizes the role of psychological and social influences on well-being.

■ One important psychological risk factor for poor health is stress, which occurs when an individual is threatened or challenged.

■ Psychologists have studied stress extensively, linking it to specific environmental events as well as to how people think about these events.

■ Another important psychological risk factor for poor health is how a person behaves. Specific ways of acting can make illness in general—as well as particular diseases, such as cardiovascular disease, cancer, and AIDS—more likely to occur.

■ Emotional conflicts also put people at risk for illnesses. For instance, the Type A behavior pattern—a style marked by excessive time urgency, competitiveness, and hostility—puts an individual at risk for heart disease.

SOCIAL INFLUENCES ON HEALTH AND ILLNESS

■ A final set of influences on health and illness includes social relationships with other people. People with a rich and supportive network of family and friends enjoy better health and longer lives than people who are socially estranged.

■ People are at increased risk for death themselves following the death of someone close to them.

■ In an important study, researchers discovered that group therapy increased the longevity of women with severe cases of breast cancer.

HEALTH AND ILLNESS IN A BIOPSYCHOSOCIAL CONTEXT

■ Influences on health include the role of the larger society, which provide norms for the appropriate experience of illness and its possible treatment.

■ Popular in many parts of the world is shamanism, or spiritual healing, which is based on a drastically different idea of illness from that assumed by Western science.

■ Growing in popularity in the United States is the use of alternative medicine.

■ Shamanism and alternative medicine deserve greater attention from the scientific establishment than they have received in the past.

KEY TERMS

health psychology	606	tumor	619	secondary appraisal	625
psychosomatic disorders	606	metastasis	619	problem-focused coping	625
humours	608	AIDS; acquired immuno-		emotion-focused coping	625
mind-body dualism	609	deficiency syndrome	619	hardiness	625
heroic medicine	609	psychoneuroimmunology	621	dispositional optimism	626
germ theory	610	stress	622	explanatory style	626
immune system	611	general adaptation		Type A behavior pattern	631
immunosuppression	613	syndrome	623	John Henryism	633
cardiovascular diseases	617	hassles	624	social support	635
cancer	618	primary appraisal	625		

Industrial-Organizational and Other Applied Psychologies

John B. Watson, the founder of behaviorism (Chapters 1 and 8), was a full professor at Johns Hopkins University before he was 30 years old. His research and his papers led to this early acclaim, and he is still honored for his pioneering contributions to psychology. Watson's career, however, was not without blemish. In 1920, a well-publicized scandal involving an affair and a divorce led to his dismissal from Johns Hopkins.

Although he continued to lecture and supervise the research of graduate students, Watson never again held a regular academic appointment. But his career as a psychologist was far from over. He accepted a job with one of the first national advertising agencies, J. Walter Thompson. This agency was interested in the possible contribution that the new field of psychology could make to the equally new field of advertising. Could psychological theories and findings be used to help sell products to consumers?

Watson had a successful career in advertising, so much so that almost every advertising agency today has psychologists on its staff. Indeed, an entire field of psychology, called consumer psychology, is concerned with explaining, predicting, and influencing the public's decisions to buy one product rather than another.

Watson made a number of contributions to the field of advertising (Goldstein & Krasner, 1987), some of them now so standard that you may be surprised to learn they can be traced to one individual. Though Watson may not have been the first person to recommend each of these practices, he was the first to base them on psychological theory and to explain, from his behaviorist perspective, how and why they were successful:

1. *Placing candy and magazines near the checkout stands of supermarkets.* Candy and magazines are called impulse products. People do not usually go to a store to buy a Nestlé's Crunch candy bar or The *National Enquirer.* Consumers buy them only when they see them and the impulse hits. Placing impulse products near a checkout stand guarantees that every customer must walk by them. Further, granted the pileup at a checkout line, almost every customer must stand in front of these products for several minutes or longer. Finally, consider that people stand in front of these products with money already in their hands. What better way to arrange circumstances so that a purchase will occur? Remember Watson's view of human beings as responsive to the stimuli in their immediate environment and his view of learning as the result of repeated associations (Chapter 8).

2. *Arousing fear.* One of the clients of J. Walter Thompson was Johnson & Johnson, of baby powder fame. Using survey data, Watson determined that the most likely consumers of Johnson & Johnson baby powder were young, upwardly mobile, middle-class mothers expecting their first child. Watson assumed that these mothers would be especially worried about disease and infection, and so Johnson & Johnson baby powder was advertised as a means of preventing calamity. The unstated but obvious

One of John Watson's advertising clients was Johnson & Johnson, of baby powder fame.

message was that if you did not buy this product and sprinkle it liberally on your child, you were courting disaster and were a bad mother. Remember the importance attached to being a parent (Chapter 10).

To this day, advertisers strike at the insecurity of parents, even going so far as to arouse fear where none previously existed, in order to sell products. Along these lines, a longtime favorite of mine is the series of television ads, run by Michelin Tire Company, that picture babies crawling among tires while voices off-screen discuss the merits of saving a few dollars by buying tires from another company. Perhaps these ads have as strong an effect on you as they do on me. After watching one, I always promise myself that I will buy Michelin tires the next day, to safeguard my children. Then I remember that I do not have any children.

3. *Arranging endorsements from experts and celebrities.* One more of Watson's innovations was to hire supposed experts to endorse products (Chapter 15). So, Dr. Holt—a forerunner of Dr. Spock and well known as the pediatrician of the Rockefeller family—was hired to extol the virtues of Johnson & Johnson baby powder. And the popularity of Pond's cold cream greatly increased when Watson arranged endorsements by the queen of Spain as well as the queen of Romania.

The United States must not have changed much over the years, as we are still fascinated by royalty. Imagine the impact Princess Di would have were she to endorse a product. In her absence, we have Michael Jordan, Jerry Seinfeld, and Ringo Starr hawking products. Even the former governors Mario Cuomo and Anne Richards have endorsed corn chips on television.

4. *Writing popular books.* Finally, John Watson was one of the first pop psychologists—individuals who present to the general public a popularized version of scientific psychology (Starker, 1989). Watson wrote a variety of articles for popular magazines, including *McCall's, Harper's,* and *Cosmopolitan.* He dispensed his advice in chatty fashion, drawing on his behaviorist ideas to tell readers how to live happier and more fulfilling lives. Nowadays, Dr. Ruth, Joyce Brothers, Scott Peck, Barbara DeAngelis, John Gray, and Bernie Siegel are following Watson's example in applying psychological ideas to concrete problems in the contemporary world.

UNDERSTANDING APPLIED PSYCHOLOGY: DEFINITION AND EXPLANATION

The topic of this chapter is **applied psychology:** the use of psychological theories and findings to help solve the sorts of problems people encounter in their everyday lives. Applied psychology is often distinguished from **basic psychology:** the pursuit of psychological knowledge for its own sake. Consider research into how students might improve their memory for information from courses (Chapter 10). This research is a good example of applied psychology. Such studies can be distinguished from investigations of how learning takes place in sea slugs (Chapter 8), research that is a good example of basic psychology.

■ **applied psychology**
use of psychological theories and findings to help solve people's practical problems

■ **basic psychology**
the pursuit of psychological knowledge for its own sake

Applied psychology is the attempt to apply theory and research to practical problems. Self-help books are one obvious example of applied psychology.

Defining Applied Psychology

The distinction between basic and applied approaches to psychology is not always so clear, however, for much of psychology is inherently practical. The way in which basic psychologists go about their business cannot help but shed light on everyday problems. For instance, investigations of classical conditioning undertaken to explore basic questions about the nature of learning (Chapter 8) leads to strategies of behavior therapy (Chapter 14). Similarly, the way applied psychologists go about their business leads to an understanding of basic questions about human nature. The MMPI, for example, was developed to aid diagnosis of psychological problems (Chapter 13) but led to a statement about the basic dimensions of personality (Chapter 12). People's behavior is best regarded as contextualized, and applied psychologists have always been aware of the particular settings in which people behave.

Consider some of the other topics discussed in previous chapters, such as pain control (Chapter 6), education (Chapters 8 and 10), intellectual assessment (Chapter 11), and health promotion (Chapter 16). One cannot easily say where the basic aspects of these topics stop and the applied aspects begin, or vice versa. Indeed, Kurt Lewin's idea of action research gave modern social psychology its character by explicitly blurring the distinction between basic psychology and applied psychology (Chapter 15).

Another way of defining applied psychology, as opposed to the rest of psychology, is in terms of where the psychologist does his or her work. The basic psychologist typically works in a university setting, doing research in a laboratory, often with introductory psychology students like you as subjects. In contrast, the applied psychologist usually works outside the university, in a business or industrial setting, in a hospital, at a school, on a playing field, or in a courtroom.

Many applied psychologists believe that most definitions of their field are overly simple. Applied psychology is not the automatic application of a basic science called psychology. As we have seen, psychology itself is a highly diverse field. One does not—because one cannot—apply the whole of psychology. Rather, one applies a particular subfield of psychology and, within this subfield, a particular theory or result.

A Brief History of Applied Psychology

Applied psychology received its biggest boost in the United States, with the approach to psychology known as functionalism (Costall, 1992). As discussed in Chapter 1, functionalists such as William James and John Dewey proposed that psychology should concern itself with the functions of the mind, with the consequences of one's mental processes. This interest resulted in a field that applied psychological theory and research to human concerns outside the laboratory.

Among the first of these practical efforts were applications to business. In 1903, Walter Dill Scott published *The Theory of Advertising,* in which he explained how the new science of psychology generated numerous suggestions for influencing the buying behavior of the general public. Scott frequently cited William James in his book, echoing the idea that people are defined by their habits. Advertisers must try to make the buying of their particular products a habit (Chapter 8). To this end, slogans should be associated with products because these provide a cognitive basis to the habit an advertiser tries to establish (Chapter 9).

Another boost to applied psychology came from American involvement in World War I. Chapter 11 described how intelligence testing first came into widespread use during World War I, in an attempt to choose the right people for military positions. Whether or not this had any direct effect on the war effort is debatable, but the immediate aftermath of this mass testing cannot be denied. Written tests soon became a widely used means of hiring and placing people in industry. Personnel selection, now a thriving concern of applied psychology, had its beginnings in the intelligence tests administered to recruits during World War I.

In sum, applied psychology is the attempt to use theory and research to solve practical problems. However, qualifications and elaborations need to be added. First, the distinction between applied psychology and basic psychology can be imprecise, particularly as these approaches have developed in the United States. American psychology—due to the influence of functionalism—is highly practical. Second, some psychologists use a simple strategy to decide whether or not psychology is applied: They look at where the psychologist in question works. If the work is done in a university laboratory, then it is basic psychology; if elsewhere, it is applied psychology. Third, a psychologist applies not psychology but rather one field of psychology. He or she uses particular techniques to go about the application, so much so that it is misleading to speak of applied psychology as singular. Rather, it is a grouping of different approaches, reflecting the applications of diverse aspects of psychology.

Applied Psychology as Biopsychosocial

Different applied psychologies are biopsychosocial because contemporary psychology itself has this character. Depending on the type of psychology that is applied and the nature of the problem to be solved, these applications emphasize biological, psychological, or social influences on behavior. In many cases, all of these influences need to be taken into account by the applied psychologist. For example, if psychologists are trying to boost an athlete's performance, they might target the athlete's aerobic capacity (a biological factor), his or her pain tolerance and concentration (psychological factors), and his or her concern with team goals (a social factor).

This chapter covers some of the important speciality fields of applied psychology: industrial-organizational psychology, engineering psychology, consumer psychology, sports psychology, environmental psychology, and psychological aspects of the legal system. The fields selected here represent but one way to divide applied psychology (Anastasi, 1979; Fagan & VandenBos, 1993; Goldstein & Krasner, 1987; Gregory & Burroughs, 1989). My goal is to give a flavor of each field, noting the area of basic psychology with which it starts and then giving examples of the types of practical uses to which it has been put.

Stop and Think

1 What is applied psychology?

2 Why has applied psychology flourished in the United States?

DOING *Applied Psychology* RESEARCH

The concerns of any psychology researcher—sampling, operationalization, validity, reliability, and generalization—are also those of the applied psychology researcher. But these concerns are addressed in different ways depending on the setting in which the research is conducted. In doing applied psychology research, one uses particular techniques to carry out one's work. A researcher must know the specific requirements for each application; instances abound of researchers who take techniques out of the laboratory and into the real world, only to find that these strategies are inappropriate in the new setting.

For example, questionnaires devised for use with college students might not work well with other research subjects. College students are quite familiar with questionnaires and usually do not need to have directions spelled out for them. Subjects who rarely encounter a questionnaire might not know what to do with it. My favorite illustration of this point—which may or may not have really happened—involves a researcher who administered a questionnaire that included an item that simply read: Sex _____. The researcher wanted to know if the respondent was a male or a female, but when he read the answers to this question, he found phone numbers, frequency estimates, and particular names, times, and places.

In general, operationalizations must be sensible for the specific people being studied. A problem occurs when research is done in a work setting and workers are asked to evaluate their jobs or employers, for they may fear—with some justification—that their responses will have consequences for their own careers. Assurances of anonymity, confidentiality, and/or nonretaliation must be persuasively made and sincerely kept if measures are to be valid.

In applied research, investigators pursue knowledge in order to evaluate a given program or procedure and to make a policy recommendation. There is always a risk that those with vested interests will dismiss the researcher's conclusions or that the researcher will conduct the research in such a way as to guarantee a desired result. Research in work settings is usually initiated by management, not labor, and so applied psychologists run the risk of seeing matters from the viewpoint of management, who pays their fees (Katzell & Austin, 1992).

Although experiments are the most valid way of determining causes and effects (Chapter 2), an applied psychologist may not always be able to conduct a fully satisfactory experiment. For ethical or practical reasons, it may be impossible to assign research participants to experimental conditions on a random basis. Or some conditions may be unable to be created. Consider, for example, a researcher interested in how best to arrange the pedals in an automobile. Some configurations of pedals—we would suspect—are quite hazardous as one drives. While it might be interesting to know this information with certainty, no researcher would want to risk the possibility that he or she is correct.

Even correlational studies can be difficult to carry out in an applied setting. Suppose a researcher is interested in whether a measure of manual dexterity successfully predicts who will be a successful surgeon. The ideal way to determine this is to give a large number of individuals the test in question and then let them perform surgical procedures that are later judged as successful or not. This strategy, obviously, cannot be pursued, but the effect is that applied research can be less informative than we would like.

Finally, applied researchers cannot let statistical significance be the overriding criterion in evaluating their studies (Chapter 2). A judgment must be made about the practical significance of a finding or conclusion, and the size of an effect takes on paramount importance in applied psychology. Many individuals who work in applied settings dismiss the relevance of basic research to their interests because the effect sizes are tiny (Schonpflug, 1993). To be taken seriously, applied psychologists must show that their research has discovered patterns that matter. For example, a study might show that an extensive training program results in better workers, but if the costs of the training are not offset by gains in productivity, an employer will not put the program into operation.

> ### Stop and Think
>
> **3** Find an example in the popular media of applied psychology research. Is this example a case study, a correlational investigation, or an experiment? What are its operationalizations? Are any confounds evident?
>
> **4** What special ethical dilemmas are faced by applied psychologists?

INDUSTRIAL-ORGANIZATIONAL PSYCHOLOGY

Industrial–organizational (IO) psychology concerns itself with improving complex work organizations. IO psychologists are interested in fitting the person to the job, and vice versa (Mowday & Sutton, 1993). They proceed by applying psychological theory and research to the topic of work.

■ **industrial-organizational (IO) psychology**
field of applied psychology concerned with improving the functioning of complex work organizations

Several speciality areas within IO psychology can be distinguished (Dorfman, 1989). It is common to split the *I* in *IO psychology* off from the *O*. So, industrial psychology, sometimes called personnel psychology, focuses on selecting and evaluating people in an organization (Schuler, Farr, & Smith, 1993). This emphasis on personnel gives industrial psychology a strong interest in individual differences. In many ways, we can look at personnel psychology as applied personality psychology (Chapter 12). Devising and administering tests for selection and evaluation are among the most typical activities of personnel psychologists.

Organizational psychology, the *O* of *IO,* focuses on the process by which workers adjust to one another and their work organization (Greenberg, 1994). Here we see interest in workers' attitudes, motivation, job satisfaction, and leader-follower relationships. Given these interests, organizational psychology is very much the application of social psychological ideas (Chapter 15).

The Meaning of Work

Whether applied psychologists are at the *I* or the *O* end of *IO psychology,* they need to be interested in the psychological significance of work. Brief and Nord (1990, p. 1) introduced their book on the psychology of work with the following observation:

> We did not set out to examine the meaning of life, but found it difficult to keep our study of the meaning of work from growing to include such an examination. In fact, given the American preoccupation with work . . . if we had assumed work and life are one, the assumption might not even have been challenged by many readers.

Industrial psychologists are usually interested in the selection of individuals for jobs and the evaluation of their performance, and organizational psychologists are concerned with how workers adjust to one another and their organization.

Work is conventionally defined in economic terms—what people do for financial compensation in order to earn a living—but this definition obscures its richer psychological meaning.

The work people do often defines who they are. An occupation does more than pay the bills; it consumes one-third to one-half of the average adult's waking hours. It provides one of our most important identities by directing our life in certain directions rather than others. "What do you do?" is a conversational gambit that could be answered in any of a number of ways, but most of us hear it as a question about our occupation.

Work as biopsychosocial.   The U.S. Department of Labor has listed more than 30,000 types of jobs in this country alone. In trying to understand the meaning of jobs to workers, psychologists have proposed dimensions with which to classify these various ways of earning a living. For example, jobs differ in terms of physical requirements, intellectual demands, and interpersonal characteristics: whether they involve goods (producing things) or services (assisting people). Work collectively is biopsychosocial, although the mix of biological, psychological, and social emphases varies across jobs (see Figure 17.1).

Work in its broadest sense must also be placed in its historical and cultural context. The meaning of work to an individual varies according to societal conditions. During a recession or depression, workers are simply grateful to be employed. During prosperous times, workers are less satisfied and more willing—because they are more able—to explore alternatives to their current jobs. If the country is at war, those who work for defense contractors are more fulfilled by their jobs than is true when the country is at peace (Turner & Miclette, 1962).

A typology of workers.   England and Whitely (1990) studied workers in six different nations with respect to:

■ the centrality of work to an individual's life
■ the goals and values preferred by a worker, ranging broadly from economic motives (good pay and job security) to expressive motives (opportunity to learn new things, harmonious relationships with other people at work, and autonomy)
■ whether work was regarded as a societal right or a societal obligation

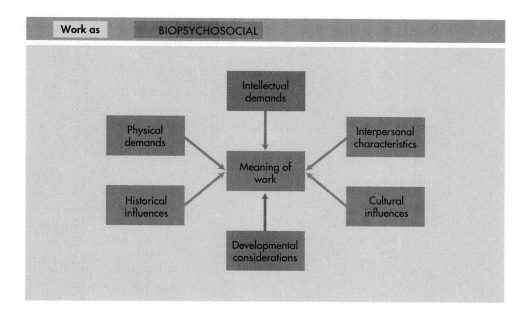

From responses to questionnaires measuring these aspects of the meaning of work, the researchers discerned several common patterns and proposed a typology of workers in terms of work's meaning.

One type of worker can be characterized as alienated. For this individual, work is not central to his or her life; it is pursued for neither economic gain nor expressive reasons; and it is not seen as fulfilling any obligation to the larger society. Another type of worker can be described as economic; the meaning of work for this individual revolves solely around good pay and high security. A third type of worker is duty-oriented. This individual regards work as highly central to his or her life, undertakes it for expressive reasons, and regards it as a societal obligation. A fourth type of worker is best described as balanced. Here work is highly central to the person's life and allows both economic and expressive goals to be satisfied.

Across all the nations studied, alienated workers in general tended to be younger and female, and they performed low-paying jobs with little variety or responsibility. As you would imagine, they rated their satisfaction with work as very low.

Economic workers in general had less education and were somewhat more likely to be males; their jobs were also low in variety and responsibility. Despite the importance of pay to these workers, they tended not to earn much money. Their satisfaction with work was also very low.

Duty-oriented workers in general were older and somewhat more likely to be females; they often worked as managers or in sales, in jobs with high variety and responsibility, and usually for good salaries. Their work satisfaction was high.

Balanced workers were usually older males with more education; they worked at a variety of jobs, usually those high in autonomy; they put in the longest hours; and they earned the highest salaries. They rated their work satisfaction as quite high.

These results are not surprising, but note that the meaning of work to an individual—as captured by his or her classification—was correlated with a range of personal and occupational characteristics, from motives to salaries. No single characteristic by itself proved to be of overriding importance in terms of its association with the meaning of work. Like the other psychological phenomena discussed in this book, the significance of work is complexly determined (Kelly & Kelly, 1994; Lundberg & Peterson, 1994).

Work in Japan versus the United States. What did England and Whitely (1990) learn about work in different nations? Let us consider just the contrasts between workers in the United States and those in Japan. These differences shed some light on the

On average, Japanese workers put in more hours at their jobs than American workers. At the same time, Japanese workers express more satisfaction with their work.

often heard charge (in both countries) that Japanese workers are "better" than those in the United States.

On average, workers in Japan put in 49 hours per week at their jobs, whereas those in the United States put in 43 hours. Japanese workers were somewhat less likely to describe their work as possessing variety (73 versus 81 percent) and as utilizing a considerable amount of their skills (65 versus 73 percent). However, Japanese workers reported much more satisfaction with their work than American workers did. They were more likely to say that they would choose the same job again if given the opportunity and that they would keep working even if they had no financial reason to do so.

These findings seem contradictory. Why were Japanese workers more satisfied with work that took more time, had (somewhat) less variety, and used (somewhat) fewer of their skills? Perhaps the answer lies in the psychological meaning of work. Workers in Japan were more likely to be classified as duty-oriented or balanced, whereas those in the United States were more likely to be classified as economic or alienated.

There are innumerable reasons for these national differences in the meaning of work and its translation into satisfaction or dissatisfaction. It is unlikely that these differences can be reduced to a handful of simple practices and procedures. Rather, we need to consider the larger cultural contexts from which the significance of work emerges if we wish to understand these differences between Japanese and American workers. Remember my discussion in Chapter 8 of the differences in education between Japan and the United States. The general points raised there apply here as well.

The United States is currently very interested in borrowing Japanese work and management techniques (Kono, 1982; Smith, Reinow, & Reid, 1984; Viau, 1990). For example, Japanese companies often encourage their workers to participate in group calisthenics. But calisthenics, in and of themselves, will not make American workers feel less alienated or more balanced in their motivation to work. The meaning of work needs to be changed in a more positive direction by undertaking innovations that make sense in terms of the culture of the United States. For instance, given the importance of the individual in the United States (Chapter 15), we can predict that jobs allowing workers to put their own identifiable spin on what they do should be more satisfying than jobs that demand uniform and anonymous performance.

The Developmental Trajectory of Work

The discussion of development in Chapter 10 emphasized the need to contextualize psychological changes across the life span. An important part of this contextualization involves an appreciation of how social and historical forces come to bear on behavior. This idea is nicely illustrated by considering how the nature of work changes as people grow older (Dex, 1991).

Depending on where a person happens to be in his or her life course, the identical job takes on drastically different meanings. For example, one of my favorite jobs was working in a hot-dog stand while I was in graduate school. I enjoyed the bantering with fellow workers and customers, the free meals, and the challenge of remembering what "the works" meant for people from New York versus Chicago versus Los Angeles. As a middle-age individual, however, I would doubtlessly loathe this job and feel alienated because I am a different person in terms of my wants and needs.

Adolescent work. In the early history of the United States, children and adolescents went to work as soon as they were able. Usually this meant assisting their family members, on farms or in shops. But with the passing of child labor laws, the presence of children and adolescents in the workplace steadily declined throughout the early part of the twentieth century. By 1940, no more than 5 percent of high school students worked during the school year. In the last few decades, matters have changed considerably (Silbereisen & Todt, 1994; Stern & Eichorn, 1989). One reason is the growth of retail stores and fast-food restaurants that employ part-time workers at low wages. Here is a societal need that adolescents can best fill, and indeed they have done so. Another reason is the general inflation that has hit our society, particularly the adolescent world. It costs a great deal of money to be a teenager today, and so economic necessity drives adolescents to work.

By some estimates, it is more common for a high school student to work during the school year than not to do so. Those adolescents from the middle and upper-middle classes are most likely to be employed because they live in suburban areas where jobs are more plentiful. Least likely to be employed are teenagers from the lower class, who live in areas where jobs are less available.

There are several important implications of the level of adolescent employment found today in the United States. First, teenagers working is an American phenomenon. Teens in Europe, Japan, or even Canada are not nearly as likely to have a job as are American teens. As a result, American adolescents do not have as much time to do schoolwork as their counterparts elsewhere (Chapter 8). Perhaps the tendency among American students for grades to drop during adolescence makes perfect sense (Kablaoui & Pautler, 1991; Schulenberg, Asp, & Petersen, 1984).

Second, the vast majority of jobs that teenagers fill are, simply put, boring. One wonders just what these jobs prepare someone to do. Further, teenage jobs are segregated by age. An adolescent rarely works directly with adults and does not develop a full understanding of what employment can mean to people in their adult lives (Steinberg, 1985).

Third, teenage work is often split between boy jobs (e.g., clearing tables, carrying newspapers, and doing lawn or construction work) and girl jobs (e.g., baby-sitting, waiting on tables, and working as a maid). Because this split occurs so early in one's working life, it ends up channeling adult males and females into sex-stereotyped jobs. Males and females might never consider that they can choose from a variety of careers, not just those regarded as "appropriate" to their gender.

The picture of the working adolescent appears bleak, but there are positive aspects, at least in principle. The lessons one might learn at work, such as the importance of responsibility, foresight, and cooperation, can help consolidate an adolescent's identity (O'Brien, Feather, & Kabanoff, 1994). These lessons can then lay the foundation for subsequent development (Chapter 10). Unfortunately, the typical jobs filled by teenagers do not measure up to this rationale. The challenge we face as a country is to

Adolescent employment is largely an American phenomenon. Middle- and upper-middle class teenagers are the most likely to work in the United States because unlike teenagers from the lower class, they live in areas where jobs are more plentiful.

discover ways to increase the likelihood that work will benefit the development of adolescents rather than harm it.

Adult work.   Adolescent work slides into adult work, gradually for those individuals who do not attend college or trade school, more abruptly for those who do (Sanford, Offord, McLeod, Boyle, Byrne, & Hall, 1994). How do people go about choosing an occupation? It is important to know that most workers do not stay with a single type of job throughout their working life. Between five and ten significant job shifts occur throughout adulthood for the typical worker, meaning that the question of occupational choice is more complicated than it may first seem. Some theorists therefore prefer to speak of an individual's career path rather than his or her career.

The range of careers to choose from is limited by factors such as gender-role socialization, family background, and education. For many young adults, these considerations combine to create a schema of legitimate versus illegitimate careers that dictates their eventual career choices. Many children follow the career paths of their parents, particularly in professional fields such as medicine and law (Mortimer, 1976).

When I talk to my students who are psychology majors, I am struck by how many have a parent who works within a social service field. Other students, who may enjoy the study of psychology just as much, never consider the possibility of majoring in psychology or pursuing a career as a psychologist because there is no family precedent for doing so.

Within the range of acceptable jobs, a worker tends to choose one that satisfies his or her basic values. The psychologist John Holland (1966, 1985) proposed an influential approach to occupational choice. He hypothesized six basic personality types, each with corresponding jobs (see Table 17.1). When personality matches the job, satisfaction is high, and work is performed well.

Some studies of worker satisfaction find that it increases with age, although the relevant factor may be experience with work rather than age itself (Avolio, Waldman, & McDaniel, 1990; Healy, Lehman, & McDaniel, 1995). In any event, older and/or more experienced workers like what they do better than younger workers do—which is hardly surprising. They typically have better jobs, with more influence and greater challenges. They are more likely to evaluate a job in terms of characteristics such as salary,

Table 17.1 Personality Types and Jobs

According to Holland (1985), the satisfaction of workers is highest when their personalities match the requirements of the jobs they hold.

Personality type	Characterization	Job examples
Realistic	Prefers objects or tools	Mechanic; contractor
Investigative	Prefers observation and study	Scientist; journalist
Artistic	Prefers creative activities	Musician; novelist
Social	Prefers aiding other people	Social worker; teacher
Enterprising	Prefers economic gain	Salesperson; stockbroker
Conventional	Prefers manipulation of information	Accountant; librarian

benefits, and security, which usually increase the longer they hold a job (Rabinowitz & Hall, 1981).

Retirement. Mandatory retirement was invented in nineteenth-century Europe by German politicians who wanted to look as if they were doing something positive for society when in fact they were doing nothing at all (Woodruff-Pak, 1988). The age of retirement was first set at 70 and later changed to 65, precisely because so few people lived to be this old. The United States followed suit in the early twentieth century. Needless to say, retirement has since become more than a cosmetic social institution.

In contemporary America are two opposing trends. First, we see ever earlier retirement for the average worker. Second, we see mandatory retirement laws thrown out altogether except for those covering a handful of occupations. It is difficult to predict what effect these trends will have on the composition of our future workforce.

Studies of worker satisfaction find that it increases with age. Older workers usually have better jobs, with more influence, greater challenges, and better pay.

Most workers retire in their early sixties. Two types of men retire early: the affluent and the ill. Keep this in mind when interpreting the consistent finding that retired individuals have a higher mortality rate than workers of the same age. Here the probable direction of causality runs from poor health to retirement, not vice versa. Among those who retire because their financial situation allows them to do so, retirement is generally a time of good health, increased social activity, and high life satisfaction. Those who fare best in retirement are the same people who fared well when working, a striking example of consistency across the life span (Palmore, 1981).

Paralleling the increase of women in the workforce over the past few decades is an increase in studies of retired women (Henretta, 1994; Perkins, 1992; Szinovacz, 1982). Like men, women today are retiring at an increasingly earlier age (Hayward, Grady, & McLaughlin, 1988). However, the factors that influence one's decision to retire vary between men and women (George, Fillenbaum, & Palmore, 1984; Hanson & Wapner, 1994; Talaga & Beehr, 1995). Many women are influenced in their own decisions to retire by the needs and wishes of their husbands and families (Reeves & Darville, 1994). And women on average retire with fewer pension benefits than men (Conway, Ahern, & Steuernagel, 1995; Handa, 1994; Jacobsen, 1994; Logue, 1991; Richardson & Kilty, 1991), meaning that with some frequency "retired" women must return to work (Perkins, 1993).

Industrial Psychology

This section describes several of the major interests of industrial psychologists. Remember the earlier characterization of industrial psychology as focusing on selecting and evaluating workers for particular jobs in an organization. The prerequisite for these activities is specifying the positions for which people are being selected.

Job analysis. Accordingly, industrial psychologists help organizations by conducting a **job analysis:** an explicit description of what people are expected to do at a particular occupation (Muysken, 1994). Job analyses specify the skills and abilities needed to perform successfully at the occupation in question.

■ **job analysis**
explicit description of what people are expected to do at a particular occupation

There are several standard procedures for performing a job analysis. Personnel psychologists may start by observing people at work, then interviewing them and their supervisors. They may undertake a survey, using questionnaires to assess various people's opinions about the required skills.

Sometimes the best way to conduct a job analysis is for personnel psychologists to do the job themselves. As you know from your own efforts in the workplace, a job title does not always tell you much about what really goes on. There is often no substitute for getting firsthand experience.

According to industrial psychologists, jobs should be characterized not just in terms of their typical demands but also in terms of **critical incidents:** specific occurrences that distinguish satisfactory workers from unsatisfactory ones (Flanagan, 1954). How a worker responds to critical incidents is usually of great interest to employers. Table 17.2 provides examples of critical incidents for college administrators (Hodinko & Whitley, 1971).

■ **critical incidents**
specific occurrences that distinguish satisfactory workers from unsatisfactory ones

Selection. As already pointed out, personnel psychologists help to recruit people for jobs (Schmidt, Ones, & Hunter, 1992; Schmitt, Borman, et al., 1993; Schmitt & Robertson, 1990). Which is a better strategy for finding employees: hiring from within the company or going outside it? Are employee referrals better or worse than newspaper ads or employment agencies? There are no simple answers here, but it appears as if employee referrals are good because they reduce turnover, yet bad because they breed

Table 17.2	Critical Incidents for College Administrators

Hodinko and Whitley (1971) were college administrators who drew on their own experiences to compile a list of critical incidents that confront people in this role. Here are the sorts of incidents they described. How might an administrator respond in each case? What do you think would be the best response? Although this list is more than 25 years old, it is still current, suggesting that the demands of college administration have not changed all that much over the years.

General area	Critical incident
Campus parking	A community college is soon to open in a confined urban area. Planners have allowed for 1,000 parking spaces, but a survey you have just completed shows that more than 3,000 individuals will need to park on campus daily.
Building takeover	A student group with a list of demands plans to take over a college building.
Drug use	You are told by campus police that known drug dealers have been seen in the student union and other campus gathering places.
Censorship of student publications	The faculty sponsor of the student humor magazine calls you in a panic, worried that an article planned for the next issue might strike some readers as racist. Should its publication be forbidden?
Contraception	Students ask that condoms be sold in vending machines on campus, but the college board of regents is opposed.

sameness in the workforce (Dorfman, 1989). These conclusions make sense in terms of the social psychological findings about friendship discussed in Chapter 15.

How should a job be portrayed to a potential applicant? Popular is a technique known as a realistic job preview (Wanous, 1980), in which the applicant is given an accurate view of a job, warts and all, rather than a rosy view that will only be dashed once work begins. Research suggests that realistic job previews reduce turnover by about 10 percent, resulting in considerable savings of time and money that would otherwise be spent in recruitment and training (McEvoy & Cascio, 1985).

Notice the parallel between realistic job previews and the training interview described in Chapter 14 as a way to give psychotherapy clients realistic views of what awaits them in therapy. Both procedures share the goal of molding expectations so that they are consistent with what actually follows. Disappointment is thereby headed off.

Many jobs will have more than one applicant, and the personnel psychologist will thus be involved in choosing which one will be hired. Virtually every major organization in the United States uses an interview as a way to select employees. Face-to-face meetings with several people in the organization take place, after which these people discuss their impressions and make a decision. Research by personnel psychologists shows that the validity of interviews as a way to assess ability—that is, to predict how well people will do at a particular job—is often poor (Arvey & Campion, 1982; Harris, 1989). Psychological principles discussed throughout this book help explain why. First, different interviewers often disagree. Their conclusions are not reliable because what they think about the applicant is more likely to reflect their own thoughts and beliefs than the applicant's actual characteristics (Chapter 9). Interviewers have their own stereotypes of a good employee, and so they try to match applicants to them. As we know, stereotypes are simplifications at best and downright wrong at worst (Chapter 15).

Jobs that rarely include women or minorities can stay that way because of the self-fulfilling nature of an interviewer's stereotypes (Morrow, 1990; Ralston, 1988). For instance, look at the historical hesitation of professional sports teams in hiring African American coaches, despite the large number of African American athletes. The reason

Should a job be portrayed to poten-
tial applicants in a realistic way?

for not hiring them simply seems to be that there have been so few in the past, and the owners of teams have trouble recognizing likely candidates. In our lifetimes, will we see a female hired to coach a team in major league baseball, basketball, or football? I suspect we will see a female president much sooner.

I should stress that some approaches to interviewing prove valid (McDaniel, Whetzel, Schmidt, & Maurer, 1994). For example, to the degree that interviewers standardize the questions they ask different applicants, validity is increased. And questions about how the applicant has handled situations in the past that are similar to those that the job in question involves yield especially useful results.

Besides interviews, selection also relies on written tests. As mentioned earlier in this chapter, work organizations started using questionnaires to select workers shortly after World War I. The debate over proper and improper uses of intelligence tests, detailed in Chapter 11, has a parallel in the use of personnel selection tests. Indeed, recent years have seen legal challenges and rulings that more explicitly limit such tests, especially when they lead to different hiring decisions concerning men versus women or those from various ethnic groups (Sackett & Wilk, 1994).

The logic behind such tests is straightforward, and it is easy in principle to specify what would be a good test. People presumably differ in characteristics that will lead to good or bad job performance. If we wish to have the best workers on a job, then we will want to know what the characteristics leading to good performance might be and how we can assess them before the job begins. If we can do all of this, then we need merely give a test and choose those who score high.

So far so good, but are such tests valid? This question involves two issues. First, what skills are necessary for a job? Second, does a test measure these skills and not irrelevant factors? The best way to answer these questions is to give a variety of people a test, hire them all, assess their performance, and then see whether the test distinguishes good and bad workers. In some cases, this process is impossible because employers might want to hire only a few people in the first place. They never get a chance to know how everyone else will perform.

An alternative strategy is to give tests to people already working in the organization and to see which questions distinguish between workers you judge as good or bad. Obviously, this strategy is not identical to choosing people before the fact. It parallels the difference between cross-sectional and longitudinal designs, as discussed in Chapter 10. Workers who are doing less well than others may answer tests in certain ways, but they might not have done so before they started.

General personality tests typically are poor predictors of job success, perhaps because they are simply that: general personality tests, measures of broad traits (Chapter 12). Traits by definition are abstract and general characteristics of people. People with different personality characteristics will approach a job in different ways, but most can still excel (or fail to do so).

The trait of conscientiousness is an exception to these conclusions because it bears a consistent relationship to job performance at most occupations (Mount, Barrick, & Strauss, 1994). This finding makes sense because reliability on the part of a worker is an obvious prerequisite for being able to do a job well. Another exception is extraversion, which research finds to be related to good performance at jobs which require social contact (Barrick & Mount, 1991,1993).

An alternative to personality tests is work-sample tests, in which prospective workers are asked to perform tasks similar to what the actual job requires: Prospective auto mechanics repair a car; prospective typists type a letter; prospective teachers conduct a class. These tests echo the point of social learning theorists such as Bandura: To assess people's personalities, you must locate them in a given setting (Chapter 12). Remember the terms introduced in Table 12.6; work-sample tests have content validity because they explicitly sample what they try to predict.

Performance evaluation.   Another concern of industrial psychologists is trying to evaluate the performance of people who already fill a job (Herbert & Doverspike, 1990; Ilgen, Barnes-Farrell, & McKellin, 1993; Matheson, Van Dyk, & Millar, 1995). Evaluation is undertaken for several purposes. It provides a basis for raises or promotions. It is used to decide which workers will survive a layoff or a corporate downsizing. In the extreme, evaluation leads to a decision to terminate a worker for unsatisfactory performance.

Merit is highly valued in the United States and figures prominently in contemporary societal debates like those involving the necessity and/or fairness of affirmative action programs (Turner & Pratkanis, 1994). The problem is that the evaluation of merit is itself a thorny matter. Industrial psychologists have grappled with the issue for decades—indeed, since the beginning of their field (Katzell & Austin, 1992).

The first step in evaluating satisfactory performance or unsatisfactory performance is defining what these mean for a given job. The ideas already described about job analyses are pertinent here. Assuming that a job's requirements can be described in a way with which most would agree, the second step is to decide how to measure whether these requirements have been met.

Various strategies are used. One of the most obvious ways to measure performance is to look at objective measures of worker output, if these exist. Assembly-line workers can be evaluated in terms of the number of units they produce in a given period and/or their lack of mistakes. Police officers can be evaluated in terms of the number of arrests they make and/or the number of successful convictions that result. All other things being equal, these are valid strategies for assessing performance.

However, all other things are usually not equal. Many workers are interdependent, meaning that their own performance—however objective its measurement—is linked to the success or failure of their fellow workers. If nothing else, the O. J. Simpson murder trial underscored to the public the degree to which police officers and prosecutors rely on one another in doing their respective jobs. The more general point is that performance reflects not simply an individual's merit but a host of other influences for which we would not want to hold the individual responsible.

Workers can be evaluated in terms of the number of units they produce, but is this a reasonable basis for evaluation, given that their performance is influenced by that of other workers?

Even if we ignore most of these other influences, objective measures of performance are still far from foolproof. Do we wish to measure a worker's typical performance or maximum performance, as might happen when he or she knows an evaluation is taking place? Even for relatively simple jobs, these different criteria are not highly correlated (Sackett, Zedeck, & Fogli, 1988), meaning that an industrial psychologist cannot interchange them.

Another strategy for measuring performance is to rely on a global rating by a supervisor. The supervisor is assumed to be familiar with the job's requirements and the worker's performance. An overall judgment is then made. For example, U.S. Civil Service workers are typically evaluated annually by their immediate supervisors, who use a rating scale ranging from outstanding to unacceptable. This system allows bias, deliberate or inadvertent, because many factors potentially influence such ratings besides a worker's actual merit. Look at Figure 17.2, which presents Landy and Farr's (1980) schematic of what occurs when even the simplest rating of a worker is made by a supervisor. Although abstract, this figure is a complex depiction of the process—which is precisely why it is included here. When the details are filled in for a particular job, the result can be overwhelming.

A more refined rating strategy asks supervisors to use several different rating scales, in order to allow them to make more subtle distinctions. A worker's performance can then be evaluated in terms of a profile of strengths and weaknesses. Often, though, the promise of this approach is not realized. Halo effects like those discussed in Chapter 12 can result in a supervisor rating a worker in similar terms across all the requested dimensions. Or a given supervisor might have a bias toward harshness or leniency, so that ratings end up reflecting more on the supervisor than on the worker in question.

■ **behaviorally anchored rating scales (BARS)**

judgments about the degree to which a worker performs particular behaviors relevant to his or her job

Yet another refinement is the use of **behaviorally anchored rating scales (BARS)** that ask not for good-versus-bad evaluations but rather for judgments about the degree to which a worker performs particular behaviors relevant to the job in question (Smith & Kendall, 1963) (see Figure 17.3). An assessment of the relative merits of these behaviors is made by management, and the worker is then given an evaluation. Advocates of BARS argue that they are more reliable and valid than other rating strategies, although the evidence for these conclusions is mixed (Landy, 1989).

Do not be left with the impression that performance evaluation is impossible. Workers, after all, do vary in how well or poorly they perform their jobs. There is no

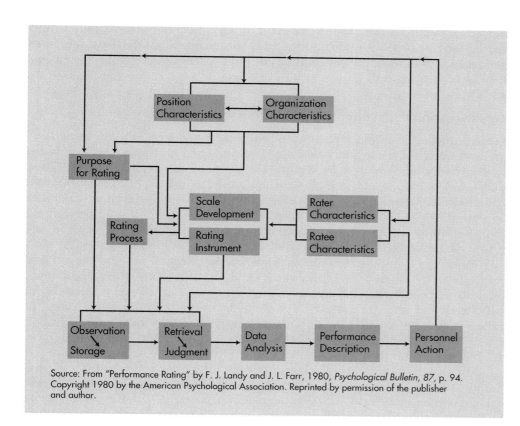

Figure 17.2
Process Model of Judging the Performance of a Worker. Judging how well a worker performs his or her job is a highly complex process, as this diagram shows.

Source: From "Performance Rating" by F. J. Landy and J. L. Farr, 1980, *Psychological Bulletin, 87*, p. 94. Copyright 1980 by the American Psychological Association. Reprinted by permission of the publisher and author.

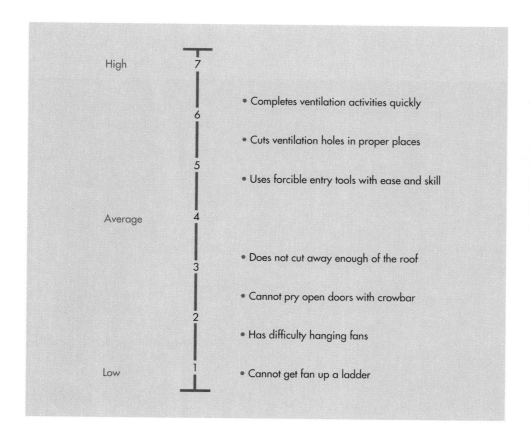

Figure 17.3
A Behaviorally Anchored Rating Scale for Firefighters. In a behaviorally anchored rating scale, a worker's performance is judged in terms of specific behaviors relevant to the job. Here is an example of such a scale for firefighters: A given individual is placed along the scale according to his or her abilities to perform these behaviors. *Source:* F. J. Landy (1989). *Psychology of work behavior* (4th ed.). Pacific Grove, CA: Brooks/ Cole, p. 140.

mystery in identifying those who fall at either extreme. All of the strategies just surveyed can be used to make reasonable judgments about performance. Just remember that performance evaluation, like performance itself, is a highly complex phenomenon and must be approached as such.

Organizational Psychology

Let us begin our discussion of organizational psychology with a look at the first investigations in this field, research known as the Hawthorne studies because it was conducted at the Hawthorne Works of the Western Electric Company outside Chicago. These studies began in 1924 and lasted for a number of years (Mayo, 1933). Their original intent was to investigate the effects of objective factors, such as illumination and length of work periods, on productivity. A consistent finding, however, derailed this original goal. Regardless of the conditions imposed on workers, those in the experimental groups did better than those in comparison conditions.

We now call this phenomenon the **Hawthorne effect.** It refers to the fact that participation in an experiment can change someone's behavior, above and beyond particular experimental manipulations. Being in an experimental group enhances the self-esteem and status of subjects as well as their willingness to work hard. The Hawthorne studies sparked concern with the social context of work and, therefore, gave rise to the entire field of organizational psychology (Chant, 1993; Diaper, 1990; Jones, 1992; Parsons, 1992).

At present, organizational psychologists study the effects on productivity of such factors as worker opinions and attitudes, job satisfaction, worker motivation, goals, communication, and modes of conflict resolution (Anastasi, 1979). Researchers rarely find simple results. Various factors combine and mingle to affect productivity, and thus organizational psychologists regard organizations as complex psychological fields (Chapter 15). This complexity provides multiple targets for intervention. The following discussion focuses on two topics of particular interest to organizational psychologists: worker satisfaction and organizational climate.

■ **Hawthorne effect**
change—above and beyond that attributable to particular experimental manipulations—in someone's behavior because he or she is participating in a workplace experiment

The Hawthorne effect was first documented in studies in the 1920s at the Hawthorne Works near Chicago. Just knowing they are in an experiment—regardless of its nature—changes how workers approach their jobs.

Worker satisfaction.   The apparent truism that satisfied workers are more productive is not supported by the evidence. Numerous reviews of the link between worker satisfaction and productivity conclude that the relationship—when it exists at all—is trivial in magnitude (Brayfield & Crockett, 1955; Das & Mital, 1994; Iaffaldano & Muchinsky, 1985; Locke, 1976; Vroom, 1964). When a correlation is found, it might be just as plausible to conclude that successful performance leads to satisfaction (Landy, 1989). Similar conclusions emerge from studies of the links between worker (dis)satisfaction and absenteeism and turnover. When relationships exist, they are trivial (Mobley, Horner, & Hollingsworth, 1978; Nicholson, Brown, & Chadwick-Jones, 1976).

The larger point is that worker satisfaction, absenteeism, turnover, and productivity are so complexly determined that we cannot reasonably expect one-to-one relationships between and among them. It does appear that work satisfaction is related to overall satisfaction with life (Davidson & Caddell, 1994; Orpen, 1978). As you know from previous chapters, a disrupted life contributes to physical and psychological problems. Dissatisfaction with work will eventually take a toll on an individual, even if it does not show up obviously or immediately at work.

The vitamin model.   It seems silly to justify why satisfaction at work is a worthy goal. The pursuit of happiness is a cherished value in our culture and is therefore worth studying in its own right. Here is what has been discovered about the sources of satisfaction at work. This discussion is based on Warr's (1987) view of the matter, which he termed the **vitamin model** of worker satisfaction, for reasons that will soon become clear.

Warr proposed that nine attributes of work need to be present in at least minimal amounts in order to produce a satisfied worker (see Table 17.3). Some of these attributes, like money and physical security, are like vitamins C and E: the more the better, or at least there is no diminishment of satisfaction with increasing amounts. Other attributes, like variety and interpersonal contact, are like vitamins A and D: necessary up to a point but potentially lethal in greater amounts. This metaphor provides a complex but sensible view of satisfaction. Its practical implication is that an employer's attempt to enrich a job—make it more satisfying—must take into account all the possible contributions to satisfaction and how these are affected by a given innovation. Too much of a given job attribute might actually decrease satisfaction, or it might push another attribute beyond its optimal level.

Flow.   This point about the importance of balancing job characteristics can be illustrated by examining a phenomenon termed **flow,** defined by Csikszentmihalyi

■ **vitamin model**
Warr's theory of worker satisfaction that specifies different attributes of work that need to be present in at least minimal amounts to produce a satisfied worker

■ **flow**
subjective feelings that accompany highly engaging activities

Table 17.3   Determinants of Worker Satisfaction

According to Warr (1987), each of these attributes of work must be present in at least a minimal amount for a worker to be satisfied. However, some of these attributes may decrease satisfaction if they are present to an extreme degree.

Attribute	**Reason attribute can be problematic in the extreme**
Money	Not a problem in the extreme
Physical safety	Not a problem in the extreme
Social status	Not a problem in the extreme
Concrete goals	Stress
Variety	Distraction
Clearly specified tasks	Limited opportunity for development
Personal responsibility	Stress
Demanding skills	Stress
Interpersonal contact	Lack of control; overcrowding

Flow takes place when a person focuses attention on the task at hand. A person's skills and the task's demands must match in order for flow to occur.

(1990) as the subjective feelings that accompany highly engaging activities. It is similar to what Maslow referred to as a peak experience (Chapter 7). Flow is not to be confused with sensual pleasure; it refers instead to the satisfying emotional engagement with what one is doing.

According to Csikszentmihalyi's studies of the flow experience, it usually occurs during activities that people enjoy, whether at work or leisure (Jackson, 1992; Wankel & Sefton, 1989). Regardless of the activity in question, flow takes place when a person focuses his or her attention on the task at hand. The task must present an above-average challenge, and the skills brought to bear must be deployed with an above-average expertise. Critically, the challenges and skills must also be in appropriate balance. Without this balance, people will not experience flow. Instead, what results is either worry (when challenges outweigh skills) or boredom (when skills outweigh challenges).

If we apply these ideas to the workplace, we predict that jobs will produce the most satisfaction when they balance their demands with a worker's abilities (Kipper, 1991). The nature of a job needs to change with time but not in a willy-nilly way. The change must be in keeping with changes in what the worker can do.

■ **organizational climate**
perception of the characteristics of an organization by its members

Organizational climate.   **Organizational climate** is the perception of an organization's characteristics by its members (Schneider, 1990). By this definition, organizational climate is a psychological phenomenon that may or may not bear a close relationship to an organization's real characteristics. So, while the size of a business can be described objectively in terms of the number of its employees, its gross profits, or the dimensions of the building where it is housed, size as perceived by those who work there might reflect its psychological feel to them.

For example, do workers know each other by name? Do they understand the rules for overtime? Can they find an inexpensive parking place? Are restrooms close to where they work? One of the important determinants of a worker's productivity is the degree to which he or she perceives the organization as supportive (Friedlander & Greenberg, 1971). To the degree that workers at the same organization share common perceptions of it, we can speak of an organizational culture (Schneider, 1985).

Theory X and Theory Y.   Organizational psychologists have devised various ways of describing and classifying organizational climates. One particularly influential formulation was presented by Douglas McGregor (1960), in his book *The Human Side of*

Enterprise. McGregor contrasted two approaches to management, termed Theory X and Theory Y, that can color the entire climate of an organization. These approaches need not be explicit in the minds of particular managers, but they are implied by the way someone goes about his or her managerial tasks. McGregor thought of these approaches as extreme examples of different climates rather than an exhaustive typology (Dwivedi & Dwivedi, 1993; Landy, 1989). However, the contrasts he drew between Theory X and Theory Y are important ones for understanding how and why people work.

Theory X is the set of assumptions that often guide traditional management: Workers are lazy and must be coerced into doing their job. In fact, Theory X assumes that people prefer to be told what to do, that they wish to avoid responsibility, that they have no ambition, and that they seek security above all other concerns.

Theory Y is a more humanistic view (Chapter 12), assuming that workers are motivated to put physical and mental effort in their work. People prefer to exercise choice and control, rather than have these imposed upon them. They seek out responsibility. Under the appropriate circumstances, workers can be counted upon to be creative and innovative. They work for a paycheck but also to fulfill less tangible needs, not least of which is the need to actualize their own potential, as workers and as people.

Can you think of employers you have had who exemplify these approaches? If your employer constantly checked up on you, monitored your coming and going, and gave you a long list of things you should not do, then you had a Theory X boss. If your employer did not look over your shoulder, asked your opinion about how to carry out various tasks, and praised your innovations, then you had a Theory Y boss. The odds are that most of you have had more personal experiences with a Theory X boss.

McGregor harshly criticized typical managerial practices, which he argued "could only have been derived from assumptions such as those of Theory X" (p. 35). In general, work is set up as if it were a form of punishment to be compensated for by satisfactions that are enjoyed away from the job. Consider the incentives provided by work organizations for their employees: salaries, bonuses, vacations, health and medical benefits, and pensions. None of these can be enjoyed at work. None of these has anything to do with work. If anything, they interfere with how people perform their jobs, by creating arbitrary status differences among workers. According to McGregor, employees would care little about minor differences in salaries and benefits if their work itself was more satisfying. But the Theory X boss assumes that work can never be satisfying, and so he or she never makes the attempt to change it.

■ **Theory X**
set of assumptions that often guide traditional management: Workers are intrinsically lazy and so must be coerced into doing their job

■ **Theory Y**
set of assumptions that guide nontraditional management: Workers are intrinsically motivated to expend physical and mental effort in their work

Theory X can be a self-fulfilling prophecy. If someone is mistrusted, then he or she may act as if this mistrust is deserved. Consider the most recent professional baseball strike, in which players and owners acted in ways that harmed everyone's best interests.

If Theory X is not as viable as Theory Y, then why has it been so popular? McGregor gave two answers. The first is historical. Not that long ago, workers functioned at what Maslow described as a deficiency level (Chapter 7). Only their most basic needs were relevant. The nature of their work—as slaves or indentured servants, in mines or sweatshops—guaranteed this. Indeed, these approaches are still business as usual in some parts of the world. Management practices originally developed to deal with workers who were in physical danger. Of necessity, managers used carrots and sticks to coerce and bribe their employees. Theory X therefore made sense. Old managerial habits have been slow to change, especially because these include the notion that one need never talk to workers about what they might prefer.

A second explanation for the persistence of Theory X is that it can be a self-fulfilling prophecy. Despite lacking initial validity, Theory X can become true if one acts as if it were (Argyris, 1975). If a worker is mistrusted and threatened, then he or she will eventually act as if this treatment were justified.

McGregor made the point that Theory Y sees the needs of the individual and those of the organization as compatible. Theory X, of course, sees workers and management locked in a struggle where the gain of one is the inevitable loss of the other. Consider the disputes in recent years that have torn apart professional baseball and other professional sports. To the onlooker, the athletes and the owners should be each other's best friends. Both sides are honored and adored beyond anyone's wildest dreams. Both sides have more money than they could possibly spend. But they butt heads periodically and refuse to compromise on trivial matters, probably because they think of labor-management relations in Theory X terms. The players go on strike, and/or the owners lock them out. Both sides lose.

Another interesting point McGregor made is that typical ways of rewarding good performance can easily backfire. An organization gives employees raises that presumably vary according to the quality of their work. Three problems exist with this common approach. First, in most cases, the quality of work is difficult to judge. As already discussed, bias creeps into performance evaluation. Second, even if the quality of work could be gauged in a foolproof fashion, the difference in actual raises—say, 3 versus 5 percent—is usually so inconsequential that it is not worth the damage to morale that it creates. Third, there is no good reason to think that merit raises really lead to better productivity. The United States, for example, has one of the biggest gaps between the highest and lowest salaries of workers, whereas Japan has one of the lowest gaps. Few would argue that productivity is superior in the United States.

Excellent organizations.   Management in recent years has become well aware of these ideas. There is a great interest in how best to tap the potential of workers. Innovations have been introduced such as employees owning the company for which they work, signing the goods they produce, and being consulted regularly by management for advice. Books like *In Search of Excellence,* by Thomas Peters and Robert Waterman (1982), have topped the best-seller list.

In Search of Excellence described a study of the most productive companies in the United States. It concluded that eight factors characterize most excellent corporations:

1. *A bias for action*: doing things and solving problems rather than simply talking about them
2. *Closeness to customers*: learning what works and what does not from the customers they serve
3. *Autonomy*: encouraging people in all parts of the company to be innovators
4. *An emphasis on workers as people*: treating employees as sources of ideas and not just pairs of hands
5. *Focus on values*: making clear the basic philosophy of an organization and treating it as more than just a slogan

6. *Sticking to what they know best*: never acquiring a business that no one knows how to run

7. *A simple organization and a lean staff*: having the most streamlined procedures possible, so that workers do not stumble over one another and/or trip on red tape

8. *A fanatical emphasis on a few core values and great flexibility with regard to everything else*: being tight with respect to what really matters and loose with everything else

These features elaborate on Theory Y to embrace the vision of the individual as conscious, purposeful, and significant, always in the process of growing and changing. Excellent corporations allow this nature to surface and serve company goals, rather than coercing and/or bribing workers into behaving according to a theory of organizational behavior that neglects their human potential.

Peters and Waterman (1982) did not find these characteristics of excellent companies surprising. They referred to them as motherhoods, meaning that they are so obviously good that none would question them. However, there must be more to their list than just common sense; otherwise, we would see more companies putting these qualities into practice (Bluedorn, 1993).

What is the barrier to making more workplaces excellent ones? Part of the problem, according to Peters and Waterman, must be laid at the feet of theorists and academics who propose managerial ideas that have nothing to do with human beings. Organizational psychologists attempt to be an exception to this criticism, by basing their recommendations firmly on what psychology has learned about people.

Stop and Think

5   Are there cohort differences in the meaning of work? Talk to younger versus older adults that you know and find out.

6   What is industrial psychology?

7   Why do people retire?

8   What are some critical incidents for a college student?

9   What is organizational psychology?

10   What is the vitamin model of worker satisfaction?

11   Describe how Theory X and Theory Y can be applied to classroom practices.

ENGINEERING PSYCHOLOGY

Every day of your life, you encounter the products of **engineering psychology,** which uses psychological theories and research to design environmental settings—typically machines—to be safe, efficient, and/or pleasurable (Fisher, 1993; Martin, 1989; Norman, 1988; Wickens, 1992). For instance, the controls and the lights on the dashboard of a car have been arranged in such a way that they are easy to see and not confusing.

When you drive a car down the street, different street signs compete for your attention. Engineering psychologists devote their efforts to how best to convey information in a symbol that will only be glimpsed. They want to minimize any ambiguity, so that you do not confuse the meaning of one sign with that of another (see Figure 17.4).

For yet another example, consider a personal computer with a word-processing program. Most programs have a menu: commands at the top or bottom of the screen. Engineering psychologists design these commands to be easy to understand and use. When complex commands are abbreviated as single letters, these should be letters with

■ engineering psychology
field of applied psychology that uses psychological theories and research to design environmental settings—usually machines—to be safe, efficient, and/or pleasurable

Engineering psychologists attempt to design controls so that they are safe and efficient.

which the full command begins: *p* for *Print*, *s* for *Save*, and *h* for *Help*. When we speak of a computer as user-friendly, we do not mean that it provides amusing graphics that bring a smile to our face. Instead, we mean that its design is psychologically informed; the computer works in a way consistent with the way we work and the way we think about our work. Macintosh computers have been so popular in part because they were the first to be explicitly designed so that their available programs and procedures resemble the way people organize their desks and their tasks (Norman, 1988). Blank screens are avoided because who works at a completely empty desk?

The dimensions of devices like chairs, light switches, and showers have been designed to fall within limits judged comfortable for the range of typical people.

Figure 17.4
Symbols for Public Information. Different symbols are used to convey information to the public, and some symbols are more efficient than others. Above each symbol is a number representing a composite of how accurately it can be recognized when seen briefly, the distance from which it can be seen, the ease with which it can be interpreted, and the correspondence between it and its meaning. The higher the number, the more efficient the symbol in these terms. *Source:* Mackett-Stout & Dewar (1981).

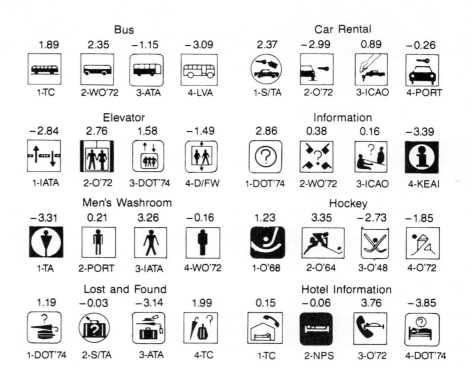

Engineering psychologists are well versed in people's dimensions, and the speciality field that studies these dimensions is called anthropometry (Roebuck, 1995). Thanks to these psychologists, we know the average reach of Americans, their eye height when sitting, and the height of their knees from the ground. One of the reasons why the armed forces have height requirements is to ensure that recruits can use the devices the military provides, whether shoes, hats, weapons, or beds.

However, engineering psychologists have learned that there is no such thing as an average person with respect to all possible bodily dimensions. For instance, Daniels (1952) studied 4,000 pilots, measuring ten relevant dimensions of their bodies. Not a single person out of the 4,000 fell between the top and bottom third on all ten dimensions. Engineering psychologists therefore try to design devices not for the nonexistent average person but rather for a range of people, typically those who fall between the fifth and ninety-fifth percentiles of each dimension.

What kinds of methods do engineering psychologists use? Obviously, they rely on surveys of bodily parts. They must also be familiar with basic findings regarding sensation and perception (Chapter 5) and cognition (Chapter 9). When they design products for people of different ages, they must additionally know about developmental changes (Chapter 10).

How bright must a display be in a cockpit in order to be visible but not distracting? How should emergencies be signaled—with a buzzer, bell, or spoken voice? Should switches move up and down or sideways?

Analogue switches are frequently used. With these switches, the amount the switch is changed or the direction it moves corresponds to changes in whatever the switch is controlling. On a stove, the switches for the burners are usually arranged in the same configuration as the burners. Other times, conventions are purely arbitrary, but then they become standardized within a culture. So, North American light switches are turned on by moving them up; in Australia, the opposite convention is followed. In Japanese and American cars, volume controls for radios are on the opposite sides.

Even simple products can be confusing if their design is at odds with the way people typically behave (Norman, 1988). For example, doors can be opened by pushing, pulling, or sliding. A well-designed door, from the perspective of its user, provides unambiguous cues about how it is to be opened. A poorly designed door leaves the user at a loss, pushing instead of pulling, or vice versa.

One more example of engineering psychology is that toy manufacturers increasingly take into account the psychological factors that make particular toys more versus less attractive to children (Chase, 1992). Have you ever bought a toy for a child, only to discover that he or she finds the box in which the toy was enclosed a more interesting play object? A toy that is appropriate for children of one age may be inappropriate—hence of no interest—to children who are slightly younger or slightly older.

Here are some generalizations about preferred toys (Feeney & Magarick, 1984). Try to make sense of them in terms of the fact that children of different ages have different physical and cognitive abilities (Chapter 10). Children like a toy they can manipulate, although it is important that they possess the required motor skills (Gramza, 1976). Small buttons or dials may prove unwieldy for extremely young children. The toy in question should provide sensory stimulation (Moosman, 1975). Children also prefer toys of moderate complexity, and the optimal complexity increases with age (Hunter, Ames, & Koopman, 1983). For many young children, the ideal toy is colorful, mobile, three-dimensional, sound-generating, and realistic (Yen, 1985).

Needless to say, toys must also be safe for the children who will play with them, and so this is an additional consideration for manufacturers informed by developmental theory and findings. One need not be a Freudian to appreciate that young children go through a period in which many objects are placed in their mouths. So, small toys or those with removable parts must be evaluated in light of this possibility.

Psychologists who study toys are often interested in the fact that many of them are sex-typed—for example, dolls for girls and trucks for boys. A preference for sex-typed toys apparently develops quite early in life, more so for boys than for girls. Sex-typing of

A preference for sex-typed toys develops early in life, more so for boys than girls.

toys also reflects the ideology of the adults who purchase them, more so for men than for women (Almqvist, 1989). Interestingly, contemporary adults in the United States are more likely to give sex-typed toys to other people's children than to their own (Fisher-Thompson, 1993).

Stop and Think

12   What is engineering psychology?

13   Think of the various items of clothing that you wear. Which fit better than others? What do you conclude about your bodily dimensions relative to those of "average" people?

14   What would be a good toy to purchase for a 3-year old child?

CONSUMER PSYCHOLOGY

■ **consumer psychology**
field of applied psychology concerned with the acquisition and consumption of goods and services

In discussing John Watson's work in applied psychology at the beginning of this chapter, I introduced the subfield of **consumer psychology:** the application of psychological theory and research to the acquisition and consumption of goods and services (Cohen & Chakravarti, 1990; Foxall, 1994; Mowen, 1989). Although consumer psychology focuses on one particular domain of behavior—buying and using things—it is an extremely broad area.

As many as 95 percent of the studies conducted by consumer psychologists examine the factors that influence the buying of particular products, and many of these studies look specifically at advertisements (Mowen, 1989). Numerous psychological factors combine to influence the impact of advertising, from needs and motives (Chapter 7) to memory and decision making (Chapter 9) to social influence (Chapter 15). Let me briefly mention some of these factors, along with representative research by consumer psychologists.

The decision to buy a product is multiply determined. Suppose you need a beverage, a laundry detergent, a soap, or a meal. There are innumerable choices you might make within each of these categories. What determines exactly which product you choose? In some cases, the actual characteristics of a particular product determine your choice, as when you buy a chocolate bar because of its taste. But advertisers do not rely on products to sell themselves; instead, they attempt to link their goods to your needs and motives.

Look at the way automobiles are advertised. A car is not simply something that gets you to work or to the country on weekends. According to advertisements, automobiles provide a way to express and actualize your true self. Why do so many men walk around wearing hats or T-shirts displaying the brand names of the vehicles they drive? Car and truck advertisements have been highly successful in their campaign to make Chevy or Ford part of someone's identity.

Henry Murray's catalog of needs (Chapter 7) has been useful to advertisers as a reminder of the range of needs that products might satisfy. For instance, beer advertisements typically appeal either to one's need to play or to one's need to achieve (McNeal, 1982). Watch television commercials for beer and see if the actors are simply having a good time (Miller Lite) or are celebrating a notable accomplishment (Löwenbräu). Beers have changed their image over the years. If you are old enough, you may remember that Miller was once sold as the champagne of bottled beer and Michelob was urged on someone for special occasions. Formerly achievement beers, these are now play beers.

In general, advertisements pair products with powerful images, and we come to associate them with one another, through classical conditioning (Chapter 8), as well as through more cognitive processes (Chapter 9). McDonald's, for instance, seems like the absolutely most fun place in the entire world, to judge by the commercials. After watching these commercials, we might learn to associate the golden arches of McDonald's with laughter and singing, and thus be led to choose McDonald's when we drive off in search of a quick hamburger.

We can speculate that if Carl Jung were alive today, he would look for evidence of archetypes not in myths but in advertisements (Chapter 12). Many of the images popular in ads today are primal and potentially universal. Commercials often feature men and women cavorting in splashing water. Is it farfetched to suggest that this image has sexual undertones?

Recall Walter Dill Scott's (1903) idea that ads are successful to the degree that they are remembered. Basic principles of memory therefore help to explain which ads are the most effective. Scott listed three key factors, all of which are well supported in recent research literature (Chapter 9).

For example, repetition is important. Ads should be repeated over and over. There is a trend in television advertising in which the same ad, or a series of related ads, are run back-to-back-to-back. Have you ever seen, for instance, the commercial in which the battery-powered toy rabbit marches tirelessly through what appear to be other commercials?

Another factor is association. Can the product be linked to other ideas or stimuli in the environment? Here we see a rationale for trademarks, slogans, and endorsements. Why do advertisers spend so much money sponsoring sporting events? One obvious answer is that they associate their product with the event in question. Virginia Slims for years underwrote women's tennis. Budweiser sponsors a variety of racing events. Never mind the fact that most tennis players do not smoke cigarettes or that most racing-car drivers do not drink, at least while racing. We think of particular products whenever we think of the sporting event they sponsor. In 1995, women's professional tennis turned down the sponsorship of a tampon company because it supposedly conveyed the "wrong image" for the sport.

Yet another key factor in advertising that Scott distinguished is what he called ingenuity, meaning the ease with which something comes to mind. As explained in

We should not drink and drive, but advertisers apparently believe that people should drink and watch others drive.

Chapter 9, items are easier to recall when they have multiple cues. Scott argued, therefore, that advertisements should link products with slogans that are ridiculous, clever, or otherwise memorable. In recent years, we have such examples of ingenuity as Bud Lite ("I love you, man"), Nike athletic shoes ("Just do it"), and the X-Files ("The truth is out there").

Stop and Think

15 Describe a current advertisement in terms of the needs to which it appeals.

16 Describe how an advertisement might be designed so that it is difficult to remember.

SPORTS PSYCHOLOGY

■ **sports psychology**
field of applied psychology concerned with physical performance, usually in the context of competitive athletics

Sports psychology is the application of psychological theory and research to physical performance, usually in the context of competitive athletics (Bakker & Whiting, 1989; Kremer, 1994; Singer, Murphey, & Tennant, 1993). Only in recent years has the subfield of sports psychology received national recognition, but it dates to at least the 1920s, when Coleman Roberts Griffith at the University of Illinois studied football stars such as Red Grange (Wiggins, 1984). In 1977, the U.S. Olympic Committee (USOC) appointed its first sports psychologist, and in subsequent years, the USOC has increasingly involved psychologists in the selection and training of the nation's elite athletes.

Although the specific applications of sports psychology often vary from sport to sport—depending on whether it is a team or an individual sport and on the particular physical skills demanded—certain concerns cut across this subfield of applied psychology. Researchers start with the general premise that athletic performance is a function of the athlete, the coach, and the particular setting (the opponent, the spectators, and the physical environment). They look at how these factors lead to good or bad performance, and they intervene to improve an athlete's performance.

One of the consistent findings is that an athlete's performance is enhanced to the degree that athletic skills are practiced over and over so that they are performed automatically, without conscious thought. This phenomenon is just one more example of the distinction between automatic and controlled processing, made in Chapter 6. For example, the practice habits of the basketball player Larry Bird were legendary. His goal was to master particular shots and passes to such a degree that he could perform them in a game without conscious thought.

As mentioned earlier, sports psychologists propose and investigate different strategies for improving performance. Both cognitive and behavioral techniques like those discussed in Chapter 14 and elsewhere in this textbook have proved useful (Goldstein & Krasner, 1987). Mental imagery in which the person rehearses in his mind how to swing a golf club or throw a football can improve actual performance (Murphy, 1990). Thought stopping—a technique for banishing anxiety-producing cognitions—can help rid the athlete of disruptive emotions. Goal setting, which pays dividends at work and school, can be just as helpful in the sports domain.

Common opinion has it that certain personality types are more likely to lead to success in sports, but research has failed to support this idea. Personality inventories such as the MMPI (Chapter 12) do not predict which athletes will succeed or fail (Fisher, 1977). Even measures of individual differences that appear obviously relevant to athletic success—such as drive, aggressiveness, determination, and mental toughness—have proved to be of little use (Martens, 1975).

Some small differences between the personalities of successful and unsuccessful athletes can be found in need for achievement, but it is still not clear whether these are a cause or a result of performance differences . For another instance, hockey and football players tolerate pain better than golfers or bowlers (Ryan & Kovacic, 1966), though this result might simply be due to frequent pain and the stimulation of endorphins (Chapter 4). Work here continues, but for the present it looks as if all types of people—personality-wise—can and do succeed at sports.

Sports psychology is still searching for an identity. A legitimate worry is that the field's focus is too much on the highly skilled athlete, and indeed, this criticism is a general one that can be made about sports in our society. While the elite athletes of our country attain ever more impressive performances and win ever more acclaim and reward, the average fitness of our citizens is declining.

We know that physical exercise is healthy for all people, both emotionally and physically (Chapters 14 and 16). Perhaps sports psychologists need to include average citizens—those of us slouching on couches throughout the land—in their attempts to motivate and involve people in physical activity. Here their efforts would entwine with those of health psychologists and clinical psychologists.

Stop and Think

17 Besides the huge amounts of money involved, why have sports psychologists been so concerned with elite athletes?

18 Compare and contrast exercise programs with psychotherapy (Chapter 14).

ENVIRONMENTAL PSYCHOLOGY

Environmental psychology concerns itself with how the physical environment affects people's thoughts, feelings, and behaviors (McAndrew, 1993; Saegert & Winkel, 1990). This field of applied psychology draws on several areas of basic psychology, especially social psychology. When the environment of concern is the workplace or mechanical devices, environmental psychology overlaps with IO psychology and engineering psychology (Carrere & Evans, 1994).

Environmental psychologists have several concerns. One is clearly social psychological in nature: How do individuals use physical space in their interactions with others (Evans & Howard, 1973; Hall, 1966; Sommer, 1969)? You probably know that people

■ **environmental psychology**
field of applied psychology concerned with how the physical environment affects people's thoughts, feelings, and behaviors

One of the concerns of environmental psychology is the way in which individuals use physical space to regulate their interactions with others. People from Middle Eastern cultures tend to stand much closer to one another while talking than most Americans or Europeans.

differ in how closely they stand next to someone else during a conversation, and that their cultural group is a determinant here. Those from Middle Eastern cultures stand much closer than many Americans or Europeans.

Another concern of environmental psychologists is cognitive: How do people think about the physical environment? To describe someone's mental representation of a physical space, psychologists have introduced the notion of a cognitive map, a direct descendant of Kurt Lewin's lifespace (see Figure 17.5). Cognitive maps are schemas: organized (and simplified) representations of the real world (Chapter 9).

Kaplan and Kaplan (1982) stressed the importance of landmarks in cognitive maps. When we think of the city where we live, we do so in terms of its landmarks: particular buildings, streets, or monuments. Landmarks denote choice points (where we turn to go to the grocery store or to the bank). They are regarded as prominent in size and distinctiveness, even if this is not entirely accurate. They are used to estimate distance. If Point A and Point B have no landmarks in between, the distance is seen as shorter than that between Point C and Point D, which have numerous landmarks in between, even if they are actually the same distance.

If landmarks are removed or altered, a person can become disoriented. For instance, I fell into the habit of finding my way to a friend's house by turning right immediately after a large orange MEN AT WORK sign, posted for months. One day the sign was removed, and I sailed right by my turn and drove for several miles before I realized something was wrong.

A third concern of environmental psychologists is the effects of environmental stressors on people. Although events such as crowding, noise, and pollution have direct physical consequences, their psychological impact is also influenced by one's sense of personal control (Evans, 1980, 1994; Evans & Joseph, 1982; Evans & Lepore, 1992, 1993; Lepore, Evans, & Palsane, 1991). We experience little discomfort when surrounded by many people as long as we have chosen to be in this situation and believe we are free to leave. Contrast a rock-and-roll concert with O'Hare Airport at Christmas. In both cases, we are crushed by other people, but stress is much more likely at O'Hare than at the concert.

Stop and Think

19 Why is environmental psychology, despite its concern with the physical world, at the same time cognitive?

20 Obtain a copy of a map of your campus. Look at the how the buildings and streets are identified. Does this map seem useful or not? How could it be improved?

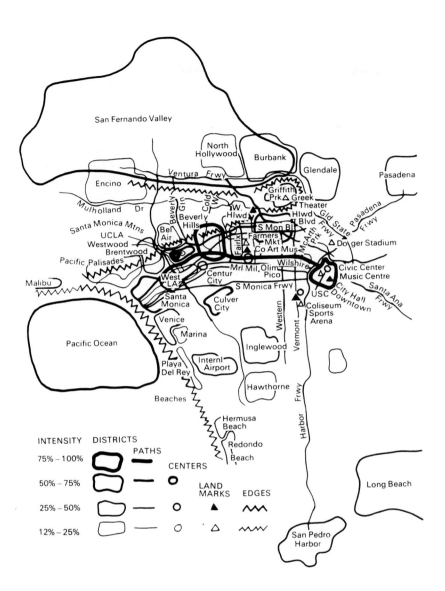

Figure 17.5
Cognitive Map of Los Angeles. This picture is not a literal map of Los Angeles but rather a psychological one. The person who holds this view of the city includes only those parts that play an important role in his or her personal life. *Source:* Gould & White (1974).

PSYCHOLOGY AND LAW

Psychology often interacts with the legal system, mainly with regard to issues of diagnosis (Chapter 13) and treatment (Chapter 14) of psychological disorders but also with respect to many other matters (Kagehiro & Laufer, 1992). When psychologists testify in court about psychological topics, they often do so as an expert witness—which means that the court recognizes them as especially knowledgeable in the case being considered (Brodsky, 1991). They are designated as experts, and so in their testimony they can include ideas from the research literature. Even if an expert has not conducted a given study herself, she can still testify about it. The court will not consider her testimony to be hearsay (Loftus, 1991).

It is unlikely that psychology and the legal system will stop trafficking with each other in the near future. But realize that tension exists between these two approaches to human conduct (Morris, 1982). Psychology is a scientific discipline based on the assumption of determinism—that what people do has causes (Chapter 1). Psychology is best equipped to offer generalizations about people. Individual cases may or may not fit these conclusions. In contrast, the legal system is based on the assumption of free will—that what people do represents their own choice, unless there are extenuating circumstances (Canali & Capurro, 1988).

Furthermore, the legal system is concerned with individual cases, not people in general. The statistical significance of results on which psychological research puts so much weight is not a criterion that makes any sense in a court of law (Chapter 2).

Finally, the legal system relies on advocacy: The prosecution and defense both try to make the strongest possible arguments. Justice is served by the interplay. The scientific ideal calls for evenhandedness on the part of individuals. However, when psychologists testify as expert witnesses, they necessarily do so as advocates. As a result, when on opposite sides of a case, they frequently disagree with one another. The general public often views this disagreement cynically, seeing psychologists and other mental health professionals as arbitrary or even mercenary. Appreciate, though, that the legal system demands advocacy. Witnesses on opposite sides of a case should be expected to disagree.

These contrasting ideas—determinism versus free will, generalities versus individual cases, scientific evenhandedness versus legal advocacy—can create a discrepancy between what psychologists do best and what those who ask psychologists to appear in court want them to do. It is not surprising that the role of psychology with regard to the legal system is controversial and in constant flux (Coleman, 1984; Havard, 1992).

Involuntary Commitment

The majority of people hospitalized for psychological problems—about 75 percent—have been voluntarily admitted (Monahan & Shah, 1989). They have given their consent to be treated. Once in the hospital, however, they do not always get to leave as readily as they arrived. The staff might decide that their condition does not allow them to be discharged, in which case their status is converted into what is known as **involuntary commitment.** The remaining 25 percent of psychiatric patients come directly into hospitals against their will, again as involuntarily committed individuals.

How does all of this occur? Procedures differ from state to state, but the process usually begins when somebody—a police officer, a mental health professional, or just an everyday person (friend, family member, fellow worker)—makes a complaint to the police or the court that the individual in question poses a danger. If this allegation is taken seriously, the police pick up the person and take him or her to a clinic or a physician for an examination.

If an emergency situation seems to be present, the court can order the person to be hospitalized for further observation. Depending on the state, the length of these emergency hospitalizations varies from a single day to several weeks. In some states, a hearing must be held to see whether further hospitalization is justified.

Holding people in a psychiatric hospital against their will is in direct conflict with our society's cherished notion of freedom of movement. As such, this procedure is not undertaken lightly. It is a formalized process, carried out under the supervision of the legal system. One of two general criteria must be documented if people are to be involuntarily committed: The person is judged to be a danger to the self or a danger to others.

A person can be involuntarily committed if he suffers some psychological disability, meaning that he needs treatment, that he is somehow dangerous to himself, and/or that he is in no position to take care of himself. Some suggest that involuntary commitment by this criterion be guided by the "thank-you test." By this test, involuntary commitment is justified if we can assume that an individual, once recovered from whatever problem he or she suffers, will thank those who carried out the commitment.

The second criterion used to justify involuntary commitment is whether the individual constitutes a danger to other people (Monahan, 1992). In the extreme, we can recognize this easily. Repeated attempts to hurt others constitute good evidence that the person is harmful. But matters are not always so clear-cut. The justification for involun-

■ **involuntary commitment**
placement of an individual in a mental hospital without his or her consent

tary commitment is not past evidence of dangerousness but a judgment that the person will be dangerous in the future.

However, psychologists cannot predict future dangerousness with any accuracy (Kress, 1979; Steadman & Keveles, 1972, 1978). This fact calls into question the very idea that the judgment of future dangerousness to others constitutes a reasonable criterion for involuntary commitment. Some suggest that the criterion be modified to mean dangerousness not for the indefinite future but for some relatively brief and specified period. This modification might well improve our ability to predict this kind of behavior (McNiel & Binder, 1987; Rofman, Askinazi, & Fant, 1980).

A more satisfactory alternative to involuntary commitment as it is currently carried out involves committing individuals to treatment as outpatients (Scheid-Cook, 1987). The individual is legally required to undergo treatment, but without the massive readjustment that hospitalization involves. We would expect that the stigma associated with being hospitalized is also substantially reduced. Research to date suggests that this alternative is promising. In one study, for instance, patients involuntarily committed to outpatient treatment fared better than comparable patients undergoing involuntary inpatient treatment (Hiday & Scheid-Cook, 1989). Notably, they were more likely to utilize aftercare services following their treatment.

Insanity Plea

A different sort of concern takes place when a person with a psychological problem finds himself accused of a crime. The legal system in the United States and most places around the world recognize that certain problems make it impossible to treat the accused individual in the same manner as an individual without such problems (Maeder, 1985). A person may have committed a crime because of his problem, in which case it makes no sense to find him guilty. Or if a defendant is flagrantly psychotic, it is impossible for him to participate in a defense of the charge. Let us consider these issues in more detail.

Insanity is not a psychological term but a legal one. Being insane is not equivalent to suffering from a DSM-IV disorder or from any particular problem specified in current diagnostic systems (Chapter 13). A psychologist or psychiatrist who testifies in court is not called upon to say that a person has a psychological problem; rather, he or she is called upon to say that the defendant fits the criteria of insanity as specified by the law. The mental health professional's task would be much easier were insanity unambiguously defined in terms of particular diagnoses and not others (Ciccone, 1992; Lewis, 1990; Reichlin, Bloom, & Williams, 1993). Instead, a person can be deemed insane in the absence of a DSM-IV diagnosis, yet sane in the presence of one.

The general idea behind an insanity plea is easy to grasp. According to the legal system's notions of right and wrong, people are responsible for their actions unless there is a reason for them not to be. People are not held accountable for the crimes they commit if there is an extenuating circumstance. That is, something must counter the argument that they freely undertook the crime in question. Being a minor is one such reason. Being intoxicated is another. Being hit in the head might also be an extenuating circumstance. Having a psychological problem that interferes with a person's ability to be responsible is yet another reason. Here we have the basis for the **insanity plea:** a defense against an accusation on the grounds that the individual was suffering from a psychological problem at the time the crime was committed.

Different states use different criteria for describing insanity, and these have changed over time (Simon & Aaronson, 1988). The various ways that insanity can be defined are less than ideal; otherwise, a consensus would have emerged long ago. A popular criterion used to judge insanity is the **American Law Institute (ALI) rule.** Its gist is that

> a person is not responsible for criminal conduct if at the time of such conduct as a result of mental disease or defect he lacks substantial capacity

■ **insanity plea**
defense against a criminal accusation on the grounds that the individual was suffering from a psychological problem at the time the crime was committed

■ **American Law Institute (ALI) rule**
currently popular criterion used to judge insanity, holding that people are not responsible for criminal conduct if at the time of a crime they did not appreciate its wrongfulness or that they could not conform their conduct to the requirements of law

Mark David Chapman shot John Lennon. Clinical psychologists argued that he was insane, but Chapman himself refused to claim that schizophrenia was the reason for his crime.

either to appreciate the criminality (wrongfulness) of his conduct or to conform his conduct to the requirements of law. (American Law Institute, 1962, p. 66)

The ALI rule has subsequently been elaborated to define a mental disease or defect as a condition that affects thoughts or emotions in such a way that behavior controls are impaired: The person cannot control what he or she does (Weiner, 1985). Also, courts have made it clear that the burden of proof for establishing insanity lies with the defense.

The ALI rule explicitly states that we cannot argue for the existence of a mental defect if the only evidence is repeated criminal activity. This gets around the problem that surrounds certain horrible crimes, like those committed by the mass murderer Jeffrey Dahmer, in which we automatically assume that the person who did such things *must* be insane. The ALI rule says no, at least not in the technical sense of being excused from a crime on the grounds that virtually no one else would have done it.

The ALI rule is favored by its adherents because it is flexible. It gives the jury or judge latitude to determine whether "appreciate" is to be used narrowly to refer to knowledge or more broadly to refer to other psychological factors, such as irresistible impulses. The phrasing of "substantial capacity" makes it explicit that the influence of mental disease or defect is to be regarded not as an either-or effect but rather as something that exists in degrees. Critics of the ALI rule point to the fact that applying it requires specific knowledge of technicalities, both psychological and legal.

Many people react strongly to the notion of the insanity plea, feeling that it is simply a way for somebody to get away with criminal conduct. Perhaps some do not understand its intent, which is not to subvert the legal system but rather to maintain its basic premise that only those fully responsible for their acts can be held accountable for them.

In any event, there have been calls for a new verdict: guilty but mentally ill (GBMI), which tries to have it both ways. In other words, we must determine first if people are sane or insane, then if they are guilty or innocent of the criminal act. It is possible for any number of combinations to exist, including insanity *and* guilt, from which this proposed verdict takes its name. Individuals who are found guilty of a crime are sentenced for the crime, whether or not they are judged to be insane.

The GBMI verdict appears to be a contradiction. If people are insane, they are not responsible for their actions; how, then, can they be punished? The GBMI verdict has considerable emotional appeal because it satisfies the public's (mistaken) belief that criminals and their lawyers frequently take advantage of the insanity plea. But the GBMI verdict is unlikely to see wide adoption. Perhaps more likely in the future is the removal of the insanity plea altogether, as several states have already done.

In any event, fewer than 1 percent of cases in the United States see a defendant offering an insanity plea (Steadman, 1980). In these, only about 25 percent of the defendants are actually acquitted by virtue of their plea. The successful defendant almost always has a history of psychological problems and warrants a DSM diagnosis, usually schizophrenia (Callahan, Steadman, McGreevy, & Robbins, 1991).

Competence to Stand Trial

In terms of the sheer numbers of people involved, many more individuals in the United States are affected by another psychological/legal decision: whether they are judged **competent to stand trial** (Bacon, 1969). Here there is a question as to whether the person can understand legal proceedings and whether she is able to contribute to her own defense. As you know from reading thus far, any of a number of psychological problems—from head injury to severe depression to schizophrenia—might make it impossible for a person to stand trial until the problem is resolved.

Competence to stand trial is not a defense against an accusation; nor is it a judgment about the person's responsibility for the act in question. Rather, it is a here-and-

■ **competence to stand trial**
ability of a person to understand legal proceedings and to contribute to his or her own defense

now judgment, one that is necessary for justice to be served. While waiting to become competent, the person is typically kept at a mental hospital. Bail is not granted. More than 90 percent of the patients deemed incompetent are eventually judged competent and complete the trial process (Pendleton, 1980).

The decision that a person is incompetent to stand trial is the result of an interview much like the one described in Chapter 14 for deciding that an individual has a problem. Focus is on the person's orientation to the present reality—that she understands the charges against her and how courts work. A thorny issue emerges here concerning the use of involuntary treatment to establish an individual's competence to stand trial. Some argue that this practice violates the constitutionally guaranteed right not to bear witness against oneself.

In the past, the judgment of incompetence to stand trial led to a bizarre state of affairs in which defendants might be judged incompetent and then kept in a mental hospital for a period much in excess of the amount of time they would have been jailed had they gone to trial and been found guilty (McGarry & Bendt, 1969). Various cases have been documented in which individuals were judged incompetent to stand trial for rather trivial crimes and then were institutionalized for literally decades. In 1972, the Supreme Court made this possibility less likely by ruling that a person cannot be confined indefinitely.

Developmental Psychology and Law

Psychologists who serve as expert witnesses may be asked to testify in child custody and visitation suits (Herman, 1990), as well as in disputed adoptions and placements in foster care (Carrieri, 1991). Remember the massive media coverage of the Woody Allen and Mia Farrow custody dispute, the struggle over Baby Jessica, and the desire by Kimberly Mays *not* to be visited by her biological parents. In each of these cases, psychological testimony was heard.

Adoptee Kimberly Mays first attracted the country's attention when she asked the court that she not be visited by her biological parents.

In cases involving children, the "best interests of the child" is one important consideration proposed by law (Maccoby & Mnookin, 1992). Most jurisdictions identify this as the overriding concern in placing a child; what will benefit the son or daughter takes precedence over what will benefit the father or mother. This principle is consistent with the general tenor of the legal system in the United States, which affords special protection to minors because they are not able to take care of themselves. Details differ from jurisdiction to jurisdiction about what constitutes the best interests of the child. Guidelines usually include the emotional bonds between the parties involved and the child; the capacity and willingness of the parties involved to raise and nurture the child; the length of time the child has lived with the parties involved; and the preference of the child, if the child is able to express a preference.

One more area in which psychologists are increasingly being called upon as expert witnesses is cases involving the alleged sexual abuse of children (Berliner & Loftus, 1992). There have been a number of well-publicized examples in recent years in which the testimony of the children proved very difficult to evaluate. What is the court to make of memories that are incomplete, inconsistent, and/or traumatic (Chapter 9)? Should a young child be subjected to harsh cross-examination? Must he or she face the accused? There are no simple answers, but developmental psychologists whose expertise includes young children exposed to trauma are in a good position to help the legal system deal with these issues (Eth, 1988; J. E. Myers, 1993; Yates, 1987).

Social Psychology and Law

Social psychologists have made several important contributions to our understanding of the legal process (Ibañez-Gracía, 1987). For example, studies show that stereotypes can introduce bias into decisions to convict or acquit defendants (Chapter 15). Physical attractiveness of defendants can inspire leniency on the part of jurors (Stewart, 1980). However, if attractiveness seems to have played a role in the crime itself, as when someone capitalizes on good looks to pull off a swindle, then jurors are more harsh (Sigall & Ostrove, 1975). In either case, justice is not blind.

Social psychologists also study what occurs during jury deliberation (Hastie, 1993; Hastie, Penrod, & Pennington, 1983). After all, juries are small groups formed in order to make a decision and are hardly immune to the processes that take place within other small groups. Most juries do not begin deliberation in agreement, although 95 percent eventually do agree on a verdict (Kalven & Zeisel, 1966). Apparently, some process of agreement unfolds. Here are some representative findings:

- Most juries arrive at the verdict initially favored by the majority of the jurors.
- When individuals in the minority prove influential, they are usually of high socioeconomic status.
- Group polarization toward harshness or leniency occurs.

Do you see how these findings are consistent with theories and studies described in Chapter 15? That juries end up with the verdict initially favored by the majority illustrates conformity in action or even groupthink. That some jurors exert more influence than others makes sense in light of research on attractiveness and social influence. That juries show group polarization is a special case of the more general tendency of group interaction to intensify initial opinions.

Perhaps the most tangible effect of social psychological research on the legal system has been in response to the decisions in some states to depart from the traditional 12-person jury. Smaller juries, some as small as 5 persons, have been deemed acceptable because there was no reason to suppose that the decisions reached by a small group would be different from those reached by a larger group.

Actually, there is plenty of reason, supplied by social psychology's investigations of conformity. Our legal system is based on the premise that one is innocent until proved guilty. This places a great deal of importance on a juror who is not convinced by the evidence. In a 12-person jury, someone in dissent is more likely to find an ally and hence be able to resist the majority. In a smaller jury, dissenters are less likely to find an ally, and this factor makes them more likely to be swayed by social forces. Citing social psychological research, the Supreme Court ended up explicitly rejecting 5-person juries.

Stop and Think

21   How do psychology and the legal system differ?

22   What is the insanity plea?

23   Why is the guilty but mentally ill verdict contradictory?

24   Speculate about the social psychological influences at work within the jury for the O. J. Simpson murder trial.

APPLIED PSYCHOLOGY IN A PERSONAL CONTEXT

We have come to the end of our introduction, and again, I would like to place the topics on focus in a larger context. Instead of the biological, psychological, and social contexts stressed throughout this book, I would like to consider the personal context of your life.

Psychology is an applied field. Whether you are working or playing, creating or consuming, thriving or ailing, your activities are affected by psychological theories and findings.

Many of you are also shaped by your own deliberate applications of psychology. Consider the recent movement in the United States toward self-help groups for people facing life challenges (Rootes & Aanes, 1992; Schubert & Borkman, 1991). Unlike the therapeutic groups discussed in Chapter 14, these do not consist of an expert therapist coordinating group activities. Rather, self-help groups are conducted by peers, those confronting the same issues. Such groups provide information and support. They sometimes organize for political action (Emerick, 1991; Hatfield, 1991). Their goal is to empower members so that they can cope without relying on traditional psychological services. Even though these groups are not directed by professional psychologists, they are informed by what psychologists have learned.

Self-help groups are available for those with medical problems, as well as psychological conditions. Alcoholics Anonymous is one of the best-known examples (Chapter 6). Other self-help groups are available for parents, children, and siblings of those with difficulties. There are also groups for people who must care for others, such as those with Alzheimer's disease, terminal cancer, or AIDS (Monahan, Greene, & Coleman, 1992). In many communities, teenage mothers have support groups available to them, as do students, adoptive parents, children from divorced families, the homeless, and victims of accidents and injuries.

Even if you never participate in a self-help group, you will still be applying psychology, by virtue of your studies in this course. And you are not alone because psychology is one of the most popular college majors and one of the most popular electives. It has been for decades.

My students often ask me, "What can one do with a degree in psychology?" I tell them sincerely, "Anything you want to do." A background in psychology is a great springboard into business and sales, law, medicine, social service, government work, and many other fields. Obviously, a background in psychology is a great springboard into psychology itself, whether you wish to pursue a career in teaching and research, or therapy, or any of the fields of applied psychology discussed in this chapter. Psychology—as has been made clear throughout this book—is a broad discipline. An education in psychology is a broad education.

Whatever you do with your life, you will be applying psychological theories and research because you are a product of what you have learned. How will you be different for having studied psychology? For starters, you will ask the types of questions that psychologists ask. You will rely on evidence to answer your questions, and you will be skeptical and cautious, realizing that evidence is never perfect, that theories are tentative hypotheses, and that you must always consider the possibility that you are wrong. You will hope that better explanations await you in the future.

You will be a different type of person as well, what psychologists refer to as psychologically minded. You will be aware that people have reasons for what they do, whether you call these motives, drives, interests, or attitudes. You will be aware that people have a mental life, filled with thoughts and dreams, hopes and wishes, passions and dreads. You will also be aware that someone's overt behavior does not correspond perfectly to his or her mental life. You will know that people have conflicts and contradictions and that sometimes their very motives may be unknown to their conscious minds.

You will know that people are at times rational but that there are limits to this rationality. You will appreciate that people are influenced by the social setting in which they find themselves, including the immediate influences of friends and family members and the more distant but equally important influences of culture, society, and history. You will be aware that people are complex, at once biological and social creatures, products of both nature and nurture. You will know that people are minds and bodies. You will know that people are who they are because of their age, cohort, gender, and ethnicity. You will know that people are the same in many ways and different in many others. The differences, however, are not necessarily fixed for life.

You will believe that at least some aspects of the human condition can be changed for the better. You will be aware that people bring their own perspectives to bear on life: You see the world from where you stand, and others do the same. Ours is perhaps a unique historical era in terms of the emphasis that we place on individuality, self-expression, and introspection. Psychology is the field of study that best mirrors this aspect of our culture. How might you apply psychology? It will be impossible for you not to do so.

SUMMARY

UNDERSTANDING APPLIED PSYCHOLOGY: DEFINITION AND EXPLANATION

■ Applied psychology is the use of psychological theories and findings to help solve people's practical problems.

■ Influenced by functionalism, applied psychology has been particularly popular in the United States.

■ Applications of psychology must be approached in biopsychosocial terms because psychology itself needs to be approached in this way.

DOING *Applied Psychology* RESEARCH

■ The concerns of any psychology researcher are the same as those of the applied psychology researcher, but they must be addressed according to the particular setting in which the research is conducted. For instance, operationalizations must be sensible for the specific people being studied.

■ Applications of psychology often involve the evaluation of jobs, workers, and employers. Assurances of anonymity, confidentiality, and nonretaliation must be made.

■ Applied researchers evaluate their studies in terms of the practical significance of a finding or conclusion, not just the statistical significance.

INDUSTRIAL-ORGANIZATIONAL PSYCHOLOGY

■ Industrial-organizational (IO) psychologists are concerned with improving the functioning of complex work organizations.

■ IO psychologists are therefore interested in the psychological significance of work, a biopsychosocial phenomenon.

■ Work has a developmental trajectory, changing in its psychological significance according to where workers are in their life span.

■ Industrial psychologists are concerned with such topics as describing what different jobs require of workers, selecting people for these jobs, and evaluating their performance once they are hired.

■ Organizational psychologists are interested in the effects on productivity of such factors as worker opinions, attitudes, motives, and satisfaction. Of special concern is organizational climate, defined as how the members of an organization perceive its characteristics.

ENGINEERING PSYCHOLOGY

■ Engineering psychologists use psychological theories and research to design environmental settings—usually machines—to be safe, efficient, and/or pleasurable.

CONSUMER PSYCHOLOGY

■ The field of consumer psychology is concerned with the acquisition and consumption of goods and services.

SPORTS PSYCHOLOGY

■ In sports psychology, psychological knowledge is applied to physical performance, usually in the context of competitive athletics.

ENVIRONMENTAL PSYCHOLOGY

■ Environmental psychologists are interested in how the physical environment affects people's thoughts, feelings, and behaviors.

■ Despite their concern with the objective environment, environmental psychologists usually take into account how people perceive environments.

PSYCHOLOGY AND LAW

■ Psychology and the legal system make different assumptions about human nature. For example, psychology assumes that what people do has causes, whereas the legal system assumes that behavior is usually undertaken freely.

■ There are nonetheless several points of contact between psychology and law, including such topics as involuntary commitment, the insanity plea, a defendant's competence to stand trial, and decisions about child custody and visitation.

APPLIED PSYCHOLOGY IN A PERSONAL CONTEXT

■ Psychology affects your personal life not just through its numerous applications but also through your study of the field, which changes the way you think about yourself and others.

KEY TERMS

STOP AND THINK ANSWERS

Chapter 1

1. Psychology is a science because it evaluates its explanations against observable evidence.

2. Behavior refers to the actions of an individual that can be observed by others.

3. The behaviors you are currently performing, of course, depend on you, but whatever actions you describe—turning pages, underlining passages in this book, staring at the clock—need in principle to be observable by someone else. So, if you are mentally repeating to yourself the definitions of terms or are daydreaming about the coming weekend, these actions are not behaviors because no one else can see them.

4. The scientific method refers to the systematic use of evidence to evaluate hypotheses.

5. Scientific psychology differs from everyday psychology in that it explicitly embraces the scientific method. Everyday psychology often does not.

6. A nonfalsifiable explanation is unscientific because evidence cannot be used to evaluate whether it is wrong.

7. Although scientific psychology tries to minimize exceptions to its generalizations, it accepts that some are inevitable because that is the nature of science.

8. The philosophical trends that led to psychology include critical empiricism, associationism, and scientific materialism. The scientific trends that led to psychology include neurology, the theory of evolution, and atomism.

9. Wilhelm Wundt is considered the first psychologist because he defined the field and established a laboratory that was used to do psychology research.

10. Gestalt psychology disagreed with the assumption of structuralism that experience is composed of simple elements. Functionalism disagreed with the static nature of structuralism, emphasizing instead the consequences of mental processes. Behaviorism disagreed with the focus of structuralism on the mind.

11. After World War II, psychology was marked by a number of trends: growth, specialization, quantification, application, globalization, the cognitive revolution, the development of neuroscience, and the emergence of the biopsychosocial perspective.

12. The cognitive revolution refers to a widespread trend in psychology, beginning in the 1960s, that emphasizes the importance of thoughts and beliefs.

13. The biopsychosocial approach assumes that all psychological phenomena should be explained in terms of relevant biological mechanisms, psychological processes, and social influences.

14. The biological context of behavior is stressed by biopsychologists. Psychological processes are of major concern to cognitive psychologists. The social context of behavior is emphasized by social psychologists and industrial-organizational psychologists.

Chapter 2

1. One operational definition of anger might be the loudness of someone's voice during a disagreement; another might be how often a person slams his or her fist on the table while making a point. These are not perfect definitions, of course, because each may be distorted by confounds.

2. Measures can be reliable without being valid. Consider a broken thermometer or a stopped clock; they give the same result on repeated occasions (reliability), but the result is rarely meaningful (lack of validity). On the other hand, a measure cannot be valid without being at least somewhat reliable.

3. A recent issue of *Time* mentioned a study of injuries to children in shopping carts; the study found that most injuries were due to the cart tipping over, whether or not the child was restrained. The sample was injured children brought to a given hospital during a given period of time. The population to which the results presumably apply is all children in societies where grocery carts are used, but can you think of how the sample may not perfectly represent this population?

4. An observational study of television and violence might involve a researcher going to a sports bar and noting if the occurrence of arguments and fistfights has any link to the type of show that is on the big-screen television (e.g., hockey games versus vegetarian cooking tips).

5. The strength of observational studies is their ability to describe behavior as it naturally occurs. The weakness is their susceptibility to researcher bias and reactivity.

6. A case study of television and violence might involve a researcher conducting extensive interviews with a highly violent individual and asking him or her about past television viewing habits.

7. The strengths of case studies include the rich detail they can provide, their usefulness as demonstrations of what can and cannot exist, and their ability to investigate rare phenomena. The weaknesses include problems with reliability due to secondhand information, the inability to identify causes, and their lack of generality.

8. A correlational investigation of television and violence might involve a researcher determining, for different U.S. cities, the correlation between the number of murders depicted on primetime shows on the city's major networks and the number of murders actually occurring in the city.

9. The strengths of correlational investigations include generality of results and the ability to study topics not otherwise able to be investigated. The weakness is a problem with identifying causes and effects.

10. An experiment investigating television and violence might involve a researcher randomly choosing one group of schoolchildren to watch violent cartoons and another group to watch *Barney,* and then measuring the number of fights each of the children starts during recess.

11. The strength of experiments is their ability to identify causes. The weaknesses include reactivity and their inapplicability to certain topics.

12. In the observational study, you would probably want to calculate the average number of arguments and fistfights that occurred during each type of television show. In the case study, you might want to calculate the correlation, across periods of the individual's life, between the amount of television seen and the number of violent acts committed. In the correlational study, you would, of course, compute the appropriate correlation coefficient. In the experiment, you would calculate and compare the average number of fights started by children in the two groups.

13. In the observational study, the researcher needs to worry that his or her presence might somehow encourage violence, that failure to intervene in those fights that do occur is morally wrong, that the anonymity of the bar's patrons is protected, and so on. In the case study, the researcher needs to be concerned that his or her investigation does not legitimize violence to the research subject by making it seem interesting or important; the researcher also needs to keep the identity of the subject (and any victims) confidential. In the correlational investigation, one of the major ethical concerns of the researcher should be that his or her conclusions might be used incorrectly for policy decisions. In the experiment, the researcher must be careful that any violence encouraged by his or her manipulation has no lasting effect on anyone.

Chapter 3

1. Consider accident-proneness. Its causes might include biological or psychological mechanisms responsible for attention (or the lack of attention); its functions might include heightened caution following accidents; its development might involve a general decrease in likelihood with age; and its evolutionary significance might involve selection for increased awareness.

2. In arguing that species had evolved, Darwin pointed to the results of the deliberate breeding of animals and plants, similar body parts across different species, and the fossil record.

3. The theory of natural selection is supported by the fact of evolution, the specific changes that have apparently occurred during evolution of different species, and occasional examples like germs, which have changed in accordance with changes in the environment.

4. The theory of natural selection would be falsified by any evidence that species do not change from one into another or evidence that the environment is irrelevant to whatever changes do occur.

5. Phenotypes—the actual characteristics of an individual—are the result of both its genetic blueprint (biological influences) and factors in its environment (psychological and social influences).

6. The Human Genome Project raises several ethical concerns. For example, are the time and effort justified when there are other pressing social needs? How will the results of the project be used? Will genetic discrimination increase? Will elective abortions increase?

7. Fitness refers to the individual's ability to survive long enough to reproduce, whereas inclusive fitness refers, in addition, to the fitness of those with whom the individual shares genes.

8. Proximate causation refers to the immediate biological or psychological mechanism that gives rise to an individual's behavior. Ultimate causation refers to how behavior contributes to survival of the individual's species.

9. Evolution is biopsychosocial because it results from the interaction between genetics and specific environments.

10. The theory of evolution by natural selection is more difficult to falsify than many other theories because the relevant evidence must be gathered over vast time periods. However, there are certainly aspects of the theory that can be falsified. Suppose there is a species in which the individuals do not vary in their characteristics? Or suppose there is a species in which all members, regardless of their characteristics, survive long enough to reproduce?

11. Some writers have made the provocative point that medical breakthroughs that have increased longevity and fertility have slowed—if not halted—the course of human evolution. Others disagree, arguing that at least minor changes in human beings—for example, changing susceptibilities to certain illnesses—are ongoing as the environment changes. The only definitive way to answer this question is to wait, perhaps tens of thousands of years, to see if the human species has a different biological character.

12. Both social Darwinism and sociobiology apply evolutionary ideas to social behavior, but social Darwinism focuses on societies as a whole, whereas sociobiology emphasizes closely related groups of individuals.

13. Ethology is concerned with the typical behavior of members of a given species as it occurs in a "natural" environment. Comparative psychology studies the behavior of members of different species, often in "artificial" situations.

14. Behavior genetics is concerned with behavioral variations within a species, whereas behavioral commonalities are the focus of other biological approaches.

15. One could argue that morning sickness among pregnant women is an evolved psychological mechanism if it is universal in the human species, present in our primate cousins, and linked to enhanced survival of eventual offspring.

Chapter 4

1. The major divisions of the nervous system are between the central and peripheral nervous systems. The peripheral nervous system in turn is divided into the somatic and autonomic nervous systems. Finally, the autonomic nervous system is divided into the sympathetic and parasympathetic nervous systems.

2. The somatic nervous system controls the skeletal muscles and the sense organs. Its causes refer to the specific neurological mechanisms responsible for its activity; its functions include physical movement and perception; its development shows a regular progression across the life span—as the result of both maturation and learning; and its evolutionary significance lies in the adaptive advantage it gave our ancestors.

3. Brain damage obviously involves biological injury and can be caused by environmental factors. Psychological or social interventions can sometimes compensate for the effects of brain damage.

4. In neural excitation, one neuron makes a second neuron more likely to fire. In neural inhibition, one neuron makes a second neuron less likely to fire.

5. The nervous system is organized in several ways: spatially, biochemically, and hierarchically.

6. Redundancy in the nervous system presumably contributes to the fitness of an individual. If parts of the brain are damaged, then other parts can take over their functions.

7. The brain is thought to have evolved by the addition of layers. Newer layers were integrated with older layers and began to regulate their functions.

8. The limbic system is involved in memory and the expression of emotions.

9. The cerebral cortex exerts final control over other brain structures and is involved in the initiation of behavior.

10. The debate over localization of function pertains to whether specific functions are located in given parts of the brain.

11. Popular descriptions of the left-right brain differences are oversimplified because the brain usually acts as a whole.

12. Researchers do not agree on exactly how experience alters the brain, but changes may occur in both the structure and the function of the brain.

13. Male-female differences in the brain may be due to innate biological differences and/or experiential differences brought about by different social conditions.

14. The endocrine system works relatively slowly through hormones that circulate in the blood. The nervous system works relatively quickly through neurotransmitters secreted into synapses between neurons.

15. The hypothalamus is one of the direct links between the nervous system and the endocrine system, and it is responsive to both neurotransmitters and hormones.

16. To demonstrate the existence of human pheromones, one would have to show that people's behavior specifically responds to chemicals that are secreted by other people.

17. Sex differences in the brain can be investigated in several ways. A researcher could determine whether injuries to specific parts of the brain have different effects for men versus women; whether electrical or chemical stimulation of the same brain structures have different effects; or whether brain images differ. Finally, a researcher could create computer models based on known brain differences between men and women and see whether these models "behave" as expected.

18. Sexual orientation could be investigated as just described (see #17) by comparing heterosexual and homosexual individuals (instead of males and females).

Chapter 5

1. The biopsychosocial resolution of the debate between the rationalists and the empiricists is that both may be right.

2. From the perspective of information processing theory, there is no clear distinction between sensation and perception. They represent different points in the processing of information.

3. An absolute threshold is the minimal amount of a stimulus that can be detected by an individual, whereas a difference threshold is the minimal difference between two stimuli that can be distinguished by an individual.

4. Weber's law holds that difference thresholds become larger as the standard becomes larger. Everyday examples include the volume of your radio, the sweetness of a dessert, and the brightness of the light on your desk.

5. Adaptation-level theory proposes that sensation is influenced not just by external stimuli but also by background stimuli and residual stimuli, which reflect the individual's psychosocial history and setting.

6. In order to argue that any given sense is the most important one, you must first decide what "important" means: necessary for survival of the individual, necessary for survival of the species, important for pleasure, important for achievement, whatever. Then you might want to obtain information comparing people with or without a given sense with respect to your definition of importance.

7. Both taste and smell are chemical senses that usually work together. However, taste is stimulated by chemicals dissolved in water, and smell by chemicals carried through the air. There are primary qualities of taste but apparently no primary qualities of smell.

8. People who lack the position senses can compensate, at least partially, by looking at the position and orientation of their body parts. They might also orient themselves with respect to the environment by attending to smells or sounds originating from known locations in the environment.

9. Perception is biopsychosocial: the product of both innate and learned factors. This conclusion supports both the rationalist and the empiricist views.

10. Illusions are of special interest to psychologists because they allow insight into perceptual tendencies that are not revealed in "ordinary" instances of perception.

11. A perceptual set refers to our tendency to perceive stimuli according to our expectations. For example, we might see random scribbles on a piece of paper as handwriting.

12. According to the research reviewed in this textbook, culture does not influence sensation.

13. If perception is defined as the psychological interpretation of sensations, then ESP is a contradiction of terms because there can be no perception without sensation. Some ESP phenomena may eventually be found to exist, but they must somehow involve sensations.

Chapter 6

1. Consciousness refers to our awareness of particular sensations, perceptions, needs, emotions, and cognitions.

2. Consciousness is the result of biological factors (the nervous system), psychological factors (learning, memory, cognition), and social factors (culture).

3. To argue that consciousness is a cultural invention, Jaynes relied on the analysis of books written thousands of years ago, which made no mention of consciousness. His conclusion may be incorrect because the books he studied were far from a thorough summary of the concepts that everyday people used at the time the books were written. Perhaps the failure of these books to mention consciousness is simply a literary convention. In contemporary mystery novels, for example, the characters are rarely described as paying federal income tax. Can we conclude that people nowadays have no concept of taxes?

4. Consciousness is difficult to study because its definition is not agreed upon.

5. The motivated unconscious describes the active keeping of information from awareness. Dissociation refers to the splitting of awareness into separate streams with little or no contact between them.

6. The unconscious might exist because the tendency to be unaware of certain unpleasant impulses provided a survival advantage to our ancestors. Perhaps awareness of one's own aggressive and sexual motives inhibits acting upon them, which affects fitness.

7. REM sleep is of special interest to psychologists because of the vivid dreams that accompany this stage.

8. In terms of information processing, lucid dreaming can be described as a top-down process, in that the dreamer's intentions dictate the content of his or her dreams.

9. Research suggests that daydreaming is virtually universal, although people have various motives: pleasure, distraction, mental rehearsal, and enhancement of motivation.

10. The mystical experience refers to a feeling of oneness with the universe and an inability to express experience in words.

11. Although psychologists agree that hypnosis is characterized by heightened suggestibility, there is an ongoing debate about whether it is a special state of consciousness.

12. Members of AA say that their Twelve Steps are not a religious belief system, but the resemblance of the Twelve Steps to Christian doctrine seems more than a coincidence.

13. Relapse prevention refers to interventions, after treatment for substance abuse, that attempt to keep the sober individual from resuming his or her use of psychoactive drugs.

14. Drug use and abuse are biopsychosocial because they involve the body, learning, cognition, emotion, motivation, and the individual's larger social setting.

Chapter 7

1. Motives refer to the causes of behavior; emotions, to the feelings that accompany our behavior.

2. A primary motive is based in biology.

3. According to Tomkins, emotions let us know our motives.

4. To demonstrate an instinct, a researcher needs to show that an animal or person displays a complex behavior in response to specific environmental stimuli without having previously learned that behavior.

5. There are motives such as mastery that have no apparent corresponding physiological need (see the discussion later in this chapter).

6. Our so-called intrinsic motives—those that lead us to behave in ways that have no apparent purpose other than the satisfaction of pursuing activities like stamp collecting or working crossword puzzles—are well explained in cognitive terms because we act on these motives only insofar as we think of them as freely chosen.

7. Dual-center theory proposes that the hypothalamus has two parts: one that excites (turns on) behavior and one that inhibits (turns off) behavior.

8. Because the TAT relies on what a person says in response to an ambiguous picture, using it to measure motivation might be confounded by the person's verbal skills or creativity.

9. In terms of Murray's list of needs, Hillary Rodham Clinton is probably high on achievement, defendance, dominance, nurturance, order, and power.

10. Communion refers to forming connections among people, and agency refers to forming separations. Some behaviors may satisfy both motives, one directly and the other indirectly. For example, if you tell your lover that you need "more space," your relationship may eventually improve (communion) because you have satisfied your individual need for privacy (agency).

11. A specific hunger leads an organism to seek food that contains specific substances, such as salt, when its body needs them.

12. Sex differs from other primary motives in that it is not necessary for individual survival.

13. Most psychologists believe that aggression is an acquired human motive because there is no evidence that it has a biological basis. Furthermore, whether or not aggression occurs depends on its consequences—that is, aggression is learned.

14. In your everyday life, you might satisfy your need for mastery by playing video games, reading mystery novels, or engaging in sports.

15. According to the James-Lange theory, emotions result from our perception of bodily responses to situations.

16. According to the Cannon-Bard theory, emotions result from the activity of our cerebral cortex.

17. According to the Schachter-Singer (two-factor) theory, emotions result from a cognitive label we place on our physiological arousal.

18. Evolutionary theories propose that we express our emotions to others through facial expressions. The James-Lange theory suggests that our facial expressions can cause emotions via physiological feedback. The Cannon-Bard theory implies that differences in left versus right facial expressions of emotion reflects brain laterality. Cognitive theories are interested in facial expressions to the degree that they provide ourselves and others with labels with which to interpret emotions.

19. The use of questionnaires to measure emotions can be confounded by the extent of people's vocabulary and their ability or willingness to identify the emotions they are experiencing.

20. It is important to distinguish the experience of emotion from its expression because different groups are socialized about how to express or inhibit specific emotions.

21. The emotion of disgust is biopsychosocial because it is based in innate responses to irritating stimuli, but its generalization to other stimuli is influenced by psychological and social factors.

Chapter 8

1. Learning takes place through instruction and practice, as when you master a folk dance after taking a special class. Performance is an observable behavior—in this case, dancing.

2. In habituation, you stop paying attention to a stimulus that never changes, like a chipped tooth or a bandage on your finger. In sensitization, you become increasingly responsive to a recurring stimulus, like a strange noise in your apartment in the middle of the night.

3. Learning is biopsychosocial because it is based in the biology of the organism and is also influenced by psychological processes such as attention and memory, as well as social factors such as cultural norms and practices.

4. Psychologists interested in learning often study animals because it is easy to do so, and traditional views hold that the findings will be the same as if they studied human beings.

5. Psychologists often use experiments because they are the best way to identify the environmental stimuli that affect learning.

6. An example from everyday life might be an aversion to a specific food that you happened to eat while you were getting the flu. The flu bug is the UCS, which caused the initial nausea, the UCR. The food paired with the flu is the CS, and the later nausea produced by the food is the CR.

7. An example from everyday life of operant conditioning might be the following scenario: You move into a new apartment and have to learn how to unlock the front door. Your movements with the key are operants, and those that lead to the reinforcer of an unlocked door become more likely in the future, while those that do not become less likely. The process by which you have learned to open the door efficiently is acquisition. You may try to open other doors with similar movements (generalization), unless these doors are different from your apartment door, in which case you do not repeat these movements (discrimination).

8. Skinner contributed to psychology by elaborating on the behaviorist perspective; specifically, he introduced important terms, theories, and methods.

9. Punishment is justified when no delay in decreasing the frequency of a behavior can be tolerated. For example, punishing a child for playing with matches is preferable to ignoring him or her. The use of punishment can be questioned when it adds nothing to the individual's repertoire of behavior.

10. Classical conditioning and operant conditioning both involve learning associations between stimuli and responses, but they differ in terms of the timing involved. In classical conditioning, one learns that given stimuli precede given behaviors. In operant conditioning, one learns that given stimuli (reinforcers or punishers) follow given behaviors.

11. People can learn novel behaviors through modeling, and the process by which this learning takes place is cognitive. Specifically, individuals must attend to the model, interpret the behavior, and evaluate the consequences.

12. Taste aversion is a good example of preparedness because it occurs quickly, usually in one trial, and may involve considerable delays. Furthermore, it makes evolutionary sense to be able to learn readily to avoid tastes that are associated with sickness because in the natural environment, most poisons or toxins enter the body through the mouth.

13. Consciousness (cognition) facilitates virtually all forms of learning by people. However, certain instances of habituation or sensitization occur automatically, without the involvement of cognition.

Chapter 9

1. Cognition refers to the mental representation of knowledge and the processes responsible for its acquisition, transformation, and utilization. Psychologists use metaphors to describe cognition because it is unobservable.

2. The social influences on memory include society's encouragement to acquire certain types of information rather than others.

3. The effect of emotion on thinking is a top-down process. Our general emotional state can influence the specifics of our cognition. Emotion may also affect the depth of processing of information. We might think "deeply" about information that is highly emotional; conversely, emotions might lead us to process information in a superficial manner.

4. In using reaction times to study cognition, researchers must be alert to the possibility that some people have quicker reflexes than others, or are more willing to pay close attention to the task at hand.

5. Thinking-aloud protocols differ from the use of introspection by the structuralists because researchers do not treat these protocols as identical to the contents of thought. Rather, these protocols are used to make inferences about cognition.

6. One limitation of artificial intelligence is that most computer simulations of thought do not allow for the influence of motivation or emotion. Another limitation is that most computer programs simulate bottom-up processes only.

7. A linear ordering is a mental representation of items in some sequence.

8. It is easy for people to create visual images because this ability aided the survival of our distant ancestors, perhaps by allowing them to rehearse responses to dangerous situations and then to enact them quickly. It is difficult for people to create olfactory images because there was no evolutionary need to do so.

9. Many familiar examples of artificial concepts come from scientific or mathematical domains. So, three sides (and only three sides) are a necessary and sufficient condition for a triangle.

10. Echoes may persist longer in sensory memory than icons because the noises we hear are usually episodic, whereas our visual experience is continuous. Imagine what the world would be like if every visual sensation lasted for ten seconds.

11. A flashbulb memory is a highly vivid and detailed memory of an emotionally charged event.

12. One way to remember the three stages of memory is with the slogan "So Simple to Learn" because the letters S-S-L correspond to the first letters in sensory memory, short-term memory, and long-term memory.

13. To solve the "problem" of finding a summer job, you need to create a problem-space in which you represent your starting point, your desired end point, and the permissible steps in between. So, you would consider your skills and the sorts of jobs you would like, and then read the want ads, mail applications, and talk to friends and family members about contacts.

14. Functional fixedness is the tendency to approach problems in the same way, even when a different approach yields a better solution.

15. According to Chomsky, a behaviorist approach to language cannot handle the fact that language is creative. If most of the sentences we say or hear are novel, how could we have learned them by trial and error?

16. Language is biopsychosocial because the ability to acquire a language is inherent in our species. In fact, there may be a critical period determined by biology during which language must be learned. Language is also influenced by psychological and social factors, because we learn only those languages to which we are exposed.

Chapter 10

1. Developmental age refers to the time at which a particular characteristic is demonstrated in life, whereas chronological age refers to age in years.

2. Development is biopsychosocial because it includes changes in biological, psychological, and social domains throughout life.

3. Researchers often use cross-sectional designs to study development because these are more efficient than longitudinal designs.

4. A cohort effect is a difference between groups of people born at different times; a cohort effect results from differing historical and social factors.

5. Behavior refers to actions that are in principle observable by others, and so behavior first appears when the fetus starts to make movements noticeable by the mother, about three months following conception.

6. An embryo will develop as a female, regardless of its sex chromosomes, unless testosterone is present.

7. The Moro reflex, which appears early in life and then disappears, presumably aided the survival of our ancestors because it ensured that they held on tightly to their caretaker when young.

8. At birth, nerve cells are not fully myelinated. As a child grows, myelin covers the nerve cells and allows motor development to proceed.

9. Increasing life expectancy in the United States has made the population—on average—older, and so parents, teachers, politicians, and so on are also older. Furthermore, there is an ever growing group of elderly individuals with special needs that society may not be prepared to meet.

10. Temperament is a biologically based style of behaving.

11. An example of everyday assimilation might be playing a video game for the first time like you play other games with which you are familiar. Accommodation, in contrast, would be a change in how you approach previous games because of your experience with the new game.

12. Object permanence is the knowledge that objects continue to exist even when out of sight.

13. The criticisms of Piaget's theory of cognitive development include (a) his research relied too much on verbal inquiry, (b) the progression through his hypothesized stages can be accelerated by training, and (c) these stages may not be as distinct as he implied.

14. Kohlberg's theory resembles Piaget's theory in that both propose universal stages through which children pass in the direction of increasing complexity and abstractness of thought.

15. The use of moral dilemmas to study moral development may be confounded by the subject's creativity or verbal ability.

16. Gilligan criticized Kohlberg's approach to moral development for its assumption of a single standard of morality, one based on rules. She argued that there also exists a morality based on the preservation of human relationships.

17. Erikson's earlier stages of psychosocial development seem to have more universality than the later stages because they are tied to the physical needs and concerns of the child.

18. Generativity refers to an individual's concern for the next generation.

19. As a measure of attachment, the Strange Situation Test may be confounded by the child's familiarity with the coming and going of caretakers.

20. Gender differences are differences between males and females due to psychological and social factors. Sex differences, in contrast, are due to biology.

21. Peer pressure does not coerce adolescents to behave in certain ways; rather, it legitimizes those behaviors already of interest.

22. On average, marital satisfaction is highest early in the marriage and after the last child leaves home.

23. One way to remove the genetic confound in the correlation between parenting style and child behavior is to study families in which the children have been adopted.

24. Research supports the existence of the reactions to death identified by Kübler-Ross but not their fixed sequence.

Chapter 11

1. Intelligence is behavior that is adaptive and purposeful.

2. Over the years, psychologists have typically measured intelligence with tests designed for this purpose.

3. The benefit of using intelligence tests is that they are simple and efficient measures.

4. Because the adaptiveness of behavior can be specified only with respect to a given environment, it is unlikely that any intelligence test can be culture-fair.

5. Binet is considered the founder of modern intelligence testing because he developed the first useful measure of intelligence, one based on complex tasks.

6. An intelligence quotient is the ratio of an individual's mental age and his or her chronological age, multiplied by 100.

7. Intelligence is biopsychosocial because all behavior—including adaptive and purposeful behavior—is influenced by biological, psychological, and social factors.

8. Intelligence research often does not recognize the biopsychosocial nature of intelligence because it takes sides in an either-or debate between nature and nurture.

9. On typical intelligence tests, Asian Americans, on average, score higher than European Americans, who, on average, score higher than African Americans.

10. Males and females, on average, score the same on measures of overall intelligence. However, the scores of men are more variable (lower *and* higher) than those of women, and men, on average, score higher on specific measures of visual-spatial and mathematical ability.

11. Organic retardation and sociocultural retardation are difficult to distinguish because individuals in impoverished environments are more likely to experience injuries, illness, malnutrition, and exposure to toxins. All of these can damage the nervous system and limit intelligence.

12. A prodigy is an individual who, early in life, shows notable accomplishments in a given domain.

13. A genius makes lasting contributions to his or her society.

14. Savants challenge traditional views of intelligence because one form of intelligence is present despite deficiencies in other skills.

15. General intelligence (g) influences all tasks, whereas specific intelligence (s) influences only a specific task.

16. Gardner's intelligences may have helped solve survival problems of our ancestors. For example, linguistic intelligence helped our ancestors communicate, spatial intelligence helped them hunt or find parking spaces, and personal intelligence facilitated life in a group.

Chapter 12

1. Whether or not height and social class are considered part of people's personality depends on their psychological representation of them. Do they believe that these characteristics set them apart from others? Are they entwined with other characteristics? Are they related to adaptation?

2. The definition of personality—psychological characteristics that are general, enduring, distinctive, integrated, and functional—include all of the biological, psychological, and social phenomena of interest to psychology.

3. Both Freud and Jung stressed the importance of unconscious motives. They differed in that Freud believed that these motives were sexual and aggressive in nature, whereas Jung did not. Furthermore, Jung theorized extensively about the collective unconscious.

4. Again, both Freud and Adler stressed the importance of unconscious motives, but they differed in that Freud emphasized biologically based motives and Adler emphasized socially based motives.

5. The neo-Freudians followed the example of Freud's theorizing by emphasizing the unconscious and taking a developmental approach to personality.

6. Erik Erikson's approach to personality is most similar to that of the neo-Freudians.

7. A recent issue of *Time* magazine described a typology of successful politicians (and successful people in general): those who reach the top by slowly working their way through the system ("lifers"), those who succeed by taking risks and being single-minded ("talents"), and those who attain success through advanced education ("mandarins").

8. The biological mechanism of extraversion might involve how an individual's nervous system responds to stimulation. An extraverted person might have higher thresholds than an introverted person, and so learns to seek out other people for stimulation.

9. Here is a description of my own personality in terms of the Big Five: above average on agreeableness and conscientiousness, below average on extraversion, and average on neuroticism and openness.

10. A personal construct is a cognitive category used to interpret experience.

11. Unconditional regard is acceptance of an individual's worth and value regardless of his or her specific behaviors.

12. Both Kelly and Rogers proposed cognitive theories of personality. Their theories differ in that Rogers assumed that all people are driven toward self-actualization, whereas Kelly did not make this assumption.

13. A familiar example of an approach-avoidance conflict is whether to finish classroom assignments or put them off.

14. Reciprocal determinism is the mutual influence among behavior, cognition, and the environment.

15. Dollard and Miller as well as Bandura emphasized learning, particularly from other people, as the key to understanding personality. Their theories differ in that Dollard and Miller stressed drives and their reduction, whereas Bandura emphasized cognition.

16. In terms of the MMPI subscales, many college students fall within the typical range for most characteristics but are slightly lower than the general population for masculinity/femininity and slightly lower for social introversion.

17. Experience sampling uses a beeper to interrupt research subjects at randomly chosen times to ask them what they are thinking, feeling, and doing at that moment.

18. A researcher could use all the personality assessment strategies to study the same individual simply by undertaking them at the same time. If the results of the different strategies agree, then the researcher can be confident that the individual's personality has been assessed. What is missing from this approach is a way to resolve or at least understand disagreements.

19. The consistency controversy refers to a debate within personality psychology concerning whether people act in consistent ways across different situations.

20. An everyday example of a trait-environment interaction might be the personality characteristic of boldness versus caution. People falling at either end of this dimension will be comfortable or not depending on how familiar a situation is to them.

Chapter 13

1. If abnormality is a fuzzy concept, then it has neither necessary nor sufficient conditions. Therefore, most operational definitions of abnormality are only approximations, more so than in other areas of research.

2. Each of the popular models of abnormality makes its own assumptions about the nature of psychological health. The biological model assumes that health exists when the individual is free from injury or illness. The psychodynamic model regards health as the use of psychological energy for useful purposes: work and love. The cognitive-behavioral model assumes that health involves the use of cognitive and behavioral skills to gain socially sanctioned reward while avoiding punishment.

3. The diathesis-stress model recognizes biological and psychological predispositions to abnormality (the diathesis) as well as its environmental triggers (the stress).

4. The currently popular New Age movement provides many examples of a magical belief system: channeling, healing crystals, aroma therapy, and so on.

5. Krafft-Ebing's research is historically important because it linked general paresis to untreated syphilis, providing one of the first clear examples of the biological approach to abnormality.

6. Freud's approach to abnormality is both biological and psychological because he theorized about psychological concepts using metaphors from neurology.

7. Watson and Rayner's research is historically important because their study of Little Albert provides an excellent example of the cognitive-behavioral approach to abnormality.

8. A convenience sample refers to research subjects chosen simply because they are readily available.

9. Research diagnostic criteria are stringent diagnostic rules used to include (or exclude) subjects in psychopathology investigations.

10. The five axes of DSM-IV are clinical syndromes, personality disorders, physical illnesses and conditions, existing stressors, and global level of functioning.

11. The benefits of diagnosis include enhanced communication and clues about etiology, prognosis, and effective treatment.

12. The drawbacks of diagnosis include disagreements among mental health professionals about theoretical assumptions, the treatment of normality and abnormality as discontinuous, occasionally poor reliability, and self-fulfilling prophecies because of labeling.

13. Anxiety disorders are biopsychosocial because they involve genetic predispositions and neurological mechanisms, psychological processes such as learning and cognition, and social influences such as modeling.

14. Hypochondriasis is an individual's preoccupation with having or contracting an illness in the absence of any medical indications.

15. Multiple personality disorder is more likely to occur among females than males because its onset typically follows prolonged childhood abuse, and females are more likely than males to be abused.

16. The symptoms of depression—emotional, motivational, physiological, behavioral, and cognitive—tend to be the opposite of those of mania.

17. The dopamine hypothesis suggests that schizophrenia is caused by excess activity of the neurotransmitter dopamine.

18. Personality disorders are difficult to diagnose reliably because they exist within a social context that is not explicitly noted in DSM-IV diagnostic criteria. Furthermore, different personality disorders are described in terms of overlapping symptoms.

Chapter 14

1. Biomedical therapies are based on a biological conception of human nature: People are physical systems produced by evolution; they develop problems because of injury or illness; and they can be helped by interventions that normalize their physiological functioning. Psychotherapies are based on a psychological conception of human nature: People are information-processing systems; they develop problems because they learned faulty cognitive, emotional, or behavioral styles; and they can be helped by interventions that encourage them to think, feel, or behave differently.

2. Over the years, therapies have been derived from theories that stressed only biological, psychological, or social factors. The absence of a biopsychosocial perspective on behavior led to the absence of any biopsychosocial therapies.

3. Psychosurgery refers to brain surgery undertaken to alleviate psychological problems.

4. Drugs that treat bipolar disorder and schizophrenia are effective only while they are taken. If the drugs are discontinued, these problems can flare up again.

5. Both client-centered therapy and psychoanalysis stress the importance of the client-therapist relationship, but client-centered therapy emphasizes consciousness and rationality, whereas psychoanalysis emphasizes the unconscious and motivation.

6. Both cognitive therapy and psychoanalysis are interested in the client's thoughts, but cognitive therapy focuses on conscious thoughts, whereas psychoanalysis focuses on unconscious thoughts.

7. Behavior therapy is a set of therapeutic strategies that are based in the psychology of learning—classical conditioning, operant conditioning, and modeling—and help a client replace undesirable habits with desirable ones.

8. Because of its emphasis on the stratified nature of gender roles in society, feminist therapy is most easily combined with approaches that recognize the social nature of problems—for example, couples therapy, family therapy, group therapy, and community psychology.

9. A placebo effect occurs when an individual improves following some treatment only because he or she expected to improve, not because the treatment itself was beneficial.

10. Meta-analysis is important for outcome research because it allows the results of different studies to be combined and an overall conclusion to be drawn.

11. Table 14.3 provides several educated guesses about which treatments are best suited for which problems, but appreciate that outcome research to date has not been fine-grained enough to draw conclusions that some therapies are superior to others for treating given problems.

12. Learning the relationship between multiplication and division is an example of education; learning multiplication tables by rote is an example of training.

13. The helping alliance refers to a relationship between client and therapist in which both believe that therapy will be helpful. Many consider it a prerequisite for successful therapy.

14. People with less severe problems are easier to help than those with more severe problems, because their disorders are less entrenched. Furthermore, when people have ample resources—material, psychological, and social—they can best be helped, and people with resources tend not to have severe problems in the first place.

Chapter 15

1. Social psychology is cognitive in nature because social influence occurs in terms of how people perceive and interpret social situations.

2. If social behavior is the result of evolved psychological mechanisms, we can expect these mechanisms to be numerous and specific, as they are in other domains of behavior.

3. If social psychology had its roots in behaviorism, overt behavior and social rewards and punishments would be emphasized. If social psychology had its roots in psychoanalysis, motivation and the unconscious would be emphasized.

4. For topics such as conformity, obedience, and helping, surveys could ask people about the occurrence of these behaviors and factors associated with them, although the researcher must be alert to the possibility that people often describe themselves in flattering terms. Perhaps such surveys could additionally ask respondents about conformity, obedience, and helping on the part of others.

5. Although the contents of social cognition typically vary across cultures, we can expect universality of the underlying processes by which the contents are acquired, represented, transformed, and used.

6. A prototype is a typical member of a category. A stereotype is an example of a prototype, in which the category is a social group and the characterization is usually oversimplified and objectionable to members of that group.

7. Attribution theory is an account of how people explain the causes of their behavior and that of others, and how their causal explanations in turn affect their social behavior.

8. Both conformity and obedience are examples of social influence, but conformity takes place between peers, whereas obedience takes place between two people of different status. Also, people usually deny the existence of their conformity, yet readily acknowledge the existence of their obedience.

9. An everyday example of deindividuation might be attending a crowded concert or sports event, feeling anonymous, and thus relaxing your inhibitions.

10. Social influence is biopsychosocial because it is predisposed by evolved psychological mechanisms—often cognitive in nature—that are pertinent to life in a group.

11. A comprehensive program to change prejudiced attitudes might combine persuasive communications (e.g., announcements in the mass media by credible individuals), counter-attitudinal behavior (e.g., nonprejudicial actions encouraged by small incentives), and group contact (e.g., desegregation of the workplace).

12. During times of severe economic competition between groups, people's basic needs for physical safety and comfort may be threatened, leading to prejudice; people's stereotyping of the competing group may be increased, leading to prejudice; and people's concern for those in their own group may be heightened, again leading to prejudice.

13. Cognitive dissonance theory is consistent with Gestalt psychology because it assumes that people are motivated to achieve a harmonious state (a good gestalt) among their thoughts.

14. Helping is biopsychosocial because its occurrence is influenced by biological relatedness, feelings of sympathy, and modeling.

15. The motives for affiliation include social comparison, the reduction of anxiety, and the desire for information about how to behave in given situations.

16. The determinants of liking include proximity, similarity, complementarity of needs, high ability, attractiveness, and reciprocity.

17. Judgment heuristics might bias an individual's calculation of his or her benefits in a relationship by overestimating the frequency of those that are easy to remember and/or highly representative (e.g., getting flowers or candy), and underestimating the frequency of those that are neither.

18. An everyday example of social loafing might be a group project or presentation for one of your college classes.

19. A recent example of groupthink might be the shutdown of the U.S. government in late 1995 and early 1996 because of disagreements between Congress and the White House about a balanced budget.

20. Leaders in the contemporary United States are often wealthy, confident, optimistic, glib, and demeaning of their opponents; these characteristics are consistent with our cultural emphases on the individual and competition.

Chapter 16

1. Everyday psychologists often take health for granted, and only try to explain illness. Their explanations sometimes overly blame the victim of illness and sometimes ignore altogether the contributions of behavior and lifestyle.

2. The benefit of a health psychologist being trained as a clinical psychologist is that he or she is expert in helping troubled individuals. The drawback is that clinical psychology is only one of many fields that is relevant to health and illness.

3. Despite the most modern medical care in the world, the United States does not have the highest life expectancy, because factors in addition to medical care determine longevity. Proper diet, exercise, and other health-promoting habits are still avoided by many Americans.

4. A recent article in a tabloid described a Haitian woman who claimed to be more than 125 years old. She attributed her longevity to a diet of red beans and rice, but the article nowhere mentioned the possibility that this woman's genetic inheritance, coupled with a fortunate avoidance of serious diseases, was important as well.

5. Contemporary medicine is biological in its approach because of the dramatic success of germ theory in combating illness during the past 100 years. However, the success of a biological approach in drastically reducing death due to infectious diseases led researchers to look for other strategies of health care that address psychological and social causes of illness.

6. A biopsychosocial perspective reminds us that all behavior has numerous

causes. Compliance with medication, for example, is influenced by a person's thoughts and beliefs about drugs, his or her motivation to follow a doctor's advice, and social factors that range from the advice of friends and family members to the compliance habits legitimized or not by the larger culture.

7. Again, I refer to the tabloid article describing a Haitian woman who claimed to be at least 125 years old (see #4). This report is a case study, and it operationalizes health/illness in terms of self-reported longevity. We can question the accuracy of her reported age either because her memory may be suspect or because her claims were exaggerated as a result of the attention they created.

8. From an evolutionary perspective, cardiovascular disease and cancer may exist because they tend to afflict older individuals who have already reproduced, and there has never been a selection advantage for individuals immune to these diseases. As for the existence of AIDS, perhaps an explanation lies in terms of the fitness of the virus that causes it. HIV kills its human hosts only after a long incubation period during which it multiplies and spreads to other people.

9. Both cancer and schizophrenia can be explained in diathesis-stress terms.

10. The opinion of many public health experts is that there will be an immunization against AIDS sooner than a cure. At least in the near future, AIDS will continue to spread unless people change the behaviors that put them at risk for this disease.

11. Psychoneuroimmunology is the interdisciplinary field that studies the mutual influences among psychological, neurological, and immunological factors.

12. Stress is biopsychosocial because both its causes and its remedies include biological, psychological, and social influences.

13. John Henryism is a personality trait reflecting the degree to which people believe they can control all events and outcomes in their lives solely through hard work and determination.

14. Social support refers to the various resources that one person can provide to another.

15. It is likely that women outlive men because of a combination of genetic, lifestyle, and social factors.

16. Although there are no guarantees, a person with cancer should think optimistically, be happy, and cultivate supportive relationships in order to live longer. Even if the quantity of his or her life is not increased, its quality will certainly be enhanced.

Chapter 17

1. Applied psychology is the use of theories and findings from psychology to help solve practical problems.

2. Applied psychology has flourished in the United States largely because it embodies functionalism.

3. A recent television story described clinical psychologists who went to a high school to talk to the students after the unexpected deaths of several of their classmates in an automobile accident. The psychologists' goal was to minimize negative reactions resulting from this tragic event by encouraging the students to express their feelings. According to the story, the intervention was successful in that the students were able to resume their personal and academic lives without developing any psychological difficulties. This example is a case study of a group, and it operationalized "success" in terms of the absence of diagnosable problems such as depression. This operationalization may be confounded by the fact that not all people with psychological problems find themselves in situations where a diagnosis can be given. Furthermore, there is no way of telling how the students would have fared without the intervention, because there was no comparison group.

4. One of the ethical dilemmas faced by many applied psychologists involves whether research participants have freely given their consent to be studied. Also, applied psychology invariably studies outcomes that are important to people, and there is always the risk that a study can have a negative impact on someone, if only because this person is in a "comparison" group that does not receive an intervention that might be beneficial.

5. There are probably cohort differences in the meaning of work that reflect the availability of jobs when a person first entered the workforce. Try to speak to people who became adults during the Great Depression, during the affluent post–World War II era, and during the current era of downsizing and cutbacks.

6. Industrial psychology is the applied field that is concerned with selecting and evaluating workers.

7. People retire for one of two reasons: Poor health forces them to retire, or economic well-being allows them to retire.

8. Some critical incidents for a college student might involve how he or she gains access to a required course that has been closed, copes with a crashed personal computer, and juggles three final exams on the same day.

9. Organizational psychology is the applied field that studies the process by which workers adjust to one another and their organization.

10. The vitamin model of worker satisfaction proposes that there are several sources of worker satisfaction. For some sources—like money and physical security—the more the better. For other sources—like interpersonal contact and variety—there is an optimal level: Too little or too much is harmful.

11. A Theory X classroom would be one in which students are treated as inherently lazy and sneaky—attendance is monitored; quizzes are frequent; plagiarism and cheating are assumed to be common. A Theory Y classroom would be one in which students are treated as inherently interested in education—attendance is not required; readings are the subject of discussions, not quizzes; students are involved in planning, carrying out, and evaluating classroom exercises and assignments.

12. Engineering psychology is the applied field that attempts to design settings—usually machines—to be safe, efficient, and/or pleasurable.

13. The odds are overwhelming that at least one item of clothing—designed for an "average" person—never fits you well. By this misfit, you can identify what is most unusual about your bodily dimensions.

14. Remember from Chapter 10 that most 3-year-olds are entering the preoperational stage of cognitive development, where they begin to think symbolically. They have established one or more social attachments. Many of their bodily movements remain unskilled. So, an appropriate toy might be one that lends itself to playing make-believe, can be cuddled, and is easy to carry and manipulate. Not surprisingly, a doll or teddy bear is therefore an excellent gift for a 3-year-old.

15. The most recent television advertisement I have seen was for Taco Bell, that in only 30 seconds made an appeal to several of my needs: hunger, efficiency, novelty, and economy. I made a run for the border!

16. A difficult-to-remember advertisement would be one that lacked repetition, associability, and ingenuity.

17. Perhaps sports psychologists have focused on elite athletes for the same reason other psychologists have focused on individuals who fall at the extremes of various characteristics or skills: Extreme examples reveal the operation of psychological processes that are difficult to discern in more typical instances.

18. Both exercise programs and psychotherapy attempt to change people's behavior and thereby their well-being. In both cases, people who are in good shape (physically or psychologically) in the first place probably benefit the most. Psychotherapy requires an expert in behavior change (the therapist), whereas an exercise program may or may not involve such a person (the trainer). When exercise programs are coordinated by a trainer, a "helping alliance" between the trainer and the client may be as important as it is in psychotherapy. Finally, participation in an exercise program is usually given a positive social value, whereas participation in psychotherapy can have a social stigma.

19. Environmental psychology pays a great deal of attention to people's thoughts and beliefs because the physical environment affects behavior at least partly in terms of how the individual thinks about it.

20. A typical campus map is difficult for users to understand because it treats all buildings and streets as equally important and is intended to be used by both drivers and pedestrians. If they are not buildings, notable landmarks may be missing altogether. A more useful map should highlight the places and pathways that are relevant to those people who need to consult a map in the first place—visitors or newcomers to a campus—and it should be designed differently for people in cars versus people on foot. Also, landmarks like statues and gardens should be conspicuously identified.

21. Psychology and the legal system differ in several basic ways concerning their approach to understanding people and their actions. Psychology assumes determinism, offers generalizations, and relies on an evenhanded use of the scientific method. In contrast, the legal system assumes free will, focuses on individuals, and relies on advocacy.

22. The insanity plea is a defense against a criminal accusation on the grounds that the individual was not psychologically responsible for the act in question.

23. The guilty but mentally ill verdict is contradictory because it holds an individual simultaneously responsible (guilty) and not responsible (mentally ill) for a crime.

24. Almost everyone agrees that the O. J. Simpson verdict was reached quickly. Perhaps the jury reached a decision so rapidly because of the operation of social psychological processes such as conformity, group polarization, and groupthink.

GLOSSARY

ablation   complete destruction or removal of some part of the brain or nervous system

abnormal psychology   field that studies people's emotional, cognitive, and/or behavioral problems

abnormality   behavior with features that include suffering, maladaptiveness, loss of control, unconventionality, and the production of discomfort among observers

absolute threshold   minimal amount of energy needed to create a detectable sensation

accommodation   modification of what is already known to fit new information

acetylcholine   neutrotransmitter involved in Alzheimer's disease

achievement motivation   need to accomplish something difficult in situations characterized by a standard of excellence

acquired motives   learned motives: achievement, power, and mastery

acquisition   in classical conditioning, the process in which the conditioned response becomes stronger through repeated pairings of the conditioned stimulus with the unconditioned stimulus

acquisition   in operant conditioning, process by which the frequency of an operant increases

action potential   electrical and chemical changes that take place when a neuron fires

action research   attempt to make scientific investigations relevant to social issues

activation-synthesis theory   theory proposing that dreams are not themselves significant but represent a person's interpretation of random activity in the brain stem during sleep

actor-observer effect   tendency to explain one's own behavior in terms of situational forces but others' behavior in terms of internal causes

acuity   ability to make visual discriminations among objects

adaptation   acclimation of photoreceptors to background illumination

adaptation-level theory   idea that sensation is affected not only by a given stimulus but also by other stimuli present and stimuli that have been experienced in the past

adrenal glands   endocrine glands that are located on top of the kidneys and control the body's response to threat and danger

affiliation   tendency to seek out other people

aggregation   assembly of individuals physically in the same place

aggression   intentionally destructive acts directed against individuals or groups

agonists   chemicals that mimic actual neurotransmitters, causing neurons to fire

agoraphobia   fear of being in a situation from which escape is difficult or embarrassing

AIDS; acquired immunodeficiency syndrome   disease characterized by pervasive immunosuppression

Alcoholics Anonymous (AA)   self-help group for recovering alcohol abusers

algorithm   approach to solving a problem that guarantees a solution

all-or-none principle   idea that neurons fire either totally or not at all

American Law Institute (ALI) rule   currently popular criterion used to judge insanity, holding that people are not responsible for criminal conduct if at the time of a crime they did not appreciate its wrongfulness or if they could not conform their conduct to the requirements of law

amnestic syndrome   memory impairment caused by a neurological problem

amplitude   height of a light wave

amplitude   height of a sound wave

amygdala   part of the limbic system that produces rage and aggression

animism   belief that inanimate objects are living beings

anorexia nervosa   deliberate restriction of calories resulting in extreme weight loss

antagonists   chemicals that occupy receptor sites of neurons and prevent the normal role of actual neurotransmitters

anterior commissure   bundle of nerve fibers that connects the two temporal lobes

antidepressants   drugs, such as tricyclics, MAO-inhibitors, and Prozac, used to treat depression and certain anxiety disorders

anxiety   emotion similar to fear except that one's sense of danger is usually not specific

anxiety disorders   disorders in which anxiety predominates

applied psychology   use of psychological theories and findings to help solve people's practical problems

approach-avoidance conflict   course of activity both attractive (because it reduces drives) and unattractive (because it produces punishment)

archetypes   according to Jung, universal symbols

artificial concept   concept defined by necessary and sufficient conditions

artificial intelligence   deliberately-created computer programs that perform tasks similar to those that people perform

assimilation   modification of new information to fit what is already known

association   relationship between two variables

association areas   parts of the cortex where higher mental activities take place

associationism   assumption that ideas are organized in the mind according to their original association in ongoing experience

atomism   assumption that complex objects are composed of a finite number of basic elements

attachment theory   idea that adults approach romantic relationships in accordance with their attachment history as infants

attention   process by which some stimuli rather than others are perceived

attitude   stable and general disposition toward an object, usually a social group

attribution theory   explanation of the role played by causal attributions in social behavior

auditory canal   connection between the outer ear and the inner ear

auditory nerve   bundle of nerves that runs from the inner ear to the brain

authoritarian parenting   style of raising children that is firm, punitive, and emotionally cold

authoritative parenting   style of raising children that involves negotiating, setting limits but explaining why, and encouraging independence

automatic processing   carrying out activities without conscious attention to them

autonomic nervous system   neurons that control the heart, lungs, and digestive organs

axons   parts of the neuron that send messages to other neurons

backward conditioning   classical conditioning in which the conditioned stimulus follows the unconditioned stimulus

barbiturates   depressants like phenobarbital that slow down activity in the entire nervous system

basic emotions   emotions experienced by people in a variety of cultures: anger, fear, sadness, disgust, surprise, curiosity, acceptance, and joy

basic psychology   the pursuit of psychological knowledge for its own sake

basilar membrane   structure that runs the length of the cochlea and has hair cells on its surface

behavior   a person's (or animal's) actions and reactions that can be observed and measured by others

behavior genetics   field that studies how genetic differences within a species are related to behavior differences

behavior therapy   therapy techniques based on the psychology of learning

behaviorally anchored rating scales (BARS)   judgments about the degree to which a worker performs particular behaviors relevant to his or her job

behaviorism   approach to psychology that explains behavior in terms of observable actions

Big Five   five personality traits thought to describe the important ways in which people differ: neuroticism, extraversion, openness, agreeableness, and conscientiousness

biomedical therapies   treatment of problems with biological interventions

biopsychosocial approach   assumption that people and their behavior are best explained in terms of relevant biological mechanisms, psychological processes, and social influences

bipolar disorder   manic-depression; mood disorder in which periods of depression alternate with periods of excessive agitation and elation

blind spot   area in the retina through which the optic nerve passes

bottleneck model   theory of attention hypothesizing a biological restriction on the amount of sensory stimulation that can be attended to

bottom-up information processing   information processing in which simple aspects of thinking are not influenced by complex ones

brightness   psychological experience of the physical intensity of light

Broca's area   brain structure involved in the production of speech

bulimia nervosa   alternation between bingeing (ingesting thousands of calories of food in a short time) and purging (ridding oneself of these calories)

cancer   group of diseases characterized by the uncontrollable growth of cells

Cannon-Bard theory of emotion   theory that emotions are produced by brain activity

capacity model   theory of attention proposing a psychological restriction on the amount of sensory stimulation that can be attended to

cardiovascular diseases   diseases involving the heart and circulatory system

case study   intensive investigation of a single subject or group

CAT scan; computerized axial tomography   three-dimensional X-ray of the brain

causal attribution   belief about the cause of some event

cell body   the neuron's largest concentration of mass, containing the nucleus of the cell

central nervous system   neurons in the brain and spinal cord

central tendency   typical value of a variable

cerebellum   structure of the hindbrain involved in coordination, balance, and muscle tone

cerebral cortex   outer layer of the forebrain

cerebral hemispheres   symmetrical halves of the forebrain

chaining   process by which a sequence of responses is learned through operant conditioning: first the last response, then the next-to-last response, and so on

chemical sense   sense that detects chemicals dissolved in water: taste and odor

chromosomes   sets of genes found in each cell of the body

chunking   process in which cognitive elements are grouped into larger wholes

classical conditioning   learning that takes place when we associate two environmental stimuli that occur together in time

client-centered therapy; person-centered therapy   approach to psychotherapy developed by Rogers that provides clients with unconditional positive regard

clinical syndromes   problems with identifiable beginnings that bring a person into therapy

cochlea   fluid-filled canals in the inner ear

cognition   psychological processes that acquire, retain, transform, and use knowledge

cognitive development   processes of change in how knowledge is gained and used

cognitive dissonance theory   Festinger's idea that when people perceive an inconsistency between their attitudes and their behaviors, they attempt to reduce it, perhaps by changing their attitudes

cognitive learning   form of learning in which an individual behaves differently as a result of acquiring new information about the relationships between responses and stimuli

cognitive map   mental representation of a physical place

cognitive revolution   beginning in the 1960s, the increasingly cognitive approach of psychology

cognitive science   interdisciplinary field concerned with knowledge

cognitive therapy   approach to psychotherapy developed by Beck that attempts to change the cognitions that cause and maintain anxiety and depression

cohort effects   differences among people that are due to prevailing historical and social conditions when they were born

collective unconscious   repository of ancestral experiences and memories that all people share

collectivity   any social category: two or more individuals who can be discussed as a whole

common traits   traits that describe all people

community psychology   approach that attempts to change social conditions in order to eliminate or minimize the causes of disorders

comparative psychology   study of behavioral similarities and differences across species

competence to stand trial   ability of a person to understand legal proceedings and to contribute to his or her own defense

complex emotions   combinations of basic emotions in ways shaped by socialization within a specific culture

compulsion   repetitive action carried out to prevent some dreaded event

concept   cognitive representation of a category of elements

concrete operations stage   Piaget's third stage of cognitive development, from ages 7 to about 11, characterized by an understanding of conservation

conditional regard   acceptance from others that depends on particular ways of behaving

conditioned response (CR)   in classical conditioning, the response produced by the conditioned stimulus after pairing with the unconditioned stimulus

conditioned stimulus (CS)   in classical conditioning, a stimulus paired with the unconditioned stimulus

conditioning   form of learning involving the acquisition of particular behaviors in the presence of particular environmental stimuli

cones   photoreceptors with a tapered shape that are responsible for vision in bright light

conformity   the changing of one's behavior to be consistent with that of others

confound irrelevant factor that distorts results in an investigation because of its unintended association with the factors of concern

conscious what one is aware of at a particular moment

consciousness awareness of one's current environment and mental life

conservation recognition that characteristics of objects or substances can stay the same even if their appearance changes

consumer psychology field of applied psychology concerned with the acquisition and consumption of goods and services

contact hypothesis idea that mere contact between different groups decreases prejudice

context-dependent recall better recall of a memory in the same setting in which it was encoded than in different settings

contingency in classical conditioning, the prediction of the subsequent occurrence of the unconditioned stimulus by the conditioned stimulus

contingency theory Fiedler's idea that the best leader for a group depends on the nature of the group

continuous reinforcement operant conditioning in which reinforcement occurs after every response

contraprepared learning learning that our evolutionary history has made difficult

control group in an experiment, the group of research subjects not exposed to a potential cause

controlled processing carrying out activities with a conscious effort to direct them

conventional reasoning Kohlberg's second stage of moral development, in which the individual justifies moral action in terms of society's rules and conventions

conversion disorder hysteria; a loss of physical functioning without a physical cause

cornea transparent membrane at the front of the eye

corpus callosum bundle of nerve fibers that is the major connection between the two cerebral hemispheres

correlation coefficient number between −1.00 and 1.00 reflecting the degree to which two variables are correlated with one another

correlational investigation research strategy that ascertains how different factors are associated with one another

counterconditioning behavior therapy techniques based on classical conditioning that replace undesirable responses to stimuli with desirable ones

couples therapy approach to psychotherapy that treats the cohabiting couple

creativity behavior that is adaptive and purposeful as well as novel

crib death; sudden infant death syndrome the death of an infant during sleep for no apparent reason except that breathing stops

critical empiricism assumption that all knowledge originates through the senses

critical incidents specific occurrences that distinguish satisfactory workers from unsatisfactory ones

cross-cultural psychology field of psychology that compares and contrasts people's behaviors across different cultures

cross-cultural psychopathology field that attempts to explain cultural influences on disorders

cross-sectional study investigation that simultaneously compares individuals of different ages

crystallized intelligence skills or knowledge formed through education or practice

culture-bound syndromes psychological disorders that occur only within specific cultures

culture-fair intelligence tests intelligence tests designed to measure abilities that are unaffected by an individual's particular background

cutaneous senses senses that respond to touch or temperature

data scientific facts

daydreaming fantasizing that one deliberately undertakes while awake

death instinct; Thanatos motive for violence and aggression

decay forgetting due to the passage of time

deception experiment experiment in which subjects are misled about its actual purpose

defense mechanisms unconscious strategies people use to defend against threat

deindividuation feelings of anonymity resulting from submersion in a group

delirium overall impairment of thinking due to biological causes imposed on an otherwise intact nervous sytem

delusions patently false beliefs

dementia overall impairment of thinking due to the compromising of the nervous system as a whole by illness or injury

dendrites parts of the neuron that receive messages from other neurons

dependent variable in an experiment, the factor assessed by the researcher following the manipulation—the potential effect

depressants psychoactive drugs that reduce awareness of external stimuli and slow down bodily functions

depressive disorder; major depression mood disorder in which one experiences excessively negative moods

depth of processing degree to which information is encoded or transformed

descriptive statistics summaries of the general characteristics and patterns of data

determinism assumption that all behaviors have causes

development physical and psychological changes that take place throughout life

diagnosis placement of people in categories according to the particular signs or symptoms of their difficulties

diathesis-stress model integrative approach that explains abnormality as due to a biological weakness (diathesis) coupled with certain environmental conditions (stress)

difference threshold; just noticeable difference (jnd) minimal distinction between two stimuli that can be discriminated

discrimination behavior resulting from prejudice

discrimination in classical conditioning, the failure of stimuli dissimilar to the conditioned stimulus to elicit the conditioned response

discrimination in operant conditioning, the process by which an organism does not behave in a new situation as it did in an old situation because the discriminative stimuli in them are dissimilar

discriminative stimulus stimulus indicating that reinforcement is (or is not) available

dispositional optimism personality dimension reflecting the expectation that good events will be plentiful in the future

dissociation splitting of consciousness into separate streams, with little or no communication between or among them

dissociative amnesia sudden inability to recall personally important information because of psychological trauma

dissociative disorder disorder characterized by discontinuities in an individual's consciousness

dissociative identity disorder; multiple personality disorder (MPD) presence within the same person of two or more distinct identities or personalities

divided attention ability to attend to different stimuli at the same time

doctrine of specific nerve energies Müller's idea that neural messages register as different sensations because they move along nerves that terminate in different areas of the brain

dominant gene gene in a pair that influences the phenotype

dopamine neurotransmitter involved in the experience of pleasure

dopamine hypothesis theory that schizophrenia results from excess activity of the neurotransmitter dopamine

double-depletion hypothesis theory of thirst proposing two causes of thirst: depletion of fluid within the cells of the body and depletion of fluid outside the cells

Down syndrome type of organic retardation caused by an extra chromosome

dream anxiety disorder   sleep disorder characterized by frequent and/or particularly distressing nightmares

drive   state of tension or arousal produced by a need

DSM-IV; Diagnostic and Statistical Manual of Mental Disorders—Fourth Edition   American Psychiatric Association's manual that contains diagnostic criteria for psychological disorders

dual-center theory   theory proposing that there are two parts (or centers) in the hypothalamus that work together to maintain the body's homeostasis

dyssomnias   problems with the amount, quality, or timing of sleep

eardrum   membrane at the end of the eardrum

echo   auditory image in sensory memory

eclectic therapy   approach to treatment that draws on a variety of techniques

ecological approach   Gibson's theory of perception emphasizing the actual environment that people perceive and the evolved psychological mechanisms that allow them to perceive it

effector   neuron that initiates some response toward the environment

ego   mental structure that allows one to satisfy needs and desires in socially acceptable ways

ego integrity   according to Erikson, the focus of later adulthood: acceptance of one's choices in life and a sense that one's dilemmas have been resolved

egocentrism   ability to see things only from one's own point of view

electroconvulsive therapy (ECT)   treatment of depression by passing a brief electric current through the brain of a patient and causing a seizure

electroencephalogram (EEG)   recording device that measures general patterns of electrical activity in the brain

electromyogram (EMG)   recording device that measures electrical activity of the muscles

electrooculogram (EOG)   recording device that measures eye movements

embryo   developing unborn child from about two weeks to two months after conception

emotion   subjective feelings in response to situations, as well as associated patterns of physiological arousal, thought, and behavior

emotion-focused coping   attempt to moderate one's emotional response to a stressful event

empiricists   philosophers who believe that particular ideas originate through experience

encoding   process by which information is placed in memory

endocrine system   set of glands that secrete hormones into the bloodstream

endorphins   pain-reducing chemicals produced in the brain that are similar to narcotics

engineering psychology   field of applied psychology that uses psychological theories and research to design environmental settings—usually machines—to be safe, efficient, and/or pleasurable

engram   as-yet-undiscovered physical changes in the body that correspond to learning

enuresis   repeated bedwetting after bladder control is achieved

environmental psychology   field of applied psychology concerned with how the physical environment affects people's thoughts, feelings, and behaviors

equipotentiality   assumption that all responses are equally able to be learned

equity theory   idea that relationships persist to the degree that both people involved believe that what they are receiving from a relationship is proportional to what they are investing

ethology   field that studies the behavior of animals in their natural environments

etiology   presumed cause of a disorder

eugenics   attempt to improve the human species through the systematic application of the theory of evolution

everyday psychology   anecdotal explanations used in the course of everyday life to account for one's own behavior or that of others

evolution   process by which species originate and change over time

evolutionary psychology   field that studies the evolved psychological mechanisms that give rise to behavior

evolved psychological mechanism   biological and/or psychological process that arose in the course of evolution to solve a survival problem of a species and still influences behavior today

excitation   process by which one neuron causes other neurons to fire

experience sampling   procedure in which research subjects are contacted at random intervals and asked to describe where they are, what they are doing, how they are feeling, and what they are thinking

experiment   research strategy in which a researcher deliberately manipulates certain events and measures the effects of those manipulations on other events

experimental group   in an experiment, the group of research subjects exposed to a potential cause

explanatory style   personality dimension reflecting how people explain the causes of bad events that befall them

explicit memory   deliberate attempt to remember information

expressed emotion   degree to which families are critical and emotionally confrontive

extinction   in classical conditioning, the loss of the power of the conditioned stimulus to elicit the conditioned response after it no longer is paired with the unconditioned stimulus

extinction   in operant conditioning, decrease in the frequency of an operant when reinforcers are withheld

factor analysis   statistical procedure for detecting patterns in a large set of correlations

family therapy   approach to psychotherapy that treats the entire family

feature detectors   cells that respond only to highly specific environmental characteristics

Fechner's law   for most sensory systems, the straight-line relationship between changes in sensation intensity, measured by the number of jnds, and changes in stimulus intensity divided by the magnitude of the stimulus already present

feminist therapy   approach to psychotherapy informed by feminist philosophy

fetus   developing unborn child from about the third month after conception until birth

field theory   Lewin's idea that people are self-regulating, dynamic systems

figure-ground relationship   tendency to organize perceptions in terms of a coherent object (the figure) within a context (the ground)

fitness   successful reproduction

fixation   failure to resolve a particular psychosexual stage so that the concerns of that stage continue to dominate one's adult personality

fixed-action patterns; instincts   unlearned behaviors, common to an entire species, that occur in the presence of certain stimuli

flashbulb memories   highly vivid recollections of emotionally charged events

flow   subjective feelings that accompany highly engaging activities

fluid intelligence   ability to adapt to new situations

forebrain   highest and newest layer of the brain

forgetting   failure of memory

formal operations stage   Piaget's final stage of cognitive development, from age 11 through adulthood, characterized by the ability to think abstractly

forward conditioning   classical conditioning in which the conditioned stimulus precedes the unconditioned stimulus

fovea   central point in the retina where a visual image is focused

free will   assumption that behavior is freely undertaken except in special cases

frequency   number of times that sound waves repeat themselves in a given period

frequency theory   explanation of hearing proposing that sound waves of different frequencies affect the firing rate of neurons in the ear

frontal lobe   region of the cortex located right behind the forehead and involved in planning and decision making

frustration-aggression hypothesis theory that all aggression is due to the failure to attain a desired goal

functional analysis identification of reinforcers and punishers by observing actual behavior and its consequences

functional fixedness tendency to persist in representing problems in a particular way, perhaps preventing their solution

functionalism approach to psychology that emphasizes the consequences of mental processes

fundamental attribution error tendency to overlook the possibility that situational forces influence behavior

GABA neurotransmitter necessary for the parasympathetic nervous system to counteract arousal

ganglia clumps of neurons

gate-control theory explanation of pain proposing that cells in the spinal cord act as a gate, blocking some pain signals from going to the brain, while letting others pass

gender differences psychological and social differences between men and women

gene microscopic mechanism of inheritance, composed of DNA molecules, passed from parents to offspring

general adaptation syndrome sequence of physiological reactions to an environmental stressor: alarm reaction, resistance, and exhaustion

general intelligence (g) type of intelligence reflected in many or all types of performance

generalization how far and how well findings from a given study can be applied

generalization in classical conditioning, the ability of stimuli similar to the conditioned stimulus to elicit the conditioned response

generalization in operant conditioning, the process by which an organism behaves in a new situation as it did in an old situation because the discriminative stimuli in them are similar

generalized anxiety disorder (GAD) disorder characterized by pervasive and chronic anxiety

generate-and-recognize model of recall theory of recall proposing that a person generates possible answers to a memory task and then attempts to recognize one as the correct answer

generativity concern with the world outside oneself and in particular the next generation

genius someone whose accomplishments exert a profound influence on contemporary and subsequent generations

genotype one's complete set of genes

germ theory idea that illnesses are caused by microorganisms (germs)

gestalt organizational principles tendencies to organize stimuli into coherent forms

Gestalt psychology approach to psychology that explains behavior in terms of the relationships or patterns among mental events

glial cells cells that hold neurons in place, provide nourishment to them, and dispose of waste material

grammar rules that allow language to be generated and understood

group set of interacting individuals who mutually influence each other

group polarization tendency of groups to make more extreme decisions than individuals

group therapy approach to psychotherapy that treats groups of people with similar problems or challenges

groupthink processes within a group that suppress criticism and preclude the consideration of alternatives, thereby resulting in disastrous decisions

habituation form of learning in which we stop paying attention to an environmental stimulus that never changes

hair cells cells in the cochlea that send neural impulses to the brain

hallucinations sensations and perceptions with no basis in reality

hallucinogens psychoactive drugs that produce hallucinations

hardiness personality dimension reflecting the ability to find meaning and challenge in the demands of life

hassles minor annoyances of everyday life

Hawthorne effect change—above and beyond that attributable to particular experimental manipulations—in someone's behavior because he or she is participating in a work place experiment

health psychology field of psychology concerned with physical well-being

helping alliance expectations shared by a client and a therapist that treatment will be helpful

heritability proportion of a trait's variation across individuals that is due to genetic factors

heroic medicine medical approach in the 1800s that treated illness by aggressive interventions such as bleeding

heuristic approach to solving a problem that is efficient but may or may not lead to a solution

hidden observer in hypnosis, the part of the mind that does not yield to the suggestions of the hypnotist and is concealed from the part of the mind that does

hierarchy of needs Maslow's idea that motives are arranged in a hierarchy reflecting the order in which they are satisfied

hindbrain lowest and oldest layer of the brain, consisting of most of the brain stem

hippocampus part of the limbic system involved in the processing of memories

homeostasis maintenance of a stable or balanced state of physiological conditions

hormones chemicals that are secreted by glands into the bloodstream and affect various bodily organs

hue color; psychological experience of the wavelength of light

Human Genome Project ongoing scientific project to locate and describe all human genes

humanistic psychology approach that looks at people in terms of their freely undertaken choices

humours bodily fluids long thought to influence physical and emotional health

hypersomnia excessive daytime sleepiness or sleep attacks not accounted for by an inadequate amount of sleep

hypnosis psychological state characterized by heightened suggestibility

hypochondriasis preoccupation with having one or more serious illnesses, when all medical evidence is to the contrary

hypothalamus structure at the top of the brain stem that controls much of the activity of the autonomic nervous system

hypothesis specific prediction tested in a scientific study

icon visual image in sensory memory

id mental structure in which one's instincts are located

illusion phenomenon in which the perception of an object is at odds with its actual characteristics

image cognitive representation much like perception except without an external stimulus

immune system bodily system that identifies and combats foreign material invading the body, including germs

immunosuppression suppression of the immune system

implicit memory unintentional recall or recognition of information

imprinting attachment formed by the young of some species to whatever moving object they first encounter

inclusive fitness fitness of an individual plus fitness of the individual's relatives

independent variable in an experiment, the factor manipulated by the researcher

industrial-organizational (IO) psychology field of applied psychology concerned with improving the functioning of complex work organizations

inferential statistics probabilistic conclusions about data

inferiority complex Adler's idea that all people feel inadequate with respect to some aspect of the self and try to compensate

information processing theory theory that explains the transformation of information

inhibition   process by which one neuron causes other neurons not to fire

insanity plea   defense against a criminal accusation on the grounds that the individual was suffering from a psychological problem at the time the crime was committed

insight   form of learning marked by a sudden understanding of the relationship among the parts of a problem that leads to a solution

insomnia   problem in initiating sleep, maintaining sleep, or not feeling rested after sleep

instinct   complex behavior that appears without having been explicitly learned

instinctive drift   blending of learning with instinctive (unlearned) tendencies

instrumental conditioning   Thorndike's term for describing operant conditioning, to emphasize his interest in responses that prove instrumental (useful) to the individual

intelligence   adaptive and purposive behavior

intelligence quotient (IQ)   ratio of one's mental age and chronological age, multiplied by 100

interaction   joint effect on behavior of traits and the environment

intermittent reinforcement   operant conditioning in which reinforcement does not occur after every response

internal reliability   degree to which different items on the same test give the same scores to an individual at the same point in time

intoxication   alteration in brain function brought about by drug use

introspection   attempt to identify the contents of thought by precisely describing one's mental experiences

introversion-extraversion   degree to which people are inwardly or outwardly oriented

involuntary commitment   placement of an individual in a mental hospital without his or her consent

iris   colored part of the eye

James-Lange theory of emotion   theory that emotions are the perception of the body's physiological responses

job analysis   explicit description of what people are expected to do at a particular occupation

John Henryism   personality dimension reflecting the belief that all events can be controlled solely through hard work and determination

kinesthetic sense   sense that detects the movement or position of muscles and joints

language   systematic way of communicating ideas or feelings using signs, sounds, gestures, or marks having symbolic significance

latent content   underlying significance to the dreamer of a dream's manifest content

lateralization   greater involvement in some behavior of one hemisphere rather than the other

law of effect   Thorndike's proposal that reward stamps in responses, whereas lack of reward stamps out responses

learned helplessness   passivity following learning that responses and outcomes are unrelated

learning   any relatively permanent change in behavior resulting from experience

lens   structure of the eye that focuses images

lesion   wound or injury to a particular part of the brain or nervous system

levels of processing model of memory   theory that the supposed stages of memory represent different depths of information processing

libido   psychological energy that drives behavior

life instinct; Eros   motive for pleasure

light   radiating energy that travels in an oscillating pattern of waves

limbic system   structures in the forebrain involved in the expression of emotions

linear ordering   cognitive representation of elements in some order

lithium   naturally occurring salt used to treat bipolar disorder

lobotomy   type of psychosurgery in which fibers connecting parts of the brain are severed, once used to treat depression and schizophrenia

localization of function   position that specific parts of the brain are responsible for given behaviors

lock-and-key theory   explanation of smell proposing that different sites on odor detectors have characteristic shapes that only certain molecules fit

long-term memory   stage of memory into which information passes from short-term memory and is held for an extremely long time

longitudinal study   investigation that follows the same individuals over a considerable period of time

loudness   psychological experience of the amplitude of sound waves

lovemap   Money's term for the gist of one's sexual orientation

mainstreaming   education of mentally retarded individuals with normal children

major tranquilizers; neuroleptics   drugs, such as Thorazine and Haldol, used to treat schizophrenia

malleus, incus, and stapes   hammer, anvil, and stirrup; three small bones in the inner ear that transmit vibrations from the eardrum to the oval window

mania   state of excessive elation and agitation

manifest content   dream images and events of which the dreamer is aware

mass action   idea that the brain acts as a whole

mastery   need to behave in a competent way

maturation   unfolding of biologically based processes of growth

medial forebrain bundle (MFB)   group of neurons that connects the middle of the brain to the top of the brain and is involved in pleasure

meditation   strategy of altering consciousness that combines a refocusing of attention with relaxation

medulla   part of the brain stem that is directly connected to the spinal cord and controls respiration and cardiac function

memory   initial acquisition and subsequent access to mental representations of knowledge

mental age   average intelligence test score of children of a given chronological age

mental map; cognitive map   cognitive representation of a physical place

mental measurement   approach to psychology that regards differences among people as primary and tries to devise measures of those differences

mental processes   occurrences within an individual's mind that cannot be directly observed by others

mental retardation   below-average general intellectual functioning existing along with deficits in adaptive behavior

meta-analysis   statistical technique that takes the results of separate experimental studies and combines them to yield an overall estimate of an experimental effect

metacognition   awareness of oneself as a cognitive being

metastasis   spread of cancer cells

midbrain   middle layer of the brain, consisting of the upper part of the brain stem

mind-body dualism   philosophical position that people's minds and bodies are altogether different

minor tranquilizers   depressants like Valium that counteract arousal of the sympathetic nervous system

mnemonics   strategies and techniques used to improve memory

modeling   type of learning that takes place by observing the behavior of others

mood disorders   disorders characterized by extreme sadness and/or elation

moral development   processes of change in judgments of the rightness or wrongness of acts

motivation   processes that arouse, direct, and maintain behavior

motor development   processes of change in the skill with which the body is used

motor projection areas   parts of the cortex that send messages to the various muscles

MRI; magnetic resonance imaging   image of magnetic activity in the brain

multiple intelligences Gardner's idea that there are several independent types of intelligence, each a biologically based set of problem-solving skills

multistore model of memory theory that memories are represented in several different ways

mutation error in the process of chromosome combination and/or replication

myelin white, fatty substance that covers some neurons, protecting the axons and speeding neural messages

mystical experience phenomenon characterized by a feeling of oneness with the universe and an inability to express experience in mere words

natural concept concept without necessary or sufficient conditions

natural selection Darwin's explanation of evolution, holding that the natural environment of a species selects which individuals survive and reproduce, passing their characteristics on to offspring

naturalistic observation research strategy in which behavior is observed as it naturally occurs

nature-versus-nurture debate controversy as to whether behavior is due to inherent biological characteristics (nature) or to learning and socialization (nurture)

need lack of a biological essential

negative afterimage perceptual phenomenon in which one stares at an object of one color, quickly looks away, and sees an image of the "opposite" color

negative reinforcement reinforcement in which a stimulus is removed after a response

neo-Freudians theorists influenced by Freud who stress people's social character rather than their sexual instincts

neural networks computer simulations of the nervous system

neuroleptics drugs that control many of the symptoms of schizophrenia

neurons individual nerve cells that compose the nervous system

neuroscience interdisciplinary field that attempts to understand behavior in biological terms

neuroticism degree to which people are moody and nervous

neurotransmitter chemical secreted by one neuron that influences a second neuron

nightmare dream with a frighetning content

non-REM sleep all stages of sleep other than REM sleep

nonfalsifiable unable to be disproved by any observable evidence

nonsense syllables sets of letters with no inherent meaning, used in memory research

norepinephrine neurotransmitter involved in depressive disorder

norms average scores for test performance, based on research with large samples

norms expectations about appropriate and inappropriate behavior

obedience doing what a person in authority tells one to do

obesity condition of being 20 percent or more in excess of what is considered a normal and healthy weight

object permanence knowledge that objects exist even when out of sight

object relations mental representations people have of themselves and others

objective tests measures in which scores are assigned according to explicit rules

obsession recurring unpleasant thought

obsessive-compulsive disorder (OCD) anxiety disorder characterized by obsessions and compulsions

occipital lobe region of the cortex located at the rear of the brain and devoted to vision

Oedipus complex according to Freud, events during the phallic stage in which children feel sexual desire for the opposite-sex parent and treat the same-sex parent as a rival

olfactory bulb structure at the base of the brain to which the olfactory nerve leads

olfactory nerve bundle of nerves leading from odor detectors to the brain

ontogeny course of development of an individual organism within its lifetime

operant behavior that is emitted spontaneously

operant chamber Skinner box; mechanized device for studying operant conditioning

operant conditioning learning that takes place when we come to associate a behavior with its consequences

operation mental process used to transform and manipulate information

operational definition concrete and specific measure of a theoretical concept

opiates; narcotics depressants derived from poppy plants or synthesized in laboratories to be chemically similar

opponent-process color theory theory that explains color vision in terms of two systems, each composed of a pair of colors that oppose each other

optic nerve bundle of neurons that lead away from the photoreceptors to the brain

organic personality syndrome persistent change in one's personality due to neurological damage

organic retardation mental retardation due to specific illness, injury, or physiological dysfunction

organic syndromes constellations of psychological symptoms associated with neurological problems

organization enduring and organized group

organizational climate perception of the characteristics of an organization by its members

orientation positioning of sense organs to best receive environmental stimulation

Ortgeist influence of a given culture on theories and research

outcome research investigation of the effectiveness of therapy

oval window membrane that focuses sound waves and makes the fluid in the cochlea move

pacinian corpuscle specialized touch receptor

panic disorder anxiety disorder characterized by recurrent panic attacks

parallel processing information processing of several stimuli at the same time

parasomnias abnormal events during sleep

parasympathetic nervous system part of the autonomic nervous system that counteracts arousal

parietal lobe region of the brain found behind the frontal lobe and in front of the occipital lobe and involved in the integration of sensory information relayed from lower parts of the brain

partial reinforcement effect resistance to extinction of responses acquired with intermittent as opposed to continuous reinforcement

participant observation research strategy in which behavior is observed as it naturally occurs by joining into it

peer pressure legitimization of activities by one's peer group

perception process by which sensory information is organized and interpreted in psychological terms

perceptual defense process by which people protect themselves by not consciously perceiving threatening stimuli

perceptual set; mental set predisposition to perceive a particular stimulus in a particular context

peripheral nervous system neurons that link the central nervous system to the senses, glands, and muscles

permissive parenting style of raising children that is loving but lax

personal construct theory Kelly's explanation of personality in terms of the categories with which people interpret their experiences

person-role merger identification with a social role to such a degree that the person becomes the role

personal traits traits that describe only some people

personality psychological characteristics of an individual that are general, enduring, distinctive, integrated, and functional

personality disorders long-standing personality styles that can make a clinical syndrome worse as well as create difficulties in their own right

personality inventory set of objective tests that attempts to measure the range of individual differences

personology   term for personality psychology that stresses the study of the person as a whole

persuasive communications   messages designed to change attitudes

PET scan; positron emission tomography   image of metabolic activity in the brain

phenomenological approach; cognitive approach   group of personality theories that stress what and how people think

phenotype   characteristics that one actually shows

pheromones   hormone-like chemicals involved in communication between individuals

phobia   anxiety disorder in which an individual shows persistent fear and avoidance of some specific object or situation

photoreceptors   nerve cells sensitive to light

phylogeny   evolution of a species or genetically related group of organisms

physical development   processes of bodily change and growth in the developing individual

pinna   outer ear

pitch   psychological experience of the frequency of sound waves

pituitary gland   endocrine gland that is located at the base of the brain and controls the secretions of many other glands

place theory   explanation of hearing proposing that sound waves of different frequencies affect different locations along the basilar membrane

polygenic inheritance   determination of characteristics by more than one gene

polygraph   so-called lie detector device that actually measures physiological arousal, which may or may not accompany the intent to deceive

pons   structure that links the hindbrain to the rest of the brain

population   larger group to which a researcher wishes to generalize from a study of a particular sample

position senses   senses that detect the movement or position of the body or its parts

positive reinforcement   reinforcement in which a stimulus is presented after a response

postconventional reasoning   Kohlberg's final stage of moral development, in which the individual justifies moral action in terms of his or her own abstract standards

post-traumatic stress disorder (PTSD)   anxiety disorder that can follow a traumatic event, and is characterized by anxiety and reexperiencing of the traumatic event

power motivation   need to have an impact on others

preconscious   whatever one can voluntarily call into awareness

preconventional reasoning   Kohlberg's first stage of moral development, in which the individual justifies moral action in terms of rewards and punishments

prejudice   prejudgment of people based solely on the group to which they belong

Premack principle   Premack's hypothesis that preferred activities act as reinforcers for less preferred activities

preoperational stage   Piaget's second stage of cognitive development, from ages 2 to 6, characterized by symbolic thinking and egocentrism

prepared learning   learning predisposed by our evolutionary history

primary appraisal   judgment about what is at stake in a stressful event

primary colors   red, green, and blue

primary motives   biologically based motives: hunger, thirst, and sex

primary reinforcer   stimulus that is reinforcing because of its inherent biological properties

proactive interference   forgetting due to interference from previously acquired information

problem   discrepancy between what one knows and what one wants to know

problem-focused coping   attempt to remove the effects of a stressful event

problem solving   reduction of the discrepancy between what one knows and what one wants to know

problem-space   cognitive representation of a problem: its initial state, its desired goal state, and the admissible operations or transformations that allow one to get from the one to the other

prodigy   child with a special skill or talent advanced far beyond what is considered normal for his or her age

prognosis   likely outcome of a disorder

projective techniques   procedures that ask research subjects to respond to ambiguous stimuli

propositional network   cognitive representation of the meaning of a concept in terms of a network of associations

prosocial behavior   acts that benefit other people while having no obvious benefits for the person who carries them out

prototype   typical example of a concept

proximate causation   how a characteristic occurs in an individual

psychoactive drugs   chemicals that affect brain activity and consciousness

psychoanalysis   approach to psychology that explains behavior in terms of unconscious conflicts and their resolutions

psychoanalytic therapy   approach to psychotherapy developed by Freud that attempts to free a person's psychic energy from symptoms

psychodynamic approach   family of theories by Freud and others that stress psychological forces and conflicts

psychodynamic therapy   approach to psychotherapy based on the assumption that problems are caused by unconscious conflicts and distortions in thinking

psychological therapies; psychotherapies   treatment of problems with psychological interventions

psychology   scientific study of behavior and mental processes

psychoneuroimmunology   interdisciplinary field concerned with the mutual influences among psychological, neurological, and immunological factors

psychophysics   field of psychology that studies the relationship between physical stimuli and psychological experience

psychosexual stages   periods of development defined by the part of the body that provides pleasure to an individual

psychosocial stages   according to Erikson, the stages people pass through during life, each characterized by a social challenge to be resolved

psychosomatic disorders   physical illnesses influenced by psychological factors

psychosurgery   treatment of problems with brain surgery

psychoticism   degree to which people are insensitive, odd, and detached

puberty   physical changes that accompany adolescence

punishment   process by which a stimulus that follows a response reduces the probability that the response will recur

pupil   opening in the colored part of the eye

purity   degree to which a sound is dominated by waves of a single frequency

purity   degree to which light is dominated by a single wavelength

random assignment   in an experiment, the process of assigning subjects to experimental and control groups on a random basis

rational-emotive therapy   approach to psychotherapy developed by Ellis that is based on the assumption that problems are caused by irrational beliefs

rationalists   philosophers who believe that particular ideas are innate

reactivity   alteration of a phenomenon by measuring it

recall   retrieval of information from memory without explicit clues

receptor   neuron that receives stimulation from the environment

recessive gene   gene in a pair that does not influence the phenotype

reciprocal determinism   idea that behavior, cognition, and the environment mutually influence each other

recognition   realization that presented information is familiar

reference group   group that provides one's identity

reflex   automatic response to an external event

refractory period   period of time after a neuron fires when it cannot fire again until its resting potential is restored

reinforcement   process by which reinforcers affect behavior

reinforcer change in the environment that follows a behavior and increases the probability that it will recur

relapse prevention strategies for preventing return of drug or alcohol problems after successful treatment for abuse or dependence

reliability consistency or stability of measures or findings

REM (rapid eye movement) sleep stage of sleep in which the eyes dart back and forth rapidly

repression removal to the unconscious

research diagnostic criteria stringent rules for including subjects in a psychopathology study

resistance unwillingness on the part of a client to accept what therapy reveals about areas of conflict

resting potential the difference in electrical charge between the inside and outside of a neuron at rest

reticular formation network of neurons centrally located in the brain and richly connected to other structures

retina structure at the back of the eye lined with nerve cells sensitive to light

retrieval process by which information is located in memory and then used

retrieval failure forgetting due to inadequate cues for retrieval

retroactive interference forgetting due to interference from subsequently acquired information

rods photoreceptors shaped like cylinders that are responsible for vision in dim light

rule abstract guideline about how to act in a certain situation

rules cognitive representations that allow examples of a concept to be generated

sample actual group of research subjects investigated in a study

saturation psychological experience of the purity of light

savant individual with mediocre or even deficient skills in most domains who possesses one extraordinarily developed ability

scaling specification of the quantitative link between a physical dimension of a stimulus and the corresponding psychological dimension

schedules of reinforcement different patterns of providing reinforcement following a response

schema organized set of beliefs

scheme mental structure that represents knowledge

schizophrenia group of psychological disorders characterized by disturbed thinking and deteriorated functioning

scientific materialism philosophical position that living things are part of the physical world

scientific method process of evaluating tentative explanations against observable evidence

script accepted sequence of social events that unfold over time

secondary appraisal judgment about the resources available to cope with a stressful event

secondary reinforcer; conditioned reinforcer stimulus that is reinforcing because of its prior association with a primary reinforcer

second-order conditioning; higher-order conditioning classical conditioning in which a stimulus comes to elicit a conditioned response after pairing with a conditioned stimulus

selective attention ability to tune in some information while tuning out other information

self-actualization full use and exploitation of one's talents, capacities, and potentialities

self-efficacy belief that one can perform a given behavior

self-serving bias tendency to take credit for one's success but not one's failure

self-theory Rogers's explanation of personality in terms of how people view themselves in relationship to their worlds

sensation process by which environmental energy is transformed into neural activity

sensitization form of learning in which we become more responsive to a stimulus we encounter repeatedly

sensorimotor stage Piaget's first stage of cognitive development, from birth to about age 2, characterized by advances in motor development and object permanence

sensory memory; sensory register brief but relatively faithful memory of sensory experiences

sensory projection areas parts of the cortex that receive information from the various senses

septum part of the limbic system that reduces rage and aggression

serial position effect better memory for items at the beginning or end of a linear ordering

serial processing information processing of one stimulus at a time

serotonin neurotransmitter involved in depressive disorder

set-point theory idea that one's body is set to maintain a certain level of fat

sex differences physical differences between males and females

sexual orientation sexual object and aim of a particular person

shaping process by which simple responses become complex ones through changing the standard for reinforcement on successive occasions

short-term memory stage of memory into which information passes from sensory memory and is held for about 15 to 20 seconds

simultaneous conditioning classical conditioning in which the conditioned stimulus and the unconditioned stimulus occur at the same time

sleep apnea temporary failure of breathing during sleep

sleep terror awakening during non-REM sleep in a state of panic and disorientation

sleep terror disorder sleep disorder characterized by frequent and/or particularly distressing sleep terrors

sleep-wake schedule disorder mismatch between a normal sleep-wake schedule for a person's environment and his or her natural sleep-wake pattern

sleepwalking disorder sleep disorder in which the individual arises from bed during sleep, yet is unresponsive to others and able to be awakened only with difficulty

social cognition cognitive representations and processes that people use to make sense of the social world

social comparison tendency to compare one's skills, aptitudes, attitudes, and values with those of others

social Darwinism application of the theory of natural selection to human societies as a whole

social development processes of change in attitudes, values, and roles

social influence ways that people affect the social behavior of one another

social learning approach group of personality theories that stress principles of learning

social loafing tendency of people in a group not to work as hard as when alone

social perception process by which people come to know about themselves and others

social psychology field that explains how individuals are influenced by the presence of others

social support benefits provided by people to one another

sociobiology application of modern evolutionary theory to social behavior

sociocultural retardation mental retardation due to social disadvantage

somatic nervous system neurons that control the skeletal muscles and sense organs

somatoform disorder disorder characterized by physical symptoms that have no actual basis in physiology

specific hungers motives to consume food containing particular substances

specific intelligence (s) type of intelligence reflected in only one type of performance

split-brain patients individuals whose corpus callosum has been severed in order to relieve severe epileptic seizures

spontaneous recovery in classical conditioning, reappearance of a conditioned response after extinction

spontaneous recovery in operant conditioning, the reappearance of an extinguished operant

sports psychology field of applied psychology concerned with physical performance, usually in the context of competitive athletics

Stanford-Binet Intelligence Scale intelligence test based on Binet's original measure and its translation into English by Terman at Stanford University

state-dependent recall better recall of a memory in the same physiological or emotional state in which it was encoded than in different states

statistical significance degree to which research results are unlikely to have occurred by chance

statistics numerical representation of data

stereotype rigid and overly simple set of beliefs about members of a social group

stimulants psychoactive drugs that increase arousal and speed up mental and physical activity

stimulus environmental energy that produces a response by an organism

storage representation of information in memory

stress complex response to environmental demands

strong method approach to solving a problem that is obvious and explicit

structuralism approach to psychology that explains behavior in terms of how experience is structured from its simpler parts

subliminal perception perception of stimuli without awareness

substance abuse difficulties or distress due to drug use

substance dependence cluster of cognitive, behavioral, and physiological symptoms that indicate severe impairment and distress due to drug use

superego mental stucture that contains one's internalization of parental and societal values

survey research strategy in which subjects are selected at random from some larger group and asked questions, the answers to which are treated as representative of the larger group

sympathetic nervous system part of the autonomic nervous system that produces arousal

synapse the gap between two neurons into which a neurotransmitter is secreted

synesthesia unusual sensory phenomenon in which stimulation of one type of sensory receptor gives rise to the experience of another sense

systems theory theoretical approach of many family therapists, who assume that families are complex wholes in which changes in one part affect all other parts

taste aversion avoidance of a stimulus with a particular taste after that taste has been associated with illness

taste buds receptors, mostly located on the tongue, that are sensitive to taste

temperament biologically based style of behaving

temporal lobe region of the cortex located near the temple and devoted to speech comprehension and memory

terminal buttons end of the axon where chemicals are secreted that influence other neurons

test-retest reliability degree to which a test gives the same scores to an individual on repeated occasions

texture gradient graduated changes in the grain of an environment that provide information about distance

thalamus structure above the hypothalamus that integrates and organizes neural messages

Thematic Apperception Test (TAT) series of ambiguous pictures about which stories are told, used to infer the strength of one's needs

theory general scientific explanation

Theory X set of assumptions that often guide traditional management: Workers are intrinsically lazy and so must be coerced into doing their job

Theory Y set of assumptions that guide nontraditional management: Workers are intrinsically motivated to expend physical and mental effort in their work

therapy treatment of psychological disorders by mental health professionals

timbre sharpness or clarity of sound

tip-of-the-tongue phenomenon experience of knowing that one has a given memory but being unable to retrieve it

tolerance need to take more of a psychoactive drug in order to produce the same effect

top-down information processing information processing in which simple aspects of thinking are influenced by complex ones

trait stable and pervasive individual difference that initiates and guides diverse behavior

trait approach group of personality theories that classifies people in terms of their stable and general individual differences

transduction process by which external energy produces neural impulses

transference tendency of clients to relate to therapists as they have related to other important individuals in their lives

transformational grammar Chomsky's linguistic theory proposing that people create sentences by performing operations (transformations) on underlying meanings

triarchic theory Sternberg's theory of intelligence in terms of its context, tasks, and mechanisms

trichromatic color theory theory that explains color vision in terms of the relative stimulation of red cones, green cones, and blue cones

tumor mass of cells

two-factor theory of emotion theory that emotions result from physiological arousal and a cognitive label placed on this arousal

Type A behavior pattern set of behaviors marked by excessive time urgency, competitiveness, and hostility and thought to increase one's risk for heart disease

typology description of personality in terms of categories

ultimate causation how a characteristic contributes to the fitness of a species

unconditional regard acceptance from others that occurs regardless of what one thinks, feels, or does

unconditioned response (UCR) in classical conditioning, the response produced by an unconditioned stimulus

unconditioned stimulus (UCS) in classical conditioning, a stimulus that produces a response as a reflex, without learning

unconscious thoughts actively kept from awareness because they are threatening

unprepared learning learning neither predisposed nor precluded by evolution

validity degree to which research studies what it claims to study

value belief that certain personal goals are preferable to others

variability variation in a variable

vestibular sense sense responsible for balancing and for detecting the position of the body in relationship to gravity

vibration theory explanation of smell proposing that once in place, molecules trigger odor detectors because they vibrate at a particular frequency

visual constancies tendencies for visual perceptions to stay constant even as visual sensations change

visual pigments chemicals contained in photoreceptors that are sensitive to light

vitamin model Warr's theory of worker satisfaction that specifies different attributes of work that need to be present in at least minimal amounts to produce a satisfied worker

vitreous humor fluid within the eyeball

wavelength distance between the peaks of two successive light waves

weak method approach to solving a problem that is neither obvious nor explicit

Weber's law for most sensory systems, the straight-line relationship between the size of the standard and the jnd

Wechsler Intelligence Scales intelligence tests that were devised by David Wechsler and yield separate verbal and performance scores

Wernicke's area brain structure involved in the comprehension of speech

withdrawal alteration in brain function brought about by the cessation of drug use

Zeitgeist influence of a given historical era on theories and research

zygote newly fertilized cell

REFERENCES

Abelson, R. P. (1972). Are attitudes necessary? In B. T. King & E. McGinnies (Eds.), *Attitudes, conflict, and social change.* New York: Academic Press.

Abramov, I., & Gordon, J. (1994). Color appearance: On seeing red—or yellow, or green, or blue. *Annual Review of Psychology, 45,* 451–485.

Abramowitz, S. I., & Murray, J. (1983). Race effects in psychotherapy. In J. Murray & P. R. Abramson (Eds.), *Bias in psychotherapy.* New York: Praeger.

Abramson, L.Y., Seligman, M. E. P., & Teasdale, J. D. (1978). Learned helplessness in humans: Critique and reformulation. *Journal of Abnormal Psychology, 87,* 49–74.

Abravanel, E., & Sigafoos, A. D. (1984). Exploring the presence of imitation during early infancy. *Child Development, 55,* 381–392.

Achenbach, T. M. (1986). Developmental perspectives on psychotherapy and behavior change. In S. L. Garfield & A. E. Bergin (Eds.), *Handbook of psychotherapy and behavior change* (3rd ed.). New York: Wiley.

Adams, D. M., & Overholser, J. C. (1992). Suicidal behavior and history of substance abuse. *American Journal of Drug and Alcohol Abuse, 18,* 343–354.

Adebimpe, V. R. (1994). Race, racism, and epidemiological surveys. *Hospital and Community Psychiatry, 45,* 27–31.

Ader, R., & Cohen, N. (1981). Conditioned immunopharmacological responses. In R. Ader (Ed.), *Psychoneuroimmunology.* New York: Academic Press.

Ader, R., & Cohen, N. (1993). Psychoneuroimmunology: Conditioning and stress. *Annual Review of Psychology, 44,* 53–85.

Adityanjee. (1994). *Jauhar:* Mass suicide by self-immolation in Waco, Texas. *Journal of Nervous and Mental Disease, 182,* 727–728.

Adler, A. (1964). Inferiority feeling and defiance and obedience. In H. L. Ansbacher & R. R. Ansbacher (Original work published 1910) (Eds.), *The individual psychology of Alfred Adler.* New York: Harper.

Adler, A. (1927). *The practice and theory of individual psychology.* New York: Harcourt, Brace, & World.

Aguirre, B. E., Quarantelli, E. L., & Mendoza, J. L. (1988). The collective behavior of fads: The characteristics, effects, and career of streaking. *American Sociological Review, 53,* 569–584.

Ainsworth, L. L. (1989). Problems with subliminal perception. *Journal of Business and Psychology, 3,* 361–365.

Ainsworth, M. D. S. (1973). The development of infant-mother attachment. In B. M. Caldwell & H. N. Ricciuti (Eds.), *Review of child development research* (Vol. 3). Chicago: University of Chicago Press.

Ainsworth, M. D. S., & Wittig, B. A. (1969). Attachment and exploratory behavior of one-year-olds in a strange situation. In B. M. Foss (Ed.), *Determinants of infant behavior* (Vol. 4). London: Methuen.

Albert, D. J., & Walsh, M. L. (1984). Neural systems and the inhibitory modulation of agonistic behavior: A comparison of mammalian species. *Neuroscience and Biobehavioral Reviews, 8,* 5–24.

Alberti, E.T., & Witryol, S. L. (1990). Children's preference for complexity as a function of perceived units in collative motivation. *Journal of Genetic Psychology, 151,* 91–101.

Alcaraz-García, M. (1993). Especificidad vs. generalidad de las respuestas autonómicas en las emociones. *Psicothema, 5,* 255–264.

Aldag, R. J., & Fuller, S. R. (1993). Beyond fiasco: A reappraisal of the group-think phenomenon and a new model of group decision processes. *Psychological Bulletin, 113,* 533–552.

Aldrich, M. S., Prokopowicz, G., Ockert, K., Hollingsworth, Z., Penney, J. B., & Albin, R. L. (1994). Neurochemical studies of human narcolepsy: Alpha-adrenergic receptor autoradiography of human narcoleptic brain and brainstem. *Sleep, 17,* 598–608.

Alessi, G. (1992). Models of proximate and ultimate causation in psychology. *American Psychologist, 47,* 1359–1370.

Alexander, F. (1939). Emotional factors in essential hypertension. *Psychosomatic Medicine, 1,* 139–152.

Alexander, F. (1950). *Psychosomatic medicine: Its principles and applications.* New York: Norton.

Alexander, I. E. (1990). *Personology: Method and content in personality assessment and psychobiography.* Durham, NC: Duke University Press.

Alexander, J. F., Holtzworth-Munroe, A., & Jameson, P. B. (1994). The process and outcome of marital and family therapy: Research review and evaluation. In A. E. Bergin & S. L. Garfield (Eds.), *Handbook of psychotherapy and behavior change* (4th ed.). New York: Wiley.

Alexander, R. D. (1990). Epigenetic rules and Darwinian algorithms: The adaptive study of learning and development. *Ethology and Sociobiology, 11,* 241–303.

Algom, D. (1992). Psychophysical analysis of pain: A functional perceptive. In H.-G. Geissler, S. W. Link, & J.T. Townsend (Eds.), *Cognition, information processing, and psychophysics: Basic issues.* Hillsdale, NJ: Erlbaum.

Allain, H. (1990). Insomnie et benzodiazépines: questions actuelles. *Psychologie Médicale, 22,* 947–961.

Allen, L. S., & Gorski, R. A. (1992). Sexual orientation and the size of the anterior commissure in the human brain. *Proceedings of the National Academy of Science, 89,* 7199–7202.

Allen, L. S., Hines, M., Shryne, J. E., & Gorski, R. A. (1989). Two sexually dimorphic cell groups in the human brain. *Journal of Neuroscience, 9,* 497–506.

Allen, P. A., & Crozier, L. C. (1992). Age and ideal chunk size. *Journals of Gerontology, 47,* 47–51.

Alliger, G. M., & Williams, K. J. (1993). Using signal-contingent experience sampling methodology to study work in the field: A discussion and illustration examining task perceptions and mood. *Personnel Psychology, 46,* 525–549.

Allport, G. W. (1937). *Personality: A psychological interpretation.* New York: Holt.

Allport, G. W. (1942). *The use of personal documents in psychological science.* New York: Social Science Research Council.

Allport, G. W. (1961). *Pattern and growth in personality.* New York: Holt, Rinehart & Winston.

Allport, G. W. (1968). The historical background of modern social psychology. In G. Lindzey & E. Aronson (Eds.), *The handbook of social psychology* (2nd ed., Vol. 1). Reading, MA: Addison-Wesley.

Allport, G. W., & Odbert, H. S. (1936). Trait-names: A psycho-lexical study. *Psychological Monographs, 47*(Whole No. 211), 171–220.

Allport, G. W., Vernon, P. E., & Lindzey, G. (1960). *A study of values* (Rev. ed.). Boston: Houghton Mifflin.

Allred, K. D., & Smith, T. W. (1991). Social cognition in cynical hostility. *Cognitive Therapy and Research, 15,* 399–412.

Almqvist, B. (1989). Age and gender differences in children's Christmas requests. *Play and Culture, 2,* 2–19.

Alvarez, G., & Fuentes, P. (1994). Recognition of facial expression in diverging socioeconomic levels. *Brain and Cognition, 25,* 235–239.

Amelang, M. (1991). Tales from Crvenka and Heidelberg: What about the empirical basis? *Psychological Inquiry, 2,* 233–236.

American Law Institute. (1962). *Model penal code: Proposed official draft.* Philadelphia: Author.

American Psychiatric Association. (1987). *Diagnostic and statistical manual of mental disorders* (3rd ed., Rev.). Washington, DC: Author.

American Psychiatric Association. (1994). *Diagnostic and statistical manual of mental disorders* (4th ed.). Washington, DC: Author.

American Psychological Association. (1992). Ethical principles of psychologists and code of conduct. *American Psychologist, 47,* 1597–1611.

American Psychological Association. (1995). *Report of the task force on the changing gender composition of psychology.* Washington, DC: Author.

Amoore, J. E. (1964). Current status of the steric theory of odor. *Annals of the New York Academy of Science, 116,* 457–476.

Anastasi, A. (1971). Note on the concepts of creativity and intelligence. *Journal of Creative Behavior, 5,* 113–116.

Anastasi, A. (1979). *Fields of applied psychology* (2nd ed.). New York: McGraw-Hill.

Anderson, J. R. (1985). *Cognitive psychology and its implications* (2nd ed.). New York: Freeman.

Andia, A. M., & Zisook, S. (1991). Gender differences in schizophrenia: A literature review. *Annals of Clinical Psychiatry, 3,* 333–340.

Andreasen, N. C. (1984). *The broken brain: The biological revolution in psychiatry.* New York: Harper & Row.

Andresen, J. (1991). Skinner and Chomsky 30 years later or, The return of the repressed. *Behavior Analyst, 14,* 49–60.

Andrews, M. F. (1978). Taste the sound of raindrops. *Journal of Creative Behavior, 12,* 151–155.

Angleitner, A., & Wiggins, J. S. (Eds.). (1986). *Personality assessment via questionnaires: Current issues in theory and measurement.* Berlin: Springer-Verlag.

Ansari, Z. A. (Ed.). (1992). *Qur'anic concepts of human psyche.* Lahore: Institute of Islamic Culture.

Anthony, S., & Gibbins, S. (1992). Characteristics of the daydreams of deaf women. *Journal of Mental Imagery, 16,* 73–88.

Antonets, V. A., Zeveke, A. V., Malysheva, G. I., & Polevaya, S. A. (1992). Sensory code redundancy of the skin analyzer. *Sensory Systems, 6,* 327–328.

Antonovsky, A. (1979). *Health, stress, and coping.* San Francisco: Jossey-Bass.

Antonucci, T. C., & Akiyama, H. (1993). Stress and coping in the elderly. *Applied and Preventive Psychology, 2,* 201–208.

Appel, J. (1963). Aversive effects of a schedule of positive reinforcement. *Journal of the Experimental Analysis of Behavior, 6,* 423–428.

Aram, J. D., & Piraino, T. G. (1978). The hierarchy of needs theory: An evaluation in Chile. *Revista Interamericana de Psicologia, 12,* 179–188.

Archer, J. (1991). The influence of testosterone on human aggression. *British Journal of Psychology, 82,* 1–28.

Argyris, C. (1975). Dangers in applying results from experimental social psychology. *American Psychologist, 30,* 469–485.

Aronson, E., & Carlsmith, J. M. (1969). Experimentation in social psychology. In G. Lindzey & E. Aronson (Eds.), *The handbook of social psychology* (Vol. 2, 2nd ed.). Reading, MA: Addison-Wesley.

Arvey, R. D., & Campion, J. E. (1982). The employment interview: A summary and review of recent research. *Personnel Psychology, 35,* 281–322.

Asch, S. E. (1956). Studies of independence and conformity: A minority of one against a unanimous majority. *Psychological Monographs, 70*(9, Whole No. 416).

Aserinsky, E., & Kleitman, N. (1953). Regularly occurring periods of eye motility and concurrent phenomena during sleep. *Science, 118,* 273–274.

Ash, D. W., & Holding, D. H. (1990). Backward versus forward chaining in the acquisition of a keyboard skill. *Human Factors, 32,* 139–146.

Atkinson, J. W. (1958). *Motives in fantasy, action, and society.* Princeton, NJ: Van Nostrand.

Atkinson, J. W., & Litwin, G. H. (1960). Achievement motive and test anxiety conceived as motive to approach success and motive to avoid failure. *Journal of Abnormal and Social Psychology, 60,* 52–63.

Atkinson, R. C. (1975). Mnemotechnics in second-language learning. *American Psychologist, 30,* 821–828.

Atkinson, R. C., & Shiffrin, R. M. (1968). Human memory: A proposed system and its control processes. In K. W. Spence & J. T. Spence (Eds.), *The psychology of learning and motivation* (Vol. 2). New York: Academic Press.

Atoum, A. O., & Farah, A. M. (1993). Social loafing and personal involvement among Jordanian college students. *Journal of Social Psychology, 133,* 785–789.

Attneave, A. (1957). Transfer of experience with a class schema to identification learning of patterns and shapes. *Journal of Experimental Psychology, 54,* 81–88.

Auerbach, C., & Leventhal, G. (1973). Evidence for all-or-none preperceptual processing in perceptual set. *Perception and Psychophysics, 14,* 24–30.

Averill, J. R. (1973). Personal control over aversive stimuli and its relationship to stress. *Psychological Bulletin, 80,* 286–303.

Avolio, B. J., Waldman, D. A., & McDaniel, M. A. (1990). Age and work performance in nonmanagerial jobs: The effects of experience and occupational type. *Academy of Management Journal, 33,* 407–422.

Avis, J. M., & Sprenkle, D. H. (1990). Outcome research on family therapy training: A substantive and methodological review. *Journal of Marital and Family Therapy, 16,* 241–264.

Axinn, W. G., & Thornton, A. (1993). Mothers, children, and cohabitation: The intergenerational effects of attitudes and behavior. *American Sociological Review, 58,* 233–246.

Backer, T. E., Batchelor, W. F., Jones, J. M., & Mays, V. M. (Eds.). (1988). Special issue: Psychology and AIDS. *American Psychologist, 43,* 835–987.

Bacon, D. L. (1969). Incompetency to stand trial: Commitment to an inclusive test. *Southern California Law Review, 42,* 444.

Baddeley, A. (1994). The magical number seven: Still magic after all these years? *Psychological Review, 101,* 353–356.

Bagby, J. W. (1957). A cross-cultural study of perceptual predominance in binocular rivalry. *Journal of Abnormal and Social Psychology, 54,* 331–334.

Bagnato, S. J., & Neisworth, J. T. (1994). A national study of the social and treatment "invalidity" of intelligence testing for early intervention. *School Psychology Quarterly, 9,* 81–102.

Baker, L. A., Vernon, P. A., & Ho, H. (1991). The genetic correlation between intelligence and speed of information processing. *Behavior Genetics, 21,* 351–367.

Bakker, F. C., & Whiting, H. T. (1989). Psychologie du sport: Théorie et pratique. *Revue Québecoise de Psychologie, 10,* 98–118.

Balay, J., & Shevrin, H. (1988). The subliminal psychodynamic activation method: A critical review. *American Psychologist, 43,* 161–174.

Balay, J., & Shevrin, H. (1989). SPA is subliminal, but is it psychodynamically activating? *American Psychologist, 44,* 1423–1426.

Baldwin, E. (1993). The case for animal research in psychology. *Journal of Social Issues, 49*(1), 121–131.

Bales, R. F. (1950). *Interaction process analysis: A method for the study of small groups.* Reading, MA: Addison-Wesley.

Bales, R. F. (1953). The equilibrium problem in small groups. In T. Parsons, R. F. Bales, & E. A. Shils (Eds.), *Working papers in the theory of action.* Glencoe, IL: Free Press.

Balkwell, C. (1981). Transition to widowhood: A review of the literature. *Family Relations, 30,* 117–128.

Ball, J. F. (1976–1977). Widow's grief: The impact of age and mode of death. *Omega, 7,* 307–333.

Baltes, P. B. (1968). Longitudinal and cross-sectional sequences in the study of age and generation effects. *Human Development, 11,* 145–171.

Bancroft, J. (1994). Homosexual orientation: The search for a biological basis. *British Journal of Psychiatry, 164,* 437–440.

Bandura, A. (1974). Behavior theories and the models of man. *American Psychologist, 29,* 859–869.

Bandura, A. (1977). Self-efficacy: Toward a unifying theory of behavior change. *Psychological Review, 84,* 191–215.

Bandura, A. (1986). *Social foundations of thought and action.* Englewood Cliffs, NJ: Prentice Hall.

Bandura, A. (1989). Regulation of cognitive processes through perceived self-efficacy. *Developmental Psychology, 25,* 729–735.

Bandura, A. (1993). Perceived self-efficacy in cognitive development and functioning. *Educational Psychologist, 28,* 117–148.

Bandura, A., Ross, D., & Ross, S. A. (1963). Imitation of film-mediated aggressive models. *Journal of Abnormal and Social Psychology, 66,* 3–11.

Banks, W. P. (1993). Problems in the scientific pursuit of consciousness. *Consciousness and Cognition: An International Journal, 2,* 255–263.

Bannister, R. C. (1979). *Social Darwinism: Science and myth in Anglo-American social thought.* Philadelphia: Temple University Press.

Baranowski, T. (1989–1990). Reciprocal determinism at the stages of behavior change: An integration of community, personal, and behavioral perspectives. *International Quarterly of Community Health Education, 10,* 297–327.

Barbarin, O. A. (1993). Emotional and social development of African American children. *Journal of Black Psychology, 19,* 381–390.

Barbera, E., & Martínez-Benlloch, I. (1989). Nuevas Perspectivas Explicativas acerca de la Vinculación Genero-Emoción. *Boletin de Psicología Spain, 23,* 49–63.

Bard, P. A. (1928). A diencephalic mechanism for the expression of rage with special reference to the sympathetic nervous system. *American Journal of Physiology, 84,* 490–515.

Barefoot, J. D., Dahlstrom, W. G., & Williams, R. B. (1983). Hostility, CHD incidence, and total mortality: A 25-year follow-up study of 255 physicians. *Psychosomatic Medicine, 45,* 559–570.

Barker, E. (1927). *National character and the factors in its formation.* London: Methuen.

Barlow, F. (1952). *Mental prodigies.* New York: Philosophical Library.

Barrick, M. R., & Mount, M. K. (1991). The Big Five personality dimensions and job performance: A meta-analysis. *Personnel Psychology, 44,* 1–26.

Barrick, M. R., & Mount, M. K. (1993). Autonomy as a moderator of the relationship between the Big Five personality dimensions and job performance. *Journal of Applied Psychology, 78,* 111–118.

Barsky, A. J. (1988). *Worried sick: Our troubled quest for wellness.* Boston: Little, Brown.

Barsky, A. J., Wyshak, G., Klerman, G. L., & Latham, K. S. (1990). The prevalence of hypochondriasis in medical outpatients. *Social Psychiatry and Psychiatric Epidemiology, 25,* 89–94.

Bartlett, F. C. (1932). *Remembering: A study in experimental and social psychology.* London: Cambridge University Press.

Bartoshuk, L. M. (1993). The biological basis of food perception and acceptance. *Food Quality and Preference, 4,* 21–32.

Bartoshuk, L. M., & Beauchamp, G. K. (1994). Chemical senses. *Annual Review of Psychology, 45,* 419–449.

Bartrop, R. W., Luckhurst, E., Lazarus, L., Kiloh, L. G., & Penny, R. (1977). Depressed lymphocyte function after bereavement. *Lancet, 97,* 834–836.

Baruch, G., Barnett, R., & Rivers, C. (1983). *Life prints: New patterns of love and work for today's woman.* New York: McGraw-Hill.

Basbaum, A. I., & Fields, H. L. (1984). Endogenous pain control systems: Brainstem spinal pathways and endorphin circuitry. *Annual Review of Neuroscience, 7,* 309–338.

Bass, B. M. (1960). *Leadership, psychology, and organizational psychology.* New York: Harper & Row.

Bates, E., Chen, S., Tzeng, O. J., Li, P., & Opie, M. (1991). The noun-verb problem in Chinese aphasia. *Brain and Language, 41,* 203–233.

Bates, M. S., & Rankin-Hill, L. (1994). Control, culture, and chronic pain. *Social Science and Medicine, 39,* 629–645.

Batson, C. D., Dyck, J. L., Brandt, J. R., Batson, J. G., Powell, A. L., McMaster, M. R., & Griffitt, C. (1988). Five studies testing two new egoistic alternatives to the empathy-altruism hypothesis. *Journal of Personality and Social Psychology, 55,* 52–77.

Batuev, A. S., & Gafurov, B. G. (1991). Chemical nature of hypothalamo-cortical activation underlying the drinking behaviour. *Fiziologicheskii Zhurnal SSSR im I. M. Sechenova, 77,* 45–51.

Baumeister, R. F. (1987). How the self became a problem: A psychological review of historical research. *Journal of Personality and Social Psychology, 52,* 163–176.

Baumrind, D. (1964). Some thoughts on the ethics of research: After reading Milgram's "Behavioral study of obedience." *American Psychologist, 19,* 421–423.

Baumrind, D. (1971). Current patterns of parental authority. *Developmental Psychology Monographs, 4*(1, Pt. 2).

Baumrind, D. (1978). Parental disciplinary patterns and social comparison in children. *Youth and Society, 9,* 239–276.

Beach, F. A. (1983). Hormones and psychological processes. *Canadian Journal of Psychology, 37,* 193–210.

Beck, A. T. (1967). *Depression: Clinical, experimental, and theoretical aspects.* New York: Hoeber.

Beck, A. T. (1976). *Cognitive therapy and the emotional disorders.* New York: International University Press.

Beck, A. T., & Emery, G. (1985). *Anxiety disorders and phobias: A cognitive perspective.* New York: Basic Books.

Beck, A. T., Freeman, A., & Associates. (1990). *Cognitive therapy of personality disorders.* New York: Guilford.

Beck, A. T., Rush, A. J., Shaw, B. F., & Emery, G. (1979). *Cognitive therapy of depression.* New York: Guilford.

Beck, A. T., Sokol, L., Clark, D. A., Berchick, R. J., & Wright, F. (1992). A crossover study of focused cognitive therapy for panic disorder. *American Journal of Psychiatry, 149,* 778–783.

Beck, S., Neeper, R., Baskin, C. H., & Forehand, R. (1983). An examination of children's perceptions of themselves and others as a function of popularity level. *Journal of Social and Clinical Psychology, 1,* 259–271.

Becker, W. C. (1964). Consequences of different types of parental discipline. In M. L. Hoffman & L. W. Hoffman (Eds.), *Review of child development research* (Vol. 1). New York: Russell Sage Foundation.

Beckstrom, J. H. (1993). *Darwinism applied: Evolutionary paths to social goals.* Westport, CT: Praeger.

Bee, H. L. (1987). *The journey of adulthood.* New York: Macmillan.

Begg, I. M., Needham, D. R., & Bookbinder, M. (1993). Do backward messages unconsciously affect listeners? No. *Canadian Journal of Experimental Psychology, 47,* 1–14.

Bekesy, G. V. (1947). The variation of phase along the basilar membrane with sinusoidal vibration. *Journal of the Acoustical Society of America, 19,* 452–460.

Bellak, L. (1986). *The thematic apperception test, the children's apperception test, and the senior apperception technique in clinical use.* Orlando, FL: Grune & Stratton.

Belloc, N. B. (1973). Relationship of health practices and mortality. *Preventive Medicine, 2,* 67–81.

Belloc, N. B., & Breslow, L. (1972). Relationship of physical health status and family practices. *Preventive Medicine, 1,* 409–421.

Bellugi, U., Poizner, H., & Klima, E. S. (1989). Language, modality, and the brain. *Trends in Neuroscience, 12,* 380–388.

Belsky, J. (1988). The "effects" of infant day care reconsidered. *Early Childhood Research Quarterly, 3,* 235–272.

Bem, D. J., & Allen, A. (1974). On predicting some of the people some of the time: The search for cross-situational consistencies in behavior. *Psychological Review, 81,* 506–520.

Benbow, S. M. (1991). ECT in late life. *International Journal of Geriatric Psychiatry, 6,* 401–406.

Bengston, V. L., Cuellar, J. B., & Ragan, P. K. (1977). Stratum contrasts and similarities in attitudes toward death. *Journal of Gerontology, 32,* 76–88.

Benjamin, L. T., Durkin, M., Link, M., & Vestal, M. (1992). Wundt's American doctoral students. *American Psychologist, 47,* 123–131.

Bennett, P., Wallace, L., Carroll, D., & Smith, N. (1991). Treating Type A behaviours and mild hypertension in middle-aged men. *Journal of Psychosomatic Research, 35,* 209–223.

Bentley, K. S., & Fox, R. A. (1991). Mothers and fathers of young children: Comparison of parenting styles. *Psychological Reports, 69,* 320–322.

Benton, D., & Wastell, V. (1986). Effects of androstenol on human sexual arousal. *Biological Psychology, 22,* 141–147.

Berk, L. E. (1989). *Child development.* Boston: Allyn & Bacon.

Berkman, L., Singer, B., & Manton, K. (1989). Black/white differences in health status and mortality among the aged. *Demography, 26,* 661–678.

Berkowitz, L. (1981). Aversive conditions as stimuli for aggression. In L. Berkowitz (Ed.), *Advances in experimental social psychology* (Vol. 15). New York: Academic Press.

Berkowitz, M. W., & Keller, M. (1994). Transitional processes in social cognitive development: A longitudinal study. *International Journal of Behavioral Development, 17,* 447–467.

Berlin, B., & Kay, P. (1969). *Basic color terms: Their universality and evolution.* Berkeley and Los Angeles: University of California Press.

Berliner, L., & Loftus, E. F. (1992). Sexual abuse accusations: Desperately seeking reconciliation. *Journal of Interpersonal Violence, 7,* 570–578.

Bermudez-Sarguera, R., & Infante-Ochoa, A. (1988). Asimetría funtional de los grandes hemisferios cerebrales en la actividad de la esfera emocional. *Revista del Hospital Psiquiátrico de La Habana, 29,* 61–68.

Bernal, M. E., & Castro, F. G. (1994). Are clinical psychologists prepared for service and research with ethnic minorities? Report of a decade of progress. *American Psychologist, 49,* 797–805.

Bernheim, K. F., & Lewine, R. R. J. (1979). *Schizophrenia.* New York: Norton.

Bernstein, B. L. (1991–1992). Central issue importance as a function of gender and ethnicity. *Current Psychology Research and Reviews, 10,* 241–252.

Berridge, K. C., & Zajonc, R. B. (1991). Hypothalamic cooling elicits eating: Differential effects on motivation and pleasure. *Psychological Science, 2,* 184–189.

Berscheid, E. (1994). Interpersonal relationships. *Annual Review of Psychology, 45,* 79–129.

Bertilson, H. S. (1990). Can aggression be justified in order to study aggression? *American Behavioral Scientist, 33,* 594–607.

Berzins, J. I. (1977). Therapist-patient matching. In A. S. Gurman & A. M. Razin (Eds.), *Effective psychotherapy: A handbook of research.* New York: Pergamon.

Betancourt, H., & Lopez, S. R. (1993). The study of culture, ethnicity, and race in American psychology. *American Psychologist, 48,* 629–637.

Bettinghaus, E. P. (1980). *Persuasive communications* (3rd ed.). New York: Holt, Rinehart & Winston.

Betzig, L. (1989). Rethinking human ethology: A response to some recent critiques. *Ethology and Sociobiology, 10,* 315–324.

Beutler, L. E., & Consoli, A. J. (1993). Matching the therapist's interpersonal stance to clients' characteristics: Contributions from systematic eclectic psychotherapy. *Psychotherapy, 30,* 417–422.

Beutler, L. E., Machado, P. P. P., & Neufeldt, S. A. (1994). Therapist variables. In A. E. Bergin & S. L. Garfield (Eds.), *Handbook of psychotherapy and behavior change* (4th ed.). New York: Wiley.

Bezirganian, S., & Cohen, P. (1992). Sex differences in the interaction between temperament and parenting. *Journal of the American Academy of Child and Adolescent Psychiatry, 31,* 790–801.

Bhatnagar, S. C., & Andy, O. J. (1989). Alleviation of acquired stuttering with human centremedian thalamic stimulation. *Journal of Neurology, Neurosurgery, and Psychiatry, 52,* 1182–1184.

Bidell, T. R., & Fischer, K. W. (1989). "Reflections on 25 years of Piagetian cognitive developmental psychology: 1963–1988": Commentary. *Human Development, 32,* 363–368.

Bierbrauer, G. (1992). Reactions to violation of normative standards: A cross-cultural analysis of shame and guilt. *International Journal of Psychology, 27,* 181–193.

Bigelow, H. J. (1850). Dr. Harlow's case of recovery from the passage of an iron bar through the head. *American Journal of Medical Science, 20,* 13–22.

Binet, A., & Simon, T. (1905). Application des méthodes nouvelles au diagnostic du niveau intellectuel chez enfants normaux et anormaux d'hospice et d'êcole primarire. *L'Année psychologique, 11,* 191–244.

Binet, A., & Simon, T. (1913). *A method of measuring the development of the intelligence of young children* (3rd ed.). Chicago: Chicago Medical Book.

Bird, C. (1940). *Social psychology.* New York: Appleton-Century-Crofts.

Bishop, J. A., & Cook, L. M. (1975, January). Moths, melanism, and clean air. *Scientific American,* pp. 90–99.

Bitterman, M. E. (1965). Phyletic differences in learning. *American Psychologist, 20,* 396–410.

Bixler, R. D., Carlisle, C. L., Hammitt, W. E., & Floyd, M. F. (1994). Observed fears and discomforts among urban students on field trips to wildland areas. *Journal of Environmental Education, 26,* 24–33.

Bjorkqvist, K. (1994). Sex differences in physical, verbal, and indirect aggression: A review of recent research. *Sex Roles, 30,* 177–188.

Black, S. L., & Biron, C. (1982). Androstenol as a human pheromone: No effect on perceived physical attractiveness. *Behavioral and Neural Biology, 34,* 326–330.

Blackwell, B. (1987). "Nightmares": Commentary. *Integrative Psychiatry, 5,* 75–76.

Blair, A. (1992). The role of primary prevention in mental health services: A review and critique. *Journal of Community and Applied Social Psychology, 2,* 77–94.

Blake, W. M., & Darling, C. A. (1994). The dilemmas of the African American male. *Journal of Black Studies, 24,* 402–415.

Blakemore, C., & Cooper, G. F. (1970). Development of the brain depends on the visual environment. *Nature, 228,* 477–478.

Blanchard, J. J., & Neale, J. M. (1992). Selective serotonin reuptake inhibitors (SSRIs) are effective in medication effects: Conceptual and methodological issues in schizophrenia research. *Clinical Psychology Review, 12,* 345–361.

Blanchard, R., Zucker, K. J., Bradley, S. J., & Hume, C. S. (1995). Birth order and sibling sex ratio in homosexual male adolescents and probably prehomosexual feminine boys. *Developmental Psychology, 31,* 22–30.

Blanes, T., Burgess, M., Marks, I. M., & Gill, M. (1993). Dream anxiety disorders (nightmares): A review. *Behavioural Psychotherapy, 21,* 37–43.

Blaney, P. H. (1986). Affect and memory: A review. *Psychological Bulletin, 99,* 229–246.

Blascovich, J. (1992). A biopsychosocial approach to arousal regulation. *Journal of Social and Clinical Psychology, 11,* 213–237.

Blasi, A. (1990). Kohlberg's theory and moral motivation. *New Directions for Child Development, 47,* 51–57.

Blass, E. M., & Hall, W. G. (1976). Drinking termination: Interactions among hydrational, orogastric, and behavioral control in rats. *Psychological Review, 83,* 356–374.

Blass, J. P., Nolan, K. A., Black, R. S., & Kurita, A. (1991). Delirium: Phenomenology and diagnosis: A neurobiologic view. *International Psychogeriatrics, 3,* 121–134.

Blennerhassett, R. (1993). The serial killer in film: An archetype for our time. *Irish Journal of Psychological Medicine, 10,* 101–104.

Bleuler, M. (1978). *The schizophrenic disorders: Long-term patient and family studies.* New Haven, CT: Yale University Press.

Bliss, E. L. (1980). Multiple personalities: Report of fourteen cases with implications for schizophrenia and hysteria. *Archives of General Psychiatry, 37,* 1388–1397.

Bliss, J. C., Crane, H. D., Mansfield, P. K., & Townsend, J. T. (1966). Information available in brief tactile presentations. *Perception and Psychophysics, 1,* 273–283.

Bliwise, D. L. (1993). Sleep in normal aging and dementia. *Sleep, 16,* 40–81.

Bloom, B. L. (1984). *Community mental health: A general introduction* (2nd ed.). Monterey, CA: Brooks/Cole.

Bloom, P. (1994). Generativity within language and other cognitive domains. *Cognition, 51,* 177–189.

Bluedorn, A. C. (1993). Pilgrim's progress: Trends and convergence in research on organizational size and environments. *Journal of Management, 19,* 163–191.

Blum, L. (1990). Universality and particularity. *New Directions for Child Development, 47,* 59–69.

Blumberg, M. S., & Wasserman, E. A. (1995). Animal mind and the argument from design. *American Psychologist, 50,* 133–144.

Blumer, D., & Benson, D. F. (1975). Personality changes with frontal lobe and temporal lobe lesions. In D. F. Benson & D. Blumer (Eds.), *Psychiatric aspects of neurological disease.* New York: Grune & Stratton.

Boakes, R. A. (1989). How one might find evidence for conditioning in adult humans. In T. Archer & L.-G. Nilsson (Eds.), *Aversion, avoidance, and anxiety.* Hillsdale, NJ: Erlbaum.

Bodenhausen, G. V., Sheppard, L. A., & Kramer, G. P. (1994). Negative affect and social judgment: The differential impact of anger and sadness. *European Journal of Social Psychology, 24,* 45–62.

Bofinger, F., Marguth, U., Pankofer, R., Seidl, O., & Ermann, M. (1993). Psychosocial aspects of longterm-surviving with AIDS. *International Conference on AIDS, 9,* 878.

Bogart, G. (1991). The use of meditation in psychotherapy: A review of the literature. *American Journal of Psychotherapy, 45,* 383–412.

Bohart, A. C. (1991). Empathy in client-centered therapy: A contrast with psychoanalysis and self psychology. *Journal of Humanistic Psychology, 31,* 34–48.

Bolles, R. C. (1967). *Theory of motivation.* New York: Harper & Row.

Boneau, C. A. (1992). Observations on psychology's past and future. *American Psychologist, 47,* 1586–1596.

Boral, G. C. (1986). Psychoendocrinology and behaviour. *Indian Journal of Psychiatry, 28,* 3–11.

Borbely, A. (1986). *Secrets of sleep.* New York: Basic Books.

Boring, E. G. (1950). *A history of experimental psychology* (2nd ed.). New York: Appleton-Century-Crofts.

Bornstein, R. F. (1993). Implicit perception, implicit memory, and the recovery of unconscious material in psychotherapy. *Journal of Nervous and Mental Disease, 181,* 337–344.

Borod, J. C. (1993). Emotion and the brain: Anatomy and theory. *Neuropsychology, 7,* 427–432.

Bouchard, T. J., & McGue, M. (1981). Familial studies of intelligence: A review. *Science, 212,* 1055–1059.

Bourne, L. E. (1966). *Human conceptual behavior.* Boston: Allyn & Bacon.

Bowd, A. D., & Shapiro, K. J. (1993). The case against laboratory animal research in psychology. *Journal of Social Issues, 49*(1), 133–142.

Bower, D. W., & Christopherson, V. A. (1977). University student cohabitation: A regional comparison of selected attitudes and behavior. *Journal of Marriage and the Family, 39,* 447–453.

Bower, G. H. (1981). Mood and memory. *American Psychologist, 36,* 129–148.

Bower, G. H., Black, J. B., & Turner, T. J. (1979). Scripts in memory for text. *Cognitive Psychology, 11,* 117–220.

Bower, G. H., & Mayer, J. D. (1989). In search of mood-dependent retrieval. *Journal of Social Behavior and Personality, 4,* 121–156.

Bowers, K. S. (1973). Situationism in psychology: An analysis and critique. *Psychological Review, 80,* 307–336.

Bowlby, J. (1969). *Attachment and loss* (Vol. 1). New York: Basic Books.

Bowmaker, J. K., & Dartnall, H. M. A. (1980). Visual pigments of rods and cones in a human retina. *Journal of Physiology, 298,* 501–511.

Boyd, J. H., Rae, D. S., Thompson, J. W., Burns, B. J., Bourdon, K. H., Locke, B. Z., & Regier, D. A. (1990). Phobia: Prevalence and risk factors. *Social Psychiatry and Psychiatric Epidemiology, 25,* 314–323.

Boyle, M. (1990). *Schizophrenia: A scientific delusion.* London: Routledge.

Boyle, R. H., & Ames, W. (1983, April 11). Too many punches, too little concern. *Sports Illustrated,* pp. 44–67.

Bozarth, J. D., & Brodley, B. T. (1991). Actualization: A functional concept in client-centered therapy. *Journal of Social Behavior and Personality, 6,* 45–59.

Bradshaw, J. L., & Nettleton, N. C. (1989). Lateral asymmetries in human evolution. *International Journal of Comparative Psychology, 3,* 37–71.

Brainerd, C. J. (1978). *Piaget's theory of intelligence.* Englewood Cliffs, NJ: Prentice Hall.

Brandon, P. R. (1991). Gender differences in young Asian Americans' educational attainments. *Sex Roles, 25,* 45–61.

Brannigan, G. G., Shahon, A. J., & Schaller, J. A. (1992). Locus of control and time orientation in daydreaming: Implications for therapy. *Journal of Genetic Psychology, 153,* 359–361.

Bransford, J. D. (1979). *Human cognition: Learning, understanding, and remembering.* Belmont, CA: Wadsworth.

Bransford, J. D., & Franks, J. J. (1971). The abstraction of linguistic ideas. *Cognitive Psychology, 2,* 331–350.

Braun, C. M., & Chouinard, M. J. (1992). Is anorexia nervosa a neuropsychological disease? *Neuropsychology Review, 3,* 171–212.

Brayfield, A. H., & Crockett, W. H. (1955). Employee attitudes and employee performance. *Psychological Bulletin, 52,* 396–424.

Brecher, E. M., & the Editors of Consumer Reports. (1972). *Licit and illicit drugs.* Mount Vernon, NY: Consumers Union.

Breedlove, S. M. (1994). Sexual differentiation of the human nervous system. *Annual Review of Psychology, 45,* 389–418.

Breetvelt, I. S., & Van Dam, F. S. (1991). Underreporting by cancer patients: The case of response-shift. *Social Science and Medicine, 32,* 981–987.

Brehm, J. (1966). *A theory of psychological reactance.* New York: Academic Press.

Breland, K., & Breland, M. (1961). The misbehavior of organisms. *American Psychologist, 16,* 681–684.

Brenneis, C. B. (1994). Belief and suggestion in the recovery of memories of childhood sexual abuse. *Journal of the American Psychoanalytic Association, 42,* 1027–1053.

Brentar, J., & Lynn, S. J. (1989). "Negative" effects and hypnosis: A critical examination. *British Journal of Experimental and Clinical Hypnosis, 6,* 75–84.

Breslau, N., & Davis, G. C. (1992). Posttraumatic stress disorder in an urban population of young adults: Risk factors for chronicity. *American Journal of Psychiatry, 149,* 671–675.

Breuer, J., & Freud, S. (1895). Studies on hysteria. *Standard edition* (Vol. 2). London: Hogarth.

Brewer, M. B., & Caporael, L. R. (1990). Selfish genes vs. selfish people: Sociobiology as origin myth. *Motivation and Emotion, 14,* 237–243.

Brewer, W. F. (1974). There is no convincing evidence for operant and classical conditioning in human beings. In W. B. Weimer & D. J. Palermo (Eds.), *Cognition and the symbolic processes.* Hillsdale, NJ: Erlbaum.

Brief, A. P., & Nord, W. R. (Eds.). (1990). *Meanings of occupational work: A collection of essays.* Lexington, MA: Lexington Books.

Briere, J., & Runtz, M. (1988). Symptomatology associated with childhood sexual victimization in a nonclinical adult sample. *Child Abuse and Neglect, 12,* 51–59.

Brigham, J. C. (1986). *Social psychology.* Boston: Little, Brown.

Briley, M., & Moret, C. (1993). Neurobiological mechanisms involved in antidepressant therapies. *Clinical Neuropharmacology, 16,* 387–400.

Brna, T. G., & Wilson, C. C. (1990). Psychogenic amnesia. *American Family Physician, 41,* 229–234.

Broadbent, D. E. (1958). *Perception and communication.* London: Pergamon.

Broca, P. (1861). Remarques sur le siège de la faculté du langage articulé, suivies d'une observation d'aphémie (perte de la parole). *Bulletin de la Société Anatomique, 36,* 330–357.

Brodsky, S. L. (1991). *Testifying in court: Guidelines and maxims for the expert witness.* Washington, DC: American Psychological Association.

Bronfenbrenner, U. (1970). *Two worlds of childhood: U.S. and U.S.S.R.* New York: Pocket Books.

Bronstein, P. A., & Quina, K. (Eds.). (1988). *Teaching a psychology of people: Resources for gender and sociocultural awareness.* Washington, DC: American Psychological Association.

Brooksbank, B. W., Brown, R., & Gustafsson, J. A. (1974). The detection of 5a-androst–16-en–3a-ol in human male axillary sweat. *Experientia, 30,* 864–865.

Brothers, L. (1990). The neural basis of primate social communication. *Motivation and Emotion, 14,* 81–91.

Browder, S. (1988, June). Is living together such a good idea? *New Woman,* pp. 120–124.

Brown v. Board of Education of Topeka, 347 U.S. 483 (1954).

Brown, A. M. (1990). Development of visual sensitivity to light and color vision in human infants: A critical review. *Vision Research, 30,* 1159–1188.

Brown, A. S. (1991). A review of the tip-of-the-tongue experience. *Psychological Bulletin, 109,* 204–223.

Brown, G. W., & Harris, T. O. (1978). *Social origins of depression.* New York: Free Press.

Brown, L. L., & Robinson, S. E. (1993). The relationship between meditation and/or exercise and three measures of self-actualization. *Journal of Mental Health Counseling, 15,* 85–93.

Brown, L. S. (1992). A feminist critique of the personality disorders. In L. S. Brown & M. Ballou (Eds.), *Personality and psychopathology: Feminist reappraisals.* New York: Guilford.

Brown, N. O. (1959). *Life against death.* Baltimore: Penguin.

Brown, P., & Jenkins, H. M. (1968). Autoshaping of the pigeon's keypecking. *Journal of the Experimental Analysis of Behavior, 11,* 1–8.

Brown, R. (1954). Mass phenomena. In G. Lindzey (Ed.), *Handbook of social psychology* (Vol. 2). Cambridge, MA: Addison-Wesley.

Brown, R., & Chiesa, M. (1990). An introduction to repertory grid theory and technique. *British Journal of Psychotherapy, 6,* 411–419.

Brown, R., & Hanlon, C. (1970). Derivational complexity and order of acquisition. In J. R. Hayes (Ed.), *Cognition and the development of language.* New York: Wiley.

Brown, R., & Kulik, J. (1977). Flashbulb memories. *Cognition, 5,* 73–99.

Brown, R., & McNeill, D. (1966). The "tip of the tongue" phenomenon. *Journal of Verbal Learning and Verbal Behavior, 5,* 325–337.

Brown, T. S. (1975). General biology of sensory systems. In B. Scharf (Ed.), *Experimental sensory psychology.* Glenview, IL: Scott, Foresman.

Browne, A., & Finkelhor, D. (1986). Impact of child sexual abuse: A review of the research. *Psychological Bulletin, 99,* 66–77.

Brownell, K. D., & Wadden, T. A. (1992). Etiology and treatment of obesity: Understanding a serious, prevalent, and refractory disorder. *Journal of Consulting and Clinical Psychology, 60,* 505–517.

Bruner, J. S. (1964). The course of cognitive growth. *American Psychologist, 19,* 1–15.

Bruyer, R. (1981). L'asymétrie du visage humain: État de la question. *Psychologica Belgica, 21,* 7–15.

Bruyer, R. (1991). Covert face recognition in prosopagnosia: A review. *Brain and Cognition, 15,* 223–235.

Bryan, J. H., & Test, M. A. (1967). Models and helping: Naturalistic studies in aiding behavior. *Journal of Personality and Social Psychology, 6,* 400–407.

Bryant, P. (1989). "Reflections on 25 years of Piagetian cognitive developmental psychology: 1963–1988": Commentary. *Human Development, 32,* 369–374.

Bryden, M. P., & MacRae, L. (1988). Dichotic laterality effects obtained with emotional words. *Neuropsychiatry, Neuropsychology, and Behavioral Neurology, 1,* 171–176.

Buchanan, G. A., & Seligman, M. E. P. (Eds.). (1995). *Explanatory style.* Hillsdale, NJ: Erlbaum.

Buck, L., & Axel, R. (1991). A novel multigene family may encode odorant receptors: A molecular basis for odor recognition. *Cell, 65,* 175–181.

Bulkley, K. (1991). Interdisciplinary dreaming: Hobson's successes and failures. *Dreaming: Journal of the Association for the Study of Dreams, 1,* 225–234.

Bulman-Fleming, M. B., & Bryden, M. P. (1994). Simultaneous verbal and affective laterality effects. *Neuropsychologia, 32,* 787–797.

Burkhardt, D. A. (1994). Light adaptation and photopigment bleaching in cone photoreceptors *in situ* in the retina of the turtle. *Journal of Neuroscience, 14,* 1091–1105.

Burling, R. (1993). Primate calls, human language, and nonverbal communication. *Current Anthropology, 34,* 25–53.

Burns, J. E. (1990). Contemporary models of consciousness: I. *Journal of Mind and Behavior, 11,* 153–171.

Burns, J. E. (1991). Contemporary models of consciousness: II. *Journal of Mind and Behavior, 12,* 407–420.

Buss, A. H., & Plomin, R. (1975). *A temperament theory of personality.* New York: Wiley.

Buss, A. H., & Plomin, R. (1984). *Temperament: Early developing personality traits.* Hillsdale, NJ: Erlbaum.

Buss, D. M. (1987). Selection, evocation, and manipulation. *Journal of Personality and Social Psychology, 53,* 1214–1221.

Buss, D. M. (1989). Sex differences in human mate preferences: Evolutionary hypotheses tested in 37 cultures. *Behavioral and Brain Sciences, 12,* 1–14.

Buss, D. M. (1990). The evolution of anxiety and social exclusion. *Journal of Social and Clinical Psychology, 9,* 196–201.

Buss, D. M. (1991). Evolutionary personality psychology. *Annual Review of Psychology, 42,* 459–491.

Buss, D. M. (1994). *The evolution of desire: Strategies of human mating.* New York: Basic Books.

Buss, D. M. (1995). Evolutionary psychology: A new paradigm for psychological science. *Psychological Inquiry, 6,* 1–30.

Buss, D. M., Larsen, R. J., Westen, D., & Semmelroth, J. (1992). Sex differences in jealousy: Evolution, physiology, and psychology. *Psychological Science, 3,* 251–255.

Buss, D., & Schmitt, D. P. (1993). Sexual Strategies Theory: An evolutionary perspective on human mating. *Psychological Review, 100,* 204–232.

Bussey, K., & Bandura, A. (1992). Self-regulatory mechanisms governing gender development. *Child Development, 63,* 1236–1250.

Butcher, J. N. (Ed.). (1995). *Clinical personality assessment: Practical approaches.* New York: Oxford University Press.

Butcher, J. N., Dahlstrom, W. G., Graham, J. R., Tellegen, A., & Kaemmer, B. (1989). *Manual for the restandardized Minnesota Multiphasic Personality Inventory: MMPI-2. An interpretative and administrative guide.* Minneapolis: University of Minnesota Press.

Butler, R., & Lewis, M. (1981). *Aging and mental health.* St. Louis: Mosby.

Buunk, B. P., Van Yperen, N. W., Taylor, S. E., & Collins, R. L. (1991). Social comparison and the drive upward revisited: Affiliation as a response to marital stress. *European Journal of Social Psychology, 21,* 529–546.

Byrne, D. (1971). *The attraction paradigm.* New York: Academic Press.

Cacioppo, J. T., & Berntson, G. G. (1992). Social psychological contributions to the decade of the brain: Doctrine of multilevel analysis. *American Psychologist, 47,* 1019–1028.

Cadoret, R. J., Troughton, E., Bagford, J., & Woodworth, G. (1990). Genetic and environmental factors in adoptee antisocial personality. *European Archives of Psychiatry and Neurological Sciences, 239,* 231–240.

Cahalan, D. (1978). Implications of American drinking practices for prevention and treatment of alcoholism. In G. A. Marlatt & P. E. Nathan (Eds.), *Behavioral approaches to alcoholism.* New Brunswick, NJ: Rutgers Center of Alcohol Studies.

Cai, Z. (1991). The functions of sleep: Further analysis. *Physiology and Behavior, 50,* 53–60.

Caillet, R. (1993). *Pain: Mechanisms and management.* Philadelphia: F. A. Davis.

Callahan, L. A., Steadman, H. J., McGreevy, M. A., & Robbins, P. C. (1991). The volume and characteristics of insanity defense pleas: An eight-state study. *Bulletin of the American Academy of Psychiatry and the Law, 19,* 389–393.

Calvin, W. H. (1983). *The throwing madonna: Essays on the brain.* New York: McGraw-Hill.

Campbell, C. B., & Hodos, W. (1991). The *Scala Naturae* revisited: Evolutionary scales and anagenesis in comparative psychology. *Journal of Comparative Psychology, 105,* 211–221.

Campbell, D. T., & Fiske, D. W. (1959). Convergent and discriminant validation by the multitrait-multimethod matrix. *Psychological Bulletin, 56,* 81–105.

Campos, J. J., Campos, R. G., & Barrett, K. C. (1989). Emergent themes in the study of emotional development and emotion regulation. *Developmental Psychology, 25,* 394–402.

Canali, O., & Capurro, P. (1988). L'atto intenzionale nella psicologia e nel diritto. *Ricerche di Psicologia, 12,* 9–35.

Cann, R. L., Stonekins, M., & Wilson, A. C. (1987). Mitochondrial DNA and human evolution. *Nature, 325,* 31–36.

Cannell, C. F., & Kahn, R. L. (1969). Interviewing. In G. Lindzey & E. Aronson (Eds.), *The handbook of social psychology* (Vol. 2, 2nd ed.). Reading, MA: Addison-Wesley.

Cannon, W. B. (1929). *Bodily changes in pain, hunger, fear, and rage.* New York: Appleton.

Cannon, W. B. (1939). *The wisdom of the body.* New York: Norton.

Cantor, N. (1980). Perceptions of situations: Situation prototypes and person-situation prototypes. In D. Magnusson (Ed.), *The situation: An interactional perspective.* Hillsdale, NJ: Erlbaum.

Cantor, N. (1990). From thought to behavior: "Having" and "doing" in the study of personality and cognition. *American Psychologist, 45,* 735–750.

Cantor, N., & Kihlstrom, J. F. (1987). *Personality and social intelligence.* Englewood Cliffs, NJ: Prentice Hall.

Cantor, N., & Mischel, W. (1977). Traits as prototypes: Effects on recognition memory. *Journal of Personality and Social Psychology, 37,* 337–344.

Cantor, N., & Mischel, W. (1979). Prototypes in person perception. In L. Berkowitz (Ed.), *Advances in experimental social psychology* (Vol. 12). New York: Academic Press.

Cantor, N., Smith, E. E., French, R. deS., & Mezzich, J. (1980). Psychiatric diagnosis as prototype categorization. *Journal of Abnormal Psychology, 89,* 181–193.

Caparros, A., & Anguera, B. (1986). Ebbinghaus y la tradición funcionalista. *Revista de Historia de la Psicología, 7,* 11–27.

Caparros-Lefebvre, D., Ruchoux, M. M., Blond, G., Petit, H., & Percheron, G. (1994). Long-term thalamic stimulation in Parkinson's disease: Postmortem anatomoclinical study. *Neurology, 44,* 1856–1860.

Caporael, L. R., & Brewer, M. B. (1991). Reviving evolutionary psychology: Biology meets society. *Journal of Social Issues, 47*(3), 187–195.

Cappella, J. N. (1993). The facial feedback hypothesis in human interaction: Review and speculation. *Journal of Language and Social Psychology, 12,* 13–29.

Caramazza, A. (Ed.). (1990). *Cognitive neuropsychology and neurolinguistics: Advances in models of cognitive function and impairment.* Hillsdale, NJ: Erlbaum.

Carlson, N. R. (1986). *Physiology of behavior* (3rd ed.). Boston: Allyn & Bacon.

Carmichael, L., Hogan, H. P., & Walter, A. A. (1932). An experimental study of the effect of language on the reproduction of visually perceived form. *Journal of Experimental Psychology, 15,* 73–86.

Carpendale, J. I., & Krebs, D. L. (1992). Situational variation in moral judgment: In a stage or on a stage? *Journal of Youth and Adolescence, 21,* 203–224.

Carr, J. E., & Tan, E. K. (1976). In search of the true amok: Amok as viewed within the Malay culture. *American Journal of Psychiatry, 133,* 1295–1299.

Carrere, S., & Evans, G. W. (1994). Life in an isolated and confined environment: A qualitative study of the role of the designed environment. *Environment and Behavior, 26,* 707–741.

Carrieri, J. R. (1991). *Child custody, foster care, and adoptions.* New York: Lexington Books.

Carroll, J. B. (1982). The measurement of intelligence. In R. J. Sternberg (Ed.), *Handbook of human intelligence.* Cambridge, England: Cambridge University Press.

Carson, R. C., Butcher, J. N., & Coleman, J. C. (1988). *Abnormal psychology and modern life* (8th ed.). Glenview, IL: Scott, Foresman.

Cartwright, R. D. (1978). *A primer on sleep and dreaming.* Reading, MA: Addison-Wesley.

Casey, B. J., Gordon, C. T., Mannheim, G. B., & Rumsey, J. M. (1993). Dysfunctional attention in autistic savants. *Journal of Clinical and Experimental Neuropsychology, 15,* 933–946.

Casey, K. L., Zumberg, M., Heslep, H., & Morrow, T. J. (1993). Afferent modulation of warmth sensation and heat pain in the human hand. *Somatosensory and Motor Research, 10,* 327–337.

Cassano, G. B., Perugi, G., Musetti, L., & Savino, M. (1990). Drug treatment of anxiety disorders. In N. Sartorius, V. Andreoli, G. Cassano, L. Eisenberg, P. Kielholz, P. Pancheri, & G. Racagni (Eds.), *Anxiety: Psychobiological and clinical perspectives.* New York: Hemisphere.

Castonguay, L. G., & Goldfried, M. R. (1994). Psychotherapy integration: An idea whose time has come. *Applied and Preventive Psychology, 3,* 159–172.

Cattell, J. M., & Farrand, L. (1896). Physical and mental measurements of the students of Columbia University. *Psychological Review, 3,* 618–648.

Cattell, R. B. (1950). *Personality: A systematic, theoretical, and factual study.* New York: McGraw-Hill.

Cattell, R. B. (1971). *Abilities: Their structure, growth, and action.* Boston: Houghton Mifflin.

Cattell, R. B., Eber, H. W., & Tatsuoka, M. (1970). *The handbook for the Sixteen Personality Factor Questionnaire.* Champaign, IL: Institute for Personality and Ability Testing.

Caumartin, S., Joseph, J. G., & Chmiel, J. (1991). Premorbid psychosocial factors associated with differential survival time in AIDS patients. *International Conference on AIDS, 7,* 324.

Cavalli-Sforza, L. L., Menozi, P., & Piazza, A. (1994). *The history and geography of human genes.* Princeton, NJ: Princeton University Press.

Ceci, S. J. (1990). On the relation between microlevel processing efficiency and macrolevel measures of intelligence: Some arguments against current reductionism. *Intelligence, 14,* 141–150.

Ceci, S. J., Ramey, S. L., & Ramey, C. T. (1990). Framing intellectual assessment in terms of a person-process-context model. *Educational Psychologist, 25,* 269–291.

Chafetz, M. D., & Buelow, G. (1994). A training model for psychologists with prescription privileges: Clinical pharmacopsychologists. *Professional Psychology: Research and Practice, 25,* 149–153.

Chang, J., & Hiebert, B. (1989). Relaxation procedures with children: A review. *Medical Psychotherapy: An International Journal, 2,* 163–176.

Chant, G. (1993). The Hawthorne effect. *Journal of the Market Research Society, 35,* 279.

Chalpin, W. F. (1991). The next generation of moderator research in personality psychology. *Journal of Personality, 59,* 143–178.

Chapman, C. R., Wilson, M. E., & Gehrig, J. D. (1976). Comparative effects of acupuncture and transcutaneous stimulation of the perception of painful dental stimuli. *Pain, 2,* 265–283.

Chase, R. A. (1992). Toys and infant development: Biological, psychological, and social factors. *Children's Environments, 9,* 3–12.

Chen, X., Rubin, K. H., & Sun, Y. (1992). Social reputation and peer relationships in Chinese and Canadian children: A cross-cultural study. *Child Development, 63,* 1336–1343.

Cherry, E. C. (1953). Some experiments on the recognition of speech, with one and with two ears. *Journal of the Acoustical Society of America, 25,* 975–979.

Cheshire, J., & Jenkins, N. (1991). Gender issues in the GCSE oral English examination: Part 2. *Language and Education, 5,* 19–40.

Chesler, P. (1972). *Women and madness.* New York: Doubleday.

Chi, M. T. H., Feltovich, P. J., & Glaser, R. (1981). Categorization and representation of physics problems by experts and novices. *Cognitive Science, 5,* 121–152.

Chiesa, M. (1992). Radical behaviorism and scientific frameworks: From mechanistic to relational accounts. *American Psychologist, 47,* 1287–1299.

Chinsky, J. M., & Rappaport, J. (1970). Brief critique of the meaning and reliability of "accurate empathy" ratings. *Psychological Bulletin, 73,* 379–382.

Chodorow, N. (1989). *Feminism and psychoanalytic theory.* New Haven, CT: Yale University Press.

Chomsky, N. (1957). *Syntactic structures.* The Hague: Mouton.

Chomsky, N. (1959). A review of B. F. Skinner's *Verbal behavior. Language, 35,* 26–58.

Chowdhury, A. N. (1991). Penis-root perception of Koro patients. *Acta Psychiatrica Scandinavica, 84,* 12–13.

Christensen, K. R., Valbak, K., & Weeke, A. (1991). Premature termination in analytic group therapy: Dropout frequencies and pretherapy predictors. *Nordisk Psykiatrisk Tidsskrift, 45,* 377–382.

Chui, H. C. (1989). Dementia: A review emphasizing clinicopathologic correlation and brain-behavior relationships. *Archives of Neurology, 46,* 806–814.

Church, A. T., & Katigbak, M. S. (1989). Internal, external, and self-report structure of personality in a non-western culture: An investigation of cross-language and cross-cultural generalizability. *Journal of Personality and Social Psychology, 57,* 857–872.

Cialdini, R. B. (1985). *Influence: Science and practice.* Glenview, IL: Scott, Foresman.

Ciccone, J. R. (1992). Murder, insanity, and medical expert witnesses. *Archives of Neurology, 49,* 608–611.

Ciminero, A. R., Calhoun, K. S., & Adams, H. E. (Eds.) (1986). *Handbook of behavioral assessment.* New York: Wiley.

Ciompi, L. (1994). Affect logic: An integrative model of the psyche and its relations to schizophrenia. *British Journal of Psychiatry, 164,* 51–55.

Clark, E. (1978). Strategies for communicating. *Child Development, 49,* 953–959.

Clark, M. S., & Mills, J. (1979). Interpersonal attraction in exchange and communal relationships. *Journal of Personality and Social Psychology, 37,* 12–24.

Clarke-Stewart, K. A. (1989). Infant day care: Maligned or malignant? *American Psychologist, 44,* 266–273.

Clarke-Stewart, K. A., & Fein, G. G. (1983). Early childhood programs. In P. H. Mussen (Ed.), *Handbook of child psychology* (Vol. 2). New York: Wiley.

Clarke-Stewart, K. A., Friedman, S., & Koch, J. (1985). *Child development: A topical approach.* New York: Wiley.

Clearing-Sky, M. (1988). A path analysis of the biopsychosocial variables related to exercise performance and adherence. *Dissertation Abstracts International, 49,* 539.

Coates, J. (1992). *Women, men, and language* (2nd ed.). New York: Longman.

Cobb, S. (1976). Social support as a moderator of life stress. *Psychosomatic Medicine, 38,* 300–314.

Cocroft, B. K., & Ting-Toomey, S. (1994). Facework in Japan and the United States. *International Journal of Intercultural Relations, 18,* 469–506.

Coe, S. P. (1981). Sociobiology: Some general considerations. *American Psychologist, 36,* 1462–1464.

Cohen, D. B. (1979). *Sleep and dreaming: Origins, nature, and functions.* Oxford: Pergamon.

Cohen, G., Conway, M. A., & Maylor, E. A. (1994). Flashbulb memories in older adults. *Psychology and Aging, 9,* 454–463.

Cohen, J. (1994). The earth is round (p < .05). *American Psychologist, 49,* 997–1003.

Cohen, J. B., & Chakravarti, D. (1990). Consumer psychology. *Annual Review of Psychology, 41,* 243–288.

Cohen, R. A., & Albers, H. E. (1991). Disruption of human circadian and cognitive regulation following a discrete hypothalamic lesion: A case study. *Neurology, 41,* 726–729.

Cohen, S. (1988). Psychosocial models of the role of social support in the etiology of physical disease. *Health Psychology, 7,* 269–297.

Cohen, S., Tyrrell, D. A., & Smith, A. P. (1991). Psychological stress and susceptibility to the common cold. *New England Journal of Medicine, 325,* 606–612.

Cohen, S., & Williamson, G. M. (1991). Stress and infectious disease in humans. *Psychological Bulletin, 109,* 5–24.

Cohen, S. I. (1988). La muerte vudu, la respuesta al stress, depression y SIDA. *Psicopatologia, 8,* 1–15.

Colace, C., Violani, C., & Solano, L. (1993). La deformazione/bizzarria onirica nella teoria freudiana del sogno: Indicazioni teoretiche e verifica di due ipotesi di ricerca in un campione di 50 sogni di bambini. *Archivio di Psicologia, Neurologia e Psichiatria, 54,* 380–401.

Colby, A., Kohlberg, L., Gibbs, J., & Lieberman, M. (1983). A longitudinal study of moral development. *Monographs of the Society for Research in Child Development, 48*(Serial No. 200).

Colby, C. L. (1991). The neuroanatomy and neurophysiology of attention. *Journal of Child Neurology, 6,* 90–118.

Coleman, L. (1984). *The reign of error: Psychiatry, authority, and law.* Boston: Beacon Press.

Collins, A. M., & Loftus, E. F. (1975). A spreading-activation theory of semantic processing. *Psychological Review, 82,* 407–428.

Condry, J., & Condry, S. (1976). Sex differences: A study of the eye of the beholder. *Child Development, 47,* 812–819.

Conn, J., & Kanner, L. (1940). Spontaneous erections in childhood. *Journal of Pediatrics, 16,* 337–340.

Conrad, R. (1963). Acoustic confusions and memory span for words. *Nature, 197,* 1029–1030.

Conrad, R. (1964). Acoustic confusions in immediate memory. *British Journal of Psychology, 55,* 75–84.

Consumer Reports (1985, February). Chocolate chip cookies, pp. 69–72.

Conte, H. R., & Karasu, T. B. (1992). A review of treatment studies of minor depression: 1980–1991. *American Journal of Psychotherapy, 46,* 58–74.

Contreas Ortiz, C. I., & Romo Santos, M. (1989). Creatividad e inteligencia: una revisión de estudios comparativos. *Revista de Psicología General y Aplicada, 42,* 251–260.

Conway, M. M., Ahern, D. W., & Steuernagel, G. A. (1995). *Women and public policy: A revolution in progress.* Washington, DC: CQ Press.

Cook, M. L., & Peterson, C. (1986). Depressive irrationality. *Cognitive Therapy and Research, 10,* 293–298.

Cook, N. M. (1989). The applicability of verbal mnemonics for different populations: A review. *Applied Cognitive Psychology, 3,* 3–22.

Cook, S. W. (1970). Motives in a conceptual analysis of attitude-related behaviors. In W. J. Arnold & D. Levine (Eds.), *Nebraska Symposium on Motivation* (Vol. 17). Lincoln: University of Nebraska Press.

Cook, S. W. (1984). The 1954 social science statement and school desegregation: A reply to Gerard. *American Psychologist, 39,* 819–832.

Cook-Degan, R. (1994). *The gene wars: Science, politics, and the human genome.* New York: Norton.

Cooper, J. R., Bloom, F. E., & Roth, R. H. (1986). *The biochemical basis of neuropharmacology* (5th ed.). New York: Oxford University Press.

Corballis, M. C. (1992). On the evolution of language and generativity. *Cognition, 44,* 197–226.

Corballis, M. C. (1994). The generation of generativity: A response to Bloom. *Cognition, 51,* 191–198.

Coren, S., Porac, C., & Ward, L. M. (1984). *Sensation and perception* (2nd ed.). Orlando, FL: Academic Press.

Corso, J. E. (1959). Age and sex differences in thresholds. *Journal of the Acoustical Society of America, 31,* 498–509.

Cortese, A. J. (1989). The interpersonal approach to morality: A gender and cultural analysis. *Journal of Social Psychology, 129,* 429–442.

Cosmides, L., & Tooby, J. (1994). Beyond intuition and instinct blindness: Toward an evolutionarily rigorous cognitive science. *Cognition, 50,* 41–77.

Costall, A. (1992). Why British psychology is not social: Frederic Bartlett's promotion of the new academic discipline. *Canadian Psychology, 33,* 633–639.

Cote, J. E. (1993). Foundations of a psychoanalytic social psychology: Neo-Eriksonian propositions regarding the relationship between psychic structure and cultural institutions. *Developmental Review, 13,* 31–53.

Coulter, H. L. (1982). *Divided legacy: The conflict between homeopathy and the American Medical Association.* Berkeley, CA: North Atlantic Books.

Cousins, N. (1981). *The anatomy of an illness.* New York: Norton.

Couvreur, V., Ansseau, M., & Franck, G. (1989). Electroconvulsive therapy and its mechanism of action. *Acta Psychiatrica Belgica, 89,* 96–109.

Cowan, P., Cowan, C., Coie, J., & Coie, L. (1978). Becoming a family: The impact of a first child's birth on the couple's relationship. In W. B. Miller & L. F. Newman (Eds.), *The first child and family formation.* Durham: University of North Carolina Press.

Cowan, W. M. (1979). The development of the brain. *Scientific American, 241,* 112–133.

Cowles, J. T. (1937). Food-tokens as incentive for learning by chimpanzees. *Comparative Psychology Monographs, 14*(No. 5).

Cox, C. M. (1926). *Genetic studies of genius: Vol. 2. The early mental traits of three hundred geniuses.* Stanford, CA: Stanford University Press.

Coyle, J. T., Price, D. L., & Delong, M. H. (1983). Alzheimer's disease: A disorder of central cholinergic innervation. *Science, 219,* 1184–1189.

Crabtree, A. (1992). Dissociation and memory: A two-hundred-year perspective. *Dissociation: Progress in the Dissociative Disorders, 5,* 150–154.

Craib, K. J., Strathdee, S. A., Hogg, R. S., Le, T. N., Montaner, J. S., O'Shaughnessy, M. V., & Schechter, M. T. (1994). AIDS mortality rates and factors related to survival in a cohort of homosexual men. *International Conference on AIDS, 10,* 317.

Craig, A. D., & Bushnell, M. C. (1994). The thermal grill illusion: Unmasking the burn of cold pain. *Science, 265,* 252–255.

Craik, F. I. M., & Lockhart, R. S. (1972). Levels of processing: A framework for memory research. *Journal of Verbal Learning and Verbal Behavior, 11,* 671–684.

Cranston, M. (1967). Francis Bacon. In P. Edwards (Ed.), *The encyclopedia of philosophy.* New York: Macmillan.

Cravens, H. (1992). A scientific project locked in time: The Terman Genetic Studies of Genius, 1920s–1950s. *American Psychologist, 47,* 183–189.

Crawford, H. J. (1994). Brain dynamics and hypnosis: Attentional and disattentional processes. *International Journal of Clinical and Experimental Hypnosis, 42,* 204–232.

Crites, L. (1991). Cross-cultural counseling in wife beating cases. *Response to the Victimization of Women and Children, 13,* 8–12.

Crits-Christoph, P. (1992). The efficacy of brief dynamic psychotherapy: A meta-analysis. *American Journal of Psychiatry, 149,* 151–158.

Cromwell, P. F., Marks, A., Olson, J. N., & Avary, D. W. (1991). Group effects on decision-making by burglars. *Psychological Reports, 69,* 579–588.

Cronshaw, S. F., & Ellis, R. J. (1991). A process investigation of self-monitoring and leader emergence. *Small Group Research, 22,* 403–420.

Crystal, J. D., & Shettleworth, S. J. (1994). Spatial list learning in black-capped chickadees. *Animal Learning and Behavior, 22,* 77–83.

Csikszentmihalyi, M. (1990). *Flow: The psychology of optimal experience.* New York: Harper & Row.

Csikszentmihalyi, M., Larson, R., & Prescott, S. (1977). The ecology of adolescent activity and experience. *Journal of Youth and Adolescence, 6,* 281–294.

Cunningham, J. D., & Antill, J. K. (1994). Cohabitation and marriage: Retrospective and predictive comparisons. *Journal of Social and Personal Relationships, 11,* 77–93.

Cunningham, M. R. (1986). Measuring the physical in physical attractiveness: Quasi-experiments on the sociobiology of female facial beauty. *Journal of Personality and Social Psychology, 50,* 925–935.

Curtiss, S. (1977). *Genie: A psycholinguistic study of a modern-day wild child.* New York: Academic Press.

Cushman, P. (1990). Why the self is empty: Toward a historically situated psychology. *American Psychologist, 45,* 599–611.

Cuzzillo, S. W. (1991). Historical contingencies in the evolution of human behavior and psychopathology. *Psychiatry, 54,* 187–207.

Cvetkovich, G., Grote, B., Bjorseth, A., & Sarkissian, J. (1975). On the psychology of adolescents' use of contraceptives. *Journal of Sex Research, 11,* 256–270.

Cytowic, R. E. (1989). Synesthesia and mapping of subjective sensory dimensions. *Neurology, 39,* 849–850.

Cytowic, R. E., & Wood, F. B. (1982). Synesthesia: I. A review of major theories and their brain basis. *Brain and Cognition, 1,* 23–35.

Dahl, R. E. (1992). The pharmacologic treatment of sleep disorders. *Psychiatric Clinics of North America, 15,* 161–178.

Dale, A. J. D. (1980). Organic mental disorders associated with infections. In H. I. Kaplan, A. M. Freedman, & B. J. Sadock (Eds.), *Comprehensive textbook of psychiatry* (Vol. 2, 3rd ed.). Baltimore: Williams & Wilkins.

Dallenbach, K. M. (1927). The temperature spots and end-organs. *American Journal of Psychology, 39,* 402–427.

Daly, M., & Wilson, M. (1983). *Sex, evolution, and human behavior* (2nd ed.). Boston: Willard Grant.

Dana, R. H., & Whatley, P. R. (1991). When does a difference make a difference? MMPI scores and African-Americans. *Journal of Clinical Psychology, 47,* 400–406.

Danesi, M. A., & Adetunji, J. B. (1994). Use of alternative medicine by patients with epilepsy: A survey of 265 epileptic patients in a developing country. *Epilepsia, 35,* 344–351.

Daniels, G. S. (1952). *The "average man"?* (Technical Note WCRD 53-7). Wright-Patterson Air Force Base, OH: Wright Air Development Center, USAF.

Darley, J. M., & Latané, B. (1968). Bystander intervention in emergencies: Diffusion of responsibility. *Journal of Personality and Social Psychology, 8,* 377–383.

Darou, W. G. (1992). Native Canadians and intelligence testing. *Canadian Journal of Counselling, 26,* 96–99.

Darwin, C. (1859). *Origin of species.* London: Murray.

Darwin, C. (1871). *The descent of man and selection in relation to sex.* New York: Appleton.

Darwin, C. (1872). *The expression of the emotions in man and animals.* London: Murray.

Das, B., & Mital, A. (1994). Production feedback and standards as moderators of the worker satisfaction–productivity relationship. *Ergonomics, 37,* 1185–1194.

Davey, G. C. L. (1994). Is evaluative conditioning a qualitatively distinct form of classical conditioning? *Behaviour Research and Therapy, 32,* 291–299.

Davidson, J. C., & Caddell, D. P. (1994). Religion and the meaning of work. *Journal for the Scientific Study of Religion, 33,* 135–147.

Davidson, J. E. (1990). Intelligence recreated. *Educational Psychologist, 25,* 337–354.

Davidson, R. J. (1984). Hemispheric asymmetry and emotion. In K. R. Scherer & P. Ekman (Eds.), *Approaches to emotion.* Hillsdale, NJ: Erlbaum.

Davies, J. C. (1991). Maslow and theory of political development: Getting to fundamentals. *Political Psychology, 12,* 389–420.

Davis, C., & Yager, J. (1992). Transcultural aspects of eating disorders: A critical literature review. *Culture, Medicine, and Psychiatry, 16,* 377–394.

Davis, J. (1984). *Endorphins: New waves in brain chemistry.* Garden City, NY: Dial.

Davis, J. N., & Bistodeau, L. (1993). How do L1 and L2 reading differ? Evidence from thinking aloud protocols. *Modern Language Journal, 77,* 459–472.

Davis, W. (1988). *Passage of darkness: The ethnobiology of the Haitian zombie.* Chapel Hill: University of North Carolina Press.

Dawkins, M. S. (1993). *Through our eyes only? The search for animal consciousness.* New York: Freeman.

de Castro, J. M. (1991). The relationship of spontaneous macronutrient and sodium intake with fluid ingestion and thirst in humans. *Physiology and Behavior, 49,* 513–519.

de Gaston, J. F., Jensen, L., & Weed, S. (1995). A closer look at adolescent sexual activity. *Journal of Youth and Adolescence, 24,* 465–479.

De Houwer, J., Baeyens, F., & Eelen, P. (1994). Verbal evaluative conditioning with undetected US presentations. *Behaviour Research and Therapy, 32,* 629–633.

de Jong, R. (1993). Multiple bottlenecks in overlapping task performance. *Journal of Experimental Psychology: Human Perception and Performance, 19,* 965–980.

de Munck, V. C. (1992). The fallacy of the misplaced self: Gender relations and the construction of multiple selves among Sri Lankan Muslims. *Ethos, 20,* 167–190.

de Raad, B., & Szirmak, Z. (1994). The search for the "Big Five" in a non-Indo-European language: The Hungarian trait structure and its relationship to the EPQ and the PTS. *Revue Européenne de Psychologie Appliquée, 44,* 17–24.

Dealberto, M. J. (1992). Les troubles du sommeil en psychiatrie: Aspects épidémiologiques. *Encéphale, 18,* 331–340.

Deaux, K. (1985). Sex and gender. *Annual Review of Psychology, 36,* 49–81.

DeCarvalho, R. J. (1990). Contributions to the history of psychology: LXIX. Gordon Allport on the problem of method in psychology. *Psychological Reports, 67,* 267–275.

DeCarvalho, R. J. (1991). Gordon Allport and humanistic psychology. *Journal of Humanistic Psychology, 31,* 8–13.

Deepak, K. K., Manchanda, S. K., & Maheshwari, M. C. (1994). Meditation improves clinicoelectroencephalographic measures in drug-resistant epileptics. *Biofeedback and Self Regulation, 19,* 25–40.

Dehaene, S., & Cohen, L. (1994). Dissociable mechanisms of subitizing and counting: Neuropsychological evidence from simultanagnosis patients. *Journal of Experimental Psychology: Human Perception and Performance, 20,* 958–975.

DeJong, W. (1975). Another look at Banuazizi and Movahedi's analysis of the Stanford Prison Experiment. *American Psychologist, 30,* 1013–1015.

DeLong, G. R. (1992). Autism, amnesia, hippocampus, and learning. *Neuroscience and Biobehavioral Reviews, 16,* 63–70.

DeLucia, P. R. (1993). A quantitative analysis of illusion magnitude predicted by several averaging theories of the Müller-Lyer illusion. *Perception and Psychophysics, 53,* 498–504.

Demb, J. (1990). Black, inner-city, female adolescents and condoms: What the girls say. *Family Systems Medicine, 8,* 401–406.

Dement, W. C. (1974). *Some must watch while some must sleep.* San Francisco: Freeman.

Dement, W. C., & Wolpert, E. (1958). The relation of eye movements, bodily motility, and external stimuli to dream content. *Journal of Experimental Psychology, 55,* 543–553.

Dennett, D. C. (1991). *Consciousness explained.* Boston: Little, Brown.

Denton, L. (1994, December). Interim report issued on memories of abuse. *The APA Monitor,* pp. 8–9.

Denton, R. E., & Kampfe, C. M. (1994). The relationship between family variables and adolescent substance abuse: A literature review. *Adolescence, 29,* 475–495.

Deregowski, J. B. (1980). Perception. In H. C. Triandis & J. J. Berry (Eds.), *Handbook of cross-cultural psychology: Basic processes* (Vol. 3). Boston: Allyn & Bacon.

DeRidder, R., & Tripathi, R. C. (Eds.) (1992). *Norm violation and intergroup relations.* New York: Oxford University Press.

Derogatis, L. R. (1991). Personality, stress, disease, and bias in epidemiological research. *Psychological Inquiry, 2,* 238–242.

Derryberry, D., & Tucker, D. M. (1992). Neural mechanisms of emotion. *Journal of Consulting and Clinical Psychology, 60,* 329–338.

Desforges, D. M., Lord, C. G., Ramsey, S. L., & Mason, J. A. (1991). Effects of structured cooperative contact on changing negative attitudes toward stigmatized social groups. *Journal of Personality and Social Psychology, 60,* 531–544.

Dethier, V. G. (1976). *The hungry fly.* Cambridge, MA: Harvard University Press.

Deutsch, G. (1992). The nonspecificity of frontal dysfunction in disease and altered states: Cortical blood flow evidence. *Neuropsychiatry, Neuropsychology, and Behavioral Neurology, 5,* 301–307.

Devolder, P. A., & Pressley, M. (1989). Metamemory across the adult lifespan. *Canadian Psychology, 30,* 578–587.

Dewey, J. (1913). *Interest and effort in education.* New York: Houghton Mifflin.

Dewsbury, D. A. (1990). Early interactions between animal psychologists and animal activists and the founding of the APA Committee on Precautions in Animal Experimentation. *American Psychologist, 45,* 315–327.

Dewsbury, D. A. (1991). "Psychobiology." *American Psychologist, 46,* 198–205.

Dewsbury, D. A. (1992). On the problems studied in ethology, comparative psychology, and animal behavior. *Ethology, 92,* 89–107.

Dewsbury, D. A. (1994). On the utility of the proximate-ultimate distinction in the study of animal behavior. *Ethology, 96,* 63–68.

Dex, S. (Ed.) (1991). *Life and work history methods: Qualitative and quantitative developments.* London: Routledge.

Diaper, G. (1990). The Hawthorne effect: A fresh examination. *Educational Studies, 16,* 261–267.

Díaz-Barriga, A. F. (1987). Operaciones de pensamiento formal: Estado actual de la teoria y la investigación. *Revista Mexicana de Psicología, 4,* 41–46.

Dickinson, A., & Balleine, B. (1994). Motivational control of goal-directed action. *Animal Learning and Behavior, 22,* 1–18.

Diener, E. (1977). Deindividuation: Causes and consequences. *Social Behavior and Personality, 5,* 143–155.

Diener, E., Fraser, S. C., Beaman, A. L., & Kelem, R. T. (1976). Effects of deindividuation variables on stealing among Halloween trick-or-treaters. *Journal of Personality and Social Psychology, 33,* 178–183.

Dienstfrey, H. (1991). Neal Miller, the dumb autonomic nervous system, and biofeedback. *Advances, 7,* 33–44.

Dillard, J. P. (1991). The current status of research on sequential-request compliance techniques. *Personality and Social Psychology Bulletin, 17,* 283–288.

Dillman, D. A. (1978). *Mail and telephone surveys: The total design method.* New York: Wiley.

Dion, K. K., Berscheid, E., & Walster, E. (1972). What is beautiful is good. *Journal of Personality and Social Psychology, 24,* 285–290.

Dixon, N. F. (1990). Perceptual and other related defenses. *Polish Psychological Bulletin, 21,* 319–330.

Dohrenwend, B. S., & Dohrenwend, B. P. (1981). Hypotheses about stress processes linking social class to various types of psychopathology. *American Journal of Community Psychology, 9,* 145–159.

Dolan, B. (1991). Cross-cultural aspects of anorexia nervosa and bulimia: A review. *International Journal of Eating Disorders, 10,* 67–79.

Dollard, J., Doob, L. W., Miller, N. E., Mowrer, O. H., & Sears, R. R. (1939). *Frustration and aggression.* New Haven: Yale University Press.

Dollard, J., & Miller, N. E. (1950). *Personality and psychotherapy: An analysis in terms of learning, thinking, and culture.* New York: McGraw-Hill.

Doman, G., Wilkinson, R., Dimancescu, M. D., & Pelligra, R. (1993). The effect of intense multi-sensory stimulation on coma arousal and recovery. *Neuropsychological Rehabilitation, 3,* 203–212.

Donald, M. (1993). Precis of *Origins of the modern mind: Three stages in the evolution of culture and cognition. Behavioral and Brain Sciences, 16,* 737–791.

Dorfman, P. (1989). Industrial and organizational psychology. In W. L. Gregory & W. J. Burroughs (Eds.), *Introduction to applied psychology.* Glenview, IL: Scott, Foresman.

Dorit, R. L., Akashi, H., & Gilbert, W. (1995). Absence of polymorphism at the ZFY locus on the human Y chromosome. *Science, 268,* 1183–1185.

Dornbusch, S. M., Carlsmith, J. M., Bushwall, S. J., Ritter, P. L., Leiderman, H., Hastorf, A. H., & Gross, R. T. (1985). Single parents, extended households, and the control of adolescents. *Child Development, 56,* 326–341.

Downey, G., & Coyne, J. C. (1990). Children of depressed parents: An integrative review. *Psychological Bulletin, 108,* 50–76.

Downs, J. F. (1990). Nudity in Japanese visual media: A cross-cultural observation. *Archives of Sexual Behavior, 19,* 583–594.

Draguns, J. G. (1989). Normal and abnormal behavior in cross-cultural perspective: Specifying the nature of their relationship. In J. J. Berman (Ed.), *Nebraska Symposium on Motivation* (Vol. 37). Lincoln: University of Nebraska Press.

Dressler, D., & Schönle, P. W. (1989). Das Narkolepsie-Syndrom: Klinik, Diagnostik, Therapie. *Fortschritte der Neurologie, Psychiatrie, 57,* 440–449.

Drout, C. E., & Vander, T. (1993). Milgram's "Obedience" film and attributions of responsibility. *Psychological Reports, 73,* 595–606.

Duckitt, J. H. (1992a). Psychology and prejudice: A historical analysis and integrative framework. *American Psychologist, 47,* 1182–1193.

Duckitt, J. H. (1992b). *The social psychology of prejudice.* New York: Praeger.

Duijker, H. C. J. (1960). *National character and national stereotypes.* Amsterdam: North-Holland.

Duijkers, T. J., Drijver, M., Kromhout, D., & James, S. A. (1988). "John Henryism" and blood pressure in a Dutch population. *Psychosomatic Medicine, 50,* 353–359.

Dujardin, K., Guerrien, A., & Leconte, P. (1990). Sleep, brain activation, and cognition. *Physiology and Behavior, 47,* 1271–1278.

Duncker, K. (1945). On problem solving. *Psychological Monographs, 58*(Whole No. 270).

Dunn, R. L., & Schwebel, A. I. (1995). Meta-analytic review of marital therapy outcome research. *Journal of Family Psychology, 9,* 58–68.

Dunne, J., & Hedrick, M. (1994). The parental alienation syndrome: An analysis of sixteen selected cases. *Journal of Divorce and Remarriage, 21,* 21–38.

Duran, E., & Duran, B. (1995). *Native American postcolonial psychology.* Albany: State University of New York Press.

Durbin, D. L., Darling, N., Steinberg, L., & Brown, B. B. (1993). Parenting style and peer group membership among European-American adolescents. *Journal of Research on Adolescence, 3,* 87–100.

Dustman, R. E., Ruhling, R. O., Russell, E. M., Shearer, D. E., Bonekat, H. W., Shigeoka, J. W., Woods, J. S., & Bradford, D. C. (1984). Aerobic exercise training and improved neuropsychological function of older individuals. *Neurobiology of Aging, 5,* 35–42.

Duxbury, L., Higgins, C., & Lee, C. (1994). Work-family conflict: A comparison by gender, family type, and perceived control. *Journal of Family Issues, 15,* 449–466.

Dweck, C. (1990). Toward a theory of goals: Their role in motivation and personality. In R. A. Dienstbier (Ed.), *Nebraska Symposium on Motivation* (Vol. 38). Lincoln: University of Nebraska Press.

Dwinell, P. L., & Higbee, J. L. (1991). Affective variables related to mathematics achievement among high-risk college freshmen. *Psychological Reports, 69,* 399–403.

Dwivedi, R. S., & Dwivedi, S. (1993, Winter). Creative orientation and theoretical assumptions among executives: An empirical study. *Abhigyan,* pp. 1–10.

Dykema, J., Bergbower, K., & Peterson, C. (1995). Pessimistic explanatory style, life events, hassles, and illness. *Journal of Social and Clinical Psychology, 14,* 357–371.

Dywan, J., & Bowers, K. S. (1983). The use of hypnosis to enhance recall. *Science, 222,* 184–185.

Eagle, M., & Wolitzky, D. (1994). Dynamic psychotherapy. In V. B. Van Hasselt & M. Hersen (Eds.), *Advanced abnormal psychology.* New York: Plenum.

Eagly, A. H. (1994). On comparing women and men. *Feminism and Psychology, 4,* 513–522.

Eagly, A. H. (1995). The science and politics of comparing women and men. *American Psychologist, 50,* 145–158.

Eagly, A. H., & Johnson, B. T. (1990). Gender and leadership style: A meta-analysis. *Psychological Bulletin, 108,* 233–256.

Eagly, A. H., & Wood, W. (1991). Explaining sex differences in social behavior: A meta-analytic perspective. *Personality and Social Psychology Bulletin, 17,* 306–315.

Eals, M., & Silverman, I. (1994). The hunter-gatherer theory of spatial sex differences: Proximate factors mediating the female advantage in recall of object arrays. *Ethology and Sociobiology, 15,* 95–105.

Earley, P. C. (1989). Social loafing and collectivism: A comparison of the United States and the People's Republic of China. *Administrative Science Quarterly, 34,* 565–581.

Eaton, J. S. (1980). The psychiatrist and psychiatric education. In H. I. Kaplan, A. M. Freedman, & B. J. Sadock (Eds.), *Comprehensive textbook of psychiatry* (Vol. 3, 3rd ed.). Baltimore: Williams & Wilkins.

Ebbinghaus, H. (1885). *Memory: A contribution to experimental psychology.* New York: Columbia University Press.

Eccles, J. S. (1985). Why doesn't Jane run? Sex differences in educational and occupational patterns. In F. D. Horowitz & M. O'Brien (Eds.), *The gifted and talented: Developmental perspectives.* Washington, DC: American Psychological Association.

Edelman, G. M. (1987). *Neural Darwinism: The theory of neuronal group selection.* New York: Basic Books.

Edgerton, R. E. (1979). *Mental retardation.* Cambridge, MA: Harvard University Press.

Edwards, G., Hensman, C., Hawker, A., & Williamson, V. (1967). Alcoholics Anonymous: The anatomy of a self-help group. *Social Psychiatry, 1,* 195–204.

Egeth, H., & Dagenbach, D. (1991). Parallel versus serial processing in visual search: Further evidence from subadditive effects of visual quality. *Journal of Experimental Psychology: Human Perception and Performance, 17,* 551–560.

Eibl-Eibesfeldt, I. (1970). *Ethology: The biology of behavior.* New York: Holt, Rinehart & Winston.

Eich, J. E. (1980). The cue-dependent nature of state dependent retrieval. *Memory and Cognition, 8,* 157–173.

Eichenbaum, H., Otto, T., & Cohen, N. J. (1994). Two functional components of the hippocampal memory system. *Behavioral and Brain Sciences, 17,* 449–517.

Einfeld, S. L. (1992). Clinical assessment of psychiatric symptoms in mentally retarded individuals. *Australian and New Zealand Journal of Psychiatry, 26,* 48–63.

Eisenberg, D. M., Kessler, R. C., Foster, C., Norlock, F. E., Calkins, D. R., & Delbanco, T. L. (1993). Unconventional medicine in the United States: Prevalence, costs, and patterns of use. *New England Journal of Medicine, 328,* 246–252.

Eisenberger, R. (1992). Learned industriousness. *Psychological Review, 99,* 248–267.

Eisler, R. M., & Blalock, J. A. (1991). Masculine gender role stress: Implications for the assessment of men. *Clinical Psychology Review, 11,* 45–60.

Eisner, G. M. (1990). Hypertension: Racial differences. *American Journal of Kidney Diseases, 16,* 35–40.

Ekehammar, B. (1974). Interactionism in psychology from a historical perspective. *Psychological Bulletin, 81,* 1026–1048.

Ekman, P. (1984). Expression and the nature of emotion. In K. Scherer & P. Ekman (Eds.), *Approaches to emotion.* Hillsdale, NJ: Erlbaum.

Ekman, P. (1986). *Telling lies.* New York: Berkley.

Ekman, P. (1992). An argument for basic emotions. *Cognition and Emotion, 6,* 169–200.

Ekman, P. (1993). Facial expression and emotion. *American Psychologist, 48,* 384–392.

Ekman, P., & Friesen, W. V. (1975). *Unmasking the face.* Englewood Cliffs, NJ: Prentice Hall.

Elder, G. H. (1969). Appearance and education in marriage mobility. *American Sociological Review, 34,* 519–533.

Eldredge, N., & Gould, S. J. (1972). Punctuated equilibria: An alternative to phyletic gradualism. In T. J. M. Schopf (Ed.), *Models in paleobiology.* San Francisco: Freeman.

Elkind, D. (1978a). *The child's reality: Three developmental themes.* Hillsdale, NJ: Erlbaum.

Elkind, D. (1978b). Understanding the young adolescent. *Adolescence, 13,* 127–134.

Ellenberger, H. F. (1970). *The discovery of the unconscious: The history and evolution of dynamic psychiatry.* New York: Basic Books.

Ellicott, A., Hammen, C., Gitlin, M., Brown, G., & Jamison, K. (1990). Life events and the course of bipolar disorder. *American Journal of Psychiatry, 147,* 1194–1198.

Elliott, F. A. (1987). Neuroanatomy and neurology of aggression. *Psychiatric Annals, 17,* 385–388.

Ellis, A. (1962). *Reason and emotion in psychotherapy.* New York: Stuart.

Ellis, G. J., & Petersen, L. R. (1992). Socialization values and parental control techniques: A cross-cultural analysis of child-rearing. *Journal of Comparative Family Studies, 23,* 39–54.

Ellis, H. C., & Ashbrook, P. W. (1989). The "state" of mood and memory research: A selective review. *Journal of Social Behavior and Personality, 4,* 1–21.

Ellis, R. J., & Cronshaw, S. F. (1992). Self-monitoring and leader emergence: A test of moderator effects. *Small Group Research, 23,* 113–129.

Ellison, C. G., & Sherkat, D. E. (1993). Obedience and autonomy: Religion and parental values reconsidered. *Journal for the Scientific Study of Religion, 32,* 313–329.

Ellsworth, P. C. (1994). William James and emotion: Is a century of fame worth a century of misunderstanding? *Psychological Review, 101,* 222–229.

Ellsworth, P. C., & Smith, C. A. (1988a). From appraisal to emotion: Differences among unpleasant feelings. *Motivation and Emotion, 12,* 271–302.

Ellsworth, P. C., & Smith, C. A. (1988b). Shades of joy: Patterns of appraisal differentiating pleasant emotions. *Cognition and Emotion, 2,* 301–331.

Ellwood, M. S., & Stolberg, A. L. (1993). The effects of family composition, family health, parenting behavior, and environmental stress on children's divorce adjustment. *Journal of Child and Family Studies, 2,* 23–36.

Elovitz, P. H. (1994). Clinton's childhood, personality, and first year in office. *Journal of Psychohistory, 21,* 257–286.

Emerick, R. E. (1991). The politics of psychiatric self-help: Political factions, interactional support, and group longevity in a social movement. *Social Science and Medicine, 32,* 1121–1128.

Emery, R. E. (1982). Interparental conflict and the children of discord and divorce. *Psychological Bulletin, 92,* 310–330.

Emmelkamp, P. M. G. (1994). Behavior therapy with adults. In A. E. Bergin & S. L. Garfield (Eds.), *Handbook of psychotherapy and behavior change* (4th ed.). New York: Wiley.

Emmelkamp, P. M. G., & Kuipers, A. (1979). Agoraphobia: A follow-up study four years after treatment. *British Journal of Psychiatry, 134,* 352–355.

Endler, N. S., & Magnusson, D. (1976). Toward an interactional theory of personality. *Psychological Bulletin, 83,* 956–974.

Endler, N. S., & Parker, J. D. (1992). Interactionism revisited: Reflections on the continuing crisis in the personality area. *European Journal of Personality, 6,* 177–198.

Engel, G. L. (1980). The clinical application of the biopsychosocial model. *American Journal of Psychiatry, 137,* 535–544.

Engels, G. I., Garnefski, N., & Diekstra, R. F. W. (1993). Efficacy of rational-emotive therapy: A quantitative analysis. *Journal of Consulting and Clinical Psychology, 61,* 1083–1090.

Engen, T. (1987). Remembering odors and their names. *American Scientist, 75,* 497–503.

England, G. W., & Whitely, W. T. (1990). Cross-national meanings of working. In A. P. Brief & W. R. Nord (Eds.), *Meanings of occupational work: A collection of essays.* Lexington, MA: Lexington Books.

Ennett, S. T., & Bauman, K. E. (1994). The contribution of influence and selection to adolescent peer group homogeneity: The case of adolescent cigarette smoking. *Journal of Personality and Social Psychology, 67,* 653–663.

Enns, C. Z. (1993). Twenty years of feminist counseling and therapy: From naming biases to implementing multifaceted practice. *Counseling Psychologist, 21,* 3–87.

Epstein, A. W. (1990). Associations and their nature: A foundation of psychodynamic science. *Journal of the American Academy of Psychoanalysis, 17,* 463–473.

Epstein, R. (1991). Skinner, creativity, and the problem of spontaneous behavior. *Psychological Science, 2,* 362–370.

Epstein, R., Kirshnit, C. E., Lanza, R. P., & Rubin, L. C. (1984). "Insight" in the pigeon: Antecedents and determinants of an intelligent performance. *Nature, 308,* 61–62.

Epstein, S. (1979). The stability of behavior: I. On predicting most of the people much of the time. *Journal of Personality and Social Psychology, 37,* 1097–1126.

Epstein, S. (1990). Comment on the effects of aggregation across and within occasions on consistency, specificity, and reliability. *Methodika, 4,* 95–100.

Epstein, S. (1992). The cognitive self, the psychoanalytic self, and the forgotten selves. *Psychological Inquiry, 3,* 34–37.

Epstein, S. (1994). Integration of the cognitive and the psychodynamic unconscious. *American Psychologist, 49,* 709–724.

Erdelyi, M. H. (1974). A new look at the New Look: Perceptual defense and vigilance. *Psychological Review, 81,* 1–25.

Erdelyi, M. H. (1985). *Psychoanalysis: Freud's cognitive psychology.* New York: Freeman.

Ericsson, K. A., & Chase, W. G. (1982). Exceptional memory. *American Scientist, 70,* 607–615.

Ericsson, K. A., & Simon, H. A. (1984). *Protocol analysis: Verbal reports as data.* Cambridge, MA: MIT Press.

Erikson, E. (1963). *Childhood and society* (2nd ed.). New York: Norton.

Erikson, E. (1968). *Identity: Youth and crisis.* New York: Norton.

Erikson, E. (1982). *The life cycle completed.* New York: Norton.

Erlenmeyer-Kimling, L., & Cornblatt, B. A. (1992). A summary of attentional findings in the New York High-Risk Project. *Journal of Psychiatric Research, 26,* 405–426.

Erlenmeyer-Kimling, L., & Jarvik, L. F. (1963). Genetics and intelligence: A review. *Science, 142,* 1477–1479.

Ernulf, K. E., & Innala, S. M. (1991). Biologiska faktorer och sexuell identitet: Vad vi vet/inte vet idag. *Nordisk Sexologi, 9,* 3–22.

Escos, J., Alados, C. L., & Boza, J. (1993). Leadership in a domestic goat herd. *Applied Animal Behaviour Science, 38,* 41–47.

Eslinger, P. J., & Grattan, L. M. (1994). Altered serial position learning after frontal lobe lesion. *Neuropsychologia, 32,* 729–739.

Eth, S. (1988). The child victim as witness in sexual abuse proceedings. *Psychiatry, 51,* 221–232.

Evans, G. W. (1980). Environmental cognition. *Psychological Bulletin, 88,* 259–287.

Evans, G. W. (1994). Working on the hot seat: Urban bus operators. *Accident Analysis and Prevention, 26,* 181–193.

Evans, G. W., & Howard, R. B. (1973). Personal space. *Psychological Bulletin, 80,* 334–344.

Evans, G. W., & Joseph, S. V. (1982). Air pollution and human behavior. *Managerial Psychology, 3,* 1–30.

Evans, G. W., & Lepore, S. J. (1992). Conceptual and analytic issues in crowding research. *Journal of Environmental Psychology, 12,* 163–173.

Evans, G. W., & Lepore, S. J. (1993). Household crowding and social support: A quasiexperimental analysis. *Journal of Personality and Social Psychology, 65,* 308–316.

Everett, J. J., Smith, R. E., & Williams, K. D. (1992). Effects of team cohesion and identifiability on social loafing in relay swimming performance. *International Journal of Sport Psychology, 23,* 311–324.

Exner, J. E. (1974–1982). *The Rorschach: A comprehensive system* (3 vols.). New York: Wiley.

Eyferth, K. (1961). Leistungen verschiedener Gruppen von Besatzungskindern in Hamburg-Wechsler Intelligenztest für Kinder (HAWIK). *Archiv für die gesamte Psychogie, 113,* 222–241.

Eysenck, H. J. (1947). *Dimensions of personality.* London: Routledge & Kegan Paul.

Eysenck, H. J. (1952). The effects of psychotherapy: An evaluation. *Journal of Consulting Psychology, 16,* 319–324.

Eysenck, H. J. (1967). *The biological basis of personality.* Springfield, IL: Thomas.

Eysenck, H. J. (1976). *Sex and personality.* Austin: University of Texas Press.

Eysenck, H. J. (1988). Personality and stress as causal factors in cancer and coronary heart disease. In M. P. Janisse (Ed.), *Individual differences, stress, and health psychology.* New York: Springer-Verlag.

Eysenck, H. J. (1990a). Genetic and environmental contributions to individual differences: The three major dimensions of personality. *Journal of Personality, 58,* 245–261.

Eysenck, H. J. (1990b). The prediction of death from cancer by means of personality/stress questionnaire: Too good to be true? *Perceptual and Motor Skills, 71,* 216–218.

Eysenck, H. J. (1991). Reply to criticisms of the Grossarth-Maticek studies. *Psychological Inquiry, 2,* 297–323.

Eysenck, H. J. (1993). "The structure of phenotypic personality traits": Comment. *American Psychologist, 48,* 1299–1300.

Eysenck, H. J., & Eysenck, S. B. G. (1975). *Manual of the Eysenck Personality Questionnaire.* San Diego: EdITS.

Faber, R. J. (1992). Money changes everything: Compulsive buying from a biopsychosocial perspective. *American Behavioral Scientist, 35,* 809–819.

Fabes, R. A., & Martin, C. L. (1991). Gender and age stereotypes of emotionality. *Personality and Social Psychology Bulletin, 17,* 532–540.

Fabrega, H. (1989). Language, culture, and the neurobiology of pain: A theoretical exploration. *Behavioural Neurology, 2,* 235–260.

Fagan, T. K., & VandenBos, G. R. (Eds.). (1993). *Exploring applied psychology: Origins and critical analyses.* Washington, DC: American Psychological Association.

Fagot, B. I. (1978). The influence of sex of child on parental reactions to toddler children. *Child Development, 49,* 459–465.

Fagot, B. I., Hagan, R., Leinbach, M. D., & Kronsberg, S. (1985). Differential reactions to assertive and communicative acts of toddler boys and girls. *Child Development, 56,* 1499–1505.

Falloon, I. R. (1992). Psychotherapy of schizophrenia. *British Journal of Hospital Medicine, 48,* 164–170.

Farley, J., & Alkon, D. L. (1985). Cellular mechanisms of learning, memory, and information storage. *Annual Review of Psychology, 36,* 419–494.

Farquhar, J. W., Maccoby, N., & Solomon, D. (1984). Community applications of behavioral medicine. In W. D. Gentry (Ed.), *Handbook of behavioral medicine.* New York: Guilford.

Fausto-Sterling, A. (1985). *Myths of gender: Biological theories about women and men.* New York: Basic Books.

Fay, A., & Lazarus, A. A. (1993). On necessity and sufficiency in psychotherapy. *Psychotherapy in Private Practice, 12,* 33–39.

Feeney, J. A., & Noller, P. (1990). Attachment style as a predictor of adult romantic relationships. *Journal of Personality and Social Psychology, 58,* 281–291.

Feeney, S., & Magarick, M. (1984). Choosing good toys for young children. *Young Children, 40,* 21–25.

Feighner, J. P., Robins, E., Guze, S. B., Woodruff, R. A., Winokur, G., & Munoz, R. (1972). Diagnostic criteria for use in psychiatric research. *Archives of General Psychiatry, 26,* 57–63.

Feingold, A. (1988). Cognitive gender differences are disappearing. *American Psychologist, 43,* 95–103.

Feingold, A. (1992a). Sex differences in variability in intellectual abilities: A new look at an old controversy. *Review of Educational Research, 62,* 61–84.

Feingold, A. (1992b). The greater male variability controversy: Science versus politics. *Review of Educational Research, 62,* 89–90.

Feingold, A. (1993a). Cognitive gender differences: A developmental perspective. *Sex Roles, 29,* 91–112.

Feingold, A. (1993b). Joint effects of gender differences in central tendency and gender differences in variability. *Review of Educational Research, 63,* 106–109.

Feingold, A. (1994a). Gender differences in personality: A meta-analysis. *Psychological Bulletin, 116,* 429–456.

Feingold, A. (1994b). Gender differences in variability in intellectual abilities: A cross-cultural perspective. *Sex Roles, 30,* 81–92.

Feinstein, C. B. (1983). Early adolescent deaf boys: A biopsychosocial approach. *Adolescent Psychiatry, 11,* 147–162.

Feldman, D. H. (1980). *Beyond universals in cognitive development.* Norwood, NJ: Ablex.

Feldman, D. H. (1993). Child prodigies: A distinctive form of giftedness. *Gifted Child Quarterly, 37,* 188–193.

Fellin, P. (1989). Perspectives on depression among black Americans. *Health and Social Work, 14,* 245–252.

Ferencik, B. M. (1992). The helping process in group therapy: A review and discussion. *Group, 16,* 113–124.

Ferguson, B., & Tyrer, B. (1988). Classifying personality disorder. In P. Tyrer (Ed.), *Personality disorders: Diagnosis, management, and course.* London: Wright.

Fergusson, D. M., Horwood, L. J., & Lynskey, M. T. (1994). Parental separation, adolescent psychopathology, and problem behaviors. *Journal of the American Academy of Child and Adolescent Psychiatry, 33,* 1122–1131.

Ferraro, K. R. (1984). Widowhood and social participation in later life: Isolation or compensation? *Research on Aging, 6,* 451–468.

Ferrell, W. R., Crighton, A., & Sturrock, R. D. (1992). Age-dependent changes in position sense in human proximal interphalangeal joints. *Neuroreport: An International Journal for the Rapid Communication of Research in Neuroscience, 3,* 259–261.

Ferveur, J. F., Stortkuhl, K. F., Stocker, R. F., & Greenspan, R. J. (1995). Genetic feminization of brain structures and changed sexual orientation in male *Drosophilia. Science, 267,* 902–905.

Festinger, L. (1954). A theory of social comparison processes. *Human Relations, 7,* 117–140.

Festinger, L. (1957). *A theory of cognitive dissonance.* Evanston: Row, Peterson.

Festinger, L., & Carlsmith, J. M. (1959). Cognitive consequences of forced compliance. *Journal of Abnormal and Social Psychology, 68,* 359–366.

Festinger, L., Pepitone, A., & Newcomb, T. M. (1952). Some consequences of deindividuation in a group. *Journal of Abnormal and Social Psychology, 47,* 382–389.

Feuerstein, M., Papciak, A., Shapiro, S., & Tannenbaum, S. (1989). The Weight Loss Profile: A biopsychosocial approach to weight loss. *International Journal of Psychiatry in Medicine, 19,* 181–192.

Fiedler, F. E. (1950). A comparison of therapeutic relationships in psychoanalytic, non-directive, and Adlerian therapy. *Journal of Consulting Psychology, 14,* 436–445.

Fiedler, F. E. (1951). Factor analysis of psychoanalytic, non-directive, and Adlerian therapeutic relationships. *Journal of Consulting Psychology, 15,* 32–38.

Fiedler, F. E. (1971). Validation and extension of the contingency model of leadership effectiveness: A review of empirical findings. *Psychological Bulletin, 76,* 128–148.

Finger, S. (1975). Child-holding patterns in Western art. *Child Development, 46,* 267–271.

Finke, J. (1990). Can psychotherapeutic competence be taught? *Psychotherapy and Psychosomatics, 53,* 64–67.

Fischer, K. W. (1987). Relations between brain and cognitive development. *Child Development, 58,* 623–632.

Fischhoff, B. (1988). Judgment and decision making. In R. J. Sternberg & E. E. Smith (Eds.), *The psychology of human thought.* Cambridge, England: Cambridge University Press.

Fishbein, D. H. (1992). The psychobiology of female aggression. *Criminal Justice and Behavior, 19,* 99–126.

Fisher, A. C. (1977). Sport personality assessment: Facts, fallacies, and perspectives. *Motor Skills: Theory into Practice, 1,* 87–97.

Fisher, D. L. (1993). Optimal performance engineering: Good, better, best. *Human Factors, 35,* 115–139.

Fisher-Thompson, D. (1993). Adult toy purchases for children: Factors affecting sex-typed toy selection. *Journal of Applied Developmental Psychology, 14,* 385–406.

Fishman, P. (1980). Interactional shitwork. *Heresies, 2,* 99–101.

Fiske, A. P. (1992). The four elementary forms of sociality: Framework for a unified theory of social relations. *Psychological Review, 99,* 689–723.

Fiske, A. P. (1993). Social errors in four cultures: Evidence about universal forms of social relations. *Journal of Cross-Cultural Psychology, 24,* 463–494.

Fiske, J. (1994). Radical shopping in Los Angeles: Race, media, and the sphere of consumption. *Media, Culture, and Society, 16,* 469.

Fiske, S. T. (1992). Thinking is for doing: Portraits of social cognition from Daguerreotype to laserphoto. *Journal of Personality and Social Psychology, 63,* 877–889.

Fiske, S. T. (1993). Social cognition and social perception. *Annual Review of Psychology, 44,* 155–194.

Fiske, S. T., & Taylor, S. E. (1984). *Social cognition.* Reading, MA: Addison-Wesley.

Fivush, R. (1991). Gender and emotion in mother-child conversations about the past. *Journal of Narrative and Life History, 1,* 325–341.

Flaherty, V. L., Cowart-Steckler, D., & Pollack, R. H. (1988). Magnitude of fixation effect as influenced by estrogen fluctuations during the menstrual cycle. *Bulletin of the Psychonomic Society, 26,* 115–117.

Flanagan, J. C. (1954). The critical incident technique. *Psychological Bulletin, 51,* 327–358.

Flavell, J. H. (1979). Metacognition and cognitive monitoring: A new area of cognitive-developmental inquiry. *American Psychologist, 34,* 906–911.

Flavell, J. H. (1981). Cognitive monitoring. In W. P. Dickson (Ed.), *Children's oral communication skills.* New York: Academic Press.

Flood, S. E., & Hellstedt, J. C. (1991). Gender differences in motivation for intercollegiate athletic participation. *Journal of Sport Behavior, 14,* 159–167.

Flores-Ortiz, Y. G. (1994). The role of cultural and gender values in alcohol use patterns among Chicana/Latina high school and university students: Implications for AIDS prevention. *International Journal of Addictions, 92,* 1149–1171.

Foa, E. B., Kozak, M. J., Steketee, G. S., & McCarthy, P. R. (1992). Treatment of depressive and obsessive-compulsive symptoms in OCD by imipramine and behaviour therapy. *British Journal of Clinical Psychology, 31,* 279–292.

Ford, C. S., & Beach, F. A. (1951). *Patterns of sexual behavior.* New York: Harper & Row.

Forehand, R., & Nousiainen, S. (1993). Maternal and paternal parenting: Critical dimensions in adolescent functioning. *Journal of Family Psychology, 7,* 213–221.

Form, W. H., & Nosow, S. (1958). *Community in disaster.* New York: Harper.

Forsyth, D. R., & Wibberly, K. H. (1993). The self-reference effect: Demonstrating schematic processing in the classroom. *Teaching of Psychology, 20,* 237–238.

Forward, J., Canter, R., & Kirsch, N. (1976). Role-enactment and deception: Alternative paradigms? *American Psychologist, 31,* 595–604.

Foulkes, D. (1985). *Dreaming: A cognitive-psychological analysis.* Hillsdale, NJ: Erlbaum.

Fowles, D. C. (1992). Schizophrenia: Diathesis-stress revisited. *Annual Review of Psychology, 43,* 303–336.

Fox, B. H. (1991). Quandaries created by unlikely numbers in some of Grossarth-Maticek's studies. *Psychological Inquiry, 2,* 242–247.

Fox, R. A., Kimmerly, N. L., & Schafer, W. D. (1991). Attachment to mother/attachment to father: A meta-analysis. *Child Development, 62,* 210–225.

Foxall, G. R. (1991). *Consumer psychology for marketing.* London: Routledge.

Francis, C. K. (1990). Hypertension and cardiac disease in minorities. *American Journal of Medicine, 88,* 3–8.

Frank, J. D. (1974). *Persuasion and healing* (Rev. ed.). New York: Schocken Books.

Frank, J. D. (1978). *Psychotherapy and the human predicament: A psychosocial approach.* New York: Schocken Books.

Frankel, F. H. (1976). *Hypnosis: Trance as a coping mechanism.* New York: Plenum.

Frankenburg, W. K., & Dodds, J. B. (1967). The Denver Developmental Screening Test. *Journal of Pediatrics, 71,* 181–191.

Franks, C. M. (1984). Behavior therapy: An overview. *Annual Review of Behavior Therapy: Theory and Practice, 10,* 1–46.

Franks, D. J. (1971). Ethnic and social status characteristics of children in EMR and LD classes. *Exceptional Children, 37,* 537–538.

Franssen, E. H., Kluger, A., Torossian, C. L., & Reisberg, B. (1993). The neurologic syndrome of severe Alzheimer's disease: Relationship to functional decline. *Archives of Neurology, 50,* 1029–1039.

Fraser, S. (Ed.) (1995). *The bell curve wars: Race, intelligence, and the future of America.* New York: Basic Books.

Frazer, J. G. (1922). *The golden bough: A study in magic and religion.* New York: Macmillan.

Free, M. D. (1991). Clarifying the relationship between the broken home and juvenile delinquency: A critique of the current literature. *Deviant Behavior, 12,* 109–167.

Freeman, S. C. (1993). Client-centered therapy with diverse populations: The universal within the specific. *Journal of Multicultural Counseling and Development, 21,* 248–254.

Freud, S. (1900). The interpretation of dreams. *Standard edition* (Vol. 4). London: Hogarth.

Freud, S. (1905). Three essays on the theory of sexuality. *Standard edition* (Vol. 7). London: Hogarth.

Freud, S. (1908). Creative writers and daydreaming. *Standard edition* (Vol. 9). London: Hogarth.

Freud, S. (1909a). Analysis of a phobia in a five-year-old boy. *Standard edition* (Vol. 10). London: Hogarth.

Freud, S. (1909b). Notes upon a case of obsessional neurosis. *Standard edition* (Vol. 10). London: Hogarth.

Freud, S. (1916). Introductory lectures on psychoanalysis. *Standard edition* (Vol. 15). London: Hogarth.

Freud, S. (1917). Mourning and melancholia. *Standard edition* (Vol. 14). London: Hogarth.

Freud, S. (1918). From the history of an infantile neurosis. *Standard edition* (Vol. 17). London: Hogarth.

Frey, R., & Adams-Webber, J. (1992). Mood-related changes in construing self and others. *International Journal of Personal Construct Psychology, 5,* 367–376.

Fridlund, A. J. (1991a). Evolution and facial action in reflex, social motive, and paralanguage. *Biological Psychology, 32,* 3–100.

Fridlund, A. J. (1991b). Sociality of solitary smiling: Potentiation by an implicit audience. *Journal of Personality and Social Psychology, 60,* 229–240.

Friedlander, F., & Greenberg, S. (1971). Effect of job attitudes, training, and organization climate on performance of the hard-core unemployed. *Journal of Applied Psychology, 55,* 187–195.

Friedman, H. L. (1992). Changing patterns of adolescent sexual behavior: Consequences for health and development. *Journal of Adolescent Health, 13,* 345–350.

Friedman, H. S., & Booth-Kewley, S. (1987). The "disease-prone personality": A meta-analytic view of the construct. *American Psychologist, 42,* 539–555.

Friedman, H. S., & DiMatteo, M. R. (1989). *Health psychology.* Englewood Cliffs, NJ: Prentice Hall.

Friedman, M. (1989). Type A behavior: Its diagnosis, cardiovascular relation, and the effect of its modification on recurrence of coronary artery disease. *American Journal of Cardiology, 64,* 12–19.

Friedman, M., & Rosenman, R. H. (1974). *Type A behavior and your heart.* New York: Knopf.

Friedman, M., Thoresen, C. E., Gill, J. J., Ulmer, D., Powell, L. H., Price, V. A., Brown, B., Thompson, L., Rabin, D. D., Breall, W. S., Bourg, E., Levy, R., & Dixon, T. (1986). Alteration of Type A behavior and its effect on cardiac recurrences in post myocardial infarction patients: Summary results of the recurrent coronary prevention project. *American Heart Journal, 112,* 653–665.

Friedman, R. C., & Downey, J. (1993). Neurobiology of sexual orientation: Current relationships. *Journal of Neuropsychiatry and Clinical Neurosciences, 5,* 131–153.

Friedman, S., Hatch, M., & Paradis, C. M. (1993). Obsessive compulsive disorder in two black ethnic groups: Incidence in an urban dermatology clinic. *Journal of Anxiety Disorders, 7,* 343–348.

Friedman, S., Paradis, C. M., & Hatch, M. (1994). Characteristics of African-American and white patients with panic disorder and agoraphobia. *Hospital and Community Psychiatry, 45,* 798–803.

Friedmann, M. S., & Goldstein, M. J. (1993). Relatives' awareness of their own expressed emotion as measured by a self-report adjective checklist. *Family Process, 32,* 459–471.

Friend, T. (1994, May 13–15). Philly hostile? 'Who asked ya?' *USA Today,* pp. 1A, 5D.

Fries, J. F., & Crapo, L. M. (1981). *Vitality and aging.* San Francisco: Freeman.

Frisby, C. L. (1993). One giant step backward: Myths of black cultural learning styles. *School Psychology Review, 22,* 535–557.

Frischholz, E. J., Braun, B. G., Sachs, R. G., Schwartz, D. R., Lewis, J., Shaeffer, D., Westergaard, C., & Pasquotto, J. (1992). Con- struct validity of the Dissociative Experiences Scale: II. Its relationship to hypnotizability. *American Journal of Clinical Hypnosis, 35,* 145–152.

Frith, C. D. (1992). Consciousness, information processing, and the brain. *Journal of Psychopharmacology, 6,* 436–440.

Fritze, J., Deckert, J., Lanczik, M., Strik, W., Struck, M., & Wodarz, N. (1992). Status of the amine hypothesis in depressive disorders. *Nervenarzt, 63,* 3–13.

Fromm, E. (1947). *Man for himself.* New York: Rinehart.

Fry, C. L. (1985). Culture, behavior, and aging in the comparative perspective. In J. E. Birren & K. W. Schaie (Eds.), *Handbook of the psychology of aging* (2nd ed.). New York: Van Nostrand.

Frymier, A. B., Klopf, D. W., & Ishii, S. (1990). Japanese and Americans compared on the affect orientation construct. *Psychological Reports, 66,* 985–986.

Fuller, R. C. (1988). *Alternative medicine and American religious life.* New York: Oxford University Press.

Funder, D. C. (1991). Global traits: A neo-Allportian approach to personality. *Psychological Science, 2,* 31–39.

Funder, D. C., & West, S. G. (1993). Consensus, self-other agreement, and accuracy in personality judgment: An introduction. *Journal of Personality, 61,* 457–476.

Fung, L. (1992). Participation motives in competitive sports: A cross-cultural comparison. *Adapted Physical Activity Quarterly, 9,* 114–122.

Furstenberg, F. F. (1990). Divorce and the American family. *Annual Review of Sociology, 16,* 379–403.

Gaertner, S. L., Rust, M. C., Dovidio, J. F., & Bachman, B. A. (1994). The contact hypothesis: The role of a common ingroup identity on reducing intergroup bias. *Small Group Research, 25,* 224–249.

Gafurov, B. G., & Batuev, A. S. (1993). The influence of stimulation of the hypothalamus on the choice of food during maintenance of rats on various salt and water diets. *Neuroscience and Behavioral Physiology, 23,* 310–315.

Gaillard, J. M. (1992). Neurobiological correlates of the unlocking of the unconscious. *International Journal of Short-Term Psychotherapy, 7,* 89–107.

Galanter, E. (1962). Contemporary psychophysics. In R. Brown, E. Galanter, E. H. Hess, & G. Mandler (Eds.), *New directions in psychology.* New York: Holt, Rinehart & Winston.

Gallistel, C. R. (1980). *The organization of action.* Hillsdale, NJ: Erlbaum.

Gallois, C. (1993). The language and communication of emotion: Universal, interpersonal, or intergroup? *American Behavioral Scientist, 36,* 309–338.

Gallup, G. (1972). *The sophisticated poll watcher's guide.* Princeton, NJ: Princeton Opinion Press.

Gallup, G. G., & Cameron, P. A. (1992). Modality specific metaphors: Is our mental machinery "colored" by a visual bias? *Metaphor and Symbolic Activity, 7,* 93–98.

Gallup, G. G., & Suarez, S. D. (1985). Alternatives to the use of animals in psychological research. *American Psychologist, 40,* 1104–1111.

Galotti, K. M. (1989). Gender differences in self-reported moral reasoning: A review and new evidence. *Journal of Youth and Adolescence, 18,* 475–488.

Galton, F. (1869). *Hereditary genius.* London: Macmillan.

Galton, F. (1888). Co-relations and their measurement. *Proceedings of the Royal Society, 45,* 135–145.

Gandelman, R. (1983). Gonadal hormones and sensory function. *Neuroscience and Biobehavioral Reviews, 7,* 1–17.

Gantt, H. (1994). Do consciousness and mental processes require physical energy? *Integrative Physiological and Behavioral Science, 29,* 77–80.

Garb, H. N. (1994). Toward a second generation of statistical prediction rules in psychodiagnosis and personality assessment. *Computers in Human Behavior, 10,* 377–394.

Garcia, J., & Koelling, R. A. (1966). The relation of cue to consequence in avoidance learning. *Psychonomic Science, 4,* 123–124.

Gardner, H. (1976). *The shattered mind.* New York: Vintage Books.

Gardner, H. (1983). *Frames of mind: The theory of multiple intelligences.* New York: Basic Books.

Gardner, H. (1985). *The mind's new science: A history of the cognitive revolution.* New York: Basic Books.

Gardner, H. (1988). Creativity: An interdisciplinary perspective. *Creativity Research Journal, 1,* 8–26.

Gardner, H. (1993). Intelligence and intelligences: Universal principles and individual differences. *Archives de Psychologie, 61,* 169–172.

Gardner, R. A., & Gardner, B. T. (1969). Teaching sign language to a chimpanzee. *Science, 165,* 664–672.

Garfield, S. L. (1994). Research on client variables in psychotherapy. In A. E. Bergin & S. L. Garfield (Eds.), *Handbook of psychotherapy and behavior change* (4th ed.). New York: Wiley.

Garner, D. M., & Wooley, S. C. (1991). Confronting the failure of behavioral and dietary treatments for obesity. *Clinical Psychology Review, 11,* 729–780.

Gasanov, G. G., & Kuliev, E. I. (1992). Neuronal activity of the ventro-medial hypothalamus under pharmacological effects modulating the motivational and emotional states. *Fiziologicheskii Zhurnal SSSR im I. M. Sechenova, 78,* 29–35.

Gasquoine, P. G. (1993). Alien hand sign. *Journal of Clinical and Experimental Neuropsychology, 15,* 653–667.

Gay, P. (1988). *Freud: A life for our time.* New York: Norton.

Gazzaniga, M. S. (1992). *Nature's mind.* New York: Basic Books.

Geary, D. C. (1995). Reflections of evolution and culture in children's cognition: Implications for mathematical development and instruction. *American Psychologist, 50,* 24–37.

Geen, R. G. (1991). Social motivation. *Annual Review of Psychology, 42,* 377–399.

Geer, J. H., & McGlone, M. S. (1990). Sex differences in memory for erotica. *Cognition and Emotion, 4,* 71–78.

Geiger, B. (1994). Stimulating moral growth in the classroom: A model. *High School Journal, 77,* 280–285.

Gelman, R. (1969). Conservation acquisition: A problem of learning to attend to relevant attributes. *Journal of Experimental Child Psychology, 7,* 167–178.

Gelman, R., & Baillargeon, R. A. (1983). A review of some Piagetian concepts. In P. H. Mussen (Ed.), *Handbook of child psychology* (Vol. 3). New York: Wiley.

Gentner, D., & Stevens, A. L. (Eds.). (1983). *Mental models.* Hillsdale, NJ: Erlbaum.

George, J. M. (1992). Extrinsic and intrinsic origins of perceived social loafing in organizations. *Academy of Management Journal, 35,* 191–202.

George, L. K., Fillenbaum, G. G., & Palmore, E. (1984). Sex differences in the antecedents and consequences of retirement. *Journal of Gerontology, 39,* 364–371.

Gergen, K. J. (1973). Social psychology as history. *Journal of Personality and Social Psychology, 26,* 309–320.

Gerrards-Hesse, A., Spies, K., & Hesse, F. W. (1994). Experimental inductions of emotional states and their effectiveness: A review. *British Journal of Psychology, 85,* 55–78.

Gerstner, C. R., & Day, D. V. (1994). Cross-cultural comparison of leadership prototypes. *Leadership Quarterly, 5,* 121–134.

Gescheider, G. A. (1988). Psychophysiological scaling. *Annual Review of Psychology, 39,* 169–200.

Gibb, C. A. (1969). Leadership. In G. Lindzey & E. Aronson (Eds.), *The handbook of social psychology* (Vol. 4, 2nd ed.). Reading, MA: Addison-Wesley.

Gibbons, F. X., & Kassin, S. M. (1987). Information consistency and perceptual set: Overcoming the mental retardation "schema." *Journal of Applied Social Psychology, 17,* 810–827.

Gibson, D. R. (1990). Relationship of socioeconomic status to logical and sociomoral judgment of middle-aged men. *Psychology and Aging, 5,* 510–513.

Gibson, E. J. (1988). Exploratory behavior in the development of perceiving, acting, and the acquiring of knowledge. *Annual Review of Psychology, 39,* 1–41.

Gibson, E. J. (1992). How to think about perceptual learning: Twenty-five years later. In H. L. Pick, P. van den Broek, & D. C. Knill (Eds.), *Cognition: Conceptual and methodological issues.* Washington, DC: American Psychological Association.

Gibson, E. J., & Walk, R. D. (1960, September). The "visual cliff." *Scientific American,* pp. 64–71.

Gibson, H. B. (1991). Can hypnosis compel people to commit harmful, immoral, and criminal acts? A review of the literature. *Contemporary Hypnosis, 8,* 129–140.

Gibson, J. J. (1979). *The ecological approach to visual perception.* Boston: Houghton Mifflin.

Gibson, J. T. (1991). Training people to inflict pain: State terror and social learning. *Journal of Humanistic Psychology, 31,* 72–87.

Gibson, K. R. (1994). Continuity theories of human language origins versus the Lieberman model. *Language and Communication, 14,* 97–114.

Gibson, R. C. (1994). The age-by-race gap in health and mortality in the older population: A social science research agenda. *Gerontologist, 34,* 454–462.

Giere, R. N. (Ed.). (1992). *Cognitive models of science.* Minneapolis: University of Minnesota Press.

Gifford, R., & Sacilotto, P. A. (1993). Social isolation and personal space: A field study. *Canadian Journal of Behavioural Science, 25,* 165–174.

Gil, T. E. (1989). Psychological etiology to cancer: Truth or myth? *Israel Journal of Psychiatry and Related Sciences, 26,* 164–185.

Gilbert, L. A. (1980). Feminist therapy. In A. Brodsky & R. T. Hare-Mustin (Eds.), *Women and psychotherapy.* New York: Guilford.

Gilgen, A. R. (1982). *American psychology since World War II.* Westport, CT: Greenwood.

Gilger, J. W., Geary, D. C., & Eisele, L. M. (1991). Reliability and validity of retrospective self-reports of the age of pubertal onset using twin, sibling, and college student data. *Adolescence, 26,* 41–53.

Gill, J. J., Price, V. A., Friedman, M., Thoreson, C. E., Powell, L. H., Ulmer, D., Brown, B., & Drews, F. R. (1985). Reduction in Type A behavior in healthy middle-aged American military officers. *American Heart Journal, 110,* 503–514.

Gill, K. G. (1970). *Violence against children.* Cambridge, MA: Harvard University Press.

Gillett, G. R. (1988). Consciousness and brain function. *Philosophical Psychology, 1,* 327–341.

Gilligan, C. (1982). *In a different voice.* Cambridge, MA: Harvard University Press.

Gitlin, M. J., Cochran, S. D., & Jamison, K. R. (1989). Maintenance lithium treatment: Side effects and compliance. *Journal of Clinical Psychiatry, 50,* 127–131.

Gladue, B. A. (1994). The biopsychology of sexual orientation. *Current Directions in Psychological Science, 3,* 150–154.

Glantz, K., & Pearce, J. K. (1989). *Exiles from Eden: Psychotherapy from an evolutionary perspective.* New York: Norton.

Glaser, R., Kiecolt-Glaser, J. K., Bonneau, R. H., Malarkey, W., Kennedy, S., & Hughes, J. (1992). Stress-induced modulation of the immune response to recombinant hepatitis B vaccine. *Psychosomatic Medicine, 54,* 22–29.

Glaser, R., Kiecolt-Glaser, J. K., Stout, J. C., Tarr, K. L., Speicher, C. E., & Holliday, J. E. (1985). Stress-related impairments in cellular immunity. *Psychiatry Research, 16,* 233–239.

Glass, A. L., & Holyoak, K. J. (1986). *Cognition* (2nd ed.). New York: Random House.

Glass, D. C. (1977). *Behavior patterns, stress, and coronary disease.* Hillsdale, NJ: Erlbaum.

Glenn, S. S., Ellis, J., & Greenspoon, J. (1992). On the revolutionary nature of the operant as a unit of behavioral selection. *American Psychologist, 47,* 1329–1336.

Glick, R. A., & Bone, S. (Eds.). (1990). *Pleasure beyond the pleasure principle.* New Haven, CT: Yale University Press.

Glucksberg, S. (1988). Language and thought. In R. J. Sternberg & E. E. Smith (Eds.), *The psychology of human thought.* Cambridge, England: Cambridge University Press.

Goddard, H. H. (1917). Mental tests and the immigrant. *Journal of Delinquency, 2,* 243–277.

Godden, D. R., & Baddeley, A. D. (1975). Context-dependent memory in two natural environments: On land and underwater. *British Journal of Psychology, 65,* 325–332.

Goffman, E. (1961). *Asylums.* Garden City, NJ: Anchor.

Goldberg, L. R. (1990). An alternative "description of personality": The Big-Five factor structure. *Journal of Personality and Social Psychology, 59,* 1216–1229.

Goldberg, L. R. (1992). The development of markers for the Big-Five factor structure. *Psychological Assessment, 4,* 26–42.

Goldberg, L. R. (1993). The structure of phenotypic personality traits. *American Psychologist, 48,* 26–34.

Goldberg, R. L., & Wise, T. N. (1990). The importance of the sense of smell in human sexuality. *Journal of Sex Education and Therapy, 16,* 236–241.

Goldberg, S. (1991). Recent developments in attachment theory and research. *Canadian Journal of Psychiatry, 36,* 393–400.

Goldman, M. J. (1991). Kleptomania: Making sense of the nonsensical. *American Journal of Psychiatry, 148,* 986–996.

Goldner, V. (1985). Feminism and family therapy. *Family Process, 24,* 31–47.

Goldsmith, H. H., & Campos, J. J. (1990). The structure of temperamental fear and pleasure in infants: A psychometric perspective. *Child Development, 61,* 1944–1964.

Goldsmith, L. T. (1992). Wang Yani: Stylistic development of a Chinese painting prodigy. *Creativity Research Journal, 5,* 281–293.

Goldstein, A., & Hilgard, E. R. (1975). Lack of influence of the morphine antagonist naloxone on hypnotic analgesia. *Proceedings of the National Academy of Sciences, 72,* 2041–2043.

Goldstein, A. P., & Krasner, L. (1987). *Modern applied psychology.* New York: Pergamon.

Goldstein, M. (1990). The Decade of the Brain: An era of promise for neurosurgery and a call to action. *Journal of Neurosurgery, 73,* 1–2.

Goldstein, M., & Deutsch, A. Y. (1992). Dopaminergic mechanisms in the pathogenesis of schizophrenia. *FASEB Journal, 6,* 2413–2421.

Goleman, D. (1995). *Emotional intelligence.* New York: Bantam.

Goleman, D., & Gurin, J. (Eds.). (1993). *Mind/body medicine: How to use your mind for better health.* Yonkers, NY: Consumer Reports Books.

Golub, A., & Johnson, B. D. (1994). A recent decline in cocaine use among youthful arrestees in Manhattan, 1987 through 1993. *American Journal of Public Health, 84,* 1250–1254.

Gomez, J., & Rodriguez, A. (1989). An evaluation of the results of a drug sample analysis. *Bulletin on Narcotics, 41,* 121–126.

Good, B. J. (1992). Culture and psychopathology: Directions for psychiatric anthropology. In T. Schwartz, G. M. White, & C. A. Lutz (Eds.), *New directions in psychological anthropology.* Cambridge, England: Cambridge University Press.

Goodman, L. A., Koss, M. P., Fitzgerald, L. F., Russo, N. F., & Keita, G. P. (1993). Male violence against women: Current research and future directions. *American Psychologist, 48,* 1054–1058.

Goodrich, T. J., Rampage, C., Ellman, B., & Halstead, K. (1988). *Feminist family therapy.* New York: Norton.

Goodwin, D. W., & Guze, S. B. (1989). *Psychiatric diagnosis* (4th ed.). New York: Oxford University Press.

Goodwin, F. K., & Jamison, K. R. (1990). *Manic-depressive illness.* New York: Oxford University Press.

Gooren, L., Fliers, E., & Courtney, K. (1990). Biological determinants of sexual orientation. *Annual Review of Sex Research, 1,* 175–196.

Gopnik, I., & Gopnik, M. (Eds.). (1986). *From models to modules: Studies in cognitive science from the McGill Workshops.* Norwood, NJ: Ablex.

Gorman, M. E. (1992). *Simulating science: Heuristics, mental models, and technoscientific thinking.* Bloomington: Indiana University Press.

Gottesman, I. I. (1991). *Schizophrenia genesis: The origins of madness.* New York: Freeman.

Gottman, J. M., & Levenson, R. W. (1992). Marital processes predictive of later dissolution: Behavior, physiology, and health. *Journal of Personality and Social Psychology, 63,* 221–233.

Gottsdanker, R. (1982). Age and simple reaction time. *Journal of Gerontology, 37,* 342–348.

Gould, P., & White, R. (1974). *Mental maps.* New York: Penguin.

Gould, S. J. (1977). *Ontogeny and phylogeny.* Cambridge, MA: Harvard University Press.

Gould, S. J. (1981). *The mismeasure of man.* New York: Norton.

Gould, S. J. (1991). Exaptation: A crucial tool for an evolutionary psychology. *Journal of Social Issues, 47*(3), 43–65.

Graddol, D., & Swann, J. (1989). *Gender voices.* Oxford: Basil Blackwell.

Graham, C. A. (1991). Menstrual synchrony: An update and review. *Human Nature, 2,* 293–311.

Graham, S. (1991). A review of attribution theory in achievement contexts. *Educational Psychology Review, 3,* 5–39.

Graham, S. (1992). "Most of the subjects were white and middle class": Trends in published research on African Americans in selected APA journals. *American Psychologist, 47,* 629–639.

Grahame-Smith, D. G. (1992). Serotonin in affective disorders. *International Clinical Psychopharmacology, 6,* 5–13.

Gramza, A. F. (1976). Responses to manipulability of a play object. *Psychological Reports, 38,* 1109–1110.

Grant, P. R. (1991). Ethnocentrism between groups of unequal power under threat in intergroup competition. *Journal of Social Psychology, 131,* 21–28.

Green, D. G., & Powers, M. K. (1982). Mechanisms of light adaptation in the rat retina. *Vision Research, 22,* 209–216.

Greenberg, J. (Ed.). (1994). *Organizational behavior: The state of the science.* Hillsdale, NJ: Erlbaum.

Greenberg, J. R., & Mitchell, S. A. (1983). *Object relations in psychoanalytic theory.* Cambridge, MA: Harvard University Press.

Greenberg, L. S., Elliott, R. K., & Lietar, G. (1994). Research on experiential psychotherapies. In A. E. Bergin & S. L. Garfield (Eds.), *Handbook of psychotherapy and behavior change* (4th ed.). New York: Wiley.

Greenberger, E., & Steinberg, L. (1981). The workplace as a context for the socialization of youth. *Journal of Youth and Adolescence, 10,* 185–210.

Greenfield, P. M., & Cocking, R. R. (Eds.). (1994). *Cross-cultural roots of minority child development.* Hillsdale, NJ: Erlbaum.

Greenhill, L. L. (1992). Pharmacologic treatment of attention deficit hyperactivity disorder. *Psychiatric Clinics of North America, 15,* 1–27.

Greer, S., Moorey, S., & Baruch, J. (1991). Evaluation of adjuvant psychological therapy for clinically referred cancer patients. *British Journal of Cancer, 63,* 257–260.

Gregg, E., & Rejeski, W. J. (1990). Social psychobiologic dysfunction associated with anabolic steroid abuse: A review. *Sport Psychologist, 4,* 275–284.

Gregory, R. L. (1966). *Eye and brain: The psychology of seeing.* New York: McGraw-Hill.

Gregory, R. L. (1986). *Odd perceptions.* London: Methuen.

Gregory, W. L., & Burroughs, W. J. (Eds.). (1989). *Introduction to applied psychology.* Glenview, IL: Scott, Foresman.

Greif, E. B. (1979). *Sex differences in parent-child conversations: Who interrupts who?* Paper presented at the annual meeting of the Society for Research in Child Development, Boston.

Grewal, D., & Marmorstein, H. (1994). Market price variation, perceived price variation, and consumers' price search decisions for durable goods. *Journal of Consumer Research, 21,* 453–460.

Griffiths, M. D. (1990). Addiction to fruit machines: A preliminary study among young males. *Journal of Gambling Studies, 6,* 113–126.

Grob, C., & Dobkin de Rios, M. (1992). Adolescent drug use in cross-cultural perspective. *Journal of Drug Issues, 22,* 121–138.

Gross, J. J. (1989). Emotional expression in cancer onset and progression. *Social Science and Medicine, 28,* 1239–1248.

Gross, J. J., & Levenson, R. W. (1993). Emotional suppression: Physiology, self-report, and expressive behavior. *Journal of Personality and Social Psychology, 64,* 970–986.

Gross, J. J., & Munoz, R. M. (1995). Emotion regulation and mental health. *Clinical Psychology: Science and Practice, 2,* 151–164.

Grossarth-Maticek, R., & Eysenck, H. J. (1991). Creative novation behaviour therapy as a prophylactic treatment for cancer and coronary heart disease: Part I. Description of treatment. *Behaviour Research and Therapy, 29,* 1–16.

Grossman, G. E., Leigh, R. J., Bruce, E. N., Huebner, W. P., & Lanska, D. J. (1989). Performance of the human vestibuloocular reflex during locomotion. *Journal of Neurophysiology, 62,* 264–272.

Grossman, H. J. (1977). *A manual on terminology and classification in mental retardation.* Washington, DC: American Association on Mental Deficiency.

Grossman, M., & Rowat, K. M. (1995). Parental relationships, coping strategies, received support, and well-being in adolescents of separated or divorced and married parents. *Research in Nursing and Health, 18,* 249–261.

Grusser, O. J. (1983). Mother-child holding patterns in Western art: A developmental study. *Ethology and Sociobiology, 4,* 89–94.

Guilford, J. P. (1967). *The nature of human intelligence.* New York: McGraw-Hill.

Guilford, J. P. (1975). Factors and factors of personality. *Psychological Bulletin, 82,* 802–814.

Guiton, M. V. (1992). François Mitterand: Personality and politics. *Psychohistory Review, 21,* 27–72.

Gulevich, G., Dement, W. C., & Johnson, L. (1966). Psychiatric and EEG observations on a case of prolonged (264-hour) wakefulness. *Archives of General Psychiatry, 15,* 29–35.

Guthrie, G. M., & Tanco, P. P. (1980). Alienation. In H. C. Triandis & J. G. Draguns (Eds.), *Handbook of cross-cultural psychology: Psychopathology* (Vol. 6). Boston: Allyn & Bacon.

Guze, S. B. (1989). Biological psychiatry: Is there any other kind? *Psychological Medicine, 19,* 315–323.

Hacker, P. M. (1990). Chomsky's problems. *Language and Communication, 10,* 127–148.

Haefely, W. E. (1990). The GABA-benzodiazepine receptor complex and anxiety. In N. Sartorius, V. Andreoli, G. Cassano, L. Eisenberg, P. Kielholz, P. Pancheri, & G. Racagni (Eds.), *Anxiety: Psychobiological and clinical perspectives.* New York: Hemisphere.

Hahdahl, K., Iversen, P. M., & Jonsen, B. H. (1993). Laterality for facial expressions: Does the sex of the subject interact with the sex of the stimulus face? *Cortex, 29,* 325–331.

Hahn, R. C., & Petitti, D. B. (1988). Minnesota Multiphasic Personality Inventory–rated depression and the incidence of breast cancer. *Cancer, 61,* 845–848.

Hajal, F. (1994). Diagnosis and treatment of lovesickness: An Islamic medieval case study. *Hospital and Community Psychiatry, 45,* 647–650.

Halford, G. S. (1989). Reflections on 25 years of Piagetian cognitive developmental psychology: 1963–1988. *Human Development, 32,* 325–357.

Hall, C., & Van de Castle, R. L. (1966). *The content analysis of dreams.* East Norwalk, CT: Appleton-Century-Crofts.

Hall, E. T. (1966). *The hidden dimension.* Garden City, NY: Doubleday.

Hall, E. T., & Hall, M. (1990). *Understanding cultural differences.* Yarmouth, ME: Intercultural Press.

Hall, G. (1983). *Behaviour: An introduction to psychology as a biological science.* London: Academic Press.

Hall, G. C. N., & Malony, H. N. (1983). Cultural control in psychotherapy with minority clients. *Psychotherapy: Theory, Research, and Practice, 20,* 131–142.

Hall, G. S. (1904). *Adolescence* (Vol. 1). New York: Appleton.

Halpern, C. T., Udry, J. R., Campbell, B., & Suchindran, C. (1993). Relationships between aggression and pubertal increases in testosterone: A panel analysis of adolescent males. *Social Biology, 40,* 8–24.

Halpern, D. F. (1992). *Sex differences in cognitive abilities* (2nd ed.). Hillsdale, NJ: Erlbaum.

Hamer, D. H., Hu, S., Magnuson, V. L., Hu, N., & Pattatucci, A. M. L. (1993). A linkage between DNA markers on the X chromosome and male sexual orientation. *Science, 261,* 321–327.

Hamill, R. J., & Rowlingson, J. C. (Eds.). (1994). *Handbook of critical care pain management.* New York: McGraw-Hill.

Hamilton, W. D. (1964). The genetical evolution of social behaviour. *Journal of Theoretical Biology, 12,* 12–45.

Hamilton, W. F. (1993). The effects of a maritally disrupted environment on the latency stage child: In respect to the formal education process. *Journal of Divorce and Remarriage, 20,* 65–74.

Handa, J. (1994). *Discrimination, retirement, and pensions.* Brookfield, VT: Avebury.

Hankin, J. R. (1994). FAS prevention strategies: Passive and active measures. *Alcohol Health and Research World, 18,* 62–66.

Hanson, K., & Wapner, S. (1994). Transition to retirement: Gender differences. *International Journal of Aging and Human Development, 39,* 189–208.

Hardaway, R. A. (1990). Subliminally activated symbiotic fantasies: Facts and artifacts. *Psychological Bulletin, 107,* 177–195.

Hardy, C. J. (1990). Social loafing: Motivational losses in collective performance. *International Journal of Sport Psychology, 21,* 305–327.

Harlow, H. F. (1958). The nature of love. *American Psychologist, 13,* 673–685.

Harlow, H. F. (1965). Sexual behavior in the rhesus monkey. In F. Beach (Ed.), *Sex and behavior.* New York: Wiley.

Harlow, R. E., & Cantor, N. (1994). Social pursuit of academics: Side effects and spillover of strategic reassurance seeking. *Journal of Personality and Social Psychology, 66,* 386–397.

Harrell, R. F., Woodyard, E. R., & Gates, A. I. (1956). The influence of vitamin supplementation of the diets of pregnant and lactating women on the intelligence of their offspring. *Metabolism, 5,* 555–562.

Harris, B. (1979). What ever happened to Little Albert? *American Psychologist, 34,* 151–160.

Harris, J. E. (1978). External memory aids. In M. M. Gruneberg, P. E. Morris, & R. N. Sykes (Eds.), *Practical aspects of memory.* London: Academic Press.

Harris, L. J. (1989). Footedness in parrots: Three centuries of research, theory, and mere surmise. *Canadian Journal of Psychology, 43,* 369–396.

Harris, M. (1985). *Good to eat: Riddles of food and culture.* New York: Simon & Schuster.

Harris, M. M. (1989). Reconsidering the employment interview: A review of recent literature and suggestions for future research. *Personnel Psychology, 42,* 691–726.

Harrison, L. D. (1992). Trends in illicit drug use in the United States: Conflicting results from national surveys. *International Journal of the Addictions, 27,* 817–847.

Harrison, P. A. (1989). Women in treatment: Changing over time. *International Journal of the Addictions, 24,* 655–673.

Hartmann, H. (1939). *Ego psychology and the problem of adaptation.* New York: International Universities Press.

Hartshorne, H., & May, M. A. (1928). *Studies in deceit.* New York: Macmillan.

Harvey, M. A., & Dym, B. (1987). An ecological view of deafness. *Family Systems Medicine, 5,* 52–64.

Hasselmo, M. E., & Bower, J. M. (1993). Acetylcholine and memory. *Trends in Neurosciences, 16,* 218–222.

Hastie, R. (Ed.). (1993). *Inside the juror: The psychology of juror decision making.* Cambridge, England: Cambridge University Press.

Hastie, R., Penrod, S. D., & Pennington, N. (1983). *Inside the jury.* Cambridge, MA: Harvard University Press.

Hatfield, A. B. (1991). The National Alliance for the Mentally Ill: A decade later. *Community Mental Health Journal, 27,* 95–103.

Hatfield, E., & Rapson, R. L. (1993). Historical and cross-cultural perspectives on passionate love and sexual desire. *Annual Review of Sex Research, 4,* 67–97.

Hatfield, E., & Sprecher, S. (1986). *Mirror, mirror: The importance of looks in everyday life.* Albany, NY: State University of New York Press.

Hathaway, S. R., & McKinley, J. C. (1943). *The Minnesota Multiphasic Personality Inventory.* Minneapolis: University of Minnesota Press.

Hatta, T., Nakaseko, M., & Yamamoto, M. (1992). Hand differences on a sensory test using tactual stimuli. *Perceptual and Motor Skills, 74,* 927–933.

Hauser, M. J. (1983). Bereavement outcome for widows. *Journal of Psychosocial Nursing and Mental Health Sevices, 21,* 22–31.

Havard, J. D. (1992). Expert scientific evidence under the adversarial system: A travesty of justice? *Journal of the Forensic Science Society, 32,* 225–235.

Hayashi, S., Kuno, T., Osawa, M., Shimizu, M., & Suetake, Y. (1992). The client-centered therapy and person-centered approach in Japan: Historical development, current status, and perspectives. *Journal of Humanistic Psychology, 32,* 115–136.

Hayes, R. L. (1994). The legacy of Lawrence Kohlberg: Implications for counseling and human development. *Journal of Counseling and Development, 72,* 261–267.

Hayes, S. C., & Hayes, L. J. (1992). Verbal relations and the evolution of behavior analysis. *American Psychologist, 47,* 1383–1395.

Hayward, M. D., Grady, W. R., & McLaughlin, S. D. (1988). The retirement process among older women in the United States: Changes in the 1970s. *Research on Aging, 10,* 358–382.

Hazan, C. C., & Shaver, P. (1987). Romantic love conceptualized as an attachment process. *Journal of Personality and Social Psychology, 52,* 511–524.

Healy, M. C., Lehman, M., & McDaniel, M. A. (1995). Age and voluntary turnover: A quantitative review. *Personnel Psychology, 48,* 335–345.

Heaven, P. C. L., Connors, J., & Stones, C. R. (1994). Three or five personality dimensions? An analysis of natural language terms in two cultures. *Personality and Individual Differences, 17,* 181–189.

Hedge, A., & Yousif, Y. H. (1992). Effects of urban size, urgency, and cost on helpfulness: A cross-cultural comparison between the United Kingdom and the Sudan. *Journal of Cross-Cultural Psychology, 23,* 107–115.

Heider, E. R. (1972). Universals in color naming and memory. *Journal of Experimental Psychology, 93,* 10–20.

Heider, F. (1944). Social perception and phenomenal causality. *Psychological Review, 51,* 358–374.

Heider, F. (1958). *The psychology of interpersonal relations.* New York: Wiley.

Heim, A. W. (1954). *The appraisal of intelligence.* London: Methuen.

Heinrichs, R. W. (1993). Schizophrenia and the brain: Conditions for a neuropsychology of madness. *American Psychologist, 48,* 221–233.

Helgeson, V. S. (1993). Implications of agency and communion for patient and spouse adjustment to a first coronary event. *Journal of Personality and Social Psychology, 64,* 807–816.

Helgeson, V. S. (1994). Relation of agency and communion to well-being: Evidence and potential explanations. *Psychological Bulletin, 116,* 412–428.

Helson, H. (1964). *Adaptation level theory.* New York: Harper & Row.

Hemphill, J. K. (1950). *Leader behavior description.* Columbus: Ohio State University Personnel Research Board.

Hemphill, J. K. (1955). Leadership behavior associated with the administrative reputation of college departments. *Journal of Educational Psychology, 46,* 385–401.

Henretta, J. C. (1994). Recent trends in retirement. *Reviews in Clinical Gerontology, 4,* 71–81.

Henry, J. A., Alexander, C. A., & Sener, E. K. (1995). Relative mortality from overdose of antidepressants. *British Medical Journal, 310,* 221–224.

Henry, R. M., & Maze, J. R. (1989). Motivation in personal construct theory: A conceptual critique. *International Journal of Personal Construct Psychology, 2,* 169–183.

Henry, W. P., Strupp, H. H., Schacht, T. E., & Gaston, L. (1994). Psychodynamic approaches. In A. E. Bergin & S. L. Garfield (Eds.), *Handbook of psychotherapy and behavior change* (4th ed.). New York: Wiley.

Herbert, G. R., & Doverspike, D. (1990). Performance appraisal in the training needs analysis process: A review and critique. *Public Personnel Management, 19,* 253–270.

Herman, J. L. (1992). *Trauma and recovery.* New York: Basic Books.

Herman, S. P. (1990). Special issues in child custody evaluations. *Journal of the American Academy of Child and Adolescent Psychiatry, 29,* 969–974.

Hermelin, B., Pring, L., & Heavey, L. (1994). Visual and motor functions in graphically gifted savants. *Psychological Medicine, 24,* 673–680.

Herringer, L. G. (1993). Consistency and variability in two personality traits over time and across situations. *Psychological Reports, 73,* 355–362.

Herrmann, C., Candas, V., Hoeft, A., & Garreaud, I. (1994). Humans under showers: Thermal sensitivity, thermoneutral sensations, and comfort estimates. *Physiology and Behavior, 56,* 1003–1008.

Herrmann, D. J., Crawford, M., & Holdsworth, M. (1992). Gender-linked differences in everyday memory performance. *British Journal of Psychology, 83,* 221–231.

Herrnstein, R. J., & Murray, C. (1994). *The bell curve: Intelligence and class structure in American Life.* New York: Free Press.

Herrnstein, R. J., Loveland, D. H., & Cable, C. (1976). Natural concepts in pigeons. *Journal of Experimental Psychology: Animal Behavior Processes, 2,* 285–302.

Hertz, D. G. (1982). Infertility and the physician–patient relationship: A biopsychosocial challenge. *General Hospital Psychiatry, 4,* 95–101.

Hertz, D. G. (1993). Bio–psycho–social consequences of migration stress: A multidimensional approach. *Israel Journal of Psychiatry and Related Sciences, 30,* 204–212.

Herzog, H., Lele, V. R., Kuwert, T., Langen, K. J., Kops, E. R., & Feinendegen, L. E. (1990–1991). Changed pattern of regional glucose metabolism during Yoga meditative relaxation. *Neuropsychobiology, 23,* 182–187.

Hes, J. P. (1958). Hypochondriasis in oriental Jewish immigrants: A preliminary report. *International Journal of Social Psychiatry, 4,* 18–23.

Hes, J. P. (1968). Hypochondriacal complaints in Jewish psychiatric patients. *Israel Annals of Psychiatry and Related Disciplines, 6,* 134–142.

Hess, R. F., & Hayes, A. (1993). Neural recruitment explains "Weber's law" of spatial position. *Vision Research, 33,* 1673–1684.

Hess, U., Kappas, A., McHugo, G. J., Lanzetta, J. T., & Kleck, R. E. (1992). The facilitative effect of facial expression on the self-generation of emotion. *International Journal of Psychophysiology, 12,* 251–265.

Hesse, F. W., Spies, K., Hänze, M., & Gerrards-Hesse, A. (1992). Experimentelle Induktion emotionaler Zustände: Alternativen zur Velten-Methode. *Zeitschrift für Experimentelle und Angewandte Psychologie, 39,* 559–580.

Hetherington, E. M. (1979). Divorce: A child's perspective. *American Psychologist, 34,* 851–858.

Hetherington, E. M., & Arasteh, J. D. (1988). *Impact of divorce, single-parenting, and stepparenting on children.* Hillsdale, NJ: Erlbaum.

Hetherington, E. M., Cox, M., & Cox, R. (1978). The aftermath of divorce. In J. Stevens & M. Mathews (Eds.), *Mother-child, father-child relations.* Washington, DC: National Association for the Education of Young Children.

Hetherington, E. M., Cox., M., & Cox, R. (1979). Stress and coping in divorce: A focus on women. In J. E. Gullahorn (Ed.), *Psychology and women: In transition.* New York: Wiley.

Hetherington, E. M., Cox., M., & Cox, R. (1982). Effects of divorce on parents and children. In M. E. Lamb (Ed.), *Nontraditional families: Parenting and child development.* Hillsdale, NJ: Erlbaum.

Heubner, A. M., & Garrod, A. C. (1993). Moral reasoning among Tibetan monks: A study of Buddhist adolescents and young adults in Nepal. *Journal of Cross-Cultural Psychology, 24,* 167–185.

Hewes, G. W. (1992). Primate communication and the gestural origin of language. *Current Anthropology, 33,* 65–84.

Heylighen, F. (1992). A cognitive-systemic reconstruction of Maslow's theory of self-actualization. *Behavioral Science, 37,* 39–58.

Hiday, V. A., & Scheid-Cook, T. L. (1989). A follow-up of chronic patients committed to outpatient treatment. *Hospital and Community Psychiatry, 40,* 52–59.

Hilgard, E. R. (1973). A neodissociation interpretation of pain reduction in hypnosis. *Psychological Review, 80,* 396–411.

Hilgard, E. R. (1977). *Divided consciousness: Multiple controls in human thought and action.* New York: Wiley.

Hilgard, E. R. (1987). *Psychology in America: A historical survey.* San Diego: Harcourt Brace Jovanovich.

Hilgard, E. R., & Hilgard, J. R. (1983). *Hypnosis in the relief of pain.* Los Altos, CA: Kaufmann.

Hill, D. L., & Mistretta, C. M. (1990). Developmental neurobiology of salt taste sensation. *Trends in Neuroscience, 13,* 188–195.

Hill, M. A. (1992). Light, circadian rhythms, and mood disorders: A review. *Annals of Clinical Psychiatry, 4,* 131–146.

Hill, R. D., Schwob, S. L., & Ottman, S. (1993). Self-generated mnemonics for number recall in young and old adults. *Perceptual and Motor Skills, 76,* 467–470.

Hillbrand, M., & Waite, B. M. (1994). The everyday experience of an institutionalized sex offender: An idiographic application of the experience sampling method. *Archives of Sexual Behavior, 23,* 453–463.

Himmelstein, J. L. (1979). The pleasure principle is not enough. *Psychoanalytic Review, 66,* 103–114.

Hines, M. (1990). Gonadal hormones and human cognitive development. In J. Balthazart (Ed.), *Hormones, brain, and behavior in vertebrates: I. Sexual differentiation, neuroanatomical aspects, neurotransmitters, and neuropeptides.* Basel: Karger.

Hirsch, J. (Ed.). (1967). *Behavior-genetic analysis.* New York: McGraw-Hill.

Hirsch-Pasek, K., Treiman, R., & Schneiderman, M. (1984). Brown and Hanlon revisited: Mothers' sensitivity to ungrammatical forms. *Journal of Child Language, 11,* 81–88.

Ho, D. Y. F. (1994). Filial piety, authoritarian moralism, and cognitive conservatism in Chinese societies. *Genetic, Social, and General Psychology Monographs, 120,* 347–365.

Hobson, J. A. (1988). *The dreaming brain.* New York: Basic Books.

Hobson, J. A., & McCarley, R. W. (1977). The brain as a dream state generator: An activation-synthesis hypothesis of the dream process. *American Journal of Psychiatry, 134,* 1335–1348.

Hobson, J. A., & Stickgold, R. (1994). Dreaming: A neurocognitive approach. *Consciousness and Cognition: An International Journal, 3,* 1–15.

Hodinko, B. A., & Whitley, S. D. (1971). *Student personnel administration: A critical incident approach.* Washington, DC: College Guidance Associates.

Hofmann, A. (1968). Psychotomimetic agents. In A. Burger (Ed.), *Drugs affecting the central nervous system* (Vol. 2). New York: Marcel Dekker.

Hogg, R. S., Strathdee, S. A., Craib, K. J., O'Shaughnessy, M. V., Montaner, J. S., & Schechter, M. T. (1994). Lower socioeconomic status and shorter survival following HIV infection. *Lancet, 344,* 1120–1124.

Hohmann, A. A., Richeport, M., Mariott, B. M., Canino, G. J., Rubio-Stipec, M., & Bird, H. (1990). Spiritism in Puerto Rico: Results of an island-wide community study. *British Journal of Psychiatry, 156,* 328–335.

Holinger, P. C. (1987). *Violent deaths in the United States: An epidemiological study of suicide, homicide, and accidents.* New York: Guilford.

Holland, J. L. (1966). *The psychology of vocational choice: A theory of personality types and model environments.* Waltham, MA: Blaisdell.

Holland, J. L. (1985). *Making vocational choices: A theory of vocational personalities and work environments* (2nd ed.). Englewood Cliffs, NJ: Prentice Hall.

Holland, P. C. (1977). Conditioned stimulus as a determinant of the form for the Pavlovian conditioned response. *Journal of Experimental Psychology: Animal Behavior Processes, 3,* 77–104.

Holland, P. C. (1980). Influence of visual conditioned stimulus characteristics on the form of Pavlovian appetitive conditioned responding in rats. *Journal of Experimental Psychology: Animal Behavior Processes, 6,* 81–97.

Hollifield, M., Katon, W., Spain, D., & Pule, L. (1990). Anxiety and depression in a village in Lesotho, Africa: A comparison with the United States. *British Journal of Psychiatry, 156,* 343–350.

Hollingshead, A. B., & Redlich, F. C. (1958). *Social class and mental illness: A community study.* New York: Wiley.

Hollingworth, L. S. (1942). *Children above 180 IQ.* New York: World Book.

Hollister, L. E., Müller-Oerlinghausen, B., Rickels, K., & Shader, R. I. (1993). Clinical uses of benzodiazepines. *Journal of Clinical Psychopharmacology, 13*(6, Suppl. 1), 1–169.

Hollon, S. D., & Beck, A. T. (1994). Cognitive and cognitive-behavioral therapies. In A. E. Bergin & S. L. Garfield (Eds.), *Handbook of psychotherapy and behavior change* (4th ed.). New York: Wiley.

Holmbeck, G. N., Crossman, R. E., Wandrei, M. L., & Gasiewski, E. (1994). Cognitive development, egocentrism, self-esteem, and adolescent contraceptive knowledge, attitudes, and behavior. *Journal of Youth and Adolescence, 23,* 168–193.

Holmes, D. S. (1984). Meditation and somatic arousal reduction: A review of the experimental evidence. *American Psychologist, 39,* 1–10.

Holmes, D. S. (1985). To meditate or rest? The answer is rest. *American Psychologist, 40,* 728–731.

Holmes, T. H., & Rahe, R. H. (1967). The Social Readjustment Rating Scale. *Journal of Psychosomatic Research, 11,* 213–218.

Holt, E. B. (1931). *Animal drive and the learning process.* New York: Holt.

Hommer, D., Weingartner, H. J., & Breier, A. (1993). Dissociation of benzodiazepine-induced amnesia from sedation by flumazenil pretreatment. *Psychopharmacology, 112,* 455–460.

Hoptman, M. J., & Davidson, R. J. (1994). How and why do the two cerebral hemispheres interact? *Psychological Bulletin, 116,* 195–219.

Horch, K. (1991). Coding of vibrotactile stimulus frequency by Pacinian corpuscle afferents. *Journal of the Acoustical Society of America, 89,* 2827–2836.

Hormuth, S. E. (1986). The sampling of experiences in situ. *Journal of Personality, 54,* 262–293.

Horn, J. M. (1968). Organization of abilities and the development of intelligence. *Psychological Review, 75,* 242–259.

Horney, K. (1937). *Neurotic personality of our times.* New York: Norton.

Horney, K. (1945). *Our inner conflicts.* New York: Norton.

Horwitz, W. A., Kestenbaum, C., Person, E., & Jarvik, L. F. (1965). Identical twins—"idiot savants"—calendar calculators. *American Journal of Psychiatry, 121,* 1075–1079.

Hough, L. M. (1992). The "Big Five" personality variables—construct confusion: Description versus prediction. *Human Performance, 5,* 139–155.

House, R. J., & Singh, J. V. (1987). Organizational behavior: Some new directions for I/O psychology. *Annual Review of Psychology, 38,* 669–718.

Howe, M. J. (1989). Separate skills or general intelligence: The autonomy of human abilities. *British Journal of Educational Psychology, 59,* 351–360.

Hu, Y., Qiuo, Y., & Zhong, G. (1990). Crossed aphasia in Chinese: A clinical survey. *Brain and Language, 39,* 347–356.

Hubel, D. H. (1979, January). The brain. *Scientific American,* pp. 45–53.

Hubel, D. H., & Wiesel, T. N. (1962). Receptive fields, binocular interaction and functional architecture in the cat's visual cortex. *Journal of Physiology, 160,* 106–154.

Hubel, D. H., & Wiesel, T. N. (1979). Brain mechanisms of vision. *Scientific American, 241,* 150–162.

Hudson, W. (1960). Pictorial depth perception in sub-cultural groups in Africa. *Journal of Social Psychology, 52,* 183–208.

Huffman, T., Chang, K., Rausch, P., & Schaffer, N. (1994). Gender differences and factors related to the disposition toward cohabitation. *Family Therapy, 21,* 171–184.

Hughes, D. J. (1991). Blending with an other: An analysis of trance channeling in the United States. *Ethos, 19,* 161–184.

Hughes, J., Smith, T. W., Kosterlitz, H. W., Fothergill, L. A., Morgan, B. A., & Morris, H. R. (1975). Identification of two related pentapeptides from the brain with potent opiate agonist activity. *Nature, 258,* 577–579.

Huizinga, J. (1950). *Homo ludens: A study of the play element in culture.* Boston: Beacon Press.

Hull, C. L. (1943). *Principles of behavior.* New York: Appleton-Century-Crofts.

Humphreys, L. G. (1988). Trends in levels of academic achievement of blacks and other minorities. *Intelligence, 12,* 231–260.

Hunt, E. (1983). On the nature of intelligence. *Science, 219,* 141–146.

Hunt, E. (1990). A modern arsenal for mental assessment. *Educational Psychologist, 25,* 223–241.

Hunt, E. (1995). The role of intelligence in modern society. *American Scientist, 83,* 356–368.

Hunt, J. M. (1982). Toward equalizing the developmental opportunities of infants and preschool children. *Journal of Social Issues, 38*(4), 163–191.

Hunt, J. M., Kernan, J. B., & Bonfield, E. H. (1992). Memory structure in the processing of advertising messages: How is unusual information represented? *Journal of Psychology, 126,* 343–356.

Hunt, N., Bruce-Jones, W., & Silverstone, T. (1992). Life events and relapse in bipolar affective disorder. *Journal of Affective Disorders, 25,* 13–20.

Hunter, M. A., Ames, E. W., & Koopman, R. (1983). Effects of stimulus complexity and familiarization time on infant preferences for novel and familiar stimuli. *Developmental Psychology, 19,* 338–352.

Hupka, R. (1981). Cultural determinants of jealousy. *Alternative Lifestyles, 4,* 310–356.

Hur, J., & Osborne, S. (1993). A comparison of forward and backward chaining methods used in teaching corsage making skills to mentally retarded adults. *British Journal of Developmental Disabilities, 39,* 108–117.

Hurford, J. R. (1991). The evolution of the critical period for language acquisition. *Cognition, 40,* 159–201.

Hurvich, L. M., & Jameson, D. (1974). Opponent processes as a model of neural organization. *American Psychologist, 29,* 88–102.

Huttenlocher, P. R. (1979). Synaptic density in human frontal cortex: Developmental changes and effects of aging. *Brain Research, 163,* 195–205.

Huyck, M. H. (1982). From gregariousness to intimacy: Marriage and friendship over the adult years. In T. M. Field, A. Huston, H. C. Quay, L. Troll, & G. E. Finley (Eds.), *Review of human development.* New York: Wiley.

Iaccino, J. F. (1993). *Left brain–right brain differences: Inquiries, evidence, and new approaches.* Hillsdale, NJ: Erlbaum.

Iaffaldano, M. T., & Muchinsky, P. M. (1985). Job satisfaction and job performance: A meta-analysis. *Psychological Bulletin, 97,* 251–273.

Ibañez-Gracía, T. (1987). Por una psicología social del derecho. *Boletín de Psicología Spain, 15,* 13–21.

Iga, M. (1981). Suicide of Japanese youth. *Suicide and Life-Threatening Behavior, 11,* 17–30.

Ilgen, D. R., Barnes-Farrell, J. L., & McKellin, D. B. (1993). Performance appraisal process research in the 1980s: What has it contributed to appraisals in use? *Organizational Behavior and Human Decision Processes, 54,* 321–368.

Imahori, T. T., & Cupach, W. R. (1994). A cross-cultural comparison of the interpretation and management of face: U.S. American and Japanese responses to embarrassing predicaments. *International Journal of Intercultural Relations, 18,* 193–219.

Ingram, D. H., & Lerner, J. A. (1992). Horney theory: An object relations theory. *American Journal of Psychoanalysis, 52,* 37–44.

Intraub, H. (1980). Presentation rate and the representation of briefly glimpsed pictures in memory. *Journal of Experimental Psychology: Human Learning and Memory, 6,* 1–12.

Irwin, C. E., & Millstein, S. G. (1986). Biopsychosocial correlates of risk-taking behaviors during adolescence: Can the physician intervene? *Journal of Adolescent Health Care, 7,* 82–96.

Ito, M. (1993). New concepts in cerebellar function. *Revue Neurologique, 149,* 596–599.

Izard, C. E. (1977). *Human emotions.* New York: Plenum.

Izard, C. E. (1992). Basic emotions, relations among emotions, and emotion-cognition relations. *Psychological Review, 99,* 561–565.

Izard, C. E. (1993). Four systems for emotion activation: Cognitive and noncognitive processes. *Psychological Review, 100,* 68–90.

Izard, C. E. (1994). Innate and universal facial expressions: Evidence from developmental and cross-cultural research. *Psychological Bulletin, 115,* 288–299.

Jablensky, A. (1989). Epidemiology and cross-cultural aspects of schizophrenia. *Psychiatric Annals, 19*, 516–524.

Jackson, L. E. (1993). Understanding, eliciting, and negotiating clients' multicultural health beliefs. *Nurse Practitioner, 18*, 30–43.

Jackson, S. A. (1992). Athletes in flow: A qualitative investigation of flow states in elite figure skaters. *Journal of Applied Sport Psychology, 4*, 161–180.

Jackson, S. W. (1986). *Melancholia and depression from Hippocratic times to modern times.* New Haven, CT: Yale University Press.

Jackson, S. W. (1994). Catharsis and abreaction in the history of psychological healing. *Psychiatric Clinics of North America, 17*, 471–491.

Jacobs, B. L. (1991). Serotonin and behavior: Emphasis on motor control. *Journal of Clinical Psychiatry, 52*, 17–23.

Jacobsen, J. P. (1994). *The economics of gender.* Cambridge, MA: Blackwell.

Jahoda, M. (1966). Geometric illusions and environment: A study in Ghana. *British Journal of Psychology, 57*, 193–199.

Jakobson, R. (1968). *Child language, aphasia, and phonological universals.* The Hague: Mouton.

James, S. A. (1984a). Coronary heart disease in black Americans: Suggestions for research on psychosocial factors. *American Heart Journal, 108*, 833–838.

James, S. A. (1984b). Socioeconomic influences on coronary heart disease in black populations. *American Heart Journal, 108*, 669–672.

James, S. A., Hartnett, S. A., & Kalsbeek, W. D. (1983). John Henryism and blood pressure differences among black men. *Journal of Behavioral Medicine, 6*, 259–278.

James, S. A., Keenan, N. L., Strogatz, D. S., Browning, S. R., & Garrett, J. M. (1992). Socioeconomic status, John Henryism, and blood pressure in black adults: The Pitt County Study. *American Journal of Epidemiology, 135*, 59–67.

James, S. A., LaCroix, A. Z., Kleinbaum, D. G., & Strogatz, D. S. (1984). John Henryism and blood pressure differences among black men: II. The role of occupational stressors. *Journal of Behavioral Medicine, 7*, 259–275.

James, S. A., Strogatz, D. S., Wing, S. B., & Ramsey, D. L. (1987). Socioeconomic status, John Henryism, and hypertension in blacks and whites. *American Journal of Epidemiology, 126*, 664–673.

James, W. (1884). What is emotion? *Mind, 4*, 188–204.

James, W. (1890). *Principles of psychology* (2 vols.). New York: Holt.

Janis, I. L. (1982). *Victims of groupthink.* Boston: Houghton Mifflin.

Janus, L. (1991). The expression of pre- and perinatal experience in cultural phenomena. *Pre- and Peri-Natal Psychology Journal, 5*, 203–220.

Jaynes, G. D., & Williams, R. M. (Eds.). (1989). *A common destiny: Blacks and American society.* Washington, DC: National Academy Press.

Jaynes, J. (1976). *The origins of consciousness in the breakdown of the bicameral mind.* Boston: Houghton Mifflin.

Jebb, R. C. (1870). *The characters of Theophrastus.* London: Macmillan.

Jefferson, J. W. (1989). Lithium: A therapeutic magic wand. *Journal of Clinical Psychiatry, 50*, 81–86.

Jefferson, J. W. (1990). Lithium: The present and the future. *Journal of Clinical Psychiatry, 51*, 17–19.

Jemmott, J. B., Helman, C., McClelland, D. C., Locke, S. C., Kraus, L., Williams, R. M., Valeri, C. R., & Jemmott, J. B. (1990). Motivational syndromes associated with natural killer cell activity. *Journal of Behavioral Medicine, 13*, 53–73.

Jendrek, M. P. (1992). Students' reactions to academic dishonesty. *Journal of College Student Development, 33*, 260–273.

Jenkins, I. H., & Frackowiak, R. S. J. (1993). Functional studies of the human cerebellum with positron emission tomography. *Revue Neurologique, 149*, 647–653.

Jenkins, N., & Cheshire, J. (1990). Gender issues in the GCSE oral English examination: Part 1. *Language and Education, 4*, 261–292.

Jensen, A. B. (1991). Psychosocial factors in breast cancer and their possible impact upon prognosis. *Cancer Treatment Reviews, 18*, 191–210.

Jensen, A. R. (1969). How much can we boost IQ and scholastic achievement? *Harvard Educational Review, 39*, 1–123.

Jerison, H. J. (1973). *Evolution of the brain and intelligence.* New York: Academic Press.

Jiranek, D. (1993). Use of hypnosis in pain management and post-traumatic stress disorder. *Australian Journal of Clinical and Experimental Hypnosis, 21*, 75–84.

John, O. P., Goldberg, L. R., & Angleitner, A. (1984). Better than the alphabet: Taxonomies of personality-descriptive terms in English, Dutch, and German. In H. J. C. Bonarius, G. L. M. van Heck, & N. G. Smid (Eds.), *Personality psychology in Europe.* Lisse, Switzerland: Swets & Zeitlinger.

Johns, G. (1994). Absenteeism estimates by employees and managers: Divergent perspectives and self-serving perceptions. *Journal of Applied Psychology, 79*, 229–239.

Johnson, G. R., Ratwik, S. H., & Sawyer, T. J. (1987). The evocative significance of kin terms in patriotic speech. In V. Reynolds, V. Falger, & I. Vine (Eds.), *The sociobiology of ethnocentrism: Evolutionary dimensions of xenophobia, discrimination, racism, and nationalism.* Athens: University of Georgia Press.

Johnson, J., Fabian, V., & Pascual-Leone, J. (1989). Quantitative hardware stages that constrain language development. *Human Development, 32*, 245–271.

Johnson, J., & Newport, E. L. (1991). Critical period effects on universal properties of language: The status of subjacency in the acquisition of a second language. *Cognition, 39*, 215–258.

Johnson, M. A., Dziurawiec, S., Ellis, H., & Morton, J. (1991). Newborns' preferential tracking of face-like stimuli and its subsequent decline. *Cognition, 4*, 1–19.

Johnson, P., Wilkinson, W. K., & McNeil, L. (1995). The impact of parental divorce on the attainment of the developmental tasks of young adulthood. *Contemporary Family Therapy: An International Journal, 17*, 249–264.

Johnson, R. C., Danko, G. P., Darvill, T. J., Bochner, S., Bowers, J. K., Huang, Y.-H., Park, J. Y., Pecjak, V., Rahim, A. R., & Pennington, D. (1989). Cross-cultural assessment of altruism and its correlates. *Personality and Individual Differences, 10*, 855–868.

Johnston, D. W. (1989). Prevention of cardiovascular disease by psychological methods. *British Journal of Psychiatry, 154*, 183–194.

Johnston, W. A., & Dark, V. J. (1986). Selective attention. *Annual Review of Psychology, 37*, 43–75.

Jones, E. E. (1990). *Interpersonal perception.* New York: Freeman.

Jones, E. E., & Davis, K. E. (1965). A theory of correspondent inferences: From acts to dispositions. In L. Berkowitz (Ed.), *Advances in experimental and social psychology* (Vol. 2). New York: Academic Press.

Jones, E. E., & Nisbett, R. E. (1972). The actor and observer: Divergent perceptions of the causes of behavior. In E. E. Jones, D. E. Kanouse, H. H. Kelley, R. E. Nisbett, S. Valins, & B. Weiner (Eds.), *Attribution: Perceiving the causes of behavior.* Morristown, NJ: General Learning Press.

Jones, S. R. (1992). Was there a Hawthorne effect? *American Journal of Sociology, 98*, 451–468.

Jordan, T. G., Grallo, R., Deutsch, M., & Deutsch, C. P. (1985). Long-term effects of enrichment: A 20-year perspective on persistence and change. *American Journal of Community Psychology, 13*, 393–414.

Joseph, R. (1992). The limbic system: Emotion, laterality, and unconscious mind. *Psychoanalytic Review, 79*, 405–456.

Judd, L. L. (1990). The decade of the brain: Prospects and challenges. *Neuropsychopharmacology, 3*, 309–310.

Judge, T. A., & Bretz, R. D. (1992). Effects of work values on job choice decisions. *Journal of Applied Psychology, 77*, 261–277.

Jung, C. G. (1907). The psychology of dementia praecox. *Collected works* (Vol. 3). New York: Pantheon.

Juraska, J. M. (1991). Sex differences in "cognitive" regions of the rat brain. *Psychoneuroendocrinology, 16*, 105–119.

Justice, A. (1985). Review of the effects of stress on cancer in laboratory animals: Importance of time of stress application and types of tumor. *Psychological Bulletin, 98*, 108–138.

Kaas, J. H. (1987). The organization of neocortex in mammals: Implications for theories of brain function. *Annual Review of Psychology, 38*, 129–151.

Kabat-Zinn, J., Massion, A. O., Kristekker, J., & Peterson, L. G. (1992). Effectiveness of a meditation-based stress reduction program in the treatment of anxiety disorders. *American Journal of Psychiatry, 149*, 936–943.

Kablaoui, B. N., & Pautler, A. J. (1991). The effects of part-time work experience on high school students. *Journal of Career Development, 17*, 195–211.

Kachele, H. (1992). Die Persönlichkeit des Psychotherapeuten und ihr Beitrag zum Behandlungsprozess. *Zeitschrift für Psychosomatische Medizin und Psychoanalyse, 38*, 227–239.

Kagan, J., Reznick, J. S., & Gibbons, J. (1989). Inhibited and uninhibited types of children. *Child Development, 60*, 838–845.

Kagehiro, D. K., & Laufer, W. S. (Eds.). (1992). *Handbook of psychology and law.* New York: Springer-Verlag.

Kagle, J. D., & Kopels, S. (1994). Confidentiality after Tarasoff. *Health and Social Work, 19*, 217–222.

Kahn, D., & Hobson, J. A. (1993). Self-organization theory of dreaming. *Dreaming: Journal of the Association for the Study of Dreams, 3,* 151–178.

Kahneman, D. (1973). *Attention and effort.* Englewood Cliffs, NJ: Prentice Hall.

Kahneman, D., Slovic, P., & Tversky, A. (Eds.). (1982). *Judgment under uncertainty: Heuristics and biases.* Cambridge, England: Cambridge University Press.

Kahneman, D., & Tversky, A. (1973). On the psychology of prediction. *Psychological Review, 80,* 237–251.

Kalechofsky, R. (1987). *The persistence of error: Essays in developmental epistemology.* Lanham, MD: University Press of America.

Kalfus, M. (1994). Phallic women and macho men: Hollywood, "The Dread of Woman," and Hillary Clinton. *Journal of Psychohistory, 21,* 287–300.

Kalinowsky, L. B. (1980). Convulsive therapies. In H. I. Kaplan, A. M. Freedman, & B. J. Sadock (Eds.), *Comprehensive textbook of psychiatry* (Vol. 3, 3rd ed.). Baltimore: Williams & Wilkins.

Kalven, H., & Zeisel, H. (1966). *The American jury.* Boston: Little, Brown.

Kambon, K. K., & Hopkins, R. (1993). An African-centered analysis of Penn et al.'s critique of the own-race preference assumption underlying Africentric models of personality. *Journal of Black Psychology, 19,* 342–349.

Kamin, L. J. (1969). Predictability, surprise, attention, and conditioning. In B. A. Campbell & R. M. Church (Eds.), *Punishment and aversive behavior.* New York: Appleton-Century-Crofts.

Kamin, L. J. (1974). *The science and politics of IQ.* Potomac, MD: Erlbaum.

Kandel, D. B. (1991). The social demography of drug use. *Milbank Quarterly, 69,* 365–414.

Kandel, E. R. (1981). Visual systems III: Physiology of the central visual pathways. In E. R. Kandel & J. H. Schwartz (Eds.), *Principles of neural science.* New York: Elsevier.

Kandel, E. R., Schwartz, J. H., & Jessell, T. M. (1991). *Principles of neural science* (3rd ed.). New York: Elsevier.

Kanner, A. D., Coyne, J. C., Schaefer, C., & Lazarus, R. S. (1981). Comparison of two modes of stress measurement: Daily hassles and uplifts versus major life events. *Journal of Behavioral Medicine, 4,* 1–39.

Kaplan, G. A., & Reynolds, P. (1988). Depression and cancer mortality and morbidity: Prospective evidence from the Alameda County Study. *Journal of Behavioral Medicine, 11,* 1–13.

Kaplan, M. (1983a). A woman's view of DSM-III. *American Psychologist, 38,* 786–792.

Kaplan, M. (1983b). The issue of sex bias in DSM-III: Comments on the articles by Spitzer, Williams, and Kass. *American Psychologist, 38,* 802–803.

Kaplan, R. M., Anderson, J. P., & Wingard, D. L. (1991). Gender differences in health-related quality of life. *Health Psychology, 10,* 86–93.

Kaplan, S., & Kaplan, R. (1982). *Cognition and environment: Functioning in an uncertain world.* New York: Praeger.

Karagiannis, D. (Ed.) (1994). *Database and expert systems applications.* Berlin: Springer-Verlag.

Karau, S. J., & Williams, K. D. (1993). Social loafing: A meta-analytic review and theoretical integration. *Journal of Personality and Social Psychology, 65,* 681–706.

Karbon, M., Fabes, R. A., Carlo, G., & Martin, C. L. (1992). Preschoolers' beliefs about sex and age differences in emotionality. *Sex Roles, 27,* 377–390.

Karney, B. R., & Bradbury, T. N. (1995). The longitudinal course of marital quality and stability: A review of theory, method, and research. *Psychological Bulletin, 118,* 3–34.

Karni, A., Tanne, D., Rubenstein, B. S., Askenasy, J. J., & Sagi, D. (1994). Dependence on REM sleep of overnight improvement of a perceptual skill. *Science, 265,* 679–682.

Kartsounis, L. D., & Warrington, E. K. (1991). Failure of object recognition due to a breakdown of figure-ground discrimination in a patient with normal acuity. *Neuropsychologia, 29,* 969–980.

Kasper, S. (1993). Neue Erfahrungen mit der Lichttherapie: Saisonal abhängige Depressionen (SAD) und weitere Indikationsgebiete. *Schweizer Archiv für Neurologie und Psychiatrie, 144,* 539–560.

Katchadourian, H. A. (1985). *Fundamentals of human sexuality* (4th ed.). New York: Holt, Rinehart & Winston.

Katz, J. N. (1993). The assessment and management of low back pain: A critical review. *Arthritis Care and Research, 6,* 104–114.

Katz, P. A., & Walsh, P. V. (1991). Modification of children's gender-stereotyped behavior. *Child Development, 62,* 338–351.

Katz, R. J. (1991). Neurobiology of obsessive compulsive disorder: A serotonergic basis of Freudian repression. *Neuroscience and Biobehavioral Reviews, 15,* 375–381.

Katzell, R. A., & Austin, J. T. (1992). From then to now: The development of industrial-organizational psychology in the United States. *Journal of Applied Psychology, 77,* 803–835.

Kaye, K., & Marcus, J. (1978). Imitation over a series of trials without feedback: Age six months. *Infant Behavior and Development, 1,* 141–155.

Kayser, V., & Guilbaud, G. (1991). Physiological relevance and time course of a tonic endogenous opioid modulation of nociceptive messages, based on the effects of naloxone in a rat model of localized hyperalgesic inflammation. *Brain Research, 567,* 197–203.

Kazarian, S. S. (1992). The measurement of expressed emotion: A review. *Canadian Journal of Psychiatry, 37,* 51–56.

Kazdin, A. E. (1994). Methodology, design, and evaluation in psychotherapy research. In A. E. Bergin & S. L. Garfield (Eds.), *Handbook of psychotherapy and behavior change* (4th ed.). New York: Wiley.

Kearney-Cooke, A., & Striegel-Moore, R. H. (1994). Treatment of childhood sexual abuse in anorexia and bulimia nervosa: A feminist psychodynamic approach. *International Journal of Eating Disorders, 15,* 305–319.

Keating, D. P. (1990). Charting pathways to the development of expertise. *Educational Psychologist, 25,* 243–267.

Keesey, R. E., & Powley, T. L. (1986). The regulation of body weight. *Annual Review of Psychology, 37,* 109–133.

Keiser, R. E., & Prather, E. N. (1990). What is the TAT? A review of ten years of research. *Journal of Personality Assessment, 55,* 800–803.

Keith, T. Z., & Benson, M. J. (1992). Effects of manipulable influences on high school grades across five ethnic groups. *Journal of Educational Research, 86,* 85–93.

Kelley, H. H. (1973). The process of causal attribution. *American Psychologist, 28,* 107–128.

Kelley, H. H. (1992). Common-sense psychology and scientific psychology. *Annual Review of Psychology, 43,* 1–23.

Kelley, H. H., & Thibaut, J. W. (1978). *Interpersonal relations: A theory of interdependence.* New York: Wiley.

Kellner, R. (1986). *Somatization and hypochondriasis.* New York: Praeger.

Kellner, R. (1990). Somatization: Theories and research. *Journal of Nervous and Mental Disease, 178,* 150–160.

Kelly, G. A. (1955). *The psychology of personal constructs.* New York: Norton.

Kelly, J. B. (1993). Current research on children's postdivorce adjustment: No simple answers. *Family and Conciliation Courts Review, 31,* 29–49.

Kelly, J. R., & Kelly, J. R. (1994). Multiple dimensions of meaning in the domains of work, family, and leisure. *Journal of Leisure Research, 26,* 250–274.

Kelly, S. F. (1993). The use of music as a hypnotic suggestion. *American Journal of Clinical Hypnosis, 36,* 83–90.

Kemp, S. (1990). *Medieval psychology.* New York: Greenwood.

Kendall, P. C., & Turk, D. C. (1984). Cognitive-behavioral strategies and health enhancement. In J. D. Matarazzo, S. M. Weiss, J. A. Herd, N. E. Miller, & S. M. Weiss (Eds.), *Behavioral health: A handbook of health enhancement and disease prevention.* New York: Wiley.

Kendall, P. C., Williams, L., Pechacek, T. F., Graham, L. E., Shisslak, C., & Herzoff, N. (1979). Cognitive-behavioral and patient education interventions in cardiac catheterization procedures: The Palo Alto medical psychology project. *Journal of Consulting and Clinical Psychology, 47,* 49–58.

Kennedy, G. (1984). *Invitation to statistics.* Oxford: Basil Blackwell.

Kenny, D. A., & Zaccaro, S. J. (1983). An estimate of variance due to traits in leadership. *Journal of Applied Psychology, 68,* 678–685.

Kenrick, D. T., Neuberg, S. L., Zierk, K. L., & Krones, J. M. (1994). Evolution and social cognition: Contrast effects as a function of sex, dominance, and physical attractiveness. *Personality and Social Psychology Bulletin, 20,* 210–217.

Kenrick, D. T., & Stringfield, D. O. (1980). Personality traits and the eye of the beholder: Crossing some traditional philosophical boundaries in the search for personality consistency in all of the people. *Psychological Review, 87,* 88–104.

Kenshalo, D. R. (Ed.). (1968). *The skin senses.* Springfield, IL: Thomas.

Kerr, S., & Jowett, S. (1994). Sleep problems in pre-school children: A review of the literature. *Child Care, Health, and Development, 20,* 379–391.

Kessler, R. C., McGonagle, K. A., Zhao, S., Nelson, C. B., Hughes, M., Eshleman, S., Wittchen, H.-U., & Kendler, K. S. (1994). Lifetime and 12-month prevalence of DSM-III-R psychiatric diagnoses in the United States. *Archives of General Psychiatry, 51,* 8–19.

Kety, S. S. (1974). From rationalization to reason. *American Journal of Psychiatry, 131,* 957–963.

Key, W. B. (1973). *Subliminal seduction*. Englewood Cliffs, NJ: Prentice Hall.

Kiecolt-Glaser, J. K., Fisher, L. D., Ogrocki, P., Stout, J. C., Speicher, C. E., & Glaser, R. (1987). Marital quality, marital disruption, and immune function. *Psychosomatic Medicine, 49*, 13–34.

Kiecolt-Glaser, J. K., Garner, W., Speicher, C. E., Penn, G. M., Holliday, J. E., & Glaser, R. (1984). Psychosocial modifiers of immunocompetence in medical students. *Psychosomatic Medicine, 46*, 7–14.

Kiecolt-Glaser, J. K., & Glaser, R. (1992). Psychoneuroimmunology: Can psychological interventions modulate immunity? *Journal of Consulting and Clinical Psychology, 60*, 569–575.

Kiecolt-Glaser, J. K., Glaser, R., Strain, E. C., Stout, J. C., Tarr, K. L., Holliday, J. E., & Speicher, C. E. (1986). Modulation of cellular immunity in medical students. *Journal of Behavioral Medicine, 9*, 5–21.

Kiecolt-Glaser, J. K., Kennedy, S., Malkoff, S., Fisher, L., Speicher, C. E., & Glaser, R. (1988). Marital discord and immunity in males. *Psychosomatic Medicine, 50*, 213–229.

Kihlstrom, J. F. (1985). Hypnosis. *Annual Review of Psychology, 36*, 385–418.

Kihlstrom, J. F. (1990). The psychological unconscious. In L. A. Pervin (Ed.), *Handbook of personality: Theory and research*. New York: Guilford.

Kihlstrom, J. F., & Harackiewicz, J. M. (1990). An evolutionary milestone in the psychology of personality. *Psychological Inquiry, 1*, 86–92.

Kimble, G. A. (1984). Psychology's two cultures. *American Psychologist, 39*, 833–839.

Kinchla, R. A. (1992). Attention. *Annual Review of Psychology, 43*, 711–742.

King, B. H., & Liston, E. H. (1990). Proposals for the mechanism of action of convulsive therapy: A synthesis. *Biological Psychiatry, 27*, 76–94.

King, B. M., & Lococo, E. C. (1990). Effects of sexually explicit textbook drawings on enrollment and family communication. *Journal of Sex Education and Therapy, 16*, 38–53.

King, N. J., Hamilton, D. I., & Murphy, G. C. (1983). The prevention of children's maladaptive fears. *Child and Family Behavior Therapy, 5*, 43–57.

Kinsey, A. C., Pomeroy, W. D., & Martin, C. E. (1948). *Sexual behavior in the human male*. Philadelphia: Saunders.

Kinsey, A. C., Pomeroy, W. D., Martin, C. E., & Gebhard, P. H. (1953). *Sexual behavior in the human female*. Philadelphia: Saunders.

Kintsch, W. (1974). *The representation of meaning in memory*. Hillsdale, NJ: Erlbaum.

Kipper, D. A. (1991). The dynamics of role satisfaction: A theoretical model. *Journal of Group Psychotherapy, Psychodrama, and Sociometry, 44*, 71–86.

Kirchler, E. (1989). Zufriedenheit unterm gemeinsamen Dach: Ein Überblick uber sozialpsychologische Untersuchungen zur Ehequalität. *Gruppendynamik, 20*, 75–94.

Kirk-Smith, M., Booth, D. A., Carroll, D., & Davies, P. (1978). Human social attitudes affected by androstenol. *Research Communications in Psychology, Psychiatry, and Behavior, 3*, 379–384.

Kirmayer, L. J., & Robbins, J. M. (1993). Cognitive and social correlates of the Toronto Alexithymia Scale. *Psychosomatics, 34*, 41–52.

Kirsch, N. L., Levine, S. P., Fallon-Krueger, M., & Jaros, L. A. (1987). Focus on clinical research: The microcomputer as an "orthotic" device for patients with cognitive deficits. *Journal of Head Trauma Rehabilitation, 2*, 77–86.

Kishton, J. M. (1994). Contemporary Eriksonian theory: A psychobiographical illustration. *Gerontology and Geriatrics Education, 14*, 81–91.

Kitamura, A. (1982). A comparative study of suicide in children and adolescents: West Germany and Japan. *Japanese Journal of Child and Adolescent Psychiatry, 23*, 124–137.

Kitano, H. H. L., Yeung, W., Chai, L., & Hatanaka, H. (1984). Asian-American interracial marriage. *Journal of Marriage and the Family, 46*, 179–190.

Kitchin, R. M. (1994). Cognitive maps: What are they and why study them? *Journal of Environmental Psychology, 14*, 1–19.

Klag, M. J., Whelton, P. K., Coresh, J., Grim, C. E., & Kuller, L. H. (1991). The association of skin color with blood pressure in U.S. blacks with low socioeconomic status. *JAMA, 265*, 599–602.

Klahr, D., Chase, W. G., & Lovelace, E. A. (1983). Structure and process in alphabetic retrieval. *Journal of Experimental Psychology: Learning, Memory, and Cognition, 9*, 462–477.

Kleinfeld, J., & Nelson, P. (1991). Adapting instruction to Native Americans' learning styles: An iconoclastic view. *Journal of Cross-Cultural Psychology, 22*, 273–282.

Kleinman, A., & Good, B. (Eds.) (1985). *Culture and depression*. Berkeley: University of California Press.

Kleinmuntz, B. (1990). Why we still use our heads instead of formulas: Toward an integrative approach. *Psychological Bulletin, 107*, 296–310.

Klerman, G. L. (1987). Clinical epidemiology of suicide. *Journal of Clinical Psychiatry, 48*, 33–38.

Klerman, G. L., Weissman, M. M., Markowitz, J. C., Glick, I., Wilner, P. J., Mason, B., & Shear, M. K. (1994). Medication and psychotherapy. In A. E. Bergin & S. L. Garfield (Eds.), *Handbook of psychotherapy and behavior change* (4th ed.). New York: Wiley.

Klink, M., & Klink, W. (1990). The influence of father caretaker speech on early language development: A case study. *Early Child Development and Care, 62*, 7–22.

Klopf, A. H., Morgan, J. S., & Weaver, S. E. (1993). A hierarchical network of control systems that learn: Modeling nervous system function during classical and instrumental conditioning. *Adaptive Behavior, 1*, 263–319.

Kluft, R. P. (1984). Treatment of multiple personality disorder: A study of 33 cases. *Psychiatric Clinics of North America, 7*, 9–29.

Kluft, R. P. (1988). The postunification treatment of multiple personality disorder: First findings. *American Journal of Psychotherapy, 42*, 212–228.

Knapp, M. J., Knopman, D. S., Soloman, P. R., & Pendlebury, W. H. (1994). A 30-week randomized controlled trial of high-dose tacrine in patients with Alzheimer's disease. *JAMA, 271*, 985–991.

Knapp, T. J. (1974). The Premack Principle in human experimental and applied settings. *Behaviour Research and Therapy, 14*, 133–147.

Knobel, M. (1990). Significance and importance of the psychotherapist's personality and experience. *Psychotherapy and Psychosomatics, 53*, 58–63.

Kobasa, S. C. (1979). Stressful life events, personality, and health: An inquiry into hardiness. *Journal of Personality and Social Psychology, 37*, 1–11.

Kobasa, S. C. (1982). Commitment and coping in stress resistance among lawyers. *Journal of Personality and Social Psychology, 42*, 707–717.

Kobasa, S. C., Maddi, S. R., & Courington, S. (1981). Personality and constitution as mediators in the stress-illness relationship. *Journal of Health and Social Behavior, 22*, 368–378.

Kobasa, S. C., Maddi, S. R., & Kahn, S. (1982). Hardiness and health: A prospective study. *Journal of Personality and Social Psychology, 42*, 168–177.

Koelega, H. S. (1994). Sex differences in olfactory sensitivity and the problem of the generality of smell acuity. *Perceptual and Motor Skills, 78*, 203–213.

Koenderink, J. J. (1993). What is a "feature"? *Journal of Intelligent Systems, 3*, 49–82.

Kohlberg, L. (1981). *Essays on moral development: Vol. 1. The philosophy of moral development*. New York: Harper & Row.

Kohlberg, L. (1984). *Essays on moral development: Vol. 2. The nature and validity of moral stages*. San Francisco: Harper & Row.

Kohlberg, L., & Gilligan, C. (1971). The adolescent as a philosopher: The discovery of the self in a postconventional world. *Daedalus, 100*, 1051–1086.

Kohler, W. (1924). *The mentality of apes*. London: Kegan Paul.

Kolb, L. C. (1982). Attachment behavior and pain complaints. *Psychosomatics, 23*, 413–425.

Kono, T. (1982). Japanese management philosophy: Can it be exported? *Long Range Planning, 15*(3), 90–102.

Koob, G. E., & Bloom, F. E. (1988). Cellular and molecular mechanisms of drug dependence. *Science, 242*, 715–723.

Korchin, S. J., & Schuldberg, D. (1981). The future of clinical assessment. *American Psychologist, 36*, 1147–1158.

Kornhaber, M., Krechevsky, M., & Gardner, H. (1990). Engaging intelligence. *Educational Psychologist, 25*, 177–199.

Korzenik, D. (1992). Gifted child artists. *Creativity Research Journal, 5*, 313–319.

Korzh, N. N., & Safuanova, O. V. (1993). The dynamics of a perceptual image and individual personal characteristics of the reflection of a colored environment. *Journal of Russian and East European Psychology, 31*, 22–36.

Koski, K. J., & Marttila, R. J. (1990). Transient global amnesia: Incidence in an urban population. *Acta Neurologica Scandinavica, 81*, 358–360.

Koss, M. P., Tromp, S., & Tharan, M. (1995). Traumatic memories: Empirical foundations, forensic, and clinical implications. *Clinical Psychology: Science and Practice, 2*, 111–132.

Kosslyn, S. M. (1980). *Image and mind*. Cambridge, MA: Harvard University Press.

Kosslyn, S. M., Alpert, N. M., Thompson, W. L., Maljkovic, V., Weise, S. B., Chabris, C. F., Hamilton, S. E., Rauch, S. L., & Buonanno, F. S. (1993). Visual mental imagery activates topographically organized visual cortex: PET investigations. *Journal of Cognitive Neuroscience, 5*, 263–287.

Koyanagi, T., Horimoto, N., Maeda, H., Kukita, J., Minami, T., Ueda, K., & Nakano, H. (1993). Abnormal behavioral patterns in the human fetus at term: Correlation with lesion sites in the central nervous system after birth. *Journal of Child Neurology, 8,* 19–26.

Kozel, N. J. (1990). Epidemiology of drug abuse in the United States: A summary of methods and findings. *Bulletin of the Pan American Health Organization, 24,* 53–62.

Kramer, A. F., Larish, J. F., & Strayer, D. L. (1995). Training for attentional control in dual task settings: A comparison of young and old adults. *Journal of Experimental Psychology: Applied, 1,* 50–76.

Kramer, D. A., & Woodruff, D. S. (1984). Categorization and metaphoric processing in young and older adults. *Research on Aging, 6,* 271–286.

Krampen, G., Effertz, B., Jostock, U., & Muller, B. (1990). Gender differences in personality: Biological and/or psychological? *European Journal of Personality, 4,* 303–317.

Krass, J., Kinoshita, S., & McConkey, K. M. (1989). Hypnotic memory and confident reporting. *Applied Cognitive Psychology, 3,* 35–51.

Krausz, E. O. (1994). Freud's devaluation of women. *Individual Psychology: Journal of Adlerian Theory, Research, and Practice, 50,* 298–313.

Krauz, V. A., Drosdov, A. L., Malyshev, S. L., & Tverdokhleb, T. V. (1988). The role of different neurotransmitter systems in control of engram production in rats. *Zhurnal Vysshel Nervnoi Deyaiel'nosti, 38,* 1107–1112.

Krebs, D. L., & Van Hesteren, F. (1994). The development of altruism: Toward an integrative model. *Developmental Review, 14,* 103–158.

Kremer, J. M. D. (1994). *Psychology in sport.* London: Taylor & Francis.

Kress, F. (1979). Evaluations of dangerousness. *Schizophrenia Bulletin, 5,* 211–217.

Kreuz, L. E., & Rose, R. M. (1972). Assessment of aggressive behavior and plasma testosterone in a young criminal population. *Psychosomatic Medicine, 34,* 321–332.

Krieger, N. (1990). Racial and gender discrimination: Risk factors for high blood pressure. *Social Science and Medicine, 30,* 1273–1281.

Kripke, D. F., Simons, R. N., Garfinkel, L., & Hammond, E. C. (1979). Short and long sleep and sleeping pills: Is increased mortality associated? *Archives of General Psychiatry, 36,* 103–116.

Krippner, S., & Hughes, W. (1970). Dreams and human potential. *Journal of Humanistic Psychology, 10,* 1–20.

Krol, N. P., de Bruyn, E. E., & Van den Bercken, J. H. (1992). Diagnostic classification by experts and novices. *Acta Psychologica, 81,* 23–37.

Krosnick, J. A., Betz, A. L., Jussim, L. J., & Lynn, A. R. (1992). Subliminal conditioning of attitudes. *Personality and Social Psychology Bulletin, 18,* 152–162.

Krull, F., & Schifferdecker, M. (1990). Inpatient treatment of conversion disorder: A clinical investigation of outcome. *Psychotherapy and Psychosomatics, 53,* 161–165.

Kübler-Ross, E. (1969). *On death and dying.* New York: Macmillan.

Kudler, H. (1989). The tension between psychoanalysis and neuroscience: A perspective on dream theory in psychiatry. *Psychoanalysis and Contemporary Thought, 12,* 599–617.

Kuhl, P. K., Williams, K. A., Lacerda, F., Stevens, K. N., & Lindblom, B. (1992). Linguistic experience alters phonetic perception in infants by 6 months of age. *Science, 255,* 606–608.

Kulik, J. A., Bangert-Drowns, R. L., & Kulik, C. C. (1984). Effectiveness of coaching for aptitude tests. *Psychological Bulletin, 95,* 179–188.

Kulik, J. A., & Mahler, H. I. (1989). Stress and affiliation in a hospital setting: Preoperative roommate preferences. *Personality and Social Psychology Bulletin, 15,* 183–193.

Kupfersmid, J. (1993). Freud's rationale for abandoning the seduction theory. *Psychoanalytic Psychology, 10,* 275–290.

Kurian, G., & Santhakumari, K. (1990). Consciousness and the left cerebral hemisphere. *Journal of Indian Psychology, 8,* 33–36.

Kurosawa, K. (1993). Self-monitoring and conformity revisited: A case for a four-factor measurement model. *Japanese Psychological Research, 35,* 19–31.

Kurtzburg, R. L., Safar, H., & Cavior, N. (1968). Surgical and social rehabilitation of adult offenders. *Proceedings of the 76th Annual Convention of the American Psychological Association, 3,* 649–650.

Kusyszyn, I. (1990). Existence, effectance, esteem: From gambling to a new theory of human motivation. *International Journal of the Addictions, 25,* 159–177.

La Vecchia, C., Lucchini, F., & Levi, F. (1994). Worldwide trends in suicide mortality, 1955–1989. *Acta Psychiatrica Scandinavica, 90,* 53–64.

Lackner, J. R. (1993). Orientation and movement in unusual force environments. *Psychological Science, 4,* 134–142.

Lackner, J. R., & DiZio, P. (1993). Multisensory, cognitive, and motor influences on human spatial orientation in weightlessness. *Journal of Vestibular Research, 3,* 361–372.

Laing, D. G., Prescott, J., Bell, G. A., Gillmore, R., James, C., Best, D. J., Allen, S., Yoshida, M., & Yarnazaki, K. (1993). A cross-cultural study of taste discrimination with Australians and Japanese. *Chemical Senses, 18,* 161–168.

Laing, R. D. (1965). *The divided self.* Baltimore: Penguin.

Laing, R. D. (1967). *The politics of experience.* New York: Pantheon.

Lakoff, R. (1975). *Language and woman's place.* New York: Harper & Row.

Lakosina, N. D., Kostiunina, Z. G., Kal'ke, A. R., & Shashkova, N. G. (1987). Pathomorphosis of hysterical neurosis. *Zhurnal Nevropatologi i Psiyhiatrii, 87,* 1684–1688.

Lambert, M. J., & Bergin, A. E. (1994). The effectiveness of psychotherapy. In A. E. Bergin & S. L. Garfield (Eds.), *Handbook of psychotherapy and behavior change* (4th ed.). New York: Wiley.

Lamminpaa, A. (1995). Alcohol intoxication in childhood and adolescence. *Alcohol and Alcoholism, 30,* 5–12.

Land, M. F., & Fernald, R. D. (1992). The evolution of eyes. *Annual Review of Neuroscience, 15,* 1–29.

Landrine, H. (1989). The politics of personality disorder. *Psychology of Women Quarterly, 13,* 325–339.

Landy, F. J. (1989). *Psychology of work behavior* (4th ed.). Pacific Grove, CA: Brooks/Cole.

Landy, F. J., & Farr, J. L. (1980). Performance rating. *Psychological Bulletin, 87,* 72–107.

Langer, E. J. (1989). *Mindfulness.* Reading, MA: Addison-Wesley.

Langer, E. J., Janis, I. L., & Wolfer, J. (1975). Reduction of psychological stress in surgical patients. *Journal of Experimental Social Psychology, 11,* 155–165.

Langlois, J. H., Ritter, J. M., Casey, R. J., & Sawin, D. B. (1995). Infant attractiveness predicts maternal behaviors and attitudes. *Developmental Psychology, 31,* 464–473.

Langlois, J. H., & Roggman, L. A. (1990). Attractive faces are only average. *Psychological Science, 1,* 115–121.

LaPiere, R. T. (1934). Attitudes and actions. *Social Forces, 13,* 230–237.

Larivee, S., Longeot, F., & Normandeau, S. (1989). Apprentissage des opérations formelles: Une récension des recherches. *Année Psychologique, 89,* 553–584.

Larsen, K. S. (1990). The Asch conformity experiment: Replication and transhistorical comparisons. *Journal of Social Behavior and Personality, 5,* 163–168.

Larsen, R. J., Kasimatis, M., & Frey, K. (1992). Facilitating the furrowed brow: An unobtrusive test of the facial feedback hypothesis applied to unpleasant affect. *Cognition and Emotion, 6,* 321–338.

Larsen, R. J., & Sinnett, L. M. (1991). Meta-analysis of experimental manipulations: Some factors affecting the Velten mood induction procedure. *Personality and Social Psychology Bulletin, 17,* 323–334.

Larson, R. (1989). Beeping children and adolescents: A method for studying time use and daily experience. *Journal of Youth and Adolescence, 18,* 511–530.

Lashley, K. S. (1929). *Brain mechanisms and intelligence.* Chicago: University of Chicago Press.

Lashley, K. S. (1950). In search of the engram. *Symposium of the Society for Experimental Biology, 4,* 454–482.

Latané, B., Williams, K., & Harkins, S. (1979). Many hands make light the work: The causes and consequences of social loafing. *Journal of Personality and Social Psychology, 37,* 822–832.

Lattal, K. A. (1992). B. F. Skinner and psychology: Introduction to the special issue. *American Psychologist, 47,* 1269–1272.

Lau, R. K., Jenkins, P., Caun, K., Forster, S. M., Weber, J. N., McManus, T. J., Harris, J. R., Jeffries, D. J., & Pinching, A. J. (1992). Trends in sexual behaviour in a cohort of homosexual men: A 7 year prospective study. *International Journal of STD and AIDS, 3,* 267–272.

Laub, J. H., & Lauritsen, J. L. (1993). Violent criminal behavior over the life course: A review of the longitudinal and comparative research. *Violence and Victims, 8,* 235–252.

Laurence, J. R., & Perry, C. (1983). Hypnotically created memory among highly hypnotizable subjects. *Science, 222,* 523–524.

Lautrey, J., & Chartier, D. (1987). Images mentales de transformations et opérations cognitives: Une revue critique des études développementales. *Année Psychologique, 87,* 581–602.

Lavie, N., & Tsal, Y. (1994). Perceptual load as a major determinant of the locus of selection in visual attention. *Perception and Psychophysics, 56,* 183–197.

Lawson, D. E. (1992). Need for safeguarding the field of intelligence testing. *Journal of Educational Psychology, 84,* 131–133. (Reprinted from *Journal of Educational Psychology, 1944, 35,* 240–247.)

Lazarus, R. S. (1966). *Psychological stress and the coping process.* New York: McGraw-Hill.

Lazarus, R. S. (1982). Thoughts on the relations between emotion and cognition. *American Psychologist, 37,* 1019–1024.

Lazarus, R. S. (1991). *Emotion and adaptation.* New York: Oxford University Press.

Lazarus, R. S., & Folkman, S. (1984). *Stress, appraisal, and coping.* New York: Springer.

Lazerson, J. (1992). Feminism and group psychotherapy: An ethical responsibility. *International Journal of Group Psychotherapy, 42,* 523–546.

Lea, D. R. (1992). Reflections on certain presuppositions which tend to limit dialogue between philosophies and psychologists. *Psychological Record, 42,* 75–86.

Leakey, R. E. (1979). Introduction. In C. Darwin, *The illustrated origin of species.* New York: Hill & Wang.

Leary, T. (1957). *Interpersonal diagnosis of personality.* New York: Ronald Press.

Leary, T. (1964). The religious experience: Its production and interpretation. *Psychedelic Review, 1,* 324–346.

Lebedeva, N. N., & Dobronravova, I. S. (1990). Organization of human EEG rhythms in special states of mind. *Zhurnal Vysshei Nervnoi Deyatel'nosti, 40,* 951–962.

Lebow, J. L., & Gurman, A. S. (1995). Research assessing couple and family therapy. *Annual Review of Psychology, 46,* 27–57.

Lee, J. A. (1988). Love-styles. In R. J. Sternberg & M. L. Barnes (Eds.), *Psychology of love.* New Haven, CT: Yale University Press.

Lee, L. A., & Heppner, P. P. (1991). The development and evaluation of a sexual harassment inventory. *Journal of Counseling and Development, 69,* 512–517.

Leff, J., & Vaughn, C. (1985). *Expressed emotion in families: Its significance for mental illness.* New York: Guilford.

Lehmann, H. E. (1980). Schizophrenia: Clinical features. In H. I. Kaplan, A. M. Freedman, & B. J. Sadock (Eds.), *Comprehensive textbook of psychiatry* (Vol. 2, 3rd ed.). Baltimore: Williams & Wilkins.

Lehrner, J. P. (1993). Gender differences in long-term odor recognition memory: Verbal versus sensory influences and the consistency of label use. *Chemical Senses, 18,* 17–26.

Lei, T. (1994). Being and becoming moral in a Chinese culture: Unique or universal? *Cross-Cultural Research: The Journal of Comparative Social Science, 28,* 58–91.

Leigh, R. J. (1994). Human vestibular cortex. *Annals of Neurology, 35,* 383–384.

Leippe, M. R., & Eisenstadt, D. (1994). Generalization of dissonance reduction: Decreasing prejudice through induced compliance. *Journal of Personality and Social Psychology, 67,* 395–413.

Leman, K. (1985). *The birth order book: Why you are the way you are.* New York: Dell.

Lemonick, M. D. (1994, September 12). The killers all around. *Time,* pp. 62–69.

Lemonick, M. D. (1995a, July 17). Glimpses of the mind. *Time,* pp. 44–52.

Lemonick, M. D. (1995b, May 22). Return to the hot zone. *Time,* pp. 62–63.

Lenneberg, E. H. (1967). *Biological foundations of language.* New York: Wiley.

Lepore, S. J., Evans, G. W., & Palsane, M. N. (1991). Social hassles and psychological health in the context of chronic crowding. *Journal of Health and Social Behavior, 32,* 357–367.

Lerner, R. M., & von Eye, A. (1992). Sociobiology and human development: Arguments and evidence. *Human Development, 35,* 12–33.

Lesgold, A. (1988). Problem solving. In R. J. Sternberg & E. E. Smith (Eds.), *The psychology of human thought.* Cambridge, England: Cambridge University Press.

Lester, D., & Arcuri, A. F. (1994). How did police officers view the Rodney King incident? *Perceptual and Motor Skills, 79,* 1382.

LeVay, S. (1991). A difference in hypothalamic structure between heterosexual and homosexual men. *Science, 253,* 1034–1037.

LeVay, S. (1993). *The sexual brain.* Cambridge, MA: MIT Press.

Levene, M. (1990). Female adolescent development: Reflections upon relational growth. *Melanie Klein and Object Relations, 8,* 31–42.

Levenson, J. L., & Bemis, C. (1991). The role of psychological factors in cancer onset and progression. *Psychosomatics, 32,* 124–132.

Levenson, R. W. (1992). Autonomic nervous system differences among emotions. *Psychological Science, 3,* 23–27.

Levenson, R. W., Carstensen, L. L., & Gottman, J. M. (1993). Long-term marriage: Age, gender, and satisfaction. *Psychology and Aging, 8,* 301–313.

Levenson, R. W., Ekman, P., Heider, K., & Friesen, W. V. (1992). Emotion and autonomic nervous system activity in the Minangkabau of West Sumatra. *Journal of Personality and Social Psychology, 62,* 972–988.

Levenson, R. W., & Gottman, J. M. (1983). Marital interaction: Physiological linkage and affective exchange. *Journal of Personality and Social Psychology, 45,* 587–597.

Levenson, R. W., & Gottman, J. M. (1985). Physiological and affective predictors of change in relationship satisfaction. *Journal of Personality and Social Psychology, 49,* 85–94.

Leventhal, H., & Tomarken, A. J. (1986). Emotion: Today's problems. *Annual Review of Psychology, 37,* 565–610.

Levine, M., Anderson, E., Ferretti, L., & Steinberg, K. (1993). Legal and ethical issues affecting clinical child psychology. *Advances in Clinical Child Psychology, 15,* 81–120.

Levit, D. B. (1991). Gender differences in ego defenses in adolescence: Sex roles as one way to understand the differences. *Journal of Personality and Social Psychology, 61,* 992–999.

Levy, J. (1976). Cerebral lateralization and spatial ability. *Behavior Genetics, 6,* 171–188.

Levy, J., & Heller, W. (1992). Gender differences in human neuropsychological function. In A. A. Gerall, H. Moltz, & I. L. Ward (Eds.), *Handbook of behavioral neurobiology: Sexual differentiation.* New York: Plenum.

Levy, S. M. (1985). *Behavior and cancer.* San Francisco: Jossey-Bass.

Levy, Y. (Ed.). (1994). *Other children, other languages: Issues in the theory of language acquisition.* Hillsdale, NJ: Erlbaum.

Lewin, K. (1951). *Field theory in social science: Selected theoretical papers.* New York: Harper.

Lewin, K., Lippett, R., & White, R. K. (1939). Patterns of aggressive behavior in experimentally created "social climates." *Journal of Social Psychology, 10,* 271–299.

Lewinsohn, P. M. (1974). A behavioral approach to depression. In R. J. Friedman & M. M. Katz (Eds.), *The psychology of depression: Contemporary theory and research.* Washington, DC: Winston-Wiley.

Lewinsohn, P. M., & Libet, J. (1972). Pleasant events, activity schedules, and depressions. *Journal of Abnormal Psychology, 79,* 291–295.

Lewinsohn, P. M., Mischel, W., Chaplin, W., & Barton, R. (1980). Social competence and depression: The role of illusory self-perceptions. *Journal of Abnormal Psychology, 89,* 203–212.

Lewis, C. A. (1993). Oral pessimism and depressive symptoms. *Journal of Psychology, 127,* 335–343.

Lewis, D. O., Lovely, R., Yeager, C., & Ferguson, G. (1988). Intrinsic and environmental characteristics of juvenile murders. *Journal of the American Academy of Child and Adolescent Psychiatry, 27,* 582–587.

Lewis, J. W. (1990). Premenstrual syndrome as a criminal defense. *Archives of Sexual Behavior, 19,* 425–441.

Lewis, R. C. (1989). The historical development of the concept of the archetype. *Quadrant, 22,* 41–53.

Lewis-Fernandez, R., & Kleinman, A. (1994). Culture, personality, and psychopathology. *Journal of Abnormal Psychology, 103,* 67–71.

Lezak, M. D. (1978). Living with the characterologically altered brain injured patient. *Journal of Clinical Psychiatry, 39,* 592–598.

Li, D., Wu, Z., Shao, D., & Liu, S. (1991). The relationship of sleep to learning and memory. *International Journal of Mental Health, 20,* 41–47.

Libet, J., & Lewinsohn, P. M. (1973). The concept of social skill with special reference to the behavior of depressed persons. *Journal of Consulting and Clinical Psychology, 40,* 304–312.

Liebowitz, M. R., Gorman, J. M., Fyer, A. J., Levitt, M., Dillon, D., Levy, G., Appleby, I. L., Anderson, S., Palij, M., Davies, S. O., & Klein, D. F. (1985). Lactate provocation of panic attacks: II. Biochemical and physiological findings. *Archives of General Psychiatry, 42,* 709–719.

Lifton, R. (1986). *The Nazi doctors.* New York: Basic Books.

Lim, T. K. (1994). Gender-related differences in intelligence: Application of confirmatory factor analysis. *Intelligence, 19,* 179–192.

Lin, E. H., & Peterson, C. (1990). Pessimistic explanatory style and response to illness. *Behaviour Research and Therapy, 28,* 243–248.

Lind, L. (1991). Thanatos: The drive without a name: The development of the concept of the death drive in Freud's writings. *Scandinavian Psychoanalytic Review, 14,* 60–80.

Lindsay, D. S. (1994). Contextualizing and clarifying criticisms of memory work. *Consciousness and Cognition: An International Journal, 3,* 426–437.

Lindstrom, K., & Hurrell, J. J. (1992). Coping with job stress by managers at different career stages in Finland and the United States. *Scandinavian Journal of Work, Environment, and Health, 18,* 14–17.

Linkins, R. W., & Comstock, G. W. (1990). Depressed mood and development of cancer. *American Journal of Epidemiology, 132,* 962–972.

Liotti, G., Ceccarelli, M., & Chouhy, A. (1993). Regole e rappresentazioni della relazione. Un confronto fra prospettive cognitivo-evoluzioniste e relazionali. *Terapia Familiare, 41,* 19–34.

Lipowski, Z. J. (1991). Delirium: How its concept has developed. *International Psychogeriatrics, 3,* 115–120.

Lipowski, Z. J. (1992). Update on delirium. *Psychiatric Clinics of North America, 15,* 335–346.

Lippa, R., & Donaldson, S. I. (1990). Self-monitoring and idiographic measures of behavioral variability across interpersonal relationships. *Journal of Personality, 58,* 465–479.

Lippmann, W. (1922). *Public opinion.* New York: Harcourt, Brace.

Lipsey, M. W., & Wilson, D. B. (1993). The efficacy of psychological, educational, and behavioral treatment: Confirmation from meta-analysis. *American Psychologist, 48,* 1181–1209.

Lister, L. (1991). Men and grief: A review of research. *Smith College Studies in Social Work, 61,* 220–235.

Littlewood, J. L., Cramer, D., Hoekstra, J., & Humphrey, G. B. (1991). Gender differences in parental coping following their child's death. *British Journal of Guidance and Counselling, 19,* 139–148.

Littlewood, R. (1990). From categories to contexts: A decade of the "new cross-cultural psychiatry." *British Journal of Psychiatry, 156,* 308–327.

Lloyd, A. T. (1990). Implications of an evolutionary metapsychology for clinical psychoanalysis. *Journal of the American Academy of Psychoanalysis, 18,* 286–306.

Lloyd, C. (1980). Life events and depressive disorder reviewed: I. Events as predisposing factors: II. Events as precipitation factors. *Archives of General Psychiatry, 37,* 529–548.

Locke, E. A. (1976). Job satisfaction and job performance: A theoretical analysis. *Organizational Behavior and Human Performance, 5,* 484–500.

Loehlin, J. C., Lindzey, G., & Spuhler, J. N. (1975). *Race differences in intelligence.* San Francisco: Freeman.

Loehlin, J. C., Willerman, L., & Horn, J. M. (1988). Human behavior genetics. *Annual Review of Psychology, 39,* 101–133.

Loftus, E. F. (1979). *Eyewitness testimony.* Cambridge, MA: Harvard University Press.

Loftus, E. F. (1991). Resolving legal questions with psychological data. *American Psychologist, 46,* 1046–1048.

Loftus, E. F. (1993). The reality of repressed memories. *American Psychologist, 48,* 518–537.

Loftus, E. F., Garry, M., Brown, S. W., & Rader, M. (1994). Near-natal memories, past-life memories, and other memory myths. *American Journal of Clinical Hypnosis, 36,* 176–179.

Loftus, E. F., & Ketcham, K. (1994). *The myth of repressed memory: False memories and allegations of sexual abuse.* New York: St. Martin's Press.

Loftus, E. F., & Loftus, G. R. (1980). On the permanence of stored information in the human brain. *American Psychologist, 35,* 409–420.

Logan, A. C., & Goetsch, V. L. (1993). Attention to external threat cues in anxiety states. *Clinical Psychology Review, 13,* 541–559.

Logan, G. D. (1980). Attention and automaticity in Stroop and primary tasks: Theory and data. *Cognitive Psychology, 12,* 523–553.

Logue, B. J. (1991). Women at risk: Predictors of financial stress for retired women workers. *Gerontologist, 31,* 657–665.

Lolas, F. (1989). Communication of emotional meaning, alexithymia, and somatoform disorders: A proposal for a diagnostic axis. *Psychotherapy and Psychosomatics, 52,* 214–219.

Long, M. A. (1993). As if day had rearranged into night: Suicidal tendencies in the poetry of Anne Sexton. *Literature and Psychology, 39,* 26–41.

Loomis, A. L., Harvey, E. N., & Hobart, G. A. (1937). Cerebral states during sleep as studied by human brain potentials. *Journal of Experimental Psychology, 21,* 127–144.

Lopez, S. R., Grover, K. P., Holland, D., Johnson, M. J., Kain, C. D., Kanel, K., Mellins, C. A., & Rhyne, M. C. (1989). Development of culturally sensitive psychotherapists. *Professional Psychology: Research and Practice, 20,* 369–376.

Lord, R. G., De Vader, C. L., & Alliger, G. M. (1986). A meta-analysis of the relation between personality traits and leadership perceptions: An application of validity generalization procedures. *Journal of Applied Psychology, 71,* 402–410.

Lorenz, K. (1937). The companion in the bird's world. *Auk, 54,* 245–273.

Lorenz, K. (1965). *Evolution and modification of behavior.* Chicago: University of Chicago Press.

Lorenz, K. (1966). *On aggression.* New York: Harcourt Brace Jovanovich.

Lovaas, O. I. (1977). *The autistic child: Language development through behavior modification.* New York: Halsted.

Lowenstein, M. K., & Field, T. (1993). Maternal depression effects on infants. *Analise Psicologica, 10,* 63–69.

Lu, Z.-L., Williamson, S. J., & Kaufman, L. (1992). Behavioral lifetime of human auditory sensory memory predicted by physiological measures. *Science, 258,* 1668–1670.

Lubart, T. I. (1990). Creativity and cross-cultural variation. *International Journal of Psychology, 25,* 39–59.

Luborsky, L. (1970). New directions in research on neurotic and psychosomatic symptoms. *American Scientist, 58,* 661–668.

Luborsky, L. (1984). *Principles of psychoanalytic psychotherapy.* New York: Basic Books.

Luborsky, L., Crits-Christoph, P., & Mellon, J. (1986). Advent of objective measures of the transference concept. *Journal of Consulting and Clinical Psychology, 54,* 39–47.

Luborsky, L., & DeRubeis, R. J. (1984). The use of psychotherapy treatment manuals: A small revolution in psychotherapy research style. *Clinical Psychology Review, 4,* 5–14.

Luborsky, L., & Spence, D. P. (1978). Quantitative research on psychoanalytic therapy. In S. L. Garfield & A. E. Bergin (Eds.), *Handbook of psychotherapy and behavior change* (2nd ed.). New York: Wiley.

Ludwig, A. O., & Ranson, S. W. (1947). A statistical followup of treatment of combat-induced psychiatric casualties. *Military Surgeon, 100,* 51–62, 169–175.

Lugassy, F. (1986–1987). Évolution actuelle des relations à l'éspace: Théorie bio-psycho-socio-génétique de l'éspace. *Bulletin de Psychologie, 40,* 503–512.

Lumsdaine, A. A., & Janis, I. L. (1953). Resistance to "counter-propaganda" produced by one-sided and two-sided "propaganda" presentations. *Public Opinion Quarterly, 17,* 311–318.

Lundberg, C. D., & Peterson, M. F. (1994). The meaning of working in U.S. and Japanese local governments at three hierarchical levels. *Human Relations, 47,* 1459–1487.

Lundrigan, P. J. (1991). Reality therapy and "method acting." *Journal of Reality Therapy, 11,* 72–75.

Luria, A. R. (1987). *The mind of a mnemonist: A little book about a vast memory.* Cambridge, MA: Harvard University Press.

Lynch, S., & Yarnell, P. R. (1973). Retrograde amnesia: Delayed forgetting after concussion. *American Journal of Psychology, 86,* 643–645.

Lynn, R. (1971). *Personality and national character.* New York: Pergamon.

Lynn, R. (1991). Race differences in intelligence: A global perspective. *Mankind Quarterly, 31,* 254–296.

Lynn, R. (1993). Sex differences in competitiveness and the valuation of money in twenty countries. *Journal of Social Psychology, 133,* 507–511.

Lynn, R. (1994). Sex differences in intelligence and brain size: A paradox resolved. *Personality and Individual Differences, 17,* 257–271.

Lynn, R., & Song, M. J. (1992). General intelligence, visuospatial and verbal abilities in Korean children. *Journal of the Indian Academy of Applied Psychology, 18,* 1–3.

Lynn, S. J., & Ruhe, J. W. (1986). The fantasy-prone person: Hypnosis, imagination, and creativity. *Journal of Personality and Social Psychology, 51,* 404–408.

Ma, H. K. (1989). "Moral orientation and moral judgment in adolescents in Hong Kong, mainland China, and England": Erratum. *Journal of Cross-Cultural Psychology, 20,* 440.

Maag, J. W., & Reid, R. (1994). Attention-deficit hyperactivity disorder: A functional approach to assessment and treatment. *Behavioral Disorders, 20,* 5–23.

Maccoby, E. E., & Jacklin, C. N. (1974). *The psychology of sex differences.* Palo Alto, CA: Stanford University Press.

Maccoby, E. E., & Mnookin, R. H. (1992). *Dividing the child: Social and legal dilemmas of custody.* Cambridge, MA: Harvard University Press.

MacDonald, K. (1991). A perspective on Darwinian psychology: The importance of domain-general mechanisms, plasticity, and individual differences. *Ethology and Sociobiology, 12,* 449–480.

Mace, C. J. (1992a). Hysterical conversion. I: A history. *British Journal of Psychiatry, 161,* 369–377.

Mace, C. J. (1992b). Hysterical conversion. II: A critique. *British Journal of Psychiatry, 161,* 378–389.

Mackett-Stout, J., & Dewar, R. (1981). Evaluation of symbolic public information signs. *Human Factors, 23,* 129–151.

MacKinnon, D. W. (1962). The personality correlates of creativity: A study of American architects. In G. S. Nielsen (Ed.), *Proceedings of the 14th International Congress of Applied Psychology* (Vol. 2). Copenhagen: Munksgaard.

Maclean, C. (1977). *The wolf children.* New York: Hill & Wang.

Macphail, E. M. (1993). *The neuroscience of animal intelligence: From the seahare to the seahorse.* New York: Columbia University Press.

Macrae, C. N., Milne, A. B., & Bodenhausen, G. V. (1994). Stereotypes as energy-saving devices: A peek inside the cognitive toolbox. *Journal of Personality and Social Psychology, 66,* 37–47.

Macrae, C. N., Stangor, C., & Milne, A. B. (1994). Activating social stereotypes: A functional analysis. *Journal of Experimental Social Psychology, 30,* 370–389.

Madden, D. J. (1990). Adult age differences in attentional selectivity and capacity. *European Journal of Cognitive Psychology, 2,* 229–252.

Madsen, P. L. (1993). Blood flow and oxygen uptake in the human brain during various states of sleep and wakefulness. *Acta Neurologica Scandinavica, 88,* 1–27.

Maeder, T. (1985). *Crime and madness: The origins and evolution of the insanity defense.* New York: Harper & Row.

Magner, L. N. (1992). *A history of medicine.* New York: Marcel Dekker.

Mair, R. G., Bouffard, J. A., Engen, T., & Morton, T. (1978). Olfactory sensitivity during the menstrual cycle. *Sensory Processes, 2,* 90–98.

Majnemer, A., Brownstein, A., Kadanoff, R., & Shevell, M. I. (1992). A comparison of neurobehavioral performance of healthy term and low-risk preterm infants at term. *Developmental Medicine and Child Neurology, 34,* 417–424.

Makin, J. W., & Porter, R. H. (1989). Attractiveness of lactating females' breast odors to neonates. *Child Development, 60,* 803–810.

Makin, P. J., & Hoyle, D. J. (1993). The Premack Principle: Professional engineers. *Leadership and Organization Development Journal, 14,* 16–21.

Malamuth, N. M., & Brown, L. M. (1994). Sexually aggressive men's perceptions of women's communications: Testing three explanations. *Journal of Personality and Social Psychology, 67,* 699–712.

Mancia, M. (1981). On the beginning of mental life in the foetus. *International Journal of Psycho-Analysis, 62,* 351–357.

Mandai, O., Guerrien, A., Sockeel, P., Dujardin, K., & Leconte, P. (1989). REM sleep modifications following a Morse code learning session in humans. *Physiology and Behavior, 46,* 639–642.

Mandler, J. M. (1992). "The importance of motor activity in sensorimotor development: A perspective from children with physical handicaps": Commentary. *Human Development, 35,* 246–253.

Manis, M. (1977). Cognitive social psychology. *Personality and Social Psychology Bulletin, 3,* 550–556.

Mann, R. D. (1959). A review of the relationships between personality and performance in small groups. *Psychological Bulletin, 56,* 241–270.

Manning, J. T. (1991). Sex differences in left-side infant holding: Results from "family album" photographs. *Ethology and Sociobiology, 12,* 337–343.

Manning, J. T., & Chamberlain, A. T. (1990). The left-side cradling preference in great apes. *Animal Behaviour, 39,* 1224–1227.

Manning, J. T., & Chamberlain, A. T. (1991). Left-side cradling and brain lateralization. *Ethology and Sociobiology, 12,* 237–244.

Manning, J. T., & Denman, J. (1994). Lateral cradling preferences in humans (*Homo sapiens*): Similarities within families. *Journal of Comparative Psychology, 108,* 262–265.

Maratos, J. (1994). Thanatos: Does it exist? *Group Analysis, 27,* 37–49.

Mardell, B. (1992). A practitioner's perspective on the implications of attachment theory for daycare professionals. *Child Study Journal, 22,* 201–232.

Marder, S. R., Wirshing, W. C., & Van Putten, T. (1991). Drug treatment of schizophrenia: Overview of recent research. *Schizophrenia Research, 4,* 81–90.

Marinkovic, K., Schell, A. M., & Dawson, M. E. (1989). Awareness of the CS-UCS contingency and classical conditioning of skin conductance responses with olfactory CSs. *Biological Psychology, 29,* 39–60.

Markides, K. S. (1989). Consequences of gender differentials in life expectancy for black and Hispanic Americans. *International Journal of Aging and Human Development, 29,* 95–102.

Markovits, H. (1993). Piaget and plasticine: Who's right about conservation? *Canadian Psychology, 34,* 233–238.

Marks, D. F., & MacAvoy, M. G. (1989). Divided attention performance in cannabis users and non-users following alcohol and cannabis separately and in combination. *Psychopharmacology, 99,* 397–401.

Marks, I. M. (1986). Epidemiology of anxiety. *Social Psychiatry, 21,* 167–171.

Marks, I. M. (1987). *Fears, phobias, and rituals.* New York: Oxford University Press.

Marks, I. M. (1990). Behavioral therapy of anxiety states. In N. Sartorius, V. Andreoli, G. Cassano, L. Eisenberg, P. Kielholz, P. Pancheri, & G. Racagni (Eds.), *Anxiety: Psychobiological and clinical perspectives.* New York: Hemisphere.

Marks, I. M., & O'Sullivan, G. (1988). Drugs and psychological treatments for agoraphobia/panic and obsessive-compulsive disorders: A review. *British Journal of Psychiatry, 153,* 650–658.

Marks, L. E. (1975). On colored-hearing synesthesia: Cross-modal translations of sensory dimensions. *Psychological Bulletin, 82,* 303–331.

Markus, H., & Kitayama, S. (1991). Culture and the self: Implications for cognition, emotion, and motivation. *Psychological Review, 98,* 224–253.

Markus, H., & Zajonc, R. B. (1985). The cognitive perspective in social psychology. In G. Lindzey & E. Aronson (Eds.), *Handbook of social psychology* (Vol. 1, 3rd ed.). New York: Random House.

Marlatt, G. A., & Gordon, J. R. (Eds.). (1985). *Relapse prevention.* New York: Guilford.

Marlatt, G. A., Baer, J. S., Donovan, D. M., & Kivlahan, D. R. (1988). Addictive behaviors: Etiology and treatment. *Annual Review of Psychology, 39,* 223–252.

Marrow, A. J. (1977). *The practical theorist: The life and work of Kurt Lewin.* New York: Teachers College Press.

Marsella, A. J. (1987). The measurement of depressive experience and disorder across cultures. In A. J. Marsella, R. M. A. Hirschfeld, & M. M. Katz (Eds.), *The measurement of depression.* New York: Guilford.

Marsella, A. J. (1988). Cross-cultural research on severe mental disorders: Issues and findings. *Acta Psychiatrica Scandinavica (Supplementum), 344,* 7–22.

Martens, R. (1975). *Social psychology and physical activity.* New York: Harper & Row.

Marti-Carbonell, M. A., Darbra, S., Garau, A., & Balada, F. (1992). Hormonas y agresión. *Archivos de Neurobiología, 55,* 162–174.

Martin, D. (1989). Engineering psychology. In W. L. Gregory & W. J. Burroughs (Eds.), *Introduction to applied psychology.* Glenview, IL: Scott, Foresman.

Martin, J. E. (1990). Bulimia: A review of the medical, behavioural and psychodynamic models of treatment. *British Journal of Occupational Therapy, 53,* 495–500.

Martinez, C., & Martin, H. W. (1966). Folk diseases among urban Mexican-Americans. *JAMA, 196,* 161–164.

Marzuk, P. M., Leon, A. C., Tardiff, K., Morgan, E. B., Stajic, M., & Mann, J. J. (1992). The effect of access to lethal methods of injury on suicide rates. *Archives of General Psychiatry, 49,* 451–458.

Masheter, C. (1990). Postdivorce relationships between exspouses: A literature review. *Journal of Divorce and Remarriage, 14,* 97–122.

Masling, J. M., Bornstein, R. F., Poynton, F., Reed, S., & Katkin, E. S. (1991). Perception without awareness and electrodermal responding: A strong test of subliminal psychodynamic activation effects. *Journal of Mind and Behavior, 12,* 33–47.

Maslow, A. H. (1970). *Motivation and personality* (2nd ed.). New York: Harper & Row.

Massaro, D. W., & Cowan, N. (1993). Information processing models: Microscopes of the mind. *Annual Review of Psychology, 44,* 383–425.

Masson, J. M. (1983). *Assault on the truth: Freud's suppression of the seduction theory.* New York: Farrar, Straus, & Giroux.

Masters, W. H. (1980). Update on sexual physiology. Unpublished paper cited in H. A. Katchadourian (1985). *Fundamentals of human sexuality.* New York: Holt, Rinehart & Winston.

Matheson, W., Van Dyk, C., & Millar, K. (1995). Performance evaluation in the human services. New York: Haworth Press.

Matin, L., & MacKinnon, G. E. (1964). Autokinetic movement: Selective manipulation of directional components by image stabilization. *Science, 143,* 147–148.

Matlin, M. W. (1988). *Sensation and perception* (2nd ed.). Boston: Allyn & Bacon.

Matsumoto, D. (1990). Cultural similarities and differences in display rules. *Motivation and Emotion, 14,* 195–214.

Matsumoto, D., & Assar, M. (1992). The effects of language on judgments of universal facial expressions of emotion. *Journal of Nonverbal Behavior, 16,* 85–99.

Matthews, K. A. (1982). Psychological perspectives on the Type A behavior pattern. *Psychological Bulletin, 91,* 293–323.

Matthies, H. (1989). Neurobiological aspects of learning and memory. *Annual Review of Psychology, 40,* 381–404.

Matthys, W., Cohen-Kettenis, P., & Berkhout, J. (1994). Boys' and girls' perceptions of peers in middle childhood: Differences and similarities. *Journal of Genetic Psychology, 155,* 15–24.

Matthysse, S. (1977). The role of dopamine in schizophrenia. In E. Usdin, D. A. Hamburg, & J. D. Barkus (Eds.), *Neuroregulators and psychiatric disorders.* New York: Oxford University Press.

Mattila, V. J., Joukamaa, M. I., & Salokangas, R. K. (1989). Retirement, aging, psychosocial adaptation, and mental health: Findings of the TURVA project. *Acta Psychiatrica Scandinavica, 80,* 356–367.

Mattlar, C.-E., Tarkkanen, P., Carlsson, A., Aaltonen, T. & Helenius, H. (1993). Personality characteristics for 83 paraplegic patients evaluated by the Rorschach method using the Comprehensive System. *British Journal of Projective Psychology, 38,* 20–30.

Maurer, D., & Maurer, C. (1988). *The world of the newborn.* New York: Basic Books.

Maurer, D., & Salapatek, P. (1976). Developmental changes in the scanning of faces by young infants. *Child Development, 47,* 523–527.

Mauro, R., Sato, K., & Tucker, J. (1992). The role of appraisal in human emotions: A cross-cultural study. *Journal of Personality and Social Psychology, 62,* 301–317.

Mavissakalian, M. (1990). Sequential combination of imipramine and self-directed exposure in the treatment of panic exposure with agoraphobia. *Journal of Clinical Psychiatry, 51,* 184–188.

May, C. (1993). Resistance to peer group pressure: An inadequate basis for alcohol education. *Health Education Research, 8,* 159–165.

Mayberry, R. I., & Eichen, E. B. (1991). The long-lasting advantage of learning sign language in childhood: Another look at the critical period for language acquisition. *Journal of Memory and Language, 30,* 486–512.

Mayer, J. D. (1993). The emotional madness of the dangerous leader. *Journal of Psychohistory, 20,* 331–348.

Maylor, E. A., Rabbit, P. M., James, G. H., & Kerr, S. A. (1990). Effects of alcohol and extended practice on divided-attention performance. *Perception and Psychophysics, 48,* 445–452.

Mayne, T. J., Norcross, J. C., & Sayette, M. A. (1994). Admission requirements, acceptance rates, and financial assistance in clinical psychology programs: Diversity across the practice-research continuum. *American Psychologist, 49,* 806–811.

Mayo, E. (1933). *The human problems of an industrial civilization.* New York: Macmillan.

Mays, V. M., Albee, G. W., & Schneider, S. F. (Eds.). (1989). *Primary prevention of AIDS: Psychological approaches.* Newbury Park, CA: Sage.

McAndrew, F. T. (1993). *Environmental psychology.* Pacific Grove, CA: Brooks/Cole.

McBride, R. L. (1983a). A JND-scale/category-scale convergence in taste. *Perception and Psychophysics, 34,* 77–83.

McBride, R. L. (1983b). Psychophysics: Could Fechner's assumption be correct? *Australian Journal of Psychology, 35,* 85–88.

McCall, R. B. (1990). Infancy research: Individual differences. *Merrill Palmer Quarterly, 36,* 141–157.

McCann, I. L., & Holmes, D. S. (1984). Influence of aerobic exercise on depression. *Journal of Personality and Social Psychology, 46,* 1142–1147.

McCarthy, M. (1990). The thin ideal, depression, and eating disorders in women. *Behaviour Research and Therapy, 28,* 205–215.

McClelland, D. C. (1961). *The achieving society.* Princeton, NJ: Van Nostrand.

McClelland, D. C. (1975). *Power: The inner experience.* New York: Wiley.

McClelland, D. C. (1982). The need for power, sympathetic activation, and illness. *Motivation and Emotion, 6,* 31–41.

McClelland, D. C. (1985). *Human motivation.* Glenview, IL: Scott, Foresman.

McClelland, D. C., & Franz, C. E. (1992). Motivational and other sources of work accomplishments in mid-life: A longitudinal study. *Journal of Personality, 60,* 679–707.

McClenney, L., & Neiss, R. (1989). Posthypnotic suggestion: A method for the study of nonverbal communication. *Journal of Nonverbal Behavior, 13,* 37–45.

McClenon, J. (1994). Surveys of anomalous experience: A cross-cultural analysis. *Journal of the American Society for Psychical Research, 88,* 117–135.

McClintock, M. K. (1971). Menstrual synchrony and suppression. *Nature, 229,* 244–245.

McConatha, J. T., Lightner, E., & Deaner, S. L. (1994). Culture, age, and gender as variables in the expression of emotions. *Journal of Social Behavior and Personality, 9,* 481–488.

McCrae, R. R., & Costa, P. T. (1987). Validation of the five-factor model of personality across instruments and observers. *Journal of Personality and Social Psychology, 52,* 81–90.

McDaniel, M. A., Whetzel, D. L., Schmidt, F. L., & Maurer, S. D. (1994). The validity of employment interviews: A comprehensive review and meta-analysis. *Journal of Applied Psychology, 79,* 599–616.

McDougall, W. (1908). *An introduction to social psychology.* London: Methuen.

McEvoy, G. M., & Cascio, W. F. (1985). Strategies for reducing employee turnover: A meta-analysis. *Journal of Applied Psychology, 70,* 342–353.

McGarry, A. L., & Bendt, R. H. (1969). Criminal vs. civil commitment of psychotic offenders: A seven year follow-up. *American Journal of Psychiatry, 125,* 1387–1394.

McGarty, C., Turner, J. C., Hogg, M. A., David, B., & Wetherell, M. S. (1992). Group polarization as conformity to the prototypical group member. *British Journal of Social Psychology, 31,* 1–19.

McGaugh, J. L., Weinberger, N. M., & Lynch, G. (Eds.). (1995). *Brain and memory: Modulation and mediation of neuroplasticity.* New York: Oxford University Press.

McGinnies, E. (1949). Emotionality and perceptual defense. *Psychological Review, 56,* 244–251.

McGregor, D. (1960). *The human side of enterprise.* New York: McGraw-Hill.

McGregor, G., & Axelrod, S. (1988). Microcomputers in the classroom: Teaching students with severe handicaps to use a computer. *Education and Treatment of Children, 11,* 230–238.

McGuffin, P., & Katz, R. (1989). The genetics of depression and manic-depressive disorder. *British Journal of Psychiatry, 155,* 294–304.

McGuire, B. E. (1990). Psychopharmacological treatments for memory impairment. *Clinical Rehabilitation, 4,* 235–244.

McGuire, W. J. (1968). Personality and susceptibility to social influence. In E. F. Borgatta & W. W. Lambert (Eds.), *Handbook of personality theory and research.* Chicago: Rand McNally.

McGurk, H., Caplan, M., Hennessy, E., & Moss, P. (1993). Controversy, theory, and social context in contemporary day care research. *Journal of Child Psychology and Psychiatry and Allied Disciplines, 34,* 3–23.

McInnes, J. M., & Treffry, J. A. (1982/1993). *Deaf-blind infants and children: A developmental guide.* Toronto: University of Toronto Press.

McKelvie, S. J., Standing, L., St. Jean, D., & Law, J. (1993). Gender differences in recognition memory for faces and cars: Evidence for the interest hypothesis. *Bulletin of the Psychonomic Society, 31,* 447–448.

McKenna, J. J. (1990). Evolution and sudden infant death syndrome (SIDS): I. Infant responsivity to parental contact. *Human Nature, 1,* 145–177.

McKenna, J. J., & Mosko, S. (1990). Evolution and the sudden infant death syndrome (SIDS): III. Infant arousal and parent-infant co-sleeping. *Human Nature, 1,* 291–330.

McKillip, J., & Riedel, S. L. (1983). External validity of matching on physical attractiveness for same and opposite sex couples. *Journal of Applied Social Psychology, 13,* 328–337.

McKim, M. K. (1993). Quality child care: What does it mean for individual infants, parents, and caregivers? *Early Child Development and Care, 88,* 23–30.

McMaster, N. L. (1990). The courts and hypnotically refreshed memory: A review of the literature. *Australian Journal of Clinical Hypnotherapy and Hypnosis, 11,* 1–9.

McNeal, J. U. (1982). *Consumer behavior: An integrative approach.* Boston: Little, Brown.

McNeill, D. (1966). Developmental psycholinguistics. In F. Smith & G. A. Miller (Eds.), *The genesis of language: A psycholinguistic approach.* Cambridge, MA: MIT Press.

McNiel, D. E., & Binder, R. L. (1987). Predictive validity of judgments of dangerousness in emergency civil commitment. *American Journal of Psychiatry, 144,* 197–200.

Mebel, B., & Dreschler-Fischer, L. (Eds.). (1994). *KI–94: Advances in artificial intelligence.* Berlin: Springer-Verlag.

Medin, D. L., & Schaffer, M. M. (1978). A context theory of classification. *Psychological Review, 85,* 207–238.

Meehl, P. E. (1954). *Clinical versus statistical prediction.* Minneapolis: University of Minnesota Press.

Meehl, P. E. (1957). When shall we use our heads instead of the formula? *Journal of Counseling Psychology, 4,* 268–273.

Meehl, P. E. (1962). Schizotaxia, schizotypy, schizophrenia. *American Psychologist, 17,* 827–838.

Meehl, P. E. (1977). Why I do not attend case conferences. In *Psychodiagnosis.* New York: Norton.

Meehl, P. E. (1989). Schizotaxia revisited. *Archives of General Psychiatry, 46,* 935–944.

Meehl, P. E. (1990). Toward an integrated theory of schizotaxia, schizotypy, and schizophrenia. *Journal of Personality Disorders, 4,* 1–99.

Meeus, W., & Raaijmakers, Q. (1989). Autoritätsgehorsam in Experimenten des Milgram-Typs: Eine Forschungsübersicht. *Zeitschrift für Sozialpsychologie, 20,* 70–85.

Megargee, E. I., & Spielberger, C. D. (Eds.). (1992). *Personality assessment in America: A retrospective on the occasion of the fiftieth anniversary of the Society for Personality Assessment.* Hillsdale, NJ: Erlbaum.

Mehta, S. D., Ward, C., & Strongman, K. (1992). Cross-cultural recognition of posed facial expressions of emotion. *New Zealand Journal of Psychology, 21,* 74–77.

Meier, A. (1993). Toward an integrated model of competency: Linking White and Bandura. *Journal of Cognitive Psychotherapy, 7,* 35–47.

Melnick, S. L., Sherer, R., Louis, T. A., Hillman, D., Rodriguez, E. M., Lackman, C., Capps, L., Brown, L. S., Carlyn, M., Korvick, J. A., & Deyton, L. (1994). Survival and disease progression according to gender of patients with HIV infection. *JAMA, 272,* 1915–1921.

Meltzoff, A. N. (1985). Immediate and deferred imitation in fourteen- and twenty-four-month-old infants. *Child Development, 56,* 62–72.

Meltzoff, A. N. (1988). Infant imitation and memory: Nine-month-olds in immediate and deferred tests. *Child Development, 59,* 217–225.

Meltzoff, A. N., & Moore, M. K. (1977). Imitation of facial and manual gestures by human neonates. *Science, 198,* 75–78.

Meltzoff, A. N., & Moore, M. K. (1994). Imitation, memory, and the representation of persons. *Infant Behavior and Development, 17,* 83–99.

Melzack, R. (1973). *The puzzle of pain.* London: Penguin.

Memmi, D., & Nguyen-Xuan, A. (1988). Une méthode d'extraction d'expertise via l'apprentissage. *Psychologie Française, 33,* 139–144.

Mendelson, M. (1974). *Psychoanalytic concepts of depression* (2nd ed.). New York: Halsted Press.

Mendes de Leon, C. F., Powell, L. H., & Kaplan, B. H. (1991). Change in coronary-prone behaviors in the Recurrent Coronary Prevention Project. *Psychosomatic Medicine, 53,* 407–419.

Mennella, J. A., Blumberg, M. S., McClintock, M. K., & Moltz, H. (1990). Inter-litter competition and communal nursing among Norway rats: Advantages of birth synchrony. *Behavioral Ecology and Sociobiology, 27,* 183–190.

Mennuti, R. B., & Creamer, D. G. (1991). Role of orientation, gender, and dilemma content in moral reasoning. *Journal of College Student Development, 32,* 241–248.

Mercer, J. R. (1973). *Labeling the retarded.* Berkeley: University of California Press.

Merluzzi, T. V., Glass, C. R., & Genest, M. (Eds.). (1981). *Cognitive assessment.* New York: Guilford.

Merrill, J., Milner, G., Owens, J., & Vale, A. (1992). Alcohol and attempted suicide. *British Journal of Addiction, 87,* 83–89.

Mesquita, B., & Frijda, N. H. (1992). Cultural variations in emotions: A review. *Psychological Bulletin, 112,* 179–204.

Meyer, J. E. (1988). "Die Freigabe der Vernichtung lebensunwerten Lebens" von Binding und Hoche im Spiegel der deutschen Psychiatrie vor 1933. *Nervenarzt, 59,* 85–91.

Mezzich, J. E., Jorge, M. R., & Salloum, I. M. (Eds.). (1994). *Psychiatric epidemiology: Assessment concepts and methods.* Baltimore: Johns Hopkins University Press.

Mikulincer, M., & Erev, I. (1991). Attachment style and the structure of romantic love. *British Journal of Social Psychology, 30,* 273–291.

Milgram, S. (1963). Behavioral study of obedience. *Journal of Abnormal and Social Psychology, 67,* 371–378.

Milgram, S. (1974). *Obedience to authority.* New York: Harper & Row.

Miller, G. A. (1956). The magical number seven, plus or minus two: Some limits on our capacity for processing information. *Psychological Review, 63,* 81–97.

Miller, J. (1991). Threshold variability in subliminal perception experiments: Fixed threshold estimates reduce power to detect subliminal effects. *Journal of Experimental Psychology: Human Perception and Performance, 17,* 841–851.

Miller, J. G. (1984). Culture and the development of everyday social explanation. *Journal of Personality and Social Psychology, 46,* 961–978.

Miller, J. G. (1994). Cultural diversity in the morality of caring: Individually oriented versus duty-based interpersonal moral codes. *Cross-Cultural Research: The Journal of Comparative Social Science, 28,* 3–39.

Miller, J. W., Petersen, R. C., Metter, E. J., Millikan, C. H., & Yanagihara, T. (1987). Transient global amnesia: Clinical characteristics and prognosis. *Neurology, 37,* 733–737.

Miller, N. E. (1978). Biofeedback and visceral learning. *Annual Review of Psychology, 29,* 373–404.

Miller, N. E. (1985). The value of behavioral research on animals. *American Psychologist, 40,* 423–440.

Miller, N. S., & Gold, M. S. (1990). Benzodiazepines: Reconsidered. *Advances in Alcohol and Substance Abuse, 8,* 67–84.

Miller, P. R. (1969). Outcasts and conformers in a girls' prison. *Archives of General Psychiatry, 20,* 700–708.

Miller, S. D., Blackburn, T., Scholes, G., White, G. L., & Mamalis, N. (1991). Optical differences in multiple personality disorder: A second look. *Journal of Nervous and Mental Disease, 179,* 132–135.

Miller, S. D., & Triggiano, P. J. (1992). The psychophysiological investigation of multiple personality disorder: Review and update. *American Journal of Clinical Hypnosis, 35,* 47–61.

Miller, S. M. (1979). Controllability and human stress: Method, evidence, and theory. *Behaviour Research and Therapy, 17,* 287–304.

Miller, T. Q., Turner, C. W., Tinsdale, R. S., Posavac, E. J., & Dugoni, B. L. (1991). Reasons for the trend toward null findings in research on Type A behavior. *Psychological Bulletin, 110,* 469–485.

Miller, W. R. (1983). Controlled drinking: A history and a clinical review. *Journal of Studies on Alcohol, 44,* 68–83.

Miller, W. R., & Hester, R. K. (1986). The effectiveness of alcohol treatment: What research reveals. In W. R. Miller & N. Heather (Eds.), *Treating addictive behaviors: Processes of change.* New York: Plenum.

Millon, T. (1990). *Toward a new personology.* New York: Wiley.

Millstein, S. G., & Irwin, C. E. (1988). Accident-related behaviors in adolescents: A biopsychosocial view. *Alcohol, Drugs, and Driving, 4,* 21–29.

Minces, J. (1991). La sexualité de la femme musulmane. *Psychanalystes, 40,* 63–70.

Mineka, S. (1985). Animal models of anxiety-based disorders: Their usefulness and limitations. In A. H. Tuma & J. D. Maser (Eds.), *Anxiety and the anxiety disorders.* Hillsdale, NJ: Erlbaum.

Mineka, S., & Henderson, R. W. (1985). Controllability and predictability in acquired motivation. *Annual Review of Psychology, 36,* 495–529.

Miranda, S. M. (1994). Avoidance of groupthink: Meeting management using group support systems. *Small Group Research, 25,* 105–136.

Mischel, W. (1968). *Personality and assessment.* New York: Wiley.

Mischel, W., & Peake, P. K. (1982). Beyond déjà-vu in the search for cross-situational consistency. *Psychological Review, 89,* 730–755.

Mischel, W., & Shoda, Y. (1994). Personality psychology has two goals: Must it be two fields? *Psychological Inquiry, 5,* 156–158.

Misumi, J., & Peterson, M. F. (1990). Psychology in Japan. *Annual Review of Psychology, 41,* 213–241.

Mitchell, J. E. (1991). A review of the controlled trials of psychotherapy for bulimia nervosa. *Journal of Psychosomatic Research, 35,* 23–31.

Mitchell, J. E., Raymond, N., & Specker, S. M. (1993). A review of the controlled trials of pharmacotherapy and psychotherapy in the treatment of bulimia nervosa. *International Journal of Eating Disorders, 14,* 229–247.

Mixon, D. (1989). *Obedience and civilization: Authorized crime and the normality of evil.* Winchester, MA: Pluto.

Mobley, W. H., Horner, S. O., & Hollingsworth, A. T. (1978). An evaluation of precursors of hospital employee turnover. *Journal of Applied Psychology, 63,* 408–414.

Modell, J. G., Mountz, J. M., & Beresford, T. P. (1990). Basal ganglia/limbic striatal and thalamocortical involvement in craving and loss of control in alcoholism. *Journal of Neuropsychiatry and Clinical Neurosciences, 2,* 123–144.

Modgil, S., & Modgil, C. (1987). *Arthur Jensen: Consensus and controversy.* New York: Falmer.

Mohammed, A. H., Henriksson, B. G., Soderstrom, S., Ebendal, T., Olsson, T., & Seckl, J. R. (1993). Environmental influences on the central nervous system and their implications for the aging rat. *Behavioural Brain Research, 57,* 183–191.

Monahan, D. J., Greene, V. L., & Coleman, P. D. (1992). Caregiver support groups: Factors affecting use of services. *Social Work, 37,* 254–260.

Monahan, J. (1992). Mental disorder and violent behavior: Perceptions and evidence. *American Psychologist, 47,* 511–521.

Monahan, J., & Shah, S. A. (1989). Dangerousness and commitment of the mentally disordered in the United States. *Schizophrenia Bulletin, 15,* 541–553.

Money, J. (1965). Psychosexual differentiation. In J. Money (Ed.), *Sex research: New directions.* New York: Holt, Rinehart & Winston.

Money, J. (1986). *Lovemaps: Clinical concepts of sexual/erotic health and pathology, paraphilia, and gender transposition in childhood, adolescence, and maturity.* New York: Irvington.

Money, J., & Ehrhardt, A. A. (1972). *Man and woman, boy and girl.* Baltimore: Johns Hopkins University Press.

Monroe, S. M., & Simons, A. D. (1991). Diathesis-stress theories in the context of life stress research: Implications for the depressive disorders. *Psychological Bulletin, 110,* 406–425.

Mook, D. G. (1987). *Motivation: The organization of action.* New York: Norton.

Moore, C. L., Dou, H., & Juraska, J. M. (1992). Maternal stimulation affects the number of motor neurons in a sexually dimorphic nucleus of the lumbar spinal cord. *Brain Research, 572,* 52–56.

Moore, S. M., & Rosenthal, D. A. (1992). The social context of adolescent sexuality: Safe sex implications. *Journal of Adolescence, 15,* 415–435.

Moorhead, G., Ference, R., & Neck, C. P. (1991). Group decision fiascoes continue: Space Shuttle Challenger and a revised groupthink framework. *Human Relations, 44,* 539–550.

Moosman, I. (1975). Preference for play materials with varying stimulus values among 3–6 year old children. *Zeitschrift für Entwicklungpsychologie und Pädagogische Psychologie, 7,* 254–267.

Moray, N. (1959). Attention in dichotic listening: Affective cues and the influence of instructions. *Quarterly Journal of Experimental Psychology, 11,* 56–60.

Morgan, C. D., & Murray, H. A. (1935). A method for investigating fantasies. *Archives of Neurology and Psychiatry, 34,* 289–306.

Morgan, M., & Grube, J. W. (1991). Closeness and peer group influence. *British Journal of Social Psychology, 30,* 159–169.

Morgan, M. J., Hole, G. J., & Glennerster, A. (1990). Biases and sensitivities in geometrical illusions. *Vision Research, 30,* 1793–1810.

Morris, D. (1967). *The naked ape.* London: Jonathan Cape.

Morris, N. (1982). *Madness and the criminal law.* Chicago: University of Chicago Press.

Morrison, J. (1990). Managing somatization disorder. *Disease-a-Month, 36,* 537–591.

Morrow, P. C. (1990). Physical attractiveness and selection decision making. *Journal of Management, 16,* 45–60.

Morse, D. R. (1993). The stressful kiss: A biopsychosocial evaluation of the origins, evolution, and societal significance of vampirism. *Stress Medicine, 9,* 181–189.

Mortimer, J. T. (1976). Social class, work, and family: Some implications of the father's occupation for family relationships and son's career decisions. *Journal of Marriage and the Family, 38,* 241–256.

Motluk, A. (1994). The sweet smell of purple. *New Scientist, 143,* 32.

Mott, F. L. (1991). Developmental effects of infant care: The mediating role of gender and health. *Journal of Social Issues, 47,* 139–158.

Mount, M. K., Barrick, M. R., & Strauss, J. P. (1994). Validity of observer ratings of the big five personality factors. *Journal of Applied Psychology, 79,* 272–280.

Mowbray, C. T., Oyserman, D., & Ross, S. (1995). Parenting and the significance of children for women with a serious mental illness. *Journal of Mental Health Administration, 22,* 189–200.

Mowday, R. T., & Sutton, R. I. (1993). Organizational behavior: Linking individuals and groups to organizational contexts. *Annual Review of Psychology, 44,* 195–229.

Mowen, J. C. (1989). Consumer psychology. In W. L. Gregory and W. J. Burroughs (Eds.), *Introduction to applied psychology.* Glenview, IL: Scott, Foresman.

Mowrer, O. H. (1950). *Learning theory and personality dynamics.* New York: Ronald Press.

Mowrer-Popiel, E., Pollard, C., & Pollard, R. (1993). An examination of factors affecting the creative production of female professors. *College Student Journal, 27,* 428–436.

Mullen, B. (1991). Group composition, salience, and cognitive representations: The phenomenology of being in a group. *Journal of Experimental Social Psychology, 27,* 297–323.

Mullen, B., Anthony, T., Salas, E., & Driskell, J. E. (1994). Group cohesiveness and quality of decision making: An integration of tests of the groupthink hypothesis. *Small Group Research, 25,* 189–204.

Mullen, B., Johnson, C., & Anthony, T. (1994). Relative group size and cognitive representations of ingroup and outgroup: The phenomenology of being in a group. *Small Group Research, 25,* 250–266.

Müller, J. (1826a). *Über die phantastischen Gesichtserscheinungen.* Coblenz: Holscher.

Müller, J. (1826b). *Zur vergleichenden Physiologie des Gesichtssinnes des Menschen und der Thiere.* Leipzig: Cnobloch.

Mumford, D. B. (1993). Somatization: A transcultural perspective. *International Review of Psychiatry, 5,* 231–242.

Mundy-Castle, A. C. (1966). Pictorial depth perception in Ghanian children. *International Journal of Psychology, 1,* 290–300.

Munk-Jorgensen, P., & Mortensen, P. B. (1992). Social outcome in schizophrenia: A 13-year follow-up. *Social Psychiatry and Psychiatric Epidemiology, 27,* 129–134.

Munro, D. (1981). Passive versus active consciousness. *American Psychologist, 36,* 432–434.

Murphy, G. (1947). *Personality: A biosocial approach to origins and structure.* New York: Harper.

Murphy, S. M. (1990). Models of imagery in sport psychology: A review. *Journal of Mental Imagery, 14,* 153–172.

Murphy, S. T., & Zajonc, R. B. (1993). Affect, cognition, and awareness: Affective priming with optimal and suboptimal stimulus exposures. *Journal of Personality and Social Psychology, 64,* 723–739.

Murray, E. A., & Mishkin, M. (1985). Amygdalectomy impairs cross-modal associations in monkeys. *Science, 228,* 604–606.

Murray, H. A. (1938). *Explorations in personality.* New York: Oxford University Press.

Murray, J. B. (1992). Posttraumatic stress disorder: A review. *Genetic, Social, and General Psychology Monographs, 118,* 313–338.

Murstein, B. I. (1963). *Theory and research in projective techniques, emphasizing the TAT.* New York: Wiley.

Murstein, B. I. (1976). *Who will marry whom.* New York: Springer.

Murstein, B. I., Chalpin, M. J., Heard, K. V., & Vyse, S. A. (1989). Sexual behavior, drugs, and relationship patterns on a college campus over thirteen years. *Adolescence, 24,* 125–139.

Murstein, B. I., Merighi, J. R., & Vyse, S. A. (1991). Love styles in the United States and France: A cross-cultural comparison. *Journal of Social and Clinical Psychology, 10,* 37–46.

Muysken, J. (Ed.). (1994). *Measurement and analysis of job vacancies: An international perspective.* Brookfield, VT: Avebury.

Mwamwenda, T. S. (1992). Studies on attainment of higher moral reasoning. *Psychological Reports, 71,* 287–290.

Myers, D. G. (1987). *Social psychology* (2nd ed.). New York: McGraw-Hill.

Myers, D. G., & Lamm, H. (1976). The group polarization phenomenon. *Psychological Bulletin, 83,* 602–627.

Myers, J. E. (1993). Expert testimony regarding child sexual abuse. *Child Abuse and Neglect, 17,* 175–185.

Myers, L. J. (1993). *Understanding an Afrocentric world view: Introduction to an optimal psychology.* Dubuque, IA: Kendall/Hunt.

Nagase, M. (1993). Language of the autistic from the perspective of cognitive science. *Italian Journal of Intellective Impairment, 6,* 13–22.

Nagata, D. K. (1993). *Legacy of injustice: Exploring the cross-generational impact of the Japanese American internment.* New York: Plenum.

Nakano, K. (1990). Effects of two self-control procedures on modifying Type A behavior. *Journal of Clinical Psychology, 46,* 652–657.

Neal, J. H. (1983). Children's understanding of their parents' divorces. In L. A. Kurdek (Ed.), *New directions for child development* (No. 19). San Francisco: Jossey-Bass.

Neher, A. (1991). Maslow's theory of motivation: A critique. *Journal of Humanistic Psychology, 31,* 89–112.

Neimark, E. D. (1982). Adolescent thought: Transition to formal operations. In B. B. Wolman & G. Strickler (Eds.), *Handbook of developmental psychology.* Englewood Cliffs, NJ: Prentice Hall.

Neimeyer, R. A., & Chapman, K. M. (1980–1981). Self-ideal discrepancy and fear of death: The test of an existential hypothesis. *Omega, 11,* 233–239.

Neisser, U. (1967). *Cognitive psychology*. Englewood Cliffs, NJ: Prentice Hall.

Neisser, U. (Ed.). (1982). *Memory observed: Remembering in natural contexts*. New York: Freeman.

Neisworth, J. T., & Bagnato, S. J. (1992). The case against intelligence testing in early intervention. *Topics in Early Childhood Special Education, 12,* 1–20.

Nelson, D. L., Schreiber, T. A., & McEvoy, C. L. (1992). Processing implicit and explicit representations. *Psychological Review, 99,* 322–348.

Nelson, M. L., & Holloway, E. L. (1990). Relation of gender to power and involvement in supervision. *Journal of Counseling Psychology, 37,* 473–481.

Nemeroff, C., & Rozin, P. (1994). The contagion concept in adult thinking in the United States: Transmission of germs and of interpersonal influence. *Ethos, 22,* 158–186.

Nemiah, J. C. (1980). Phobic disorder (phobic neurosis). In H. I. Kaplan, A. M. Freedman, & B. J. Sadock (Eds.), *Comprehensive textbook of psychiatry* (Vol. 2, 3rd ed.). Baltimore: Williams & Wilkins.

Nesse, R. M. (1990). Evolutionary explanations of emotions. *Human Nature, 1,* 261–289.

Nestadt, G. R., Romanoski, A. J., Samuels, J. F., Folstein, M. F., & McHugh, P. R. (1992). The relationship between personality and DSM-III axis I disorders in the population: Results from an epidemiological survey. *American Journal of Psychiatry, 149,* 1228–1233.

Neugarten, B. L. (1970). Adaptation and the life cycle. *Journal of Geriatric Psychiatry, 4,* 71–87.

Neuliep, J. W., & Crandall, R. (1993). Everyone was wrong: There are lots of replications out there. *Journal of Social Behavior and Personality, 8,* 1–8.

Nguyen, N. A., & Williams, H. L. (1989). Transition from East to West: Vietnamese adolescents and their parents. *Journal of the American Academy of Child and Adolescent Psychiatry, 28,* 505–515.

Nicholson, N., Brown, C. A., & Chadwick-Jones, J. K. (1976). Absence from work and job satisfaction. *Journal of Applied Psychology, 61,* 728–737.

Nickerson, R. A., & Adams, M. J. (1979). Long-term memory for a common object. *Cognitive Psychology, 11,* 287–307.

Nielsen, T. (1993). Angst-indlaering. En gammel teori med nye "biopsykosociale modifikationer." *Psyke & Logos, 14,* 74–105.

Nielsen, T. A., & Powell, R. A. (1989). The "dream-lag" effect: A 6-day temporal delay in dream content incorporation. *Psychiatric Journal of the University of Ottawa, 14,* 561–565.

Nisan, M., & Kohlberg, L. (1982). Universality and variation in moral judgment: A longitudinal and cross-sectional study in Turkey. *Child Development, 53,* 865–876.

Nisbett, R. E., & Wilson, T. D. (1977). Telling more than we can know: Verbal reports on mental processes. *Psychological Review, 84,* 231–259.

Nissani, M. (1990). A cognitive reinterpretation of Stanley Milgram's observations on obedience to authority. *American Psychologist, 45,* 1384–1385.

Nock, S. L. (1995). A comparison of marriages and cohabiting relationships. *Journal of Family Issues, 16,* 53–76.

Nofzinger, E. A., Buysse, D. J., Reynolds, C. F., & Kupfer, D. J. (1993). Sleep disorders related to another mental disorder (nonsubstance/primary): A DSM-IV literature review. *Journal of Clinical Psychiatry, 54,* 244–255.

Nolen-Hoeksema, S. (1987). Sex differences in unipolar depression: Theory and evidence. *Psychological Bulletin, 101,* 259–282.

Norman, D. A. (1988). *The design of everyday things*. New York: Doubleday.

Norman, W. T. (1963). Toward an adequate taxonomy of personality attributes: Replicated factor structure in peer nomination personality ratings. *Journal of Abnormal and Social Psychology, 66,* 574–583.

Norris, F. H. (1992). Epidemiology of trauma: Frequency and impact of different potentially traumatic events on different demographic groups. *Journal of Consulting and Clinical Psychology, 60,* 409–418.

Norton, A. J. (1983). Family life cycle: 1980. *Journal of Marriage and the Family, 45,* 267–275.

Novak, M. A., & Harlow, H. F. (1975). Social recovery of monkeys isolated for the first year of life: I. *Developmental Psychology, 11,* 453–465.

Nuckolls, C. W. (1992). Toward a cultural history of the personality disorders. *Social Science and Medicine, 35,* 37–47.

Nuechterlein, K. H., Dawson, M. E., Gitlin, M., Ventura, J., Goldstein, M. J., Snyder, K. S., Yee, C. M., & Mintz, J. (1992). Developmental processes in schizophrenic disorders: Longitudinal studies of vulnerability and stress. *Schizophrenia Bulletin, 18,* 387–425.

Numan, I. M., Barklind, K. S., & Lubin, B. (1981). Correlates of depression in chronic dialysis patients: Morbidity and mortality. *Research in Nursing and Health, 4,* 295–297.

Nunes, E. V., Frank, K. A., & Kornfeld, D. S. (1987). Psychologic treatment for the Type A behavior pattern and for coronary heart disease: A meta-analysis of the literature. *Psychosomatic Medicine, 49,* 159–173.

Nunn, O. B., & Hazler, R. J. (1990). The affective component of early moral development: Does it deserve greater emphasis? *Journal of Human Behavior and Learning, 7,* 28–33.

Nunns, C. G., & Bluen, S. D. (1992). The impact of behavioral modeling on self-reports on White supervisors in two South African mines. *Journal of Applied Behavioral Science, 28,* 433–444.

Nyamathi, A., & Vasquez, R. (1989). Impact of poverty, homelessness, and drugs on Hispanic women at risk for HIV infection. *Hispanic Journal of Behavioral Sciences, 11,* 299–314.

Nyborg, E. (1992). Det ubevidste i den analytiske psykologi. *Psyke & Logos, 13,* 87–98.

O'Brien, G. E., Feather, N. T., & Kabanoff, B. (1994). Quality of activities and the adjustment of unemployed youth. *Australian Journal of Psychology, 46,* 29–34.

O'Connell, A. N., & Russo, N. F. (Eds.). (1983). *Models of achievement: Reflections of eminent women in psychology*. New York: Columbia University Press.

O'Connell, A. N., & Russo, N. F. (Eds.). (1988). *Models of achievement: Reflections of eminent women in psychology* (Vol. 2). Hillsdale, NY: Erlbaum.

O'Connell, R. A., Mayo, J. A., Flatow, L., Cuthbertson, B., & O'Brien, B. E. (1991). Outcome of bipolar disorder on long-term treatment with lithium. *British Journal of Psychiatry, 159,* 123–129.

O'Connor, B. P. (1991). How a relationship between thinking and feeling may give rise to a variety of human behaviors. *Genetic, Social, and General Psychology Monographs, 117,* 29–48.

O'Hare, J. J. (1991). Perceptual integration. *Journal of the Washington Academy of Sciences, 81,* 44–59.

O'Leary, A. (1990). Stress, emotion, and human immune function. *Psychological Bulletin, 108,* 363–382.

O'Leary, K. D., & Smith, D. A. (1991). Marital interactions. *Annual Review of Psychology, 42,* 191–212.

O'Malley, S. (1979, October 7). Can the method survive the madness? *New York Times Magazine*, pp. 32–34+.

Offer, D., & Sabshin, M. (Eds.). (1991). *The diversity of normal behavior*. New York: Basic Books.

Ohira, H., & Kurono, K. (1993). Facial feedback effects on impression formation. *Perceptual and Motor Skills, 77,* 1251–1258.

Olds, J., & Milner, P. (1954). Positive reinforcement produced by electrical stimulation of septal area and other regions of rat brain. *Journal of Comparative and Physiological Psychology, 47,* 419–427.

Olfman, S. (1994). Gender, patriarchy, and women's mental health: Psychoanalytic perspectives. *Journal of the American Academy of Psychoanalysis, 22,* 259–271.

Oliansky, A. (1991). A confederate's perspective on deception. *Ethics and Behavior, 1,* 253–258.

Oliner, S. P., & Oliner, P. M. (1988). *The altruistic personality: Rescuers of Jews in Nazi Europe*. New York: Free Press.

Ollendick, T. H., & King, N. J. (1991). Origins of childhood fears: An evaluation of Rachman's theory of fear acquisition. *Behaviour Research and Therapy, 29,* 117–123.

Olson, J. M., & Zanna, M. P. (1993). Attitudes. *Annual Review of Psychology, 44,* 117–154.

Olton, D. S., & Raffaele, K. C. (1990). Long-term effects of cholinergic agonists on memory. *National Institute on Drug Abuse Research Monograph Series, 97,* 37–47.

Omer, H. (1993). The integrative focus: Coordinating symptom- and person-oriented perspectives in therapy. *American Journal of Psychotherapy, 47,* 283–295.

Oppawsky, J. (1991). The effects of parental divorce on children in West Germany: From the view of the children. *Journal of Divorce and Remarriage, 16,* 291–304.

Orne, M. T., & Wender, P. H. (1968). Anticipatory socialization for psychotherapy. *American Journal of Psychiatry, 124,* 1202–1211.

Ornstein, R. E. (Ed.). (1973). *Nature of human consciousness*. San Francisco: Freeman.

Ornstein, R. E. (1977). *The psychology of consciousness* (2nd ed.). New York: Harcourt Brace Jovanovich.

Ornstein, R. E. (1988). *Psychology: The study of human experience* (2nd ed.). San Diego: Harcourt Brace Jovanovich.

Ornstein, R. E., & Thompson, R. (1984). *The amazing brain*. Boston: Houghton Mifflin.

Orpen, C. (1978). Work and nonwork satisfaction: A causal-correlational analysis. *Journal of Applied Psychology, 63,* 530–532.

Ortmann, J., Genefke, I. K., Jakobsen, L., & Lunde, I. (1987). Rehabilitation of torture victims: An interdisciplinary treatment model. *American Journal of Social Psychiatry, 7,* 161–167.

Osborne, R. E., Karlin, J. E., Baumann, D. J., Osborne, M., & Nelms, D. (1993). A social comparison perspective of treatment seeking by the homeless. *Journal of Social Distress and the Homeless, 2,* 135–153.

Ots, T. (1990). The angry liver, the anxious heart, and the melancholy spleen: The phenomenology of perceptions in Chinese culture. *Culture, Medicine, and Psychiatry, 14,* 21–58.

Otto-Salaj, L. L., Nadon, R., Hoyt, I. P., Register, P. A., & Kihlstrom, J. F. (1992). Laterality of hypnotic response. *International Journal of Clinical and Experimental Hypnosis, 40,* 12–20.

Overholser, J. C. (1992). Aggregation of personality measures: Implications for personality disorder research. *Journal of Personality Disorders, 6,* 267–277.

Overmier, J. B., & Seligman, M. E. P. (1967). Effects of inescapable shock upon subsequent escape and avoidance learning. *Journal of Comparative and Physiological Psychology, 63,* 23–33.

Owen, D. (1985). *None of the above*. Boston: Houghton Mifflin.

Owen, I. (1990). Re-emphasizing a client-centered approach. *Counselling, 1,* 92–94.

Paccosi, S. (1985). Ipnosi ed edonica olfattoria. *Rivista Internazionale di Psicologia e Ipnosi, 26,* 177–180.

Packard, V. (1957). *The hidden persuaders*. New York: David McKay.

Page, A. C. (1994). Blood-injury phobia. *Clinical Psychology Review, 14,* 443–461.

Palfai, T. P., & Salovey, P. (1992). The influence of affect on self-focused attention: Conceptual and methodological issues. *Consciousness and Cognition: An International Journal, 1,* 306–339.

Palmore, E. (1981). *Social patterns in normal aging*. Durham, NC: Duke University Press.

Panksepp, J. (1986). The neurochemistry of behavior. *Annual Review of Psychology, 37,* 77–107.

Paradis, C. M., Hatch, M., & Friedman, S. (1994). Anxiety disorders in African Americans: An update. *Journal of the National Medical Association, 86,* 609–612.

Paranjpe, A. C., Ho, D. Y. F., & Rieber, R. W. (Eds.). (1988). *Asian contributions to psychology*. New York: Praeger.

Parish, T. S., & McCluskey, J. J. (1994). The relationship between parenting styles and young adults' self-concepts and evaluations of parents. *Family Therapy, 21,* 223–226.

Parisi, T. (1987). Why Freud failed: Some implications for neurophysiology and sociobiology. *American Psychologist, 42,* 235–245.

Park, W. (1990). A review of research on groupthink. *Journal of Behavioral Decision Making, 3,* 229–245.

Parke, R. D., & Collmer, W. C. (1978). Child abuse: An interdisciplinary analysis. In E. M. Hetherington (Ed.), *Review of child development research* (Vol. 5). Chicago: University of Chicago Press.

Parkinson, B., & Manstead, A. S. (1993). Making sense of emotion in stories and social life. *Cognition and Emotion, 7,* 295–323.

Parmelee, P. A., Katz, I. R., & Lawton, M. P. (1992). Depression and mortality among institutionalized aged. *Journal of Gerontology, 47,* 3–10.

Parsons, C. D., & Wakeley, P. (1991). Idioms of distress: Somatic responses to distress in everyday life. *Culture, Medicine, and Psychiatry, 15,* 111–132.

Parsons, H. M. (1992). Hawthorne: An early OBM experiment. *Journal of Organizational Behavior Management, 12,* 27–43.

Pashler, H. (1992). Attentional limitations in doing two tasks at the same time. *Current Directions in Psychological Science, 1,* 44–48.

Patten, B. M. (1990). The history of memory arts. *Neurology, 40,* 346–352.

Patterson, C. H. (1986). *Theories of counseling and psychotherapy* (4th ed.). New York: Harper & Row.

Patterson, F. (1978). Conversations with a gorilla. *National Geographic, 154,* 438–465.

Paul, G. L. (1966). *Insight versus desensitization in psychotherapy: An experiment in anxiety reduction*. Stanford, CA: Stanford University Press.

Paul, G. L. (1967). Insight vs. desensitization in psychotherapy two years after termination. *Journal of Counseling Psychology, 31,* 333–348.

Paulhus, D. L., & Lim, D. T. K. (1994). Arousal and evaluative extremity in social judgments: A dynamic complexity model. *European Journal of Social Psychology, 24,* 89–99.

Paykel, E. (1974). Life stress and psychiatric disorder: Applications of the clinical approach. In P. S. Dowrenwend & B. P. Dowrenwend (Eds.), *Stressful life events: Their nature and effects*. New York: Wiley.

Payne, K. (1989). Elephant talk. *National Geographic, 176,* 264–277.

Pearce, R. K., Seeman, P., Jellinger, K., & Tourtellotte, W. W. (1990). Dopamine uptake sites and dopamine receptors in Parkinson's disease and schizophrenia. *European Neurology, 30,* 9–14.

Pelletier, K. R., & Herzing, D. L. (1989). Psychoneuroimmunology: Toward a mindbody model. *Advances, 5*(1), 27–56.

Pendleton, L. (1980). Treatment of persons found incompetent to stand trial. *American Journal of Psychiatry, 137,* 1098–1100.

Penfield, W., & Jasper, H. (1954). *Epilepsy and the functional anatomy of the human brain*. Boston: Little, Brown.

Penfield, W., & Rasmussen, T. (1952). *The cerebral cortex of man*. New York: Macmillan.

Peng, X. T., Kandel, A., & Wang, P. (1991). Concepts, rules, and fuzzy reasoning: A factor space approach. *IEEE Transactions on Systems, Man, and Cybernetics, 21,* 194–205.

Pennebaker, J. W., Hughes, C. F., & O'Heeron, R. C. (1987). The psychophysiology of confession: Linking inhibitory and psychosomatic processes. *Journal of Personality and Social Psychology, 52,* 781–793.

Pennebaker, J. W., & O'Heeron, R. C. (1984). Confiding in others and illness rate among spouses of suicide and accidental-death victims. *Journal of Abnormal Psychology, 93,* 473–476.

Perkins, K. (1992). Psychosocial implications of women and retirement. *Social Work, 37,* 526–532.

Perkins, K. (1993). Working-class women and retirement. *Journal of Gerontological Social Work, 20,* 129–146.

Perkins, R. J. (1982). Catatonia: The ultimate response to fear? *Australian and New Zealand Journal of Psychiatry, 16,* 282–287.

Perlmutter, P. (1992). *Divided we fall: A history of ethnic, religious, and racial prejudice in America*. Ames: Iowa State University Press.

Perpina, C., & Baños, R. M. (1989). Historia del Tratamiento Conductual de la Obesidad Una Historia de Excusas. *Boletin de Psicología Spain, 25,* 103–127.

Perrett, D. I., May, K. A., & Yoshikawa, S. (1994). Facial shape and judgments of female attractiveness. *Nature, 368,* 239–242.

Perry, E. K., & Perry, R. H. (1993). Neurochemical pathology and therapeutic strategies in degenerative dementia. *International Review of Psychiatry, 5,* 363–380.

Persky, H. (1983). Psychosexual effects of hormones. *Medical Aspects of Human Sexuality, 17,* 74–101.

Persky, V. W., Kempthorne-Rawson, J., & Shekelle, R. B. (1987). Personality and risk of cancer: 20-year follow-up of the Western Electric Study. *Psychosomatic Medicine, 49,* 435–449.

Persons, J. B. (1986). The advantages of studying psychological phenomena rather than psychiatric diagnoses. *American Psychologist, 41,* 1252–1260.

Pervin, L. A. (1994). A critical analysis of current trait theory. *Psychological Inquiry, 5,* 103–113.

Peterka, R. J., Black, F. O., & Schoenhoff, M. B. (1990–1991). Age-related changes in human vestibulo-ocular and optokinetic reflexes: Pseudorandom rotation tests. *Journal of Vestibular Research, 1,* 61–71.

Peters, T. J., & Waterman, R. H. (1982). *In search of excellence: Lessons from America's best-run companies*. New York: Warner.

Peterson, B. E., & Stewart, A. J. (1993). Generativity and social motives in young adults. *Journal of Personality and Social Psychology, 65,* 186–198.

Peterson, C. (1988). Explanatory style as a risk factor for illness. *Cognitive Therapy and Research, 12,* 117–130.

Peterson, C. (1991). Meaning and measurement of explanatory style. *Psychological Inquiry, 2,* 1–10.

Peterson, C. (1992). *Personality* (2nd ed.). Fort Worth, TX: Harcourt Brace Jovanovich.

Peterson, C. (1996). *The psychology of abnormality*. Fort Worth, TX: Harcourt Brace.

Peterson, C., & Bossio, L. M. (1991). *Health and optimism*. New York: Free Press.

Peterson, C., Colvin, D., & Lin, E. H. (1992). Explanatory style and helplessness. *Social Behavior and Personality, 20,* 1–14.

Peterson, C., Maier, S. F., & Seligman, M. E. P. (1993). *Learned helplessness: A theory for the age of personal control*. New York: Oxford.

Peterson, C., & Seligman, M. E. P. (1984). Causal explanations as a risk factor for depression: Theory and evidence. *Psychological Review, 91,* 347–374.

Peterson, C., & Stunkard, A. J. (1989). Personal control and health promotion. *Social Science and Medicine, 28,* 819–828.

Peterson, L. R., & Peterson, M. J. (1959). Short-term retention of individual items. *Journal of Experimental Psychology, 58,* 193–198.

Peterson, M. A., & Gibson, B. S. (1994a). Must figure-ground organization precede object recognition? An assumption in peril. *Psychological Science, 5,* 253–259.

Peterson, M. A., & Gibson, B. S. (1994b). Object recognition contributions to figure-ground organization: Operations on outlines and subjective contours. *Perception and Psychophysics, 56,* 551–564.

Petty, R. E., & Cacioppo, J. T. (1986). *Central and peripheral routes to persuasion: Theory and research.* New York: Springer-Verlag.

Pfenninger, D. T., & Klion, R. E. (1994). Fitting the world to constructs: The role of activity in meaning making. *Journal of Constructivist Psychology, 7,* 151–161.

Philliber, W. W., & Hiller, D. V. (1983). Relative occupational attainments of spouses and later changes in marriage and wife's work experience. *Journal of Marriage and the Family, 46,* 161–170.

Phillips, D. P., & Brugge, J. F. (1985). Progress in neurophysiology of sound localization. *Annual Review of Psychology, 36,* 245–274.

Piaget, J. (1926). *The language and thought of the child.* New York: Harcourt, Brace.

Piaget, J. (1928). *Judgment and reasoning in the child.* New York: Harcourt, Brace.

Piaget, J. (1929). *The child's conception of the world.* New York: Harcourt, Brace.

Piaget, J. (1932). *Moral judgment of the child.* New York: Harcourt, Brace.

Piaget, J. (1950). *The psychology of intelligence.* New York: Harcourt, Brace.

Piaget, J., & Inhelder, B. (1969). *The origin of the idea of chance in children.* New York: Norton.

Pinard, L., & Minde, K. (1991). The infant psychiatrist and the transplant team. *Canadian Journal of Psychiatry, 36,* 442–446.

Pinker, S. (1994). *The language instinct.* New York: HarperPerennial.

Pinsky, J. J. (1978). Chronic, intractable, benign pain: A syndrome and its treatment with intensive short-term group psychotherapy. *Journal of Human Stress, 4,* 17–21.

Pitman, R. K., van der Kolk, B. A., Orr, S. P., & Greenberg, M. S. (1990). Naloxone-reversible analgesic response to combat-related stimuli in posttraumatic stress disorder: A pilot study. *Archives of General Psychiatry, 47,* 541–544.

Pittman, T. S., & Heller, J. F. (1987). Social motivation. *Annual Review of Psychology, 38,* 461–489.

Pledge, D. S. (1992). Marital separation/divorce: A review of individual responses to a major life stressor. *Journal of Divorce and Remarriage, 17,* 151–181.

Plomin, R. (1986). Behavioral genetic methods. *Journal of Personality, 54,* 226–261.

Plomin, R. (1987). Genetics of intelligence. In S. Modgil & C. Modgil (Eds.), *Arthur Jensen: Consensus and controversy.* New York: Falmer.

Plomin, R. (1994). Nature, nurture, and social development. *Social Development, 3,* 37–53.

Plomin, R., & Nesselroade, J. R. (1990). Behavioral genetics and personality change. *Journal of Personality, 58,* 191–220.

Plomin, R., & Rende, R. (1991). Human behavioral genetics. *Annual Review of Psychology, 42,* 161–190.

Plomin, R., Scheier, M. F., Bergeman, C. S., & Pedersen, N. L. (1992). Optimism, pessimism, and mental health: A twin/adoption analysis. *Personality and Individual Differences, 13,* 921–930.

Plude, D. J., Enns, J. T., & Brodeur, D. (1994). The development of selective attention: A life-span overview. *Acta Psychologica, 86,* 227–272.

Plutchik, R. (1962). *The emotions: Facts, theories, and a new model.* New York: Random House.

Plutchik, R. (1980). *Emotion: A psychoevolutionary synthesis.* New York: Harper & Row.

Plutchik, R. (1984). Emotions: A general psychoevolutionary theory. In K. R. Scherer & P. Ekman (Eds.), *Approaches to emotion.* Hillsdale, NJ: Erlbaum.

Pohl, R. F. (1990). Position effects in chunked linear orders. *Psychological Research, 52,* 68–75.

Pollack, M. H., Otto, M. W., Rosenbaum, J. F., Sachs, G. S., O'Neil, C., Asher, R., & Meltzer-Brody, S. (1990). Longitudinal course of panic disorder: Findings from the Massachusetts General Hospital Naturalistic Study. *Journal of Clinical Psychiatry, 51,* 12–16.

Pollitt, E. (1994). Poverty and child development: Relevance of research in developing countries to the United States. *Child Development, 65,* 283–295.

Porter, D., & Neuringer, A. (1984). Music discrimination by pigeons. *Journal of Experimental Psychology: Animal Behavior Processes, 10,* 138–148.

Porter, R. H. (1991). Human reproduction and the mother-infant relationship. In T. V. Getchell, R. L. Doty, L. M. Bartoshuk, & J. B. Snow (Eds.), *Smell and taste in health and disease.* New York: Raven Press.

Posner, M. I. (1978). *Chronometric explorations of mind.* Hillsdale, NJ: Erlbaum.

Posner, M. I., Petersen, S. E., Fox, P. T., & Raichle, M. E. (1988). Localization of cognitive operations in the human brain. *Science, 240,* 1627–1631.

Poulin-Dubois, D., & Heroux, G. (1994). Movement and children's attributions of life properties. *International Journal of Behavioral Development, 17,* 329–347.

Powell, L. H., & Thoreson, C. E. (1988). Effects of Type A behavioral counseling and severity of prior acute myocardial infarction on survival. *American Journal of Cardiology, 62,* 1159–1163.

Premack, A. J., & Premack, D. (1972). Teaching language to an ape. *Scientific American, 277,* 92–99.

Premack, D. (1965). Reinforcement theory. In D. Levine (Ed.), *Nebraska Symposium on Motivation* (Vol. 13). Lincoln: University of Nebraska Press.

Presti, D. E., Ary, D. V., & Lichtenstein, E. (1992). The context of smoking initiation and maintenance: Findings from interviews with youths. *Journal of Substance Abuse, 4,* 35–45.

Preuschoft, S. (1992). "Laughter" and "smile" in Barbary macaques *(Macaca sylvanus). Ethology, 91,* 220–236.

Price, D. D. (1988). *Psychological and neural mechanisms of pain.* New York: Raven Press.

Pridham, K. F., Chang, A. S., & Chiu, Y. M. (1994). Mothers' parenting self-appraisals: The contribution of perceived infant temperament. *Research in Nursing and Health, 17,* 381–392.

Priebe, S., & Gruyters, T. (1993). The role of the helping alliance in psychiatric community care: A prospective study. *Journal of Nervous and Mental Disease, 181,* 552–557.

Prigatano, G. P., & Schacter, D. L. (Eds.). (1991). *Awareness of deficit after brain injury: Clinical and theoretical issues.* New York: Oxford University Press.

Prince, M. (1924). *The unconscious.* New York: Macmillan.

Prior, M. (1992). Childhood temperament. *Journal of Child Psychology and Psychiatry and Allied Disciplines, 33,* 249–279.

Prochaska, J. O. (1984). *Systems of psychotherapy: A transtheoretical analysis* (2nd ed.). Homewood, IL: Dorsey.

Provine, R. R. (1992). Contagious laughter: Laughter is a sufficient stimulus for laughs and smiles. *Bulletin of the Psychonomic Society, 30,* 1–4.

Provine, R. R., & Yong, Y. L. (1991). Laughter: A stereotyped human vocalization. *Ethology, 89,* 115–124.

Pruzinsky, T., & Borkovec, T. D. (1990). Cognitive and personality characteristics of worriers. *Behaviour Research and Therapy, 28,* 507–512.

Pugh, J. F. (1991). The semantics of pain in Indian culture and medicine. *Culture, Medicine, and Psychiatry, 15,* 19–43.

Purifoy, F. E., Grodsky, A., & Giambra, L. M. (1992). The relationship of sexual daydreaming to sexual activity, sexual drive, and sexual attitudes for women across the life-span. *Archives of Sexual Behavior, 21,* 369–385.

Purtilo, D. T., & Purtilo, R. B. (1989). *A survey of human diseases* (2nd ed.). Boston: Little, Brown.

Putnam, F. W. (1989). *Diagnosis and treatment of multiple personality disorder.* New York: Guilford.

Putnam, F. W., Guroff, J. J., Silberman, E. K., Barban, L., & Post, R. M. (1986). The clinical phenomenology of multiple personality disorder: Review of 100 recent cases. *Journal of Clinical Psychiatry, 47,* 285–293.

Putnam, F. W., Zahn, T. P., & Post, R. M. (1990). Differential autonomic nervous system activity in multiple personality disorder. *Psychiatry Research, 31,* 251–260.

Pylyshyn, Z. W. (1984). *Computation and cognition: Toward a foundation for cognitive science.* Cambridge, MA: MIT Press.

Pyryt, M. C. (1993). The fulfillment of promise revisited: A discriminant analysis of factors predicting success in the Terman study. *Roeper Review, 15,* 178–179.

Quinn, T. J., & Wilson, B. R. (1989). Somatotype and Type A behavior in college-age adults. *Psychological Reports, 65,* 15–18.

Rabin, A. I. (Ed.). (1968). *Projective techniques in personality assessment: A modern introduction.* New York: Springer.

Rabinowitz, S., & Hall, D. T. (1981). Changing correlates of job involvement in three career stages. *Journal of Vocational Behavior, 18,* 138–144.

Rachman, S. J. (1994). Pollution of the mind. *Behaviour Research and Therapy, 32,* 11–314.

Rachman, S. J., & Hodgson, R. J. (1980). *Obsessions and compulsions.* Englewood Cliffs, NJ: Prentice Hall.

Rachman, S. J., & Wilson, G. T. (1980). *The effects of psychological therapy* (2nd ed.). New York: Pergamon.

Radner, D. (1989). *Animal consciousness.* Buffalo, NY: Prometheus Books.

Rado, S. (1956). *Psychoanalysis and behavior.* New York: Grune & Stratton.

Ragland, D. R., & Brand, R. J. (1988a). Coronary heart disease mortality in the Western Collaborative Group Study: Follow-up experience of 22 years. *American Journal of Epidemiology, 127,* 462–475.

Ragland, D. R., & Brand, R. J. (1988b). Type A behavior and mortality from coronary heart disease. *The New England Journal of Medicine, 318,* 65–69.

Raichle, M. E. (1994). Images of the mind: Studies with modern imaging techniques. *Annual Review of Psychology, 45,* 333–356.

Rainey, D. W., Santilli, N. R., & Fallon, K. (1992). Development of athletes' conceptions of sport officials' authority. *Journal of Sport and Exercise Psychology, 14,* 392–404.

Rakos, R. F. (1992). Achieving the just society in the 21st century: What can Skinner contribute? *American Psychologist, 47,* 1499–1506.

Ralston, S. M. (1988). The effect of applicant race upon personnel selection decisions: A review with recommendations. *Employee Responsibilities and Rights Journal, 1,* 215–226.

Rankin, C. H., & Broster, B. S. (1992). Factors affecting habituation and recovery from habituation in the nematode *Caenorhabditis elegans. Behavioral Neuroscience, 106,* 239–246.

Rao, B. S., Disraju, T., & Raju, T. R. (1993). Neuronal plasticity induced by self-stimulation rewarding experience in rats: A study on alteration in dendritic branching in pyramidal neurons of hippocampus and motor cortex. *Brain Research, 627,* 216–224.

Rape, R. N., & Bush, J. P. (1994). Psychological preparation for pediatric oncology patients undergoing painful procedures: A methodological critique of the research. *Children's Health Care, 23,* 51–67.

Rapoport, J. (1989). *The boy who couldn't stop washing: The experience and treatment of obsessive-compulsive disorders.* New York: Dutton.

Rappaport, Z. H. (1992). Psychosurgery in the modern era: Therapeutic and ethical aspects. *Medicine and Law, 11,* 449–453.

Raskin, R., & Novacek, J. (1991). Narcissism and the use of fantasy. *Journal of Clinical Psychology, 47,* 490–499.

Rasmussen, S. A., & Eisen, J. L. (1992). The epidemiology and differential diagnosis of obsessive compulsive disorder. *Journal of Clinical Psychiatry, 53,* 4–10.

Rastam, M. (1994). Anorexia nervosa: Recent research findings and implications for clinical practice. *European Child and Adolescent Psychiatry, 3,* 197–207.

Raven, J. C. (1948). The comparative assessment of intellectual ability. *British Journal of Psychology, 39,* 12–19.

Reber, A. S. (1992). The cognitive unconscious: An evolutionary perspective. *Consciousness and Cognition: An International Journal, 1,* 93–133.

Redding, R. E. (1990). Metacognitive instruction: Trainers teaching thinking skills. *Performance Improvement Quarterly, 3,* 27–41.

Reed, G. M., Kemeny, M. E., Taylor, S. E., Wang, H. Y., & Visscher, B. R. (1994). Realistic acceptance as a predictor of decreased survival time in gay men with AIDS. *Health Psychology, 13,* 299–307.

Reed, T. E., & Jensen, A. R. (1992). Conduction velocity in a brain nerve pathway of normal adults correlates with intelligence level. *Intelligence, 16,* 259–272.

Reeves, J. B., & Darville, R. L. (1994). Social contact patterns and satisfaction with retirement of women in dual-career/earner families. *International Journal of Aging and Human Development, 39,* 163–175.

Reich, J. H. (1986). The epidemiology of anxiety. *Journal of Nervous and Mental Disease, 174,* 129–136.

Reich, J. H. (1987). Sex distribution of DSM-III personality disorders in psychiatric outpatients. *American Journal of Psychiatry, 144,* 485–488.

Reich, J. H. (1989). Update on instruments to measure DSM-III and DSM-III-R personality disorders. *Journal of Nervous and Mental Disease, 177,* 366–370.

Reich, J. H., & Green, A. I. (1991). Effect of personality disorders on outcome of treatment. *Journal of Nervous and Mental Disease, 179,* 74–82.

Reichlin, S. M., Bloom, J. D., & Williams, M. H. (1993). Excluding personality disorders from the insanity defense: A follow-up study. *Bulletin of the American Academy of Psychiatry and the Law, 21,* 91–100.

Reillo, M. (1990). Psychosocial factors associated with prognosis in AIDS. *International Conference on AIDS, 6,* 179.

Rescorla, R. A. (1988). Pavlovian conditioning: It's not what you think it is. *American Psychologist, 43,* 151–160.

Rest, J. R. (1983). Morality. In P. H. Mussen (Ed.), *Handbook of child psychology* (Vol. 3). New York: Wiley.

Reynolds, M., Mayman, M., & Peterson, C. (1995). *Illusory mental health and distress in a clinical population.* Unpublished manuscript, University of Michigan.

Reynolds, V., Falger, V., & Vine, I. (Eds.). (1987). *The sociobiology of ethnocentrism: Evolutionary dimensions of xenophobia, discrimination, racism, and nationalism.* Athens: University of Georgia Press.

Ricciuti, H. N. (1993). Nutrition and mental development. *Current Directions in Psychological Science, 2,* 43–46.

Rice, M. L. (1989). Children's language acquisition. *American Psychologist, 44,* 149–156.

Rich, J. M. (1993). Discipline and moral development. *High School Journal, 76,* 139–144.

Richardson, V., & Kilty, K. M. (1991). Adjustment to retirement: Continuity vs. discontinuity. *International Journal of Aging and Human Development, 33,* 151–169.

Richman, B. (1993). On the evolution of speech: Singing as the middle term. *Current Anthropology, 34,* 721–722.

Rickels, K. (1981). Benzodiazepines: Use and misuse. In D. F. Klein & J. Rabkin (Eds.), *Anxiety: New research and changing concepts.* New York: Raven.

Rienzi, B. M., & Scrams, D. J. (1991). Gender stereotypes for paranoid, antisocial, compulsive, dependent, and histrionic personality disorders. *Psychological Reports, 69,* 976–978.

Riley, D. M., Sobell, L. C., Leo, G. I., Sobell, M. B., & Klajner, E. (1987). Behavioral treatment of alcohol problems: A review and a comparison of behavioral and nonbehavioral studies. In W. M. Cox (Ed.), *Treatment and prevention of alcohol problems: A resource manual.* New York: Academic Press.

Ring, K. (1967). Experimental social psychology: Some sober questions about some frivolous values. *Journal of Experimental Social Psychology, 3,* 113–123.

Roach-Higgins, M. E., & Eicher, J. B. (1992). Dress and identity. *Clothing and Textiles Research Journal, 10,* 1–8.

Robiner, W. N., Arbisi, P. A., & Edwall, G. E. (1994). The basis for the doctoral degree for psychology licensure. *Clinical Psychology Review, 14,* 227–254.

Robins, L. N., Helzer, J. E., Weissman, M. M., Orvaschel, H., Gruenberg, E., Burke, J. D., & Regier, D. A. (1984). Lifetime prevalence of specific psychiatric disorders in three sites. *Archives of General Psychiatry, 41,* 949–958.

Robinson, J. P., Shaver, P. R., & Wrightsman, L. S. (Eds.). (1991). *Measures of personality and social psychological attitudes.* San Diego: Academic Press.

Rodin, J., & Wack, J. T. (1984). The relationship between cigarette smoking and body weight: A health promotion dilemma? In J. D. Matarazzo, S. M. Weiss, J. A. Herd, N. E. Miller, & S. M. Weiss (Eds.), *Behavioral health: A handbook of health enhancement and disease prevention.* New York: Wiley.

Rodseth, L., Wrangham, R. W., Harrigan, A. M., & Smuts, B. (1991). The human community as a primate society. *Current Anthropology, 32,* 221–254.

Roebuck, J. A. (1995). *Anthropometric methods: Designing to fit the human body.* Santa Monica, CA: Human Factors and Ergonomic Society.

Roesler, T. A., & McKenzie, N. (1994). Effects of childhood trauma on psychological functioning in adults sexually abused as children. *Journal of Nervous and Mental Disease, 182,* 145–150.

Roffman, R. A., Gillmore, M. R., Gilchrist, L. D., Mathias, S. A., & Krueger, L. (1990). Continuing unsafe sex: Assessing the need for AIDS prevention counseling. *Public Health Reports, 105,* 202–208.

Rofman, E. S., Askinazi, C., & Fant, E. (1980). The prediction of dangerous behavior in emergency civil commitment. *American Journal of Psychiatry, 137,* 1061–1064.

Rogers, C. R. (1942). *Counseling and psychotherapy: Newer concepts in practice.* Boston: Houghton Mifflin.

Rogers, C. R. (1951). *Client-centered therapy: Its current practice, implications, and theory.* Boston: Houghton Mifflin.

Rogers, C. R. (1970). *Carl Rogers on encounter groups.* New York: Harper & Row.

Roggman, L. A., Langlois, J. H., Hubbs-Tait, L., & Rieser-Danner, L. A. (1994). Infant day-care, attachment, and the "file drawer problem." *Child Development, 65,* 1429–1443.

Roitblat, H. L., & von Fersen, L. (1992). Comparative cognition: Representations and processes in learning and memory. *Annual Review of Psychology, 43,* 671–710.

Rokeach, M. (1973). *The nature of human values.* New York: Free Press.

Rokeach, M. (1979). *Understanding human values: Individual and social.* New York: Free Press.

Rolland, J. P. (1993). Validité de construct de "marqueurs" des dimensions de personnalite du modele en cinq facteurs. *Revue Européenne de Psychologie Appliquée, 43,* 317–338.

Rollin, B. E. (1986). Animal consciousness and scientific change. *New Ideas in Psychology, 4,* 141–152.

Romanes, G. J. (1882). *Animal intelligence.* London: Kegan Paul.

Rootes, L. E., & Aanes, D. L. (1992). A conceptual framework for understanding self-help groups. *Hospital and Community Psychiatry, 43,* 379–381.

Rorschach, H. (1942). *Psychodiagnostics: A diagnostic test based on perception.* Berne: Huber.

Rosch, E. (1975). Cognitive representations of semantic categories. *Journal of Experimental Psychology: General, 104,* 192–233.

Rosch, E., & Mervis, C. B. (1975). Family resemblances: Studies in the internal structure of categories. *Cognitive Psychology, 7,* 573–605.

Rosch, E., Mervis, C. B., Gray, W., Johnson, D., & Boyes-Braem, P. (1976). Basic objects in natural categories. *Cognitive Psychology, 8,* 382–439.

Rose, R. M., Gordon, T. P., & Bernstein, I. S. (1972). Plasma testosterone levels in the male rhesus: Influences of sexual and social stimuli. *Science, 178,* 643–645.

Rose, S. (1993). *The making of memory: From molecules to mind.* New York: Anchor.

Rosen, A. J. (1986). Schizophrenic and affective disorders: Rationale for a biopsychosocial treatment model. *Integrative Psychiatry, 4,* 173–177.

Rosenhan, D. L. (1973). On being sane in insane places. *Science, 179,* 250–258.

Rosenhan, D. L., & Seligman, M. E. P. (1989). *Abnormal psychology* (2nd ed.). New York: Norton.

Rosenthal, N. E., Sack, D. A., Gillin, J. C., Lewy, A. J., Goodwin, F. K., Davenport. Y., Mueller, P. S., Newsome, D. A., & Wehr, T. A. (1984). Seasonal affective disorder: A description of the syndrome and preliminary findings with light therapy. *Archives of General Psychiatry, 41,* 72–80.

Rosenthal, R. R., & Jacobson, L. (1968). *Pygmalion in the classroom.* New York: Holt, Rinehart & Winston.

Rosenzweig, M. R. (1984). Experience, memory, and the brain. *American Psychologist, 39,* 365–376.

Roskies, E., Seraganian, P., Oseasohn, R., Hanley, J. A., Collu, R., Martin, N., & Smilga, C. (1986). The Montreal Type A Intervention Project: Major findings. *Health Psychology, 5,* 45–69.

Ross, C. A., Joshi, S., & Currie, R. (1990). Dissociative experiences in the general population. *American Journal of Psychiatry, 147,* 1547–1552.

Ross, C. A., Miller, S. D., Bjornson, L., Reagor, P., Fraser, G. A., & Anderson, G. (1991). Abuse histories in 102 cases of multiple personality disorder. *Canadian Journal of Psychiatry, 36,* 97–101.

Ross, C. A., Miller, S. D., Reagor, P., Bjornson, L., Fraser, G. A., & Anderson, G. (1990). Structured interview data on 102 cases of multiple personality disorder from four centers. *American Journal of Psychiatry, 147,* 596–601.

Ross, L. (1977). The intuitive psychologist and his shortcomings: Distortions in the attribution process. In L. Berkowitz (Ed.), *Advances in experimental social psychology* (Vol. 10). New York: Academic Press.

Ross, L., & Nisbett, R. E. (1991). *The person and the situation: Perspectives of social psychology.* Philadelphia: Temple University Press.

Roth, G., & Ekblad, S. (1993). Migration and mental health: Current research issues. *Nordic Journal of Psychiatry, 47,* 185–189.

Rothbart, M. K., & Ahadi, S. A. (1994). Temperament and the development of personality. *Journal of Abnormal Psychology, 103,* 55–66.

Rothschild, A. J. (1988). Biology of depression. *Medical Clinics of North America, 72,* 765–790.

Rowan, J. (1992). What is humanistic psychotherapy? *British Journal of Psychotherapy, 9,* 74–83.

Rowe, D. C., & Osgood, D. W. (1984). Heredity and sociology theories of delinquency: A reconsideration. *American Sociological Review, 49,* 526–540.

Rowe, D. C., & Plomin, R. (1981). The Burt controversy: A comparison of Burt's data on IQ with data from other studies. *Behavior Genetics, 8,* 81–84.

Rozin, P. (1968). Are carbohydrate and protein intakes separately regulated? *Journal of Comparative and Physiological Psychology, 65,* 23–29.

Rozin, P. (1984). Disorders of the nervous system. In D. L. Rosenhan & M. E. P. Seligman, *Abnormal psychology.* New York: Norton.

Rozin, P., & Fallon, P. (1987). A perspective on disgust. *Psychological Review, 94,* 23–41.

Rozin, P., & Kalat, J. W. (1971). Specific hungers and poison avoidance as adaptive specializations of learning. *Psychological Review, 78,* 459–486.

Rozin, P., Lowery, L., & Ebert, R. (1994). Varieties of disgust faces and the structure of disgust. *Journal of Personality and Social Psychology, 66,* 870–881.

Rubin, D. C., & Kontis, T. S. (1983). A schema for common cents. *Memory and Cognition, 11,* 335–341.

Rubin, J., Provenzano, F., & Luria, Z. (1974). The eye of the beholder: Parents' views on sex of newborns. *American Journal of Orthopsychiatry, 44,* 512–519.

Rubin, R. B., Fernandez-Collado, C., & Hernandez-Sampieri, R. (1992). A cross-cultural examination of interpersonal communication motives in Mexico and the United States. *International Journal of Intercultural Relations, 16,* 145–157.

Rubin, Z. (1973). *Liking and loving: An invitation to social psychology.* New York: Holt, Rinehart & Winston.

Rumbaugh, D. M. (1990). Comparative psychology and the great apes: Their competency in learning, language, and numbers. *Psychological Record, 40,* 15–39.

Rumelhart, D. E., Lindsay, P. H., & Norman, D. A. (1972). A process model for long-term memory. In E. Tulving & W. Donaldson (Eds.), *Organization of memory.* New York: Academic Press.

Rumelhart, D. E., McClelland, J. L., & the PDP Research Group (1986). *Parallel distributed processing: Explorations in the microstructure of cognition: Vol. 1. Foundations.* Cambridge, MA: MIT Press.

Runco, M. A. (1992). Children's divergent thinking and creative ideation. *Developmental Review, 12,* 233–264.

Runyan, W. M. (1981). Why did Van Gogh cut off his ear? The problem of alternative explanations in psychobiology. *Journal of Personality and Social Psychology, 40,* 1070–1077.

Rusbult, C. E. (1980). Commitment and satisfaction in romantic associations: A test of the investment model. *Journal of Experimental Social Psychology, 16,* 172–186.

Rusbult, C. E., Zembrodt, I. M., & Gunn, L. K. (1982). Exit, voice, loyalty, and neglect: Responses to dissatisfaction in romantic relationships. *Journal of Personality and Social Psychology, 43,* 1230–1242.

Rushen, J. P. (1985). The scientific status of animal consciousness. *Applied Animal Behaviour Science, 13,* 387–390.

Rushton, J. P. (1985). Differential K theory: The sociobiology of individual and group differences. *Personality and Individual Differences, 6,* 441–452.

Rushton, J. P. (1988). Race differences in behaviour: A review and evolutionary analysis. *Personality and Individual Differences, 9,* 1009–1024.

Rushton, J. P. (1989). Genetic similarity, human altruism, and group selection. *Behavioral and Brain Sciences, 12,* 503–559.

Russell, J. A. (1991). Culture and the categorization of emotions. *Psychological Bulletin, 110,* 426–450.

Russell, J. A. (1993). Forced-choice response format in the study of facial expression. *Motivation and Emotion, 17,* 41–51.

Russell, J. A. (1994). Is there universal recognition of emotion from facial expressions? A review of the cross-cultural studies. *Psychological Bulletin, 115,* 102–141.

Russell, R. J. H., & Wells, P. A. (1994). Predictors of happiness in married couples. *Personality and Individual Differences, 17,* 313–321.

Rutkowski, G. K., Gruder, C. L., & Romer, D. (1983). Group cohesiveness, social norms, and bystander intervention. *Journal of Personality and Social Psychology, 44,* 545–552.

Rutman, E. M. (1990). Studies of attention development in ontogenesis. *Voprosy Psikhologii, 4,* 161–167.

Rutter, M. (1993). An overview of developmental neuropsychiatry. *Educational and Child Psychology, 10,* 4–11.

Ryan, E. D., & Kovacic, C. R. (1966). Pain tolerance and athletic participation. *Journal of Personality and Social Psychology, 2,* 383–390.

Ryle, G. (1949). *The concept of mind.* London: Hutchinson.

Rymer, R. (1993). *Genie: An abused child's flight from silence.* New York: HarperCollins.

Sackett, P. R., & Wilk, S. L. (1994). Within-group norming and other forms of score adjustment in preemployment testing. *American Psychologist, 49,* 929–954.

Sackett, P. R., Zedeck, S., & Fogli, M. A. (1988). Relationship between measures of typical and maximum job performance. *Journal of Applied Psychology, 67,* 10–17.

Sacks, O. (1984). *A leg to stand on.* New York: Harper & Row.

Saegert, S., & Winkel, G. H. (1990). Environmental psychology. *Annual Review of Psychology, 41,* 441–477.

Saling, M. M., Abrams, R., & Chesler, H. (1983). A photographic survey of lateral cradling preferences in black and white women. *South African Journal of Psychology, 13,* 135–136.

Saling, M. M., & Bonert, R. (1983). Lateral cradling preferences in female preschoolers. *Journal of Genetic Psychology, 142,* 149–150.

Saling, M. M., & Cooke, W. L. (1984). Cradling and transport of infants by South African mothers: A cross-cultural study. *Current Anthropology, 25,* 333–335.

Samms, M., Hari, R., Rif, J., & Knuutila, J. (1993). The human auditory sensory memory trace persists about 10 sec: Neuromagnetic evidence. *Journal of Cognitive Neuroscience, 5,* 363–370.

Sandberg, D. A., & Lynn, S. J. (1992). Dissociative experiences, psychopathology and adjustment, and child and adolescent maltreatment in female college students. *Journal of Abnormal Psychology, 101,* 717–723.

Sandín, B. (1990). Factores de predisposición en los trastornos de ansiedad. *Revista de Psicologia General y Aplicada, 43,* 343–351.

Sanford, M., Offord, D. R., McLeod, K., Boyle, M., Byrne, C., & Hall, B. (1994). Pathways into the work force: Antecedents of school and work force status. *Journal of the American Academy of Child and Adolescent Psychiatry, 33,* 1036–1046.

Sanguiliano, I. (1978). *In her time.* New York: William Morrow.

Sarason, I. G. (Ed.). (1980). *Test anxiety: Theory, research, and applications.* Hillsdale, NJ: Erlbaum.

Sarbin, T. R., & Coe, W. C. (1972). *Hypnosis: A social psychological analysis of influence communication.* New York: Holt, Rinehart & Winston.

Sarbin, T. R., & Mancuso, J. C. (1980). *Schizophrenia: Medical diagnosis or moral verdict?* New York: Pergamon.

Satoh, Y. (1994). Developmental changes of self-disgust during adolescence. *Japanese Journal of Educational Psychology, 42,* 253–260.

Savage-Rumbaugh, E. S. (1990). Language acquisition in a nonhuman species: Implications for the innateness debate. *Developmental Psychobiology, 23,* 599–620.

Savage-Rumbaugh, E. S. (1993). How does evolution design a brain capable of learning language? *Monographs of the Society for Research in Child Development, 58,* 243–252.

Scarborough, E., & Furumoto, L. (1987). *Untold lives: The first generation of American women psychologists.* New York: Columbia University Press.

Scarr, S. (1988). Race and gender as psychological variables: Social and ethical issues. *American Psychologist, 43,* 56–59.

Scarr, S., & Weinberg, R. A. (1976). IQ test performance of black children adopted by white families. *American Psychologist, 31,* 726–739.

Schab, F. R. (1991). Odor memory: Taking stock. *Psychological Bulletin, 109,* 242–251.

Schachere, K. (1990). Attachment between working mothers and their infants: The influence of family processes. *American Journal of Orthopsychiatry, 60,* 19–34.

Schachter, S. (1959). *The psychology of affiliation.* Stanford, CA: Stanford University Press.

Schachter, S., & Singer, J. E. (1962). Cognitive, social, and physiological determinants of emotional state. *Psychological Review, 65,* 379–399.

Schacter, D. L., & Tulving, E. (1994). *Memory systems 1994.* Cambridge, MA: MIT Press.

Schaie, K. W. (1965). A general model for the study of developmental problems. *Psychological Bulletin, 64,* 92–107.

Schank, R. C., & Abelson, R. P. (1977). *Scripts, plans, goals, and understanding.* Hillsdale, NJ: Erlbaum.

Scheff, T. J. (1966). *Being mentally ill: A sociological theory.* Chicago: Aldine.

Scheflin, A. W. (1994). Forensic hypnosis: Unanswered questions. *Australian Journal of Clinical and Experimental Hypnosis, 22,* 25–37.

Scheid-Cook, T. L. (1987). Commitment of the mentally ill to outpatient treatment. *Community Mental Health Journal, 23,* 173–182.

Scheier, M. F., & Carver, C. S. (1985). Optimism, coping, and health: Assessment and implications of generalized outcome expectancies. *Health Psychology, 4,* 219–247.

Scheier, M. F., & Carver, C. S. (1987). Dispositional optimism and physical well-being: The influence of generalized outcome expectancies on health. *Journal of Personality, 55,* 169–210.

Scheier, M. F., Matthews, K. A., Owens, J. F., Magovern, G. J., Lefebvre, R. C., Abbott, R. A., & Carver, C. S. (1989). Dispositional optimism and recovery from coronary artery bypass surgery: The beneficial effects on physical and psychological well-being. *Journal of Personality and Social Psychology, 57,* 1024–1040.

Scherer, K. R., & Wallbott, H. G. (1994). Evidence for universality and cultural variation of differential emotion response patterning. *Journal of Personality and Social Psychology, 66,* 310–328.

Schiffman, S. S. (1977). Food recognition by the elderly. *Journal of Gerontology, 32,* 586–592.

Schildkraut, J. J. (1965). The catecholamine hypothesis of affective disorders: A review of supporting evidence. *American Journal of Psychiatry, 122,* 509–522.

Schleifer, S. J., Keller, S. E., Siris, S. G., Davis, K. L., & Stein, M. (1985). Depression and immunity. *Archives of General Psychiatry, 42,* 129–133.

Schmale, A. H., & Iker, H. P. (1971). Hopelessness as a predictor of cervical cancer. *Social Science and Medicine, 5,* 95–100.

Schmidt, F. L., Ones, D. S., & Hunter, J. E. (1992). Personnel selection. *Annual Review of Psychology, 43,* 627–670.

Schmitt, M. (1992). Interindividuelle Konsistenzunterschiede als Herausforderung für die differentielle psychologie. *Psychologische Rundschau, 43,* 30–45.

Schmitt, N., Borman, W. C., and the Society for Industrial and Organizational Psychology (Eds.). (1993). *Personnel selection in organizations.* San Francisco: Jossey-Bass.

Schmitt, N., & Robertson, I. (1990). Personnel selection. *Annual Review of Psychology, 41,* 289–319.

Schneider, B. (1985). Organizational behavior. *Annual Review of Psychology, 36,* 573–611.

Schneider, B. (Ed.). (1990). *Organizational climate and culture.* San Francisco: Jossey-Bass.

Schneider, D. J. (1991). Social cognition. *Annual Review of Psychology, 42,* 527–561.

Schneider, E. L. (1991). Attachment theory and research: Review of the literature. *Clinical Social Work Journal, 19,* 251–266.

Schneider, W. H. (1992). After Binet: French intelligence testing, 1900–1950. *Journal of the History of the Behavioral Sciences, 28,* 111–132.

Schnell, L., & Schwab, M. E. (1990). Axonal regeneration in the rat spinal cord produced by an antibody against myelin-associated neurite growth inhibitors. *Nature, 343,* 269–272.

Schnitzer, M. L. (1990). Critique of linguistic knowledge. *Language and Communication, 10,* 95–125.

Schofield, W. (1964). *Psychotherapy: The purchase of friendship.* Englewood Cliffs, NJ: Prentice Hall.

Schonpflug, W. (1993). Applied psychology: Newcomer with a long tradition. *Applied Psychology: An International Review, 42,* 5–30.

Schotte, D. E., & Stunkard, A. J. (1987). Bulimia vs bulimic behaviors on a college campus. *JAMA, 258,* 1213–1215.

Schrodinger, E. (1994). On the relationship of four-color theory to three-color theory. *Color Research and Application, 19,* 37–47.

Schubert, M. A., & Borkman, T. J. (1991). An organizational typology for self-help groups. *American Journal of Community Psychology, 19,* 769–787.

Schulenberg, J. E., Asp, C. E., & Petersen, A. C. (1984). School from the young adolescent's perspective: A descriptive report. *Journal of Early Adolescence, 4,* 107–130.

Schuler, H., Farr, J. L., & Smith, M. (Eds.). (1993). *Personnel selection and assessment: Individual and organizational perspectives.* Hillsdale, NJ: Erlbaum.

Schull, J. (1990). Are species intelligent? *Behavioral and Brain Sciences, 13,* 63–109.

Schulman, B. M. (1994). Worklessness and disability: Expansion of the biopsychosocial perspective. *Journal of Occupational Rehabilitation, 4,* 113–122.

Schulman, P., Keith, D., & Seligman, M. E. P. (1993). Is optimism heritable? A study of twins. *Behaviour Research and Therapy, 31,* 569–574.

Schulz, R., & Aderman, D. (1974). Clinical research and the stages of dying. *Omega, 5,* 137–143.

Schwartz, B. (1984). *Psychology of learning and behavior* (2nd ed.). New York: Norton.

Schwartz, B., & Reisberg, D. (1991). *Learning and memory.* New York: Norton.

Schwartz, G. E. (1972). Voluntary control of human cardiovascular integration and differentiation through feedback and reward. *Science, 175,* 90–93.

Schwartz, G. E. (1975). Biofeedback, self-regulation, and the patterning of physiological processes. *American Scientist, 63,* 314–324.

Scott, J. P., & Fuller, J. L. (1965). *Genetics and the social behavior of the dog.* Chicago: University of Chicago Press.

Scott, W. A. (1957). Attitude change through reward of verbal behavior. *Journal of Abnormal and Social Psychology, 55,* 72–75.

Scott, W. A. (1959). Attitude acquisition by response reinforcement: Replication and extension. *Sociometry, 22,* 328–335.

Scott, W. D. (1903). *The theory of advertising.* Boston: Small & Maynard.

Sears, D. O., & Kinder, D. R. (1985). Whites' opposition to busing: On conceptualizing and operationalizing group conflict. *Journal of Personality and Social Psychology, 38,* 1141–1147.

Seeley, E. (1992). Human needs and consumer economics: The implications of Maslow's theory of motivation for consumer expenditure patterns. *Journal of Socio-Economics, 21,* 303–324.

Seeman, J. (1989). Toward a model of positive health. *American Psychologist, 44,* 1099–1109.

Segal, N. L. (1990). The importance of twin studies for individual differences research. *Journal of Counseling and Development, 68,* 612–622.

Segal, S. J., & Fusella, V. (1970). Influence of imaged pictures and sounds in detection of visual and auditory signals. *Journal of Experimental Psychology, 83,* 458–474.

Segall, M. H., Campbell, D. T., & Herskovitz, M. J. (1963). Cultural differences in the perception of geometric illusions. *Science, 139,* 769–771.

Segall, M. H., Campbell, D. T., & Herskovitz, M. J. (1966). *The influence of culture on visual perception.* Indianapolis: Bobbs-Merrill.

Seibert, P. S., & Ellis, H. C. (1991). A convenient self-referencing mood induction procedure. *Bulletin of the Psychonomic Society, 29,* 121–124.

Selfe, L. (1977). *Nadia: A case of extraordinary drawing ability in an autistic child.* London: Academic Press.

Seligman, M. E. P. (1970). On the generality of the laws of learning. *Psychological Review, 77,* 406–418.

Seligman, M. E. P. (1974). Depression and learned helplessness. In R. J. Friedman & M. M. Katz (Eds.), *The psychology of depression: Contemporary theory and research.* Washington, DC: Winston.

Seligman, M. E. P. (1975). *Helplessness: On depression, development, and death.* San Francisco: Freeman.

Seligman, M. E. P. (1994, October 2). *Gene environment covariation.* Message posted on Helplessness Electronic Mailbase.

Seligman, M. E. P. (1995). The effectiveness of psychotherapy: The *Consumer Reports* study. *American Psychologist, 50,* 965–974.

Seligman, M. E. P., & Maier, S. F. (1967). Failure to escape traumatic shock. *Journal of Experimental Psychology, 74,* 1–9.

Selye, H. (1956). *The stress of life.* New York: McGraw-Hill.

Serrano, J. A. (1993). Working with chronically disabled children's families: A biopsychosocial approach. *Child and Adolescent Mental Health Care, 3,* 157–168.

Sestoft, D. (1991). The relative antidepressant efficacy of bilateral compared with non-dominant unilateral electroconvulsive therapy: A review. *Nordisk Psykiatrisk Tidsskrift, 45,* 207–213.

Severino, S. K., Bucci, W., & Creelman, M. L. (1989). Cyclical changes in emotional information processing in sleep and dreams. *Journal of the American Academy of Psychoanalysis, 17,* 555–577.

Shaffer, D. R., Pegalis, L. J., & Cornell, D. P. (1992). Gender and self-disclosure revisited: Personal and contextual variations in self-disclosure to same-sex acquaintances. *Journal of Social Psychology, 132,* 307–315.

Shafter, R. (1992). Women and masochism: An introduction to trends in psychoanalytic thinking. *Issues in Ego Psychology, 15,* 56–62.

Shah, M., & Jeffery, R. W. (1991). Is obesity due to overeating and inactivity, or to a defective metabolic rate? A review. *Annals of Behavioral Medicine, 13,* 73–81.

Shanker, S. G. (1994). Ape language in a new light. *Language and Communication, 14,* 59–85.

Shapiro, K. J. (1990). Animal rights versus humanism: The charge of speciesism. *Journal of Humanistic Psychology, 30,* 9–37.

Shapiro, Y., & Gabbard, G. O. (1994). A reconsideration of altruism from an evolutionary and psychodynamic perspective. *Ethics and Behavior, 4,* 23–42.

Sharp, C. W., & Freeman, C. P. (1993). The medical complications of anorexia nervosa. *British Journal of Psychiatry, 162,* 452–462.

Shaver, K. G. (1975). *An introduction to attribution processes.* Cambridge, MA: Winthrop.

Shaw, M. E. (1981). *Group dynamics: The psychology of small group behavior.* New York: McGraw-Hill.

Shea, M. T., Pilkonis, P. A., Beckham, E., Collins, J. F., Elkin, I., Sotsky, S. M., & Docherty, J. P. (1990). Personality disorders and treatment outcome in the NIMH Treatment of Depression Collaborative Research Program. *American Journal of Psychiatry, 147,* 711–718.

Shedler, J., & Block, J. (1990). Adolescent drug use and psychological health: A longitudinal inquiry. *American Psychologist, 45,* 612–630.

Shedler, J., Mayman, M., & Manis, M. (1993). The *illusion* of mental health. *American Psychologist, 48,* 1117–1131.

Sheehan, P. W., & Tilden, J. (1983). Effects of suggestibility and hypnosis on accurate and distorted retrieval from memory. *Journal of Experimental Psychology: Learning, Memory, and Cognition, 9,* 283–293.

Sheldon, W. H. (1940). *The varieties of human physique.* New York: Harper.

Sheldon, W. H. (1942). *The varieties of temperament.* New York: Harper.

Shepard, R. N., & Cooper, L. A. (1992). Representation of colors in the blind, color-blind, and normally sighted. *Psychological Science, 3,* 97–104.

Sherif, M. (1937). An experimental approach to the study of attitudes. *Sociometry, 1,* 90–98.

Sherif, M. (1966). *In common predicament: Social psychology of intergroup conflict and cooperation.* Boston: Houghton Mifflin.

Sherif, M., & Hovland, C. I. (1961). *Social judgment: Assimilation and contrast effects in communication and attitude change.* New Haven, CT: Yale University Press.

Sherwood, N. (1993). Effects of nicotine on human psychomotor performance. *Human Psychopharmacology: Clinical and Experimental, 8,* 155–184.

Shiina, K. (1991). Conceptualization of concept "concept": On the relation between artificial categories and conceptual representations. *Japanese Journal of Psychonomic Science, 10,* 15–32.

Shilling, L. E. (1984). *Perspectives on counseling theories.* Englewood Cliffs, NJ: Prentice Hall.

Shimberg, M. E. (1929). An investigation into the validity of norms with special reference to urban and rural groups. *Archives of Psychology, No.* 104.

Shoda, Y., Mischel, W., & Wright, J. C. (1993). The role of situational demands and cognitive competencies in behavior organization and personality coherence. *Journal of Personality and Social Psychology, 65,* 1023–1035.

Shoda, Y., Mischel, W., & Wright, J. C. (1994). Intraindividual stability in the organization and patterning of behavior: Incorporating psychological situations into the idiographic analysis of personality. *Journal of Personality and Social Psychology, 67,* 674–687.

Sholomii, K. M., Chuprikova, N. I., & Zakharova, S. A. (1989). Memory functioning when forming "natural" concepts. *Psikologicheskii Zhurnal, 10,* 99–109.

Shorter, E. (1992). *From paralysis to fatigue: A history of psychosomatic illness in the modern era.* New York: Free Press.

Shostak, M. (1981). *Nisa: The life and words of a !Kung woman.* Cambridge: Harvard University Press.

Shukla, G. D. (1989). Electro-convulsive therapy: A review. *Indian Journal of Psychiatry, 31,* 97–115.

Shweder, R. A., & Sullivan, M. A. (1993). Cultural psychology: Who needs it? *Annual Review of Psychology, 44,* 497–523.

Shvyrkov, V. B. (1988). A systems-evolutionary approach to the study of the brain, mind, and consciousness. *Psikologicheskii Zhurnal, 9,* 132–148.

Sicoly, F. (1992). Estimating the accuracy of decisions based on cutting scores. *Journal of Psychoeducational Assessment, 10,* 26–36.

Siegel, D. M., & McDaniel, S. H. (1991). *The Frog Prince:* Tale and toxicology. *American Journal of Orthopsychiatry, 61,* 558–562.

Siegel, L. S. (1993). Amazing new discovery: Piaget was wrong. *Canadian Psychology, 34,* 239–245.

Siegel, S. (1983). Classical conditioning, drug tolerance, and drug dependence. In R. G. Smart, F. B. Glaser, & Y. Israel (Eds.), *Research advances in alcohol and drug problems* (Vol. 7). New York: Plenum.

Sigall, H., & Ostrove, N. (1975). Beautiful but dangerous: Effects of offender attractiveness and nature of the crime on juridic judgment. *Journal of Personality and Social Psychology, 31,* 410–414.

Silbereisen, R. K., & Noack, P. (1988). On the constructive role of problem behavior in adolescence. In N. Bolger, A. Caspi, G. Downey, & M. Moorehouse (Eds.), *Person and context: Developmental processes.* Cambridge, England: Cambridge University Press.

Silbereisen, R. K., & Todt, E. (Eds.). (1994). *Adolescence in context: The interplay of family, school, peers, and work in adjustment.* New York: Springer-Verlag.

Silberman, M. A., & Snarey, J. (1993). Gender differences in moral development during early adolescence: The contribution of sex-related variations in maturation. *Current Psychology: Developmental, Learning, Personality, Social, 12,* 163–171.

Silverman, L. H., Bronstein, A., & Mendelsohn, E. (1976). The further use of the subliminal psychodynamic activation method for the experimental study of the clinical theory of psychoanalysis: On the specificity of relationships between manifest psychopathology and unconscious conflict. *Psychotherapy: Theory, Research, and Practice, 13,* 2–16.

Silverstein, A. M. (1989). *A history of immunology.* San Diego: Academic Press.

Silverstein, S. M. (1993). Methodological and empirical considerations in assessing the validity of psychoanalytic theories of hypnosis. *Genetic, Social, and General Psychology Monographs, 119,* 5–54.

Silverstone, P. H. (1990). Depression increases mortality and morbidity in acute life-threatening medical illness. *Journal of Psychosomatic Research, 34,* 651–657.

Simek, T. C., O'Brien, R. M., & Figlerski, L. B. (1994). Contracting and chaining to improve the performance of a college golf team: Improvement and deterioration. *Perceptual and Motor Skills, 78,* 1099–1105.

Simon, H. A., & Chase, W. G. (1973). Skill in chess. *American Scientist, 61,* 394–403.

Simon, H. A., & Gilmartin, K. (1973). A simulation of memory for chess positions. *Cognitive Psychology, 5,* 29–46.

Simon, R. J., & Aaronson, D. E. (1988). *The insanity defense: A critical assessment of law and policy in the post-Hinckley era.* New York: Praeger.

Simonov, P. V. (1989). Experimental neuropsychology and its importance for human brain research. *Human Physiology, 15,* 161–167.

Simonton, D. K. (1984). *Genius, creativity, and leadership: Historiometric methods.* Cambridge, MA: Harvard University Press.

Simonton, D. K. (1992). Gender and genius in Japan: Feminine eminence in masculine culture. *Sex Roles, 27,* 101–119.

Simonton, D. K. (1993). Blind variations, chance configurations, and creative genius. *Psychological Inquiry, 4,* 225–228.

Simonton, D. K. (1994). *Greatness: Who makes history and why.* New York: Guilford.

Simpson, C. (1991). Colour perception: Cross-cultural linguistic translation and relativism. *Journal for the Theory of Social Behaviour, 21,* 409–430.

Simpson, E. (1974). Moral development research: A case study of scientific cultural bias. *Human Development, 17,* 81–105.

Sinclair, R. C., Hoffman, C., Mark, M. M., & Martin, L. L. (1994). Construct accessibility and the misattribution of arousal: Schachter and Singer revisited. *Psychological Science, 5,* 15–19.

Sinclair, R. C., Mark, M. M., Enzle, M. E., & Borkovec, T. D. (1994). Toward a multiple-method view of mood induction: The appropriateness of a modified Velten mood induction technique and the problems of procedures with group assignment to conditions. *Basic and Applied Social Psychology, 15,* 389–408.

Singer, J. L. (1966). *Daydreaming.* New York: Random House.

Singer, J. L. (1975). *The inner world of daydreaming.* New York: Harper & Row.

Singer, J. L. (1984). *The human personality.* San Diego: Harcourt Brace Jovanovich.

Singer, R. N., Murphey, M., & Tennant, L. K. (Eds.). (1993). *Handbook of research on sport psychology.* New York: Macmillan.

Sitzman, B. T. (1993). ICU psychosis: Organic, psychosocial, or both? *Psychiatric Forum, 16,* 33–39.

Skinner, B. F. (1956). A case history in scientific method. *American Psychologist, 11,* 221–233.

Skinner, B. F. (1957). *Verbal behavior.* New York: Appleton-Century-Crofts.

Sklar, L. S., & Anisman, H. (1979). Stress and coping factors influence tumor growth. *Science, 205,* 513–515.

Sklar, L. S., & Anisman, H. (1981). Stress and cancer. *Psychological Bulletin, 89,* 369–406.

Slama-Cazacu, T. (1992). When does child language learning begin? A (still) challenging question. *Revue Roumaine de Psychologie, 36,* 93–104.

Slater, A. (1992). The visual constancies in early infancy. *Irish Journal of Psychology, 13,* 412–425.

Slobin, D. I. (1979). *Psycholinguistics* (2nd ed.). Glenview, IL: Scott, Foresman.

Slote, W. H. (1992). Oedipal ties and the issue of separation-individuation in traditional Confucian societies. *Journal of the American Academy of Psychoanalysis, 20,* 435–453.

Slyker, J. P., & McNally, R. J. (1991). Experimental induction of anxious and depressed moods: Are Velten and musical procedures necessary? *Cognitive Therapy and Research, 15,* 33–45.

Smilkstein, G. (1984). Prediction of pregnancy complications: An application of the biopsychosocial model. *Social Science and Medicine, 18,* 315–321.

Smith, C. A., & Ellsworth, P. C. (1985). Patterns of cognitive appraisal in emotion. *Journal of Personality and Social Psychology, 48,* 813–838.

Smith, C. A., & Ellsworth, P. C. (1987). Patterns of appraisal and emotion related to taking an exam. *Journal of Personality and Social Psychology, 52,* 475–488.

Smith, C. P. (Ed.). (1992). *Handbook of thematic analysis.* New York: Cambridge University Press.

Smith, C. U. (1993). Evolutionary biology and psychiatry. *British Journal of Psychiatry, 162,* 149–153.

Smith, C., & Lapp, L. (1991). Increases in number of REMs and REM density in humans following an intensive learning period. *Sleep, 14,* 325–330.

Smith, D. C., & Maher, M. F. (1991). Healthy death. *Counseling and Values, 36,* 42–48.

Smith, H. L., Reinow, F. D., & Reid, R. A. (1984). Japanese management: Implications for nursing administration. *Journal of Nursing Administration, 14*(9), 33–39.

Smith, K. H., & Rogers, M. (1994). Effectiveness of subliminal messages in television commercials: Two experiments. *Journal of Applied Psychology, 79,* 866–874.

Smith, M. L., & Glass, G. V. (1977). The meta-analysis of psychotherapy outcome studies. *American Psychologist, 32,* 752–760.

Smith, M. L., Glass, G. V., & Miller, T. I. (1980). *The benefits of psychotherapy.* Baltimore: Johns Hopkins University Press.

Smith, P. B., Peterson, M., Misumi, J., & Bond, M. (1992). A cross-cultural test of the Japanese PM leadership theory. *Applied Psychology: An International Review, 41,* 5–19.

Smith, P. C., & Kendall, L. M. (1963). Retranslation of expectancies: An approach to the construction of unambiguous anchors for rating scales. *Journal of Applied Psychology, 47,* 149–155.

Smith, S. B. (1983). *The great mental calculators.* New York: Columbia University Press.

Smith, S. S., & Richardson, D. (1983). Amelioration of deception and harm in psychological research: The important role of debriefing. *Journal of Personality and Social Psychology, 45,* 1075–1082.

Snarey, J. R. (1985). Cross-cultural universality of social-moral development: A critical review of Kohlbergian research. *Psychological Bulletin, 97,* 202–232.

Snyder, M. (1983). The influence of individuals on situations: Implications for understanding the links between personality and social behavior. *Journal of Personality, 51,* 497–516.

Snyder, M., & Gangestad, S. (1982). Choosing social situations: Two investigations of self-monitoring processes. *Journal of Personality and Social Psychology, 43,* 123–135.

Sogon, S., & Masutani, M. (1989). Identification of emotion from body movements: A cross-cultural study of Americans and Japanese. *Psychological Reports, 65,* 35–46.

Solomon, D. A., & Bauer, M. S. (1993). Continuation and maintenance pharmacotherapy for unipolar and bipolar mood disorders. *Psychiatric Clinics of North America, 16,* 515–540.

Solomon, I. (1994). Analogical transfer and "functional fixedness" in the science classroom. *Journal of Educational Research, 87,* 371–377.

Somervell, P. D., Leaf, P. J., Weissman, M. M., Blazer, D. G., & Bruce, M. L. (1989). The prevalence of major depression in black and white adults in five United States communities. *American Journal of Epidemiology, 130,* 725–735.

Sommer, R. (1969). *Personal space.* Englewood Cliffs, NJ: Prentice Hall.

Sommerhoff, G., & MacDorman, K. (1994). An account of consciousness in physical and functional terms: A target for research in the neurosciences. *Integrative Physiological and Behavioral Science, 29,* 151–181.

Sontag, S. (1979). *Illness as metaphor.* New York: Vintage Books.

Sontag, S. (1988). *AIDS and its metaphors.* New York: Farrar, Straus, & Giroux.

Soubbotskiy, Y. V. (1987). Development in children of the object permanence concept. *Voprosy Psikhologii, 6,* 139–149.

Southwick, C. H., Pal, B. C., & Siddiqui, M. F. (1972). Experimental studies of social intolerance in wild rhesus monkeys. *American Zoologist, 12,* 651–652.

Sowden, S., & Blades, M. (1994). A comparison of children's performance on different linear-ordering tasks. *Journal of Genetic Psychology, 155,* 493–502.

Spacapan, S., & Oskamp, S. (Eds.). (1992). *Helping and being helped: Naturalistic studies.* Newbury Park, CA: Sage.

Spearman, C. (1904). "General intelligence" objectively determined and measured. *American Journal of Psychology, 15,* 201–292.

Spears, R., Lea, M., & Lee, S. (1990). De-individuation and group polarization in computer-mediated communication. *British Journal of Social Psychology, 29,* 121–134.

Spencer, H. (1864). *Social statics.* New York: Appleton.

Sperling, G. (1960). The information available in brief visual presentations. *Psychological Monographs, 74,* 1–29.

Sperry, L. (1989). Assessment in marital therapy: A couples-centered biopsychosocial approach. *Individual Psychology: Journal of Adlerian Theory, Research, and Practice, 45,* 546–551.

Sperry, L. (1990). Personality disorders: Biopsychosocial descriptions and dynamics. *Individual Psychology: Journal of Adlerian Theory, Research, and Practice, 46,* 193–202.

Sperry, R. W. (1969). A modified concept of consciousness. *Psychological Review, 76,* 532–536.

Sperry, R. W. (1976). Changing concepts of consciousness and free will. *Perspectives in Biology and Medicine, 20,* 9–19.

Sperry, R. W. (1987). Structure and significance of the consciousness revolution. *Journal of Mind and Behavior, 8,* 37–65.

Sperry, R. W. (1993). The impact and promise of the cognitive revolution. *American Psychologist, 48,* 878–885.

Spiegel, D., Bloom, J. R., Kraemer, H., & Gottheil, E. (1989). Effect of psychosocial treatment on survival of patients with metastatic breast cancer. *Lancet, 109,* 888–891.

Spitzer, L., & Rodin, J. (1981). Human eating behavior: A critical review of studies in normal weight and overweight individuals. *Appetite, 2,* 293–329.

Spitzer, R. L. (1975). On pseudoscience in science, logic in remission, and psychiatric diagnosis. *Journal of Abnormal Psychology, 84,* 442–452.

Springer, S. P., & Deutsch, G. (1985). *Left brain, right brain* (Rev. ed.). New York: Freeman.

Springer, S. P., & Deutsch, G. (1993). *Left brain, right brain* (4th ed.). New York: Freeman.

Squire, L. R., & Ojemann, J. G. (1992). Activation of the hippocampus in normal humans: A functional anatomical study of memory. *Proceedings of the National Academy of Sciences, 89,* 1837–1841.

Staats, A. W., & Staats, C. K. (1958). Attitudes established by classical conditioning. *Journal of Abnormal and Social Psychology, 57,* 37–40.

Staddon, J. E. R. (1993). *Behaviorism: Mind, mechanism, and society.* London: Duckworth.

Stallone, D. D., & Stunkard, A. J. (1991). The regulation of body weight: Evidence and clinical implications. *Annals of Behavioral Medicine, 13,* 220–230.

Standage, K. (1989). Structured interviews and the diagnosis of personality disorders. *Canadian Journal of Psychiatry, 34,* 906–912.

Stander, V., & Jensen, L. (1993). The relationship of value orientation to moral cognition: Gender and cultural differences in the United States and China explored. *Journal of Cross-Cultural Psychology, 24,* 42–52.

Stanford, L. D., & Hynd, G. W. (1994). Congruence of behavioral symptomatology in children with ADD/H, ADD/WO, and learning disabilities. *Journal of Learning Disabilities, 27,* 243–253.

Starker, S. (1989). *Oracle at the supermarket: The American preoccupation with self-help books.* New Brunswick, NJ: Transaction Publishers.

Staum, M. J., & Brotons, M. (1992). The influence of auditory subliminals on behavior: A series of investigations. *Journal of Music Therapy, 29,* 130–185.

Steadman, H. J. (1980). Insanity acquittals in New York State, 1965–1978. *American Journal of Psychiatry, 137,* 321–326.

Steadman, H. J., & Keveles, C. (1972). The community adjustment and criminal activity of the Baxtrom patients: 1966–1970. *American Journal of Psychiatry, 129,* 304–310.

Steadman, H. J., & Keveles, C. (1978). The community adjustment and criminal activity of Baxtrom patients. *American Journal of Psychiatry, 135,* 1218–1220.

Steadman, J. H., & McCloskey, G. T. (1987). The prospect of surrogate mothering: Clinical concerns. *Canadian Journal of Psychiatry, 32,* 545–550.

Stebbins, W. C. (1980). The evolution of hearing in the mammals. In A. N. Pupper & R. R. Fay (Eds.), *Comparative studies of hearing in vertebrates.* New York: Springer-Verlag.

Steinberg, L. (1985). *Adolescence.* New York: Knopf.

Stellar, E. (1954). The physiology of motivation. *Psychological Review, 61,* 5–22.

Stemmer, N. (1990). Skinner's *Verbal Behavior,* Chomsky's review, and mentalism. *Journal of the Experimental Analysis of Behavior, 54,* 307–315.

Stern, D., & Eichorn, D. (1989). *Adolescence and work: Influences of social structure, labor markets, and culture.* Hillsdale, NJ: Erlbaum.

Stern, J. B., & Fodor, I. G. (1989). Anger control in children: A review of social skills and cognitive behavioral approaches to dealing with aggressive children. *Child and Family Behavior Therapy, 11,* 1–20.

Stern, M., & Karraker, K. H. (1989). Sex stereotyping of infants: A review of gender labeling studies. *Sex Roles, 20,* 501–522.

Stern, R. S. (1978). Obsessive thoughts: The problem of therapy. *British Journal of Psychiatry, 133,* 200–205.

Stern, W. (1914). *The psychological methods of testing intelligence.* Baltimore: Warwick & York.

Sternberg, R. J. (1985). *Beyond IQ: A triarchic theory of human intelligence.* Cambridge, England: Cambridge University Press.

Sternberg, R. J. (1986). *Intelligence applied.* San Diego, CA: Harcourt Brace Jovanovich.

Sternberg, R. J. (1988). Applying cognitive theory to the testing and teaching of intelligence. *Applied Cognitive Psychology, 2,* 231–255.

Sternberg, R. J., & Salter, W. (1982). Conceptions of intelligence. In R. J. Sternberg (Ed.), *Handbook of human intelligence.* Cambridge, England: Cambridge University Press.

Sternberg, R. J., & Smith, E. E. (Eds.) (1988). *The psychology of human thought.* Cambridge, England: Cambridge University Press.

Stevens, A., & Coupe, P. (1978). Distortions in judged spatial relations. *Cognitive Psychology, 10,* 422–437.

Stevens, J. C. (1989). Food quality reports from noninstitutionalized aged. *Annals of the New York Academy of Sciences, 561,* 87–93.

Stevenson, H. W., & Stigler, J. W. (1992). *The learning gap: Why our schools are failing and what we can learn from Japanese and Chinese education.* New York: Summit.

Stewart, J. E. (1980). Defendant's attractiveness as a factor in the outcome of criminal trials: An observational study. *Journal of Applied Social Psychology, 10,* 348–361.

Stigler, J. W. (1984). "Mental abacus": The effect of abacus training on Chinese children's mental calculation. *Cognitive Psychology, 16,* 145–176.

Stoddard, A., Zapka, J., & McCuskar, J. (1992). Social support relationships with drug use and AIDS protective behavior. *International Conference on AIDS, 8,* 228.

Stodgill, R. M. (1948). Personal factors associated with leadership. *Journal of Psychology, 23,* 1–14.

Stodgill, R. M. (1969). Validity of leader behavior descriptions. *Personnel Psychology, 22,* 153–158.

Stoffregen, T. A., & Becklen, R. C. (1989). Dual attention to dynamically structured naturalistic events. *Perceptual and Motor Skills, 69,* 1187–1201.

Stoller, R. J. (1985). *Observing the erotic imagination.* New Haven, CT: Yale University Press.

Stoner, J. A. F. (1961). *A comparison of individual and group decisions involving risk.* Unpublished master's thesis, Massachusetts Institute of Technology.

Straton, D. (1990). Catharsis reconsidered. *Australian and New Zealand Journal of Psychiatry, 24,* 543–551.

Strauss, S. (1989). "Reflections on 25 years of Piagetian cognitive developmental psychology: 1963–1988": Commentary. *Human Development, 32,* 379–382.

Stravynski, A., & Greenberg, D. (1992). The psychological management of depression. *Acta Psychiatrica Scandinavica, 85,* 407–414.

Streissguth, A. P. (1994). A long-term perspective of FAS. *Alcohol Health and Research World, 18,* 74–81.

Stricker, G., & Healey, B. J. (1990). Projective assessment of object relations: A review of the empirical literature. *Psychological Assessment, 2,* 219–230.

Stroebe, M. S., & Stroebe, W. (1983). Who suffers more? Sex differences in health risks of the widowed. *Psychological Bulletin, 93,* 279–301.

Stroebe, W., & Stroebe, M. S. (1987). *Bereavement and health: The psychological and physical consequences of partner loss.* Cambridge, England: Cambridge University Press.

Strom, A. (1980). *Norwegian concentration camp survivors.* New York: Humanities Press.

Strube, M. J., & Garcia, J. E. (1981). A meta-analytical investigation of Fiedler's contingency model of leadership effectiveness. *Psychological Bulletin, 90,* 307–321.

Studd, M. V., & Gattiker, U. E. (1991). The evolutionary psychology of sexual harassment in organizations. *Ethology and Sociobiology, 12,* 249–290.

Stunkard, A. J., Harris, J. R., Pedersen, N. L., & McClearn, G. E. (1990). The body-mass index of twins who have been reared apart. *New England Journal of Medicine, 322,* 1483–1487.

Stuss, D. T., & Benson, D. F. (1986). *The frontal lobes.* New York: Raven Press.

Subotnik, R. F., Karp, D. E., & Morgan, E. R. (1989). High IQ children at midlife: An investigation into the generalizability of Terman's genetic studies of genius. *Roeper Review, 11,* 139–144.

Sudakov, K. V. (1994). The pacemaker of dominant motivation. *Neuroscience and Behavioral Physiology, 24,* 260–266.

Sue, S., & Okazaki, S. (1990). Asian-American educational achievements: A phenomenon in search of an explanation. *American Psychologist, 45,* 913–920.

Sue, S., & Zane, N. (1987). The role of culture and cultural techniques in psychotherapy: A critique and reformulation. *American Psychologist, 42,* 37–45.

Sue, S., Zane, N., & Young, K. (1994). Research on psychotherapy with culturally diverse populations. In A. E. Bergin & S. L. Garfield (Eds.), *Handbook of psychotherapy and behavior change* (4th ed.). New York: Wiley.

Suedfeld, P. (Ed.). (1971). *Attitude change: The competing views.* Chicago: Aldine-Atherton.

Sullivan, H. S. (1947). *Conceptions of modern psychiatry.* Washington, DC: William Alonson White Psychiatric Foundation.

Sullivan, L. (1994). The unseen design. *Psychoanalytic Review, 81,* 175–198.

Sulloway, F. J. (1979). *Freud, biologist of the mind.* New York: Basic Books.

Sumerlin, J. R., & Norman, R. L. (1992). Self-actualization and homeless men: A known-groups examination of Maslow's hierarchy of needs. *Journal of Social Behavior and Personality, 7,* 469–481.

Sun, S., & Meng, Z. (1993). An experimental study of examining "facial feedback hypothesis." *Acta Psychologica Sinica, 25,* 277–283.

Sundberg, N. D., Taplin, J. R., & Tyler, L. E. (1983). *Introduction to clinical psychology.* Englewood Cliffs, NJ: Prentice Hall.

Surrey, J. L. (1990). Mother-blaming and clinical theory. *Women and Therapy, 10,* 83–87.

Sutton, S. R. (1982). Fear-arousing communications: A critical examination of theory and research. In J. R. Eiser (Ed.), *Social psychology and behavioral medicine.* Chichester: Wiley.

Suzuki, K., & Arashida, R. (1992). Geometrical haptic illusions revisited: Haptic illusions compared with visual illusions. *Perception and Psychophysics, 52,* 329–335.

Suzuki, T. (1993). Reexamination of children's spatial egocentrism. *Japanese Journal of Educational Psychology, 41,* 470–480.

Svartberg, M., & Stiles, T. C. (1991). Comparative effects of short-term psychodynamic psychotherapy: A meta-analysis. *Journal of Consulting and Clinical Psychology, 59,* 704–714.

Swanson, H. L. (1988). Learning disabled children's problem solving: Identifying mental processes underlying intelligent performance. *Intelligence, 12,* 261–278.

Sweet, A. A., & Loizeaux, A. L. (1991). Behavioral and cognitive treatment methods: A critical comparative review. *Journal of Behavior Therapy and Experimental Psychiatry, 22,* 159–185.

Sweeting, H. N., & Gilhooly, M. L. (1990). Anticipatory grief: A review. *Social Science and Medicine, 30,* 1073–1080.

Swensen, C. H., Eskew, R. W., & Kohlhepp, K. A. (1981). Stage of family life cycle, ego development, and the marriage relationship. *Journal of Marriage and the Family, 43,* 841–853.

Swets, J. A., & Bjork, R. A. (1990). Enhancing human performance: An evaluation of "New Age" techniques considered by the U.S. Army. *Psychological Science, 1,* 85–86.

Szasz, T. S. (1961). *The myth of mental illness.* New York: Hoeber.

Szinovacz, M. (Ed.). (1982). *Women's retirement: Policy implications of recent research.* Beverly Hills, CA: Sage.

Tadmor, C. S., & Brandes, J. M. (1994). Biopsychosocial profiles of pregnant women at high or low risk to encounter preterm birth. *Journal of Community Psychiatry, 22,* 231–247.

Tajfel, H. (1969). Social and cultural factors in perception. In G. Lindzey & E. Aronson (Eds.), *The handbook of social psychology* (2nd ed., Vol. 3). Reading, MA: Addison-Wesley.

Talaga, J. A., & Beehr, T. A. (1995). Are there gender differences in predicting retirement decisions? *Journal of Applied Psychology, 80,* 16–28.

Tan, E. K., & Carr, J. E. (1977). Psychiatric sequelae of Amok. *Culture, Medicine, and Psychiatry, 1,* 59–67.

Tankard, J. W. (1984). *The statistical pioneers.* Cambridge, MA: Schenkman.

Tannenbaum, A. (1992). Early signs of giftedness: Research and commentary. *Journal for the Education of the Gifted, 15,* 104–133.

Tanner, D. (1972). *Secondary education.* New York: Macmillan.

Tasker, F. L., & Richards, M. P. M. (1994). Adolescents' attitudes toward marriage and marital prospects after parental divorce: A review. *Journal of Adolescent Research, 9,* 340–362.

Taube, C. A., Burns, B. J., & Kessler, L. (1984). Patients of psychiatrists and psychologists in office-based practice: 1980. *American Psychologist, 39,* 1435–1447.

Tavris, C. (1992). *The mismeasure of woman.* New York: Simon & Schuster.

Tavris, C. (1994). "Meeting at the crossroads: Women's psychology and girls' development": Reply. *Feminism and Psychology, 4,* 350–352.

Taylor, A. (1993). Night terrors. *Journal of Contemporary Psychotherapy, 23,* 121–125.

Taylor, R. B., Denham, J. R., & Ureda, J. W. (1982). *Health promotion: Principles and clinical applications.* Norwalk, CT: Appleton-Century-Crofts.

Taylor, S. E. (1985). Adjustments to threatening events: A theory of cognitive adaptation. *American Psychologist, 38,* 1161–1173.

Taylor, S. L., O'Neal, E. C., Langley, T., & Butcher, A. H. (1991). Anger arousal, deindividuation, and aggression. *Aggressive Behavior, 17,* 193–206.

Teglasi, H. (1993). *Clinical use of story telling: Emphasizing the T.A.T. with children and adolescents.* Boston: Allyn & Bacon.

Teicher, M. H., Glod, C. A., Surrey, J., & Swett, C. (1993). Early childhood abuse and limbic system ratings in adult psychiatric outpatients. *Journal of Neuropsychiatry and Clinical Neurosciences, 5,* 301–306.

Tellegen, A., Lykken, D. T., Bouchard, T. J., Wilcox, K. J., Segal, N. L., & Rich, S. (1988). Personality similarity in twins reared apart and together. *Journal of Personality and Social Psychology, 54,* 1031–1039.

Temperley, J. (1993). Is the Oedipus complex bad news for women? *Free Associations, 4,* 265–275.

Tennov, D. (1973). Feminism, psychotherapy, and professionalism. *Journal of Contemporary Psychotherapy, 5,* 107–111.

Terman, L. M. (1916). *The measurement of intelligence.* Boston: Houghton Mifflin.

Terman, L. M. (1925). *Genetic studies of genius:* Vol. 1. *Mental and physical traits of a thousand gifted children.* Stanford, CA: Stanford University Press.

Terman, L. M., Dickson, V. E., Sutherland, A. H., Franzen, R. H., Tupper, C. R., & Fernald, G. (1923). *Intelligence tests and school reorganization.* Yonkers, NY: World Book.

Terrace, H. S. (1985). In the beginning was the "name." *American Psychologist, 40,* 1011–1028.

Tesser, A., & Shaffer, D. R. (1991). Attitudes and attitude change. *Annual Review of Psychology, 41,* 479–523.

Tester, K. (1991). *Animals and society: The humanity of animal rights.* London: Routledge.

Thau, K., Meszaros, K., & Simhandl, C. A. (1993). The use of high dosage lithium carbonate in the treatment of acute mania: A review. *Lithium, 4,* 149–159.

Thayer, S., & Saarni, C. (1975). Demand characteristics are everywhere (anyway): A comment on the Stanford Prison Experiment. *American Psychologist, 30,* 1015–1016.

Thomas, A., & Chess, S. (1977). *Temperament and development*. New York: Bruner-Mazel.

Thomas, D. (1995, February 21). The world's firstborn: Guiness's record-holder turns 120 in France. *The Washington Post*, p. D1.

Thomas, E. L., & Robinson, H. A. (1972). *Improving reading in every class: A sourcebook for teachers*. Boston: Allyn & Bacon.

Thomas, K. R., & Kaplan, S. P. (1994). Greenberg's two-factor safety and effectance drive theory: Implications for rehabilitation. *Journal of Applied Rehabilitation Counseling, 25,* 3–6.

Thomas, R. M. (Ed.). (1988). *Oriental theories of human development: Scriptural and popular beliefs from Hinduism, Buddhism, Confucianism, Shinto, and Islam*. New York: Lang.

Thomas, V. J., & Rose, F. D. (1991). Ethnic differences in the experience of pain. *Social Science and Medicine, 32,* 1063–1066.

Thompson, J. M., Baxter, L. R., & Schwartz, J. M. (1992). Freud, obsessive-compulsive disorder, and neurobiology. *Psychoanalysis and Contemporary Thought, 15,* 483–505.

Thompson, L. (1995, June 12). Search for a gay gene. *Time*, pp. 60–61.

Thompson, R. F. (1976). The search for the engram. *American Psychologist, 31,* 209–227.

Thompson, R. F. (1986). The neurobiology of learning and memory. *Science, 233,* 941–947.

Thompson, R. F. (1993). *The brain: A neuroscience primer* (2nd ed.). New York: Freeman.

Thompson, S. (1981). Will it hurt less if I can control it? A complex answer to a simple question. *Psychological Bulletin, 90,* 89–101.

Thoreson, C. E., & Powell, L. H. (1992). Type A behavior pattern: New perspectives on theory, assessment, and intervention. *Journal of Consulting and Clinical Psychology, 60,* 595–604.

Thorndike, E. L. (1911). *Animal intelligence: Experimental studies*. New York: Macmillan.

Thorndike, R. L., Hagan, E., & Sattler, J. (1986). *Stanford-Binet* (4th ed.). Chicago: Riverside.

Thorndike, R. M. (1990). Origins of intelligence and its measurement. *Journal of Psychoeducational Assessment, 8,* 223–230.

Thurstone, L. L. (1938). Primary mental abilities. *Psychometric Monographs* (No. 1).

Thurstone, L. L., & Thurstone, T. C. (1941). Factorial studies of intelligence. *Psychometric Monographs* (No. 2).

Tien, A. Y., & Eaton, W. W. (1992). Psychopathologic precursors and sociodemographic risk factors for the schizophrenia syndrome. *Archives of General Psychiatry, 49,* 37–46.

Timberlake, W., & Allison, J. (1974). Response deprivation: An empirical approach to instrumental performance. *Psychological Review, 81,* 146–164.

Timberlake, W., & Farmer-Dougan, V. A. (1991). Reinforcement in applied settings: Figuring out ahead of time what will work. *Psychological Bulletin, 110,* 379–391.

Timbrook, R. E., & Graham, J. R. (1994). Ethnic differences on the MMPI–2? *Psychological Assessment, 6,* 212–217.

Tinbergen, N. (1951). *The study of instinct*. Oxford: Clarendon.

Tinbergen, N. (1968). On war and peace in animals and man. *Science, 160,* 1411–1418.

Tippett, L. J. (1992). The generation of visual images: A review of neuropsychological research and theory. *Psychological Bulletin, 112,* 415–432.

Tischer, B. (1988). Ein Verfahren zur Messung der vokalen Kommunikation von Gefühlen. *Sprache und Kognition, 7,* 205–216.

Tolman, E. C. (1948). Cognitive maps in rats and men. *Psychological Review, 55,* 189–208.

Tolman, E. C. (1959). Principles of purposive behavior. In S. Koch (Ed.), *Psychology: A study of a science* (Vol. 2). New York: McGraw-Hill.

Tomer, A. (1992). Death anxiety in adult life: Theoretical perspectives. *Death Studies, 16,* 475–506.

Tomkins, S. S. (1962). *Affect, imagery, consciousness* (Vol. 1). New York: Springer.

Tomkins, S. S. (1963). *Affect, imagery, consciousness* (Vol. 2). New York: Springer.

Tomkins, S. S. (1982). *Affect, imagery, consciousness* (Vol. 3). New York: Springer.

Tomkins, S. S. (1984). Affect theory. In K. S. Scherer & P. Ekman (Eds.), *Approaches to emotion*. Hillsdale, NJ: Erlbaum.

Tomlinson-Keasey, C., & Little, T. D. (1990). Predicting educational attainment, occupational achievement, intellectual skill, and personal adjustment among gifted men and women. *Journal of Educational Psychology, 82,* 442–455.

Toneatto, A., Sobell, L. C., & Sobell, M. B. (1992). Gender issues in the treatment of abusers of alcohol, nicotine, and other drugs. *Journal of Substance Abuse, 4,* 209–218.

Toner, H. L., & Gates, G. R. (1985). Emotional traits and recognition of facial expression of emotion. *Journal of Nonverbal Behavior, 9,* 48–66.

Tooby, J., & Cosmides, L. (1989). Adaptation versus phylogeny: The role of animal psychology in the study of human behavior. *International Journal of Comparative Psychology, 2,* 175–188.

Tooby, J., & Cosmides, L. (1990a). On the universality of human nature and the uniqueness of the individual: The role of genetics and adaptation. *Journal of Personality, 58,* 17–68.

Tooby, J., & Cosmides, L. (1990b). The past explains the present: Emotional adaptations and the structure of ancestral environments. *Ethology and Sociobiology, 11,* 375–424.

Torgersen, S. (1983). Genetic factors in anxiety disorders. *Archives of General Psychiatry, 43,* 222–226.

Toribio, J. (1993). Why there still has to be a theory of consciousness. *Consciousness and Cognition: An International Journal, 2,* 28–47.

Torrey, E. F. (1986). *Witchdoctors and psychiatrists: The common roots of psychotherapy and its future*. Northvale, NJ: Aronson.

Treffert, D. A. (1989). *Extraordinary people: Understanding "idiot savants."* New York: Harper & Row.

Tronick, E. Z., Morelli, G. A., & Ivey, P. K. (1992). The Efe forager infant and toddler's pattern of social relationships: Multiple and simultaneous. *Developmental Psychology, 28,* 568–577.

Trudeau, M., Overbury, O., & Conrod, B. (1990). Perceptual training and figure-ground performance in low vision. *Journal of Visual Impairment and Blindness, 84,* 204–206.

Tryon, G. S., & Kane, A. S. (1990). The helping alliance and premature termination. *Counselling Psychology Quarterly, 3,* 233–238.

Tryon, R. C. (1940). Genetic differences in maze learning in rats. *Yearbook of the National Society for Studies in Education, 39,* 111–119.

Trzepacz, P. T. (1994). The neuropathogenesis of delirium: A need to focus our research. *Psychosomatics, 35,* 374–391.

Tseng, M. H., & Cermak, S. A. (1993). The influence of ergonomic factors and perceptual-motor abilities on handwriting performance. *American Journal of Occupational Therapy, 47,* 919–926.

Tsirul'nikov, E. M. (1992). New suggestions for a classification of somatic sensitivity. *Sensory Systems, 6,* 310–313.

Tuljapurkar, S., Li, N., & Feldman, M. W. (1995). High sex ratios in China's future. *Science, 267,* 874–876.

Tulving, E. (1985). How many memory systems are there? *American Psychologist, 40,* 385–398.

Tulving, E. (1986). What kind of hypothesis is the distinction between episodic and semantic memory? *Journal of Experimental Psychology: Learning, Memory, and Cognition, 12,* 307–311.

Tuorila, H., Pangborn, R. M., & Schutz, H. G. (1990). Choosing a beverage: Comparison of preferences and beliefs related to the reported consumption of regular vs. diet sodas. *Appetite, 14,* 1–8.

Turnbull, C. (1962). *The forest people*. New York: Simon & Schuster.

Turner, A. N., & Miclette, A. L. (1962). Sources of satisfaction in repetitive work. *Occupational Psychology, 36,* 215–231.

Turner, H. A., Hays, R. B., & Coates, T. J. (1993). Determinants of social support among gay men: The context of AIDS. *Journal of Health and Social Behavior, 34,* 37–53.

Turner, M. E., & Pratkanis, A. R. (1994). Affirmative action as help: A review of recipient reactions to preferential selection and affirmative action. *Basic and Applied Social Psychology, 15,* 43–69.

Turner, R. H. (1978). The role and the person. *American Journal of Sociology, 84,* 1–23.

Tury, F., & Szabo, P. (1991). Bulimia nervosa. Irodalmi attekintes. *Psychiatria Hungarica, 6,* 43–59.

Tzeng, O. J., Chen, S., & Hung, D. L. (1991). The classifier problem in Chinese aphasia. *Brain and Language, 41,* 184–202.

Ucros, C. G. (1989). Mood state-dependent memory: A meta-analysis. *Cognition and Emotion, 3,* 139–169.

Ulbaek, I. (1990). Sprog og kognition i evolutionshistorien. *Psyke & Logos, 11,* 32–64.

Umoren, J. A. (1992). Maslow's hierarchy of needs and OBRA 1987: Toward need satisfaction by nursing home residents. *Educational Gerontology, 18,* 657–670.

Unyk, A. M., Trehub, S. E., Trainor, L. J., & Schellenberg, E. G. (1992). Lullabies and simplicity: A cross-cultural perspective. *Psychology of Music, 20,* 15–28.

U.S. Department of Commerce. (1995). *Statistical abstract of the United States*. Washington, DC: Author.

U.S. Department of Health and Human Services. (1986). *Coping with AIDS*. DHHS Publication No. (ADM) HHS–85–1432.Washington, DC: U.S. Government Printing Office.

U.S. Department of Health and Human Services. (1988). *Understanding AIDS*. DHHS Publication No. (CDC) HHS–88–8404. Washington, DC: U.S. Government Printing Office.

U.S. Department of Health and Human Services. (1992). *Health United States 1991*. Hyattsville, MD: Author.

Vaillant, G. E. (1977). *Adaptation to life*. Boston: Little, Brown.

Vaillant, G. E. (1978). Natural history of male psychological health: IV. What kinds of men do not get psychosomatic illness? *Psychosomatic Medicine, 40,* 420–431.

Vaillant, G. E. (1983). *The natural history of alcoholism*. Cambridge, MA: Harvard University Press.

Vaillant, G. E. (1993). *The wisdom of the ego*. Cambridge, MA: Harvard University Press.

Vaillant, G. E., & Vaillant, C. O. (1990). Natural history of male psychological health: A 45-year study of predictors of successful aging. *American Journal of Psychiatry, 147,* 31–37.

Valatx, J. L. (1989). Rêve et mémoire: Approche neurobiologique. *Études Psychothérapiques, 20,* 103–107.

Valenstein, E. S. (1986). *Great and desperate cures*. New York: Basic Books.

Valkenburg, P. M., & van der Voort, T. H. A. (1994). Influence of TV on daydreaming and creative imagination: A review of research. *Psychological Bulletin, 116,* 316–339.

van der Pompe, G., & de Heus, P. (1993). Work stress, social support, and strains among male and female managers. *Anxiety, Stress, and Coping: An International Journal, 6,* 215–229.

Van Heck, G. L., Perugini, M., Caprara, G.V., & Froger, J. (1994).The Big Five as tendencies in situations. *Personality and Individual Differences, 16,* 715–731.

Van Ijzendoorn, M. H. (1992). Intergenerational transmission of parenting: A review of studies in nonclinical populations. *Developmental Review, 12,* 76–99.

Vandereycken, W. (1994). Emergence of bulimia nervosa as a separate diagnostic entity: Review of the literature from 1960 to 1979. *International Journal of Eating Disorders, 16,* 105–116.

VanderVoort, D. J., & Fuhriman, A. (1991).The efficacy of group therapy for depression: A review of the literature. *Small Group Research, 22,* 320–338.

Velten, E. (1968). A laboratory task for induction of mood state. *Behaviour Research and Therapy, 6,* 473–482.

Venneri, A., Stucci, V., Cubelli, R., & Nichelli, P. (1993). L'effetto dell'-elaborazione semantica sulla rievocazione e sul riconoscimento. *Giornale Italiano di Psicologia, 20,* 603–620.

Verbrugge, L. M. (1989). Recent, present, and future health of American adults. *Annual Review of Public Health, 10,* 333–361.

Vernon, P. A. (1982). *The abilities and achievements of Orientals in North America.* New York: Academic Press.

Vernon, P. A. (1983). Speed of information processing and general intelligence. *Intelligence, 7,* 53–70.

Vernon, P. A. (1990a). An overview of chronometric measures of intelligence. *School Psychology Review, 19,* 399–410.

Vernon, P. A. (1990b). The use of biological measures to estimate behavioral intelligence. *Educational Psychologist, 25,* 293–304.

Vernon, P. A. (1991). Studying intelligence the hard way. *Intelligence, 15,* 389–395.

Vernon, P. A., & Mori, M. (1992). Intelligence, reaction times, and peripheral nerve conduction velocity. *Intelligence, 16,* 273–288.

Vernon, P. A., & Weese, S. E. (1993). Predicting intelligence with multiple speed of information-processing tests. *Personality and Individual Differences, 14,* 413–419.

Vernon, P. E. (1979). *Intelligence: Heredity and environment*. San Francisco: Freeman.

Vgontzas, A. N., Kales, A., Bixler, E. O., & Vela-Bueno, A. (1993). "Sleep disorders related to another mental disorder (nonsubstance/ primary): A DSM-IV literature review": Commentary. *Journal of Clinical Psychiatry, 54,* 256–259.

Vialle, W. (1994). "Termanal" science? The work of Lewis Terman revisited. *Roeper Review, 17,* 32–38.

Viau, J. J. (1990). Theory Z: "Magic potion" for decentralized management? *Nursing Management, 21*(12), 34–36.

Vidyasagar, P., & Mishra, H. (1993). Effect of modelling on aggression. *Indian Journal of Clinical Psychology, 20,* 50–52.

Villarruel, A. M., & Ortiz de Montellano, B. (1992). Culture and pain: A Mesoamerican perspective. *Advances in Nursing Science, 15,* 21–32.

Vining, D. R. (1986). Social versus reproductive success:The central theoretical problem of human sociobiology. *Behavioral and Brain Sciences, 9,* 167–216.

Visintainer, M.,Volpicelli, J. R., & Seligman, M. E. P. (1982).Tumor rejection in rats after inescapable or escapable shock. *Science, 216,* 437–439.

Vitaliano, P. P., Maiuro, R. D., Russo, J., & Mitchell, E. S. (1988). A biopsychosocial model of medical student distress. *Journal of Behavioral Medicine, 11,* 311–331.

Vogel, D. A., Lake, M. A., Evans, S., & Karraker, K. H. (1991). Children's and adults' sex-stereotyped perceptions of infants. *Sex Roles, 24,* 605–616.

Vollhardt, L. T. (1991). Psychoneuroimmunology: A literature review. *American Journal of Orthopsychiatry, 61,* 35–47.

von Sydow, K. (1992). Weibliche Sexualität im mittleren und höheren Erwachsenenalter: Übersicht über vorliegende Forschungsarbeiten. *Zeitschrift für Gerontologie, 25,* 113–127.

Vonderheide, S. G., & Mosher, D. L. (1988). Should I put in my diaphragm? Sex-guilt and turn-offs. *Journal of Psychology and Human Sexuality, 1,* 97–111.

Vroom,V. (1964). *Work and motivation*. New York: Wiley.

Vygotsky, L. S. (1962). *Thought and language*. Cambridge, MA: MIT Press.

Vygotsky. L. S. (1978). *Mind in society: The development of higher psychological processes*. Cambridge, MA: MIT Press.

Wachs, T. D., & Desai, S. (1993). Parent-report measures of toddler temperament and attachment: Their relation to each other and to the social microenvironment. *Infant Behavior and Development, 16,* 391–396.

Walker, L. J. (1984). Sex differences in the development of moral reasoning: A critical review. *Child Development, 55,* 677–691.

Walker, S. G., & Watson, G. L. (1994). Integrative complexity and British decisions during the Munich and Polish crises. *Journal of Conflict Resolution, 38,* 3–23.

Wallace, B. (1984). Apparent equivalence between perception and imagery in the production of various visual illusions. *Memory and Cognition, 12,* 156–162.

Wallace, J. (1985). Predicting the onset of compulsive drinking in alcoholics: A biopsychosocial model. *Alcohol, 2,* 589–595.

Wallach, H. (1987). Perceiving a stable environment when one moves. *Annual Review of Psychology, 38,* 1–27.

Wallach, M. A. (1985). Creativity testing and giftedness. In F. D. Horowitz & M. O'Brien (Eds.), *The gifted and talented: Developmental perspectives*. Washington, DC: American Psychological Association.

Wallerstein, J. S. (1991). The long-term effects of divorce on children: A review. *Journal of the American Academy of Child and Adolescent Psychiatry, 30,* 349–360.

Wallerstein, J. S., & Blakeslee, S. (1989). *Second chances: Men, women, and children a decade after divorce*. New York: Ticknor & Fields.

Wallerstein, J. S., & Kelley, J. (1974).The effects of parental divorce: The adolescent experience. In E. Anthony & A. Koupernik (Eds.), *The child in his family: Children as a psychiatric risk* (Vol. 3). New York: Wiley.

Walster, E., Walster, G. W., & Berscheid, E. (1978). *Equity: Theory and research*. Boston: Allyn & Bacon.

Wang, Z.-M. (1993). Psychology in China: A review dedicated to Li Chen. *Annual Review of Psychology, 44,* 87–116.

Wang, Z.W., Crowe, R. R., & Noyes, R. (1992). Adrenergic receptor genes as candidate genes for panic disorder: A linkage study. *American Journal of Psychiatry, 149,* 470–474.

Wankel, L. M., & Sefton, J. M. (1989). A season-long investigation of fun in youth sports. *Journal of Sport and Exercise Psychology, 11,* 355–366.

Wanous, J. P. (1980). *Organizational entry: Recruitment, selection, and socialization of newcomers*. Reading, MA: Addison-Wesley.

Ward, C. A. (1989). Possession and exorcism: Psychopathology and psychotherapy in a magico-religious context. In C. A. Ward (Ed.), *Altered states of consciousness and mental health: A cross-cultural perspective*. Newbury Park, CA: Sage.

Ward, L. M., & Davidson, K. P. (1993).Where the action is: Weber fractions as a function of sound pressure at low frequencies. *Journal of the Acoustical Society of America, 94,* 2587–2594.

Warr, P. B. (1987). *Work, unemployment, and mental health*. Oxford: Clarendon Press.

Wartel, S. G. (1991). Clinical considerations for adults abused as children. *Families in Society, 72,* 157–163.

Wason, P. C. (1966). Reasoning. In B. M. Foss (Ed.), *New horizons in psychology.* Harmondsworth: Penguin.

Wasserman, E. A. (1993). Comparative cognition: Beginning the second century of the study of animal intelligence. *Psychological Bulletin, 113,* 211–228.

Wasserman, P. D. (1989). *Neural computing: Theory and practice.* New York: Van Nostrand Reinhold.

Watkins, C. E. (1992). Research activity with Adler's theory. *Individual Psychology: Journal of Adlerian Theory, Research, and Practice, 48,* 107–108.

Watson, J. B. (1913). Psychology as the behaviorist views it. *Psychological Review, 20,* 158–177.

Watson, J. B. (1925). *Behaviorism.* New York: Norton.

Watson, J. B., & Rayner, R. (1920). Conditioned emotional reactions. *Journal of Experimental Psychology, 3,* 1–14.

Watson, R. E. L. (1983). Premarital cohabitation versus traditional courtship: Their effects on subsequent marital adjustment. *Family Relations, 32,* 139–147.

Watson, R. I. (1973). Investigation into deindividuation using a cross-cultural survey technique. *Journal of Personality and Social Psychology, 25,* 342–345.

Waugh, N. C., & Norman, D. A. (1965). Primary memory. *Psychological Review, 72,* 89–104.

Weaver, C. A. (1993). Do you need a "flash" to form a flashbulb memory? *Journal of Experimental Psychology: General, 122,* 39–46.

Webb, W. B. (1975). *Sleep, the gentle tyrant.* Englewood Cliffs, NJ: Prentice Hall.

Weber, S. J., & Cook, T. D. (1972). Subject effects in laboratory research: An examination of subject roles, demand characteristics, and valid inference. *Psychological Bulletin, 77,* 273–295.

Wechsler, D. (1939). *The measurement of adult intelligence.* Baltimore: Williams & Wilkins.

Weddell, R. A. (1994). Effects of subcortical lesion site on human emotional behavior. *Brain and Cognition, 25,* 161–193.

Weeks, D. J. (1988). *Eccentrics: The scientific investigation.* London: Stirling University Press.

Wehmeyer, M. L. (1992). Developmental and psychological aspects of the savant syndrome. *International Journal of Disability, Development, and Education, 39,* 153–163.

Wehner, T., & Stadler, M. (1994). The cognitive organisation of human errors: A Gestalt theory perspective. *Applied Psychology: An International Review, 43,* 565–584.

Weiffenbach, J. M., Tylenda, C. A., & Baum, B. J. (1990). Oral sensory changes in aging. *Journal of Gerontology, 45,* 121–125.

Weil, A. (1972). *The natural mind: A new way of looking at drugs and the higher consciousness.* Boston: Houghton Mifflin.

Weil, A. (1988). *Health and healing* (Rev. ed.). Boston: Houghton Mifflin.

Weinberger, J., & Hardaway, R. (1990). Separating science from myth in subliminal psychodynamic activation. *Clinical Psychology Review, 10,* 727–756.

Weinberger, J., & Silverman, L. H. (1990). Testability and empirical verification of psychoanalytic dynamic propositions through subliminal psychodynamic activation. *Psychoanalytic Psychology, 7,* 299–339.

Weinberger, M., Hiner, S. L., & Tierney, W. M. (1987). In support of hassles as a measure of stress in predicting health outcomes. *Journal of Behavioral Medicine, 10,* 19–31.

Weiner, B. (1978). Achievement strivings. In H. London & J. E. Exner (Eds.), *Dimensions of personality.* New York: Wiley.

Weiner, B. (1985). *Human motivation.* New York: Springer-Verlag.

Weiner, B. (1986). *An attributional theory of motivation and emotion.* New York: Springer-Verlag.

Weiner, B. A. (1985). Mental disability and the criminal law. In S. J. Brakel, J. Parry, & B. A. Weiner (Eds.), *The mentally disabled and the law.* Chicago: American Bar Foundation.

Weiner, H. (1977). *Psychobiology and human disease.* New York: Elsevier.

Weinstein, N. D. (1989). Optimistic biases about personal risks. *Science, 246,* 1232–1233.

Weinstein, S., & Sersen, E. A. (1961). Tactual sensitivity as a function of handedness and laterality. *Journal of Comparative and Physiological Psychology, 54,* 665–669.

Weisberg, R. W. (1986). *Creativity: Genius and other myths.* New York: Freeman.

Weissman, M. M. (1984). The psychological treatment of depression: An update of clinical trials. In J. B. Williams & R. L. Spitzer (Eds.), *Psychotherapy research: Where are we and where should we go?* New York: Guilford.

Weissman, M. M., Bland, R., Joyce, R. R., Newman, S., Wells, J. E., & Wittchen, H. U. (1993). Sex differences in rates of depression: Cross-national perspectives. *Journal of Affective Disorders, 29,* 77–84.

Weller, A., & Weller, L. (1992). Menstrual synchrony in female couples. *Psychoneuroendocrinology, 17,* 171–177.

Weller, A., & Weller, L. (1993). Menstrual synchrony between mothers and daughters and between roommates. *Physiology and Behavior, 53,* 943–949.

Weller, A., & Weller, L. (1995). The impact of social interaction factors on menstrual synchrony in the workplace. *Psychoneuroendocrinology, 20,* 21–31.

Weller, L., & Weller, A. (1993). Human menstrual synchrony: A critical assessment. *Neuroscience and Biobehavioral Reviews, 17,* 427–439.

Welsh, D. H., Bernstein, D. J., & Luthans, F. (1992). Application of the Premack principle of reinforcement to the quality performance of service employees. *Journal of Organizational Behavior Management, 13,* 9–32.

Wenxi, C. (1994). A mathematical approach to difference limen. *Journal of General Psychology, 121,* 283–293.

Wernicke, C. (1874). *Der aphsiche symptomenkomplex.* Breslau, Poland: Cohn & Weigert.

Wertheimer, M. (1912). Experimentelle Studien über das Sehen von Bewegung. *Zeitschrift für Psychologie, 60,* 321–378.

Wertheimer, M. (1979). *A brief history of psychology* (Rev. ed.). New York: Holt, Rinehart & Winston.

Westen, D. (1991). Social cognition and object relations. *Psychological Bulletin, 109,* 429–455.

Westergaard, G. C., & Suomi, S. J. (1993). Hand preference in the use of nut-cracking tools by tufted capuchin monkeys *(Cebus apella). Folia Primatologica, 61,* 38–42.

Westover, S. A., & Lanyon, R. I. (1990). The maintenance of weight loss after behavioral treatment: A review. *Behavior Modification, 14,* 123–137.

Wever, E. G. (1949). *Theory of hearing.* New York: Wiley.

Whalen, R. E., & Simon, N. G. (1984). Biological motivation. *Annual Review of Psychology, 35,* 257–276.

Whisman, M. A. (1993). Mediators and moderators of change in cognitive therapy of depression. *Psychological Bulletin, 114,* 248–265.

Whissell, C. M. (1985). The role of the face in human emotion: First system or one of many? *Perceptual and Motor Skills, 61,* 3–12.

Whitaker, A., Johnson, J., Shaffer, D., Rapoport, J. L., Kalikow, K., Walsh, B. T., Davies, M., Braiman, S., & Dolinsky, A. (1990). Uncommon troubles in young people: Prevalence estimates of selected psychiatric disorders in a nonreferred adolescent population. *Archives of General Psychiatry, 47,* 487–496.

White, B. L. (1967). An experimental approach to the effects of experience on early human behaviors. In J. P. Hill (Ed.), *Minnesota symposium on child psychology* (Vol. 1). Minneapolis: University of Minnesota Press.

White, C. L., & Burke, P. J. (1987). Ethnic role identity among black and white college students: An interactionist approach. *Sociological Perspectives, 30,* 310–331.

White, N. M., & Milner, P. M. (1992). The psychobiology of reinforcers. *Annual Review of Psychology, 43,* 443–471.

White, R. W. (1959). Motivation reconsidered: The concept of competence. *Psychological Review, 66,* 297–333.

White, S. D., & DeBlassie, R. R. (1992). Adolescent sexual behavior. *Adolescence, 27,* 183–191.

Whiting, J. W. M., & Child, I. L. (1953). *Child training and personality: A cross-cultural study.* New Haven, CT: Yale University Press.

Whittington, H. G. (1985). The biopsychosocial model applied to chronic pain. *Journal of Operational Psychology, 16,* 1–8.

Whorf, B. L. (1956). *Language, thought, and reality.* Cambridge, MA: MIT Press.

Wickens, C. D. (1992). *Engineering psychology and human performance* (2nd ed.). New York: HarperCollins.

Wicker, A. W. (1969). Attitudes versus actions: The relationship of verbal and overt behavioral responses to attitude objects. *Journal of Social Issues, 25*(4), 41–78.

Wicker, A. W. (1971). An examination of the "other variables" explanation of attitude-behavior inconsistency. *Journal of Personality and Social Psychology, 19*, 18–30.

Wicker, F. W., Brown, G., Wiehe, J. A., Hagen, A. S., & Reed, J. L. (1993). On reconsidering Maslow: An examination of the deprivation/dominance proposition. *Journal of Research in Personality, 27*, 118–133.

Wickett, J. C., Vernon, P. A., & Lee, D. H. (1994). *In vivo* brain size, head perimeter, and intelligence in a sample of healthy adult females. *Personality and Individual Differences, 16*, 831–838.

Wickizer, T., Maynard, C., Atherly, A., Frederick, M., Koepsell, T., Krupski, A., & Stark, K. (1994). Completion rates of clients discharged from drug and alcohol treatment programs in Washington State. *American Journal of Public Health, 84*, 215–221.

Wiggins, D. K. (1984). The history of sport psychology in North America. In J. M. Silva & R. S. Weinberg (Eds.), *Psychological foundations of sport.* Champaign, IL: Human Kinetics.

Wilhite, S. C., & Payne, D. E. (1992). *Learning and memory: The basis of behavior.* Boston: Allyn & Bacon.

Wilkie, T. (1993). *Perilous knowledge: The human genome project and its implications.* Berkeley: University of California Press.

Wilkinson, W. K. (1992). The cognitive and social-emotional correlates of color deficiency in children: A literature review and analysis. *Adolescence, 27*, 603–611.

Willerman, L., & Cohen, D. B. (1990). *Psychopathology.* New York: McGraw-Hill.

Williams, C. A. (1990). Biopsychosocial elements of empathy: A multidimensional model. *Issues in Mental Health Nursing, 11*, 155–174.

Williams, L., Bischoff, R., & Ludes, J. (1992). A biopsychosocial model for treating infertility. *Contemporary Family Therapy: An International Journal, 14*, 309–322.

Williams, R. H., & Stockmyer, J. (1987). *Unleashing the right side of the brain: The LARC creativity program.* Lexington, MA: Stephen Greene Press.

Williams, S., & Taormina, R. J. (1992). Group polarization on business decisions in Singapore. *Journal of Social Psychology, 132*, 265–267.

Williams, S., & Taormina, R. J. (1993). Unanimous versus majority influences on group polarization in business decision making. *Journal of Social Psychology, 133*, 199–205.

Willoughby, B., Hogg, R. S., Strathdee, S. A., Craib, K. J., Zadra, J., Montaner, J. S., & Schechter, M. T. (1994). Is low social support a risk factor for subsequent HIV disease progression? *International Conference on AIDS, 10*, 322.

Wilson, C., & Brewer, N. (1993). Individuals and groups dealing with conflict: Findings from police on patrol. *Basic and Applied Social Psychology, 14*, 55–67.

Wilson, E. O. (1975). *Sociobiology: The new synthesis.* Cambridge, MA: Harvard University Press.

Wilson, E. O. (1978). *On human nature.* Cambridge, MA: Harvard University Press.

Wilson, M. A., & Languis, M. L. (1990). A topographic study of differences in the P300 between introverts and extraverts. *Brain Topography, 2*, 269–274.

Wimer, R. E., & Wimer, C. C. (1985). Animal behavior genetics: A search for the biological foundations of behavior. *Annual Review of Psychology, 36*, 171–218.

Winch, R. F. (1958). *Mate selection: A study of complementary needs.* New York: Harper & Row.

Winett, R. A., King, A. C., & Altman, D. G. (1989). *Health psychology and public health: An integrative approach.* Elmsford, NY: Pergamon.

Winn, K. I., Crawford, D. W., & Fischer, J. L. (1991). Equity and commitment in romance versus friendship. *Journal of Social Behavior and Personality, 6*, 301–314.

Winogrond, I. R. (1984). Sensory changes with age: Impact on psychological well-being. *Psychiatric Medicine, 2*, 1–26.

Winter, D. A. (1993). Slot rattling from law enforcement to lawbreaking: A personal construct theory exploration of police stress. *International Journal of Personal Construct Psychology, 6*, 253–267.

Winter, D. G. (1973). *The power motive.* New York: Free Press.

Winter, D. G. (1988). The power motive in women—and men. *Journal of Personality and Social Psychology, 54*, 510–519.

Winter, D. G. (1991). A motivational model of leadership: Predicting long-term management success from TAT measures of power motivation and responsibility. *Leadership Quarterly, 2*, 67–80.

Winter, D. G. (1993). Power, affiliation, and war: Three tests of a motivational model. *Journal of Personality and Social Psychology, 65*, 532–545.

Wise, R. A., & Bozarth, M. A. (1987). A psychostimulant theory of addiction. *Psychological Review, 94*, 469–492.

Wissler, C. L. (1901). The correlation of mental and physical tests. *Psychology Review Monograph Supplement, 3*(No. 6).

Witkin, M. J. (1981). *Provisional patient movement and selective administrative data, state and county mental hospitals, by state: United States, 1977.* Washington, DC: NIMH.

Wittgenstein, L. (1953). *Philosophical investigations.* New York: Macmillan.

Wober, M. (1975). *Psychology in Africa.* London: International African Institute.

Wolf, F. A. (1985). The quantum physics of consciousness: Toward a new psychology. *Integrative Psychiatry, 3*, 236–242.

Wolfe, J. B. (1936). Effectiveness of token-rewards for chimpanzees. *Comparative Psychology Monographs, 12*(No. 60).

Wolfe, T. (1969). *The electric Kool-Aid acid test.* New York: Bantam.

Wolpe, J. (1958). *Psychotherapy by reciprocal inhibition.* Stanford, CA: Stanford University Press.

Wolpe, J., & Rachman, S. (1960). Psychoanalytic "evidence": A critique based on Freud's case of Little Hans. *Journal of Nervous and Mental Disease, 131*, 135–147.

Wong, P. T. (1989). Personal meaning and successful aging. *Canadian Psychology, 30*, 516–525.

Wood, B., Boyle, J. T., Watkins, J. B., & Nogueira, J. (1988). Sibling psychological status and style as related to the disease of their chronically ill brothers and sisters: Implications for models of biopsychosocial interaction. *Journal of Developmental and Behavioral Pediatrics, 9*, 66–72.

Wood, J. M., Bootzin, R. R., Kihlstrom, J. F., & Schacter, D. L. (1992). Implicit and explicit memory for verbal information presented during sleep. *Psychological Science, 3*, 236–239.

Wood, N., & Cowan, N. (1995). The cocktail party phenomenon revisited: How frequent are attention shifts to one's name in an irrelevant auditory channel? *Journal of Experimental Psychology: Learning, Memory, and Cognition, 21*, 255–260.

Wood, W., Wong, F. Y., & Chachere, G. (1991). Effects of media violence on viewers' aggression in unconstrained social interaction. *Psychological Bulletin, 109*, 371–383.

Woodruff-Pak, D. (1988). *Psychology and aging.* Englewood Cliffs, NJ: Prentice Hall.

Woodruff-Pak, D., Logan, C. G., & Thompson, R. F. (1990). Neurobiological substrates of classical conditioning across the life span. *Annals of the New York Academy of Sciences, 608*, 150–178.

Woodward, B. (1985). *Wired: The short life and fast times of John Belushi.* New York: Pocket Books.

Woody, C. D. (1986). Understanding the cellular basis of memory and learning. *Annual Review of Psychology, 37*, 433–493.

Wright, L. (1994). *Remembering Satan.* New York: Knopf.

Wright, L. (1988). The Type A behavior pattern and coronary artery disease. *American Psychologist, 43*, 2–14.

Wright, L., Newman, R. A., Meyer, D., & May, K. (1993). Gender differences in negative affectivity among university faculty members. *Professional Psychology: Research and Practice, 24*, 497–499.

Wright, R. H. (1977). Odor and molecular vibration: Neural coding of olfactory information. *Journal of Theoretical Biology, 64*, 473–502.

Wright, R. H. (1982). *The sense of smell.* Boca Raton, FL: CRC Press.

Wuillemin, D., Richardson, B., & Lynch, J. (1994). Right hemisphere involvement in processing later-learned languages in multilinguals. *Brain and Language, 46*, 620–636.

Wyatt, J. K., & Bootzin, R. R. (1994). Cognitive processing and sleep: Implications for enhancing job performance. *Human Performance, 7*, 119–139.

Wyatt, R. J., Alexander, R. C., Egan, M. F., & Kirch, D. G. (1988). Schizophrenia, just the facts: What do we know, how well do we know it? *Schizophrenia Research, 1*, 3–18.

Yacker, N., & Weinberg, S. L. (1990). Care and justice moral orientation: A scale for its assessment. *Journal of Personality Assessment, 55*, 18–27.

Yalch, R. F. (1991). Memory in a jingle jungle: Music as a mnemonic device in communicating advertising slogans. *Journal of Applied Psychology, 76*, 268–275.

Yalom, I. D. (1995). *The theory and practice of group psychotherapy* (4th ed.). New York: Basic Books.

Yankelovich, D. (1981). *New rules.* New York: Random House.

Yates, A. (1987). Should young children testify in cases of sexual abuse? *American Journal of Psychiatry, 144,* 476–480.

Yee, A. H., Fairchild, H. H., Weizmann, F., & Wyatt, G. E. (1993). Addressing psychology's problems with race. *American Psychologist, 48,* 1132–1140.

Yen, A. (1985). Characteristics of toys preferred by young children. *Information on Psychological Sciences, 2,* 51–52.

Ying, Y., & Zhang, X. (1992). Personality structure in rural and urban Chinese peoples. *Bulletin of the Hong Kong Psychological Society, 28–29,* 81–93.

Yogman, M. W. (1981). Development of the father-infant relationship. In H. Fitzgerald, B. Lester, & M. W. Yogman (Eds.), *Theory and research in behavioral pediatrics* (Vol. 1). New York: Plenum.

Young, L. R., Oman, C. M., Merfeld, D., Watt, D., Roy, S., DeLuca, C., Balkwill, D., Christie, J., Groleau, N., Jackson, D. K., Law, G., Modestino, S., & Mayer, W. (1993). Spatial orientation and posture during and following weightlessness: Human experiments on Spacelab Life Sciences. *Journal of Vestibular Research, 3,* 231–239.

Youniss, J., & Haynie, D. L. (1992). Friendship in adolescence. *Journal of Developmental and Behavioral Pediatrics, 13,* 59–66.

Youniss, J., & Smollar, J. (1985). *Adolescent relations with mothers, fathers, and friends.* Chicago: University of Chicago Press.

Zabik, J. E., Sprague, J. E., & Odio, M. (1993). Interactive dopaminergic and noradrenergic systems in the regulation of thirst in the rat. *Physiology and Behavior, 54,* 29–33.

Zajonc, R. B. (1976). Family configuration and intelligence. *Science, 192,* 227–229.

Zajonc, R. B. (1980). Feeling and thinking: Preferences need no inferences. *American Psychologist, 35,* 151–175.

Zajonc, R. B. (1985). Emotion and facial efference: A theory reclaimed. *Science, 228,* 15–21.

Zajonc, R. B., Murphy, S. T., & Ingelhart, M. (1989). Feeling and facial efference: Implications of the vascular theory of emotion. *Psychological Review, 96,* 395–416.

Zatzick, D. F., Marmar, C. R., Weiss, D. S., & Metzler, T. (1994). Does trauma-linked dissociation vary across ethnic groups? *Journal of Nervous and Mental Disease, 182,* 576–582.

Zborowski, M. (1969). *People in pain.* San Francisco: Jossey-Bass.

Zebrowitz, L. A. (1990). *Social perception.* Pacific Grove, CA: Brooks/Cole.

Zelvys, V. I. (1990). Obscene humor: What the hell? *Humor: International Journal of Humor Research, 3,* 323–332.

Zencius, A., Wesolowski, M. D., & Burke, W. H. (1990). A comparison of four memory strategies with traumatically brain-injured clients. *Brain Injury, 4,* 33–38.

Zerbe, K. J. (1990). Through the storm: Psychoanalytic theory in the psychotherapy of the anxiety disorders. *Bulletin of the Menninger Clinic, 54,* 171–183.

Zigler, E. F., & Berman, W. (1983). Discerning the future of early childhood intervention. *American Psychologist, 38,* 894–906.

Zigler, E. F., & Frank, M. (Eds.) (1988). *The parental leave crisis.* New Haven, CT: Yale University Press.

Zimbardo, P. G. (1972). *The Stanford Prison Experiment: A slide-tape presentation.* Stanford, CA: Author.

Zimbardo, P. G. (1991). *The psychology of attitude change and social influence.* Philadelphia: Temple University Press.

Zimmer, J. W., & Hocevar, D. J. (1994). Effects of massed versus distributed practice of test taking on achievement and test anxiety. *Psychological Reports, 74,* 915–919.

Zimmerman, D., & West, C. (1975). Sex roles, interruptions, and silences in conversation. In B. Thorne & N. Henley (Eds.), *Language and sex: Difference and dominance.* Rowley, MA: Newbury House.

Zohary, E., & Hochstein, S. (1989). How serial is serial processing in vision? *Perception, 18,* 191–200.

Zonderman, A. B., Costa, P. T., & McCrae, R. R. (1989). Depression as a risk factor for cancer morbidity and mortality in a nationally representative sample. *JAMA, 262,* 1191–1195.

Zucker, R. A., & Gomberg, E. S. (1986). Etiology of alcoholism reconsidered: The case for a biopsychosocial process. *American Psychologist, 41,* 783–793.

Zuckerman, M., & Brody, N. (1988). Oysters, rabbits, and people: A critique of "Race differences in behaviour" by J. P. Rushton. *Personality and Individual Differences, 9,* 1025–1033.

Zuckerman, M., & Lubin, B. (1965). *Handbook for the Multiple Affect Adjective Check List.* San Diego: Educational and Industrial Testing Service.

Zuelzer, M., & Maas, J. W. (1994). An integrated conception of the psychology and biology of superego development. *Journal of the American Academy of Psychoanalysis, 22,* 195–209.

Zuk, G. H. (1991). Is divorce a major trauma? *Journal of the American Academy of Child and Adolescent Psychiatry, 30,* 1022.

Zuschlag, M. K., & Whitbourne, S. K. (1994). Psychosocial development in three generations of college students. *Journal of Youth and Adolescence, 23,* 567–577.

Zwyghuizen-Doorenbos, A., Roehrs, T. A., Lipschutz, L., Timms, V., & Roth, T. (1990). Effects of caffeine on alertness. *Psychopharmacology, 100,* 36–39.

ACKNOWLEDGMENTS

Cover Illustration: 261/269/I/PIP FEMALE TORSO II by Kasimir Malevich; Russian State Museum, St. Petersburg/A. Burkatousky/Superstock.

Photo Credits: All photos not credited are the property of Addison-Wesley Educational Publishers Inc. Positions of photographs are shown in abbreviated form as follows: top (t), bottom (b), center (c), left (l), right (r).

Table of Contents: vii © Van Gogh Museum, Amsterdam/Superstock; viii © Palazzo Vecchio, Florence/E.T. Archive, London/Superstock; ix © Christie's London/Superstock; x © Superstock; xi © Lerner Fine Art Collection/Superstock; xii © Christie's, London/Superstock; xii © Private Collection/Superstock; xiii © Superstock; xiv © National Portrait Gallery, London/Superstock"; xv © National Gallery, Budapest/E.T. Archive, London/Superstock; xvi © Private Collection/Superstock; xvii © Russian State Museum, St. Petersburg/A. Burkatousky/Superstock; xviii © Russian State Museum, St. Petersburg/A. Burkatousky/Superstock; xix © Private Collection/Superstock; xx © Superstock; xxi © Private Collection/Superstock; xxii © Lerner Fine Art Collection/Superstock.

Preface: xxviii © Jeff Greenberg/Unicorn Stock; xxix © Superstock; xxxvii Courtesy of the Author.

Chapter One: 2 © Van Gogh Museum, Amsterdam/Superstock; 6 (l) © Bob Daemmrich/The Image Works; 6 (r) © Barbara J. Feigles/Stock Boston 8 © Reuters/Bettmann 12 © The Bettmann Archive 13 © Culver Pictures 14 (t) © The Ferdinand Hamburger, Jr. Archives of the Johns Hopkins University 14 (b) © The Bettmann Archive 18 (t) © Archives of the History of American Psychology, University of Akron, Akron, Ohio 18 (b) © Superstock; 21 © UPI/Bettmann; 23 (r) © Frank Siteman/Stock Boston; 23 (t) © The Gorilla Foundation; 23 (b) © Superstock.

Chapter Two: 30 © Palazzo Vecchio, Florence/E.T. Archive, London/Superstock 32 © Superstock 34 © Bob Daemmrich/The Image Works 37 © Herb Snitzer/Stock Boston 38 © Frank Clarkson/Gamma Liason 42 © Bill Bachmann/Photo Researchers 44 © Jim Amos/Photo Researchers 48 © Culver Pictures; 52 © Richard Pasley/Stock Boston; 54 Courtesy Alexandria Milgram, Riverdale, NY; 58 © Brown Brothers.

Chapter Three: 60 © Christie's London/Superstock; 62 © Superstock; 63 © Owen Franken/Stock Boston; 66 © Cerry Cooke/Animals/Animals; 67 © Royal College of Surgeons of England; 68 © Joel Gordon; 69 © Howard Sochurek; 69 © Howard Sochurek; 71 © W. K. Fletcher/Photo Researchers; 73 © Petit Format/Nestlé/Science Source/Photo Researchers 76G David L. Arnold/National Geographic Society Image Collection; 84 © Wesley Bocxe/Photo Researchers; 87 © H. Dratch/The Image Works; 89 © David R. Frazier Photolibrary/Photo Researchers.

Chapter Four: 94 © Superstock; 96 © Warren Anatomical Museum; 99 © Jeff Greenberg/The Picture Cube; 101 © Peter Vandermark/Stock Boston; 104 © Gary Retherford/Photo Researchers; 105 © J. Pickerell/The Image Works; 112 © Sidney/Monkmeyer Press; 117 © Superstock; 121 © Carlin/Arcive Photos 1226476; 125 © J. Berndt/Stock Boston; 127 © James King-Holmes/Science Photo Library/Photo Researchers; 130 © Hank Morgan/Science Source/Photo Researchers; 130 © Brookhaven National Laboratory; 131Clinique Ste Catherine/CNRI/Science Photo Library/Photo Researchers.

Chapter Five: 136 © Lerner Fine Art Collection/Superstock; 138 © Lee Balterman/The Picture Cube; 140 © The Bettmann Archive; 141 © Robert Aschenbrenner/Stock Boston; 142 © The Granger Collection; 145 © Archive Photos/Jeff Robbins/Reuters; 146 © Al Cook/Stock Boston;

150 © Bob Daemmrich/Stock Boston; 154 © Bob Burch/Photobank, Inc.; 163 © Ken Kerbs/Monkmeyer Press; 165 © D. Ogust/The Image Works; 168 © Tom Mackie/Tony Stone Images; 169 © Enrico Ferorelli; 173 © 1996 M.C. Escher/Cordon Art-Baarn-Holland. All Rights Reserved.

Chapter Six: 180 © Christie's, London/Superstock; 182 © Paul Chesley/Tony Stone Images 1826476.WADE.468; 184 © Robert Frerck/Tony Stone Worldwide; 187 © Ron Chapple/FPG; 191 © Chromosohm/Sohm/Stock Boston; 192 © Christopher Springman; 198 The Museum of Modern Art, New York. Acquired through the Lillie P. Bliss Bequest. Photograph © 1996 The Museum of Modern Art, New York.; 201 © Alan Oddie/Photo Edit; 204 © Brian Smith/Stock Boston; 206 Tibor Hirsch/Photo Researchers; 208 Courtesy News and Publication Service, Stanford University; 210 Paula Lerner/The Picture Cube; 213 © Bachmann/Photo Researchers; 215 © Kate Denny/Photo Edit; 217 © Archive photos.

Chapter Seven: 220 © Private Collection/Superstock; 222 © Kobal Collection; 224 © Oxford Scientific Films/Animals/Animals; 227 © Peter Menzel/Stock Boston; 228 Photograph by J.A. Stevenson. Supplied by Neal E. Miller, Dept. of Psychology, Yale Unviersity; 230 © Merrim/Monkmeyer Press; 234 © Jeff Greenberg/Photo Edit; 236 © Earl Dotter/Impact Visuals; 239 © Deborah Davis/Photo Edit; 243 © Reuters/Bettmann; 245 © Robert Brenner/Photo Edit; 251 © Myrleen Ferguson Cate/Photo Edit; 257 © Philip J. Griffiths/Magnum Photos; 260 © Michael Krasowitz/FPG.

Chapter Eight: 262 © Superstock; 263 © Cheryl Woike Kucharzak; 265 © Bob Daemmrich/Stock Boston; 267 © Will & Deni McIntyre/Photo Researchers; 268 © The Bettmann Archive; 271 © Alan Carey/Photo Reseachers; 273 © M. Siluk/The Image Works; 274 Prof. Benjamin Harris, University of Wisconsin, Parkside; 276 © Mulvehill/The Image Works; 278 © Falk/Monkmeyer 280 © Michelle Bridwell/Photo Edit; 284 © Peter Glass/Monkmeyer Press; 285 © Bob Daemmrich/The Image Works; 288 © Jack Spratt/The Image Works; 290 © Lew Merrim/Monkmeyer Press; 293 Courtesy of Albert Bandura, Stanford University, CA.; 296 © J.P. Laffont/Sygma; 297 © A. Hudalic/Saola/Gamma Liaison; 301 © Michael Dwyer/Stock Boston; 301 © Frank Pedrick/The Image Works.

Chapter Nine: 306 © National Portrait Gallery, London/Superstock; 308 © Steve Bloom; 312 © Bob Daemmrich/Stock Boston; 313 © Grant LeDuc/Monkmeyer Press; 318 © Richard Reed/Unicorn Stock Photos; 321 © Granitsas/The Image Works; 321 © Neubauer/Monkmeyer Press CUT © F. Pedrick/The Image Works; 323 © Sidney/Monkmeyer Press; 326 © Bob Daemmrich/Stock Boston; 331 © Tom McCarthy/The Picture Cube, Inc.; 336 © Byron/Monkmeyer Press; 339 © R. Lord/The Image Works; 342 © Bob Daemmrich/Stock Boston.

Chapter Ten: 350 © National Gallery, Budapest/E.T. Archive, London/Superstock; 352 (all) © Henry Gris/FPG; 356 © Ed Carreon/Sipa Press; 366 © Lew Merrim/ Monkmeyer; 366 © Lew Merrim/Monkmeyer; 368 © Nathan Nourok; 373 © UPI/Bettmann Newsphotos; 375 © UPI/Bettmann Newsphotos; 377 © Mike Mazzaschi/Stock Boston; 378 © Martin Rogers/Tony Stone Worldwide; 381 © Andy Sacks/Tony Stone Worldwide; 383 © Tony Freeman/Photo Edit; 385Bob Daemmrich/Stock Boston; 388 © W. Hill, Jr./The Image Works; 390 ©David Young-Wolff/Photo Edit; 393 © UPI/Bettmann.

Chapter Eleven: 396 © Private Collection/Superstock; 398 © Stephen Collins/Photo Researchers; 400 © Russell D. Curtis/Photo Researchers; 402 ©The Bettmann Archive; 409National Archives; 411Edward Clark/Life Magazine © Time Inc.; 412 © John Carter/Photo Researchers; 415 © Bob

Daemmrich/The Image Works; 418 © Russell D. Curtis/Photo Researchers; 420 © MacPherson/Monkmeyer; 422 © Florent Flipper/Unicorn Stock Photos; 426 © The Kobal Collection; 431 © AP/Wide World; 431 © Ulf Anderson/Gamma Liaison; 431Paul Robertson; 431 © Bob Daemmrich/Stock Boston; 432Courtesy of Robert J. Sternberg, Dept. of Psychology, Yale University; 434 © Paul Murphy/Unicorn Stock Photos.

Chapter Twelve: 438 © Russian State Museum, St. Petersburg/A. Burkatousky/Superstock; 441 Jonathan Daniel/Allsport USA; 444 © Shackman/Monkmeyer Press; 447 © David J. Sams/Stock Boston; 449 (t) © Ed Malitsky/The Picture Cube; 449 (b) © UPI/Bettmann; 450 © The Bettmann Archive; 452 © Robert W. Ginn/Unicorn Stock Photos; 453 © UPI/Bettmann; 455 (Cattell) © Topham/The Image Works; 455 (Eysenk) Courtesy Institute of Psychiatry, London, England; 457 © Keystone/The Image Works; 459 © Reuters/Sam Mircovich/Archive Photos; 460 © The Bettmann Archive; 462 © Robert Ginn/Photo Edit; 465 © Jean Higgins/Unicorn Stock Photos; 473 © David J. Sams/Stock Boston; 474 © C. Gatewood/The Image Works; 477 © Kerbs/Monkmeyer.

Chapter Thirteen: 480 © Russian State Museum, St. Petersburg/A. Burkatousky/Superstock; 483 © Bruce M. Wellman/Stoc Boston; 487 © The Bettmann Archive; 490 © Hazel Hankin/Stock Boston; 492 © Will & Deni McIntyre/Photo Researchers; 495 © Robert Brenner/Photo Edit; 496 © Bettmann; 498 © C. Schmeiser/Unicorn Stock Photos; 502 © David Young-Wolff/Photo Edit; 506 ©David Young-Wolff/Photo Edit; 511AP/Wide World; 513 © Brookhaven National Lab; 515 © AP/WIDE WORLD; 517 © Reuters/Bettmann.

Chapter Fourteen: 520 © Private Collection/Superstock; 523 © Brian Smith/Stock Boston; 533 © J. Griffin/The Image Works; 536 © Paul Murphy/Unicorn Stock Photos; 537 © Tom McCarthy/Unicorn Stock Photos; 539 © LeDuc/Monkmeyer Press; 543 © Bob Daemmrich/The Image Works; 550 © Billy E. Barnes/Stock Boston; 551 © Stephen Frisch/Stock Boston; 554 © R. Sidney/The Image Works.

Chapter Fifteen: 558 © Superstock; 560 © Reuters/LA Daily News-POOL/Archive Photos; 561 © Corbis-Bettmann; 563 © Jeff Isaac Greenberg/Photo Edit; 567 © The Bettmann Archive; 568 © Will McIntyre/Photo Researchers; 571 © Superstock; 575 © Susan McCartney/Photo Researchers; 581 © J. Pickerell/FPG; 583 © Sue Ford/Science Photo Library/Photo Researchrs; 584 © Rhoda Sidney/Stock Boston; 586 © Jeffry Myers/FPG; 590 © Spencer Grant/Photo Researchers; 592 © Joe Polillio/Gamma Liaison; 595 © David Graham/Black Star; 598 (t) © Mark Reinstein/FPG; 598 (l) © Topham/The Image Works; 598 (r) © DPA/The Image Works.

Chapter Sixteen: 604 © Private Collection/Superstock; 607 © Joseph Nettis/Photo Researchers; 610 © Florent Flipper/Unicorn Stock Photos; 613 © Biology Media/Science Source/Photo Researchers; 615 © Ed Lallo/Gamma Liaison; 618 © Prof. P. Motta/Dept. of Anatomy/University La Sapienza, Rome/Science Photo Library/Photo Researchers; 618 © Prof. P. Motta, G. Macchiarelli, S.A. Nottola/Science Photo Library/Photo Researchers; 620 © AP/Wide World; 622 © Christopher Brown/Stock Boston; 625 © Peter Vadnai/The Stock Market; 627 © David Weintraub/Photo Researchers; 629 © Jay Foreman/Unicorn Stock Photos; 631 © Richard Hutchings/Photo Researchers; 634 © Rob Crandall/Stock Boston; 637 © Goodman/Monkmeyer; 639 © Jeff Greenberg/Unicorn Stock Photos.

Chapter Seventeen: 642 © Lerner Fine Art Collection/Superstock; 644Courtesy Johnson & Johnson; 646 © Dion Ogust/The Image Works; 650 © James L. Fly/Unicorn Stock Photos; 652 © Superstock; 654 © Stpehen Frisch/Stock Boston; 655 © D. Ogust/The Image Works; 658 © Eric R. Berndt/Unicorn Stock Photos; 660 © George Haung/Photo Researchers; 664 © Cecile Treal/Gamma Liaison; 665 © Gamma Liaison; 668 © David R. Frazier/Photo Researchers; 672 © Dean Abramson/Stock Boston; 674 © Azzi/Woodfin Camp & Associates; 678 © AP/Wide World.

NAME INDEX

Aaltonen, T., 205
Aanes, D. L., 681
Aaronson, D. E., 677
Abelson, R. P., 570, 580
Abramov, I., 152
Abramowitz, S. I., 551
Abrams, R., 61
Abramson, L. Y., 508
Abravanel, E., 376
Achenbach, T. M., 470
Adam, 78
Adams-Webber, J., 461
Adams, D. M., 507
Adams, H. E., 466
Adams, J., 317, 400
Adams, M. J., 329
Adebimpe, V. R., 511
Ader, R., 275, 621
Aderman, D., 391
Adetunji, J. B., 639
Adityanjee, 451
Adler, A., 450$–$52, 518
Aesop, 188
Aguirre, B. E., 576
Ahadi, S. A., 26
Ahern, D. W., 656
Ainsworth, L. L., 189
Ainsworth, M. D. S., 379
Akashi, H., 78
Akiyama, H., 26
Alados, C. L., 597
Albee, G. W., 629
Albers, H. E., 113
Albert, D. J., 112
Albert, L., 274–75, 488, 500
Alberti, E. T., 172
Albin, R. L., 111
Alcaraz-García, M., 252
Aldag, R. J., 596
Aldrich, M. S., 111
Alessi, G., 278
Alexander, C. A., 527
Alexander, F., 630–33
Alexander, I. E., 464
Alexander, J. F., 537
Alexander, R. C., 24
Alexander, R. D., 295
Algom, D., 176
Alkon, D. L., 120
Allain, H., 199
Allen, A., 474–75
Allen, L. S., 121
Allen, P. A., 327
Allen, W., 679
Alliger, G. M., 470, 599
Allison, J., 285
Allport, G. W., 40, 453–55, 474, 560, 571
Allred, K. D., 566
Almqvist, B., 670
Altman, D. G., 614
Alvarez, G., 252
Amelang, M., 634
Ames, E. W., 669
Ames, W., 111–12
Amoore, J. E., 159
Anastasi, A., 428, 647, 662
Anderson, E., 552
Anderson, G., 504

Anderson, J. P., 91
Anderson, J. R., 316–18, 335
Andia, A. M., 511
Andreasen, N. C., 103, 496
Andresen, J., 341
Andrews, M. F., 140
Andy, O. J., 113
Angleitner, A., 457, 464
Anguera, B., 324
Anisman, H., 626
Ansari, Z. A., 19
Ansseau, M., 508
Anthony, S., 205
Anthony, T., 577, 596
Antill, J. K., 387
Antonets, V. A., 160
Antonovsky, A., 244
Antonucci, T. C., 26
Appel, J., 287
Aram, J. D., 246
Arashida, R., 172
Arasteh, J. D., 384
Arbisi, P. A., 549
Archer, J., 242
Arcuri, A. F., 560
Argyris, C., 666
Aristotle, 10, 146, 439, 608, 611
Aronson, E., 563
Arvey, R. D., 657
Ary, D. V., 294
Asch, S. E., 573, 577
Aserinsky, E., 193
Ash, D. W., 282
Ashbrook, P. W., 332
Askenasy, J. J., 196
Askinazi, C., 677
Asp, C. E., 653
Assar, M., 257
Atkinson, J. W., 242–43
Atkinson, R. C., 325, 334
Atoum, A. O., 595
Attneave, A., 320
Auerbach, C., 173
Austin, J. T., 648, 659
Avary, D. W., 597
Averill, J. R., 177
Avis, J. M., 538
Avolio, B. J., 654
Axel, R., 159
Axelrod, S., 282
Axinn, W. G., 387

Bach, J. S., 300
Bachman, B. A., 585
Backer, T. E., 620
Bacon, D. L., 678
Bacon, F., 31–32
Baddeley, A., 327, 331
Baer, J. S., 214
Baeyens, F., 298
Bagby, J. W., 174
Bagford, J., 515
Bagnato, S. J., 402, 408
Baillargeon, R. A., 369
Baker, L. A., 414
Bakker, F. C., 672
Balada, F., 241
Balay, J., 189

Baldwin, E., 55
Bales, R. F., 598–99
Balkwell, C., 391
Ball, J. F., 391
Balleine, B., 226
Baltes, P. B., 369
Bancroft, J., 133
Bandura, A., 293, 462–63, 476, 536, 659
Bangert-Drowns, R. L., 411
Banks, W. P., 185
Bannister, R. C., 80
Baños, R. M., 235
Baranowski, T., 463
Barban, L., 505
Barbarin, O. A., 392
Barbera, E., 256
Bard, P. A., 252
Barefoot, J. D., 632
Barker, E., 441
Barkley, C., 606
Barklind, K. S., 623
Barlow, F., 423
Barnes-Farrell, J. L., 659
Barnett, R., 387
Barrett, K. C., 256
Barrick, M. R., 659
Barsky, A. J., 502, 616
Bartlett, F. C., 328
Barton, R., 469
Bartoshuk, L. M., 157–58
Bartrop, R. W., 636
Baruch, G., 387
Baruch, J., 638
Basbaum, A. I., 177
Baskin, C. H., 173
Bass, B. M., 598
Batchelor, W. F., 620
Bates, E., 118
Bates, M. S., 177
Batson, C. D., 587
Batuev, A. S., 228
Bauer, M. S., 528
Baum, B. J., 143
Bauman, K. E., 385
Baumann, D. J., 145
Baumeister, R. F., 184
Baumrind, D., 54, 388
Baxter, L. R., 476
Beach, F. A., 134, 142, 177, 240
Beaman, A. L., 575
Beauchamp, G. K., 158
Beavis and Butt-Head, 303
Beck, A. T., 466, 498–500, 508–10, 515, 534–35
Beck, S., 173
Becker, W. C., 389
Becklen, R. C., 166
Beckstrom, J. H., 84
Bee, H. L., 376
Beehr, T. A., 656
Begg, I. M., 190
Bekesy, G. V., 157
Bellak, L., 467
Belloc, N. B., 628
Bellugi, U., 118
Belsky, J., 380
Belushi, J., 209
Bem, D. J., 474–75
Bemis, C., 634

SUBJECT INDEX

Schema, 318-20, 566
Scheme, 365
Schizoid personality disorder, 514
Schizophrenia, 23-25, 103, 481-82, 510-14
  hallucinations and delusions of, 186, 511, 513
  symptoms of thought disorder in, 511
Schizotypal personality disorder, 514, 515
Scholastic Aptitude Test (SAT), 397-98, 399, 402, 410-11
School, adolescent social development and, 384
Science, Bacon's contribution to, 31-32
Scientific materialism, 11, 183
Scientific method, 5, 31, 32
Scientific psychology, 6-8
Scientific trends, 11
Scripts, 570
Seasonal affective disorder, 530
Secondary appraisal, 625
Secondary (conditioned) reinforcers, 283
Secondary sexual characteristics, 361, 363
Second-order conditioning, 272
Secure attachment, 593-94
Seizures, EEGs of, 129
Selection, personnel, 647, 656-59
Selection (interaction type), 474
Selective attention, 164, 186
Selective serotonin reuptake inhibitors, 528
Selectivity of perception, 164-66
Self
  invention of, 184
  loss of, 575-76
Self-actualization, 246, 460-61
Self-aggrandizement, 566
Self-criticism and crisis of 1960s and 1970s, 17-18
Self-doubt, autonomy vs., 374
Self-efficacy, 463
Self-fulfilling prophecy, Theory X as, 665, 666
Self-help groups, 681
Self-image, attitude-behavior consistency and, 581
Self-monitoring, 475
Self-reports, 469-70
Self-serving bias, 569
Self-theory, 460-61
Self-understanding, 531
Semantic memory, 328, 329
Senility, 369
Sensation, 138-63, 175-7. *See also* Perception;
    Sensory systems
  culture and, 175
  defined, 138
  information processing theory and, 140-41
  knowledge of world and, 139-40
  psychophysics research and, 141-45
Sensitization, 265
Sensorimotor stage of cognitive development, 366, 368
Sensory memory (sensory register), 325-27
Sensory projection areas, 116, 117
Sensory systems, 146-63
  aging and, 89-90, 142-43
  cutaneous senses, 142, 160-61, 176
  evolution and development of, 146-47, 156
  hearing, 142, 154-57
  position senses, 161-63
  smell, 142, 158-60, 346
  taste, 142, 143, 157-58, 175
  vision, 137-38, 147-54
Sentience need, 230
Separation, attachment and reaction to, 379
Septum, 112
Serial position effect, 324
Serial processing, 310-11, 312
Serotonin, 103, 104, 507-8, 528, 530

Set-point theory, 234-35
Sex
  aggression and, 224-25
  need for, 230
Sex differences, 380. *See also* Gender differences
  in brain, 121-23
  physical development of, 358-59
Sex glands, 359
Sex hormones, 237, 241, 242, 561
Sexism, 578
Sex organs, 359
Sex-typing of toys, 669-70
Sexual abuse, 504, 679
Sexual activity
  AIDS and, 629-30
  cultural norms of, 258
Sexual behavior, 237
Sexual characteristics, secondary, 361, 363
Sexual development, 239-41, 385-86
Sexual harassment, 87
Sexual-identity disorders, 482
Sexuality, 237-41
Sexually transmitted disease, 386
  AIDS, 386, 605-6, 619-21, 629-30, 635-36
  syphilis, 487, 628
Sexual orientation, 132-34, 238-39, 240, 241
  defined, 132
  heritability of, 132-33
  neurological basis of, 133
Sexual revolution, 386
Shamanism, 638-39, 640
Shape constancy, 170
Shaping, 281-82
Shock therapy, 527-28
Short-term memory, 325, 327-28
Similarity
  liking and, 591
  principle of, 166
Simultaneous conditioning, 271
Single-parent family, 388
Siriono, sexual socialization among, 240
Six-hour retardation, 422
Sixteen Personality Factor Inventory, 468
Size constancy, 170
Skin, sense of touch and, 160-61
Skinner box, 278-79, 286
Sleep, 191-200
  dreams and, 193-95, 197-98
  functions of, 195-97
  non-REM, 193
  REM, 193-94, 196
  research on, 191-92
  stages of, 192-93
Sleep apnea, 199, 200
Sleep deprivation, 195
Sleep disorders, 198-200, 482
Sleep spindles, 192
Sleep terror, 194
Sleep terror disorder, 199, 200
Sleep-wake schedule disorder, 199, 200
Sleepwalking disorder, 199, 200
Smell, sense of, 142, 158-60, 346
Smell memory, 346
Smiles, 82
Snakes, fear of, 86, 88
Social advocacy, community psychology and, 539
Social class
  intelligence and, 415
  schizophrenia and, 23-25
  therapy approaches and, 552, 553
Social cognition, 560-61, 565-72
  attitudes. See Attitudes
  contents vs. processes of, 565

defined, 560
  general principles of, 565-66
  social description, 566-67
  social evaluation, 570-71
  social explanation, 567-70
  social influence and, 560-61, 577
Social comparison, 590
Social Darwinism, 79-80
Social development, 373-92
  adolescent, 381-86
  adult, 386-92
  defined, 373
  Erikson's theory of, 373-76
  in infants and children, 376-81
Social errors, 565
Social exchange, 591-93
Social influence(s), 560-61, 572-78
  on anxiety disorders, 501
  conformity, 572-74, 680
  defined, 560
  deindividuation, 575-76
  on health, 618, 635-38
  helping behavior and, 589
  in jury deliberation, 680
  on language acquisition, 343-44
  on learning, 292-94
  obedience to authority and, 53-54, 55, 574-75, 600
  person-role merger, 576
  on schizophrenia, 512
  social cognition and, 560-61, 577
  training people to inflict pain, 600-601
Socialization, 132
  aggression and, 242
  defined, 373
  gender and, 346, 381, 419, 477
  sexual, 240
Social learning approach to personality, 443, 461-63
Social loafing, 595-96
Social perception, 565, 567-71
Social phobia, 494-95, 544-46
Social psychology, 25, 559-603. *See also*
    Environmental psychology; Social cognition;
    Social influence(s)
  attraction, 589-94
  defined, 559-60
  diversity of social settings and, 561
  evolutionary explanations of social behavior, 561
  group processes, 594-600
  helping (prosocial behavior), 587-89
  history of, 561-62
  law and, 679-80
  prejudice and discrimination, 418, 578-87
  research in, 562-65
  social processes in biopsychosocial context, 600-601
Social relationships, 450-51
Social skills training, 289-90
Social support, health and, 635-36
Social worker, clinical, 523
Sociobiology, 84-85, 561
Sociocultural retardation, 422
Socioeconomic status. *See* Social class
Solution, problem, 338-39
Somatic nervous system, 97
Somatoform disorders, 482, 501-3
Sound, 142, 154-55, 157
Source traits, 455, 476
Spatial ability, sex differences in, 122
Spatial organization of nervous system, 105
Spatial thinking, 346
Specialization within psychology, 17